FOURTH EDITION

CRIMINAL JUSTICE
IN ACTION

Larry K. Gaines
California State University
San Bernardino

Roger LeRoy Miller
Institute for University Studies,
Arlington, Texas

THOMSON
WADSWORTH

Australia • Canada • Mexico • Singapore • Spain
United Kingdom • United States

THOMSON
WADSWORTH

Criminal Justice in Action
Fourth Edition
Larry K. Gaines and Roger LeRoy Miller

Editor-in-Chief: Eve Howard
Acquisitions Editor: Chris Caldiera
Development Editor: Sherry Symington
Assistant Editor: Jana Davis
Editorial Assistant: Jennifer Walsh
Marketing Communications Manager: Linda Yip
Advertising Project Manager: Stacey Purviance
Technology Production Manager: Susan DeVanna
Permissions Editor: Joo Hee Lee
Print/Media Buyer: Doreen Suruki
Project Manager, Editorial Production: Ann Borman

Photo Research: Anne Sheroff
Copyeditor: Pat Lewis
Proofreader: Suzie Franklin DeFazio
Indexer: Bob Marsh
Interior and Cover Designer: Lisa Buckley
Cover images: Bullet hole: ©age fotostock/Superstock; Jail bars: BrandXPictures/Alamy; Fingerprint: Getty Images/TRBfoto; Cop in car: ©Palmer/Kane, Inc./Workbook Stock; Scales of justice: Comstock Images/Alamy;
Text & Cover Printer: C&C Offset Printing Co., Ltd
Compositor: Parkwood Composition Service

Library of Congress Control Number: 2005933013
Student Edition: ISBN-13: 978-0-495-09342-8
ISBN-10: 0-495-093424
Instructor's Edition: ISBN-10: 0-495-18687-2
Student Paperback Edition: ISBN-13: 978-0-495-18686-1
ISBN-10: 0-495-18686-4

Thomson Higher Education
10 Davis Drive
Belmont, CA 94002-3098
USA

For more information about our products, contact us at:
Thomson Learning Academic Resource Center
1-800-423-0563
For permission to use material from this text or product, submit a request online at http://www.thomsonrights.com. Any additional questions about permissions can be submitted by e-mail to **thomsonrights@thomson.com**

Chapter opening credits:
Ch 1 © PETER FOLEY/EPA /Landov;
Ch 2 © Catherine Karnow/CORBIS;
Ch 3 © EPA/ARMANDO ARORIZO /Landov;
Ch 4 © AP Photo/Don Murray;
Ch 5 © Thomas Dworzak / Magnum Photos;
Ch 6 © AP Photo/Julie Jacobson;
Ch 7 © Ruaridh Stewart/ZUMA/CORBIS;
Ch 8 © Reuters/Bo Rader/The Wichita Eagle/Pool/Landov;
Ch 9 © AP Photo/Brian Ray, Pool;
Ch 10 © AP Photo/Mark Humphrey;
Ch 11 © AP Photo/Dave Martin, File;
Ch 12 © AP Photo/Coshocton Tribune, Dante Smith;
Ch 13 © AP Photo/Ted S. Warren;
Ch 14 © Fat Chance Productions/CORBIS;
Ch 15 © AP Photo/Matt Houston;
Ch 16 © AP Photo/Michael Dwyer;
Ch 17 © William B. Plowman/Getty Images

Chapter-ending information guides you to Criminal JusticeNow™ and www.cjinaction.com

A "Test Preparation Online" section included at the end of each chapter reminds you to visit www.cjinaction.com to access both **Criminal JusticeNow™** and the Book Companion Web Site— and gives you tips on how to use these great tools to develop the targeted study habits that spell success for you.

"Concept Builder" learning modules

"Concept Builder" prompts at the beginning of every chapter in this book guide you to the Book Companion Web Site, where you'll find a three-step "Concept Builder" learning module that reinforces in-text material by:

- Defining the concept
- Providing a practical example of the concept
- Asking you to apply your new understanding of the concept

Web links in the margins throughout every chapter

These references in the margins throughout the book include the names of Web sites with brief descriptions of what the sites contain—giving you many opportunities to enrich your study of chapter-related topics. We suggest that you access these links through www.cjinaction.com.

Also Available

Careers in Criminal Justice 3.0 Interactive CD-ROM
See the inside back endpaper of this book for details

Test Preparation Online

Criminal JusticeNow

Go to **www.cjinaction.com** and click on Criminal JusticeNow for access to this powerful online study tool. You will get a **personalized study plan** based on your responses to a diagnostic pretest. Once you have mastered the material with the help of interactive learning tools, video clips with questions, an integrated e-book, and more, you can take a posttest to confirm you are ready to move on to the next chapter.

Book Companion Web Site

At the book companion Web site (**www.cjinaction.com**), you will find many resources in addition to Criminal JusticeNow to aid you in studying for your exams. For example, under Chapter Resources you will find the G... Glossary, Learning... Builder, Essay Ques... test yourself with i... tion. Check out th...

Suggested Read

Kelly, Caitlin, **Blown Away:** ... Pocket Books, 2004. At leas... States are women, but fem... from the gun control debat... situation by taking a hard... spective. In the course of ir... sides of the debate, Kelly ge... der issue. Women—partic... traditionally been at the fo... ity of firearms. At the sam... smaller and physically weak... a gun, in the words of the... levels the field in a life-thre...

Scott Peterson's guilt

may have seemed clear to mem... homicide is not so cut and dried. In... son must have intended to commit... Peterson obviously knew of Conner'... woman without knowing she is carry... if, as occurred in Kentucky recently,... light and kills a woman and her unb... for two deaths? In South Carolina,... unborn child because she smoked... homicide laws to be interpreted to a... or drinking alcohol—during pregna...

CONCEPT BUILDER

Society has become less tolerant of crime, and especially of certain types of crime. Visit **www.cjinaction.com** for an interactive exploration of how such intolerance affects crime policies.

See the **Computer Crime and Intellectual Property Section** of the U.S. Department of Justice for a wealth of information on cyber crimes. Find this Web site by clicking on *Web Links* under *Chapter Resources* at **www.cjinaction.com**.

CONTENTS IN BRIEF

CONTENTS

PART TWO The Police and Law Enforcement

CHAPTER FIVE FEATURES

CHAPTER SIX FEATURES

CHAPTER 7

Police and the Constitution:
The Rules of Law Enforcement   202

CHAPTER SEVEN FEATURES

PART THREE   Criminal Courts

CHAPTER 8
Courts and the Quest for Justice   240

CHAPTER EIGHT FEATURES

CHAPTER 9

Pretrial Procedures: The Adversary System in Action   272

CHAPTER NINE FEATURES

PART FOUR   Corrections

CHAPTER 12
Probation and Community Corrections   388

CHAPTER 13

Prisons and Jails   418

CHAPTER THIRTEEN FEATURES

CJ IN FOCUS: MYTH VERSUS REALITY
Does Placing Criminals in Prison
Reduce Crime?   425

CJ AND TECHNOLOGY
The Electronic Head Count   432

CAREERS IN CJ
Penny Lucero: Warden   435

CJ IN FOCUS: LANDMARK CASES
Bell v. Wolfish   440

CHAPTER 14

Behind Bars: The Life of an Inmate 452

PART FIVE   Special Issues

CHAPTER 15

The Juvenile Justice System   488

CHAPTER FIFTEEN FEATURES

CJ IN FOCUS: LANDMARK CASES
In re Gault   494

CJ IN FOCUS: A QUESTION OF ETHICS
Interrogating Children   500

MASTERING CONCEPTS
The Juvenile Justice System versus the Criminal Justice System   503

CAREERS IN CJ
Cathy Wasseman: Public Defender: Juvenile Courts   505

OUTSIDE THE BOX
Young Women's Support Project   508

CJ AND TECHNOLOGY
The Electronic Hall Monitor   510

Preface

Crime and justice. These two issues have come to dominate our culture, from the halls of Congress, to prime-time television, to the blogosphere. They are also the twin pillars of a degree in criminal justice, one of the fastest-growing majors in American higher education. Criminal justice programs across the nation are offering students a combination of theory, practical experience, and "ripped from the headlines" immediacy that make criminal justice one of the most exciting and rewarding areas of study in academia. The practical benefits of the criminal justice major are also evident: a "foot in the door" to dozens of professional fields including law enforcement, corrections administration, and probation and parole, as well as a strong foundation for a graduate degree in law or a career in social work or private security.

In this, the Fourth Edition of *Criminal Justice in Action,* we continue to blend the bedrock theoretical principles of criminal justice with up-to-date research and high-interest examples of what is happening in the world of crime and crime prevention right now. Students just entering the discipline of criminal justice are facing a dizzying array of challenges in a field that has seen epochal changes in the past few years. Consider the following:

- With the creation of the U.S. Department of Homeland Security and the reorganization of the Federal Bureau of Investigation, the "war on terror" has led to the most extensive shift in how the federal government views and fights crime since World War II. These changes have affected every level of the criminal justice system, including local police departments, which must now take responsibility for areas of law enforcement that had previously been handled by federal agencies.
- For the first time ever, those incarcerated throughout the United States exceeded 2 million, and the number is rising. While this inmate population explosion reflects the public will, prison and jail overcrowding has reached the point at which alternatives to "lock 'em up" policies are badly needed. Consequently, corrections officials are turning to treatment and rehabilitation programs to an extent not seen in this country for many years.
- New technologies have influenced nearly every aspect of the criminal justice process. DNA techniques have allowed police to solve increased numbers of crimes, sometimes years after they have occurred, but have also provided evidence that many people have been wrongly convicted and imprisoned.
- The public's view of the criminal justice system is increasingly being molded by how the popular media portray it. Have the media been accurate? If not, is there anything we can do about it? How do we teach our students to become more critical consumers of the media?

These are the kinds of issues that face students going into the field of criminal justice today. Undoubtedly, as this nation confronts the challenge of terrorism on our soil, the role of the criminal justice system will expand and evolve. What is certain is that major new questions involving the trade-off between increased security and diminished civil liberties will be at the forefront of the public debate.

A Complete Learning Experience

While the text of *Criminal Justice in Action,* Fourth Edition, is filled with numerous eye-catching, instructive, and penetrating features, we have not stopped there. You will notice that the first page of every chapter starts with the chapter outline and learning objectives. The following page has an introduction in the form of a case study and an appropriate photo. The pedagogy continues all the way through to the end of each chapter, with the pedagogical devices listed below:

- **Criminal Justice in Action:** Every chapter ends with this important feature. It deals with major issues and controversies that require several pages to explain.
- **Outside the Box:** Of all the resources expanded to prevent and control crime, none is more important than the industriousness and creativity shown by the employees of the criminal justice system. This new feature highlights and analyzes the strategies of those who are thinking "outside the box" when it comes to crime and justice.
- **You Be the Judge:** Students are put into the position of a judge in a hypothetical criminal case (based, though, on an actual court case). The facts of the case are presented with alternative possible outcomes. The student is asked to make a decision as if he or she were the judge. What the courts actually ruled in each case can be found by the student in Appendix B at the end of the text.
- **International CJ:** Because it is sometimes easier to teach by comparison, in this feature we present students with information about how our criminal justice system compares with those of other countries.
- **CJ and Technology:** Since the criminal justice field is changing so rapidly because of technology, we made sure that the student could not miss learning about the important technology issues confronted by practitioners in the field today.
- **CJ and the Media:** Many aspects of the criminal justice system have invaded the media. We felt that this feature was important to reveal these "invasions" while at the same time commenting on their accuracy.
- **Careers in CJ:** Most students reading this book are planning a career in criminal justice. We have provided them with an insight into some of these careers by offering first-person accounts of what it is like to work in the criminal justice professions.
- **CJ in Focus:** This generic feature title covers important topics such as excerpts from significant Supreme Court cases and the age-old struggle between the need to protect society and the rights of individuals.
- **Mastering Concepts:** This feature helps students to master essential concepts of criminal justice. Because it is often important to compare and contrast two similar concepts to assist the student to understand them, many of the concept summaries are based on comparisons.
- **In-Margin Online Features:** Our teaching/learning package offers numerous opportunities for using online technology in the classroom. In the margins, you will find links to various Web sites that illuminate a particular subject in the corresponding text. This feature gives students access to up-to-date information on criminal justice topics, as well as providing an introduction to the massive amounts of information on crime and justice on the Internet. Each chapter also starts with a *Concept Builder* that leads students to an interactive critical-thinking exploration of a key topic.

Challenges for the Future: Terrorism and Cyber Crime

Because of the growing and obvious importance of terrorism and cyber crime in the criminal justice system, we have devoted most of Chapter 17 to these issues. The discussion focuses on the steps taken by American law enforcement personnel to combat these threats, as well as efforts to protect the public against terrorists and cyber criminals while at the same time protecting the nation's commitment to civil liberties. Chapter 17 also provides a "wrap-up" of the course, closing the textbook with a brief look to the immediate future of the criminal justice system.

The Supplements

Our entire team—the two authors plus numerous individuals at Wadsworth—have put together a complete teaching package. In this package you will find:

FOR THE INSTRUCTOR:

Instructor's Resource Manual with Test Bank By David Struckhoff, Loyola University—Chicago. One of the most comprehensive resource manuals ever provided to accompany *Criminal Justice in Action,* this manual includes detailed outlines, chapter summaries, key terms, student research activities, lecture and discussion ideas, and a test bank containing over 1,000 questions.

Criminal Justice Video Library Qualified adopters can select from a variety of videos, including exclusive *CNN Today* videos for Introduction to Criminal Justice, Criminology, Juvenile Delinquency, and Corrections, as well as *America's New War: CNN Looks at Terrorism,* Volumes I and II, all of which are tied to chapters of the selected texts; an exclusive *Introduction to Criminal Justice* video from the Films for the Humanities, Volumes II and III; thirty-one dynamic *Court TV* videos profiling some of the most famous and current cases in the judicial system; the *A&E American Justice* Series; and ABC News videos. Many videos are available on both VHS and DVD. **http://www.cj.wadsworth.com/videos**

Criminal Justice Faculty Development: Teaching Professors to Teach, **Second Edition** This completely revised booklet provides valuable tips on teaching the introduction to criminal justice course with suggested articles, work sheets, and sample syllabi.

Introduction to Criminal Justice Transparency Masters Enhance your lectures with images from the text that highlight some of the most important concepts in criminal justice.

ExamView® Computerized Testing This fully integrated suite of computerized test creation, delivery, and reporting tools enables you to help students enhance their test performance, and allows you to deliver tests that can be customized to fit your needs.

WebTutor ToolBox for WebCT and Blackboard Designed specifically for *Criminal Justice in Action.* Combines easy-to-use course management tools with content from this text's companion Web site. Ready to use as soon as you log on—or, customize WebTutor ToolBox with Web links, images, and other resources.

Multimedia Manager for Criminal Justice: A Microsoft® PowerPoint® Tool The Multimedia Manager for Criminal Justice is an important instrument that instructors can utilize to prepare for class lectures. More than 450 color images are included on this invaluable reference to aid instructors in visually representing to students the main concepts and ideas contained in the text.

JoinIn™ on TurningPoint®   You have access to book-specific JoinIn™ content for classroom response systems. This allows you to assess your students' progress with instant in-class quizzes and polls. With TurningPoint® software you can pose questions and display students' answers seamlessly within the Microsoft® PowerPoint® slides of your own lecture, in conjunction with the "clicker" hardware of your choice.

Thomson InSite for Writing and Research™—with Turnitin plagiarism checker! InSite features a full suite of writing, peer review, online grading, and e-portfolio applications. It is an all-in-one tool that helps instructors manage the flow of papers electronically and allows students to submit papers and peer reviews online. Also included in the suite is Turnitin, an "originality checker" that offers a simple solution for instructors who want a strong deterrent against plagiarism, as well as encouragement for students to employ proper research techniques. Access is available for packaging with each copy of this book. For more information, visit **http://insite.thomson.com**.

FOR THE STUDENT:

Web Site to Accompany *Criminal Justice in Action*, Fourth Edition   Students and instructors will have access to the book-specific Web site that includes chapter links, discussions, Internet projects, homework, quizzes, scavenger hunts, and instructor resources. **http://www.cjinaction.com**

Criminal JusticeNow™   This online study tool offers students support for mastering the course with a pretest to assess your understanding of the material. You are then given a personalized study plan that offers interactive, visual, and audio resources to help you master what you need to know. Also, you can use the integrated online text just like a printed textbook; or read the text pages only when your study plan sends you there. You can then take a posttest to check your progress. For students who need access to Criminal JusticeNow, visit **http://1pass.thomson.com** to purchase electronic access.

Careers in Criminal Justice Interactive CD-ROM   This engaging self-exploration provides an interactive discovery of careers in criminal justice. The CD-ROM furnishes personalized results from a self-assessment of interests and strengths to help steer students to careers based on their profiles. Students gather information on various careers from job descriptions, salaries, employment requirements, and actual video profiles of criminal justice professionals.

The Wadsworth Criminal Justice Resource Center   Designed to help students easily locate the latest and most relevant information in the field of criminal justice, this Web site features fascinating links, conference and job listings, grant information, links to book-specific sites with additional student resources, and much more. **http://cj.wadsworth.com**

Crime Scenes CD-ROM   An interactive CD-ROM featuring six vignettes that allows students to play various roles as they explore all aspects of the criminal justice system such as policing/investigation, courts, and sentencing and corrections. Awarded the gold medal in higher education and silver medal for video interface by *New Media* magazine's *Invision* Awards.

Study Guide   By David Struckhoff, Loyola University—Chicago. Includes chapter objectives, outlines, summaries, key terms and concepts, and a multitude of test questions in true/false, multiple-choice, matching, and essay formats.

InfoTrac® College Edition   This online database offers continuously updated, full-length articles from nearly five thousand journals and periodicals. By doing a simple key-word search, users can quickly generate a powerful list of related articles from thousands of possibilities, then select relevant articles to explore and/or print out for reference or for further study.

The Criminal Justice Internet Investigator III   This colorful trifold brochure lists the most popular Internet addresses for criminal justice–related Web sites, including URLs for corrections, victimization, crime prevention, high-tech crime, policing, courts, investigations, juvenile justice, research, and fun sites.

Internet Activities for Criminal Justice, **Second Edition**   This guide teaches students the best practices for utilizing the Internet for research and includes criminal justice–specific activities.

Internet Guide for Criminal Justice, **Second Edition**   Intended for the novice user, the first half of this eighty-page booklet explains the background and vocabulary necessary for navigating the Web, while the second half is customized for criminal justice–related Web sites as well as Internet project ideas.

Seeking Employment in Criminal Justice and Related Fields, **Fourth Edition**   This new edition is designed to help students develop a job-search strategy and provides information on résumés, cover letters, and interview techniques; it also furnishes extensive details about a wide range of criminal justice professions.

Acknowledgments

Throughout the creation of the four editions of this text, we have been aided by literally hundreds of experts in various criminal justice fields and by professors throughout the country, as well as by numerous students who have used the text. We list below the reviewers and survey respondents for this Fourth Edition, followed by the class-test participants and reviewers for the first three editions. We sincerely thank all who participated on the revision of *Criminal Justice in Action.* We believe that the Fourth Edition responds even more to the needs of today's criminal justice instructors and students alike because we have taken into account the constructive comments and criticisms of our reviewers and the helpful suggestions of our survey respondents.

REVIEWERS AND SURVEY RESPONDENTS FOR THE FOURTH EDITION

We are grateful for the participation of the reviewers who read and reviewed portions of our manuscript throughout its development, and for those who gave us valuable insights through their responses to our survey.

David L. Anderson
Louisiana State University—
Shreveport

Tammy Anderson
University of Delaware

Thomas E. Baker
University of Scranton

Shannon Barton
Indiana State University

Lee Roy Black
California University of
Pennsylvania

John K. Bordell
Kansas Wesleyan University

Sandy Boyd
College of Marin

Robert Boyer
Luzerne County Community
College

Timothy M. Bray
University of Texas—Dallas

Frank W. Budd
Weber State University

Frank Butler
Temple University

Charles Chastain
University of Arkansas at
Little Rock

James J. Chriss
Cleveland State University

Ellen G. Cohn
Florida International University

William Crawley
Grand Valley State University

Chris De Lay
University of Louisiana at Lafayette

Richard H. De Lung
Wayland Baptist University

Jo-Ann Della-Giustina
John Jay College of Criminal Justice

Frank J. Drummond
Modesto Junior College

Michael T. Eskey
Troy State University

Peter Galie
Canisius College

Donna F. Gaughan
Prince George's Community College

Paul Gregory
Western Michigan University

Deborah Henderson
Arizona State University

Nancy A. Horton
University of Maryland—Eastern Shore

G. G. Hunt
Wharton County Junior College

Al Ingham
Western New England College

Robert Jerin
Endicott College

James M. Johnson
Virginia Union University

Howard Jordan
Hostos College

Joseph Kibitlewski
International College

Lloyd Klein
Bemidji State University

Francis Kollmann
Suffolk County Community College

David Kotajarvi
Lakeshore Technical College

Betsey Wright Kreisel
Central Missouri State University

James Lasley
California State University, Fullerton

Deborah Laufersweiler-Dwyer
University of Arkansas at Little Rock

Larry Linville
North Virginia Community College

Neal W. Lippold
Waubonsee Community College

Arnold C. Lyerly
Community College of Southern Nevada

Larry Mays
New Mexico State University

James J. Mazza
Middlesex Community College

Joe Morris
Northwestern State University

Thomas R. O'Connor
North Carolina Wesleyan College

Peter Parilla
University of St. Thomas

William R. Parks II
University of South Carolina—Spartanburg

Mike Penrod
Kirkwood Community College

Heather Perfetti
Murray State University

Michael Polakowski
University of Arizona

Byron Quivey
Chipola Junior College

James T. Santor
Community College of Southern Nevada

Jim Smith
West Valley College

John Song
Buffalo State College

Domenick Stampone
Raritan Valley Community College

Sally Velzen
Itasca Community College

Ross A. Wolf
University of Central Florida

Kevin C. Woods
Becker College

Thanks to the Career Education Criminal Justice Advisory Board for their valuable inputs and contributions to the Wadsworth Criminal Justice Team:

Adell Newman
Chair, School of Criminal Justice
Kaplan College

Nancy Oesch
Criminal Justice Department Chair
Florida Metropolitan University

Kathryn Sellers
Criminal Justice Program Director
Virginia College

Jim Walney
Criminal Justice Program Director
ICM School of Business & Medical Careers

CLASS-TEST PARTICIPANTS

We also want to acknowledge the participation of the professors and their students who agreed to class-test portions of the text. Our thanks go to:

Tom Arnold
College of Lake County

Paula M. Broussard
University of Southwestern Louisiana

Mike Higginson
Suffolk Community College

Andrew Karmen
John Jay College of Criminal Justice

Fred Kramer
John Jay College of Criminal Justice

Anthony P. LaRose
Western Oregon University

Anne Lawrence
Kean University

Jerry E. Loar
Walters State Community College

Phil Reichel
University of Northern Colorado

Albert Sproule
Allentown College

Gregory B. Talley
Broome Community College

Karen Terry
John Jay College of Criminal Justice

Angelo Tritini
Passaic County Community College

Gary Uhrin
Westmoreland County Community College

Robert Vodde
Fairleigh Dickinson University

REVIEWERS OF THE FIRST, SECOND, AND THIRD EDITIONS

We appreciate the assistance of the following reviewers whose guidance helped create the foundation for this best seller. We are grateful to all.

Angela Ambers-Henderson
Montgomery County Community College

Judge James Bachman
Bowling Green State University

Tom Barclay
University of South Alabama

Julia Beeman
University of North Carolina at Charlotte

Anita Blowers
University of North Carolina at Charlotte

John Bower
Bethel College

Steven Brandl
University of Wisconsin—Milwaukee

Charles Brawner III
Heartland Community College

Susan Brinkley
University of Tampa

Paula Broussard
University of Southwestern Louisiana

Michael Brown
Ball State College

Joseph Bunce
Montgomery College—Rockville

James T. Burnett
SUNY, Rockland Community College

Ronald Burns
Texas Christian University

Paul Campbell
Wayne State College

Dae Chang
Wichita State University

Steven Chermak
Indiana University

Charlie Chukwudolue
Northern Kentucky University

Monte Clampett
Asheville-Buncome Community College

John Cochran
University of South Florida

Mark Correia
University of Nevada—Reno

John del Nero
Lane Community College

John Dempsey
Suffolk County Community College

Tom Dempsey
Christopher Newpoint University

Joyce Dozier
Wilmington College

M. G. Eichenberg
Wayne State College

Frank L. Fischer
Kankakee Community College

Frederick Galt
Dutchess Community College

James Gilbert
University of Nebraska—Kearney

Dean Golding
West Chester University of Pennsylvania

Debbie Goodman
Miami-Dade Community College

Donald Grubb
Northern Virginia Community College

Sharon Halford
Community College of Aurora

Michael Hallett
Middle Tennessee State University

Mark Hansel
Moorhead State University

Michelle Heward
Weber State University

Dennis Hoffman
University of Nebraska—Omaha

Richard Holden
Central Missouri State University

Ronald Holmes
University of Louisville

Marilyn Horace-Moore
Eastern Michigan University

Matrice Hurrah
Shelby State Community College

Nicholas Irons
County College of Morris

Michael Israel
Kean University

J. D. Jamieson
Southwest Texas State University

James Jengeleski
Shippensburg University

Paul Johnson
Weber State University

Casey Jordan
Western Connecticut State University

Matthew Kanjirathinkal
Texas A & M University—Commerce

Bill Kelly
University of Texas—Austin

John H. Kramer
Pennsylvania State University

Kristen Kuehnle
Salem State University

Karl Kunkel
Southwest Missouri State

Barry Latzer
John Jay College of Criminal Justice

Deborah Laufersweiler-Dwyer
University of Arkansas at Little Rock

Paul Lawson
Montana State University

Nella Lee
Portland State University

Walter Lewis
St. Louis Community College—Meramec

Faith Lutze
Washington State University

Richard Martin
Elgin Community College

Richard H. Martin
University of Findlay

William J. Mathias
University of South Carolina

Bill Matthias
University of South Carolina—Columbia

Janet McClellan
Southwestern Oregon Community College

Pat Murphy
State University of New York—Geneseo

Rebecca Nathanson
Housatonic Community Technical College

Michael Palmiotto
Wichita State University

Rebecca D. Petersen
University of Texas, San Antonio

Gary Prawel
Monroe Community College

Mark Robarge
Mansfield University

Matt Robinson
Appalachian State University

Debra Ross
Buffalo State College

William Ruefle
University of South Carolina

Gregory Russell
Washington State University

John Scheb II
University of Tennessee—Knoxville

Ed Selby
Southwestern College

Ronald Sopenoff
Brookdale Community College

Katherine Steinbeck
Lakeland Community College

Kathleen M. Sweet
St. Cloud State University

Gregory Talley
Broome Community College

Karen Terry
John Jay College of Criminal Justice

Lawrence F. Travis III
University of Cincinnati

Kimberly Vogt
University of Wisconsin—La Crosse

Robert Wadman
Weber State University

Ron Walker
Trinity Valley Community College

John Wyant
Illinois Central College

Others were instrumental in bringing this Fourth Edition to fruition. We continue to appreciate the extensive research efforts of Shawn G. Miller and the additional legal assistance of William Eric Hollowell. Sherry Symington, our developmental editor, provided equal parts elbow grease and creative energy; it was a pleasure to work with her. Editor Chris Caldeira supplied crucial guidance to the project through her suggestions and recommendations. Editor in chief Eve Howard and CEO Susan Badger provided key support. At the production end, we once again feel fortunate to have enjoyed the services of our tireless production manager, Ann Borman, who oversaw virtually all aspects of this book. How she was able to make all of the schedules on time never ceased to amaze us. Additionally, we wish to thank the designer of this new edition, Lisa Buckley, who has created what we believe to be the most dazzling and student-friendly design of any text in the field. Photo researcher Anne Sheroff went to great lengths to satisfy our requests, and we sincerely appreciate her efforts. We are also thankful for the services of all those at Parkwood Composition who worked on the Fourth Edition, particularly Debbie Mealey. The eagle eyes of Pat Lewis, who did expert double duty as copy editor and proofreader, and Suzie Franklin DeFazio, proofer extraordinaire, were invaluable.

A special word of thanks must also go to the team responsible for the extensive multimedia package included in this project, including technology project manager Susan DeVanna, writers Robert C. De Lucia of John Jay College of Criminal Justice and Kelli Stevens of Texas Christian University, Larry Bassi of SUNY Brockport, and Carolyn Dennis of Mount Olive College. In addition, we appreciate the work of David Struckhoff of Loyola University—Chicago, who developed the Instructor's Resource Manual and Student Study Guide; as well as the aid of editorial assistant Jennifer Walsh, who pitched in to ensure the timely publication of the supplements. A final thanks to all of the great people in marketing and advertising who helped to get the word out about the book, including marketing manager Terra Schultz, who has been tireless in her attention to this project; Joy Westberg for her excellent writing skills; and advertising project manager Stacey Purviance for keeping everything on track.

Any criminal justice text has to be considered a work in progress. We know that there are improvements that we can make. Therefore, write us with any suggestions that you may have.

L. K. G.
R. L. M.

Dedication

This book is dedicated to my good friend
and colleague, Lawrence Walsh, of the
Lexington, Kentucky Police Department.
When I was a rookie, he taught me about
policing. When I became a researcher,
he taught me about the practical
applications of knowledge. He is truly
an inspiring professional in our field.

L.K.G.

To Clyde,

Your advice and help
for so many years
cannot be repaid with
a simple dedication.
But thanks for everything,
nonetheless.

R.L.M.

Criminal Justice Today

Chapter outline

- What Is Crime?
- The Criminal Justice System
- Values of the Criminal Justice System
- Issues in Criminal Justice Today
- Criminal Justice in Action—Coming to Grips with Gangs

Chapter objectives

After reading this chapter, you should be able to:

1 Describe the two most common models of how society determines which acts are criminal.
2 Define crime and the different types of crime.
3 Outline the three levels of law enforcement.
4 List the essential elements of the corrections system.
5 Explain the difference between the formal and informal criminal justice processes.
6 Describe the layers of the "wedding cake" model.
7 Contrast the crime control and due process models.
8 List the major issues in criminal justice today.

Criminal JusticeNow

Optimize your study time and master key chapter concepts with *Criminal JusticeNow*, an online study tool that provides you with a *personalized study plan*. Check out the "Test Preparation Online" section at the end of the chapter for additional information.

Husbands and Lives

Teresa Keeler was maneuvering down a narrow mountain road near Stockton, California, when another car driven by Robert Keeler, her ex-husband, suddenly blocked the path. Robert demanded to know if she was pregnant by her new boyfriend, a man named Ernst Vogt. Teresa ignored the question. Robert dragged her out of the vehicle and, seeing her swollen belly, said, "I'm going to stomp it out of you." He kneed Teresa in the abdomen and proceeded to beat her unconscious. Later, at the hospital, Teresa delivered a stillborn baby girl with a fractured skull.

More than three decades later, Robert Keeler's actions on that winter day in 1969 would have major consequences for Scott Peterson, a fertilizer salesman from Modesto, California, after the body of his wife, Laci, washed up on the coast of San Francisco Bay. Following Keeler's arrest, state officials tried to charge him with the murder of "Baby Girl Vogt." The California Supreme Court dismissed the charge, ruling that an unborn child was not a human being and therefore could not be murdered under state law. In response to public anger at this result, the state legislature changed its definition of murder to "the unlawful killing of a human being, *or a fetus,* with malice aforethought." [Emphasis added.]

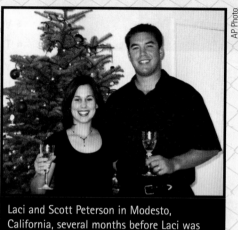

AP Photo

Laci and Scott Peterson in Modesto, California, several months before Laci was found dead and Scott was charged with her murder and the murder of their unborn son.

Thus, after law enforcement officials determined that Peterson was responsible for the death of Laci, who was eight months pregnant with a son (to be named Conner) when she was killed, they could charge him with not one murder, but two. The difference was no small matter: under state law, a person found guilty of a single murder may not be sentenced to death, but a double-murder charge is a "special circumstance" under which capital punishment is possible. As it turned out, in 2004 a California jury decided that Peterson did deserve the ultimate punishment for his crimes, and he is now awaiting execution on San Quentin State Prison's death row.

Scott Peterson's guilt may have seemed clear to members of that particular jury, but the issue of fetal homicide is not so cut and dried. In Chapter 4, you will learn that in most cases a person must have intended to commit a crime to be guilty of that crime. In this case, Peterson obviously knew of Conner's existence, but what if a person attacks a pregnant woman without knowing she is carrying a child and unwittingly harms the fetus? What if, as occurred in Kentucky recently, a driver under the influence of drugs runs a red light and kills a woman and her unborn baby?[1] Should the driver be held responsible for two deaths? In South Carolina, a mother was found guilty of the murder of her unborn child because she smoked crack cocaine while pregnant.[2] Do we want fetal homicide laws to be interpreted to apply to the mother's behavior—such as smoking or drinking alcohol—during pregnancy?

The Peterson trial raised a number of other concerns. It attracted an incredible amount of public attention, raising the prospect that the defendant was being unfairly "tried in the media," a subject we will discuss in Chapter 10. Furthermore, prosecutors were unable to present any "hard" evidence against Peterson; that is, they had no murder weapon, no witnesses, nothing to place the defendant at the scene of the crime, and no confession from Peterson himself. Instead, they relied on circumstantial evidence such as Peterson's admission that he was fishing in San Francisco Bay on the day his wife was murdered, an affair he was having at the time of the murder, and gruesome photos of Laci and Conner's decomposed bodies. We will explore these procedural strategies in Chapter 10 as well. Finally, many observers, even if they agree that Peterson is guilty, do not think he should be executed. As we shall see in Chapter 11, capital punishment is one of the most hotly debated topics in the United States today.

As you proceed through this textbook, you will see that few aspects of the criminal justice system are ever simple, even though you may have clear opinions about them. In this first chapter, we will introduce you to the criminal justice system by discussing its structure, the values that it is designed to promote, and the most challenging issues it faces today.

Chai Vang was charged with multiple counts of murder after a confrontation that led to the deaths of six hunters in the woods of northern Wisconsin on November 21, 2004. Vang, a Hmong immigrant, claims that some of the hunters taunted him with racial slurs before the killings occurred. Why do we need to know the circumstances surrounding a crime before deciding on the proper punishment?

WHAT IS CRIME?

A year before Laci Peterson's body washed ashore, Jerold and Keya Ponder were convicted of second degree murder for killing Zaneta Browne in Rochester, New York. Browne was pregnant with twins at the time of her death, but the Ponders were not charged with any crime related to that fact.[3] New York is one of eighteen states that still subscribe to the "born alive" rule, which holds that a person must be born before he or she can be murdered.[4] All other states have passed legislation that allows for an unborn child to be a victim of criminal activity, but the laws vary widely in their particulars. In California, for example, the term *fetus* means "beyond the embryonic state of seven to eight weeks."[5] Five states rely on the United States Supreme Court's definition of *viability* (at the end of the second trimester of pregnancy) to determine when a fetus becomes a person for homicide purposes.[6] Other jurisdictions punish third parties for killing a fetus at any time of its development, an interpretation adopted in the Unborn Victims of Violence Act, a federal law passed in 2004 largely as a result of the Peterson case.[7]

Hence, in some states, Scott Peterson could not have been charged with a crime for causing his unborn son's death. This is not the only inconsistency in our nation's murder laws. In Chapter 4, you will see that a person must be considered sane to be convicted of homicide and that, in general, killing another may be justified when it is done for self-protection. In some circumstances, described in Chapter 6, law enforcement officers may kill in the line of duty without the threat of criminal penalties. The state may sanction killing in times of war or as punishment.

When, then, is homicide considered murder? The easy answer is when it meets the legal conditions that designate it as such. Therefore, a *crime* can be defined as a wrong against society proclaimed by law and, if committed under certain circumstances, punishable by society. The problem with this definition, however, is that it obscures the complex nature of societies. A society is not static—it evolves and changes, and its concept of criminality evolves and changes as well. Different societies can have vastly different ideas of what constitutes a "wrong." In Singapore, for

○ CONCEPT BUILDER

Society has become less tolerant of crime, and especially of certain types of crime. Visit **www.cjinaction.com** for an interactive exploration of how such intolerance affects crime policies.

Consensus Model
A criminal justice model in which the majority of citizens in a society share the same values and beliefs. Criminal acts are those acts that conflict with these values and beliefs and are deemed harmful to society.

Conflict Model
A criminal justice model in which the content of criminal law is determined by the groups that hold economic, political, and social power in a community.

example, until recently the sale of chewing gum was illegal; many Americans found this law incomprehensible.

To more fully understand the concept of crime, it will help to examine the two most common models of how society "decides" which acts are criminal: the consensus model and the conflict model.

The Consensus Model

The **consensus model** assumes that as people gather together to form a society, its members will naturally come to a basic agreement with regard to shared norms and values. Those individuals whose actions deviate from the established norms and values are considered to pose a threat to the well-being of society as a whole and must be sanctioned (punished). The society passes laws to control and prevent deviant behavior, thereby setting the boundaries for acceptable behavior within the group.[8] Use of the term *consensus* implies that a majority of the citizens agree on what activities should be outlawed and punished as crimes.

The consensus model, to a certain extent, assumes that a diverse group of people can have similar *morals;* that is, they share an ideal of what is "right" and "wrong." Consequently, as public attitudes toward morality change, so do laws. In colonial times, those found guilty of adultery were subjected to corporal punishment; a century ago, one could walk into a pharmacy and purchase heroin. Today, social attitudes have shifted to consider adultery a personal issue, beyond the purview of the state, and to consider the sale of heroin a criminal act. When a consensus does not exist as to whether a certain act falls within the parameters of acceptable behavior, a period of uncertainty ensues as society struggles to formalize its attitudes as law. (For an example of the consensus model at work, see the feature *International CJ—Doctor-Assisted Death and the Dutch.*)

The Conflict Model

Those who reject the consensus model do so on the ground that moral attitudes are not absolute. In large, democratic societies such as the United States, different segments of society will inevitably have different value systems and shared norms. According to the **conflict model,** these different segments—separated by social class, income, age, and race—are engaged in a constant struggle with each other for control of society. The victorious groups exercise their power by codifying their value systems into criminal laws.[9]

Consequently, what is deemed criminal activity is determined by whichever group happens to be holding power at any given time. Because certain groups do not have access to political power, their interests are not served by the criminal justice system. To give one example, the penalty (five years in prison) for possession of 5 grams of crack cocaine is the same as for possession of 500 grams of powder cocaine. This 1:100 ratio has had widespread implications for inner-city African Americans, who are statistically more likely to get caught using crack cocaine than are white suburbanites, who appear to favor the illicit drug in its powdered form.[10]

An Integrated Definition of Crime

Considering both the consensus and conflict models, we can construct a definition of crime that will be useful throughout this textbook. For our purposes, crime is an action or activity that is:

1 Punishable under criminal law, as determined by the majority of a society or, in some cases, a powerful minority.

2 Considered an *offense against society as a whole* and prosecuted by public officials, not by victims and their relatives or friends.

INTERNATIONAL CJ

Doctor–Assisted Death and the Dutch

In 2001, the Netherlands became the first nation to legalize physician-assisted suicide and euthanasia ("mercy killing"). The new law simply formalized practices that had been taking place since 1973, when this European nation's courts decided that doctors can help terminate a patient's life if certain conditions are met: the patient must explicitly request such an action, the request must be voluntary, and the patient's suffering must be unbearable and without any hope of improvement. The law requires youths aged twelve to sixteen to obtain parental consent before requesting assisted suicide. From the age of sixteen, all patients have the right to discuss the matter with their doctors without obtaining their parents' approval.

In explaining why the Netherlands accepts actions that many other countries would consider objectionable, observers point to several characteristics of Dutch society. First, doctors hold exalted positions, and their actions are rarely questioned. Not only are doctors authorized to terminate "meaningless" lives, but they are also expected to do so. Second, the country lacks a strong religious influence, which might place the question of assisted suicide in a different moral perspective. As it is, hopelessly ill patients who fail to request euthanasia are seen as adhering to outdated ethical values. Third, and most important, is the Dutch emphasis on personal autonomy; the choice to die is considered the responsibility of the individual, not of the state.

In 1998, an elderly Oregon woman whose breast cancer left her unable to breathe easily became the first American to legally

On April 10, 2000, thousands of protesters gather outside the Upper House of Parliament in The Hague, Netherlands, as Dutch government officials debate the legalization of euthanasia.

commit suicide with the aid of a doctor. Oregon's Death with Dignity Act—which is modeled in many respects after the Dutch system—was upheld by a federal court ruling in 2002 that reconfirmed each state's authority to legalize assisted suicide. As of April 2005, 208 people have ended their lives with a physician's help in Oregon, which is still the only state that allows such a practice.

FOR CRITICAL ANALYSIS
What social attitudes make it unlikely that physician-assisted suicide and euthanasia will become widely accepted in this country?

---

3 Punishable by statutorily determined sanctions that bring about the loss of personal freedom or life.

At this point, it is important to understand the difference between crime and **deviance,** or behavior that does not conform to the norms of a given community or society. Deviance is a subjective concept; some segments of society may think that smoking marijuana or killing animals for clothing and food is deviant behavior. Deviant acts become crimes only when a majority is willing to accept that those acts should be punished—as is the situation today in the United States with using illegal drugs but not with eating meat. Furthermore, not all crimes are considered particularly deviant; little social disapprobation is attached to those who fail to follow the letter of parking laws. In essence, criminal law reflects those acts that we, as a society, agree are so unacceptable that steps must be taken to prevent them from occurring.

Deviance
Behavior that is considered to go against the norms established by society.

Types of Crime

The manner in which crimes are classified depends on their seriousness. Federal, state, and local legislation has provided for the classification and punishment of hundreds of thousands of different criminal acts, ranging from jaywalking to first degree murder. For general purposes, we can group criminal behavior into six categories: violent crime, property crime, public order crime, white-collar crime, organized crime, and high-tech crime.

Violent Crime Crimes against persons, or **violent crimes,** have come to dominate our perspectives on crime. There are four major categories of violent crime:

- *Murder,* or the unlawful killing of a human being.
- *Sexual assault,* or *rape,* which refers to coerced actions of a sexual nature against an unwilling participant.
- *Assault and battery,* two separate acts that cover situations in which one person physically attacks another (battery) or, through threats, intentionally leads another to believe that he or she will be physically harmed (assault).
- *Robbery,* or the taking of money, personal property, or any other article of value from a person by means of force or fear.

As you will see in Chapter 4, these violent crimes are further classified by *degree,* depending on the circumstances surrounding the criminal act. These circumstances include the intent of the person committing the crime, whether a weapon was used, and (in cases other than murder) the level of pain and suffering experienced by the victim.

Property Crime The most common form of criminal activity is **property crime,** or those crimes in which the goal of the offender is some form of economic gain or the damaging of property. Pocket picking, shoplifting, and the stealing of any property that is not accomplished by force are covered by laws against *larceny/theft. Burglary* refers to the unlawful entry of a structure with the intention of committing a serious crime such as theft. *Motor vehicle theft* describes the theft or attempted theft of a motor vehicle, including all cases in which automobiles are taken by persons not having lawful access to them. The willful and malicious burning of a home, automobile, commercial building, or any other construction, known as *arson,* is also a property crime.

Public Order Crime The concept of **public order crimes** is linked to the consensus model discussed earlier. Historically, societies have always outlawed activities that are considered contrary to public values and morals. Today, the most common public order crimes include public drunkenness, prostitution, gambling, and illicit drug use. These crimes are sometimes referred to as *victimless crimes* because they often harm only the offender. As you will see throughout this textbook, however, that term is rather misleading. Public order crimes may create an environment that gives rise to property and violent crimes.

White-Collar Crime Business-related crimes are popularly referred to as **white-collar crimes.** The term *white-collar crime* is broadly used to describe an illegal act or series of acts committed by an individual or business entity using some nonviolent means to obtain a personal or business advantage. Figure 1.1 lists various types of white-collar crime; note that certain property crimes fall into this category when committed in a corporate context.

Although it is difficult to know the exact extent of the problem, the Association of Certified Fraud Examiners estimates that white-collar crime might cost U.S. corporations as much as $66 billion a year.[11] Penalties for this activity, however, have generally been light. Between 1991 and 2001, the average sentence for a white-collar crime was around 20 months, about one-fourth the average sentence for a drug offense.[12] During a seven-month period in 2001–2002, however, four of the six largest bankruptcies in U.S. history took place, fueled by a frenzy of corporate misconduct. The result was a concerted effort to change the perception that white-collar criminals receive only a "slap on the wrist." President George W. Bush formed a corporate fraud task force to consolidate law enforcement efforts against white-collar crime, and the U.S. Congress passed a law that greatly increased the criminal penalties for business-related wrong-

FIGURE 1.1

White-Collar Crime

Embezzlement	A form of employee fraud in which an individual uses his or her position within a corporation to *embezzle*, or steal, the corporation's funds, property, or other assets. Pilferage is a less serious form of employee fraud in which the individual steals items from the workplace.
Mail and Wire Fraud	This umbrella term covers all schemes to intentionally deceive in a business environment that involve the use of mail, radio, television, the Internet, or a telephone.
Credit-Card and Check Fraud	This form of white-collar crime involves obtaining credit-card numbers through a variety of schemes (such as stealing them from the Internet) and using the numbers for personal gain. Check fraud includes writing checks that are not covered by bank funds, forging checks, and stealing traveler's checks.
Insurance Fraud	Insurance fraud involves making false claims in order to collect insurance payments under false pretenses. Faking an injury in order to receive payments from a workers' compensation program, for example, is a form of insurance fraud.
Securities Fraud	This area covers illegal activity in the stock market. It includes stockbrokers who steal funds from their clients and *insider trading*, which is the illegal trading in a stock by someone (or on behalf of someone) who has inside knowledge about the company in question.
Bribery	Also known as *influence peddling*, bribery occurs in the business world when somebody within a company sells influence, power, or information to a person outside the company who can benefit. A county official, for example, could give a construction company a lucrative county contract to build a new jail. In return, the construction company would give a sum of money, also known as a *kickback*, to the official.
Consumer Fraud	This term covers a wide variety of activities designed to defraud consumers, from selling counterfeit art to offering "free" items, such as electronic devices or vacations, that include a number of hidden charges.
Tax Evasion	The practice by which taxpayers either underreport (or do not report) their taxable income or otherwise purposely attempt to evade a tax liability.

doing.[13] (See the feature *CJ in Focus—A Question of Ethics: Getting Tough on White-Collar Crime* on the next page.)

Organized Crime White-collar crime involves the use of legal business facilities and employees to commit illegal acts. For example, a bank teller can't embezzle unless she is hired first as a legal employee of the bank. In contrast, **organized crime** describes illegal acts by illegal organizations, usually geared toward satisfying the public's demand for unlawful goods and services. Organized crime broadly implies a conspiratorial and illegal relationship among any number of persons engaged in unlawful acts. More specifically, groups engaged in organized crime employ criminal tactics such as violence, corruption, and intimidation for economic gain. The hierarchical structure of organized crime operations often mirrors that of legitimate businesses, and, like any corporation, these groups attempt to capture a sufficient percentage of any given market to make a profit. For organized crime, the traditional preferred markets are gambling, prostitution, illegal narcotics, and loan sharking (lending money at higher-than-legal interest rates), along with more recent ventures into counterfeiting and credit-card scams.[14]

Organized Crime
A conspiratorial relationship among any number of persons engaged in the market for illegal goods or services, such as illicit drugs or firearms.

High-Tech Crime The newest typology of crime is directly related to the increased use of computers in everyday life. The Internet, with approximately 800 million users

Getting Tough on White-Collar Crime

"The business pages of American newspapers should not read like a scandal sheet," lectured President George W. Bush to a group of Wall Street professionals. "At this moment America's greatest economic need is higher ethical standards." During the summer of 2002, the world of commerce did seem to be suffering from an ethical crisis. Corporate fraud involving billions of dollars had been uncovered at giant companies such as Enron, Xerox, Adelphia, and WorldCom. One in five American workers said they knew of colleagues who had lied on expense reports, stolen items from supply cabinets, accepted personal gifts from clients, or skimmed money from cash sales. The country appeared to be suffering from an epidemic of white-collar crime, causing many to believe that we were somehow less ethical as a people than we used to be.

As we will see throughout this textbook, perception often drives legislation. In this instance, the scandals of 2002 led to tough new laws to prevent and punish white-collar crimes. Under the new sentencing guidelines, the maximum punishment for wire and mail fraud, the most common white-collar crimes, increased from five to twenty years. Today, a corporate executive whose fraudulent activity causes a 50-cent drop in his company stock value faces a stiffer penalty (eleven years in prison) than a person convicted of selling forty grams of heroin (three years) or voluntary manslaughter (ten years).

The new guidelines, combined with a greater willingness to convict on the part of juries, have resulted in much harsher punishments for white-collar wrongdoers than they would previously have received. Fifteen years ago, Ivan Boesky was sentenced to only three years in prison for a securities fraud scheme that made him $50 million richer. In 2004, James Olis, an executive with the energy company Dynegy, was given twenty-four years for "cooking the books" to gain $472,000. That same year,

In 2004–2005, businesswoman and television personality Martha Stewart served five months in federal prison as punishment for lying to federal investigators about a stock sale.

AP Photo/Louis Lanzano

celebrity homemaker and businesswoman Martha Stewart was sentenced to five months in prison even though she had not, at first, done anything wrong. Instead, she was convicted of obstructing justice for lying to federal officials concerning a stock transaction. As one observer noted, "If I were someone on Wall Street, this [trend] would send a chill through my spine."

FOR CRITICAL ANALYSIS
Some observers have suggested that the prospect of going to prison is more of a deterrent for those who may commit white-collar crimes than those who may commit violent or property crimes. Why might this be true? Why might this not be true?

---

worldwide, is the site of numerous *cyber crimes,* such as selling pornographic materials, soliciting minors, and defrauding consumers with bogus financial investments. The dependence of businesses on computer operations has left corporations vulnerable to sabotage, fraud, embezzlement, and theft of proprietary data. (See Figure 1.2 for a description of several types of cyber crimes.)

THE CRIMINAL JUSTICE SYSTEM

See the **Computer Crime and Intellectual Property Section** of the U.S. Department of Justice for a wealth of information on cyber crimes. Find this Web site by clicking on *Web Links* under *Chapter Resources* at **www.cjinaction.com**.

Defining which actions are to be labeled "crimes" is only the first step in safeguarding society from criminal behavior. Institutions must be created to apprehend alleged wrongdoers, determine whether these persons have indeed committed crimes, and punish those who are found guilty according to society's wishes. These institutions combine to form the *criminal justice system.* As we begin our examination of the American criminal justice system in this introductory chapter, it is important to have an idea of its purpose.

The Purpose of the Criminal Justice System

In 1967, the President's Commission on Law Enforcement and Administration of Justice stated that the criminal justice system is obliged to enforce accepted standards of conduct so as to "protect individuals and the community."[15] Given this general mandate, we can further separate the purpose of the modern criminal justice system into three general goals:

1 To control crime
2 To prevent crime
3 To provide and maintain justice

Though many observers differ on the precise methods of reaching them, the first two goals are fairly straightforward. By arresting, prosecuting, and punishing wrongdoers, the criminal justice system attempts to *control* crime. In the process, the system also hopes to *prevent* new crimes from taking place. The prevention goal is often used to justify harsh punishments for wrongdoers, which some see as deterring others from committing similar criminal acts. The third goal—of providing and maintaining justice—is more complicated, largely because *justice* is a difficult concept to define. Broadly stated, justice means that all citizens are equal before the law and that they are free from arbitrary arrest or seizure as defined by the law.[16] In other words, the idea of justice is linked with the idea of fairness. Above all, we want our laws and the means by which they are carried out to be fair.

Justice and fairness are subjective terms; different people may have different concepts of what is just and fair. If a woman who has been beaten by her husband retaliates by killing him, what is her just punishment? Reasonable persons could disagree, with some thinking that the homicide was justified and she should be treated leniently, and others insisting that she should not have taken the law into her own hands. Police officers, judges, prosecutors, prison administrators, and other employees of the criminal justice system must decide what is "fair." Sometimes, their course of action is obvious; often, as we shall see, it is not.

Society places the burden of controlling crime, preventing crime, and determining fairness on those citizens who work in the three main institutions of the criminal justice system: law enforcement, courts, and corrections. In the next section, we take an introductory look at these institutions and their role in the criminal justice system as a whole.

The Structure of the Criminal Justice System

To understand the structure of the criminal justice system, one must understand the concept of **federalism,** which means that government powers are shared by the national (federal) government and the states. The framers of the U.S. Constitution, fearful of tyranny and a too-powerful central government, chose the system of federalism as a compromise. The appeal of federalism was that it allowed for state powers and local traditions while establishing a strong national government capable of handling large-scale problems.

The Constitution gave the national government certain express powers, such as the power to coin money, raise an army, and regulate interstate commerce. All other powers were left to the states, including police power, which allows the states to enact

---

FIGURE 1.2

Types of Cyber Crimes

Cyber Crime against Persons
- *Obscene Material and Pornography:* The selling, posting, and distributing of obscene material such as pornography, indecent exposure, and child pornography.
- *Cyberstalking:* The act of using a computer and the Internet to continually attempt to contact and/or intimidate another person.
- *Cyber Harassment:* The harassment of a person through electronic mail, on chat sites, or by printing information about the person on Web sites.

Cyber Crime against Property
- *Hacking:* The act of using programming abilities with malicious intent.
- *Cracking:* The act of using programming abilities in an attempt to gain unauthorized access to a computer or network.
- *Piracy:* Copying and distributing software or other items belonging to someone else over the Internet.
- *Viruses:* The creation and distribution of harmful computer programs.

Cyber Crime against the Government
- *Cyberterrorism:* The use of a computer and/or the Internet to further political goals of terrorism against a country and its citizens.

Source: Susan Brenner and Rebecca Cochran, University of Dayton School of Law at **www.cybercrimes.net**.

Federalism

A form of government in which a written constitution provides for a division of powers between a central government and several regional governments. In the United States, the division of powers between the federal government and the fifty states is established by the Constitution.

whatever laws are necessary to protect the health, morals, safety, and welfare of their citizens. As the American criminal justice system has evolved, the ideals of federalism have ebbed somewhat; in particular, federal involvement has expanded significantly. Crime is still, however, for the most part a local concern, and the majority of all employees in the criminal justice system work for local government (see Figure 1.3).

Law Enforcement The ideals of federalism can be clearly seen in the local, state, and federal levels of law enforcement. Though agencies from the different levels will cooperate if the need arises, they have their own organizational structures and tend to operate independently of one another. In addition to this brief introduction, each level of law enforcement will be covered in more detail in Chapters 5, 6, and 7.

Local Law Enforcement On the local level, the duties of law enforcement agencies are split between counties and municipalities. The chief law enforcement officer of most counties is the county sheriff. The sheriff is usually an elected post, with a two- or four-year term. In some areas, where city and county governments have merged, there is a county police force, headed by a chief of police. The bulk of local police officers—nearly 500,000—are employed by municipalities. The majority of these forces consist of fewer than ten officers, though a large city such as New York can have a police force of more than 35,000.

Local police are responsible for the "nuts and bolts" of law enforcement work. They investigate most crimes and attempt to deter crime through patrol activities. They apprehend criminals and participate in trial proceedings, if necessary. Local police are also charged with "keeping the peace," a broad set of duties that includes crowd and traffic control and the resolution of minor conflicts between citizens. In many areas, local police have the added obligation of providing social services such as dealing with domestic violence and child abuse.

State Law Enforcement Hawaii is the only state that does not have a state law enforcement agency. Generally, there are two types of state law enforcement agencies, those designated simply as "state police" and those designated as "highway patrols." State highway patrols concern themselves mainly with infractions on public highways and freeways. Other state law enforcers include fire marshals, who investigate suspicious fires and educate the public on fire prevention; and fish, game, and watercraft wardens, who police a state's natural resources and often oversee its firearms laws. Some states also have alcoholic beverage control officers plus agents who investigate welfare and food stamp fraud.

Federal Law Enforcement The enactment of new national gun, drug, and violent crime laws over the past thirty years has led to an expansion in the size and scope of

FIGURE 1.3

Local, State, and Federal Employees in Our Criminal Justice System

Source: Bureau of Justice Statistics, *Justice Expenditure and Employment Extracts, 1999* (Washington, D.C.: U.S. Department of Justice, 2002), Table 5.

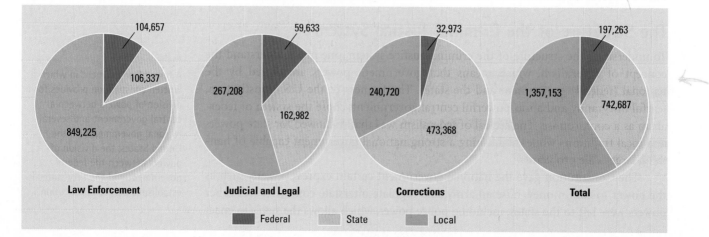

| Law Enforcement | Judicial and Legal | Corrections | Total |

104,657 / 106,337 / 849,225 — Law Enforcement

59,633 / 267,208 / 162,982 — Judicial and Legal

32,973 / 240,720 / 473,368 — Corrections

197,263 / 1,357,153 / 742,687 — Total

Federal   State   Local

Louisiana State Police officers patrol the streets of New Orleans following the destruction caused by Hurricane Katrina in late August 2005. State-level law enforcement agencies are often among the first responders to natural disasters and other emergencies. What are some of the other common duties of state law enforcement agencies?

the federal government's participation in the criminal justice system. Federal agencies with police powers include the Federal Bureau of Investigation (FBI), the Drug Enforcement Administration (DEA), the U.S. Secret Service, and the Bureau of Alcohol, Tobacco, Firearms and Explosives (ATF). In fact, almost every federal agency, including the postal and forest services, has some kind of police power. On November 25, 2002, President George W. Bush created the Department of Homeland Security, which combines the police powers of twenty-two federal agencies in order to protect the United States from terrorist attacks. The crucial law enforcement role of this new department will be examined in detail in Chapters 5 and 17.

The Courts The United States has a *dual court system;* that is, we have two independent judicial systems, one on the federal level and one on the state level. In practice, this translates into fifty-two different court systems: one federal court system and fifty different state court systems, plus the District of Columbia system. The federal system consists of district courts, circuit courts of appeals, and the United States Supreme Court. The state systems include trial courts at the local and state levels, intermediate courts of appeals, and state supreme courts.

The *criminal court* and its work group—the judge, prosecutors, and defense attorneys—are charged with the weighty responsibility of determining the innocence or guilt of criminal suspects. We will cover these important participants, their roles in the criminal trial, and the court system as a whole in Chapters 8, 9, 10, and 11.

Corrections Once the court system convicts and sentences an offender, she or he is delegated to the corrections system. Depending on the seriousness of the crime and their individual needs, offenders are placed on probation, incarcerated, or transferred to community-based corrections facilities.

- *Probation,* the most common correctional treatment, allows the offender to return to the community and remain under the supervision of an agent of the court known as a probation officer. While on probation, the offender must follow certain rules of conduct. If probationers fail to follow these rules, they may be incarcerated.

- If the offender's sentence includes a period of incarceration, he or she will be remanded to a corrections facility for a certain amount of time. *Jails* hold those convicted of minor crimes with relatively short sentences, as well as

Patrick Connolly
Supervisory Special Agent, FBI
Coordinator, Joint Terrorism Task Force

In the course of my twenty-three years with the Federal Bureau of Investigation, I've held many jobs with many titles, with my most recent being Supervisory Special Agent and Coordinator for the Joint Terrorism Task Force. The FBI clearly has an important mission to prevent another attack like that of September 11, 2001, which is why the antiterrorism function of the Bureau is so important. However, the FBI is not alone in this mission. In fact, the Joint Terrorism Task Force includes representatives from more than thirty agencies—including federal, state, and local intelligence and law enforcement agencies.

The training of the FBI members selected for the task force is not different from the standard training. The Special Agents go through fifteen to sixteen weeks of training at the FBI Academy at the U.S. Marine Corps base at Quantico, Virginia. I went through the Academy early in my career but now the training has been refocused to increase the emphasis on international terrorism. There is also a great deal of emphasis on providing timely and relevant training on current terrorism issues to all members of the task force.

In my work with the Bureau, I've been responsible for investigations in every area of FBI jurisdiction—including terrorism, organized crime, drugs/alien smuggling, violent crime, white-collar crime, and civil rights. Most of these investigations were long term and targeted criminal enterprises. We used sophisticated investigative techniques, such as wiretaps and undercover operations. In addition, I've served as a hostage negotiator, police instructor, legal adviser, and crisis management coordinator.

I also oversaw our FBI Detainee operation at the military prison at the U.S. Naval Base at Guantánamo Bay, Cuba. There, hundreds of individuals who had been involved with the Taliban and the war in Afghanistan were detained for questioning. Working at Guantánamo made it especially clear to me how important the FBI's role was in preventing attacks in the United States, although there has since been controversy over the appropriateness of detaining so many for so long. A key challenge in the area of antiterrorism is to balance individual liberties with national security. This is always a fine line but I feel that the FBI in general and the Joint Terrorism Task Force in particular have been very successful at achieving that balance.

My background includes a law degree (J.D.) and experience working as a prosecutor in Howard County, Maryland. Before that, I had spent about seven years in other jobs and two years in the Army. All of these experiences helped me in making the career switch from attorney to FBI Special Agent.

What is the hardest part about my job? Paperwork can be a challenge since everything has to be so carefully documented. You may eventually have to turn over records for legal proceedings. Also, all FBI employees are subject to a high level of scrutiny by FBI management, the judiciary, the media, and Congress.

Courtesy of Patrick Connolly

Patrick Connolly

What advice would I give a job seeker looking for a position in the FBI? Get a college degree in any subject that interests you because the FBI is looking for individuals with expertise in a wide range of areas. For example, if you're interested in fields that range from criminal justice, to biology, to psychology, to business administration, there are relevant jobs in the FBI. Also, if you're especially interested in terrorism, you can access much unclassified information to educate yourself. For example, just exploring the Web will yield much information about terrorist groups, ideologies, and tactics. Of course, it's necessary to evaluate this material carefully, and to use a variety of resources.

Most positions in the FBI now require at least a bachelor's degree and three years of full-time related experience. However, given the number of applicants for each position, you would have a better chance with a master's degree. You must also have the highest ethics, not only because that's a core value, but you may end up testifying under oath at a trial.

Overall, I have found the job very fulfilling. Every day is different and the FBI is involved in important matters ranging from informing policy on a national level to vindicating victims. I retired very recently from the FBI and now teach administration of justice at MiraCosta College in Oceanside, California.

Go to the Careers in Criminal Justice Interactive CD *for a video of Patrick Connolly discussing his career and more profiles in the field of criminal justice. Also check the list at the end of the table of contents for career profiles in the book.*

those awaiting trial or involved in certain court proceedings. *Prisons* house those convicted of more serious crimes with longer sentences. Generally speaking, counties and municipalities administer jails, while prisons are the domain of federal and state governments.

- *Community-based corrections* have increased in popularity, as jails and prisons have been plagued with problems of overcrowding. Community-based correctional facilities include halfway houses, residential centers, and work-release centers; they operate on the assumption that all convicts do not need, and are not benefited by, incarceration in jail or prison.

The majority of those inmates released from incarceration are not finished with the correctional system. The most frequent type of release from a jail or prison is *parole,* in which an inmate, after serving part of his or her sentence in a correctional facility, is allowed to serve the rest of the term in the community. Like someone on probation, a parolee must conform to certain conditions of freedom, with the same consequences if these conditions are not followed. Issues of probation, incarceration, community-based corrections, and parole will be covered in Chapters 12, 13, and 14.

The Criminal Justice Process

In its 1967 report, the President's Commission on Law Enforcement and Administration of Justice asserted that the criminal justice system

> is not a hodgepodge of random actions. It is rather a continuum—an orderly progression of events—some of which, like arrest and trial, are highly visible and some of which, though of great importance, occur out of public view.[17]

> "What is legal is not necessarily—not even usually—about what is right, just, or ethical. It is about order. Similarly, 'justice' is a process that makes things work, not necessarily a result that is good or moral or ethical."
>
> —Charles R. Gregg, President, Houston Bar Association (1995)

The commission's assertion that the criminal justice system is a "continuum" is one that many observers would challenge.[18] Some liken the criminal justice system to a sports team, which is the sum of an indeterminable number of decisions, relationships, conflicts, and adjustments.[19] Such a volatile mix is not what we generally associate with a "system." For most, the word *system* indicates a certain degree of order and discipline. That we refer to our law enforcement agencies, courts, and correctional facilities as part of a "system" may reflect our hopes rather than reality.

Just as there is an idealized image of the criminal justice system as a smooth continuum, there also exists an idealized version of the *criminal justice process,* or the procedures through which the criminal justice system meets the expectations of society. Professor Herbert Packer, for example, compared the idealized criminal justice process to an assembly line,

> down which moves an endless stream of cases, never stopping, carrying the cases to workers who stand at fixed stations and who perform on each case as it comes by the same small but essential operation that brings it one stop closer to being a finished product, or, to exchange the metaphor for the reality, a closed file.[20]

As Packer himself was wont to point out, the daily operations of criminal justice are not nearly so perfect. In this textbook, the criminal justice process will be examined as the end product of literally thousands of decisions made by the police, courtroom workers, and correctional administrators. It should become clear that, in fact, the criminal justice process functions as a continuous balancing act between its formal and informal nature, both of which are discussed in the following subsections.

The Formal Criminal Justice Process
In Packer's image of assembly-line justice, each step of the process "involves a series of routinized operations whose success is gauged primarily by their tendency to pass the case along to a successful conclusion."[21] These "routinized" steps are detailed in the foldout exhibit in this chapter.

The Informal Criminal Justice Process Each step described in the foldout exhibit is the result of a series of decisions that must be made by those who work in the criminal justice system. This **discretion**—which can be defined as the authority to choose between and among alternative courses of action—leads to the development of the informal criminal justice process, discussed below.

Discretionary Basics One New York City public defender called his job "a pressure cooker." That description could apply to the entire spectrum of the criminal justice process. Law enforcement agencies do not have the staff or funds to investigate *every* crime; they must decide where to direct their restricted resources. Increasing caseloads and a limited amount of time in which to dispose of them constrict many of our nation's courts. Overcrowding in prisons and jails affects both law enforcement agencies and the courts—there is simply not enough room for all convicts.

The criminal justice system uses discretion to alleviate these pressures. Police decide whether to arrest a suspect; prosecutors decide whether to prosecute; magistrates decide whether there is sufficient probable cause for a case to go to a jury; judges decide on sentencing; and so on. (See Figure 1.4 for a rundown of some of the most important discretionary decisions.) Collectively, these decisions are said to produce an *informal criminal justice system* because discretion is informally exercised by the individual and is not enclosed by the rigid confines of the law. Even if prosecutors believe that a suspect is guilty, they may decide not to prosecute if the case is weak or if they know that the police erred in the investigative process. In most instances, prosecutors will not squander the scarce resource of court time on a case they might not win. Some argue that the informal process has made our criminal justice system more just. Given the immense pressure of limited resources, the argument goes, only rarely will an innocent person end up before a judge and jury.[22]

Of course, not all discretionary decisions are dictated by the scarcity of resources. Sometimes, discretion is based on political considerations, such as when a police administrator orders a crackdown on public order crimes because of citizen complaints. Furthermore, employees of the criminal justice system may make decisions based on their personal values or morality, which, depending on what those personal and moral values are, may make the system less just in the eyes of some observers. For that reason, discretion is closely connected to questions of *ethics* in criminal justice and will be discussed in that context throughout this textbook.

The "Wedding Cake" Model of Criminal Justice Some believe that the prevailing informal approach to criminal justice creates a situation in which all cases are not treated equally. They point to the highly publicized O. J. Simpson trial of 1994, during which the defendant was treated differently than most double-murder suspects. To describe this effect, criminal justice researchers Lawrence M. Friedman and Robert V. Percival came up with a **"wedding cake" model** of criminal justice.[23] This model posits that discretion comes to bear depending on the relative importance of a particular case to the decision makers. Like any wedding cake, Friedman and Percival's model has the smallest layer at the top and the largest at the bottom (see Figure 1.5).

Discretion

The ability of individuals in the criminal justice system to make operational decisions based on personal judgment instead of formal rules or official information.

"Wedding Cake" Model

A wedding cake–shaped model that explains why different cases receive different treatment in the criminal justice system. The cases at the "top" of the cake receive the most attention and have the greatest effect on public perception of criminal justice, while those cases at the "bottom" are disposed of quickly and virtually ignored by the media.

FIGURE 1.4

Discretion in the Criminal Justice System

Criminal justice officials must make decisions every day concerning their duties. The officials listed below must decide whether to make the following decisions, or how to make them.

Police	• Enforce laws • Investigate specific crimes • Search people or buildings • Arrest or detain people
Prosecutors	• File charges against suspects brought to them by the police • Drop cases • Reduce charges
Judges	• Set conditions for pretrial release • Accept pleas • Dismiss charges • Impose sentences
Correctional Officials	• Assign convicts to prison or jail • Punish prisoners who misbehave • Reward prisoners who behave well

Source: U.S. Department of Justice, Bureau of Justice Statistics, *Report to the Nation on Crime and Justice*, 2d ed. (Washington, D.C.: Government Printing Office, 1988), 59.

Gordon Randall Steidl is pictured with his wife, Patty, left, and his mother, Barbara, as he walks out of the Danville Correction Center in 2004 after spending seventeen years behind bars for a crime he apparently did not commit. Since Steidl's 1987 conviction for the stabbing deaths of newlyweds Dyke and Karen Rhoads, an important witness who said she saw Steidl kill the couple recanted, and Illinois law enforcement officials admitted that police made numerous errors while investigating the crime. How can criminal justice procedure be seen as a system of "checks and balances" in which discretionary errors are eventually corrected?

1 The "top" layer consists of a handful of "celebrity" cases that attract the most attention and publicity. Recent examples of top level cases include the trials of Scott Peterson, discussed in the chapter opening; musician Michael Jackson, accused of child molestation; and Dennis Rader, the BTK serial killer.

2 The second layer consists of "high-profile" felonies. A **felony** is a serious crime such as murder, rape, or burglary that in most states is punishable either by death or by incarceration for a period longer than one year. This layer includes crimes committed by persons with criminal records, crimes in which the victim was seriously injured, and crimes in which a weapon was used, as well as crimes in which the offender and victim were strangers. These types of felonies are considered "high profile" because they usually draw a certain amount of public attention, which places pressure on the prosecutors to bring the case to trial instead of accepting a guilty plea for a lesser sentence.

3 The third layer consists of "ordinary" felonies, which include less violent crimes such as burglaries and thefts or even robberies in which no weapon was used. Because of the low profile of the accused—usually a first-time offender who has had a prior relationship with his or her victim—these "ordinary" felonies often do not receive the full formal process of a trial.

4 Finally, the fourth layer consists of **misdemeanors,** or crimes less serious than felonies. Misdemeanors include petty offenses such as shoplifting, disturbing the peace, and violations of local ordinances; they are usually punishable by fines, probation, or short jail times. More than three-quarters of all arrests made by police are for misdemeanors.

The irony of the wedding cake model is that the cases on the top level come closest to meeting our standards of ideal criminal justice. In these celebrity trials, we

Felony
A serious crime punishable by death or by imprisonment in a federal or state corrections facility for more than a year.

Misdemeanor
Any crime that is not a felony; punishable by a fine or by confinement for up to a year.

I. The celebrated cases

II. Serious or "high-profile" felonies

III. Less serious or "ordinary" felonies

IV. Misdemeanors

FIGURE 1.5
The Wedding Cake Model

get to see committed (and expensive) attorneys argue minute technicalities of the law, sometimes for days on end. The further one moves down the layers of the cake, the more informal the process becomes. Though many of the cases in the second layer are brought to trial, only rarely does this occur for the less serious felonies in the third level of the wedding cake. By the fourth level, cases are dealt with almost completely informally, and the end goal appears to be speed rather than what can be called "justice."

Public fascination with celebrity cases obscures a truth of the informal criminal justice process: trial by jury is relatively rare (only about 3 percent of those arrested for felonies go to trial), and most cases are disposed of with an eye more toward convenience than ideals of justice or fairness. Consequently, the summary of the criminal justice system provided by the wedding cake model is much more realistic than the impression many Americans have obtained from the media.

VALUES OF THE CRIMINAL JUSTICE SYSTEM

If the general conclusion of the wedding cake model—that some defendants are treated differently than others—bothers you, then you probably question the values of the system. Just as individuals have values—a belief structure governing individual conduct—our criminal justice system can be said to have values, too. These values form the foundation for Herbert Packer's two models of the criminal justice system.

Crime Control and Due Process: To Punish or Protect?

In his landmark book, *The Limits of the Criminal Sanction*, Packer introduced two models for the American criminal justice system: the crime control model and the due process model.[24] The underlying value of the crime control model is that the most important function of the criminal justice process is to punish and repress criminal conduct. Though not in direct conflict with crime control, the underlying values of the due process model focus more on protecting the rights of the accused through legal constraints on police, courts, and corrections.

The Crime Control Model   Under the **crime control model,** law enforcement must be counted on to control criminal activity. "Controlling" criminal activity is at best difficult, and probably impossible. For the crime control model to operate successfully, Packer writes, it

> must produce a high rate of apprehension and conviction, and must do so in a context where the magnitudes being dealt with are very large and the resources for dealing with them are very limited.[25]

In other words, the system must be quick and efficient. In the ideal crime control model, any suspect who most likely did not commit a crime is quickly jettisoned from the system, while those who are transferred to the trial process are convicted as quickly as possible. It was in this context that Packer referred to the criminal justice process as an assembly line.

The crime control model also assumes that the police are in a better position than the courts to determine the guilt of arrested suspects. Therefore, not only should judges operate on a "presumption of guilt" (that is, any suspect brought before the

Crime Control Model
A criminal justice model that places primary emphasis on the right of society to be protected from crime and violent criminals. Crime control values emphasize speed and efficiency in the criminal justice process; the benefits of lower crime rates outweigh any possible costs to individual rights.

court is more likely guilty than not), but as few restrictions as possible should be placed on police investigative and fact-gathering activities. The crime control model relies on the informality in the criminal justice system, as discussed earlier.

The Due Process Model Packer likened the **due process model** to an obstacle course instead of an assembly line. Rather than expediting cases through the system, as is preferable in the crime control model, the due process model strives to make it more difficult to prove guilt. It rests on the belief that it is more desirable for society that ninety-nine guilty suspects go free than that a single innocent person be condemned.[26]

The due process model is based on the assumption that the absolute efficiency that is the goal of the crime control model can be realized only if the power of the state is absolute. Because fairness, and not efficiency, is the ultimate goal of the due process model, it rejects the idea of a criminal justice system with unlimited powers. As a practical matter, the model also argues that human error in any process is inevitable; therefore, the criminal justice system should recognize its own fallibility and take all measures necessary to ensure that this fallibility does not impinge on the rights of citizens.

Finally, whereas the crime control model relies heavily on the police, the due process model relies just as heavily on the courts and their role in upholding the legal procedures of establishing guilt. The due process model is willing to accept that a person who is factually guilty will go free if the criminal justice system does not follow legally prescribed procedures in proving her or his culpability.[27] Therefore, the due process model relies on formality in the criminal justice system. *Mastering Concepts* on the following page compares and contrasts the two models.

Due Process Model
A criminal justice model that places primacy on the right of the individual to be protected from the power of the government. Due process values hold that the state must prove a person's guilt within the confines of a process designed to safeguard personal liberties as enumerated in the Bill of Rights.

Which Model Prevails Today?

Though both the crime control and the due process models have always been present to a certain degree, during different time periods one has taken precedence over the other. The twentieth century saw an ebb and flow between them. The influx of immigrants and problems of urbanization in the early 1900s caused somewhat of a panic within the American upper class. Considering that most, if not all, politicians and legal theorists were members of this class, it not surprising that crime control principles prevailed during the first half of the last century.

The Pendulum Swings As the nation became more secure and prosperous in the 1950s and 1960s, a "due process revolution" took place. Under the leadership of Chief Justice Earl Warren, the United States Supreme Court significantly expanded the rights of the accused. Following a series of landmark cases that will be referred to throughout this textbook (some of which are featured in the timeline on the back of the foldout exhibit at the end of this chapter), suspected offenders were guaranteed, among other things, that an attorney would be provided to them by the state if they could not afford one[28] and that they would be notified of their right to remain silent and retain counsel on being arrested.[29] The 1960s also saw severe limits placed on the power of the police, as the Court required law enforcement officers to strictly follow specific guidelines on gathering evidence or risk having that evidence invalidated.[30]

Rising crime rates in the late 1970s and early 1980s led to increased pressure on politicians and judges to get "tough on crime." This certainly slowed down the due process revolution and perhaps returned the principles of the crime control model to our criminal justice system. In 1984, for example, three Supreme Court cases restored to police some of the freedoms they had enjoyed in the first half of the century. Even if evidence was obtained illegally, the Court ruled, it could be admitted at trial if the police officers could prove they would have obtained the evidence legally anyway.[31]

MASTERING CONCEPTS

Crime Control Model versus Due Process Model

Crime Control Model	Due Process Model
Goals of the Criminal Justice System	**Goals of the Criminal Justice System**
• Deter crime. • Protect citizens from crime. • Incapacitate criminals. • Provide quick and efficient justice.	• Protect the individual against the immense power of the state. • Rehabilitate those convicted of crimes.
Goals Can Best Be Met by:	**Goals Can Best Be Met by:**
• Promoting discretion and limiting bureaucratic red tape in criminal justice institutions. • Making it easier for police to arrest criminals. • Reducing legal restrictions on proving guilt in a criminal trial.	• Limiting state power by assuring the constitutional rights of the accused. • Providing even guilty offenders with full protection of the law, and allowing those offenders to go free if due process procedures are not followed. • Assuring that all accused criminals receive the same treatment from the law, regardless of class, race, gender, or sexual orientation. • Protecting the civil rights of prisoners.
Favored Policies	**Favored Policies**
• More police. • More jails and prisons. • Harsher penalties (including increased use of the death penalty) and longer sentences.	• Open the criminal justice process to scrutiny by the media and public. • Abolish the death penalty. • Limit police powers to arbitrarily search, interrogate, and seize criminal suspects. • Limit discretion and formalize criminal justice procedures so that all suspects and convicted offenders receive the same treatment. • Increase funding for rehabilitation and education programs in jails and prisons.
View of Criminality	**View of Criminality**
• Wrongdoers are responsible for their own actions. • Wrongdoers have violated the social contract and can therefore be deprived of many of the rights afforded to law-abiding citizens.	• Criminal behavior can be attributed to social and biological factors. • Criminals can be rehabilitated and returned to the community.
Case in Point	**Case in Point**
• *Ohio v. Robinette* (519 U.S. 33 [1996]), which allows police greater freedom to search the automobile of a driver stopped for speeding.	• *Mapp v. Ohio* (367 U.S. 643 [1961]), which invalidates evidence improperly gathered by the police, even if the evidence proves the suspect's guilt.

Furthermore, the Court created the "good faith" exception to evidence-gathering rules, which basically allowed illegally obtained evidence to be admitted if the police officers were unaware that they were acting unconstitutionally.[32] According to many criminal law experts, this trio of cases resulted in the values of crime control gaining undue leverage.[33] (The role of the Bill of Rights in determining police power will be covered in Chapter 7.)

Responding to Terrorism The values of the criminal justice system are reflected not only in court decisions, but also in public policy. On September 11, 2001, terrorists hijacked four commercial airliners and used the planes to kill 3,021 people in New York City, northern Virginia, and rural Pennsylvania. Broadly defined as the random use of staged violence to achieve political goals, **terrorism** suddenly became a crucial issue in criminal justice, as

Terrorism
The use or threat of violence to achieve political objectives.

will be evident throughout this textbook. Six weeks after the attacks, President George W. Bush signed the USA PATRIOT Act into law.[34] In an effort to prevent future strikes, the law strengthened the ability of federal law enforcement agencies to investigate and incarcerate suspects; thus, it represented a dramatic shift toward the crime control model (see Figure 1.6). The USA PATRIOT Act has been strongly criticized as going "too far" and endangering the due process rights of many Americans. If these measures do indeed represent the will of the public, as expressed by its elected officials, crime control values will continue to dominate the criminal justice system in the immediate future.

See **Foundations of Inquiry: Terrorism** for information concerning federal, state, local, and international efforts to combat terrorism. Find this Web site by clicking on *Web Links* under *Chapter Resources* at **www.cjinaction.com**.

ISSUES IN CRIMINAL JUSTICE TODAY

"Crime can't be solved; it can only be controlled," noted James Alan Fox, professor of criminal justice at Northeastern University in Boston.[35] Professor Fox was striking a cautionary note in response to news that the nation's crime rate dropped again in 2004, continuing a trend that has persisted for almost fifteen years. As we shall learn in Chapter 2, experts who study crime rates, known as criminologists, have a number of theories as to why these rates rise and fall. For example, many criminologists feel that a drop in crime behavior is inevitable as the "baby boomers"—the large number of people born between 1946 and 1964—grow older and therefore become less likely to commit crimes.[36] Law enforcement agents have their own ideas on the subject, of course. A spokesperson for the Chicago Police Department attributed a decrease in the city's murder rate to police strategies that target "gangs, drugs, and guns."[37]

Indeed, where crime figures are not so rosy, the explanation can often be found in gangs, drugs, and guns. In 2004, the homicide rate in Washington, D.C., was at its lowest level in two decades, yet the number of victims under age eighteen doubled from 2003.[38] Nationwide, about 16 percent of all persons arrested for violent crimes each year are juveniles, making them the age group most likely to be involved in such crimes.[39] While most other indicators of crime dropped dramatically between 1993 and 2004, the number of drug abuse violations increased 21.7 percent.[40] Finally, the number of firearm homicides in the United States rose 8 percent from 2000 to 2004.[41] Many criminal justice experts blame these grim statistics on the proliferation of gangs in the United States and neighboring countries, a topic that will be covered in the *Criminal Justice in Action* feature at the end of this chapter.

FIGURE 1.6

Key Provisions of the USA PATRIOT Act

The 342-page USA PATRIOT Act of 2001 is designed to strengthen the hand of law enforcement in its efforts to deter terrorism on American soil. Some of the law's most important provisions are listed below.

- Creates a new crime of "domestic terrorism," defined as acts that "appear to be intended . . . to influence the policy of a government by intimidation or coercion."
- Expands the definition of "engage in terrorist activity" to include not only the use of weapons but also the provision of material support by such activities as fund-raising for suspected terrorist organizations.
- Allows for easier detention and removal of noncitizens suspected of terrorist activities.
- Gives law enforcement agents greater ability to use surveillance and wiretap methods, conduct searches, track Internet use, and access private records when investigating terrorist activity.
- Reduces the amount of suspicion law enforcement agents need before apprehending a terrorist suspect.

Source: USA PATRIOT Act of 2001.

Fear of Crime

Despite the "gangs, drugs, and guns" situation, crime statistics, which will be the focus of Chapter 3, show that the United States is a safer place for most citizens than it has been in decades. This does not mean, however, that most Americans feel safe. Indeed, fear of crime often operates independently of crime data. From 1993 to 1998, for example, the national crime rate dropped nearly 20 percent to the lowest level since the 1970s, yet nearly half of those polled by Gallup in 1998 said they felt more threatened by crime than they were five years earlier.[42] In a 2004 survey by the organization, 94 percent of the respondents labeled crime as a "serious" problem in the United States.[43]

> "The fear of burglars is not only the fear of being robbed, but also the fear of a sudden and unexpected clutch out of the darkness."
>
> —Elias Canetti, Austrian novelist (1962)

Media and Fear In fact, the odds of dying in a criminal attack are about the same as the odds of dying from an accidental fall.[44] Most people, however, have a greater fear of walking down a dark alleyway than climbing up a stepladder. When it comes to fear of crime, researchers have found that perceived vulnerability is more important than actual risk.[45] No single factor plays a greater role in this "perceived vulnerability" than the media.

More than half a century ago, when the modern media were in their infancy, researcher Edwin H. Sutherland noted the ability of mass communications to increase fear through the dissemination of publicity.[46] The propensity of the media—especially television—to condense any act into its most graphic aspects without providing any context has had a much-discussed effect on public perception. For example, polls show that most parents believe that random shootings are a serious threat to their children's safety at school, a perception only strengthened by incidents such as the 2005 slaying of ten people by a sixteen-year-old student at Red Lake High School in Minnesota. In fact, as we shall see in Chapter 15, the chances of a student being injured by gunfire at school are minuscule. A report by Building Blocks for Youth singles out intense media coverage of school shootings as having a particularly strong effect on perceptions of juvenile crime.[47]

Crime News The media can also distort reality by the subjects they choose to cover. Again according to Gallup, in the winter of 2005 the two most important crime issues for Americans were the sexual molestation of children and the illegal use or sale of methamphetamines, or "crystal meth."[48] Both subjects, which were of greater concern than violent crime or terrorism, had recently been the focus of intense media coverage. One survey of a hundred local news programs found that seventy-two began their broadcasts with a crime-related story and that one-third of all stories concerned crime or crime control.[49] Widespread coverage of violence on such local programs can have a particularly strong effect on fear of crime, as it gives viewers the impression that their communities are unsafe.[50]

Crime and Punishment

Citizen interest in crime does not just influence television ratings. It also galvanizes politicians, who understand that public perception of their effectiveness in "fighting" crime is often the key to success in elections. So, responding to the worries noted above, legislatures in almost half of the states have placed limits on over-the-counter sales of medicines containing pseudoephedrine—an ingredient in crystal meth—while in 2005 Florida lawmakers continued a national trend of imposing harsher punishments on sex offenders who prey on children.[51]

The Growing Prison Population The present criminal justice landscape has been greatly influenced by a number of "get tough on crime" laws passed by federal, state, and local politicians in response to the crime wave of the late 1980s and early 1990s. The result has been a rising number of inmates in U.S. prisons and jails, a trend that has continued even as crime rates have dropped over the last decade. As Figure 1.7 on the next page shows, the prisoner population in this country has steadily grown over the past two decades, reaching its latest peak of 2,267,787 in 2004.[52] Tough sentencing laws, which we will discuss in Chapter 11, are one explanation that has been offered for this increase. More stringent laws against illegal drugs—addressed in Chapter 16—have also had a large impact. In fact, drug offenders now represent more than half of all inmates in federal prisons.

The drugs laws have had particularly disastrous consequences for African Americans and women. Even though African Americans make up only 13 percent of the general population in the United States, the number of black men in state and federal prisons (842,500) is significantly larger than the number of white men (695,800).[53] According to the U.S. Department of Justice, 60 percent of those African Americans in federal prisons were locked up for drug offenses.[54] The incarceration rate of women, which is growing faster than that for men, is also fueled by drug abuse. Sixty-five percent of white women and 63 percent of African American women behind bars were arrested on drug charges.[55] The question of whether these figures reflect purposeful bias on the part of certain members of the criminal justice community will be addressed at various points in this textbook.

Traffic runs smoothly southbound on the 110 Freeway toward downtown Los Angeles, an area that was terrorized by a series of highway shootings that left four motorists dead during the spring of 2005. Although police believed the violence to be random, news reports that the shootings were part of a gang initiation rite set many drivers on edge. What effect can the media have on public fear of crime in this type of situation?

Diversion and Execution During the 1990s, states and the federal government were willing to spend seemingly limitless amounts to house the steady flow of inmates. The bleaker economic climate of the early 2000s, however, has had a dampening effect on the prison boom. As a result, a number of states have decided to grant early release to prisoners, not because of a change in the political climate, but because their budgets cannot accommodate "tough on crime" public policies. State officials are also trying to divert offenders from correctional facilities through special courts that promote rehabilitation rather than punishment for drug offenses, domestic violence, and other specific crimes. We will examine these policies and their ramifications on the nation's prisons and jails in Chapters 13 and 14.

One area where the political climate does seem to be changing is capital punishment. Alone among Western nations, the United States continues to rely on the death penalty as punishment for the most heinous crimes. By October 2005, the states and the federal government had executed 384 convicts in the new century. In two recent cases, however, the United States Supreme Court abolished the death penalty for mentally ill[56] and juvenile offenders.[57] Due in part to these decisions, the number of people sentenced to death in 2004 fell to the lowest level in nearly thirty years, a situation we will explore in Chapter 11.

New Directions in Law Enforcement

Another reason that so many offenders are finding themselves locked away may be the performance of law enforcement. The crime wave of the late 1980s and early 1990s forced police departments to be more creative, resulting in a crackdown on "quality of

FIGURE 1.7

Prison and Jail Populations in the United States, 1985–2004

Sources: Bureau of Justice Statistics, *Correctional Populations in the United States, 1995* (Washington, D.C.: U.S. Department of Justice, June 1997), Table 1.1, page 12; and Bureau of Justice Statistics, *Prisoners in 2004* (Washington, D.C.: U.S. Department of Justice, October 2005), 2.

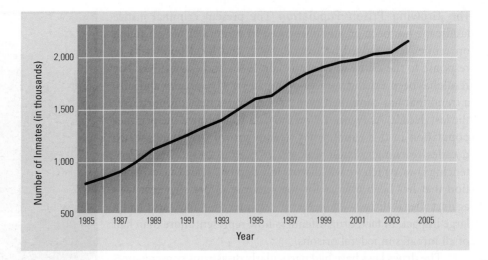

life" crimes and a recommitment to a strategy known as "community policing." In Chapter 6, we will see how these efforts are credited for the dramatic downturn in crime over the past decade.

Changing Tactics The events of September 11, 2001, to a certain extent, also served as a "wake-up call" for those agencies and individuals whose duty is to thwart future attacks while at the same time fighting conventional crime. Law enforcement agencies are searching for new strategies to help them become more efficient at fighting domestic and international crime. Increasingly, officials are turning to the following three approaches to achieve that goal:

- *Cooperation.* One of the greatest hindrances to effective crime fighting has been the unwillingness of federal, state, and local law enforcement agencies to cooperate with each other. In the past several years, however, federal agencies such as the FBI and the Central Intelligence Agency (CIA) have begun sharing information to a much greater extent, and "antiterrorist task forces" combining federal, state, and local police agents have become common. Databases have allowed agencies to share important information with each other as well.

- *Globalization.* With American security being threatened by persons and groups that operate outside our borders, law enforcement agencies have been forced to broaden the scope of their operations. The FBI has engaged in numerous searches for terrorist suspects in countries such as Pakistan and Afghanistan, while New York City police officers have been assigned to the Middle East to protect New York from future attacks.

- *Militarization.* For most of this nation's history, the idea of the U.S. military becoming involved in crime prevention has been rejected as improper, dangerous, and even unconstitutional. Now, however, the "war" against terrorism has led to a reconsideration of this stance, though many observers are still uneasy with the prospect of a military police force.

DNA Profiling Police investigators are also enjoying the benefits of perhaps the most effective new crime-fighting tool since fingerprint identification became available a century ago: DNA profiling. This technology allows law enforcement agents to identify a suspect from body fluid evidence, such as blood, saliva, or semen, or biological evidence, such as hair strands or fingernail clippings. By collecting DNA from persons convicted of certain felonies and storing that information in databases, investigators have been able to reach across hundreds of miles and back through time to catch wrongdoers. In 2005, for example, New York law enforcement agents ran a DNA check on a pair of underpants that were the only evidence remaining from a thirty-two-year-old unsolved sexual assault. Not only did they find a match, but they were also able to identify the suspect as the same person wanted in at least twenty-four other rapes in New York, New Jersey, and Maryland.[58]

For many observers, however, DNA profiling raises troubling privacy issues. How far are we as a society willing to go, they ask, in allowing the government to collect personal information for crime control purposes? In 2005, law enforcement agents asked every male citizen of the small beach community of Truro, Massachusetts, to provide a DNA sample to aid in the (ultimately successful) investigation of a three-year-old murder.[59] That same year, the federal government announced plans to create a high-tech ID card that would be issued to Americans as their current driver's licenses expire. The card would included a chip containing information verifying a person's identity and would be required for those who want to use airplanes, trains, courthouses, parks, monuments, and other areas under government control. (To learn more about identification methods and crime control, see the feature *CJ and Technology—Biometrics* on the following page.)

Technology: Fighting and Fueling Crime

Finally, as technology has become more advanced, high-tech crime has become big business. According to the annual Computer Crime and Security Survey, more than half of the large corporations and governmental organizations polled reported that the security of their computer systems had been breached within the past year, causing financial losses of more than $141 million.[60] The Internet has become a veritable web of criminal activity, as users have learned to take advantage of the anonymity and access it provides as cover for illegal drug and weapon sales, terrorist activity, gambling, and child pornography. *Identity theft*, in which an imposter steals personal information such as a Social Security number or a credit-card number and uses that information for personal monetary gain, is perhaps the fastest-growing crime in the United States. The Federal Trade Commission estimates that 10 million Americans are victims of identity theft each year, with losses approaching $50 billion.[61]

The moment of impact as United Airlines Flight 175 crashes into the World Trade Center south tower at 9:03 on the morning of September 11, 2001. To the left, the World Trade Center north tower burns after being hit by American Airlines Flight 11 approximately fifteen minutes earlier. This attack, along with a simultaneous one on the Pentagon in Washington, D.C., cost more than three thousand lives and brought the horrors of terrorism into the lives of all Americans. What freedoms do you think the nation would be willing to give up to prevent such attacks in the future?

AP Photo/Carmen Taylor

Biometrics

How much privacy are we willing to give up to be safer? How much safer will we be if we give up some of our privacy? In light of law enforcement efforts to combat terrorism, these questions have become much more important for Americans in recent years. The quandary is particularly pronounced when it comes to biometrics—the science of identifying a person through his or her unique physical characteristics. This technology may be our most effective way to control access to sensitive sites such as airports, power plants, and computer networks, but it also gives the government unprecedented ability to monitor the activities of all citizens.

The most common biometric is the human face. Computerized face-recognition systems use a camera to record from thirty to eighty "markers" on a subject's face, such as cheekbone formation, the width of the nose bridge, and the space between the eyes. Earlier biometric systems examined the hand—measuring shape, size, and other characteristics such as the design of veins on the palm—but today the technology is more likely to focus on a single finger and its print. Another popular method is eye scanning, in which the minute details of the retina or the iris provide a very reliable biometric.

IMPERFECTIONS IN THE SYSTEM

Under the US-VISIT program that started in 2004, all foreigners entering the United States on visas are subject to "multibiometric" face and hand scans. Within several years, all new passports issued to U.S. citizens will be embedded with a chip that contains biometric information. These systems will be used not to identify persons, but to verify their identities; that is, to verify that the traveler is who she or he claims to be and not a terrorist suspect. In the first year of US-VISIT, U.S. border agents arrested or denied entry to 372 people who had criminal records or had violated immigration laws. None of those apprehended were linked to terrorism, however, causing some to question whether the program is worth its $700 million price tag.

Another worry with biometrics is the error rate. Even if such systems are accurate 99.9 percent of the time, they will generate thousands of false alarms every day. Each such alarm will require a law enforcement response, including searches, questioning, and detention of the suspect. Thus, even a small number would severely tax security resources. In addition, there is no guarantee that biometrics will protect against a terrorist attack. All nineteen of the September 11, 2001, hijackers entered the country legally and therefore would not have been detained even if a perfect biometric system had been in place.

IN THE FUTURE

With biometrics, the question is not "if" but "when" the technology will become an accepted part of everyday life. At some point, for example, face-recognition systems will allow hidden cameras to verify the identities of thousands of people shopping in a mall or taking a stroll in a city park. Police officers will be able to take a photo of a suspect and instantaneously check the biometrics against a database of millions of people. Thus, two issues will dominate the future of the technology. First, how can we ensure that the government stays within the limits set by the U.S. Constitution in its biometric operations? Second, how can we limit criminal use of biometrics? While the theft of a credit card or photo ID can be a serious inconvenience, imagine the ramifications of someone stealing the electronic representation of a fingerprint or retina.

For more information on biometrics and other CJ technologies, click on Crime and Technology *under* Book Resources *at* **www.cjinaction.com**.

At the same time, however, technology offers law enforcement agents a wealth of crime-fighting devices to combat both high-tech and conventional crime. Almost every chapter of this textbook will contain some information on technology and the criminal justice system, and we will explore the subject in great depth in Chapter 17.

Coming to Grips with Gangs

Since the fall of 2001, the American criminal justice system has mobilized to protect the nation against terrorism. Federal, state, and local governments have shifted scarce resources to the terrorist beat, and homeland security has become the new watchword in law enforcement. Although nobody questions the need for aggressive antiterrorist action, some experts are expressing concern that more traditional criminals are taking advantage of the lack of attention. In particular, a wave of street gang violence is threatening to overwhelm local police departments in many communities. "Outside of New York, al Qaeda isn't killing people [in the United States]; gang violence is," points out William Bratton, chief of the Los Angeles Police Department.[62] In this *Criminal Justice in Action* feature, we will explore the causes and consequences of gang violence and see why many of those in law enforcement, including homeland security officials, see it as the "sleeping tiger" of crime.

Gang Violence in the United States

Like most other indicators of criminal activity, gang-related homicides decreased in the late 1990s. That trend has reversed itself in the 2000s, however: between 1999 and 2002, gang killings increased by more than 50 percent.[63] According to the U.S. Department of Justice, there are now 30,000 street gangs with more than 800,000 members in the United States.[64] (A *street gang* can be defined as any group of people who form an allegiance for a common purpose and engage in violent, unlawful, or criminal activity.) The Los Angeles metropolitan area alone is believed to house more than 700 different gangs with 110,000 members, a group responsible for about half of the city's homicides.[65]

Like other upsurges in violent gang activity over the past several decades, particularly in the late 1980s, the latest increase is closely related to the illegal drug trade and the use of firearms to protect that trade. The difference, according to some experts, is that more people are becoming involved in gangs for purely economic reasons, rather than for the cultural or territorial motives that have historically fueled gang membership.[66] (We will look at why people join gangs as part of the larger discussion of juvenile crime in Chapter 15.) One of every three gangs runs drug-dealing operations, and according to a spokesperson for the Chicago Police Department, the modern street gang is "much more violent than the Mafia ever was."[67] In addition, some researchers believe that major gangs have "weapons superiority" over most police forces, making it very difficult for law enforcement to control their illegal activities.[68]

Mara Salvatrucha

Although "Super Gangs" such as the Bloods, Crips, Latin Kings, and Gangster Disciples are still responsible for their share of gang-related criminal activity in the United States, a relative newcomer has gained the attention of the law enforcement community because of its rapid growth

A heavily tattooed former member of Mara Salvatrucha languishes in a high-security cell at the Penitenceria Nacional near Tegucigalpa, Honduras. Efforts by Central American law enforcement agencies to "crack down" on gang violence often drive Honduran, Salvadoran, and Guatemalan gang members to the United States.

AP Photo/Ginnette Riquelme

and brutality. The Mara Salvatrucha (MS-13), which translates to "Gang of Salvadoran Guys," has its roots in the civil wars of El Salvador in the 1980s. To escape the violence, thousands of immigrants fled to the United States, particularly to Los Angeles. Their children found themselves easy prey for the established local gangs and formed MS-13 as a protective measure. The gang soon became involved in crime rings of its own, and American authorities responded by deporting the members—and their violent gang culture—en masse back to Central America.

Between 70,000 and 100,000 gang members now operate in El Salvador, Honduras, Guatemala, and Mexico, where they have killed thousands of people over the past decade.[69] MS-13, in particular, has gained a reputation for attacking the wives and other female family members of rivals. In 2003, the El Salvadoran government responded with Article 332, which makes gang membership illegal.[70] Furthermore, as part of Operation *Super Mano Duro* ("Super Firm Hand"), Salvadoran police were given the freedom to arrest anyone they believed to be a gang member, often based on nothing more than a suspect's clothes or tattoos.

MS-13 reacted to Article 332 with shocking violence. On December 23, 2004, six gang members with assault rifles boarded a bus in the northern city of San Pedro Sula and killed twenty-eight passengers, including six children, to protest the crackdown. The law enforcement measures have been very popular with the populace, however, and gang activity dropped off significantly following their implementation. "Before Firm Hand, taxis wouldn't even drive here. It was too dangerous," said one resident of a high-crime neighborhood in Ilopango, El Salvador. "But now you don't even see the gangs."[71]

Coming "Home"

One reason that MS-13 is now less visible in El Salvador is that many members escaped that government's firm hand by returning to the gang's birthplace: the United States. Today, federal officials estimate that as many as 10,000 MS-13 members are scattered among thirty-three states. The gang's presence is driving up crime rates in cities such as Los Angeles and Chicago and introducing acts of violence into more suburban areas. In July 2003, for example, the body of Brenda "Smiley" Paz, a former MS-13 gang member turned FBI informant, was found in the Shenandoah Valley of Virginia. Paz had been stabbed repeatedly and nearly decapitated by a strong slash to the throat. Almost a year later, in the same area, three teenage MS-13 members slashed a sixteen-year-old rival gang member with machetes, severing four fingers on one hand and a thumb on the other.[72]

American law enforcement agencies cannot respond with an Operation *Super Mano Duro* of their own. Under most circumstances, the Fourth Amendment to the U.S. Constitution does not allow police officers to make arrests on the basis of a suspect's appearance alone. This does not mean, however, that officials are completely handcuffed when it comes to street gangs. In 2005, the FBI organized a nationwide task force to target MS-13, the first of its type to concentrate on a single gang. On March 15 of that year, in cooperation with local police departments, federal authorities arrested 103 "Salvatruchas," in the first of what promises to be many large-scale operations against the gang.[73]

Looking at the Law

As you will see throughout this textbook, direct law enforcement action is only one way to combat crime. Another way is to deter criminal behavior by enacting laws that raise the "cost" of committing a crime in the first place. Four states—California, Florida, Indiana, and Missouri—have recently passed legislation making those individuals involved in gang-related murders eligible for the death penalty.[74] In Chapter 11, we will discuss competing theories of whether harsh punishments, in general, and capital punishment, in particular, deter crime.

Jurisdictions can also pass legislation to control behavior that may not be criminal in itself but can lead to future crime. A number of communities have "antiloitering" laws that allow police to disperse groups of people on public sidewalks and arrest those who raise specific suspicions. The United States Supreme Court, however, struck down a Chicago ordinance that prohibited people from gathering in groups "with no apparent purpose" because it gave police officers too much freedom to decide whether a suspect's purpose was apparent or not.[75] Such laws are too similar in spirit to an operation like *Super Mano Duro*, a distinction we will discuss in much more detail in Chapter 7.

Finally, sometimes the criminal justice system turns to supplementary areas of the law for help. For example, many members of MS-13 and other predominantly Hispanic street gangs have violated U.S. immigration law by entering the country illegally. Thus, officials can use the "immigration hammer" to detain these suspects without proving that they have committed any crime. Then, instead of going through the costly and time-consuming process of a criminal trial (covered in Chapters 9, 10, and 11), authorities can simply return the gang members to their homelands. Of course, this policy has negative consequences for countries such as El Salvador, which once again must deal with an onslaught of hardened criminals. It may also have an impact on the fight against terrorism.

American and foreign officials fear that groups such as al Qaeda will seek out MS-13 and other gangs from Central America and Mexico. After all, many of the gangs' members have made successful clandestine crossings of the U.S. border and might be willing to help others do so for the right price.[76]

Making Sense of the Gang Problem

1 Do you think that police officers should have more authority to stop and even arrest someone that they think may be a gang member, even if there is no evidence that a specific crime has been committed? What are the pros and cons of giving American police the same power their El Salvadoran counterparts enjoyed under Operation *Super Mano Duro?*

2 Should the U.S. Congress pass a law making membership alone in street gangs illegal? What are some of the problems that this type of legislation might cause?

3 The governments of El Salvador, Guatemala, and Honduras would prefer that U.S. officials not deport dangerous gang members back to their countries. In general, how much should U.S. officials consider the consequences for other countries when making criminal justice decisions?

Chapter Summary

1 **Describe the two most common models of how society determines which acts are criminal.** The consensus model argues that the majority of citizens will agree on which activities should be outlawed and punished as crimes; it rests on the assumption that a diverse group of people can have similar morals. In contrast, the conflict model argues that in a diverse society, the dominant groups exercise power by codifying their value systems into criminal laws.

2 **Define crime and the different types of crime.** Crime is any action punishable under criminal statutes and is considered an offense against society. Therefore, alleged criminals are prosecuted by the state rather than by victims. Crimes are punishable by sanctions that bring about a loss of personal freedom or, in some cases, fines. There are six groups of crimes: (a) violent crimes—murder, rape, assault, battery, robbery; (b) property crimes—pocket picking, shoplifting, larceny/theft, burglary, and arson; (c) public order crimes—public drunkenness, prostitution, gambling, and illicit drug use; (d) white-collar crime—fraud and embezzlement; (e) organized crime—crime undertaken by a number of persons who operate their activities much as legal businesses do; and (f) high-tech crime—sabotage, fraud, embezzlement, and theft of proprietary data from computer systems as well as cyber crimes, such as selling child pornography over the Internet.

3 **Outline the three levels of law enforcement.** Because we have a federal system of government, law enforcement occurs at the (a) federal and the (b) state levels and within the states at (c) local levels. Because crime is mostly a local concern, most employees in the criminal justice system work for local governments. Agencies at the federal level include the FBI, the DEA, and the U.S. Secret Service, among others.

4 **List the essential elements of the corrections system.** Criminal offenders are placed on probation, incarcerated in a jail or prison, transferred to community-based corrections facilities, or released on parole.

5 **Explain the difference between the formal and informal criminal justice processes.** The formal criminal justice process involves procedures such as booking, setting bail, and the like. For every step in the formal process, though, someone has discretion, and such discretion leads to an informal process. Even when prosecutors believe that a suspect is guilty, they have the discretion not to prosecute, for example.

6 **Describe the layers of the "wedding cake" model.** The top layer consists of celebrity cases, which are most highly publicized; the second layer involves high-profile felonies, such as rape and murder; the third layer consists of property crimes such as larcenies and burglaries; the fourth layer consists of misdemeanors.

7 **Contrast the crime control and due process models.** The crime control model assumes that the criminal justice system is designed to protect the public from criminals; thus, its most important function is to punish and repress criminal conduct. The due process model presumes that the accused are innocent and provides them with the most complete safeguards, usually within the court system.

8 **List the major issues in criminal justice today.** (a) The proliferation of gangs, guns, and drugs; (b) fear of crime; (c) terrorism; (d) "tough on crime" politicians and legislation; (e) the ever-expanding prison population; (f) possible bias against minorities and women in the criminal justice system; (g) the death penalty; (h) new law enforcement tactics; and (i) the role of technology.

 STORIES FROM THE STREET

Go to the *Stories from the Street* feature at **www.cjinaction.com** to hear Larry Gaines tell insightful stories related to this chapter and his experiences in the field.

Key Terms

✗ conflict model   6
✗ consensus model   6
✗ crime control model   18
   deviance   7

   discretion   16
✗ due process model   19
✗ federalism   11
✗ felony   17

✗ misdemeanor   17
   organized crime   9
✗ property crime   8
✗ public order crime   8

   terrorism   20
✗ violent crime   8
   "wedding cake" model   16
   white-collar crime   8

Questions for Critical Analysis

1 How is it possible to have a consensus about what should or should not be illegal in a country with several hundred million adults from all races, religions, and walks of life?
2 Why are criminals prosecuted by the state, through its public officials, rather than by the victims themselves?
3 Why are public order crimes sometimes referred to as victimless crimes?
4 At what political level is most law enforcement carried out? Relate your answer to the concept of federalism.
5 Assume that all of the officials involved in the criminal justice process were deprived of most of the discretion they now have. What might some of the results be?

6 What effect do the media—particularly local news coverage—have on the public's perception of crime and fears concerning crime?
7 How can a weak economy influence the number of people kept in prisons and jails?
8 What is the name of the federal legislation passed in 2001 to aid the federal government's efforts to combat terrorism? What are some of the "tools" this law gives to law enforcement officers to aid their antiterrorism efforts?

Test Preparation Online

Criminal JusticeNow

Go to **www.cjinaction.com** and click on *Criminal JusticeNow* for access to this powerful online study tool. You will get a *personalized study plan* based on your responses to a diagnostic pretest. Once you have mastered the material with the help of interactive learning tools, video clips with questions, an integrated e-book, and more, you can take a posttest to confirm you are ready to move on to the next chapter.

Book Companion Web Site

At the book companion Web site (**www.cjinaction.com**), you will find many resources in addition to *Criminal JusticeNow* to aid you in studying for your exams. For example, under *Chapter Resources*, you will find the *Chapter Outline, Chapter Summary, Flashcards, Glossary, Learning Objectives, Lecture Presentations, Concept Builder, Essay Questions*, and a *Tutorial Chapter Quiz*. You can also test yourself with interactive *Online Reviews* of each chapter section. Check out the *Web Links* to access the Web sites mentioned in the text, as well as many others. You can also access recent perspectives by clicking on *CJ in the News* and *Terrorism Update* under *Course Resources*.

Suggested Readings

Hutton, Donald B., and Anna Mydlarz, *Guide to Homeland Security Careers*, Hauppage, NY: Barron's Educational Series, 2003. Since the September 11, 2001, terrorist attacks, the field of homeland security has become the fastest-growing area of the American criminal justice system. This book provides a wealth of practical information for those interested in making homeland security a profession. It describes career opportunities not only in law enforcement but also in biomedical technology, disaster assistance, cyber technology, and other areas. Hutton and Mydlarz include information on internships and student study programs, as well as dozens of addresses, phone numbers, and e-mail addresses that will help the reader obtain additional information about homeland security opportunities. The authors also give practical advice, such as how to organize an effective résumé and prepare for a job interview.

Penzler, Otto, and Thomas H. Cook, eds., *The Best American Crime Writing 2004*, New York: Vintage Books, USA, 2005. This annual collection provides twenty of the best stories the criminal justice world has to offer. The 2004 edition includes articles on the art of the police interrogation, a registered sex offender's perspective on sex offender notification laws, and a look inside the (somewhat stomach-turning) routine of a crime scene clean-up team. This year's collection also has a strong selection of international stories, involving subjects ranging from the disappearance of three hundred women in Juárez, Mexico, to law enforcement aspects of the Israeli-Palestinian conflict.

Notes

1. John Cheves, "Viable Fetus Is a Person, Court Says State Ruling Applies to Homicide Law," *Lexington Herald-Leader* (June 18, 2004), A1.
2. "Lawyers Challenge Child Abuse Conviction," *Columbia Slate* (July 29, 2004), B3.
3. Gene Warner, "Peterson Case Points Up Contentious Legal Issue Here," *Buffalo News* (May 4, 2003), B1.
4. N.Y [Penal] Sections 125.00, 125.05 (Consol. 2003).
5. *People v. Davis,* 872 P.2d 591 (Calif. 1994).
6. *Roe v. Wade,* 410 U.S. 113, 159 (1973).
7. Unborn Victims of Violence Act of 2004, Pub. L. No. 108-212.
8. Herman Bianchi, *Justice as Sanctuary: Toward a New System of Crime Control* (Bloomington: Indiana University Press, 1994), 72.
9. George B. Vold, *Theoretical Criminology* (New York: Oxford Press, 1994), 72.
10. United States Sentencing Commission, *Special Report to Congress: Cocaine and Federal Sentencing Policy* (Washington, D.C.: Government Printing Office, 1995), 184–187.
11. *2004 Report to the Nation: Occupational Fraud and Abuse* (Austin, TX: Association of Certified Fraud Examiners, 2004), 8.
12. U.S. Sentencing Commission, "Monitoring Data Files 1995–2002," at **http://www.ussc.gov/linktop.htm**.
13. Sarbanes-Oxley Act of 2002, Pub. L. No. 107-24, 116 Stat. 745 (2002).
14. Chicago Crime Commission, *The New Faces of Organized Crime* (Chicago: Chicago Crime Commission, 1997).
15. President's Commission on Law Enforcement and Administration of Justice, *The Challenge of Crime in a Free Society* (Washington, D.C.: Government Printing Office, 1967), 7.
16. John Rawls, *A Theory of Justice* (Cambridge, MA: Belknap Press of Harvard University Press, 1971), 60–61.
17. President's Commission on Law Enforcement and Administration of Justice, 7.
18. John Heinz and Peter Manikas, "Networks among Elites in a Local Criminal Justice System," *Law and Society Review* 26 (1992), 831–861.
19. James Q. Wilson, "What to Do about Crime: Blaming Crime on Root Causes," *Vital Speeches* (April 1, 1995), 373.
20. Herbert Packer, *The Limits of the Criminal Sanction* (Stanford, CA: Stanford University Press, 1968), 154–173.
21. *Ibid.*
22. Daniel Givelber, "Meaningless Acquittals, Meaningful Convictions: Do We Reliably Acquit the Innocent?" *Rutgers Law Review* 49 (Summer 1997), 1317.
23. Lawrence M. Friedman and Robert V. Percival, *The Roots of Justice* (Chapel Hill, NC: University of North Carolina Press, 1981).
24. Packer, 154–173.
25. *Ibid.*
26. Givelber, 1317.
27. Guy-Uriel E. Charles, "Fourth Amendment Accommodations: (Un) Compelling Public Needs, Balancing Acts, and the Fiction of Consent," *Michigan Journal of Race and Law* (Spring 1997), 461.
28. *Gideon v. Wainwright,* 372 U.S. 335 (1963). Many United States Supreme Court cases will be cited in this book, and it is important to understand these citations. *Gideon v. Wainwright* refers to the parties in the case that the Court is reviewing. "U.S." is the abbreviation for *United States Reports,* the official publication of United States Supreme Court decisions. "372" refers to the volume of the *United States Reports* where the case appears, and "335" refers to the page number. The citation ends with the year the case was decided in parentheses. Most, though not all, case citations in this book will follow this formula. For general information on how to read case citations and find court decisions, see the appendix at the end of this chapter.
29. *Miranda v. Arizona,* 384 U.S. 436 (1966).
30. *Mapp v. Ohio,* 367 U.S. 643 (1961).
31. *Nix v. Williams,* 467 U.S. 431 (1984).
32. *Massachusetts v. Sheppard,* 468 U.S. 981 (1984); and *United States v. Leon,* 468 U.S. 897 (1984).
33. James P. Fleissner, "Glide Path to an 'Inclusionary Rule,'" *Mercer Law Review* 48 (Spring 1997), 1023.
34. Uniting and Strengthening America by Providing Appropriate Tools Required to Intercept and Obstruct Terrorism (USA PATRIOT) Act of 2001, Pub. L. No. 107-56, 115 Stat. 272 (2001).
35. Associated Press Online, "Survey Shows Drop in Murders for 2004" (January 1, 2005).
36. Bernard Harcourt, "Reflecting on the Subject: A Critique of the Social Influence Conception of Deterrence, the Broken Windows Theory, and Order Maintenance Policing New York Style," *Michigan Law Review* (1998), 331–339.
37. Associated Press Online.
38. Kristen A. Lee, "As Juvenile Homicides Soar, Washington Starts a Plan," *New York Times* (April 2, 2005), A9.
39. Federal Bureau of Investigation, *Crime in the United States, 2004* (Washington, D.C.: U.S. Department of Justice, 2005), Table 38, page 290.
40. *Ibid.,* Table 32, page 284.
41. *Ibid.,* Figure 2.9, page 19.
42. Gallup/CNN/*USA Today* Poll, October 23–25, 1998.
43. See **http://www.gallup.com/poll/content/default.aspx?ci=16123**.
44. National Security Council, "What Are the Odds of Dying?" at **http://www.nsc.org/lrs/statinfo/odds.htm**.
45. Beverly L. Stiles, Shaheem Halim, and Howard B. Kaplan, "Fear of Crime among Individuals with Physical Limitations," *Criminal Justice Review* (Autumn 2003), 233–234.
46. Edwin H. Sutherland, "The Diffusion of Sexual Psychopath Laws," *American Journal of Sociology* 56 (1950), 142–148.
47. Lori Dorfman and Vincent Schiraldi, *Off Balance: Youth, Race, and Crime in the News* (Washington, D.C.: Justice Policy Institute, April 2001), 1.

48. See **http://www.gallup.com/poll/content/ default.aspx?ci=16123**.

49. Paul Klite, Robert A. Bardwell, and Jason Salzman, *Baaad News: Local TV News in America* (Denver, CO: Rocky Mountain Media Watch, 1997), 23.

50. Ted Chiricos, Kathy Padgett, and Marc Getz, "Fear, TV News, and the Reality of Crime," *Criminology* (May 2000), 755.

51. J. R. Gonzales, "S.C. Tries to Stem Spread of Meth," *Columbia Slate* (April 28, 2005), B1; and Matthew Waite, "Molesters Face More Time in Prison," *St. Petersburg Times* (April 26, 2005), 1B.

52. Bureau of Justice Statistics, *Prison and Jail Inmates at Midyear 2004* (Washington, D.C.: U.S. Department of Justice, April 2005), 2.

53. Bureau of Justice Statistics, *Prisoners in 2002* (Washington, D.C.: U.S. Department of Justice, July 2003), 11.

54. See **http://www.albany.edu/sourcebook/pdf/t653.pdf**.

55. *Ibid.*

56. *Atkins v. Virginia,* 536 U.S. 304 (2002).

57. *Roper v. Simmons,* 125 S.Ct. 1183 (2005).

58. Julia Preston, "After 32 Years, Clothing Yields a DNA Key to Dozens of Rapes," *New York Times* (April 27, 2005), A1.

59. Pam Belluck, "DNA Test Leads, At Last, to Arrest in Cape Cod Case," *New York Times* (April 16, 2005), A1.

60. Lawrence A. Gordon, Martin P. Loeb, William Lucyshyn, and Robert Richardson, *2004 CSI/FBI Computer and Security Survey* (San Francisco: Computer Security Institute, 2005), 8, 10.

61. Arthur Kane, "Facial Scanning Targets ID Theft," *Denver Post* (January 5, 2005), A1.

62. Chitra Ragavan and Monika Guttman, "Terror on the Streets," *U.S. News and World Report* (December 13, 2004), 22.

63. William Christeson and Sanford Newman, *Caught in the Crossfire: Arresting Gang Violence by Investing in Kids* (Washington, D.C.: Fight Crime: Invest in Kids, 2004), 5.

64. "The Growing Gang Problem," *Economist* (February 26, 2005), 80.

65. Ginger Thompson, "Shuttling between Nations, Latino Gangs Confound the Law," *New York Times* (September 26, 2004), 14.

66. H. Mitchell Caldwell and Daryl Fisher-Ogden, "Stalking the Jets and the Sharks: Exploring the Constitutionality of the Gang Death Penalty Enhancer," *George Mason Law Review* (Spring 2004), 601.

67. "The Growing Gang Problem."

68. Jeffrey Fagan, "Gangs, Drugs, and Neighborhood Change," in *Gangs in America,* 2d ed., ed. Ronald Huff (Thousand Oaks, CA: Sage Publications, 1996), 61.

69. Thompson, 1.

70. *Ibid.*

71. Chris Kraul, "El Salvador Comes to Grips with Gangs," *Los Angeles Times* (December 13, 2004), A1.

72. Ragavan and Guttman, 23.

73. Joe Mozingo, "Going after the Gangs," *Miami Herald* (April 12, 2005), A1.

74. Cal. Penal Code Section 190.2(22) (West 1999); Fla. Stat. Ann. Section 921.141(5)(n)(West 2001); Ind. Code Ann. Section 35-50-2-9(b)(1)(I) (Mich. Supp. 2003); Mo. Ann. Stat. Section 565.032 (2)(17) (West 1999).

75. *Chicago v. Morales,* 527 U.S. 41 (1999).

76. "The Growing Gang Problem."

Chapter One Appendix

How to Read Case Citations and Find Court Decisions

Many important court cases are discussed throughout this book. Every time a court case is mentioned, you will be able to check its citation using the endnotes on the final pages of the chapter. Court decisions are recorded and published on paper and on the Internet. When a court case is mentioned, the notation that is used to refer to, or to *cite,* the case denotes where the published decision can be found.

State courts of appeals decisions are usually published in two places, the state reports of that particular state and the more widely used *National Reporter System* published by West Group. Some states no longer publish their own reports. The *National Reporter System* divides the states into the following geographic areas: Atlantic (A. or A.2d), South Western (S.W., S.W.2d, or S.W.3d), North Eastern (N.E. or N.E.2d), North Western (N.W. or N.W.2d), Southern (So. or So.2d), and Pacific (P., P.2d, or P.3d). The *2d* and *3d* in these abbreviations refer to the *Second Series* and *Third Series,* respectively.

Federal trial court decisions are published unofficially in West's *Federal Supplement* (F.Supp. or F.Supp.2d), and opinions from the circuit courts of appeals are reported unofficially in West's *Federal Reporter* (F., F.2d, or F.3d). Opinions from the United States Supreme Court are reported in the *United States Reports* (U.S.), the *Lawyers' Edition of the Supreme Court Reports* (L.Ed.), West's *Supreme Court Reporter* (S.Ct.), and other publications. The *United States Reports* is the official publication of United States Supreme Court decisions. It is published by the federal government. Many early decisions are missing from these volumes. The citations of the early volumes of the *United States Reports* include the names of the actual reporters, such as Dallas, Cranch, or Wheaton. *McCulloch v. Maryland,* for example, is cited as 17 U.S. (4 Wheat.) 316. Only after 1874 did the present citation system, in which cases are cited based solely on their volume and page numbers in the *United States Reports,* come into being. The *Lawyers' Edition of the Supreme Court Reports* is an unofficial and more complete edition of Supreme Court decisions. West's *Supreme Court Reporter* is an unofficial edition of decisions dating from October 1882. These volumes contain headnotes and numerous brief editorial statements of the law involved in the case.

State courts of appeals decisions are cited by giving the name of the case; the volume, name, and page number of the state's official report (if the state publishes its own reports); and the volume, unit, and page number of the *National Reporter.* Federal court citations are also listed by giving the name of the case and the volume, name, and page number of the reports. In addition to the citation, this textbook lists the year of the decision in parentheses. Consider, for example, the case *Miranda v. Arizona,* 384 U.S. 436 (1966). The Supreme Court's decision in this case may be found in volume 384 of the *United States Reports* on page 436. The case was decided in 1966.

CHAPTER TWO

Causes of Crime

Chapter outline

- Exploring the Causes of Crime
- Victimology and Victims of Crime
- Criminology from Theory to Practice
- Criminal Justice in Action—The Ever-Elusive Serial Killer

Chapter objectives

After reading this chapter, you should be able to:

1 Explain why classical criminology is based on choice theory.
2 Contrast positivism with classical criminology.
3 List and describe the three theories of social structure that help explain crime.
4 List and briefly explain the three branches of social process theory.
5 Describe how life course criminology differs from the other theories addressed in this chapter.
6 Discuss the evolution of victimology from its beginnings in the 1940s until today.
7 Explain why some criminologists believe the connection between alcohol and victimization is unique.
8 List the arguments for and against greater legal protection of victims' rights.

Criminal JusticeNow 🖥

Optimize your study time and master key chapter concepts with *Criminal JusticeNow*, an online study tool that provides you with a *personalized study plan*. Check out the "Test Preparation Online" section at the end of the chapter for additional information.

Out of the Blue

In his more than two decades at the Jeep assembly plant in Toledo, Ohio, Myles Meyers had never given his colleagues any reason to think of him as a dangerous person. On the evening of January 26, 2005, however, the fifty-four-year-old metal finisher walked into the plant with a shotgun hidden under his coat. Brandishing the weapon, he ordered co-worker Yiesha Martin to call his boss and two other supervisors into her office. He told her he planned to shoot them. "Myles, why are you doing this? You don't have to go out this way," Martin remembers telling him. "Yes, I do," he replied.

That night, Meyers ended up killing his boss, Roy Thacker, and wounding two other plant employees

On January 26, 2005, Myles Meyers, an employee at a Jeep plant in Toledo, Ohio, shot three co-workers, one fatally, before killing himself with a bullet to the head.

AP Photo/Dept. of Motor Vehicles

before taking his own life. The morning before, Meyers had met with several superiors, including Thacker and one of the other victims, to discuss his job performance. Even though the meeting ended amicably and no disciplinary action was taken, Meyers apparently felt he was being unfairly singled out over numerous problems in the body shop.

Meyers also had concerns in his personal life. He had recently separated from his wife, and a month before the shootings he had been arrested when police found illegally obtained prescription drugs, a bag of marijuana, and a loaded firearm in his car during a traffic stop. Still, his violent outburst shocked his family and friends. "We are trying to understand why this happened," said his stepdaughter, "but we may never know."

The carnage at the Jeep plant in Toledo was hardly uncommon. In an average year, about 18,000 employees suffer injuries from assault, and more than 600 are murdered while on the job.[1] One out of every six violent crimes committed in the United States occurs in the workplace.[2] The U.S. Centers for Disease Control has called workplace violence a "national epidemic."[3]

In one respect, though, workplace violence is atypical: it seems to follow a pattern. According to data collected by James Alan Fox of Northeastern University in Boston, 73 percent of those persons convicted for workplace homicide are white, more than half are over age thirty-five, and almost all are male.[4] These criminals tend to be hypersensitive to criticism and often respond violently when disciplined.[5] Researchers also note that usually several "trigger" events lead up to a workplace murder, which, in most instances, is carried out with a firearm.[6] Do these factors provide us with any clues as to the underlying causes of Myles Meyers's behavior?

The study of crime, or **criminology,** is rich with different theories as to why people commit crimes. In this chapter, we will discuss the most influential of these theories, some of which complement each other and some of which do not. We will also look at the various factors most commonly, if not always correctly, associated with criminal behavior. Finally, this chapter will address the question of relevance: What effect do theories of why wrongdoing occurs have on efforts to control and prevent crime?

CONCEPT BUILDER

To what extent should a person be held responsible for his or her behavior? Visit **www.cjinaction.com** for an interactive exploration of this idea in relation to causes of crime.

Criminology
The scientific study of crime and the causes of criminal behavior.

EXPLORING THE CAUSES OF CRIME

Criminologists, or researchers who study the causes of crime, warn against using models to predict violent behavior. After all, not every middle-aged white man who has a grudge against his employers and owns a gun is a potential criminal, and it would be wrong to treat them as such. Studies may show a *correlation* between these factors and workplace violence, but very few criminologists would go as far as to claim that these factors *cause* such violent behavior. Correlation between two variables means that they tend to vary together. Causation, in contrast, means that one variable is responsible for the change in the other. Research shows, for example, that ice cream sales and crime rates both rise in the summer. Thus, there is a correlation between ice cream sales and crime. Nobody would seriously suggest, though, that increased sales of ice cream cause the boost in crime rates.

This is the quandary in which criminologists find themselves. One can say that there is a correlation between violent workplace crime and certain characteristics of the lives of violent workplace criminals. But we cannot say what actually caused Myles Meyers to kill Roy Thacker without knowing much more about his background and environment, and possibly not even then. Consequently, the question that is the underpinning of criminology—what causes crime?—has yet to be fully answered. Certainly, criminologists have uncovered a wealth of information concerning a different, and more practically applicable, inquiry: Given a certain set of circumstances, why do individuals commit certain crimes? Various schools of criminology have developed numerous theories of crime causation, the most widely recognized of which we will examine in the following sections.

Crime and Free Will: Choice Theories of Crime

For the purposes of the American criminal justice system, the answer to why a person commits a crime is rather straightforward: because that person chooses to do so. This application of **choice theory** to criminal law is not absolute; if a defendant can prove that she or he lacked the ability to make a rational choice, in certain circumstances the defendant will not be punished as harshly for a crime as would normally be the case. But such allowances are relatively recent. From the early days of this country, the general presumption in criminal law has been that behavior is a consequence of free will.

Theories of Classical Criminology An emphasis on free will and human rationality in the realm of criminal behavior has its roots in **classical criminology.** Classical theorists believed that crime was an expression of a person's rational decision-making process: before committing a crime, a person would weigh the benefits of the crime against the costs of being apprehended. Therefore, if punishments were stringent enough to outweigh the benefits of crime, they would dissuade people from committing the crime in the first place.

The earliest popular expression of classical theory came in 1764 when the Italian Cesare Beccaria (1738–1794) published his *Essays on Crime and Punishments*. Beccaria criticized existing systems of criminal law as irrational and argued that criminal procedures should be more consistent with human behavior. He believed that, to be just, criminal law should reflect three truths:

1 All decisions, including the decision to commit a crime, are the result of rational choice.

2 Fear of punishment can have a deterrent effect on the choice to commit crime.

3 The more swift and certain punishment is, the more effective it will be in controlling crime.[7]

Beccaria believed that any punishment that purported to do anything other than deter crime was cruel and arbitrary. This view was shared by his contemporary, Britain's

Choice Theory
A school of criminology that holds that wrongdoers act as if they weigh the possible benefits of criminal or delinquent activity against the expected costs of being apprehended. When the benefits are greater than the expected costs, the offender will make a rational choice to commit a crime or delinquent act.

Classical Criminology
A school of criminology based on the belief that individuals have free will to engage in any behavior, including criminal behavior. To deter criminal behavior, society must hold wrongdoers responsible for their actions by punishing them.

Utilitarianism

An approach to ethical reasoning in which the "correct" decision is the one that results in the greatest amount of good for the greatest number of people affected by that decision.

Positivism

A school of the social sciences that sees criminal and delinquent behavior as the result of biological, psychological, and social forces. Because wrongdoers are driven to deviancy by external factors, they should not be punished but treated to lessen the influence of those factors.

Carolyn Correa, pictured here, surrendered to the Philadelphia Police Department in 2004. Seven years earlier, Correa allegedly caused a fire as part of a plan to kidnap a ten-day-old baby named Delimar Vera (who was eventually returned to her mother). According to choice theory, what "costs" and "benefits" would Correa consider before deciding to commit the crimes of arson and kidnapping? Do you believe that criminal behavior can be the result of such a rational decision-making process?

Jeremy Bentham (1748–1832). In 1789, Bentham pronounced that "nature has placed man under the governance of two sovereign masters, *pain* and *pleasure*." Bentham applied his theory of **utilitarianism** to the law by contending that punishment should use the threat of pain against criminal individuals to assure the pleasure of society as a whole.[8] As a result, Bentham felt that punishment should have four goals:

1 To prevent all crime.
2 When it cannot prevent crime, to assure that a criminal will commit a lesser crime to avoid a harsher punishment.
3 To give the criminal an incentive not to harm others in the pursuit of crime.
4 To prevent crime at the least possible cost to society.[9]

Positivism and Modern Rational Theory By the end of the nineteenth century, the positivist school of criminologists had superseded classical criminology. According to **positivism,** criminal behavior is determined by biological, psychological, and social forces and is beyond the control of the individual. The Italian physician Cesare Lombroso (1835–1909), an early adherent of positivism who is known as the "Father of Criminology," believed that criminals were throwbacks to the savagery of early humankind and could therefore be identified by certain physical characteristics such as sharp teeth and large jaws. He also theorized that criminality was similar to mental illness and could be genetically passed down from generation to generation in families that had cases of insanity, syphilis, epilepsy, and even deafness. Such individuals, according to Lombroso and his followers, had no free choice when it came to wrong-doing—their criminality had been predetermined at birth.

Positivist theory lost credibility as crime rates began to climb in the 1970s. If crime was caused by external factors, critics asked, why had the proactive social programs of the 1960s not brought about a decrease in criminal activity? An updated version of classical criminology, known as *rational choice theory,* found renewed acceptance. James Q. Wilson, one of the most prominent critics of the positivist school, sums up rational choice theory as follows:

> At any given moment, a person can choose between committing a crime and not committing it. The consequences of committing a crime consist of rewards (what psychologists call "reinforcers") and punishments; the consequences of not committing the crime also entail gains and losses. The larger the ratio of the net rewards of crime to the net rewards of [not committing a crime], the greater the tendency to commit a crime.[10]

According to rational choice theory, we can hypothesize that criminal actions, including acts of violence and drug abuse, are committed *as if* individuals had this ratio in mind.

The Seduction of Crime In expanding on rational choice theory, sociologist Jack Katz has stated that the "rewards" of crime may be sensual as well as financial. The inherent danger of criminal activity, according to Katz, increases the "rush" a criminal experiences on successfully committing a crime. Katz labels the rewards of this "rush" the *seduction of crime.*[11] For example, serial killer John Wayne Gacy claims to have "realized that death was the ultimate thrill" after murdering the first of his more than thirty victims.[12] Katz believes that seemingly "senseless" crimes can be explained by rational choice theory only if the intrinsic reward of the crime itself is considered.

Choice Theory and Public Policy The theory that wrongdoers choose to commit crimes is a cornerstone of the American criminal justice system. Because crime is seen as the end result of a series of rational choices, policymakers have reasoned that severe punishment can deter criminal activity by adding another variable to the

A Criminologist at Work

Despite its vaunted position in modern criminology, rational choice theory is viewed with suspicion by many criminologists. If the decision to commit a crime is based on a rational consideration of the costs and benefits of the crime, what happens if the person making the decision is not capable of rationality? The question is particularly relevant given that as many as 75 percent of violent offenders may be under the influence of alcohol or drugs when they commit their crimes.

M. Lyn Exum, a professor of criminal justice at the University of North Carolina in Charlotte, decided to test the "robustness" of rational choice theory in light of high intoxicant use among criminals. Exum recruited eighty-four male college students for what they believed would be an experiment concerning the effects of alcohol on brain functions. In fact, Exum planned to measure the impact of alcohol and anger on the decision to engage in physical assault. The participants were randomly divided into "alcohol" and "no alcohol" groups, with the members of the "alcohol" group given 1.5 ounces of vodka (diluted with orange juice) per 40 pounds of body weight. Then, without the participants' knowledge, the test group was split into "anger" and "no anger" categories. Exum induced the desired emotions from those in the "anger" set by falsely accusing them of arriving thirty minutes late to the laboratory and threatening to withhold their $25 payment as a result.

Once the desired physical and mental states had been reached, each participant was presented with the following hypothetical situation:

> You return from the restroom in a bar to find "Joe" flirting with your girlfriend. After a brief argument, "Joe" pushes you. How likely are you to physically assault "Joe" in retaliation?

Exum found that those in the "anger/alcohol" group were significantly more likely to choose a violent outcome to the scenario than those in the "sober/calm" group. To Exum, this outcome suggests "there is no single rational choice model that underlies the decision to engage in physical assault."

FOR CRITICAL ANALYSIS

What is your opinion of Professor Exum's methods and conclusion? How do you think the participants' demographics (all male, all college students, 76 percent Caucasian) affect the results, if at all?

---

decision-making process. Supporters of the death penalty—now used by thirty-eight states and the federal government—emphasize its deterrent effects, and legislators have used harsh mandatory sentences to control illegal drug use and trafficking. (To see why one expert questions choice theory as a basis for criminal policy, see the feature *Outside the Box—A Criminologist at Work.*)

"Born Criminal": Biological and Psychological Theories of Crime

As we have seen, Cesare Lombroso believed in the "criminal born" man and woman and was confident that he could distinguish criminals by their apelike physical features. Such far-fetched notions have long been relegated to scientific oblivion. But many criminologists do believe that *trait theories* have validity. These theories suggest that certain biological or psychological traits in individuals could incline them toward criminal behavior given a certain set of circumstances. "All behavior is biological," points out geneticist David C. Rowe of the University of Arizona. "All behavior is represented in the brain, in its biochemistry, electrical activity, structure, and growth and decline."[13]

Biochemical Conditions and Crime One trait theory is that biochemical conditions can influence criminal behavior. These conditions can be genetic or brought about through environmental contacts. An example of the latter occurred in 1979, when Dan White was accused of murdering San Francisco Mayor George Moscone and Supervisor Harvey Milk. White successfully pleaded the "Twinkie defense"—that he should not be held accountable for his actions because he had suffered a major "mood disturbance" caused in part by an addiction to high-sugar junk food.[14]

 The **American Society of Criminology** will keep you updated on the hot issues in criminology. Find its Web site by clicking on *Web Links* under *Chapter Resources* at **www.cjinaction.com.**

In 2004, a North Carolina judge found that Yvonne Chapman was not guilty of murder for drowning her six-month-old son because she was suffering from *postpartum psychosis* at the time of her actions. This temporary illness, believed to be partly caused by the hormonal changes that women experience after childbirth, triggers abnormal behavior in a small percentage of new mothers.[15] Criminal activity in males has also been linked to hormones—specifically *testosterone,* which controls secondary sexual characteristics (such as the growth of facial and pubic hair and the change of voice pitch) and has been linked to traits of aggression. Testing of inmate populations has shown that those incarcerated for violent crimes have higher testosterone levels than other prisoners.[16] High testosterone levels have also been used to explain the age-crime relationship, as the average testosterone level of men under the age of twenty-eight is double that of men between thirty-one and sixty-six years old.[17]

Genetics and Crime Some criminologists might contend that Katz's "seduction of crime" provides more support for a modern, gene-based, evolutionary theory of crime than for rational choice theory. In other words, the seduction of crime represents an ancestral urge—which is stronger in some people than others—to commit acts that are considered crimes only in modern society.

Behavioral Genes Recently, psychologist Leda Cosmides and anthropologist John Tooby have advocated a "Swiss army knife model" to explain how genetics influences brain activity. According to this model, humans have evolved special modules and networks in their brains that dispose them toward certain behavioral patterns.[18] Criminologists such as Lee Ellis and Anthony Walsh have suggested that some of these behavior patterns, which at one time were beneficial to human survival, have now become antisocial and have had sanctions imposed on them by society. In prehistoric eras, for example, extreme sexual aggressiveness in males toward a large number of females would have diversified a community's gene pool. Now laws against sexual assault and rape restrict such behavior.[19]

> "Crime is a fact of the human species, a fact of that species alone, but it is above all the secret aspect, impenetrable and hidden. Crime hides, and by far the most terrifying things are those which elude us."
> —Georges Bataille, French novelist (1965)

Another theory suggests that a person's genetic make-up may contribute to personality traits associated with criminal behavior. Researchers have hunted in vain for a "crime gene," or a genetic abnormality that could conclusively predict criminal behavior. In 2002, however, British criminologist Terrie Moffitt and several colleagues published results of a study that linked violent behavior to the absence of the gene for a protein called monoamine oxidase-A (MAOA).[20] This protein helps adjust a person's mood by regulating the molecules that carry "command signals" from one cell to another. Following more than five hundred men in New Zealand from birth to their late twenties, Moffitt and her team found that 12 percent of these males had *both* low levels of MAOA and had been abused as children. This group of 12 percent accounted for 85 percent of the entire sample who showed signs of overly aggressive behavior and 44 percent of those who had been convicted of violent crimes.

Because people who have been abused as children generally exhibit higher levels of antisocial behavior than those who have not—regardless of their MAOA supply—these findings are hardly decisive. Nor will they affect the consistent view of the courts that medical evidence has not been able to establish a causal relationship between genetic defects and criminal behavior.[21] Nevertheless, the efforts of Moffitt and her colleagues have spurred interest in the possibility that a "crime gene" does exist.

Twin Studies Because genes are inherited, some researchers have turned to *twin studies* to determine the relationship between genetics and criminal behavior. If the two are linked, then twins should exhibit similar antisocial tendencies. The problem with twin studies is that most twins grow up in the same environment, so it is difficult to determine whether their behavior is influenced by their genes or by their surroundings. To overcome this difficulty, criminologists compare identical twins, known as MZ twins, and fraternal twins of the same sex, known as DZ twins. Because MZ twins are genetically identical while DZ twins share only half of their genes, the latter should be less likely to have similar behavior patterns than the former.

Indeed, some studies seem to support this hypothesis. Researcher Karl Christiansen, for example, examined nearly four thousand male twin pairs and found that 52 percent of MZ pairs exhibited similar behavior patterns compared to only 22 percent for DZ pairs.[22] As is often the frustrating case in criminology, however, other studies seem to refute the idea that genetics is more important than environment in determining delinquent behavior. Research by criminologist David Rowe shows that nontwin siblings resemble each other in terms of delinquency to the same extent as twins do.[23] Consequently, though twin studies have contributed much to the discussion of trait theories, they have not proved conclusive in determining the effect of genetics on criminal behavior.[24]

Brain Activity and Crime The study of brain activity, or *neurophysiology,* has also found a niche in criminology. Some criminologists hypothesize that criminal behavior can be influenced by neurological defects that are acquired early in life. Neurophysiological studies of crime have relied on *electroencephalographic (EEG)* scans of brain activity. An EEG records the series of electric oscillations, or waves, given off by the part of the brain that controls functions such as learning and memory. These brain waves are measured according to their frequency and strength, and certain patterns of brain waves can be associated with criminal behavior. (For more information on "brain mapping" procedures, see the feature *CJ and Technology—Mapping Crime in the Brain* on the next page.) One study of a random sample of 333 subjects referred for an EEG found that those who exhibited lifelong patterns of violence had an incidence of EEG abnormality of 65 percent, three times higher than the same trait in those who had been charged with only one violent offense.[25]

Psychology and Crime For all of his accomplishments in the field of psychology, Sigmund Freud (1856–1939) rarely turned his attention to the causes of crime. His followers, however, have proposed a *psychoanalytic theory* for criminal behavior. This theory rests on the belief that the human personality is made up of three parts:

1 The *id,* which controls sexual urges.
2 The *ego,* which controls behavior that leads to the fulfillment of the id.
3 The *superego,* which is directly related to the conscience and determines which actions are right and wrong, in the context of a person's environment.

Psychoanalytic theorists contend that people who exhibit criminal behavior have an overdeveloped ego or an underdeveloped superego. A strong ego leads to such feelings of guilt that a person commits a crime in order to be punished; alternatively, a weak superego means that a person cannot control his or her violent urges.

Several years ago, Andrea P. Yates methodically drowned her five children, aged six months to seven years, in the family bathtub. A state psychiatrist found that Yates, shown here in a Houston courtroom, suffered from severe depression with "psychotic features." After her arrest, Yates told doctors that she saw Satan in the walls of her jail cell. What if Yates's psychological problems could be successfully treated? Do you believe that she should still be severely punished for her crimes?

AP Photo/Steve Ueckert, Pool

Mapping Crime in the Brain

During the trial of John Hinckley, Jr., who attempted to assassinate President Ronald Reagan in 1981, the defense offered the jury a black-and-white photo of Hinckley's brain. This picture, the defense claimed, showed that Hinckley was schizophrenic and not responsible for his actions. In a controversial decision, the defendant was found not guilty by reason of insanity.

Twenty years later, "brain mapping" techniques make the black-and-white photo of Hinckley's brain look like the drawing of a child. By placing electrodes on a subject's scalp, scientists can use computerized electroencephalography (CEEG) to measure the brain's spontaneous electrical activity, or its electrical response to visual and auditory stimuli. Using CEEG, scientists can present a color-coded display of brain activity. Other neuro-imaging measures include positron emission computer tomography (PET scanning), which produces a computerized image of molecular variations in brain metabolism, and magnetic resonance imaging (MRI), which depicts the brain's form and structure by bombarding it with magnetic fields and radio waves.

Scans that measure brain activity can be particularly helpful in identifying *attention deficit/hyperactivity disorder (ADHD)*, a condition most commonly found in children of elementary school age. The symptoms of ADHD include an inability to concentrate and a tendency to be impulsive and hyperactive. The condition—which is believed to affect between 3 and 5 percent of the children in the United States—is associated with substance abuse, learning disabilities, and delinquency. Observers believe that because those who suffer from ADHD perform poorly in school, they are at much greater risk of developing antisocial and delinquent behavioral patterns. Brain scans can identify ADHD in "problem" children and lead to treatment that lessens the risk of future criminality.

Centers for Disease Control

An MRI scan showing the human brain.

IN THE FUTURE

The use of brain scanning to show a proclivity toward criminal behavior or as a defense strategy in criminal trials is dismissed as "junk science" by many criminologists. A number of studies, though, have established that certain brain patterns are associated with criminal behavior. As scientific methods improve, brain mapping may allow physicians to "predict" crime—with all the controversial implications that ability would bring.

For more information on brain scans and other CJ technologies, click on Web Links under Chapter Resources at **www.cjinaction.com.**

Because these theories are based on often untestable hypotheses rather than empirical data, psychological explanations for criminal behavior are quite controversial. During the middle of the twentieth century, the concept of the criminal as *psychopath* (used interchangeably with the term *sociopath*) gained a great deal of credence. The psychopath was seen as a person who had somehow lost her or his "humanity" and was unable to experience human emotions such as love or regret, to control criminal impulses, or to understand the consequences of her or his decisions.[26] Over the past few decades, the concept of psychopathy has lost standing, as criminologists have criticized the notion that emotions can be "measured."

Trait Theory and Public Policy Whereas choice theory justifies punishing wrongdoers, biological and psychological views of criminality suggest that antisocial behavior should be identified and treated before it manifests itself in first-time or further criminal activity. Though the focus on treatment diminished somewhat in the 1990s, rehabilitation practices in corrections have made somewhat of a comeback over the past few years. Some offenders are treated with mood-altering drugs to control their antisocial behavior, and nearly all corrections facilities offer group or individual therapy to help prisoners address possible root causes of their criminal predilections.

Sociological Theories of Crime

The problem with trait theory, many criminologists contend, is that it falters when confronted with certain crime patterns. Why is the crime rate in Detroit, Michigan, twenty-five times that of Sioux Falls, South Dakota? Do high levels of air pollution cause an increase in abnormal brain activity or higher levels of testosterone? As no evidence has been found that would suggest that biological factors can be so easily influenced, several generations of criminologists have instead focused on social and physical environmental factors in their study of criminal behavior.

The Chicago School The importance of sociology in the study of criminal behavior was established by a group of scholars who were associated with the Sociology Department at the University of Chicago in the early 1900s. These sociologists, known collectively as the Chicago School, gathered empirical evidence from the slums of the city that showed a correlation between conditions of poverty, such as inadequate housing and poor sanitation, and high rates of crime. Chicago School members Ernest Burgess (1886–1966) and Robert Ezra Park (1864–1944) argued that neighborhood conditions, be they of wealth or poverty, had a much greater determinant effect on criminal behavior than ethnicity, race, or religion.[27] The methods and theories of the Chicago School, which stressed that humans are social creatures whose behavior reflects their environment, have had a profound effect on criminology over the past century.

The study of crime as correlated to social structure revolves around three specific theories: (1) social disorganization theory, (2) strain theory, and (3) cultural deviance theory.

Social Disorganization Theory Park and Burgess introduced an *ecological* analysis of crime to criminology. Just as ecology studies the relationships between animals and their environments, the two Chicago School members studied the relationship between inner-city residents and their environment. In addition, Clifford Shaw and Henry McKay, contemporaries of the Chicago School and researchers in juvenile crime, popularized the idea of ecology in criminology through **social disorganization theory.** This theory states that crime is largely a product of unfavorable conditions in certain communities.[28]

Studying juvenile delinquency in Chicago, Shaw and McKay discovered certain "zones" that exhibited high rates of crime. These zones were characterized by "disorganization," or a breakdown of the traditional institutions of social control such as family, school systems, and local businesses. In contrast, in the city's "organized" communities, residents had developed certain agreements about fundamental values and norms. Shaw and McKay found that residents in high-crime neighborhoods had to a large degree abandoned these fundamental values and norms. Also, a lack of social controls had led to increased levels of antisocial, or criminal, behavior.[29] According to social disorganization theory, ecological factors that lead to crime in these neighborhoods are perpetuated by continued elevated levels of high school dropouts, unemployment, deteriorating infrastructures, and single-parent families. (See Figure 2.1 on the following page to better understand social disorganization theory.)

Recently, some criminologists questioned the usefulness of conventional social disorganization theory. As Robert J. Sampson, a sociologist from Harvard University, has pointed out, the "ideal typical neighborhoods" characterized by close-knit ties between residents on which Shaw and McKay based their research are no longer common in the United States.[30] Social bonds between people who live in the same area are weakening, meaning that members of any given community have less influence on each other than in the past. Furthermore, the concept of the neighborhood as a

See **Crime Times** for an online publication dedicated to understanding the role brain dysfunction plays in criminal behavior. Find this Web site by clicking on *Web Links* under *Chapter Resources* at **www.cjinaction.com**.

Social Disorganization Theory
The theory that deviant behavior is more likely in communities where social institutions such as the family, schools, and the criminal justice system fail to exert control over the population.

The Problem: Poverty
The Consequences:
Formation of isolated impoverished areas, racial and ethnic discrimination, lack of legitimate economic opportunities.

→ *Leads to* →

The Problem: Social Disorganization
The Consequences:
Breakdown of institutions such as school and the family.

→ *Leads to* →

The Problem: Breakdown of Social Control
The Consequences:
Peer groups replace family and educators as primary influences on youth; formation of gangs.

↓ *Leads to* ↓

The Problem: Criminal Careers
The Consequences:
The majority of youths "age out" of crime, start families, and, if they can, leave the neighborhood. Those who remain still adhere to the values of the impoverished-area culture and become career criminals.

← *Leads to* ←

The Problem: Cultural Transmission
The Consequences:
The younger juveniles inherit the values of delinquency and crime from their older siblings and friends, establishing a deep-rooted impoverished-area culture.

← *Leads to* ←

The Problem: Criminal Areas
The Consequences:
Rise of crime in poverty-stricken neighborhood; delinquent behavior becomes socially acceptable for youths; outside investment and support shun the area.

FIGURE 2.1

The Stages of Social Disorganization Theory

Social disorganization theory holds that crime is related to the environmental pressures that exist in certain communities or neighborhoods. These areas are marked by the desire of many of their inhabitants to "get out" at the first possible opportunity. Consequently, residents tend to ignore the important institutions in the community, such as business and education, causing further erosion and an increase in the conditions that lead to crime.

Source: Adapted from Larry J. Siegel, *Criminology*, 8th ed. (Belmont, CA: Thomson/Wadsworth, 2003), 183.

Strain Theory

The assumption that crime is the result of frustration felt by individuals who cannot reach their financial and personal goals through legitimate means.

Anomie

A condition in which the individual suffers from the breakdown or absence of social norms. According to this theory, this condition occurs when a person is disconnected from these norms or rejects them as inconsistent with his or her personal goals.

distinct place, separate and different from other neighborhoods, is no longer helpful in most contemporary cities.[31] Sampson and those who agree with him do not think the ideas of the Chicago School should be abandoned, but rather feel that they should not be limited by reliance on traditional notions of neighborhood and community.

Strain Theory Another self-perpetuating aspect of disorganized neighborhoods is that once residents gain the financial means to leave a high-crime community, they usually do so. This desire to escape the inner city is related to the second branch of social structure theory: **strain theory.** Most Americans have similar life goals, which include gaining a certain measure of wealth and financial freedom. The means of attaining these goals, however, are not universally available. Many citizens do not have access to the education or training necessary for financial success. This often results in frustration and anger, or *strain.*

Strain theory has its roots in the works of French sociologist Emile Durkheim (1858–1917) and his concept of **anomie** (derived from the Greek word for "without norms"). Durkheim believed that *anomie* resulted when social change threw behavioral norms into a flux, leading to a weakening of social controls and an increase in deviant behavior.[32] Another sociologist, American Robert K. Merton, expanded on Durkheim's ideas in his own theory of strain. Merton believed that *anomie* was caused by a social structure in which all citizens have similar goals without equal means to achieve them.[33] One way to alleviate this strain is to gain wealth by the means that are available to the residents of disorganized communities: drug trafficking, burglary, and other criminal activities.

In the 1990s, Robert Agnew of Emory University in Atlanta, Georgia, updated this line of criminology with his *general strain theory,* or GST.[34] Agnew reasoned that of all "strained" individuals, very few actually turn to crime to relieve the strain. GST tries to determine what factors, when combined with strain, actually lead to criminal activity. By the early 2000s, Agnew and other criminologists settled on the factor of *negative emotionality,* a term used to cover personality traits of those who are easily frustrated, quick to lose their tempers, and disposed to blame others for their own problems.[35] Thus, GST mixes strain theory with aspects of psychological theories of crime.

Cultural Deviance Theory Combining, to a certain extent, social disorganization and strain theories, **cultural deviance theory** asserts that people adapt to the values of the

Robert Agnew
Criminologist

I had no plans to become a criminologist when I began my Ph.D. program in sociology at the University of North Carolina. In fact, I never took a course in criminology during my undergraduate days. The turning point came when I had to pick my dissertation subject. I discovered a survey that had some excellent measures of the relationship between a person's social environment and later delinquent behavior. I had my topic: the impact of social environment on delinquency.

My research led to the "strain" or *anomie* theories that said when a person stumbles in achieving financial success or middle-class status due to social factors beyond his or her control, he or she may turn to crime. That is, if you didn't have access to a good education because your local school was poor, or perhaps your parents just didn't have the money to send you to college, or you couldn't land a good job because of your background, you might respond to these kinds of frustrations by turning to crime. While strain theory made a lot of sense to me, I felt that the theory was incomplete.

When I looked around me, it was easy to spot other sources of frustration and anger, such as harassment by peers, conflict with parents or romantic partners, poor grades in school, or poor working conditions. In addition, strain theory did not explain why some people reacted to strain by turning to crime, while others did not.

My dissertation proposed additional sources of strain besides failure to achieve monetary success. I continued to research this topic after I joined the faculty at Emory University. I drew on strain theory, social psychology, and my own experiences to develop a new "general strain theory" [see note 34].

I outlined sources of strain as the loss of "positively valued stimuli" such as romantic relationships, or the threat of "negatively valued stimuli" such as an insult or physical assault. I also pointed out that monetary success was just one among many "positively valued goals" that might cause strain when not achieved.

Finally, I noted that people who experience strain may turn to crime for several reasons—crime might allow them to achieve their monetary and status goals, protect positively valued stimuli, escape negative stimuli, achieve revenge against wrongs, or simply to deal with the strain (such as taking drugs to forget problems).

Courtesy of Robert Agnew

Robert Agnew

I think that general strain theory is important because it significantly expands the scope of strain theory and—in doing so—it has helped generate new interest in strain theories of crime.

I've explored a number of factors that influence whether a person will respond to strain by turning to crime, including coping skills and resources, social support, and association with delinquent peers [see note 35].

If you are planning to do research on strain theory or on the causes of crime more generally, first familiarize yourself with relevant literature. Ask yourself whether a particular theory or argument makes sense—does it jibe with your experiences and your observations of others? If not, you may want to suggest an extension or revision in the theory.

Likewise, ask yourself whether the empirical tests of the theory make sense—are adequate samples employed, are all major concepts measured, and so on. It is not as difficult to make an original contribution as you might think.

Go to the Careers in Criminal Justice Interactive CD *for more profiles in the field of criminal justice.*

---

subculture to which they belong. A **subculture** (a subdivision that exists within the dominant culture) has its own standards of behavior, or norms. By definition, a disorganized neighborhood is isolated from society at large, and the strain of this isolation encourages the formation of subcultures within the slum. According to cultural deviance theory, members of low-income subcultures are more likely to conform to value systems that celebrate behavior, such as violence, that directly confronts the value system of society at large and therefore draws criminal sanctions.

Social Structure Theory and Public Policy If criminal behavior can be explained by the conditions in which certain groups of people live, then it stands to reason that changing those conditions can prevent crime. Indeed, government programs to decrease unemployment, reduce poverty, and improve educational facilities in

Cultural Deviance Theory
A branch of social structure theory based on the assumption that members of certain subcultures reject the values of the dominant culture through deviant behavior patterns.

Subculture
A group exhibiting certain values and behavior patterns that distinguish it from the dominant culture.

Social Process Theories
A school of criminology that considers criminal behavior to be the predictable result of a person's interaction with his or her environment. According to these theories, everybody has the potential for wrongdoing. Those who act on this potential are conditioned to do so by family or peer groups, or institutions such as the media.

Learning Theory
The hypothesis that delinquents and criminals must be taught both the practical and emotional skills necessary to partake in illegal activity.

Theory of Differential Association
Sutherland's theory that criminality is the result of the values an individual is exposed to by family, friends, and other members of the community. When these values favor deviant behavior over conventional norms, criminal activity is more likely.

Control Theory
A series of theories that assume that all individuals have the potential for criminal behavior, but are restrained by the damage that such actions would do to their relationships with family, friends, and members of the community. Criminality occurs when these bonds are broken or nonexistent.

low-income neighborhoods have been justified to a degree as part of large-scale attempts at crime prevention.

Family, Friends, and the Media: Social Processes of Crime

Some criminologists find class theories of crime overly narrow. Surveys that ask people directly about their criminal behavior have shown that the criminal instinct is pervasive in middle- and upper-class communities, even if it is expressed differently. Anybody, these criminologists argue, has the potential to act out criminal behavior, regardless of class, race, or gender.

Psychologist Philip Zimbardo conducted a well-known, if rather unscientific, experiment to make this point. Zimbardo placed an abandoned automobile with its hood up on the campus of Stanford University. The car remained in place, untouched, for a week. Then, the psychologist smashed the car's window with a sledgehammer. Within minutes, passerbys had joined in the destruction of the automobile, eventually stripping its valuable parts.[36] **Social process theories** function on the same basis as Zimbardo's "interdependence of decisions experiment": the potential for criminal behavior exists in everyone and will be realized depending on an individual's interaction with various institutions and processes of society. There are three main branches of social process theory: (1) learning theory, (2) control theory, and (3) labeling theory.

Learning Theory Popularized by Edwin Sutherland in the 1940s, **learning theory** contends that criminal activity is a learned behavior. In other words, a criminal is taught both the practical methods of crime (such as how to pick a lock) and the psychological aspects of crime (how to deal with the guilt of wrongdoing). Sutherland's **theory of differential association** held that individuals are exposed to values from family and peers such as school friends or co-workers. If the dominant values one is exposed to favor criminal behavior, then that person is more likely to mimic such behavior.[37] Sutherland concentrated particularly on familial relations, believing that a child was more likely to commit crimes if she or he saw an older sibling or a parent doing so.

Recently, learning theory has been expanded to include the growing influence of the media. In the latest in a long series of studies, psychologists at the University of Michigan's Institute for Social Research released data in 2003 showing that exposure to high levels of televised violence erodes a natural aversion to violence and increases aggressive behavior among young children.[38] Such findings have spurred a number of legislative attempts to curb violence on television.[39] (To see how another medium has come under scrutiny for its violent tendencies, see the feature *CJ and the Media—Shoot to Thrill.*)

Control Theory Criminologist Travis Hirschi focuses on the reasons why individuals *do not* engage in criminal acts, rather than why they do. According to Hirschi, social bonds promote conformity to social norms. The stronger these social bonds—which include attachment to, commitment to, involvement with, and belief in societal values—the less likely that any individual will commit a crime.[40] **Control theory** holds that although we all have the potential to commit crimes, most of us are dissuaded from doing so because we care about the opinions of our family and peers. James Q. Wilson and George Kelling describe control theory in terms of the "broken windows" effect. Neighborhoods in poor condition are filled with cues of lack of social control (for example, broken windows) that invite further vandalism and other deviant behavior.[41] If these cues are removed, according to Wilson and Kelling, so is the implied acceptance of crime within a community.

Shoot to Thrill

Sixteen-year-old William Buckner and his fourteen-year-old stepbrother Joshua had been playing video games for hours, and they were bored. To make things a little more interesting, they took a pair of .22 caliber shotguns from their home in Newport, Tennessee, and started randomly shooting at tractor-trailers on nearby Interstate 40. One of their blasts struck motorist Aaron Hamel in the head, killing him. Another seriously injured Kimberly Bede in a separate car.

The stepbrothers told authorities that they had gotten the idea for their antics from Grand Theft Auto (GTA), the best-selling video game in history and, because of its violent content, one of the most controversial. In the various versions of GTA, characters, among other activities, solicit and beat prostitutes, attack police officers, shoot ambulance drivers, spray people with machine-gun bullets, and fire randomly at large automobiles. Several months after the shootings, the Buckner family filed a $246 million lawsuit against the makers of GTA, claiming that the game's producers should have known that their product could lead young players to copy what they see on the screen.

www.rockstargames.com/sanandreas

CAUSE AND EFFECT?

Can video games cause violent behavior? There may be some connection between this particular form of entertainment and aggressive behavior among juveniles. Various studies have shown that video games act both as "operant conditioners" (in which players are rewarded for violence) and as "stimulus addiction" (in which players come to crave the positive emotional response they get from virtual violence). Douglas Gentile of Iowa State University recently observed more than six hundred Minnesota junior high students and found that teenagers with nonaggressive personalities who played violent video games were ten times more likely to get into a physical fight than those who did not play the games.

The problem with such studies, say critics, is that they are "probabilistic." In other words, the research may show that some people are probably more likely to act violently after playing a violent video game, but it does not establish any proof that the games cause violent behavior. In the legal realm, the research has not been strong enough to overcome the First Amendment protection of freedom of speech, and courts have overturned laws designed to regulate the video game industry in Georgia, Indiana, Missouri, and Washington State.

Labeling Theory A third social process theory, **labeling theory,** focuses on perceptions of criminal behavior rather than the behavior itself. Labeling theorists study how being labeled a criminal—a "whore," or a "junkie," or a "thief"—affects that person's future behavior. Sociologist Howard Becker contends that deviance is

> a consequence of the application by others of rules and sanctions to an offender. The deviant is one to whom that label has successfully been applied; deviant behavior is behavior that people so label.[42]

Such labeling, some criminologists believe, becomes a self-fulfilling prophecy. Someone labeled a "junkie" will begin to consider himself or herself a deviant and continue the criminal behavior for which he or she has been labeled. Following this line of reasoning, the criminal justice system is engaged in artificially creating a class of criminals by labeling victimless crimes such as drug use, prostitution, and gambling as "criminal."

Social Process Theory and Public Policy Because adult criminals are seen as too "hardened" to unlearn their criminal behavior, crime prevention policies associated with social process theory focus on juvenile offenders. Many youths, for example, are diverted from the formal juvenile justice process to keep them from being labeled "delinquent." Furthermore, many schools have implemented programs that attempt to steer children away from crime by encouraging them to "just say no" to drugs and stay

Labeling Theory
The hypothesis that society creates crime and criminals by labeling certain behavior and certain people as deviant. The stigma that results from this social process excludes a person from the community, thereby increasing the chances that she or he will adopt the label as her or his identity and engage in a pattern of criminal behavior.

in school. As we shall see in Chapter 6, implementation of Wilson and Kelling's "broken windows" principles has been credited with lowering the violent crime rate in New York and a number of other major cities.

Social Conflict Theories

A more recent movement in criminology focuses not on psychology, biology, or sociology, but on *power*. Those who identify power—seen as the ability of one person or group of persons to control the economic and social positions of other people or groups—as the key component in explaining crime entered the mainstream of American criminology during the 1960s. These theorists saw social ills such as poverty, racism, sexism, and destruction of the environment as the "true crimes," perpetrated by the powerful, or ruling, classes. Burglary, robbery, and even violent crimes were considered reactions by the powerless against laws that were meant to repress, not protect, them. Supporters of these ideas aligned themselves with Marxist, radical, conflict, and feminist schools of criminology. Collectively, they have constructed the **social conflict theories** of crime causation.

> "The common argument that crime is caused by poverty is a kind of slander on the poor."
>
> —H. L. Mencken, American journalist (1956)

Marxism versus Capitalism The genesis of social conflict theory can be found in the political philosophy of Karl Marx (1818–1883). Though he did not concentrate on crime in his writings, Marx's belief that a capitalist economic system necessarily produces income inequality and leads to exploitation of the working classes has been adopted by social conflict theorists.[43] These criminologists generally hold that crime is the natural result of class inequality as identified by Marx.

For this reason, social conflict theory is often associated with a critique of our capitalist economic system. Capitalism is seen as leading to high levels of violence and crime because of the disparity of income that results. The poor commit property crimes for reasons of need and because, as members of a capitalist society, they desire the same financial rewards as everybody else. They commit violent crimes because of the frustration and rage they feel when these rewards seem unattainable. Laws, instead of reflecting the values of society as a whole, reflect only the values of the segment of society that has achieved power and is willing to use the criminal justice system as a tool to keep that power.[44] Thus, the harsh penalties for "lower-class" crimes such as burglary can be seen as a means of protecting the privileges of the "haves" from the aspirations of the "have-nots."

The Social Reality of Crime It is important to note that, according to social conflict theory, power is not synonymous with wealth. Women and members of minority groups can be wealthy and yet still be disassociated from the benefits of power in our society. Richard Quinney, one of the most influential social conflict theorists of the past thirty years, encompasses issues of race, gender, power, and crime in a theory known as the **social reality of crime**.[45] For Quinney, along with many of his peers, criminal law does not reflect a universal moral code, but instead is a set of "rules" through which those who hold power can control and subdue those who do not. Any conflict between the "haves" and the "have-nots," therefore, is bound to be decided in favor of the "haves," who make the law and control the criminal justice system. Following this reasoning, Quinney sees violations of the law not as inherently criminal acts, but rather as political ones—as revolutionary acts against the power of the state.

Thinking along racial lines, many observers would assert that African Americans as a group have been "have-nots" since the colonial period. Today, the median income of an African American male is nearly $10,000 less than that of a white male. In 2005,

Social Conflict Theories
A school of criminology that views criminal behavior as the result of class conflict. Certain behavior is labeled illegal not because it is inherently criminal, but because the ruling class has an economic or social interest in restricting such behavior in order to protect the status quo.

Social Reality of Crime
The theory that criminal laws are designed by those in power (the rich) to help them keep power at the expense of those who do not have power (the poor).

only three of the nation's five hundred most profitable companies had a black chief executive.[46] Similarly, women have run up against what has been called the "glass ceiling" as they attempt to assume positions of power in corporations: only eight major U.S. corporations have a female chief executive.[47] Furthermore, those women most likely to be arrested and imprisoned have exactly the characteristics—low income, often raising children without the aid of a partner—that social conflict theorists would predict.

Those who perceive the criminal justice system as an instrument of social control point to a number of historical studies and statistics to support their argument. In the nineteenth century, nearly three-quarters of female inmates had been incarcerated for sexual misconduct; they were sent to institutions such as New York's Western House of Refuge at Albion to be taught the virtues of "true" womanhood.[48] Today, approximately 90,000 women are arrested each year for prostitution. After the Civil War, many African Americans were driven from the South by "Jim Crow laws" designed to keep them from attaining power in the postwar period. Today, the criminal justice system performs a similar function. One out of every eleven adult black males is incarcerated on any given day, and one out of every three black males between the ages of eighteen and thirty-four is either in prison, in jail, or on probation or parole.[49]

Social Conflict Theory and Public Policy Given its radical nature, social conflict theory has had a limited impact on public policy. Even in the aftermath of situations in which class conflict has had serious and obvious repercussions, such as the Los Angeles riots of 1991, few observers feel that enough has been accomplished to improve the conditions that led to the violence. Indeed, many believe that the best hope for a shift in the power structure is the employment of more women and minorities in the criminal justice system itself.

Looking Back to Childhood: Life Course Theories of Crime

Over the past decade, a number of criminologists have begun to fill a gaping hole in the study of the causes of crime. As Francis T. Cullen and Robert Agnew put it, "throughout much of the history of American criminology, scholars simply ignored the fact that humans have a childhood."[50] Instead, the bulk of research on youthful offending has focused on teenagers.

This emphasis on adolescents has occurred for two very good reasons. First, because adolescents and young adults commit proportionally more crimes than any other age groups, criminologists have tended to focus on what happens during these years. Second, studying the behavior patterns of juveniles into adulthood is difficult enough. Extending these studies back to childhood is an even more daunting task.

Nevertheless, childhood may hold the key to many questions criminologists have been asking for years. The other theories we have studied in this chapter tend to attribute criminal behavior to factors—such as unemployment or poor educational performance—that take place long after an individual's personality has been established. Practitioners of **life course criminology** believe that lying, stealing, bullying, and other conduct problems that occur in childhood are the strongest predictors of future criminal behavior and have been seriously undervalued in the examination of why crime occurs.[51]

Self-Control Theory Focusing on childhood behavior raises the question of whether conduct problems established at a young age can be changed as one grows toward adulthood. Michael Gottfredson and Travis Hirschi, whose 1990 publication *A General Theory of Crime* is one of the foundations of life course criminology, think not.[52] Gottfredson and Hirschi believe that criminal behavior is linked to "low self-control,"

Life Course Criminology
The study of crime based on the belief that behavioral patterns developed in childhood can predict delinquent and criminal behavior later in life.

a personality trait that is formed before a child reaches the age of ten and can usually be attributed to poor parenting.[53]

Someone with low self-control is generally impulsive, thrill seeking, and likely to solve problems with violence rather than his or her intellect. Gottfredson and Hirschi think that once low self-control has been established, it will persist; that is, childhood behavioral problems are not "solved" by positive developments later in life, such as healthy personal relationships or a good job.[54] Thus, these two criminologists ascribe to what has been called the *continuity theory of crime,* which essentially says that once negative behavior patterns have been established, they cannot be changed.

The Possibility of Change Not all of those who practice life course criminology follow the continuity theory. Terrie Moffitt, for example, notes that youthful offenders can be divided into two groups. The first group are life-course-persistent offenders; they are biting playmates at age five, skipping school at ten, stealing cars at sixteen, committing violent crimes at twenty, and perpetrating fraud and child abuse at thirty.[55] The second group are adolescent-limited offenders; as the name suggests, their "life of crime" is limited to the teenage years.[56]

So, according to Moffitt, change is possible, if not for the life-course-persistent offenders (who are saddled with psychological problems that lead to continued social failure and misconduct), then for the adolescent-limited offenders. Robert Sampson and John Laub take this line of thinking one step further. While acknowledging that "antisocial behavior is relatively stable" from childhood to old age, Sampson and Laub have gathered a great deal of data showing, in their opinion, that offenders may experience "turning points" when they are able to veer off the road to a life of crime.[57]

Life Course Criminology and Public Policy As we will see in Chapter 15, the American public often seems of two minds as to how to treat juvenile offenders. The American juvenile justice system was created with an eye toward rehabilitating wayward youths, but in recent years it has become more of an instrument to punish them. Though it is too early to determine how life course criminology will affect public policy in this area, certain patterns are rather predictable. On the one hand, politicians who want to continue to "get tough" with juvenile delinquents will point to continuity theories to promote the view that "once a criminal, always a criminal"—no matter what the age. On the other hand, those who favor rehabilitation will use research such as that done by Sampson and Laub to argue that the juvenile justice system's primary purpose should be to provide the "turning points" that these troubled youths so badly need. (See *Mastering Concepts* for a review of the theories discussed so far in this chapter.)

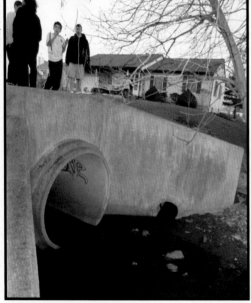

Onlookers stand over a drainage pipe in Woodbridge, New Jersey, where, on March 26, 2003, police found the body of three-year-old Amir Beeks. A ten-year-old was eventually accused of beating Meeks with a baseball bat and sexually assaulting the toddler before abandoning him in the ditch. Why might the fact that neighbors described the adolescent as a "bully" who threw rocks, picked fights, and vandalized cars be of interest to those who subscribe to life course criminology theory?

AP Photo/Mike Derer

Emerging Theories in Criminology

The six theories described so far form the bedrock of criminological study, but the field is in no way limited to these basic principles. Criminologists such as Anthony Walsh, a professor of criminal justice at Boise State University, are constantly challenging accepted theories on crime with new insights and research. Walsh believes that "biological factors do not operate in an environmental vacuum, nor do environmental factors operate in a biological vacuum."[58] Consequently, he advocates a "biosocial" model of crime, combining aspects of trait and sociological theories to explain antisocial behavior. Other emerging theories in criminology include racial threat theory, differential coercion theory, and convict criminology.

MASTERING CONCEPTS

The Causes of Crime

Choice Theories

Crime is the result of rational choices made by those who decide to engage in criminal activity for the rewards it offers. The rewards may be financial or they may be psychological—criminals enjoy the "rush" that comes with committing a crime. According to choice theorists, the proper response to crime is harsh penalties, which force potential criminals to weigh the benefits of wrongdoing against the costs of punishment if they are apprehended.

Biological and Psychological Trait Theories

Criminal behavior is explained by biological and psychological attributes of the individual. Those who support biological theories of crime believe that the secret to crime is locked in the human body: in genes, brain disorders, reaction to improper diet or allergies, and so on. Psychological attempts to explain crime are based on the study of personality and intelligence and the development of a person's behavioral patterns during infancy.

Sociological Theories

Crime is not something a person is "born to do." Instead, it is the result of the social conditions under which a person finds himself or herself. Those who are socially disadvantaged—because of poverty or other factors such as racial discrimination—are more likely to commit crimes because other avenues to "success" have been closed off. High-crime areas will develop their own cultures that are in constant conflict with the dominant culture and create a cycle of crime that claims the youth who grow up in the area and go on to be career criminals.

✓ Social Process Theories

The major influence on any individual is not society in general, but the interactions that dominate everyday life. Therefore, individuals are drawn to crime not by general factors such as "society" or "community," but by family, friends, and peer groups. Crime is "learned behavior"; the "teacher" is usually a family member or friend. Everybody has the potential to become a criminal. Those who form positive social relationships instead of destructive ones have a better chance of avoiding criminal activity. Furthermore, if a person is labeled "delinquent" or "criminal" by the authority figures or organizations in his or her life, there is a greater chance he or she will create a personality and actions to fit that label.

Social Conflict Theories

Criminal laws are a form of social control. Through these laws, the dominant members of society control the minority members, using institutions such as the police, courts, and prisons as tools of oppression. Crime is caused by the conflict between the "haves" and "have-nots" of society. The poor commit crimes because of the anger and frustration they feel at being denied the benefits of society.

✓ Life Course Theories

Even though criminal behavior usually begins after the age of fourteen, the factors that lead to that behavior start much earlier. To fully understand why crime occurs, then, criminologists must better understand conduct problems of early childhood and how those problems lead to or predict later wrongdoing. The most pressing question becomes whether early misbehavior necessarily leads to a life of crime, or whether it can be used as a warning signal to prevent such a future from taking place.

Racial Threat Theory Sometimes, new criminological theories result from dramatic developments in the "real world" of crime. Over the past few decades, for example, the increased imprisonment of African Americans has led to the resurgence of *racial threat theory*. First developed to describe the reaction of many whites to the growing social, economic, and political power of blacks in the 1960s,[59] today the theory focuses on the relationship between modern racism and the amount of control the criminal justice system exerts on the African American population. Specifically, a number of studies have linked increases in black residency to increases in the size and funding of local police departments and higher arrest and incarceration rates for African Americans in those areas.[60]

> "It is not racism that makes whites uneasy about blacks moving into their neighborhoods . . . it is fear. Fear of crime, of drugs, of gangs, of violence."
>
> —James Q. Wilson, criminologist (1992)

Differential Coercion Theory In 2000, Professor Mark Colvin of Kent State University presented his *differential coercion theory* to the criminological community.[61] Building on aspects of strain and self-control theories, Colvin focuses on various types of force that compel a person to engage in delinquent or criminal behavior. This force can be either physical, in the form of a direct attack, or nonphysical, in the form of threats, criticism, teasing, whining, yelling, or negative commands. According to Colvin, the degree (from no coercion to very strong coercion) and the frequency of the coercion a young person is subjected to will have a significant impact on the likelihood that he or she will engage in misconduct.[62]

Over the past several years, criminologists have tested and expanded on differential coercion theory. One study, conducted by Colvin himself with colleagues James D. Unnever and Francis T. Cullen, showed that while family-related coercion was significantly related to delinquency, those youths exposed to peer coercion—"bullying"—did not show high rates of misbehavior.[63] Another research group investigated the effect of having an antisocial romantic partner and found that this form of coercion increased levels of criminality in both men and women.[64] As coercion theory continues to gain acceptance, many criminologists are questioning its public-policy implications: If "negative" coercion breeds crime, can "positive" coercion in the form of constructive role models reduce crime?[65]

Criminology professor Stephen C. Richards of Northern Kentucky University is a self-described "convict criminologist." During the 1980s, Richards spent three years in prison after being found guilty of conspiracy to distribute marijuana. He feels his time behind bars provided a "sort of crash course in studying the reality of prisons." What other kinds of "real-life" backgrounds do you think would be helpful in researching and teaching criminal justice topics?

© Mark Lyons

Convict Criminology A third "new" criminology highlights the messenger as much as the message. A group of nearly thirty criminology professors and graduate students who have served prison time are promoting the benefits of *convict criminology* research. These former inmates reject what they see as the antiseptic approach of mainstream criminology in favor of an approach that relies on experience and a comfort level with those elements of society who have committed crimes and served time in correctional facilities.[66] Daniel S. Murphy, a criminology professor at Appalachian State University in Boone, North Carolina, who spent five years in federal prison for a drug offense, thinks that he and other convict criminologists feel more at ease with inmates than traditional researchers do and therefore are more likely to engage them on a one-on-one level. "In some ways it's easier to sit in your office and look at government statistics," he says.[67]

This school of research is primarily concerned with corrections issues, such as the use—or overuse—of incarceration as a crime-fighting tool and the dehumanizing conditions in many prisons and jails. Some critics of the movement find the convict criminologists *too* focused on prisons and prison life, to the exclusion of the other facets of the field that have been discussed in this chapter. But, in general, the consensus appears to be that the unique insights of ex-inmates can only enrich the body of criminological knowledge.[68]

✳ VICTIMOLOGY AND VICTIMS OF CRIME

Since its founding days, criminology has focused almost exclusively on one-half of the crime equation: the offender. If you review our discussion of criminology up to this point, you will find little mention of the other half: the victim. Indeed, it was not until after World War II (1939–1945) that the scientific study of crime victims began to appeal to academicians, and only in the last several decades has **victimology** become an essential component of criminology.[69] The growing emphasis on the victim has had a profound impact on the police, the courts, and corrections administrators in this country. Accordingly, Andrew Karmen, a professor of sociology at the John Jay College of Criminal Justice in New York City, has defined *victimology* as the study of "relationships between victims and offenders [and] the interactions between victims and the criminal justice system."[70]

The Experience of Being a Victim

Although he never used the term *victimology* to describe his work, the German criminologist Hans von Hentig (1887–1974) has been credited with introducing the notion that increased attention needed to be paid to the victim's role in crime.[71] In his 1948 book, *The Criminal and His Victim,* von Hentig described the victim as one of the "causative elements" of the crime, consciously or unconsciously provoking the criminal act through his or her behavior.[72] The theory that the victim played an active role in his or her own victimization continued to dominate victimology for several decades.[73] Starting in the 1970s, however, the "art of blaming the victim" came under heavy criticism, and criminologists began to concentrate on the physical, emotional, and economic damages suffered by individuals as a result of crime.

Taking into account factors ranging from lost wages to medical costs to psychological trauma, Ross Macmillan of the University of Minnesota has estimated that an adolescent victim of crime will lose about $240,000 over the course of her or his lifetime.[74] A number of studies have also shown that victimization results in mental health problems and substance abuse, as crime victims struggle to deal with the psychological aftermath of the experience.[75] Furthermore, data show that the same persons tend to be both victims and offenders, suggesting that being a victim may lead to future criminal wrongdoing.[76]

Factors of Victimization

The proliferation of data on crime victims has been invaluable in the development of victimology. Resources such as the National Crime Victimization Survey, which you will learn more about in the next chapter, allow "victimologists" to pinpoint those persons who are most at risk to be victimized by crime. As Figure 2.2 on the next page shows, certain demographic groups—particularly young, low-income African Americans—are statistically more vulnerable than others. Without suggesting that these groups cause their own victimization, criminologists can explore how aspects of an individual's life affect the possibility of being a crime victim.[77]

Victimology
A school of criminology that studies why certain people are the victims of crimes and the optimal role for victims in the criminal justice system.

FIGURE 2.2
Crime Victims in
the United States

According to the U.S. Department
of Justice, African Americans,
households with annual incomes
of less than $7,500, and
teenagers between the ages of
sixteen and nineteen are most
likely to be victims of violent
crime in this country.

Source: Bureau of Justice Statistics,
Criminal Victimization, 2003
(Washington, D.C.: U.S. Department of
Justice, 2004), 4, 6.

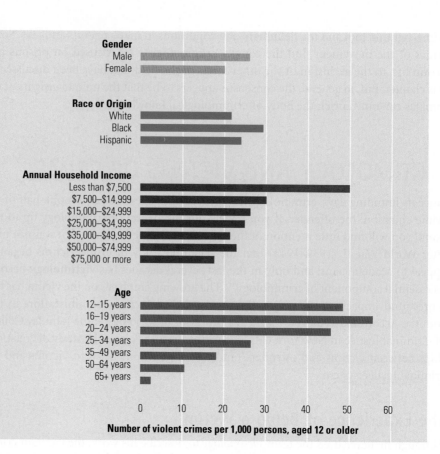

Alcohol and Victimization In the introduction to this chapter, we discussed the differences between correlations and causes. Due to the complexities of their field, criminologists are usually reluctant to declare that any one factor causes a certain result. Richard B. Felson and Keri B. Burchfield of Penn State University, however, believe that alcohol consumption has a causal effect on victimization under certain circumstances.[78] After examining victimization surveys, Felson and Burchfield found that "frequent and heavy drinkers" are at a great risk of assault when they are drinking, but do not show abnormal rates of victimization when they are sober. The authors hypothesize that drinking causes aggressive and offensive behavior, particularly in intoxicated men, which in turn triggers violent reactions in those around them.

Women and Victimization The discipline of victimology has been particularly informative in expanding the knowledge of female victims of crime. Although female offending rates are on the rise, the vast majority of offenders are men. Consequently, traditional criminology has centered primarily on male criminal behavior. As Figure 2.2 shows, however, victimization rates of men and women are comparable, a fact reflected in a wide range of studies concerning female victims.

The research conducted by Felson and Burchfield, for example, shows that the relationship between alcohol and sexual assault is unaffected by the gender of the victim.[79] These findings are somewhat at odds with a tenet of social conflict theory, which holds that men are motivated to rape drunk women to punish them for socially unacceptable ("unladylike") behavior such as drinking heavily. Rather, alcohol affects judgment and leads to risky behavior by both male and female victims of sexual assault.

A study published by Janet L. Lauritsen and Robin J. Schaum of the University of Missouri–St. Louis has similarly expanded our understanding of women at risk of violent crime.[80] Though much research has focused on the victim's race, ethnicity, or economic status, Lauritsen and Schaum believe that family structure and the family composition of a community may provide more consistent clues to the actual threat of violence faced by women. They found that young women who are raising children without the help of a partner and who live in communities with a higher concentration of other single-mother households suffer consistently elevated victimization rates, regardless of their race or income level. Lauritsen and Schaum's results may be partly explained by the difficulty these women have in forming the community ties that, in the eyes of social disorganization theorists, help protect individuals against crime.

Protecting Victims' Rights

Female victims of crime, particularly sexual assault, have been integral to perhaps the most remarkable aspect of victimology: its transformation from a solely academic discipline to the basis for a political movement.[81] Historically, victims of crime were virtually absent from the criminal justice system. Once the crime was committed, the victim's role in the process was generally limited to appearing as a witness for the prosecution. In criminal trials, the state brings charges against the defendant "in the name of the people," effectively reducing the victim to an afterthought. "[T]he purpose of the criminal trial is not to stand by the victim," says Stephen J. Schulhofer, a professor at the New York University School of Law. "The purpose of the trial is to determine whether the defendant is factually and legally responsible for an offense."[82]

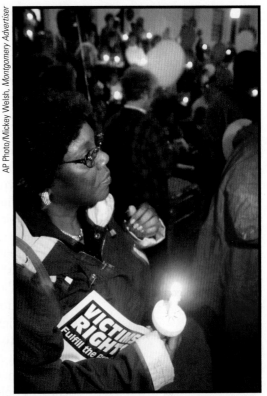

Nell Rankins, whose daughter was murdered, holds a candle at the Victims of Crime and Leniency vigil on the steps of the Public Safety Building in Montgomery, Alabama. What have been some of the results of these kinds of efforts to give victims and their families a greater voice in the criminal justice system?

The Victims' Rights Movement A large number of Americans, particularly victims themselves, do not agree with Schulhofer. Advocates of victims' rights speak of *system revictimization,* a term used to describe the frustration of victims.[83] "The system saw me as a piece of evidence, like a fingerprint or a photograph, not as a feeling, thinking human being," said one rape victim.[84] Indeed, the modern victims' rights movement began with the opening of rape-crisis centers by feminist groups in the early 1970s. Since then, hundreds of grassroots organizations have been formed to deal with the needs of victims. Some, such as Parents of Murdered Children, are primarily concerned with the emotional state of victims. Others, such as Mothers Against Drunk Driving, concentrate on lobbying legislators for victims' rights laws.

State Laws Much of this effort has focused on state-level protection, and the impact has been impressive. State legislators have passed nearly 30,000 victim-related laws over the past twenty years, and thirty-two state constitutions now include protections for the rights of crime victims.[85] These laws generally focus on three areas:

- Enabling the victim to receive restitution from the person who committed the crime.
- Allowing the victim to participate in the criminal prosecution and sentencing of the offender (a topic we will explore in Chapters 9 and 11).
- Protecting the victim from harassment or abuse from the criminal justice process (such as intrusive interviews by the police).[86]

This legislation often gives the victim a legal ground on which to challenge the actions of police, judges, and corrections officials. In Arizona, for example, a state parole board granted a rapist parole without notifying his victim of the parole hearing. The woman challenged the decision, noting that the state constitution gave her the right to be present at any such proceeding. Citing this failure to notify the victim, the Arizona

See the **National Organization for Victim Assistance,** an advocacy organization for victims' rights. Find its Web site by clicking on *Web Links* under *Chapter Resources* at **www.cjinaction.com.**

As you will see throughout this textbook, the U.S. Constitution provides defendants in criminal proceedings with a number of protective rights. Those who support a Victims' Rights Amendment believe that the document should be "evened out" to give those who have suffered at the hands of wrongdoers more of a voice in the criminal justice system. For more information on the crucial issues in the dispute over victims' rights laws, click on *Great Debates* under *Book Resources* at **www.cjinaction.com.**

Supreme Court ordered a new parole hearing at which she was given a chance to tell her "side of the story." The parole decision was reversed, and the offender was sent back to prison.[87]

Federal Laws Despite decisions such as the Arizona parole board's reversal, many observers feel that state laws do not go far enough in protecting victims' rights. A large-scale study carried out by federal government researchers found that these laws are not consistently observed. Fewer than 60 percent of victims were notified of their offender's sentencing hearing, and fewer than 40 percent were told that the offender was going to be released from jail before trial.[88]

Many victims' advocates feel that the U.S. Constitution is at the root of the problem. Though the Constitution provides numerous rights for criminal defendants, its articles and amendments never mention crime victims. A long and intense effort to insert a Victims' Rights Amendment into the Constitution was finally abandoned in 2004, defeated by concerns that the amendment would place "enormous new burdens" on law enforcement agencies and possibly make it more difficult for the criminal justice system to effectively punish wrongdoers.[89] Even those who favor more rights for victims also worried that an amendment would impinge on the constitutional rights of the accused to a fair trial, a subject we will study in more detail in Chapter 10.

Instead, supporters of the amendment had to settle for new federal legislation that President George W. Bush signed into law on October 31, 2004.[90] The statute gives victims of violent crime a core set of procedural rights in federal courts, including the right to be "reasonably protected" from the accused offender, the right to be involved in all public proceedings involving the victim, and the right to "be treated with fairness and with respect for the victim's dignity and privacy." (For a discussion of how one European country has dealt with this issue, see the feature *International CJ—Victims' Rights in Germany*.)

CRIMINOLOGY FROM THEORY TO PRACTICE

You have almost completed the only chapter in this textbook that deals primarily with theory. What follows will concentrate on the more practical and legal aspects of the criminal justice system: how law enforcement agencies fight crime, how our court systems determine guilt or innocence, and how we punish those who are found guilty. As our discussion of victimology's influence on victims' rights legislation shows, however, criminology can play a crucial role in the criminal justice system. Perhaps the most influential criminological contribution to crime fighting in the past half century was *Delinquency in a Birth Cohort,* published by the pioneering trio of Marvin Wolfgang, Robert Figlio, and Thorsten Sellin in 1972. This research established the idea of the **chronic offender,** or career criminal, by showing that a small group of juvenile offenders—6 percent—was responsible for a disproportionate amount of the violent crime attributed to a group of nearly 10,000 young males: 71 percent of the murders, 82 percent of the robberies, 69 percent of the aggravated assaults, and 73 percent of the rapes.[91] Further research has supported the idea of a "chronic 6 percent,"[92] and law enforcement agencies and district attorneys' offices have devised specific strategies to apprehend and prosecute repeat offenders, with dozens of local police agencies forming career criminal units to deal with the problem. Legislators have also reacted to this research: habitual offender laws that provide harsher sentences for repeat offenders have become quite popular. We will discuss these statutes, including the controversial "three-strikes-and-you're-out" laws, in Chapter 11.

Chronic Offender
A delinquent or criminal who commits multiple offenses and is considered part of a small group of wrongdoers who are responsible for a majority of the antisocial activity in any given community.

INTERNATIONAL CJ

Victims' Rights in Germany

American supporters of victims' rights might well look with envy at the criminal justice system of Germany. According to one German official, the aim of victim protection laws in his country is to "stop a person aggrieved because of a criminal act from being a mere object of the proceedings." Rather, in Germany the victim is "made a player in the proceedings with rights he [or she] can assert [in court]."

Specifically, Chapter Two of the German Federal Code of Criminal Procedure codifies the victim's right to "join a public prosecution as a private accessory prosecutor." In essence, this means that a victim (or, in the case of murder, a victim's parents, children, siblings, and/or spouse) can choose to become a "secondary accuser" in a German criminal trial and receive treatment equal to the defendant's. The victim is permitted to use a "victim attorney," or *Opferanwalt,* and this attorney has the same access to evidence and the same ability to obtain information regarding the crime as the state's attorney and the defense attorney. If the victim is unable to afford an *Opferanwalt,* the government will provide one at no cost.

Initially, critics of this system, known as *Nebenklager,* worried that its costs would be too burdensome for German society. The procedure is, however, limited by two factors. First, it is available only to victims of serious, violent crimes such as murder, assault, kidnapping, and rape. Second, the procedure is optional. So far, only sexual-assault victims have decided to invoke *Nebenklager* in large numbers. In fact, it is now standard practice for German police to inform rape victims of their right to participate in the trial.

FOR CRITICAL ANALYSIS

Why do you think victims of sexual assault have been more likely than victims of other violent crimes to take advantage of the opportunities provided by the *Nebenklager* procedure? In general, could such a system operate effectively in the United States?

There is a sense, however, that criminology has not done enough to make our country a safer place. Eminent criminologist James Q. Wilson, for one, has criticized his peers for trying to understand crime rather than reduce it.[93] Many criminal justice practitioners also argue that too much of the research done by criminologists is inaccessible for them. As Sarah J. Hart, director of the National Institute of Justice, has noted, an overwhelmed police chief simply does not have the time or patience to wade through the many scientific journals in which crime research appears.[94]

These criticisms notwithstanding, John H. Laub of the American Society of Criminology defends modern criminology's practical benefits.[95] He points out that the work of Clifford Shaw and Henry McKay (see page 43) focused law enforcement efforts on the community, while Travis Hirshi's research in the 1960s on the root causes of delinquency has had a wide impact on the juvenile justice system. As we will discuss further in Chapter 6, Wilson himself (in collaboration with George Kelling) developed the "broken windows" theory, which reshaped police strategy in the 1990s and 2000s. Indeed, in the opinion of many observers, researchers know more today about "what works" in criminology than at any other time in our nation's history.[96] (For a discussion of one area in which criminologists remain somewhat unsure of themselves, see the *Criminal Justice in Action* feature starting on the next page.)

The Ever-Elusive Serial Killer

Criminologists do not pull their theories out of thin air. They study the conduct of groups of people, known as *cohorts*, to test different ideas about why crime occurs. Preferably, members of a cohort will share certain characteristics, such as age, income, or background, and, as a general rule, the larger the cohort, the better. The cohort used in the groundbreaking "chronic 6 percent" study mentioned on page 56, for example, contained nearly 10,000 males born in Philadelphia in 1945. When a cohort is small and ill defined, however, any conclusions drawn from the behavior of its members will be of minimal value. In some instances, as our discussion of the serial killer phenomenon in this *Criminal Justice in Action* feature will show, overreliance on limited crime data can have tragic results.

Breaking the Mold

Dennis L. Rader hardly fit the profile of the serial killer. He had a stable family life: married for thirty-four years with two children. He had a steady job: working for the municipality of Park City, Kansas, as a compliance officer. He was well respected by his friends and neighbors: Cub Scout leader and regular churchgoer. And yet, in August 2005, a judge sentenced Rader, also known as the "BTK" killer, to ten consecutive life terms in prison

AP Photo/Court TV, Pool

On June 27, 2005, Dennis Rader, also known as the BTK killer, admitted to killing ten people in the Wichita, Kansas, area between 1974 and 1991. "If you've read much about serial killers, they go through what they call different phases," Radar told the Sedgwick (Kansas) County District Court. "In the trolling stage, basically, you're looking for a victim. You can be trolling for months or years, but once you lock in on a certain person, you become a stalker."

for a series of murders he committed between 1974 and 1991. "We've rarely seen serial killers so well integrated into the community," noted Michael Rustigan, a criminologist at San Francisco State University.[97]

Rader is only one of several serial killers to confound expectations in recent years. Robert L. Yates, a married Army veteran and factory worker with five children, was convicted in 2000 for murdering thirteen prostitutes in and around Spokane, Washington. Derrick Todd Lee killed two of his seven female victims after being investigated and disregarded by law enforcement officials looking for a white or Hispanic man who had a "low level of sophistication in interacting with women"—stereotypical characteristics of serial murderers. Lee, who is African American and apparently charmed his way into the homes of his targets in Baton Rouge, Louisiana, was not arrested until DNA evidence linked him to a slaying in 2003.[98] "We all think we know what the bogeyman looks like, but we don't," says Professor Tomas Guillen of Seattle University.[99]

Violence for Violence's Sake

The public has been fascinated with these "bogeymen" since Jack the Ripper set off a media frenzy in late nineteenth-century London, England, with several brutal murders of prostitutes. Criminology professionals, however, still believe our knowledge of serial murderers is inadequate. Even the Federal Bureau of Investigation's (FBI's) definition of the crime—a series of two or more killings, having common characteristics such as to suggest the reasonable possibility that the crimes were committed by the same offender or offenders—is controverted, with some criminologists believing that even one murder can be a serial killing.[100]

The problem lies with serial killers' motives. Most violent crime is *instrumental*, meaning that the violence is used to achieve some purpose, such as an armed robber shooting a convenience store clerk to get access to the cash register. In contrast, most serial murders are *affective*. In other words, the "thrill of the kill"—the "rush" described by Jack Katz on page 38—is the sole purpose of the crime. Furthermore, the victim-offender relationship in serial killings is unusual in that the victim rarely has any established ties to her or his murderer. Hence, the crimes seem random unless one can understand the mental processes behind the slayings.[101]

Finally, a serial killer is often very well organized compared to other types of criminals. He or she fantasizes about the murder and plans it with a high degree of care, often choosing the victim with the sole purpose of evading capture. Keith Jesperson, who has been tied to eight murders in five states and boasts of as many as 160 victims, said that time and distance were the keys to his craft. He would meet a victim in one place and then dispose of the body somewhere else, where nobody would be searching for the missing person. "The longer it takes to find a body, the better," he told a reporter.[102]

"Linkage Blindness"

These factors—lack of comprehensible motive, no ties to the victim, and a high degree of planning—make serial killers very difficult to catch. In addition, serial killers often prey on those persons University of Houston criminologist Steven Eggers refers to as "the less dead" because they live on the edges of society and draw less police attention when they vanish.[103] Serial killer Keith Jesperson said he sought out "lot lizards," his term for drug users, prostitutes, and hitchhikers who frequent truck stops, for this very reason.[104]

In focusing on this particular type of victim, serial killers exploit a weakness in law enforcement that Eggers calls "linkage blindness."[105] Most local police departments do not communicate with each other and therefore have no means of knowing when similar murders occur in different geographic areas. Consequently, a serial killer can avoid detection simply by crossing county or state lines.

Law enforcement is trying to fight "linkage blindness" with innovations such as the FBI's Violent Criminal Apprehension Program (ViCAP), a nationwide information center that collects and analyzes data on violent crimes that are apparently random, motiveless, or sexually oriented. With the proper software, local police departments can access this database and compare local crimes to similar crimes nationwide. DNA technology, which will be discussed in more detail in Chapter 6, has also proved invaluable in serial murder cases. As noted earlier, DNA evidence was instrumental in the capture of the Baton Rouge serial killer Derrick Todd Lee, and a DNA sample taken in 2001 led to the arrest of Gary Ridgway, the so-called Green River killer, and his conviction in the deaths of forty-eight women.

Self-Proclaimed Celebrities

Even with programs such as ViCAP and advances in DNA technology, law enforcement officers usually rely on a surprising source in their fight against serial killers—the suspects themselves. Many serial killers seem to have a need to be in the public eye. David Berkowitz, the famed "Son of Sam" who murdered six people in New York City in the mid-1970s, wrote letters to the press during his killing spree and continues to do so from his prison cell. Herebito Seda was dubbed the New York Zodiac Killer after he mailed handwritten notes to the media outlining his plan to kill one person for each sign of the zodiac in the early 1990s.

Police would probably never have found Dennis Rader, the "BTK" killer, were it not for his love of the limelight. Following his first murders in 1974, Rader began sending letters with graphic descriptions of his crimes and poems to media outlets in Wichita, Kansas. In one, he complained, "How many do I have to kill before I get my name in the paper or some national attention?" He even coined his own nickname, which stands for Bind, Torture, Kill. Eventually, the letters stopped, and hopes of determining Rader's identity faded. Then, in March 2004, Rader reopened his communication with the press and police, taking credit for an unsolved 1986 killing. On February 16, 2005, local television station KSAS received a package from Rader that included a lilac-colored computer disk. The disk was traced to a computer at Rader's church, which led police to his doorstep.

The Problem

Criminologist James Alan Fox believes that this craving for celebrity comes from serial killers' need to distinguish themselves in a way not possible in their everyday lives.[106] Given the high number of serial murderers who have not sought public attention, however, this insight applies only to certain offenders. Therein lies the problem, and challenge, for criminology when it comes to serial killers: each killer is unique and therefore is unable to provide many clues to the actions of the others.

Making Sense of Serial Killers

1. The FBI and many criminologists have turned to "psychological autopsies" to learn more about serial killers. This process, developed to determine the state of mind of suicide victims, explores the behavior, thoughts, feelings, and relationships of an individual through a series of interviews with people who knew the serial killer and, in these cases, the criminals themselves. What, if any, practical benefits do you think psychological autopsies might provide when it comes to understanding serial killers?

2. In 1992, Jeffrey Dahmer was convicted of killing sixteen men and boys in Milwaukee, Wisconsin. During his trial, it came out that Dahmer would "zombify" his dead victims by pouring chemicals into their bodies, have sex with the corpses, and eat various body parts. At the same time, he planned each murder very carefully and avoided detection for years. After reviewing the sections on choice and biological theories of crime in this chapter (see pages 37–42), do you think that someone like Dahmer has "control" over his actions? Do you think the fact that a criminal may have psychological problems should affect the severity of her or his punishment? Explain your answer.

Chapter Summary

1 Explain why classical criminology is based on choice theory. Choice theory holds that those who commit crimes choose to do so. Classical criminology is based on a model of a person rationally making a choice before committing a crime—weighing the benefits against the costs.

2 Contrast positivism with classical criminology. Whereas classical theorists believe criminals make rational choices, those of the positivist school believe that criminal behavior is determined by psychological, biological, and social forces that the individual cannot control.

3 List and describe the three theories of social structure that help explain crime. Social disorganization theory states that crime is largely a product of unfavorable conditions in certain communities, or zones of disorganization. The strain theory argues that most people seek increased wealth and financial security and that the strain of not being able to achieve these goals legally leads to criminal behavior. Finally, cultural deviance theory asserts that people adapt to the values of the subculture—which has its own standards of behavior—to which they belong.

4 List and briefly explain the three branches of social process theory. (a) Learning theory, which contends that people learn to be criminals from their family and peers. (b) Control theory, which holds that most of us are dissuaded from a life of crime because we place importance on the opinions of family and peers. (c) Labeling theory, which holds that a person labeled a "junkie" or a "thief" will respond by remaining whatever she or he is labeled.

5 Describe how life course criminology differs from the other theories addressed in this chapter. The five other theories addressed in this chapter link criminal behavior to factors—such as unemployment or poor schools—that affect an individual long after his or her personality has been established. Life course theories focus on behavioral patterns of childhood such as bullying, lying, and stealing as predictors of future criminal behavior.

6 Discuss the evolution of victimology from its beginnings in the 1940s until today. When criminologists first began studying the victims of crimes after World War II, they theorized that the victim played an active role in her or his victimization. This line of thinking remained popular for several decades. In the 1970s, however, victims' rights groups began to criticize the "blame the victim" tendency in criminology, and researchers turned their attention to the experience of being a victim and the victim's role in the criminal justice system.

7 Explain why some criminologists believe the connection between alcohol and victimization is unique. In general, criminologists are unwilling to say that a factor causes victimization or crime. Rather, they focus on correlations between data and actions. Research has shown, however, that people who abuse alcohol are much more likely to be the victim of an assault when they are drinking than when they are sober. Thus, some criminologists suggest that victimization may be a direct result of alcohol intake.

8 List the arguments for and against greater legal protection of victims' rights. (a) Those who have been the target of crimes also suffer from "system revictimization" due to the thoughtlessness of the criminal justice system. Even though the majority of state constitutions contain provisions to protect victims' rights, these laws are not consistently observed. Only federal legislation, in the form of an amendment to the U.S. Constitution or otherwise, will adequately protect a victim's interests. (b) Victims are excluded from the trial process because it is designed to determine the guilt or innocence of the accused. Because the defendant is in an adversarial relationship with the government, he or she needs the legal protections provided in the Constitution and elsewhere. The victim is not "on trial," so providing equal protection would only "bog down" the criminal justice system.

STORIES FROM THE STREET

Go to the *Stories from the Street* feature at **www.cjinaction.com** to hear Larry Gaines tell insightful stories related to this chapter and his experiences in the field.

Key Terms

anomie   44
choice theory   37
chronic offender   56
classical criminology   37
control theory   46
criminology   36

cultural deviance theory   44
labeling theory   47
learning theory   46
life course criminology   49
positivism   38
social conflict theories   48

social disorganization theory   43
social process theories   46
social reality of crime   48
strain theory   44
subculture   45

theory of differential association   46
utilitarianism   38
victimology   53

Questions for Critical Analysis

1 What is one possible reason for higher crime rates in low-income communities?

2 If you believe that fear of punishment can have a deterrent effect on criminal activity, to what view of human behavior are you subscribing?

3 If you believe that criminals learn how to be criminals, to what theory are you subscribing?

4 Why have social conflict theories had a limited impact on public policy in the United States?

5 Why is it important for criminologists to study the behavior of preadolescents?

6 Why do some convict criminologists believe they have an advantage over their mainstream colleagues?

7 What factors contributed to the victims' rights movement becoming politically successful?

8 What is a chronic offender, and why is this sort of person of interest to criminologists?

Test Preparation Online

Criminal JusticeNow

Go to **www.cjinaction.com** and click on *Criminal JusticeNow* for access to this powerful online study tool. You will get a *personalized study plan* based on your responses to a diagnostic pretest. Once you have mastered the material with the help of interactive learning tools, video clips with questions, an integrated e-book, and more, you can take a posttest to confirm you are ready to move on to the next chapter.

Book Companion Web Site

At the book companion Web site (**www.cjinaction.com**), you will find many resources in addition to *Criminal JusticeNow* to aid you in studying for your exams. For example, under *Chapter Resources,* you will find the *Chapter Outline, Chapter Summary, Flashcards, Glossary, Learning Objectives, Lecture Presentations, Concept Builder, Essay Questions,* and a *Tutorial Chapter Quiz.* You can also test yourself with interactive *Online Reviews* of each chapter section. Check out the *Web Links* to access the Web sites mentioned in the text, as well as many others. You can also access recent perspectives by clicking on *CJ in the News* and *Terrorism Update* under *Course Resources.*

Suggested Readings

Cote, Suzette, ed., *Criminological Theories: Bridging the Past to the Future,* Thousand Oaks, CA: Sage Publications, 2002. This anthology covers all the major criminological theories, including articles on social, biological, and cultural causes of crime. It also offers a criminological perspective on white-collar crime and investigates feminist criminal theory. Though most of the thirty-six articles were originally published in scholarly journals, they have been edited in this edition to make them accessible to students interested in delving deeper into the various explanations of criminal behavior.

Meadows, Robert J., and Julie Kuehnel, *Evil Minds: Understanding and Responding to Violent Predators,* Upper Saddle River, NJ: Prentice Hall, 2004. Meadows, a criminal justice professor, and Kuehnel, a psychologist, take a detailed look at the "monsters" in our society to explore the fields of criminology and victimology. Using case studies of various serial killers, mass murderers, pedophiles, and rapists, the authors examine the important questions that criminologists deal with every day: Who becomes a violent predator? How did they get that way? What should we do to stop them? Meadows and Kuehnel also focus on female violent predators, comparing and contrasting them with their male counterparts.

Notes

1. Bureau of Labor Statistics, *National Census of Fatal Occupational Injuries in 2002* (Washington, D.C.: U.S. Department of Labor, 2003), 1.
2. Amy D. Whitten and Deanne M. Mosley, "Caught in the Crossfire: Employers' Liability for Workplace Violence," *Mississippi Law Journal* (2000), 506.
3. Anne Fisher, "How to Prevent Violence at Work," *Fortune* (February 21, 2005), 42.
4. Stephanie Armour, "Death in the Workplace: The Mind of a Killer," *USA Today* (July 15, 2004), 2A.
5. Thomas Capozzoli and Steve McVey, *Managing Violence in the Workplace* (Delray Beach, FL: St. Lucie Press, 1996), 26–27.
6. Ibid., 23–24.
7. James Q. Wilson and Richard J. Hernstein, *Crime and Human Nature: The Definitive Study of the Causes of Crime* (New York: Simon & Schuster, 1985), 515.
8. Ibid.
9. Jeremy Bentham, *An Introduction to the Principles of Morals and Legislation,* ed. W. Harrison (Oxford: Basil Blackwell, 1948).
10. Wilson and Hernstein, 44.
11. Jack Katz, *Seductions of Crime: Moral and Sensual Attractions of Doing Evil* (New York: Basic Books, 1988).
12. Quoted in Tim Cahill, *Buried Dreams: Inside the Mind of a Serial Killer* (New York: Bantam Books, 1986), 349.
13. David C. Rowe, *Biology and Crime* (Los Angeles: Roxbury, 2002), 2.
14. "Ex-Supervisor Held Unable to Tell Right from Wrong," *New York Times* (May 8, 1979), A16.
15. Katherine L. Wisner, Barbara L. Parry, and Catherine M. Piontek, "Postpartum Depression," *New England Journal of Medicine* (July 18, 2002), 194–199.
16. L. E. Kreuz and R. M. Rose, "Assessment of Aggressive Behavior and Plasma Testosterone in a Young Criminal Population," *Psychosomatic Medicine* 34 (1972), 321–332.
17. H. Persky, K. Smith, and G. Basu, "Relation of Psychological Measures of Aggression and Hostility to Testosterone Production in Men," *Psychosomatic Medicine* 33 (1971), 265, 276.
18. Leda Cosmides and John Tooby, "Cognitive Adaptations for Social Exchange," in *The Adapted Mind: Evolutionary Psychology and the Generation of Culture,* ed. Jerome H. Berkow, Leda Cosmides, and John Tooby (New York: Oxford University Press, 1992).
19. Lee Ellis and Anthony Walsh, "Gene-Based Evolutionary Theories in Criminology," *Criminology* 35 (May 1997), 229–276.

20. Avshalom Caspi, Joseph McClay, Terrie E. Moffitt, and Jonathan Mill, "Role of Genotype in the Cycle of Violence in Maltreated Children," *Science* (August 2, 2002), 851–854.

21. *State v. Roberts,* 14 Wash.App. 733–744, 544 P. 2d 758 (1976).

22. Sarnoff A. Mednick and Karl O. Christiansen, eds., *Biosocial Bases in Criminal Behavior* (New York: Gardner Press, 1977).

23. David C. Rowe, "Genetic and Environmental Components of Antisocial Behavior: A Study of 265 Twin Pairs," *Criminology* 24 (1986), 513–532.

24. Alison Pike and Robert Plomin, "Importance of Nonshared Environmental Factors for Childhood and Adolescent Psychopathology," *Journal of the American Academy of Child and Adolescent Psychopathology* 35 (May 1996), 560.

25. D. Williams, "Neural Factors Related to Habitual Aggression," *Brain* 92 (1969), 503.

26. Hervey M. Cleckley, *The Mask of Sanity,* 4th ed. (St. Louis: Mosby, 1964.)

27. Robert Park, Ernest Burgess, and Roderic McKenzie, *The City* (Chicago: University of Chicago Press, 1929).

28. Clifford R. Shaw, Henry D. McKay, and Leonard S. Cottrell, *Delinquency Areas* (Chicago: University of Chicago Press, 1929).

29. Clifford R. Shaw and Henry D. McKay, *Report on the Causes of Crime, Vol. 2: Social Factors in Juvenile Delinquency* (Washington, D.C.: National Commission on Law Observance and Enforcement, 1931).

30. Robert. J. Sampson, "Transcending Tradition: New Directions in Community Research, Chicago Style," *Criminology* (May 2002), 216–217.

31. Jeffrey D. Morenoff, Robert J. Sampson, and Stephen W. Raudenbush, "Neighborhood Inequality, Collective Efficacy, and the Spatial Dynamics of Urban Violence," *Criminology* (August 2001), 517–560.

32. Emile Durkheim, *The Rules of Sociological Method,* trans. Sarah A. Solovay and John H. Mueller (New York: Free Press, 1964).

33. Robert K. Merton, *Social Theory and Social Structure* (New York: Free Press, 1957). See the chapter on "Social Structure and *Anomie.*"

34. Robert Agnew, "Foundation for a General Strain Theory of Crime and Delinquency," *Criminology* 30 (1992), 47–87.

35. Robert Agnew, Timothy Brezina, John Paul Wright, and Francis T. Cullen, "Strain, Personality Traits, and Delinquency: Extending General Strain Theory," *Criminology* (February 2002), 43–71.

36. Philip G. Zimbardo, "The Human Choice: Individuation, Reason, and Order versus Deindividuation, Impulse, and Chaos," in *Nebraska Symposium on Motivation,* ed. William J. Arnold and David Levie (Lincoln, NE: University of Nebraska Press, 1969), 287–293.

37. Edwin H. Sutherland, *Criminology,* 4th ed. (Philadelphia: Lippincott, 1947).

38. L. Rowell Huesmann, Jessica Moise-Titus, Cheryl-Lynn Podolski, and Leonard D. Eron, "Longitudinal Relations between Children's Exposure to TV Violence and Their Aggressive and Violent Behavior in Young Adulthood: 1977–1992," *Developmental Psychology* (March 2003), 201.

39. Telecommunications Act of 1996, 47 U.S.C. Section 303 (1999).

40. Travis Hirschi, *Causes of Delinquency* (Berkeley: University of California Press, 1969).

41. James Q. Wilson and George L. Kelling, "Broken Windows," *Atlantic Monthly* (March 1982), 29.

42. Howard S. Becker, *Outsiders: Studies in the Sociology of Deviance* (New York: Free Press, 1963).

43. Lawrence L. Shornack, "Conflict Theory and the Family," *International Social Science Review* 62 (1987), 154–157.

44. Robert Meier, "The New Criminology: Continuity in Criminology Theory," *Journal of Criminal Law and Criminology* 67 (1977), 461–469.

45. Richard Quinney, *The Social Reality of Crime* (Boston: Little, Brown, 1970).

46. Star Parker, "Frozen in a Time Warp," *Cincinnati Post* (February 21, 2005), A12.

47. Dave Carpenter, "Going Gray: Is It a Blessing or a Curse?" *Miami Herald* (April 18, 2005), GB6.

48. Nicole Hahn Rafter, *Partial Justice: Women, Prisons, and Social Control* (New Brunswick, NJ: Transaction Publishers, 1990).

49. John A. Coleman, "Book Review: *Urban Injustice: How Ghettos Happen,*" *America* (December 1, 2002), 20.

50. Francis T. Cullen and Robert Agnew, *Criminological Theory, Past to Present: Essential Readings,* 2d ed. (Los Angeles: Roxbury Publishing Co., 2003), 12.

51. *Ibid.,* 443.

52. Michael R. Gottfredson and Travis Hirschi, *A General Theory of Crime* (Stanford, CA: Stanford University Press, 1990).

53. *Ibid.,* 90.

54. *Ibid.*

55. Terrie Moffitt, "Adolescent-Limited and Life-Course-Persistent Antisocial Behavior: A Developmental Taxonomy," *Psychological Review* 100 (1993), 679–680.

56. *Ibid.,* 674.

57. Robert J. Sampson and John H. Laub, *Crime in the Making: Pathways and Turning Points through Life* (Cambridge, MA: Harvard University Press, 1993), 11.

58. Anthony Walsh, *Biosocial Criminology: Introduction and Integration* (Cincinnati, OH: Anderson, 2002), vii.

59. Hubert M. Blaylock, *Toward a Theory of Minority-Group Relations* (New York: Capricorn Books, 1967).

60. These studies are discussed in Ted Chiricos, Kelly Welch, and Marc Gertz, "Racial Typification of Crime and Support for Punitive Measures," *Criminology* (May 1, 2004), 359–390.

61. Mark Colvin, *Crime and Coercion: An Integrated Theory of Chronic Criminality* (New York: Palgrave Macmillan, 2000).

62. James D. Unnever, Mark Colvin, and Francis T. Cullen, "Crime and Coercion: A Test of Core Theoretical Propositions," *Journal of Research in Crime and Delinquency* (August 2004), 245–246.

63. *Ibid.,* 256–258.

64. Ronald L. Simons, Eric Stewart, Leslie C. Gordon, Rand D. Conger, and Glen H. Elder, Jr., "A Test of Life-Course Explanations for Stability and Change in Antisocial Behavior from Adolescence to Young Adulthood," *Criminology* (May 1, 2002), 401–434.

65. Mark Colvin, Francis T. Cullen, and Thomas Vander Ven, "Coercion, Social Support, and Crime: An Emerging Theoretical Consensus," *Criminology* (February 1, 2002), 19–42.

66. Jeffrey Ian Ross and Stephen C. Richards, *Convict Criminology* (Belmont, CA: Wadsworth, 2003), 6.

67. Quoted in John Railey, "ASU Professor Has Insider's Insight on Criminology," *Winston-Salem Journal* (September 28, 2003), 1.

68. Warren St. John, "Professors with a Past," *New York Times* (August 9, 2003), B7.

69. Ezzat A. Fattah, "Victimology: Past, Present, and Future," *Criminologie* (2000), 18.

70. Andrew Karmen, *Crime Victims: An Introduction to Victimology* (Belmont, CA: Wadsworth, 2003).

71. Fattah, 22.

72. Hans von Hentig, *The Criminal and His Victim* (New Haven, CT: Yale University Press, 1948), 436.

73. Emilio C. Viano, "Victimology: The Study of the Victim," *Victimology* (1976), 1.

74. Ross Macmillan, "Adolescent Criminalization and Income Deficits in Adulthood," *Criminology* (May 2000), 574.

75. Scott Menard, *Short- and Long-Term Consequences of Adolescent Victimization* (Washington, D.C.: Office of Juvenile Justice and Delinquency Prevention, February 2002), 2.

76. Robert J. Sampson and Janet L. Lauritsen, "Deviant Lifestyles, Proximity to Crime, and the Offender-Victim Link in Personal Violence," *Journal of Research in Crime and Delinquency* 27 (1990), 110–139.

77. Fattah, 30.

78. Richard B. Felson and Keri B. Burchfield, "Alcohol and the Risk of Physical and Sexual Assault Victimization," *Criminology* (November 1, 2004), 837.

79. *Ibid.*

80. Janet L. Lauritsen and Robin J. Schaum, "The Social Ecology of Violence against Women," *Criminology* (May 1, 2004), 323.

81. Fattah, 25.

82. Stephen J. Schulhofer, "The Trouble with Trials; the Trouble with Us," *Yale Law Journal* (1995), 840.

83. Victor-Hugo Schulze, "In the Cold No Longer: A Primer on Victims' Rights," *Nevada Lawyer* (April 2001), 14, 15.

84. Prepared Testimony of Christine Long before the House Judiciary Committee's Constitution Subcommittee, February 10, 2000.

85. David Beatty and Trudy Gregorie, "Implementing Victims' Rights," *Corrections Today* (August 1, 2003), 81.

86. Gessner H. Harrison, "The Good, the Bad, and the Ugly: Arizona's Courts and the Crime Victims' Bill of Rights," *Arizona State Law Journal* (Summer 2002), 531.

87. *Ibid.*

88. Dean G. Kirkland, David Beatty, and Susan Smith Howley, *The Rights of Crime Victims—Does Legal Protection Make a Difference?* (Washington, D.C.: National Institute of Justice, December 1998).

89. Kelly McMurry, "Victims' Rights Movement Rises in Power," *Trial* (July 1, 1997), 12.

90. Justice for All Act of 2004, Pub. L. No. 108-405, Title I, Section 102.

91. Marvin Wolfgang, Robert Figlio, and Thorsten Sellin, *Delinquency in a Birth Cohort* (Chicago: University of Chicago Press, 1972).

92. Lawrence W. Sherman, "Attacking Crime: Police and Crime Control," in *Modern Policing,* ed. Michael Tonry and Norval Morris (Chicago: University of Chicago Press, 1992), 159.

93. James Q. Wilson, "What to Do about Crime," *Commentary* (September 1994), 25–34.

94. Sarah J. Hart, "A New Way of Doing Business at the NIJ," *Law Enforcement News* (January 15/31, 2002), 9.

95. John H. Laub, "The Life Course of Criminology in the United States: The American Society of Criminology 2003 Presidential Address," *Criminology* (February 1, 2004), 1.

96. Richard Rosenfeld, "Book Review: *The Limits of Crime Control,*" *Journal of Criminal Law and Criminology* (Fall 2002).

97. Sharon Cohen, "Suspect in BTK Serial Killer Case Lived a Remarkably Stable Life, Criminologists Say," *AP Alert—Kansas* (March 1, 2005).

98. Steve Ritea and Stephanie A. Stanley, "Why Didn't They Put the Pieces Together Sooner?" *New Orleans Picayune* (June 1, 2003), 1.

99. "Expert: Spokane Slayings Suspect Does Not Fit Serial Killer Profile," *Augusta Chronicle* (April 28, 2000), A6.

100. Mike Barber, "Serial Killers: They're Not Always Who We Think," *Seattle Post-Intelligencer* (February 21, 2003), A1.

101. Alan C. Brantley and Robert H. Kosky, Jr., "Serial Murder in the Netherlands: A Look at Motivation, Behavior, and Characteristics," *FBI Law Enforcement Bulletin* (January 1, 2005), 26.

102. Quoted in Lewis Kamb, "In Their Own Words: The Twisted Art of Murder," *Seattle Post-Intelligencer* (February 22, 2003), A1.

103. Quoted in Mike Barber, "Serial Killers Prey on 'The Less Dead,'" *Seattle Post-Intelligencer* (February 20, 2003), A1.

104. Quoted in Kamb.

105. Quoted in Barber, "Serial Killers Prey on 'The Less Dead.'"

106. Quoted in Matt Sedensky, "Experts: Serial Killers Crave Power, Resort to Violence to Achieve It," *AP Alert—Missouri* (February 28, 2005).

CHAPTER THREE

Defining and Measuring Crime

Chapter objectives

After reading this chapter, you should be able to:

1 Discuss the primary goals of civil law and criminal law and explain how these goals are realized.

2 Explain the differences between crimes *mala in se* and *mala prohibita.*

3 Identify the publication in which the FBI reports crime data and list the three ways it does so.

4 Distinguish between Part I and Part II offenses as defined in the Uniform Crime Report (UCR).

5 Describe some of the shortcomings of the UCR as a crime-measuring tool.

6 Distinguish between the National Crime Victimization Survey and self-reported surveys.

7 Identify some of the reasons given to explain the high rate of delinquent and criminal behaviors by adolescents and young adults.

8 Explain some of the links between income level and crime.

9 Discuss how crime statistics explain the rising number of women incarcerated in the United States.

Criminal JusticeNow ⏎

Optimize your study time and master key chapter concepts with *Criminal JusticeNow,* an online study tool that provides you with a *personalized study plan.* Check out the "Test Preparation Online" section at the end of the chapter for additional information.

Taking Memos in St. Louis

Danielle
Geekie was hurrying down South Broadway in St. Louis, Missouri, late on a cold January night. She had missed her bus and was trying to beat the curfew of the women's shelter where she was staying. Before she reached her destination, however, Geekie says a man carrying a gun accosted her. He took her purse and called her "lucky" because he did not take her life. St. Louis Police Officer Joyce Wesley responded to Geekie's 911 call from a nearby liquor store, but never filed an "incident report" concerning the attack. Instead, Officer Wesley detailed the event in an informal "Crime Memo Data Sheet." As a result, the apparent armed robbery of Geekie was never registered in the city's official crime records. Instead, the data sheet wound up in a drawer at the Central Park Station.

According to a January 2005 article in the *St. Louis Post-Dispatch*, city police officers wrote more than three thousand such memos in 2004, with some describing serious crimes such as burglaries, armed robberies, thefts, and rapes. In response to strong public criticism

St. Louis police officers, such as the one pictured above, have come under criticism for underreporting the amount of crime in the city.

generated by the newspaper article, the St. Louis Police Department denied that the practice was widespread. Police Chief Joe Mokwa insisted that no more than 490 memos had been taken down during the previous year. Furthermore, a source inside the police department told the *Post-Dispatch* that the memos were a valuable tool that allowed officers to avoid wasting time following up claims they believed to be false. Indeed, in her memo, Officer Wesley wrote that Geekie "was attempting to get a police report to justify her late arrival at the shelter."

What difference does
it make that the incident involving Danielle Geekie, and perhaps many other similar ones, were not officially reported? Perhaps St. Louis officials merely wanted to create the impression that their city was a safe place in order to attract new residents and businesses. Such a motive would be unethical, certainly, but what effect could it have on the safety of the citizens of St. Louis? In fact, as we will see in this chapter, definitions and measurements of crime are tools that help fight crime, and these tools are only as useful as they are reliable. Although the St. Louis Police Department's use of memos was not illegal, it did clearly violate federal standards for crime reporting. As a consequence of the officers' actions, if the *St. Louis Post-Dispatch*'s calculations were correct, the city's official 2004 crime rate was about six percentage points lower than it should have been.[1]

Even with complete cooperation from police departments, the collection of crime data is not an exact science. In the early 2000s, after almost a decade of falling crime rates, data collected by one method—which relies on police reports—indicated that rates had

Andrew Cutraro/St. Louis Post-Dispatch

66

begun to rise.[2] At the same time, according to data collected by another method—which relies on victims' reports—crime rates were at their lowest levels in thirty years.[3] Today, both methods are showing a small but steady decline for almost all types of crime except homicide, which increased each year from 1999 to 2003 before declining in most parts of the country in 2004.[4] Crime data also raise numerous questions. Why have murder rates stubbornly failed to conform to the waning numbers for other violent and property crimes? Are criminals killing criminals with more regularity? Have drug gangs

Former professional basketball player Jayson Williams, center, was charged with manslaughter in the shooting death of his limousine driver, Costas Christofi. In 2003, while the criminal trial was ongoing, Williams paid Christofi's family $2.75 million to settle a civil wrongful death lawsuit. How does this case highlight the differences between civil law and criminal law?

moved to rural areas with less of a police presence, giving them free rein to "battle it out" on the streets of small-town America? Does the proliferation of firearms contribute to these figures, or does an armed citizenry reduce violent crime? We will start our examination of these subjects with an overview of how crimes are classified, move on to the various methods of measuring crime, and end with a discussion of some statistical trends that give us a good idea of the "state of crime" in the United States today.

CLASSIFICATION OF CRIMES

The huge body of the law may be broken down according to various classifications. Three of the most important distinctions can be made between (1) civil law and criminal law, (2) felonies and misdemeanors, and (3) crimes *mala in se* and *mala prohibita*.

Civil Law and Criminal Law

All law can be divided into two categories: civil law and criminal law. As U.S. criminal law has evolved, it has diverged from U.S. civil law. The two categories of law are distinguished by their primary goals. The criminal justice system is concerned with protecting society from harm by preventing and prosecuting crimes. A crime is an act so reprehensible that it is considered a wrong against society as a whole, as well as against the individual victim.[5] Therefore, the state prosecutes a person who commits a criminal act. If the state is able to prove that a person is guilty of a crime, the government will punish her or him with imprisonment or fines, or both.

Civil law, which includes all types of law other than criminal law, is concerned with disputes between private individuals and between entities. Proceedings in civil lawsuits are normally initiated by an individual or a corporation (in contrast to criminal proceedings, which are initiated by public prosecutors). Such disputes may involve, for example, the terms of a contract, the ownership of property, or an automobile accident. Under civil law, the government provides a forum for the resolution of torts, or private wrongs, in which the injured party, called the *plaintiff*, tries to prove that a wrong has been committed by the accused party, or the *defendant*. (Note that the

Civil Law
The branch of law dealing with the definition and enforcement of all private or public rights, as opposed to criminal matters.

accused party in both criminal and civil cases is known as the defendant.) Most civil cases involve a request for monetary damages in recognition that a wrong has been committed. If, for example, a driver runs a red light and hits a pedestrian, the pedestrian could file a civil suit asking for monetary compensation for the "pain and suffering" caused by his or her injuries. (See *Mastering Concepts* for a comparison of civil and criminal law.)

Although criminal law proceedings are completely separate from civil law proceedings in the modern legal system, the two systems do have some similarities. Both attempt to control behavior by imposing sanctions on those who violate the law. Furthermore, criminal and civil law often supplement each other. In certain instances, a victim may file a civil suit against an individual who is also the target of a criminal prosecution by the government.

Because the burden of proof is much greater in criminal trials than civil ones, it is usually easier to win monetary damages than a criminal conviction.[6] After shooting

> "The good of the people is the greatest law."
> —Cicero, Roman philosopher (106–43 B.C.E.)

sixteen-year-old exchange student Yoshihiro Hattori of Japan, for example, Rodney Pearis was acquitted of manslaughter charges by a Louisiana jury. Pearis claimed he thought Hattori—who mistook the defendant's home for the site of a Halloween party—was an intruder. After the criminal trial, however, Hattori's family brought a civil suit against Pearis and was awarded more than $650,000 in damages. While the government had been unable to prove *beyond a reasonable doubt* (the burden of proof in criminal cases) that Pearis had intended to kill Hattori, the civil trial established that a *preponderance of the evidence* (the burden of proof in civil cases) showed this to be the case.

Felonies and Misdemeanors

Depending on their degree of seriousness, crimes are classified as felonies or misdemeanors. Felonies are serious crimes punishable by death or by imprisonment in a federal or state penitentiary for one year or longer (though some states, such as North Carolina, consider felonies to be punishable by at least two years' incarceration). The Model Penal Code, a general guide for criminal law that you will learn more about in the next chapter, provides for four degrees of felony:

1 Capital offenses, for which the maximum penalty is death.
2 First degree felonies, punishable by a maximum penalty of life imprisonment.
3 Second degree felonies, punishable by a maximum of ten years' imprisonment.
4 Third degree felonies, punishable by a maximum of five years' imprisonment.[7]

MASTERING CONCEPTS

Civil Law versus Criminal Law

Issue	Civil Law	Criminal Law
Area of concern	Rights and duties between individuals	Offenses against society as a whole
Wrongful act	Harm to a person or business entity	Violation of a statute that prohibits some type of activity
Party who brings suit	Person who suffered harm (plaintiff)	The state
Party who responds	Person who supposedly caused harm (defendant)	Person who allegedly committed crime (defendant)
Standard of proof	Preponderance of the evidence	Beyond a reasonable doubt
Remedy	Damages to compensate for the harm	Punishment (fine or incarceration)

Degrees of Murder Though specifics vary from state to state, some general rules apply when grading crimes. For example, most jurisdictions punish a burglary that involves a nighttime forced entry into

> "Crime, like virtue, has its degrees."
>
> —Jean Racine, French playwright (1639–1699)

a home more seriously than one that takes place during the day and involves a non-residential building or structure. Murder in the first degree occurs under two circumstances:

1 When the crime is *premeditated,* or considered beforehand by the offender, instead of being a spontaneous act of violence.

2 When the crime is *deliberate,* meaning that it was planned and decided on after a process of decision making. Deliberation does not require a lengthy planning process; a person can be found guilty of first degree murder even if she or he made the decision to murder only seconds before committing the crime.

Second degree murder occurs when no premeditation or deliberation was present, but the offender did have *malice aforethought* toward the victim. In other words, the offender acted with wanton disregard of the consequences of his or her actions. The difference between first and second degree murder is clearly illustrated in a case involving a California man who beat a neighbor to death with a partially full brandy bottle. The crime took place after Ricky McDonald, the victim, complained to Kazi Cooksey, the offender, about the noise coming from a late-night barbecue Cooksey and his friends were holding. The jury could not find sufficient evidence that Cooksey's actions were premeditated, but he certainly acted with wanton disregard of his victim's safety. Therefore, the jury convicted Cooksey of second degree murder rather than first degree murder.

A homicide committed without malice toward the victim is known as *manslaughter* and is usually punishable by up to fifteen years in prison. *Voluntary manslaughter* occurs when the intent to kill may be present, but malice was lacking. Voluntary manslaughter covers crimes of passion, in which the emotion of an argument between two friends may lead to a homicide. Voluntary manslaughter can also occur when the victim provoked the offender to act violently. *Involuntary manslaughter* covers incidents in which the offender's acts were negligent, even though there was no intent to kill. In 2005, for

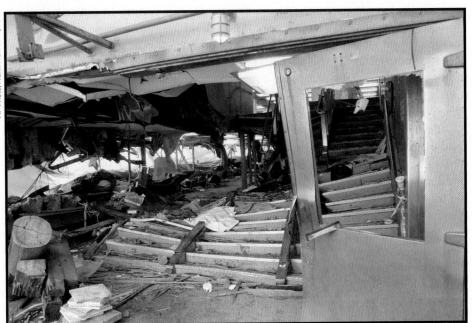

AP Photo/Frank Franklin II, Pool

As this photo shows, substantial damage was done to the interior of the Staten Island (New York) ferry *Andrew J. Barberi* when it crashed into a concrete pier in 2003. Eleven commuters died in the accident, which occurred after assistant captain Richard Smith, made drowsy by pain medication, lost consciousness at the ship's controls. Smith pleaded guilty to eleven counts of involuntary manslaughter in 2004. Why was involuntary manslaughter the proper charge in this instance? What purpose is served by punishing people for what they *intended* to occur rather than for what *actually* occurred?

example, Vanessa McGlumphy of Springfield Township, Ohio, was convicted of involuntary manslaughter for failing to protect her thirteen-month-old daughter from an abusive boyfriend. Even though there was no evidence that McGlumphy intended for her child to die at the boyfriend's hands, a jury felt that she was responsible for the girl's death nonetheless.

Degrees of Misdemeanor Under federal law and in most states, any crime that is not a felony is considered a misdemeanor. Misdemeanors are crimes punishable by a fine or by confinement for up to a year. If imprisoned, the guilty party goes to a local jail instead of a penitentiary. Disorderly conduct and trespassing are common misdemeanors. Like felonies, misdemeanors are graded by level of seriousness. In Illinois, for example, misdemeanors are either Class A (confinement for up to a year), Class B (not more than six months), or Class C (not more than thirty days).

Most states similarly distinguish between *gross misdemeanors,* which are offenses punishable by thirty days to a year in jail, and *petty misdemeanors,* or offenses punishable by fewer than thirty days in jail. The least serious form of crime is a *violation* (such as a traffic offense), which is punishable only by a small fine and does not appear on the wrongdoer's criminal record. Whether a crime is a felony or a misdemeanor can also determine whether the case is tried in a magistrate's court (for example, by a justice of the peace) or in a general trial court (for example, superior court).

Probation and community service are often imposed on those who commit misdemeanors, especially juveniles.[8] Also, most states have decriminalized all but the most serious traffic offenses. These infractions are treated as civil proceedings, and civil fines are imposed. In many states, the violator has "points" assessed against her or his driving record.

Mala in Se and Mala Prohibita

Criminologists often express the social function of criminal law in terms of *mala in se* or *mala prohibita* crimes. A criminal act is referred to as **mala in se** if it would be considered wrong even if there were no law prohibiting it. *Mala in se* crimes are said to go against "natural laws"; that is, against the "natural, moral, and public" principles of a society.[9] Murder, rape, and theft are examples of *mala in se* crimes. These crimes are generally the same from country to country or culture to culture. In contrast, the term **mala prohibita** refers to acts that are considered crimes only because they have been codified as such through statute—"human-made" laws. A *mala prohibita* crime is considered wrong only because it has been prohibited; it is not inherently a wrong, though it may reflect the moral standards of a society at a given time.[10] Thus, the definition of a *mala prohibita* crime can vary from country to country or even from state to state. Bigamy could be considered a *mala prohibita* crime.

Some observers believe that the distinction between *mala in se* and *mala prohibita* is problematic. In many instances, it is difficult to define a "pure" *mala in se* crime; that is, it is difficult to separate a crime from the culture that has deemed it a crime.[11] Even murder, in certain cultural circumstances, is not considered a criminal act. In a number of poor, traditional areas of the Middle East and Asia, for example, the law excuses "honor killings" in which men kill female family members suspected of sexual indiscretion. Our own legal system excuses homicide in extreme situations, such as self-defense or when a law enforcement agent kills in the course of upholding the law. Therefore, all "natural" laws can be seen as culturally specific. Similar difficulties occur in trying to define a "pure" *mala prohibita* crime.[12] (For an example of how different cultures have different views on crime, see the feature *International CJ—The World's Oldest Profession.*)

Mala in Se
A descriptive term for acts that are inherently wrong, regardless of whether they are prohibited by law.

Mala Prohibita
A descriptive term for acts that are made illegal by criminal statute and are not necessarily wrong in and of themselves.

The World's Oldest Profession

Bridgette does not think that prostitution should exist. "I know there are a lot of women suffering in that business," she says. Her opinion might come as a surprise to her clients, given that Bridgette, who lives and works in Belgium, is herself a prostitute. "I'm making good money," she admits. Part of the reason for her success is that prostitution is legal in Belgium. In fact, about 80,000 people pay for sex every day there, more than go to the movies.

The situation in Belgium is hardly unique. According to the Protection Project (**http://www.protectionproject.org**), prostitution is legal (though often heavily regulated) in more than 150 countries, including most members of the European Union. Indeed, in the past several years, both Germany and the Netherlands have passed legislation that treats prostitutes like any other workers, collecting taxes on their sex profits in return for health care, unemployment insurance, and pensions.

In the United States, state laws have made the buying and selling of sex illegal almost everywhere. In part, these laws are designed to prevent the illegal activities that are said to go along with prostitution, such as organized crime, drug use, trafficking in women from other countries, and the spread of sexually transmitted diseases. The main driving force behind the legislation, however, is public morality: prostitution is widely believed to go against America's "social fabric." Indeed, in the seven Nevada counties that have legalized prostitution, criminal problems associated with the practice are almost nonexistent, and thanks to strict testing regulations, the rate of AIDS and other sexually transmitted diseases among registered prostitutes in the state is practically zero.

Molly Luft has been a prostitute for thirty years and operates one of the best-known legal brothels in Berlin, Germany.

REUTERS/Manuela Hartling/Landov

FOR CRITICAL ANALYSIS

Is prostitution a *mala in se* crime or a *mala prohibita* crime? Explain your answer, and discuss whether the practice should be legalized more broadly in the United States. How does the fact that illicit trafficking in women who are forced into the sex trade is much more common in countries such as the Netherlands and Germany than in the United States affect your argument?

THE UNIFORM CRIME REPORT

Suppose that a firefighter dies while fighting a fire at an office building. Later, police discover that the building manager intentionally set the fire. All of the elements of the crime of arson are certainly met, but can the manager be charged with murder? In some jurisdictions, the act might be considered a form of manslaughter, but according to the U.S. Department of Justice, "arson-related deaths and injuries of police officers and firefighters due to the hazardous natures of their professions" are not murders.[13]

The distinction is important because the Department of Justice provides the most far-reaching and oft-cited set of national crime statistics. Each year, the department releases the **Uniform Crime Report (UCR).** Since its inception in 1930, the UCR has attempted to measure the overall rate of crime in the United States by organizing

Uniform Crime Report (UCR)
An annual report compiled by the FBI to give an indication of criminal activity in the United States. The FBI collects data from local, state, and federal law enforcement agencies in preparing this report.

"crimes known to the police."[14] To produce the UCR, the Federal Bureau of Investigation (FBI) relies on the voluntary participation of local law enforcement agencies. These agencies—approximately 17,000 in total, covering 95 percent of the population—base their information on three measurements:

1 The number of persons arrested.
2 The number of crimes reported by victims, witnesses, or the police themselves.
3 The number of officers and support law enforcement specialists.[15]

Once this information has been sent to the FBI, the agency presents the crime data in three ways:

1 As a *rate* per 100,000 people. In 2004, for example, the crime index rate was 4,011. In other words, for every 100,000 inhabitants of the United States, 4,011 *index crimes* (explained below) were reported to the FBI. This statistic is known as the *crime rate* and is often cited by media sources when discussing the level of crime in the United States.
2 As a *percentage* change from the previous year or other time periods. From 2003 to 2004, there was a 2.1 percent drop in the crime index rate.
3 As an *aggregate*, or total, number of crimes. In 2004, the FBI recorded 11,763,509 index crimes.[16]

The Department of Justice publishes these data annually in *Crime in the United States.* Along with the basic statistics, this publication offers an exhaustive array of crime information, including breakdowns of crimes committed by city, county, and other geographic designations and by the demographics (gender, race, age) of the individuals who have been arrested for crimes.

The Crime Index

The UCR divides the criminal offenses it measures into two major categories: Part I and Part II offenses. Part I offenses, or **index crimes,** are those crimes that, due to their seriousness and frequency, are recorded by the FBI to give a general idea of the "crime picture" in the United States in any given year. For a description of the eight index crimes, see Figure 3.1.

The index crime rate is hardly constant. As you can see in Figure 3.2, the last two decades have witnessed "peaks" (the early and late 1980s) and "valleys" (the mid-1980s and the present) in the index crime rate. As we have seen, the reasons for these fluctuations are a matter of great debate among those who study crime in the United States; some point to social conditions such as poverty and education, while others see the rates as a reflection of criminal laws and the efforts of law enforcement agencies.

Index crimes are those most likely to be covered by the media and, consequently, inspire the most fear of crime in the population. These crimes have come to dominate crime coverage to such an extent that, for most Americans, the first image that comes to mind at the mention of "crime" is one person physically attacking another person or a robbery taking place with the use or threat of force.[17] Furthermore, in the stereotypical crime, the offender and the victim usually do not know each other.

Given the trauma of violent crimes, this perception is understandable. It is not, however, accurate. According to UCR statistics, a friend or acquaintance of the victim commits at least 43 percent of the homicides in the United States.[18] Furthermore, as is evident from Figure 3.3 on page 74, the majority of index crimes committed are property crimes. Notice that 53.2 percent of all reported index crimes are larceny-thefts, and nearly another 13.2 percent are burglaries.[19]

The **Federal Bureau of Investigation** posts many of its statistical findings, including the Uniform Crime Report. Find its Web site by clicking on *Web Links* under *Chapter Resources* at **www.cjinaction.com**.

Index Crimes
Those crimes reported annually by the FBI in its Uniform Crime Report. Index crimes include murder, rape, robbery, aggravated assault, burglary, larceny, motor vehicle theft, and arson. Also known as Part I offenses.

FIGURE 3.1

Part I Index Crime Offenses

Every month local law enforcement agencies voluntarily provide information on serious offenses in their jurisdiction to the FBI. These serious offenses are known as Part I offenses, or index crimes, and are defined here. The FBI collects data on Part I offenses in order to present an accurate picture of criminal activity in the United States.

Criminal homicide. a. Murder and nonnegligent manslaughter: the willful (nonnegligent) killing of one human being by another. Deaths caused by negligence, attempts to kill, assaults to kill, suicides, accidental deaths, and justifiable homicides are excluded. Justifiable homicides are limited to: (1) the killing of a felon by a law enforcement officer in the line of duty; and (2) the killing of a felon, during the commission of a felony, by a private citizen. **b. Manslaughter by negligence:** the killing of another person through gross negligence. Traffic fatalities are excluded. While manslaughter by negligence is a Part I crime, it is not included in the Crime Index.

Forcible rape. The carnal knowledge of a female forcibly and against her will. Included are rapes by force and attempts or assaults to rape. Statutory offenses (no force used—victim under age of consent) are excluded.

Robbery. The taking or attempting to take anything of value from the care, custody, or control of a person or persons by force or threat of force or violence and/or by putting the victim in fear.

Aggravated assault. An unlawful attack by one person on another for the purpose of inflicting severe or aggravated bodily injury. This type of assault usually is accompanied by the use of a weapon or by means likely to produce death or great bodily harm. Simple assaults are excluded.

Burglary—breaking or entering. The unlawful entry of a structure to commit a felony or a theft. Attempted forcible entry is included.

Larceny-theft (except motor vehicle theft). The unlawful taking, carrying, leading, or riding away of property from the possession or constructive possession of another. Examples are thefts of bicycles or automobile accessories, shoplifting, pocket picking, or the stealing of any property or article that is not taken by force and violence or by fraud. Attempted larcenies are included. Embezzlement, "con" games, forgery, worthless checks, and the like, are excluded.

Motor vehicle theft. The theft or attempted theft of a motor vehicle. A motor vehicle is self-propelled and runs on the surface and not on rails. Specifically excluded from this category are motorboats, construction equipment, airplanes, and farming equipment.

Arson. Any willful or malicious burning or attempt to burn, with or without intent to defraud, a dwelling house, public building, motor vehicle or aircraft, personal property of another, and the like.

Source: "Appendix II: Offenses in Uniform Crime Reporting," in Federal Bureau of Investigation, *Crime in the United States, 2004* (Washington, D.C.: U.S. Department of Justice, 2005), 505.

Part II Offenses

Not only do violent crimes represent the minority of index crimes, but index crimes are far outweighed by **Part II offenses,** or those crimes that can be designated as either misdemeanors or felonies. While information gathered on index crimes reflects those offenses "known," or reported to the FBI by local agencies, Part II offenses are measured only by arrest data. In 2004, the FBI recorded more than 2.2 million arrests for index crimes in the United States. That same year, more than 11.5 million arrests for Part II offenses took place.[20] In other words, a Part II offense was about five times more common than an index crime (for a description of Part II offenses and their rates, see Figure 3.4 on page 75). Such statistics have prompted Marcus Felson, a professor at Rutgers University School of Criminal Justice, to comment that "most crime is very ordinary."[21]

Part II Offenses
All crimes recorded by the FBI that do not fall into the category of Part I offenses. Include both misdemeanors and felonies.

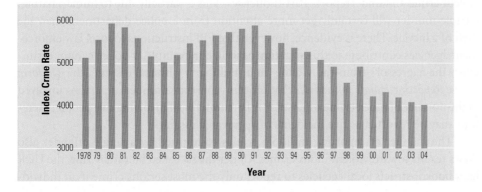

FIGURE 3.2
Index Crime Rates

These data chart the rate of index crimes per 100,000 inhabitants in the United States from 1978 to 2004.

Source: Federal Bureau of Investigation, *Crime in the United States, 2004* (Washington, D.C.: U.S. Department of Justice, 2005), X.

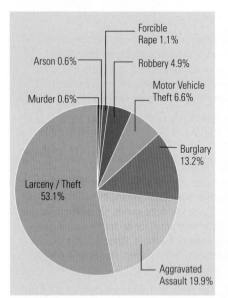

FIGURE 3.3
Composition of
Part I Index Crimes

Source: Federal Bureau of Investigation, *Crime in the United States, 2004* (Washington, D.C.: U.S. Department of Justice, 2005), Table 29, page 280.

The UCR: A Flawed Method?

Even though the UCR is the predominant source of crime data in the country, there are numerous questions about the accuracy of its findings. These criticisms focus on the methods by which the UCR statistics are collected by local law enforcement agencies and reported to the FBI.

Discretionary Distortions For the UCR to be accurate, citizens must report criminal activity to the police, and the police must then pass this information on to the FBI. Criminologists have long been aware that neither can be expected to perform these roles with consistency.[22] Citizens may not report a crime for any number of reasons, including fear of reprisal, embarrassment, or a personal bias in favor of the offender. Many also feel that police cannot do anything to help them in the aftermath of a crime, so they do not see the point of involving law enforcement agents in their lives. Surveys of crime victims reveal that only 50 percent of violent crimes and 39 percent of property crimes were reported to the police in 2004.[23] Studies have also shown that police underreport crimes in certain instances, such as when the offense has occurred within a family or the victim does not want the offender to be charged.[24] Also, as we saw in the introduction to this chapter, police departments may have official or unofficial policies that keep crime rates artificially low.

Furthermore, the FBI and local law enforcement agencies do not always interpret index crimes in the same manner. FBI guidelines, for example, define forcible rape as the "carnal knowledge" of a woman "forcibly and against her will." Although some local agencies may strictly adhere to this definition, others may define rape more loosely—listing any assault on a woman as a rape. Furthermore, different jurisdictions have different definitions of rape. In Alabama, rape occurs only in cases where the woman offers "earnest resistance" to sexual intercourse,[25] and in a number of other jurisdictions, the courts require proof that the victim physically opposed her attacker's advances. A number of jurisdictions have also expanded their definition of the crime to include the possibility that males can be raped.

These factors influence the arrest decision, as police officers are more likely to make arrests that can be *cleared*. An arrest is cleared when the suspect is charged with a particular crime and turned over to the court for trial. With law enforcement agents in different jurisdictions operating under different definitions of rape, or any other crime, their reports to the FBI for UCR purposes may be misleading. Indeed, when a police department in Alabama and a police department in Oregon both report a rape to the federal agency, they may not be describing the same act. Given that the UCR incorporates reports from 17,000 different local agencies, varying methods of defining offenses could have a significant effect on the overall outcome.

Overreporting Violent Crime Many observers also believe that the UCR overreports violent crime and underreports Part II offenses. This is partially due to human nature; a triple murder will certainly get more attention from a police department than the theft of a bicycle. There is evidence, however, that FBI instructions to local law enforcement agencies contribute to this situation as well. For example, if police cannot distinguish the aggressors from the victims in a multiparty physical dispute, the *Uniform Crime Reporting Handbook* advises that officers report the number of persons involved as the number of index crime offenses.[26] A barroom brawl involving five people, therefore, may be reported as five incidents of aggravated assault.

The manner of reporting multiple crimes committed by a single offender also skews results toward violent index crimes. Under the so-called hierarchy rule, the UCR handbook instructs local agencies to report only the most serious crime if an individ-

FIGURE 3.4

Part II Crime Offenses

Offense	Estimated Annual Arrests	Offense	Estimated Annual Arrests
Drug abuse violations	1,749,712	Offenses against family and children	125,955
Driving under the influence	1,432,524	Stolen property	129,280
Other assaults	1,285,501	Runaways	118,966
Disorderly conduct	683,850	Forgery and counterfeiting	119,410
Liquor laws	613,922	Sex offenses (except forcible rape and prostitution)	91,395
Drunkenness	550,795	Prostitution and commercialized vice	90,231
Fraud	282,864	Vagrancy	36,082
Vandalism	276,543	Embezzlement	17,386
Weapons	177,330	Gambling	10,916
Curfew and loitering law violations	138,685	Suspicion	3,554

Curfew and loitering laws (persons under age eighteen)—Offenses relating to violations of local curfew or loitering ordinances where such laws exist.

Disorderly conduct—Breach of the peace.

Driving under the influence—Driving or operating any vehicle or common carrier while drunk or under the influence of liquor or narcotics.

Drug abuse violations—State and/or local offenses relating to the unlawful possession, sale, use, growing, and manufacturing of narcotic drugs. The following drug categories are specified: opium or cocaine and their derivatives (morphine, heroin, codeine); marijuana; synthetic narcotics—manufactured narcotics that can cause true addiction (Demerol, methadone); and dangerous nonnarcotic drugs (barbiturates, benzedrine).

Drunkenness—Offenses relating to drunkenness or intoxication. Excluded is "driving under the influence."

Embezzlement—Misappropriation or misapplication of money or property entrusted to one's care, custody, or control.

Forgery and counterfeiting—Making, altering, uttering, or possessing, with intent to defraud, anything false in the semblance of that which is true. Attempts are included.

Fraud—Fraudulent conversion and obtaining money or property by false pretenses. Included are confidence games and bad checks, except forgeries and counterfeiting.

Gambling—Promoting, permitting, or engaging in illegal gambling.

Liquor laws—State and/or local liquor law violations, except "drunkenness" and "driving under the influence." Federal violations are excluded.

Offenses against the family and children—Nonsupport, neglect, desertion, or abuse of family and children.

Other assaults (simple)—Assaults and attempted assaults where no weapon is used and that do not result in serious or aggravated injury to the victim.

Prostitution and commercialized vice—Sex offenses of a commercialized nature, such as prostitution, keeping a bawdy house, procuring, or transporting women for immoral purposes. Attempts are included.

Runaways (persons under age eighteen)—Limited to juveniles taken into protective custody under provisions of local statutes.

Sex offenses (except forcible rape, prostitution, and commercialized vice)—Statutory rape and offenses against chastity, common decency, morals, and the like. Attempts are included.

Stolen property: buying, receiving, possessing—Buying, receiving, and possessing stolen property, including attempts.

Suspicion—No specific offense; suspect released without formal charges being placed.

Vagrancy—Vagabondage, begging, loitering, and the like.

Vandalism—Willful or malicious destruction, injury, disfigurement, or defacement of any public or private property, real or personal, without consent of the owner or persons having custody or control.

Weapons: carrying, possessing, and the like—All violations of regulations or statutes controlling the carrying, using, possessing, furnishing, and manufacturing of deadly weapons or silencers. Included are attempts.

Source: Federal Bureau of Investigation, *Crime in the United States, 2004* (Washington, D.C.: U.S. Department of Justice, 2005), Table 29, pages 280, 505–506.

ual has committed a number of crimes in a single crime "spree." So, if a person steals an automobile, robs a convenience store, and then kills the store clerk, only the murder will be recorded for the UCR.[27]

The National Incident-Based Reporting System

In the 1980s, well aware of the various criticisms of the UCR, the Department of Justice began seeking ways to revise its data-collecting system. The result was the National Incident-Based Reporting System (NIBRS). In the NIBRS, local agencies collect data

Victim Surveys
A method of gathering crime data that directly surveys participants to determine their experiences as victims of crime.

on each single crime occurrence within twenty-two offense categories made up of forty-six specific crimes called Group A offenses (see Figure 3.5 for a list of NIBRS offense categories). These data are recorded on computerized record systems provided—though not completely financed—by the federal government.

Though the NIBRS became available to local agencies in 1989, fifteen years later only 29 states had been NIBRS certified, with 10 other states in the process of testing the new process.[28] Even in its still-limited form, however, criminologists have responded enthusiastically to the NIBRS because the system provides information about four "data sets"—offenses, victims, offenders, and arrestees—unavailable through the UCR. The NIBRS also presents a more complete picture of crime by monitoring all criminal "incidents" reported to the police, not just those that lead to an arrest.[29] Furthermore, because jurisdictions involved with the NIBRS must identify bias motivations of offenders, the procedure is very useful in studying hate crimes, a topic we will address in the next chapter.[30]

ALTERNATIVE MEASURING METHODS

The shortcomings of the UCR have led to other attempts to collect data that better measure crime in the United States. Two of the most highly regarded methods, along with their shortcomings, are discussed below.

Victim Surveys

One alternative source of data collecting attempts to avoid the distorting influence of the "intermediary," or the local police agencies. In **victim surveys,** criminologists or other researchers ask the victims of crime directly about their experiences, using techniques such as interviews or mail and phone surveys. The first large-scale victim survey took place in 1966, when members of 10,000 households answered questionnaires

---

FIGURE 3.5

NIBRS Offense Categories

The NIBRS collects data on each single incident and arrest within twenty-two offense categories made up of these forty-six specific crimes, called Group A offenses.

1. Arson
2. Assault Offenses—Aggravated Assault, Simple Assault, Intimidation
3. Bribery
4. Burglary/Breaking and Entering
5. Counterfeiting/Forgery
6. Destruction/Damage/Vandalism of Property
7. Drug/Narcotic Offenses—Drug/Narcotic Violations, Drug Equipment Violations
8. Embezzlement
9. Extortion/Blackmail
10. Fraud Offenses—False Pretenses/Swindle/Confidence Game, Credit Card/Automatic Teller Machine Fraud, Impersonation, Welfare Fraud, Wire Fraud
11. Gambling Offenses—Betting/Wagering, Operating/Promoting/ Assisting Gambling, Gambling Equipment Violations, Sports Tampering
12. Homicide Offenses—Murder and Nonnegligent Manslaughter, Negligent Manslaughter, Justifiable Homicide
13. Kidnapping/Abduction
14. Larceny/Theft Offenses—Pocket Picking, Purse Snatching, Shoplifting, Theft from Building, Theft from Coin-Operated Machine or Device, Theft from Motor Vehicle, Theft of Motor Vehicle Parts or Accessories, All Other Larceny
15. Motor Vehicle Theft
16. Pornography/Obscene Material
17. Prostitution Offenses—Prostitution, Assisting or Promoting Prostitution
18. Robbery
19. Sex Offenses, Forcible—Forcible Rape, Forcible Sodomy, Sexual Assault with an Object, Forcible Fondling
20. Sex Offenses, Nonforcible—Incest, Statutory Rape
21. Stolen Property Offenses (Receiving and the like)
22. Weapon Law Violations

Source: The Federal Bureau of Investigation.

as part of the President's Commission on Law Enforcement and the Administration of Justice. The results indicated a much higher victimization rate than had been previously expected, and researchers felt the process gave them a better understanding of the **dark figure of crime,** or the actual amount of crime that occurs in the country.

Dark Figure of Crime
A term used to describe the actual amount of crime that takes place. The "figure" is "dark," or impossible to detect, because a great number of crimes are never reported to the police.

The National Crime Victimization Survey Criminologists were so encouraged by the results of the 1966 experiment that the federal government decided to institute an ongoing victim survey. The result was the National Crime Victimization Survey (NCVS), which started in 1972. Conducted by the U.S. Bureau of the Census in cooperation with the Bureau of Justice Statistics of the Justice Department, the NCVS conducts an annual survey of more than 40,000 households with nearly 75,000 occupants over twelve years of age. Participants are interviewed twice a year concerning their experiences with crimes in the prior six months. As you can see in Figure 3.6, the questions cover a wide array of possible victimization.

Supporters of the NCVS highlight a number of aspects in which the victim survey is superior to the UCR:

1 It measures both reported and unreported crime.
2 It is unaffected by police bias and distortions in reporting crime to the FBI.
3 It does not rely on victims directly reporting crime to the police.[31]

Most important, some supporters say, is that the NCVS gives victims a voice in the criminal justice process.

Reliability of the NCVS Even supporters of the NCVS would not, however, claim that the process is infallible. For one thing, there is no guarantee that those who answer

---

FIGURE 3.6

Sample Questions from the NCVS *(National Crime Victimization Survey)*

36a. Was something belonging to YOU stolen, such as:
  a. Things that you carry, like luggage, a wallet, purse, briefcase, book—
  b. Clothing, jewelry, or cell phone—
  c. Bicycle or sports equipment—
  d. Things in your home—like a TV, stereo, or tools—
  e. Things from outside your home, such as a garden hose or lawn furniture—
  f. Things belonging to children in the household—
  g. Things from a vehicle, such as a package, groceries, camera, or CDs—
  h. Did anyone ATTEMPT to steal anything belonging to you?

41a. Has anyone attacked or threatened you in any of these ways:
  a. With any weapon, for instance, a gun or knife—
  b. With anything like a baseball bat, frying pan, scissors, or stick—
  c. By something thrown, such as a rock or bottle—
  d. Include any grabbing, punching, or choking,
  e. Any rape, attempted rape, or other type of sexual attack—
  f. Any face-to-face threats—OR
  g. Any attack or threat or use of force by anyone at all? Please mention it even if you are not certain it was a crime.

42a. People often don't think of incidents committed by someone they know. Other than the incidents already mentioned, did you have something stolen from you OR were you attacked or threatened by:
  a. Someone at work or school—
  b. A neighbor or friend—
  c. A relative or family member—
  d. Any other person you've met or known?

43a. Incidents involving forced or unwanted sexual acts are often difficult to talk about. Have you been forced or coerced to engage in unwanted sexual activity by—
  a. someone you didn't know before—
  b. a casual acquaintance—OR
  c. someone you know well—

44a. During the last 6 months (other than any incidents already mentioned), did you call the police to report something that happened to YOU which you thought was a crime?

45a. During the last 6 months (other than any incidents already mentioned), did anything which you thought was a crime happen to YOU, but you did NOT report to the police?

Source: U.S. Department of Justice, *National Crime Victimization Survey 2004* (Washington, D.C.: Bureau of Justice Statistics, 2004).

the questionnaire will do so accurately. For reasons of shame, forgetfulness, or fear of reprisal, a participant may not give a completely true picture of her or his recent history. Also, as with any survey research, the manner in which the questions are asked can have a distorting effect on the answers.[32] Consider the following two questions:

1 Have you ever been the victim of a rape?
2 Were you knifed, shot, or attacked with some other weapon? Did someone try to attack you in some other way?

The second question is, in fact, one that the NCVS has used in the past to measure rape. Surveyors expected, or hoped, that victims of rape would answer accordingly, as they had been "attacked in some other way." On the one hand, the first question was more direct and may have elicited more "yes" answers. On the other hand, because of the stigma attached to the word *rape,* it may have discouraged participants from answering truthfully. As a result of complaints that the vagueness of the second question led rape to be seriously underreported in the NCVS (see Question 43a of the revised version in Figure 3.6 on page 77), in the early 1990s the surveyors altered their methods of gaining information concerning sexual assaults (see *Outside the Box—The National College Women Sexual Victimization Survey*).

Victim surveys also present a number of other potential problems. Many citizens are not well versed in the terminology of criminal justice, and a person may not know, for example, that a break-in that occurred at her home while she was at the movies is a burglary and not a robbery. (Remember that *burglary* refers to breaking into a structure with the intention to commit a felony, whereas *robbery* is the illegal taking of property using force or the threat of force.) There are also a number of crimes that victim surveys cannot record, such as drug use or gambling, for legal reasons, and murder, for more obvious ones.[33]

OUTSIDE THE BOX

The National College Women Sexual Victimization Survey

Researchers have long been aware that young women who live on college campuses are at greater risk for rape and other forms of sexual assault than are other women of a comparable age. Many of these same experts also believe that the National Crime Victimization Survey (NCVS), even with its improvements, does not adequately measure the problem. To test this hypothesis, the Department of Justice sponsored a survey called "The National College Women Sexual Victimization Survey" (NCWSV) that varied the process used by the NCVS.

Both surveys follow a two-stage format that relies on responses to "screen questions" to determine victimization. If the respondent answers "yes" to one of these questions, then a more detailed incident report is filled out. As you can see in Figure 3.6, the NCVS "screen question" asks respondents if they have been "attacked or threatened" and then follows with a short list of cue responses that includes "rape, attempted rape, or other type of sexual attack." In contrast, the NCWSV uses much more specific screen questions, such as "Since the school year began . . . has anyone made you have sexual intercourse by using force or

threatening to harm you? Just so there is no mistake, by intercourse I mean putting a penis in your vagina."

The results were dramatic. Female students were more than ten times more likely to tell a NCWSV researcher that they were raped than one utilizing the NCVS. The NCWSV found that 350 women—about 2 percent of all female college students—are raped every year on campuses with 10,000 or more students. The authors of the report believe that, because of the sensitive nature of sexual assault, "graphically descriptive screen questions are needed to prompt reluctant victims" to report being victims of sexual assault. Along the same lines, the survey also estimated that, because of embarrassment, self-blame, or other reasons, only about 5 percent of all rapes or attempted rapes of college women are reported to law enforcement officials.

FOR CRITICAL ANALYSIS

Why might someone be more likely to answer "yes" to the NCWSV screen question concerning rape than to the NCVS screen question? Do you think that more graphic descriptions of other crimes would also result in higher rates of positive responses?

Self-Reported Surveys

Based on many of the same principles as victim surveys, but focusing instead on offenders, **self-reported surveys** are a third source of data for criminologists. In this form of data collection, persons are asked directly—through personal interviews or questionnaires, or over the telephone—about specific criminal activity to which they may have been a party. Though not implemented on the scale of the UCR or NCVS, self-reported surveys are most useful in situations in which the group to be studied is already gathered in an institutional setting, such as a juvenile facility or a prison. One of the most widespread self-reported surveys in the United States, the Drug Use Forecasting Program, collects information on narcotics use from arrestees who have been brought into booking facilities.

Such studies can also be particularly helpful in finding specific information about groups of subjects. When professors Peter B. Wood, Walter R. Grove, James A. Wilson, and John K. Cochran wanted to learn how criminals "felt" when committing crimes, for example, they used self-reported surveys. By comparing these results to those gathered from a group of male students at a state university, the researchers were able to draw conclusions on the "high" a criminal experiences during a crime.[34]

A "Giant" Dark Figure Because there is no penalty for admitting to criminal activity in a self-reported survey, subjects tend to be more forthcoming in discussing their behavior. The researchers mentioned above found that a significant number of the students interviewed admitted to committing minor crimes for which they had never been arrested. This fact points to the most striking finding of self-reported surveys: the dark figure of crime, referred to earlier in the chapter as the *actual* amount of crime that takes place, appears to be much larger than the UCR or NCVS would suggest.

The first major self-reported survey, conducted by James S. Wallerstein and Clement J. Wyle in 1947, queried 1,020 men and 678 women from a wide spectrum of different backgrounds on their participation in a number of crimes. Ninety-nine percent of the participants admitted to committing at least one of the crimes referenced by Wallerstein and Wyle.[35] When alcohol offenses, recreational drug use, truancy, and petty theft are factored in, self-reported surveys consistently show that almost everybody has committed at least one crime in their lifetime.[36]

Besides their usefulness in determining the criminal behavior of the average American, self-reported surveys are also valued for their ability to target specific criminological subjects. For example, to test a theory that drug use by parents leads to a greater possibility of drug use in their children, researchers can do a self-reported survey with a cross section of drug users. Also, self-reported surveys allow researchers to control aspects of the data collection themselves, thereby assuring that race, class, and gender will not bias the results.

Reliability of Self-Reported Surveys Again, despite these advantages there are a number of perceived disadvantages with self-reported surveys. A subject's personality or beliefs often affect the manner in which he or she answers questions. If a person sees criminal behavior as something to be ashamed of, he or she may downplay such behavior. In contrast, a person who sees criminal behavior as positive may exaggerate the truth to impress the questioner.

For the same reason that a participant has nothing to lose by telling the truth, she or he has nothing to gain by telling the truth, either. The effects of lying on self-reported surveys can be dramatic. In a self-reported survey of juveniles, researchers Thomas Gray and Eric Walsh tested their subjects with urinalysis as well as asking them about their drug use. Less than 33 percent of the juveniles who tested positive for marijuana also admitted to using the drug, and only 15 percent of those who tested

Self-Reported Surveys
A method of gathering crime data that relies on participants to reveal and detail their own criminal or delinquent behavior.

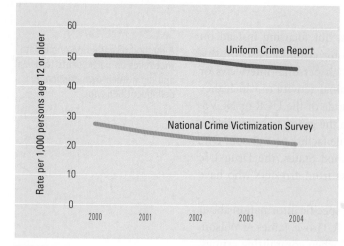

FIGURE 3.7

Comparing Violent Crime Data, 2000–2004

According to both the Uniform Crime Report (UCR) and the National Crime Victimization Survey (NCVS), violent crime in the United States has declined steadily during the 2000s.

Sources: Federal Bureau of Investigation, and U.S. Bureau of Justice Statistics.

positive for cocaine were truthful about their habits.[37] These types of results have led many criminologists to conclude that self-reported surveys are skewed by many of the same inaccuracies that plague the other collection methods.

CRIME TRENDS TODAY

Crime rates as measured by the NCVS tend to run higher than those measured by the UCR, primarily because NCVS data include crimes not reported to the police.[38] Nevertheless, for the most part, the nation's two most important crime surveys have tracked each other over the past several decades: after reaching record highs in the early 1990s, the amount of criminal activity dropped dramatically throughout the rest of that decade and has continued to decline steadily in the new millennium (see Figure 3.7). Indeed, we are now in a period in which crimes rates have remained "impressively flat," in the words of Alfred Blumstein, a criminologist at Carnegie Mellon University in Pittsburgh, Pennsylvania.[39]

Thanks to the efforts of government law enforcement agencies, educational institutions, and private individuals, more data on crime are available today than at any time in this nation's history. These figures provide a crucial litmus test for the criminological theories discussed in the previous chapter and help us to establish a detailed picture of crime trends. Sometimes, however, the data raise as many questions as they answer.

The Countertrend in Murder Rates

Can a place be both safer and deadlier at the same time? According to crime statistics, this appears to be the case in many cities: overall violent crime rates have decreased, but murder rates are on the rise. In Baltimore, Maryland, for example, the violent crime rate has plummeted 40 percent since 1999, but the number of murders within the city limits has grown each year of the 2000s.[40] In fact, the thirty-two murders in January 2005 were the most in a single month for Baltimore since 1973.[41] A number of other cities, including New York, Boston, Washington, D.C., and Los Angeles, have also seen disturbing increases in murder rates over the past several years.

Nationally, the number of murders in this country has risen since 2000 and the murder rate has declined only 0.8 percent, compared to significant decreases in robbery, aggravated assault, and property crime numbers.[42] Because no other crime can be measured as accurately, homicide statistics are of great interest to law enforcement experts, and, as we shall see in the rest of this section, a number of theories have been offered to explain the failure of murder rates to conform with other indicators of crime.

The Geography of Crime

As we discussed in the previous chapter, many criminologists believe that a breakdown of community values has led to high levels of social disorganization in America's cities, which in turn which have led to higher rates of crime in more heavily populated areas (see pages 43 to 44). This theory finds support in the crime data. According to the Bureau of Justice Statistics, nearly 19 percent of all households in urban areas in the United States were victimized by violent or property crimes in 2003, compared to only

12 percent of households in rural areas.[43] FBI data show that violent crime and property crime rates are 63 and 60 percent greater, respectively, in counties with the highest population density than in those with the lowest.[44]

Homicide rates are consistently higher in large U.S. cities than in rural areas as well. Surprisingly, however, the number of murders has skyrocketed in cities with populations under 10,000—jumping 15.7 percent between 2002 and 2003. By comparison, those figures rose only 0.2 percent in cities with more than one million residents in the same time period.[45] Professor Alfred Blumstein of Carnegie Mellon University attributes this phenomenon to a shift in illegal drug activity from large cities to smaller ones, where the law enforcement presence is less pronounced.[46] Indeed, when criminologists want to explain crime rates, they often turn to drugs, guns, and gangs.

Illegal Drugs and Crime

Many observers blamed the explosion of violent crime that shook this country in the late 1980s and early 1990s on the widespread use and sale of crack cocaine at the time.[47] Today, rising murder rates are still seen as a reflection of illegal drug activity. Indeed, Baltimore officials point out that about 90 percent of the city's homicide victims have criminal records, typically for drug-related convictions. In other words, as one official commented, "Baltimore is actually a very safe city if you are not involved in the drug trade."[48] Nationally, about 5 percent of all homicides are drug related;[49] in 2004, there were 1,745,712 arrests for drug violations in the United States, up from about 581,000 in 1980.[50]

The drug-crime relationship has also proved to be a rich field of study for social conflict theorists (see pages 48–49). The fact that a disproportionate number of those arrested and imprisoned for drug crimes in this country are low-income minorities supports the basic contention of these criminologists that crime is more a matter of who you are than what you have done. Furthermore, because members of this "underclass" are more likely to be unemployed and live in disorganized neighborhoods, both the sale (as an alternative to poverty) and use (as a means of escaping harsh reality) of illegal drugs are attractive options for them.[51] Issues concerning illegal drugs and the "war" to restrict their use will be addressed in Chapter 16.

Age and Crime: The Peak Years

Officials in Boston attribute the recent rise in murders in that city in part to the growing number of young people involved in drug-related gang activity.[52] In fact, the strongest statistical determinant of criminal behavior appears to be age. Criminal behavior peaks during the teenage years. For most offenses, rates are at their highest around ages seventeen and eighteen (a few years later for violent crime).[53] As Figure 3.8 shows, criminal activity begins to decline as a person grows older; 85 percent of former delinquents are no longer involved in wrongdoing by the time they reach age twenty-eight.[54]

Why is the crime rate dramatically higher for young people? There is no single, simple answer. As already noted, biological theories of crime point to high testosterone levels in young males, which increase levels of aggression and violence (see page 40). Adolescents are also more susceptible to peer pressure, and sociological and social process theories of crime in this area are backed by studies showing that juvenile delinquents tend to socialize with other juvenile delinquents.[55] A recent survey conducted by researchers from Columbia

Rock musician Courtney Love in Los Angeles Superior Court on May 25, 2004. Love pled guilty to being under the influence of cocaine in connection with an incident in which police found her breaking the windows of her boyfriend's house. Some criminologists believe that people using drugs or alcohol cannot make "clearheaded" decisions about whether to engage in criminal behavior. How does this conclusion subvert the choice theory of crime (see page 37)?

AP Photo/Nick Ut

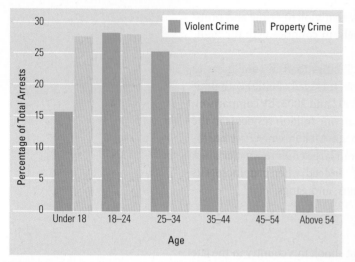

FIGURE 3.8

Percentage of Arrests by Age

As this graph shows, the majority of those persons arrested for property crimes in the United States are under twenty-five years old, and more violent crimes are committed by eighteen- to twenty-four-year-olds than by any other age group.

Source: Federal Bureau of Investigation, *Crime in the United States, 2004* (Washington, D.C.: U.S. Department of Justice, 2005), Table 38, pages 290–291.

University found that juveniles who were frequently bored were 50 percent more likely than other teenagers to abuse illegal drugs and alcohol, and those who received more than $25 a week in spending money were twice as likely to get high or drunk as those who received less than that amount.[56]

Criminologists call possible sources of juvenile delinquency such as boredom and too much pocket money *risk factors.* Common risk factors cited by those who study juvenile delinquency include poor parental supervision, poor academic achievement, weapon carrying, gang membership, and low intelligence. No single risk factor can predict delinquency, and the consensus seems to be that the more risk factors that are present in the life of any juvenile, the better are his or her chances of offending.[57] As we saw in Chapter 2, life course theories of crime have convinced a number of criminologists to begin searching for risk factors in early childhood, without waiting until a person has reached adolescence and entered the juvenile justice system. We will take a comprehensive look at juvenile delinquency and crime in Chapter 15.

Guns and Crime

Since at least the 1930s, young people have committed more violent crimes than have their elders. Starting nearly two decades ago, however, such rates have increased *significantly.* Between 1985 and 1992, homicide rates went up by 50 percent for white males aged fourteen to seventeen and tripled for African Americans of the same age.[58] This sharp increase has been linked to the role guns play in juvenile criminal behavior. The rise in gun ownership among gang members in high-crime urban areas has been well documented,[59] but these high rates of violence also reflect a growing pattern of gun ownership among suburban youths as well.[60]

According to government figures, 66 percent of all homicides in 2004 were committed with a firearm. In addition, 41 percent of all robberies and 19 percent of all aggravated assaults were carried out by someone brandishing a gun.[61] Victims' rights groups and gun control advocates argue that America's high rates of violence reflect the ease with which firearms are available to its citizens; hence, they push for legislation to restrict the ability to sell and purchase such weapons. Criminologists have struggled to determine the actual impact of our firearm laws. Some argue that the relative ease with which most Americans can purchase firearms increases rates of gun violence, while others claim that gun ownership deters would-be criminals who are afraid of being shot in the act.[62] (For a discussion of gun policies and their possible impact on violent crimes, go to the feature *Criminal Justice in Action—The Link between Guns and Crime* at the end of the chapter.)

Crime, Race, and Poverty

The issue of guns and crime is widely debated on the Internet. The **Coalition to Stop Gun Violence** offers the pro-gun control view, while the **National Rifle Association** provides arguments against gun control. Find their Web sites by clicking on *Web Links* under *Chapter Resources* at **www.cjinaction.com**.

Homicide data also produce disturbing results when race is taken into account. According to government statistics, African Americans are about six times more likely to be murder victims than Caucasians, and blacks are about seven times more likely to commit murder than whites.[63] In general, poor people and members of minority groups commit more crimes—and are more often the victims of crimes—than wealthier people and whites. But the relationship among race, income level, and crime is much more complicated than any generalization. Studies have shown that, even in low-income neighborhoods, the rate of violent crime is associated much more strongly with family disorganization (lack of a father in the household, family members committing crimes) than with race.[64] Furthermore, even when income levels are similar, juveniles and young adults from households in which the father is absent are twice as likely to be incarcerated as those from two-parent families.[65]

Class and Crime The highest crime rates in the United States are consistently recorded in the low-income, urban neighborhoods with the highest unemployment rates. Lack of education, another handicap most often faced by low-income citizens, also seems to correlate with criminal activity. Forty-one percent of all inmates in state and federal prisons failed to obtain a high school diploma, compared to 18 percent in the population at large.[66]

It might seem logical that those who believe they lack a legal opportunity to gain the consumer goods and services that dominate American culture would turn to illegal methods to do so. But, logic aside, many criminologists are skeptical of such an obvious class-crime relationship. After all, poverty does not *cause* crime; the majority of residents in low-income neighborhoods are law abiding. Furthermore, higher-income citizens are also involved in all sorts of criminal activities and are more likely to commit white-collar crimes, which are not included in statistics on violent crime.

In addition, self-reported surveys have shown that as far as less serious crimes are concerned, the behavior of lower-, middle-, and upper-class criminals differs very little.[67] These findings tend to support the theory that high crime rates in low-income communities are at least partly the result of a greater willingness of police to arrest poor citizens, and of the court system to convict them.

Race and Crime The class-crime relationship and the class-race relationship are invariably linked. Official crime data seem to indicate a strong correlation between minority status and crime: African Americans—who make up 13 percent of the population—constitute 37 percent of those arrested for violent crimes and 29 percent of those arrested for property crimes.[68] Furthermore, African Americans are victims of violent crime at a rate of 26 per 1,000, compared to 21 per 1,000 for whites.[69]

The racial differences in the crime rate are one of the most controversial areas of the criminal justice system (see the feature *CJ in Focus—Myth versus Reality: Race Stereotyping and Crime* on the following page). At first glance, crime statistics seem to support the idea that the subculture of African Americans in the United States is

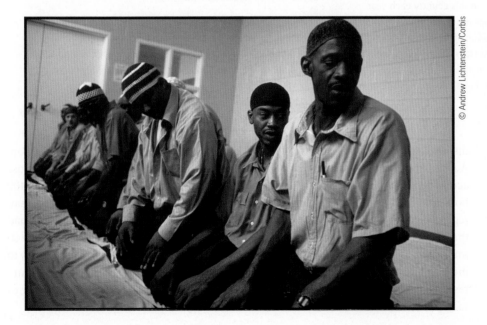

A group of African American Muslims attend a prayer session in a Virginia state prison. According to the latest statistics, an African American male born in 2001 in the United States has a one in three chance of going to prison at some point in his life. The national average for American men of all races is one in fifteen. What do these types of statistics tell us about the relationship between race and crime?

© Andrew Lichtenstein/Corbis

CJ IN FOCUS/MYTH VERSUS REALITY

Race Stereotyping and Crime

In an effort to study the effect of race on perception, Birt Duncan gathered 104 white undergraduate students at the University of California and had them observe an argument between two people in which one person shoved the other. The undergraduates were randomly assigned to view one of four different conditions: (1) white shover/African American victim, (2) white shover/white victim, (3) African American shover/white victim, and (4) African American shover/African American victim. The students were then asked to rate the behavior of the person who did the shoving.

Duncan found that when the shover was African American and the victim was white, 75 percent of the students considered the shove to be "violent behavior" and 6 percent saw it as "playing around." In contrast, when the shover was white and the victim black, only 17 percent characterized the shove as violent while 42 percent saw it as playful.

THE MYTH

The results of Duncan's study are not, in the end, surprising. Racial stereotyping is not an aberration in our society. Negative stereotypes of minorities, especially African Americans, label them as prone to violence and more likely to be criminals or members of gangs than others.

THE REALITY

According to the University of Maryland's Katheryn K. Russell, the best-kept secret in criminology is that the United States has a "white crime" problem. Whites, Russell points out, are the subject of about two-thirds of the arrests in this country each year. Russell believes that public and academic obsession with "black crime" has severely limited discussion of "white crime." This fascination can be explained, at least from a criminological standpoint, by the different *proportional* involvement of racial minorities in crime. As Figure 3.9 shows, although white involve-

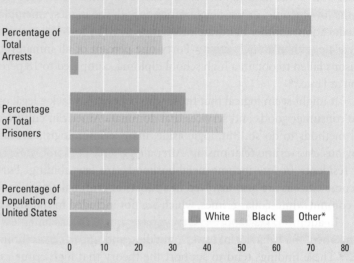

*Includes American Indians, Native Alaskans, Asian Americans, and Pacific Islanders

NOTE: For purposes of crime statistics, government agencies distinguish between race and ethnicity. Hispanic Americans are seen as a separate ethnicity, not a separate race. Therefore, most crime statistics will make a distinction between "white non-Hispanic" and "black non-Hispanic" if they aim to draw conclusions about ethnicity in the criminal justice system.

FIGURE 3.9

Crime and Race in the United States

Sources: U.S. Census, U.S. Department of Justice, Federal Bureau of Investigation.

ment in crime is high, it is "relatively" low given the percentage of the American population that is of white, European descent. In contrast, minorities have a disproportionate involvement in crime—especially as a percentage of prison and jail inmates—based on their population statistics.

FOR CRITICAL ANALYSIS

According to Figure 3.9, although African Americans are arrested at less than half the rate of whites, they comprise almost 30 percent more of the prison population. How might this statistical anomaly be explained?

disposed toward criminal behavior. Not all of the data, however, support that assertion. A number of crime-measuring surveys show consistent levels of crime and drug abuse across racial lines.[70] In addition, a study of nearly 900 African American children (400 boys and 467 girls) from neighborhoods with varying income levels showed that, regardless of the different factors often cited by criminologists, family income level had the only significant correlation with violent behavior. The authors of the study were so impressed by the results that they called on their colleagues to make greater efforts to include African American families living outside urban neighborhoods in future research in order to give a more complete—and perhaps less stereotypical—picture of race and crime in this country.[71]

Another point to remember when reviewing statistical studies of minority offenders and victims is that they tend to focus on *race,* which distinguishes groups based on physical characteristics such as skin color, rather than *ethnicity,* which denotes national or cultural background. Thus, the bulk of criminological research in this area has focused on the differences between European Americans and African Americans, both because the latter have been the largest minority group in the United States for most of its history and because the racial differences between the two groups are easily identifiable. Americans of Hispanic descent have either been excluded from many crime studies or been linked with whites or blacks based on racial characteristics.[72] Other minority groups, such as Asian Americans, Native Americans, and immigrants from the South Pacific or Eastern Europe, have been similarly underreported in crime studies.

Women and Crime

To put it bluntly, crime is an overwhelmingly male activity. More than 65 percent of all murders involve a male victim and a male perpetrator; in only 2.4 percent of homicides are both the offender and the victim female.[73] Only 24 percent of those persons arrested in the United States in 2004 were women.[74] A closer look at the statistics, however, shows that rates of female criminality are growing. Between 1995 and 2004, arrests of women nationwide rose by 9 percent. During that same period, arrests of men declined 8.9 percent.[75] The women's prison population topped 100,000 for the first time in 2003, and the incarceration rate for females is increasing at nearly twice that for males.

The vast majority of women are prosecuted for nonviolent crimes, usually drug-related offenses. In fact, drug-related crimes account for nearly two-thirds of the women sent to prison each year (violent crimes account for only about 3 percent).[76] The habitual offender statutes and mandatory sentencing for drug crimes that have accompanied the "war on drugs," which we will discuss in Chapter 11, have been particularly influential. In the 1980s, many of the women now in prison would not have been arrested or would have received light sentences for their drug-related wrongdoing. When women do kill, the patterns are distinct as well: the victim is usually a male partner, and a woman is likely to kill in response to physical aggression or threats of physical aggression by her partner.[77]

The Link between Guns and Crime

Approximately 30,000 Americans are killed each year by guns in incidents ranging from suicide to homicide. As noted earlier, according to the most recent FBI statistics, firearms are used in about two-thirds of murders and 41 percent of robberies in the United States.[78] Roughly speaking, there is one gun per person in this country, and half of our households own at least one firearm.[79] The link between guns and violent behavior seems obvious, but drawing conclusions from statistics is often problematic. As we will see in this *Criminal Justice in Action* feature, there is considerable debate as to whether there is, in fact, any causal relationship between the prevalence of firearms in our society and their use in criminal activity and, if so, whether gun control laws can affect this relationship.

Do Guns Mean More Crime?

On February 25, 2005, David Hernandez Arroyo opened fire with an AK-47 assault rifle outside a courthouse in Tyler, Texas. In the barrage, Arroyo, who was apparently angry about being sued for unpaid child support, killed his ex-wife and Mark Wilson, a bystander. According to witnesses, Arroyo would probably have killed his son, David, Jr., as well if Wilson had not protected the young man by returning fire with a handgun of his own.

As often happens when the issue of gun control is involved, the incident was interpreted differently by opposing sides. Those who favor greater restrictions on firearms saw the shootings as a reflection of a society addicted to guns and violence and continued to voice their displeasure with a U.S. Congress that had failed to renew a decade-old ban on assault weapons several months earlier. They cited a study conducted by the Brady Center to Prevent Gun Violence that found a 66 percent drop in the use of assault weapons to commit crimes in the five years after the ban was enacted in 1994 when compared with the five years prior to the law's implementation.[80]

Those who want to curtail government regulation of firearms saw an act of heroism by Wilson, a gun enthusiast who had legally purchased his weapon and had a permit to carry it in public. To underscore the deterrent effect of an armed citizenry, they cited research done by John Lott of the American Enterprise Institute in communities that had recently passed "right-to-carry" laws, which allow an adult applicant to be granted a concealed-weapons permit unless he or she is a felon or has a history of mental illness. Lott estimated that such legislation reduced homicide by 8 percent,

sexual assault by 5 percent, aggravated assault by 7 percent, and robbery by 3 percent, attributing these declines in part to fewer "helpless victims" in the "right-to-carry" states.[81]

Do Guns Mean More Crime? Part II

The problem with these and many other studies concerning the gun-crime relationship is that evidence disputing their findings is readily available. Research conducted under the auspices of the U.S. Department of Justice discovered only a small decline in the number of crimes involving assault weapons following the ban, and the researchers noted that even this minor reduction had been offset by an increase in crimes committed by other guns allowed under the law.[82] Meanwhile, John Lott's conclusions have been widely criticized among criminologists, many of whom believe that concealed-carry laws have little effect on criminal activity. John Donohue of Stanford University even provided data showing that areas with newly passed concealed-carry laws saw an increase in crime.[83]

In fact, several years ago a task force created by the U.S. Centers for Disease Control examined fifty-one studies that attempted to measure the influence of gun control laws on violent crime. The conclusion? "Insufficient evidence" on the effect of these laws.[84] As Gary Kleck of Florida State University's School of Criminology and Criminal Justice points out, gun ownership among criminals *may* increase crime, and gun ownership among non-criminals *may* decrease crime, but until a reliable method for measuring these two factors exists, it will be virtually impossible to understand the true impact of gun levels on crime and violence rates.[85]

The Brady Bill

For government and law enforcement agencies, the important question is not "Do guns cause crime?" but rather, "How can we keep people from using guns to commit crimes?" Statistically, most guns will never inflict harm on another human being. Only 1.1 percent of all handguns and 0.1 percent of "long guns" (shotguns, rifles, and the like) in the United States are involved in criminal activity each year.[86] The challenge, therefore, is first to determine who might use a gun to commit a crime and then to keep the gun out of that person's hands.

In general, a criminal obtains a firearm in one of three ways: by stealing it, by purchasing it from a gun

Peggy Landry of New Orleans is pictured here proudly showing off her handgun and concealed-weapon license. Thanks to a law passed recently by the Louisiana legislature, Landry and other citizens of the state are allowed to open fire on a person "who is reasonably believed" to be using "unlawful force" or making an "unlawful entry" into a car they happen to be driving. What might be some of the drawbacks of such a law?

dealer, or by purchasing it from a private citizen.[87] As it is almost impossible to control the private gun market among law-abiding citizens, and law enforcement agencies already expend a great deal of energy trying to control traffic in stolen guns, most recent gun control laws focus on gun dealers.

To that end, Congress passed the Brady Handgun Violence Prevention Act in 1993.[88] Commonly known as the Brady Bill, this measure requires local law enforcement agencies to conduct background checks of potential handgun purchasers. From the effective date of the Brady Bill until December 31, 2003, approximately 1.1 million gun-purchase applications were rejected. Nearly 60 percent of the denials were based on felony convictions or indictments found during the background check, with another 13 percent due to domestic violence misdemeanors.[89] Thus, it seems clear that, since 1994, hundreds of thousands of potentially dangerous would-be buyers were denied the opportunity to purchase a firearm.

And yet, further research shows that the Brady Bill has had no measurable impact on murders committed with guns or on overall homicide trends.[90] Law enforcement officials believe this seeming inconsistency is easily explained: anyone who is going to commit a crime with a gun is not going to get a permit for the weapon in the first place. There are about 15,000 serious gun crimes in New York each year, for example, but the state's licensed firearm owners commit very few of them. "You could count them on one hand," says a local weapons expert.[91]

The Brady Bill has also been criticized for not going far enough. The law requires background checks only for those who purchase guns from federally licensed firearms dealers. It does not cover purchases made at gun shows or from private citizens, which represent between 30 and 40 percent of the market.[92] Indeed, a number of states have enacted much more restrictive gun control laws than are required under the Brady Bill. Reacting to the fatal shootings at Columbine High School, in 2001 Colorado became the twentieth state to require background checks for all public gun sales, including sales at gun shows. In Massachusetts, gun dealers may not sell a firearm unless it has a safety device that enables a user to know whether the gun is loaded and a "trigger lock" designed to prevent accidental shootings. That state also banned all sales of "Saturday night specials," cheap handguns that are often used in crimes. Some jurisdictions are also looking into "user identification" technology that would prevent anyone but the owner of a handgun from firing the weapon.

Fingerprinting Firearms

Perhaps the most important development in this area is the ability of the federal government to "fingerprint" guns. Today, almost every gun is manufactured with a serial number, and firearm companies provide the Bureau of Alcohol, Tobacco, Firearms and Explosives (ATF) with detailed information concerning the marks made on shell casings by every weapon they produce. With this information, the ATF can "trace" a gun used in a crime to its original owner and the store where it was purchased. This technology, developed in Canada, is being used in twenty-seven countries, including Australia, Germany, Spain, and

Sweden. In this country, only two states, Maryland and New York, require that ballistics data be gathered on every handgun made and sold within state lines. Public pressure to require more firearm fingerprinting increased after the sniper shootings in the Washington, D.C., area in 2002. Supporters of the technology argue that a national database would have led law enforcement agents to the suspects much more quickly, perhaps even before all of their eighteen victims had been killed or injured.

Making Sense of the Link between Guns and Crime

1 One criminologist has suggested that arrest report forms include a space for police officers to indicate whether the suspect possessed a weapon at the time of arrest and what type of weapon it was. How would this information increase our understanding of the relationship between guns and crime?

2 In a single year, guns are used to murder about 15 people in Japan, 30 people in Great Britain, 100 people in Canada, and about 11,000 in the United States. Are these figures relevant for the gun control debate in our country? Explain your answer.

3 A recent report by the Maryland State Police's forensic sciences division shows that the ballistic fingerprinting system required in Maryland and New York has not solved a single crime in its four years of existence. Why might the ability to trace a gun to its original owner and the store where it was purchased *not* be very helpful in tracking down a person who used the weapon to commit a crime?

Chapter Summary

1 Discuss the primary goals of civil law and criminal law and explain how these goals are realized. Civil law is designed to resolve disputes between private individuals and other entities such as corporations. In these disputes, one party, called the plaintiff, tries to gain monetary damages by proving that the accused party, or defendant, is to blame for a tort, or wrongful act. In contrast, criminal law exists to protect society from criminal behavior. To that end, the government prosecutes defendants, or persons who have been charged with committing a crime.

2 Explain the differences between crimes *mala in se* and *mala prohibita*. A criminal act is *mala in se* if it is inherently wrong, while a criminal act *mala prohibita* is illegal only because it goes against the "natural, moral, and public" principles of society. It is sometimes difficult to distinguish between these two sorts of crimes because what may be considered a *mala in se* crime in one culture may not go against the "natural laws" of another.

3 Identify the publication in which the FBI reports crime data and list the three ways it does so. Every year the FBI releases the Uniform Crime Report (UCR), in which it presents different crimes as (a) a rate per 100,000 people; (b) a percentage change from the previous year; and (c) an absolute, or aggregate, number.

4 Distinguish between Part I and Part II offenses as defined in the Uniform Crime Report (UCR). Part I offenses are always felonies and include the most violent crimes. They are called index crimes and yield the index crime rate. Part II offenses can be either misdemeanors or felonies and constitute the majority of crimes committed.

5 Describe some of the shortcomings of the UCR as a crime-measuring tool. To collect its data, the Uniform Crime Report (UCR) relies on citizens reporting crimes to the police and the police passing this information on to the FBI. If either fails to do so, the UCR will not accurately reflect criminal activity in the United States. Furthermore, the FBI and local law enforcement agencies do not always define crimes in the same manner, leading to inconsistencies in the data. Finally, the UCR tends to overreport violent crimes and underreport more common offenses.

6 Distinguish between the National Crime Victimization Survey and self-reported surveys. The NCVS involves an annual survey of more than 40,000 households conducted by the Bureau of the Census along with the Bureau of Justice Statistics. The survey queries citizens on crimes that have been committed against them. As such, the NCVS includes crimes not necessarily reported to police. Self-reported surveys, in contrast, involve asking individuals about criminal activity to which they may have been a party.

7 Identify some of the reasons given to explain the high rate of delinquent and criminal behavior by adolescents and young adults. (a) Young males have high levels of testosterone, which increases aggression; (b) adolescents are more susceptible to peer pressure and, therefore, can be convinced to misbehave by friends and peers; (c) teenagers often seek the "thrill" of crime or delinquency to alleviate boredom; and (d) risk factors such as lack of parental supervision, poor academic achievement, weapon carrying, and gang membership increase the likelihood of criminal behavior.

STORIES FROM THE STREET

Go to the *Stories from the Street* feature at **www.cjinaction.com** to hear Larry Gaines tell insightful stories related to this chapter and his experiences in the field.

8 Explain some of the links between income level and crime. Statistically, poor people commit more crimes, and are victims of more crimes, than those in the middle- and upper-income levels. Evidence shows, however, that income is not as important as other factors such as family disorganization, lack of education, and lack of employment. Indeed, the vast majority of all residents in low-income neighborhoods are law abiding.

9 Discuss how crime statistics explain the rising number of women incarcerated in the United States. Experts believe that many women are arrested and given harsh punishments for activity that would not have placed them behind bars several decades ago. For the most part, this activity is nonviolent: drug-related offenses account for about two out of every three women sent to prison every year. Only about 2 percent of women are incarcerated for violent crimes.

Key Terms

civil law 67
dark figure of crime 77
index crimes 72

mala in se 70
mala prohibita 70
Part II offenses 73

self-reported surveys 79
Uniform Crime Report
(UCR) 71

victim surveys 76

Questions for Critical Analysis

1 Give an example of how one person could be involved in a civil lawsuit and a criminal lawsuit for the same action.

2 What is the difference between a felony and a misdemeanor?

3 Two fathers, John and Phil, get in a heated argument following a dispute between their sons in a Little League baseball game. They come to blows and John strikes Phil in the temple, killing him. Will John be charged with voluntary manslaughter or involuntary manslaughter? What other details might you need to be sure of your answer?

4 Why is murder considered a *mala in se* crime? What argument can be made that murder is not a *mala in se* crime?

5 What is the distinction between the crime rate and crime in America?

6 Although Part II offenses constitute the bulk of crimes, Part I offenses get the most publicity. Is this necessarily irrational? Why or why not?

7 Why might self-reported surveys be the best method of learning the dark figure of crime?

8 How have some experts explained the failure of murder rates to decline along with other indicators of violent and property crimes over recent years?

9 How do self-reported surveys give lie to the stereotype that someone from a low-income neighborhood is more likely to engage in criminal activity than someone from a high-income neighborhood?

Test Preparation Online

Criminal JusticeNow

Go to **www.cjinaction.com** and click on *Criminal JusticeNow* for access to this powerful online study tool. You will get a *personalized study plan* based on your responses to a diagnostic pretest. Once you have mastered the material with the help of interactive learning tools, video clips with questions, an integrated e-book, and more, you can take a posttest to confirm you are ready to move on to the next chapter.

Book Companion Web Site

At the book companion Web site (**www.cjinaction.com**), you will find many resources in addition to *Criminal JusticeNow* to aid you in studying for your exams. For example, under *Chapter Resources*, you will find the *Chapter Outline, Chapter Summary, Flashcards, Glossary, Learning Objectives, Lecture Presentations, Concept Builder, Essay Questions,* and a *Tutorial Chapter Quiz.* You can also test yourself with interactive *Online Reviews* of each chapter section. Check out the *Web Links* to access the Web sites mentioned in the text, as well as many others. You can also access recent perspectives by clicking on *CJ in the News* and *Terrorism Update* under *Course Resources.*

Suggested Readings

Kelly, Caitlin, *Blown Away: American Women and Guns,* New York: Pocket Books, 2004. At least 17 million gun owners in the United States are women, but female voices have been notably lacking from the gun control debate. In this book, Kelly tries to rectify the situation by taking a hard look at the issue from a feminine perspective. In the course of interviewing numerous women on both sides of the debate, Kelly gets to the heart of gun control as a gender issue. Women—particularly mothers of gun victims—have traditionally been at the forefront of efforts to limit the availability of firearms. At the same time, given that women are usually smaller and physically weaker than those who would attack them, a gun, in the words of the author, "is the only weapon that truly levels the field in a life-threatening confrontation."

Spitzer, Robert J., *The Politics of Gun Control,* 3d ed., New York: Chatham House Publishers, 2004. It is impossible to understand the gun control debate in the United States without understanding the nation's "gun culture." The author's many insights help explain why crime statistics are often the last thing people bring up when they talk about guns. Rather, the American mythology of the gun dominates the words and actions of politicians and citizens alike. Along with sections on the Second Amendment, the National Rifle Association, and the Brady Bill, Spitzer relies on international models in providing his own solution to the political problem of gun violence.

Notes

1. Jeremy Kohler, "Special Report: Crime Statistics: What Crime?" *St. Louis Post-Dispatch* (January 16, 2005), A01.

2. Federal Bureau of Investigation, *Crime in the United States, 2001* (Washington, D.C.: U.S. Department of Justice, 2002), 1.

3. Bureau of Justice Statistics, *Criminal Victimization, 2002* (Washington, D.C.: U.S. Department of Justice, 2003), 1.

4. Update with 2004 UCR.

5. Robert W. Drane and David J. Neal, "On Moral Justifications for the Tort/Crime Distinction," *California Law Review* 68 (1980), 398.

6. Gail Heriot, "An Essay on the Civil-Criminal Distinction with Special Reference to Punitive Damages," *Journal of Contemporary Legal Issues* 7 (1996), 43.

7. Model Penal Code Section 1.04 (2).

8. Advisory Task Force on the Juvenile Justice System, *Final Report* (Minneapolis, MN: Minnesota Supreme Court, 1994), 5–11.

9. *Black's Law Dictionary*, 6th ed. (St. Paul, MN: West Publishing Co., 1990), 959.

10. *Ibid.*, 960.

11. Johannes Andenaes, "The Moral or Educative Influence of Criminal Law," *Journal of Social Issues* 27 (Spring 1971), 17, 26.

12. Stuart P. Green, "Why It's a Crime to Tear the Tag Off a Mattress," *Emory Law Journal* 46 (Fall 1997), 1533–1614.

13. Federal Bureau of Investigation, *Uniform Crime Reporting Handbook* (Washington, D.C.: U.S. Department of Justice, 1992), 30.

14. Federal Bureau of Investigation, *Crime in the United States, 2004* (Washington, D.C.: U.S. Department of Justice, 2005), 1.

15. *Ibid.*

16. *Ibid.*, 11–64.

17. Jeffrey Reiman, *The Rich Get Richer and the Poor Get Prison*, 4th ed. (Boston: Allyn & Bacon, 1995), 59–60.

18. *Crime in the United States*, 2004, Figure 2.4, page 21.

19. *Ibid.*, Table 29, page 280.

20. *Ibid.*

21. Marcus Felson, *Crime in Everyday Life* (Thousand Oaks, CA: Pine Forge Press, 1994), 3.

22. Donald J. Black, "Production of Crime Rates," *American Sociological Review* 35 (1970), 733–748.

23. Bureau of Justice Statistics, *Crime Victimization, 2004* (Washington, D.C.: U.S. Department of Justice, 2005), 1.

24. Victoria W. Schneider and Brian Weirsma, "Limits and Use," in Doris Layton MacKenzie, Phyllis Jo Baunach, and Roy R. Robergs, eds., *Measuring Crime: Large-Scale, Long-Range Efforts* (Albany, NY: State University of New York Press, 1990), 21–27.

25. Alabama Code Sections 13A-6-60(8), 13A-6-61(a)(1) (1994).

26. William Chambliss, *Exporting Criminology* (New York: Macmillan, 1988), 30.

27. *Uniform Crime Reporting Handbook*, 33.

28. *Crime in the United States, 2004*, 5.

29. Lisa Stolzenberg, Stewart J. D'Alessio, and David Eitle, "A Multilevel Test of Racial Threat Theory," *Criminology* (August 1, 2004), 680.

30. Steven F. Messner, Suzanne McHugh, and Richard B. Felson, "Distinctive Characteristics of Assaults Motivated by Bias," *Criminology* (August 1, 2004), 585.

31. Victor E. Kappeler, Mark Blumberg, and Gary W. Potter, *The Mythology of Crime and Criminal Justice*, 2d ed. (Prospect Heights, IL: Waveland Press, 1993), 31.

32. Alfred D. Biderman and James P. Lynch, *Understanding Crime Statistics: Why the UCR Diverges from the NCVS* (New York: Springer-Verlag, 1991).

33. L. Edward Vells and Joseph Rankin, "Juvenile Victimization: Convergent Validation of Alternative Measurements," *Journal of Research in Crime and Delinquency* 32 (1995), 287–307.

34. Peter B. Wood, Walter R. Grove, James A. Wilson, and John K. Cochran, "Nonsocial Reinforcement and Criminal Conduct: An Extension of Learning Theory," *Criminology* 35 (May 1997), 335–366.

35. James S. Wallerstein and Clement J. Wyle, "Our Law-Abiding Law Breakers," *Probation* 35 (April 1947), 107–118.

36. Michael Hindelang, "Causes of Delinquency: A Partial Replication and Extension," *Social Problems* 20 (1973), 471–487.

37. Thomas Gray and Eric Walsh, *Maryland Youth at Risk: A Study of Drug Use in Juvenile Detainees* (College Park, MD: Center for Substance Abuse Research, 1993).

38. Bureau of Justice Statistics, *Crime and Victimization in the Three Largest Metropolitan Areas, 1980–1998* (Washington, D.C.: U.S. Department of Justice, March 2005), 1.

39. Quoted in Fox Butterfield, "Violent Crime Dropped by 3 Percent in 2003," *New York Times* (May 25, 2004), A18.

40. Stephen Braun, "Bleak Math of Killings Clouds Baltimore's Anti-Crime Effort," *Los Angeles Times* (February 9, 2005), A14.

41. James Dao, "Baltimore Streets Meaner," *New York Times* (February 9, 2005), A1.

42. *Crime in the United States*, 2004, 15, 31, 37, 41.

43. Bureau of Justice Statistics, *Crime and the Nation's Households, 2003* (Washington, D.C.: U.S. Department of Justice, October 2004), 3.

44. *Crime in the United States, 2004*, Table 18, page 253.

45. Butterfield, "Violent Crime Dropped by 3 Percent in 2003."

46. *Ibid.*

47. James Alan Fox and Jack Levin, *The Will to Kill: Making Sense of Senseless Murder* (Needham, MA: Allyn & Bacon, 2001), 33–37.

48. Dao, "Baltimore Streets Meaner."

49. See **http://www.ojp.usdoj.gov/bjs/dcf/duc.htm**.

50. *Crime in the United States, 2004*, Table 29, page 280.

51. Celia C. Lo, "An Application of Social Conflict Theory to Arrestees' Use of Cocaine and Opiates," *Journal of Drug Issues* (January 1, 2003), 237.

52. Kevin Cullen, "Boston Recalls a Worse Era, but Murders Still Shake City," *Boston Globe* (August 8, 2004), A1.

53. Robert Agnew, *Juvenile Delinquency: Causes and Control* (Los Angeles: Roxbury Publishing Co., 2001), 1–3.

54. Avshalom Caspi and Terrie Moffitt, "The Continuity of Maladaptive Behavior: From Description to Understanding in the Study of Antisocial Behavior," in Dante Cicchetti and Donald J. Cohen, eds., *Manual of Developmental Psychology* (New York: John Wiley, 1995), 493.

55. Delbert S. Elliot and Scott Menard, "Delinquent Friends and Delinquent Behavior: Temporal and Developmental Patterns," in Rolf Loeber and David P. Farrington, eds., *Delinquency and Crime: Current Theories* (Thousand Oaks, CA: Sage Publications, 1996), 47–66.

56. *National Survey of American Attitudes on Substance Abuse VIII: Teens and Parents* (New York: National Center on Addiction and Substance Abuse at Columbia University, August 2003), 2.

57. Rolf Loeber, David P. Farrington, and David Petechuk, *Child Delinquency: Early Intervention and Prevention* (Washington, D.C.: Office of Juvenile Justice and Delinquency Prevention, May 2003), 6–9.

58. James Q. Wilson, "What to Do about Crime," *Commentary* (September 1994), 25–35.

59. Beth Bjerregaard and Alan J. Lizotte, "Gun Ownership and Gang Membership," *Journal of Criminal Law and Criminology* (Fall 1995), 37–58.

60. Joseph F. Sheley and Victoria E. Brewer, *Public Health Reports* (January-February 1995), 18–27.

61. *Crime in the United States, 2004,* 19, 36, 38.

62. Scott H. Decker, Leanne Fiftal Alarid, and Charles M. Katz, *Controversies in Criminal Justice: Contemporary Readings* (Los Angeles: Roxbury Publishing Co., 2003), 36–37.

63. See **http://www.ojp.usdoj.gov/bjs/homicide/race.htm**.

64. James Q. Wilson, "The Family Way," *The Wall Street Journal* (January 7, 2003), A12.

65. *Ibid.*

66. Caroline Wolf Harlow, *Education and Correctional Populations* (Washington, D.C.: Bureau of Justice Statistics, January 2003), 1.

67. Charles Tittle and Robert Meier, "Specifying the SES/Delinquency Relationship," *Criminology* 28 (1990), 270–301.

68. *Crime in the United States, 2004,* Table 43, page 298.

69. *Crime Victimization, 2004,* Table 4, page 6.

70. Arthur H. Garrison, "Disproportionate Minority Arrests: A Note on What Has Been Said and How It Fits Together," *New England Journal on Criminal and Civil Confinement* (Winter 1997), 29.

71. Eric A. Stewart, Ronald L. Simons, and Rand D. Donger, "Assessing Neighborhood and Social Psychological Influences on Childhood Violence in an African American Sample," *Criminology* (November 2002), 801–829.

72. Margaret Farnworth, Raymond H. C. Teske, Jr., and Gina Thurman, "Ethnic, Racial, and Minority Disparity in Felony Court Processing," in *Race and Criminal Justice,* ed. Michael J. Lynch and E. Britt Patterson (New York: Harrow & Heston, 1991), 55–57.

73. See **http://www.ojp.usdoj.gov/bjs/homicide/gender.htm**.

74. *Crime in the United States, 2004,* Table 42, page 297.

75. *Ibid.,* Table 33, page 285.

76. *Sourcebook of Criminal Justice Statistics, 2003* (Bureau of Justice Statistics, 2004), Table 6.56, page 519.

77. Meda Chesney-Lind, "The Forgotten Offender," *Corrections Today* 60 (1998), 70.

78. *Crime in the United States, 2004,* 19, 36.

79. Franklin E. Zimring, "Firearms, Violence, and the Potential Impact of Firearms Control," *Journal of Law, Medicine, and Ethics* (Spring 2004), 37.

80. *On Target: The Impact of the 1994 Federal Assault Weapon Act* (Washington, D.C.: Brady Center to Prevent Gun Violence, March 2004), 2.

81. John R. Lott, Jr., "Does Allowing Law-Abiding Citizens to Carry Concealed Handguns Save Lives?" *Valparaiso University Law Review* (Spring 1997), 355; and John R. Lott, Jr., and David Muster, "Crime, Deterrence, and Right to Carry Concealed Handguns," *Journal of Legal Studies* (1997), 1.

82. National Institute of Justice, *Impacts of the 1994 Assault Weapons Ban: 1994–96* (Washington, D.C.: U.S. Department of Justice, March 1999), 8–9.

83. John J. Donohue, "Guns, Crime, and the Impact of State Right-to-Carry Laws," *Fordham Law Review* (November 2004), 623.

84. "First Reports Evaluating the Effectiveness of Strategies for Preventing Violence: Firearm Laws," *Morbidity and Mortality Weekly Report* (Washington, D.C.: U.S. Centers for Disease Control, October 3, 2003), 11–20.

85. Gary Kleck, "Measures of Gun Ownership Levels for Macro-Level Crime and Violence Research," *Journal of Research in Crime and Delinquency* (February 2004), 33.

86. Gary Kleck, *Targeting Guns* (New York: Aldine de Gruyter, 1997), 8.

87. Jerry J. Phillips, "The Relation of Constitutional and Tort Law to Gun Injuries and Deaths in the United States," *Connecticut Law Review* (Summer 2000), 1342.

88. Pub. L. No. 103-159, 107 Stat. 1536 (1993); codified as amended at 18 U.S.C. Sections 922(s)–(t) (1995).

89. Bureau of Justice Statistics, *Background Checks for Firearm Transfers, 2003* (Washington, D.C.: U.S. Department of Justice, September 2004), 1.

90. Philip J. Cook and Jens Ludwig, "Principles for Effective Gun Policy," *Fordham Law Review* (November 2004), 589.

91. Jordan Carleo-Evangelist, "Gun Control Advocates Mourn the Loss of Assault Weapons Ban, but Opponents Says Laws Like It Accomplish Little," *Albany Times Union* (October 17, 2004), A1.

92. Jens Ludwig and Philip J. Cook, "Homicide and Suicide Rates Associated with Implementation of the Brady Handgun Violence Prevention Act," *Journal of the American Medical Association* 284 (August 2, 2000), 585–591.

CHAPTER FOUR

Inside Criminal Law

Chapter outline

- The Development of American Criminal Law
- Written Sources of American Criminal Law
- The Purposes of Criminal Law
- The Elements of a Crime
- Defenses under Criminal Law
- Procedural Safeguards
- Criminal Justice in Action—Punishing Hate

Chapter objectives

After reading this chapter, you should be able to:

1   Explain precedent and the importance of the doctrine of *stare decisis.*
2   List the four written sources of American criminal law.
3   Explain the two basic functions of criminal law.
4   Delineate the elements required to establish *mens rea* (a guilty mental state).
5   Explain how the doctrine of strict liability applies to criminal law.
6   List and briefly define the most important excuse defenses for crimes.
7   Describe the four most important justification criminal defenses.
8   Distinguish between substantive and procedural criminal law.
9   Explain the importance of the due process clause in the criminal justice system,

Criminal JusticeNow

Optimize your study time and master key chapter concepts with *Criminal JusticeNow*, an online study tool that provides you with a *personalized study plan*. Check out the "Test Preparation Online" section at the end of the chapter for additional information.

Spreading the Risk

Ashley McMillan was twenty-three years old and recently divorced when she started dating Anthony Whitfield. After several months, she ended the relationship because he had been cheating on her. Soon after, she heard a rumor that he was infected with human immunodeficiency virus (HIV), the virus that can lead to acquired immune deficiency syndrome (AIDS). McMillan filed a report with the Oklahoma City Police Department, saying she wanted to bring criminal charges against Whitfield. The Oklahoma City police, however, took no action.

Eight years later, in 2004, McMillan (who did not contract the virus) was saddened but not surprised to learn that Whitfield, now living in Washington State, had been charged with deliberately exposing seventeen women to HIV by having unprotected sex with them. Local health officials first became aware of Whitfield's dangerous behavior when a large number of women who tested positive for HIV listed him as a recent sex partner. Whitfield, who was infected during a prison rape in the early 1990s, had been issued a cease-and-desist order that required him to wear a condom during any sexual act and inform his partners of his condition.

Ron Soliman/The Olympian

Anthony Whitfield was found guilty on seventeen counts of assault in the first degree with sexual motivation for knowingly exposing numerous sexual partners to HIV, the virus that causes AIDS.

By his own admission, Whitfield tossed the document in the trash and exposed another woman two days later.

A judge in Thurston County, Washington, found Whitfield guilty on seventeen counts of first degree assault with sexual motivation and sentenced him to 178 years in prison. McMillan wonders what "might have been" if the Oklahoma City police had taken action when they had the chance. "I've been walking around for eight years wondering if this guy is still on the loose and infecting women out there," she says. "The chain reaction has got to be amazing."

Was the law fair to Anthony Whitfield? In this chapter, we will learn that a defendant must have a guilty mental state, or *mens rea*, to have committed a crime. Arguably, Whitfield did not have this mental state if he did not intentionally attempt to infect his partners with HIV. According to his attorney, Whitfield used women for shelter, money, and sex but never intended to harm them. Nonetheless, it is important to carefully consider the words in the statute under which Whitfield was charged. The criminal code of Washington declares that a person is guilty of first degree assault if he or she "with intent to inflict great bodily harm: administers, exposes, or transmits . . . the human immunodeficiency virus."[1]

A close reading of the law—particularly the word *exposes*—shows that prosecutors did not need to prove that Whitfield had infected anyone. They only needed to prove that he knew he was HIV-positive and had engaged in unprotected sex "with

CONCEPT BUILDER

Mental state or intent (*mens rea*) is essential in many criminal cases and can affect sentencing dispositions. Visit **www.cjinaction.com** for an interactive exploration of this key topic.

intent to inflict great bodily harm." In the eyes of the judge, Whitfield provided sufficient proof of this intent by remarking to friends on two different occasions, "If I had AIDS, I'd give it to everyone I could."[2] Generally, of course, risky sexual behavior is not a criminal offense. As the *Whitfield* case suggests, however, criminal law must be flexible enough to encompass acts that are not obviously criminal, yet still pose a threat to society and therefore, in the eyes of some, deserve punishment. In this chapter, we will examine how these "threats to society" are identified and focus on the guidelines that determine how the criminal justice system resolves and punishes criminal guilt.

THE DEVELOPMENT OF AMERICAN CRIMINAL LAW

Given its various functions, a single definition of *law* is difficult to establish. To the Greek philosopher Aristotle (384–322 B.C.E.), law was a "pledge that citizens of a state will do justice to one another." Aristotle's mentor, Plato (427–347 B.C.E.), saw the law as primarily a form of social control. The British jurist Sir William Blackstone (1723–1780) described law as "a rule of civil conduct prescribed by the supreme power in a state, commanding what is right, and prohibiting what is wrong." In the United States, jurist Oliver Wendell Holmes, Jr. (1841–1935), contended that law was a set of rules that allowed one to predict how a court would resolve a particular dispute.

> "Justice?—You get justice in the next world, in this world you have the law."
>
> —William Gaddis, American novelist (1994)

The Conception of Law

Although these definitions vary in their particulars, they are all based on the following general observation: *law* consists of enforceable rules governing relationships among individuals and between individuals and their society.[3] Searching back into history, several sources for modern American law can be found in the rules laid out by ancient societies. One of the first known sets of written law was created during the reign of Hammurabi (1792–1750 B.C.E.), the sixth king of the ancient empire of Babylon. The Code of Hammurabi set out crimes and their punishments based on *lex Talionis,* or "an eye for an eye." This concept of retribution is still important and will be discussed in Chapter 11.

Another ancient source of law can be found in the Mosaic Code of the Israelites (1200 B.C.E.). According to tradition, Moses—acting as an intermediary for God—presented the code to the tribes of Israel. The two sides entered into a covenant, or contract, in which the Israelites agreed to follow the code and God agreed to protect them as the chosen people. Besides providing the basis for Judeo-Christian teachings, the Mosaic Code is also reflected in modern American law, as evident by similar prohibitions against murder, theft, adultery, and perjury.

Modern law also owes a debt to the Code of Justinian, promulgated throughout the Roman Empire in the sixth century. This code collected many of the laws that Western society had produced. It was influential in the development of the civil law systems of the European continent. To some extent, it also influenced the common law of England.

English Common Law

The English system of law as it stands today was solidified during the reign of Henry II (1154–1189). Henry sent judges on a specific route throughout the country known as a *circuit.* These circuit judges established a **common law** in England; that is, they

See the **Legal Information Institute** for an overview of criminal law and links to an extensive number of documents relating to criminal justice. Find its Web site by clicking on *Web Links* under *Chapter Resources* at **www.cjinaction.com**.

Common Law
The body of law developed from custom or judicial decisions in English and U.S. courts and not attributable to a legislature.

Precedent

A court decision that furnishes an example of authority for deciding subsequent cases involving similar facts.

Stare Decisis

(pronounced *ster*-ay dih-*si-ses*). A common law doctrine under which judges are obligated to follow the precedents established under prior decisions.

solidified a national law in which legal principles applied to all citizens equally, no matter where they lived or what the local customs had dictated in the past. When confusion about any particular law arose, the circuit judges could draw on English traditions, or they could borrow from legal decisions made in other European countries. Once a circuit judge made a ruling, other circuit judges faced with similar cases generally followed that ruling. Each interpretation became part of the law on the subject and served as a legal **precedent**—a decision that furnished an example or authority for deciding subsequent cases involving similar legal principles or facts. Over time, a body of general rules that prescribed social conduct and that was applied throughout the entire English realm was established, and subsequently it was passed on to British colonies, including those in the New World that would eventually become the thirteen original states.

What is important about the formation of the common law is that it developed from the customs of the people rather than simply the will of a ruler. As such, the common law came to reflect the social, religious, economic, and cultural values of the people. All the while, a system of sheriffs, courts, juries, and lawyers accompanied the development of the common law.

Stare Decisis

The practice of deciding new cases with reference to precedents is the basis for a doctrine called **stare decisis** ("to stand on decided cases"). Under this doctrine, judges are obligated to follow the precedents established within their jurisdictions.[4] For example, any decision of a particular state's highest court will control the outcome of future cases on that issue brought before all of the lower courts within that same state (unless preempted by the federal Constitution). All United States Supreme Court decisions on issues involving the U.S. Constitution are normally binding on *all* courts because the U.S. Constitution is the supreme law of the land and the Court is its final interpreter.

Controlling precedents in a jurisdiction are referred to as *binding authorities*, as are statutes or other laws that must be followed. In contrast, in civil law systems, which rely primarily on legislation and custom rather than case law, precedent is not binding. (To see the extent to which common law and the doctrine of *stare decisis* have been adopted in other countries, see Figure 4.1.)

The doctrine of *stare decisis* helps the court system to be more efficient because if other courts have carefully examined a similar case, their legal reasoning and opinions can serve as a guide. This does not mean, however, that the system is rigid. The United States Supreme Court, for example, will sometimes rule against precedent set in a previous Court decision. It does so when there have been sufficient changes in society to warrant departing from the doctrine of *stare decisis*. In general, however, the judicial system is slow to change, and courts rarely alter major points of law. The doctrine of *stare decisis* leads to stability in the law, allowing people to predict how the law will be applied in given circumstances.

George Washington, standing at right, presided over the Constitutional Convention of 1787. The convention resulted in the U.S. Constitution, the source of a number of laws that continue to form the basis of our criminal justice system today.

The Granger Collection

WRITTEN SOURCES OF AMERICAN CRIMINAL LAW

Originally, common law was *uncodified;* that is, it relied primarily on judges following precedents, and the body of the law was not written down in any single place. Uncodified law, however, presents a number of drawbacks, not the least being that citizens have difficulty learning which acts are illegal and understanding the procedures that must be followed to establish innocence or guilt. Consequently, U.S. history has seen the development of several written sources of American criminal law, also known as "substantive" criminal law. These sources include:

1 The U.S. Constitution and the constitutions of the various states.

2 Statutes, or laws, passed by Congress and by state legislatures, plus local ordinances.

3 Regulations, created by regulatory agencies, such as the federal Food and Drug Administration.

4 Case law (court decisions).

We describe each of these important written sources of law in the following pages (see Figure 4.2 on the next page).

Constitutional Law

The federal government and the states have separate written constitutions that set forth the general organization and powers of, and the limits on, their respective governments. **Constitutional law** is the law as expressed in these constitutions.

The U.S. Constitution is the supreme law of the land. As such, it is the basis of all law in the United States. Any law that violates the Constitution, as ultimately determined by the United States Supreme Court, will be declared unconstitutional and will not be enforced. The Tenth Amendment, which defines the powers and limitations of the federal government, reserves to the states all powers not granted to the federal government. Under our system of federalism (see Chapter 1), each state also has its own constitution. Unless they conflict with the U.S. Constitution or a federal law, state constitutions are supreme within their respective borders. (You will learn more about how constitutional law applies to our criminal justice system in later chapters.)

Statutory Law

Statutes enacted by legislative bodies at any level of government make up another source of law, which is generally referred to as **statutory law.** *Federal statutes* are laws that are enacted by the U.S. Congress. *State statutes* are laws enacted by state legislatures, and statutory law also includes the ordinances passed by cities and counties. A federal statute, of course, applies to all states. A state statute, in contrast, applies only within that state's borders. City or county ordinances (statutes) apply only to those jurisdictions where they are enacted. As mentioned, statutory law found by the Supreme Court to violate the U.S. Constitution will be overturned. In the late 1980s, for example, the Court ruled that any state laws banning the burning of the American flag were unconstitutional because they impinged on the individual's right to freedom of expression.[5]

Common Law and State Statutes Even though the body of statutory law has expanded greatly since the beginning of this nation, thus narrowing the applicability of common law doctrines, there is significant overlap between statutory law and common law. For example, many statutes essentially codify existing common law rules. Therefore, the courts, when interpreting the statutes, often rely on the common law as

---

FIGURE 4.1

Selected Countries with Civil and Common Law Systems

Civil Law	Common Law
Argentina	Australia
Austria	Bangladesh
Brazil	Canada
Chile	Ghana
China	India
Egypt	Israel
Finland	Jamaica
France	Kenya
Germany	Malaysia
Greece	New Zealand
Indonesia	Nigeria
Iran	Singapore
Italy	United Kingdom
Japan	United States
Mexico	Zambi
Poland	
South Korea	
Sweden	
Tunisia	
Venezuela	

The United States was not the only country to adopt the basics of English common law and *stare decisis.* Many of Britain's former colonies have assimilated elements of common law to complement their traditional legal practices. As this figure shows, however, a number of countries operate under civil legal systems (not be confused with the classification of civil versus criminal law, which was explained in Chapter 3). Civil law systems rely primarily on legislation (usually called codes) rather than case law and *stare decisis.* In a country with a civil law system, the courts normally refer only to legislation on the subject. The decisions of civil law judges do not necessarily set precedents for later cases.

Constitutional Law
Law based on the U.S. Constitution and the constitutions of the various states.

Statutory Law
The body of law enacted by legislative bodies.

FIGURE 4.2

Sources of American Law

1 **Constitutional law** The law as expressed in the U.S. Constitution and the various state constitutions. The U.S. Constitution is the supreme law of the land. State constitutions are supreme within state borders to the extent that they do not violate the U.S. Constitution or a federal law.

2 **Statutory law** Laws or ordinances created by federal, state, and local legislatures and governing bodies. None of these laws can violate the U.S. Constitution or the relevant state constitution. Uniform laws, when adopted by a state legislature, become statutory law in that state.

3 **Administrative law** The rules, orders, and decisions of federal or state government administrative agencies. Federal administrative agencies are created by enabling legislation enacted by the U.S. Congress. Agency functions include rulemaking, investigation and enforcement, and adjudication.

4 **Case law and common law doctrines** Judge-made law, including interpretations of constitutional provisions, of statutes enacted by legislatures, and of regulations created by administrative agencies. The common law—the doctrines and principles embodied in case law—governs all areas not covered by statutory law (or agency regulations issued to implement various statutes).

a guide to what the legislators intended. In some instances, statutory law has brought common law principles more in line with modern criminal theory. Under common law, for example, the law of rape applied only when the victim was a female. Today, many states recognize that both genders may be the targets of sexual assault. Under common law, burglary was defined as the breaking and entering of a dwelling during the nighttime. State legislatures, in contrast, generally have defined burglary as occurring at any time. They have extended it to apply to structures beyond dwellings and even to automobiles.

Model Penal Code Until the mid–twentieth century, state statutes were disorganized, inconsistent, and generally inadequate for modern society. In 1952, the American Law Institute began to draft a uniform penal code in hopes of solving this problem. The first Model Penal Code was released ten years later and has had a broad effect on state statutes.[6] Though not a law itself, the code defines the general principles of criminal responsibility and codifies specific offenses; it is the source for many of the definitions of crime in this textbook. The majority of the states have adopted parts of the Model Penal Code into their statutes, and some states, such as New York, have adopted a large portion of the Code.[7]

It is important to keep in mind that there are essentially fifty-two different criminal codes in this country—one for each state, the District of Columbia, and the federal government. Even if a state has adopted a large portion of the Model Penal Code, there may be certain discrepancies. Indeed, a state's criminal code often reflects specific values of its citizens, which may not be in keeping with those of the majority of other states. New Mexico and Louisiana, for example, are the only states where cockfighting is still legal. Sometimes, old laws remain on the books even though they are clearly anachronistic and are rarely, if ever, enforced: in Oklahoma, a person can be sentenced to thirty days in jail for "injuring fruit," and a hundred counties in North Carolina prohibit swearing.[8]

Administrative Law

A third source of American criminal law consists of **administrative law**—the rules, orders, and decisions of regulatory agencies. A regulatory agency is a federal, state, or local government agency established to perform a specific function. The Occupational Safety and Health Administration (OSHA), for example, oversees the safety and health of American workers; the Environmental Protection Agency (EPA) is concerned with protecting the natural environment; and the Food and Drug Administration (FDA) regulates food and drugs produced in the United States. Disregarding certain laws created by regulatory agencies can be a criminal violation. Many modern federal statutes, such as the Clean Air Act, designate authority to a specific regulatory agency, such as the EPA, to promulgate regulations to which criminal sanctions are attached. The number of criminal investigators employed by the EPA has grown from six in 1982 to more than 150 at present. These investigators are involved in nearly 500 law enforcement cases each year.[9]

Administrative Law
The body of law created by administrative agencies (in the form of rules, regulations, orders, and decisions) in order to carry out their duties and responsibilities.

Case Law

As is evident from the earlier discussion of the common law tradition, another basic source of American law consists of the rules of law announced in court decisions. These rules of law include interpretations of constitutional provisions, of statutes enacted by legislatures, and of regulations created by administrative agencies. Today, this body of law is referred to variously as the common law, judge-made law, or **case law.**

Case law relies to a certain extent on how courts interpret a particular statute. If you wanted to learn about the coverage and applicability of a particular statute, for example, you would need to locate the statute and study it. You would also need to see how the courts in your jurisdiction have interpreted the statute—in other words, what precedents have been established in regard to that statute. The use of precedent means that judge-made law varies from jurisdiction to jurisdiction. (To learn about the sources of criminal law in many parts of the Muslim world, see *International CJ— Sharia and Islamic Law* on the following page.)

Case Law
The rules of law announced in court decisions. Case law includes the aggregate of reported cases that interpret judicial precedents, statutes, regulations, and constitutional provisions.

THE PURPOSES OF CRIMINAL LAW

Why do societies need laws? Many criminologists believe that criminal law has two basic functions: one relates to the legal requirements of a society, and the other pertains to its need to maintain and promote social values.

Protect and Punish: The Legal Function of the Law

The primary legal function of the law is to maintain social order by protecting citizens from *criminal harm.* This term refers to a variety of harms that can be generalized to fit into two categories:

1 Harms to individual citizens' physical safety and property, such as the harm caused by murder, theft, or arson.
2 Harms to society's interests collectively, such as the harm caused by unsafe foods or consumer products, a polluted environment, or poorly constructed buildings.[10]

The first category is self-evident, although even murder has different degrees, or grades, of offense to which different punishments are assigned. The second, however, has proved more problematic, for it is difficult to measure society's "collective" interests. Often, laws passed to reduce such harms seem overly intrusive and marginally necessary. An extreme example would seem to be the Flammable Fabrics Act, which makes it a crime for a retailer to willfully remove a precautionary instruction label from a mattress that is protected with a chemical fire retardant.[11] Yet even in this example, a criminal harm is conceivable. Suppose a retailer removes the tags before selling a large number of mattresses to a hotel chain. Employees of the chain then unknowingly wash the mattresses with an agent that lessens their flame-resistant qualities. After the mattresses have been placed in rooms, a guest falls asleep while smoking a cigarette, starting a fire that burns down the entire hotel and causes several deaths.[12]

Maintain and Teach: The Social Function of the Law

If criminal laws against acts that cause harm or injury to others are almost universally accepted, the same cannot be said for laws that criminalize "morally" wrongful activities that may do no obvious, physical harm outside the families of those involved. Why criminalize gambling or prostitution if the participants are consenting?

INTERNATIONAL CJ

Sharia and Islamic Law

Despite the influence of Judeo-Christian doctrine on our legal system, the U.S. Constitution, in the words of Thomas Jefferson, created a "wall of separation of Church and State." In contrast, Islamic law, one of the three major legal systems in the world along with civil law and common law, is primarily based on the Koran (Qur'an).

The Koran is the most important source of *sharia*, a term that can be translated as "path" and refers to the laws and way of life provided to Muhammad by Allah. For most Muslims, *sharia* is a guide to religious activities such as prayer and fasting. Many Muslim countries have also adopted *sharia* as their civil law, allowing it to govern marriages, inheritance, the formation of contracts, and other matters. A few countries also use *sharia* as the basis for criminal law, a practice that has drawn criticism from their own citizens and human rights activists in the West.

Under the strictest interpretation of *sharia*, the penalty for a first theft is amputation of the right hand. After a second conviction for that crime, the offender loses the left foot. An unmarried person who has sexual intercourse is to receive one hundred lashes from a whip, while the punishment for adultery is burial to the waist and stoning to death. In Nigeria, a man and woman who were not married were recently sentenced to death for telling each other, "I like you."

Sharia forms the basis for criminal law in Saudi Arabia and Iran and was widely used in Afghanistan under the Taliban before 2003. Recently, it has spread to countries such as Nigeria and Pakistan, where it has come into conflict with constitutional governments. In

Zafran Bibi, after a Pakistani court overturned her sentence to death by stoning for adultery in 2002.

Pakistan, for example, a local *sharia* court convicted a woman who had been raped of adultery and sentenced her to death by stoning. Bowing to public outrage, an Islamic appeals court eventually overturned the decision.

AP Photo/Tariq Aziz

FOR CRITICAL ANALYSIS

Depending on how it is interpreted, *sharia* can be particularly harsh on women, and many women's rights groups from Western nations have worked to change these laws. What are the possible drawbacks when a person from one culture tries to change the traditions of another culture? Do you think that foreign governments should pressure countries that implement strict *sharia* to modify their criminal laws?

Expressing Public Morality The answer lies in the social function of criminal law. Many observers believe that the main purpose of criminal law is to reflect the values and norms of society, or at least of those segments of society that hold power. Legal scholar Henry Hart has stated that the only justification for criminal law and punishment is "the judgment of community condemnation."[13]

Take, for example, the misdemeanor of bigamy, which occurs when someone knowingly marries a second person without terminating her or his marriage to an original husband or wife. Apart from moral considerations, there would appear to be no victims in a bigamous relationship, and indeed many societies have allowed and continue to allow bigamy to exist. In the American social tradition, however, as John L. Diamond of the University of California's Hastings College of the Law points out:

> Marriage is an institution encouraged and supported by society. The structural importance of the integrity of the family and a monogamous marriage requires unflinching enforcement of the criminal laws against bigamy. The immorality is not in choosing to do wrong, but in transgressing, even innocently, a fundamental social boundary that lies at the core of social order.[14]

When discussing the social function of criminal law, it is important to remember that a society's views of morality change over time. Puritan New England society not only had strict laws against adultery, but also considered lying and idleness to be criminal acts.[15] Today, such acts may carry social stigmas, but only in certain extreme circumstances do they elicit legal sanctions. Furthermore, criminal laws aimed at minority groups, which were once widely accepted in the legal community as well as society at large, have increasingly come under question. (See the feature *CJ in Focus—Landmark Cases:* Lawrence v. Texas.)

Teaching Societal Boundaries Some scholars believe that criminal laws not only express the expectations of society, but "teach" them as well. Professor Lawrence M. Friedman of Stanford University thinks that just as parents teach children behavioral norms through punishment, criminal justice "'teaches a lesson' to the people it punishes, and to society at large." Making burglary a crime, arresting burglars, placing them in jail—each step in the criminal justice process reinforces the idea that burglary is unacceptable and is deserving of punishment.[16]

CJ IN FOCUS/LANDMARK CASES

Lawrence v. Texas

Police officers in Houston arrested John Geddes Lawrence and Tyron Garner for violating a Texas law that prohibits individuals of the same sex from engaging in "deviate sexual intercourse." Lawrence and Garner challenged the law as unconstitutional because it banned sexual practices—in this case, sodomy—by homosexual couples that are lawful when performed by a man and a woman. The Texas Supreme Court upheld the statute, relying on the United States Supreme Court's decision in *Bowers v. Hardwick* (1986), which preserved a similar state law (since repealed) in Georgia. Lawrence and Garner appealed to the Supreme Court, in essence telling the highest court in the land that it had been mistaken when it ruled on the *Bowers* case and asking it to reconsider.

> *Lawrence v. Texas*
> United States Supreme Court
> 522 U.S. 1064 (2003)
> http://laws.findlaw.com/us/000/02-102.html

In the words of the court . . .
Justice KENNEDY, majority opinion

* * * *

The laws involved in *Bowers* and here are, to be sure, statutes that purport to do no more than prohibit a particular sexual act. Their penalties and purposes, though, have more far-reaching consequences, touching upon the most private human conduct, sexual behavior, and in the most private of places, the home. The statutes do seek to control a personal relationship that, whether or not entitled to formal recognition in the law, is within the liberty of persons to choose without being punished as criminals.

This, as a general rule, should counsel against attempts by the State, or a court, to define the meaning of the relationship or to set its boundaries absent injury to a person or abuse of an institution the law protects. It suffices for us to acknowledge that

adults may choose to enter upon this relationship in the confines of their homes and their own private lives and still retain their dignity as free persons. * * * The liberty protected by the Constitution allows homosexual persons the right to make this choice.

* * * *

When homosexual conduct is made criminal by the law of the State, that declaration in and of itself is an invitation to subject homosexual persons to discrimination both in the public and in the private spheres. The central holding of *Bowers* has been brought in question by this case, and it should be addressed. Its continuance as precedent demeans the lives of homosexual persons.

* * * *

The petitioners are entitled to respect for their private lives. The State cannot demean their existence or control their destiny by making their private sexual conduct a crime.

DECISION
Overturning its earlier *Bowers* decision, the Court ruled that the Texas antisodomy law was unconstitutional, at the same time invalidating similar statutes in three other states—Kansas, Oklahoma, and Missouri.

FOR CRITICAL ANALYSIS
Nine states still have laws on the books that make sodomy illegal for both heterosexual and homosexual partners. How do you think one of these laws would fare if brought before the Supreme Court today? Have the morals of American society changed to the point where any law criminalizing consensual sexual conduct between adults is outdated?

For more information and activities related to this case, click on Landmark Cases *under* Book Resources *at* **www.cjinaction.com.**

Corpus Delicti
The body of circumstances that must exist for a criminal act to have occurred.

This teaching function can also be seen in traffic laws. There is nothing "natural" about most traffic laws; Americans drive on the right side of the street, the British on the left side, with no obvious difference in the results. These laws, such as stopping at intersections, using headlights at night, and following speed limits, do lead to a more orderly flow of traffic and fewer accidents—certainly socially desirable goals. Various forms of punishment for breaking traffic laws teach drivers the "social" order of the road.

THE ELEMENTS OF A CRIME

In fictional accounts of police work, the admission of guilt is often portrayed as *the* crucial element of a criminal investigation. Although an admission is certainly useful to police and prosecutors, it alone cannot establish the innocence or guilt of a suspect. Criminal law normally requires that the **corpus delicti,** a Latin phrase for "the body of the crime," be proved before a person can be convicted of wrongdoing.[17] *Corpus delicti* can be defined as "proof that a specific crime has actually been committed by someone."[18] It consists of the basic elements of any crime, which include (1) *actus reus*, or a guilty act; (2) *mens rea*, or a guilty intent; (3) concurrence, or the coming together of the criminal act and the guilty mind; (4) a link between the act and the legal definition of the crime; (5) any attendant circumstances; and (6) the harm done, or result of the criminal act. (See *Mastering Concepts* for an example showing some of the various elements of a crime.)

Criminal Act: *Actus Reus*

Suppose Mr. Smith walks into a police department and announces that he just killed his wife. In and of itself, the confession is insufficient for conviction unless the police find Mrs. Smith's corpse, for example, with a bullet in her brain and establish through

---

MASTERING CONCEPTS

The Elements of a Crime

Carl Robert Winchell walked into the SunTrust Bank in Volusia County, Florida, and placed a bag containing a box on a counter. Announcing that the box held a bomb, he demanded to be given an unspecified amount of money. After being provided with several thousand dollars in cash, Winchell fled, leaving the box behind. A Volusia County Sheriff's Office bomb squad subsequently determined that the box did not in fact contain any explosive device. Winchell was eventually arrested and charged with robbery.

Winchell's actions were criminal because they satisfy the three elements of a crime:

1 *Actus reus*—The physical act of a crime took place. In this case, Winchell committed bank robbery.

2 *Mens rea*—The offender must intentionally, knowingly, or willingly commit the criminal act. In this case,

Winchell obviously planned to rob the SunTrust Bank using the false threat of a bomb.

3 A **concurrence** of *actus reus* and *mens rea*—The criminal act must be the result of the offender's intention to commit that particular criminal act. In this case, the robbery was the direct result of Winchell's intent to take property using the threat of the fake bomb. If, in addition, a bank customer had died of a heart attack during the robbery attempt, Winchell could not have been charged with first degree murder because he did not intend to harm anyone.

Note that the fact that there was no bomb in the box has no direct bearing on the three elements of the crime. It could, however, lead to Winchell receiving a lighter punishment than if he had used a real bomb.

evidence that Mr. Smith fired the gun. (This does not mean that an actual dead body has to be found in every homicide case. Rather, it is the fact of the death that must be established in such cases.)

Most crimes require an act of *commission;* that is, a person must *do* something in order to be accused of a crime. The prohibited act is referred to as the **actus reus,** or guilty act. Furthermore, the act of commission must be voluntary. For example, if Mr. Smith had an epileptic seizure while holding a hunting rifle and accidentally shot his wife, he would normally not be held criminally liable for her death. (See *You Be the Judge—A Voluntary Act?*)

In some cases, an act of *omission* can be a crime, but only when a person has a legal duty to perform the omitted act. One such legal duty is assumed to exist based on a "special relationship" between two parties, such as a parent and child, adult children and their aged parents, and spouses.[19] Those persons involved in contractual relationships with others, such as physicians and lifeguards, must also perform legal duties to avoid criminal penalty. Minnesota, Rhode Island, Vermont, and Wisconsin have even passed "duty to aid" statutes requiring their citizens to report criminal conduct and help victims of such conduct if possible.[20] Another example of a criminal act of omission is failure to file a federal income tax return when required by law to do so.

The *guilty act* requirement is based on one of the premises of criminal law—that a person is punished for harm done to society. Planning to kill someone or to steal a car may be wrong, but the thoughts do no harm and are therefore not criminal until they are translated into action. Of course, a person can be punished for attempting murder or robbery, but normally only if he or she took substantial steps toward the criminal objective. Furthermore, the punishment for an *attempt* normally is less severe than if the act had succeeded.

Mental State: *Mens Rea*

A wrongful mental state—**mens rea**—is as necessary as a wrongful act in establishing guilt. The mental state, or requisite *intent,* required to establish guilt of a crime is indicated in the applicable statute or law. For theft, the wrongful act is the taking of

Actus Reus
(pronounced *ak*-tus *ray*-uhs). A guilty (prohibited) act. The commission of a prohibited act is one of the two essential elements required for criminal liability, the other element being the intent to commit a crime.

Mens Rea
(pronounced *mehns ray*-uh). Mental state, or intent. A wrongful mental state is as necessary as a wrongful act to establish criminal liability.

YOU BE THE JUDGE

A Voluntary Act?

THE FACTS
On a bright, sunny afternoon, Emil was driving on Delaware Avenue in Buffalo, New York. As he was making a turn, Emil suffered an epileptic seizure and lost control of his automobile. The car careened onto the sidewalk and struck a group of six schoolgirls, killing four of them. Emil knew that he was subject to epileptic attacks that rendered him likely to lose consciousness.

THE LAW
An "act" committed while one is unconscious is in reality not an act at all. It is merely a physical event or occurrence over which the defendant has no control; that is, such an act is involuntary. If the defendant

voluntarily causes the loss of consciousness by, for example, using drugs or alcohol, however, then he or she will usually be held criminally responsible for any consequences.

YOUR DECISION
Emil was charged in the deaths of the four girls. He asked the court to dismiss the charges, as he was unconscious at the time of the accident and therefore had not committed a voluntary act. In your opinion, is there an *actus reus* in this situation, or should the charges against Emil be dismissed?

[To see how the appellate court in New York ruled in this case, go to Example 4.1 in Appendix B.]

Negligence
A failure to exercise the standard of care that a reasonable person would exercise in similar circumstances.

another person's property, and the required mental state involves both the awareness that the property belongs to another and the desire to deprive the owner of it.

The Categories of *Mens Rea* A guilty mental state includes elements of purpose, knowledge, negligence, and recklessness.[21] A defendant is said to have *purposefully* committed a criminal act when he or she desires to engage in certain criminal conduct or to cause a certain criminal result. For a defendant to have *knowingly* committed an illegal act, he or she must be aware of the illegality, must believe that the illegality exists, or must correctly suspect that the illegality exists but fail to do anything to dispel (or confirm) his or her belief. Criminal **negligence** involves the mental state in which the defendant grossly deviates from the standard of care that a reasonable person would use under the same circumstances. The defendant is accused of taking an unjustified, substantial, and foreseeable risk that resulted in harm. In Texas, for example, a parent commits a felony if she or he fails to secure a loaded firearm or leaves it in such a manner that it could easily be accessed by a child.[22]

A defendant who commits an act *recklessly* is more blameworthy than one who is criminally negligent. The Model Penal Code defines criminal recklessness as "consciously disregard[ing] a substantial and unjustifiable risk."[23] Some courts, particularly those adhering to the Model Penal Code, will not find criminal recklessness on the part of a defendant who was subjectively unaware of the risk when she or he acted.

Criminal Liability Intent plays an important part in allowing the law to differentiate among varying degrees of criminal liability for similar, though not identical, guilty acts. The role of intent is clearly seen in the different classifications of homicide, defined generally as the willful killing of one human being by another. It is important to emphasize the word *willful,* as it precludes deaths caused by accident or negligence and those deemed justifiable. A death that results from negligence or accident normally is considered a private wrong and a matter for civil law, although some statutes allow for culpable negligence, which permits certain negligent homicides to be criminalized. As we saw in Chapter 3, when the act of killing is willful, deliberate, and premeditated (planned beforehand), it is considered first degree murder. When premeditation does not exist but intent does, the act is considered second degree murder. (See Figure 4.3 for an example of the different homicide statutes in Florida.)

Different degrees of criminal liability for various categories of homicide lead to different penalties. The distinction between murder and manslaughter was evident in the punishment given to Kevin Kelly, a resident of Manassas, Virginia, who left his twenty-one-month-old daughter buckled in the family van for more than seven hours. With the temperature inside the car rising to 140 degrees, the child eventually died of heatstroke. Local prosecutors had the option of charging Kelly with murder, but could find no

FIGURE 4.3

Florida Homicide Statutes (Excerpts)

782.02 Justifiable use of deadly force.
The use of deadly force is justifiable when a person is resisting any attempt to murder such person or to commit any felony upon him or her or upon or in any dwelling house in which such person shall be.

782.03 Excusable homicide.
Homicide is excusable when committed by accident and misfortune in doing any lawful act by lawful means with usual ordinary caution, and without any unlawful intent, or by accident and misfortune in the heat of passion, upon any sudden and sufficient provocation, or upon a sudden combat, without any dangerous weapon being used and not done in a cruel or unusual manner.

782.04 Murder.
(1)(a) The unlawful killing of a human being:

1. When perpetrated from a premeditated design to effect the death of the person killed or any human being;

2. When committed by a person engaged in the perpetration of, or in the attempt to perpetrate, any: [such acts as arson, robbery, burglary, etc.]; . . .

is murder in the first degree and constitutes a capital felony, ...

(2) The unlawful killing of a human being, when perpetrated by any act imminently dangerous to another and evincing a depraved mind regardless of human life, although without any premeditated design to effect the death of any particular individual, is murder in the second degree and constitutes a felony of the first degree, punishable by imprisonment for a term of years not exceeding life . . . .

782.07 Manslaughter; aggravated manslaughter of an elderly person or disabled adult; aggravated manslaughter of a child.
(1) The killing of a human being by the act, procurement, or culpable negligence of another, without lawful justification according to the provisions of Chapter 776 and in cases in which such killing shall not be excusable homicide or murder, according to the provisions of this chapter, is manslaughter, a felony of the second degree, ...

indication that he had *intentionally* killed his daughter. Instead, the evidence showed that Kelly, who has twelve other children, forgot where he had placed the girl. Kelly was charged with involuntary manslaughter; found guilty, he was sentenced to spend one day in jail each year for seven years. A murder conviction, in contrast, could have brought the death penalty.

Strict Liability For certain crimes, criminal law holds the defendant to be guilty even if intent to commit the offense is lacking. These acts are known as **strict liability crimes** and generally involve endangering the public welfare in some way.[24] Drug control statutes, health and safety regulations, and traffic laws are all strict liability laws. To a certain extent, the concept of strict liability is inconsistent with the traditional principles of criminal law, which hold that *mens rea* is required for an act to be criminal. The goal of strict liability laws is to protect the public by eliminating the possibility that wrongdoers could claim ignorance or mistake to absolve themselves of criminal responsibility.[25] Thus, a person caught dumping waste in a protected pond or driving 70 miles per hour in a 55 miles-per-hour zone cannot plead a lack of intent in his or her defense.

One of the most controversial strict liability crimes is statutory rape, in which an adult engages in a sexual relationship with a minor. In most states, even if the minor consents to the sexual act, the crime still exists because, being underage, he or she is considered incapable of making a rational decision on the matter.[26] Therefore, statutory rape has been committed even if the adult was unaware of the minor's age or was misled to believe that the minor was older.

Accomplice Liability Under certain circumstances, a person can be charged with and convicted of a crime that he or she did not actually commit. This occurs when the suspect has acted as an *accomplice* to a crime; that is, he or she has helped another person commit the crime. Generally, to be found guilty as an accomplice a person must have the "dual intent" (1) to aid the person who committed the crime and (2) that such aid would lead to the commission of the crime.[27] As for the *actus reus*, the accomplice must have helped the primary actor in either a physical sense (for example, by providing the getaway car) or a psychological sense (for example, by encouraging her or him to commit the crime).[28]

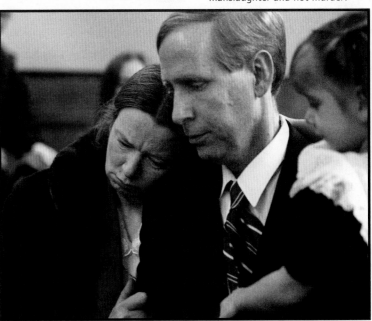

Kevin Kelly with wife and daughter leaving a Prince William County courtroom in Manassas, Virginia. Kelly was convicted of involuntary manslaughter for accidentally forgetting his infant child in the family van, where she eventually died of heatstroke. Why did prosecutors charge Kelly with manslaughter and not murder?

AP Photo/Tracy A. Woodward, Pool

In some states, a person can be convicted as an accomplice even without intent if the crime was a "natural and probable consequence" of his or her actions.[29] Suppose that Jim and Mary enter Frank's home with the goal of burglary. Frank walks in on them while they are carrying out his television, and Jim shoots and kills Frank with a shotgun. Mary could be charged as an accomplice to murder because it is reasonably foreseeable that if one illegally enters another's home with a dangerous weapon, a homicide could occur.

Concurrence

According to criminal law, there must be *concurrence* between the guilty act and the guilty intent. In other words, the guilty act and the guilty intent must occur together.[30] Suppose, for example, that a woman intends to murder her husband with poison in order to collect his life insurance. Every evening, this woman drives her husband home from work. On the night she plans to poison him, however, she swerves to avoid a cat crossing the road and runs into a tree. She survives the accident, but her husband is killed. Even though her intent was realized, the incident would be considered an accidental death because she had not planned to kill him by driving the car into a tree.

Causation

Criminal law also requires that the criminal act cause the harm suffered. In Michigan, for example, two defendants were convicted of murder even though their victim died several years after the initial crime. In the course of that robbery, the defendants had shot the victim in the heart and abdomen and abandoned him in a sewer. Though the victim survived, his heart remained very weak. Four years later, the victim collapsed during a basketball game and died. Medical examination established that his heart failed as a direct result of the earlier injury, and the Michigan Supreme Court ruled that, despite the passing of time, the defendants' criminal act had been the cause of the man's death.[31] (It is interesting to contrast this decision with the historical rule that a victim's death must occur within a year and a day from the date of the defendant's crime.)

Attendant Circumstances

In certain crimes, attendant circumstances—also known as accompanying circumstances—are relevant to the *corpus delicti.* Most states, for example, differentiate between simple assault and the more serious offense of aggravated assault depending on whether the defendant used a weapon such as a gun or a knife while committing the crime. Criminal law also classifies degrees of property crimes based on the amount stolen. According to federal statutes, robbing a bank of less than $100 is a misdemeanor, while taking any amount over $100 is a felony.[32] As we shall see in the *Criminal Justice in Action* feature at the end of this chapter, many states use the concept of attendant circumstances to impose harsher penalties on certain crimes, known as *hate crimes,* that are committed because of a characteristic of the victim.

Harm

For most crimes to occur, some harm must have been done to a person or to property. A certain number of crimes are actually categorized depending on the harm done to the victim, regardless of the intent behind the criminal act. Take two offenses, both of which involve one person hitting another in the back of the head with a tire iron. In the first instance, the victim dies, and the offender is charged with murder. In the second, the victim is only knocked unconscious, and the offender is charged with battery. Because the harm in the second instance was less severe, so was the crime with which the offender was charged, even though the act was exactly the same. Furthermore, most states have different degrees of battery depending on the extent of the injuries suffered by the victim.

Many acts are deemed criminal if they could do harm that the laws try to prevent. Such acts are called **inchoate offenses.** They exist when only an attempt at a criminal act was made. If Jenkins solicits Peterson to murder Jenkins's business partner, this is an inchoate offense on the part of Jenkins, even though Peterson fails to carry out the act. Conspiracies also fall into the category of inchoate offenses; in 2003, the United States Supreme Court ruled that a person could be convicted of criminal conspiracy even though police intervention made the completion of the illegal plan impossible.[33]

Inchoate Offenses
Conduct deemed criminal without actual harm being done, provided that the harm that would have occurred is one the law tries to prevent.

DEFENSES UNDER CRIMINAL LAW

Driving at a speed more suited to a highway, George R. Weller plowed his Buick through a crowded farmers' market in Santa Monica, California, killing ten people in the process. Weller, who was eighty-seven years old at the time of the incident, claimed that he had confused the gas pedal for the brake and then panicked, making him temporarily unable to stop the vehicle. In 2004, a state superior court judge showed little sympathy, ordering Weller to stand trial on ten counts of vehicular manslaughter.

Weller had little chance of successfully arguing that he was not guilty because of "momentary confusion," but a number of other defenses can be raised in the course of a criminal trial. These defenses generally rely on one of two arguments: (1) the defendant is not responsible for the crime, or (2) the defendant was justified in committing the crime.

Insanity

A defense for criminal liability that asserts a lack of criminal responsibility. According to the law, a person cannot have the requisite state of mind to commit a crime if she or he did not know at the time of the act that it was wrong, or did not know the nature and quality of the act.

Criminal Responsibility and the Law

The idea of responsibility plays a significant role in criminal law. In certain circumstances, the law recognizes that a person is not responsible for wrongdoing because he or she does not meet certain mental conditions. In many jurisdictions, for example, children under a specific age are believed to be incapable of committing crimes because they are too young to understand the ramifications of their actions. Thus, *infancy* is an "excuse" defense that argues that the accused's wrongdoing should be excused because he or she lacked the capacity to be held liable for the crime. Other important excuse defenses include insanity, intoxication, and mistake.

Insanity After Deanna Laney used rocks to bludgeon two of her sons—aged six and eight—to death and maim the third in his crib, she told authorities that she had been ordered by God to kill her children as a test of her faith. In 2004, a jury in Tyler, Texas, found that Laney was so divorced from reality that she could not be found guilty of murder, even though her first act after the killings was to call 911. As a result, the defendant was sent to a mental hospital rather than to prison. Thus, **insanity** may be a defense to a criminal charge when the defendant's state of mind is such that she or he cannot claim legal responsibility for her or his actions.

Measuring Sanity Although criminal law has accepted the idea that an insane person cannot be held responsible for criminal acts, society has long debated what standards should be used to measure sanity for the purposes of a criminal trial. One of the oldest tests for insanity resulted from a case in 1843 in which Daniel M'Naughten shot and killed Edward Drummond in the belief that Drummond was Sir Robert Peel, the British prime minister. At trial, M'Naughten claimed that he was suffering from delusions at the time of the murder, and he was found not guilty by reason of insanity. In response to public outcry over the decision, the British court established

Brian David Mitchell, center, sings the Christmas hymn "Oh Come, Oh Come, Immanuel" in Salt Lake City's Third District Court. Judge Judith Atherton removed Mitchell, facing charges of kidnapping fourteen-year-old Elizabeth Smart, from the courtroom seven times for disruptive behavior during his competency hearings in the summer of 2005. Why might a defendant feign mental imbalance during court proceedings?

AP Photo/Rick Egan, Pool

M'Naughten Rule

A common law test of criminal responsibility derived from *M'Naughten's* case in 1843 that relies on the defendant's inability to distinguish right from wrong.

Irresistible Impulse Test

A test for the insanity defense under which a defendant who knew his or her action was wrong may still be found insane if he or she was nonetheless unable, as a result of a mental deficiency, to control the urge to complete it.

Durham Rule

A test of criminal responsibility adopted in a 1954 case: "an accused is not criminally responsible if his unlawful act was the product of mental disease or mental defect."

Substantial Capacity Test

From the Model Penal Code, a test that states that a person is not responsible for criminal behavior if when committing the act "as a result of mental disease or defect he [or she] lacks substantial capacity either to appreciate the wrongfulness of his [or her] conduct or to conform his [or her] conduct to the requirements of the law."

the **M'Naughten rule.** Also known as the right-wrong test, the *M'Naughten* rule states that a person is legally insane and therefore not criminally responsible if, at the time of the offense, he or she was not able to distinguish between right and wrong.[34]

As Figure 4.4 shows, twenty-two states still use a version of the *M'Naughten* rule. Several other jurisdictions, reacting to criticism of the *M'Naughten* rule as too narrow, have supplemented it with the less restrictive **irresistible impulse test.** Under this combined approach, a person may be found insane even if he or she was aware that a criminal act was "wrong," provided that some "irresistible impulse" resulting from a mental deficiency drove him or her to commit the crime.[35] Under the **Durham rule,** established by the District of Columbia Federal Court of Appeals in 1954, a jury is expected to decide whether the criminal act was the product of a mental defect or disease.[36] For this reason, the rule is referred to as the *products test.* The *Durham* rule fell out of favor, however, as judges struggled to determine exactly what constituted a "mental defect or disease," and today all federal courts and about two-fifths of the states use the **substantial capacity test** to determine sanity. Characterized as a modern improvement on the *M'Naughten* test, substantial capacity guidelines state that:

> A person is not responsible for criminal conduct if at the time of such conduct as a result of mental disease or defect he [or she] lacks substantial capacity either to appreciate the wrongfulness of his [or her] conduct or to conform his [or her] conduct to the requirements of the law.[37]

The key element of this rule is that it requires only a lack of "substantial capacity" to release a defendant from criminal responsibility. This standard is considerably easier to meet than the "right-wrong" requirements of the *M'Naughten* rule or the irresistible impulse test.

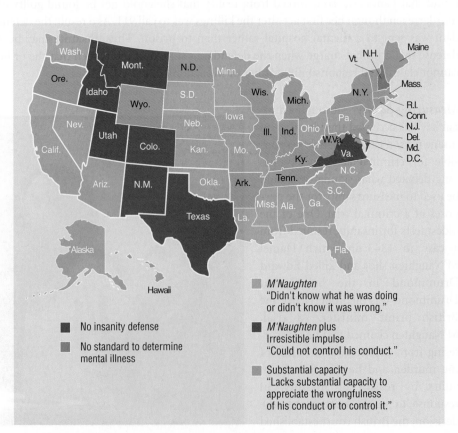

FIGURE 4.4
Insanity Defenses

Source: Bureau of Justice Statistics, *State Court Organization, 1998* (Washington, D.C.: U.S. Department of Justice, 2000), 257–259.

Are Too Many Criminals Found Not Guilty by Reason of Insanity?

To many Americans, it seems likely that any person who commits a gruesome murder or any other sort of violent crime has psychological problems. The question, then, is, how do we balance the need to punish such a person with the possibility that he or she may be seriously ill?

THE MYTH

The American system of criminal justice answers this question by stating that a person may not be tried for an offense if that person cannot be held legally responsible for her or his actions. Because of the publicity surrounding the insanity defense, many people are under the impression that it is a major loophole in our system, allowing criminals to be "let off" no matter how heinous their crimes.

THE REALITY

In fact, the insanity defense is raised in only about 1 percent of felony trials, and is successful only one out of every four times it is raised. The reason: it is extremely difficult to prove insanity under the law. For example, after drowning her five children in a bathtub, Andrea Pia Yates entered a plea of not guilty by reason of insanity. The success of this strategy seemed inevitable to many observers, who felt that only an insane woman could systematically kill her children as Yates had done. Indeed, Yates was on antipsychotic medication throughout her trial. Nonetheless, the prosecutors were able to convince a Houston jury that Yates understood her actions were "wrong," and she was found guilty of murder and sentenced to life in prison. (Yates was granted a new trial on appeal due to an unrelated matter.) Even if Yates had succeeded with the insanity defense, she would not have been "let off" in the sense that she would have been set free. Many defendants found not guilty by reason of insanity spend more time in mental hospitals than criminals who are convicted of similar acts spend in prison.

FOR CRITICAL ANALYSIS

What do the relatively limited use and success rate of the insanity defense indicate about the impact of public opinion on criminal law?

Guilty but Mentally Ill In 1981, John Hinckley was found not guilty of the attempted murder of President Ronald Reagan by reason of insanity. Due to the media attention garnered by this and other high-visibility cases, many Americans see the insanity defense as an easy means for violent criminals to "cheat" the criminal justice system. In fact, this public perception is faulty. The insanity defense is rarely entered and is even less likely to result in an acquittal, as it is difficult to prove.[38] (See the feature *CJ in Focus—Myth versus Reality: Are Too Many Criminals Found Not Guilty by Reason of Insanity?*) Psychiatry is far more commonly used in the courtroom to determine the "competency" of a defendant to stand trial. If a judge believes that the defendant is unable to understand the nature of the proceedings or to assist in his or her own defense, the trial will not take place. When competency hearings (which may also take place after the initial arrest and before sentencing) reveal that the defendant is in fact incompetent, the court may decide to place the defendant under treatment. Once competency has been restored to the defendant, the proceedings may recommence.[39]

Nevertheless, public backlash against the insanity defense caused seven state legislatures to pass "guilty but mentally ill" statutes. Under these laws, a defendant is guilty but mentally ill if

> at the time of the commission of the act constituting the offense, he [or she] had the capacity to distinguish right from wrong . . . but because of mental disease or defect he [or she] lacked sufficient capacity to conform his [or her] conduct to the requirements of the law.[40]

In other words, the laws allow a jury to determine that a defendant is "mentally ill," though not insane, and therefore criminally responsible for her or his actions.

Defendants found guilty but mentally ill generally spend the early years of their sentences in a psychiatric hospital and the rest of the time in prison, or they receive treatment while in prison.

Intoxication The law recognizes two types of **intoxication,** whether from drugs or from alcohol: *voluntary* and *involuntary.* Involuntary intoxication occurs when a person is physically forced to ingest or is injected with an intoxicating substance, or is unaware that a substance contains drugs or alcohol. Involuntary intoxication is a viable defense to a crime if the substance leaves the person unable to form the mental state necessary to understand that the act committed while under the influence was wrong.[41] In Colorado, for example, the murder conviction of a man who shot a neighbor was overturned on the basis that the jury in the initial trial was not informed of the possibility of involuntary intoxication. At the time of the crime, the man had been taking a prescription decongestant that contained phenylpropanolamine, which has been known to cause psychotic episodes.

Voluntary drug or alcohol intoxication is also used to excuse a defendant's actions, though it is not a defense in itself. Rather, it is used when the defense attorney wants to show that the defendant was so intoxicated that *mens rea* was negated. In other words, the defendant could not possibly have had the state of mind that a crime requires. Many courts are reluctant to allow voluntary intoxication arguments to be presented to juries, however. After all, the defendant, by definition, voluntarily chose to enter an intoxicated state.

> "You know how it is, Dr. Ellsworth. You go to a party, have a few drinks, somebody gets killed."
>
> —Letter from a death row inmate to Professor Phoebe Ellsworth, University of Michigan (1999)

Twelve states have eliminated voluntary intoxication as a possible defense, a step that has been criticized by many legal scholars but was upheld by the United States Supreme Court in *Montana v. Egelhoff* (1996).[42] The case concerned a double murder committed by James Allen Egelhoff, who was extremely drunk at the time of the crime. Egelhoff was convicted on two counts of deliberate homicide, which is defined by Montana law as "knowingly" or "purposefully" causing the death of another human being.[43] Egelhoff appealed his conviction, arguing that the state statute prohibiting evidence of voluntary intoxication kept his attorneys from showing the jury that he was too inebriated to "knowingly" or "purposefully" commit the murders.[44] The Court allowed Egelhoff's conviction, ruling that states were constitutionally within their rights to abolish the voluntary intoxication defense.

Mistake Everyone has heard the saying, "Ignorance of the law is no excuse." Ordinarily, ignorance of the law or a *mistaken idea* about what the law requires is not a valid defense.[45] A few years ago, for example, Gilbert A. Robinson appealed his conviction for possession of sexually explicit photographs of teenage boys, claiming he did not know that such an act had become illegal. Chief Judge Juan R. Torruella del Valle of the Fifth Circuit Court of Appeals upheld Robinson's conviction, stating that child pornography is "inherently deleterious" and that the "probability of regulation is so great that anyone who is aware that he is in possession of [it] . . . must be presumed to be aware of the regulation."[46]

In some states, however, that rule has been modified. People who claim that they honestly did not know that they were breaking a law may have a valid defense if (1) the law was not published or reasonably known to the public or (2) the person relied on an official statement of the law that was erroneous.[47]

A *mistake of fact,* as opposed to a *mistake of law,* operates as a defense if it negates the mental state necessary to commit a crime. If, for example, Oliver mis-

---

Intoxication
A defense for criminal liability in which the defendant claims that the taking of intoxicants rendered him or her unable to form the requisite intent to commit a criminal act.

takenly walks off with Julie's briefcase because he thinks it is his, there is no theft. Theft requires knowledge that the property belongs to another. The mistake of fact defense has proved very controversial in rape and sexual assault cases, where the accused claims that the sex was consensual while the alleged victim claims it was coerced.

Duress
Unlawful pressure brought to bear on a person, causing the person to perform an act that he or she would not otherwise perform.

Justification Criminal Defenses and the Law

In certain instances, a defendant will accept responsibility for committing an illegal act, but contend that—given the circumstances—the act was justified. In other words, even though the guilty act and the guilty intent are present, the particulars of the case relieve the defendant of criminal liability. In 2004, for example, there were 666 "justified" killings of felons who were in the process of committing a felony: 437 were killed by law enforcement officers, and 229 by private citizens.[48] Four of the most important justification defenses are duress, self-defense, necessity, and entrapment.

Duress **Duress** exists when the *wrongful* threat of one person induces another person to perform an act that she or he would otherwise not perform. In such a situation, duress is said to negate the *mens rea* necessary to commit a crime. For duress to qualify as a defense, the following requirements must be met:

1 The threat must be of serious bodily harm or death.
2 The harm threatened must be greater than the harm caused by the crime.
3 The threat must be immediate and inescapable.
4 The defendant must have become involved in the situation through no fault of his or her own.[49]

When ruling on the duress defense, courts often examine whether the defendant had the opportunity to avoid the threat in question. Two narcotics cases illustrate this point. In the first, the defendant claimed that an associate threatened to kill him and his wife unless he participated in a marijuana deal. Although this contention was proved true during the course of the trial, the court rejected the duress defense because the defendant made no apparent effort to escape, nor did he report his dilemma to the police. In sum, the drug deal was avoidable—the defendant could have made an effort to extricate himself, but he did not, thereby surrendering the protection of the duress defense.[50]

In the second case, a taxi driver in Bogotá, Colombia, was ordered by a passenger to swallow cocaine-filled balloons and take them to the United States. The taxi driver was warned that if he refused, his wife and three-year-old daughter would be killed. After a series of similar threats, the taxi driver agreed to transport the drugs. On arriving at customs at the Los Angeles airport, the defendant consented to have his stomach X-rayed, which led to discovery of the contraband and his arrest. During trial, the defendant told the court that he was afraid to notify the police in Colombia because he believed them to

Special agents examine the body of Brian Douglas Wells, who was killed after robbing a bank in Summit Township, Pennsylvania, when a bomb attached to his neck detonated. Before his death, Wells told state troopers that the explosive device was used to force him to commit the crime. If this is true, and he had survived, would Wells have been able to claim duress as a defense?

Self-Defense
The legally recognized privilege to protect one's self or property from injury by another. The privilege of self-defense only covers acts that are reasonably necessary to protect one's self or property.

GREAT DEBATES

The "battered woman defense" goes to the heart of the debate over the justifiable use of force. Does an abused woman who strikes against her abuser without provocation deserve the law's protection? Or, is deadly self-defense justified only if the threat of danger is immediate? For an in-depth discussion of the issues that inform this debate, click on *Great Debates* under *Book Resources* at **www.cjinaction.com**.

be corrupt. The court accepted his duress defense, on the grounds that it met the four requirements listed above and the defendant had notified American authorities when given the opportunity to do so.[51]

Justifiable Use of Force—Self-Defense A person who believes he or she is in danger of being harmed by another is justified in defending himself or herself with the use of force, and any criminal act committed in such circumstances can be justified as **self-defense.** Other situations that also justify the use of force include the defense of one's dwelling, the defense of other property, and the prevention of a crime. In all these situations, it is important to distinguish between deadly and nondeadly force. Deadly force is likely to result in death or serious bodily harm.

Generally speaking, people can use the amount of nondeadly force that seems necessary to protect themselves, their dwellings, or other property or to prevent the commission of a crime. Deadly force can be used in self-defense if there is a *reasonable belief* that imminent death or bodily harm will otherwise result, if the attacker is using unlawful force (an example of lawful force is that exerted by a police officer), if the defender has not initiated or provoked the attack, and if there is no other possible response or alternative way out of the life-threatening situation.[52] Deadly force normally can be used to defend a dwelling only if the unlawful entry is violent and the person believes deadly force is necessary to prevent imminent death or great bodily harm or—in some jurisdictions—if the person believes deadly force is necessary to prevent the commission of a felony (such as arson) in the dwelling. (See the feature *You Be the Judge—Justifying a Shooting*.)

Necessity In 2005, Charley Charles tried to defend his illegal possession of a firearm by saying he needed the weapon for protection. More than twenty years earlier, Charles had set his six-year-old son on fire, and he claimed that members of the community still wanted to harm him for this heinous act. Unimpressed, a Mississippi jury

---

YOU BE THE JUDGE

Justifying a Shooting

THE FACTS
Bernhard was riding a subway train in New York City when four young men approached and asked him for $5. Bernhard tried to avoid the young men, afraid that they were looking to harass him. When one of the men, Troy, again asked for $5, Bernhard pulled out a handgun and shot and injured each of the four men. Bernhard later told police that he was afraid of being physically attacked. He was charged with attempted murder, assault, and reckless endangerment.

THE LAW
Under New York law, a person is justified in using physical force in self-defense when he or she "reasonably believes" that force is going to be used against him or her; the force used in self-defense may be of the degree that the person "reasonably believes to be necessary."

YOUR DECISION
The key question under this law is whether Bernhard reasonably believed that he was in danger of being attacked. In other words, it does not matter if the four young men had no intention of doing anything but teasing him; what matters is what Bernhard expected to happen. Do you think he was justified in shooting Troy and his friends, or is Bernhard guilty on all charges? What factors must be taken into consideration when determining whether Bernhard was acting "reasonably"?

[To see how a New York jury decided Bernhard's fate, go to Example 4.2 in Appendix B.]

found him guilty for being a felon in possession of a handgun.[53] The **necessity** defense is valid under other circumstances, however. According to the Model Penal Code, the necessity defense is justifiable if "the harm or evil sought to be avoided by such conduct is greater than that sought to be prevented by the law defining the offense charged."[54] For example, in one case a convicted felon was threatened by an acquaintance with a gun. The felon grabbed the gun and fled the scene, but subsequently he was arrested under a statute that prohibits convicted felons from possessing firearms. In this situation, the necessity defense was valid because the defendant's crime avoided a "greater evil."[55] The one crime for which the necessity defense is not viable is murder.[56]

Entrapment **Entrapment** is a justification defense that criminal law allows when a police officer or government agent deceives a defendant into wrongdoing. Although law enforcement agents can legitimately use various forms of subterfuge—such as informants or undercover agents—to gain information or apprehend a suspect in a criminal act, the law places limits on these strategies. Police cannot persuade an innocent person to commit a crime, nor can they coerce a suspect into doing so, even if they are certain she or he is a criminal.

The guidelines for determining entrapment were established in the 1932 case of *Sorrells v. United States.*[57] The case, which took place during Prohibition when the sale of alcoholic beverages was illegal, involved a federal law enforcement agent who repeatedly urged the defendant to sell him bootleg whiskey. The defendant initially rejected the agent's overtures, stating that he "did not fool with whiskey." Eventually, however, he sold the agent a half-gallon of the substance and was summarily convicted of violating the law. The United States Supreme Court held that the agent had improperly induced the defendant to break the law and reversed his conviction.

In *Sorrells,* the Supreme Court set the precedent for taking a "subjective" view of entrapment. In other words, the Court decided that entrapment occurs if a defendant who is not predisposed to commit a crime is enticed to do so by an agent of the government.[58] In the 1992 case of *Jacobson v. United States,*[59] for example, the U.S. Postal Inspection Service targeted the defendant as a potential purchaser of child pornography. Over a period of more than two years, postal agents sent the defendant seven letters inquiring about his sexual preferences, two sex catalogues, and two sexual-attitude surveys, all from fictitious persons and organizations. Eventually, the defendant ordered a publication called "Boys Who Love Boys" and was arrested and convicted for breaking child-pornography laws.[60] The Court overturned the conviction, ruling that entrapment had taken place because the defendant had shown no predisposition to order the illicit publication in the absence of the government's efforts. (For an overview of justification and excuse defenses, see Figure 4.5 on the following page.)

PROCEDURAL SAFEGUARDS

To this point, we have focused on **substantive criminal law,** which defines the acts that the government will punish. We will now turn our attention to **procedural criminal law.** (The section that follows will provide only a short overview of criminal procedure. In later chapters, many other constitutional issues will be examined in more detail.) Criminal law brings the force of the state, with all its resources, to bear against the individual. Criminal procedures, drawn from the ideals stated in the Bill of Rights, are designed to protect the constitutional rights of individuals and to prevent the arbitrary use of power by the government.

Necessity
A defense against criminal liability in which the defendant asserts that circumstances required her or him to commit an illegal act.

Entrapment
A defense in which the defendant claims that he or she was induced by a public official—usually an undercover agent or police officer—to commit a crime that he or she would otherwise not have committed.

Substantive Criminal Law
Law that defines the rights and duties of individuals with respect to each other.

Procedural Criminal Law
Rules that define the manner in which the rights and duties of individuals may be enforced.

The **American Civil Liberties Union** defines its mission with the slogan, "Defending the Bill of Rights." To find its Web site, click on *Web Links* under *Chapter Resources* at **www.cjinaction.com**.

FIGURE 4.5

Justification and Excuse Defenses

Justification Defenses: Based on a defendant admitting that he or she committed the particular criminal act, but asserting that, under the circumstances, the criminal act was justified.

Duress
<u>The Defendant Must Prove That:</u> He or she performed the criminal act under the use or threat of use of unlawful force against his or her person that a reasonable person would have been unable to resist.

<u>Situation in Which the Defense Has Been Attempted:</u> A mother assists her boyfriend in committing a burglary after he threatens to kill her children if she refuses to do so.

Self-Defense
<u>The Defendant Must Prove That:</u> He or she acted in a manner to defend himself or herself, others, or property, or to prevent the commission of a crime.

<u>Situation in Which the Defense Has Been Attempted:</u> A husband awakes to find his wife standing over him, pointing a shotgun at his chest. In the ensuing struggle, the firearm goes off, killing the wife.

Necessity
<u>The Defendant Must Prove That:</u> The criminal act he or she committed was necessary in order to avoid a harm to himself or herself or another that was greater than the harm caused by the act itself.

<u>Situation in Which the Defense Has Been Attempted:</u> Four people physically remove a friend from her residence on the property of a religious cult, arguing that the crime of kidnapping was justified in order to remove the victim from the damaging influence of cult leaders.

Entrapment
<u>The Defendant Must Prove That:</u> She or he was encouraged by agents of the state to engage in a criminal act she or he would not have engaged in otherwise.

<u>Situation in Which the Defense Has Been Attempted:</u> The owner of a boat marina agrees to allow three federal drug enforcement agents, posing as drug dealers, to use his dock to unload shipments of marijuana from Colombia.

Excuse Defenses: Based on a defendant admitting that she or he committed the criminal act, but asserting that she or he cannot be held criminally responsible for the act due to lack of criminal intent.

Age
<u>The Defendant Must Prove That:</u> Because he or she was under a statutorily determined age, he or she did not have the maturity to make the decisions necessary to commit a criminal act.

<u>Situation in Which the Defense Has Been Attempted:</u> A fourteen-year-old takes a handgun from his backpack at school and begins shooting at fellow students, killing three. (In such cases, the offender is often processed by the juvenile justice system rather than the criminal justice system.)

Insanity
<u>The Defendant Must Prove That:</u> At the time of the criminal act, he or she did not have the necessary mental capacity to be held responsible for his or her actions.

<u>Situation in Which the Defense Has Been Attempted:</u> A man with a history of mental illness pushes a woman in front of an oncoming subway train, which kills her instantly.

Intoxication
<u>The Defendant Must Prove That:</u> She or he had diminished control over her or his actions due to the influence of alcohol or drugs.

<u>Situation in Which the Defense Has Been Attempted:</u> A woman who had been drinking malt liquor and vodka stabs her boyfriend to death after a domestic argument. She claims to have been so drunk as to not remember the incident.

Mistake
<u>The Defendant Must Prove That:</u> He or she did not know that his or her actions violated a law (this defense is very rarely even attempted), or that he or she violated the law believing a relevant fact to be true when, in fact, it was not.

<u>Situation in Which the Defense Has Been Attempted:</u> A woman, thinking that her divorce in another state has been finalized when it was not, marries for a second time, placing herself in a situation in which she has committed bigamy.

The Bill of Rights

For various reasons, proposals related to the rights of individuals were rejected during the framing of the U.S. Constitution in 1787. In fact, the original constitution contained only three provisions that referred to criminal procedure. Article I, Section 9, Clause 2 states that the "Privilege of the Writ of Habeas Corpus shall not be suspended." As will be discussed in Chapter 10, a writ of *habeas corpus* is an order that requires jailers to bring a person before a court or judge and explain why the person is being held in prison. Article I, Section 9, Clause 3 holds that no "Bill of Attainder or ex post facto Law shall be passed." A bill of attainder is a legislative act that targets a particular person or group for punishment without a trial, while an *ex post facto* law operates retroactively, making an event or action illegal though it took place before the law was passed. Finally, Article III, Section 2, Clause 3 maintains that the "Trial of all Crimes" will be by jury and "such Trial shall be held in the State where the said crimes shall have been committed."

Amending the Constitution The need for a written declaration of rights of individuals eventually caused the first Congress to draft twelve amendments to the Constitution and submit them for approval by the states. Ten of these amendments, commonly known as the **Bill of Rights,** were adopted in 1791. Since then, seventeen more amendments have been added.

The Bill of Rights, as interpreted by the United States Supreme Court, has served as the basis for procedural safeguards of the accused in this country. These safeguards include the following:

1 The Fourth Amendment protection from unreasonable searches and seizures.
2 The Fourth Amendment requirement that no warrants for a search or an arrest can be issued without probable cause.
3 The Fifth Amendment requirement that no one can be deprived of life, liberty, or property without "due process" of the law.
4 The Fifth Amendment prohibition against *double jeopardy* (trying someone twice for the same criminal offense).
5 The Fifth Amendment guarantee that no person can be required to be a witness against (incriminate) himself or herself.
6 The Sixth Amendment guarantees of a speedy trial, a trial by jury, a public trial, the right to confront witnesses, and the right to a lawyer at various stages of criminal proceedings.
7 The Eighth Amendment prohibitions against excessive bails and fines and cruel and unusual punishments. (For the full text, see Appendix A.)

As part of heightened airport security following the September 11, 2001, terrorist attacks, a police officer leads a bomb-sniffing dog through Boston's Logan Airport. Other measures included increased scrutiny of luggage, a ban on customer parking within three hundred feet of a terminal, and not allowing anyone without a ticket past airline checkpoints. Which amendments in the Bill of Rights apply to these measures and why?

Expanding the Constitution The Bill of Rights offered citizens protection only against the federal government. Shortly after the end of the Civil War, in 1868, three-fourths of the states ratified the Fourteenth Amendment to expand the protections of the Bill of Rights. For our purposes, the most important part of the amendment reads:

> No State shall make or enforce any law which shall abridge the privileges or immunities of citizens of the United States, nor shall any State deprive any person of life, liberty, or property, without due process of the law; nor deny to any person within its jurisdiction the equal protection of the laws.

The United States Supreme Court did not immediately interpret the Fourteenth Amendment as extending the procedural protections of the Bill of Rights to people who had been charged with breaking state criminal law. Indeed, it would be nearly a hundred years before those accused of crimes on the state level would enjoy all the same protections as those accused of breaking federal laws.[61] As these protections are crucial to criminal justice procedures in the United States, they will be afforded much

Bill of Rights
The first ten amendments to the U.S. Constitution.

more attention in Chapter 6, with regard to police action, and in Chapter 10, with regard to the criminal trial.

Due Process

Both the Fifth and Fourteenth Amendments provide that no person should be deprived of "life, liberty, or property without due process of the law." This **due process clause** basically requires that the government not act unfairly or arbitrarily. In other words, the government cannot rely on individual judgment and impulse when making decisions, but must stay within the boundaries of reason and the law. Of course, disagreements as to the meaning of these provisions have plagued courts, politicians, and citizens since this nation was founded, and will undoubtedly continue to do so.

To understand due process, it is important to consider its two types: procedural due process and substantive due process.

Procedural Due Process According to **procedural due process,** the law must be carried out by a *method* that is fair and orderly. It requires that certain procedures be followed in administering and executing a law so that an individual's basic freedoms are never violated.

For example, the United States Supreme Court requires that schools follow certain procedures before suspending students for misconduct. The Court has held that a student facing a suspension of ten days or less must be given oral or written notice of the charges against him or her. Furthermore, if the student denies the charges, he or she must be given an explanation of the evidence of misconduct and an opportunity to present his or her side of the story.[62] In criminal law, procedural due process prevents a host of unfair practices, such as forced confessions, denial of counsel, and unreasonable searches.

Substantive Due Process Fair procedures would obviously be of little use if they were used to administer unfair laws. For example, suppose a law requires everyone to wear a red shirt on Mondays. You wear a blue shirt on Monday, and you are arrested, convicted, and sentenced to one year in prison. The fact that all proper procedures were followed and your rights were given their proper protections would mean very little because the law that you broke was unfair and arbitrary.

Thus, **substantive due process** requires that the laws themselves be reasonable. The idea is that if a law is unfair or arbitrary, even if properly passed by a legislature, it must be declared unconstitutional. In the 1930s, for example, Oklahoma instituted the Habitual Criminal Sterilization Act. Under this statute, a person who had been convicted of three felonies could be "rendered sexually sterile" by the state (that is, the person would no longer be able to produce children). The United States Supreme Court held that the law was unconstitutional, as there are "limits to the extent which a legislatively represented majority may

Due Process Clause
The provisions of the Fifth and Fourteenth Amendments to the Constitution that guarantee that no person shall be deprived of life, liberty, or property without due process of law. Similar clauses are found in most state constitutions.

Procedural Due Process
A provision in the Constitution that states that the law must be carried out in a fair and orderly manner.

Substantive Due Process
The constitutional requirement that laws used in accusing and convicting persons of crimes must be fair.

Ahmed Omar Abu Ali, far left, watches as his defense attorney makes a point in the U.S. Courthouse in Alexandria, Virginia. Abu Ali, an American citizen, spent twenty months in prison in Saudi Arabia, where he was arrested on terrorism charges. He claims that the U.S. government consented to his detention in the Middle Eastern nation, where officials do not recognize due process rights and torture is common. How does the due process clause protect those accused of crimes in the United States from being tortured?

AP Photo/Dana Verkouteren

conduct biological experiments at the expense of the dignity and personality and natural powers of a minority."[63]

The Supreme Court's Role in Due Process As the last example suggests, the United States Supreme Court often plays the important role of ultimately deciding when due process has been violated and when it has not. (See Figure 4.6 for a list of important Supreme Court due process cases.) This is not a role that the Court has always embraced. As noted earlier, for much of its history the Court did not apply the Bill of Rights to criminal procedures in state trials. Until relatively recently most justices have felt that due process rights were not violated if state procedures were fair and, therefore, there was no need to burden the states with the Bill of Rights.[64]

This line of thinking changed in the early 1960s, when the Court—presided over by Chief Justice Earl Warren—began to *incorporate* the procedural safeguards in the Bill of Rights, meaning that they were now applicable to the states. Between 1961 and 1968, the Warren Court incorporated the right to a jury trial,[65] the right of the accused to confront witnesses at trial,[66] the right against self-incrimination,[67] the right to counsel,[68] and the right to be free from cruel and unusual punishment, among others.[69]

Challenges to Due Process The due process clause does not, however, automatically doom laws that may infringe on procedural or substantive rights. In certain circumstances, the lawmaking body may be able to prove that its interests are greater than the due process rights of the individual, and in those cases the statute may be upheld. In 2003, for example, a U.S. appeals court upheld the immediate suspension of a kindergarten student who said, "I'm going to shoot you," to classmates during recess. Although, as we saw earlier, in most cases a school must follow certain steps before suspending a student, the court in this instance felt that the kindergarten's interest in

FIGURE 4.6

Important United States Supreme Court Due Process Decisions

Year	Issue	Amendment Involved	Court Case
1948	Right to a public trial	VI	*In re Oliver*, 333 U.S. 257
1949	No unreasonable searches and seizures	IV	*Wolf v. Colorado*, 338 U.S. 25
1961	Exclusionary rule	IV	*Mapp v. Ohio*, 367 U.S. 643
1963	Right to a lawyer in all criminal felony cases	VI	*Gideon v. Wainwright*, 372 U.S. 335
1964	No compulsory self-incrimination	V	*Malloy v. Hogan*, 378 U.S. 1
1964	Right to have counsel when taken into police custody and subject to questioning	VI	*Escobedo v. Illinois*, 378 U.S. 478
1965	Right to confront and cross-examine witnesses	VI	*Pointer v. Texas*, 380 U.S. 400
1966	Right to an impartial jury	VI	*Parker v. Gladden*, 385 U.S. 363
1966	Confessions of suspects not notified of due process rights ruled invalid	V	*Miranda v. Arizona*, 384 U.S. 436
1967	Right to a speedy trial	VI	*Klopfer v. North Carolina*, 386 U.S. 21
1967	Juveniles have due process rights, too	V	*In re Gault*, 387 U.S. 1
1968	Right to a jury trial ruled a fundamental right	VI	*Duncan v. Louisiana*, 391 U.S. 145
1969	No double jeopardy	V	*Benton v. Maryland*, 395 U.S. 784

Forced Competency

After Hessam Ghane was arrested for possessing enough cyanide capable of, in the words of one government official, "killing 800 to 1,000" people, it seemed that only one factor could keep him out of prison: his mental health. Ghane suffered from a severe delusional disorder that prevented him from understanding the nature of the proceedings against him. Hence, it was unlikely that Ghane would be found competent to stand trial as he could not meaningfully participate in those proceedings. To remedy the situation, a Missouri court ordered that Ghane be involuntarily medicated with antipsychotic drugs that would render him competent to stand trial. Ghane's attorneys argued that this order violated their client's due process rights.

As already mentioned, there are two types of due process rights: substantive and procedural. The nation's courts have consistently held that a person has a constitutionally protected, substantive "liberty interest" from unwanted bodily intrusions by the government, including being forced to take antipsychotic medication. Under procedural due process law, however, this liberty interest must always be balanced against the state's interest—here, the state's interest in rendering a defendant competent to

stand trial. In 2003, the United States Supreme Court ruled that forced medication in these circumstances is allowed only if the government can prove that the defendant committed a "serious" crime and that the successful use of the drugs will not cause any harmful side effects.

So, even though defendants such as Ghane do have substantive due process rights to be free from unwanted bodily intrusions, the government can satisfy the due process clause if it follows the correct procedure as determined by the Supreme Court. In this case, because Missouri prosecutors could not prove that antipsychotic drugs were likely to help Ghane achieve competency, an appeals court ruled that his due process rights had been violated.

FOR CRITICAL ANALYSIS
Some observers argue that, under the Supreme Court test, forcibly making a defendent competent to stand trial will always have the "harmful side effect" of exposing her or him to punishment—especially if that punishment is the death penalty. Critique this argument.

limiting this kind of violent speech was more important than the student's due process rights.[70] (For a further explanation of how procedural and substantive rights work in tandem, see the feature *CJ in Focus—The Balancing Act: Forced Competency.*)

The U.S. court system, including the Supreme Court, is more likely to defer to the government in times of national crisis. The Court was powerless in 1861, when President Abraham Lincoln suspended constitutional guarantees of *habeas corpus* at the start of the Civil War.[71] During World War II, in perhaps its most widely criticized decision of the twentieth century, the Court gave its approval to the federal government's rounding up of Japanese American citizens and confining them in "relocation" camps.[72] Finally, since the September 11, 2001, terrorist attacks, the U.S. Department of Justice has moved to limit the due process rights of suspected terrorists and certain types of immigrants. Although some of the lawsuits arising out of this strategy have yet to reach the Court, some observers feel that the federal government is overstepping the bounds of the Constitution by limiting access to counsel, the right to confront hostile witnesses, and a number of other due process rights. These issues will be explored in more detail in Chapter 17.

Punishing Hate

In this chapter, we have seen that a crime, as traditionally understood, has two basic elements: an *actus reus* and a *mens rea*. Criminal law, however, is not set in stone; it changes with the values of the society it is meant to protect. Under certain circumstances, many state penal codes have expanded to include a third element: motive. In most cases, a person's motive for committing a crime is irrelevant—a court will not try to read the accused's mind. But, as we will discuss in this *Criminal Justice in Action* feature, when the motive involves hate or bias, many jurisdictions have decided that the harm done by the crime is more serious and, therefore, the punishment should be as well.

A Brutal Crime

Twenty-one-year-old James Maestas and several friends had just finished their meal at a Denny's in Santa Fe, New Mexico, on February 27, 2005, when the trouble started. A group of young men verbally accosted Maestas and a male companion in the parking lot outside the restaurant and then followed them to a nearby La Quinta Inn. At that point, according to court records, the group attacked Maestas and his friend, shouting, "Let's [beat] these fag-

Hate Crime Law
A statute that provides for greater sanctions against those who commit crimes motivated by animosity against an individual or a group based on race, ethnicity, religion, gender, sexual orientation, disability, or age.

gots up" among other homophobic slurs.[73] One of the attackers allegedly pinned Maestas to the pavement and punched him in the face until he lost consciousness. Maestas suffered a broken nose, a concussion, and lung injuries so severe that he had to be placed on a respirator to help him breathe.

Maestas was one of the approximately 7,600 Americans who are victims of violent crimes motivated by hate or bias each year.[74] Only two years before the incident in Santa Fe, New Mexico became the forty-sixth state to pass a **hate crime law.** In general, hate crime laws provide for greater sanctions against those who commit crimes motivated by animosity against a person based on race, ethnicity, religion, gender, sexual orientation, disability, or age (see Figure 4.7). Under New Mexico's new law, the punishment for most felonies is increased by one year if the prosecution can prove that the crime was motivated by hate.[75] So, for example, Isaia Medina, who was charged with four felonies, including aggravated battery, in connection with Maestas's beating, faces four extra years of imprisonment if found guilty on all counts.

Penalty Enhancement Statutes

The concept of a hate crime as a measurable, definable criminal act, separate from other criminal acts, is a relatively new one. The Uniform Crime Report did not start measuring hate crimes until 1992, and the National Crime Victimization Survey did not ask questions relating to crimes of "bigotry and prejudice" until 1997.[76] Due to the

FIGURE 4.7
Offenses Motivated by Bias

In 2004, the Federal Bureau of Investigation reported 7,649 bias-motivated offenses. This chart shows the percentage distribution of the motivating factors.

Source: Adapted from Federal Bureau of Investigation, *Crime in the United States, 2004* (Washington, D.C.: U.S. Department of Justice, 2005), Figure 2.17, page 65.

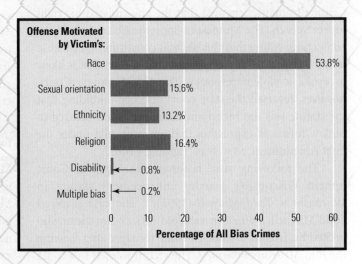

lack of a federal hate crime statute, the full weight of prosecuting these crimes has fallen on those states that have passed relevant laws. In general, these laws are based on a model created by the Anti-Defamation League (ADL) in 1981. The ADL model was centered around the concept of "penalty enhancement": just as someone who robs a convenience store using a gun will face a greater penalty than if he or she had been unarmed, so will someone who commits a crime because of prejudice against her or his victim or victims.[77]

The specifics of hate crime legislation vary from jurisdiction to jurisdiction. Not all states follow the penalty enhancement model, preferring instead to create new categories of crimes committed "because of" or "by reason of" the victim's characteristics. Some states do not specify which groups are protected by the legislation, while others list some aspects, such as race, but not others, such as mental or physical disability. Furthermore, some states establish training in dealing with hate crimes for law enforcement personnel. A number of police departments have created specialized bias units to prevent hate crimes and collect data on them. Despite the lack of federal hate crime legislation, in 2003 federal prosecutors decided to seek the death penalty for Darrell David Rice, who allegedly murdered two hikers in Shenandoah National Park because they were lesbians.[78]

Supreme Court Rulings

The legal basis for hate crime legislation was established by two cases heard by the United States Supreme Court in the early 1990s. In *R.A.V. v. St. Paul* (1992),[79] the Court reviewed a case involving a group of white teenagers who burned a cross on the lawn of an African American family in St. Paul, Minnesota. One of the youths, who had been arrested and convicted under the city's Bias-Motivated Crime Ordinance, claimed that the law violated his right to free speech. The Minnesota Supreme Court upheld the conviction, ruling that the law was constitutional because it applied only to "fighting words," or speech that is likely to evoke a violent response. The U.S. Supreme Court, however, reversed the state court's decision, holding that the statute was too broad and therefore could be used to outlaw forms of expression that are protected under the First Amendment, as well as "fighting words."

The following year, however, the Supreme Court upheld Wisconsin's penalty enhancement statute in *Wisconsin v. Todd Mitchell* (1993).[80] The case involved Todd Mitchell, a nineteen-year-old African American who incited his friends to attack a white teenager after viewing the film *Mississippi Burning*. The victim was left in a coma for two days, and Mitchell was convicted of felony aggra-

In Santa Fe, New Mexico, participants express themselves during a candlelight vigil for James Maestas, who had been severely beaten on February 27, 2005, in what local police reported as an attack on a gay man.

vated battery and sentenced to two years in prison, plus an additional two years under the state's hate crime law. The Court upheld the statute, reasoning that the results of hate crime, such as community fear, justify harsher punishments. Furthermore, it ruled that speech could be used as evidence of motive, and because motive is an integral part of sentencing, hate speech could be used to augment sentences. The Court clarified this ruling in *Apprendi v. New Jersey* (2000),[81] holding that motive must be an element of any hate crime law and that, like any other element of a crime, it must be proved beyond a reasonable doubt.

Questioning Hate Laws

Many of those who question the validity of hate crime legislation do so on First Amendment grounds. Punish Todd Mitchell for his acts, they say, but not for his beliefs, which he has a constitutional right to hold. Some of these opponents also question laws that seem to indicate that some victims are worthy of more protection than others. They find it disturbing that Mitchell would have received a lesser sentence if he and his friends had beaten an African American youth instead of a white youth.[82]

In addition, Brian S. MacNamara of the John Jay College of Criminal Justice in New York City points out that it is difficult enough to establish the *mens rea* of someone who has committed a criminal act without trying to establish his or her motivation.[83] MacNamara envisions court cases becoming bogged down as prosecutors try to establish the defendant's levels of prejudice and bias, a difficult task considering the deep psychological and sociological roots of such feelings. Law enforcement officials are also wary of the demands of hate crime legislation. "I'm very fearful of the concept of thought police," said a commander in the Kenosha (Wisconsin) police department. "It makes me nervous."[84]

Making Sense of Hate Crime Laws

1 According to Professor MacNamara, "Every individual's safety and personal property should be afforded the same protections under the law, regardless of the subjective motivation of those who seek to do them harm." What is your opinion of this statement, which questions the foundation of hate crime laws?

2 Why do you suppose that motive is usually not considered in criminal law? Why might determining motive be difficult?

3 How does society suffer a greater "harm" from crimes motivated by bias than from those driven by greed, jealousy, or some other emotion?

Chapter Summary

1 **Explain precedent and the importance of the doctrine of *stare decisis*.** Precedent is a common law concept in which one decision becomes the example or authority for deciding future cases with similar facts. Under the doctrine of *stare decisis,* judges in a particular jurisdiction are bound to follow precedents of that same jurisdiction. The doctrine of *stare decisis* leads to efficiency in the judicial system.

2 **List the four written sources of American criminal law.** (a) The U.S. Constitution and state constitutions; (b) statutes passed by Congress and state legislatures (plus local ordinances); (c) administrative agency regulations; and (d) case law.

3 **Explain the two basic functions of criminal law.** The primary function is to protect citizens from harms to their safety and property and from harms to society's interest collectively. The second function is to maintain and teach social values as well as social boundaries; for example, laws against bigamy and speed limits.

4 **Delineate the elements required to establish *mens rea* (a guilty mental state).** (a) Purpose, (b) knowledge, (c) negligence, or (d) recklessness.

5 **Explain how the doctrine of strict liability applies to criminal law.** Strict liability crimes do not allow the alleged wrongdoer to claim ignorance or mistake to avoid criminal responsibility; for example, exceeding the speed limit and statutory rape.

6 **List and briefly define the most important excuse defenses for crimes. Insanity**—different tests of insanity can be used including (a) the *M'Naughten* rule (right-wrong test); (b) the irresistible impulse test; (c) the *Durham* rule, also called the products test, where the criminal act was the product of a mental defect or disease; and (d) the substantial capacity test. **Intoxication**—voluntary and involuntary, the latter being a possible crimi-

nal defense. **Mistake**—sometimes valid if the law was not published or reasonably known or if the alleged offender relied on an official statement of the law that was erroneous. Also, a mistake of fact may negate the mental state necessary to commit a crime.

7 **Describe the four most important justification criminal defenses. Duress**—requires that (a) the threat is of serious bodily harm or death, (b) the harm is greater than that caused by the crime; (c) the threat is immediate and inescapable; and (d) the defendant became involved in the situation through no fault of his or her own. **Justifiable use of force**—the defense of one's person, dwelling, or property, or the prevention of a crime. **Necessity**—justifiable if the harm sought to be avoided is greater than that sought to be prevented by the law defining the offense charged. **Entrapment**—if the criminal action was induced by certain governmental persuasion or trickery.

8 **Distinguish between substantive and procedural criminal law.** The former concerns questions about what acts are actually criminal. The latter concerns procedures designed to protect the constitutional rights of individuals and to prevent the arbitrary use of power by the government.

9 **Explain the importance of the due process clause in the criminal justice system.** The due process clause acts to limit the power of government. In the criminal justice system, the due process clause requires that certain procedures be followed to ensure the fairness of criminal proceedings and that all criminal laws be reasonable and in the interest of the public good.

STORIES FROM THE STREET

Go to the *Stories from the Street* feature at **www.cjinaction.com** to hear Larry Gaines tell insightful stories related to this chapter and his experiences in the field.

Key Terms

✓ *actus reus* 103
administrative law 98
✓ Bill of Rights 115
✓ case law 99
common law 95
✓ constitutional law 97
corpus delicti 102
✓ due process clause 116

duress 111
Durham rule 108
entrapment 113
hate crime law 119
inchoate offenses 106
✓ insanity 107 ~~basic def~~
✓ intoxication 110
irresistible impulse test 108

✓ *mens rea* 103
M'Naughten rule 108
necessity 113
negligence 104
✓ precedent 96
✓ procedural criminal law 113
✓ procedural due process 116
✓ self-defense 112

✓ *stare decisis* 96
statutory law 97
✓ strict liability crimes 105
substantial capacity test 108
substantive criminal
law 113
✓ substantive due
process 116

Questions for Critical Analysis

1 Why is the common law said to be uncodified?
2 How does *stare decisis* contribute to the efficiency of a court system?
3 What is the Model Penal Code, and how has it contributed to criminal law in the United States?
4 Give an example of how the criminal justice system teaches societal boundaries.
5 Many people are careless. At what point can such carelessness be deemed criminal negligence?
6 Assume you are planning to pay someone to set fire to an old barn (arson) for the insurance money. Before you get a chance to carry out your plan, you accidentally drop a

tool on another metal object, creating a spark that ignites some dry hay and burns the barn down. What essential element of a crime is missing in your actions?
7 What test is most often used for insanity, and how does it differ from other tests?
8 Why would a defense attorney admit that a client had voluntarily gotten drunk before an accident in which she hit and killed a pedestrian?
9 Under what circumstances is the use of deadly force a justified criminal defense?
10 How has the United States Supreme Court incorporated the due process clause?

Test Preparation Online

Criminal JusticeNow

Go to **www.cjinaction.com** and click on *Criminal JusticeNow* for access to this powerful online study tool. You will get a *personalized study plan* based on your responses to a diagnostic pretest. Once you have mastered the material with the help of interactive learning tools, video clips with questions, an integrated e-book, and more, you can take a posttest to confirm you are ready to move on to the next chapter.

Book Companion Web Site

At the book companion Web site (**www.cjinaction.com**), you will find many resources in addition to *Criminal JusticeNow* to aid you in studying for your exams. For example, under *Chapter Resources*, you will find the *Chapter Outline, Chapter Summary, Flashcards, Glossary, Learning Objectives, Lecture Presentations, Concept Builder, Essay Questions,* and a *Tutorial Chapter Quiz.* You can also test yourself with interactive *Online Reviews* of each chapter section. Check out the *Web Links* to access the Web sites mentioned in the text, as well as many others. You can also access recent perspectives by clicking on *CJ in the News* and *Terrorism Update* under *Course Resources.*

Suggested Readings

Duhl, Robert Alan, *How Democratic Is the American Constitution?* New Haven, CT: Yale University Press, 2002. In this thin volume, Yale University professor Duhl challenges the democratic credentials of the U.S. Constitution. From its inception, Duhl notes, the Constitution was stained by several "undemocratic elements," including the acceptance of slavery and limitation of voting rights to white males. Though these elements have been removed, Duhl points out that some of the most sacred aspects of our modern political system—federalism, the bicameral legislature, judicial review, and the electoral college—often contradict "the will of the people." Most disturbing, Duhl suggests that the framers "rigged" the Constitution to discourage democratic reform.

Healy, Gene, ed., *Go Directly to Jail: The Criminalization of Almost Everything,* Washington, D.C.: The Cato Institute, 2004. The six essays in this book explore an overlooked phenomenon of the modern criminal justice system: the dramatic increase in new federal criminal law. For most of our nation's history, most criminal law was created on the state or local level; only the most serious crimes were prosecuted by the federal government. Today, however, the federal criminal code catalogues four thousand crimes, many of them involving behavior that is not obviously criminal. In one of the many examples in this book, a businessman was sentenced to eight years in prison for shipping lobster tails to Honduras in clear plastic bags instead of paper ones, as required by both Honduran and, as it turns out, American criminal law. The authors represented in *Go Directly to Jail* are worried that this increase in federal power threatens many of our basic freedoms.

Notes

1. Revised Code of Washington, Chapter 9A.36.011 (2005).
2. Associated Press Wire Reports, "Man Guilty in Serial HIV Assault Case" (November 8, 2004).
3. Roger LeRoy Miller and Gaylord A. Jentz, *Business Law Today, Comprehensive Edition,* 7th ed. (St. Paul, MN: West Publishing Co., 2007), 2–3.
4. *Neff v. George,* 364 Ill. 306, 4 N.E.2d 388, 390, 391 (1936).
5. *Texas v. Johnson,* 491 U.S. 397 (1989).
6. Joshua Dressler, *Understanding Criminal Law,* 2d ed. (New York: Richard D. Irwin, 1995), 22–23.
7. *Ibid.,* 23.
8. Jim Yardley, "Unmarried and Living Together, Till the Sheriff Do Us Part," *New York Times* (March 25, 2000), A7.
9. Chris Bowman, "EPA Pumps Up Its Record," *Sacramento Bee* (July 7, 2003), 1A.
10. Joel Feinberg, *The Moral Limits of the Criminal Law: Harm to Others* (New York: Oxford University Press, 1984), 221–232.
11. Flammable Fabrics Act, 15 U.S.C. Section 1196 (1994).
12. Stuart P. Green, "Why It's a Crime to Tear the Tag Off a Mattress," *Emory Law Journal* 46 (Fall 1997), 1533–1614.
13. Henry M. Hart, Jr., "The Aims of the Criminal Law," *Law & Contemporary Problems* 23 (1958), 405–406.
14. John L. Diamond, "The Myth of Morality and Fault in Criminal Law Doctrine," *American Criminal Law Review* 34 (Fall 1996), 111.
15. Lawrence M. Friedman, *Crime and Punishments in American History* (New York: Basic Books, 1993), 34.
16. *Ibid.,* 10.
17. Thomas A. Mullen, "Rule without Reason: Requiring Independent Proof of the *Corpus Delicti* as a Condition of Admitting Extrajudicial Confession," *University of San Francisco Law Review* 27 (1993), 385.
18. *Hawkins v. State,* 219 Ind. 116, 129, 37 N.E.2d 79 (1941).
19. David C. Biggs, "'The Good Samaritan Is Packing': An Overview of the Broadened Duty to Aid Your Fellowman, with the Modern Desire to Possess Concealed Weapons," *University of Dayton Law Review* 22 (Winter 1997), 225.
20. Minn. Stat. Ann. Section 604A.01; R.I. Gen. Laws Section 11-56-1 (1956); Vt. Stat. Ann. Tit. 12, Section 519 (2000); and Wis. Stat. Section 940.34 (West 2000).
21. Model Penal Code Section 2.02.
22. Texas Penal Code Section 46.13 (1995).
23. Model Penal Code Section 2.02 (c).
24. *Black's Law Dictionary,* 1423.
25. *United States v. Dotterweich,* 320 U.S. 277 (1943).
26. *State v. Stiffler,* 763 P.2d 308, 311 (Idaho Ct. App. 1988).
27. *State v. Harrison,* 425 A.2d 111 (1979).
28. Richard G. Singer and John Q. LaFond, *Criminal Law: Examples and Explanations* (New York: Aspen Law & Business, 1997), 322.
29. *State v. Linscott,* 520 A.2d 1067 (1987).
30. *Morissette v. United States,* 342 U.S. 246, 251–252 (1952).
31. *People v. Harding,* 443 Mich. 699–703, 506 N.W.2d 486–487 (1994).
32. Federal Bank Robbery Act, 18 U.S.C.A. Section 2113.
33. *United States v. Jiminez Recio,* 537 U.S. 270 (2003).
34. *M'Naughten's Case,* 10 Cl.&F. 200, Eng.Rep. 718 (1843). Note that the name of the rule is also spelled M'Naghten and McNaughten.
35. Joshua Dressler, *Cases and Materials on Criminal Law,* 2d ed. (St. Paul, MN: West Group, 1999), 599.
36. 214 F.2d 862 (D.C. Cir. 1954).
37. Model Penal Code Section 401 (1952).
38. Stephen Lally, "Making Sense of the Insanity Plea," *Washington Post Weekly Edition* (December 1, 1997), 23.
39. Bruce J. Winick, "Presumptions and Burdens of Proof in Determining Competency to Stand Trial: An Analysis of *Medina v. California* and the Supreme Court's New Due Process Methodology in Criminal Cases," *University of Miami Law Review* 47 (1993), 817.
40. South Carolina Code Ann. Section 17-24-20(A) (Law. Co-op. Supp. 1997).
41. Lawrence P. Tiffany and Mary Tiffany, "Nosologic Objections to the Criminal Defense of Pathological Intoxication: What Do the Doubters Doubt?" *International Journal of Law and Psychiatry* 13 (1990), 49.
42. 518 U.S. 37 (1996).
43. Mont. Code Ann. Section 45-5-102 (1997).
44. Mont. Code Ann. Section 45-2-203 (1997).
45. Kenneth W. Simons, "Mistake and Impossibility, Law and Fact, and Culpability: A Speculative Essay," *Journal of Criminal Law and Criminology* 81 (1990), 447.
46. *United States v. Robinson,* 119 F.3d 1205 (5th Cir. 1997).
47. *Lambert v. California,* 335 U.S. 225 (1957).
48. Federal Bureau of Investigation, *Crime in the United States, 2004* (Washington, D.C.: U.S. Department of Justice, 2005), 24.
49. Craig L. Carr, "Duress and Criminal Responsibility," *Law and Philosophy* 10 (1990), 161.
50. *United States v. May,* 727 F.2d 764 (1984).
51. *United States v. Contento-Pachon,* 723 F.2d 691 (1984).
52. *People v. Murillo,* 587 N.E.2d 1199, 1204 (Ill. App. Ct. 1992).
53. "Pariah's Sorry State Fails as His Defense," *Sun Herald* (Biloxi, Mississippi), (February 9, 2005), C3.
54. Model Penal Code Section 3.02.
55. *United States v. Paolello,* 951 F.2d 537 (3d Cir. 1991).
56. *People v. Petro,* 56 P.2d 984 (Cal. Ct. App. 1936); and *Regina v. Dudley and Stephens,* 14 Q.B.D. 173 (1884).
57. 287 U.S. 435 (1932).
58. Kenneth M. Lord, "Entrapment and Due Process: Moving toward a Dual System of Defenses," *Florida State University Law Review* 25 (Spring 1998), 463.
59. 503 U.S. 540 (1992).
60. Fred Warren Bennett, "From *Sorrells* to *Jacobson:* Reflections on Six Decades of Entrapment Law and Related Defenses in Federal Court," *Wake Forest Law Review* 27 (1992), 829.
61. Henry J. Abraham, *Freedom and the Court: Civil Liberties in the United States,* 7th ed. (New York: Oxford University Press, 1998), 38–41.

62. *Goss v. Lopez,* 419 U.S. 565 (1975).

63. *Skinner v. Oklahoma,* 316 U.S. 535, 546–547 (1942).

64. William J. Stuntz, "The Substantive Origins of Criminal Procedure," *Yale Law Journal* 105 (1995), 440.

65. *Duncan v. Louisiana,* 391 U.S. 145 (1968).

66. *Pointer v. Texas,* 380 U.S. 400 (1965).

67. *Malloy v. Hogan,* 378 U.S. 1 (1964).

68. *Gideon v. Wainwright,* 372 U.S. 335 (1963).

69. *Robinson v. California,* 370 U.S. 660 (1962).

70. *"S.G.V. Sayreville Board of Education et al.,* No. 02-2384," *New Jersey Law Journal* (July 14, 2003), 139.

71. Alfred H. Kelley and Winfred A. Harbison, *The American Constitution: Its Origins and Developments,* 7th ed. (New York: Norton, 1991), 441–448.

72. *Korematsu v. United States,* 323 U.S. 214 (1944).

73. Jeremy Pawloski, "Five of Six Suspects in Beating Were Arraigned Friday," *Albuquerque Journal* (March 19, 2005).

74. *Crime in the United States, 2004,* 66.

75. Section 31-18B-3(A) NMSA (2003).

76. "Statement of the Anti-Defamation League on Bias-Motivated Crime and H.R. 1082—The Hate Crimes Prevention Act," *Chicano-Latino Law Review* (Spring 2000), 56.

77. Steve M. Freeman, "Hate Crime Laws: Punishment Which Fits the Crime," *Annual Survey of American Law* 4 (1992/93), 581–585.

78. Jen McCaffery, "Prosecutors Allowed to Seek Death Penalty in Park Slaying Case," *Roanoke Times & World News* (February 1, 2003), B4.

79. 505 U.S. 377 (1992).

80. 508 U.S. 476 (1993).

81. 530 U.S. 4666 (2000).

82. Nat Hentoff, "Letting Loose the Hate Crimes Police," *The Village Voice* (July 13, 1993).

83. Brian S. MacNamara, "New York's Hate Crimes Act of 2000: Problematic and Redundant Legislation Aimed at Subjective Motivation," *Albany Law Review* (2003), 519.

84. Quoted in Hentoff.

CHAPTER FIVE

Law Enforcement Today

Chapter outline

- A History of the American Police
- Law Enforcement Agencies
- Private Security
- The Responsibilities of the Police
- The Role of Discretion in Policing
- Criminal Justice in Action—The Police and Domestic Violence

Chapter objectives

After reading this chapter, you should be able to:

1. Describe the first systems of law enforcement in colonial America.
2. Tell how the patronage system affected policing.
3. Indicate the results of the Wickersham Commission.
4. List five main types of law enforcement agencies.
5. List some of the most important law enforcement agencies under the control of the Department of Homeland Security.
6. Identify the six investigative priorities of the FBI.
7. Analyze the importance of private security today.
8. List the four basic responsibilities of the police.
9. Indicate why patrol officers are allowed discretionary powers.
10. Explain how some jurisdictions have reacted to perceived leniency to perpetrators of domestic violence.

Criminal JusticeNow

Optimize your study time and master key chapter concepts with *Criminal JusticeNow*, an online study tool that provides you with a *personalized study plan*. Check out the "Test Preparation Online" section at the end of the chapter for additional information.

Heroes or Bums?

As the black Chevrolet Suburban made its slow way toward downtown Atlanta, Georgia, on the morning of March 12, 2005, people lined the streets to cheer. They knew that the sport utility vehicle, escorted by a number of police cars, contained Brian Nichols, the prime suspect in a killing spree that had started slightly more than twenty-four hours earlier when he overpowered a sheriff's deputy at the Fulton County Courthouse and stole her firearm. Nichols, the defendant in a rape trial, used the gun to kill three people— the judge presiding over his case, a court reporter, and another sheriff's deputy who tried to keep him from escaping. Over the course of the next day, Nichols apparently hijacked several vehicles and murdered a federal customs agent before taking a woman hostage at her residence in the Bridgewater Luxury Apartment Homes.

Even though a team of law enforcement officers managed to apprehend Nichols without further bloodshed, Atlanta law enforcement agencies came under a great deal of scrutiny following the incident. The Fulton County Sheriff's Department, which was responsible for security at the courthouse, was criticized for allowing

Law enforcement agents huddle to discuss strategy after the apprehension of shooting suspect Brian Nichols in Duluth, Georgia, on March 12, 2005.

Nichols to arm himself and escape so easily. Many citizens wondered how the Atlanta Police Department could have "lost" Nichols for an entire day, including the twelve hours he reportedly spent wandering around a crowded mall. In fact, most of the acclaim for Nichols's capture went to Ashley Smith, the hostage, who appeared to have talked him into surrendering. "We did expect a fight . . . either that or suicide," said U.S. Marshal Richard V. Mecum. "We never counted on [her]."

The cheers and jeers showered on Atlanta's finest following Brian Nichols's arrest should have come as no surprise. Law enforcement agencies receive much of the credit when the news concerning crime in this country is good, and the bulk of the blame when it is bad. Police officers are the most visible representatives of our criminal justice system; indeed, they symbolize the system for many Americans who may never see the inside of a courtroom or a prison cell. The police are entrusted with immense power to serve and protect the public good: the power to use weapons and the power to arrest. But that same power alarms many citizens, who fear that it may be turned arbitrarily against them. The role of the police is constantly debated as well. Is their primary mission to fight crime, or should they also be concerned with the social conditions that presumably lead to crime?

This chapter will lay the foundation for our study of law enforcement agents and the work that they do. A short history of policing will be followed by an examination of the many different agencies that make up the American law enforcement system. We

ⓘ CONCEPT BUILDER

Is policing considered a profession or a trade? Visit **www.cjinaction.com** for an interactive exploration of this key topic.

will also look at the various responsibilities of police officers and discuss the crucial role of discretion in law enforcement.

A HISTORY OF THE AMERICAN POLICE

Although modern society relies on law enforcement officers to control and prevent crime, in the early days of this country police services had little to do with crime control. The policing efforts in the first American cities were directed toward controlling certain groups of people (mostly slaves and Native Americans), delivering goods, regulating activities such as buying and selling in the town market, maintaining health and sanitation, controlling gambling and vice, and managing livestock and other animals.[1] Furthermore, these police services were for the most part performed by volunteers, as a police force was an expensive proposition. Most communities simply could not afford to pay a group of law enforcement officers.[2]

> "Every society gets the kind of criminal it deserves. What is equally true is that every community gets the kind of law enforcement it insists on."
>
> —Robert Kennedy, U.S. attorney general (1964)

Eventually, of course, as the populations of American cities grew, so did the need for public order and the willingness to devote resources to the establishment of formal police forces. Policing in the United States and in England evolved along similar lines, and many of our policing institutions have their roots in English tradition. Consequently, we will begin our discussion of the history of American police with a look back at its English beginnings.

English Roots

Before William the Conqueror invaded the island in 1066, the dominant system of law enforcement in Anglo-Saxon England was the **tithing system.** Every male was enrolled in a group of ten families, which was called a *tithing*. If one person in the tithing committed a crime, then every person in the group was responsible for paying the fine. The theory was that this obligation would be an incentive for the tithing to engage in collective community policing. Later, ten tithings were joined together to form a *hundred*, whose top law official was the *reeve*. Finally, the hundreds were consolidated into *shires* (the equivalent of modern counties), and the law enforcement official became known as the **shire-reeve.** As the phonetics suggest, this official is the earliest example of what is now the county sheriff.

The Role of the Constable In 1326, the office of the **justice of the peace** was established to replace the shire-reeve. Over the next centuries, in most English cities the justice of the peace, with the help of a constable, came to oversee various law enforcement activities, including organizing the night watch, investigating crimes, and securing criminals for trial. In the countryside, the hundred was replaced by the parish, which corresponded to the territory served by a particular church and included its members. Under the *parish constable system*, the parish hired a person to oversee criminal justice for its parishioners.

The London Experiments By the mid-1700s, London, England—one of the largest cities in the Western world—still did not have an organized system of law enforcement. Crime was endemic to city life, and the government's only recourse was to *read the riot act* (call in the military when the lawbreaking became unbearable). Such actions were

Tithing System
In Anglo-Saxon England, a system of law enforcement in which groups of ten families, known as tithings, were collectively responsible for law and order within their groups.

Shire-Reeve
The chief law enforcement officer in an early English shire, or county. The forerunner of the modern sheriff.

Justice of the Peace
Established in fourteenth-century England, a government official who oversaw various aspects of local law enforcement. The post eventually became strictly identified with judicial matters.

FIGURE 5.1

Fundamental Principles of the Metropolitan Police Act of 1829

The first modern police force was established in London by the Metropolitan Police Act of 1829. Sir Robert Peel, the politician who pushed through the legislation, wanted a police force that would provide citizens with "the full and complete protection of the law" and "check the increase of crime." To fulfill these objectives, Peel's early police were guided by the basic principles listed here.

1 The police force must be organized along military lines.
2 Police administrators and officers must be under government control.
3 Emphasis must be placed on hiring qualified persons and training them properly.
4 New police officers must complete a probationary period; if they fail to meet standards during this time, they will not be hired as permanent officers.
5 Police personnel should be assigned to specific areas of the city for a specific time period.
6 Police headquarters must be centrally located in the city.
7 Police officers must maintain proper appearances at all times in order to gain and keep the respect of citizens.
8 Individual police officers should be able to control their temper and refrain from violence whenever possible.
9 Police records must be kept in order to measure police effectiveness.

widely unpopular, as the townspeople did not appreciate being disciplined (and fired on) by soldiers whose salaries they were paying. Furthermore, the soldiers proved unreliable peacemakers, as they were hesitant to use force against their fellow London citizens. Despite rampant crime in the city, most Londoners were not in favor of a police force under the control of the city government. English history is rife with instances in which the king or some other government official abused military power by turning it against the citizens. Therefore, the citizenry were wary of any formal, armed organization that could restrict their individual liberties.

This mistrust began to ebb in 1829, when British Home Secretary Sir Robert "Bobbie" Peel pushed the Metropolitan Police Act through Parliament. This legislation has had a lasting impact, as many of its operating goals were similar to those of modern police forces (see Figure 5.1 for a summary of the act). Under the terms of this act, the London Metropolitan Police was formed. One thousand members strong at first, the members of this police force were easily recognizable in their uniforms that included blue coats and top hats. Under Peel's direction, the "bobbies," as the police were called in honor of their founder, had four specific operating philosophies:

1 To reduce tension and conflict between law enforcement officers and the public.

2 To use nonviolent means (they did not carry firearms) in keeping the peace, with violence to be used only as a last resort. This point was crucial because, as mentioned earlier, the English were suspicious of armed government military organizations. Being unarmed, the bobbies could hardly be confused with soldiers.

3 To relieve the military from certain duties, such as controlling urban violence. (Peel specifically hoped that his police would be less inclined to use excessive force than the military had been.)

4 To be judged on the absence of crime rather than through high-visibility police action.[3]

London's police operation was so successful that it was soon imitated in smaller towns throughout England and, eventually, in the United States.

The Early American Police Experience

In colonial America and immediately following the American Revolution, law enforcement virtually mirrored the English system. Constables and night watchmen were taken from the ranks of ordinary citizens. The governor of each colony hired a sheriff in each county to oversee the formal aspects of law enforcement, such as selecting juries and managing jails and prisons.[4] These colonial appointees were not always of the highest moral character. In 1730, the Pennsylvania colony felt the need to pass laws specifically prohibiting sheriffs from extorting money from prisoners or selling "strong liquors" to "any person under arrest."[5]

The First Police Department In 1801, Boston became the first American city to acquire a formal night watch; the watchmen were paid 50 cents a night. For the next three decades, most major cities went no further than the watch system. Finally, facing the same pressures as London, major American metropolitan areas began to form "reactive patrol units" geared toward enforcing the law and preventing crime.[6] In 1833, Philadelphia became the first city to employ both day and night watchmen. Five years later, working from Sir Robert Peel's model, Boston formed the first organized police department, consisting of six full-time officers. In 1844, New York City set the foundation for the modern police department by combining its day and night watches under the control of a single police chief. By the onset of the Civil War in 1861, a number of American cities, including Baltimore, Boston, Chicago, Cincinnati, New Orleans, and Philadelphia, had similarly consolidated police departments, modeled on the Metropolitan Police of London.

A horse-drawn police wagon used by the New York City Police Department, circa 1886. In the 1880s a number of American cities introduced patrol wagons, which transported prisoners and drunks and also performed ambulance duties. Along with signal service, or "call boxes," the police wagon represented a "revolution" in police methods. If a patrol officer made an arrest far from headquarters, he could now call the station and request a police wagon to pick up and deliver the arrested person (instead of having to deliver the arrestee himself).

Like their modern counterparts, many early police officers were hard working, honest, and devoted to serving and protecting the public. On the whole, however, in the words of historian Samuel Walker, "The quality of American police service in the nineteenth century could hardly have been worse."[7] This poor quality can be attributed to the fact that the recruitment and promotion of police officers were intricately tied into the politics of the day. Police officers received their jobs as a result of political connections, not because of any particular skills or knowledge. Whichever political party was in power in a given city would hire its own cronies to run the police department; consequently, the police were often more concerned with serving the interests of the political powers than with protecting the citizens.[8]

The Spoils System Corruption was rampant during this *political era* of policing, which lasted roughly from 1840 to 1930. (See Figure 5.2 on the next page for an overview of the three eras of policing, which are discussed in this chapter and referred to throughout the book.) Police salaries were relatively low; thus, many police officers saw their positions as opportunities to make extra income through any number of illegal activities. Bribery was common, as police would use their close proximity to the people to request "favors," which went into the police officers' own pockets or into the coffers of the local political party as "contributions."[9] This was known as the **patronage system,** or the "spoils system," because to the political victors went the spoils.

The political era also saw police officers take an active role in providing social services for their bosses' constituents. In many instances, this role even took precedence over law enforcement duties. Politicians realized that they could attract more votes by offering social services to citizens than by arresting them, and they required the police departments under their control to act accordingly.

The Modernization of the American Police

The abuses of the political era of policing did not go unnoticed. But it was not until 1929 that President Herbert Hoover appointed the national Commission on Law Observance and Enforcement to assess the American criminal justice system. The Wickersham Commission, named after its chairman, George Wickersham, focused on two areas of American policing that were in need of reform: (1) police brutality and (2) "the corrupting influence of politics." According to the commission, this reform

Patronage System

A form of corruption in which the political party in power hires and promotes police officers, receiving job-related "favors" in return.

	1840 1850 1860 1870 1880 1890 1900 1910 1920 1930 1940 1950 1960 1970 1980 1990 2000 2010

	The Political Era	The Reform Era	The Community Era
Time Period	1840 to 1930	1930 to 1980	1980 to present
Primary Function of Police	Provide range of social services to citizenry	Crime control	Continue to control crime while providing a broader range of social services
Organization	Decentralized	Centralized	Decentralized, with specialized units and task forces
Police/Community Relationship	Intimate	Professional and distant	Return to intimate
Tactics	Patrolling neighborhoods on foot	Patrolling neighborhoods in cars, rapid response to emergency calls for service (911 calls)	Foot patrol, problem solving, and public relations
Strategic Goal	Satisfy the needs of citizens and political bosses	Crime control	Improve the quality of life of citizens
Strategic Weakness	Widespread police corruption and brutality	Lack of communication with citizens fostered mistrust and community violence (riots)	An overreliance on police officers to solve all of society's problems

FIGURE 5.2

The Three Eras of American Policing

George L. Kelling and Mark H. Moore have separated the history of policing in the United States into three distinct periods. Above is a brief summarization of these three eras.

Source: Adapted from George L. Kelling and Mark H. Moore, "From Political to Reform to Community: The Evolving Strategy of Police," in *Community Policing: Rhetoric or Reality*, ed. Jack R. Greene and Stephen D. Mastrofski (New York: Praeger Publishers, 1991), 14–15, 22–23; plus authors' updates. Reproduced with permission of Greenwood Publishing Group, Inc., Westport, Connecticut.

Professional Model

A style of policing advocated by August Vollmer and O. W. Wilson that emphasizes centralized police organizations, increased use of technology, and a limitation of police discretion through regulations and guidelines.

should come about through higher personnel standards, centralized police administrations, and the increased use of technology.[10] Reformers of the time took the commission's findings as a call for the professionalization of American police and initiated the progressive (or *reform*) era in American policing.

Professionalism In truth, the Wickersham Commission was not groundbreaking. Many of its recommendations echoed the opinions of one of its contributors—August Vollmer, the police chief of Berkeley, California, from 1905 until 1932. Known as "the father of modern police administration," Vollmer pioneered the training of potential police officers in institutions of higher learning. The first program to grant a degree in law enforcement, at San Jose State College (now a university), was developed under Vollmer.

Along with increased training, Vollmer also championed the use of technology in police work. His Berkeley police department became the first in the nation to use automobiles to patrol city streets and to hire a scientist to assist in solving crimes.[11] Furthermore, Vollmer believed that police could prevent crime by involving themselves in the lives of *potential* criminals, which led to his establishing the first juvenile crime unit in the nation.

Vollmer's devotion to modernism was also apparent in the career of his most successful protégé, police reformer O. W. Wilson, who promoted a style of policing known as the **professional model.** In an attempt to remove politics from police work, Wilson stressed the need for efficiency through bureaucracy and technology.

Administrative Reforms Under the professional model, police chiefs, who had been little more than figureheads during the political era, took more control over their departments. A key to these efforts was the reorganization of police departments in many major cities. To improve their control over operations, police chiefs began to add midlevel positions to the force. These new officers, known as majors or assistant chiefs, could develop and implement crime-fighting strategies and more closely supervise individual officers. Police chiefs also tried to consolidate their power by bringing large areas of a city under their control so that no local ward, neighborhood, or politician could easily influence a single police department.

Finally, police chiefs set up special units such as criminal investigation, vice, and traffic squads with jurisdiction-wide power. Previously, all police powers within a precinct were controlled by the politicians in that precinct. By creating specialized units that worked across all precincts, the police chiefs increased their own power at the expense of the political bosses.

Technological innovations on all fronts—including patrol cars, radio communications, public records systems, fingerprinting, toxicology (the study of poisons), and forensics (the application of chemistry to the examination of physical evidence)— allowed police operations to move even more quickly toward O. W. Wilson's professional model. By the 1950s, America prided itself on having the most modern and professional police force in the world. (The pace of technological innovation continues to this day, as you can see in the feature *CJ and Technology—Going Wireless* on the following page.) As efficiency became the goal of the reform-era police chief, however, relations with the community suffered. Instead of being members of the community, police officers were now seen almost as intruders, patrolling the streets in the anonymity of their automobiles. The drawbacks of this perception—and the professional model in general—would soon become evident.

Turmoil in the 1960s The 1960s was one of the most turbulent decades in American history. The civil rights movement, though not inherently violent, intensified feelings of helplessness and impoverishment in African American communities. These frustrations resulted in civil unrest, and many major American cities experienced race riots in the middle years of the decade.

Even though police brutality often provided the spark for riots—and there is little question that police departments often overreacted to antiwar demonstrations during the Vietnam era (1964–1975)—it would

> "He may be a very nice man. But I haven't got the time to figure that out. All I know is, he's got a uniform and a gun and I have to relate to him that way."
>
> —James Baldwin, American author (1971)

be simplistic to blame the strife of the 1960s on the police. The rioters were reacting to social circumstances that they found unacceptable. Their clashes with the police were the result rather than the cause of these problems. Many observers, however, believed that the police *contributed* to the disorder. The National Advisory Commission on Civil Disorders stated bluntly that poor relations between the police and African American communities were partly to blame for the violence that plagued many of those communities.[12] In striving for professionalism, the police appeared to have lost touch with the citizens they were supposed to be serving. To repair their damaged relations with a large segment of the population, police would have to rediscover their community roots.

Returning to the Community

The beginning of the third era in American policing, the *community era,* may have started with several government initiatives that took place in 1968. Of primary importance was the Omnibus Crime Control and Safe Streets Act, which was passed that year.[13] Under this act, the federal government provided state and local police departments with funds to create a wide variety of police-community programs. Most large-city police departments established entire units devoted to community relations, implementing programs that ranged from summer recreation activities for inner-city youths to "officer-friendly" referral operations that encouraged citizens to come to the police with their crime concerns.

Going Wireless

Despite the many technological advances that have transformed police work since August Vollmer sent out the first patrol cars in the early 1900s, law enforcement agents have always faced one important limitation. Any information taken down on paper by a police officer in the field—such as speeding tickets or arrest warrants—would have to be refiled when he or she returned to the station. Time that could be better spent on providing services to citizens was taken up with paperwork that, essentially, had already been done.

Thanks to a new technology known as wireless-fidelity, or Wi-Fi, police departments can set up wide-area networks (WANs) that connect computer systems via directional antennas. Each of these antennas has a radius of fifteen to thirty miles, and they can be chained together to create large areas of coverage. Any police officer with a laptop or dashboard computer that has the proper network card (and an antenna on the roof of the patrol car) can use this wireless technology to link up not only with local police headquarters, but also with other law enforcement agencies, courtrooms, and government departments. The potential for Wi-Fi as an information transmitter goes well beyond saving police officers from having to fill out an arrest report twice. Jail authorities could, for example, use Wi-Fi to send a mug shot of an escaped convict to all law enforcement agencies in the immediate vicinity.

IN THE FUTURE

Today, Wi-Fi systems are often limited by the range of the antennas or "access points." Thus, if a patrol car moves out of range of an access point, the police officer will enter a "dead zone" with no wireless access. Some systems have developed a back-up plan in which the connection is immediately reestablished through a cellular WAN (using the same technology as a cellular phone), but many experts worry that any information transferred in this manner can easily be intercepted by someone with the proper tools. The scope of this problem may be reduced, however, as more WANs use satellite links, which both increase their range and protect against information theft. Furthermore, until 2002 the Federal Communications Commission required all WANs to be licensed. Now that the networks are unregulated, it will be much easier for law enforcement agencies to create and use them.

AP Photo/Nick Ut

The "ISBS" is a wireless device that can record a fingerprint at the scene of an investigation and then send the image to be checked against a database.

For more information on wireless-fidelity and other CJ technologies, click on Web Links *under* Chapter Resources *at* **www.cjinaction.com**.

In the 1970s, as this vital rethinking of the role of the police was taking place, the country was hit by a crime wave. Thus, police administrators were forced to combine efforts to improve community relations with aggressive and innovative crime-fighting strategies. At first, these strategies were *reactive;* that is, they focused on reducing the amount of time the police took to react to crime—how quickly they were able to reach the scene of a crime, for example. Eventually, police departments began to focus on *proactive* strategies—that is, strategies aimed at stopping crimes before they are committed. A dedication to proactive strategies led to widespread acceptance of *community policing* in the 1980s. Community policing is based on the notion that meaningful interaction between officers and citizens will lead to a partnership in preventing and fighting crime.[14] Though the idea of involving members of the community in this manner is hardly new—a similar principle was set forth by Sir Robert Peel—innovative tactics in community policing, many of which will be discussed in Chapter 6, have had a significant impact on modern police work.

LAW ENFORCEMENT AGENCIES

Another aspect of modern police work is the "multilayering" of law enforcement. For example, a wide network of local, state, and federal law enforcement agencies was involved in the extensive hunt for Brian Nichols across the Atlanta area, mentioned in the introduction to this chapter. Included in the search were hundreds of law enforcement agents from the Atlanta and Fulton County police, the Fulton County Sheriff's Department, the Metropolitan Atlanta Rapid Transit Authority, the Georgia Bureau of Investigation, the Georgia State Patrol, the Federal Bureau of Investigation (FBI), the Bureau of Alcohol, Tobacco, Firearms and Explosives, and the U.S. Marshals Service.

The manhunt illustrates how many agencies can become involved in a single incident. There are over 14,000 law enforcement agencies in the United States, employing more than 970,000 people.[15] The various agencies include:

- 3,088 sheriffs' departments.
- 1,332 special police agencies, limited to policing parks, schools, airports, and so on.
- 49 state police departments, with Hawaii being the one exception.
- 70 federal law enforcement agencies.

Each level has its own set of responsibilities, which we shall discuss starting with local police departments.

Municipal Law Enforcement Agencies

According to the FBI, there are 3.5 state and local police officers for every 1,000 citizens in the United States.[16] This average somewhat masks the discrepancies between the police forces in urban and rural America. As noted in Chapter 1, the vast majority of all police officers work in small and medium-sized police departments (see Figure 5.3 on the next page). While the New York City Police Department has more than 40,000 employees, almost 680 small towns have only one police officer.[17]

Of the three levels of law enforcement, municipal agencies have the broadest authority to apprehend criminal suspects, maintain order, and provide services to the community. Whether the local officer is part of a large force or the only law enforcement officer in the community, he or she is usually responsible for a wide spectrum of duties, from responding to noise complaints to investigating homicides. Much of the criticism of local police departments is based on the belief that local police are too underpaid or poorly trained to handle these various responsibilities. Reformers have suggested that residents of smaller American towns would benefit from greater statewide coordination of local police departments.[18]

Sheriffs and County Law Enforcement

A vestige of the English shire-reeve discussed earlier in the chapter, the **sheriff** is still an important figure in American law

Sheriff
The primary law enforcement officer in a county, usually elected to the post by a popular vote.

A local police officer operates a roadblock as part of the search for Jason Lee Wheeler, who killed a Lake County (Florida) sheriff's deputy and wounded two others on February 9, 2005. The search for Wheeler, which ended successfully later that day, involved members of the U.S. Marshals Service, the Orlando Police Department, and the Seminole, Orange, and Brevard County Sheriff's Departments. Why would local law enforcement agencies seek the aid of federal law enforcement agencies in a situation such as this one?

AP Photo/Phil Sandlin

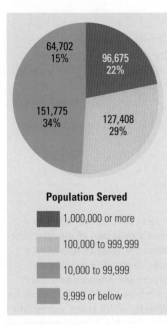

Population Served

■ 1,000,000 or more

■ 100,000 to 999,999

■ 10,000 to 99,999

■ 9,999 or below

FIGURE 5.3
Full-Time Police Personnel,
by Size of Population Served

Source: Bureau of Justice Statistics,
Local Police Departments, 2000
(Washington, D.C.: U.S. Department of
Justice, January 2003), Table 3, p. 3.

Coroner
The medical examiner of a county,
usually elected by popular vote.

enforcement. Almost every one of the more than three thousand counties in the United States (except those in Alaska) has a sheriff. In every state except Rhode Island and Hawaii, sheriffs are elected by members of the community for two- or four-year terms and are paid a salary set by the state legislature or county board. As elected officials who do not necessarily need a background in law enforcement, modern sheriffs resemble their counterparts from the political era of policing in many ways. Simply stated, the sheriff is also a politician. When a new sheriff is elected, she or he will sometimes repay political debts by appointing new deputies or promoting those who have given her or him support. This high degree of instability and personnel turnover in many states is seen as one of the weaknesses of county law enforcement.[19]

Size and Responsibility of Sheriffs' Departments Like municipal police forces, sheriffs' departments vary in size. The largest is the Los Angeles County Sheriff's Department, with more than 8,400 full-time employees. Of the 3,088 sheriffs' departments in the country, twelve employ more than 1,000 officers, while eleven have only one.[20]

The image of the sheriff as a powerful figure patrolling vast expanses is not entirely misleading. Most sheriffs' departments are assigned their duties by state law. Almost 90 percent of all sheriffs' departments have the primary responsibility for investigating violent crimes in their jurisdictions. Other common responsibilities of a sheriff's department include:

- Protecting the public.
- Maintaining the county jail.
- Carrying out civil and criminal processes within county lines, such as serving eviction notices and court summonses.
- Keeping order in the county courthouse.
- Collecting taxes.
- Enforcing orders of the court, such as overseeing the sequestration of a jury during a trial.[21]

It is easy to confuse sheriffs' departments and local police departments. As Figure 5.4 shows, both law enforcement agencies are responsible for many of the same tasks, including crime investigation and routine patrol. There are differences, however, also evident in Figure 5.4: sheriffs' departments are more likely to be involved in county court and jail operations and to perform certain services such as search and rescue. Local police departments, for their part, are more likely to perform traffic-related functions than are sheriffs' departments.

The County Coroner Another elected official on the county level is the **coroner,** or medical examiner. Duties vary from county to county, but the coroner has a general mandate to investigate "all sudden, unexplained, unnatural, or suspicious deaths" reported to the office. The coroner is ultimately responsible for determining the cause of death in these cases. Coroners also perform autopsies and assist other law enforcement agencies in homicide investigations.[22] In certain rare circumstances, such as when the sheriff is arrested or otherwise forced to leave his or her post, the coroner becomes the leading law enforcement officer of the county.

State Police and Highway Patrols

The most visible state law enforcement agency is the state police or highway patrol agency. Historically, state police agencies were created for four reasons:

1 To assist local police agencies, which often did not have adequate resources or training to handle their law enforcement tasks.

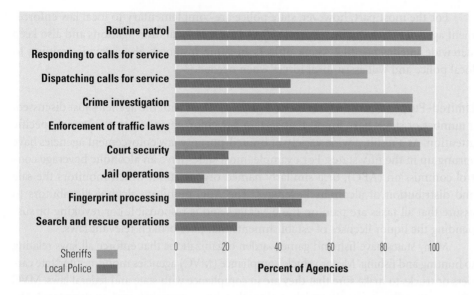

FIGURE 5.4

The Functions of Sheriffs' and Local Police Departments

Sheriffs' and local police departments perform many of the same functions. As you see here, however, the emphasis is often different. Sheriffs' departments are much more involved in operating local jails, while police departments are more likely to deal with traffic control.

Source: Bureau of Justice Statistics, *Sheriffs' Departments, 1997* (Washington, D.C.: U.S. Department of Justice, February 2000), 14.

2 To investigate criminal activities that crossed jurisdictional boundaries (such as when bank robbers committed a crime in one county and then fled to another part of the state).

3 To provide law enforcement in rural and other areas that did not have local or county police agencies.

4 To break strikes and control labor movements.

The first statewide police organization was the Texas Rangers. When this organization was initially created in 1835, the Rangers' primary purpose was to patrol the border with Mexico as scouts for the Republic of Texas Army. The Rangers evolved into a more general-purpose law enforcement agency, and in 1874 they were commissioned as police officers and given law enforcement duties. The Arizona Rangers (created in 1901) and the New Mexico Mounted Police (1905) were formed in a similar manner.

The Difference between the State Police and Highway Patrols Today, there are twenty-three state police agencies and twenty-six highway patrols in the United States. State police agencies have statewide jurisdiction and are authorized to perform a wide variety of law enforcement tasks. Thus, they provide the same services as city or county police departments and are limited only by the boundaries of the state. Such full-service state police agencies exist in Virginia, Michigan, Texas, New Mexico, Louisiana, Oregon, New York, Kentucky, Pennsylvania, and Rhode Island.

In contrast, highway patrols have limited authority. They are limited either by their jurisdiction or by the specific types of offenses they have the authority to control. As their name suggests, most highway patrols concentrate primarily on regulating traffic; specifically, they enforce traffic laws and investigate traffic accidents. Furthermore, they usually limit their activity to patrolling state and federal highways. States such as Florida, Georgia, Ohio, Nevada, and North Carolina have highway patrols.

Trying to determine what state agency has which duties can be confusing. The Washington State Highway Patrol, despite its name, also has state police powers. In addition, thirty-five states have investigative agencies that are independent of the state police or highway patrol. Such agencies are usually found in states with highway patrols, and they have the primary responsibility of investigating criminal activities. For example, in addition to its highway patrol, Oklahoma runs a State Bureau of Investigation and a State Bureau of Narcotics and Dangerous Drugs. Each state has its own methods of determining the jurisdictions of these various organizations.

Nearly every law enforcement agency hosts a Web site. To find the home pages of the **Pennsylvania State Police** and the **Washington State Highway Patrol,** click on *Web Links* under *Chapter Resources* at **www.cjinaction.com**.

For the most part, however, state police are complementary to local law enforcement agencies. They maintain crime labs to assist in local investigations and also keep statewide intelligence files. State officers in some instances also provide training to local police and will assist local forces when needed.[23]

Limited-Purpose Law Enforcement Agencies Even with the agencies just discussed, a number of states have found that certain law enforcement areas need more specific attention. As a result, a wide variety of limited-purpose law enforcement agencies have sprung up in the fifty states. For example, most states have an alcoholic beverage control commission (ABC), or a similarly named organization, which monitors the sale and distribution of alcoholic beverages. The ABC monitors alcohol distributors to assure that all taxes are paid on the beverages and is responsible for revoking or suspending the liquor licenses of establishments that have broken relevant laws.

Many states have fish and game warden organizations that enforce all laws relating to hunting and fishing. Motor vehicle compliance (MVC) agencies monitor interstate carriers or trucks to make sure that they are in compliance with state and federal laws. MVC officers generally operate the weigh stations that are commonly found on interstate highways. Other limited-purpose law enforcement agencies deal with white-collar and computer crime, regulate nursing homes, and provide training to local police departments.

Federal Law Enforcement Agencies

Statistically, employees of federal agencies do not make up a large part of the nation's law enforcement force. In fact, the New York City Police Department has nearly half as many employees as all of the federal law enforcement agencies combined.[24] The influence of these federal agencies, however, is substantial. Unlike local police departments, which must deal with all forms of crime, federal agencies have been authorized, usually by Congress, to enforce specific laws or attend to specific situations. The U.S. Coast Guard, for example, patrols the nation's waterways, while U.S. Postal Inspectors investigate and prosecute crimes perpetrated through the use of the U.S. mails. In response to the terrorist attacks of September 11, 2001, the Federal Aviation Administration has resurrected a program that places law enforcement agents on passenger aircraft. (See the feature *International CJ—Sky Marshals Fly Again.*)

As mentioned in Chapter 1, the most far-reaching reorganization of the federal government since World War II took place in 2002 and 2003. These changes, particularly the formation of the Department of Homeland Security, have had a profound effect on federal law enforcement. (See Figure 5.5 for the new federal law enforcement "lineup.") We will address the most important agencies in this section, grouping them according to the federal department or bureau to which they report.

The Department of Homeland Security On November 25, 2002, President George W. Bush signed the Homeland Security Act.[25] This legislation created the Department of Homeland Security (DHS), a new cabinet-level department designed to coordinate federal efforts to protect the United States against international and domestic terrorism. The new department has no new agencies; rather, twenty-two existing agencies were shifted under the control of the secretary of homeland security, a post now held by Michael Chertoff. For example, the Transportation Security Administration, which was formed in 2001 to revive the Federal Air Marshals program placing undercover federal agents on commercial flights, was moved from the Department of Transportation to the DHS. The Directorate of Customs and Border Security, the U.S. Customs Service, and the U.S. Secret Service are the three most visible agencies under the direction of the DHS.

See the **U.S. Department of Homeland Security** for information on how this branch of federal law enforcement is fighting terrorism. Find its Web site by clicking on *Web Links* under *Chapter Resources* at **www.cjinaction.com**.

Sky Marshals Fly Again

In 1970, more than thirty years before terrorists commandeered four commercial aircraft and used them as weapons against American citizens in New York and Washington, D.C., hijackers in Europe carried out a somewhat similar plot. A coordinated group of terrorists took over four commercial airplanes, managing to divert three of the jets to the Middle Eastern country of Jordan. The fourth plane, operated by El Al, Israel's national airline, did not reach Jordan, however. One hijacker was killed and another apprehended as security guards regained control of the aircraft, allowing it to land safely in London. The presence of a law enforcement agent on the El Al flight was no accident. Operating in one of the most volatile areas of the world, the airline (which is operated by Israel's government) incorporates a number of security measures into its day-to-day operations. One of these measures is that every El Al flight has at least one plainclothes sky marshal on board.

In the wake of the September 11, 2001, terrorist attacks in the United States, many politicians seized on the idea of duplicating Israel's sky marshal program on American air carriers as a "new" way to combat hijackings. In fact, the U.S. Federal Aviation Administration (FAA) formed its own sky marshal program in the 1970s, in response to a series of airplane hijackings to Cuba. As

the perceived threat lessened over the past three decades, though, many of the specially trained agents were allowed to leave the program.

At the time of the terrorist attacks, only thirty-two sky marshals were still employed. Subsequently, the Bush administration announced a plan to combine a revamped air marshals program with the new immigration security bureau under the Department of Homeland Security. The intent was to make 5,000 armed federal agents available to protect commercial flights, although by 2005 only about 2,200 had been deployed. In particular, government officials would like to be able to quickly deploy a large number of sky marshals when intelligence reports indicate a hijacking may be imminent.

FOR CRITICAL ANALYSIS

Several European nations, including Britain, Portugal, Denmark, Sweden, and Norway, have refused to allow U.S. sky marshals on their airlines. Why might pilots from these countries balk at the idea of armed law enforcement agents on airplanes? How insistent should the U.S. government be on the posting of sky marshals on international flights when there might be a terrorist risk?

The Directorate of Customs and Border Security One of the most significant effects of the Homeland Security Act was the termination of the Immigration and Naturalization Service (INS), which had monitored and policed the flow of immigrants into the United States since 1933. The INS faced particular criticism in the aftermath of the terrorist attacks on Washington, D.C., and New York City after it became

FIGURE 5.5
Federal Law Enforcement Agencies

A number of federal agencies employ law enforcement officers who are authorized to carry firearms and make arrests. The most prominent ones are under the control of the U.S. Department of Homeland Security, the U.S. Department of Justice, or the U.S. Department of the Treasury.

Source: Bureau of Justice Statistics, *Federal Law Enforcement Officers, 2002* (Washington, D.C.: U.S. Department of Justice, August 2003), 1–2, 5.

DEPARTMENT OF HOMELAND SECURITY
U.S. Secret Service
U.S. Customs Service
U.S. Customs and Border Protection
U.S. Immigration and Customs Enforcement

DEPARTMENT OF JUSTICE
Federal Bureau of Investigation
U.S. Marshals Service
Bureau of Alcohol, Tobacco, Firearms and Explosives
Drug Enforcement Administration

DEPARTMENT OF THE TREASURY
Internal Revenue Service

0   3,000   6,000   9,000   12,000   15,000
Number of officers

AP Photo/Ron Edmonds

President George W. Bush promotes the Department of Homeland Security, a large federal agency designed to protect the United States against terrorist attacks. Considering that the United States already has a federal crime-fighting agency—the FBI— why might a Department of Homeland Security be necessary?

clear that several of the hijackers were in the country illegally at the time.[26] The architects of the Homeland Security Act hoped that separating the functions of the old INS into several new bureaus would cure some of the inefficiency problems that had plagued the INS since its inception.

Before the formation of the DHS, the INS was responsible for enforcing our immigration laws and for providing immigration benefits. Now, according to the dictates of the Homeland Security Act, U.S. Citizenship and Immigration Services processes applications for immigration benefits, and the Directorate of Customs and Border Security oversees the two bureaus responsible for immigration law enforcement:

1   *U.S. Customs and Border Protection (CBP)* polices the flow of goods and people across the United States' international borders with Mexico and Canada. In 2004, CBP agents seized more than $2.6 billion worth of illegal drugs and intercepted more than 50,000 undocumented immigrants being smuggled across the borders.[27]

2   *U.S. Immigration and Customs Enforcement (ICE)* implements laws concerning customs and immigration inside the United States.[28]

Even before September 11, 2001, a large number of illegal immigrants and huge amounts of illicit drugs entered the United States via Mexico and Canada. Government officials hope that the reorganization of the INS will help control these traditional concerns of immigration services and protect against terrorist attacks.

U.S. Border Patrol   Much of the burden for policing both the Mexican and Canadian borders between official ports of entry falls on the U.S. Border Patrol, a part of the CBP. In 2003, the Border Patrol caught nearly 1.1 million people entering the country illegally and seized more than $1.6 billion worth of illegal narcotics.[29] Today, about ten thousand Border Patrol agents guard twenty different sectors along the borders, almost double the number ten years earlier.

Particular attention is being paid to the Canadian border. As recently as 2001, the 4,200-mile border was policed by only 300 Border Patrol agents. One of the first moves made by the CBP after its inception was to raise that number to well over 1,000.

The flash point of immigration enforcement, however, remains the line between Mexico and the United States. Under the CBP, the Border Patrol hopes not only to restrict the flow of contraband and illegal aliens across the Rio Grande, but also to limit the human tragedy that is a side effect of this traffic. In 2004, 191 people died while trying to enter the United States illegally from Mexico; many of them perished from heat exposure. In response, the federal government added hundreds of new agents and three surveillance helicopters, as well as solar-power rescue beacons that send a radio distress signal when activated, to an area on the Arizona border known as the "devil's corridor" because of its high death rate.

Border Patrol agents frisk illegal aliens captured in Nogales, Arizona. Starting in 1994, Operation Gatekeeper increased the number of Border Patrol agents in the southwestern United States from 800 to 2,300, resulting in a dramatic increase in the number of illegal aliens captured and returned to Mexico. The increase in agents also appears to have led to an increase in violent confrontations between agents and illegal aliens. Do you believe society benefits from efforts to keep illegal aliens out of the country? Is the use of force to carry out these efforts justifiable?

U.S. Customs Service The U.S. Customs Service, which stations agents at every port of entry and exit to the United States, moved from the Department of the Treasury to the Directorate of Customs and Border Security. Customs agents have widespread authority to investigate and search all international passengers, including those arriving on airplanes, ships, or other forms of transportation. Furthermore, the Customs Service is responsible for ensuring that proper tariffs and taxes have been paid on all goods imported into the United States. It collects more than $20 billion a year in these duties and fees.

Before September 11, 2001, the primary goal of the Customs Service was to prevent the smuggling of contraband (anything that is unlawful to produce or possess), while allowing the free flow of goods to encourage commerce between the United States and its trading partners. Today, the bureau is asked to balance these economic concerns against the need for security. This has placed a particular burden on the agents at the Mexican and Canadian borders, who have been on continual "high alert" since the terrorist attacks. Around 1.3 million people in 350,000 cars, trucks, and buses cross at border posts each day, and at the most popular routes, Customs agents have between thirty seconds and two minutes to decide whether a vehicle and its passengers are suspicious. If they took any longer, the resulting lines at the border stops would make travel across the borders nearly impossible.[30]

The U.S. Secret Service When created in 1865, the Secret Service was primarily responsible for combating currency counterfeiters. In 1901, the agency was given the added responsibility of protecting the president of the United States, the president's family, the vice president, the president-elect, and former presidents. These duties have remained the cornerstone of the agency, with several expansions. After a number of threats against presidential candidates in the 1960s and early 1970s, including the shootings of Robert Kennedy and Governor George Wallace of Alabama, in 1976 Secret Service agents became responsible for protecting those political figures as well.

In addition to its special plainclothes agents, the agency also directs two uniformed groups of law enforcement officers. The Secret Service Uniformed Division protects the grounds of the White House and its inhabitants, and the Treasury Police Force polices the Treasury Building in Washington, D.C. This responsibility includes investigating threats against presidents and those running for presidential office.

To aid its battle against counterfeiters and forgers of government bonds, the agency has the use of a laboratory at the Bureau of Engraving and Printing in the nation's capital.

The Department of Justice The U.S. Department of Justice, created in 1870, is still the primary federal law enforcement agency in the country. With the responsibility of enforcing criminal law and supervising the federal prisons, the Justice Department plays a leading role in the American criminal justice system. To carry out its responsibilities to prevent and control crime, the department has a number of law enforcement agencies, including the Federal Bureau of Investigation, the federal Drug Enforcement Administration, the Bureau of Alcohol, Tobacco, Firearms and Explosives, and the U.S. Marshals Service.

The Federal Bureau of Investigation (FBI) Initially created in 1908 as the Bureau of Investigation, this agency was renamed the **Federal Bureau of Investigation (FBI)** in 1935. One of the primary investigative agencies of the federal government, the FBI has jurisdiction over nearly two hundred federal crimes, including sabotage, espionage (spying), kidnapping, extortion, interstate transportation of stolen property, bank robbery, interstate gambling, and civil rights violations. Note that the FBI is not considered a "national" police force. In general, law enforcement is seen as the responsibility of state and local governments. There is no doubt, however, that the agency plays a crucial role in today's law enforcement landscape. With its network of agents across the country and the globe, the FBI is uniquely positioned to combat worldwide criminal activity such as terrorism and drug trafficking. Furthermore, in times of national emergency the FBI is the primary arm of federal law enforcement. Within hours after the terrorist attacks on September 11, 2001, more than 7,000 FBI employees in 57 different countries had begun an intense search for those responsible.

Today, the FBI has more than 28,000 employees and an annual budget of over $5 billion. The agency has six investigative priorities: (1) terrorism, (2) organized crime, (3) cyber crime, (4) foreign intelligence operations in the United States, (5) federal drug offenses, and (6) white-collar crime.[31] The agency also offers valuable assistance to local and state law enforcement agencies. The FBI's Identification Division maintains a huge database of fingerprint information and offers assistance in finding missing persons and identifying the victims of fires, airplane crashes, and other disfiguring disasters. The services of the FBI Laboratory, the largest crime laboratory in the world, are available at no charge to other agencies. Finally, the FBI's National Crime Information Center (NCIC) provides lists of stolen vehicles and firearms, missing license plates, vehicles used to commit crimes, and other information to local and state law enforcement officers who may access the NCIC database.

The Drug Enforcement Administration (DEA) With a $1.8 billion budget and more than 4,000 special agents, the Drug Enforcement Administration (DEA) is one of the fastest-growing law enforcement agencies in the country. The mission of the DEA is to enforce domestic drug laws and regulations and to assist other federal and foreign agencies in combating illegal drug manufacture and trade on an international level. The agency also enforces the provisions of the Controlled Substances Act, which governs the manufacture, distribution, and dispensing of legal drugs, such as prescription drugs.

As we shall see in Chapter 16, the federal government has had a role in policing the manufacture and sale of illicit drugs since 1914. The first federal drug agency, the Federal Bureau of Narcotics (FBN), was established in 1930 under President Herbert Hoover. The FBN's main priorities were cocaine and opiates such as heroin. As the level of illegal drug use expanded over the decades, and international trafficking became a

Jim Rice
Federal Bureau of Investigation (FBI)

Jim Rice

Growing up in a small town in rural West Virginia, I always knew that I wanted to be an FBI agent. There were probably a lot of other kids in America who shared this dream, but the murder of a woman who at one time was my babysitter convinced me to do everything that I could to make my dream of becoming a law enforcement officer come true.

I received a B.S. in biology from John Marshall University in West Virginia and subsequently earned a master's degree in biochemistry from there as well. During college, I worked at several part-time jobs, loading trucks and bagging groceries, and also served in the Coast Guard as a reservist.

Following college, I went to work for the West Virginia State Police (WVSP) as a forensic toxicologist, a job that prepared me well for my current position with the FBI. These four years were well spent, because it was an interesting and challenging job and also because the FBI seeks to attract candidates who are competitive and who bring a specialty or work experience to the job.

I joined the FBI as a Special Agent in 1988 and spent the first sixteen weeks of my Bureau career at the FBI Academy in Quantico, Virginia, as do all new agents. The FBI Academy is similar to a small college campus, with classrooms, dormitories, a cafeteria, and a gymnasium, with hundreds of students in residence at any given time, including new agents, experienced agents who are back for a week or two of specialized training, and police officers from all over the country and the world.

Following graduation from the FBI Academy, agents are subject to transfer to one of the fifty-six field offices in the United States for their first assignment. I was sent to the Indianapolis (Indiana) office, where I was assigned to a "reactive squad," which handled violent criminal violations, such as bank robberies, fugitives, kidnappings, and extortions.

It was during my time in Indianapolis that I worked on a case that had a major impact on me and reaffirmed that the FBI was the right career choice for me. A young boy was kidnapped by an adult family friend and driven cross-country in the subject's truck. The FBI had surveillances on a number of locations in the

Midwest, including the home of the subject's relatives in Indianapolis. After many long hours of surveillance in the cold and rain, our team found a truck that matched the description of the subject's truck, parked beside a house in a desolate part of the city. We continued the surveillance on the truck and finally, the subject and the victim emerged from the house. As they drove off in the truck, our team followed discreetly at a distance until the order came from the lead agent to move in and conduct a tactical car stop. The subject was arrested and the boy was rescued, frightened but unharmed, and reunited with his parents.

A rotational transfer brought me to the Washington, D.C., field office in 1992, where I joined the SWAT team and worked on a "safe streets gang task force" and then on a cold case homicide squad. Soon thereafter, a joint terrorism task force was formed to address domestic terrorism matters in the nation's capital, an area filled with symbolic targets for would-be terrorist activities.

I volunteered to be part of this task force in late 1992 and was promoted to the position of Supervisory Special Agent of the squad in 1998. My duties include the operational and emergency response to incidents of domestic terrorism; bombings and bomb threats; chemical, biological, and nuclear incidents; and security for special events, such as presidential inaugurations and the fiftieth anniversary celebration of NATO, which brought dozens of heads of state to Washington in 1999 without incident.

Go to the Careers in Criminal Justice Interactive CD *for more profiles in the field of criminal justice.*

more pressing problem, several additional agencies were formed to deal with drug enforcement. Then, in 1970 Congress passed the comprehensive Drug Abuse Prevention and Control Act,[32] which gave Congress the authority to regulate interstate commerce of legal drugs. With the Bureau of Narcotics and Dangerous Drugs (a successor to the FBN), the U.S. Customs Service, the FBI, and hundreds of state and local law enforcement agencies all working to enforce drug laws—as well as the government's new responsibility with regard to legal drugs—it was evident that a new "superagency" was needed. In 1973, by order of President Richard Nixon, the DEA was formed.

Today, DEA agents often work in conjunction with local and state authorities to prevent illicit drugs from reaching communities. The agency also conducts extensive operations with law enforcement entities in other drug-producing countries. In the DEA's

"Operation Jump Start," for example, American agents joined with their counterparts in Colombia and Guatemala to disrupt an operation to smuggle illegal drugs concealed in car batteries into the southwestern United States. The operation culminated in 2005 with the seizure of $1 million in cash, 176 pounds of cocaine, and 48 pounds of heroin, along with the arrest of 100 people linked to the trafficking organization.[33] Like the FBI, the DEA operates a network of six regional laboratories used to test and categorize seized drugs. Local law enforcement agencies have access to the DEA labs and often use them to ensure that information about particular drugs that will be presented in court is accurate and up to date. In recent years Congress has given the FBI more authority to enforce drug laws, and the two agencies now share a number of administrative controls.

The Bureau of Alcohol, Tobacco, Firearms and Explosives (ATF) As its name suggests, the Bureau of Alcohol, Tobacco, Firearms and Explosives (ATF) is primarily concerned with the illegal sale, possession, and use of firearms and the control of untaxed tobacco and liquor products. The Firearms Division of the agency has the responsibility of enforcing the Gun Control Act of 1968, which sets the circumstances under which firearms may be sold and used in this country. The bureau also regulates all gun trade between the United States and foreign nations and collects taxes on all firearm importers, manufacturers, and dealers. In keeping with these duties, the ATF is also responsible for policing the illegal use and possession of explosives. Furthermore, the ATF is charged with enforcing federal gambling laws.

Because it has jurisdiction over such a wide variety of crimes, especially those involving firearms and explosives, the ATF is a constant presence in federal criminal investigations. Since 1982, for example, the agency has been working in conjunction with the FBI to prevent the bombing of abortion clinics. Recently, the agency, along with the FBI, has begun to place undercover informants inside antiabortion groups to gain information about proposed bombings. Furthermore, the ATF has been active in forming multijurisdictional drug task forces with other federal and local law enforcement agencies to investigate drug crimes involving firearms.

The U.S. Marshals Service The oldest federal law enforcement agency is the U.S. Marshals Service. In 1789, President George Washington assigned thirteen U.S. Marshals to protect his attorney general. That same year, Congress created the office of the U.S. Marshals and Deputy Marshals. Originally, the U.S. Marshals acted as the main law enforcement officers in the western territories. Following the Civil War, when most of these territories had become states, these agents were assigned to work for the U.S. district courts, where federal crimes are tried. The relationship between the U.S. Marshals Service and the federal courts continues today and forms the basis for the officers' main duties, which include:

1 Providing security at federal courts for judges, jurors, and other courtroom participants.
2 Controlling property that has been ordered seized by federal courts.

Bureau of Alcohol, Tobacco, Firearms and Explosives (ATF) agent Doug Moore observes the remains of a warehouse in Salt Lake City, Utah. Officials suspected ecoterrorism as the cause of the suspicious fire. Why might the ATF be involved in investigating this sort of crime?

AP Photo/Douglas C. Pizac

3 Protecting government witnesses who place themselves in danger by testifying against the targets of federal criminal investigations. This protection is sometimes accomplished by relocating the witnesses and providing them with different identities.

4 Transporting federal prisoners to detention institutions.

5 Investigating violations of federal fugitive laws.[34]

The Department of the Treasury The Department of the Treasury, formed in 1789, is mainly responsible for all financial matters of the federal government. It pays all the federal government's bills, borrows money, collects taxes, mints coins, and prints paper currency. The largest bureau of the Treasury Department, the Internal Revenue Service (IRS), is concerned with violations of tax laws and regulations. The bureau has three divisions, only one of which is involved in criminal investigations. The examination branch of the IRS audits the tax returns of corporations and individuals. The collection division attempts to collect taxes from corporations or citizens who have failed to pay the taxes they owe. Finally, the criminal investigation division investigates cases of tax evasion and tax fraud. Criminal investigation agents can make arrests. The IRS has long played a role in policing criminal activities such as gambling and selling drugs for one simple reason: those who engage in such activities almost never report any illegally gained income on their tax returns. Therefore, the IRS is able to apprehend them for tax evasion. The most famous instance of this took place in the 1920s, when the IRS finally arrested famed crime boss Al Capone—responsible for numerous violent crimes—for not paying his taxes.

PRIVATE SECURITY

Even with increasing numbers of local, state, and federal law enforcement officers, the police do not have the ability to prevent every crime. Recognizing this, many businesses and citizens have decided to hire private guards for their properties and homes. In fact, more than $100 billion a year is spent worldwide on **private security.** In the United States, estimates place the figure at $12 billion.[35] More than 10,000 firms employing around 2 million people provide private security services in the United States.

Privatizing Law Enforcement

In the eyes of the law, a private security guard is the same as any other private person when it comes to police powers such as being able to arrest or interrogate a person suspected of committing a crime. Ideally, a security guard—lacking the training of a law enforcement agent—should only observe and report criminal activity unless use of force is needed to prevent a felony.[36]

Citizens' Arrests Any private citizen (including private security guards) may perform a "citizen's arrest" under certain circumstances, however. The California Penal Code, for example, allows a private person to arrest another:

- For a public offense committed in his or her presence.
- When the person arrested has committed a felony, even if it was not in the arrester's presence, if he or she has reasonable cause to believe that the person committed the felony.[37]

Obviously, these are not very exacting standards, and, in reality, private security guards have many, if not most, of the same powers to prevent crime that a police officer does.

Private Security

The practice of private corporations or individuals offering services traditionally performed by police officers.

The Deterrence Factor As a rule, however, private security is not designed to "replace" law enforcement. It is intended to deter crime rather than stop it.[38] A uniformed security guard patrolling a shopping mall parking lot or a bank lobby has one primary function—to convince a potential criminal to search out a shopping mall or bank that does not have private security. For the same reason, many citizens hire security personnel to drive marked cars through their neighborhoods, making them a less attractive target for burglaries, robberies, vandalism, and other crimes.

Problems with Private Security

Despite the proliferation of private security, many questions remain about this largely unregulated industry. In late 2004, four security guards accidentally asphyxiated Peter James Lawrence to death outside a nightclub in Las Vegas, Nevada. The security guards were trying to subdue Lawrence, who reacted violently when he was asked to stop bothering an ex-girlfriend.[39] The only requirement for becoming a security guard in Nevada is four hours of training.[40]

Lack of Standards As there are no federal regulations regarding private security, each state has its own rules for employment as a security guard. In several states, including California and Florida, prospective guards must have at least forty hours of training. Thirty states, however, have no specific training requirements, and ten states do not regulate the private security industry at all. By comparison, Spain mandates 160 hours of theoretical training, 20 hours of practical training, and 20 hours of annual continuing education for anybody hoping to find employment as a security guard.[41]

The quality of employees is also a problem for the U.S. private security industry. In a widely publicized incident in 2005, the Maryland Port Administration fired the company that was providing private security services for the Port of Baltimore after discovering that the security guards abandoned their posts during the night, often slept on the job, and sometimes never even bothered to show up for work.[42] Part of the problem is the profession's high turnover rate; save for those employed by the largest firms, private security is often a second job offering few career prospects. Furthermore, given the low pay (see Figure 5.6) and lack of benefits such as health insurance, paid vacation time, and sick days, the industry does not always attract highly qualified and motivated recruits.[43] "At those wages," notes one industry specialist, "you're competing with McDonald's."[44] To make matters worse, fewer than half of the states require a fingerprint check for applicants, making it relatively easy for a person with a criminal record in one state to obtain a security guard position in another.[45]

The security industry will find it much easier to uncover past convictions of employees and job applicants thanks to the Private Security Officer Employment Authorization Act of 2004.[46] The legislation, which authorizes the FBI to provide background checks for security firms, was spurred by congressional concern over possible terrorist attacks on shipping ports, water treatment facilities, telecommunications facilities, power plants, and other strategic targets that are often secured by private guards. At present, only twenty-two states require private security officers to be put through a federal background check, but industry experts hope this legislation will spur more jurisdictions to pass similar laws.

Continued Growth in the Industry Issues surrounding private security promise to gain even greater prominence in the criminal justice system, as indicators point to higher rates of growth for the industry. The Hallcrest Report II, a far-reaching overview of private security trends funded by the National Institute of Justice, identifies four factors driving this growth:

1 An increase in fear on the part of the public triggered by the growing rate of crime, either real or perceived.

2 The problem of crime in the workplace.

3 Budget cuts in states and municipalities that have forced reductions in the number of public police, thereby raising the demand for private ones.

4 A rising awareness of private security products (such as home burglar alarms) and service as cost-effective protective measures.[47]

Another reason is fear of terrorism. The U.S. Bureau of Labor Statistics reported that nearly 15,000 new security guards were hired between September 11, 2001, and October 11, 2001.[48] The bureau predicts that private security will expand by 21 to 35 percent by 2008.[49]

THE RESPONSIBILITIES OF THE POLICE

Some law enforcement officials welcome the massive influx of private security. Private firms, they believe, may be able to relieve the constant budget and staffing pressures that public police forces face.[50] The problem with this theory, however, is that public and private police have different basic functions. For a private security firm, the primary goal is to protect property. As noted earlier, that often means persuading a criminal to choose an alternative target for a burglary or some other crime. As a manager at one private security company noted, "We're a business, not a law enforcement agency."[51]

The goal of public law enforcement, in contrast, is to stop crimes, not simply shift them from one location to another—which is not to say that preventing crime is the only duty of a police officer. For the most part, the incidents that make up a police officer's daily routine would not make it onto television dramas such as *Law and Order*. Besides catching criminals, police spend a great deal of time on such mundane tasks as responding to noise complaints, confiscating firecrackers, and poring over paperwork. Sociologist Egon Bittner warned against the tendency to see the police primarily as agents of law enforcement and crime control. A more inclusive accounting of "what the police do," Bittner believed, would recognize that they provide "situationally justified force in society."[52] In other words, the function of the police is to solve any problem that may *possibly*, though not *necessarily*, require the use of force.

Within Bittner's rather broad definition of "what the police do," we can pinpoint four basic responsibilities of the police:

1 To enforce laws.
2 To provide services.
3 To prevent crime.
4 To preserve the peace.

As will become evident over the next two chapters, there is a great deal of debate among legal and other scholars and law enforcement officers over which responsibilities deserve the most police attention and what methods should be employed by the police in meeting those responsibilities.

FIGURE 5.6
Average Salaries in Law Enforcement

In New York City, servers in restaurants, landscapers, hotel desk clerks, and domestic workers all earn more than private security guards. Nationwide, as this figure shows, security guards are the lowest paid of the "protective service occupations."

Source: Bureau of Labor Statistics.

Baltimore Sun Photo © Amy Davis

Police officers struggle to capture one of nine American bison that escaped from a farm in Stevenson, Maryland, in April 2005. Law enforcement agents provide a number of services to the community that have little to do with fighting crime.

Enforcing Laws

In the public mind, the primary role of the police is to enforce society's laws—hence, the term *law enforcement officer*. In their role as "crime fighters," police officers have a clear mandate to seek out and apprehend those who have violated the law. The crime-fighting responsibility is so dominant that all police activity—from the purchase of new automobiles to a plan to hire more minority officers—must often be justified in terms of its law enforcement value.[53]

Police officers also primarily see themselves as crime fighters, or "crook catchers," a perception that often leads people into what they believe will be an exciting career in law enforcement. Although the job certainly offers challenges unlike any other, police officers normally do not spend the majority of their time in law enforcement duties. After surveying a year's worth of dispatch data from the Wilmington (Delaware) Police Department, researchers Jack Greene and Carl Klockars found that officers spent only about half of their time enforcing the law or dealing with crimes. The rest of their time was taken up with order maintenance, providing services, traffic patrol, and medical assistance.[54] Furthermore, information provided by the Uniform Crime Report shows that most arrests are made for "crimes of disorder" or public annoyances rather than violent or property crimes.[55] In 2004, for example, police made almost 6 million arrests for drunkenness, liquor law violations, disorderly conduct, vagrancy, loitering, and other minor offences, but only about 600,000 arrests for violent crimes.[56]

Providing Services

The popular emphasis on crime fighting and law enforcement tends to overshadow the fact that a great deal of a police officer's time is spent providing services for the community. The motto "To Serve and Protect" has been adopted by thousands of local police departments, and the *Law Enforcement Code of Ethics* recognizes the duty "to serve the community" in its first sentence.[57] The services that police provide are numerous—a partial list would include directing traffic, performing emergency medical procedures, counseling those involved in domestic disputes, providing directions to tourists, and finding lost children. Along with firefighters, police officers are among the first public servants to arrive at disaster scenes to conduct search and rescue operations. This particular duty adds considerably to the dangers faced by law enforcement agents (discussed in more detail in Chapter 6). In the aftermath of Hurricane Katrina, which struck the southeastern United States in 2005, New Orleans police officers had to dodge snipers' bullets as they tried to restore order to the beleaguered city. As mentioned earlier, a number of police departments have adopted the strategy of community policing, and as a consequence, many officers find themselves providing assistance in areas that have not until recently been their domain.[58] For example, police are required to deal with the problems of the homeless and the mentally ill to a greater extent than in past decades.

Preventing Crime

Perhaps the most controversial responsibility of the police is to *prevent* crime. According to Jerome Skolnick of the University of California at Berkeley, there are two predictable public responses when crime rates begin to rise in a community. The first is to punish convicted criminals with stricter laws and more severe penalties. The second is to demand that the police "do something" to prevent crimes from occurring in the first place. Is it, in fact, possible for the police to "prevent" crimes? The strongest response that Professor Skolnick is willing to give to this question is "maybe."[59]

On a limited basis, police can certainly prevent some crimes. If a rapist is dissuaded from attacking a solitary woman because a patrol car is cruising the area, then the police officer behind the wheel has prevented a crime. In general, however, the deterrent effects of police presence are unclear. Carl Klockars has written that the "war on crime" is a war that the police cannot win because they cannot control the factors—such as unemployment, poverty, immorality, inequality, political change, and lack of educational opportunities—that lead to criminal behavior in the first place.[60] As we shall see in the next chapter, many police stations have adopted the idea of community policing in an attempt to better prevent crime.

> "That's the only thing that made me feel safe last night when I came home from work."
>
> —Penny Baily, resident of Indianapolis, commenting on the police car patrolling her neighborhood (1996)

Preserving the Peace

To a certain extent, the fourth responsibility of the police, that of preserving the peace, is related to preventing crime. Police have the legal authority to use the power of arrest, or even force, in situations in which no crime has yet occurred, but might occur in the immediate future.

In the words of James Q. Wilson, the police's peacekeeping role (which Wilson believes is the most important role of law enforcement officers) often takes on a pattern of simply "handling the situation."[61] For example, when police officers arrive on the scene of a loud late-night house party, they may feel the need to disperse the party and even arrest some of the party goers for disorderly conduct. By their actions, the officers have lessened the chances of serious and violent crimes taking place later in the evening. The same principle is often used when dealing with domestic disputes, which, if escalated, can lead to homicide. Such situations are in need of, to use Wilson's terminology again, "fixing up," and police can use the power of arrest, or threat, or coercion, or sympathy, to do just that.

The basis of Wilson and George Kelling's zero-tolerance theory is similar: street disorder—such as public drunkenness, urination, and loitering—signals to both law-abiding citizens and criminals that the law is not being enforced and therefore leads to more violent crime. Hence, if police preserve the peace and "crack down" on the minor crimes that make up street disorder, they will in fact be preventing serious crimes that would otherwise occur in the future.[62] Some law enforcement experts believe the police should take on even greater responsibilities. (For a discussion of one such responsibility, see *CJ in Focus—The Balancing Act: Policing Illegal Immigrants* on p. 150.)

THE ROLE OF DISCRETION IN POLICING

Though the responsibilities just discussed provide a helpful overview of "what police do," they also highlight the ambiguity of a police officer's duties. To say, for example, that highway patrol officers have a responsibility to enforce speed laws is to oversimplify their "real" job. In fact, most highway patrol officers would not find it feasible to

Policing Illegal Immigrants

On a cold night in March 2005, police officers in Spirit Lake, Iowa, pulled over a van because of a traffic violation. Inside, they found ten citizens of Mexico who had been living and working in the United States illegally. Even though the passengers were lawbreakers, the Spirit Lake officers had no authority to arrest them. Unable to enforce immigration laws, the police had to hand the illegal immigrants over to federal authorities—an arrangement that satisfies many local and state law enforcement agents but also one that other criminal justice professionals would like to change.

State and local law enforcement officers have several reasons for being reluctant to implement federal immigrations laws. First, most local police departments are not equipped or trained to enforce these often-complex statutes. Second, many officers worry that immigrants might be wary of cooperating with the police if the latter were involved in immigration enforcement. "If we were to question everybody's status, it would literally hurt our ability to solve crimes," noted one San Jose, California, police sergeant.

A NEED FOR COOPERATION?

The enforcement of immigration laws is the responsibility of U.S. Immigration and Customs Enforcement, which, as mentioned earlier, is part of the Department of Homeland Security (DHS). Only about 5,500 federal agents are assigned to immigration enforcement. A number of officials at the DHS believe they need the help of the nation's 600,000 state and local law enforcement agents to control the estimated 8 million illegal immigrants, an issue that has taken on greater importance in light of domestic terrorism concerns. To further cooperation in this area, the DHS has empowered police officers in Alabama and Florida to arrest and detain illegal immigrants, and similar programs are being considered in Arkansas, Connecticut, Oklahoma, and parts of California.

THE PROBLEM OF POSSIBLE PROFILING

These programs, though limited, have drawn criticism because of fear that they will cause police officers to target people on the basis of race or ethnicity. In practice, however, this has not been a problem. Colonel W. M. Coppage, director of the Alabama Department of Public Safety, says that his officers run background checks only on people arrested for other crimes or stopped for traffic violations. "You can't just say hey, 'There's somebody that may be Hispanic,' and stop them or say, 'There's someone from the Middle East,' and stop them," Coppage explains.

FOR CRITICAL ANALYSIS

Why would an illegal immigrant be wary of reporting criminal activity to a police officer if that officer had authority to enforce immigration laws? Can you think of any reasons that a *legal* immigrant might similarly be discouraged from seeking help from or cooperating with local police?

hand out speeding tickets to every driver who exceeds the posted speed limit. Furthermore, depending on the circumstances, a patrol officer may decide not to issue a ticket to a driver who has been pulled over. Rather, most officers selectively enforce speed laws, ticketing only those who significantly exceed the limit or drive so recklessly that they endanger other drivers. As noted in Chapter 1, when police officers use their judgment in deciding which offenses to punish and which to ignore, they are said to be using *discretion*. Whether this discretion applies to speed limits or any other area of the law, it is a crucial aspect of policing.

Justification for Police Discretion

One of the ironies of law enforcement is that patrol officers—often the lowest-paid members of an agency with the least amount of authority—have the greatest amount of discretionary power. Part of the explanation for this is practical. Patrol officers spend most of the day on the streets, beyond the control of their supervisors. Usually, only two people are present when a patrol officer must make a decision: the officer and the possible wrongdoer. In most cases, the law enforcement officer has a great deal of freedom to take the action that he or she feels best corresponds to the situation.[63]

This is not to say that police discretion is misplaced. In general, courts have recognized that a patrol officer is in a unique position to be allowed discretionary powers:

- Police officers are considered trustworthy and are therefore assumed to make honest decisions, regardless of contradictory testimony by a suspect.

- Experience and training give officers the ability to determine whether certain activity poses a threat to society, and to take any reasonable action necessary to investigate or prevent such activity.
- Due to the nature of their jobs, police officers are extremely knowledgeable in human, and by extension criminal, behavior.
- Police officers may find themselves in danger of personal, physical harm and must be allowed to take reasonable and necessary steps to protect themselves.[64]

Dr. Anthony J. Pinizzotto, a psychologist with the FBI, and Charles E. Miller, an instructor in the bureau's Criminal Justice Information Services Division, take the justification for discretion one step further, arguing that many police officers have a "sixth sense" that helps them handle on-the-job challenges. Pinizzotto and Miller believe that although "intuitive policing" is often difficult to explain to those outside law enforcement, it is a crucial part of policing and should not be discouraged by civilian administrators.[65]

Making the Decision

In deciding how to apply the law to any particular situation, police officers generally consider three factors. First, and most important, is the nature of the criminal act. The less serious a crime, the more likely a police officer is to ignore it. A person driving 60 miles per hour in a 55-miles-per-hour zone, for example, is much less likely to be ticketed than someone doing 80 miles per hour. A second factor often considered is the attitude of the wrongdoer toward the officer. A motorist who is belligerent toward a highway patrol officer is much more likely to be ticketed than one who is contrite and apologetic. Third, departmental policy can place limits on discretion.[66] If a police chief decides that all motorists who exceed the speed limit by 10 miles will be ticketed, that policy will influence the patrol officer's decisions.

One of the most controversial areas of police discretion is the decision of whether to engage in a high-speed pursuit of a fleeing suspect. Although such drastic action is often necessary, the results can be tragic: between 1994 and 2002, police chases caused 3,146 deaths, one-third of which involved drivers of other cars or pedestrians who were present merely as "innocent bystanders."[67] As a result, according to the U.S. Department of Justice, more than 90 percent of the nation's local police departments have implemented police pursuit policies, with 57 percent restricting the discretion of officers to engage in a high-speed chase.[68] (For a discussion of another area where police discretion has been limited, see the chapter-ending *Criminal Justice in Action* feature starting on the next page.)

The Police and Domestic Violence

A factor that often influences police discretion is the relationship between the person committing the criminal act and the victim. The closer this relationship, the less likely many police officers are to respond to the victim's complaints and arrest the wrongdoer.[69] This tendency is often evident in police action (or lack thereof) concerning *domestic violence*. The statistics surrounding this crime speak volumes as to the extent of the problem in the United States. According to the National Violence Against Women Survey, of the estimated 5.9 million physical assaults against women that occur each year, current or former husbands, cohabiting partners, or dates commit 76 percent.[70] The U.S. Department of Justice has found that about one-third of all female homicide victims are killed by a husband, former husband, or boyfriend.[71] In all, intimate partner violence causes more than 2 million injuries each year to American women aged eighteen and over.[72] For most of this nation's history, the police role in domestic violence was limited to "calming" the situation, a short-term response that did little to prevent future violence. Today, as we shall see in this feature, more is expected.

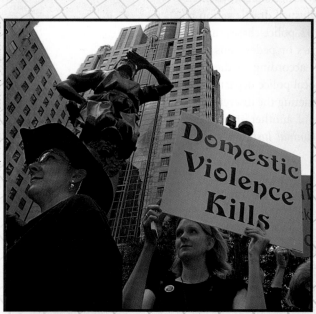

Women in Charlotte, North Carolina, take part in a silent march to mark the start of Domestic Violence Awareness Week. Pressure from activist citizens played a large role in the passage of state mandatory arrest laws for those who commit domestic violence.

The Problem: Lack of Police Involvement in "Family Matters"

As we will discuss in more detail in Chapter 7, police have a great deal of discretion in deciding whether to make an arrest. Basically, if a police officer has good reason (known as "probable cause") to believe that a person has committed a crime or is about to commit a crime, that officer can arrest the suspect.

Historically, police officers have been hesitant to make arrests when the dispute involves a "family matter," even when faced with strong evidence that domestic violence has taken place. This hesitancy has been obvious in studies such as the one conducted by James J. Fyfe of Temple University, David Klinger of the University of Houston, and Jeanne Flavin of Fordham University with regard to the Chester (Pennsylvania) Police Department.[73] The researchers found that Chester police were less likely to arrest male felony assailants who had attacked former or present female partners than other males who had committed similarly violent acts against strangers. Among the cases that did not lead to arrests were 4 attacks on domestic partners with guns, 38 attacks involving cutting instruments (including one with an ax), and 27 attacks with blunt instruments such as baseball bats or hammers. In one incident that did not result in arrest, a woman was held by her feet over a second-floor landing and dropped on her head.

A number of factors have been considered to explain this leniency. Many police officers see domestic violence cases as the responsibility of social-service providers, not law enforcement officers. Furthermore, officers are often uncomfortable with the intensely private nature of domestic disputes.[74] Finally, even when a police officer does arrest the abuser, the victim often chooses to drop the charges.

The Response: Mandatory Arrest Policies

Whatever the reasons for this reluctance to arrest domestic abusers, many jurisdictions have responded by severely limiting police discretion in domestic violence cases. Today, 72 percent of police departments have *mandatory arrest policies*, under which a police officer *must* arrest a person who has battered a spouse or domestic partner. No discretion in involved.[75]

Several early studies encouraged the implementation of these policies. In the landmark Minneapolis Domestic

Violence Experiment of 1983, the Minneapolis Police Department and Professors Lawrence Sherman and Richard Berk attempted to determine the consequences of police inaction in domestic violence cases. The researchers found that the most effective deterrent to repeat incidents of battering was the arrest of the batterer.[76] A similar project in Duluth, Minnesota, had similar results, with rates of rearrest of domestic abusers dropping to levels as low as 16 percent seven to twelve months after the initial arrest.[77]

The theory behind mandatory arrest policies is relatively straightforward: they act as a deterrent to criminal behavior. Costs are imposed on a person who is arrested. He or she must go to court and face the possibility of time in jail. Arrest may also lead to humiliation, loss of a job, and separation from family and friends. To avoid these unpleasant consequences, the argument goes, potential abusers will not act in a manner that increases the risk that they will be arrested.

Questioning Mandatory Arrests

Despite the popularity of mandatory arrest policies, not all of the evidence supports limiting police discretion in this manner. The National Institute of Justice commissioned studies in six other cities to verify the findings of the Minneapolis experiment. In only one of the sites—Miami, Florida—were researchers able to match the Minneapolis results.[78]

More troubling are findings by Professor Sherman that led him to conclude that "mandatory arrests in domestic violence cases may cause more violence against women in the long run."[79] After completing a research project in Milwaukee, Wisconsin, Sherman found that while arrest deterred employed men from committing domestic violence, being arrested increased repeat violence by 44 percent in unemployed men.[80] Thus, it seems that only those who have "more to lose" by being arrested (such as their jobs, standing in the community, and so on) are likely to be deterred by arrest. As Sherman noted, "Mandatory arrest puts us in the moral dilemma of reducing violence against women who are relatively well off [living with or married to an employed assailant], at the price of increasing violence against women whose abusers are unemployed."[81]

A Return to Discretion?

Mandatory arrest policies also raise other questions. For the most part, the police rely on the victim to report incidents of domestic abuse. Under certain circumstances, the risk that the abuser will be arrested may actually keep the victim from calling the police. A victim in a low-income family might not want to lose the wages that the abuser provides. Similarly, immigrant victims might not want to run the risk that they or their abusers will be deported.[82]

Furthermore, what if a victim uses force to protect himself or herself against an abuser? Statistics show that in jurisdictions with mandatory arrest policies, arrests of women under domestic abuse charges have increased dramatically. These women may be less willing to report domestic violence in the future, fearing that they themselves will be arrested again for "abusing" their attackers in self-defense.[83]

Finally, research shows that most domestic violence suspects do not continue to harm intimate partners, whether they are arrested or not. As with other types of crimes, a relatively small number of high-rate repeat offenders are largely responsible for the problem. Consequently, any policy that requires the arrest of *all* suspects would appear to be a poor use of a police department's limited resources. Instead, law enforcement efforts should focus on protecting those persons most at risk because of a particularly dangerous spouse or partner.[84]

To reduce some of the harsher effects of mandatory arrest policies and resolve some of these inconsistencies, Professors Sherman and Berk favor a policy of "presumption of arrest." In other words, after finding evidence of domestic violence, police should make an arrest unless there are "good, clear reasons why an arrest would be counterproductive."[85] Of course, it would be up to the police officers to determine whether these "good, clear reasons" exist, in effect returning to them the ability and the responsibility of using discretion to make the final decision.

Making Sense of Police Discretion and Domestic Violence

1 What reasons can be given to support widespread police discretion in general? What reasons can be given to limit police discretion in general?

2 Why might police officers welcome mandatory arrest policies or any other limitation on their discretionary abilities?

3 Can you think of any other reasons why a victim might *not* call the police if she or he was sure that it would result in the arrest of the abuser?

Chapter Summary

1 Describe the first systems of law enforcement in colonial America. Constables and night watchmen were drawn from the ranks of ordinary citizens. Each colony had a sheriff in each county who selected juries and managed incarcerations. Local citizens assisted sheriffs in peace-keeping duties.

2 Tell how the patronage system affected policing. During the political era of policing (1840–1930), bribes paid by citizens and business owners often went into the coffers of the local political party. This became known as the patronage system.

3 Indicate the results of the Wickersham Commission. The Wickersham Commission of 1929 called for reform to eliminate police brutality and the corrupting influence of politics. The result was the professionalization of American police, sometimes called the progressive era in American policing. Potential police officers began to be trained in institutes of higher learning. Another result was the increased use of technology in police work.

4 List five main types of law enforcement agencies. (a) Municipal police departments; (b) sheriffs' departments; (c) special police agencies, such as those limited to school protection or airport security; (d) state police departments (in all states except Hawaii); and (e) federal law enforcement agencies.

5 List some of the most important law enforcement agencies under the control of the Department of Homeland Security. (a) The Directorate of Customs and Border Security, which oversees U.S. Customs and Border Protection, U.S. Immigration and Customs Enforcement, the U.S. Border Patrol, and the U.S. Customs Service; and (b) the U.S. Secret Service.

6 Identify the six investigative priorities of the FBI. (a) Terrorism, (b) organized crime, (c) cyber crime, (d) foreign intelligence operations in the United States, (e) federal drug offenses, and (f) white-collar crime.

7 Analyze the importance of private security today. In the United States, businesses and citizens spend $12 billion a year on private security, more than double the amount spent on public law enforcement. Heightened fear of crime and increased crime in the workplace have fueled the growth in spending on private security.

8 List the four basic responsibilities of the police. (a) To enforce laws, (b) to provide services, (c) to prevent crime, and (d) to preserve the peace.

9 Indicate why patrol officers are allowed discretionary powers. Police officers are considered trustworthy and able to make honest decisions. They have experience and training. They are knowledgeable in criminal behavior. Finally, they must be able to have the discretion to reasonably protect themselves.

10 Explain how some jurisdictions have reacted to perceived leniency to perpetrators of domestic violence. Some jurisdictions have instituted mandatory arrest policies, requiring a police officer to arrest a person who has battered a spouse or domestic partner. Such policies eliminate police officers' discretion.

STORIES FROM THE STREET

Go to the *Stories from the Street* feature at **www.cjinaction.com** to hear Larry Gaines tell insightful stories related to this chapter and his experiences in the field.

Key Terms

coroner 136
Federal Bureau of
  ✓ Investigation (FBI) 142

justice of the peace 129
patronage system 131
private security 145

professional model 132
sheriff 135
shire-reeve 129

tithing system 129

Questions for Critical Analysis

1 What was the major problem faced by the earliest formal American police departments? Why did it occur?

2 Increased professionalism in police forces has been made possible by two-way radios, telephones, and automobiles. In what way has society *not* benefited from this increased professionalism? Explain your answer.

3 The latest era in policing has been called the community era and dates from the 1980s. How does this "new" era differ from the era of professionalism?

4 To what extent are state police complementary to, rather than substitutes for, local law enforcement agencies?

5 What economic and security concerns does the U.S. Customs Service need to balance, and how does it do so?

6 Besides the FBI's six principal investigative priorities, how does that agency benefit local policing units?

7 Why do experts believe that the private security industry will continue to grow for the foreseeable future?

8 Which of the four basic responsibilities of the police do you think is most important? Why?

9 Is it ever possible to completely eliminate discretion in policing? Explain.

Test Preparation Online

Criminal JusticeNow

Go to **www.cjinaction.com** and click on *Criminal JusticeNow* for access to this powerful online study tool. You will get a *personalized study plan* based on your responses to a diagnostic pretest. Once you have mastered the material with the help of interactive learning tools, video clips with questions, an integrated e-book, and more, you can take a posttest to confirm you are ready to move on to the next chapter.

Book Companion Web Site

At the book companion Web site (**www.cjinaction.com**), you will find many resources in addition to *Criminal JusticeNow* to aid you in studying for your exams. For example, under *Chapter Resources*, you will find the *Chapter Outline, Chapter Summary, Flashcards, Glossary, Learning Objectives, Lecture Presentations, Concept Builder, Essay Questions,* and a *Tutorial Chapter Quiz.* You can also test yourself with interactive *Online Reviews* of each chapter section. Check out the *Web Links* to access the Web sites mentioned in the text, as well as many others. You can also access recent perspectives by clicking on *CJ in the News* and *Terrorism Update* under *Course Resources.*

Suggested Readings

Powers, Richard G., *Broken: The Troubled Past and Uncertain Future of the FBI*, New York: Free Press, 2004. Following the terrorist attacks of September 11, 2001, no law enforcement agency came under more criticism than the FBI. In this book, popular historian Powers tries to explain how the bureau's institutional culture, fostered over years of political intrigue and infighting, hindered its abilities to detect the looming threat of terrorism. Though *Broken* is not an outright attack on the FBI, it does highlight the agency's many flaws and raises numerous questions as to whether America's foremost federal crime-fighting unit should be allowed to continue in its present form.

Wadman, Robert C., and William Thomas Allison, *To Protect and Serve: A History of Police in America*, Upper Saddle River, NJ: Prentice Hall, 2003. This book offers a comprehensive and readable look at the development of law enforcement in the United States. In particular, it focuses on the challenge of maintaining law and order in a democratic society, a task that American law enforcement agencies have been dealing with since the earliest days of the nation. The authors also provide a strong survey of the recent history of our police forces, from the increased emphasis on professionalism, to police and technology, to the main issues facing law enforcement in the twenty-first century.

Notes

1. M. K. Nalla and G. R. Newman, "Is White-Collar Crime Policing, Policing?" *Policing and Society* 3 (1994), 304.
2. Richard Maxwell Brown, "Vigilante Policing," in *Thinking about Police*, ed. Carl Klockars and Stephen Mastrofski (New York: McGraw-Hill, 1990), 66.
3. Peter K. Manning, *Police Work* (Cambridge, MA: MIT Press, 1977), 82.
4. Carol S. Steiker, "Second Thoughts about First Principles," *Harvard Law Review* 107 (1994), 820.
5. Lawrence M. Friedman, *Crime and Punishment in American History* (New York: Basic Books, 1993), 29.
6. Mark H. Moore and George L. Kelling, "'To Serve and Protect': Learning from Police History," *Public Interest* 70 (1983), 53.
7. Samuel Walker, *The Police in America: An Introduction* (New York: McGraw-Hill, 1983), 7.
8. Moore and Kelling, 54.
9. Mark H. Haller, "Chicago Cops, 1890–1925," in *Thinking about Police*, ed. Carl Klockars and Stephen Mastrofski (New York: McGraw-Hill, 1990), 90.
10. William J. Bopp and Donald O. Shultz, *A Short History of American Law Enforcement* (Springfield, IL: Charles C Thomas, 1977), 109–110.
11. Roger G. Dunham and Geoffrey P. Alpert, *Critical Issues in Policing: Contemporary Issues* (Prospect Heights, IL: Waveland Press, 1989).
12. National Advisory Commission on Civil Disorders, *Report* (Washington, D.C.: U.S. Government Printing Office, 1968), 157–160.
13. 18 U.S.C.A. Sections 2510–2521.
14. Jayne Seagrave, "Defining Community Policing," *American Journal of Police* 1 (1996), 1–22.
15. Federal Bureau of Investigation, *Crime in the United States, 2004* (Washington, D.C.: U.S. Department of Justice, 2005), 369.
16. *Ibid.*
17. Matthew J. Hickman and Brian A. Reaves, *Local Police Departments, 2000* (Washington, D.C.: U.S. Department of Justice, January 2003), 2.
18. G. Robert Blakey, "Federal Criminal Law," *Hastings Law Journal* 46 (April 1995), 1175.
19. Vern L. Folley, *American Law Enforcement* (Boston: Allyn & Bacon, 1980), 228.
20. Matthew J. Hickman and Brian A. Reaves, *Sheriffs' Offices, 2000* (Washington, D.C.: U.S. Department of Justice, January 2003), 2.
21. *Ibid.*, 10–14.
22. *Black's Law Dictionary*, 982.
23. Robert Borkenstein, "Police: State Police," *Encyclopedia of Crime and Justice*, ed. Sanford H. Kadish (New York: Free Press, 1983), 1131.
24. Brian A. Reaves and Lynn M. Bauer, *Federal Law Enforcement Officers, 2002* (Washington, D.C.: U.S. Department of Justice, August 2003), 1.
25. Pub. L. No. 107-296, 116 Stat. 2135.
26. "A New Look at USA's Porous Borders," *Law Enforcement News* (December 15–31, 2001), 8.

27. Press Release, "U.S. Customs and Border Protection Made Over 56,000 Illegal Drug Seizures, Nearly 2.2 Million Pounds, in FY2004," U.S Customs and Border Protection (January 11, 2005); and Press Release, "FY 2004: U.S. Customs and Border Protection Apprehends Large Amount of Narcotics, Thousands of Undocumented Migrants," U.S. Customs and Border Protection (January 18, 2005).

28. Reaves and Bauer, 5.

29. *Yearbook of Immigration Statistics: 2003* (Washington, D.C.: U.S. Department of Homeland Security, 2004), Tables 35, 38.

30. Tim Weiner, "Border Customs Agents Are Pushed to the Limit," *New York Times* (July 25, 2002), A14.

31. "Feds Have a Plan if Terrorists Strike," *UPI Online* (February 19, 1998).

32. Pub. L. No. 91-513, 84 Stat. 1242 (1970), codified as amended at 21 U.S.C. Section 801 (1994).

33. Jerry Seper, "U.S. Breaks Up International Drug Ring," *Washington Times* (February 16, 2005), A06.

34. **http://www.usdoj.gov/marshals/factsheets/general.htm**.

35. Elizabeth E. Joh, "The Paradox of Private Policing," *Journal of Criminal Law and Criminology* (Fall 2004), 49.

36. John B. Owens, "Westec Story: Gated Communities and the Fourth Amendment," *American Criminal Law Review* (Spring 1997), 1138.

37. Cal. Penal Code Section 837 (West 1995).

38. Bruce L. Benson, "Guns, Crime, and Safety," *Journal of Law and Economics* (October 2001), 725.

39. "Security Guards Won't Face Criminal Charges in Death outside Strip Night Club," *Las Vegas Review-Journal* (January 24, 2005), 2B.

40. See **http://www.seiu.org/building/security/legislation/security_report_card/allstates_report.cfm**.

41. Jeremy Bagott, "Security Standards Putting Public at Risk," *Chicago Tribune* (February 24, 2003), 15.

42. Brock N. Meeks, "Are 'Rent-a-Cops' Threatening Security?" *MSNBC Online* (March 9, 2005).

43. Mimi Hall, "Private Security Guards: Homeland Defense's Weak Link," *USA Today* (January 23, 2003), A1.

44. Meeks.

45. "Don Walker, CPP, Former President of ASIS International, Testifies before U.S. House of Representatives' Subcommittee on Crime, Terrorism and Homeland Security," *Business Wire* (March 31, 2004).

46. Pub. L. 108-458, Section 6402(d)(2) (2004).

47. William C. Cunningham, John J. Strauchs, and Clifford W. Van Meter, *The Hallcrest Report II: Private Security Trends, 1970 to 2000* (Boston: Butterworth-Heinemann, 1990), 236.

48. Cameron Conant, "Private Security Firms See Improved Status, Job Growth in Recent Months," *Grand Rapids Press* (December 15, 2001), D4.

49. Bagott, 15.

50. Ronnie L. Paynter, "Privatization: Something to Think About?" *Law Enforcement Technology* (September 2000), 6.

51. Ronald L. Soble, "Private Firms on Patrol: Security Is Big Business," *Los Angeles Times* (May 21, 1985), Section 1, page 1.

52. Egon Bittner, *The Functions of the Police in a Modern Society,* Public Health Service Publication No. 2059 (Chevy Chase, MD: National Institute of Mental Health, 1970), 38–44.

53. Carl Klockars, "The Rhetoric of Community Policing," in *Community Policing: Rhetoric or Reality,* ed. Jack Greene and Stephen Mastrofski (New York: Praeger Publishers, 1991), 244.

54. Jack R. Greene and Carl B. Klockars, "What Do Police Do?" in *Thinking about Police,* 2d ed., ed. Carl B. Klockars and Stephen B. Mastrofski (New York: McGraw-Hill, 1991), 273–284.

55. John S. Dempsey and Linda S. Forst, *An Introduction to Policing,* 3d ed. (Belmont, CA: Thomson Wadsworth, 2005), 110.

56. *Crime in the United States, 2004,* Table 29, page 280.

57. Reprinted in *Police Chief* (January 1990), 18.

58. Eric J. Scott, *Calls for Service: Citizen Demand and Initial Police Response* (Washington, D.C.: U.S. Government Printing Office, 1981), 28–30.

59. Jerome H. Skolnick, "Police: The New Professionals," *New Society* (September 5, 1986), 9–11.

60. Klockars, 250.

61. James Q. Wilson, *Varieties of Police Behavior: The Management of Law and Order in Eight Communities* (Cambridge, MA: Harvard University Press, 1968).

62. James Q. Wilson and George L. Kelling, "Broken Windows," *Atlantic Monthly* (March 1982), 29.

63. A. J. Reiss, Jr., "Police Organization in the Twentieth Century," in *Modern Policing,* ed. Michael Tonry and Norval Morris (Chicago: University of Chicago Press, 1992), 51–98.

64. C. E. Pratt, "Police Discretion," *Law and Order* (March 1992), 99–100.

65. "More than a Hunch," *Law Enforcement News* (September 2004), 1.

66. Herbert Jacob, *Urban Justice* (Boston: Little, Brown, 1973), 27.

67. Frederick Rivara and Chris Mack, "Motor Vehicle Crash Deaths Related to Police Pursuits in the United States," *Injury Prevention* (April 2004), 93–95.

68. Hickman and Reaves, 21.

69. Stephen D. Mastrofski, Jeffrey B. Snipes, Roger B. Parks, and Christopher D. Maxwell, "The Helping Hand of the Law: Police Control of Citizens on Request," *Criminology* 38 (May 2000), 307.

70. "Intimate Partner Violence: Fact Sheet," Centers for Disease Control and Prevention Web site, at **http://www.cdc.gov/ncipc/factsheets/ipvfacts.htm**.

71. Callie Marie Rennison, *Intimate Partner Violence, 1993–2001* (Washington, D.C.: U.S. Department of Justice, February 2003), 1.

72. "Intimate Partner Violence: Fact Sheet."

73. James J. Fyfe, David A. Klinger, and Jeanne M. Flavin, "Differential Police Treatment of Male-on-Female Spousal Violence," *Criminology* 35 (August 1997), 455–473.

74. L. Craig Parker, Robert D. Meier, and Lynn Hunt Monahan, *Interpersonal Psychology for Criminal Justice* (St. Paul, MN: West Publishing Co., 1989), 113.

75. Hickman and Reaves, 67.

76. Lawrence W. Sherman and Ellen G. Cohn, "The Impact of Research on Legal Policy: The Minneapolis Domestic Violence Experiment," *Law and Society Review* 23 (1989), 261.

77. Ellen Pence, "The Duluth Domestic Abuse Intervention Project," *Hamline Law Review* 6 (1983), 258.

78. J. David Hirschel and Ira W. Hutchison, "Realities and Implications of the Charlotte Spousal Abuse Experiment," in *Do Arrests and Restraining Orders Work?* ed. Eve S. Buzawa and Carl G. Buzawa (Thousand Oaks, CA: Sage Publications, 1996), 54–55.

79. Franklyn W. Dunford *et al.,* "The Role of Arrest in Domestic Assault: The Omaha Police Experiment," *Criminology* 28 (1990), 167.

80. *Ibid.*

81. Quoted in Roger Worthington, "Value of Mandatory Arrest for Women Beaters Questioned," *Chicago Tribune* (November 19, 1991), C5.

82. Donna Coker, "Shifting Power for Battered Women: Law, Material Resources, and Poor Women of Color," *University of California at Davis Law Review* (Summer 2000), 1042.

83. Cecelia M. Expenoza, "No Relief for the Weary: VAWA Relief Denied for Battered Immigrants," *Marquette Law Review* 83 (1999), 163.

84. Christopher D. Maxwell, Joel H. Garner, and Jeffrey A. Fagan, "The Effect of Arrest on Intimate Partner Violence: New Evidence," in *Domestic Violence Research: Summaries for Justice Professionals* (Washington, D.C.: U.S. Department of Justice, December 2003), 36–37.

85. Lawrence W. Sherman and Richard A. Berk, "The Specific Deterrence Effects of Arrest for Domestic Assault," *American Society Review* 49 (1984), 270.

CHAPTER SIX

Challenges to Effective Policing

Chapter outline

- Recruitment and Training: Becoming a Police Officer
- Police Organization
- Refocusing on the Community
- Law Enforcement in the Field
- "Us versus Them": Issues in Modern Policing
- Police Ethics
- Criminal Justice in Action—The DNA Revolution

Chapter objectives

After reading this chapter, you should be able to:

1 Identify the differences between the police academy and field training as learning tools for recruits.
2 Explain some of the benefits of a culturally diverse police force.
3 Describe the theory behind a differential response strategy of responding to calls for service.
4 Explain community policing and its strategies.
5 Describe two types of problem-solving policing.
6 List the three primary purposes of police patrol.
7 Indicate some investigation strategies that are considered aggressive.
8 Determine when police officers are justified in using deadly force.
9 Identify the three traditional forms of police corruption.
10 Explain what an ethical dilemma is and name four categories of ethical dilemmas typically facing a police officer.

Criminal JusticeNow

Optimize your study time and master key chapter concepts with *Criminal JusticeNow*, an online study tool that provides you with a *personalized study plan*. Check out the "Test Preparation Online" section at the end of the chapter for additional information.

LAPD Blues

Most citizens of South Los Angeles agreed that eighth-grader Devin Brown should not have been driving a stolen car at 4 o'clock in the morning on February 6, 2005. What happened after patrol officers saw the maroon Toyota Camry run a red light, however, had members of this predominantly black community frustrated and furious with local law enforcement—again.

On spotting the traffic infraction, Los Angeles Police Department (LAPD) officers Steve Garcia and Dana Grant tried to pull Brown over. After a three-minute chase, the African American boy apparently lost control of the automobile, and it skidded up onto a sidewalk. The officers parked their car behind the Toyota, which suddenly reversed direction and crashed against the police cruiser. Officer Garcia then fired ten shots at Brown, killing him in the process.

Devin's death came only a week after prosecutors decided not to file criminal charges against an LAPD officer who had been captured on videotape striking an African American man with a heavy aluminum flashlight. A month earlier, a jury found that two other local police officers had been wrongfully fired after slamming a black teenager on the hood of a patrol car—another

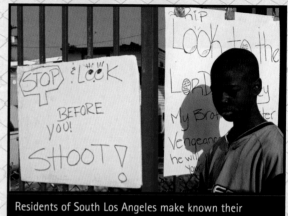

Residents of South Los Angeles make known their displeasure with local law enforcement tactics in the wake of the 2005 police shooting of eighth-grader Devin Brown.

incident caught on video. Although there was no reported violence in the wake of Brown's shooting, memories of the 1992 Los Angeles riots are still strong in the community. That show of collective aggression erupted after four white police officers were acquitted on charges stemming from the beating of black motorist Rodney King. "They put these [police officers] out here who they know don't like us," said one resident who was taking part in a demonstration against the LAPD. Even if Brown "was doing wrong," she added, "that doesn't give them the right to kill him that way."

A community is in trouble

when people start referring to themselves as "us" and law enforcement agents as "them." Ideally, police would like to be seen as an integral part of society, with the same goals of crime prevention and public safety as everybody else. When the relationship between police officers and those they serve is marked by ill will and distrust, those goals will be very difficult to reach. At the time of Devin Brown's death, LAPD policy permitted officers to use their weapons to defend themselves or others from death or serious injury; it specifically allowed officers to consider a vehicle a deadly weapon.[1] Under the circumstances, Officer Garcia could have reasonably considered the moving Toyota a threat to his life, and there was no indication he was aware of the color of Brown's skin. Because of past incidents, however, many of the city's African American residents were absolutely unwilling to give Garcia the benefit of the doubt.

Most Americans cannot imagine the on-the-job situations that the average law enforcement agent faces daily. As James Fyfe of Temple University explains, by telling police officers that we expect them to eradicate crime, we are putting them in a "no win war." Like some soldiers in such combat, Fyfe adds, "they commit atrocities."[2] In this chapter, we will examine some of these "atrocities," such as police brutality and corruption. We will also consider the possible causes of police misconduct and review the steps that are being taken to limit these problems. Our discussion begins with a look at how a person becomes a police officer—a process that can have a significant impact on the quality of law enforcement in communities such as South Los Angeles and in the United States as a whole.

RECRUITMENT AND TRAINING: BECOMING A POLICE OFFICER

In 1961, police expert James H. Chenoweth commented that the methods used to hire police officers had changed little since 1829 when the Metropolitan Police of London was created.[3] The past forty-five years, however, have seen a number of improvements on the original model. Efforts have been made to diversify police rolls, and recruits in most police departments undergo a substantial array of tests and screens—discussed below—to determine their aptitude. Furthermore, annual starting salaries of up to $50,000, along with the opportunities offered by an interesting profession in the public service field, have attracted a wide variety of applicants to police work. (To learn what a police officer can expect to earn in his or her first year on the job, see Figure 6.1.)

Basic Requirements

The selection process involves a number of steps, and each police department has a different method of choosing candidates. Most agencies, however, require at a minimum that a police officer:

- Be a U.S. citizen.
- Not have been convicted of a felony.

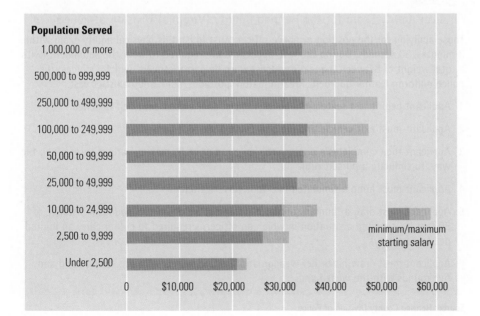

FIGURE 6.1

Average Annual Salary for Entry-Level Officers by Size of Population Served

Source: Matthew J. Hickman and Brian A. Reaves, *Local Police Departments 2000* (Washington, D.C.: U.S. Department of Justice, January 2003), Table 14, page 8.

- Have or be eligible to have a driver's license in the state where the department is located.
- Be at least twenty-one years of age.
- Meet weight and eyesight requirements.

Beyond these minimum requirements, police departments usually engage in extensive background checks, including drug tests; a review of the applicant's educational, military, and driving records; credit checks; interviews with spouses, acquaintances, and previous employers; and a Federal Bureau of Investigation (FBI) search to determine whether the applicant has been convicted of any criminal acts.[4] Police agencies generally require certain physical attributes in applicants: normally, they must be able to pass a physical agility or fitness test. (For an example of one such test, see Figure 6.2.)

Age is also a factor, as few departments will accept candidates younger than twenty-one years of age or older than forty-five. In some departments, the applicant must take a polygraph (lie-detector) exam in conjunction with the background check. The results of the polygraph exam are often compared to the information from the background check to ensure that the applicant has not been deceptive. According to one study, around 20 percent of the nearly 70,000 persons who apply for police jobs annually are rejected because they lied during the screening process.[5]

Educational Requirements One of the most dramatic differences between today's police recruits and those of several generations ago is their level of education. In the 1920s, when August Vollmer began promoting the need for higher education in police officers, few had attended college. By the 1990s, 65 percent of police officers had some college credits and 25 percent were college graduates.[6] Today, 83 percent of all local police departments require at least a high school diploma, and 8 percent require a degree from a two-year college.[7] Recruits with college or university experience are generally thought to have an advantage in hiring and promotion.

Not all police observers believe, however, that education is a necessity for police officers. In the words of one police officer, "effective street cops learn their skills on the job, not in a classroom."[8] By emphasizing a college degree, say some, police departments discourage those who would make solid officers but lack the education necessary to apply for positions in law enforcement.

The **Oakland Police Academy,** located in Auburn Hills, Michigan, is a full-service police training facility. To visit its Web site, click on *Web Links* under *Chapter Resources* at **www.cjinaction.com**.

FIGURE 6.2

Physical Agility Exam for the Henrico County (Virginia) Division of Police

Those applying for the position of police officer must finish this physical agility exam within 3 minutes, 30 seconds. During the test, applicants are required to wear the equipment (with a total weight of between 9 and 13 pounds) worn by patrol officers, which includes: the police uniform; leather gun belt; firearm; baton; portable radio; and ballistics vest.

1 Applicant begins test seated in a police vehicle, door closed, seat belt fastened.

2 Applicant must exit vehicle and jump or climb a six-foot barrier.

3 Applicant then completes a one-quarter mile run or walk, making various turns along the way (to simulate a pursuit run).

4 Applicant must jump a simulated five-foot culvert/ditch.

5 Applicant must drag a "human simulator" (dummy) weighing 175 pounds a distance of 50 feet (to simulate a situation in which an officer is required to pull or carry an injured person to safety).

6 Applicant must draw his or her weapon and fire five rounds with the strong hand and five rounds with the weak hand.

Source: Henrico County Division of Police.

Training Almost every state requires that police recruits pass through a training period during which they are taught the basics of police work and are under constant observation by superiors. The training period usually has two components: the police academy and field training. On average, local police departments require 1,054 hours of training—637 hours in the classroom and 417 hours in the field.[9]

The *police academy,* run by either the state or a police agency, provides recruits with a controlled, militarized environment in which they receive their introduction to the world of the police officer. They are taught the laws of search, seizure, arrest, and interrogation; how and when to use weapons; the procedures of securing a crime scene and interviewing witnesses; first aid; self-defense; and other essentials of police work. About four in five police academies also provide terrorism-related training to teach recruits how to respond to terrorist incidents including those involving weapons of mass destruction.[10] Academy instructors evaluate the recruits' performance and send intermittent progress reports to police administrators.

Field training takes place outside the confines of the police academy. A recruit is paired with an experienced police officer known as a field training officer (FTO). The goal of field training is to help rookies apply the concepts they have learned in the academy "to the streets," with the FTO playing a supervisory role to make sure that nothing goes awry. According to many, the academy introduces recruits to the formal rules of police work, but field training gives the rookies their first taste of the informal rules. In fact, the initial advice to recruits from some FTOs is along the lines of "O.K., kid. Forget everything you learned in the academy. You're in the real world now." Nonetheless, the academy is a critical component in the learning process, as it provides rookies with a road map to the job.

> **Field Training**
> The segment of a police recruit's training in which he or she is removed from the classroom and placed on the beat, under the supervision of a senior officer.

Recruiting Members of Minority Groups and Women

For many years, the typical American police officer was white and male. As recently as 1968, African Americans represented only 5 percent of all sworn officers in the United States, and the percentage of "women in blue" was even less.[11] Only within the past twenty-five years has this situation been addressed, and only within the past decade have many police departments actively tried to recruit women, African Americans, Hispanics, Asian Americans, and other members of minority groups. An estimated 17 percent of the recruits who completed training in 2002 were female, and 27 percent were members of a minority group.[12]

Discrimination and the Law Initially, external pressures drove law enforcement agencies to take these steps. The 1964 Civil Rights Act and its 1972 amendments guaranteed minorities and women equal access to jobs in law enforcement, and the Equal Employment Opportunity Act of 1972 set the stage for affirmative action in hiring and promotion. Court decisions also played a role: in several cases in the 1970s, the United States Supreme Court ruled that police departments could be held in violation of federal law if their hiring and promotion policies were tainted by racial discrimination.[13]

The Benefits of a Culturally Diverse Police Force Not all of the efforts to increase minority representation in law enforcement are simply the result of orders from Congress and the Supreme Court. Many departments, particularly those in urban areas, have realized that a culturally diverse police force can offer a number of benefits, including improved community relations and higher levels of service.[14]

Recruits experience a training session at the New York Police Academy. Why are police academies an important part of the learning process for a new police officer?

Piotr Redlinski/CORBIS

For example, after a series of racially motivated riots in 1967, Detroit decided to institute quotas to increase its percentage of black police officers—which had been 5 percent in a city that was more than 50 percent African American. In defending itself during a court case that challenged the constitutionality of these quotas, the city argued that it needed a representative police force to fulfill its duties to the citizens of Detroit. The Sixth Circuit Court of Appeals agreed, noting that the presence of a "mostly white police force in minority communities can be a 'dangerous irritant' which can trigger" a destructive response.[15] In 1986, United States Supreme Court Justice John Paul Stevens agreed, stating that police administrators "might reasonably conclude that an integrated police force could develop a better relationship and thereby do a more effective job of maintaining law and order than a force composed of white officers."[16]

As efforts to recruit African Americans, Hispanics, and other minorities have improved, their numbers on the nation's police forces have grown steadily, if not dramatically. Minority representation as a whole increased from 17 percent in 1990 to 22.7 percent in 2000 (see Figure 6.3). The number of police officers who are African American rose from 10.5 percent to 11.7 percent, and the number of Hispanic or Latino officers increased from 5.2 percent to 8.3 percent.[17] Nevertheless, blacks, Hispanics and other minorities are still underrepresented as law enforcement personnel in most jurisdictions, including those metropolitan areas with large minority populations.[18]

Women in Policing If anything, the barriers against women in law enforcement have been greater than those facing racial and ethnic minorities. As of 1946, only 141 out of 417 American cities had any policewomen at all, and it was not until 1968 that a city—Indianapolis—had two female patrol officers on the force.[19] During the 1990s, however, the number of women in law enforcement increased by 59 percent to about 47,000 (though they still account for only 12.5 percent of sworn personnel).[20] In 2003 and 2004, four of the nation's largest cities—Boston, Detroit, Milwaukee, and San Francisco—named a woman to the post of police chief. (See the feature *CJ in Focus— Myth versus Reality: Women Make Bad Cops.*)

Unlike with members of minority groups, a law enforcement agency can legally discriminate against women in recruitment and hiring. Often, the instrument of this discrimination is the physical fitness test. In California, for example, by state law all applicants must scale a six-foot wall to be considered for a police job. Officials estimate that this requirement eliminates half the women who apply because they do not possess the physical strength to get over the wall.[21] Overall, agencies without a physical agility test have 31 percent more female police officers than those agencies that require such a test.[22]

In 2002, the Third Circuit Court of Appeals upheld a Pennsylvania law that requires transit police officers to run 1.5 miles in twelve minutes. Even though the effect of this test is to discriminate against female applicants, 93 percent of whom fail the test, the court ruled that the requirement is legal because it represents a reasonable "minimum qualification" that any applicant, regardless of gender, needs to be able to meet to serve the citizens of Pennsylvania.[23] Of course, police departments that value a diverse force may adjust their physical fitness tests to level the playing field. The Champaign (Illinois) Police Department, for example, requires male

FIGURE 6.3
Female and Minority Police Officers, 1990 and 2000

Source: Matthew J. Hickman and Brian A. Reaves, *Local Police Departments 2000* (Washington, D.C.: U.S. Department of Justice, January 2003), Figure 2, page 4.

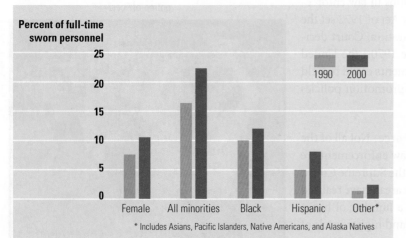

Percent of full-time sworn personnel

1990 2000

Female   All minorities   Black   Hispanic   Other*

* Includes Asians, Pacific Islanders, Native Americans, and Alaska Natives

Women Make Bad Cops

Since the formation of the earliest police departments in the nineteenth century, policing has been seen as "man's work." Only men were considered to have the physical strength necessary to deal with the dangers of the street.

THE MYTH

The perception that women are not physically strong enough to be effective law enforcement officers prevails both in the public mind and within police forces themselves. Criminologist Susan Martin has found that policewomen are under "constant pressure to demonstrate their competence and effectiveness vis-à-vis their male counterparts." One female police officer describes her experience:

Copyright © Dwayne Newton/PhotoEdit

Two members of the San Francisco (California) Police Department.

> I got a call. They send another male officer and then another male officer. The attitude is—get a *guy.* I'm there with the one male officer and when the other guy shows up, the first male officer says to the second, this is right in front of me—"I'm glad you came."

THE REALITY

A number of studies have shown, however, that policewomen can be as effective as men in most situations, and often more so. Citizens appear to prefer dealing with a female police officer rather than a male during service calls—especially those that involve domestic violence. In general, policewomen are less aggressive and more likely to reduce the potential for a violent situation by relying on verbal skills rather than their authority as law enforcement agents. According to a study conducted by the National Center for Women & Policing, payouts in lawsuits for claims of brutality and misconduct involving male officers exceed those involving females by a ratio of 43 to 1.

FOR CRITICAL ANALYSIS

Anecdotal evidence tells us that policewomen continue to face a great deal of bias from male police officers and that sexual harassment still occurs in many departments. What effect might a "male-dominated" police department have on attempts to recruit and keep women as law enforcement officers? What steps can the heads of police departments take to improve the situation?

---

applicants to run 1.5 miles in thirteen minutes and female applicants to complete the course in sixteen minutes.[24]

POLICE ORGANIZATION

Studies have shown that female police officers are particularly effective in the area of community relations.[25] Consequently, police administrators have an incentive to recruit more women, because "connecting" with the public has become an important organizational objective for law enforcement agencies. Police departments are indeed organizations, and like most organizations, they have missions, goals, structures, managers, workers, and clients.[26]

The model of the modern police department is bureaucratic. In a **bureaucracy,** formal rules govern an individual's actions and relationships with co-employees. The

Bureaucracy

A hierarchically structured administrative organization that carries out specific functions.

ultimate goal of any bureaucracy is to reach its maximum efficiency—in the case of a police department, to provide the best service for the community within the confines of its limited resources such as staff and budget. Although some police departments are experimenting with alternative structures based on a partnership between management and the officers in the field,[27] most continue to rely on the hierarchical structure described below.

The Structure of the Police Department

Each police department is organized according to its environment: the size of its jurisdiction, the type of crimes it must deal with, and the demographics of the population it must police. A police department in a racially diverse city often faces different challenges than a department in a homogeneous one. Geographic location also influences police organization. The make-up of the police department in Miami, Florida, for example, is partially determined by the fact that the city is a gateway for illegal drugs from Central and South America. The department directs a high percentage of its resources to special drug-fighting units and has formed cooperative partnerships with federal agencies such as the FBI and the U.S. Customs Service in an effort to stop the flow of narcotics and weapons into the South Florida area.

Whatever the size or location of a police department, it needs a clear rank structure and strict accountability to function properly.[28] One of the goals of the police reformers, especially beginning in the 1950s, was to lessen the corrupting influence of politicians. The result was a move toward a militaristic organization of police.[29] As you can see in Figure 6.4, a typical police department is based on a chain of command that leads from the police chief down through the various levels of the department. In this formalized structure, all persons are aware of their place in the chain and of their duties and responsibilities within the organization.

FIGURE 6.4

The Command Chain of the Lombard (Illinois) Police Department

The Lombard (Illinois) Police Department is made up of sixty-eight sworn law enforcement officers and thirty-two civilians. As you can see, the chain of command runs from the chief of police down to crossing guards and part-time secretaries.

Source: Lombard Police Department.

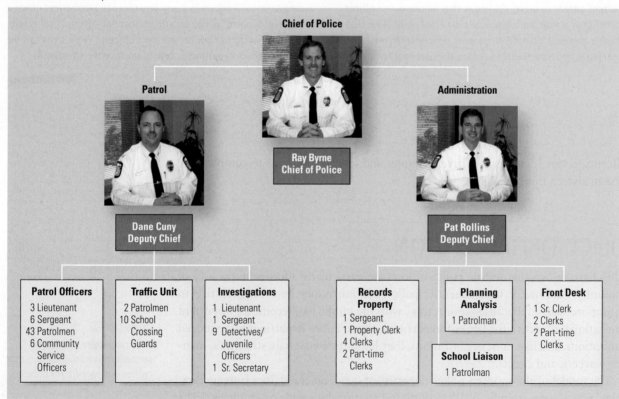

Chief of Police
Ray Byrne, Chief of Police

Patrol — Dane Cuny, Deputy Chief

Administration — Pat Rollins, Deputy Chief

Patrol Officers	Traffic Unit	Investigations	Records Property	Planning Analysis	Front Desk
3 Lieutenant	2 Patrolmen	1 Lieutenant	1 Sergeant	1 Patrolman	1 Sr. Clerk
6 Sergeant	10 School	1 Sergeant	1 Property Clerk		2 Clerks
43 Patrolmen	Crossing	9 Detectives/	4 Clerks	**School Liaison**	2 Part-time
6 Community	Guards	Juvenile	2 Part-time	1 Patrolman	Clerks
Service		Officers	Clerks		
Officers		1 Sr. Secretary			

Delegation of authority is a critical component of the chain of command, especially in larger departments. The chief of police delegates authority to division chiefs, who delegate authority to commanders, and so on down through the organization. This structure creates a situation in which nearly every member of a police department is directly accountable to a superior. As was the original goal of police reformers, these links encourage discipline and control and lessen the possibility that any individual police employee will have the unsupervised freedom to abuse her or his position.[30] In keeping with the need to delegate authority, police departments in large cities divide their jurisdictions into *precincts*. The precinct commander is then held responsible by his or her superiors at police headquarters for the performance of the officers in the precinct.

Striving for Efficiency

If the ultimate goal of a bureaucratic organization is efficiency, have police bureaucracies made departments more efficient? This question is difficult to answer. On the whole, any bureaucracy responds best to statistical measures. In the era of professional policing, the double yardsticks of statistical efficiency for police have been (1) response time and (2) arrest rates.

Response Time and Efficiency Though police do not like to think of themselves as being at "the beck and call" of citizens, that is essentially the *modus operandi* of many law enforcement officers. All departments practice **incident-driven policing,** in which calls for service are the primary instigators of action. Between 40 and 60 percent of police activity is the result of 911 calls or other citizen requests, which means that only about half of such activity is initiated by a police officer in the field.[31]

The speed with which the police respond to calls for service has traditionally been seen as a crucial aspect of crime fighting and crime prevention. The ideal scenario in incident-driven policing is as follows: a citizen sees a person committing a crime and calls 911; the police arrive quickly and catch the perpetrator in the act. Or, a citizen who is the victim of a crime, such as a mugging, calls 911 as soon as possible, and the police arrive to catch the mugger before she or he can flee the immediate area of the crime. Although, as we shall see, such scenarios are quite rare in real life, **response time,** or the time elapsed between the instant a call for service is received and the instant the police arrive on the scene, has become a benchmark for police efficiency.

Differential Response Many police departments have come to realize that overall response time is not as critical as response time for the most important calls. In Los Angeles, for example, the response time for "emergencies"—including shootings, knifings, and robberies—is 6.7 minutes. Urgent nonemergency calls such as car break-ins and other property crimes that do not involve any danger to life are answered in 10.5 minutes, and calls considered routine have a response time of more than 26 minutes.[32]

The Los Angeles police have instituted a **differential response** strategy, in which the department distinguishes

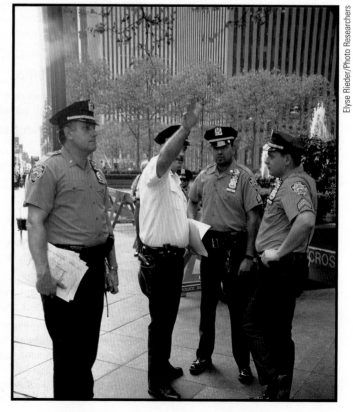

A lieutenant (in the white shirt) gives instructions to two sergeants. To the extreme left, a patrol officer appears to be awaiting instructions. How do the delegation of authority and the chain of command contribute to police efficiency?

Elyse Rieder/Photo Researchers

among different calls for service so that it can respond more quickly to the most serious incidents. Suppose, for example, that a police department receives two calls for service at the same time. The first caller reports that her house is in the process of being robbed, and the second says that he has returned home to find his automobile missing. If the department has instituted a differential response strategy, the robbery in progress—a "hot" crime—will receive immediate attention. The missing automobile—a "cold" crime that could have been committed several hours earlier—will receive attention "as time permits," and the caller may even be asked to make an appointment to come to the station. (See Figure 6.5 for possible responses to calls to a 911 operator.)

Another attempt to alleviate the pressures on 911 systems has been the introduction of the alternative number 311 for citizens who have nonemergency requests for police service. New York City implemented its 311 system in March of 2003, and within months it was receiving 17,000 calls a day and had reduced the load on the city's 911 system by 300 calls daily.[33] Today, more than twenty metropolitan areas have instituted 311 systems.[34] Although these programs have significantly reduced the workload of 911 operators, no evidence has been presented to date showing that they reduce response times for 911 emergency calls.[35]

Arrest Rates and Efficiency The other measure of police efficiency, arrest rates, also seems logical. The more arrests a police department makes, the fewer the number of criminals there should be on the streets of the community.

Again, practice does not necessarily follow theory. The amount of crime is not a function of arrest rates; self-reported surveys show that many, if not most, criminal

FIGURE 6.5

Putting the Theory of Differential Response into Action

Differential response strategies are based on a simple concept: treat emergencies like emergencies and nonemergencies like nonemergencies. As you see, calls for service that involve "hot crimes" will be dealt with immediately, while those that report "cold crimes" will be dealt with at some point in the future.

"Hot" Calls for Service—Immediate Response

Complaint to 911 Officer	Rationale
"I just got home from work, and I can see someone in my bedroom through the window."	Possibility that the intruder is committing a crime.
"My husband has a baseball bat, and he's says he's going to kill me."	Crime in progress.
"A woman in a green jacket just grabbed my purse and ran away."	Chances of catching the suspect are increased with immediate action.

"Cold" Calls for Service—Alternative Response

Complaint to 911 Officer	Rationale
"I got to my office about two hours ago, but I just noticed that the fax machine was stolen at some point during the night."	The crime occurred at least two hours earlier.
"The guy in the apartment above me has been selling pot for years, and I'm sick and tired of it."	Not an emergency situation.
"My husband came home late two nights ago with a black eye, and I finally got him to admit that he didn't run into a doorknob. Larry Smith smacked him."	Past crime with a known suspect who is unlikely to flee.

Source: Adapted from John S. Dempsey, *An Introduction to Policing*, 2d ed. (Belmont, CA: West/Wadsworth Publishing, 1999), Table 8.1, page 175.

acts do not lead to arrests. To make a generalization, police will never be able to make an arrest for *every* crime that is committed. Observers have offered other, more specific reasons for a possible disconnect between arrest rates and crime rates. One explanation is that, given the amount of paperwork each arrest forces on a police officer, more arrests mean less time for crime prevention.[36] Perhaps arrest rates and crime rates would prove more consistent if all arrests were made for serious crimes. But, as we have discussed, this is not the case. Most arrests are for misdemeanors, not felonies. Furthermore, arrests are poor predictors of incarceration: one study found that nearly sixty times more Americans are arrested than are sent to prison each year.[37]

In sum, it is difficult to measure the effectiveness of the police. Even crime rates are at least partially determined by elements beyond police control, such as the sociological, biological, and psychological factors discussed in Chapter 2. Hence, crime rates cannot be relied on as definitive indicators of the job a police department is doing.

REFOCUSING ON THE COMMUNITY

An additional measure of police effectiveness, which has only recently been recognized, is *citizen satisfaction*. As all businesspersons know, the customers are the most important people in any service industry (which includes police work), and the greater the effort to listen to customers' concerns, the greater their level of satisfaction will be. In analyzing the results of a foot patrol experiment in Flint, Michigan, in which the police department made a concerted effort to forge bonds with citizens, Robert Trojanowicz of Michigan State University found a significant increase in citizen confidence in police performance.[38]

This strategy of increasing police presence in the community has been part of, in the words of George Kelling, a "quiet revolution" in American law enforcement over the past two decades.[39] This revolution has been fueled by the emergence of two theories of police strategy, now combined under the umbrella term of *community policing*: community-oriented policing and problem-oriented policing. Though conceptually different, both theories are based on the philosophy that to prevent and control crime effectively, police need to form partnerships with members of the community.

Community Policing

For all its negative associations, the political era of policing (discussed in Chapter 5) did have characteristics that many observers have come to see as advantageous. During the nineteenth century, police were much more involved in the community than they were after the reforms. Police officers performed many duties that today are associated with social services, such as operating soup kitchens and providing lodging for homeless people. They also played a more direct role in keeping public order by "running in" drunks and intervening in minor disturbances.[40]

Return to the Community To a certain extent, **community policing** advocates a return to this understanding of the police mission. In general, community policing can be defined as an approach that promotes community-police partnerships, proactive problem solving, and community engagement to address issues such as fear of crime and the causes of crime in a particular area.[41] In the reform era, the police were, in a sense, detached from the community. They did their jobs to the best of their ability, but were more concerned with making arrests or speedily answering calls for service than learning about the problems or concerns of the citizenry. In their efforts to eliminate police corruption, administrators put more emphasis on segregating the police from the

Community Policing
A policing philosophy that emphasizes community support for and cooperation with the police in preventing crime. Community policing stresses a police role that is less centralized and more proactive than reform-era policing strategies.

public than on cooperatively working with citizens to resolve community problems. Under community policing, patrol officers have much more freedom to improvise. They are expected to develop personal relationships with residents and to encourage those residents to become involved in making the community a safer place. (See *Mastering Concepts—The Professional Model of Policing versus Community Policing.*)

Thinking Locally Local initiatives have played a significant role in the community era of policing. Responding to citizen requests, law enforcement administrators in Worcester, Massachusetts, implemented a "split-force" police department in early 2005.[42] Officers of one branch respond to 911 service calls, while those assigned to the other, called the Community Impact Division, are not tied to radio calls and are therefore "free to interact with the community."[43] Community Impact officers patrol specific areas on foot or bicycle and are expected to meet frequently with crime-watch groups and school administrators to discuss their crime-related problems.

The Columbia (South Carolina) Police Department has taken the idea of community involvement to the extreme with its adoption of the Japanese *koban* system. A *koban* is a mini–police station where police officers live as well as work. The initial *koban* in Columbia was set up more than a decade ago on Lady Street, which runs through one of the city's high-crime neighborhoods. Two volunteer police officers stay rent free in the upper floor of the building, while the lower floor is a police station/community center. Residents are encouraged to come to the *koban* to report crimes, and it also serves as a work station for social and educational services. According to Charles Austin, Columbia's police chief, the *koban* is a sign to residents that the police have "a vested stake in the community."[44]

MASTERING CONCEPTS

The Professional Model of Policing versus Community Policing

The past sixty years have seen two dominant trends in the style of American policing. The first was the professional model, designed to reduce corruption and improve performance by emphasizing efficiency. The second, community policing, was a reaction against the professional model, which many thought went too far in relying on statistics and technology. The main characteristics of these two trends are summarized below.

Professional Model of Policing

- The separation of policing from politics.
- Reduced emphasis on the social-service function of police, with resources and strategies directed toward crime control.
- Limits placed on police discretion; emphasis placed on following guidelines and respecting the authority of the law.
- Centralized, bureaucratic police departments.
- The promotion of a certain distance between police officers and citizens, also the result of increased use of automobile patrols as opposed to foot patrols.
- Main strategies:
  1. Rapid response to calls for service, made possible by technological innovations such as the two-way radio.
  2. Preventive patrol, which attempts to use police presence to deter criminal activity.

Community Policing

- Although professionalism is still valued, it is tempered by recognition that police serve the community and its citizens, as well as the ideal of the law.
- Decentralized, less bureaucratic police departments, allowing more authority and discretion to rest in the hands of police officers.
- Recognition that crime control is only one function of law enforcement, to be included with crime prevention and the provision of social services.
- A more intimate relationship between police and citizens, which comes from understanding that police officers can do only so much to fight crime; ultimately, they need the cooperation of the community to be successful.
- Main strategies:
  1. Return to foot patrol to "reconnect" with the community.
  2. Problem solving, which treats crimes not just as isolated incidents but as "problems" that can be "solved" with innovative, long-term approaches.

These programs and others across the country typify the essence of community policing. First, they show how the police can engage in problem solving as opposed to only responding to calls for service. Second, they are examples of how the police are attempting to forge partnerships with neighborhoods or community groups. Finally, the programs illustrate how the police can engage the community by encouraging citizens' active involvement in crime and disorder problems.

Problem-Solving Policing

Problem solving, a key component of community policing, has its roots in **problem-solving policing,** which was introduced by Herman Goldstein of the Police Executive Research Forum in the late 1970s. Goldstein's basic premise was that police departments were devoting too many of their resources to reacting to calls for service and too few to "acting on their own initiative to prevent or reduce community problems."[45] To rectify this situation, problem-solving policing moves beyond simply responding to incidents and attempts instead to control or even solve the root causes of criminal behavior.

Goldstein's theory was in direct contrast to the reform-era theories of policing, discussed in the previous chapter.[46] Goldstein was suggesting that patrol officers must become intimately involved with citizens. For example, instead of responding to a call concerning illegal drug use by simply arresting the offender—a short-term response— the patrol officers should also look at the long-term implications of the situation. They should analyze the pattern of similar arrests in the area and interview the arrestee to determine the reasons, if any, that the site had been selected for drug activity.[47] Then additional police actions should be taken to prevent further drug sales at the identified location.

Hot Spots According to the tenets of reform-era policing, patrol officers should be spread evenly throughout a precinct, giving each citizen the same level of service. Many observers find this shortsighted, at best. Professor Lawrence Sherman compares it to giving every citizen an equal dose of penicillin—whether that person is sick or not.[48]

Some say a more practical response is for police to concentrate on **hot spots,** or areas of high criminal activity. Minneapolis police discovered, for example, that 100 percent of the robberies in a certain year occurred in only 2 percent of the city's ZIP codes.[49] Similarly, law enforcement officials in Jersey City, New Jersey, found that fifty-six hot spots of drug activity (occupying 4.4 percent of the city's street sections) accounted for 45 percent of the city's narcotics sales arrests and 46 percent of emergency calls for service.[50]

In both cases, the city's police department took part in experiments in which extra patrol coverage—in brief bursts of activity—was directed to a select number of the hot spots. In Minneapolis, robbery rates in the targeted hot spots fell by more than 20 percent, and in both cities, calls for service reporting public disorder also decreased. Neither police department, however, concluded that the hot spots experiment had

Redlands (California) police officer Stephen Crane takes part in a one-legged jumping race with neighborhood children. The race was sponsored by Redlands's Risked Focus Policing Program, which works to reduce juvenile delinquency in the community. How can establishing friendly relations with citizens help law enforcement agencies reduce crime?

Problem-Solving Policing
A policing philosophy that requires police to identify potential criminal activity and develop strategies to prevent or respond to that activity.

Hot Spots
Concentrated areas of high criminal activity that draw a directed police response.

decreased overall crime. Criminals had simply moved to other areas, or "scattered like cockroaches in the light," as one observer put it.[51]

Crime Mapping Many police departments are using *crime mapping* technology to locate and identify hot spots. A new generation of geographic information systems (GISs) provides departments with colored maps that allow them to easily spot patterns of crime and determine where increased coverage is needed. With the press of a button, GIS software can find and predict crime patterns by matching variables such as time of day, type of crime, and type of weapon used.

Broken Windows: Popularizing Community Policing

If Herman Goldstein introduced the idea of problem-solving policing, James Q. Wilson and George L. Kelling brought it widespread attention. Many observers believe that Wilson and Kelling set the modern wave of community policing in motion with their 1982 article in *Atlantic Monthly* entitled "Broken Windows."[52]

The Broken Windows Theory In "Broken Windows," Wilson and Kelling argued that reform-era police strategies focused on violent crime to the detriment of the vital police role of promoting the quality of life in neighborhoods. As a result, many American communities, particularly in large cities, had fallen into a state of disorder and disrepute, with two very important consequences. First, these neighborhoods—with their broken windows, dilapidated buildings, and lawless behavior by citizens—send out "signals" that criminal activity is tolerated. Second, this disorder promotes fear among law-abiding citizens, dissuading them from leaving their homes or attempting to improve their surroundings.

The **broken windows theory,** therefore, is based on "order maintenance" of neighborhoods by cracking down on "quality-of-life" crimes such as panhandling, public drinking and urinating, loitering, and graffiti painting. Only by encouraging police diligence with regard to these quality-of-life crimes, the two professors argued, could American cities be rescued from rising crime rates.

Community policing played a prominent role in Wilson and Kelling's article. To reduce fear and crime, they insisted, police had to rely on the cooperation of the citizens. Many cities have found that a crucial step in "reconnecting" with the community has been the reintroduction of foot patrols in high-crime neighborhoods. Studies have shown that foot patrol officers pay more attention to "order maintenance crimes" such as drunkenness, vagrancy, and panhandling than do patrol officers in police cars. Although these crimes are not serious, they do increase fear of crime in a community.

Crackdowns In many American cities, the implementation of the broken windows theory has been accompanied by aggressive patrol tactics known as "crackdowns." When police intensely focus their energies on a particular crime or set of crimes in a given area, they are said to be conducting a "crackdown." Crackdowns, which are related to the "hot spot" tactics discussed earlier, are typically used to solve a significant crime or disorder problem in an area.

For example, Worcester's Community Impact Division, working on tips from residents, has established "impact areas" that are targeted by police officers. One such area, just off Main Street downtown, saw seventy arrests and 143 citations by traffic, gang, and vice squads on a single day in March 2004.[53] New York City, which experienced a dramatic drop in violent crime in the 1990s, is often held up as the ultimate example of what can be accomplished when the broken windows theory and aggressive police actions are combined. (See the feature *Outside the Box—Compstat*.)

Compstat

What makes crime rates drop and rise? According to Lawrence M. Friedman, Stanford University professor of law, "the honest answer is that no one knows." Many law enforcement experts, however, credit a system instituted in New York City in the mid-1990s for much of the success police departments have had fighting crime in recent years. The system is known as Compstat, and it starts with beat officers reporting the exact location of crimes and other crime-related information—such as crack houses and abandoned cars—to department officials. These reports are then fed into a database, which prepares grids of a particular city or neighborhood and highlights areas with a high incidence of violent crime, drug dealing, and so on (see Figure 6.6).

William Bratton, New York's police commissioner from 1994 to 1996, and his deputy commissioner, Jack Maple, modeled the earliest version of Compstat after England's use of radar to target and shoot down German Luftwaffe bombers in World War II. Twice a week, Maple would hold a meeting of all precinct chiefs and place pressure on those who presided over high-crime neighborhoods by showing them exactly where the problems were the worst. Compstat allowed these officers to apply "zero-tolerance" strategies to these "hot spots," cracking down on minor offenses such as loitering and aggressively searching for illegal weapons.

After New York experienced record-breaking crime lows in the late 1990s, the "gospel" of Compstat spread throughout the nation as other cities became eager to replicate the Big Apple's successes. Bratton wound up as chief of police in Los Angeles, and other New York Police Department officers took similar positions in large metropolitan areas (Miami, Baltimore), midsized cities (Raleigh, North Carolina; Ann Arbor, Michigan), and smaller communities (Sarasota, Florida; Lawrence, Massachusetts). The results have been heartening—major crimes dropped nearly 40 percent in Baltimore between 2000 and 2004, 43 percent in Lawrence between 1999 and 2004, and 13 percent in Raleigh during that time period.

FOR CRITICAL ANALYSIS

Along with community policing, computer-run systems such as Compstat are considered the two pillars of "The New Policing." How do you think that the two approaches can be combined for greatest effect? Note that the New York Police Department has been criticized for ignoring many of the practices of community policing in its aggressive crime-fighting strategies.

FIGURE 6.6
Compstat Maps

These Compstat maps of the Rampart area of Los Angeles show the location of gang-related crimes and narcotics arrests over a four-week period.

Source: *The Police Chief,* January 2004, p. 18.

The Continued Impact of Community Policing The community policing "revolution" shows no signs of abating. The Office of Community Oriented Policing Services, a branch of the U.S. Department of Justice, has distributed close to $9 billion in grants to law enforcement agencies in the past decade to promote the strategy.[54] About two-thirds of all local police departments, employing 86 percent of all police officers in the country, have full-time community policing officers.[55] The "broken windows" theory now has proponents all over the globe and has influenced public policy in places such as Mexico and Honduras.

Some law enforcement officials worry that community policing has become so widespread that it has lost any coherence as a useful policing philosophy. More than half of the police chiefs and sheriffs in a survey conducted by the National Institute of Justice were unclear about the actual meaning of "community policing,"[56] leading one observer to joke that Professor Kelling's revolution is even quieter than had been expected.[57] Generally, however, the trend toward community policing is regarded as having a positive impact—if for no other reason than that it forces police departments to consider the complex relationship between law enforcement agents and the community.

> "We have a hard enough time dealing with real crime, let alone somebody's fantasy of it."
> —Los Angeles patrol officer, complaining about the difficulty in implementing community policing programs (1998)

LAW ENFORCEMENT IN THE FIELD

Community policing is one of the *field services* that police officers perform. Also known as "operations" or "line services," field services include patrol activities, investigations, and special operations. According to Henry M. Wrobleski and Karen M. Hess, most police departments are "generalists"; that is, police officers are assigned to general areas and perform all field service functions within the boundaries of their beats. Larger departments may be more specialized, with personnel assigned to specific types of crime, such as drugs or white-collar crime, rather than geographic locations. Smaller departments, which make up the bulk of local law enforcement agencies, rely almost exclusively on general patrol.[58]

Police on Patrol: The Backbone of the Department

One of the great ironies of the police organization is that the people lowest on the hierarchical "stepladder"—the patrol officers—are considered the most valuable members of the force. (Many patrol officers, considering their pay and work hours, would call the situation unjust, not ironic.) As many as two-thirds of the *sworn officers,* or those officers authorized to make arrests and use force, in some large police departments are patrol officers, and every department has a patrol unit.

"Life on the street" is not easy. Patrol officers must be able to handle any number of difficult situations, and experience is often the best and, despite training programs, the only teacher. As one patrol officer commented:

> You never stop learning. You never get your street degree. The person who says . . . they've learned it all is the person that's going to wind up dead or in a very compromising position. They've closed their minds.[59]

It may take a patrol officer years to learn when a gang is "false flagging" (trying to trick rival gang members into the open) or what to look for in a suspect's eyes to sense if he or she is concealing a weapon. This learning process is the backdrop to a number of different general functions that a patrol officer must perform on a daily basis.

Live Scanner Broadcasts allow you to listen in on radio reports from police officers in the field over the Internet. To find its Web site, click on *Web Links* under *Chapter Resources* at **www.cjinaction.com**.

The Purpose of Patrol As was mentioned earlier, patrol officers do not spend a great deal of time chasing, catching, and handcuffing suspected criminals. The vast majority of patrol shifts are completed without a single arrest.[60] Officers spend a great deal of time meeting with other officers, taking breaks, and patrolling with the goal of preventing crime in general rather than any specific crime or criminal activity.

As Samuel Walker noted, the basic purposes of the police patrol have changed very little since 1829, when Sir Robert Peel founded the modern police department. These purposes include:

The most common law enforcement agent is the patrol officer, who is responsible for deterring and preventing crime as well as providing social services. Given that most patrol shifts end without an officer making a single arrest, what activities take up most of a patrol officer's time?

1 The deterrence of crime by maintaining a visible police presence.
2 The maintenance of public order and a sense of security in the community.
3 The twenty-four-hour provision of services that are not crime related.[61]

The first two goals—deterring crime and keeping order—are generally accepted as legitimate police functions. The third, however, has been more controversial.

As noted in Chapter 5, the community era has seen a resurgence of the patrol officer as a provider of community services, many of which have little to do with crime. The extent to which noncrime incidents dominate patrol officers' time is evident in the Police Services Study, a survey of 26,000 calls to police in sixty different neighborhoods. The study found that only one out of every five calls involved the report of criminal activity.[62] (See Figure 6.7 on the following page.)

There is some debate over whether community services should be allowed to dominate patrol officers' duties. The question, however, remains: If the police do not handle these problems, who will? Few cities have the financial resources to hire public servants to deal specifically with, for example, finding shelter for homeless persons. Furthermore, the police are the only public servants on call twenty-four hours a day, seven days a week, making them uniquely accessible to citizen needs.

Patrol Activities To recap, the purposes of police patrols are to prevent and deter crime and also to provide social services. How can the police best accomplish these goals? Of course, each department has its own methods and strategies, but William Gay, Theodore Schell, and Stephen Schack are able to divide routine patrol activity into four general categories:

1 *Preventive patrol.* By maintaining a presence in a community, either in a car or on foot, patrol officers attempt to prevent crime from occurring. This strategy, which O. W. Wilson called "omnipresence," was a cornerstone of policing philosophy and still takes up roughly 40 percent of patrol time.
2 *Calls for service.* Patrol officers spend nearly a quarter of their time responding to 911 calls for emergency service or other citizen problems and complaints.

FIGURE 6.7

Calls for Service

Over a period of two years, the Project on Policing Neighborhoods gathered information on calls for service in Indianapolis, Indiana, and St. Petersburg, Florida. As you can see, the largest portion of these calls involved disputes where no violence or threat of violence existed. Be aware also that nearly two-thirds of the nonviolent dispute calls and nearly half of the assault calls answered by police dealt with domestic confrontations.

Description of Violation	Percentage of Total Calls
NONSERIOUS CRIME CALLS	
Nonviolent disputes	41.7
Public disorder (drunk, disorderly, begging, prostitution, etc.)	11.1
Assistance (missing persons, traffic accident, damaged property, etc.)	9.8
Minor violations (shoplifting, trespassing, traffic/parking offense, refusal to pay, etc.)	4.5
SERIOUS CRIME CALLS	
Assaults (using violence against a person, kidnapping, child abuse, etc.)	26.0
Serious theft (motor vehicle theft, burglary, purse snatching, etc.)	5.1
General disorder (illicit drugs, fleeing police, leaving the scene of of an accident, etc.)	1.8

Source: Stephen D. Mastrofski, Jeffrey B. Snipes, Roger B. Parks, and Christopher D. Maxwell, "The Helping Hand of the Law: Police Control of Citizens on Request," *Criminology* 38 (May 2000), Table 5, page 328.

3 *Administrative duties.* Paperwork takes up nearly 20 percent of patrol time.

4 *Officer-initiated activities.* Incidents in which the patrol officer initiates contact with citizens, such as stopping motorists and pedestrians and questioning them, account for 15 percent of patrol time.[63]

The category estimates made by Gay, Schell, and Schack are not universally accepted. Professor of law enforcement Gary W. Cordner argues that administrative duties account for the largest percentage of patrol officers' time and that when these officers are not consumed with paperwork and meetings, they are either answering calls for service (which takes up 67 percent of the officers' time on the street) or initiating activities themselves (the remaining 33 percent).[64]

> **"One night . . . it was so slow that three patrol cars showed up for a dispute between two crackheads over a shopping cart."**
> —Marcus Laffey, New York police officer (2000)

Indeed, there are dozens of academic studies that purport to answer the question of how patrol officers spend their days and nights. Perhaps it is only fair, then, to give a police officer the chance to describe the duties patrol officers perform. In the words of Anthony Bouza, a former police chief:

[Patrol officers] hurry from call to call, bound to their crackling radios, which offer no relief—especially on summer weekend nights. . . . The cops jump from crisis to crisis, rarely having time to do more than tamp one down sufficiently and leave for the next. Gaps of boredom and inactivity fill the interims, although there aren't many of these in the hot months. Periods of boredom get increasingly longer as the nights wear on and the weather gets colder.[65]

Bouza paints a picture of a routine beat as filled with "noise, booze, violence, drugs, illness, blaring TVs, and human misery." This may describe the situation in high-crime

Lois Perillo
Bicycle Community Policing Officer

A career in law enforcement first entered my mind when I saw a recruitment poster hanging in a very bohemian San Francisco restaurant. It depicted a United Nations of women in uniform and encouraged that I join them. I did. However, the hiring process, inclusive of background checks and written, oral, physical, and polygraph testing, took two years. Concerned with my ability to scale the six-foot wall, I talked my way into a specialized physical prep class designed for female firefighter candidates. To stay motivated, I enrolled in a preacademy study class and I hunkered down for the wait.

In late June 1994, I received a letter from the San Francisco Police Department: my academy class was to begin in four weeks. By July, my hair was significantly shorter, and I was starching a gray rookie uniform weekly and polishing my brass and shoes daily. Those of us who could write easily were forced to do pushups, and those whose pushup style was one hand behind their backs were compelled to write. After three months, my star was pinned to my navy blue wool uniform by the chief of police, and I was off to four years of midnights before falling into the daylight and community policing.

I credit my fall to Valerie, one of the very first San Francisco community officers, who was about to move to another department when she recruited me to join the Community Police Officer Program, or C.P.O.P, as her replacement. I left the darkness of Mission Police Station's midnight watch, bought a very good pair of sunglasses, and began my adjustment to days. Soon, I was investigating a stalking incident on my beat. The suspect kept eluding us until I went undercover, riding a bicycle. We caught the guy, found he was affected by dementia, and placed him in mental-health treatment. My career as S.F.P.D.'s first bicycle community officer had begun.

At first we rode our personal bicycles with rubber bands around pant legs to protect ourselves from chain snags. After ten years of bicycles on the beat, we are now fully funded with departmental supplies, equipment, and uniforms.

As a bicycle community officer, I don't just lock 'em up and go to court to testify. I am charged to be a problem solver and to

stem repeat calls to dispatch. For example, after catching graffiti vandals in the act, I contracted with the teens and their parents that they remove their markings in lieu of facing arrest. I managed a crime alert system that merchants use to share information and hopefully avert criminal activity. I helped organize the community to encourage a judge to compel a once ever

Courtesy of Lois Perillo

Lois Perillo

present, panhandling heroin addict to choose drug treatment over jail time. And when Headquarters called me into action, I've switched into cop and robber mode to chase and catch bike thieves, shoplifters, burglars, and drug dealers on my bike.

Though it doesn't fit on my gun belt like the other tools I carry, the bicycle is an asset to my job and helps me expand my potential; it is a barrier breaker. Children and adults approach me easily, making my duties flow smoothly. My responsibilities include daily bicycle patrol, ongoing contact with residents and merchants, and liaison with other city departments. I frequent community meetings and crime prevention talks. I listen to neighborhood concerns and prioritize my response according to the issues, assisting in residents' empowerment. I maintain voice mail at the station, shortcutting community calls to dispatch for issues that are not time sensitive, yet require a police response. I share information with the community by writing the Police Beat column for the local paper, *The Noe Valley Voice*, which posts to the Web. As with all police officers, I answer radio calls for service, take reports, comfort the aggrieved, bandage wounds, collect evidence, and arrest suspects. I think of myself as an old-fashioned beat officer (with the plus of my bicycle) who was fortunate enough to fall into my life's work.

Go to the Careers in Criminal Justice Interactive CD for more profiles in the field of criminal justice.

neighborhoods, but it certainly does not represent the reality for the majority of patrol officers in the United States. Duties that all patrol officers have in common, whether they work in Bouza's rather nightmarish city streets or in the quieter environment of rural America, include controlling traffic, conducting preliminary investigations, making arrests, and patrolling public events.

Preventive Patrol and the Kansas City Experiment On the night of May 7, 2004, members of the Boston Police Department, along with law enforcement officers from a number of other agencies, flooded several of the city's most dangerous neighborhoods. Within several hours, the officers made twenty-seven arrests (most on drug

Directed Patrol
Patrol strategies that are designed to respond to a specific criminal activity at a specific time.

General Patrol
Patrol strategies that rely on police officers monitoring a certain area with the goal of detecting crimes in progress or preventing crime due to their presence. Also known as random or preventive patrol.

charges), recovered three firearms and one knife, and issued more than 100 moving violations. This type of activity is a **directed patrol.** Such patrols are specifically designed to deal with crimes that commonly occur in certain locations and under circumstances that provide police with opportunity for preparation.

Most police work, in contrast, is done on **general patrol,** during which officers make the rounds of a specific area with the purpose of carrying out the various patrol functions. Every police department in the United States patrols its jurisdiction using automobiles; in addition, 62 percent utilize foot patrols, 43 percent bicycle patrols, 12 percent motorcycle patrols, 3 percent boat patrols, and 2 percent horse patrols.[66] In a sense, general patrols are random because the officers spend a substantial amount of their shifts hoping to notice any crimes that may be occurring.

Testing Preventive Patrol Theories in Kansas City Some observers have compared a patrol officer to a scarecrow because of the hope that the officer's presence alone will deter any would-be criminals from attempting a crime.[67] The theory of *preventive patrol* was tested by the Kansas City Preventive Patrol Experiment, conducted in 1972 and 1973.[68] With the cooperation of the local police department, a team of researchers chose three areas, each comprising five beats, with similar crime statistics. Over the course of twelve months, the police applied different patrol strategies to each designated area:

- On the *control* beats, normal preventive measures were taken, meaning that a single automobile drove the streets when not answering a call for service.
- On the *proactive* beats, the level of preventive measures was increased, with automobile patrols being doubled and tripled.
- On the *reactive* beats, preventive patrol was eliminated entirely, and patrol cars only answered calls for service.

Before, during, and after the experiments, the researchers also interviewed residents of the three designated areas to determine their opinion of police service and fear of crime.

The results of the Kansas City experiment were somewhat shocking. Researchers found that increasing or decreasing preventive patrol had little or no impact on crimes, public opinion of the effectiveness of police, police response time, traffic accidents, or reports of crime to police.[69]

Interpreting the Kansas City Experiment Criminologists were, and continue to be, somewhat divided on how to interpret these results. For some, the Kansas City experiment and other similar data proved that patrol officers, after a certain threshold, were not effective in preventing crime, and therefore scarce law enforcement resources should be diverted to other areas. "It makes about as much sense to have police patrol routinely in cars to fight crime as it does to have firemen patrol routinely in fire trucks to fight fire," noted University of Delaware professor Carl Klockars.[70]

Others saw the experiment as proving only one conclusion in a very specific set of circumstances and were unwilling to accept the results as universal. Professor James Q. Wilson, for example, said that the study showed only that random patrols in marked automobiles were of questionable value and that it proved nothing about other types of police presence such as foot patrols or patrols in unmarked automobiles.[71]

Indeed, despite the Kansas City Preventive Patrol Experiment, most modern police departments continue to assign officers to random, preventive patrols. Such patrols bring local governments revenue through traffic tickets and also are believed to reassure citizens. The lasting benefit of the Kansas City study, according to researchers Robert Sheehan and Gary Cordner, seems to be that it has freed police departments

The Eye in the Sky

The most effective preventive control strategy would be to completely blanket an area with police officers, stationing them at every street corner, every subway stop, and every office lobby in a city. Of course, no police department in the country has the resources to provide that kind of coverage. A number of cities, however, have opted for the next best option: surveillance cameras. Following the lead of London, which has placed more than 150,000 cameras throughout its public places, officials in Los Angeles, Washington, D.C., Chicago, New Orleans, and Palm Springs, California, have installed video cameras on city streets to supplement normal patrol activities. Many of these cameras can pan, tilt, and zoom, giving law enforcement agents the ability to monitor all activity within the device's view.

ONE STEP FURTHER

Inevitably, however, the old problem of scarce resources arises— the more cameras a city installs, the more personnel are needed to operate those cameras. Chicago hopes to solve this dilemma with a computer program that creates "smart" surveillance cameras. This software has the ability to scrutinize the movement of people within view of the camera's eye and alert the city's 911 emergency center if any of them act suspiciously. So, for example, if someone is wandering aimlessly near a potential terrorist target, or parks a car on the shoulder of a highway, or places a package on the ground or a bench and walks away with it within range of the camera, Chicago law enforcement would be notified immediately. Then, a human observer would take over surveillance duties with the ability to magnify the images of the suspect up to 400 times. "Cameras are the equivalent of hundreds of sets of eyes," says Chicago Mayor Richard M. Daley. "They're the next best thing to having police officers stationed at every potential trouble spot."

IN THE FUTURE

One limitation of surveillance cameras—even the "smart" ones used in Chicago—is their stationary nature. If a suspect goes around the corner, the camera cannot follow. The Draganfly Predator is another matter. A smaller version of the drones used by the Central Intelligence Agency in Afghanistan and Iraq, this radio-controlled device has a six-foot wingspan, can soar to 8,000 feet, and transmits full-color video images to monitors on the ground. Plus, the Draganfly Predator costs only $750—an important consideration for any possible law enforcement use.

For more information on police surveillance cameras and other CJ technologies, click on Crime and Technology *under* Book Resources *at* **www.cjinaction.com.**

from their reliance on the random patrol.[72] In light of the study, police departments realized that they could divert patrol officers from their traditional patrol duties without setting off an increase in crime. Therefore, administrators felt free to experiment with alternative strategies and tactics. (An extreme example of this experimentation is discussed in the feature *CJ and Technology—The Eye in the Sky.*)

Police Investigations

Investigation is the second main function of police, along with patrol. Whereas patrol is primarily preventive, investigation is reactive. After a crime has been committed and the patrol officer has gathered the preliminary information from the crime scene, the responsibility of finding "who dunnit" is delegated to the investigator, most commonly known as the **detective.** Today, detectives make up about 15 percent of the personnel in the average midsized and large-city police department.[73] Detectives have not been the focus of nearly as much reform attention as their patrol counterparts, mainly because the scope of the detective's job is limited to law enforcement, with less emphasis given to social services or order maintenance.

The job is not a glamorous one, however. Detectives spend much of their time investigating common crimes such as burglaries and are more likely to be tracking down stolen property than a murderer. They must also prepare cases for trial, which involves a great deal of time-consuming paperwork. Furthermore, a landmark Rand Corporation study estimated that more than 97 percent of cases that are "solved" can be attributed to a patrol officer making an arrest at the scene, witnesses or victims identifying the perpetrator, or detectives undertaking routine investigative procedures that could easily be

Detective

The primary police investigator of crimes.

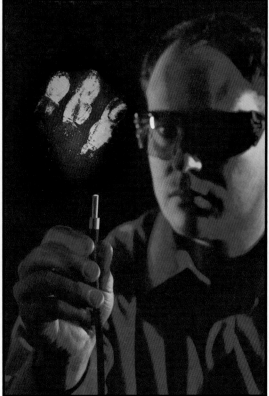

A special light designed to illuminate fingerprints is tested at Sandia National Laboratories in Livermore, California. Fingerprints—the result of sweat and grease from the pores of the skin—bloodstains, footprints, tire impressions, fiber from clothing, hair and skin samples, and weapons are important types of physical evidence that help police officers investigate crimes and convict offenders.

performed by clerical personnel.[74] "There is no Sherlock Holmes," said one investigator. "The good detective on the street is the one who knows all the weasels and one of the weasels will tell him who did it."[75]

The Detection Function A detective division in the larger police departments usually has a number of sections. These sections often include crimes against persons, such as homicide or sexual assault, and crimes against property, such as burglary and robbery. Many departments have separate detective divisions that deal exclusively with *vice,* a broad term that covers a number of public order crimes such as prostitution, gambling, and pornography. In the past, vice officers have also been primarily responsible for narcotics violations, but many departments now devote entire units to that growing social and legal problem.

The ideal case for any detective, of course, is one in which the criminal stays on the scene of the crime, has the weapon in his or her hands when apprehended, and, driven by an overriding sense of guilt, confesses immediately. Such cases are, needless to say, rare. University of Cincinnati criminal justice professor John E. Eck, in attempting to improve the understanding of the investigative process, concluded that investigators face three categories of cases:

- *Unsolvable cases,* or weak cases that cannot be solved regardless of investigative effort.
- *Solvable cases,* or cases with moderate evidence that can be solved with considerable investigative effort.
- *Already solved cases,* or cases with strong evidence that can be solved with minimum investigative effort.[76]

Eck found that the "unsolvable cases," once identified as such, should not be investigated because the effort would be wasted, and that the "already solved cases" require little additional effort or time on the part of detectives. Therefore, Eck concluded, the investigation resources of a law enforcement agency should primarily be aimed at "solvable cases." Further research by Steven G. Brandl and James Frank found that detectives had relatively high success rates in investigating burglary and robbery cases for which a moderate level of evidence was available.[77] Thus, the Rand study cited above may be somewhat misleading, in that investigators can routinely produce positive results as long as they concentrate on those cases that potentially can be solved. (To learn the factors that help law enforcement agents solve cases, see Figure 6.8.)

Cold Case Investigations When police officers found James Evans Ridgeway's rotting corpse in a pile of leaves in 1979, none of the solvability factors listed in Figure 6.8 were present, and the case grew cold. In 2005, however, Cumberland County (New Jersey) officials reopened the investigation in light of new evidence and ordered Ridgeway's body exhumed.[78] The term *cold case* refers to a crime that has been unsolved for a long period of time. Cold case squads, such as the one that examined Ridgeway's remains, have become more common in the past decade thanks to advances in forensic science.[79] DNA testing, in particular, has revolutionized cold case investigating, and it will be the topic of the *Criminal Justice in Action* feature at the end of this chapter.

Aggressive Investigation Strategies Detective bureaus also have the option of implementing more aggressive strategies. For example, if detectives suspect that a person was involved in the robbery of a Mercedes-Benz parts warehouse, one of them

FIGURE 6.8

Solvability Factors

During their investigations of crimes, officers with the Rochester, New York, Police Department pay close attention to the *solvability factors* listed here. Without any of these factors present, the chances of determining who committed the crime are minimal.

1 Are there any eyewitnesses to the crime?

2 Has the suspect been identified by name or otherwise?

3 Where did the crime occur?

4 Is a description of the suspect available?

5 If the crime is a property crime, does the stolen property have any recognizable marks, numbers, or other identifiable characteristics?

6 Do the particulars of the crime match any other crimes committed recently?

7 Is there significant physical evidence (bodily fluids, hair, fingerprints) at the crime scene?

8 Has a vehicle involved with the crime been identified?

9 Will additional investigative work or media assistance increase the probability of solving the crime?

10 Is it possible that someone other than the suspect is responsible for the crime?

Source: Adapted from Ronald F. Becker, *Criminal Investigation*, 2d ed. (Sudbury, MA: Jones and Bartlett Publishers, 2005), 145.

might pose as a "fence"—or purchaser of stolen goods. In what is known as a "sting" operation, the suspect is deceived into thinking that the detective (fence) wants to buy stolen car parts; after the transaction takes place, the suspect can be arrested.

Perhaps the most dangerous and controversial operation a detective can undertake is to go *undercover,* or to assume a false identity in order to obtain information concerning illegal activities. Though each department has its own guidelines on when undercover operations are necessary, all that is generally required is the suspicion that illegal activity is taking place. (As you may recall from the discussion of entrapment in Chapter 4, police officers are limited in what they can do to convince the target of an undercover operation to participate in the illegal activity.) Today, undercover officers are most commonly used to infiltrate large-scale narcotics operations or those run by organized crime. Undercover operations, though extremely dangerous, can be very successful. In 2005, a two-year undercover stint by an FBI agent led to the arrests of thirty-two suspected mob figures.

In some cases, a detective bureau may not want to take the risk of exposing an officer to undercover work or may believe that an outsider cannot infiltrate an organized crime network. When the police need access and information, sometimes they turn to a **confidential informant (CI).** A CI is a person who is involved in criminal activity and gives information about the activity and those who engage in it to the police. The United States Supreme Court, in *Rovario v. United States* (1957),[80] held that the state has a confidential informant privilege, which means that it is not required to disclose the identity of an informant unless a court finds that such information is needed to determine the guilt or innocence of a suspect.

The Military and Law Enforcement

By law, the U.S. military cannot participate in domestic criminal law investigations. According to the Posse Comitatus Act (PCA) of 1878, anyone who uses a branch of the military to carry out the law may be punished by a fine or two years' imprisonment.[81]

Confidential Informant (CI)
A human source for police who provides information concerning illegal activity in which he or she is involved.

CORBIS/Bettmann

New York detective Mary Glatzke, wearing a gray wig and the nonthreatening clothes of a civilian, sits on a park bench. By posing as a "Muggable Mary," Detective Glatzke is using herself as bait to lure would-be robbers. This sort of undercover strategy hopes to deter crime as well as catch criminals in the act. What might be some of the deterrent effects of Detective Glatzke's assignment?

The statute reflects the wish of lawmakers, both at the time it was passed and today, that armed soldiers never be used by the federal government to oppress the citizenry. The act does, however, allow the use of the military in law enforcement when so authorized by the U.S. Congress. To fight the "war on drugs," for example, in 1981 Congress created an exception to the PCA and encouraged the military to share equipment and information with law enforcement agencies fighting the illegal drug trade in Central and South America and Southeast Asia.[82]

Some believe that American law enforcement has already adopted a "culture of paramilitarism."[83] As mentioned earlier in the chapter, most police departments in the United States are organized according to a military structure of command. Police officers who operate near military bases often train with soldiers, and military equipment is becoming more widely available to law enforcement agencies. In the early 2000s, nine different police departments began using Forward Looking Infrared Technology, a viewer mounted in a police car that allows officers to "see in the dark" by noting differences in heat as small as one-tenth of one degree Fahrenheit.[84]

In addition, about 85 percent of police departments serving a population of more than 250,000 operate a Special Weapons and Tactics (SWAT) team.[85] These special operations units are more heavily armed than regular police officers and use military tactics to respond to particularly dangerous circumstances such as hostage situations, barricaded suspects, and drug raids. The most significant challenge to the separation of military and police, however, has come as law enforcement reorganizes to combat terrorism. In 2002, President George W. Bush called on Congress to effectively eliminate the PCA by allowing military personnel to arrest, search, and seize terrorism suspects on American soil.[86]

"US VERSUS THEM": ISSUES IN MODERN POLICING

▶ GREAT DEBATES

Many observers insist that the threat of terrorism is the greatest danger ever faced by this nation and that the military should be given greater powers, including the power to engage in law enforcement, in the interests of national security. For a closer look at this argument, as well as an explanation of the role the military has played in American law enforcement, click on *Great Debates* under *Book Resources* at **www.cjinaction.com**.

Several years ago, Richard Herzog, a King's County (Washington) sheriff's deputy, was killed trying to restrain a man who had been running naked in traffic. When the man, named Ronald Matthews, turned and attacked, Herzog pulled out his pepper spray instead of his firearm. Matthews knocked Herzog to the ground, grabbed his holstered handgun, and shot him several times. In the days following his death, the question on the minds of the law enforcement community in Seattle was, "Why didn't Herzog draw his gun?" The answer, for many, came down to racial politics. County Executive Ron Sims, the highest-ranking African American in the city, had no doubt that Herzog had been inhibited in using his weapon because he was white and Matthews was black. Several killings of black suspects by white police officers in the months before Herzog's death—and the ensuing criticism—had, Sims said, made police officers afraid to protect themselves in situations involving African Americans.[87] Racial tension is one of the many on-the-job issues that make law enforcement such a challenging and often difficult career. When faced with these issues, sometimes police officers make the right decisions, and sometimes they make the wrong ones. In the worst-case scenario, as with Deputy Herzog, even a seemingly "right" decision may have an unexpected outcome.

> "The police subculture permits and sometimes demands deception of courts, prosecutors, defense attorneys, and defendants."
>
> —Jerome Skolnick, professor of law, University of California at Berkeley (1966)

Police Subculture

At a press conference after Richard Herzog's death, King County Sheriff Dave Reichert vented his frustrations. "We are sick and tired of being nitpicked about decisions we make every day," said Reichert.[88] His words encapsulate the bitterness toward civilians that often marks **police subculture,** a broad term used to describe the basic assumptions and values that permeate law enforcement agencies and are taught to new members of a law enforcement agency as the proper way to think, perceive, and act.[89] Every organization has a subculture, with values shaped by the particular aspects and pressures of that organization. In the police subculture, those values are formed in an environment characterized by danger, stress, boredom, and violence.

The Core Values of Police Subculture From the first day on the job, rookies begin the process of **socialization,** in which they are taught the values and rules of police work. This process is aided by a number of rituals that are common to the law enforcement experience. Police theorist Harry J. Mullins believes that the following rituals are critical to the police officer's acceptance, and even embrace, of police subculture:

- Attending a recruit academy.
- Working with a senior officer, who passes on the "lessons" of police work and life to the younger officer.
- Making the initial felony arrest.
- Using force to make an arrest for the first time.
- Using or witnessing deadly force for the first time.
- Witnessing major traumatic incidents for the first time.[90]

Each of these rituals makes it clear to the police officer that this is not a "normal" job. The only other people who can understand the stresses of police work are fellow officers, and consequently law enforcement officers tend to insulate themselves from civilians. Eventually, the insulation breeds mistrust, and the police officer develops an "us versus them" outlook toward those outside the force.[91]

In turn, this outlook creates what sociologist William Westly called the **blue curtain,** also known as the "blue wall of silence" or simply "the code."[92] This curtain separates the police from the civilians they are meant to protect.

Police Cynicism A cynic is someone who universally distrusts human motives and expects nothing but the worst from human behavior. **Police cynicism** is characterized by a rejection of the ideals of truth and justice—the very values that an officer is sworn to uphold.[93] As cynical police officers lose respect for the law, they replace legal rules with those learned in the police subculture, which are believed to be more reflective of "reality." The implications for society can be an increase in police misconduct, corruption, and brutality.[94]

Police cynicism is exacerbated by a feeling of helplessness—to report another officer's wrongdoing is a severe breach of the blue wall of silence. As one officer said:

> If you were to challenge somebody for something that was going on, they would say: "Listen, if the supervisor isn't saying anything, what the hell are you interjecting for? What are you, a rat?" You've gotta work with a lot of these guys. You go on a gun job, the next thing you know, you got nobody following you up the stairs.[95]

Police Subculture
The values and perceptions that are shared by members of a police department and, to a certain extent, by all law enforcement agents. These values and perceptions are shaped by the unique and isolated existence of the police officer.

Socialization
The process through which a police officer is taught the values and expected behavior of the police subculture.

Blue Curtain
A metaphorical term used to refer to the value placed on secrecy and the general mistrust of the outside world shared by many police officers.

Police Cynicism
The suspicion that citizens are weak, corrupt, and dangerous. This outlook is the result of a police officer being constantly exposed to civilians at their worst and can negatively affect the officer's performance.

The officer's statement highlights one of the reasons why police subculture resonates beyond department walls—he has basically admitted that he will not report wrongdoing by his peers. In this manner, police subculture influences the actions of police officers, sometimes to the detriment of society. In the next two sections, we will examine two areas of the law enforcement work environment that help create police subculture and must be fully understood if the cynical nature of police subculture is ever to be changed: (1) the danger of police work and (2) the need for police officers to establish and maintain authority.[96]

The Physical and Mental Dangers of Police Work

Police officers face the threat of physical harm every day. According to the U.S. Department of Justice, police have the most dangerous job in the United States, with 261 of every 1,000 officers targets of nonfatal violence each year.[97] In the two-year period 2003–2004, more than 300 police officers were killed in the line of duty.

In addition to physical dangers, police work entails considerable mental pressure and stress. According to the U.S. Bureau of Labor Statistics, policing is one of the ten most stressful occupations in the country, along with firefighting, driving a taxi, and being a surgeon.[98] The social isolation police officers must deal with also leads to one of the highest divorce rates of any job, which exacerbates the problem. Stress, in turn, contributes to other problems. Law enforcement officers are 300 percent more likely to suffer from alcoholism than the average American.[99] The average life expectancy of a police officer is fifty-seven years, compared to seventy-one for the general public—a statistic that can be attributed to police officers' top ranking among professions in rates of heart disease, hypertension, and diabetes.[100]

Greg Owen kisses the coffin of his father, Birmingham (Alabama) Police Officer Carlos Owen, one of three officers fatally shot when they tried to serve an arrest warrant at a reputed "crack house" on June 17, 2004. About 150 police officers die on duty each year, most from gunfire, automobile accidents, and vehicular assault. What are some of the other occupational threats that police officers face on a daily basis?

Authority and the Use of Force

If the police subculture is shaped by the dangers of the job, it often finds expression through authority. The various symbols of authority that decorate a police officer—including the uniform, badge, nightstick, and firearm—establish the power she or he holds over civilians. For better or for worse, both police officers and civilians tend to equate terms such as *authority* and *respect* with the ability to use force. Near the turn of the twentieth century, a police officer stated that his job was to "protect the good people and treat the crooks rough."[101] Implicit in the officer's statement is the idea that to do the protecting, he had to do some roughing up as well. This attitude toward the use of force is still with us today. Indeed, it is generally accepted that not only is police use of force inevitable, but that police officers who are unwilling to use force in certain circumstances cannot do their jobs effectively.

The "Misuse" of Force In general, the use of physical force by law enforcement personnel is very rare, occurring in only about 1.5 percent of police-public encounters.[102] Still, the Department of Justice estimates that law enforcement officers threatened to use force or used force in encounters with about 664,500 Americans in 2002.[103] (See Figure 6.9.) Of

AP Photo/Haraz Ghanbari

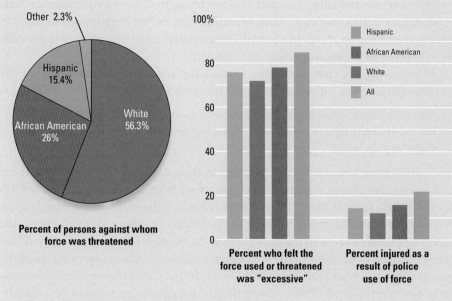

Percent of persons against whom force was threatened

Other 2.3%
Hispanic 15.4%
African American 26%
White 56.3%

Hispanic
African American
White
All

Percent who felt the force used or threatened was "excessive"

Percent injured as a result of police use of force

FIGURE 6.9

The Use of Force by Police against Suspects

Of the approximately 45 million Americans who came into contact with police officers in 2002, about 1.5 percent reported the use or threat of force. As you can see, whites had more total forceful contacts with the police, but minorities were more likely to suffer "excessive" force and injuries.

Source: Bureau of Justice Statistics, *Contacts between Police and the Public* (Washington, D.C.: U.S. Department of Justice, February 2005), 16, 18.

course, police officers are often justified in using force to protect themselves or other citizens. At the same time, few observers would be naïve enough to believe that police are *always* justified in the use of force. How, then, is "misuse" of force to be defined?

One attempt to qualify excessive force that has been lauded by legal scholars, if not necessarily by police officers, was offered by the Christopher Commission. Established in Los Angeles in 1992 after the beating of African American motorist Rodney King, the commission advised that "an officer may resort to force only where he or she faces a credible threat, and then may only use the minimum amount necessary to control the subject."[104]

The Phoenix Study Terms such as *credible* and *necessary* are, of course, quite subjective, rendering these definitions too vague to be practical. To better understand the subject, the Phoenix (Arizona) Police Department, in partnership with Rutgers University and Arizona State University, conducted a study to measure how often police officers used force. The results showed that police used some form of "physical force"—defined as any "weaponless tactic" (such as kicking or shoving) or the threatened or actual use of any weapon—in 22 percent of the surveyed arrests.[105] The study also examined the predictors of force; that is, the factors that were present in the situations where force was used. As one might expect, the study found that the best predictor of police use of force was the suspect's use of force.[106]

Types of Force To comply with the various, and not always consistent, laws concerning the use of force, a police officer must understand that there are two kinds of force: *nondeadly force* and *deadly force*. Most force used by law enforcement is nondeadly force. In most states, the use of nondeadly force is regulated by the concept of **reasonable force,** which allows the use of nondeadly force when a reasonable person would assume that such force was necessary. In contrast, **deadly force** is force that an objective police officer realizes will place the subject in direct threat of serious injury or death.

The United States Supreme Court and Use of Force The United States Supreme Court set the limits for the use of deadly force by law enforcement officers in *Tennessee v. Garner* (1985).[107] The case involved an incident in which Memphis police officer

Reasonable Force
The degree of force that is appropriate to protect the police officer or other citizens and is not excessive.

Deadly Force
Force applied by a police officer that is likely or intended to cause death.

Elton Hymon shot and killed a suspect who was trying to climb over a fence after stealing ten dollars from a residence. Hymon testified that he had been trained to shoot to keep a suspect from escaping, and indeed Tennessee law at the time allowed police officers to apprehend fleeing suspects in this manner.

In reviewing the case, the Court focused not on Hymon's action but on the Tennessee statute itself, ultimately finding it unconstitutional:

> When the suspect poses no immediate threat to the officer and no threat to others, the use of deadly force is unjustified. . . . It is not better that all felony suspects die than that they escape.[108]

The Court's ruling forced twenty-three states to change their fleeing felon rules. It did not, however, completely eliminate police discretion in such situations; police officers may use deadly force if they have probable cause to believe that the fleeing suspect poses a threat of serious injury or death to the officers or others. (We will discuss the concept of probable cause in the next chapter.) In essence, the Court recognized that police officers must be able to make split-second decisions without worrying about the legal ramifications. Four years after the *Garner* case, the Court tried to clarify this concept in *Graham v. Connor* (1989), stating that the use of any force should be judged by the "reasonableness of the moment."[109] In 2004, the Court modified this rule by suggesting that an officer's use of force could be "reasonable" even if, by objective measures, the force was not needed to protect the officer or others in the area.[110] (See *You Be the Judge—Justified Force?*)

Nonlethal Weapons Regardless of any legal restrictions, violent confrontations between officers and suspects are inevitable. To decrease the likelihood that such con-

YOU BE THE JUDGE

Justified Force?

THE FACTS
Officer Brosseau of the Puyallup (Washington) Police Department answered a 911 call reporting that Haugen and two other men were fighting in front of Haugen's mother's home. Brosseau knew that a warrant was out for Haugen's arrest on drug charges. When Brosseau arrived on the scene, Haugen fled. After a forty-five-minute chase, Haugen managed to circle around and jump in his Jeep Cherokee, which was parked in front of the house. He locked the doors and began fumbling for the keys as Brosseau approached the vehicle. Believing that Haugen was searching for a weapon, Brosseau smashed the driver's side window of the Jeep with her handgun and tried to grab the keys out of Haugen's hands, striking him on the head with her weapon in the process. Despite the officer's efforts, Haugen succeeded in starting the car and began to drive away. Brosseau then fired a shot through the car window, hitting Haugen in the back and puncturing his lung. Brosseau later testified that she shot Haugen because she feared for the safety of other police officers and citizens in the area.

THE LAW
The United States Supreme Court has ruled that cases involving the use of police force should be decided by observing all the circumstances surrounding the incident and then determining whether the police officer was "reasonable" in the use of force. In other words, would a reasonable police officer in this officer's shoes have been justified in using force?

YOUR DECISION
Haugen has sued Officer Brosseau for using excessive and unnecessary force. Under the circumstances, was Brosseau justified in firing at Haugen?

[To see how the United States Supreme Court decided this case, go to Example 6.1 in Appendix B.]

frontations will result in death or serious injury, many police departments use *nonlethal weapons,* which are designed to subdue but not seriously harm suspects. More than 90 percent of local police departments authorize the use of Oleoresin capsicum, or OC pepper spray.[111] An organic substance that combines ingredients such as resin and cayenne pepper, OC causes a sensation "similar to having sand or needles" in the eyes when sprayed into a suspect's face. Other common nonlethal weapons include tear gas, water cannons, and 37-mm pistols that fire wood, rubber, beanbags, or polyurethane bullets.

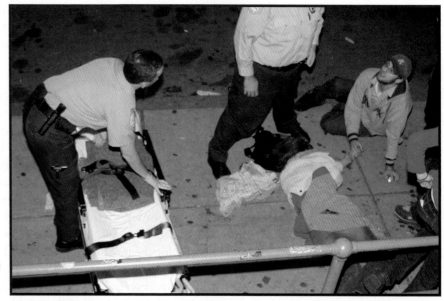

Twenty-one-year-old college student Victoria Snelgrove lies unconscious on Lansdowne Street in downtown Boston after being struck in the eye by a projectile designed to disperse pepper spray on impact. A Boston police officer had fired the object to help break up a crowd of unruly Boston Red Sox fans on October 21, 2004. How can the use of supposedly "nonlethal" weapons increase the risk that police officers will accidentally kill or seriously injure a civilian?

Even nonlethal weapons can raise safety concerns, and these have intensified with the increased use of Tasers—handheld electronic stun guns that fire blunt darts up to twenty-five feet, delivering 50,000 volts into their targets for a span of about five seconds. More than 5,000 local police departments employ the Taser, and many law enforcement agents credit its use with reducing the number of fatal shootings by police in their jurisdictions.[112] According to a report by Amnesty International, however, 103 Taser-related deaths occurred in the United States and Canada between June 2001 and March 2005.[113] Critics of the Taser insist that it poses a deadly threat to any target whose heart is weak because of cocaine use or disease and are calling for further research to be done on the stun gun's safety. To date, no federal or state law enforcement agencies have adopted the Taser, though the U.S. military employs the device.

Racial and Ethnic Biases in Policing

In its guidelines for the use of deadly force by undercover officers, the New York Police Department warns its officers not to be victims of symbolic opponent syndrome, defined as a "preconceived notion that places suspects into a 'BAD GUY' category because of race, nationality, grooming, or mode of dress."[114] The warning may seem self-evident, but it addresses a clear problem in law enforcement today. The Department of Justice study cited earlier reports that police officers are almost three times more likely to use force when coming into contact with African Americans than with whites and more than twice as likely with Hispanics as with whites.[115] Furthermore, Malcolm D. Holmes of the University of Wyoming has determined that in some of the nation's largest cities blacks and Hispanics are significantly more likely than whites to file civil rights complaints alleging police brutality.[116]

The "Just Us" System These experiences have led some to believe that the United States has, in practice, not a justice system but a "just us" system. Following the shooting described in the opening of this chapter, 81 percent of those African Americans polled believed that the police would have handled the incident differently "if Devin Brown had been a white teenager driving in a middle-class neighborhood."[117] In the next chapter's discussion of racial profiling, we will see that many African Americans believe that they are often targeted for a particular "offense"—DWB, or "driving while black." Since the September 11, 2001, terrorist attacks, Muslims living in the United

States have also felt that they are being singled out for law enforcement attention. This perception is strengthened by such actions as the FBI directive in 2003 ordering field supervisors to count the mosques and Muslim populations in their areas as part of their antiterrorism duties.

Police Attitudes and Discretion Such attitudes, say critics, lead to unnecessary harassment of members of minority groups by police and arouse ill will toward law enforcement in many minority neighborhoods. A greater police presence in these neighborhoods is not automatic evidence of law enforcement bias, however. As we learned earlier in the chapter, the primary operational tactic of all metropolitan police forces is responding to calls for service. According to research by law enforcement expert Richard J. Ludman, the greater police presence in these communities is mainly the result of calls for service from residents, which, in turn, are caused by higher local crime rates. Indeed, Randall Kennedy believes that such "selective law enforcement" should be, and for the most part is, welcomed by those who live in high-crime areas and appreciate the added protection.[118]

Furthermore, as several experts point out, cultural differences often exist between police officers and the residents of the neighborhoods they patrol. One survey found that police working in minority areas perceived higher levels of abuse and less respect from those citizens than from those in nonminority areas.[119] In looking at police abuse in Inglewood, California, the *Los Angeles Times* found that most of the victims claimed they were assaulted after "contempt of cop" incidents, such as not immediately following orders or verbally challenging the officer.[120] Judging someone's demeanor is often a subjective task and can be influenced by a lack of communication between two people of different backgrounds—another reason why it is so important for police departments to attract members of minority groups, as noted in our discussion of recruiting strategies.

Police Corruption

Police corruption has been a concern since the first organized American police departments. As you recall from Chapter 5, a desire to eradicate, or at least limit, corruption was one of the motivating factors behind the reform movement of policing. For general purposes, **police corruption** can be defined as the misuse of authority by a law enforcement officer "in a manner designed to produce personal gain." Corrupt police officers fall into two categories: "grass eaters" and "meat eaters." "Grass eaters" are involved in passive corruption; they simply accept the payoffs and opportunities that police work can provide. As the name implies, "meat eaters" are more aggressive in their quest for personal gain, initiating and going to great lengths to carry out corrupt schemes.

Types of Corruption Certain forms of corruption have been endemic to police work since its inception. These traditional forms of corruption include:

1 *Bribery,* in which the police officer accepts money or other forms of payment in exchange for "favors," which may include allowing a certain criminal activity to continue or misplacing a key piece of evidence before a trial. Related to bribery are *payoffs,* in which an officer demands payment from an individual or a business in return for certain services.

2 *Shakedowns,* in which an officer attempts to coerce money or goods from a citizen or criminal.

3 *Mooching,* in which the police officer accepts free "gifts" such as cigarettes, liquor, or services in return for favorable treatment of the gift giver.

Police Corruption
The abuse of authority by a law enforcement officer for personal gain.

Police corruption can also involve overzealous crime-fighting methods and efforts to keep such misconduct behind the "blue curtain" discussed earlier in the chapter. In 2003, for example, a jury found four Miami (Florida) police officers guilty of corruption for planning to plant firearms on unarmed suspects to justify using deadly force against them as well as misleading investigators and lying under oath to protect each other.

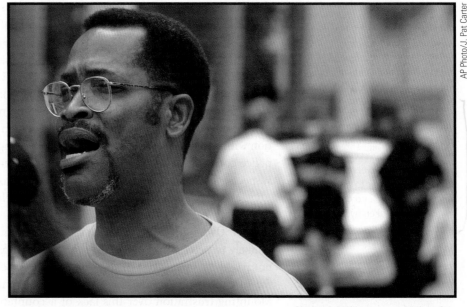

Nathaniel Wilcox, an organizer for People United to Lead the Struggle for Equality, speaks to the press following the conviction of four former Miami, Florida, police officers for corruption in 2003. Pressure from public interest groups plays a crucial role in efforts to "police the police."

Corruption in Police Subculture

There is no single reason that police corruption occurs. In covering corrupt behavior by a group of Miami police officers known as the Miami River Cops, journalist John Dorschner highlighted some of the factors that lead to unethical behavior, including a lack of proper training, a lack of supervision, and the fact that most officers can double or triple their salaries through corrupt activities.[121]

Lawrence Sherman identifies several stages in the moral decline of police officers.[122] In the first stage, the officers accept minor gratuities, such the occasional free meal from a restaurant on their beats. These gratuities gradually evolve into outright bribes, in which the officers receive the gratuity for overlooking some violation. For example, a law officer may accept pay from a bar owner to ensure that the establishment is not investigated for serving alcohol to minors. In the final stage, officers no longer passively accept bribes, but actively seek them out, to the point where the officers may even force the other party to pay for unwanted police services. This stage often involves large amounts of money and may entail protection of or involvement in drug, gambling, or prostitution organizations.

The insulating effects of police subculture also contribute to corruption by making it difficult to uncover. The Knapp Commission, which investigated police corruption in New York City in the 1970s, highlighted the "code of silence" that exists in police departments, a code that brands anybody within the department who exposes corrupt behavior as a traitor. "The rookie who comes into the department," it was noted, "is faced with the situation where it is easier for him to become corrupt than to remain honest."[123]

Police Accountability

Even in a police department with excellent recruiting methods, state-of-the-art ethics and discretionary training programs, and a culturally diverse workforce that nearly matches the make-up of the community, the problems discussed earlier in this chapter are bound to occur. The question then becomes—given the inevitability of excessive force, corruption, and other misconduct—*who shall police the police?*

Internal Investigations "The minute the public feels that the police department is not investigating its own alleged wrongdoing well, the police department will not be able to function credibly in even the most routine of matters," says Sheldon Greenberg, a professor of police management at Johns Hopkins University.[124] The mechanism for

Internal Affairs Unit (IAU)
A division within a police department that receives and investigates complaints of wrongdoing by police officers.

Citizen Oversight
The process by which citizens review complaints brought against individual police officers or police departments. The citizens often do not have the power to discipline misconduct, but can recommend that action be taken by police administrators.

Ethics
The rules or standards of behavior governing a profession; aimed at ensuring the fairness and rightness of actions.

Samuel Walker, professor of criminal justice at the University of Nebraska, is one of the nation's leading experts on the **Best Practices in Police Accountability.** Click on *Web Links* under *Chapter Resources* at **www.cjinaction.com** for access to his Web site.

these investigations within a police department is the **internal affairs unit (IAU)**. In many smaller police departments, the police chief conducts internal affairs investigations, while midsized and large departments have a team of internal affairs officers.

As much as police officers may resent internal affairs units, most realize that it is preferable to settle disciplinary matters in house. The alternatives may be worse. Police officers are criminally liable for any crimes they might commit, and city and state governments can be held civilly liable for wrongdoing by their police officers. Over the past decade, drug dealers and gang members filed more than 200 lawsuits in connection with a spate of wrongdoing by an elite Los Angeles antigang unit. As a result of the police corruption, which included planting evidence and physically abusing criminal suspects, the courts eventually overturned 100 convictions. By 2005, the city of Los Angeles had paid an estimated $70 million to settle the lawsuits.[125]

Citizen Oversight Despite the large sums of money involved, such civil suits are unlikely to deter police corruption for two reasons. First, the misbehaving officers do not pay the damages out of their own pockets. Second, in the vast majority of cases, the offending officers do not face disciplinary measures within the department.[126] Mounting frustration over this lack of accountability has led many communities to turn to an external procedure for handling citizens' complaints known as **citizen oversight.** In this process, citizens—people who are not sworn officers and, by inference, not biased in favor of law enforcement officers—review allegations of police misconduct or brutality. According to Samuel Walker, nearly one hundred cities now operate some kind of review procedure by an independent body.[127] For the most part, citizen review boards can only recommend action to the police chief or other executive. They do not have the power to discipline officers directly. Police officers generally resent this intrusion by civilians, and most studies have shown that civilian review boards are not widely successful in their efforts to convince police chiefs to take action against their subordinate officers.[128]

POLICE ETHICS

Police corruption is intricately connected with the ethics of law enforcement officers. **Ethics** has to do with fundamental questions of the fairness, justice, rightness, or wrongness of any action. Given the significant power that police officers hold, society expects very high standards of ethical behavior from them. These expectations are summed up in the *Police Code of Conduct,* which was developed by the International Association of Chiefs of Police in 1989.

To some extent, the *Police Code of Conduct* is self-evident: "A police officer will not engage in acts of corruption or bribery." In other aspects, it is idealistic, perhaps unreasonably so: "Officers will never allow personal feelings, animosities, or friendships to influence official conduct." The police working environment—rife with lying, cheating, lawbreaking, and violence—often does not allow for such ethical absolutes.

Ethical Dilemmas

Some police actions are obviously unethical, such as the behavior of a Pennsylvania officer who paid a woman he was dating $500 to pretend to be an eyewitness in a murder trial. The majority of ethical dilemmas that a police officer will face are not so clear-cut. Joycelyn M. Pollock and Ronald F. Becker, both members of the Criminal

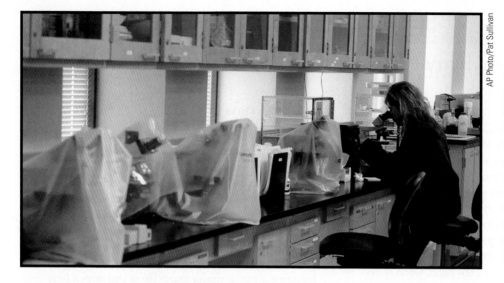

The Houston Police Crime Lab, pictured here, has become notorious for its poor efficiency and management. The lab's DNA section was shut down in 2002, plagued by problems such as waterlogged rape kits and rats eating through evidence boxes. Crime lab officials had even refused to take disciplinary action against two lab employees who fabricated scientific evidence in several high-profile cases, including one murder trial. What pressures might lead law enforcement administrators to tolerate, or even support, such a poor ethical working environment?

Justice Department at Southwest Texas State University, define an ethical dilemma as a situation in which law enforcement officers:

- Do not know the right course of action;
- Have difficulty doing what they consider to be right; and/or
- Find the wrong choice very tempting.[129]

These ethical dilemmas can occur often in police work, and it is how an officer deals with them that determines to what extent he or she is behaving ethically. (For further discussion of the difficult ethical situations that police officers face, see the feature *CJ in Focus—A Question of Ethics: The Dirty Harry Problem* on the following page.)

Elements of Ethics

Pollock and Becker, both of whom have extensive experience as ethics instructors for police departments, further identify four categories of ethical dilemmas, involving discretion, duty, honesty, and loyalty.[130]

- *Discretion.* The law provides rigid guidelines for how police officers must act and how they cannot act, but it does not offer guidelines for how officers *should* act in many circumstances. As mentioned in Chapter 5, police officers often use discretion to determine how they should act, and ethics plays an important role in guiding discretionary actions.
- *Duty.* The concept of discretion is linked with **duty,** or the obligation to act in a certain manner. Society, by passing laws, can make a police officer's duty more clear and, in the process, help eliminate discretion from the decision-making process. But an officer's duty will not always be obvious, and ethical considerations can often supplement "the rules" of being a law enforcement agent.
- *Honesty.* Of course, honesty is a critical attribute for an ethical police officer. A law enforcement agent must make hundreds of decisions in a day, and most of them require him or her to be honest in order to properly do the job.
- *Loyalty.* What should a police officer do if he or she witnesses a partner using excessive force on a suspect? The choice often sets loyalty against ethics, especially if the officer does not condone the violence.

Duty
The moral sense of a police officer that she or he should apply authority in a certain manner.

The Dirty Harry Problem

Do the ends justify the means? This is one of the most difficult and complex ethical questions, and one that is particularly crucial for police officers. Should they take steps that they know to be illegal in order to achieve a positive goal?

In addressing this moral dilemma, the University of Delaware's Carl B. Klockars turns to one of the most popular police dramas of all time, the 1971 film *Dirty Harry*. In this movie, Detective Harry Callahan, played by Clint Eastwood, faces a situation in which a young girl has been kidnapped by a psychotic killer named Scorpio. Demanding $200,000 in ransom, Scorpio has buried the girl alive, leaving her just a few hours' worth of oxygen. Callahan manages to find Scorpio, and in his efforts to learn the location of the girl, he shoots and then tortures the kidnapper. Although Callahan eventually gets the information out of Scorpio, it is too late. By the time he finds the girl, she has suffocated.

Assuming for argument's sake that Callahan was able to save the girl, would he have been justified in taking such drastic measures? After all, Callahan, like all officers, took an oath to obey the U.S. Constitution, which certainly does not permit the torture of suspects. Following proper procedure, Callahan should have arrested Scorpio and advised him of his right to an attorney. If Scorpio had exercised his right, the attorney would certainly have reminded him of his right to remain silent, and Callahan would have had no chance to save the little girl. In fact, Callahan committed a crime himself by assaulting Scorpio. Given all these factors, was the detective justified in doing what he did in order to save a life?

According to Klockars:

[The] core scene in *Dirty Harry* should only be understood as a dramatic example of a far more common problem: real, everyday, routine situations in which police officers know they can only achieve good ends by employing dirty means. Each time a police officer considers deceiving a suspect into confessing by telling him that his fingerprints were found at the scene or that a conspirator has already confessed, each time a police officer considers adding some untrue details to his account of probable cause to legitimate a crucial stop or search [he or she] faces a Dirty Harry problem.

Klockars calls the effects of the Dirty Harry problem on police officers "devastating." On the one hand, if the officers decide not to use dirty means, they must face the consequences: perhaps a suspect the officers know is guilty will be set free to commit further crimes. On the other hand, if the officers do abandon rules and procedures to serve the law, they are essentially breaking the very laws that they took an oath to uphold. The Dirty Harry problem, Klockars says, makes policing the most "morally corrosive occupation."

FOR CRITICAL ANALYSIS

Are police ever justified in using unlawful methods, no matter what good may ultimately be achieved? What do you believe is the proper solution to the Dirty Harry problem?

Although there is no easy "formula" to guide police officers through ethical challenges, Linda S. Miller of the Midwest Regional Community Policing Institute and Karen M. Hess of Normandale Community College have come up with three questions that can act as personal "checks" for police officers. Miller and Hess suggest that officers, when considering a particular action, ask themselves:

1 Is it legal?

2 Is it balanced?

3 How does it make me feel about myself?[131]

The DNA Revolution

One prosecutor likened it to "the finger of God." Another government representative called it "a miracle of justice." A third said that it "has become one of the most significant tools ever imagined in law enforcement." Each of these criminal justice experts was referring to deoxyribonucleic acid (DNA) fingerprinting, a relatively new procedure that has revolutionized the art of the criminal investigation. In this *Criminal Justice in Action* feature, we will examine the pros of this technology, celebrated by many, as well as its cons, highlighted by a worried few.

The DNA "Miracle" at Work

In 1994, Charlotte Stewart was bludgeoned to death in her apartment in the Bronx. Investigators found a great deal of physical evidence at the scene of the crime, including drops of the intruder's blood on the floor, a bloody rag that he had used after cutting himself, and the murder weapon, a two-foot African statue owned by the victim. At the time, however, the local police did not have the means to determine the source of the blood, and Stewart's murder, one of more than 1,500 in New York City that year, was forgotten.

Ten years later, however, local police began systematically retesting all evidence in unsolved cases that predated

the advent of DNA fingerprinting in the late 1990s. The result: a match between DNA embedded in the decade-old bloody rag and the DNA of Stewart's nephew, a man named Richard Jackson who had seven prior arrests and had just been released after nine years in prison for a stabbing. Jackson had not been a suspect at the time of the crime, but he was quickly arrested for his aunt's murder. "Every detective dreams of solving a case like this," said Chief Joseph Reznick, commander of the New York Police Department's Fugitive Enforcement Division, after Jackson's apprehension in 2004.[132]

DNA, which is the same in each cell of a person's body, provides a "genetic blueprint" or "code" for every living organism. DNA "profiling" is useful in criminal investigations because no two people, save for identical twins, have the same genetic code. Therefore, lab technicians, using the process described in Figure 6.10, can compare the DNA sample of a suspect such as Jackson to the evidence found at the crime scene. If the match is negative, it is certain that the two samples did not come from the same source. If the match is positive, the lab will determine the odds that the DNA sample could have come from somebody other than the subject. These odds are so high—sometimes reaching 30 billion to one—that a match is practically conclusive.[133]

FIGURE 6.10

Unlocking Evidence in DNA

Deoxyribonucleic acid, or DNA, is the genetic material that carries the code for all living cells. DNA is useful to crime solvers thanks to the discovery that the DNA of one person is different from the DNA of all other persons (except identical twins). Through DNA profiling, a process explained here, forensic scientists test DNA samples to see if they match the DNA profile of a known criminal or other test subject.

1. Collection of Samples. DNA samples can be taken from a number of sources, including saliva, blood, hair, or skin. These samples are labeled and shipped to a forensic lab.

2. Extraction and Purification. At the lab, the sample is mixed with chemicals that break open the cells and let the DNA seep out. The broken cell fragments are removed from the mixture, and the remains are placed in a test tube. This tube is then spun very quickly, which makes the pure DNA sink to the bottom.

3. Separation and Binding The double helix is then separated into two single strands. Lab technicians add "probes" to the single strands. These probes are short pieces of single-stranded DNA: A pairs with T and C pairs with G. Because the probes are tagged with radioactivity, technicians follow them as they form connections, and figure out the strand of the original DNA sample. (For example, whenever a T probe connects, it connects with an A strand, and so on.)

4. Replication. DNA samples are very small and difficult to see. Consequently, scientists have invented a way to "photocopy" them using a process called polymerase chain reaction (PCR). In PCR, when a probe attaches itself to a rung in the original DNA, it very quickly creates a large number of copies of the new pair. (Imagine that the probe acts like a finger pressing the "copy" button on a photocopying machine, producing repeated patterns such as ATGCTAGCAT, and so on.)

5. Identification. Next, technicians place a drop containing millions of DNA fragments at one end of a sheet of gel. An electric current is then run through the sheet, a process that pulls the DNA fragments across the gel. The larger a fragment is, the slower it will move. In order to measure these movements, the DNA fragments are tagged with dye, and they show up as colored bands when exposed to ultraviolet light.

6. Matching. Normally, a crime lab will analyze thirteen places on a person's DNA in the profiling process. These thirteen markers will be compared to a suspect's DNA profiles that are already on file. If a match is found for each of the thirteen markers, there is almost no chance that the two DNA samples did not come from the same person.

193

A Wealth of Evidence

The initial use of DNA to establish criminal guilt took place in Britain in 1986; the FBI used it for the first time in the United States two years later. The process begins when forensic technicians gather blood, semen, skin, saliva, or hair from the scene of the crime. Blood cells and sperm are rich in DNA, making them particularly useful in murder and rape cases, but DNA has also been extracted from sweat, skin cells, and saliva on dirty laundry, eyeglasses, and used envelope seals.[134] Once a suspect is identified, her or his DNA can be tested to determine whether she or he can be placed at the crime scene. In 2005, for example, Illinois investigators were able to determine that Bart Ross was responsible for killing Michael Lefkow and Donna Humphrey—the husband and mother of U.S. District Judge Joan Lefkow—because of his saliva on a cigarette butt found near the bodies. This key piece of evidence ended intense police and media speculation that the victims had been murdered by white supremacists angered at rulings made against their interests by Judge Lefkow.

Databases and Cold Hits

The ability to "dust" for genetic information on such a wide variety of evidence, as well as that evidence's longevity and accuracy, greatly increases the "solvability" factors discussed earlier in the chapter. Indeed, as the Richard Jackson and Bart Ross cases show, police no longer need a witness or even a suspect to solve crimes. What they do seem to need, however, is a database. The blood on the rag in Charlotte Stewart's apartment was traced to Jackson only because, as a convicted felon, his DNA had automatically been entered into the national Combined DNA Index System (CODIS). Operated by the FBI since 1998, CODIS gives local and state law enforcement agencies access to the DNA profiles of a wide variety of persons who have been convicted of homicide and sexual assault. Today, CODIS contains DNA records of more than 2.1 million people.[135]

Jackson's arrest is an example of what police call a *cold hit*, the process in which the police "find a suspect out of nowhere" by matching DNA evidence from a crime scene against the contents of a database.[136] In 2004, this process was used to link Chester D. Turner, imprisoned for rape, to the unrelated murders of twelve women that occurred in California between 1987 and 1998. As of February 2005, CODIS had aided almost 1,000 investigations in that state[137] and produced 20,200 cold hits nationwide.[138]

The Many Uses of DNA

The cold hits made on Chester D. Turner were particularly welcome news for David Allen Jones, who was released in March 2004 after spending nine years in prison for three of the murders actually committed by Turner. Jones's situation underscores the fact that DNA fingerprinting is as effective at proving innocence as it is at determining guilt. Also in 2004, DNA evidence freed Bruce Goodman, who spent nineteen years in Utah State Prison after being wrongly convicted of raping and murdering his girlfriend in 1984. Jones and Goodman are only two of nearly 160 persons exonerated by DNA evidence as of April 2005.[139]

Police investigators have even started to turn the DNA microscope on nonviolent crimes such as burglaries and car thefts, which previously were ignored because they did not produce DNA-rich evidence such as blood, semen, or saliva. New high-sensitivity crime labs can create a genetic profile using only six cells' worth of DNA, compared to the 150 cells needed for the more common variety of testing.[140] A test run of this new system in New York City identified twenty-three suspects linked to thirty-four property crimes. Proponents of expanding expensive DNA fingerprinting to property crimes believe it will have a "broken windows" effect (see page 172) of its own by stopping nonviolent offenders before they turn violent.[141]

Privacy Concerns

All fifty states have passed legislation requiring the collection of DNA samples from convicted sex offenders, and most require such samples from any person convicted of a violent felony.[142] If the benefits of DNA databases are so evident, many observers ask, why not expand the range of collection? Some states have already begun to do so. Arizona, Kansas, and Oregon require juveniles found delinquent of certain sex offenses to submit DNA samples.[143] Louisiana and Virginia collect DNA from everyone arrested for a felony, a practice California will begin in 2009.[144]

As much as the prospect of ever-increasing DNA databases may encourage law enforcement professionals, it frightens many civil libertarians. The main issue concerns personal privacy, which the United States Supreme Court has identified as a "fundamental right" guaranteed by our Constitution.[145] Having been found guilty of a crime by a jury, convicted felons are said to have relinquished their right to privacy. But what of those who have only been arrested and have not been convicted? Do they have a right to keep certain information that DNA testing can reveal—such as a genetic predisposition to disease—private? Observers such as Barry Steinhardt, associate director of the American Civil Liberties Union, are troubled by laws that allow DNA searches before conviction.[146] Steinhardt and his allies point out that about 50,000 people a year are arrested but never prosecuted for felonies in California alone and, therefore, requiring all arrestees to submit DNA imposes a heavy burden on possibly innocent citizens. Further, he is worried that the law will encourage police officers to make "pretextual" arrests solely for the purpose of collecting DNA from suspects whom the officers do not have enough evidence to arrest.[147]

The issue of privacy was at the heart of a lawsuit brought by a convicted sex offender against the state of Connecticut.[148] The convict argued that the state did not have reasonable cause to store his DNA in its database because it could not be sure that he would commit another crime. Therefore, he argued, the DNA collection was an illegal search.[149] The U.S. Court of Appeals for the Second Circuit rejected this argument, holding that Connecticut's interest in protecting its citizens from possible sex offenders was greater than an individual convict's interest in keeping his or her blood from being tested.[150] When the U.S. Court of Appeals for the Ninth Circuit reached a similar conclusion in a similar case in 2004, it meant that every U.S. circuit court of appeals in the nation had upheld DNA collection as a constitutional practice.[151]

Making Sense of DNA Profiling

1 Do you agree that the positive impact of DNA profiling on crime-fighting efforts outweighs an individual's interest in privacy? Why or why not?

2 How far should the government be allowed to go in collecting DNA samples from citizens? Should such methods be limited to felons convicted of violent crimes? To anybody convicted of any felony? To those who have only been arrested?

3 Considering how successful DNA is in identifying criminals, should those accused or convicted of crimes automatically be given access to DNA material in preparing their defense? What might be the pros and cons of such a policy? In making your answer, be aware that only three states—Illinois, Minnesota, and New York—have laws that require courts to honor such a request. In most other states, judges can deny such a request under most circumstances.

Chapter Summary

1 Identify the differences between the police academy and field training as learning tools for recruits. The police academy is a controlled environment where police recruits learn the basics of policing from instructors in classrooms. In contrast, field training takes place in the "real world": the recruit is taken on patrol with an experienced police officer. In the field, the recruit learns to apply the lessons he or she received at the academy.

2 Explain some of the benefits of a culturally diverse police force. Members of an integrated police force are more likely to develop strong relationships with the community, which may allow them to do a more effective job of maintaining law and order. Specifically, a predominantly white department can be a "dangerous irritant" in minority neighborhoods during times of crisis.

3 Describe the theory behind a differential response strategy of responding to calls for service. A differential response strategy allows a police department to distinguish among calls for service so that officers may respond to important calls more quickly. Therefore, a "hot" crime, such as a burglary in progress, will receive more immediate attention than a "cold" crime, such as a missing automobile that disappeared several days earlier.

4 Explain community policing and its strategies. Community policing involves proactive problem solving and a community-police partnership in which the community engages itself along with the police to address crime and the fear of crime in a particular geographic area. Strategies include sending police officers to schools, opening community intervention offices for high-risk youths, and encouraging police officers to live in high-crime neighborhoods.

5 Describe two types of problem-solving policing. (a) By concentrating on *hot spots,* or areas of high criminal activity, police can prepare specific strategies for combating those crimes; and (b) *crime mapping* allows law enforcement officials to identify geographic areas that are likely to be susceptible to certain types of crimes, and deploy personnel to those areas accordingly.

6 List the three primary purposes of police patrol. (a) The deterrence of crime, (b) the maintenance of public order,

STORIES FROM THE STREET

Go to the *Stories from the Street* feature at **www.cjinaction.com** to hear Larry Gaines tell insightful stories related to this chapter and his experiences in the field.

and (c) the provision of services that are not related to crime.

7 Indicate some investigation strategies that are considered aggressive. Using undercover officers is considered an aggressive (and often dangerous) investigative technique. The use of informants is also aggressive, but involves danger for those who inform.

8 Determine when police officers are justified in using deadly force. Police officers must make a reasonable judgment in determining when to use force that will place the suspect in threat of injury or death; that is, given the circumstances, the officer must reasonably assume that the use of such force is necessary to avoid serious injury or death to the officer or someone else.

9 Identify the three traditional forms of police corruption. The three traditional forms are bribery, shakedowns, and mooching.

10 Explain what an ethical dilemma is and name four categories of ethical dilemmas typically facing a police officer. An ethical dilemma is a situation in which police officers (a) do not know the right course of action; (b) have difficulty doing what they consider to be right; and/or (c) find the wrong choice very tempting. The four types of ethical dilemmas involve (a) discretion, (b) duty, (c) honesty, and (d) loyalty.

Key Terms

✓ blue curtain   183
✓ broken windows theory   172
  bureaucracy   165
✓ citizen oversight   190
✓ community policing   169
  confidential informant
     (CI)   181
✓ deadly force   185
✓ delegation of authority   167
  detective   179
  differential response   167
  directed patrol   178
✓ duty   191
✓ ethics   190
  field training   163
  general patrol   178
  hot spots   171
  incident-driven policing   167
  internal affairs unit
     (IAU)   190
  police corruption   188
  police cynicism   183
  police subculture   183
  problem-solving
     policing   171
✓ reasonable force   185
✓ response time   167
  socialization   183

Questions for Critical Analysis

1 In what sense have police departments' physical standards been used to discriminate against women?

2 Contrast the community policing model with the professional policing model.

3 The Kansas City Preventive Patrol Experiment involved control beats, proactive beats, and reactive beats. Did the results of that experiment show any benefits to increasing preventive police patrol? If yes, how? If not, why not?

4 Relate the concept of "broken windows" to high-crime neighborhoods and potential ways to combat crime in such neighborhoods.

5 What are the various experiences that rookie police officers undergo that make them aware they are not in a "normal" job?

6 How does the police subculture affect police officers?

7 Under what circumstances can a police officer legally shoot a suspect who is trying to escape a crime scene?

8 How does the police subculture contribute to police corruption?

Test Preparation Online

Criminal JusticeNow

Go to **www.cjinaction.com** and click on *Criminal JusticeNow* for access to this powerful online study tool. You will get a *personalized study plan* based on your responses to a diagnostic pretest. Once you have mastered the material with the help of interactive learning tools, video clips with questions, an integrated e-book, and more, you can take a posttest to confirm you are ready to move on to the next chapter.

Book Companion Web Site

At the book companion Web site (**www.cjinaction.com**), you will find many resources in addition to *Criminal JusticeNow* to aid you in studying for your exams. For example, under *Chapter Resources*, you will find the *Chapter Outline, Chapter Summary, Flashcards,*

Glossary, Learning Objectives, Lecture Presentations, Concept Builder, Essay Questions, and a *Tutorial Chapter Quiz.* You can also test yourself with interactive *Online Reviews* of each chapter section. Check out the *Web Links* to access the Web sites mentioned in the text, as well as many others. You can also access recent perspectives by clicking on *CJ in the News* and *Terrorism Update* under *Course Resources.*

Suggested Readings

Klinger, David, *Inside the Kill Zone: A Cop's Eye View of Deadly Force*, San Francisco: Jossey-Bass, 2004. When the author was a twenty-three-year-old Los Angeles police officer, he shot and killed a man who had attacked his partner. In this book, Klinger describes how taking another person's life changed his own and also interviews numerous other law enforcement agents involved in fatal shootings. Though media coverage of police shootings tends to focus on the outrage felt by the victim's family and the community, Klinger is more interested in presenting the emotions of the officers before, during, and after these violent encounters. The stories drive home a harsh reality of life as a police officer: every day, the possibility exists that you will have to kill.

Queen, William, *Under and Alone: The True Story of the Undercover Agent Who Infiltrated America's Most Violent Outlaw Motorcycle Gang,* New York: Random House, 2005. The author, a special agent with the Bureau of Alcohol, Tobacco, Firearms and Explosives (ATF), spent twenty-eight months as "Billy St. John," a member of the Mongol Nation. The California-based motorcycle gang was heavily involved in a wide variety of crimes from drug dealing, to weapons trafficking, to murder, and during his undercover stint, Queen lived in constant danger of discovery and serious harm to his own well-being. Undercover operations are among the most effective strategies available to law enforcement, but, as is evident from Queen's story, they also take a tremendous toll on the agents involved. Besides the physical dangers, undercover agents must also deal with the emotional stress of knowing that they must betray those who, though criminals, often become trusted friends. The book gives the sense that Queen identified more with his bearded, beer-swilling Mongol companions than with his buttoned-down, bureaucratic colleagues at the ATF and was even, at times, tempted to "switch sides"—turn in his badge and ride off into a life of crime.

Notes

1. Richard Winton, "Broad Review of LAPD Use of Force Urged," *Los Angeles Times* (February 15, 2005), B3.
2. Quoted in Gordon Witkin, "When the Bad Guys Are Cops," *U.S. News and World Report* (September 11, 1995), 22.
3. James H. Chenoweth, "Situational Tests: A New Attempt at Assessing Police Candidates," *Journal of Criminal Law, Criminology and Police Science* 52 (1961), 232.
4. Matthew J. Hickman and Brian A. Reaves, *Local Police Departments 2000* (Washington, D.C.: U.S. Department of Justice, January 2003), 10.
5. Frank Horvath, "Polygraphic Screening Candidates for Police Work in Large Police Agencies in the United States: A Survey of Practices, Policies, and Evaluative Comments," *American Journal of Police* 12 (1993), 67–86.
6. David L. Carter and Allen D. Sapp, "College Education and Policing: Coming of Age," *FBI Law Enforcement Bulletin* 61 (1992), 8.
7. Hickman and Reaves, 11.
8. D. P. Hinkle, "College Degree: An Impractical Prerequisite for Police Work," *Law and Order* (July 1991), 105.
9. Hickman and Reaves, 11.
10. Bureau of Justice Statistics, *State and Local Law Enforcement Training Academies, 2002* (Washington, D.C.: U.S. Department of Justice, January 2005), 18.
11. National Advisory Commission on Civil Disorder, *Report* (Washington, D.C.: U.S. Government Printing Office, 1968), Chapter 11.
12. *State and Local Law Enforcement Training Academies, 2002,* 8.
13. *Griggs v. Duke Power Co.,* 401 U.S. 424 (1971); and *Abermarle Paper Co. v. Moody,* 422 U.S. 405 (1975).
14. Corrine Streit, "Recruiting Minority Officers," *Law Enforcement Technology* (February 2001), 70–75.
15. *Detroit Police Officers' Association v. Young,* 608 F.2d 671, 675 (1979).
16. *Wygant v. Jackson Board of Education,* 476 U.S. 314 (1986).
17. Hickman and Reaves, 4.
18. National Research Council of the National Academies, *Fairness and Effectiveness in Policing: The Evidence* (Washington, D.C.: National Academies Press, 2004), 82.
19. Lawrence M. Friedman, *Crime and Punishment in American History* (New York: Basic Books, 1993), 364–365.
20. Hickman and Reaves, 4.
21. Liz Tascio, "Women Recruits Meet High Standard," *Contra Costa Times* (March 16, 2003), 4.
22. Kimberly A. Lonsway, "Tearing Down the Wall: Problems with Consistency, Validity, and Adverse Impact of Physical Agility Testing in Police Selection," *Police Quarterly* (2003), 237.
23. *Lanning v. SEPTA,* No. 01-1040 (3d Cir. 2002).
24. "DOJ Decides Suit Is a Bad Fit," *Law Enforcement News* (October 31, 2001), 1.
25. Penny E. Harrington, *Recruiting and Retaining Women: A Self-Assessment Guide for Law Enforcement* (Los Angeles: National Center for Women & Policing, 2001), 22–27.
26. Larry K. Gaines and Gary W. Cordner, *Policing Perspectives: An Anthology* (Los Angeles: Roxbury Publishing Co., 1999), 351.
27. H. Nees, "Policing 2001," *Law and Order* (January 1990), 257–264.
28. Peter K. Manning, *Police Work: The Social Organization of Policing,* 2d ed. (Prospect Heights, IL: Waveland Press, 1997), 96.
29. Samuel Walker, *The Police in America: An Introduction,* 2d ed. (New York: McGraw-Hill, 1992), 16.
30. George L. Kelling and Mark H. Moore, "From Political to Reform to Community: The Evolving Strategy of Police," in *Community Policing: Rhetoric or Reality,* ed. Jack Greene and Stephen Mastrofski (New York: Praeger Publishers, 1988), 13.

31. Henry M. Wrobleski and Karen M. Hess, *Introduction to Law Enforcement and Criminal Justice,* 7th ed. (Belmont, CA: Wadsworth/Thomson Learning, 2003), 173.

32. Patrick McGreevy, "LAPD's Response Time Gauged," *Los Angeles Times* (February 16, 2005), B3.

33. "311 Is Not Just for Urban Areas Anymore," *Law Enforcement News* (August 31, 2003), 1.

34. See **http://www.911dispatch.com/information/311map.html**.

35. Office of Justice Programs, *Managing Calls to Police with 911/311 Systems* (Washington, D.C.: U.S. Department of Justice, February 2005), 4.

36. Lawrence W. Sherman, "Attacking Crime: Police and Crime Patrol," in *Modern Policing,* ed. Michael H. Tonry and Norval Morris, vol. 16 of *Crime and Justice: A Review of Research* (Chicago: University of Chicago Press, 1992), 335.

37. *Ibid.,* 338.

38. Robert Trojanowicz, *An Evaluation of the Neighborhood Foot Patrol Program in Flint, Michigan* (East Lansing, MI: Michigan State University, 1982), 85–87.

39. George Kelling, "Police and Community: The Quiet Revolution," in *Perspectives on Policing* (Washington, D.C.: National Institute of Justice, 1988).

40. Mark H. Moore and George L. Kelling, "'To Serve and Protect': Learning from Police History," *Public Interest* (Winter 1983), 54–57.

41. A. Steven Dietz, "Evaluating Community Policing: Quality Police Service and Fear of Crime," *Policing: An International Journal of Police Strategies and Management* 20 (1997), 83–100.

42. Martin Luttrell, "New Vehicles to Help City's Community Policing Effort," *Worcester Telegram & Gazette* (February 18, 2005), B1.

43. "The Worcester Police Department Community Policing Initiative," page 6, available at **http://www.ci.worcester.ma.us/wpd/pdf/PolicingInitiative.pdf**.

44. "Fighting Crime, Japanese Style," *Economist* (August 7, 1999), 24.

45. Herman Goldstein, "Improving Policing: A Problem-Oriented Approach," *Crime and Delinquency* 25 (1979), 236–258.

46. Kelling and Moore, 12.

47. Bureau of Justice Assistance, *Problem-Oriented Drug Enforcement: A Community-Based Approach for Effective Policing* (Washington, D.C.: Office of Justice Programs, 1993), 5.

48. Sherman, 331–332.

49. Lawrence W. Sherman, Patrick R. Gartin, and Michael E. Buerger, "Hot Spots of Predatory Crime: Routine Activities and the Criminology of Place," *Criminology* 27 (1989), 27–55.

50. National Institute of Justice Research Preview, *Policing Drug Hot Spots* (Washington, D.C.: Office of Justice Programs, January 1996).

51. Brian J. Taylor, "The Screening of America," *Reason* (May 1, 1997), 44.

52. James Q. Wilson and George L. Kelling, "Broken Windows," *Atlantic Monthly* (March 1982), 29–38.

53. Milton J. Valencia, "Police Have Impact on Main Street," *Worcester Telegram & Gazette* (March 14, 2004), A1.

54. Office of Community Oriented Policing Services, *Promising Strategies from the Field: A National Overview* (Washington, D.C.: U.S. Department of Justice, 2002), 1.

55. Hickman and Reaves, 15.

56. National Institute of Justice Research Preview, *Community Policing Strategies* (Washington, D.C.: Office of Justice Programs, November 1995).

57. Jihong Zhao and Quint C. Thurman, "Community Policing: Where Are We Now?" *Crime and Delinquency* (July 1997), 345–357.

58. Wrobleski and Hess, 119.

59. Connie Fletcher, "What Cops Know," *On Patrol* (Summer 1996), 44–45.

60. David H. Bayley, *Police for the Future* (New York: Oxford University Press, 1994), 20.

61. Walker, 103.

62. Eric J. Scott, *Calls for Service: Citizens Demand an Initial Police Response* (Washington, D.C.: National Institute of Justice, 1981), 28–30.

63. William G. Gay, Theodore H. Schell, and Stephen Schack, *Routine Patrol: Improving Patrol Productivity,* vol. 1 (Washington, D.C.: National Institute of Justice, 1977), 3–6.

64. Gary W. Cordner, "The Police on Patrol," in *Police and Policing: Contemporary Issues,* ed. Dennis Jay Kenney (New York: Praeger Publishers, 1989), 60–71.

65. Anthony V. Bouza, *The Police Mystique: An Insider's Look at Cops, Crime, and the Criminal Justice System* (New York: Plenum Press, 1990), 27.

66. Hickman and Reaves, 10.

67. Dale O. Cloninger, "Enforcement Risks and Deterrence: A Reexamination," *Journal of Socio-Economics* 23 (1994), 273.

68. George L. Kelling, Tony Pate, Duane Dieckman, and Charles Brown, *The Kansas City Preventive Patrol Experiment: A Summary Report* (Washington, D.C.: The Police Foundation, 1974), 3–4.

69. *Ibid.*

70. Carl B. Klockars and Stephen D. Mastrofski, "The Police and Serious Crime," in *Thinking about Police,* ed. Carl Klockars and Stephen Mastrofski (New York: McGraw-Hill, 1990), 130.

71. James Q. Wilson, *Thinking about Crime* (New York: Basic Books, 1983), 65–66.

72. Robert Sheehan and Gary W. Cordner, *Introduction to Police Administration,* 2d ed. (Cincinnati, OH: Anderson, 1989), 367–368.

73. U.S. Bureau of Labor Statistics, "Police and Detectives," in *Occupational Outlook Handbook,* at **http://www.bls.gov/oco/ocos160.htm**.

74. Peter W. Greenwood and Joan Petersilia, *The Criminal Investigation Process: Summary and Policy Implications* (Santa Monica, CA: Rand Corporation, 1975).

75. Fletcher, 46.

76. John E. Eck, *Solving Crimes: The Investigation of Burglary and Robbery* (Washington, D.C.: Police Executive Research Forum, 1983).

77. Steven G. Brandl and James Frank, "The Relationship between Evidence, Detective Effort, and the Disposition of Burglary and Robbery Investigations," *American Journal of Police* 1 (1994), 149–168.

78. Jacqueline L. Urgo, "Breathing Life into a 25-Year-Old Unsolved Death," *Philadelphia Inquirer* (April 3, 2005), B3.

79. John S. Dempsey, *An Introduction to Policing*, 3d ed. (Belmont, CA: Thomson Wadsworth, 2005), 173.

80. 353 U.S. 53 (1957).

81. Army Appropriations Act, Ch. 263, Section 15, 20 Stat. 145 (1878), codified as amended at 18 U.S.C. Section 1385 (2000).

82. Military Cooperation with Law Enforcement Officials Act of 1981, Pub. L. No. 97-86, Section 905, 95 Stat. 1115, codified as amended at 10 U.S.C. Sections 371–378 (1998).

83. Diane Cecilia Weber, *Warrior Cops: The Ominous Growth of Paramilitarism in American Police Departments*, Cato Institute Briefing Paper No. 50 (1999), at **http://www. cato.org/pubs/briefs/bp-050es.html**.

84. Raytheon Corporation, *NightSight Field Assessment: Creative Technology Solutions to Law Enforcement Problems* (Rockville, MD: National Criminal Justice Reference Service, 2002), 2.

85. Hickman and Reaves, 13.

86. Scott Lindlaw, "U.S. Mulls Military's Domestic Role," *Associated Press* (July 22, 2002).

87. Timothy Egan, "Killing of White Deputy Quiets Protests over Police Shootings of 2 Blacks," *New York Times* (July 13, 2002), A7.

88. *Ibid.*

89. Edgar H. Schein, *Organizational Culture and Leadership* (San Francisco: Jossey-Bass, 1985), 9.

90. Harry J. Mullins, "Myth, Tradition, and Ritual," *Law and Order* (September 1995), 197.

91. John Van Maanen, "Observations on the Making of a Policeman," *Human Organization* 32 (1973), 407–418.

92. William Westly, *Violence and the Police: A Sociological Study of Law, Custom, and Morality* (Cambridge, MA: MIT Press, 1970).

93. Wallace Graves, "Police Cynicism: Causes and Cures," *FBI Law Enforcement Bulletin* (June 1996), 16–21.

94. Robert Regoli, *Police in America* (Washington, D.C.: R. F. Publishing, 1977).

95. Bob Herbert, "A Cop's View," *New York Times* (March 15, 1998), 17.

96. Jerome H. Skolnick, *Justice without Trial: Law Enforcement in a Democratic Society* (New York: Wiley, 1966), 44.

97. Detis T. Duhart, *Violence in the Workplace, 1993–99* (Washington, D.C.: U.S. Department of Justice, December 2001), 1.

98. Les Krantz, *Job-Related Almanac* (New York: World Almanac, 1998).

99. James Hibberd, "Police Psychology," *On Patrol* (Fall 1996), 26.

100. "Dispatches," *On Patrol* (Summer 1996), 25.

101. Friedman, 362.

102. National Research Council of the National Academies, 67.

103. Bureau of Justice Statistics, *Contacts between Police and the Public* (Washington, D.C.: U.S. Department of Justice, February 2005), v.

104. Independent Commission on the Los Angeles Police Department, *Report of the Independent Commission on the Los Angeles Police Department* (1991), ix.

105. Joel Garner, John Buchanan, Tom Schade, and John Hepburn, *Research in Brief: Understanding the Use of Force by and against the Police* (Washington, D.C.: Office of Justice Programs, November 1996), 5.

106. *Ibid.*, 1.

107. 471 U.S. 1 (1985).

108. 471 U.S. 1, 11 (1985).

109. 490 U.S. 386 (1989).

110. *Brosseau v. Haugen,* 125 S.Ct. 596 (2004).

111. Hickman and Reaves, 22.

112. Charisse Jones, "Police Say Taser Shocks Are Replacing Deadly Shots," *USA Today* (July 14, 2004), 2A.

113. "Amnesty Criticizes Taser's Safer Pitch," *Arizona Daily Star* (April 1, 2005), A7.

114. Cited in Peter Noel, "I Thought He Had a Gun," *Village Voice* (July 13, 1998), 41.

115. Bureau of Justice Statistics, *Contacts between Police and the Public,* 16.

116. Malcolm D. Holmes, "Minority Threat and Police Brutality: Determinants of Civil Rights Criminal Complaints in U.S. Municipalities," *Criminology* 38 (May 2000), 361.

117. "Police Shooting Widens Racial Gap," *Los Angeles Times* (March 3, 2005), A2.

118. Randall L. Kennedy, "*McCleskey v. Kemp,* Race, Capital Punishment, and the Supreme Court," *Harvard Law Review* 101 (1988), 1436–1438.

119. Douglas A. Smith, "Minorities and the Police: Attitudinal and Behavioral Questions," *Race and Criminal Justice,* ed. Michael J. Lynch and E. Britt Patterson (New York: Harrow & Heston, 1991), 28–30.

120. Matt Lait and Scott Glover, "Inglewood Police Accused of Abuse in Other Cases," *Los Angeles Times* (July 15, 2002), A1.

121. J. Dorschner, "Police Deviance: Corruption and Controls," in *Critical Issues in Policing, Contemporary*

Readings, ed. Roger G. Dunham and Geoffrey P. Albert (Prospect Heights, IL: Waveland Press, 1989), 249–285.

122. Lawrence W. Sherman, "Becoming Bent: Moral Careers of Corrupt Policemen," in *Police Corruption: A Sociological Perspective,* ed. Lawrence W. Sherman (Garden City, NY: Doubleday, 1974), 191–208.

123. Knapp Commission, *Report on Police Corruption* (New York: Brazilier, 1973).

124. Quoted in Jennifer Dukes and Loren Keller, "Can Police Be Police to Selves?" *Omaha World-Herald* (February 22, 1998), 1A.

125. AP Alert—California, "L.A. Police Corruption Settlements Estimates to Reach $70 Million," *Associated Press* (March 31, 2005).

126. National Research Council of the National Academies, 279, 289.

127. "Roster of Civilian Oversight Agencies in the U.S.," National Association for Civilian Oversight of Law Enforcement, at **http://www.nacole.org**.

128. Hazel Glenn Beh, "Municipal Liability for Failure to Investigate Citizen Complaints against Police," *Fordham Urban Law Journal* 23 (Winter 1998), 209.

129. Jocelyn M. Pollock and Ronald F. Becker, "Ethics Training Using Officers' Dilemmas," *FBI Law Enforcement Bulletin* (November 1996), 20–28.

130. *Ibid.*

131. Linda S. Miller and Karen M. Hess, *Police in the Community: Strategies for the 21st Century,* 2d ed. (Belmont, CA: Wadsworth Publishing, 1998), 81.

132. Shaila K. Dewan, "Review of DNA Evidence Leads to Arrest in '94 Death," *New York Times* (October 9, 2004), B15.

133. Judith E. Lewter, "The Use of Forensic DNA in Criminal Cases in Kentucky as Compared with Other Selected States," *Kentucky Law Journal* (1997–1998), 223.

134. National Institute of Justice, *NIJ Special Report: Using DNA to Solve Cold Cases* (Washington, D.C.: U.S. Department of Justice, July 2002), 21.

135. Richard Roesler, "Legislators Seek to Expand Collection of Convicts' DNA Databanks to Help Solve Crimes," *The (Spokane) Spokesman-Review* (February 20, 2005), 1A.

136. Christi Parsons and Steve Mills, "State to Collect DNA Data from All New Felons," *Chicago Tribune* (August 23, 2002), 1.

137. CODIS statistics at **http://www.fbi.gov/hq/lab/codis/ca.htm**.

138. CODIS statistics at **http://www.fbi.gov/hq/lab/codis/success.htm**.

139. See **http://www.innocentproject.org**.

140. Shaila K. Dewan, "New York, to Catch Burglars, Works on a Better DNA Trap," *New York Times* (May 26, 2004), A1.

141. Shaila K. Dewan, "Police Try Extending DNA Testing to Different Crimes," *New York Times* (October 26, 2004), A25.

142. Victor M. Manuel, "DNA Data Base and Data Base Expansion Laws," *Western State University Law Review* (Spring 2004), 340–341.

143. Ariz. Rev. Stat. Ann. Sections 13-4438, 31-282 (West 2002); Kan. Stat. Ann. Section 21-2511(a) (Cum. Supp. 2002); Or. Rev. Stat. Section 419C.473(1) (1999).

144. Jason D. Plemons, "Prop. 69 Opens DNA Database," *Fresno Bee* (October 31, 2004), B1.

145. *Katz v. United States,* 389 U.S. 347 (1967).

146. Barry Steinhardt, "Law Opens Door to Abuse," *USA Today* (January 2, 2001), 10A.

147. *Ibid.*

148. *Roe v. Marcotte,* 193 F.3d 76 (2d Cir. 1999).

149. *Ibid.*

150. *Ibid.,* 82.

151. *United States v. Kincade,* 345 F.3d 1000 (9th Cir. 2004).

Police and the Constitution:

The Rules of Law Enforcement

Chapter outline

- The Fourth Amendment
- Stops and Frisks
- Arrests
- Lawful Searches and Seizures
- The Interrogation Process and *Miranda*
- The Identification Process
- Criminal Justice in Action—Racial Profiling and the Constitution

Chapter objectives

After reading this chapter, you should be able to:

1 Outline the four major sources that may provide probable cause.
2 Explain the exclusionary rule and the exceptions to it.
3 Distinguish between a stop and a frisk, and indicate the importance of the case *Terry v. Ohio.*
4 List the four elements that must be present for an arrest to take place.
5 List the four categories of items that can be seized by use of a search warrant.
6 Explain when searches can be made without a warrant.
7 Describe how the USA PATRIOT Act of 2001 changed the guidelines for electronic surveillance of suspected terrorists.
8 Recite the *Miranda* warning.
9 Indicate situations in which a *Miranda* warning is unnecessary.
10 List the three basic types of police identification.

Criminal JusticeNow

Optimize your study time and master key chapter concepts with *Criminal JusticeNow*, an online study tool that provides you with a *personalized study plan.* Check out the "Test Preparation Online" section at the end of the chapter for additional information.

The Case of the Sniffing Dog
Roy Caballes

thought that he was going to catch a break. After all, he had not been driving *that* fast down Interstate 80—71 miles per hour in a 65-mile-per-hour zone—and the Illinois state trooper who pulled him over looked as though he was only going to issue a warning. When another officer showed up with a drug-sniffing dog, however, Caballes's luck ran out. The dog eagerly signaled toward the trunk of Caballes's car, where the troopers found $250,000 worth of marijuana. Caballes was eventually found guilty of drug trafficking and sentenced to twelve years in prison and fined $256,136.

Caballes's lawyers argued that their client's conviction should be overturned because his arrest was improper. According to the United States Supreme Court, law enforcement agents must have a reason to think that a crime has been committed before they can search a person or property. In this case, Caballes had been stopped for speeding, which is not a crime, and the police had no reason to suspect any further criminal activity. If such searches were allowed, predicted the lawyers, police would have almost unlimited power to conduct "roving, suspicionless" investigations of citizens.

In 2005, the Supreme Court disagreed and upheld the conviction. The Illinois troopers did not act randomly; they correctly pulled Caballes over for a traffic

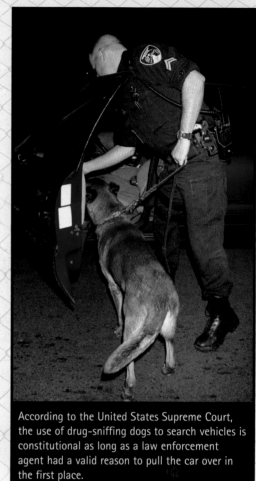

Mario Villafuerte/Getty Images

According to the United States Supreme Court, the use of drug-sniffing dogs to search vehicles is constitutional as long as a law enforcement agent had a valid reason to pull the car over in the first place.

violation. So, said Justice John Paul Stevens, as long as a traffic stop is "lawful at its inception" and the suspect is not detained for an unreasonable amount of time, the use of a drug-sniffing dog in this manner is perfectly constitutional.

Note that the Supreme Court's decision was not unanimous.[1] Two justices felt that the search of Roy Caballes's trunk was unreasonable, with Justice Ruth Bader Ginsburg warning that the ruling cleared the way for "dog-accompanied drug sweeps on parked cars along sidewalks and in parking lots."[2] In effect, each member of the Court was forced to weigh Caballes's personal freedoms against the ability of the Illinois state troopers to combat illegal drugs. This balance between the need for effective law enforcement and the rights of American citizens under the U.S. Constitution has been, and remains, a controversial issue. Many observers feel that courts go too far in protecting the rights of the accused, but others believe that police have been given a dangerous amount of leeway in using their powers. In this chapter we will examine the extent to which police behavior is controlled by the law, starting with a discussion of the constitutional principles on which such control is grounded.

THE FOURTH AMENDMENT

In *Illinois v. Caballes,* the Supreme Court did not address the defendant's illegal activity. Rather, it ruled that the state troopers had not overstepped their boundaries of authority in searching the trunk. To understand these boundaries, law enforcement officers must understand the Fourth Amendment, which reads as follows:

> The right of the people to be secure in their persons, houses, papers, and effects, against unreasonable searches and seizures, shall not be violated, and no Warrants shall issue, but upon probable cause, supported by Oath or affirmation, and particularly describing the place to be searched, and the persons or things to be seized.

This amendment contains two critical legal concepts: a prohibition against *unreasonable* **searches and seizures** and the requirement of *probable cause* to issue a warrant (see Figure 7.1).

Reasonableness

Law enforcement personnel use searches and seizures to look for and collect the evidence they need to convict individuals suspected of crimes. As you have just read, when police are conducting a search or seizure, they must be *reasonable.* Though courts have spent innumerable hours scrutinizing the word, no specific meaning for "reasonable" exists. A thesaurus can provide useful synonyms—logical, practical, sensible, intelligent, plausible—but because each case is different, those terms are relative.

In the *Caballes* case, the Supreme Court rejected the argument that the search had been so unreasonable as to violate the Fourth Amendment's prohibition against unreasonable searches and seizures. That does not mean that the state troopers' actions would have been reasonable under any circumstances. What if, after issuing the warning, the state trooper had forced Caballes to wait an hour before the arrival of the second officer and the drug-sniffing dog? The officers' conduct would almost certainly have been considered unreasonable.

CONCEPT BUILDER

Probable cause is often misunderstood by the general public and at times is even difficult for law enforcement officials to establish. Visit **www.cjinaction.com** for an interactive exploration of this key topic.

Searches and Seizures
The legal term, as found in the Fourth Amendment of the U.S. Constitution, that generally refers to the searching for and the confiscating of evidence by law enforcement agents.

FIGURE 7.1

The Meaning of Unreasonable Searches and Seizures and Probable Cause

Unreasonable Searches and Seizures

The Fourth Amendment provides that individuals have the right to be "secure in their persons" against "unreasonable searches and seizures" conducted by government agents. In practice, this means that law enforcement officers are required to obtain a search warrant prior to any search and seizure. Basically, the search warrant is the acknowledgment by a judge that probable cause exists for law enforcement officers to search for or take a person or property. In other words, the search and seizure must be "reasonable."

Probable Cause

Before a search can take place or an individual can be arrested, the requirement of probable cause must be met. Probable cause exists if there is a substantial likelihood that (1) a crime was committed and (2) the individual committed the crime. Note that probable cause involves a *likelihood*—not just a possibility—that the suspect committed the crime. Probable cause must exist before police can get an arrest warrant or a search warrant from a judge.

Probable Cause

The concept of reasonableness is linked to **probable cause.** The Supreme Court has ruled, for example, that any arrest or seizure is unreasonable unless it is supported by probable cause.[3] The burden of probable cause requires more than mere suspicion on a police officer's part; that officer must know of facts and circumstances that would reasonably lead to "the belief that an offense has been or is being committed."[4]

Sources of Probable Cause If no probable cause existed when a police officer took a certain action, it cannot be retroactively applied. If, for example, a police officer stops a person for jaywalking and then (without the help of a drug-sniffing dog) finds several ounces of marijuana in that person's pocket, the arrest for marijuana possession would probably be disallowed. Remember, suspicion does not equal probable cause. If, however, an informant had tipped the officer off that the person was a drug dealer, probable cause might exist and the arrest could be valid. Informants are one of several sources that may provide probable cause. Others include:

1 *Personal observation.* Police officers may use their personal training, experience, and expertise to infer probable cause from situations that may not be obviously criminal. If, for example, a police officer observes several people in a car slowly circling a certain building in a high-crime area, that officer may infer that the people are "casing" the building in preparation for a robbery. Probable cause could be established for detaining the suspects.

2 *Information.* Law enforcement officers receive information from victims, eyewitnesses, informants, and official sources such as police bulletins or broadcasts. Such information, as long as it is believed to be reliable, is a basis for probable cause.

3 *Evidence.* In certain circumstances, which will be examined later in this chapter, police have probable cause for a search or seizure based on evidence—such as a shotgun—in plain view.

4 *Association.* In some circumstances, if the police see a person with a known criminal background in a place where criminal activity is openly taking place, they have probable cause to stop that person. Generally, however, association is not adequate to establish probable cause.[5]

Michigan state and federal law enforcement officers take part in a predawn raid of a Detroit residence. Before taking such action, the officers must receive permission from a judge or magistrate in the form of a search warrant. Ideally, the judicial official will issue such a warrant only if the law enforcement agency involved can provide probable cause that an illegal activity is taking place in the dwelling. How does the need to provide probable cause in such instances limit police power?

AP Photo, *Detroit News*/Charles V. Tines

The Probable Cause Framework In a sense, the concept of probable cause allows police officers to do their job effectively. Most arrests are made without a warrant because most arrests are the result of quick police reaction to the commission of a crime. Indeed, it would not be practical to expect a police officer to obtain a warrant before making an arrest on the street. Thus, probable cause provides a framework that limits the situations in which police officers can make arrests, but also gives officers the freedom to act within that framework. In 2003, the Supreme Court reaffirmed this freedom by ruling that Baltimore (Maryland) police officers acted properly when they arrested all three passengers of a car in which cocaine had been hidden in the back seat. "A reasonable officer," wrote then Chief Justice William H. Rehnquist, "could conclude that there was probable cause to believe" that the defendant, who had been sitting in the front seat, was in "possession" of the illicit drug despite his protestations to the contrary.[6]

Once an arrest is made, the arresting officer must prove to a judge that probable cause existed. In *County of Riverside v. McLaughlin* (1991),[7] the Supreme Court ruled that this judicial determination of probable cause must be made within forty-eight hours after the arrest, even if this two-day period includes a weekend or holiday.

The Exclusionary Rule

Historically, the courts have looked to the Fourth Amendment for guidance in regulating the activity of law enforcement officers, as the language of the Constitution does not expressly do so. The courts' most potent legal tool in this endeavor is the **exclusionary rule,** which prohibits the use of illegally seized evidence. According to this rule, any evidence obtained by an unreasonable search or seizure is inadmissible (may not be used) against a defendant in a criminal trial.[8] Even highly incriminating evidence, such as a knife stained with the victim's blood, usually cannot be introduced at a trial if illegally obtained. Furthermore, any physical or verbal evidence police are able to acquire by using illegally obtained evidence is known as the **fruit of the poisoned tree** and is also inadmissible. For example, if the police use the existence of the bloodstained knife to get a confession out of a suspect, that confession will be excluded as well.

One of the implications of the exclusionary rule is that it forces police to gather evidence properly. If they follow appropriate procedures, they are more likely to be rewarded with a conviction. If they are careless or abuse the rights of the suspect, they are unlikely to get a conviction. Critics of the exclusionary rule, however, argue that its strict application may permit guilty people to go free because of police carelessness or innocent errors (for an example, see the feature *CJ in Focus—The Balancing Act: Excluding Justice?* on the following page).

Establishing the Exclusionary Rule The exclusionary rule is applied to all evidence presented in federal courts as a result of the decision in *Weeks v. United States.*[9] For almost fifty years after this 1914 case, however, state courts continued to allow illegally obtained evidence, and federal courts could do so if the evidence had been obtained by state officers. This practice was known rather sarcastically as the *silver platter doctrine,* because such evidence handed the prosecution a conviction "on a silver platter." The only exception to the silver platter doctrine was when police actions were so extreme that they "shocked the conscience" of the court.

The "shocks the conscience" standard was established in *Rochin v. California* (1952).[10] In this case, police officers entered Rochin's home without a warrant and saw him place what they thought were narcotics in his mouth. The police tried to forcibly expel the items from Rochin. When this failed, they took him to the hospital and had his stomach pumped. This action produced two tablets of morphine. Rochin was convicted of possession of illegal drugs and sentenced to sixty days in jail. The Supreme Court overturned his conviction on the ground that the police officers' actions violated Rochin's Fourth Amendment due process rights; Justice Felix Frankfurter compared the police's methods to the "rack and screw."

The *Rochin* decision did not make the exclusionary rule applicable to all state cases. Instead, the Supreme Court ruled that it applied only in cases that involved serious police misconduct. The silver platter doctrine was finally eliminated nine years later by the Court's decision in *Mapp v. Ohio* (1961).[11] This case involved an illegal search and seizure conducted by Cleveland (Ohio) police officers. Whereas the Court

Exclusionary Rule
A rule under which any evidence that is obtained in violation of the accused's rights under the Fourth, Fifth, and Sixth Amendments, as well as any evidence derived from illegally obtained evidence, will not be admissible in criminal court.

Fruit of the Poisoned Tree
Evidence that is acquired through the use of illegally obtained evidence and is therefore inadmissible in court.

Excluding Justice?

After the disappearance of fourteen-year-old Destiny Thetford, Harris County (Texas) sheriff's deputies focused their attention on her half brother, Nicholas Thetford, who had a prior sexual relationship with the girl. Nicholas eventually confessed that he had stabbed Destiny to death and placed her body in a drainage ditch. He also implicated a friend, Robert Kaupp, in the murder, but without further evidence Nicholas's statement did not provide enough probable cause for Kaupp's arrest.

Nevertheless, a group of deputies stormed into Kaupp's bedroom at 3 A.M. One of the officers shone a flashlight in the seventeen-year-old's face and said, "[W]e need to go and talk." Kaupp replied, "Okay," and the officers handcuffed him and took him to the police station dressed only in a T-shirt and boxer shorts. At the station, Kaupp initially denied any involvement in the murder, but after being told of Nicholas's confession, he admitted to participating in the crime. Kaupp was eventually found guilty of murder and sentenced to fifty-five years in prison. The United States Supreme Court, however, found that by forcibly transporting the teenager to the police station, the deputies acted as if they had arrested him, and they had done so without probable cause. Consequently, Kaupp's confession was the fruit of an illegal arrest, and because of the exclusionary rule, it was invalid.

The Court's decision highlighted the conflicts inherent in the exclusionary rule. On the one hand, the rule does deter police from violating an individual's constitutional rights and acts as a clear demonstration that law enforcement officers are not above the law. On the other hand, the exclusionary rule imposes costs on society. By his own admission, however obtained, Kaupp was partly responsible for the heinous murder of a young girl. A number of admittedly guilty defendants have been placed back on the streets because of this rule. Furthermore, the rule weakens public confidence in American courts by giving victims and other members of society the perception that "the truth" is less important than procedure in the criminal justice system.

FOR CRITICAL ANALYSIS

Do you think there are other means of ensuring proper police behavior that would be more effective than the exclusionary rule? What if police officers were subject to criminal sanctions for improperly gathering evidence? What if the victim of an unlawful search and seizure or arrest could sue a police officer in civil court?

---

had previously been hesitant to apply the exclusionary rule to a decision made in state courts, the *Mapp* case signaled a new willingness to apply the Fourth Amendment to both federal and state law enforcement officers.[12]

Exceptions to the Exclusionary Rule Critics of the exclusionary rule have long maintained that the costs to society of losing critical evidence are higher than the benefits of deterring police misconduct. In recent decades, a number of Supreme Court decisions have mirrored this view and provided exceptions to the exclusionary rule. The **"inevitable discovery" exception** was established in the wake of the disappearance of ten-year-old Pamela Powers of Des Moines, Iowa, on Christmas Eve, 1968. The police's primary suspect in the case, a religious fanatic named Robert Williams, was tricked by a detective into leading police to the site where he had buried Powers. Specifically, the detective convinced Williams that if he did not lead police to the body, he would soon forget where it was buried. This would deny his victim a "Christian burial." Initially, in *Brewer v. Williams* (1977),[13] the Court ruled that the evidence (Powers's body) had been obtained illegally because Williams's attorney had not been present during the interrogation that led to his admission. The state of Iowa appealed this decision. In *Nix v. Williams* (1984),[14] the Court reversed itself, ruling that the evidence was admissible because the body would have eventually ("inevitably") been found by lawful means.

The scope of the exclusionary rule was further diminished in the wake of the Supreme Court's ruling in *United States v. Leon* (1984).[15] The case involved evidence that had been seized by police on the authority of a search warrant that had been

"Inevitable Discovery" Exception

The legal principle that illegally obtained evidence can be admitted in court if police using lawful means would have "inevitably" discovered it.

improperly issued by a magistrate. In allowing the evidence, the Court created a **"good faith" exception** to the exclusionary rule. Under this exception, evidence acquired by a police officer using a technically incorrect search warrant is admissible if the officer was unaware of the error. In this situation, the officer is said to have acted in "good faith." By the same token, if police officers use a search warrant that they know to be technically incorrect, the good faith exception does not apply and the evidence can be suppressed.

"Good Faith" Exception
The legal principle, established through court decisions, that evidence obtained with the use of a technically faulty search warrant is admissible during trial if the police acted in good faith when they sought the warrant from a judge.

STOPS AND FRISKS

Several years ago, an off-duty Miami–Dade County police officer named Aaron Campbell was driving on the Florida turnpike when he was pulled over by two Orange County deputies, allegedly for changing lanes without properly signaling. A fistfight ensued. At the resulting trial, Campbell claimed that he was stopped because he fit a drug courier profile in use by the deputies; he was an African American and had South Florida license plates. A circuit judge agreed, ruling that Campbell had been stopped illegally.[16]

The problem was not that the deputies had stopped Campbell. Law enforcement officers are expected to stop and question people if there is a suspicion of illegal behavior. The problem was that the Orange County deputies did not have a "reasonable" suspicion that Campbell was breaking the law. Instead, they had only a "mere" suspicion based on the drug courier profile—without any other specific facts. (See the feature *Criminal Justice in Action—Racial Profiling and the Constitution* at the end of the chapter.) When reasonable suspicion exists, police officers are well within their rights to *stop and frisk* a suspect. In a stop and frisk, law enforcement officers (1) briefly detain a person they reasonably believe to be suspicious, and (2) if they believe the person to be armed, proceed to pat down, or "frisk," that person's outer clothing.[17]

A police officer frisks a suspect in Lockhart, Texas. What is the main purpose behind a frisk? When are police justified in frisking someone who has been detained?

John Boykin/PhotoEdit

The Elusive Definition of Reasonable Suspicion

Like so many elements of police work, the decision of whether to stop a suspect is based on the balancing of conflicting priorities. On the one hand, a police officer feels a sense of urgency to act when he or she believes that criminal activity is occurring or is about to occur. On the other hand, law enforcement agents do not want to harass innocent individuals, especially if doing so runs afoul of the U.S. Constitution. In stop-and-frisk law, this balancing act rests on the fulcrum of reasonable suspicion.

Terry v. Ohio   The precedent for the ever-elusive definition of a "reasonable" suspicion in stop-and-frisk situations was established in *Terry v. Ohio* (1968).[18] In that case, a detective named McFadden observed two men (one of whom was Terry) acting strangely in downtown Cleveland. The men would walk past a certain store, peer into the window, and then stop at a street corner and confer. While they were talking, another man joined the conversation and then left quickly. Several minutes later the three men met again at another corner a few blocks away. Detective McFadden believed the trio was planning to break into the store.

FindLaw has a handy summary of the many laws regarding police procedure that can be traced to the Fourth Amendment. Find its Web site by clicking on *Web Links* under *Chapter Resources* at **www.cjinaction.com**.

He approached them, told them who he was, and asked for identification. After receiving a mumbled response, the detective frisked the three men and found handguns on two of them, who were tried and convicted of carrying concealed weapons.

The Supreme Court upheld the conviction, ruling that Detective McFadden had reasonable cause to believe that the men were armed and dangerous and that swift action was necessary to protect himself and other citizens in the area.[19] The Court accepted McFadden's interpretation of the unfolding scene as based on objective facts and practical conclusions. It therefore concluded that his suspicion was reasonable. In the Florida case described above, the deputies' reasons for stopping Campbell—his race and place of car registration—were not seen as reasonable.

The "Totality of the Circumstances" Test For the most part, the judicial system has refrained from placing restrictions on police officers' ability to make stops. In the *Terry* case, the Supreme Court did say that an officer must have "specific and articulable facts" to support the decision to make a stop, but added that the facts may be "taken together with rational inferences."[20] The Court has consistently ruled that because of their practical experience, law enforcement agents are in a unique position to make such inferences and should be given a good deal of freedom in doing so.

In the years since the *Terry* case was decided, the Court has settled on a "totality of the circumstances" test to determine whether a stop is based on reasonable suspicion.[21] In 2002, for example, the Court ruled that a U.S. Border Patrol agent's stop of a minivan in Arizona was reasonable.[22] On being approached by the Border Patrol car, the driver had stiffened, slowed down his van, and avoided making eye contact with the agent. Furthermore, the children in the van waved at the officer in a mechanical manner, as if ordered to do so. The agent pulled over the van and found 128 pounds of marijuana. In his opinion, Chief Justice William Rehnquist pointed out that such conduct might have been unremarkable on a busy city highway, but on an unpaved road thirty miles from the Mexican border it was enough to reasonably arouse the agent's suspicion.[23] The justices also made clear that the need to prevent terrorist attacks is part of the "totality of the circumstances" and, therefore, law enforcement agents will have more leeway to make stops near U.S. borders.

Informants and Reasonable Suspicion A "bare-bones" anonymous tip is at the opposite end of the reasonable suspicion spectrum from a situation that meets the "totality of the circumstances" test. In 2000, the Supreme Court overturned a conviction based on such a "bare-bones" tip. An anonymous caller had told the Miami–Dade County (Florida) police that a young African American male standing at a bus stop was illegally carrying a handgun. Even though the information was correct, the police officer who made the stop and subsequent arrest had no reason other than the anonymous tip to suspect criminal activity.[24]

This restriction does not prevent tips from informants from being valuable resources for police officers. The Court has held that a tip from a *known* informant who had provided reliable information in the past is sufficient to justify a *Terry* stop, even if there is no other supporting evidence to make the stop.[25] Furthermore, an anonymous tip can pass the "totality of the circumstances" test if it is specific enough and the police verify it with their own observations.[26]

A Stop

The terms *stop* and *frisk* are often used in concert, but they describe two separate acts. A **stop** takes place when a law enforcement officer has reasonable suspicion that a criminal activity is about to take place. Because an investigatory stop is not an arrest, there are limits to the extent police can detain someone who has been stopped. For

Stop
A brief detention of a person by law enforcement agents for questioning. The agents must have a reasonable suspicion of the person before making a stop.

example, in one situation an airline traveler and his luggage were detained for ninety minutes while the police waited for a drug-sniffing dog to arrive. The Supreme Court ruled that the initial stop of the passenger was constitutional, but that the ninety-minute wait was excessive.[27]

In 2004, the Court held that police officers could require suspects to identify themselves during a stop that is otherwise valid under the *Terry* ruling.[28] The case involved a Nevada rancher who was fined $250 for refusing to give his name to a police officer investigating a possible assault. The defendant argued that such requests force citizens to incriminate themselves against their will, which is prohibited, as we shall see later in the chapter, by the Fifth Amendment. Justice Anthony Kennedy wrote, however, that "asking questions is an essential part of police investigations" that would be made much more difficult if officers could not determine the identity of a suspect.[29] The ruling validated "stop-and-identify" laws in twenty states and numerous cities and towns.

A Frisk

The Supreme Court has stated that a **frisk** should be a protective measure. Police officers cannot conduct a frisk as a "fishing expedition" simply to try to find items besides weapons, such as illegal narcotics, on a suspect.[30] A frisk does not necessarily follow a stop and in fact may occur only when the officer is justified in thinking that the safety of police officers or other citizens may be endangered.

Again, the question of reasonable suspicion is at the heart of determining the legality of frisks. In the *Terry* case, the Court accepted that Detective McFadden reasonably believed that the three suspects posed a threat. The suspects' refusal to answer McFadden's questions, though within their rights because they had not been arrested, provided him with sufficient motive for the frisk.

ARRESTS

As in the *Terry* case, a stop and frisk may lead to an **arrest.** An arrest is the taking into custody of a citizen for the purpose of detaining him or her on a criminal charge. It is important to understand the difference between a stop and an arrest. In the eyes of the law, a stop is a relatively brief intrusion on a citizen's rights, whereas an arrest—which involves a deprivation of liberty—is deserving of a full range of constitutional protections, which we shall discuss throughout the chapter (see *Mastering Concepts—The Difference between a Stop and an Arrest* on the next page). Consequently, while a stop can be made based on reasonable suspicion, a law enforcement officer needs probable cause, as defined earlier, to make an arrest.[31]

Elements of an Arrest

When is somebody under arrest? The easy—and incorrect—answer would be whenever the police officer says so. In fact, the state of being under arrest is dependent not only on the actions of the law enforcement officers but also on the perception of the suspect. Suppose Mr. Jones is stopped by plainclothes detectives, driven to the police station, and detained for three hours for questioning. During this time, the police never tell Mr. Jones he is under arrest, and in fact, he is free to leave at any time. But if Mr. Jones or any other reasonable person *believes* he is not free to leave, then, according to the Supreme Court, that person is in fact under arrest and should receive the necessary constitutional protections.[32]

Frisk
A pat-down or minimal search by police to discover weapons; conducted for the express purpose of protecting the officer or other citizens, and not to find evidence of illegal substances for use in a trial.

Arrest
To take into custody a person suspected of criminal activity. Police may use only reasonable levels of force in making an arrest.

MASTERING CONCEPTS

The Difference between a Stop and an Arrest

Both stops and arrests are considered seizures because both police actions involve the restriction of an individual's freedom to "walk away." Both must be justified by a showing of reasonableness as well. You should be aware, however, of the differences between a stop and an arrest.

The stop is an important part of police activity. Police officers therefore have the right to stop and frisk a person if they suspect that a crime is about to be committed. Police may stop those who are acting strangely, do not "fit" the time or place, are known to associate with criminals, or are loitering. They may also stop a person who reasonably fits a description of a person who is wanted in conjunction with a crime. During a stop, police can interrogate the person and make a limited search of his or her outer clothing. If anything occurs during the stop, such as the discovery of an illegal weapon, then officers may arrest the person. If an arrest is made, the suspect is now in police custody and is protected by the U.S. Constitution in a number of ways that will be discussed later in the chapter.

	STOP	ARREST
Justification	Reasonable suspicion	Probable cause
Warrant	None	Required in some, though not all, situations
Intent of Officer	The investigation of suspicious activity	To make a formal charge against the suspect
Search	May frisk, or "pat down," for weapons	Full search for weapons and evidence
Scope of Search	Outer clothing only	Area within the suspect's immediate control, or "reach"

Criminal justice professor Rolando V. del Carmen of Sam Houston State University has identified four elements that must be present for an arrest to take place:

1 The *intent* to arrest. In a stop, though it may entail slight inconvenience and a short detention period, there is no intent on the part of the law enforcement officer to take the person into custody. Therefore, there is no arrest. As intent is a subjective term, it is sometimes difficult to determine whether the police officer intended to arrest. In situations when the intent is unclear, courts often rely—as in our hypothetical case of Mr. Jones—on the perception of the arrestee.[33]

2 The *authority* to arrest. State laws give police officers the authority to place citizens under custodial arrest, or take them into custody. Like other state laws, the authorization to arrest varies among the fifty states. Some states, for example, allow off-duty police officers to make arrests, while others do not.

3 *Seizure or detention.* A necessary part of an arrest is the detention of the subject. Detention is considered to have occurred as soon as the arrested individual submits to the control of the officer, whether peacefully or under the threat or use of force.

4 The *understanding* of the person that she or he has been arrested. Through either words—such as "you are now under arrest"—or actions, the person taken into custody must understand that an arrest has taken place. If a subject has been forcibly subdued by the police, handcuffed, and placed in a patrol car, that subject is believed to understand that an arrest has been made. This understanding may be lacking if the person is intoxicated, insane, or unconscious.[34]

Arrests with a Warrant

When law enforcement officers have established probable cause to arrest an individual who is not in police custody, they obtain an **arrest warrant** for that person. An arrest warrant contains information such as the name of the person suspected and the crime he or she is suspected of having committed. (See Figure 7.2 for an example of an arrest warrant.) Judges or magistrates issue arrest warrants after first determining that the law enforcement officers have indeed established probable cause.

There is a perception that an arrest warrant gives law enforcement officers the authority to enter a dwelling without first announcing themselves. This is not accurate. In *Wilson v. Arkansas* (1995),[35] the Supreme Court reiterated the common law requirement that police officers must knock and announce their identity and purpose before entering a dwelling. Under certain conditions, known as **exigent circumstances,** law enforcement officers need not announce themselves. These circumstances include situations in which the officers have a reasonable belief of any of the following:

- The suspect is armed and poses a strong threat of violence to the officers or others inside the dwelling.

Arrest Warrant
A written order, based on probable cause and issued by a judge or magistrate, commanding that the person named on the warrant be arrested by the police.

Exigent Circumstances
Situations that require extralegal or exceptional actions by the police. In these circumstances, police officers are justified in not following procedural rules, such as those pertaining to search and arrest warrants.

FIGURE 7.2
Example of an
Arrest Warrant

Warrantless Arrest
An arrest made without first seeking a warrant for the action; permitted under certain circumstances, such as when the arresting officer has witnessed the crime or has a reasonable belief that the suspect has committed a felony.

- Persons inside the dwelling are in the process of destroying evidence or escaping because of the presence of the police.
- A felony is being committed at the time the officers enter.[36]

The Court clarified "knock and announce" law with its decision in *United States v. Banks* (2003).[37] The defendant in that case, a suspected drug dealer, argued that Las Vegas (Nevada) police acted unconstitutionally by breaking down his door only fifteen to twenty seconds after announcing themselves. (He claimed he was in the shower and did not hear them.) Justice David H. Souter wrote that the reasonableness of police action depends on the circumstances of each individual case, and in this instance the police acted properly because the "prudent dealer" will keep cocaine near a toilet or sink for quick and easy disposal.[38] The case's outcome might have been different, Souter added, if the police had been looking for a stolen piano.[39]

Arrests without a Warrant

Arrest warrants are not always required, and in fact, most arrests are made on the scene without a warrant.[40] A law enforcement officer may make a **warrantless arrest** if:

1 The offense is committed in the presence of the officer; or
2 The officer has knowledge that a crime has been committed and probable cause to believe the crime was committed by a particular suspect.[41]

The type of crime also comes to bear in questions of arrests without a warrant. As a general rule, officers can make a warrantless arrest for a crime they did not see if they have probable cause to believe that a felony has been committed. For misdemeanors, the crime must have been committed in the presence of the officer for a warrantless arrest to be valid. According to a 2001 Supreme Court ruling involving a Texas mother who was handcuffed, taken away from her two young children, and placed in jail for failing to wear her seat belt, even an arrest for a misdemeanor that involves "gratuitous humiliations" imposed by a police officer "exercising extremely poor judgment" is valid as long as the officer can satisfy probable cause requirements.[42]

In certain situations, warrantless arrests are unlawful even though a police officer can establish probable cause. In *Payton v. New York* (1980),[43] for example, the Supreme Court held that when exigent circumstances do not exist and the suspect does not give consent to enter a dwelling, law enforcement officers cannot force themselves in for the purpose of making a warrantless arrest. The *Payton* ruling was expanded to cover the homes of third parties when, in *Steagald v. United States* (1981),[44] the Court ruled that if the police wish to arrest a criminal suspect in another person's home, they cannot enter that home to arrest the suspect without first obtaining a search warrant, a process we will discuss in the following section.

LAWFUL SEARCHES AND SEIZURES

How far can law enforcement agents go in searching and seizing private property? Consider the steps taken by Jenny Stracner, an investigator with the Laguna Beach (California) Police Department. After receiving information that a suspect, Greenwood, was engaged in drug trafficking, Stracner enlisted the aid of the local trash collector in procuring evidence. Instead of taking Greenwood's trash bags to be incinerated, the collector agreed to give them to Stracner. The officer found enough drug paraphernalia in the garbage to obtain a warrant to search Greenwood's home. Subsequently, he was arrested and convicted on narcotics charges.[45]

Remember, the Fourth Amendment is quite specific in forbidding unreasonable searches and seizures. Were Stracner's search of Greenwood's garbage and her seizure of its contents "reasonable"? The Supreme Court thought so, holding that Greenwood's garbage was not protected by the Fourth Amendment.[46]

The Role of Privacy in Searches

A crucial concept in understanding search and seizure law is *privacy.* By definition, a **search** is a governmental intrusion on a citizen's reasonable expectation of privacy. The recognized standard for a "reasonable expectation of privacy" was established in *Katz v. United States* (1967).[47] The case dealt with the question of whether the defendant was justified in his expectation of privacy in the calls he made from a public phone booth. The Supreme Court held that "the Fourth Amendment protects people, not places." Katz prevailed.

In his concurring opinion, Justice John Harlan, Jr., set a two-pronged test for a person's expectation of privacy:

1 The individual must prove that she or he expected privacy, and

2 Society must recognize that expectation as reasonable.[48]

Accordingly, the Court agreed with Katz's claim that he had a reasonable right to privacy in a public phone booth. (Remember, however, that the *Terry* case allows for conditions under which a person's privacy rights are superseded by a reasonable suspicion on the part of a law enforcement officer that a threat to public safety is present.)

In contrast, in *California v. Greenwood* (1988),[49] described above, the Court did not believe that the suspect had a reasonable expectation of privacy when it came to his garbage bags. The Court noted that when we place our trash on a curb, we expose it to any number of intrusions by "animals, children, scavengers, snoops, and other members of the public."[50] In other words, if Greenwood had truly intended for the contents of his garbage bags to remain private, he would not have left them on the side of the road. To give another example, in the case featured in this chapter's opening, the Court ruled that no one has a legitimate privacy interest in possessing illegal drugs or other contraband such as explosives in the trunk of his or her car.[51]

Search and Seizure Warrants

To protect against charges that they have unreasonably infringed on privacy rights during a search, law enforcement officers can obtain a **search warrant.** (See Figure 7.3 on the next page for an example of a search warrant.) Similar to an arrest warrant, a search warrant is a court order that authorizes police to search a certain area. Before a judge or magistrate will issue a search warrant, law enforcement officers must provide:

- Information showing probable cause that a crime has been or will be committed.
- Specific information on the premises to be searched, the suspects to be found and the illegal activities taking place at those premises, and the items to be seized.

Search

The process by which police examine a person or property to find evidence that will be used to prove guilt in a criminal trial.

Search Warrant

A written order, based on probable cause and issued by a judge or magistrate, commanding that police officers or criminal investigators search a specific person, place, or property to obtain evidence.

In the winter of 2005, Major League Baseball Commissioner Bud Selig answered questions concerning the league's new steroid testing program. Members of U.S. Congress had threatened to come up with their own antisteroid measures if Selig and the players' union failed to do so. Why might a federally mandated random drug-testing program of professional baseball players—for steroids or any other illegal substances—run afoul of the Fourth Amendment's ban on unreasonable searches?

AP Photo/Roy Dabner

United States District Court

_____DISTRICT OF_____

In the Matter of the Search of

(Name, address or brief description of person or property to be searched)

SEARCH WARRANT

CASE NUMBER:

TO:_____and any Authorized Officer of the United States

Affidavit(s) having been made before me by_____who has reason to

_____ Affiant

believe that ☐ on the person of or ☐ on the **premises known as** (name, description and/or location)

in the_____District of_____there is now

concealed a certain person or property, namely (describe the person or property)

I am satisfied that the affidavit(s) and any recorded testimony establish probable cause to believe that the person or property so described is now concealed on the person or premises above-described and establish grounds for the issuance of this warrant.

YOU ARE HEREBY COMMANDED to search on or before_____

_____ Date

(not to exceed 10 days) the person or place named above for the person or property specified, serving this warrant and making the search (in the daytime — 6:00 A.M. to 10:00 P.M.) (at any time in the day or night as I find reasonable cause has been established) and if the person or property be found there to seize same, leaving a copy of this warrant and receipt for the person or property taken, and prepare a written inventory of the person or property seized and promptly return this warrant to_____

as required by law. U.S Judge or Magistrate

_____at_____

Date and Time Issued City and State

_____ _____

Name and Title of Judicial Officer Signature of Judicial Officer

The purpose of a search warrant is to establish, before the search takes place, that a _probable cause to search_ justifies infringing on the suspect's reasonable expectation of privacy.

Particularity of Search Warrants The members of the First Congress specifically did not want law enforcement officers to have the freedom to make "general, exploratory" searches through a person's belongings.[52] Consequently, the Fourth Amendment requires that a warrant describe with "particularity" the place to be searched and the things—either people or objects—to be seized.

This "particularity" requirement places a heavy burden on law enforcement officers. Before going to a judge to ask for a search warrant, they must prepare an **affidavit** in which they provide specific, written information on the property that they wish to search and seize. They must know the specific address of any place they wish to search; general addresses of apartment buildings or office complexes are not sufficient. Furthermore, courts generally frown on vague descriptions of goods to be seized. "Stolen goods" would most likely be considered unacceptably imprecise; "1 Lexmark E330 laser printer" would be preferred.

A **seizure** is the act of taking possession of a person or property by the government because of a (suspected) violation of the law. In general, four categories of items can be seized by use of a search warrant:

1 Items that resulted from the crime, such as stolen goods.
2 Items that are inherently illegal for anybody to possess (with certain exceptions), such as narcotics and counterfeit currency.

Affidavit

A written statement of facts, confirmed by the oath or affirmation of the party making it and made before a person having the authority to administer the oath or affirmation.

Seizure

The forcible taking of a person or property in response to a violation of the law.

3 Items that can be called "evidence" of the crime, such as a bloodstained sneaker or a ski mask.

4 Items used in committing the crime, such as an ice pick or a printing press used to make counterfeit bills.[53]

Reasonableness during a Search and Seizure No matter how "particular" a warrant is, it cannot provide for all the conditions that are bound to come up during its service. Consequently, the law gives law enforcement officers the ability to act "reasonably" during a search and seizure in the event of unforeseeable circumstances. For example, if a police officer is searching an apartment for a stolen Lexmark E330 laser printer and notices a vial of crack cocaine sitting on the suspect's bed, that contraband is considered to be in "plain view" and can be seized. (See the feature *You Be the Judge—A Valid Search?*)

Note that if law enforcement officers have a search warrant that authorizes them to search for a stolen laser printer, they would *not* be justified in opening small drawers. Because a printer could not fit in a small drawer, an officer would not have a basis for reasonably searching one. Officers are restricted in terms of where they can look by the items they are searching for.

Searches and Seizures without a Warrant

Although the Court has established the principle that searches conducted without warrants are *per se* (by definition) unreasonable, it has set "specifically established" exceptions to the rule.[54] In fact, most searches, like most arrests, take place in the absence of a judicial order. Warrantless searches and seizures can be lawful when police are in "hot pursuit" of a subject or when they search bags of trash left at the curb for regular collection. Because of the magnitude of smuggling activities in "border areas" such as airports, seaports, and international boundaries, a warrant is normally not needed to search property in those places. The two most important circumstances in which a

YOU BE THE JUDGE

A Valid Search?

THE FACTS

Baltimore police officers obtained a valid warrant to search Larry's apartment for marijuana. Larry's address, as described on the warrant, was "the premises known as 2036 Park Avenue third floor apartment." When the officers conducted the search, they reasonably believed that there was only one apartment on the third floor of the building. In fact, the third floor was divided into two apartments, the second one rented by Harold. Before the officers became aware that they were actually searching Harold's apartment, for which they had no warrant, they discovered illegal drugs there. Harold was eventually charged with possession of heroin with intent to distribute.

THE LAW

To prevent general searches, the Fourth Amendment requires warrants to describe with particularity "the place to be searched." Police officers are required to make a "reasonable effort" to make sure that the place they are searching is the place specified in the warrant.

YOUR DECISION

Harold claims that the evidence against him is invalid, because "the officers, not having a warrant for [his] apartment, had no right to go into that apartment." Do you agree?

[To see how the United States Supreme Court ruled in this case, go to Example 7.1 in Appendix B.]

warrant is not needed, though, are (1) searches incidental to an arrest and (2) consent searches.

Searches Incidental to an Arrest The most frequent exception to the warrant requirement involves **searches incidental to arrests,** so called because nearly every time police officers make an arrest, they also search the suspect. As long as the original arrest was based on probable cause, these searches are valid for two reasons, established by the Supreme Court in *United States v. Robinson* (1973):[55]

1 The need for a police officer to find and confiscate any weapons a suspect may be carrying.

2 The need to protect any evidence on the suspect's person from being destroyed.

Law enforcement officers are, however, limited in the searches they may make during an arrest. These limits were established by the Supreme Court in *Chimel v. California* (1969).[56] In that case, police arrived at Chimel's home with an arrest warrant but not a search warrant. Even though Chimel refused their request to "look around," the officers searched the entire three-bedroom house for nearly an hour, finding stolen coins in the process. Chimel was convicted of burglary and appealed, arguing that the evidence of the coins should have been suppressed.

The Supreme Court held that the search was unreasonable. In doing so, the Court established guidelines as to the acceptable extent of searches incidental to an arrest. Primarily, the Court ruled that police may search any area within the suspect's "immediate control" to confiscate any weapons or evidence that the suspect could destroy. The Court found, however, that there was no justification

> for routinely searching rooms other than that in which the arrest occurs—or, for that matter, for searching through all desk drawers or other closed or concealed areas in that room itself. Such searches, in the absence of well-recognized exceptions, may be made only under the authority of a search warrant.

The exact interpretation of the "area within immediate control" has been left to individual courts, but in general it has been taken to mean the area within the reach of the arrested person. Thus, the Court is said to have established the "arm's reach doctrine" in its *Chimel* decision.

Searches with Consent **Consent searches,** the second most common type of warrantless searches, take place when individuals give law enforcement officers permission to search their persons, homes, or belongings. (For an overview of the circumstances under which warrantless searches are allowed, see *Mastering Concepts—Exceptions to the Requirement That Officers Have a Search Warrant.*) The consent must, however, be *voluntary.* If a person has been physically threatened or otherwise coerced into giving consent, the search is invalid.[57] The standard for consent searches was set in *Schneckcloth v. Bustamonte* (1973),[58] in which, after being asked, the defendant told police officers to "go ahead" and search his car. A packet of stolen checks found in the trunk was ruled valid evidence because the driver consented to the search.

Critics of consent searches hold that such searches are rarely voluntary because most citizens are intimidated by police and will react to a request

Several years ago, New York City implemented a plan that allows police officers to seize the cars of people arrested for driving with blood alcohol levels of .10 or higher. As "specifically established" exceptions to search and seizure law, such seizures are considered constitutional. Are you in favor of this method of controlling drunk drivers? What might be some of the practical problems that New York police officers may encounter while enforcing this policy?

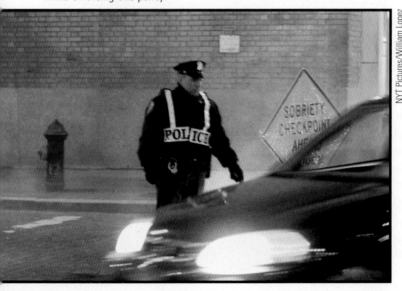

NYT Pictures/William Lopez

MASTERING CONCEPTS

Exceptions to the Requirement That Officers Have a Search Warrant

In many circumstances, it would be impractical for police officers to leave a crime scene, go to a judge, and obtain a search warrant before conducting a search. Therefore, under a number of circumstances a search warrant is not required.

Exception	Circumstance Not Requiring a Warrant
Incident to Lawful Arrest	Police officers may search the area within immediate control of a person after they have arrested him or her.
Consent	Police officers may search a person without a warrant if that person voluntarily agrees to be searched and has the legal authority to authorize the search.
Stop and Frisk	Police officers may frisk, or "pat down," a person if they suspect that the person may be involved in criminal activity or pose a danger to those in the immediate area.
Hot Pursuit	If police officers are in "hot pursuit" or chasing a person they have probable cause to believe committed a crime, and that person enters a building, the officers may search the building without a warrant.
Automobile Exception	If police officers have probable cause to believe that an automobile contains evidence of a crime, they may, in most instances, search the vehicle without a warrant.
Plain View	If police officers are legally engaged in police work and happen to see evidence of a crime in "plain view," they may seize it without a search warrant.
Abandoned Property	Any property, such as a hotel room that has been vacated or contraband that has been discarded, may be searched and seized by police officers without a warrant.
Border Searches	Law enforcement officers on border patrol do not need a warrant to search vehicles crossing the border.
Inevitable Discovery	Evidence that has been illegally obtained (without the necessary warrant) may be admitted as evidence if the prosecution can prove that it would have "inevitably" been found by lawful means.

for permission to make a search as if it were an order.[59] Furthermore, most citizens are unaware that they have the option *not* to comply with a request for a search. Thus, if a police officer asks to search a citizen's car after issuing a speeding ticket, the citizen is well within her or his rights to refuse. According to the United States Supreme Court in *Florida v. Bostick* (1991),[60] as long as police officers do not improperly coerce a suspect to cooperate, they are not *required* to inform the person that he or she has a choice in the matter.

Consequently, in *Ohio v. Robinette* (1996),[61] the Court held that police officers do *not* need to notify citizens that they are "free to go" after an initial stop when no arrest is involved. Similarly, in 2002, the Court ruled that the inside of a bus is not an inherently coercive environment and thus officers do not need to advise passengers that they can refuse to be searched.[62] The significance of this line of cases is underscored by data presented in connection with the *Robinette* ruling: in the two years leading up to that case, four hundred Ohio drivers were convicted of narcotics offenses that resulted directly from search requests that could have been denied but were not.[63]

Searches of Automobiles

Though the *Chimel* case limited the scope of searches and seizures incident to an arrest in most circumstances, the Supreme Court has not been as restrictive concerning searches in arrests involving automobile passengers. In *New York v. Belton* (1981),[64] the Supreme Court held that when police officers lawfully arrest a person driving a car, they can legally

A police officer searches a car in front of the Capitol building in Washington, D.C. According to the United States Supreme Court, under some circumstances the Fourth Amendment to the U.S. Constitution does not require police officers to obtain a warrant before searching an automobile. What is the reasoning behind this "movable vehicle exception"?

make a warrantless search of the car's entire front and back compartments. This expansive interpretation of "the area within immediate control" is indicative of the Supreme Court's lenient view of automobile searches.

The "Movable Vehicle Exception"

In *Carroll v. United States* (1925),[65] the Supreme Court ruled that the law would distinguish among automobiles, homes, and persons in questions involving police searches. In the years since *Carroll*, the Court has established that the Fourth Amendment does not require police to obtain a warrant to search automobiles or other movable vehicles when they have probable cause to believe that a vehicle contains contraband or evidence of criminal activity.[66] The reasoning behind such leniency is straightforward: requiring a warrant to search an automobile places too heavy a burden on police officers. By the time the officers could communicate with a judge and obtain the warrant, the suspects could drive away and destroy any evidence. Consequently, the Supreme Court has consistently held that someone in a vehicle does not have the same reasonable expectation of privacy as someone at home or even in a phone booth.

A number of rulings, including the dog-sniffing case discussed at the beginning of the chapter, have increased police powers in these situations. In *Whren v. United States* (1996),[67] the Supreme Court ruled that the "true" motivation of police officers in making traffic stops was irrelevant as long as they had probable cause to believe that a traffic law had been broken. In other words, police may stop a car they believe to be transporting drugs in order to issue a speeding citation. The fact that the officers are using the speeding ticket as a pretext to search for drugs (and would not have stopped the driver otherwise) does not matter, as long as the driver actually was speeding. One year later, in *Maryland v. Wilson* (1997),[68] the Court further expanded police power by ruling that an officer may order passengers as well as the driver out of a car during a traffic stop; the Court reasoned that the danger to an officer is increased when there is a passenger in the automobile.

"Individualized Suspicion" Nevertheless, the "movable vehicle exception" has not provided police officers with complete freedom in searching automobiles. Recently, the Supreme Court overturned a roadblock system in Indianapolis, Indiana, that was designed to discover illegal drugs in automobiles. At the roadblocks, a police officer would check a driver's license and registration and then subject the automobile to a "sniff search" by a dog specially trained to find narcotics.[69] Because the Court had, in prior cases, upheld checkpoints designed to apprehend drunk drivers[70] and illegal aliens,[71] the city of Indianapolis felt that its practice was constitutionally acceptable.

But, in *City of Indianapolis v. Edmond* (2000),[72] the Court distinguished the behavior being regulated in the earlier cases from the illegal behavior the city sought to uncover. Governments, the Court noted, have a special interest in protecting citizens from the dangers of drunks on the road and in controlling the flow of illegal immigrants across their borders. General searches for drugs, however, do not serve any specific purpose beyond general crime control. Therefore, the Fourth Amendment does not allow the police to stop drivers without any "individualized suspicion" that they have broken the law, in this case by possessing drugs.[73]

In 2004, however, the Court made two rulings that further confused the concept of "individualized suspicion." The first involved a defendant who was arrested for drunk driving in Lombard, Illinois, at a roadblock set up to question citizens about a hit-and-run accident.[74] The second involved government agents at the Mexican border who removed the gas tank of the defendant's car, finding packets of marijuana in the process.[75] Although neither roadblock seemed to meet the requirements established in the *City of Indianapolis* case, the Court upheld both arrests—in the first instance because the law enforcement purpose of the roadblock was to gather information, not to discover criminal activity,[76] and in the second instance because a driver's expectation of privacy is "less at the border than it is in the interior [of the United States.]"[77]

The Plain View Doctrine

Though police must have probable cause to search luggage in an automobile's trunk, no such protection applies to contraband *in plain view.* For example, suppose a traffic officer pulls over a person for speeding, looks in the driver's side window, and clearly sees what appears to be a bag of heroin resting on the passenger seat. In this instance, under the **plain view doctrine,** the officer would be justified in seizing the drugs without a warrant.

The plain view doctrine was first enunciated by the Supreme Court in *Coolidge v. New Hampshire* (1971).[78] The Court ruled that law enforcement officers may make a warrantless seizure of an item if four criteria are met:

1 The item is positioned so as to be detected easily by an officer's sight or some other sense.

2 The officer is legally in a position to notice the item in question.

3 The discovery of the item is inadvertent; that is, the officer had not intended to find the item.

4 The officer immediately recognizes the illegal nature of the item. No interrogation or further investigation is allowed under the plain view doctrine.

(For a discussion of how the plain view doctrine is being tested by new technology, see *CJ and Technology—X-Ray Eyes and the Fourth Amendment* on the next page.)

Electronic Surveillance and the Fight against Terrorism

During the course of a criminal investigation, law enforcement officers may decide to use *electronic surveillance,* or electronic devices such as wiretaps or hidden microphones ("bugs"), to monitor and record conversations, observe movements, and trace or record telephone calls.

Basic Rules: Consent and Probable Cause Given the invasiveness of electronic surveillance, the Supreme Court has generally held that the practice is prohibited by the Fourth Amendment. In *Burger v. New York* (1967),[79] however, the Court ruled that it was permissible under certain circumstances. That same year, *Katz v. United States* (discussed earlier) established that recorded conversations are inadmissible as evidence unless certain procedures are followed.

In general, law enforcement officers can use electronic surveillance only if:

1 Consent is given by one of the parties to be monitored; or

2 There is a warrant authorizing the use of the devices.[80]

Plain View Doctrine
The legal principle that objects in plain view of a law enforcement agent who has the right to be in a position to have that view may be seized without a warrant and introduced as evidence.

X-Ray Eyes and the Fourth Amendment

Suppose a detective enters a room with a warrant to search for a handgun used in a murder. The weapon is resting on a table and is immediately seized. Hidden in a closed drawer, however, is a packet of heroin. Under the plain view doctrine, the detective would most likely not have the right to search the drawer and seize the heroin. What if that detective could somehow see into the drawer without opening it? How would the plain view doctrine then apply?

A cop with X-ray eyes sounds like something out of a science fiction novel, but in fact courts around the country are already struggling with such situations. Thanks to thermal imagers, also known as forward-looking infrared devices (FLIR), law enforcement agents now have the ability to look through walls.

THE THERMAL IMAGER AT WORK

Every object with a temperature above absolute zero emits infrared radiation, which cannot be seen by the naked eye. A thermal imager, however, can detect this radiation and project its reading onto a screen. The devices have been most commonly used in missing person searches—with our high body temperature, humans are easy targets for thermal imagers. Only recently have the devices been put to use by law enforcement agencies. Thermal imagers can be particularly effective in detecting marijuana grown indoors because marijuana plants require considerable heat to survive.

The question for the courts has been whether, in the absence of a warrant, an infrared search of a dwelling is in violation of Fourth Amendment protections of privacy. In one marijuana case, in which police used a helicopter fitted with FLIR devices, a Hawaii court ruled that no reasonable expectation of privacy was involved. The court held that the FLIR device measured only heat emanating from the defendant's house and that this "abandoned heat" was not subject to privacy laws because the defendants had not tried to prevent its escape. A Pennsylvania court, ruling on a similar case, rejected the "abandoned heat" justification because thermal imaging allowed the police to see what otherwise would have been hidden to them. The Pennsylvania court warned that thermal imaging "can extract information from within a person's home, the place most deserving of protection from government intrusion."

IN THE FUTURE

The Supreme Court settled the issue by ruling that the use of a thermal imaging device by police was a search and was therefore subject to the Fourth Amendment. The Court's ruling covered not only these devices but also *any* technology that allows police to gain knowledge that would otherwise be impossible to obtain without entering the home. This does not mean that this technology is lost to law enforcement agents, but it does require them to obtain a warrant before using it.

For more information on thermal imaging and other CJ technologies, click on Crime and Technology *under* Book Resources *at* **www.cjinaction.com.**

Note that the consent of only one of the parties being monitored is needed to waive the reasonable expectation of privacy. The Court has ruled that people whose conversations have been recorded by supposed friends who turn out to be police informers have not been subjected to an unreasonable search.[81] Therefore, at least theoretically, a person always assumes the risk that whatever he or she says to someone else may be monitored by the police. A number of states do, however, have statutes that forbid private citizens from tape-recording another person's conversation without her or his knowledge. In Maryland, for example, such an act is a felony.

If consent exists, then law enforcement officers are not required to obtain a warrant before engaging in electronic surveillance. In most other instances, however, a warrant is required. For the warrant to be valid, it must:

1 Detail with "particularity" the conversations that are to be overheard.

2 Name the suspects and the places that will be under surveillance.

3 Show with probable cause that a specific crime has been or will be committed.[82]

Once the specific information has been gathered, the law enforcement officers must end the electronic surveillance immediately.[83] In any case, the surveillance cannot last more than thirty days without a judicial extension.

Searches of Computer Data In general, courts will apply the same Fourth Amendment tests to surveillance of information stored in computers, such as data files or e-mails, as to any other forms of electronic communication.[84] The level of constitutional protection for e-mails may not be as high as many Internet users think, however. In 2000, Yahoo!, Inc., an Internet service provider (ISP), provided law enforcement agents with e-mails from a client named Dale Robert Bach, who was suspected of involvement in child pornography. Police officers used the e-mails as the basis to obtain a warrant to search the suspect's home, where they found further evidence of wrongdoing that led to Bach's arrest. A federal court upheld the result,[85] but failed to address a crucial question: Do e-mail users have a reasonable expectation of privacy in stored files that have been revealed to a third party such as an ISP? How courts address this issue in the future will have a large impact on police officers' ability to access e-mail communications in criminal investigations.[86]

Electronic Surveillance and National Security The federal government has long struggled with how to apply the basic rules for electronic surveillance to the area of national security. In the late 1970s, responding to concerns that the Federal Bureau of Investigation (FBI) had too much power to "spy" on domestic religious and political groups, Congress passed legislation restricting this power. Under the Foreign Intelligence Surveillance Act (FISA), government agents could wiretap or otherwise bug a target only if there was probable cause that the target was a foreign infiltrator.[87]

New Rules The USA PATRIOT Act of 2001 amended the FISA. This new legislation, as noted earlier in this textbook, was a legislative response to the terrorist attacks of September 11, 2001. It effectively did away with the probable cause requirements of the FISA, allowing agents to procure a warrant for electronic surveillance as long as the surveillance serves a "significant purpose" in gathering foreign intelligence.[88] Under the old rules, for example, an FBI agent could not randomly surf the Internet looking for signs of wrongdoing because there was no "particularity" to support a showing of probable cause that terrorist activity was taking place. Under the new guidelines, the agent can search Web sites and chat rooms randomly because this activity might serve the significant purpose of providing leads to future terrorist attacks.[89]

The "Sneak and Peak" Provision Opponents of the USA PATRIOT Act have focused on Section 213 of the legislation. This provision allows law enforcement agents to search a person's home and seize property without immediately notifying the target of the search if the agents have "reasonable" cause to believe that notification would (1) endanger public safety, (2) lead to destruction of evidence, or (3) jeopardize an ongoing investigation.[90] By removing the traditional "probable cause" requirement for search warrants, Section 213 provides police officers with greater leeway to conduct secret, or "sneak and peak," searches of a person's home or property without that person being aware of the search.

Another controversial aspect of Section 213 is that it applies to *all* federal criminal investigations, not just those involving terrorism.[91] Between April 2003 and January 2005, the U.S. Department of Justice used Section 213 delayed-notification warrants 108 times to investigate not only terrorist activities but also drug trafficking, organized crime, and child-pornography operations.[92] The government defends these warrants as a valuable crime-fighting tool that keeps suspects from fleeing or destroying evidence.[93] Critics, however, contend that the legislation has "severely undermined the protections guaranteed by the Fourth Amendment" for a wide range of criminal suspects.[94]

Interrogation
The direct questioning of a suspect to gather evidence of criminal activity and try to gain a confession.

THE INTERROGATION PROCESS AND *MIRANDA*

After the Pledge of Allegiance, there is perhaps no recitation that comes more readily to the American mind than the *Miranda* warning:

> You have the right to remain silent. If you give up that right, anything you say can and will be used against you in a court of law. You have the right to speak with an attorney and to have the attorney present during questioning. If you so desire and cannot afford one, an attorney will be appointed for you without charge before questioning.

The *Miranda* warning is not a mere prop. It strongly affects one of the most important aspects of any criminal investigation—the **interrogation,** or questioning of a suspect from whom the police want to get information concerning a crime and perhaps a confession.

The Legal Basis for *Miranda*

The Fifth Amendment guarantees protection against self-incrimination. A defendant's choice *not* to incriminate himself or herself cannot be interpreted as a sign of guilt by a jury in a criminal trial. A confession, or admission of guilt, is by definition a statement of self-incrimination. How, then, to reconcile the Fifth Amendment with the critical need of law enforcement officers to gain confessions? The answer lies in the concept of *coercion*. When torture or brutality is involved, it is relatively easy to determine that a confession was improperly coerced and is therefore invalid.

Setting the Stage for *Miranda* The Supreme Court first recognized that a confession could not be physically coerced in a 1936 case concerning a defendant who was beaten and whipped until confessing to a murder.[95] It was not until 1964, however, that the Court specifically recognized that the accused's due process rights should be protected during interrogation. That year, the Court heard the case of *Escobedo v. Illinois*,[96] which involved a convicted murderer who had incriminated himself during a four-hour questioning session at a police station. Police officers ignored the defendant's requests to speak with his lawyer, who was actually present at the station while his client was being interrogated. The Court overturned the conviction, setting forth a five-pronged test that essentially established that if police are interrogating a suspect in custody, they cannot deny the suspect's request to speak with an attorney and must warn the suspect of his or her constitutional right to remain silent under the Fifth Amendment. If any one of the five prongs was not satisfied, the suspect had effectively been denied his or her right to counsel under the Sixth Amendment.[97]

The *Miranda* Case The limitations of the *Escobedo* decision quickly became apparent. All five

A Los Angeles police officer reads a handcuffed "suspect" his *Miranda* rights (explained on the next page) during a training exercise. Does a police officer need to take this action every time he or she arrests a suspect? If not, under what circumstances must an officer administer the *Miranda* warning?

of the prongs had to be satisfied for the defendant to enjoy the Sixth Amendment protections it offered. In fact, the accused rarely request counsel, rendering the *Escobedo* test irrelevant no matter what questionable interrogation methods the police used to elicit their confessions. Consequently, two years later, the Supreme Court handed down its *Miranda* decision,[98] establishing the **Miranda rights** and introducing the concept of what University of Columbia law professor H. Richard Uviller called *inherent coercion;* that is, even if a police officer does not lay a hand on a suspect, the general atmosphere of an interrogation is in and of itself coercive.[99]

Though the *Miranda* case is best remembered for the procedural requirement it spurred, at the time the Supreme Court was more concerned about the treatment of suspects during interrogation. (See the feature *CJ in Focus—Landmark Cases:* Miranda v. Arizona on p. 226.) The Court found that routine police interrogation strategies, such as leaving suspects alone in a room for several hours before questioning them, were inherently coercive. Therefore, the Court reasoned, every suspect needed protection from coercion, not just those who had been physically abused. The *Miranda* warning is a result of this need. In theory, if the warning is not given to a suspect before an interrogation, the fruits of that interrogation, including a confession, are invalid.

When a *Miranda* Warning Is Required

As we shall see, a *Miranda* warning is not necessary under several conditions, such as when no questions are asked of the suspect. Generally, *Miranda* requirements apply only when a suspect is in **custody.** In a series of rulings since *Miranda,* the Supreme Court has defined custody as an arrest or a situation in which a reasonable person would not feel free to leave.[100] Consequently, a **custodial interrogation** occurs when a suspect is under arrest or is deprived of her or his freedom in a significant manner. Remember, a *Miranda* warning is only required *before* a custodial interrogation takes place.

When a *Miranda* Warning Is Not Required

A *Miranda* warning is not necessary in a number of situations:

1 When the police do not ask the suspect any questions that are *testimonial* in nature. Such questions are designed to elicit information that may be used against the suspect in court. "Routine booking questions," such as the suspect's name, address, height, and eye color, however, are an exception to this rule. Even though answering these questions may provide incriminating evidence (especially if the person answering is a prime suspect), the Supreme Court has held that they are absolutely necessary if the police are to do their jobs.[101] (Imagine the officer not being able to ask a suspect her or his name.)

2 When the police have not focused on a suspect and are questioning witnesses at the scene of a crime.

3 When a person volunteers information before the police have asked a question.

4 When the suspect has given a private statement to a friend or some other acquaintance. *Miranda* does not apply to these statements as long as the government did not orchestrate the situation.

5 During a stop and frisk, when no arrest has been made.

6 During a traffic stop.[102]

Furthermore, suspects can *waive* their Fifth Amendment rights and speak to a police officer, but only if the waiver is made voluntarily. Silence on the part of a suspect does not mean that his or her *Miranda* protections have been relinquished. To waive their

Miranda **Rights**
The constitutional rights of accused persons taken into custody by law enforcement officials. Following the United States Supreme Court's decision in *Miranda v. Arizona*, on taking an accused person into custody, the arresting officer must inform the person of certain constitutional rights, such as the right to remain silent and the right to counsel.

Custody
The forceful detention of a person, or the perception that a person is not free to leave the immediate vicinity.

Custodial Interrogation
The questioning of a suspect after that person has been taken in custody. In this situation, the suspect must be read his or her *Miranda* rights before interrogation can begin.

Miranda v. Arizona

Ernesto Miranda, a produce worker, was arrested in Phoenix, Arizona, in 1963 and charged with kidnapping and rape. After being identified by the victim in a lineup, Miranda was taken into an interrogation room and questioned for two hours by detectives. At no time was Miranda informed that he had a right to have an attorney present. When the police emerged from the session, they had a signed statement by Miranda confessing to the crimes. He was subsequently convicted and sentenced to twenty to thirty years in prison. After the conviction was confirmed by the Arizona Supreme Court, Miranda appealed to the United States Supreme Court, claiming that he had not been warned that any statement he made could be used against him, and that he had a right to counsel during the interrogation. The *Miranda* case was one of four examined by the Court that dealt with the question of coercive questioning.

Ernesto Miranda

Miranda v. Arizona
United States Supreme Court
384 U.S. 436 (1966)
http://laws.findlaw.com/US/384/436.html

IN THE WORDS OF THE COURT . . .
Chief Justice WARREN, majority opinion

* * * *

The cases before us raise questions which go to the roots of our concepts of American criminal jurisprudence: the restraints society must observe consistent with the Federal Constitution in prosecuting individuals for crime. More specifically, we deal with the admissibility of statements obtained from an individual who is subjected to custodial police interrogation and the necessity for procedures which assure that the individual is accorded his privilege under the Fifth Amendment to the Constitution not to be compelled to incriminate himself.

* * * *

As for the procedural safeguards to be employed, unless other fully effective means are devised to inform accused persons of their right of silence and to assure a continuous opportunity to exercise it, the following measures are required. Prior to any questioning, the person must be warned that he has a right to remain silent, that any statement he does make may be used as evidence against him, and that he has a right to the presence of an attorney, either retained or appointed. The defendant may waive effectuation of these rights, provided the waiver is made voluntarily, knowingly and intelligently. * * * The mere fact that he may have answered some questions or volunteered some statements on his own does not deprive him of the right to refrain from answering any further inquiries until he has consulted with an attorney and thereafter consents to be questioned.

* * * *

It is obvious that such an interrogation environment is created for no purpose other than to subjugate the individual to the will of his examiner. This atmosphere carries its own badge of intimidation. To be sure, this is not physical intimidation, but it is equally destructive of human dignity. The current practice of incommunicado interrogation is at odds with one of our Nation's most cherished principles—that the individual may not be compelled to incriminate himself. Unless adequate protective devices are employed to dispel the compulsion inherent in custodial surroundings, no statement obtained from the defendant can truly be the product of his free choice.

DECISION

The Court overturned Miranda's conviction, stating that police interrogations are, by their very nature, coercive and therefore deny suspects their constitutional right against self-incrimination by "forcing" them to confess. Consequently, any person who has been arrested and placed in custody must be informed of his or her right to be free from self-incrimination and to be represented by counsel during any interrogation. In other words, suspects must be told that they *do not have to* answer police questions. To accomplish this, the Court established the *Miranda* warning, which must be read prior to questioning a suspect in custody.

FOR CRITICAL ANALYSIS

What is meant by the phrase "coercion can be mental as well as physical"? What role does the concept of "mental coercion" play in Chief Justice Warren's opinion?

For more information and activities related to this case, click on Landmark Cases *under* Book Resources *at* **www.cjinaction.com**.

rights, suspects must state—either in writing or orally—that they understand those rights and that they will voluntarily answer questions without the presence of counsel.

To ensure that the suspect's rights are upheld, prosecutors are required to prove by a preponderance of the evidence that the suspect "knowing and intelligently" waived his or her *Miranda* rights.[103] To make the waiver perfectly clear, police will ask suspects two questions in addition to giving the *Miranda* warning:

1 Do you understand your rights as I have read them to you?

2 Knowing your rights, are you willing to talk to another law enforcement officer or me?

If the suspect indicates that she or he does not want to speak to the officer, thereby invoking her or his right to silence, the officer must *immediately* stop any questioning.[104] Similarly, if the suspect requests a lawyer, the police can ask no further questions until an attorney is present.[105] The suspect must be clear about this intention, however. In *Davis v. United States* (1994),[106] the Supreme Court upheld the interrogation of a suspect after he said, "Maybe I should talk to a lawyer." The Court found that this statement was too ambiguous, stating that it did not want to force police officers to "read the minds" of suspects who make vague declarations.

> "The psychological games that are played during an interrogation . . . are difficult at best to understand: assured by authorities you don't remember things, being led to doubt your own memory, having things suggested to you only to have those things pop up in a conversation a short time later but from your own lips."
>
> —Peter Reilly, who confessed while under police interrogation to having murdered his mother (1995)

The Law Enforcement Response to *Miranda*

When the *Miranda* decision was first handed down, many people, particularly police officials, complained that it distorted the Constitution by placing the rights of criminal suspects above the rights of society as a whole.[107] In the four decades since the ruling, however, law enforcement agents have adapted to the *Miranda* restrictions, and strategies to work within their boundaries have become a standard part of police training.

Policing around *Miranda* After an extensive on-site study of police interrogation tactics, Richard A. Leo, a criminologist from the University of California at Irvine, noted a pattern of maneuvers that officers use to convince suspects to voluntarily waive their *Miranda* rights. Leo identifies three such strategies:

- The *conditioning* strategy is geared toward creating an environment in which the suspect is encouraged to think positively of the interrogator and thus is conditioned to cooperate. The interrogator will offer the suspect coffee or a cigarette and make pleasant small talk. These steps are intended to lower the suspect's anxiety level and generate a sense of trust that is conducive to a *Miranda* waiver and confession.

- The *deemphasizing* strategy tries to downplay the importance of *Miranda* protections, giving the impression that the rights are unimportant and can be easily waived. For example, one officer told a suspect, "I need to advise you of your rights. It's a formality. I'm sure you've watched television with the cop shows and you hear them say their rights so you can probably recite this better than I can, but it's something I need to do and we can get this out of the way before we talk about what happened."

- When using the *persuasion* strategy, an officer will explicitly try to convince the suspect to waive her or his rights. Commonly, the detective will tell suspects that waiving the rights is the only way they will be able to get their side of the story out. Otherwise, the detective continues, only the victim's side of the story will be considered during the trial.[108]

(To learn how these interrogation tactics are being spread abroad, see *International CJ—Building a Police Force for Iraq* on the next page.)

Building a Police Force for Iraq

Lieutenant Hussein al-Saedi of the Nasr police station in a poor section of Baghdad, Iraq, remembers the good old days. "Before, we used to bring the guy, we beat him, hung him by a hook on the ceiling, and he would confess to every single criminal act he committed since he was a toddler," he says. "Before, it was much better. Before, we used to solve these cases in one night."

"Before," in al-Saedi's words, refers to the time prior to the fall of Saddam Hussein in the spring of 2003 and the establishment of a provisional government in Iraq. Under the leadership of the United States, one of the main goals of this temporary government is to create a modern police force for the country. To that end, the U.S. government has spent hundreds of millions of dollars and recruited a former New York City police commissioner to help organize Baghdad's police departments on the American model.

The fledgling security forces face a number of challenges: lack of equipment, lack of training, and lack of recruits. Six months after the end of the war, for example, the sixty police officers at the Nasr police station had forty-four guns, two cars, and three radios that could be used only every other day because of weak batteries. The Iraqi concept of the rule of law was also somewhat different from the American approach, as is evident in al-Saedi's view of the best way to gain a confession.

In an attempt to remove torture from the Iraqi police's list of interrogation tactics, American officials set up a police academy in Baghdad with the goal of training 5,500 officers in the "human rights" approach to policing. Corporal Zuhair Mudthafir came away from the three-week course with a favorable impression of police methods in the United States. "You know, the Americans have genius officers who find ways to extract confessions from defendants without beating them," he said.

FOR CRITICAL ANALYSIS
Why is it important to train Iraqi police officers in "human rights" as well as other policing strategies? Why should the United States impose its idea of what constitutes a fair interrogation on Iraq's police force?

The Problem of False Confessions In a number of instances, the police appear to have become *too* skilled at gaining confessions. In 2002, the reopening of the Central Park jogger case focused national attention on the phenomenon of false confessions. Thirteen years after an investment banker was raped and severely beaten while jogging in New York City, a judge overturned the convictions of four young men who had confessed to attacking the woman. DNA evidence showed that another person was responsible for the crime.

About 20 percent of wrongful convictions in recent years can be attributed to false confessions.[109] Experts point to a number of reasons why people admit to a crime they did not commit. Saul Kassin, a professor of psychology at Williams College, suggests that the police tactics described above amount to a form of legal coercion, with some suspects more susceptible than others. Many times, a person will confess in the absence of any wrongdoing because he or she is hungry, frightened, or exhausted.[110] In the Central Park jogger case, several "risk factors" for a false confession were present, including the age of the subjects (the five defendants were between fourteen and sixteen years old) and the interrogation methods (they had been in custody for between fourteen and thirty hours).

GREAT DEBATES

Should government agents be allowed to use "any means necessary," including torture, to get information out of suspected terrorists? Or, does the U.S. Constitution protect them just as it would any other arrested criminals? To better understand the debate surrounding military interrogation tactics, click on *Great Debates* under *Book Resources* at **www.cjinaction.com**.

The Future of *Miranda*

In 2001, the Supreme Court made a strong ruling in favor of the continued importance of *Miranda*. In *Dickerson v. United States*,[111] the Court rejected the application of a little-known law passed by Congress in 1968 that allowed police in federal cases to use incriminatory statements even if the suspect had not been read the warning. "*Miranda* has become embedded in routine police practice to the point where the warnings have become part of our national culture," wrote Chief Justice William Rehnquist in his opinion. The chief justice added that *Miranda* was a "constitutional rule" that Congress could not overturn by passing a law.[112]

The Erosion of *Miranda* Despite these strong words, many legal scholars believe that a series of Supreme Court rulings have slowly eroded *Miranda*'s protections. According to legal scholar Alan M. Dershowitz, the Court has carved "out so many exceptions that [*Miranda*] is falling of its own weight."[113] (See Figure 7.4 for a run-down of the Court rulings that have weakened *Miranda* over the past several decades.)

The latest such decision, issued in 2004, involved a Colorado case in which the defendant had voluntarily told the police the location of his gun (which, being an ex-felon, he was not allowed to possess) without being read his rights.[114] The Court upheld the conviction, finding that *Miranda* warnings are merely *prophylactic*. In other words, they are only intended to prevent violations of the Fifth Amendment. Because only the gun, and not the defendant's testimony, was presented at trial, the police had

---

FIGURE 7.4

Supreme Court Decisions Eroding *Miranda* Rights

Rhode Island v. Innis (446 U.S. 291 [1980]). In this case the Supreme Court clarified its definition of an interrogation, which it said could extend only to "actions or words" that the police "should have known were reasonably likely to elicit an incriminating response." In making this ruling, the Court allowed as evidence an admission made by a suspect as to where a shotgun he had used in a crime was hidden. The suspect confessed after police mentioned that there was a possibility that a handicapped child might find the firearm, given that a home for such children was nearby. This was not, the Court ruled, an interrogation and therefore *Miranda* rights were not necessary.

New York v. Quarles (467 U.S. 649 [1984]). This case established the "public-safety" exception to the *Miranda* rule. It concerned a police officer who, after feeling an empty shoulder holster on a man he had just arrested, asked the suspect the location of the gun without informing him of his *Miranda* rights. The Court ruled that the gun was admissible as evidence and that the need for police officers to protect the public is more important than a suspect's *Miranda* rights.

Moran v. Burbine (475 U.S. 412 [1986]). This case established that police officers are not required to tell suspects undergoing custodial interrogation that their attorney is trying to reach them. The Court ruled that events that the suspect could have no way of knowing about have no bearing on his ability to waive his *Miranda* rights.

Illinois v. Perkins (496 U.S. 292 [1990]). Perkins was a suspected murderer in prison on an unrelated drug charge who admitted to the murder in order to impress his cellmate, who happened to be an undercover police officer. The Court ruled that even though the undercover officer goaded Perkins into making the admission, the defendant was not being subjected to a custodial interrogation; indeed, he eagerly bragged to his cellmate, describing the murder in detail in order to impress. *Miranda* does not protect suspects from their own foolishness.

Arizona v. Fulminante (499 U.S. 279 [1991]). In this very important ruling, the Court held that a conviction is not automatically overturned if the suspect was coerced into making a confession. If the other evidence introduced at the trial is strong enough to justify a conviction without the confession, then the fact that the confession was illegally gained can be, for all intents and purposes, ignored.

Davis v. United States (512 U.S. 452 [1994]). This case involved a suspect who, instead of demanding that he be provided with his *Miranda* right to an attorney, said, "Maybe I should talk to a lawyer" during his custodial interrogation. The Court ruled that a suspect must unequivocally and assertively state his right to counsel in order to stop police questioning. Furthermore, police officers are not required to try and decipher the suspect's intentions in such cases.

Texas v. Cobb (532 U.S. 162 [2001]). When a suspect refuses to waive his or her *Miranda* rights, a police officer cannot lawfully continue the interrogation until the suspect's attorney arrives on the scene. In this case, however, the Court held that a suspect may be questioned without the presence of a lawyer if the interrogation does not focus on the crime for which he or she was arrested, but does touch on another, closely related, offense.

not violated his constitutional rights. In essence, the Court was ruling that the "fruit of the poisoned tree" doctrine, discussed earlier in this chapter, does not ban the admission of physical evidence that is discovered based on voluntary statements by a suspect who has not been "Mirandized."[115]

Recording Confessions *Miranda* may eventually find itself obsolete regardless of any decisions made in the courts. A relatively new trend in law enforcement has been for agencies to record interrogations and confessions either on videotape or digitally. Thomas P. Sullivan, a former U.S. attorney in Chicago, and his staff interviewed members of 238 law enforcement agencies from thirty-eight states that record custodial interviews of felony suspects.[116] Sullivan found almost universal praise for the procedure, with police officers saying the technology saved money and time, created valuable evidence to use in court, and made it more difficult for defense attorneys to claim that their clients were illegally coerced. One member of the San Diego (California) police department told Sullivan, "I've never met a detective who didn't like it."[117] Some scholars have suggested that recording all custodial interrogations would satisfy the Fifth Amendment's prohibition against coercion and in the process render the *Miranda* warning unnecessary.

> "Every prosecutor in the country hated the day it came down . . . but after a decade even those who were strongly [against the ruling] had come to the conclusion, 'Hey, we can live with this.' It would be chaos to ever go back."
>
> —Charles E. Moylan, former Maryland state's attorney, commenting on *Miranda* (1999)

THE IDENTIFICATION PROCESS

A confession is a form of self-identification; the suspect has identified herself or himself as the guilty party. If police officers are unable to gain a confession, they must use other methods to link the suspect with the crime. In fact, to protect against false admissions, police must do so even if the suspect confesses.

Essential Procedures

Unless police officers witness the commission of the crime themselves, they must establish the identity of the suspect using three basic types of identification procedures:

1 *Showups,* which occur when a suspect who matches the description given by witnesses is apprehended near the scene of the crime within a reasonable amount of time after the crime has been committed. The suspect is usually returned to the crime scene for possible identification by witnesses.

2 *Photo arrays,* which occur when no suspect is in custody but the police have a general description of the person. Witnesses and victims are shown "mug shots" of people with police records that match the description. Police will also present witnesses and victims with pictures of people they believe might have committed the crime.

3 *Lineups,* which entail lining up several physically similar people, one of whom is the suspect, in front of a witness or victim. The police may have each member of the lineup wear clothing similar to that worn by the criminal and say a phrase that was used during the crime. These visual and oral cues are designed to help the witness identify the suspect.

As with the other procedures discussed in this chapter, constitutional law governs the identification process, though some aspects are more tightly restricted than others. The

Sixth Amendment right to counsel, for example, does not apply during showups or photo arrays. In showups, the police often need to establish a suspect quickly, and it would be unreasonable to expect them to wait for an attorney to arrive. According to the Supreme Court in *United States v. Ash* (1973),[118] however, the police must be able to prove this need for immediate identification, perhaps by showing that it was necessary to keep the suspect from fleeing the state. As for photo arrays, courts have found that any procedure that does not require the suspect's presence does not require the presence of his or her attorney.[119] The lack of an attorney does not mean that police can "steer" a witness toward a positive identification with statements such as "Are you sure this isn't the person you saw robbing the grocery store?" Such actions would violate the suspect's due process rights.

Nontestimonial Evidence

Some observers feel that the standard **booking** procedure—the process of recording information about the suspect immediately after arrest—infringes on a suspect's Fifth Amendment rights. During booking, the suspect is photographed and fingerprinted, and blood samples may be taken. If these samples lead to the suspect's eventual identification, according to some, they amount to self-incrimination. In *Schmerber v. California* (1966),[120] however, the Supreme Court held that such tests are not the equivalent of *testimonial* self-incrimination (where the suspect testifies verbally against himself or herself) and therefore do not violate the Fifth Amendment.

Using similar legal reasoning, the Court has also determined that voice and handwriting samples gathered by police may be used to identify a suspect.[121] The Court has, however, set some limits on the use of nontestimonial evidence. In the early 1980s, Ralph Watkinson of Richmond, Virginia, shot a man who had assaulted him and then fled the scene of the crime. Police found Rudolph Lee a few blocks away bleeding from a bullet wound beneath his collarbone. Watkinson identified Lee as the assailant, and the local prosecutor tried to get a court order to remove the bullet from Lee's body to match it with Watkinson's gun. In *Winston v. Lee* (1985),[122] the Court ruled that the surgery required was "highly intrusive" and was offensive to Lee's "human dignity." Therefore, the bullet was not allowed as nontestimonial evidence in the trial.

Booking
The process of entering a suspect's name, offense, and arrival time into the police log following her or his arrest.

See **Officer.com** for a wealth of information on the identification process and other law enforcement issues. Find this Web site by clicking on *Web Links* under *Chapter Resources* at **www.cjinaction.com**.

James Shaffer/PhotoEdit

Lineups are one of the primary means police have of identifying suspects. As you can see, in a lineup several people with similar appearances are placed so that a victim or witness can study them. The victim or witness is then asked to point out the one that most closely resembles the person who committed the crime. Lineup identifications are generally considered most valuable if they take place within several hours after the crime has been committed. Why is timing so important with regard to a lineup?

Racial Profiling and the Constitution

As noted earlier in this chapter, the Fourth Amendment protects persons against "unreasonable searches and seizures." Nowhere in the Constitution, however, did the framers explain the term *unreasonable*. Thus, the participants in the criminal justice system have been left to find their own coherent and useful definition. Initially, as you will recall, the burden is on the police officer to decide whether his or her actions are reasonable, a decision that—in the absence of a warrant—will be reviewed in a court. In recent years, the question of reasonableness in the context of police stops and counterterrorism strategies has become intertwined with the troubling specter of racism in our nation's law enforcement agencies. In this *Criminal Justice in Action* feature, we will explore the question of whether it is possible for law enforcement to do its job without taking into account observable features of people such as race or ethnicity. The Supreme Court has essentially left this question unanswered, creating a vacuum that has been filled by lawsuits, controversy, and frustration.

By the Numbers

Though it is often difficult to determine whether an individual officer acted reasonably in a particular situation, patterns of police behavior can provide a clearer picture. A survey of several million police-civilian contacts in Texas found that two-thirds of the state law enforcement agencies searched African Americans and Hispanics more frequently after a traffic stop than they searched whites. Of these agencies, 71 percent searched blacks at least 50 percent more frequently than whites, and 90 percent searched Hispanics at least 50 percent more frequently than whites.[123] In Milton, Massachusetts, minorities received 58 percent of traffic tickets even though they made up only about 16 percent of drivers.[124] In San Diego, California, police searched 49.8 percent of vehicles with Hispanic drivers after a traffic stop, compared to 28.7 percent for whites.[125]

These statistics are seen as proof that the local police are using *racial profiling* in deciding which motorists to stop and search. Racial profiling occurs when a police action is initiated by the race, ethnicity, or national origin of the suspect, rather than by any evidence or information that the suspect has broken the law. Although it is rare to find a law enforcement agency that has an official policy of racial profiling, many observers feel that the practice is widespread.

The "Rational Discrimination" Argument

This belief is only encouraged by statements such as the one made by Colonel Carl. A. Williams, superintendent of the New Jersey State Police. In answering charges that his officers targeted nonwhite motorists, Williams replied, "Two weeks ago, the president of the United States went to Mexico to talk . . . about drugs. He didn't go to Ireland. He didn't go to England."[126]

In other words, Williams (who subsequently resigned) felt that his officers were justified in stopping nonwhite motorists because they were more likely to be breaking the law. This line of thinking, known as "rational discrimination," relies on statistics that show a correlation between race and crime. Because minorities, the argument goes, are more likely to commit crimes, police are justified in making group distinctions.[127]

David Cole, a professor at Georgetown University Law Center, and John Lamberth, an associate professor of psychology at Temple University, refute the idea of "rational discrimination." If blacks are more likely to be carrying drugs than whites, Cole and Lamberth say, then police should find drugs more often on the African Americans that

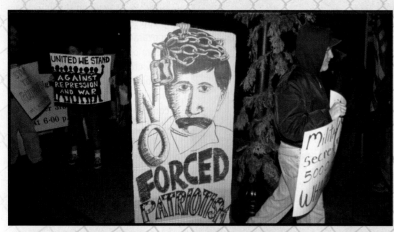

Demonstrators in front of Dearborn, Michigan, city hall protest racial profiling against Arab Americans in the "war on terrorism." Following the September 11, 2001, attacks, the U.S. government requested interviews with nearly six hundred Middle Eastern men in eastern Michigan.

© Richardson Morris/Gamma

they stop than on the whites that they stop.[128] This is not always the case. In Texas, for example, almost equal percentages of black and white drivers who were stopped were actually in possession of drugs or other contraband, and whites were slightly more likely than Hispanics to be arrested for possession.[129] In contrast, nationwide statistics show that African Americans (5.8 percent) and Hispanics (5.2 percent) who are stopped are more likely than whites (2 percent) to be arrested.[130]

Does Profiling "Work"?

Given the mistrust of law enforcement agents that racial profiling arouses in minority communities, it would seem in society's best interest to eradicate the practice. This may prove difficult, however. As Jerome H. Skolnick has explained, stereotyping is integral to the world of law enforcement. A police officer's job is essentially to investigate behavior that appears to her or him to be out of the ordinary or "different." Race is a very strong cue toward indicating "differences." Consequently, police officers may believe that they are acting "reasonably" in relying on race as an indication of criminal behavior.[131] Furthermore, law enforcement agents are often given "suspect descriptions" that include the characteristic of race. In these situations, discretionary profiling would not seem to have any impact on their actions.

Some observers also argue that, under certain circumstances, racial profiling "works." In the late 1990s, the Street Crimes Unit, a branch of the New York Police Department known for its aggressive tactics, came under a great deal of criticism. Over a two-year period, the unit made 45,000 stop and frisks. Only 22 percent of the stops led to arrests, and 90 percent of them involved members of a minority group.[132] In response to these figures and the 2002 shooting death of an immigrant from West Africa named Amadou Diallo, the Street Crimes Unit was disbanded.

Criminologists James Q. Wilson and Heather Mac Donald argue that the Street Crimes Unit's strategy actually made New York City a safer place. Those 45,000 stop and frisks, they point out, resulted in the seizure of 2,500 illegal guns, a ratio of one firearm confiscated for every eighteen stops. "No doubt some people regarded the stop as worse than an inconvenience and some stops may have been hard to justify," Wilson and Mac Donald write. "But the hassle factor has to be evaluated in the light of the great gains: 2,500 fewer dangerous weapons in dangerous hands."[133]

Terrorist Profiling

While the term *racial profiling* initially referred primarily to police stops of African Americans and Hispanics, in the past few years it has also come to be associated with counter-

terrorism efforts and their effects on the Muslim community. In the weeks following the September 11, 2001, terrorist attacks, federal law enforcement agents apprehended nearly 2,000 males of Islamic background for questioning. Only five of these suspects were ever charged with any crime. The U.S. Department of Justice targeted nearly 8,000 young Muslim men visiting the United States for interviews, and the U.S. Treasury Department raided a number of homes and offices of Arab Americans believed to be associating with terrorist groups. Many observers doubted the federal government's assertion that all these persons were targeted because they had some connection with terrorist activity. Indeed, it appeared that the suspects were chosen primarily on the basis of their nationality, religion, or, in some instances, their names. One FBI spokesperson admitted, "The only thing a lot of these people are guilty of is having the Arabic version of Bob Jones for a name."[134]

Again, though civil liberties groups and Muslim organizations have denounced these tactics, many observers support them as a "commonsense" approach to fighting terrorism. Just as detectives gather information on suspects most likely to have committed a particular crime, they argue, counterterrorist agents must "detail profile" to determine the most likely terrorists. These details include race, gender, and national origin, as well as behavioral traits such as enrollment at a flying school or participation in anti-American activities abroad or in the United States. No single detail would label someone a terrorist suspect, but a combination could be enough to meet reasonable suspicion standards. Plus, a poll conducted by Cornell University in 2004 found that 44 percent of those citizens surveyed supported some restrictions on the civil liberties of Muslim Americans, with 29 percent specifically in favor of racial profiling to prevent another terrorist attack.[135]

The *Whren* Effect

Those looking to the United States Supreme Court for answers to the questions raised by racial profiling have been disappointed. In 2001, the Court refused to hear an appeal of a case brought by a group of African American students in Oneonta, New York, who were "rounded up" and questioned following an assault in the area.[136] The best clues to the Court's view of racial profiling come from its decision in *Whren v. United States* (1996),[137] a case discussed on page 220.

In the *Whren* case, the Court ruled that the subjective intentions of the police, including any motives based on racial stereotyping or bias, are irrelevant under Fourth Amendment analysis.[138] As long as police have objective probable cause to believe a traffic violation or other wrongdoing has occurred, any other reasons for the stop will not be considered. Thus, if a suspect was driving over the speed limit or was not wearing a seat belt, then a police officer's decision to stop that driver is constitutional, even if there is proof that the "real" reason for the stop was the driver's race. The Court explained that it is already very difficult to define such terms as *reasonable* and *probable cause.* To try to measure the motivation of a law enforcement agent would be more difficult still.[139]

Protecting Minorities (Sometimes)

In the absence of guidance from the courts, jurisdictions have had to make their own decisions on what steps to take to combat possible racial stereotyping. In 2003, for example, the California Highway Patrol announced that its officers would no longer use minor traffic violations as a pretext for searching automobiles for illegal drugs. Statistics showed that in certain parts of the state African Americans and Hispanics were three times more likely than whites to be the targets of such stops and searches.[140] Today, twenty-nine states have passed laws concerning racial profiling, though forty-six states still do not explicitly ban profiling based on religion and thirty-five do not ban profiling of pedestrians or motorists.[141]

The administration of President George W. Bush has also issued guidelines designed to eradicate racial profiling in the seventy federal law enforcement agencies. Under the guidelines, a Drug Enforcement Administration officer cannot focus on a certain neighborhood simply because of its racial make-up. The guidelines do, however, provide an exception in "narrow" cases when race and ethnicity help "identify terrorist threats and stop potential catastrophic attacks."[142]

Making Sense of Racial Profiling

1 Do you agree with the Supreme Court's reasoning in the *Whren* decision? What might be some of the practical consequences of allowing the suspect's race to be a factor in the "reasonableness" test of the Fourth Amendment?

2 According to the U.S. Department of Justice, 60.8 percent of all traffic stops involve male drivers. Why do you think there is such a discrepancy in the gender make-up of these stops? Does it reflect a pattern of "gender profiling"? Why or why not?

3 Revisit the arguments made in this feature in favor of some level of racial profiling. Do you agree with these positions? Are there any circumstances in which stereotyping—racial or otherwise—might be useful in fighting crime or terrorism?

Chapter Summary

1 Outline the four major sources that may provide probable cause. (a) Personal observation, usually due to an officer's personal training, experience, and expertise; (b) information, gathered from informants, eyewitnesses, victims, police bulletins, and other sources; (c) evidence, which often has to be in plain view; and (d) association, which generally must concern a person with a known criminal background who is seen in a place where criminal activity is openly taking place.

2 Explain the exclusionary rule and the exceptions to it. This rule, established federally in *Weeks v. United States* and at the state level in *Mapp v. Ohio,* prohibits the use of illegally seized evidence, or evidence obtained by an unreasonable search and seizure in an inadmissible way. Exceptions to the exclusionary rule are the "inevitable discovery" exception established in *Nix v. Williams* and the "good faith" exception established in *United States v. Leon.*

3 Distinguish between a stop and a frisk, and indicate the importance of the case *Terry v. Ohio.* Though the terms *stop* and *frisk* are often used in concert, a stop is the separate act of detaining a suspect when an officer reasonably believes that a criminal activity is about to take place. A frisk is the physical "pat-down" of a suspect. In *Terry v. Ohio,* the Supreme Court ruled that an officer must have "specific and articulable" facts before making a stop, but those facts may be "taken together with rational inferences."

4 List the four elements that must be present for an arrest to take place. (a) Intent, (b) authority, (c) seizure or detention, and (d) the understanding of the person that he or she has been arrested.

5 List the four categories of items that can be seized by use of a search warrant. (a) Items resulting from a crime, such as stolen goods; (b) inherently illegal items; (c) evidence of the crime; and (d) items used in committing the crime.

STORIES FROM THE STREET

Go to the *Stories from the Street* feature at **www.cjinaction.com** to hear Larry Gaines tell insightful stories related to this chapter and his experiences in the field.

6 Explain when searches can be made without a warrant. Searches and seizures can be made without a warrant if they are incidental to an arrest (but they must be reasonable); when they are made with voluntary consent; when they involve the "movable vehicle exception"; when property has been abandoned; and when items are in plain view, under certain restricted circumstances (see *Coolidge v. New Hampshire*).

7 Describe how the USA PATRIOT Act of 2001 changed the guidelines for electronic surveillance of suspected terrorists. Under the old surveillance guidelines, law enforcement agents needed probable cause of a crime to engage in counterterrorism. Under the USA PATRIOT Act of 2001, agents are free to search for leads or clues to terrorist activities if such surveillance serves a "significant purpose." The "significant purpose" standard is much easier to meet than "probable cause."

8 Recite the *Miranda* warning. You have the right to remain silent. If you give up that right, anything you say can and will be used against you in a court of law. You have the right to speak with an attorney and to have the attorney present during questioning. If you so desire and cannot afford one, an attorney will be appointed for you without charge before questioning.

9 Indicate situations in which a *Miranda* warning is unnecessary. (a) When no questions that are testimonial in nature are asked of the suspect; (b) when there is no suspect and witnesses in general are being questioned at the scene of a crime; (c) when a person volunteers information before the police ask anything; (d) when a suspect has given a private statement to a friend without the government orchestrating it; (e) during a stop and frisk when no arrests have been made; and (f) during a traffic stop.

10 List the three basic types of police identification. (a) Showups, (b) photo arrays, and (c) lineups.

Key Terms

affidavit 216
arrest 211
arrest warrant 213
booking 231
consent searches 218
custodial interrogation 225
custody 225

exclusionary rule 207
exigent circumstances 213
frisk 211
fruit of the poisoned tree 207
"good faith" exception 209
"inevitable discovery" exception 208

interrogation 224
Miranda rights 225
plain view doctrine 221
probable cause 206
search 215
search warrant 215
searches and seizures 205

searches incidental to arrests 218
seizure 216
stop 210
warrantless arrest 214

Questions for Critical Analysis

1 What are the two most significant legal concepts contained in the Fourth Amendment, and why are they important?

2 Suppose that a police officer stops a person who "looks funny." The person acts strangely, so the police officer decides to frisk him. The officer feels a bulge in the suspect's coat pocket, which turns out to be a bag of cocaine. Would the arrest for cocaine possession hold up in court? Why or why not?

3 What continues to be the best indicator of probable cause in the face of no hard-and-fast definitions?

4 How does the expression "fruit of the poisoned tree" relate to the issue of searches and seizures?

5 Is it possible for a person legally to be under arrest without an officer indicating to that person that she or he is in fact under arrest? Explain.

6 Are there any circumstances in which an officer can make a warrantless arrest for a crime that is a misdemeanor? Explain.

7 What is the difference between an arrest warrant and a search warrant?

8 "A person always assumes the risk that her or his conversation may be monitored by the police." Is there any truth to this statement? Why or why not?

9 Describe some of the interrogation strategies that police officers use to gain confessions within the guidelines set down by the Supreme Court's *Miranda* decision.

10 What circumstances have led some states to videotape interrogations, and why have some jurisdictions decided not to do so?

Test Preparation Online

Criminal JusticeNow

Go to **www.cjinaction.com** and click on *Criminal JusticeNow* for access to this powerful online study tool. You will get a *personalized study plan* based on your responses to a diagnostic pretest. Once you have mastered the material with the help of interactive learning tools, video clips with questions, an integrated e-book, and more, you can take a posttest to confirm you are ready to move on to the next chapter.

Book Companion Web Site

At the book companion Web site (**www.cjinaction.com**), you will find many resources in addition to *Criminal JusticeNow* to aid you in studying for your exams. For example, under *Chapter Resources*, you will find the *Chapter Outline, Chapter Summary, Flashcards, Glossary, Learning Objectives, Lecture Presentations, Concept Builder, Essay Questions*, and a *Tutorial Chapter Quiz*. You can also test yourself with interactive *Online Reviews* of each chapter section. Check out the *Web Links* to access the Web sites mentioned in the text, as well as many others. You can also access recent perspectives by clicking on *CJ in the News* and *Terrorism Update* under *Course Resources*.

Suggested Readings

Parenti, Christian, *Soft Cage: Surveillance in America from Slavery to the War on Terror*, New York: Basic Books, 2003. For most of this nation's history, government surveillance of American citizens has been justified in the name of national security. In this book, Parenti explores the political and sociological underpinnings for "Big Brother" in the United States. He contends that an eighteenth-century slave pass, designed to keep track of the movement of slaves, and modern Social Security cards perform the same function of population control. Not surprisingly, the author strongly believes that although surveillance is justified as a means of crime control, its actual purpose is to limit civil liberties and other freedoms guaranteed to American citizens under the U.S. Constitution.

Stuart, Gary L., *Miranda: The Story of America's Right to Remain Silent*, Tucson, AZ: University of Arizona Press, 2004. Did you know that Ernesto Miranda, the defendant in perhaps the most famous criminal case in American history, was knifed to death in a bar fight in Phoenix ten years after his case appeared before the Supreme Court, that his murderer was arrested by the same police officers who had initially arrested Miranda many years earlier, and that the man confessed to the crime after being read his *Miranda* rights? The author, with his deep roots in the Arizona legal scene and personal ties to many of the principals in the *Miranda* case, provides the definitive history of the right to remain silent in this country. He also looks to the future of the *Miranda* rights, particularly in the context of the post-9/11 landscape and the interrogation of terrorist suspects.

Notes

1. *Illinois v. Caballes*, 125 S.Ct. 834 (2005).
2. *Ibid.*, 853.
3. *Michigan v. Summers*, 452 U.S. 692 (1981).
4. *Brinegar v. United States*, 338 U.S. 160 (1949).
5. Rolando V. del Carmen, *Criminal Procedure for Law Enforcement Personnel* (Monterey, CA: Brooks/Cole Publishing Co., 1987), 63–64.
6. *Maryland v. Pringle*, 540 U.S. 366 (2003).
7. 500 U.S. 44 (1991).
8. *United States v. Leon*, 468 U.S. 897 (1984).
9. 232 U.S. 383 (1914).
10. 342 U.S. 165 (1952).
11. 367 U.S. 643 (1961).
12. Potter Stewart, "The Road to *Mapp v. Ohio* and Beyond: The Origins, Development, and Future of the Exclusionary Rule in Search-and-Seizure Cases," *Columbia Law Review* 83 (October 1983), 1365.
13. 430 U.S. 387 (1977).
14. 467 U.S. 431 (1984).
15. 468 U.S. 897 (1984).
16. "Jury's Mixed Verdict in Cop Trial," *UPI Online* (April 3, 1998).
17. Karen M. Hess and Henry M. Wrobleski, *Police Operation: Theory and Practice* (St. Paul, MN: West Publishing Co., 1997), 122.
18. 392 U.S. 1 (1968).
19. *Ibid.*, 20.
20. *Ibid.*, 21.
21. See *United States v. Cortez*, 449 U.S. 411 (1981); and *United States v. Sokolow*, 490 U.S. 1 (1989).
22. *United States v. Arvizu*, 534 U.S. 266 (2002).
23. *Ibid.*, 270.
24. *Florida v. J.L.*, 529 U.S. 266, 274 (2000).
25. *Adams v. Williams*, 407 U.S. 143 (1972).
26. *Alabama v. White*, 496 U.S. 325 (1990).
27. *United States v. Place*, 462 U.S. 696 (1983).
28. *Hibel v. Sixth Judicial District Court*, 124 S.Ct. 2451 (2004).
29. *Ibid.*, 2459.
30. *Minnesota v. Dickerson*, 508 U.S. 366 (1993).
31. Rolando V. del Carmen and Jeffrey T. Walker, *Briefs of Leading Cases in Law Enforcement*, 2d ed. (Cincinnati, OH: Anderson, 1995), 38–40.
32. *Florida v. Royer*, 460 U.S. 491 (1983).

33. See also *United States v. Mendenhall,* 446 U.S. 544 (1980).
34. del Carmen, *Criminal Procedure,* 97–98.
35. 514 U.S. 927 (1995).
36. Linda J. Collier and Deborah D. Rosenbloom, *American Jurisprudence,* 2d ed. (Rochester, NY: Lawyers Cooperative Publishing, 1995), 122.
37. 540 U.S. 31 (2003).
38. *Ibid.,* 527.
39. *Ibid.,* 528.
40. Wayne R. LeFave and Jerold H. Israel, *Criminal Procedure* (St. Paul, MN: West Publishing Co., 1985), 141–144.
41. David Orlin, Jacob Thiessen, Kelli C. McTaggart, Lisa Toporek, and James Pearl, "Warrantless Searches and Seizures," in "Twenty-sixth Annual Review of Criminal Procedure," *Georgetown Law Journal* 85 (April 1997), 847.
42. *Atwater v. City of Lago Vista,* 532 U.S. 318, 346–347 (2001).
43. 445 U.S. 573 (1980).
44. 451 U.S. 204 (1981).
45. *California v. Greenwood,* 486 U.S. 35 (1988).
46. *Ibid.*
47. 389 U.S. 347 (1967).
48. *Ibid.,* 361.
49. 486 U.S. 35 (1988).
50. *Ibid.*
51. *Illinois v. Caballes,* 834.
52. *Coolidge v. New Hampshire,* 403 U.S. 443, 467 (1971).
53. del Carmen, *Criminal Procedure,* 158.
54. *Katz v. United States,* 389 U.S. 347, 357 (1967).
55. 414 U.S. 234–235 (1973).
56. 395 U.S. 752 (1969).
57. *Bumper v. North Carolina,* 391 U.S. 543 (1968).
58. 412 U.S. 218 (1973).
59. Ian D. Midgley, "Just One Question before We Get to *Ohio v. Robinette:* 'Are You Carrying Any Contraband . . . Weapons, Drugs, Constitutional Protections . . . Anything Like That?'" *Case Western Reserve Law Review* 48 (Fall 1997), 173.
60. 501 U.S. 429 (1991).
61. 519 U.S. 33 (1996).
62. *United States v. Drayton,* 536 U.S. 194 (2002).
63. Linda Greenhouse, "Supreme Court Upholds Police Methods in Vehicle Drug Searches," *New York Times* (November 19, 1996), A23.
64. 453 U.S. 454 (1981).
65. 267 U.S. 132 (1925).
66. *United States v. Ross,* 456 U.S. 798, 804–809 (1982); and *Chambers v. Maroney,* 399 U.S. 42, 44, 52 (1970).
67. 517 U.S. 806 (1996).
68. 519 U.S. 408 (1997).
69. Linda Greenhouse, "Supreme Court Bars Traffic Stops That Are Intended as Drug Checks," *New York Times* (November 29, 2000), A1.
70. *Michigan Department of State Police v. Sitz,* 496 U.S. 455 (1990).
71. *United States v. Martinez-Fuerte,* 428 U.S. 556 (1976).
72. 531 U.S. 32 (2000).
73. *Ibid.*
74. *Illinois v. Lidster,* 124 S.Ct. 885 (2004).
75. *United States v. Flores-Montano,* 124 S.Ct. 1582 (2004).
76. *Illinois v. Lidster,* 889.
77. *United States v. Flores-Montano,* 1586.
78. 403 U.S. 443 (1971).
79. 388 U.S. 42 (1967).
80. 18 U.S.C. Sections 2510(7), 2518(1)(a), 2516 (1994).
81. *Lee v. United States,* 343 U.S. 747 (1952).
82. Christopher K. Murphy, "Electronic Surveillance," in "Twenty-Sixth Annual Review of Criminal Procedure," *Georgetown Law Journal* (April 1997), 920.
83. *United States v. Nguyen,* 46 F.3d 781, 783 (8th Cir. 1995).
84. *United States v. Chan,* 830 F.Supp. 531, 535 (N.D. Cal. 1993).
85. *United States v. Bach,* 310 F.3d 1063 (8th Cir. 2002).
86. Francisco J. Navarro, "*United States v. Bach* and the Fourth Amendment in Cyberspace," *Albany Law Journal of Science and Technology* (2003), 246.
87. Foreign Intelligence Surveillance Act of 1978, Pub. L. No. 95-511, 92 Stat. 1783, codified at 50 U.S.C. Sections 1801–1811 (2000).
88. Uniting and Strengthening America by Providing Appropriate Tools Required to Interrupt and Obstruct Terrorism Act of 2001, Pub. L. No. 107-56, 115 Stat. 272, codified as amended at 50 U.S.C.A. Sections 1801–1811 (West 2000 & Supp. 2002).
89. David Hardin, "The Fuss over Two Small Words: The Unconstitutionality of the USA PATRIOT Act Amendments to FISA under the Fourth Amendment," *George Washington Law Review* (April 2003), 291.
90. 18 U.S.C. Section 3103a (2003).
91. *Ibid.*
92. Eric Lichtblau, "Justice Department Defends PATRIOT Act before Senate Hearings," *New York Times* (April 5, 2005), A21.
93. *Delayed-Notice Search Warrants: A Vital and Time Honored Tool for Fighting Crime* (Washington, D.C.: U.S. Department of Justice, September 2004), 1–8.
94. Nathan H. Seltzer, "When History Matters Not: The Fourth Amendment in the Age of the Secret Search," *Criminal Law Bulletin* (March–April 2004), 143.
95. *Brown v. Mississippi,* 297 U.S. 278 (1936).
96. 378 U.S. 478 (1964).
97. *Ibid.,* at 490–491.
98. *Miranda v. Arizona,* 384 U.S. 436 (1966).
99. H. Richard Uviller, *Tempered Zeal* (Chicago: Contemporary Books, 1988), 188–198.
100. *Orozco v. Texas,* 394 U.S. 324 (1969); *Oregon v. Mathiason,* 429 U.S. 492 (1977); and *California v. Beheler,* 463 U.S. 1121 (1983).
101. *Pennsylvania v. Muniz,* 496 U.S. 582 (1990).
102. del Carmen, *Criminal Procedure,* 267–268.
103. *Moran v. Burbine,* 475 U.S. 412 (1986).
104. *Michigan v. Mosley,* 423 U.S. 96 (1975).
105. *Fare v. Michael C.,* 442 U.S. 707, 723–724 (1979).

106. 512 U.S. 452 (1994).

107. Patrick Malone, "You Have the Right to Remain Silent: *Miranda* after Twenty Years," *American Scholar* 55 (1986), 367.

108. Richard A. Leo, "The Impact of *Miranda* Revisited," *Journal of Criminal Law and Criminology* 86 (Spring 1996), 621–692.

109. Shaila K. Dewan, "New York Police Resist Videotaping Interrogations," *New York Times* (September 2, 2002), A21.

110. Saul Kassin, "False Confessions and the Jogger Case," *New York Times* (November 1, 2002), A31.

111. 530 U.S. 428 (2000).

112. *Ibid.*, 443.

113. Alan M. Dershowitz, "A Requiem for the Exclusionary Rule," in *Taking Liberties: A Decade of Hard Cases, Bad Laws, and Bum Raps* (Chicago: Contemporary Books, 1988), 10.

114. *United States v. Patane*, 124 S.Ct. 2620 (2004).

115. *Ibid.*, 2629.

116. Thomas P. Sullivan, *Police Experiences with Recording Custodial Interrogations* (Chicago: Northwestern University School of Law Center on Wrongful Convictions, Summer 2004), 4.

117. *Ibid.*, 7.

118. 413 U.S. 300 (1973).

119. *United States v. Barker*, 988 F.2d 77, 78 (9th Cir. 1993).

120. 384 U.S. 757 (1966).

121. *United States v. Dionisio*, 410 U.S. 1 (1973); and *United States v. Mara*, 410 U.S. 19 (1973).

122. 470 U.S. 753 (1985).

123. Dwight Steward and Molly Totman, *Don't Mind If I Take a Look, Do Ya? An Examination of Consent Searches and Contraband Hit Rates at Texas Traffic Stops* (Austin, TX: Texas Criminal Justice Coalition, February 2005), 4.

124. "Nationwide, Profiling Controls Still Rankle," *Law Enforcement News* (June 2004), F1.

125. Gary Cordner, Brian Williams, and Alfredo Velasco, *Vehicle Stops in San Diego: 2001* (San Diego, CA: San Diego Police Department, 2002), 34.

126. Quoted in Jackson Toby, "'Racial Profiling' Doesn't Prove Cops Are Racist," *Wall Street Journal* (March 11, 1999), A22.

127. Dinesh D'Souza, *The End of Racism: Principles for a Multiracial Society* (New York: Free Press, 1995), 284.

128. David Cole and John Lamberth, "The Fallacy of Racial Profiling," *New York Times* (May 13, 2001), 13.

129. Steward and Totman, 5.

130. Bureau of Justice Statistics, *Contacts between Police and the Public: Findings from the 2002 National Survey* (Washington, D.C.: U.S. Department of Justice, April 2005), 7.

131. Jerome H. Skolnick, *Justice without Trial: Law Enforcement in Democratic Society*, 3d ed. (New York: Macmillan, 1994), 80.

132. Melanie Lefkowitz, "Policy Set on the Street," *Newsday* (March 14, 2002), A3.

133. James Q. Wilson and Heather Mac Donald, "Profiles in Courage," *Wall Street Journal* (January 10, 2002), A12.

134. Patrick McDonnell, "Nation's Frantic Dragnet Entangles Many Lives," *Los Angeles Times* (November 7, 2001), A1.

135. William Kates, "Many Would Limit Some Rights of Muslims," *Philadelphia Inquirer* (December 19, 2004), A32.

136. "High Court Doesn't Want to Face Up to Profiling Appeal," *Law Enforcement News* (October 31, 2001), 7.

137. 517 U.S. 806 (1996).

138. *Ibid.*, 813.

139. Tracey Maclin, "Race and the Fourth Amendment," *Vanderbilt Law Review* 51 (March 1998), 377.

140. Maura Dolan and John M. Glionna, "CHP Settles Lawsuit over Claims of Racial Profiling," *Los Angeles Times* (February 28, 2003), A1.

141. *Threat and Humiliation: Racial Profiling, Domestic Security, and Human Rights in the United States* (New York: Amnesty International USA, 2004), 6.

142. Eric Lichtblau, "Bush Issues Racial Profiling Ban but Exempts Security Inquiries," *New York Times* (June 18, 2003), A1.

CHAPTER EIGHT

Courts and the Quest for Justice

Chapter outline

- Functions of the Courts
- The Basic Principles of the American Judicial System
- State Court Systems
- The Federal Court System
- Judges in the Court System
- The Courtroom Work Group
- Criminal Justice in Action—The Long Arm of the Law

Chapter objectives

After reading this chapter, you should be able to:

1 Define and contrast the four functions of the courts.
2 Define *jurisdiction* and contrast geographical and subject-matter jurisdiction.
3 Explain the difference between trial and appellate courts.
4 Outline the several levels of a typical state court system.
5 Outline the federal court system.
6 Explain briefly how a case is brought to the Supreme Court.
7 List the actions that a judge might take prior to an actual trial.
8 Explain the difference between the selection of judges at the state level and at the federal level.
9 List and describe the members of the courtroom work group.
10 Explain the consequences of excessive caseloads.

Criminal JusticeNow

Optimize your study time and master key chapter concepts with *Criminal JusticeNow*, an online study tool that provides you with a *personalized study plan*. Check out the "Test Preparation Online" section at the end of the chapter for additional information.

Trial and Errors

It ended
with an apology. On September 1, 2004, fourteen months after he was charged with sexually assaulting a nineteen-year-old employee of the Lodge & Spa in Cordillera, Colorado, basketball star Kobe Bryant told his accuser that he was sorry for his behavior on that night and for "the consequences she has suffered in the past year." Bryant also apologized to his accuser's parents and family members and to his own family and supporters. He even apologized to the people of Eagle, Colorado, who had endured a full-fledged media circus in connection with the case.

Of course, an apology is not the same as an admission of guilt, and Bryant still maintained that the sexual relations between him and his accuser were consensual. For her part, the young woman continued to assert that Bryant had placed her in a chokehold and forced her to have sex. Nevertheless, Colorado law enforcement officials were compelled to drop the charges when Bryant's

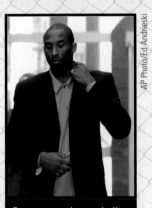

Prosecutors dropped all sexual-assault charges against professional basketball player Kobe Bryant, shown here entering the Justice Center in Eagle, Colorado, after his accuser refused to participate in court proceedings.

AP Photo/Ed Andrieski

accuser informed them that she would no longer participate in the proceedings.

Her decision did not come as a complete surprise. Several months earlier, the accuser's mother had written an angry letter to District Judge W. Terry Ruckriegle, asking him to protect her daughter, who had been receiving death threats. Even though courts are legally required to protect the privacy of alleged rape victims, the young woman's identity became widely known after court personnel mistakenly posted her name on the Internet—four times. In another gaffe, a court employee erroneously e-mailed the media transcripts of a closed hearing that featured testimony suggesting that the accuser had had sex with someone else besides Bryant on the night of the alleged rape. "I thought she needed to get the hell out of the case," said one of the young woman's attorneys. "The criminal justice system was about to throw her under the bus."

Did Kobe Bryant's accuser
suffer unfairly at the hands of the criminal justice system? Certainly, the court erred grievously in failing to protect her privacy, and future victims of sexual assault may think twice about filing charges after seeing the humiliations faced by this young woman. In the end, however, Bryant's apology may have been the most that she could have obtained even if the case had actually gone to trial. Bryant's lawyers were going to present evidence that the young woman had had multiple sexual partners in the days surrounding her encounter with their client, raising the possibility that someone other than Bryant was responsible for any physical evidence of a rape. According to one legal expert, there was "no way" that Bryant would be found guilty in the face of this evidence.[1]

After the case of "the people versus Kobe Bryant" was dismissed, Eagle County District Attorney Mark Hurlbert bemoaned, "Today, justice is sadly interrupted."[2] Of

◈ CONCEPT BUILDER

Justice is an elusive ideal, yet central to how society deals with law violators. What exactly is justice? Visit **www.cjinaction.com** for an interactive exploration of this key topic.

course, justice can mean different things to different people—Bryant and his supporters no doubt felt that justice had been served by the dismissal. Famed jurist Roscoe Pound characterized "justice" as society's demand "that serious offenders be convicted and punished," while at the same time "the innocent and unfortunate are not oppressed."[3] We can expand on this noble, if idealistic, definition. Citizens expect their courts to discipline the guilty, provide deterrents for illegal activities, protect civil liberties, and rehabilitate criminals—all simultaneously. Over the course of the next four chapters, we shall examine these lofty goals and the extent to which they can be reached. We start with a discussion of how courts in the United States work.

FUNCTIONS OF THE COURTS

Simply stated, a court is a place where arguments are settled. The argument may be between the federal government and a corporation accused of violating environmental regulations, between business partners, between a criminal and the state, or between any other number of parties. The court provides an environment in which the basis of the argument can be decided through the application of the law.

Courts have extensive powers in our criminal justice system: they can bring the authority of the state to seize property and to restrict individual liberty. Given that the rights to own property and to enjoy personal freedom are enshrined in the U.S. Constitution, a court's *legitimacy* in taking such measures must be unquestioned by society. This legitimacy is based on two factors: impartiality and independence.[4] In theory, each party involved in a courtroom dispute must have an equal chance to present its case and must be secure in the belief that no outside factors are going to influence the decision rendered by the court. In reality, as we shall see over the next four chapters, it does not always work that way.

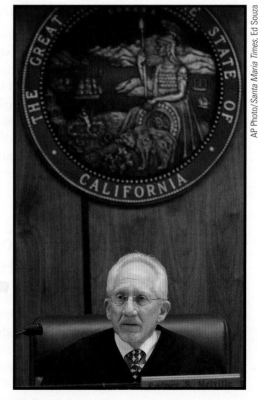

Santa Barbara (California) Superior Court Judge Rodney Melville presided over the high-profile 2005 criminal trial in which a jury found Michael Jackson not guilty of child molestation charges. Judge Melville refused to allow cameras into the courtroom—just one of the many decisions that judges make as "gatekeepers" of the American court system.

AP Photo/Santa Maria Times, Ed Souza

Due Process and Crime Control in the Courts

As mentioned in Chapter 1, the criminal justice system has two sets of underlying values: due process and crime control. Due process values focus on protecting the rights of the individual; crime control values stress the punishment and repression of criminal conduct.[5] The competing nature of these two value systems is often most evident in the nation's courts.

The Due Process Function The primary concern of early American courts was to protect the rights of the individual against the power of the state. Memories of injustices suffered at the hands of the British monarchy were still strong, and most of the procedural rules that we have discussed in this textbook were created with the express purpose of giving the individual a "fair chance" against the government in any courtroom proceedings. Therefore, the due process function of the courts is to protect individuals from the unfair advantages that the government—with its immense resources—automatically enjoys in legal battles. Seen in this light, constitutional guarantees such as the right to counsel, the right to a jury trial, and protection from self-incrimination are equalizers in the "contest" between the state and the individual. The idea that the two sides in a courtroom dispute are adversaries is, as we shall see in the next chapter, fundamental in American courts.

The Crime Control Function Advocates of crime control distinguish between the court's obligation to be fair to the accused and its obligation to be fair to society.[6] The crime control function of the courts emphasizes punishment and retribution—criminals must suffer for the harm done to society, and it is the courts' responsibility to see that they do so. Given this responsibility to protect the public, deter criminal behavior,

> "The judge is condemned when the criminal is acquitted."
>
> —Publius Syrus, Roman philosopher (42 B.C.E.)

and "get criminals off the streets," the courts should not be concerned solely with giving the accused a fair chance. Rather than using due process rules as "equalizers," the courts should use them as protection against blatantly unconstitutional acts. For example, a detective who beats a suspect with a tire iron to get a confession has obviously infringed on the suspect's constitutional rights. If, however, the detective uses trickery to gain a confession, the court should allow the confession to stand because it is not in society's interest that law enforcement agents be deterred from outwitting criminals.

The Rehabilitation Function

A third view of the court's responsibility is based on the "medical model" of the criminal justice system. In this model, criminals are analogous to patients, and the courts perform the role of doctors who dispense "treatment."[7] The criminal is seen as sick, not evil, and therefore treatment is morally justified. Of course, treatment varies from case to case, and some criminals require harsh penalties such as incarceration. In other cases, however, it may not be in society's best interest for the criminal to be punished according to the formal rules of the justice system. Perhaps the criminal can be rehabilitated to become a productive member of society and thus save taxpayers the costs of incarceration or other punishment.

The Bureaucratic Function

To a certain extent, the crime control, due process, and rehabilitation functions of a court are secondary to its bureaucratic function. In general, a court may have the goal of protecting society or protecting the rights of the individual, but on a day-to-day basis that court has the more pressing task of dealing with the cases brought before it. Like any bureaucracy, a court is concerned with speed and efficiency, and loftier concepts such as justice can be secondary to a judge's need to wrap up a particular case before six o'clock so that administrative deadlines can be met. Indeed, many observers feel that the primary adversarial relationship in the courts is not between the two parties involved but between the ideal of justice and the reality of bureaucratic limitations.[8]

THE BASIC PRINCIPLES OF THE AMERICAN JUDICIAL SYSTEM

One of the most often cited limitations of the American judicial system is its complex nature. In truth, the United States does not have a single judicial system, but fifty-two different systems—one for each state, the District of Columbia, and the federal government. As each state has its own unique judiciary with its own set of rules, some of which may be in conflict with the federal judiciary, it is helpful at this point to discuss the basics—jurisdiction, trial and appellate courts, and the dual court system.

Jurisdiction

In Latin, *juris* means "law," and *diction* means "to speak." Thus, **jurisdiction** literally refers to the power "to speak the law." Before any court can hear a case, it must have jurisdiction over the persons involved in the case or its subject matter. The jurisdiction of every court, even the United States Supreme Court, is limited in some way.

Geographical Jurisdiction One limitation is geographical. Generally, a court can exercise its authority over residents of a certain area. A state trial court, for example, normally has jurisdictional authority over crimes committed in a particular area of the state, such as a county or a district. A state's highest court (often called the state supreme court) has jurisdictional authority over the entire state, and the United States Supreme Court has jurisdiction over the entire country. (For a global perspective on this issue, see the feature *International CJ—Jurisdiction and the International Criminal Court* on the following page.)

Domestic Jurisdiction Determining which court has geographical jurisdiction can sometimes be complicated. Take the cases of John Allen Muhammad and John Lee Malvo. Although media attention focused on their sniper activities in the Washington, D.C., area in the fall of 2002, the two were charged with killing fourteen people and injuring several others in Alabama, Georgia, Louisiana, and Washington State, as well as in Maryland, Virginia, and the District of Columbia.

Almost immediately after Muhammad and Malvo were arrested, the question became: Where would they stand trial? Technically, each jurisdiction in which they had committed a crime had jurisdiction. The entity in the best position to give an answer was the federal government, which had custody over the pair and therefore the power to decide where their first trials would take place. Maryland authorities argued that because more people were killed in their state—six—than in any other jurisdiction, they should have "first crack" at the alleged snipers. The U.S. Department of Justice, however, wanted Muhammad and Malvo to receive the death penalty if found guilty, and felt that Virginia had, in the words of then Attorney General John Ashcroft, "the best law, the best facts, and the best range of available penalties."[9] Both were subsequently found guilty in Virginia courts, with Muhammad being sentenced to death and Malvo—a juvenile and therefore not eligible for execution—receiving two life sentences.

In 2005, however, Virginia sent the two convicts across state lines to Maryland, where officials hope to try them together for all six murders that took place there. Ultimately, Maryland prosecutors are seeking the same punishments as were meted out in Virginia: capital punishment for Muhammad and life imprisonment for Malvo. Critics called the action an expensive exercise in futility, but state officials insisted that the families of the duo's Maryland victims deserved the same "sense of closure" as their Virginia counterparts.[10] In addition, as we will see in Chapter 10, guilty verdicts can be appealed and reversed, and any further convictions in Maryland would serve as "insurance" against that possibility in Virginia.

International Jurisdiction Policy concerns also play a large role in questions of international geographical jurisdiction. Although many countries have agreed to *extradite* (give up or deliver) suspects when asked to do so, the decision is fraught with extralegal concerns. A number of European countries, for example, will not extradite suspects to the United States if the accused could face the death penalty at trial. In 2005, Great Britain refused to send Babar Ahmed, a computer programmer suspected of raising money for terrorist organizations over the Internet, to the United States until it received assurances that he would not be executed if found guilty. Law enforcement officials estimate that between 2,500 and 3,000 fugitives fleeing murder charges in the

Jurisdiction and the International Criminal Court

The United States has a long history of supporting international prosecution of the most heinous of crimes. In 1946, the United States was the guiding force behind the Nuremberg Trials, which established that individuals could be convicted for war crimes and crimes against humanity. (The trials resulted in Nazi leaders being found guilty of the extermination of millions of Jews.) Over the past decade, the United States has provided funds and information to international tribunals set up to punish the instigators of genocide in Rwanda and the Balkans. Yet, when the International Criminal Court (ICC)—the world's first permanent court for the prosecution of war criminals—was created on April 11, 2002, the United States refused to take part.

This decision earned the United States a great deal of international criticism, especially from the nations of the European Union. For the Bush administration, however, it was a matter of jurisdiction. The ICC assumes jurisdiction over acts of genocide, crimes against humanity, and war crimes committed by individuals regardless of nationality. In theory, this means that any American, from a high-ranking government official to soldiers in the field, could be accused of committing a crime against humanity by the court's chief prosecutor. Because the United States is currently the world's only superpower, with military operations in dozens of countries at any one time, the administration worries that Americans will be easy targets for frivolous accusations. Furthermore, as some constitutional scholars have pointed out, the ICC does not provide for a trial by jury, as guaranteed to any American charged with committing a crime by the Bill of Rights.

Supporters of the ICC counter that the United States overestimates the risks of seeing its citizens hauled before the court, as the court's jurisdiction is only "secondary"; that is, the court will prosecute only in situations in which the home country of the accused is unable or unwilling to do so. Regardless of this argument, the United States has insisted that it will not cooper-

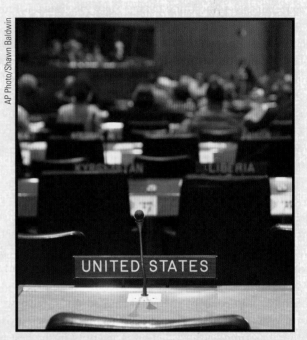

AP Photo/Shawn Baldwin

The United States chair remains empty during the first meeting of the International Criminal Court at United Nations headquarters in New York City on September 3, 2002.

ate with the ICC unless Americans are given immunity from its jurisdiction, a request that has been rejected by most participating nations.

FOR CRITICAL ANALYSIS

Do you agree with the Bush administration's position against the ICC? Which is more important—protecting the rights of Americans (to trial by jury, for example), or cooperating with the international community in fighting the crimes over which the ICC has jurisdiction?

United States are presently hiding out in Mexico, which similarly refuses to extradite any suspect who might be punished with the death penalty or life imprisonment.[11] (For a more in-depth discussion of international jurisdiction, see the *Criminal Justice in Action* feature at the end of this chapter.)

Subject-Matter Jurisdiction Jurisdiction over subject matter also acts as a limitation on the types of cases a court can hear. State court systems include courts of *general (unlimited) jurisdiction* and courts of *limited jurisdiction*. Courts of general jurisdiction have no restrictions on the subject matter they may address, and therefore deal with the most serious felonies and civil cases. Courts of limited jurisdiction, also known as lower courts, handle misdemeanors and civil matters under a certain amount, usually $1,000. To alleviate caseload pressures in lower courts, many states have created special subject-matter courts that only dispose of cases involving a specific crime. For example, a number of jurisdictions have established drug courts to

Photo by Getty Images

Ahmed Omar Saeed, who is presumed to have planned the kidnapping and murder of American journalist Daniel Pearl in 2002, is escorted into the provincial high court in Karachi, Pakistan. The United States sought Saeed's extradition, but Pakistani government officials refused, insisting that the suspect stand trial in the country where his crime took place. (Saeed was eventually convicted and sentenced to death.) What reasons might a country have for refusing an extradition request?

handle an overload of illicit narcotics arrests, and California has created twelve courts that deal specifically with domestic violence offenders.

Trial and Appellate Courts

Another distinction is between courts of original jurisdiction and courts of appellate, or review, jurisdiction. Courts having *original jurisdiction* are courts of the first instance, or **trial courts.** Almost every case begins in a trial court. It is in this court that a trial (or a guilty plea) takes place, and the judge imposes a sentence if the defendant is found guilty. Trial courts are primarily concerned with *questions of fact;* that is, they are designed to determine exactly what events occurred that are relevant to questions of the defendant's guilt or innocence.

Courts having *appellate jurisdiction* act as reviewing courts, or **appellate courts.** In general, cases can be brought before appellate courts only on appeal by one of the parties in the trial court. Note that because of constitutional protections against being tried twice for the same crime, prosecutors who lose in *criminal* trial court *cannot* appeal the verdict. An appellate court does not use juries or witnesses to reach its decision. Instead, its judges make a decision on whether the case should be *reversed* and *remanded,* or sent back to the court of original jurisdiction for a new trial. Appellate judges present written explanations for their decisions, and these **opinions** of the court are the basis for a great deal of the precedent in the criminal justice system.

It is important to understand that appellate courts do not determine the defendant's guilt or innocence—they only make judgments on questions of procedure. In other words, they are concerned with *questions of law* and normally accept the facts as established by the trial court. Only rarely will an appeals court question a jury's decision. Instead, the appellate judges will review the manner in which the facts and evidence were provided to the jury and rule on whether errors were made in the process.

The Dual Court System

Like many other aspects of American government, the structure of the judicial system was the result of a compromise. During the framing of the U.S. Constitution, two camps emerged with different views on the courts. The Anti-Federalists,

Trial Courts
Courts in which most cases usually begin and in which questions of fact are examined.

Appellate Courts
Courts that review decisions made by lower courts, such as trial courts; also known as *courts of appeals.*

Opinions
Statements by the court expressing the reasons for its decision in a case.

interested in limiting the power of the federal government, wanted the Supreme Court to be the only *national* court, with the states handling the majority of judicial work. The Federalists, dedicated to ensuring that the states did not have too much power, wanted all cases to be heard in federal courts. Both sides eventually made concessions, and the outcome is reflected in the **dual court system** that we have today (see Figure 8.1).[12]

Federal and state courts both have limited jurisdiction. Generally, federal courts deal with acts that violate federal law, and state courts deal with acts that violate state law. The distinction is not, however, always clear. A number of crimes—such as kidnapping and transportation of narcotics—are deemed illegal by both federal and state statutes, and persons accused of such crimes can be tried in either court system. In these instances, federal and state prosecutors must decide among themselves who will handle the case—a decision based on a number of factors, including the notoriety of the crime and the relative caseloads of the respective court systems. Often, the prosecutors will "steer" a suspect toward the harsher penalty. Thus, if the punishment for a particular crime is more severe under federal law than state law, then law enforcement officials may decide to try the defendant in federal court (and vice versa).

STATE COURT SYSTEMS

Typically, a state court system includes several levels, or tiers, of courts. State courts may include (1) lower courts, or courts of limited jurisdiction; (2) trial courts of general jurisdiction; (3) appellate courts; and (4) the state's highest court. As previously mentioned, each state has a different judicial structure, in which different courts have different jurisdictions, but there are enough similarities to allow for a general discussion. Figure 8.2 shows a typical state court system.

Courts of Limited Jurisdiction

Most states have local trial courts that are limited to trying cases involving minor criminal matters, such as traffic violations, prostitution, and drunk and disorderly conduct. Although these minor courts usually keep no written record of the trial proceedings and cases are decided by a judge rather than a jury, defendants have the same rights as

FIGURE 8.1
The Dual Court System

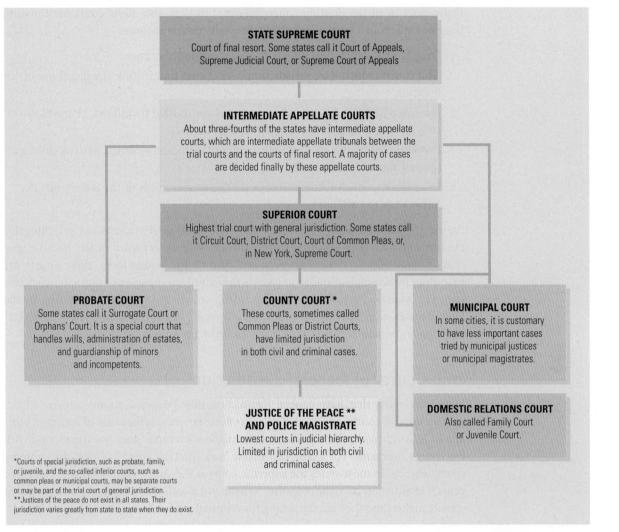

FIGURE 8.2
A Typical State Court System

those in other trial courts. The majority of all minor criminal cases are decided in these lower courts. Courts of limited jurisdiction can also be responsible for the preliminary stages of felony cases. Arraignments, bail hearings, and preliminary hearings often take place in these lower courts.

Magistrate Courts One of the earliest courts of limited jurisdiction was the *justice court,* presided over by a *justice of the peace,* or JP. In the early days of this nation, JPs were found everywhere in the country. One of the most famous JPs was Judge Roy Bean, the "hanging judge" of Langtry, Texas, who presided over his court at the turn of the twentieth century. Today, more than half the states have abolished justice courts, though JPs still serve a useful function in some cities and rural areas, notably in Texas. The jurisdiction of justice courts is limited to minor disputes between private individuals and to crimes punishable by small fines or short jail terms. The equivalent of a county JP in a city is known as a **magistrate** or, in some states, a municipal court judge. Magistrate courts have the same limited jurisdiction as do justice courts in rural settings. In most jurisdictions, magistrates are responsible for providing law enforcement agents with search and seizure warrants, discussed in Chapter 7.

Specialty Courts Many states have created **specialty courts** that have jurisdiction over very narrowly defined areas of criminal justice. Not only do these courts remove

Magistrate
A public civil officer or official with limited judicial authority within a particular geographical area, such as the authority to issue an arrest warrant.

Specialty Courts
Lower courts that have jurisdiction over one specific area of criminal activity, such as illegal drugs or domestic violence.

many cases from the existing court systems, but they also allow court personnel to become experts in a particular subject. Specialty courts include:

1 Drug courts, which deal only with illegal substance crimes.
2 Gun courts, which have jurisdiction over crimes that involve the illegal use of firearms.
3 Juvenile courts, which specialize in crimes committed by minors. (We will discuss juvenile courts in more detail in Chapter 15.)
4 Domestic courts, which deal with crimes of domestic violence, such as child and spousal abuse.
5 Elder courts, which focus primarily on the special needs of the elderly victims rather than the offenders.

As we will see in Chapter 12, many state and local governments are searching for cheaper alternatives to locking up nonviolent offenders in prison or jail. Because specialty courts offer a range of treatment options for wrongdoers, these courts are becoming increasingly popular in today's more budget-conscious criminal justice system. For example, about two thousand drug courts are presently operating in the United States, a number that is expected to increase as the financial benefits of diverting drug law violators from correctional facilities become more evident.

Trial Courts of General Jurisdiction

State trial courts that have general jurisdiction may be called county courts, district courts, superior courts, or circuit courts. In Ohio, the name is the court of common pleas and in Massachusetts, the trial court. (The name sometimes does not correspond with the court's functions. For example, in New York the trial court is called the supreme court, whereas in most states the supreme court is the state's highest court.) Courts of general jurisdiction have the authority to hear and decide cases involving many types of subject matter, and they are the setting for criminal trials (discussed in Chapter 10).

State Courts of Appeals

Every state has at least one court of appeals (known as an appellate, or reviewing, court), which may be an intermediate appellate court or the state's highest court. About three-fourths have intermediate appellate courts. The highest appellate court in a state is usually called the supreme court, but in both New York and Maryland, the highest state court is called the court of appeals. The decisions of each state's highest court on all questions of state law are final. Only when issues of federal law or constitutional procedure are involved can the United States Supreme Court overrule a decision made by a state's highest court.

THE FEDERAL COURT SYSTEM

The federal court system is basically a three-tiered model consisting of (1) U.S. district courts (trial courts of general jurisdiction) and various courts of limited jurisdiction, (2) U.S. courts of appeals (intermediate courts of appeals), and (3) the United States Supreme Court.

Unlike state court judges, who are usually elected, federal court judges—including the justices of the Supreme Court—are appointed by the president of the United States, subject to the approval of the Senate. All federal judges receive lifetime appointments (because under Article III of the Constitution they "hold their offices during Good Behavior").

U.S. District Courts

On the lowest tier of the federal court system are the U.S. district courts, or federal trial courts. These are the courts in which cases involving federal laws begin, and a judge or jury decides the case (if it is a jury trial). Every state has at least one federal district court, and there is one in the District of Columbia. The number of judicial districts varies over time, primarily owing to population changes and corresponding caseloads. At the present time, there are ninety-four judicial districts. The federal system also includes other trial courts of limited jurisdiction, such as the tax court and the court of international trade.

U.S. Courts of Appeals

In the federal court system, there are thirteen U.S. courts of appeals—also referred to as U.S. circuit courts of appeals. The federal courts of appeals for twelve of the circuits hear appeals from the district courts located within their respective judicial circuits (see Figure 8.3). The Court of Appeals for the Thirteenth Circuit, called the Federal Circuit, has national appellate jurisdiction over certain types of cases, such as cases involving patent law and cases in which the U.S. government is a defendant. The decisions of the circuit courts of appeals are final unless a further appeal is pursued and granted; in that case, the matter is brought before the Supreme Court.

FIGURE 8.3
Geographical Boundaries of the Federal Circuit Courts of Appeals

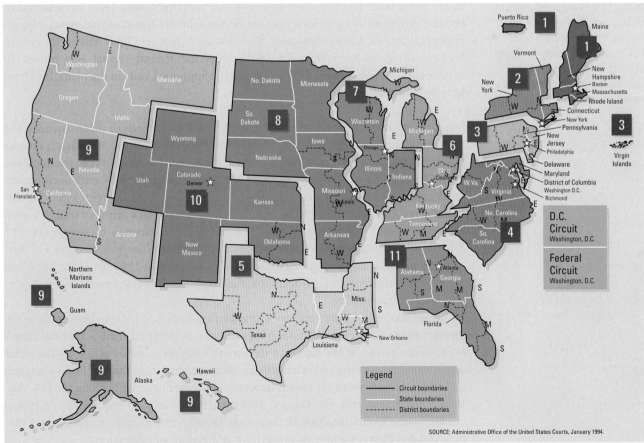

SOURCE: Administrative Office of the United States Courts, January 1994.

Supreme Court Justice Antonin Scalia, pictured here, is a prominent advocate of the legal philosophy of "originalism," which holds that judges should follow the original intent or purpose of the framers of the U.S. Constitution when deciding cases. An opposing viewpoint favors the idea of a "Living Constitution" whose meaning grows and evolves with society. Which perspective do you find more convincing? Explain your answer.

AP Photo/Evan Vucci

The **Supreme Court of the United States** provides an up-to-date record of its decisions and the most important issues that it considers. Visit the Court's Web site by clicking on *Web Links* under *Chapter Resources* at **www.cjinaction.com**.

The United States Supreme Court

Alexander Hamilton, writing in *Federalist Paper* No. 78 (1788), predicted that the United States Supreme Court would be the "least dangerous branch" of the federal government because it had neither the power of the purse nor the power of the sword (that is, it could not raise any revenue, and it lacked an enforcement agency).[13] Unless the other two branches of the government—the president and Congress—would accept its decisions, the Court would be superfluous.

In the Supreme Court's earliest years, it appeared that Hamilton's prediction would come true. The first chief justice of the Supreme Court, John Jay, resigned to become governor of New York because he thought the Court would never play an important role in American society. The next chief justice, Oliver Ellsworth, quit to become an envoy to France. In 1801, when the federal capital was moved to Washington, no one remembered to include the Supreme Court in the plans. It did not have its own meeting space until 1835.[14]

Interpreting and Applying the Law Despite these early bouts of inconsequence, the Supreme Court has come to dominate the country's legal culture. Although it reviews fewer than 0.5 percent of the cases decided in the United States each year, the decisions of the Supreme Court profoundly affect our lives. The impact of Court decisions on the criminal justice system is equally far-reaching: *Gideon v. Wainwright* (1963)[15] established every American's right to be represented by counsel in a criminal trial; *Miranda v. Arizona* (1966)[16] transformed pretrial interrogations; *Furman v. Georgia* (1972)[17] ruled that the death penalty was unconstitutional; and *Gregg v. Georgia* (1976)[18] spelled out the conditions under which it could be allowed. As you have no doubt noticed from references in this textbook, the Court has addressed nearly every important facet of criminal law.

The Supreme Court "makes" criminal justice policy in two important ways: through judicial review and through its authority to interpret the law. *Judicial review* refers to the power of the Court to determine whether a law or action by the other branches of the government is constitutional. For example, in the late 1980s Congress and several state legislatures passed laws criminalizing the act of burning the U.S. flag. In two separate decisions—*Texas v. Johnson* (1989)[19] and *United States v. Eichman* (1990)[20]—the Court invalidated these laws as unconstitutional on the ground that they violated First Amendment protections of freedom of expression.

As the final interpreter of the Constitution, the Court must also determine the meaning of certain statutory provisions when applied to specific situations. Deciding what the framers of the Constitution or a legislative body meant by a certain phrase or provision is never easy, and inevitably, at least to some extent, the personal attributes of the justices come into play during the process. For example, those justices who oppose the death penalty for ideological reasons have tended to interpret the Eighth Amendment prohibition against "cruel and unusual punishment" as sufficient constitutional justification to outlaw the execution of criminals by the state.[21]

Jurisdiction of the Supreme Court The United States Supreme Court consists of nine justices—a chief justice and eight associate justices. The Court has original, or trial, jurisdiction only in rare instances (set forth in Article III, Section 2, of the Constitution). In other words, only rarely does a case originate at the Supreme Court level. Most of the Court's work is as an appellate court. The Supreme Court has appellate authority over cases decided by the U.S. courts of appeals, as well as over some cases decided in the state courts when federal questions are at issue.

Which Cases Reach the Supreme Court? There is no absolute right to appeal to the United States Supreme Court. Although thousands of cases are filed with the Supreme Court each year, on average the Court hears fewer than one hundred. With a **writ of certiorari** (pronounced sur-shee-uh-*rah*-ree), the Supreme Court orders a lower court to send it the record of a case for review. A party can petition the Supreme Court to issue a writ of *certiorari*, but whether the Court will do so is entirely within its discretion.

More than 90 percent of the petitions for writs of *certiorari* (or "certs," as they are popularly called) are denied. A denial is not a decision on the merits of a case, nor does it indicate agreement with the lower court's opinion. Therefore, the denial of the writ has no value as a precedent.[22] The Court will not issue a writ unless at least four justices approve of it. This is called the **rule of four.** Although the justices are not required to give their reasons for refusing to hear a case, most often the discretionary decision is based on whether the legal issue involves a "substantial federal question." Political considerations aside, if the justices do not feel the case addresses an important federal law or constitutional issue, they will vote to deny the writ of *certiorari.*

Supreme Court Decisions Like all appellate courts, the Supreme Court normally does not hear any evidence. The Court's decision in a particular case is based on the written record of the case and the written arguments (briefs) that the attorneys submit. The attorneys also present **oral arguments**—arguments presented in person rather than on paper—to the Court, after which the justices discuss the case in *conference*. The conference is strictly private—only the justices are allowed in the room.

When the Court has reached a decision, the chief justice, if in the majority, assigns the task of writing the Court's opinion to one of the justices. When the chief justice is not in the majority, the most senior justice voting with the majority assigns the writing of the Court's opinion. The opinion outlines the reasons for the Court's decision, the rules of law that apply, and the decision.

Often, one or more justices who agree with the Court's decision may do so for different reasons than those outlined in the majority opinion. These justices may write **concurring opinions** setting forth their own legal reasoning on the issue. Frequently, one or more justices disagree with the Court's conclusion. These justices may write **dissenting opinions** outlining the reasons why they feel the majority erred. Although a dissenting opinion does not affect the outcome of the case before the Court, it may be important later. In a subsequent case concerning the same issue, a justice or attorney may use the legal reasoning in the dissenting opinion as the basis for an argument to reverse the previous decision and establish a new precedent.

Writ of *Certiorari*
A request from a higher court asking a lower court for the record of a case. In essence, the request signals the higher court's willingness to review the case.

Rule of Four
A rule of the United States Supreme Court that the Court will not issue a writ of *certiorari* unless at least four justices approve of the decision to hear the case.

Oral Arguments
The verbal arguments presented in person by attorneys to an appellate court. Each attorney presents reasons why the court should rule in his or her client's favor.

Concurring Opinions
Separate opinions prepared by judges who support the decision of the majority of the court but who want to make or clarify a particular point or to voice disapproval of the grounds on which the decision was made.

Dissenting Opinions
Separate opinions in which judges disagree with the conclusion reached by the majority of the court and expand on their own views about the case.

JUDGES IN THE COURT SYSTEM

Supreme Court justices are the most visible and best-known American jurists, but in many ways they are unrepresentative of the profession as a whole. Few judges enjoy three-room office suites fitted with a fireplace and a private bath, as do the Supreme Court justices. Few judges have four clerks to assist them. Few judges get a yearly vacation that stretches from July to September. Most judges, in fact, work at the lowest level of the system, in criminal trial courts, where they are burdened with overflowing caseloads and must deal daily with the detritus of society.

One thing a Supreme Court justice and a criminal trial judge in any small American city do have in common is the expectation that they will be just. Of all the participants in the criminal justice system, no single person is held to the same high standards as the judge. From her or his lofty perch in the courtroom, the judge is counted on to be "above the fray" of the bickering defense attorneys and prosecutors. When the other courtroom contestants rise at the entrance of the judge, they are placing the burden of justice squarely on the judge's shoulders.

The Roles and Responsibilities of Trial Judges

One of the reasons that judicial integrity is considered so important is the amount of discretionary power a judge has over the court proceedings. As you can see in Figure 8.4, nearly every stage of the trial process includes a decision or action to be taken by the presiding judge.

Before the Trial A great deal of the work done by a judge takes place before the trial even starts, free from public scrutiny. These duties, some of which you have seen from a different point of view in the section on law enforcement agents, include determining the following:

1 Whether there is sufficient probable cause to issue a search or arrest warrant.

FIGURE 8.4
The Role of the Judge in the Criminal Trial Process

In the various stages of a felony case, judges must undertake the actions described here.

1. Pre-Arrest
• Decide whether law enforcement officers have provided sufficient probable cause to justify a search or arrest warrant.

2. Initial Appearance
• Inform the suspect of the charges against him or her and of his or her rights.
• Review the charges to see if probable cause exists that the suspect committed the crime; if not, the judge will dismiss the case.
• Set the amount of bail (or deny bail) and determine any other conditions of pretrial release.

3. Preliminary Hearing
• Based on evidence provided by the prosecution and defense, decide whether there is probable cause that the suspect committed the crime.
• Continue to make sure that the defendant's constitutional rights are not being violated.

4. Arraignment
• Ensure that the defendant has been informed of the charges against him or her.
• Ensure that the defendant understands the plea choices before him or her (to plead guilty, not guilty, or *nolo contendere*).

5. Plea Bargain
• Assist with the plea bargaining process, if both sides are willing to "make a deal."
• If the defendant decides to plead guilty in return for charges being lessened, ensure that the defendant understands the nature of the plea bargain and has not been pressured into pleading guilty by his or her attorney.

6. Pretrial Motions
• Rule on pretrial motions presented by the defense.
• Decide whether to grant continuances (the postponement of the trial to allow more time for gathering evidence).

7. Trial
• Ensure that proper procedure is followed in jury selection.
• "Officiate" at the trial, making sure that both the prosecutor and the defense follow procedural rules in presenting evidence and questioning witnesses.
• Explain points of law that affect the case to the jury.
• Provide jury instructions, or instruction to jurors on the meaning of the laws applicable to the case.
• Receive the jury's final verdict of guilty or not guilty.

8. Sentencing
• If the verdict is "guilty," impose the sentence on the convict.

2 Whether there is sufficient probable cause to authorize electronic surveillance of a suspect.

3 Whether enough evidence exists to justify the temporary incarceration of a suspect.

4 Whether a defendant should be released on bail, and if so, the amount of the bail.

5 Whether to accept pretrial motions by prosecutors and defense attorneys.

6 Whether to accept a plea bargain.

During these pretrial activities, the judge takes on the role of the *negotiator*.[23] As most cases are decided through plea bargains rather than through trial proceedings, the judge often offers his or her services as a negotiator to help the prosecution and the defense "make a deal." The amount at which bail is set is often negotiated as well. Throughout the trial process, the judge usually spends a great of time in his or her *chambers*, or office, negotiating with the prosecutors and defense attorneys.

During the Trial When the trial starts, the judge takes on the role of *referee*. In this role, she or he is responsible for seeing that the trial unfolds according to the dictates of the law and that the participants in the trial do not overstep any legal or ethical bounds. In this role, the judge is expected to be neutral, determining the admissibility of testimony and evidence on a completely objective basis. The judge also acts as a *teacher* during the trial, explaining points of law to the jury. If the trial is not a jury trial, then the judge must also make decisions concerning the guilt or innocence of the defendant. If the defendant is found guilty, the judge must decide on the length of the sentence and the type of sentence. (Different types of sentences, such as incarceration, probation, and other forms of community-based corrections, will be discussed in Chapters 12 through 15.)

The Administrative Role Judges are also *administrators;* that is, they are responsible for the day-to-day functioning of their courts. A primary administrative task of a judge is scheduling. Each courtroom has a **docket,** or calendar of cases, and it is the judge's responsibility to keep the docket current. This entails not only scheduling the trial, but also setting pretrial motion dates and deciding whether to grant attorneys' requests for *continuances,* or additional time to prepare for a case. Judges must also keep track of the immense paperwork generated by each case and manage the various employees of the court. In some instances, judges are even responsible for the budgets of their courtrooms.[24] In 1939, Congress, recognizing the burden of such tasks, created the Administrative Office of the United States Courts to provide administrative assistance for federal court judges.[25] Most state court judges, however, do not have the luxury of similar aid, though they are supported by a court staff.

Selection of Judges

In the federal court system, all judges are appointed by the president and confirmed by the Senate. It is difficult to make a general statement about how judges are selected in state court systems, however, because the procedure varies widely from state to state. In some states, such as Delaware, all judges are appointed by the governor and confirmed by the upper chamber of the state legislature. In other states, such as Arkansas, all judges are elected on a partisan ballot, meaning they must be affiliated with a political party and that affiliation is noted on the ballot. In still other states, such as Kentucky, all judges are elected on a nonpartisan ballot, where no party affiliation is required. Finally, some states, such as Missouri, select judges based on a subjective definition of merit. Figure 8.5 (p. 257) shows the variety in the procedures for selecting judges.

Docket
The list of cases entered on a court's calendar and thus scheduled to be heard by the court.

Richard S. Gebelein
Superior Court Judge

When I began my undergraduate studies, I was very much interested in the sciences. Indeed, I ultimately obtained a B.S. in mathematics, with minors in chemistry and physics. During college, however, I began to think that I would like to work in a career where I was directly involved with people. Thus, I decided that I would attend law school. I obtained my J.D. from Villanova but was really unsure of what type of law I wanted to practice.

I began my legal career as a law clerk in the Delaware Court of Chancery. Observing many good trial lawyers that year, I decided I would like to do trial practice, or litigation as it's called. My first position was as a deputy attorney general in Delaware's Department of Justice. There I prosecuted criminal cases as well as defending the state in civil actions. I left the Justice Department and became Delaware's chief deputy public defender. In that role, I defended serious criminal charges, including murder. After a short time in private law practice I was elected Delaware Attorney General in 1978. After returning to private practice, I was appointed by the governor to my current position as a superior court judge. I was reappointed to a second twelve-year term in 1996.

As a superior court judge, I try both civil and criminal cases as well as hear appeals from administrative boards and agencies. I am currently assigned to do primarily criminal work. The large majority of all criminal cases are resolved by pleas so a large part of my work is taking those pleas, assuring that the defendant knows what he or she is doing, and then sentencing the defendant. In superior court these are usually serious felony charges. In those cases where there is no plea, it is my job to ensure that the defendant receives a fair trial. That means I rule on evidence issues and instruct the jury as to the law to be applied in the case. In some cases the jury will be waived, and then I must decide the facts as well as the law.

Our criminal justice system depends on the lawyers and the judge performing their different functions fairly and effectively. Thus, the responsibilities of each participant are great. Our system only works if each participant actively and aggressively fulfills the duties of his or her office.

The seriousness and reality of those duties came home to me several years ago when I was assigned to try the case of Delaware's first serial killer. The case was an extremely high profile case that resulted in almost daily headlines. It was not an

easy case in that there were many difficult evidence issues. These included the attempt to use DNA identification for the first time in Delaware as well as an evidence suppression issue involving the key evidence that broke the case. Luckily, both the prosecutors and the defense lawyers were

Richard S. Gebelein

excellent and did their jobs professionally. After a long trial and lengthy jury deliberations, the defendant was convicted of two counts of first degree murder. The jury could not reach a verdict on the third count of murder. A penalty trial was held, and the jury could not reach a unanimous recommendation of death, thereby causing a life sentence to be imposed by law.

But this was not the end of the case, as evidence was developed during the trial to link the defendant directly to a fourth murder. He was reindicted for that murder as well as the undecided murder from the first trial. The defendant waived a jury trial for this second case, and I had to try the case as to both facts and law. After conviction, I then had to hear the penalty phase. Nothing in my training prepared me to make the solitary decision that his crimes demanded the death penalty. Nothing really can prepare you to announce in front of the defendant's family, mother, wife, and child that he is to die by lethal injection.

This one hard decision, this one hard act makes it crystal clear why it is absolutely essential that good, bright, and ethical people participate as lawyers and judges in our criminal justice system. It is critical that every defendant be assured a fair trial, and that means a good, energetic effective defense lawyer; an ethical, effective prosecutor; and a fair judge. These are not easy jobs, but if they are done right, you can feel satisfaction that you are doing your part to ensure justice in America.

Go to the Careers in Criminal Justice Interactive CD for more profiles in the field of criminal justice.

The two key concepts in discussing methods of selecting judges are *independence* and *accountability*.[26] Those who feel that judicial fairness is dependent on the judges' belief that they will not be removed from office as the result of an unpopular ruling support methods of selection that include appointment.[27] In contrast, some observers feel that judges are "politicians in robes" who make policy decisions every time they step to the bench. Following this line of thought, judges should be held accountable to

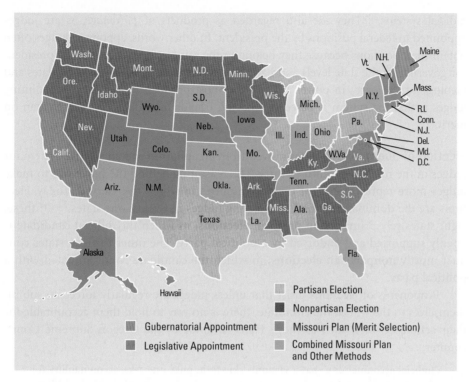

FIGURE 8.5
Methods of Judicial Selection in the Fifty States

Most states use a variety of methods to select their judges, with different procedures in different jurisdictions. The information presented here, therefore, identifies the predominant method in each state.

Source: American Judicature Society.

those who are affected by their decisions and therefore should be chosen through elections, as legislators are.[28] The most independent, and therefore least accountable, judges are those who hold lifetime appointments. They are influenced neither by the temptation to make popular decisions to impress voters nor by the need to follow the ideological or party line of the political bosses who provided them with their posts.

Appointment of Judges   Article II, Section 2, of the Constitution authorizes the president to appoint the justices of the Supreme Court with the advice and consent of the Senate. Subsequent laws enacted by Congress provide that the same procedure is used for appointing judges to the lower federal courts as well.

On paper, the appointment process is relatively simple. After selecting a nominee, the president submits the name to the Senate for approval. The Senate Judiciary Committee then holds hearings and makes its recommendation to the Senate, where a majority vote is needed to confirm the nomination. In practice, the process does not always proceed smoothly. If the members of the minority party in the Senate consider the political views of a nominee too "extreme," they can block a vote on that nominee by instituting a *filibuster*—a procedural device in which senators refuse to give up the floor during debate. The filibuster has become a more common method of blocking judicial nominees in recent years. Whereas the Senate confirmed 92 percent of the federal circuit court nominees of President Jimmy Carter (1977–1981), President Bill Clinton (1991–1999) had only a 70 percent success rate, and, as of President George W. Bush's fifth year in office, only 69 percent of his nominees were confirmed.[29] Republican anger over the Democrats' use of the filibuster to prevent a final vote on ten of President Bush's most important (and controversial) judicial nominees almost led to the abolition of the filibuster in the spring of 2005 before the two parties reached a compromise.

Three states, as well as Puerto Rico, employ similar selection methods, with the governor offering nominees for the approval of the state legislature. Judges in these states, as would be expected, serve longer terms than their counterparts in nonappointment judicial systems.[30] They are also regarded as products of *patronage,* as are judges appointed to federal positions by the president. In other words, appointed judges often obtain their positions because they belong to the same political party as the president (or governor, at the state level) and have been active in supporting the candidates and ideology of the party in power. One of the most prevalent criticisms of appointing judges is that the system is based on "having friends in high places" rather than on merit.[31]

Election of Judges Most states moved from an appointive to an elective system for judges in the mid–nineteenth century. The reasoning behind the move was to make judges more representative of the communities in which they served. Today, elections are the dominant method of selecting judges in twenty-one states.[32] Of these, eight states rely primarily on **partisan elections,** in which the judicial candidate is openly supported and endorsed by a political party. The other thirteen states conduct mostly **nonpartisan elections,** in which the candidate is not affiliated with a political party.

Proponents of elections insist that unless judges are regularly forced to submit themselves to the will of the electorate, there is no way to hold them accountable for their actions. Critics, such as Judge Hans A. Linde of the Oregon Supreme Court, counter:

> "Judicial accountability" has a virtuous ring to it, until one asks, accountability for what? For judging fairly and impartially, for conscientious attention to law and facts, for staying awake, sober, and courteous to the parties, witnesses, and court personnel—in short, for performing according to the classic model of judging? Or does it mean accountability for decisions in controversial cases?[33]

The answer to Judge Linde's rhetorical question, at least in his mind, is that the public will hold a judge accountable for making popular rulings, not "correct" ones. In recent years, many elected judges have felt pressure to hand out harsher sentences to convicted criminals in order to appear "tough on crime." (See the feature *CJ in Focus—A Question of Ethics: Judging Judicial Elections.*)

Merit Selection In 1940, Missouri became the first state to combine appointment and election in a single merit selection. When all jurisdiction levels are counted, twenty-four states and the District of Columbia now utilize the **Missouri Plan,** as merit selection has been labeled. The Missouri Plan consists of three basic steps:

- When a vacancy on the bench arises, candidates are nominated by a nonpartisan committee of citizens.
- The names of the three most qualified candidates are sent to the governor or executive of the state judicial system, and that person chooses who will be the judge.
- A year after the new judge has been installed, a "retention election" is held so that voters can decide whether the judge deserves to keep the post.[34]

The goal of the Missouri Plan is to eliminate partisan politics from the selection procedure, while at the same time giving the citizens a voice in the process. One noted drawback of the merit system—and indeed of any elective method of selecting judges—is that voters may lack knowledge not only of the issues of a judicial election, but of who the candidates are in the first place. A poll in Michigan found that nine out of ten voters could not identify any sitting state supreme court justice, and an equal number did not know how many justices served on the state's highest court or the length of their term in office.[35] (For a review of the different selection processes, see *Mastering Concepts—The Selection of State and Federal Judges* on page 261.)

Judging Judicial Elections

Challenger George Weaver wanted incumbent Leah Sears's seat, and he was not going to let a little thing like the truth stand in his way. His campaign released a brochure and television commercial claiming that Sears would legalize same-sex marriages, referred to traditional moral values as "pathetic and disgraceful," and called the electric chair "silly." None of these contentions happened to be true, but nobody should have been surprised. These are politicians, and they stretch the truth all the time, right?

Wrong. George Weaver was not a candidate for political office. He was seeking Leah Sears's seat on the Supreme Court of Georgia. When the state judicial ethics board ordered Weaver to stop distributing the misleading materials, he sued, and a federal court upheld his First Amendment right to make false and misleading statements, just like a politician.

A THREAT TO IMPARTIALITY

Until recently, judicial elections were relatively silent affairs, as many judges thought it unseemly to engage in traditional electioneering. This is no longer the case. Set free by a 2002 United States Supreme Court ruling that a state law could not keep judicial candidates from "announcing their views on disputed legal and political issues," judges are acting and spending more like their political counterparts. In 2004, two candidates for a seat on the Illinois Supreme Court raised $10 million—topping the fund-raising tally of nineteen of the thirty U.S. Senate races that year. Overall, more than $45 million was spent on state supreme court campaigns in 2004, and twice as many television attack ads were broadcast as in 2002.

Many observers feel that this trend is disastrous for the American judicial system. They point out that judges are not "representatives of the people" in the same sense as politicians. Instead, judges are representatives of the law and must often make unpopular legal decisions if legal precedent so dictates. This independence is threatened when judges feel pressured to put forth rulings for political, rather than legal, reasons. In one case study of the Louisiana Supreme Court, a justice admitted that he often voted in favor of executing defendants to counter potential criticism that he was "soft on crime." Another study found that Pennsylvania trial judges handed out harsher sentences as the calendar moved closer to reelection time. Critics of judicial electioneering also point out that judges may feel obligated to "repay" campaign contributors with favorable rulings. For example, Texans for Public Justice discovered that, over a four-year period, the Texas Supreme Court was four times more likely to accept petitions filed by lawyers, parties, or law firms that had contributed to one of the justices' recent campaigns than those filed by an entity that had not made such contributions.

FOR CRITICAL ANALYSIS

The solution to these problems, whether real or perceived, would be to do away with the election of judges. What is your position on the election of local and state judges? Should citizens have the right to vote for judicial positions? Should a judge reflect the will of the people or the will of the law?

© Jeff Danziger

Diversity on the Bench

Another criticism of the Missouri Plan is that the members of the selection committees, who are mostly white, upper-class attorneys, nominate mostly white, upper-class attorneys.[36] Similar criticisms, however, have been leveled at the federal judiciary and at judges in states that do not use the Missouri Plan. Indeed, of the nearly 900 federal judges, only about 10 percent are African American, 7 percent are Hispanic, and 1 percent are Asian American.[37] Of the 108 justices who have served on the United States Supreme Court, only two have been African American: Thurgood Marshall (1970–1991) and Clarence Thomas (1991–present). State judiciaries show similar patterns. The discrepancy is particularly striking in areas with diverse populations. In California, where minority groups make up a majority of the population (54 percent), only 17 percent of state court judges are African American, Hispanic, or Asian American.[38] Women are also underrepresented on the bench. Only about one in five federal judges is a woman.[39] Only two women have been appointed to the Supreme Court: Sandra Day O'Connor (1981–2005) and Ruth Bader Ginsburg (1993–present).

The Impact of Past Discrimination

Edward Chen, a federal magistrate judge for the Northern District of California, identifies a number of reasons for the low minority representation on the bench. Past discrimination in law schools has limited the pool of experienced minority attorneys who have the political ties, access to "old boy" networks, and career opportunities that lead to judgeships.[40] Only recently, as increased numbers of minorities have graduated from law schools, have rates of minority judges begun to creep slowly upward.

The Benefits of Diversity Traditionally, efforts to diversify American judges by race, ethnicity, and gender have been met with resistance from those who argue that because judges must be impartial, it makes no difference whether a judge is black, Asian, Hispanic, or white.[41]

Sherrilyn A. Ifill of the University of Maryland School of Law rejects this argument. She believes that "diversity on the bench" can only enrich our judiciary by introducing a variety of voices and perspectives into what are perhaps the most powerful positions in the criminal justice system. By the same token, Ifill credits the lack of diversity in many trial and appeals courts with a number of harmful consequences, such as more severe sentences for minority youths than for white youths who have committed similar crimes, disproportionate denial of bail to minority defendants, and the disproportionate imposition of the death penalty on minority defendants accused of killing white victims.[42]

Ronnie L. White became the first African American to hold the post of chief justice of the Missouri Supreme Court in 2003. "I truly believe that within the judicial department, we need to work a little bit harder to try and place people of color within our organization," said Judge White on taking his post. What are some of the benefits of diversity on the bench?

Judicial Conduct

The question of judicial accountability is further complicated by the gulf between what the public expects of judges and what the law expects of judges. The public wants judges to administer justice, while the law demands that they make sure proper legal procedures and rules have been followed. Sometimes, proper judicial conduct leads to what we would call injustice—setting a guilty person free. For example, a judge may know that a conviction is justified but overturn it anyway because tainted evidence contributed to the jury's finding. Consequently, for judges, proper behavior does not necessarily lead to justice, a concept many citizens have a difficult time accepting.

Judicial Ethics During the nineteenth century, the American public showed little enthusiasm for formal regulation of judicial conduct—as long as judges were competent, their ethics and honesty were of secondary concern.[43] It was not until the 1920s, when the entire criminal justice system was being reformed, that the American Bar Association (ABA) created the first code to regulate judicial behavior. The ABA's Canons of Judicial Ethics was updated in 1972 and 1990, and today the Model Code of Judicial Conduct forms the basis for judicial conduct codes in forty-seven states and the District of Columbia.[44]

MASTERING CONCEPTS

The Selection of State and Federal Judges

Federal Judges

The president nominates a candidate to the U.S. Senate.

⬇

The Senate Judiciary Committee holds hearings concerning the qualifications of the candidate and makes its recommendation to the full Senate.

⬇

The full Senate votes to confirm or reject the president's nomination.

State Judges

Partisan Elections
Judicial candidates, supported by and affiliated with political parties, place their names before the voters for consideration for a particular judicial seat.

⬇

The electorate votes to decide who will retain or gain the seat.

Executive Appointment
The governor nominates a candidate to the state legislature.

⬇

The legislature votes to confirm or reject the governor's nomination.

Nonpartisan Elections
Judicial candidates, not supported by or affiliated with political parties, place their names before the voters for consideration for a particular judicial seat.

⬇

The electorate votes to decide who will retain or gain the seat.

Missouri Plan
A nominating commission provides a list of worthy candidates.

⬇

An elected official (usually the governor) chooses from the list submitted by the commission.

⬇

A year later, a "retention election" is held to allow voters to decide whether the judge will stay on the bench.

The essence of the Code of Judicial Conduct is to prevent conduct that would "tend to reduce public confidence in the integrity and impartiality of the judiciary."[45] Consequently, the judicial ethics codes disfavor not only obviously illegal and corrupt activities such as bribery but also personal conduct that is lawful yet gives the appearance of impropriety. Rhode Island, for example, saw two successive state supreme court chief justices resign because of **judicial misconduct.** The first, Chief Justice Thomas Fay, stepped down because of allegations that he used his position to help a relative and friends, and the second, Chief Justice Joseph Bevilacqua, was under investigation for associating with organized crime figures.

The Removal of Judges The ABA's Code of Judicial Conduct is not a binding document; it merely offers a model of judicial ethics. As the states adopted aspects of the code, however, they also developed procedures for removing those guilty of judicial misconduct from office. Nearly every state has a *judicial conduct commission,* which consists of lawyers, judges, and other prominent citizens and is often a branch of the state's highest court. This commission investigates charges of judicial misconduct and may recommend removal if warranted by the circumstances. The final decision to discipline a judge must generally be made by the state supreme court.[46]

On average, about ten state judges are removed from office each year. Recent examples include St. Joseph County (Michigan) Circuit Judge James Noecker, who lost his seat after driving his car into the side of a convenience store while intoxicated, fleeing the scene, and lying to investigators about the accident. Such transgressions, however deplorable, would be unlikely to result in a similar outcome if committed by a federal

Judicial Misconduct
A general term describing behavior that diminishes public confidence in the judiciary. This behavior includes obviously illegal acts, such as bribery, and conduct that gives the appearance of impropriety, such as consorting with known felons.

Impeached

As authorized by Article I of the Constitution, the House of Representatives votes on impeachment; if the vote passes, the matter is sent to the Senate for a vote to remove the president, vice president, or civil officers (such as federal judges) of the United States.

Courtroom Work Group

The social organization consisting of the judge, prosecutor, defense attorney, and other court workers. The relationships among these persons have a far-reaching impact on the day-to-day operations of any court.

judge. Appointed under Article II of the U.S. Constitution, federal judges can be removed from office only if found guilty of "Treason, Bribery, or other high Crimes and Misdemeanors." Before a federal judge can be **impeached,** the U.S. House of Representatives must be presented with specific charges of misconduct and vote on whether these charges merit further action. If the vote passes in the House by a simple majority (50 percent), the U.S. Senate—presided over by the chief justice of the United States Supreme Court—holds a trial on the matter. At the conclusion of this trial, a two-thirds majority vote is required in the Senate for the removal of a federal judge.

This disciplinary action is extremely rare; only eleven federal judges have been impeached and convicted in the nation's history. Most recently, in 1989, federal judges Alcee Hastings and Walter Nixon were both removed from office—Hastings for accepting a $150,000 bribe and lying to a grand jury and Nixon for lying to a grand jury. In 1993, Judge Robert Collins resigned before he could be impeached for receiving a $100,000 bribe from a marijuana smuggler.

THE COURTROOM WORK GROUP

Television dramas often depict the courtroom as a battlefield, with prosecutors and defense attorneys spitting fire at each other over the loud and insistent protestations of a frustrated judge. Consequently, many people are somewhat disappointed when they witness a real courtroom at work. Rarely does anyone raise his or her voice, and the courtroom professionals appear—to a great extent—to be cooperating with each other. In Chapter 6, we discussed the existence of a police subculture, based on the shared values of law enforcement agents. A courtroom subculture exists as well, centered on the **courtroom work group.** The most important feature of any work group is that it is a *cooperative* unit, whose members establish shared values and methods that help the group efficiently reach its goals. Though cooperation is not a concept usually associated with criminal courts, it is in fact crucial to the adjudication process.[47]

Members of the Courtroom Work Group

The courtroom work group is made up of those individuals who are involved with the defendant from the time she or he is arrested until sentencing. The most prominent members are the judge, the prosecutor, and the defense attorney (the latter two will be discussed in detail in the next chapter). Three other court participants complete the work group:

1 The *bailiff of the court* is responsible for maintaining security and order in the judge's chambers and the courtroom. Bailiffs lead the defendant in and out of the courtroom and attend to the needs of the jurors during the trial. A bailiff, often a member of the local sheriff's department but sometimes an employee of the court, also delivers summonses in some jurisdictions.

2 The *clerk of the court* has an exhausting list of responsibilities. Any plea, motion, or other matter to be acted on by the judge must go through the clerk. The large amount of paperwork generated during a trial, including transcripts, photographs, evidence, and any other records, is maintained by the clerk. The clerk also issues subpoenas for jury duty and coordinates the jury selection process. In the federal court system, judges select clerks, while state clerks are either appointed or, in nearly a third of the states, elected.

3 *Court reporters* record every word that is said during the course of the trial. They also record any *depositions,* or pretrial question-and-answer sessions in which a party or a witness answers an attorney's questions under oath.

Formation of the Courtroom Work Group

The premise of the work group is based on constant interaction that fosters relationships among the members. As legal scholar David W. Neubauer describes:

> Every day, the same group of courthouse regulars assembles in the same courtroom, sits or stands in the same places, and performs the same tasks as the day before. The types of defendants and the nature of the crimes they are accused of committing also remain constant. Only the names of the victim, witnesses, and defendants are different.[48]

After a period of time, the members of a courtroom work group learn how the others operate. The work group establishes patterns of behavior and norms, and cooperation allows the adjudication process to function informally and smoothly.[49] In some cases, the members of the work group may even form personal relationships, which only strengthen the courtroom culture.

One way in which the courtroom work group differs from a traditional work group at a company such as Microsoft Corporation is that each member answers to a different sponsoring organization. Although the judge has ultimate authority over a courtroom, he or she is not the "boss" of the attorneys. The prosecutor is hired by the district attorney's office; the defense attorney by a private individual or the public defender's office; the judge by the court system itself.

Each member of the work group is under pressure from his or her sponsoring organization to carry out certain tasks.[50] A judge, for example, needs to take care of the cases on her or his docket, or else a backlog will accumulate. A defense attorney—under constant pressure to attain the best results—usually has many clients and often cannot spend too much time on a single case. A prosecutor must win convictions. Within the courtroom work group, each member relies on the others to help alleviate these pressures. If a defense attorney disrupts the trial routine with unnecessary motions or unreasonably rejects sentence bargains for his or her client, all members of the work group become less efficient in performing their roles. (See Figure 8.6 on the following page for an overview of the relationships among the main participants in the courtroom work group.)

The Judge in the Courtroom Work Group

The judge is the dominant figure in the courtroom and therefore exerts the most influence over the values and norms of the work group. A judge who runs a "tight ship" follows procedure and restricts the freedom of attorneys to deviate from regulations, while a *"laissez-faire"* judge allows more leeway to members of the work group. A judge's personal philosophy also affects the court proceedings. If a judge has a reputation for being "tough on crime," both prosecutors and defense attorneys will alter their strategies accordingly. In fact, a lawyer may be able to manipulate the system to "shop" for a judge whose philosophy best fits the attorney's goals in a particular case.[51] If a lawyer is caught trying to influence the assignment of judges, she or he is said to be "corrupting judicial independence" and may face legal proceedings.

Although preeminent in the work group, a judge must still rely on other members of the group. To a certain extent, the judge is the least informed member of the trio; like a juror, the judge learns the facts of the case as they are presented by the attorneys. If the attorneys do not properly present the facts, then the judge is hampered in making rulings. Furthermore, if a judge deviates from the norms of the work group—by,

> "A judge is not supposed to know anything about the facts . . . until they have been presented in evidence and explained to him at least three times."
>
> —Lord Chief Justice Parker, British judge (1961)

JUDGE

Official Responsibility: To make sure that proper legal procedure is followed before, during, and after a trial

Job Pressures: Large caseloads, little time; the administrative burden of managing case dockets

• Be prepared

• Negotiate pleas when justified

• Refrain from engaging in time-consuming arguments with prosecutor

• Refrain from filing time-consuming motions

• Grant continuances when extra time is needed to get client to pay fees

• Grant continuances when extra time is needed to prepare case

• Be prepared

• Negotiate pleas when justified

• Refrain from engaging in time-consuming arguments with defense attorney

Persuade clients to accept "reasonable" plea bargains

Negotiate a sentence that is favorable to client

DEFENSE ATTORNEY

Official Responsibility: To advocate for the client's innocence

Job Pressures: Earning a living by having a large number of clients; get best outcome for client with limited resources

PROSECUTOR

Official Responsibility: To convict those guilty of crimes against society

Job Pressures: More cases than time to dispose of all of them; satisfy public expectations that criminals will be punished

• Provide access to witnesses, police reports, and other information that is unavailable due to limited resources

• Be accommodating when extra time is needed to prepare case

FIGURE 8.6

The Courtroom Work Group and Incentives to Cooperate

The major figures of the courtroom work group—judges, prosecutors, and defense attorneys—benefit from a certain degree of cooperation. As you can see, one of the primary considerations of each of the three principals is to dispose of cases as quickly as possible.

for example, refusing to grant continuances—the other members of the work group can "discipline" the judge. Defense attorneys and prosecutors can request further continuances, fail to produce witnesses in a timely matter, and slow down the proceeding through a general lack of preparedness. The delays caused by such acts can ruin a judge's calendar—especially in large courts—and bring pressure from the judge's superiors.

Assembly-Line Justice

In discussing the goals of the courtroom work group, several general concepts figure prominently—efficiency, cooperation, rapidity, and socialization. One aim of the work group, however, is glaring in its absence: justice. One of the main criticisms of the American court system is that it has sacrificed the goal of justice for efficiency. Some observers claim that only the wealthiest can afford to receive justice as promised by the Constitution, while the rest of society is left with a watered-down version of *assembly-line justice.*

The Impact of Excessive Caseloads Given the caseloads that most courts face, some degree of assembly-line justice seems inevitable. A quick survey of the nation's court system provides clear examples of the extent of the problem and its consequences. Approximately two out of every three states are consistently behind on their dockets. In Tennessee, each criminal court judge handles between 2,300 and 4,800 cases a year.[52] Murder cases in Boston, Massachusetts, commonly take between fifteen and twenty-four months to reach trial, thanks to overcrowded courts.[53] In Tacoma, Washington, a felony conviction that would have sent one Bruce Eric Smith to prison for life was overturned because prosecutors took too long to start his trial. The prob-

In recent years, many jurisdictions have created specialty courts such as the Juvenile and Family Court of Orange County, California, the entrance of which is shown here. How do such specialty courts relieve the caseload burden of overloaded criminal courts?

lem: no available courtrooms. As a result of the delay, Smith was set free, only to be rearrested when, in an attempt to flee police after an alleged rape, he rammed his vehicle into another car, killing the driver.[54]

The federal court system faces many of the same problems. Caseloads in federal criminal courts increased by almost 50 percent between 1994 and 2003, spurred by an almost 70 percent increase in drug cases.[55] The lack of resources to deal with excessive caseloads is generally recognized as one of the most critical issues facing both federal and state law enforcement agencies and courtrooms.[56]

The Courtroom Work Group and Overloaded Courts A judge's worth is increasingly measured by her or his ability to keep the "assembly line" of cases moving, rather than by the quality of her or his judicial work. Consequently, the judicial process is accused of being "careless and haphazard" and of routinely supporting decisions made on the basis of incomplete information. Though definitive statistics on the subject have never been adequately gathered, many observers feel that assembly-line justice affects the actions of others in the criminal justice system as well:

- Beyond filling out a crime report, police officers often do not investigate misdemeanors and less serious felonies unless the offender was caught in the act.
- Police officers often are encouraged to obtain confessions—using whatever means necessary—from defendants, rather than find incriminating evidence, because a confession is more likely to lead to conviction.
- Prosecutors often press charges for misdemeanors and nonviolent felonies only when the case is a "slam dunk"—that is, when conviction is certain.
- To wrap up cases quickly, prosecutors generally bargain reduced sentences for guilty verdicts; as a result, criminals spend less time in prison than is in society's best interests.[57]

If the public is under the impression that police, judges, and lawyers are more interested in speed than in justice, the pressure of caseloads may also lead to loss of respect for the criminal justice system as a whole.

The Long Arm of the Law

Our criminal justice system was not designed for exportation. Historically, American criminal law has been based on the premise that where a crime took place was the most important factor in determining a court's jurisdiction over that crime. (Remember, *jurisdiction* refers to the power of a court to hear and decide a case.) Today, limiting the law by such territorial concerns is as outdated as it is impractical. How could such notions of jurisdiction apply to, say, the case of Ludwig Feinberg, an American citizen living in Russia who arranged to sell a diesel submarine to drug runners so that they could deliver illegal narcotics from Panama to the West Coast of the United States? Or to a terrorist who plans to launch an attack on the United States without ever setting foot on American soil? In this *Criminal Justice in Action* feature, we will explore how the concept of jurisdiction has evolved to help the United States and other countries deal with the globalization of crime.

Criminal "Education"

When John W. Seljan was arrested at Los Angeles International Airport in 2003, the eighty-six-year-old American citizen had been taking three trips a year to Southeast Asia for twenty years. His primary goal on these excursions, as he had told federal investigators, was to "educate" small children about their sexuality. A letter to a nine-year-old girl living in the Philippines that was found on Seljan at the time of his arrest stated, "Honey, I miss our love-making and that's what life is all about."[58]

For years, law enforcement agents have been aware that Americans travel to developing countries, mostly in Latin America and Southeast Asia, for the express purpose of engaging in sex with minors. Although these countries usually have stringent laws against such activity, travelers run little risk of arrest and prosecution by the local authorities. One major obstacle is corruption among law enforcement officers, who often profit by participating in or protecting the lucrative child sex trade. Furthermore, few of these countries have the personnel or expertise to aggressively attack the problem.[59] Aarti Kapoor, who works with a Cambodian group that assists young prosti-

A warning to tourists who travel to countries in Latin America and Southeast Asia for the purpose of engaging in sex with underage prostitutes.

tutes and sexual abuse victims, says that "U.S. law enforcement represents the only hope of finding justice" in her country.[60]

A Necessary and Proper Law

Under what authority can U.S. law enforcement apprehend American citizens who commit their crimes on foreign soil? By tradition and law, most crime is prosecuted on the national level, not the international level. Even when U.S. personnel work in concert with their counterparts in Cambodia, the Philippines, Thailand, Sri Lanka, Mexico, and elsewhere to stop sex crimes against children, how can American courts assert jurisdiction over the targets of these investigations?

The answer to this question lies in the U.S. Constitution, which gives Congress the power to "make all laws that are necessary and proper." U.S. courts have interpreted this to mean that Congress can expand the jurisdiction of American courts when it is in the nation's best interests to do so. Reacting to domestic and international outcry over the fate of young victims of America's sexual tourists, Congress decided to pass legislation to deal with the problem. In 2004, John W. Seljan became the first person found guilty under the PROTECT Act (Prosecuting Remedies and Tools Against the Exploitation of Children Today Act of 2003).[61] This law makes it a crime for any U.S. citizen to travel abroad and have sex with a minor. It also explicitly allows American courts to exercise jurisdiction when the prohibited behavior—the sex act itself—occurs in a foreign country.[62]

Matters of Jurisdiction

The extraterritorial jurisdictional aspects of the PROTECT Act hardly break new ground. Although territory remains the foundation for criminal jurisdiction, international law has provided courts in the United States and other countries with several other bases for expanding their reach, including:

- *Objective territorial principle of jurisdiction.* Acts committed outside a jurisdiction but intended to produce detrimental effects within that jurisdiction are treated as if they were committed within national boundaries.[63]
- *Nationality principle of jurisdiction.* A nation can subject its citizens to its laws for conduct that occurs on foreign soil.[64]
- *Protective principle of jurisdiction.* A nation has jurisdiction over crimes that occur outside its boundaries but threaten its "security, territorial integrity, or political independence."[65]
- *Passive personality theory.* A court has jurisdiction over a crime if the victim is a citizen of its territory, regardless of where the crime is committed or the nationality of the offender.[66]
- *Universal jurisdiction.* International law considers some crimes so heinous that any country may have jurisdiction if one of its citizens is the target or perpetrator of such a crime, or if she or he has committed the crime and is afterward found within that country's borders. In general, the U.S. government believes that war crimes, crimes against humanity (such as genocide), torture, and hijacking/piracy fall under universal jurisdiction.[67]

The PROTECT Act, along with similar laws passed by the legislatures of twenty-three other countries, is firmly supported by the nationality principle. Even though Seljan and the other four Americans prosecuted under the law as of 2006 did not commit a criminal act in the United States, they fall under the jurisdiction of U.S. courts because of their status as American citizens and the fact that their behavior would have been criminal had it occurred within U.S. borders.

Fighting Drugs and Terrorism

The current trend, both legislatively and judicially, has been to extend federal criminal jurisdiction. This expansion is seen as necessary to aid U.S. law enforcement against the two main international crimes of our times: the illegal drug trade and terrorism. In the early 1990s, for example, the U.S. government became convinced that a Mexican doctor named Humberto Alvarez-Machain had participated in the torture-murder of an undercover Drug

Enforcement Administration (DEA) officer in Mexico. The DEA, in cooperation with Mexican law enforcement, arranged for Alvarez-Machain to be kidnapped and brought to the United States to stand trial. In a highly controversial ruling, the United States Supreme Court held that American courts had jurisdiction over Alvarez-Machain even though he had been forcibly abducted and transported across the border against his will.[68]

The objective territorial principle (and perhaps the protective principle as well) clearly gives the United States and other nations jurisdiction over terrorist acts that are planned and initiated outside a country but are designed to have impact inside that country. Evidence shows that preparations for the terrorist attacks on New York City and Washington, D.C., on September 11, 2001, took place in Germany, Malaysia, Afghanistan, Pakistan, and the United Arab Emirates. Post–September 11 legislation specifically states that U.S. extraterritorial jurisdiction extends to any person who engages in international terrorism ("activities that involve violent acts or acts dangerous to human life that are a violation of the criminal laws of the United States or of any State") or uses or conspires to use weapons of mass destruction against the United States or U.S. citizens abroad.[69] Thus, federal courts have jurisdiction over all people who took part in those planning sessions for September 11, even if they never set foot in the United States.

Making Sense of International Jurisdiction

1. Some critics think that incidents such as the Alvarez-Machain kidnapping and legislation such as the PROTECT Act indicate that the United States is expanding its criminal jurisdiction beyond its national borders too aggressively. What limitations, if any, do you think should be placed on the U.S. government's ability to prosecute its citizens or citizens of other countries for acts committed outside the United States? Why?

2. The U.S. Coast Guard stops a boat filled with marijuana in international waters off the coast of California. The boat is not registered in the United States, and the captain is a citizen of Portugal. What facts would have to be proved to give a U.S. court jurisdiction over this case?

3. In the late 1990s, American citizen John Walker Lindh converted to Islam and traveled to the Middle East to engage in terrorist training alongside Taliban and al Qaeda operatives. In 2002, Lindh was captured in Afghanistan by U.S. troops and returned to his native land where he faced charges for aiding terrorist organizations and conspiring to kill Americans abroad. Under what theory discussed in this feature does a U.S. court have jurisdiction over Lindh, and why?

Chapter Summary

1 **Define and contrast the four functions of the courts.** The four functions are (a) due process, (b) crime control, (c) rehabilitation, and (d) bureaucratic. The most obvious contrast is between the due process and crime control functions. The former is mainly concerned with the procedural rules that allow each accused individual to have a "fair chance" against the government in a criminal proceeding. For crime control, the courts are supposed to impose enough "pain" on convicted criminals to deter criminal behavior. For the rehabilitation function, the courts serve as "doctors" who dispense "treatment." In their bureaucratic function, courts are more concerned with speed and efficiency.

2 **Define *jurisdiction* and contrast geographical and subject–matter jurisdiction.** Jurisdiction relates to the power of a court to hear a particular case. Courts are typically limited in geographical jurisdiction; for example, to a particular state. Some courts are restricted in subject matter, such as a small-claims court, which can hear only cases involving civil matters under a certain amount.

3 **Explain the difference between trial and appellate courts.** Trial courts are courts of the first instance, where a case is first heard. Appellate courts review the proceedings of a lower court. Appellate courts do not have juries.

4 **Outline the several levels of a typical state court system.** (a) At the lowest level are courts of limited jurisdiction, (b) next are trial courts of general jurisdiction, (c) then appellate courts, and (d) finally, the state's highest court.

5 **Outline the federal court system.** (a) At the lowest level are the U.S. district courts in which trials are held, as well as various minor federal courts of limited jurisdiction; (b) next are the U.S. courts of appeals, otherwise known as circuit courts of appeal; and (c) finally, the United States Supreme Court.

6 **Explain briefly how a case is brought to the Supreme Court.** Cases decided in U.S. courts of appeals, as well as cases decided in the highest state courts (when federal questions arise), can be appealed to the Supreme Court. If at least four justices approve of a case filed with the Supreme Court, the Court will issue a writ of *certiorari*, ordering the lower court to send the Supreme Court the record of the case for review.

7 **List the actions that a judge might take prior to an actual trial.** Trial judges may do the following before an actual trial: (a) issue search or arrest warrants, (b) authorize electronic surveillance of a suspect, (c) order the temporary incarceration of a suspect, (d) decide whether a suspect should be released on bail and the amount of that bail, (e) accept or reject pretrial motions by prosecutors and defense attorneys, and (f) accept or reject a plea bargain.

8 **Explain the difference between the selection of judges at the state level and at the federal level.** The president nominates all judges at the federal level, and the Senate must approve the nominations. A similar procedure is used in some states. In other states, all judges are elected on a partisan ballot or on a nonpartisan ballot. Some states use merit selection, or the Missouri Plan, in which a citizen committee nominates judicial candidates, the governor or executive of the state judicial system chooses among the top three nominees, and a year later a "retention election" is held.

9 **List and describe the members of the courtroom work group.** (a) The judge; (b) the prosecutor, who brings charges in the name of the people (the state) against the accused; (c) the defense attorney; (d) the bailiff, who is responsible for maintaining security and order in the judge's chambers and the courtroom; (e) the clerk, who accepts all pleas, motions, and other matters to be acted on by the judge; and (f) court reporters, who record what is said during a trial as well as at depositions.

10 **Explain the consequences of excessive caseloads.** Excessive caseloads have led to assembly-line justice. Such a criminal justice system increases the possibility that (a) police officers will not investigate crimes unless the offender was caught in the act; (b) officers will seek only confessions, rather than spending time finding incriminating evidence; (c) prosecutors will press charges in criminal cases only when conviction is certain; and (d) plea bargaining will be common.

> **STORIES FROM THE STREET**
> Go to the *Stories from the Street* feature at **www.cjinaction.com** to hear Larry Gaines tell insightful stories related to this chapter and his experiences in the field.

Key Terms

appellate courts 247
concurring opinions 253
courtroom work group 262
dissenting opinions 253
docket 255
dual court system 248
impeached 262
judicial misconduct 261
jurisdiction 245
magistrate 249
Missouri Plan 258
nonpartisan elections 258
opinions 247
oral arguments 253
partisan elections 258
rule of four 253
specialty courts 249
trial courts 247
writ of *certiorari* 253

Questions for Critical Analysis

1 "The primary adversarial relationship in the courts is not between the plaintiff (prosecutor, or state) and defendant, but rather between the ideal of justice and the reality of bureaucratic limitations." Explain why you agree or disagree with this statement.

2 Which court has virtually unlimited geographical and subject-matter jurisdiction? Why is this so?

3 How did we end up with a dual court system?

4 Federal judges and justices typically hold office for many years. Why is this so?

5 What effect does the Supreme Court's refusal to issue a writ of *certiorari* have on lower courts' decisions?

6 What are some of the various functions that a judge undertakes during a trial? What function does a judge assume when presiding over a trial that is not a jury trial?

7 Many states, even those using the merit system, elect their judges. What is the main drawback of using elections to select or maintain judges in office?

8 How does a courtroom work group differ from the management of a corporation?

9 What is "universal jurisdiction"? According to the U.S. government, what crimes fall under universal jurisdiction?

Test Preparation Online

Criminal JusticeNow

Go to **www.cjinaction.com** and click on *Criminal JusticeNow* for access to this powerful online study tool. You will get a *personalized study plan* based on your responses to a diagnostic pretest. Once you have mastered the material with the help of interactive learning tools, video clips with questions, an integrated e-book, and more, you can take a posttest to confirm you are ready to move on to the next chapter.

Book Companion Web Site

At the book companion Web site (**www.cjinaction.com**), you will find many resources in addition to *Criminal JusticeNow* to aid you in studying for your exams. For example, under *Chapter Resources,* you will find the *Chapter Outline, Chapter Summary, Flashcards, Glossary, Learning Objectives, Lecture Presentations, Concept Builder, Essay Questions,* and a *Tutorial Chapter Quiz.* You can also test yourself with interactive *Online Reviews* of each chapter section. Check out the *Web Links* to access the Web sites mentioned in the text, as well as many others. You can also access recent perspectives by clicking on *CJ in the News* and *Terrorism Update* under *Course Resources.*

Suggested Reading

Bogira, Steve, *Courtroom 302: A Year behind the Scenes in an American Criminal Courthouse,* New York: Knopf, 2005. The finer ideals of the American court system take a beating in this impressive work of legal journalism. After a year detailing the day-to-day happenings at the Cook County Criminal Courthouse in Chicago ("the biggest and busiest felony courthouse in the nation"), the author's point is clear: a flood of nonviolent drug offenders has turned our lower-level courts into an assembly-line grind in which the protections promised by the U.S. Constitution do not stand a chance. Rather than pass easy judgment on an obviously broken system, Bogira interviews judges, prosecutors, defense attorneys, defendants, witnesses, and police guards in an effort to understand where the American courts went wrong and what can be done to fix them.

O'Connor, Sandra Day, and Craig Joyce, *The Majesty of the Law: Reflections of a Supreme Court Justice,* New York: Random House, 2003. O'Connor, the first female Supreme Court justice, offers an insider's view of the nation's highest court. O'Connor also profiles the justices that she feels have had the greatest impact on the modern Court, including John Marshall, Warren Burger, and Thurgood Marshall. As might be expected, hot-button issues such as the death penalty, abortion rights, and affirmative action are discussed in a way to avoid controversy, but this book does provide an interesting perspective on the evolution of the Court and those who have sat on its bench.

Notes

1. "Bryant's Accuser Testifies on Her Sex Life," *USA Today* (March 25, 2004), 3A.

2. Tom Kenworthy and Patrick O'Driscoll, "Judge Dismisses Bryant Rape Case," *USA Today* (September 2, 2004), 1A.

3. Roscoe Pound, "The Administration of Justice in American Cities," *Harvard Law Review* 12 (1912).

4. Russell Wheeler and Howard Whitcomb, *Judicial Administration: Text and Readings* (Englewood Cliffs, NJ: Prentice Hall, 1977), 3.

5. Herbert Packer, *The Limits of the Criminal Sanction* (Stanford, CA: Stanford University Press, 1968), 154–173.

6. Herbert Packer, "The Courts, the Police and the Rest of Us," *Criminal Law, Criminology & Political Science* 57 (1966), 238–239.

7. Larry J. Siegal, *Criminology: Instructor's Manual,* 6th ed. (Belmont, CA: West/Wadsworth Publishing Co., 1998), 440.

8. Gerald F. Velman, "Federal Sentencing Guidelines: A Cure Worse than the Disease," *American Criminal Law Review* 29 (Spring 1992), 904.

9. "State, Feds Should Help Pay Costs of Sniper Trials," *Virginian-Pilot & Ledger Star* (September 30, 2003), B8.

10. William Wan, "Snipers to Be Tried in Maryland," *Baltimore Sun* (May 11, 2005), 1A.

11. Lisa Friedman, "Bill Highlights Mexican Policy," *(Los Angeles) Daily News* (May 17, 2005), N7.

12. David W. Neubauer, *America's Courts and the Criminal Justice System,* 5th ed. (Belmont, CA: Wadsworth Publishing Co., 1996), 41.

13. Alexander Hamilton, The Federalist, No. 78 in Clinton Rossiter, ed., *The Federalist Papers* (New York: New American Library, 1961), 467–470.

14. G. Edward White, *History of the Supreme Court, Volumes III–IV: The Marshall Court and Cultural Change* (New York: Oxford University Press, 1988), 157–200.

15. 372 U.S. 335 (1963).

16. 384 U.S. 436 (1966).

17. 408 U.S. 238 (1972).

18. 428 U.S. 153 (1976).

19. 491 U.S. 397 (1989).

20. 496 U.S. 310 (1990).

21. Mark Alan Ozimek, "The Case for a More Workable Standard in Death Penalty Jurisprudence: *Atkins v. Virginia* and Categorical Exemptions under the Imprudent 'Evolving Standards of Decency' Doctrine," *University of Toledo Law Review* (Spring 2003), 651.

22. *Singleton v. Commissioner of Internal Revenue,* 439 U.S. 940 (1978).

23. Barry R. Schaller, *A Vision of American Law: Judging Law, Literature, and the Stories We Tell* (Westport, CT: Praeger, 1997).

24. Harlington Wood, Jr., "Judiciary Reform: Recent Improvements in Federal Judicial Administration," *American University Law Review* 44 (June 1995), 1557.

25. Pub. L. No. 76-299, 53 Stat. 1223, codified as amended at 28 U.S.C. Sections 601–610 (1988 & Supp. V 1993).

26. Patrick Emery Longan, "Judicial Professionalism in a New Era of Judicial Selection," *Mercer Law Review* (Spring 2005), 913.

27. Andrew F. Hanssen, "Learning about Judicial Independence: Institutional Change in the State Courts," *Journal of Legal Studies* (2004), 431–474.

28. Brian P. Anderson, "Judicial Elections in West Virginia," *West Virginia Law Review* (Fall 2004), 243.

29. Bob Deans, "Senate Showdown: Nominee Fights May Diminish Faith in Courts," *Atlanta Journal-Constitution* (May 19, 2005), A12.

30. Daniel R. Deja, "How Judges Are Selected: A Survey of the Judicial Selection Process in the United States," *Michigan Bar Journal* 75 (September 1996), 904.

31. Edmund V. Ludwig, "Another Case against the Election of Trial Judges," *Pennsylvania Lawyer* 19 (May/June 1997), 33.

32. *Judicial Selection in the States* (Des Moines, IA: American Judicature Society, 2003), 1–2.

33. Quoted in Daniel Burke, "Code of Judicial Conduct Canon 7B(1)(c): Toward the Proper Regulation of Speech in Judicial Campaigns," *Georgetown Journal of Legal Ethics* 81 (Summer 1993), 181.

34. James E. Lozier, "The Missouri Plan a.k.a. Merit Selection Is the Best Solution for Selecting Michigan's Judges," *Michigan Bar Journal* 75 (September 1996), 918.

35. William Ballenger, "In Judicial Wilderness, Even Brickley's Not Safe," *Michigan Politics* 28 (1996), 1–3.

36. Richard A. Watson and Rondal G. Downing, *The Politics of the Bench and Bar: Judicial Selection under the Missouri Nonpartisan Court Plan* (New York: John Wiley & Sons, 1969).

37. **http://www.allianceforjustice.org/judicial/judicial_ selection_resources/selection_database/by CourtRaceGender.asp**.

38. "Survey Finds Bar Makeup Is Shifting, but Slowly," *California State Bar Journal* (November 2001), 1.

39. **http://www.allianceforjustice.org/judicial/judicial_ selection_resources/selection_database/ byCourtRaceGender.asp**.

40. Edward M. Chen, "The Judiciary, Diversity, and Justice for All," *California Law Review* (July 2003), 1109.

41. Theresa B. Beiner, "The Elusive (but Worthwhile) Quest for a Diverse Bench in the New Millennium," *University of California at Davis Law Review* (February 2003), 599.

42. Sherrilyn A. Ifill, "Racial Diversity on the Bench: Beyond Role Models and Public Confidence," *Washington and Lee Law Review* (Spring 2000), 405.

43. Shirley S. Abrahamson, *Foreword to Judicial Conduct and Ethics* (Charlottesville, VA: Michie Co., 1990), vi–vii.

44. American Bar Association, *Model Code of Judicial Conduct* (Chicago: ABA, August 1990).

45. ABA Commission on Ethics and Professional Responsibility, Informal Opinion 1468 (1981).

46. John Gardiner, "Preventing Judicial Misconduct: Defining the Role of Conduct Organizations," *Judicature* 70 (1986), 113–121.

47. Roy B. Fleming, Peter F. Nardulli, and James Eisenstein, *The Craft of Justice: Politics and Work in Criminal Court Communities* (Philadelphia: University of Pennsylvania Press, 1992).

48. Neubauer, 41.

49. Alissa P. Worden, "The Judge's Role in Plea Bargaining: An Analysis of Judges' Agreement with Prosecutors' Sentencing Recommendations," *Justice Quarterly* 10 (1995), 257–278.

50. Neubauer, 72.

51. Kimberly Jade Norwood, "Shopping for Venue: The Need for More Limits," *University of Miami Law Review* 50 (1996), 295–298.

52. "Overcrowded Courts Are Threat to City and Justice," *Tennessean-Nashville* (May 1, 2003), 16.

53. Jeff Lemberg, "A Year Later, Facing Life after Death," *Boston Globe* (November 17, 2002), 1.

54. Stacey Burns, "Free Felon in Fatal Car Chase," *Morning News Tribune* (January 12, 2002), A1.

55. **http://www.albany.edu/sourcebook/pdf/t58.pdf**.

56. *2004 Annual Report of the Director* (Washington, D.C.: The Administrative Office of the U.S. Courts, 2005), 3.

57. Malcolm Feeley, *Felony Arrests: Their Prosecution and Disposition in New York Courts* (New York: Vera Institute, 1981), xii.

58. Nick Madigan, "Man, 86, Convicted under New Law against Americans Who Go Abroad to Molest Minors," *New York Times* (November 11, 2004), A11.

59. Sara K. Andrews, "U.S. Domestic Prosecution of the American International Sex Tourist: Efforts to Protect Children from Sexual Exploitation," *Journal of Criminal Law and Criminology* (Winter 2004), 415.

60. Eric Lichtblau and James Dao, "U.S. Able to Prosecute Americans Who Commit Sex Crimes Overseas," *New York Times* (June 8, 2004), A16.

61. Pub. L. No. 108-21, 117 Stat. 650 (2003).

62. 18 U.S.C. Section 2423(c) (2005).

63. *Strassheim v. Daily,* 221 U.S. 280 (1911).

64. *Jones v. United States,* 137 U.S. 202 (1890).

65. "Draft Convention on Jurisdiction with Respect to Crime by Harvard Research in International Law," *American Journal of International Law* (Supp. 1935), Article 7.

66. *Restatement (Second) of the Foreign Relations Law of the United States,* Section 30(2) (1965).

67. Frank Turkheimer, "Globalization of U.S. Law Enforcement: Does the U.S. Constitution Come Along?" *Houston Law Review* (Summer 2002), 324.

68. *United States v. Alvarez-Machain,* 504 U.S. 655 (1992).

69. 18 U.S.C. Sections 2331(1)(A) and 2332a(a)(1)-(3) (2002).

CHAPTER NINE

Pretrial Procedures:
The Adversary System in Action

Chapter outline

- The Prosecution
- The Defense Attorney
- Truth, Victory, and the Adversary System
- Pretrial Detention
- Establishing Probable Cause
- The Prosecutorial Screening Process
- Pleading Guilty
- Going to Trial
- Criminal Justice in Action—Is Justice for Sale?

Chapter objectives

After reading this chapter, you should be able to:

1 List the different names given to public prosecutors and the general powers that they have.
2 Contrast the prosecutor's roles as an elected official and as a crime fighter.
3 Delineate the responsibilities of defense attorneys.
4 Indicate the three types of defense allocation programs.
5 List the three basic features of an adversary system of justice.
6 Identify the steps involved in the pretrial criminal process.
7 Indicate the three influences on a judge's decision to set bail.
8 Explain how a prosecutor screens potential cases.
9 List and briefly explain the different forms of plea bargaining agreements.
10 Indicate the ways that both defense attorneys and prosecutors can induce plea bargaining.

Criminal JusticeNow

Optimize your study time and master key chapter concepts with *Criminal JusticeNow*, an online study tool that provides you with a *personalized study plan*. Check out the "Test Preparation Online" section at the end of the chapter for additional information.

A Fair Trade?

At first, Emily Lyons wanted Eric Rudolph to die. Lyons was on duty as a nurse at New Woman All Women Health Care, an abortion clinic in Birmingham, Alabama, on January 29, 1998, when a bomb rigged by Rudolph detonated at the facility. The blast killed an off-duty police officer and embedded nails in Lyons's body. "The crime deserves the punishment of death," said Lyons, who is blind in one eye and still suffers numerous other health problems because of her injuries. In April 2005, however, Rudolph pleaded guilty to four bombings: the explosion in Birmingham, an attack at the 1996 Summer Olympics in Atlanta, Georgia, and strikes on an abortion clinic and gay nightclub in Atlanta in 1997. Combined, these acts of violence claimed two lives and injured 150 people. In return for his plea, Rudolph will spend the rest of his life in prison rather than face the possibility of the death penalty at trial.

Authorities escort handcuffed serial bomber Eric Rudolph from the federal courthouse in Huntsville, Alabama.

AP Photo/Haraz Ghanbari

Despite her strong conviction that Rudolph deserved to be executed, Lyons, along with many of his other victims, supported the compromise. Rudolph had hidden more than 250 pounds of dynamite in the mountains of western North Carolina and would not reveal the whereabouts of the explosives unless prosecutors took the death penalty off the table. Because dynamite destabilizes as it ages, authorities worried that the cache represented a serious public health threat and urged the victims to accept the offer. "I watched what my wife went through," said Jeffrey Lyons, Emily's husband, explaining how the hidden dynamite convinced the couple to soften their stance on Rudolph's death. "I did not want to have someone come up to me and say, 'My mother looks like your wife because you held out for the [death] sentence you wanted.'"

"Justice has prevailed," announced Carl Truscott, director of the Bureau of Alcohol, Tobacco, Firearms and Explosives, after the announcement of Eric Rudolph's plea bargain.[1] Not everyone agreed. Ted Riner, a Georgia state trooper who was injured by the bomb at the Olympics, said, "I'm very much shocked at what they have done, letting him plead off on it."[2] John Hawthorne, whose wife, Alice, was killed in the same explosion, said he would not have signed off on the plea deal if he had known that Rudolph would celebrate his "victory" by gloating in the press.[3] Even Emily Lyons said she was "nauseated" by the outcome.[4]

Though sensitive to the feelings of Emily Lyons and the other victims, federal law enforcement officials seemed pleased with the result. U.S. Attorney David E. Nahmias pointed out that the agreement removed the public safety threat posed by the concealed explosives.[5] Even if Rudolph had received the death penalty, the appeals process would have dragged on for many years, a scenario that would have been extremely trying for

▶ CONCEPT BUILDER

Having the power or authority to make decisions and to have latitude in choices is an integral aspect of the criminal justice system. Visit **www.cjinaction.com** for an interactive exploration of this key topic.

his victims and cost the federal government millions of dollars. In fact, prosecutors and defendants are constantly "making deals" just like the one between Rudolph and the federal government. The *formal* adversary process of the trial is the exception rather than the rule in American courts. More than 95 percent of those charged with a felony in this country opt, as Rudolph did, for the *informal* process. That is, they plead guilty, thereby avoiding a trial and serving, in almost all instances, a lighter sentence.[6] Indeed, most prosecutors, defense attorneys, and judges could not imagine a system in which plea bargaining was not the predominant means of resolving cases.

Given, then, that the vast majority of cases never go to trial, is it realistic to claim that the United States even has an adversary system? In this chapter, we will attempt to answer this question by examining the actions of the courtroom work group with regard to plea bargaining, bail, and other pretrial procedures. We will start with a discussion of the two main combatants of the adversary system: the prosecutor and the defense attorney.

THE PROSECUTION

Criminal cases are tried by **public prosecutors,** who are employed by the government. The public prosecutor in federal criminal cases is called a U.S. attorney. In cases tried in state or local courts, the public prosecutor may be referred to as a *prosecuting attorney, state prosecutor, district attorney, county attorney,* or *city attorney.* Given their great autonomy, prosecutors are generally considered the most dominant figures in the American criminal justice system. In some jurisdictions, the district attorney is the chief law enforcement officer, with broad powers over police operations. Prosecutors have the power to bring the resources of the state against the individual and hold the legal keys to meting out or withholding punishment.[7] Ideally, this power is balanced by a duty of fairness and a recognition that the prosecutor's ultimate goal is not to win cases, but to see that justice is done. In *Berger v. United States* (1935), Justice George Sutherland called the prosecutor

> in a peculiar and very definite sense the servant of the law, the twofold aim of which is that guilt shall not escape or innocence suffer. He may prosecute with earnestness and vigor—indeed, he should do so. But, while he may strike hard blows, he is not at liberty to strike foul ones. It is as much his duty to refrain from improper methods calculated to produce a wrongful conviction as it is to use every legitimate means to bring about a just one.[8]

The Office of the Prosecutor

When he or she is acting as an *officer of the law* during a criminal trial, there are limits on the prosecutor's conduct, as we shall see in the next chapter. During the pretrial process, however, prosecutors hold a great deal of discretion in deciding the following:

1 Whether an individual who has been arrested by the police will be charged with a crime.
2 The level of the charges to be brought against the suspect.
3 If and when to stop the prosecution.[9]

There are more than eight thousand prosecutor's offices around the country—serving state, county, and municipal jurisdictions. Even though the **attorney general** is the chief law enforcement officer in any state, she or he has limited (and in some states, no) control of prosecutors within the state's boundaries.

Public Prosecutors
Individuals, acting as trial lawyers, who initiate and conduct cases in the government's name and on behalf of the people.

Attorney General
The chief law officer of a state; also, the chief law officer of the nation.

Each jurisdiction has a chief prosecutor who is sometimes appointed but more often elected. As an elected official, he or she typically serves a four-year term, though in some states, such as Alabama, the term is six years. In smaller jurisdictions, the chief prosecutor has several assistants, and they work closely together. In larger ones, the chief prosecutor may have numerous *assistant prosecutors,* many of whom he or she will rarely meet. Assistant prosecutors—for the most part young attorneys recently graduated from law school—may be assigned to particular sections of the organization, such as criminal prosecutions in general or areas of *special prosecution,* such as narcotics or gang crimes. (See Figure 9.1 for the structure of a typical prosecutor's office.)

The Prosecutor as Elected Official

The chief prosecutor's autonomy is not complete: as an elected official, she or he must answer to the voters. (There are exceptions: U.S. attorneys are nominated by the president and approved by the Senate, and chief prosecutors in Alaska, Connecticut, New Jersey, Rhode Island, and the District of Columbia are either appointed or hired as members of the attorney general's office.) The prosecutor may be part of the political machine; in many jurisdictions the prosecutor must declare a party affiliation and is expected to reward fellow party members with positions in the district attorney's office if elected. The post is often seen as a "stepping-stone" to higher political office, and many prosecutors have gone on to serve in legislatures or as judges. Arlen Specter, a Republican senator from Pennsylvania; Ron Castille, who sits on the state's supreme court; and Ed Rendell, a former mayor of Philadelphia and now governor of the state, all served as Philadelphia district attorneys early in their careers.

Prosecutors are also subject to community pressures. As antidrug sentiment becomes more prevalent around the country, for example, many prosecutors feel obliged to aggressively prosecute and charge narcotics law offenders.[10] Several years ago, voters in Lake County (Michigan) went so far as to recall David Woodruff, their local prosecutor. Woodruff had come under intense criticism for negotiating a plea

FIGURE 9.1
The Baltimore City
State's Attorney's Office

Source: Baltimore City State's
Attorney's Office.

John Esmerado
Assistant Prosecutor

My name is John G. Esmerado. I am an assistant prosecutor in Elizabeth, New Jersey, for the county of Union. My current responsibilities are twofold. Primarily, I represent the state of New Jersey at trial. With a detective staff, I investigate crime by interviewing witnesses, searching out evidence, and asking people questions in court to establish beyond a reasonable doubt that a defendant committed a crime. Trial work is incredibly fun. It requires vast amounts of pretrial preparation. Once it starts, however, it moves at lightning speed. Trials are strategic chess games of facts and law as well as all-out mental combat, a blitzkrieg of sorts, to find the truth. My secondary responsibility is to act as legal adviser to the police. Many times during the week and periodically in the early morning hours while the world sleeps, detectives call to discuss problematic cases. They arrest someone and are not clear what the appropriate charges are. I listen to the facts and authorize certain complaints and ask the detectives to pursue additional facts to help make the case stronger for trial.

Recently, I was confronted with a moral dilemma. I was asked to participate as the second prosecutor in a death penalty trial. As a Catholic, I was ambivalent at best about the use of the death penalty by the state. I consulted the *Gospel of Life* and other Church teachings on the topic as well as my own conscience. The defendant was charged with hiring a hit man to kill his longtime girlfriend. The defendant had served a previous state prison sentence for threatening the same woman in the past. The defendant was no angel and had a lengthy criminal record. After much soul searching, I consented to work on the case with the premier assistant prosecutor in the office, Regina Caulfield. After a three-week trial, we secured a conviction for first degree murder for hire. The guilt phase of the trial was over. We had one week off to prepare for the penalty phase. I began to have doubts about the whole process. Was this really fair to both the defen-

dant and the victim's family? Is death a legitimate tool in the prosecutor's arsenal of justice? After a four-day hearing and a day and a half of deliberation, the jury returned a verdict for life and not for death. The victim's family was disappointed. I was relieved.

Courtesy John Esmerado

John Esmerado

As a prosecutor, I have always sought to do what is right and just. Incoming data support the conclusion that the current system with all its Byzantine rules cannot function properly. Jurors disregard legal instructions, while defense attorneys engender emotional sympathy for the defendant's upbringing, and victims are offered little, if any, opportunity to place their loss before the jury. Death must be reevaluated by the entire criminal justice community.

Immediately after this trial, I took some time off, grew a beard, and gained weight. I was depressed. For the first time in my career I had participated in something I did not wholly believe in. Since that time, I found my razor, exercise consistently, and have firmly resolved not to participate in another capital case.

In summary, I am glad to have a job that provides an outlet for my desire to do good. Sometimes, when I am working late at night, for free, on a case, I say to myself, "This is the greatest job in the world." I receive a salary to find the truth. I help people in crisis, people subject to violence, confront their attackers and ultimately bring some form of closure. Truth, justice, and the American way, a job far too important to leave to Superman cartoons, is the job of the prosecutor every day in and out of court.

Go to the Careers in Criminal Justice Interactive CD *for more profiles in the field of criminal justice.*

bargain with Daryl Dwayne Henderson, who had murdered his ex-girlfriend and shot her three-year-old son in the eye. Community members, particularly the victims' family, were outraged that Woodruff's deal had given Henderson a chance to spend only twenty-five years in prison.

The Prosecutor as Crime Fighter

One of the reasons the prosecutor's post is a useful first step in a political career is that it is linked to crime fighting. Thanks to savvy public relations efforts and television police dramas such as *Law and Order*—with its opening line, "In the criminal justice system, the people are represented by two separate yet equally important groups: the police who investigate crime and the district attorneys who prosecute the offenders"—prosecutors are generally seen as law enforcement agents. Indeed, the prosecutors and

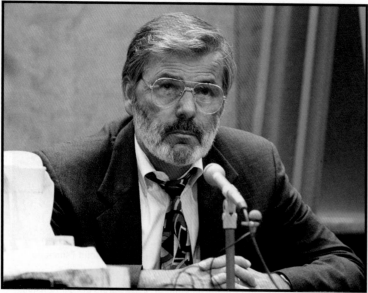

In 2004, the Arizona Supreme Court disbarred former Pima County District Attorney Kenneth Peasley for knowingly presenting false evidence in a capital punishment case. Peasely is the first American prosecutor to lose his law license for deceiving a death penalty jury. Why is it harmful to the criminal justice system when a prosecutor places his or her own personal goals above the ideals of fair play?

the police do have a symbiotic relationship. Prosecutors rely on police to arrest suspects and gather sufficient evidence, and police rely on prosecutors to convict those who have been apprehended.

Police-Prosecutor Conflict Despite, or perhaps because of, this mutual dependency, the relationship between the two branches of law enforcement is often strained. Part of this can be attributed to different backgrounds. Most prosecutors come from middle- or upper-class families, while police are often recruited from the working class. Furthermore, prosecutors are required to have a level of education that is not attained by most police officers.

More important, however, is a basic divergence in the concept of guilt. For a police officer, a suspect is guilty if he or she has in fact committed a crime. For a prosecutor, a suspect is guilty if enough evidence can be legally gathered to prove such guilt in a court of law.[11] In other words, police officers often focus on *factual guilt,* whereas prosecutors are ultimately concerned with *legal guilt.*[12] Thus, police officers will feel a great deal of frustration when a suspect they "know" to be guilty is set free. Similarly, a prosecutor may become annoyed when police officers do not follow the letter of the law in gathering evidence, thereby effectively ruining the chances of conviction.

Attempts at Cooperation Tension arising from these grievances can hamper crime control efforts. As a result, a number of jurisdictions are trying to achieve better police-prosecutor relations. A key step in the process seems to be improving communications between the two groups. In San Diego, for example, the district attorney has a permanent office in the police department for the express purpose of counseling officers on legal questions. From the office, a deputy district attorney (DDA) acts as a human legal reference book, advising police officers on how to write a search warrant, what steps they can take to help solidify a prosecutor's case, and other issues. The DDA will even sit in on morning briefings, giving updates on how changes in the law may affect police work.

THE DEFENSE ATTORNEY

The media provide most people's perception of defense counsel: the idealistic public defender who nobly serves the poor, the "ambulance chaser," or the celebrity attorney in the $3,000 suit. These stereotypes, though not entirely fictional, tend to obscure the crucial role that the **defense attorney** plays in the criminal justice system. Most persons charged with crimes have little or no knowledge of criminal procedure. Without assistance, they would be helpless against a government prosecutor. By acting as a staunch advocate for her or his client, the defense attorney (ideally) assures that the government proves every point against that client beyond a reasonable doubt, even for cases that do not go to trial. In sum, the defense attorney provides a counterweight against the state in our adversary system. (See the feature *Outside the Box—The Myth of Fingerprints.*)

Defense Attorney
The lawyer representing the defendant.

OUTSIDE THE BOX

The Myth of Fingerprints

For nearly a century, police and prosecutors have relied on fingerprints as a powerful tool to link suspects to crimes. Today, however, defense attorneys are challenging this traditional weapon of forensic science, saying that it is not really "scientific" at all.

When forensic scientists compare a fingerprint lifted from a crime scene and one taken from a suspect, they are looking for "points of similarity." Today, these experts will usually declare a match if there are between eight and sixteen points of similarity between the two samples. Many defense attorneys claim that this method is flawed. First, prints found at crime scenes tend to be incomplete, which means that examiners do not compare whole fingerprints but rather fragments of fingerprints. So, while it may be true that no two fingerprints are alike, it also may *not* be true that fragments of fingerprints are always similar or identical. Second, fingerprint evidence found at crime scenes requires treatment with chemicals or illumination with ultraviolet light to make it clear enough to work with. Is it scientifically acceptable to compare this "altered" print with a "clean" one obtained from a suspect in controlled circumstances?

No research on the frequency of erroneous police fingerprint identification has ever been attempted. In recent years, however, a number of high-profile cases have suggested the fallibility of fingerprint matches. In 2002, a woman who had been identified as a murder victim by a fingerprint examiner with the Las Vegas Police Department showed up five weeks later, very much alive. In 2004, the Federal Bureau of Investigation identified fifteen matching points between prints on a plastic bag found at the site of a terrorist bombing in Madrid, Spain, and those of an American lawyer named Brandon Mayfield. The lawyer spent two weeks in detention before the agency realized that there was, in fact, no match and released him. That same year, DNA evidence freed a Massachusetts man whose conviction for shooting a

These two fingerprints were taken from different people. Still, they have five common points of similarity.

police officer was based on fingerprints lifted from a glass of water found near the scene of the crime. He languished in prison for six years before the mistake was detected. Defense attorneys are using these cases to challenge the fail-safe reputation of fingerprint matches as evidence.

FOR CRITICAL ANALYSIS

According to defense attorneys (and many others), fingerprint identification is sometimes untrustworthy because it relies on a determination made by a fingerprint examiner, who depends on her or his experience—rather than any scientific method—to decide if the two prints match. These critics want judges to inform juries that fingerprint examiners are expert witnesses offering their opinions, not scientists presenting certain facts. What difference would such instructions have on how juries respond to fingerprint evidence, and how would the use of fingerprint identification as a crime-fighting tool be affected?

The Responsibilities of the Defense Attorney

The Sixth Amendment right to counsel is not limited to the actual criminal trial. In a number of instances, the United States Supreme Court has held that defendants are entitled to representation as soon as their rights may be denied, which, as we have seen, includes the custodial interrogation and lineup identification procedures.[13] Therefore, the primary responsibility of the defense attorney is to represent the defendant at the various stages of the custodial process, such as arrest, interrogation, lineup, and arraignment. Other responsibilities include:

> "Look at the stakes. In civil law, if you screw up, it's just money. Here, it's the client—his life, his time in jail—and you never know how much time people have in their life."
>
> —Criminal defense attorney Stacey Richman (2001)

- Investigating the incident for which the defendant has been charged.
- Communicating with the prosecutor, which includes negotiating plea bargains.

Public Defenders
Court-appointed attorneys who are paid by the state to represent defendants who are unable to hire private counsel.

- Preparing the case for trial.
- Submitting defense motions, including motions to suppress evidence.
- Representing the defendant at trial.
- Negotiating a sentence, if the client has been convicted.
- Determining whether to appeal a guilty verdict.[14]

The Public Defender

Generally speaking, there are two different types of defense attorneys: (1) private attorneys, who are hired by individuals, and (2) **public defenders,** who work for the government. The distinction is not absolute, as many private attorneys hire out as public defenders, too. The modern role of the public defender was established by the Supreme Court's interpretation of the Sixth Amendment in *Gideon v. Wainwright* (1963).[15] In that case, the Court ruled that no defendant can be "assured a fair trial unless counsel is provided for him," and therefore the state must provide a public defender to those who cannot afford to hire one for themselves. Subsequently, the Court extended this protection to juveniles in *In re Gault* (1967)[16] and those faced with imprisonment for committing misdemeanors in *Argersinger v. Hamlin* (1972).[17] The impact of these decisions has been substantial: more than 80 percent of felony defendants in the country's largest counties and 66 percent of felony defendants in federal courts are represented by publicly paid counsel.[18]

Defense Counsel Programs In most areas, the county government is responsible for providing indigent defendants with attorneys. Three basic types of programs are used to allocate defense counsel:

1 *Assigned counsel programs,* in which local private attorneys are assigned clients on a case-by-case basis by the county.

2 *Contracting attorney programs,* in which a particular law firm or group of attorneys is hired to regularly assume the representative and administrative tasks of indigent defense.

3 *Public defender programs,* in which the county assembles a salaried staff of full-time or part-time attorneys and creates a public (taxpayer-funded) agency to provide services.[19]

Jurisdictions can use several of these programs concurrently. In the most recent published survey, 63 percent of state court prosecutors' offices used assigned counsel, 29 percent contracted out their defense counsel, and 68 percent had public defender programs.[20]

Effectiveness of Public Defenders Many observers believe that public defenders, assigned counsel, and contracted lawyers do not provide an acceptable level of defense to indigents. (When is a defendant indigent? See the feature *You Be the Judge—Indigent or Not?*) Although there is certainly a great deal of anecdotal evidence to support this contention, a recent study by researchers Roger A. Hanson, Brian J. Ostrom, and Ann A. Jones suggests that the outcome of a criminal case is not greatly affected by the private or public nature of the defense attorney. In the courts covered by the study, 95 percent of the defendants with public counsel and 91 percent of those with private counsel resolved their cases via a guilty plea.[21] Additional research by the U.S. Department of Justice revealed that, if found guilty, defendants with private counsel were 10 percent more likely to be sent to prison than those represented by public counsel.[22] (In the chapter-ending *Criminal Justice in Action* feature, we will take a closer look at the quality of legal representation provided to low-income defendants, or the lack thereof.)

The **National Association of Criminal Defense Lawyers** represents more than ten thousand lawyers and advocates on a number of issues relating to the criminal justice system. To find its Web site, click on *Web Links* under *Chapter Resources* at **www.cjinaction.com.**

YOU BE THE JUDGE

Indigent or Not?

THE FACTS

Noel, a student at the University of Hawaii, was charged with driving under the influence of alcohol (DUI). Noel claimed that he did not have the resources to hire an attorney and asked the state to provide him with one. At the time he was arrested, Noel had $32 in his bank account and $1.50 in pocket money. He also had a 1971 Volkswagen sedan with a value of $1,000.

THE LAW

Hawaii law provided that an "indigent" person was entitled to free counsel if charged with an offense punishable by imprisonment for thirty days or more. (DUI in Hawaii carried a maximum penalty of one year in jail.)

YOUR DECISION

The trial judge ruled that because Noel could have sold his car to get money for an attorney, he was not indigent under Hawaii's law. Do you agree?

[To see how the Hawaii Supreme Court ruled in this case, go to Example 9.1 in Appendix B.]

The Attorney–Client Relationship

To defend a client effectively, a defense attorney must have access to all the facts concerning the case, including those that may be harmful to the defense. To promote the unrestrained flow of information between the two parties, laws of **attorney-client privilege** have been constructed. These laws require that communications between a client and his or her attorney be kept confidential, unless the client consents to disclosure. The scope of this privilege is not all encompassing, however. In *United States v. Zolin* (1989),[23] the Supreme Court ruled that attorneys may disclose the contents of a conversation with a client if the client has provided information concerning a crime that has yet to be committed.

The implied trust between an attorney and her or his client is not usually in question when the attorney has been hired directly by the defendant—as an "employee," the attorney well understands her or his duties. Relationships between public defenders and their clients, however, are often marred by suspicion on both sides. As Northwestern University's Jonathan D. Casper discovered while interviewing indigent defendants, many of them feel a certain amount of respect for the prosecutor. Like police officers, prosecutors are just "doing their job" by trying to convict the defendant. In contrast, the defendants' view of their own attorneys can be summed up in the following exchange between Casper and a defendant:

> Did you have a lawyer when you went to court the next morning?
> No, I had a public defender.[24]

This attitude is somewhat understandable. Given the caseloads that most public defenders carry, they may have as little as five or ten minutes to spend with a client before appearing in front of a judge. How much, realistically, can a public defender learn about the defendant in that time?[25] Furthermore, the defendant is well aware that the public defender is being paid by the same source as the prosecutor and the judge. Almost a decade ago, "Unabomber" Ted Kaczynski acted on impulses felt by many defendants when he requested the right to defend himself, complaining that his public counsel was "supping from the same trough" as the prosecution.[26]

The situation handcuffs the public defenders as well. With so little time to spend on each case, they cannot validate the information provided by their clients. If the defendant says he or she has no prior offenses, the public defender often has no choice but to believe the client. Consequently, many public defenders later find that their

GREAT DEBATES

One question that has troubled defense attorneys and legal ethicists is whether a lawyer has a duty to defend a client he or she knows to be guilty. To better understand the issues in this debate, click on *Great Debates* under *Book Resources* at **www.cjinaction.com**.

Attorney–Client Privilege

A rule of evidence requiring that communications between a client and his or her attorney be kept confidential, unless the client consents to disclosure.

clients have deceived them. In addition to the low pay and high pressures of the job, a client's lack of cooperation and disrespect can limit whatever satisfaction a public defender may find in the profession.[27]

TRUTH, VICTORY, AND THE ADVERSARY SYSTEM

In strictly legal terms, three basic features characterize the **adversary system:**

1 A neutral and passive decision maker, either the judge or the jury.
2 The presentation of evidence from both parties.
3 A highly structured set of procedures (in the form of constitutional safeguards) that must be followed in the presentation of that evidence.[28]

Some critics of the American court system believe that it has been tainted by overzealous prosecutors and defense attorneys. Gordon Van Kessel, a professor at Hastings College of Law in California, complains that American lawyers see themselves as "prize fighters, gladiators, or, more accurately, semantic warriors in a verbal battle," and bemoans the atmosphere of "ritualized aggression" that is endemic to the courts.[29]

Our discussion of the courtroom work group in the last chapter, however, seems to belie this image of "ritualized aggression." As political scientists Herbert Jacob and James Eisenstein have written, "pervasive conflict is not only unpleasant; it also makes work more difficult."[30] The image of the courtroom work group as "negotiators" rather than "prize fighters" seems to be supported by the fact that more than nine out of every ten cases conclude with negotiated "deals" rather than trials. Jerome Skolnick of the University of California at Berkeley has found that work group members grade each other according to "reasonableness"[31]—a concept criminal justice scholar Abraham S. Blumberg has embellished by labeling the defense attorney a "double agent." Blumberg believes that a defense attorney is likely to cooperate with the prosecutor in convincing a client to accept a negotiated plea of guilty because the defense attorney's main object is to finish the case quickly so as to collect the fee and move on.[32]

Perhaps, then, the most useful definition of the adversary process tempers Professor Van Kessel's criticism with the realities of the courtroom work group. University of California at Berkeley law professor Malcolm Feeley observes:

> In the adversary system the goal of the advocate is not to determine truth but to win, to maximize the interests of his or her side within the confines of the norms governing the proceedings. This is not to imply that the theory of the adversary process has no concern for the truth. Rather, the underlying assumption of the adversary process is that truth is most likely to emerge as a by-product of vigorous conflict between intensely partisan advocates, each of whose goal is to win.[33]

Blumberg takes a more cynical view when he calls the court process a "confidence game" in which "victory" is achieved when a defense attorney—with the implicit aid of the prosecutor and judge—is able to persuade the defendant to plead guilty.[34] As you read the rest of the chapter, which deals with pretrial procedures, keep in mind Feeley's and Blumberg's contentions concerning "truth" and "victory" in the American courts.

Adversary System

A legal system in which the prosecution and defense are opponents, or adversaries, and present their cases in the light most favorable to themselves. The court arrives at a just solution based on the evidence presented by the contestants and determines who wins and who loses.

Defense attorney Thomas Mesereau, Jr., has represented a number of celebrities, including Michael Jackson, Robert Blake, and Mike Tyson, and often appears on national television to discuss high-profile cases. What are some of the responsibilities of a defense attorney?

AP Photo/Carlo Allegri, Pool

PRETRIAL DETENTION

After an arrest has been made, the first step toward determining the suspect's guilt or innocence is the **initial appearance** (for an overview of the entire process, see Figure 9.2). During this brief proceeding, a magistrate (see Chapter 8) informs the defendant of the charges that have been brought against him or her and explains his or her constitutional rights—particularly, the right to remain silent (under the Fifth Amendment) and the right to be represented by counsel (under the Sixth Amendment). At this point, if the defendant cannot afford to hire a private attorney, a public defender may be appointed, or private counsel may be hired by the state to

Initial Appearance
An accused's first appearance before a judge or magistrate following arrest; during the appearance, the defendant is informed of the charges, advised of the right to counsel, told the amount of bail, and given a date for the preliminary hearing.

FIGURE 9.2
The Steps Leading to a Trial

Booking
After arrest, at the police station, the suspect is searched, photographed, fingerprinted, and allowed at least one telephone call. After the booking, charges are reviewed, and if they are not dropped, a complaint is filed and a judge or magistrate examines the case for probable cause.

Initial Appearance
The suspect appears before the judge, who informs the suspect of the charges and of his or her rights. If the suspect requests a lawyer, one is appointed. The judge sets bail (conditions under which a suspect can obtain release pending disposition of the case).

Grand Jury
A grand jury determines if there is probable cause to believe that the defendant committed the crime. The federal government and about half of the states require grand jury indictments for at least some felonies.

Preliminary Hearing
A court proceding in which the prosecutor presents evidence and the judge determines whether there is probable cause to hold the defendant over for trial.

Indictment
An indictment is the charging instrument issued by the grand jury.

Information
An information is the charging instrument issued by the proecutor.

Arraignment
The suspect is brought before the trial court, informed of the charges, and asked to enter a plea.

Plea Bargain
A plea bargain is a prosecutor's promise of concessions (or promise to seek concessions) in return for the defendant's guilty plea. Concessions include a reduced charge and/or a lesser sentence.

Guilty Plea
In most jurisdictions, most cases that reach the arraignment stage do not go to trial but are resolved by a guilty plea, often as the result of a plea bargain. The judge sets the case for sentencing.

Trial
If the defendant refuses to plead guilty, he or she proceeds to either a jury trial (in most instances) or a bench trial.

represent the defendant. As the U.S. Constitution does not specify how soon a defendant must be brought before a magistrate after arrest, it has been left to the judicial branch to determine the timing of the initial appearance. The Supreme Court has held that the initial appearance must occur "promptly," which in most cases means within forty-eight hours of booking.[35]

In misdemeanor cases, a defendant may decide to plead guilty and be sentenced during the initial appearance. Otherwise, the magistrate will usually release those charged with misdemeanors on their promise to return at a later date for further proceedings. For felony cases, however, the defendant is not permitted to make a plea at the initial appearance because a magistrate's court does not have jurisdiction to decide felonies. Furthermore, in most cases the defendant will be released only if she or he posts **bail**—an amount paid by the defendant to the court and retained by the court until the defendant returns for further proceedings. Defendants who cannot afford bail are generally kept in a local jail or lockup until the date of their trial, though many jurisdictions are searching for alternatives to this practice because of overcrowded incarceration facilities.

The Purpose of Bail

Bail is provided for under the Eighth Amendment. The amendment does not, however, guarantee the right to bail. Instead, it states that "excessive bail shall not be required." This has come to mean that in all cases except those involving a capital crime (where bail is prohibited), the amount of bail required must be reasonable compared with the seriousness of the wrongdoing. It does *not* mean that the amount of bail must be within the defendant's ability to pay.

The vagueness of the Eighth Amendment has encouraged a second purpose of bail: to protect the community from a defendant's committing another crime before trial. To achieve this purpose, a judge can simply set bail at a level the suspect cannot possibly afford. As we shall see, several states and the federal government have passed laws that allow judges to detain suspects deemed a threat to the community without going through the motions of setting relatively high bail.

Setting Bail

There is no uniform system for pretrial detention; each jurisdiction has its own *bail tariffs*, or general guidelines concerning the proper amount of bail. For misdemeanors, the police usually follow a preapproved bail schedule created by local judicial authorities. In felony cases, the primary responsibility to set bail lies with the judge. Figure 9.3 shows typical bail amounts for various offenses.

The Judge and Bail Setting Bail tariffs can be quite extensive. In Illinois, for example, a judge is required to take thirty-eight different factors into account when setting bail: fourteen involve the crime itself, two refer to the evidence gathered, four to the defendant's record, nine to the defendant's flight risk and immigration status, and nine to the defendant's general character.[36] For the most part, however, judges are free to use such tariffs as loose guidelines, and they have a great deal of discretion in setting bail according to the circumstances in each case.

Extralegal factors may also play a part in bail setting. University of New Orleans political scientist David W. Neubauer has identified three contexts that may influence a judge's decision-making process:[37]

Bail
The amount or conditions set by the court to ensure that an individual accused of a crime will appear for further criminal proceedings. If the accused person provides bail, whether in cash or by means of a bail bond, then she or he is released from jail.

FIGURE 9.3
Average Bail Amounts for Various Felonies

These figures represent the median bail figures for the seventy-five largest counties in the nation.

Source: Adapted from Bureau of Justice Statistics, *Federal Defendants in Large Urban Counties* (Washington, D.C.: U.S. Department of Justice, November 2001), Table 16, page 18.

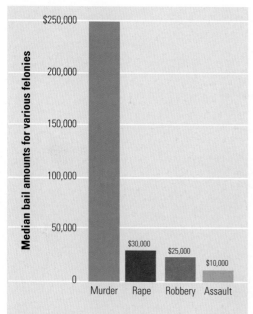

1 *Uncertainty.* To a certain extent, predetermined bail tariffs are unrealistic, given that judges are required to set bail within forty-eight hours of arrest. It is often difficult to get information on the defendant in that period of time, and even if a judge can obtain a "rap sheet," or list of prior arrests ("priors"), she or he will probably not have an opportunity to verify its accuracy. Due to this uncertainty, most judges have no choice but to focus primarily on the seriousness of the crime in setting bail.

2 *Risk.* There is no way of knowing for certain whether a defendant released on bail will return for his or her court date, or whether he or she will commit a crime while free. Judges are aware of the criticism they will come under from police groups, prosecutors, the press, and the public if a crime is committed during that time. Consequently, especially if she or he is up for reelection, a judge may prefer to "play it safe" and set a high bail to detain a suspect or refuse outright to offer bail when legally able to do so. In general, risk aversion also dictates why those who are charged with a violent crime such as murder are usually less likely to be released prior to trial than those who are charged with property crimes such as larceny or motor vehicle theft (see Figure 9.4).

3 *Overcrowded jails.* As we will discuss in detail in Chapter 13, many of the nation's jails are overcrowded. This may force a judge to make a difficult distinction between those suspects she or he believes must be detained and those who might need to be detained. To save jail space, a judge might be more lenient in setting bail for members of the latter group.[38]

Prosecutors, Defense Attorneys, and Bail Setting Though the judge has ultimate discretion in setting bail, the prosecutor and, to a lesser extent, the defense attorney can influence his or her decision. If the two sides disagree on the question of bail, a judge will usually side with the prosecutor. In many cases, given the uncertainty mentioned above, a trusted prosecutor can be a useful source of information for the judge. A hearing in Brigham City, Utah, provides a fairly typical example of the extent of the adversary process in determining pretrial detention. The defense attorney for a man charged with rape and sexual abuse asserted that his client was not a risk to the community. The prosecutor countered that the defendant had been accused of an average of one sexual offense every ten days over a three-month period. Not surprisingly, the judge denied bail.

Defense attorneys have a number of incentives for wanting their clients to be free on bail before a trial. A defendant who shows that she or he can function in the community without committing any further crimes may reduce her or his chances of conviction or at least impress on the judge the feasibility of a lighter sentence. Furthermore, a defendant free on bail is able to assist in the preparation for her or his defense by helping to gather evidence and personally steering the defense attorney toward favorable witnesses. Finally, a client free on bail is more likely to be able to earn income to pay legal bills.

The Benefits of Bail In a classic study of Philadelphia conviction rates, legal scholar

FIGURE 9.4
The Likelihood of Pretrial Release

Source: Bureau of Justice Statistics, *Felony Defendants in Large Urban Counties, 2000* (Washington, D.C.: U.S. Department of Justice, December 2003), Table 13, page 16.

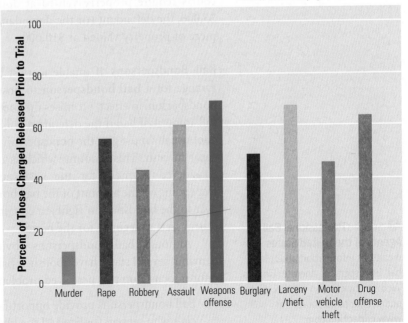

Caleb Foote found that 67 percent of those suspected of violent crimes who had been released on bail were acquitted, compared to 25 percent of those who had been jailed before their trials.[39] More recent research by Marian R. Williams of the Criminal Justice Program at Bowling Green State University also shows that convicted offenders who have been denied bail are more likely to be incarcerated and to receive longer sentences.[40] (Critics of these types of studies point out, though, that they rarely control completely for the fact that those not released on bail were likely to be more violent and to have more extensive prior criminal records than those granted bail.)

Given these benefits, one would think that defense attorneys would fight vigorously for low bail for their clients. This is not the case, however. Most courtroom work groups establish "rules of the game" that determine the levels at which bail will be set for particular crimes, and judges, prosecutors, and defense attorneys do not spend a great deal of time contesting the matter.[41]

Gaining Pretrial Release

Earlier, we mentioned that many jurisdictions are looking for alternatives to the bail system. One of the most popular options is **release on recognizance (ROR)**. This is used when the judge, based on the advice of trained personnel, decides that the defendant is not at risk to "jump" bail and does not pose a threat to the community. The defendant is then released at no cost with the understanding that he or she will return at the time of the trial. The Vera Institute, a nonprofit organization in New York City, introduced the concept of ROR as part of the Manhattan Bail Project in the 1960s, and such programs are now found in nearly every jurisdiction. When properly administered, ROR programs seem to be successful, with less than 5 percent of the participants failing to show for trial.[42]

Posting Bail Those suspected of committing a felony, however, are rarely released on recognizance. These defendants may post, or pay, the full amount of the bail in cash to the court. The money will be returned when the suspect appears for trial. Given the large amount of funds involved, and the relative lack of wealth of many criminal defendants, a defendant can rarely post bail in cash. Another option is to use personal property as collateral. These *property bonds* are also rare because most courts require property valued at double the bail amount. Thus, if bail is set at $5,000, the defendant (or the defendant's family and friends) will have to produce a piece of property valued at $10,000.

Bail Bondspersons If unable to post bail with cash or property, a defendant may arrange for a **bail bondsperson** to post a bail bond on the defendant's behalf. The bondsperson, in effect, promises the court that he or she will turn over to the court the full amount of bail if the defendant fails to return for further proceedings. The defendant usually must give the bondsperson a certain percentage of the bail (often 10 percent) in cash. This amount, which is often not returned to the defendant later, is considered payment for the bondsperson's assistance and assumption of risk. Depending on the amount of the bail bond, the defendant may also be required to sign over to the bondsperson rights to certain property (such as a car, a valuable watch, or other asset) as security for the bond.

Although bail bondspersons obviously provide a service for which there is demand, several states have abolished bail bonding for profit.[43] The rationale for such reform focuses on two perceived problems with the practice.

1 Bail bondspersons provide opportunities for corruption, as they may bribe officials who set bail (police and the like) to inflate the bail.

See the **Professional Bail Agents of the United States** for a wealth of information about how bail bondspersons operate. Find its Web site by clicking on *Web Links* under *Chapter Resources* at **www.cjinaction.com**.

2 Because they can refuse to post a bail bond, bail bondspersons are, in essence, making a business decision concerning a suspect's pretrial release. This is considered the responsibility of a judge, not a private individual with a profit motive.[44]

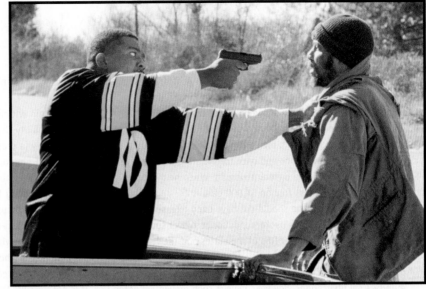

Beau Cabell, *The Macon Telegraph*

The states that have banned bail bondspersons have established an alternative known as **ten percent cash bail.** This process, pioneered in Chicago in the early 1960s, requires the court, in effect, to take the place of the bondsperson. An officer of the court will accept a deposit of 10 percent of the bail amount, refundable when the defendant appears at the assigned time.[45] A number of jurisdictions allow for both bail bondspersons and ten percent cash bail, with the judge deciding whether a defendant is eligible for the latter.

In Macon, Georgia, bounty hunter Cedric Miller takes aim at Stan Bernard Rouse. Miller, a former Macon narcotics cop, is often paid substantial sums by bail bondspersons to capture bond-jumping clients.

Bounty Hunters Supreme Court Justice Robert Jackson once called the possibility that an accused person would not return to face trial "a calculated risk which the law takes as the price of our system of justice."[46] This risk is often taken by bail bondspersons, who suffer a monetary loss if a suspect skips bail. To protect their financial interests, bail bondspersons sometimes hire a *bounty hunter* to retrieve a client who has skipped bail. Under a Supreme Court decision issued in 1873, bounty hunters have almost unlimited power to apprehend someone who has signed a bail contract, including imprisoning the fugitive and breaking and entering into his or her house.[47]

Despite the police powers involved, bounty hunting is essentially unregulated in most of the United States. Only seven states require that bounty hunters be licensed, while another seven states restrict their activities and four (Illinois, Kentucky, Oregon, and Wisconsin) have banned the practice outright. This lack of control becomes an issue when a bounty hunter uses deadly force improperly, as occurred in 2004 when Mark Smith killed Michael Robinson in Butler County, Pennsylvania. Smith shot Robinson after the fugitive swiped at him with a "shiny silver object" that turned out to be a toenail clipper. Following the incident, the Pennsylvania legislature began discussing a bill that would require all state bounty hunters to be licensed and take lethal weapons training.[48]

Bail Reform and Preventive Detention

Release on recognizance programs and ten percent cash bail were the result of a movement in the 1960s to reform the bail system. As various researchers produced empirical proof that pretrial detention increased the odds of conviction and led to longer sentences, reformers began to point out that this created an imbalance of justice between the wealthy and the poor.[49] Those who could afford to post bail were convicted less frequently and spent less time in jail than those who could not. Furthermore, the conditions in pretrial detention centers were considerably worse than the conditions in prison, and the cost of maintaining these centers was becoming prohibitive.

Ten Percent Cash Bail
An alternative to traditional bail in which defendants may gain pretrial release by posting 10 percent of their bond amount to the court instead of seeking a bail bondsperson.

Innocent on Bail?

Sylvia Hernandez was stabbed to death in Austin, Texas, by Leonard Saldana, her common law husband. Saldana, it turned out, had been arrested a month earlier for violating a court order to keep away from Hernandez. He had been jailed nineteen times in ten years, including four times for assaults involving domestic violence and once for violating a protective court order concerning a different woman. When he murdered Hernandez, Saldana was free on $4,000 bail.

In retrospect, Saldana should not have been released for such a small amount, given his background. Concern over such situations has convinced three-fifths of the states and the federal government to pass laws that allow judges to confine suspects before trial without bail if there is a threat of harm to the community. Civil libertarians, however, believe such preventive detention laws unjustly sacrifice the individual's right to be presumed innocent to a generally unsubstantiated government interest in pretrial detention. Supreme Court Justice Thurgood Marshall, in his dissent in the case in which the Bail Reform Act of 1984 was upheld, wrote that the denial of due process in such judicial decisions was "consistent with the usage of tyranny and the excesses of what bitter experience teaches us to call the police state."

The main criticism of preventive detention is that it presumes a certain ability to predict future criminal activity on the basis of past activity (a presumption that is usually not allowed in criminal trials). Criminologist Charles Ewing has concluded that statistical predictions about violent criminal behavior are "much more likely to be wrong than right." Some observers believe preventive detention will be used indiscriminately by judges who do not want to risk being criticized for freeing a suspect who goes on to commit a crime while out on bail. Furthermore, though it is possible to measure how many suspects eligible to be detained under these laws committed violent crimes after being released, it is not possible to determine how many of those who were detained would *not* have committed crimes if freed.

FOR CRITICAL ANALYSIS
Given the relatively low rate of criminal activity by suspects who have been released pending trial, are preventive detention laws justified?

The Bail Reform Acts In response to these concerns, Congress passed the Bail Reform Act of 1966.[50] Though the new law did not place statutory restrictions on the discretionary powers of federal judges, it did strongly suggest that judges implement a wide range of "conditions of release" for suspects who qualified.[51]

The Bail Reform Act of 1966 was criticized for concentrating on ways of increasing pretrial release, while failing to give judges the ability to detain suspects who posed a danger to the community.[52] Although judges have always had the *de facto* power to do just that by setting prohibitively high bails for dangerous defendants, thirty states have passed **preventive detention** laws that allow judges to deny bail to suspects with prior records of violence or nonappearance for trial. The Bail Reform Act of 1984 similarly states that federal offenders can be held without bail to assure "the safety of any other person and the community."[53]

The Constitutionality of Bail Critics of the 1984 act believe that it violates the U.S. Constitution by allowing the freedom of a citizen to be restricted before he or she has been proved guilty in a court of law. For many, the act also brings up the troubling issue of *false positives*—erroneous predictions that defendants, if given pretrial release, would commit a crime, when in fact they would not. (See the feature *CJ in Focus—The Balancing Act: Innocent on Bail?*) In *United States v. Salerno* (1987),[54] however, the Supreme Court upheld the act's premise. Then Chief Justice William Rehnquist wrote that preventive detention was not a "punishment for dangerous individuals" but a "potential solution to a pressing social problem." Therefore, "there is no doubt that preventing danger to the community is a legitimate . . . goal." In fact, about 16 percent of released defendants are rearrested before their trials begin, 7 percent for violent felonies.[55]

Preventive Detention
The retention of an accused person in custody due to fears that she or he will commit a crime if released before trial.

ESTABLISHING PROBABLE CAUSE

Once the initial appearance has been completed and bail has been set, the prosecutor must establish *probable cause;* that is, the prosecutor must prove that a crime was committed and link the defendant to that crime. There are two formal procedures for establishing probable cause at this stage of the pretrial process: preliminary hearings and grand juries.

The Preliminary Hearing

During the **preliminary hearing,** the defendant appears before a judge or magistrate who decides whether the evidence presented is sufficient for the case to proceed to trial. Normally, every person charged by warrant has a right to this hearing within a reasonable amount of time after his or her initial arrest[56]—typically, no later than ten days if the defendant is in custody or within thirty days if he or she has gained pretrial release.

The Preliminary Hearing Process The preliminary hearing is conducted in the manner of a mini-trial. Typically, a police report of the arrest is presented by a law enforcement officer, supplemented with evidence provided by the prosecutor. Because the burden of proving probable cause is relatively light (compared to proving guilt beyond a reasonable doubt), prosecutors rarely call witnesses during the preliminary hearing, saving them for the trial. During this hearing, the defendant has a right to be represented by counsel, who may cross-examine witnesses and challenge any evidence offered by the prosecutor. In most states, defense attorneys can take advantage of the preliminary hearing to begin the process of **discovery,** in which they are entitled to have access to any evidence in the possession of the prosecution relating to the case. Discovery is considered a keystone in the adversary process, as it allows the defense to see the evidence against the defendant prior to making a plea.

Waiving the Hearing The preliminary hearing often seems rather perfunctory, although in some jurisdictions it replaces grand jury proceedings. It usually lasts no longer than five minutes, and the judge or magistrate rarely finds that probable cause does not exist. In one study, only 2 percent of the cases were dismissed by the judicial official at this stage in the process.[57] For this reason, defense attorneys commonly advise their clients to waive their right to a preliminary hearing. Once a judge has ruled affirmatively on probable cause, the defendant is bound over to the grand jury in many jurisdictions. If the grand jury believes there are grounds for a trial, it issues an *indictment.* In other jurisdictions, the government prosecutor issues an **information,** which replaces the police complaint as the formal charge against the defendant for the purposes of a trial.

The Grand Jury

The federal government and about half of the states require a grand jury to make the decision as to whether a case should go to trial. A **grand jury** is a group of citizens called to decide whether probable cause exists. Grand juries are *impaneled,* or created, for a period of time usually not exceeding three months. During that time, the grand jury sits in closed (secret) session and hears only evidence presented by the prosecutor—the defendant cannot present evidence at this hearing. The prosecutor presents to the grand jury whatever evidence the state has against the defendant, including photographs, documents, tangible objects, the testimony of witnesses, and other

Preliminary Hearing
An initial hearing in which a magistrate decides if there is probable cause to believe that the defendant committed the crime with which he or she is charged.

Discovery
Formal investigation prior to trial. During discovery, the defense uses various methods to obtain information from the prosecution to prepare for trial.

Information
The formal charge against the accused issued by the prosecutor after a preliminary hearing has found probable cause.

Grand Jury
The group of citizens called to decide whether probable cause exists to believe that a suspect committed the crime with which she or he has been charged.

Indictment

A charge or written accusation, issued by a grand jury, that probable cause exists to believe that a named person has committed a crime.

items. If the grand jury finds that probable cause exists, it issues an **indictment** (pronounced in-*dyte*-ment) against the defendant. Like an information in a preliminary hearing, the indictment becomes the formal charge against the defendant. As Figure 9.5 shows, some states require a grand jury to indict for certain crimes, while in other states a grand jury indictment is optional.

The "Shield" and the "Sword" The grand jury has a long history in the United States, having been brought over from England by the colonists and codified in the Fifth Amendment to the U.S. Constitution. Historically, it has acted as both a "shield" and a "sword" in the criminal justice process. By giving citizens the chance to review government charges of wrongdoing, it "shields" the individual from the power of the state. At the same time, the grand jury offers the government a "sword"—the opportunity to provide evidence against the accused—in its efforts to fight crime and protect society.[58]

A "Rubber Stamp" Today, the protective function of the grand jury is in doubt—critics say that the "sword" aspect works too well and the "shield" aspect not at all. Statistically, the grand jury is even more prosecutor friendly than the preliminary hearing. Defendants are indicted at a rate of more than 99 percent,[59] leading to the common characterization of the grand jury as little more than a "rubber stamp" for the prosecution. Certainly, the procedural rules of the grand jury favor prosecutors. The exclusionary rule (see Chapter 7) does not apply in grand jury investigations, so prosecutors can present evidence that would be disallowed at any subsequent trial. Furthermore, because the grand jury is given only one version of the facts—the prosecution's—it is likely to find probable cause. In the words of one observer, a grand jury would indict a "ham sandwich" if the government asked it to do so.[60] As a result of these concerns, more than half of the jurisdictions have abolished grand juries.

FIGURE 9.5
State Grand Jury Requirements

As you can see, in some states a grand jury indictment is required to charge an individual with a crime, while in others it is either optional or prohibited. When a grand jury is not used, the discretion of whether to charge is left to the prosecutor, who must then present his or her argument at the preliminary hearing (discussed earlier in the chapter).

Source: Bureau of Justice Statistics, *State Court Organization 1998* (Washington, D.C.: U.S. Department of Justice, June 2000), 283–285.

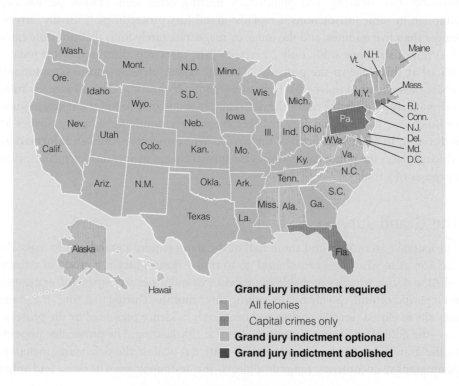

Japan's All-Powerful Prosecutors

Prosecutors in the United States are generally believed to have a great deal of charging discretion. The discretionary power of American prosecutors, however, does not equal that of their Japanese counterparts. With the ability to "cherry pick" their cases, prosecutors in Japan routinely have annual conviction rates of over 99.9 percent.

THE "CONFESSION MILL"
One observer described the Japanese courts as a "confession mill." Unlike the American system, Japan has no arraignment procedure during which the accused can plead guilty or innocent. Instead, the focus of the Japanese criminal justice system is on extracting confessions of guilt: police can hold and question suspects for up to twenty-three days without pressing charges. Furthermore, the suspect has no absolute right to counsel during the interrogation, and police are often able to get confessions that make for open-and-shut convictions. The prosecutor also has the "benevolent" discretion to drop the case altogether if the suspect expresses remorse.

The extraordinarily high conviction rate is also a product of Japanese culture. To fail in an attempt to convict results in a loss of face, not only for the individual prosecutor but also for the court system as a whole. The Japanese Justice Ministry estimates that, to avoid the risk of losing, prosecutors decline to press charges against 35 percent of indictable suspects each year. Japanese judges—there are no juries—contribute to the high conviction rate by rarely questioning the manner in which prosecutors obtain confessions.

NO PLEA BARGAINING
Interestingly, given the amount of prosecutorial discretion, the Japanese criminal justice system does not allow for plea bargaining. The Japanese see the practice of "trading" a guilty plea for a lesser sentence as counterproductive, as a defendant may be tempted to confess to crimes she or he did not commit if the prosecution has a strong case. For the Japanese, a confession extracted after twenty-three days of interrogation may be "voluntary," but a confession gained through a promise of leniency is "forced" and therefore in conflict with the system's goals of truth seeking and accuracy.

FOR CRITICAL ANALYSIS
Explain the fundamental differences between the American and Japanese criminal justice systems. Do you think the lack of a comparable adversarial system weakens or strengthens the Japanese system in comparison with the American one?

THE PROSECUTORIAL SCREENING PROCESS

Some see the high government success rates in pretrial proceedings as proof that prosecutors successfully screen out weak cases before they get to a grand jury or preliminary hearing. If, however, grand juries have indeed abandoned their traditional duties in favor of "rubber stamping" most cases set in front of them, and preliminary hearings are little better, what is to keep prosecutors from using their charging powers indiscriminately? Nothing, say many observers. Once the police have initially charged a defendant with committing a crime, the prosecutor can prosecute the case as it stands, reduce or increase the initial charge, file additional charges, or dismiss the case. In a system of government and law that relies on checks and balances, asked legal expert Kenneth Culp Davis, why should the prosecutor be "immune to review by other officials and immune to review by the courts?"[61] (For information on another prosecutor-friendly system, see the feature *International CJ—Japan's All-Powerful Prosecutors.*)

Though American prosecutors have far-ranging discretionary charging powers, it is not entirely correct to say that they are unrestricted. Controls are indirect and informal, but they do exist.

Case Attrition

Prosecutorial discretion includes the power *not* to prosecute cases. Figure 9.6 on the next page depicts the average outcomes of one hundred felony arrests in the United States. As you can see, of the sixty-five adult arrestees brought before the district attorney, only thirty-five were prosecuted, and only eighteen of these prosecutions led to incarceration. Consequently, only one in three and a half adults arrested for a felony

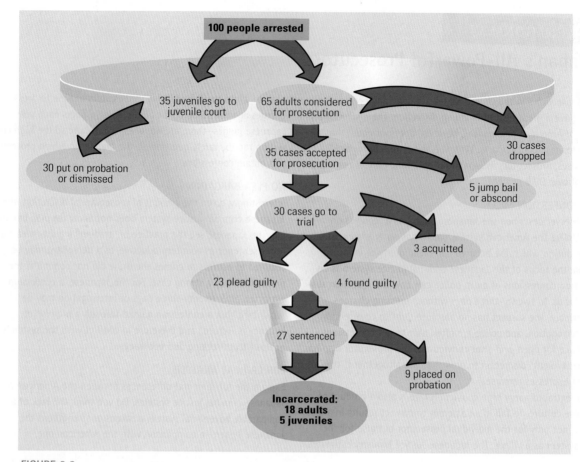

FIGURE 9.6

Following One Hundred Felony Arrests: The Criminal Justice Funnel

Source: Brian Reaves and Pheny Smith, *Felony Defendants in Large Urban Counties, 1992* (Washington D.C.: Bureau of Justice Statistics, 1995).

sees the inside of a prison or jail cell. This phenomenon is known as **case attrition,** and it is explained in part by prosecutorial discretion.

About half of those adult felony cases brought to prosecutors by police are dismissed through a *nolle prosequi.* Why are these cases "nolled," or not prosecuted by the district attorney? In the section on law enforcement, you learned that the police do not have the resources to arrest every lawbreaker in the nation. Similarly, district attorneys do not have the resources to prosecute every arrest. They must choose how to distribute their scarce resources. In some cases, the decision is made for them, such as when police break procedural law and negate important evidence. This happens rarely—less than 1 percent of felony arrests are dropped because of the exclusionary rule, and almost all of these are the result of illegal drug searches.[62]

Most prosecutors have a *screening process* for deciding when to prosecute and when to "noll." This process varies a bit from jurisdiction to jurisdiction, but most prosecutors consider several factors in making the decision:

- The most important factor in deciding whether to prosecute is not the prosecutor's belief in the guilt of the suspect, but whether there is *sufficient evidence for conviction.*[63] If prosecutors have strong physical evidence and a number of reliable and believable witnesses, they are quite likely to prosecute.

> "Let me tell you, you can paint pictures and get people indicted for just about anything."
>
> —Alfonse D'Amato, former U.S. senator from New York (1996)

Case Attrition

The process through which prosecutors, by deciding whether to prosecute each person arrested, effect an overall reduction in the number of persons prosecuted. As a result, the number of persons convicted and sentenced is much smaller than the number of persons arrested.

- Prosecutors also tend to establish *case priorities.* In other words, everything else being equal, a district attorney will prose-cute a rapist instead of a jaywalker because the former presents a greater threat to soci-ety than does the lat-ter. A prosecutor will also be more likely to prosecute someone with an extensive record of wrongdoing than a first-time offender. Often, in coordination with the police, a district attor-ney's office will target a single area of crime, such as drug use or drunk driving.

- Sometimes a case is dropped even when it involves a serious crime and a wealth of evidence exists against the suspect. These situations usually involve *uncooperative victims.* In the early 2000s, about 54 percent of domestic violence cases in South Carolina never made it to circuit court because the victims were missing or uncooperative. In response, the state's attorney general issued a general order that prosecutors were not to drop such cases unless there was no evidence other than the victim's testimony.[64]

- *Unreliability of victims* can also affect a charging decision. If the victim in a rape case is a crack addict and a prostitute, while the defendant is the chief executive officer of a large corporation, prosecutors may be hesitant to have a jury decide which one is more trustworthy.

- A prosecutor may be willing to drop a case, or reduce the charges, against a *defendant who is willing to testify against other offenders.* In New Jersey, for example, prosecutors are allowed to waive mandatory sentencing laws for low-level drug traffickers who agree to "snitch," or give the police information on major narcotics suppliers.[65]

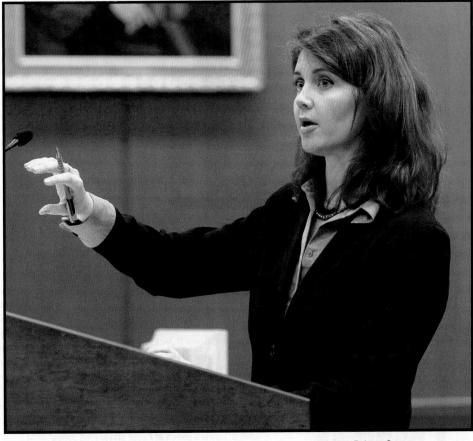

In 2005, Fulton County prosecutor Anna Green tries to convince the Georgia Supreme Court that her office should be allowed to charge James Sullivan for the murder of his wife. Federal prosecutors, in contrast, had already indicted Sullivan for hiring someone else to commit the crime. Why would different prosecutors' offices come up with different charges for the same act?

Politics and personal beliefs can also play a role in prosecutorial action. In 2005, for example, Kansas Attorney General Phil Kline, an outspoken opponent of abortion, made national headlines when he demanded the medical records of ninety women and girls who had undergone the procedure. Though Kline justified the request as a search for evidence of statutory rape, many observers believe that his actual targets were doctors who performed abortions after the twenty-second week of pregnancy, a pro-cedure that is against Kansas law.[66] (For more insight on how prosecutors make a charging decision, see Figure 9.7 on the following page.)

Tom Pidgeon/Getty Images

FIGURE 9.7
Prosecutors at Work
On November 19, 2004, an ugly brawl involving players from the Indiana Pacers professional basketball team and fans took place at The Palace of Auburn Hills, Michigan. Oakland County prosecutors reviewed ten video feeds and read through more than 1,000 pages of documents before deciding the criminal charges that would stem from the incident.

Defendant: **John F.. Green, fan**
Actions: **Threw a plastic cup at Pacer player Ron Artest, which, according to prosecutors, touched off the brawl**
Charge: **Misdemeanor assault and battery***

Defendant: **Ron Artest, Pacer**
Actions: **Went into the stands and knocked over fan Michael Ryan whom he mistakenly believed was responsible for tossing the plastic cup. Artest punched several other fans during the melee, but prosecutors believed his attack on Ryan was the only altercation that was not self-defense (see page 112)**
Charge: **Misdemeanor assault and battery**

Defendant: **Bryan D.Jackson, fan**
Actions: **Threw a folding chair at Pacer players**
Charge: **Felonious assault****

Defendant: **David Wallace, fan**
Actions: **Threw a punch at Pacer player Fred Jones**
Charge: **Misdemeanor assault and battery**

Defendant: **Jermaine O'Neal, Pacer**
Actions: **Threw usher Melvin Kendziorski over a courtside table and punched fan Michael Haddad, who ran onto the court during the brawl**
Charge: **Two counts of misdemeanor assault and battery**

Defendant: **John Frederick Anderson, fan**
Actions: **Threw a drink at Pacer player Jermaine O'Neal**
Charge: **Misdemeanor assault and battery**

Defendant: **William Paulson, fan**
Actions: **Threw a drink at Pacer players**
Charge: **Misdemeanor assault and battery**

Defendant: **David Harrison, Pacer**
Actions: **Threw a punch at fan John Frederick Anderson**
Charge: **Misdemeanor assault and battery**

Defendant: **Stephen Jackson, Pacer**
Actions: **Went into the stands and punched fan William Paulson**
Charge: **Misdemeanor assault and battery**

Defendant: **Anthony Johnson, Pacer**
Actions: **Threw a punch at fan Michael Haddad**
Charge: **Misdemeanor assault and battery**

*Misdemeanor assault and battery: Intent to commit violence, the present ability to carry out the intent, and the act done, with no other punishment available. Maximum penalty: 93 days in jail or $500 fine, or both.

**Felonious assault: Assault with a gun, revolver, pistol, knife, iron bar, club, brass knuckles, or other dangerous weapon without intending to commit murder or to inflict great bodily harm. Maximum penalty: 4 years' imprisonment or $2,000 fine, or both.

Source: Michigan Penal Code. Photos: AP

Prosecutorial Charging and the Defense Attorney

For the most part, there is little the defense attorney can do when the prosecutor decides to charge a client. If a defense attorney feels strongly that the charge has been made in violation of the defendant's rights, he or she can, however, submit *pretrial motions* to the court requesting that a particular action be taken to protect his or her client. Pretrial motions include the following:

1 Motions to suppress evidence gained illegally.
2 Motions for a change of venue because the defendant cannot receive a fair trial in the original jurisdiction.
3 Motions to invalidate a search warrant.
4 Motions to dismiss the case because of a delay in bringing it to trial.
5 Motions to obtain evidence that the prosecution may be withholding.

As we shall soon see, defense attorneys sometimes use these pretrial motions to pressure the prosecution into offering a favorable deal for their client.

PLEADING GUILTY

Based on the information (delivered during the preliminary hearing) or indictment (handed down by the grand jury), the prosecutor submits a motion to the court to order the defendant to appear before the trial court for an **arraignment.** Due process of law, as guaranteed by the Fifth Amendment, requires that a criminal defendant be informed of the charges brought against her or him and be offered an opportunity to respond to those charges. The arraignment is one of the ways in which due process requirements are satisfied by criminal procedure law.

At the arraignment, the defendant is informed of the charges and must respond by pleading not guilty or guilty. In some but not all states, the defendant may also enter a plea of **nolo contendere,** which is Latin for "I will not contest it." The plea of *nolo contendere* is neither an admission nor a denial of guilt. (The consequences for someone who pleads guilty and for someone who pleads *nolo contendere* are the same in a criminal trial, but the latter plea cannot be used in a subsequent civil trial as an admission of guilt.) Most frequently, the defendant pleads guilty to the initial charge or to a lesser charge that has been agreed on through *plea bargaining* between the prosecutor and the defendant. If the defendant pleads guilty, no trial is necessary, and the defendant is sentenced based on the crime he or she has admitted committing.

Plea Bargaining in the Criminal Justice System

Plea bargaining usually takes place after the arraignment and before the beginning of the trial. In its simplest terms, it is a process by which the accused, represented by the defense counsel, and the prosecutor work out a mutually satisfactory disposition of the case, subject to court approval. Plea bargaining agreements can take several different forms:

• *Charge bargaining.* In charge bargaining, the defendant pleads guilty in exchange for a reduction of the charges. A felony burglary charge, for example, could be reduced to the lesser offense of breaking and entering. The more serious the initial charge, the more an accused has to gain by bargaining: pleading guilty to second degree murder can save the defendant from the risk of being convicted of first degree murder, which carries the death penalty in some states.

Arraignment

A court proceeding in which the suspect is formally charged with the criminal offense stated in the indictment. The suspect enters a plea (guilty, not guilty, *nolo contendere*) in response.

Nolo Contendere

Latin for "I will not contest it." A criminal defendant's plea, in which he or she chooses not to challenge, or contest, the charges brought by the government. Although the defendant may still be sentenced or fined, the plea neither admits nor denies guilt.

Plea Bargaining

The process by which the accused and the prosecutor work out a mutually satisfactory conclusion to the case, subject to court approval. Usually, plea bargaining involves the defendant's pleading guilty to a lesser offense in return for a lighter sentence.

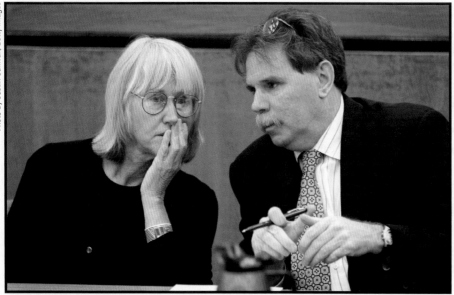

Photo by Justin Sullivan/Getty Images

Sara Jane Olson, left, in a Sacramento, California, courtroom. In 2003, Olson, a former member of the Symbionese Liberation Army, was sentenced to six years in prison after pleading guilty to being involved in a 1975 murder carried out by other members of the group. Olson later told reporters that she was innocent of the charges but had made "a deal" to avoid a possible life sentence if found guilty at trial.

- *Sentence bargaining.* In sentence bargaining, the defendant pleads guilty in exchange for a lighter sentence, which may include a shorter prison term or probation. In most jurisdictions, the judge makes the final decision on whether to accept this agreement; the prosecutor can only recommend a lighter sentence. The prosecutor may also suggest that the defendant be placed in a counseling program, such as a drug rehabilitation center, in return for the guilty plea.
- *Count bargaining.* A person can be charged with multiple counts, either for committing multiple crimes or for different aspects of a single incident. A person who goes on a killing spree that results in seven deaths, for example, would be charged with seven counts of first degree murder. A person who breaks into a home, sexually assaults the inhabitants, and then takes their credit cards could be charged with counts of rape, aggravated burglary, misdemeanor theft, felony theft, and criminal use of a credit card. In count bargaining, a defendant pleads guilty in exchange for a reduction in the counts against him or her.

In a sense, count bargaining is a form of sentence bargaining. If a person is convicted of multiple counts, her or his prison time is calculated by combining the attendant sentence of each count (which is why some criminals are sentenced to a seemingly ridiculously long prison term, well past their life expectancy). If a count is dropped, so is the prison time that goes with it.

In *Santobello v. New York* (1971),[67] the Supreme Court held that plea bargaining "is not only an essential part of the process but a highly desirable part for many reasons." Many observers would agree, but with ambivalence. They understand that plea bargaining offers the practical benefit of saving court resources, but question whether it is the best way to achieve justice.[68] Given the pressures placed on the court system, many participants conclude that plea bargaining is, in fact, an ethically acceptable means of determining the defendant's fate.

Motivations for Plea Bargaining

Given the high rate of plea bargaining—see Figure 9.8—it follows that the prosecutor, defense attorney, and defendant each have strong reasons to engage in the practice.

Prosecutors and Plea Bargaining In most cases, a prosecutor has a single goal after charging a defendant with a crime: conviction. If a case goes to trial, no matter how certain a prosecutor may be that the defendant is guilty, there is always a chance that a jury or judge will disagree. Plea bargaining removes this risk. Furthermore, the prosecutorial screening process described earlier in the chapter is not infallible. Sometimes, a prosecutor will find that the evidence against the accused is weaker than first thought or will uncover new information that changes the complexion of the case. In these sit-

Violent Offense   **Property Offense**   **Drug Offense**

FIGURE 9.8
Rates of Plea Bargaining

As you can see, most convictions are gained when the defendant pleads guilty.

Source: Bureau of Justice Statistics, *State Court Sentencing of Convicted Felons, 2000* (Washington, D.C.: U.S. Department of Justice, June 2003), Table 4.2, page 43.

uations, the prosecutor may decide to drop the charges or, if he or she still feels that the defendant is guilty, turn to plea bargaining to "save" a questionable case.

The prosecutor's role as an administrator also comes into play. She or he may be interested in the quickest, most efficient manner to dispose of caseloads, and plea bargains reduce the time and money spent on each case. Personal philosophy can affect the proceedings as well. A prosecutor who feels that a mandatory minimum sentence for a particular crime, such as marijuana possession, is too strict may plea bargain in order to lessen the penalty. Similarly, some prosecutors will consider plea bargaining only in certain instances—for burglary and theft, for example, but not for more serious felonies such as rape and murder.[69]

Defense Attorneys and Plea Bargaining Political scientist Milton Heumann has said that the most important thing that a defense attorney learns is that "most of his [or her] clients are guilty."[70] Given this stark reality, favorable plea bargains are often the best a defense attorney can do for clients, aside from helping them to gain acquittals. Some have suggested that defense attorneys have other, less savory motives for convincing a client to plead guilty, such as a desire to increase profit margins by quickly disposing of cases[71] or a wish to ingratiate themselves with the other members of the courtroom work group by showing their "reasonableness."[72] In other cases, a defense attorney may want to go to trial, even though it is *not* in the client's best interest, to win publicity or gain work experience.[73]

Defendants and Plea Bargaining The plea bargain allows the defendant a measure of control over his or her fate. When Eric Rudolph accepted the deal offered by prosecutors, as discussed in the introduction to this chapter, he guaranteed that he would not be executed and could live out the rest of his years in prison. The benefits of plea bargaining are tangible. As Figure 9.9 on p. 298 shows, defendants who plea bargain receive significantly lighter sentences on average than those who are found guilty at trial.

Victims and Plea Bargaining One of the major goals of the victims' rights movement, discussed in Chapter 2, has been to increase the role of victims in the plea bargaining process. In recent years, the movement has had some success in this area. About half of the states now allow for victim participation in plea bargaining. Many have laws similar to North Carolina's statute that requires the district attorney's office to offer victims "the opportunity to consult with the prosecuting attorney" and give their views on "plea possibilities."[74] On the federal level, the Crime Victims' Rights Act (see page 55) grants victims the right to be "reasonably heard" during the process.[75] If they choose, prosecutors can provide victims with more of a voice. Recall that in the

FIGURE 9.9
Sentencing Outcomes
for Guilty Pleas

Source: Adapted from Bureau of Justice Statistics, *State Court Sentencing of Convicted Felons, 2000* (Washington, D.C.: U.S. Department of Justice, June 2003), Table 4.5.

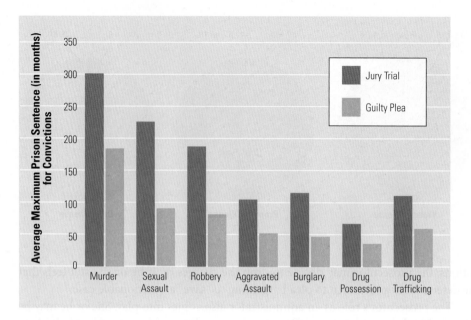

chapter introduction we saw how federal officials allowed victims of Eric Rudolph's bombing to dictate the course of the plea negotiations.

Plea Bargaining and the Adversary System

One criticism of plea bargaining is that it subverts the adversary system, the goal of which is to determine innocence or guilt. Although plea bargaining does value negotiation over conflict, it is important to remember that it does so in a context in which legal guilt has already been established. Even within this context, plea bargaining is not completely divorced from the adversary process.

Strategies to Induce a Plea Bargain Earlier, we pointed out that the most likely reason why a prosecutor does not bring charges is the lack of a strong case. This is also the most common reason why a prosecutor agrees to a plea bargain once charges have been brought. Defense attorneys are well aware of this fact and often file numerous pretrial motions in an effort to weaken the state's case. Even if the judge does not accept the motions, the defense may hope that the time required to process them will wear on the prosecutor's patience. As one district attorney has said, "the usual defense strategy today is to bring in a stack of motions as thick as a Sunday newspaper; defense attorneys hope that we won't have the patience to ride them out."[76]

Prosecutors have their own methods of inducing a plea bargain. The most common is the ethically questionable practice of *overcharging;* that is, charging the defendant with more counts than may be appropriate. There are two types of overcharging:

1 In *horizontal overcharging,* the prosecutor brings a number of different counts for a single criminal incident.

2 In *vertical overcharging,* the prosecutor raises the level of a charge above its proper place. For example, the facts of the case warrant a charge of battery, but the prosecutor charges the defendant with attempted murder.

After overcharging, prosecutors allow themselves to be "bargained down" to the correct charge, giving the defense attorney and the defendant the impression that they have achieved some sort of victory.

Protecting the Defendant Watching the defense attorney and the prosecutor maneuver in this manner, the defendant often comes to the conclusion that the plea bargaining process is a sort of game with sometimes incomprehensible rules.[77] The Supreme Court is also aware of the potential for taking advantage of the defendant in plea bargaining and has taken steps to protect the accused. Until *Boykin v. Alabama* (1969),[78] judges would often accept the defense counsel's word that the defendant wanted to plead guilty. In that case, the Court held that the defendant must make a clear statement that he or she accepts the plea bargain. As a result, many jurisdictions now ask the accused to sign a ***Boykin* form** waiving his or her right to a trial. A statement in which the defendant admits exactly what crime he or she committed must accompany this guilty plea. (For other important cases involving plea bargaining procedures, see Figure 9.10.)

Boykin Form
A form that must be completed by a defendant who pleads guilty; the defendant states that she or he has done so voluntarily and with full comprehension of the consequences.

Is Plea Bargaining Inevitable?

Observers on both sides of the criminal justice "fence" feel that the compromises inherent in plea bargaining make the process unjust. Those interested in protecting due process believe that negotiated pleas deny defendants the stricter procedural protections of a criminal trial.[79] Furthermore, the practice gives innocent people an incentive to plead guilty if they feel that the evidence is against them. For their part, those committed to crime control believe that plea bargaining allows dangerous criminals to "beat the

> "I pleaded guilty on second degree murder because they said there is too much evidence, but I ain't shot no man, but I take the fault for the other man. . . . I just pleaded guilty because they said if I didn't they would gas me for it, and that is all."
>
> —Henry Alford, who claimed that he pleaded guilty to a murder charge only because he faced the threat of the death penalty if the case went to trial (1970)

FIGURE 9.10

Notable United States Supreme Court Decisions on Plea Bargaining

The constitutional justification of the plea bargain as an accepted part of the criminal justice process has been fortified by these Supreme Court rulings.

Brady v. United States (397 U.S. 742 [1970]). In this case, the defendant entered a guilty plea in order to avoid the death penalty. In allowing this action, the Court ruled that plea bargains are a legitimate part of the adjudication process as long as they are entered into voluntarily and the defendant has full knowledge of the consequences of pleading guilty.

North Carolina v. Alford (400 U.S. 25 [1970]). Although maintaining he was innocent of the first degree murder for which he was charged, Alford pleaded guilty to second degree murder in order to avoid the possibility of the death penalty that came with the original charges. After being sentenced to thirty years in prison, Alford argued that he was forced to plea bargain because of the threat of the death penalty. The Court refused to invalidate Alford's guilty plea, stating that plea bargains are valid even if the defendant claims innocence, as long as the plea was entered into voluntarily.

Santobello v. New York (404 U.S. 257 [1971]). This case focused on the prosecutor's role in the plea bargain process. The Court ruled that if a prosecutor promises a more lenient sentence in return for the defendant's guilty plea, the promise must be kept.

Bordenkircher v. Hayes (434 U.S. 357 [1978]). A Kentucky prosecutor told Hayes that if he entered a guilty plea, the prosecutor would recommend a light sentence. If not, he would indict Hayes under the state's habitual offender act, which carried the possibility of life imprisonment. The Court ruled that prosecutors are within their rights to threaten defendants with harsher sentences in order to induce a guilty plea.

Ricketts v. Adamson (483 U.S. 1 [1987]). In return for a reduction of charges, Ricketts agreed to plead guilty and to testify against a co-defendant in a murder case. When the co-defendant's conviction was reversed on appeal, Ricketts refused to testify a second time. Therefore, the prosecutor rescinded his offer of leniency. The Court ruled that the prosecutor's action was justified, and that defendants must uphold their side of the plea bargain in order to receive its benefits.

United States v. Mezzanatto (513 U.S. 196 [1995]). The Court ruled that a prosecutor can refuse to plea bargain with a defendant unless the defendant agrees that any statements made by him or her during the bargaining process can be used against him or her in a possible trial. In other words, if the defendant admits to committing the crime during plea bargain negotiations, and then decides to plead not guilty, the prosecution can use the admission as evidence during the trial.

system" by negotiating for lighter sentences than they deserve; consequently, these observers feel that it undermines the deterrent effects of punishment.[80]

It is not easy to combat these criticisms. Instead, proponents of plea bargaining argue that although it may not be the ideal solution to problems such as overwhelming caseloads, it is the best one available under the circumstances. In a 1970 speech to the American Bar Association, then Supreme Court Chief Justice Warren Burger said:

> The consequences of what might seem on its face a small percentage change in the rate of guilty pleas can be tremendous. A reduction from 90 percent to 80 percent in guilty pleas requires the assignment of twice the judicial manpower and facilities—judges, court reporters, bailiffs, clerks, jurors and courtrooms. A reduction to 70 percent trebles this demand.[81]

Was Chief Justice Burger correct in stating, essentially, that the court system could not function without plea bargaining? Several jurisdictions have tested this assumption by banning the procedure. In the 1970s, the city of El Paso, Texas, had to abandon the experiment after its caseloads increased by 250 percent within three years.[82] Around the same time, Alaska went through a five-year plea bargaining ban without a significant jump in trials, as did Bronx County, New York, in the 1990s. In both those jurisdictions, however, prosecutors and defense attorneys sidestepped the prohibition with implicit rather than explicit plea negotiations.[83] Consequently, it does seem that plea bargaining is a necessary—and permanent—part of the criminal justice system.

GOING TO TRIAL

The pretrial process does not inexorably lead to a guilty plea. Just as prosecutors, defense attorneys, and defendants have reasons to negotiate, they may also be motivated to take a case to trial. If either side is confident in the strength of its arguments and evidence, it will obviously be less likely to accept a plea bargain. Both prosecutors and defense attorneys may favor a trial to gain publicity, and sometimes public pressure after an extremely violent or high-profile crime will force a chief prosecutor (who is, remember, normally an elected official) to take a weak case to trial. Also, some defendants may insist on their right to a trial, regardless of their attorneys' advice. In the next chapter, we will examine what happens to the roughly 10 percent of indictments that do lead to the courtroom.

Is Justice for Sale?

Earlier in the chapter, we described plea bargaining as an opportunity for the defendant to have some control over his or her fate. This assumes that the defendant has the benefit of a competent defense attorney who is able to assess the pros and cons of the plea and provide expert aid and advice. Sadly, this level of counsel is often unavailable to a large class of defendants—those who cannot pay for their own lawyer and must instead rely on our nation's overworked and underfunded public defenders. As we close this chapter, we will examine the contention that, despite the stated objectives of the United States Supreme Court, defendants get only the justice they can afford, not the justice they deserve.

Gideon v. Wainwright

In the landmark case of *Gideon v. Wainwright* (1963),[84] the Supreme Court unanimously held that "any person haled into court, who is too poor to hire a lawyer, cannot be assured a fair trial unless counsel is provided for him." It seems to be "an obvious truth," wrote Justice Hugo Black, that "lawyers in criminal cases are necessities, not luxuries."[85] For the most part, the letter of the *Gideon* case has been followed in the forty years since Justice Black wrote those words. Many observers claim, however, that the spirit of the decision has been abandoned in America's courts—that, in fact, a person's ability to receive justice is directly related to how much money he or she is able to spend. "If you're the average poor person, you are going to be herded through the criminal justice system about like an animal is herded through the stockyards," says Stephen Bright, the director of the Southern Center for Human Rights in Atlanta, Georgia.[86]

Working for the Minimum Wage

The Sixth Amendment to the U.S. Constitution provides that all criminal defendants have a right to the assistance of counsel for their defense. The *Gideon* decision assured that right for indigent defendants who could not afford to hire a lawyer. Today, more than eight out of every ten Americans accused of a felony use a publicly appointed defense attorney. As spending for new prisons and law enforcement personnel has increased over the last decade, however, the budgets for public defenders were slashed. Although Congress approved a pay hike for defense attorneys in federal courts in 1986, most of the country's

ninety-four federal districts have yet to implement the raise due to Congress's refusal to appropriate the necessary funds. Therefore, defense lawyers in those districts are still paid an hourly rate of $65 for courtroom time and $45 for out-of-court time—barely enough to cover the costs of maintaining a law office. Even in the districts that have provided the extra wages, these defense attorneys still receive considerably less than the standard hourly billing rate charged by private attorneys, which ranges from around $180 to $270 depending on the level of experience.[87]

The contrast is even more pronounced in some states. Massachusetts, for example, limits the compensation paid to court-appointed attorneys to $30 an hour for district court cases, $39 an hour for superior court cases, and $54 an hour for murder cases.[88] Considering the wages from private clients that these lawyers lose every hour they work for the state, a Massachusetts defense attorney who spends an average amount of time preparing for a murder case is being paid less than the national minimum wage. Michigan's fee schedule for indigent defense counsel provides a maximum of $225 for investigation and preparation for cases in which the defendant faces a life sentence, $45 for a single client meeting (no matter how many meetings are actually required), and no more than $108 per day for trial fees. In practice, this has meant that assigned counsel earn as little as $6.14 an hour.[89] A report by the Texas state bar commission pointed out that the fees provided for public defenders in that state barely cover a lawyer's overhead, and this low level of compensation "often translates into a disincentive to provide maximum performance."[90]

Public defenders are often overworked as well. Guidelines set by the National Advisory Commission on Criminal Justice Standards and Goals recommend that a public defender's caseload each year should not exceed 150 felony cases and 400 misdemeanor cases. In Louisiana's Calcasieu Parish, *part-time* public defenders handle 590 felonies and 150 misdemeanors annually.[91] Sometimes, there simply are not enough lawyers to meet the needs of poor defendants. Twelve thousand indigent defendants a year in Riverside County, California, plead guilty without ever speaking to a lawyer, while in Oregon thousands of nonviolent misdemeanor and low-level felony cases are dismissed due to lack of available court-appointed attorneys.[92]

Under pressure of continued budget cuts, some regions are contracting out their defense work. In this "low-bid contracting," one or more attorneys agree to represent all or a portion of a jurisdiction's caseload for a fixed price. For example, McDuffie County (Georgia) officials decided that the $46,000 the county was spending annually on indigent defense was too much. They allowed local attorneys to bid on the service and awarded a contract to Bill Wheeler, whose $25,000 was the lowest bid submitted. Wheeler continued to maintain a private practice as he took on the county's caseload.[93]

"You Get What You Pay For"

Critics of low-bid contracting argue that by emphasizing price over quality, officials are sacrificing the constitutional guarantees of indigent defendants. The contracts also clearly create a conflict of interest between the client and the attorney, who has a strong incentive to do the least amount of work possible on each case.[94] In the first three years that he held McDuffie County's contract, for example, Wheeler tried one felony case and entered 213 guilty pleas. In that time span, he entered only three pretrial motions for his defendants. This is remarkable, considering that pretrial motions are one of the primary weapons defense attorneys have to protect their clients. Furthermore, the quality of some public defenders may be unacceptable. In a recent Louisiana murder trial, not only did the court-appointed defense attorney spend only eleven minutes preparing for trial on a charge that carries a mandatory life sentence, but she also represented the victim's father and had been representing the victim at the time of his death. Not surprisingly, the defendant was found guilty.[95]

Such behavior raises a crucial question: When a lawyer does such a poor job, has she or he essentially denied her or his client the Sixth Amendment right to assistance of counsel? In *Strickland v. Washington* (1984),[96] the Supreme Court set up a two-pronged test to determine whether constitutional requirements have been met. To prove that prior counsel was not sufficient, a defendant must show (1) that counsel's performance was deficient, *and* (2) that this deficiency *more likely than not* caused the defendant to lose the case. In practice, it has been very difficult to prove the second prong because the prosecution can always argue that the defendant would have lost the case even if his or her lawyer had not been asleep, drunk, or otherwise incapacitated.[97]

Some observers have called for the Supreme Court to abandon the *Strickland* test when the lawyer's behavior is so reprehensible that there is no possibility of a "fair trial." Some lower courts seem to be moving in this direction. In 2000, a federal judge in Texas ruled that Calvin Burdine, who had spent sixteen years on death row for a murder conviction, did not receive a fair hearing because his

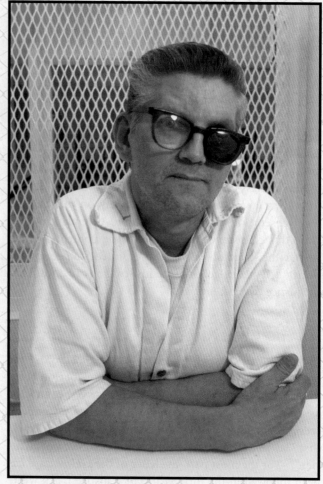

Calvin Jerold Burdine, age forty-six, was freed in 2000 after spending sixteen years on death row in Texas for murder. U.S. District Judge David Hittner overturned Burdine's conviction because his lawyer allegedly slept through long portions of his 1984 trial.

defense lawyer slept for periods as long as ten minutes during the trial.[98] A few years later, a U.S. district court judge vacated the guilty plea of a fifteen-year-old convicted of murdering two octogenarians in their Quincy, Washington, farmhouse. The most incriminating piece of evidence in the case—a recording of the defendant admitting he went to the victims' home intending to shoot them—turned out to have been doctored by local police, a fact that the defendant's attorney could not have failed to notice had he actually listened to the tape.[99] In both cases, the defendants had been appointed counsel.

Paying to Defend the Poor

Many observers believe that the federal government should share the financial burden of our indigent defender system.[100] At the present time, the load falls directly on state and local governments, which must cope with more

AP Photo/Brett Coomer

volatile revenue streams and often cut funds to public defender programs in times of fiscal crisis. In the absence of such a policy change, which does not appear to be forthcoming, other attempts are being made to improve the situation. Quitman County, located in rural Mississippi, has sued the state to improve the level of legal service for its indigent defendants. The lawsuit claims that while the state pays upwards of $13 billion a year to prosecute criminal cases, in Quitman County two attorneys are paid $1,350 a month to represent every person who cannot afford his or her own defense.[101] Similar suits have been filed in Connecticut, Illinois, Indiana, and Louisiana, based on the idea that poor defendants are not being provided with the effective assistance of counsel as required by the Constitution.

A number of states are taking steps to increase the flow of funds to public defender systems. The Georgia legislature has decided to spend $60 million a year to create and maintain a public defender system that will provide representation for all felony and juvenile cases. In 2001, the Texas legislature pledged state financial aid to local public defender programs for the first time in its history.[102] For the most part, however, legal scholars believe the promise of "equal justice for all" inherent in the Constitution and the *Gideon* ruling is not being fulfilled. Few would dispute the assertion of one observer, who stated, "If O. J. Simpson [who spent nearly $6 million on his defense] had been a poor black man in a different part of Los Angeles County, he would be on death row now."[103]

Making Sense of the Sixth Amendment Right to Counsel

1 Why is it important for indigent defendants to have counsel that is as effective as if they had paid for it themselves? Is this a reasonable goal for state, local, and federal governments?

2 Do you think that criminal defense counsel should *automatically* be deemed ineffective if the attorney does not show up for trial? What if the attorney is under the influence of drugs or alcohol during the trial? What if the attorney is asleep for portions of the trial? Should it matter if he or she sleeps for only a few seconds?

3 In the American judicial system, indigent defendants are assigned counsel by the court. In England, by contrast, they have the right to select their own lawyers, which means that public defenders must compete with each other and private attorneys for cases. How would the use of this method affect the level of service to indigent defendants in the United States? Which country do you think has the better system, and why?

Chapter Summary

1 **List the different names given to public prosecutors and the general powers that they have.** At the federal level, the prosecutor is called the U.S. attorney. In state and local courts, the prosecutor may be referred to as the prosecuting attorney, state prosecutor, district attorney, county attorney, or city attorney. Prosecutors in general have the power to decide when and how the state will pursue an individual suspected of criminal wrongdoing. In some jurisdictions, the district attorney is also the chief law enforcement officer, holding broad powers over police operations.

2 **Contrast the prosecutor's roles as an elected official and as a crime fighter.** In most instances, the prosecutor is elected and therefore may feel obliged to reward members of her or his party with jobs. To win reelection or higher political office, the prosecutor may feel a need to bow to community pressures. As a crime fighter, the prosecutor is dependent on the police, and indeed prosecutors are generally seen as law enforcement agents. Prosecutors, however, generally pursue cases only when they believe there is sufficient legal guilt to obtain a conviction.

3 **Delineate the responsibilities of defense attorneys.** (a) Representation of the defendant during the custodial process; (b) investigation of the supposed criminal incident; (c) communication with the prosecutor (including plea bargaining); (d) preparation of the case for trial; (e) submission of defense motions; (f) representation of the defendant at trial; (g) negotiation of a sentence after conviction; and (h) appeal of a guilty verdict.

4 **Indicate the three types of defense allocation programs.** (a) Assigned counsel programs, which use local private attorneys; (b) contracting attorney programs; and (c) public defender programs.

5 **List the three basic features of an adversary system of justice.** (a) A neutral decision maker (judge or jury); (b) presentation of evidence from both parties; and (c) a

STORIES FROM THE STREET

Go to the *Stories from the Street* feature at **www.cjinaction.com** to hear Larry Gaines tell insightful stories related to this chapter and his experiences in the field.

highly structured set of procedures that must be used when evidence is presented.

6 Identify the steps involved in the pretrial criminal process. (a) Suspect taken into custody or arrested; (b) initial appearance before a magistrate, at which time the defendant is informed of his or her constitutional rights and a public defender may be appointed or private counsel may be hired by the state to represent the defendant; (c) the posting of bail or release on recognizance; (d) preventive detention, if deemed necessary to ensure the safety of other persons or the community, or regular detention, if the defendant is unable to post bail; (e) preliminary hearing (mini-trial), at which the judge rules on whether there is probable cause and the prosecutor issues an information; or in the alternative (f) grand jury hearings, after which an indictment is issued against the defendant if the grand jury finds probable cause; (g) arraignment, in which the defendant is informed of the charges and must respond by pleading not guilty or guilty (or in some cases *nolo contendere*); and (h) plea bargaining.

7 Indicate the three influences on a judge's decision to set bail. (a) Uncertainty about the character and past criminal history of the defendant; (b) the risk that the defendant will commit another crime if out on bail; and

(c) overcrowded jails, which may influence a judge to release a defendant on bail.

8 Explain how a prosecutor screens potential cases. (a) Is there sufficient evidence for conviction? (b) What is the priority of the case? The more serious the alleged crime, the higher the priority. The more extensive the defendant's criminal record, the higher the priority. (c) Are the victims cooperative? Violence against family members often yields uncooperative victims; therefore, these cases are rarely prosecuted. (d) Are the victims reliable? (e) Might the defendant be willing to testify against other offenders?

9 List and briefly explain the different forms of plea bargaining agreements. (a) Charge bargaining, in which the charge is reduced to a lesser crime; (b) sentence bargaining, in which a lighter sentence is obtained; (c) count bargaining, in which a certain number or most of the multiple counts are eliminated.

10 Indicate the ways that both defense attorneys and prosecutors can induce plea bargaining. Defense attorneys can file numerous pretrial motions in an effort to weaken the state's case. Prosecutors can engage in horizontal or vertical overcharging, so they can be "bargained down" in the process of plea bargaining.

Key Terms

adversary system 282	*Boykin* form 299
arraignment 295	case attrition 292
attorney general 275	defense attorney 278
attorney-client privilege 281	discovery 289
bail 284	grand jury 289
bail bondsperson 286	indictment 290

information 289	public defenders 280
initial appearance 283	public prosecutors 275
nolo contendere 295	release on recognizance
plea bargaining 295	(ROR) 286
preliminary hearing 289	ten percent cash bail 287
preventive detention 288	

(handwritten annotation: state's attorneys)

Questions for Critical Analysis

1 Why are public prosecutors considered the most dominant figures in the American criminal justice system?

2 Which of the three basic types of programs used to allocate defense counsel in criminal cases has aroused the most criticism recently?

3 Is it true that there is no concern for truth in our adversary system of justice? Explain your answer.

4 During an initial appearance, can defendants plead guilty of having committed a felony? Why or why not?

5 What are the arguments against preventive detention?

6 What is the distinction between a preliminary hearing and an initial appearance?

7 If grand juries indict almost all criminal defendants brought before them, why do we use grand juries?

8 What is case attrition, and why does it occur?

9 Is plea bargaining inevitable?

Test Preparation Online

Criminal JusticeNow

Go to **www.cjinaction.com** and click on *Criminal JusticeNow* for access to this powerful online study tool. You will get a *personalized study plan* based on your responses to a diagnostic pretest. Once you have mastered the material with the help of interactive learning tools, video clips with questions, an integrated e-book, and more, you can take a posttest to confirm you are ready to move on to the next chapter.

Book Companion Web Site

At the book companion Web site (**www.cjinaction.com**), you will find many resources in addition to *Criminal JusticeNow* to aid you in studying for your exams. For example, under *Chapter Resources*, you will find the *Chapter Outline, Chapter Summary, Flashcards, Glossary, Learning Objectives, Lecture Presentations, Concept Builder, Essay Questions*, and a *Tutorial Chapter Quiz*. You can also test yourself with interactive *Online Reviews* of each chapter section. Check out the *Web Links* to access the Web sites mentioned in the text, as well as many others. You can also access recent perspectives by clicking on *CJ in the News* and *Terrorism Update* under *Course Resources*.

Suggested Readings

Delsohn, Gary, *The Prosecutors: A Year in the Life of a District Attorney's Office,* New York: Dutton, 2003. A reporter for the *Sacramento Bee,* the author spent a year following assistant district attorneys in that city. Delsohn shows how life in a district attorney's office is dominated by statistics: number of trials completed, number of trials won, and number of trials lost. Not surprisingly, sometimes "justice" gets mislaid in the mix. The author follows six specific cases, including those of a Ukrainian immigrant who murdered his family and a doctor who killed his young daughter by throwing her out a window. The book is particularly strong in detailing the struggles between prosecutors and defense attorneys, the "foot soldiers" of the American adversary system.

Lewis, Anthony, *Gideon's Trumpet,* New York: Vintage Books, 1989. This classic account of one of the most important United States Supreme Court decisions of the twentieth century has sold nearly one million copies since it was first published in 1964. Lewis, a renowned journalist, tells the story of Clarence Earl Gideon, a petty criminal who was charged with breaking and entering a pool hall in Panama City, Florida, in 1961. Gideon requested a court-appointed lawyer, as he could not afford to hire one. At the time, Florida provided counsel for indigent defendants only in capital cases, and Gideon's request was denied. Following his conviction, Gideon sat down in his prison cell and wrote a letter to the Supreme Court, in which he claimed his due process rights had been denied. Eventually, some of the most respected lawyers in the nation joined Gideon's defense team and, in the end, changed the course of American legal history. Today, if it seems obvious that all defendants have the right to counsel, it is only because of the dramatic steps taken by a true underdog more than four decades ago.

Notes

1. Ellen Barry, "Plea Deal Is Reached in Olympic Bombing," *Los Angeles Times* (April 9, 2005), A28.
2. *Ibid.*
3. Shaila Dewan, "Bomber Offers Guilty Pleas, and Defiance," *New York Times* (April 14, 2005), A23.
4. Associated Press Wire, "Eric Rudolph Pleads to Ala. Bombing" (April 13, 2005).
5. Dewan.
6. Bureau of Justice Statistics, *Federal Criminal Case Processing, 2002 with Trends, 1982–2002* (Washington, D.C.: U.S. Department of Justice, January 2005), Table 5, page 11.
7. Bennett L. Gershman, "Abuse of Power in the Prosecutor's Office," in *Criminal Justice 92/93,* ed. John J. Sullivan and Joseph L. Victor (Guilford, CT: The Dushkin Publishing Group, 1991), 117–123.
8. 295 U.S. 78 (1935).
9. Celesta Albonetti, "Prosecutorial Discretion: The Effects of Uncertainty," *Law and Society Review* 21 (1987), 291–313.
10. Eric Blumenson and Eva Nilson, "Policing for Profit: The Drug War's Hidden Economic Agenda," *University of Chicago Law Review* 35 (1998), 65.
11. Malcolm M. Feeley and Mark H. Lazerson, "Police-Prosecutor Relationships: An Interorganizational Perspective," in *Empirical Theories about Court,* ed. Keith O. Boyum and Lynn Mather (New York: Longman, 1983), 229–232.
12. Herbert Packer, *Limits of the Criminal Sanction* (Stanford, CA: Stanford University Press, 1968), 166–167.
13. *Gideon v. Wainwright,* 372 U.S. 335 (1963); *Massiah v. United States,* 377 U.S. 201 (1964); *United States v. Wade,* 388 U.S. 218 (1967); *Argersinger v. Hamlin,* 407 U.S. 25 (1972); and *Brewer v. Williams,* 430 U.S. 387 (1977).

14. Larry Siegel, *Criminology,* 6th ed. (Belmont, CA: West/Wadsworth Publishing Co., 1998), 487–488.
15. 372 U.S. 335 (1963).
16. 387 U.S. 1 (1967).
17. 407 U.S. 25 (1972).
18. Bureau of Justice Statistics, *Defense Counsel in Criminal Cases* (Washington, D.C.: U.S. Department of Justice, November 2000), 1.
19. Bureau of Justice Statistics, *State Funded Indigent Defense Services, 1999* (Washington, D.C.: U.S. Department of Justice, September 2001), 3.
20. *Ibid.,* 4.
21. Roger A. Hanson, Brian J. Ostrom, and Ann A. Jones, "Effective Adversaries for the Poor," in *The Japanese Adversary System in Context,* ed., Malcolm M. Feeley and Setsuo Miyazawa (New York: Palgrave Macmillan, 2002), 89, 102.
22. Bureau of Justice Statistics, *Defense Counsel in Criminal Cases,* 3–4.
23. 491 U.S. 554 (1989).
24. Jonathan D. Casper, *American Criminal Justice: The Defendant's Perspective* (Englewood Cliffs, NJ: Prentice Hall, 1972), 101.
25. *Ibid.,* 106.
26. William Finnegan, "Defending the Unabomber," *New Yorker* (March 16, 1998), 61.
27. Anthony Platt and Randi Pollock, "Channeling Lawyers: The Careers of Public Defenders," in *The Potential for Reform in Criminal Justice,* ed. Herbert Jacob (Newbury Park, CA: Sage, 1974).
28. Johannes F. Nijboer, "The American Adversary System in Criminal Cases: Between Ideology and Reality," *Cardozo Journal of International and Comparative Law* 5 (Spring 1997), 79.
29. Gordon Van Kessel, "Adversary Excesses in the American Criminal Trial," *Notre Dame Law Review* 67 (1992), 403.
30. James Eisenstein and Herbert Jacob, *Felony Justice* (Boston: Little, Brown, 1977), 24.
31. Jerome Skolnick, "Social Control in the Adversary System," *Journal of Conflict Resolution* 11 (1967), 52–70.
32. Abraham S. Blumberg, "The Practice of Law as Confidence Game: Organizational Cooption of a Profession," *Law and Society Review* 4 (June 1967), 115–139.
33. Malcolm Feeley, "The Adversary System," in *Encyclopedia of the American Judicial System,* ed. Robert J. Janosik (New York: Scribners, 1987), 753.
34. Blumberg, 115.
35. *Riverside County, California v. McLaughlin,* 500 U.S. 44 (1991).
36. Illinois Ann. Stat. Chapter 725, Paragraph 5/110-5.
37. David W. Neubauer, *America's Courts and the Criminal Justice System,* 5th ed. (Belmont, CA: Wadsworth Publishing Co., 1996), 179–181.
38. Roy Flemming, C. Kohfeld, and Thomas Uhlman, "The Limits of Bail Reform: A Quasi Experimental Analysis," *Law and Society Review* 14 (1980), 947–976.
39. Caleb Foote, "Compelling Appearance in Court: Administration of Bail in Philadelphia," *University of Pennsylvania Law Review* 102 (1954), 1031–1052.
40. Marian R. Williams, "The Effect of Pretrial Detention on Imprisonment Decisions," *Criminal Justice Review* (Autumn 2003), 299–300, 313.
41. Frederic Suffet, "Bail Setting: A Study of Courtroom Interaction," *Crime and Delinquency* 12 (1966), 318.
42. Wayne H. Thomas, Jr., *Bail Reform in America* (Berkeley, CA: University of California Press, 1976), 4.
43. Andrew D. Patrick, "Running from the Law," *Vanderbilt Law Review* (January 1999), 172.
44. John S. Goldkamp and Michael R. Gottfredson, *Policy Guidelines for Bail: An Experiment in Court Reform* (Philadelphia: Temple University Press, 1985), 18.
45. Thomas, 7.
46. *Stack v. Boyle,* 342 U.S. 1, 7–8 (1951).
47. *Taylor v. Taintor,* 83 U.S. (16 Wall.) 366 (1873).
48. Jeremy Boren, "Bill Would Set Rules for Bounty Hunters," *Pittsburgh Tribune Review* (March 21, 2005), A1.
49. Esmond Harmsworth, "Bail and Detention: An Assessment and Critique of the Federal and Massachusetts Systems," *New England Journal on Criminal and Civil Confinement* 22 (Spring 1996), 213.
50. 18 U.S.C. Section 3146(b) (1966).
51. Harmsworth, 213.
52. Thomas C. French, "Is It Punitive or Is It Regulatory?" *University of Toledo Law Review* 20 (Fall 1988), 189.
53. 18 U.S.C. Sections 3141–3150 (Supp. III 1985).
54. 481 U.S. 739 (1987).
55. Bureau of Justice Statistics, *Felony Defendants in Large Urban Counties, 2000* (Washington, D.C.: U.S. Department of Justice, December 2003), Table 21, page 22.
56. *Gerstein v. Pugh,* 420 U.S. 103 (1975).
57. David W. Neubauer, *Criminal Justice in Middle America* (Morristown, NJ: General Learning Press, 1974).
58. Andrew D. Leipold, "Why Grand Juries Do Not (and Cannot) Protect the Accused," *Cornell Law Review* 80 (January 1995), 260.
59. Robert L. Misner, "In Partial Praise of Boyd: The Grand Jury as Catalyst for Fourth Amendment Change," *Arizona State Law Review* (Fall 1997), 805.
60. New York Court of Appeals Judge Sol Wachtler, quoted in David Margolik, "Law Professor to Administer Courts in State," *New York Times* (February 1, 1985), B2.
61. Kenneth C. Davis, *Discretionary Justice: A Preliminary Inquiry* (Baton Rouge, LA: Louisiana State University Press, 1969), 189.
62. Barbara Boland, Paul Mahanna, and Ronald Scones, *The Prosecution of Felony Arrests, 1988* (Washington, D.C.: Bureau of Justice Statistics, 1992).
63. *Ibid.*
64. Rick Brundrett, "Study Ranks S.C. Worst in Nation for Rate of Women Killed by Men," *Columbia Slate* (September 26, 2003), A1.

65. Kathy B. Carter, "Court Orders Statewide Drug Penalties, Ending County Disparities," *Newark Star-Ledger* (February 20, 1998), 46.

66. Jodi Wigoren, "Kansas Prosecutor Demands Files on Later-Term Abortions," *New York Times* (February 25, 2005), A1.

67. 404 U.S. 257 (1971).

68. Fred C. Zacharias, "Justice in Plea Bargaining," *William and Mary Law Review* 39 (March 1998), 1121.

69. Albert W. Alschuler, "The Prosecutor's Role in Plea Bargaining," *University of Chicago Law Review* 36 (1968), 52.

70. Milton Heumann, *Plea Bargaining: The Experiences of Prosecutors, Judges, and Defense Attorneys* (Chicago: University of Chicago Press, 1978), 58.

71. Albert W. Alschuler, "The Defense Attorney's Role in Plea Bargaining," *Yale Law Journal* 84 (1975), 1200.

72. Stephen J. Schulhofer, "Plea Bargaining as Disaster," *Yale Law Journal* 101 (1992), 1987.

73. Kevin Cole and Fred C. Zacharias, "The Agony of Victory and the Ethics of Lawyer Speech," *Southern California Law Review* 69 (1996), 1660–1663.

74. N.C. Gen. Stat. Section 15A-832(f) (2003).

75. 18 U.S.C. Section 3771 (2004).

76. Alschuler, "The Prosecutor's Role in Plea Bargaining," 53.

77. Casper, 77–81.

78. 395 U.S. 238 (1969).

79. Stephen A. Saltzburg, "Lawyers, Clients, and the Adversary System," *Mercer Law Review* 37 (1986), 651–655.

80. Douglas A. Smith, "The Plea Bargaining Controversy," *Journal of Criminal Law and Criminology* 77 (1986), 949.

81. Warren Burger, "Address to the American Bar Association Annual Convention," *New York Times* (August 11, 1970), 24.

82. Robert A. Weninger, "The Abolition of Plea Bargaining: A Case Study of El Paso County, Texas," *UCLA Law Review* 35 (December 1987), 265.

83. Michael L. Rubinstein, Stevens H. Clarke, and Teresa White Carns, *Alaska Bans Plea Bargaining* (Washington, D.C.: National Institute of Justice, 1980), 117–119; and Roland Acevedo, "Is a Ban on Plea Bargaining an Ethical Abuse of Discretion? A Bronx County, New York, Case Study," *Fordham Law Review* (1995), 987, 999–1000.

84. 372 U.S. 335, 344 (1963).

85. *Ibid.*

86. Quoted in Bob Herbert, "Cheap Justice," *New York Times* (March 1, 1998), 15.

87. *2004 Survey of Law Firm Economics* (Philadelphia: Altman Weil, 2004), 83.

88. Jonathan Saltzman, "Suit Seeks Pay Raise for Public Defenders," *Boston Globe* (June 29, 2004), B1.

89. E. E. Edwards, "Getting around *Gideon:* The Illusion of Effective Assistance of Counsel," *Champion* (January/February 2004), 4.

90. Allen K. Butcher and Michael K. Moore, *Muting Gideon's Trumpet: The Crisis in Indigent Criminal Defense in Texas* (2000), available at **http://www.uta.edu/pols/moore/ indigent/last.pdf**.

91. Edwards, 4.

92. Bill Rankin, "Right to a Lawyer Still Not a Given for Poor Defendants," *Atlanta Journal-Constitution* (March 24, 2003), B1.

93. Adele Bernhard, "Take Courage: What the Courts Can Do to Improve the Delivery of Criminal Defense Services," *University of Pittsburgh Law Review* (Winter 2002), 293.

94. Catherine Beane, "*Gideon* Shattered: Justice Stands Still in Avoyelles Parish, Louisiana," *Champion* (March 2004), 6.

95. Catherine Beane, "Indigent Defense: Separate and Unequal," *Champion* (May 2004), 54.

96. 466 U.S. 668 (1984).

97. *Burnett v. Collins,* 982 F.2d 922, 930 (5th Cir. 1993).

98. Ross E. Milloy, "Judge Frees Texas Inmate Whose Lawyer Slept at Trial," *New York Times* (March 2, 2000), A19.

99. Ken Armstrong, Florangela Davila, and Justin Mayo, "The Empty Promise of Equal Defense Part 1: A Case Study in Incompetence," *Seattle Times* (April 4, 2004), A1.

100. American Bar Association Standing Committee on Legal Aid and Indigent Defendants, *Gideon's Broken Promise: America's Continuing Quest for Equal Justice* (Washington, D.C.: American Bar Association, December 2004), vi.

101. Reed Branson, "Poor County Sues Miss., Says Indigent Get Unequal Defense," *Commercial Appeal* (April 28, 2003), A1.

102. American Bar Association Standing Committee on Legal Aid and Indigent Defendants, 31–32.

103. M. A. Stapleton, "Crisis Seen in Privatizing Public Defender Work," *Chicago Daily Law Bulletin* (October 15, 1997), 1.

CHAPTER TEN

The Criminal Trial

Chapter outline

- Special Features of Criminal Trials
- Jury Selection
- The Trial
- The Final Steps of the Trial and Postconviction Procedures
- Criminal Justice in Action—Rape Shield Laws

Chapter objectives

After reading this chapter, you should be able to:

1 Identify the basic protections enjoyed by criminal defendants in the United States.
2 List the three requirements of the Speedy Trial Act of 1974.
3 Explain what "taking the Fifth" really means.
4 List the requirements normally imposed on potential jurors.
5 Contrast challenges for cause and peremptory challenges during *voir dire*.
6 List the standard steps in a criminal jury trial.
7 Explain the difference between testimony and real evidence; between lay witnesses and expert witnesses; and between direct and circumstantial evidence.
8 List possible affirmative defenses.
9 Delineate circumstances in which a criminal defendant may in fact be tried a second time for the same act.
10 List the six basic steps of an appeal.

Criminal JusticeNow

Optimize your study time and master key chapter concepts with *Criminal JusticeNow,* an online study tool that provides you with a *personalized study plan.* Check out the "Test Preparation Online" section at the end of the chapter for additional information.

Same Story, Different Ending

There is no doubt

that Peter Sakarias and Tuano Waidla were responsible for the death of Viivi Piirisild. The pair broke into the victim's North Hollywood, California, home while she was away. When Piirisild returned and walked into her living room, they attacked her. Waidla used a hatchet and Sakarias a kitchen knife. According to the coroner, Piirisild died of a combination of wounds inflicted by the intruders.

The two men were tried separately on charges of first degree murder. Waidla went first, and during his trial Los Angeles prosecutor Steven K. Ipsen told the jury that the defendant had planned the attack and had been "dominant" over his accomplice, Sakarias. Ipsen pointed out that Waidla had wielded the hatchet—"the more devastating" of the weapons—and delivered the "death blow" that killed Piirisild. Because he was responsible for the decisive strike, the prosecutor

In 2005, the California Supreme Court overturned the death sentence of Peter Sakarias, pictured here, because of prosecutorial inconsistency.

AP Photo/California Dept. Corrections

argued, Waidla deserved the death penalty, a request to which the jury complied.

Eight months later, Sakarias went on trial, and, once again, Ipsen was the lead prosecutor. This time, however, he presented an interpretation of the events that differed dramatically from what he had said at Waidla's trial. Following the initial attack, Ipsen told this jury, the two men dragged a still-living Piirisild into a back bedroom, where Sakarias took the hatchet from his partner and ended the victim's life with a death blow of his own. Furthermore, Ipsen said there was "no evidence" that Waidla was the "dominant personality" between the two men. After his trial, Sakarias, too, was sentenced to death, an outcome that was eventually overturned by the California Supreme Court in March 2005 because of the court's displeasure with Ipsen's conflicting interpretations of the facts surrounding Piirisild's murder.

According to some, including at least one member of the California Supreme Court, Steven Ipsen had not strayed outside the ethical boundaries of his profession. In his dissent, Justice Marvin R. Baxter wrote that prosecutors have the duty to make the best case against each defendant and that, so long as they do not falsify evidence, contradictory theories of the crime are acceptable.[1] Nonetheless, in the last chapter we learned that a prosecutor's main goal should be to "seek justice," not to convict as many defendants as possible using whatever means necessary. For the remaining members of the court, Ipsen's reliance on contradictory theories deprived both Tuano Waidla and Peter Sakarias of their right to a fair trial. The justices decided to let Waidla's sentence stand, given the "great weight" of the evidence against him.[2] But they reduced Sakarias's punishment to life in prison, leaving the Los Angeles district attorney's office with the decision of whether to seek the death penalty against him again.[3]

Fairness is, of course, a crucial component of the criminal trial. Protection against the arbitrary abuse of power is at the heart of the U.S. Constitution, and the right to a

🔵 CONCEPT BUILDER

Did you know that the words "presumption of innocence" are not found in the U.S. Constitution? How did this concept become a part of the American legal system? Visit **www.cjinaction.com** for an interactive exploration of this key topic.

criminal trial before a jury is one means of assuring this protection. In this chapter, we will examine the fairness of the criminal trial in the context of the current legal environment. Because "fairness" can only be defined subjectively, we will also make an effort to look into the effect human nature has on the adversary process. Trials may be based on fact finding, but as Judge Jerome Frank once sardonically asserted, when it comes to a jury, "facts are guesses."[4]

SPECIAL FEATURES OF CRIMINAL TRIALS

Civil trials (see Chapter 4) and criminal trials have many similar features. In both types of trials, attorneys from each side select a jury, make their opening statements to the court, examine and cross-examine witnesses, and summarize their positions in closing arguments. The jury is charged (instructed), and if it reaches a verdict, the trial comes to an end.

The principal difference is that in civil trials, the adversaries are persons (including corporations, which are legal persons, and businesses), one of whom often is seeking a remedy in the form of damages from the other. In a criminal trial, it is the state, not the victim of the crime, that brings the action against an alleged wrongdoer.[5] Criminal trial procedures reflect the need to protect criminal defendants against the power of the state by providing them with a number of rights. Many of the significant rights of the accused are spelled out in the Sixth Amendment, which reads, in part, as follows:

> In all criminal prosecutions, the accused shall enjoy the right to a speedy and public trial, by an impartial jury of the State and the district wherein the crime shall have been committed, . . . and to be informed of the nature and cause of the accusation; to be confronted with the witnesses against him; to have compulsory process for obtaining witnesses in his favor; and to have the Assistance of Counsel for his defense.

In this section, we will examine the aspects of the criminal trial that make it unique, beginning with two protections explicitly stated in the Sixth Amendment: the right to a speedy trial by an impartial jury. (See the feature *International CJ—China's Re-Education System* on the next page for a discussion of a country that restricts the right to trial in ways that would not be possible under the U.S. Constitution.)

A "Speedy" Trial

As you have just read, the Sixth Amendment requires a speedy trial for those accused of a criminal act. The reason for this requirement is obvious: depending on various factors, the defendant may lose his or her right to move freely and may be incarcerated prior to trial. Also, the accusation that a person has committed a crime jeopardizes that person's reputation in the community. If the defendant is innocent, the sooner the trial is held, the sooner his or her innocence can be established in the eyes of the court and the public.

Reasons for Delay As the preceding chapter made clear, there are numerous reasons for delay in bringing a defendant to trial. In defending the rights of the accused, a defense attorney may use a number of legal tactics, including pretrial motions and plea negotiations. Court congestion also contributes to the problem; many jurisdictions do not have enough judges and courtroom space to meet the needs of the system. This situation has been aggravated by the recent increase in drug-related arrests, which threatens to create judicial "gridlock" in certain metropolitan courthouses.[6]

China's Re-Education System

According to the United States Supreme Court, the Sixth Amendment gives criminal defendants the absolute right to trial by an impartial jury for all "serious" crimes, that is, crimes punishable by a prison sentence of more than six months. In the People's Republic of China, in contrast, approximately 300,000 people are incarcerated in nearly 300 labor camps, where they can be held for as long as four years without ever seeing the inside of a courtroom. Through the country's system of "re-education through labor" *(laojiao)*, public authorities can sentence those caught committing "minor" infractions to three years in a labor camp, with a possible one-year extension, without the need for a formal trial.

Under Chinese law, *laojiao* may serve as punishment not only for those who commit minor criminal acts such as drug use, prostitution, larceny, or "disturbance of public order," but also for those who "behave disruptively on purpose" or "are able-bodied, but have refused to work for a long period." In recent years, the practice has come under particular scrutiny because of its use against pro-democracy organizers and practitioners of the Falun Gong spiritual movement, of whom nearly 20,000 have been incarcerated at the labor camps.

Pressure from international human rights groups and a desire for greater commercial ties with Europe have caused the Chinese government to signal that it may reconsider the use of *laojiao*. There is even talk of abolishing it in the near future. Many Chinese officials, however, will strongly resist any plans for reform. They insist that the system is indispensable for maintaining public order.

FOR CRITICAL ANALYSIS
Review the discussion of the "broken windows theory" on page 172. What are the similarities between this American strategy for controlling crime and China's re-education through labor system?

The Definition of a Speedy Trial The Sixth Amendment does not specify what is meant by the term *speedy*. The United States Supreme Court has refused to quantify "speedy" as well, ruling instead in *Barker v. Wingo* (1972)[7] that only in situations in which the delay is unwarranted and proved to be prejudicial can the accused claim a violation of Sixth Amendment rights.

As a result, all fifty states have their own speedy-trial statutes.[8] For example, the Illinois Speedy Trial Act states that a defendant must be tried within 120 days of arrest unless both the prosecution and the defense agree otherwise. A defendant does not automatically go free if her or his trial is not "speedy" enough. There must be judicial action. In 2004, for example, a Philadelphia judge ordered the release of seven men, some of whom had been charged with murder and kidnapping, because they had spent six or more years in jail awaiting trial. According to Pennsylvania law, trials must start within one year of arrest.[9]

At the national level, the Speedy Trial Act of 1974[10] (amended in 1979) specifies time limits for those in the federal court system. This act requires:

1 No more than thirty days between arrest and indictment.
2 No more than ten days between indictment and arraignment.
3 No more than sixty days between arraignment and trial.

Federal law allows extra time for hearings on pretrial motions, mental competency examinations, and other procedural actions.

Note that the Sixth Amendment's guarantee of a speedy trial does not apply until a person has been accused of a crime. Citizens are protected against unreasonable delays before accusation by *statutes of limitations,* which are legislative time limits that require prosecutors to charge a defendant with a crime within a certain amount of time after the illegal act took place. If the statute of limitations on a particular crime is ten years, and the police do not identify a suspect until ten years and one day after the criminal act occurred, then that suspect cannot be charged with that particular offense.

The Role of the Jury

The Sixth Amendment also states that anyone accused of a crime shall be judged by "an impartial jury." In *Duncan v. Louisiana* (1968),[11] the Supreme Court solidified this right by ruling that in all felony cases, the defendant is entitled to a **jury trial.** The Court has, however, left it to the individual states to decide whether juries are required for misdemeanor cases.[12] If the defendant waives her or his right to trial by jury, a **bench trial** takes place in which a judge decides questions of legality and fact, and no jury is involved.

Jury Size The predominant American twelve-person jury is not the result of any one law—the Constitution does not require that the jury be a particular size. Historically, the number was inherited from the size of English juries, which was fixed at twelve during the fourteenth century.

In 1970, responding to a case that challenged Florida's practice of using a six-person jury in all but capital cases, the Supreme Court ruled that the accused did not have the right to be heard by a twelve-person jury. Indeed, the Court labeled the number twelve "a historical accident, wholly without significance except to mystics."[13] In *Ballew v. Georgia* (1978),[14] however, the Court did strike down attempts to use juries with fewer than six members, stating that a jury's effectiveness was severely hampered below that limit. About half the states allow fewer than twelve persons on criminal juries, though only for misdemeanor cases. In federal courts, defendants are entitled to have the case heard by a twelve-member jury unless both parties agree in writing to a smaller jury.

Unanimity In most jurisdictions, jury verdicts in criminal cases must be *unanimous* for **acquittal** or conviction. As will be explained in more detail later, if the jury cannot reach unanimous agreement on whether to acquit or convict the defendant, the result is a *hung jury,* and the judge may order a new trial.

Again, the Supreme Court has not held that unanimity is a rigid requirement. It has declared that jury verdicts must be unanimous in federal criminal trials, but has given states leeway to set their own rules.[15] Five states—Louisiana, Montana, Oklahoma, Oregon, and Texas—permit nonunanimous trial verdicts, though none allow more than three dissenting votes for convictions by twelve-person juries.

The Privilege against Self-Incrimination

In addition to the Sixth Amendment, which specifies the protections we have just discussed, the Fifth Amendment to the Constitution also provides important safeguards for the defendant. The Fifth Amendment states that no person "shall be compelled in any criminal case to be a witness against himself." Therefore, a defendant has the right *not* to testify at a trial if to do so would implicate him or her in the crime. Witnesses may also refuse to testify on this ground. For example, if a witness, while testifying, is asked a question and the answer would reveal her or his own criminal wrongdoing, the witness may "take the Fifth." In other words, she or he can refuse to testify on the ground that such testimony may be self-incriminating. This rarely occurs, however, as witnesses are often granted immunity before testifying, meaning that no information they disclose can be used to bring criminal charges against them. Witnesses who have been granted immunity cannot refuse to answer questions on the basis of self-incrimination.

It is important to note that not only does the defendant have the right to "take the Fifth," but also that the decision to do so should not prejudice the jury in the prosecution's favor. The Supreme Court came to this controversial decision while reviewing *Adamson v. California* (1947),[16] a case involving the convictions of two defendants

Jury Trial
A trial before a judge and a jury.

Bench Trial
A trial conducted without a jury, in which a judge makes the determination of the defendant's guilt or innocence.

Acquittal
A declaration following a trial that the individual accused of the crime is innocent in the eyes of the law and thus absolved from the charges.

Beyond a Reasonable Doubt
The standard used to determine the guilt or innocence of a person charged with a crime. To be guilty of a crime, a suspect must be proved guilty "beyond and to the exclusion of a reasonable doubt."

who had declined to testify in their own defense against charges of robbery, kidnapping, and murder. The prosecutor in *Adamson* frequently and insistently brought this silence to the notice of the jury in his closing argument, insinuating that if the pair had been innocent, they would not have been afraid to testify. The Court ruled that such tactics effectively invalidated the Fifth Amendment by using the defendants' refusal to testify against them. Now judges are required to inform the jury that an accused's decision to remain silent cannot be held against him or her.

The Presumption of a Defendant's Innocence

The presumption in criminal law is that a defendant is innocent until proved guilty. The burden of proving guilt falls on the state (the public prosecutor). Even if a defendant did in fact commit the crime, she or he will be "innocent" in the eyes of the law unless the prosecutor can substantiate the charge with sufficient evidence to convince a jury (or judge in a bench trial) of the defendant's guilt.[17] Sometimes, especially when a case involves a high-profile violent crime, pretrial publicity may have convinced many members of the community—including potential jurors—that a defendant is guilty. In these instances, a judge has the authority to change the venue of the trial to ensure an unbiased jury. In 2004, for example, the judge moved the trial of Scott Peterson, who had been charged with the murder of his pregnant wife, Laci, from the couple's hometown of Modesto, California, to San Mateo County, south of San Francisco.

A Strict Standard of Proof

In a criminal trial, the defendant is not required to prove his or her innocence. As mentioned earlier, the burden of proving the defendant's guilt lies entirely with the state. Furthermore, the state must prove the defendant's guilt **beyond a reasonable doubt;** that is, the prosecution must show that, based on all the evidence, the defendant's guilt is clear and unquestionable. In *In re Winship* (1970),[18] a case involving the due process rights of juveniles, the Supreme Court ruled that the Constitution requires the reasonable doubt standard because it reduces the risk of convicting innocent people and therefore reassures Americans of the law's moral force and legitimacy.

This high standard of proof in criminal cases reflects a fundamental social value—the belief that it is worse to convict an innocent individual than to let a guilty one go free. The consequences to the life, liberty, and reputation of an accused person from an erroneous conviction for a crime are enormous, and this has been factored into the process. Placing a high standard of proof on the prosecutor reduces the margin of error in criminal cases (at least in one direction).

JURY SELECTION

The initial step in a criminal trial involves choosing the jury. The framers of the Constitution ensured that the importance of the jury would not be easily overlooked. The right to a trial by jury is explicitly mentioned no fewer than three times in the Constitution: in Article III, Section 2; in the Sixth Amendment; and again in the Seventh Amendment. The use of a peer jury not only provided safeguards against the abuses of state power that the framers feared, but also gave Americans a chance—and a duty—to participate in the criminal justice system.

In the early years of the country, a jury "of one's peers" meant a jury limited to white, landowning males. Now, as the process has become fully democratized, there are

Collins E. Ijoma
Trial Court Administrator

I moved to the United States from Nigeria in 1976 to complete my college education, majoring in accounting and business administration. I earned a master's degree in public administration from Seton Hall University in 1982 with a concentration in public budgeting and finance. I was immensely interested in public service but was not particularly aware of the judiciary as a potential employer. My first job in the court system was by accident rather than design. After completing a graduate internship with the Essex County government, I had the opportunity to seek permanent employment with the county-funded judiciary. I was first employed in the Trial Court Administrator's Office in Newark, New Jersey, as the court finance officer in 1983. Much of my education in court administration was gained through the Institute for Court Management of the National Center for State Courts. I pursued this program of professional development from 1984 through 1991 when I graduated as a fellow of ICM.

My initial position offered many opportunities to learn about court management and the workings of a large urban court system. My primary concentration was in human resources, budget, and finance. As a state court, funded by the county, we had to continually justify and fight for positions, space, and equipment. Our court was growing rapidly, and we needed additional resources to allow for an effective and efficient operation. In 1985, I was promoted to director of personnel. I had direct responsibility for all personnel programs, policies, and practices. My association with professional organizations, including the National Association for Court Administration, the American Judicature Society, the Mid-Atlantic Association for Court Administration, and the American Society for Public Administration, was critical to my professional development. The knowledge gained combined with experience helped me to successfully seek the position of assistant trial court administrator and my present position as trial court administrator.

As the trial court administrator, I serve principally as the chief administrative officer for the largest trial and municipal court system in New Jersey. We provide technical and managerial sup-

port to the court (over sixty superior court judges and thirty-six municipal court judges) on such matters as personnel, program development, case flow, resources, and facilities management. This description may sound "highfalutin" considering that most people can only describe a court in terms of a judge, one or two courtroom staff, and a few other employees associated with the visible activities in

Collins E. Ijoma

the courthouse. Obviously, there is a lot more going on behind the scenes of which the average citizen is not aware. For example, besides directing case flow for the four major divisions (criminal, civil, family, and probation), the work involved in managing personnel programs for more than 1,200 employees, information systems and technology infrastructure, maintaining records of proceedings, coordination of transcription, grand and petit jury operations, and court interpreting, to mention but a few examples, is enormous. The modern court needs dedicated professionals in each of these areas.

One thing that keeps me going and enthused about this profession is the resolve and dedication of our judges and staff. The family division embraces a host of issues, and in some cases those who seek help are hurting and desperate. The court may be their only hope. We are also actively engaged in pursuing new ways to offer and manage dispute resolution. Some of these include drug courts to give nonviolent drug offenders a chance at rehabilitation rather than going to jail, complimentary dispute resolution to reach more satisfactory conclusions in less time and at a lower cost to litigants, and creative uses of volunteers to assist in the work of the court and create a positive connection to the community.

Go to the Careers in Criminal Justice Interactive CD for more profiles in the field of criminal justice.

still questions about what "a jury of one's peers" actually means and how effective the system has been in providing the necessary diversity in juries.

Initial Steps: The Master Jury List and *Venire*

The main goal of jury selection is to produce a cross section of the population in the jurisdiction where the crime was committed. Sometimes, a defense attorney may argue that his or her client's trial should be moved to another community to protect against undue prejudice. In practice, judges, mindful of the intent of the Constitution, are hesitant to grant such pretrial motions.

This belief that trials should take place in the community where the crime was committed is central to the purpose of selecting a jury of the defendant's "peers." The United States is a large, diverse nation, and the outlook of its citizens varies accordingly. Two very different cases, one tried in rural Maine and the other in San Francisco, illustrate this point.[19] In Maine, the defendant had accidentally shot and killed a woman standing in her backyard; he had mistaken her white mittens for a deer's tail. His attorney argued that it was the responsibility of the victim to wear bright-colored clothing in the vicinity of hunters during hunting season. The jury agreed, and the defendant was acquitted of manslaughter. In the San Francisco case, two people were charged with distributing sterile needles to intravenous drug users. Rather than denying that the defendants had distributed the needles, the defense admitted the act but insisted that it was necessary to stem the transmission of AIDS and, thus, to save lives. The jury voted 11–1 to acquit, causing a mistrial.

These two outcomes may surprise or even anger people in other parts of the country, but they reflect the values of the regions where the alleged crimes were committed. Thus, a primary goal of the jury selection process is to ensure that the defendant is judged by members of her or his community—peers in the true sense of the word.

The Master Jury List Besides having to live in the jurisdiction where the case is being tried, there are very few restrictions on eligibility to serve on a jury. State legislatures generally set the requirements, and they are similar in most states. For the most part, jurors must be

1 Citizens of the United States.
2 Over eighteen years of age.
3 Free of felony convictions.
4 Of the necessary good health to function in a jury setting.
5 Sufficiently intelligent to understand the issues of a trial.
6 Able to read, write, and comprehend the English language.

The **master jury list,** sometimes called the *jury pool,* is made up of all the eligible jurors in a community. This list is usually drawn from voter-registration lists or driver's license rolls, which have the benefit of being easily available and timely.

Increasing Jury List Diversity The drawback of tying master jury lists to voter-registration lists is that the practice has tended historically to exclude the poor, racial minorities, the young, and the uneducated (in other words, the same groups who are less likely to vote). Also, it has been surmised that some people don't vote for the express reason of keeping their names off the master jury list. These people may not be able to afford to miss work at the low pay offered jurors—less than $30 per day on average—or simply may not want to deal with the inconvenience of jury duty.

A number of states have taken steps to increase the diversity of the master jury list. Both Arizona and New York access welfare and unemployment rolls to find potential jurors, and Arizona also canvasses phone books and water service customer lists for that purpose. California uses Social Security rolls and tax returns as sources of names. In Florida and elsewhere, lists of persons with driver's licenses are also consulted. According to New Mexico's constitution, non-English-speaking citizens cannot be eliminated from jury lists simply because of their lack of language skills.[20] (In every other state, however, potential jurors may be automatically removed if they cannot speak or understand English.)

Master Jury List
The list of citizens in a court's district from which a jury can be selected; often compiled from voter-registration lists, driver's license lists, and other sources.

Venire   The next step in gathering a jury is to draw together the **venire** (Latin for "to come"). The *venire* is composed of all those people who are notified by the clerk of the court that they have been selected for jury duty. Those selected to be part of the *venire* are ordered to report to the courthouse on the date specified by the notice.

Some people are excused from answering this summons. Persons who do not meet the qualifications listed earlier in this section either need not appear in court or, in some states, must appear only in order to be officially dismissed. Also, people in some professions, including teachers, physicians, and judges, can receive exemptions due to the nature of their work. Each court sets its own guidelines for the circumstances under which it will excuse jurors from service, and these guidelines can be as strict or as lenient as the court desires.

Voir Dire

At the courthouse, prospective jurors are gathered, and the process of selecting those who will actually hear the case begins. This selection process is not haphazard. The court ultimately seeks jurors who are free of any biases that may affect their willingness to listen to the facts of the case impartially. To this end, both the prosecutor and the defense attorney have some input into the ultimate make-up of the jury. Each attorney questions prospective jurors in a proceeding known as **voir dire** (French for "to speak the truth"). During *voir dire*, jurors are required to provide the court with a significant amount of personal information, including home address, marital status, employment status, arrest record, and life experiences.

The *voir dire* process involves both written and oral questioning of potential jurors. Attorneys fashion their inquiries in such a manner as to uncover any biases on the parts of prospective jurors and to find persons who might identify with the plights of their respective sides. As one attorney noted, though a lawyer will have many chances to talk to a jury as a whole, *voir dire* is his or her only chance to talk with the individual jurors. (To better understand the specific kinds of questions asked during this process, see Figure 10.1 on the following page.)

Challenging Potential Jurors   During *voir dire*, the attorney for each side may exercise a certain number of challenges to prevent particular persons from serving on the jury. Both sides can exercise two types of challenges: challenges "for cause" and peremptory challenges.

If a defense attorney or prosecutor concludes that a prospective juror is unfit to serve, the attorney may exercise a **challenge for cause** and request that that person not be included on the jury. Attorneys must provide the court with a sound, legally justifiable reason for why potential jurors are "unfit" to serve. For example, jurors can be challenged for cause if they are mentally incompetent, do not speak English, or are proved to have a prior link—be it personal or financial—with the defendant or victim.

Jurors can also be challenged if they are outwardly biased in some way that would prejudice them for or against the defendant. In the 2003 case of Clara Harris, who drove over and killed her husband after catching him in an extramarital affair in Houston, for example, one potential juror was dismissed because she announced she could "emotionally relate" to Harris's action. Another was turned away after admitting that she had hit her own husband with a car after discovering that he had a mistress. A third was disallowed because he had assaulted his unfaithful wife.[21] The Supreme Court has ruled that individuals may also be legally excluded from a jury in a capital case if they would under no circumstances vote for a guilty verdict if it carried the death penalty.[22] At the same time, potential jurors cannot be challenged for cause if they have "general objections" or have "expressed conscientious or religious scruples"

FIGURE 10.1

Sample Juror Questionnaire

In 2005, a former University of South Florida professor named Sami Al-Arian went on trial with three co-defendants for allegedly financing and supporting the Palestinian Islamic Jihad, a terrorist group. In the excerpts from the juror questionnaire listed here, notice how both the prosecution and the defense are interested in gauging a potential juror's opinions on issues important to a trial involving an alleged terrorist with ties to the Middle East.

28. Have you or any children or relatives served in the recent war in Iraq, in Desert Storm or in military operations in Afghanistan and other areas of the Middle East?

Yes ___ No ___

31. Have you had any unpleasant experiences with Muslims, Palestinians, or Arabs?

Yes ___ No ___ If Yes, please explain:

32. Do you believe that Muslims, Palestinians, Arabs, or Israelis are disproportionately more violent than other religious or ethnic groups?

Yes ___ No ___ If Yes, what gives you that impression?

36. Do you think Palestinians were responsible for the attack on the United States on September 11, 2001?

Yes ___ No ___ Don't Know ___ If Yes, please explain:

67. Have you or any family members or close friends had any personal experience with acts of terrorism?

Yes ___ No ___ If Yes, please explain:

72. Do you believe that the protections of free speech in a democracy extend both to citizens and noncitizens?

Yes ___ No ___ If not, please explain:

73. Do you believe that the criticism of United States foreign policy is protected free speech under the First Amendment to the U.S. Constitution?

Yes ___ No ___ Please explain:

74. Can a person criticize the United States government and still be patriotic?

Yes ___ No ___ Please explain:

Source: *St. Petersburg Times* (May 18, 2005), 1B.

against capital punishment.[23] The final responsibility for deciding whether a potential juror should be excluded rests with the judge, who may choose not to act on an attorney's request.

Peremptory Challenges

Voir dire challenges to exclude potential jurors from serving on the jury without any supporting reason or cause.

Peremptory Challenges Each attorney may also exercise a limited number of **peremptory challenges.** These challenges are based *solely* on an attorney's subjective reasoning; that is, the attorney is usually not required to give any legally justifiable reason for wanting to exclude a particular person from the jury. Because of the rather random nature of peremptory challenges, each state limits the number that an attorney may utilize: between five and ten for felony trials (depending on the state) and ten and twenty for capital trials (also depending on the state). Once an attorney's peremptory challenges are used up, he or she must accept forthcoming jurors, unless a challenge for cause can be used.

An attorney's decision to exclude a juror may sometimes seem whimsical. One state prosecutor who litigated drug cases was known to use a peremptory challenge whenever he saw a potential juror with a coffee mug or backpack bearing the insignia of the local public broadcasting station. The attorney presumed that this was evidence that the potential juror had donated money to the public station, and that anybody who would do so would be too "liberal" to give the government's case against a drug offender a favorable hearing.[24] Lawyers have been known to similarly reject potential jurors for reasons of demeanor, dress, and posture. (See the feature *You Be the Judge— The Sympathetic Juror.*)

Race and Gender Issues in Jury Selection

The Sixth Amendment guarantees the right to an *impartial* jury. But, as researcher Jeremy W. Barber notes, it is in the best interests of neither the defense nor the prosecution to seek an impartial jury.[25] In fact, the goal of the attorneys' peremptory challenges is to create a *partial* jury—partial, that is, toward or against the defendant. If the jury turns out to be impartial, it may be that the efforts of the two sides have balanced each other out.

For many years, prosecutors used their peremptory challenges as an instrument of *de facto* segregation in juries. Prosecutors were able to keep African Americans off juries in cases in which an African American was the defendant. The argument that African Americans—or members of any other minority group—would be partial toward one of their own was tacitly supported by the Supreme Court. Despite its own assertion, made in *Swain v. Alabama* (1965),[26] that blacks have the same right to appear on a jury as whites, the Court mirrored the apparent racism of society as a whole by protecting the actions of many prosecutors.

YOU BE THE JUDGE

The Sympathetic Juror

THE FACTS

Alan is a prosecutor in West Palm Beach, Florida. During *voir dire* for the trial of Jason, who was indicted for assaulting a police officer, Alan used one of his peremptory challenges to dismiss Robert. Alan said that he reasoned that because Robert was a pastor, he was more likely to be sympathetic to defendants. Therefore, Alan did not want Robert on the jury, and a trial judge allowed the challenge to stand. Jason was convicted, and on appeal he argued that Robert had in fact been denied a seat on the jury because, like Jason, he was African American.

THE LAW

Generally, an attorney is not required to give any reason for dismissing a juror through a peremptory challenge. The United States

Supreme Court has ruled, however, that the rationale for a peremptory challenge cannot be the juror's race. According to Florida law, a "trial judge's ruling on the 'genuineness' of a peremptory challenge will be affirmed on appeal unless clearly erroneous."

YOUR DECISION

Does the law allow an attorney to use a peremptory challenge when he or she believes the juror may be "too sympathetic"? Can religious leaders as a group be excluded on these grounds? Was the trial judge's decision "clearly erroneous"?

[To see how the District Court ruled in this case, go to Example 10.1 in Appendix B.]

The *Batson* Reversal The Supreme Court reversed this policy in 1986 with *Batson v. Kentucky*.[27] In this case, the Court declared that the equal protection clause prohibits prosecutors from using peremptory challenges to strike possible jurors on the basis of race. Under *Batson,* the defendant must prove that the prosecution's use of a peremptory challenge was racially motivated. Doing so requires a number of legal steps.[28]

1 First, the defendant must make a *prima facie* case that there has been discrimination during *venire*. (*Prima facie* is Latin for "at first sight"; legally, it refers to a fact that is presumed to be true unless contradicted by evidence.)

2 To do so, the defendant must show that he or she is a member of a recognizable racial group and that the prosecutor has used peremptory challenges to remove members of this group from the jury pool.

3 Then, the defendant must show that these facts and other relevant circumstances raise the possibility that the prosecutor removed the prospective jurors solely because of their race.

4 If the court accepts the defendant's charges, the burden shifts to the prosecution to prove that its peremptory challenges were race neutral. If the court finds against the prosecution, it rules that a *Batson* violation has occurred. (For a closer look at the *Batson* decision, see *CJ in Focus—Landmark Cases:* Batson v. Kentucky.)

The Court has revisited the issue of race a number of times in the years since *Batson.* In *Powers v. Ohio* (1991),[29] it ruled that a defendant may contest race-based peremptory challenges even if the defendant is not of the same race as the excluded jurors. In *Georgia v. McCollum* (1992),[30] the Court placed defense attorneys under the same restrictions as prosecutors when making race-based peremptory challenges.

> "A jury consists of twelve persons chosen to decide who has the better lawyer."
> —Robert Frost, American poet (1874–1963)

Then, in 2003, the Court stayed the execution of Thomas Miller-El by the state of Texas, giving Miller-El the chance to argue that prosecutors had violated his rights by striking ten of eleven potential black jurors because of their race.[31] (The only African American juror approved by the prosecution had stated that, in his opinion, the correct punishment for murderers was to "pour some honey on them and stake them out over an ant bed.") The Court sent the case back to the Fifth Circuit Court of Appeals to determine whether the jury selection process had been tainted by racial bias. After the appellate court once again let Miller-El's conviction stand, the Court overturned the sentence in 2005.[32] Although this ruling made no new law, it did express the Court's willingness to intervene when the jury selection process is marred by obvious discrimination.

Women on the Jury Given the *Batson* precedent, it seemed inevitable that the Supreme Court would eventually address another issue: whether women were constitutionally protected from peremptory challenges based on their gender.[33] The exclusion of women has been more codified than the exclusion of racial groups. At the end of World War II, twenty-one states still prohibited female jurors, and the last state to end this practice—Alabama—did not do so until 1966.

In *J.E.B. v. Alabama ex rel. T. B.* (1994),[34] the Supreme Court extended *Batson* to cover gender bias in jury selection. The case was a civil suit for paternity and child support brought by the state of Alabama. Prosecutors used nine of their ten challenges to remove men from the jury, while the defense made similar efforts to remove women. When challenged, the state defended its actions on what it called the rational belief that men and women might have different views on the issues of paternity and child support. The Court held this to be unconstitutional under the equal protection clause.

Batson v. Kentucky

James Kirkland Batson, an African American, had been charged with second degree burglary and receipt of stolen goods. In the jury selection process for Batson's trial, the prosecutor used his peremptory challenges to strike the only four African Americans in the *venire,* resulting in an all-white jury. Batson was convicted. In appealing his conviction, Batson claimed that by removing the potential jurors on the basis of their race, the prosecution had denied him his right to a jury drawn from a cross section of the community. Previously, the Supreme Court had ruled that racially discriminatory peremptory challenges could not be proved in a single case, but had to be shown as a pattern over a period of time. With *Batson,* however, the Court would reject this ruling.

Batson v. Kentucky
United States Supreme Court
476 U.S. 79 (1986)
http://laws.findlaw.com/US/476/79.html

In the words of the court . . .
Justice Powell, majority opinion

* * * *

More than a century ago, the Court decided that the State denies a black defendant equal protection of the laws when it puts him on trial before a jury from which members of his race have been purposefully excluded. [*Strauder v. West Virginia,* 100 U.S. 303 (1880).] That decision laid the foundation for the Court's unceasing efforts to eradicate racial discrimination in the procedures used to select the venire from which individual jurors are drawn.

* * * *

Purposeful racial discrimination in selection of the venire violates a defendant's right to equal protection because it denies him the protection that a trial by jury is intended to secure. "The very idea of a jury is a body . . . composed of the peers or equals of the person whose rights it is selected or summoned to determine; that is, of his neighbors, fellows, associates, persons having the same legal status in society as that which he holds."

* * * *

The harm from discriminatory jury selection extends beyond that inflicted on the defendant and the excluded juror to touch the entire community. Selection procedures that purposefully exclude black persons from juries undermine public confidence in the fairness of our system of justice.

* * * *

The reality of [peremptory challenges], amply reflected in many state- and federal-court opinions, shows that the challenge may be, and unfortunately at times has been, used to discriminate against black jurors. By requiring trial courts to be sensitive to the racially discriminatory use of peremptory challenges, our decision enforces the mandate of equal protection and furthers the ends of justice. In view of the heterogeneous population of our Nation, public respect for our criminal justice system and the rule of law will be strengthened if we ensure that no citizen is disqualified from jury service because of his race.

DECISION

The Court overturned Batson's conviction and remanded the case, holding that prosecutors could not constitutionally use peremptory challenges to strike potential jurors based solely on their race. It also rejected the notion that African American jurors, as a whole, are unable to impartially consider a case against an African American defendant. To protect against discrimination, the Court set standards by which a defendant could prove that the jury in his or her trial had been tainted by racially motivated peremptory challenges.

FOR CRITICAL ANALYSIS

In this ruling, the Court (a) states a belief that diverse juries are necessary to ensure fair trials and (b) rejects the notion that a juror's race will influence his or her judgment. Some observers, while noting the obvious drawbacks of discrimination in jury selection, have labeled this the "*Batson* Paradox." How could these two opinions contradict each other when applied to a potential *Batson* violation?

For more information and activities related to this case, click on Landmark Cases *under* Book Resources *at* **www.cjinaction.com**.

Alternate Jurors

Because unforeseeable circumstances or illness may necessitate that one or more of the sitting jurors be dismissed, the court may also seat several *alternate jurors* who will hear the entire trial. Depending on the rules of the particular jurisdiction, two or three alternate jurors may be present throughout the trial. If a juror has to be excused in the middle of the trial, an alternate may take his or her place without disrupting the proceedings.

THE TRIAL

Once the jury members are seated, the judge swears in the jury and the trial itself can begin. A rather pessimistic truism among attorneys is that every case "has been won or lost when the jury is sworn." This reflects the belief that a juror's values are the major, if not dominant, factor in the decision of guilt or innocence.[35]

In actuality, it is difficult to predict how a jury will go about reaching a decision. Despite a number of studies on the question, researchers have not been able to provide any definitive answers. Sometimes, jurors in a criminal trial will follow instructions to find a defendant guilty unless there is a reasonable doubt, and sometimes they seem to follow instinct or prejudice and apply the law any way they choose.[36]

Opening Statements

Attorneys may choose to open the trial with a statement to the jury, though they are not required to do so. In these **opening statements,** the attorneys give a brief version of the facts and the supporting evidence that they will present during the trial. Because some trials can drag on for weeks or even months, it is extremely helpful for jurors to hear a summary of what will unfold. In short, the opening statement is a kind of "road map" that describes the destination that each attorney hopes to reach and outlines how she or he plans to reach it. The danger for attorneys is that they will offer evidence during the trial that might contradict an assertion made during the opening statement. This may cause jurors to disregard the evidence or shift their own narrative further away from the narrative being offered by the attorney.[37] In *United States v. Dinitz* (1976),[38] the Supreme Court ruled that attorneys are limited in the opening statements to subjects they believe will be presented in the trial itself.

The Role of Evidence

Once the opening statements have been made, the prosecutor begins the trial proceedings by presenting the state's evidence against the defendant. Courts have complex rules about what types of evidence may be presented and how the evidence may be brought out during the trial. **Evidence** is anything that is used to prove the existence or nonexistence of a fact. For the most part, evidence can be broken down into two categories: testimony and real evidence. **Testimony** consists of statements by competent witnesses. **Real evidence,** presented to the court in the form of exhibits, includes any physical items—such as the murder weapon or a bloodstained piece of clothing—that affect the case.

Rules of evidence are designed to ensure that testimony and exhibits presented to the jury are relevant, reliable, and not unfairly prejudicial against the defendant. One of the tasks of the defense attorney is to challenge evidence presented by the prosecution by establishing that the evidence is not reliable. Of course, the prosecutor also tries to demonstrate the irrelevance or unreliability of evidence presented by the defense. The final decision on whether evidence is allowed before the jury rests with the judge, in keeping with his or her role as the "referee" of the adversary system. (See the feature *CJ and Technology—The Imperfect Science of Lie Detection* for an example of how difficult it can be to get certain information admitted into evidence.)

Testimonial Evidence A person who is called to testify on factual matters that would be understood by the average citizen is referred to as a **lay witness.** If asked about the condition of a victim of an assault, for example, a lay witness could relate certain facts, such as "she was bleeding from her forehead" or "she lay unconscious on the ground for several minutes." A lay witness could not, however, give information about the

The Imperfect Science of Lie Detection

Jimmy Ray Slaughter was running out of options. He had been sentenced to death nearly fifteen years earlier for the murder of his girlfriend and their eleven-month-old daughter, and numerous appeals had failed to overturn the conviction. Finally, he put his faith in Dr. Lawrence Farwell and the memory and encoding related multifaceted electroencephalographic response (MERMER) lie-detection test. For a MERMER examination, the suspect wears a headband equipped with sensors that can measure brain waves denoting familiarity with aspects of a crime. According to Dr. Farwell, the results of Slaughter's MERMER test showed, with 99.9 percent accuracy, that the defendant did not know specifically where the murders took place, where his girlfriend's body was lying in their home, or what she was wearing. He concluded that Slaughter had not been at the scene of the crime and was therefore innocent.

Even though the Federal Bureau of Investigation has used MERMER technology when interrogating suspects, an Oklahoma clemency board rejected its results in this case, and Slaughter was executed on March 15, 2005. Slaughter's fate highlights the uncertain status of lie-detector tests in the criminal justice system. Although police and prosecutors use the tests extensively to gain information and determine probable cause for arrest, the results of lie-detector exams are infrequently allowed as evidence in court. New Mexico has the only state court system that routinely permits evidence gleaned from polygraphs, which measure changes in a suspect's pulse, breathing rate, perspiration, and blood pressure to establish whether he or she is telling the truth. All other states and the federal government admit polygraph evidence at the discretion of the judge. No jurisdiction allows the presentation of voice stress analysis—which measures tremors in a person's voice—as evidence of truth telling, though the method is also often used by law enforcement officers.

Although studies have shown that polygraphs can be highly effective, the procedure is plagued by problems that render its results, for the most part, inadmissible as evidence. Personal characteristics of the suspect can have considerable influence on test results: a good actor can suppress physical signs of lying, and a nervous suspect may exhibit these very signs even when telling the truth. Consequently, the polygraph is not fail-proof and, therefore, is not reliable enough for the tastes of most judges. Furthermore, judges worry that jurors may be overly impressed with the "quasi-scientific" nature of a polygraph and give its findings more weight than other, more reliable evidence.

IN THE FUTURE

Given that a reliable lie-detector test would transform not only the criminal justice system but also many other areas of society, Dr. Lawrence Farwell (who invented MERMER) is not alone in trying to improve on the polygraph. Scientists at the University of Pennsylvania have come up with two new lie-detection procedures. The first, called functional magnetic resonance imaging, measures areas of the brain that light up when the test subject is being dishonest. The second—known as the "cognosensor"—beams infrared light through a subject's skull to measure changes in cranial blood flow that supposedly occur when one is lying. Like MERMER, however, these techniques are far from gaining the scientific credibility necessary for admissibility in court.

For more information on MERMER and other CJ technologies, click on Crime and Technology *under* Book Resources *at* **www.cjinaction.com**.

medical extent of the victim's injuries, such as whether she suffered from a fractured skull or internal bleeding. Coming from a lay witness, such testimony would be inadmissible. When the matter in question requires scientific, medical, or technical skill beyond the scope of the average person, prosecutors and defense attorneys may call an **expert witness** to the stand. The expert witness is an individual who has professional training, advanced knowledge, or substantial experience in a specialized area, such as medicine, computer technology, or ballistics. The rules of evidence state that expert witnesses may base their opinions on three types of information:

1 Facts or data of which they have personal knowledge.
2 Material presented at trial.
3 Secondhand information given to the expert outside the courtroom.[39]

Expert witnesses are considered somewhat problematic for two reasons. First, they may be chosen for their "court presence"—whether they speak well or will appear sympathetic to the jury—rather than their expertise. Second, attorneys pay expert witnesses for their services. Given human nature, the attorneys expect a certain measure of cooperation from an expert they have hired, and an expert witness has an interest in

Expert Witness
A witness with professional training or substantial experience qualifying her or him to testify on a certain subject.

The job of the prosecution is to remove any traces of doubt concerning the defendant's guilt. This task can prove more difficult when the alleged crime took place many years earlier, as was the case in the 2002 trial of Kenneth K. Behrel, the longtime chaplain of the St. James School near Hagerstown, Maryland. Behrel was eventually found guilty of sexually molesting a male student in the early 1980s. A key piece of evidence in Behrel's trial was a black footlocker containing pornography that his victim had described to police officers. Is this footlocker direct evidence or circumstantial evidence of any wrongdoing?

Direct Evidence

Evidence that establishes the existence of a fact that is in question without relying on inference.

Circumstantial Evidence

Indirect evidence that is offered to establish, by inference, the likelihood of a fact that is in question.

Relevant Evidence

Evidence tending to make a fact in question more or less probable than it would be without the evidence. Only relevant evidence is admissible in court.

satisfying the attorneys so that he or she will be hired again.[40] Under these circumstances, some have questioned whether the courts can rely on the professional nonpartisanship of expert witnesses.[41]

Direct versus Circumstantial Evidence Two types of testimonial evidence may be brought into court: direct evidence and circumstantial evidence. **Direct evidence** is evidence that has been witnessed by the person giving testimony. "I saw Bill shoot Chris" is an example of direct evidence. **Circumstantial evidence** is indirect evidence that, even if believed, does not establish the fact in question but only the degree of likelihood of the fact. In other words, circumstantial evidence can create an inference that a fact exists.

Suppose, for example, that the defendant owns a gun that shoots bullets of the type found in the victim's body. This circumstantial evidence, by itself, does not establish that the defendant committed the crime. Combined with other circumstantial evidence, however, it may do just that. For instance, if other circumstantial evidence indicates that the defendant had a motive for harming the victim and was at the scene of the crime when the shooting occurred, the jury might conclude that the defendant committed the crime.

Prosecutors take a risk if the *only* evidence they present is circumstantial. In the spring of 2005, prosecutors and many other legal experts were shocked when a California jury acquitted actor Robert Blake of killing his wife, Bonny Lee Bakely. The case against Blake seemed strong: Bakely was shot as she sat in a car outside the restaurant where the couple had just had dinner, two stuntmen testified that the defendant had asked them to kill his wife two months before her death, and there were no other suspects. All of the evidence against Blake was circumstantial, however. The prosecution did not produce any eyewitnesses and could not link Blake to the murder weapon, a Walther P-38 handgun. In the end, the circumstantial evidence was not enough to convince the jury of Blake's guilt beyond a reasonable doubt.[42]

Relevance Evidence will not be admitted in court unless it is relevant to the case being considered. **Relevant evidence** is evidence that tends to prove or disprove a fact in question. Forensic proof that the bullets found in a victim's body were fired from a gun discovered in the suspect's pocket at the time of arrest, for example, is certainly relevant. The suspect's prior record, showing a conviction for armed robbery ten years earlier, is, as we shall see in the next subsection, irrelevant to the case at hand and in most instances will be ruled inadmissible by the judge.

Prejudicial Evidence Evidence may be excluded if it would tend to distract the jury from the main issues of the case, mislead the jury, or cause jurors to decide the issue on an emotional basis. In American trial courts, this rule precludes prosecutors from using prior purported criminal activities or actual convictions to show that the defendant has criminal propensities or an "evil character."[43]

This concept is codified in the Federal Rules of Evidence, which state that evidence of "other crimes, wrongs, or acts is not admissible to prove the character of a person in order to show action in conformity therewith." Such evidence is allowed only when it does not apply to character construction and focuses instead on "motive, opportunity, intent, preparation, plan, knowledge, identity, or absence of mistake or accident."[44]

Though this legal concept has come under a great deal of criticism, it is consistent with the presumption-of-innocence standards discussed earlier. Presumably, if a prosecutor is allowed to establish that the defendant has shown antisocial or even violent

Peeping Juries

The jurors at Michael Jackson's 2005 trial had to expect to be subjected to a certain amount of sexually explicit material during the court proceedings. After all, the pop star was charged with four counts of molesting a twelve-year-old boy. Some of them had to be a bit surprised, however, to be spending one Wednesday morning looking at seventy-five large-screen projections of sex acts and nude photos taken from magazines, photographs, and videos found at Jackson's Wonderland ranch. Among the featured publications: *Playboy, Hustler, Plumpers, Purely 18, Live Young Girls,* and *Finally Legal.*

Jackson's defense team argued vigorously that the photos had no relevance to the current case, especially considering that none of the pictures featured boys or young men. In most instances, this argument would have succeeded. In general, evidence of a defendant's bad moral character is not admissible in court, as it unfairly prejudices the jury against him or her. This follows the bedrock principle of American law that the accused should be tried only for what he or she did, and not for who he or she is. A decade before Jackson's trial, however, the California legislature enacted Section 1108 of the California Evidence Code, which allows prosecutors to use a defendant's history of sexual misconduct to show a present inclination to commit sex crimes. According to legislative records, this change was based on the belief, shared by many state lawmakers, that sexual criminals are more likely than other criminals to be repeat offenders and, therefore, evidence of past misbehavior is a legitimate predictor of future behavior. (As we will see in Chapter 14, many criminologists do not hold this opinion.)

Section 1108 places almost no limits on the type of prior acts that can be offered at trial. Thus, presiding Judge Rodney S. Melville of the Santa Barbara County Superior Court ruled that the jury could construe Jackson's interest in pornography as evidence of a pattern of sexual deviancy. Potentially even more damaging to the defendant's case was Judge Melville's decision that the prosecution could present evidence of five previous incidents in which Jackson was accused of engaging in inappropriate behavior with young boys. Two of the incidents led to civil suits

REUTERS/Lucy Nicholson/Landov

Michael Jackson reacts to supporters after his 2003 arrest on charges of child molestation.

that the pop star paid more than $22 million to settle in the early 1990s. Again, for the most part, prosecutors are not allowed to bring up prior convictions or arrests, much less civil suits or mere allegations, because of the prejudicial effect such evidence tends to have on juries. Under Section 1108, however, this type of evidence is admissible in sex crime trials. (Despite the damaging nature of the evidence that the prosecutors were able to get in the courtroom, the jury acquitted Jackson of all charges.)

FOR CRITICAL ANALYSIS
Does Section 1108 infringe on the rights of those accused of sex crimes in California? Explain your answer.

character traits, this will prejudice the jury against the defendant. While discussing a 1930 murder case, New York Court of Appeals Chief Judge Benjamin Cardozo addressed the issue thusly:

> With only the rough and ready tests supplied by their experience of life, the jurors were to look into the workings of another's mind, and discover its capacities and disabilities, its urges and inhibitions, in moments of intense excitement. Delicate enough and subtle is the inquiry, even in the most favorable conditions, with every warping influence excluded. There must be no blurring of the issues by evidence illegally admitted and carrying with it in its admission an appeal to prejudice and passion.[45]

(For a discussion of how the rules of evidence were applied in one of the most high-profile cases of the past decade, see the feature *CJ in Focus—The Balancing Act: Peeping Juries.*)

Authentication
Establishing the genuineness of an item that is to be introduced as evidence in a trial.

Direct Examination
The examination of a witness by the attorney who calls the witness to the stand to testify.

Hearsay
An oral or written statement made by an out-of-court declarant that is later offered in court by a witness (not the declarant) concerning a matter before the court. Hearsay usually is not admissible as evidence.

Authentication of Evidence At trial, an attorney must lay the proper foundation for the introduction of certain evidence, such as documents, exhibits, and other objects, and must demonstrate to the court that the evidence is competent; that is, the evidence is what the attorney claims. The process by which this is accomplished is referred to as **authentication.** The authentication requirement relates to relevance because something offered in evidence is relevant to the case only if it is authentic, or genuine.

Commonly, evidence is authenticated by the testimony of witnesses. For example, if an attorney wants to introduce an autopsy report as evidence in a case, he or she can have the report authenticated by the testimony of the medical examiner who signed it. By the same token, before drugs taken from a crime scene can be admitted as evidence, the law enforcement agent who collected them will be required to testify that they are in fact the same drugs.

The rules of evidence require authentication because certain types of evidence, such as exhibits and objects, cannot be cross-examined by opposing counsel, as witnesses can, yet such evidence may have a significant effect on the jury. (The cross-examination process will be examined later in the chapter.) The authentication requirement provides a safeguard against the introduction of nonverified evidence that may strongly influence the outcome of the case.

The Prosecution's Case

Because the burden of proof is on the state, the prosecution is generally considered to have a more difficult task than the defense. The prosecutor attempts to establish guilt beyond a reasonable doubt by presenting the *corpus delicti* ("body of the offense" in Latin) of the crime to the jury. The *corpus delicti* is simply a legal term that refers to the substantial facts that show a crime has been committed. By establishing such facts through the presentation of evidence, the prosecutor hopes to convince the jury of the defendant's guilt.

As was mentioned earlier, this evidence must be relevant and nonprejudicial. For example, a prosecutor might not be allowed to show the jury graphic photographs of the victim in a murder trial. Such photographs could elicit emotional responses from jurors and prejudice them against the defendant who is to be presumed innocent.[46] This is not to say, however, that evidence is never used for emotional effect. A prosecutor may, for example, place the murder weapon on a table in plain view of the jury, forcing the jurors to consider that a violent crime has in fact taken place and to focus on their duty to ensure that the guilty party is punished.

Direct Examination of Witnesses Witnesses are crucial to establishing the prosecutor's case against the defendant. The prosecutor will call witnesses to the stand and ask them questions pertaining to the sequence of events that the trial is addressing. This form of questioning is known as **direct examination.** During direct examination, the prosecutor will usually not be allowed to ask *leading questions*—questions that might suggest to the witness a particular desired response. A leading question might be something like "So, Mrs. Williams, you noticed the defendant threatening the victim with a broken beer bottle?" If Mrs. Williams answers "yes" to this question, she has, in effect, been "led" to the conclusion that the defendant was, in fact, threatening with a broken beer bottle. (A properly worded query would be, "Mrs. Williams, please describe the defendant's manner toward the victim during the incident.") The fundamental purpose behind testimony is to establish what actually happened, not what the trial attorneys would like the jury to believe happened.

Hearsay When interviewing a witness, both the prosecutor and the defense attorney will make sure that the witness's statements are based on the witness's own knowledge and not hearsay. **Hearsay** can be defined as any testimony given in court about a statement made by someone else. Literally, it is what someone heard someone else say. For the most part, hearsay is not admissible as evidence. It is excluded because the listener may have misunderstood what the other person said, and without the opportunity of cross-examining the originator of the statement, the misconception cannot be challenged.

There are a number of exceptions to the hearsay rule, and as a result, a good deal of hearsay evidence is allowed before the jury. For example, a hearsay statement is usually admissible if there seems to be little risk of a lie. Therefore, a statement made by someone who believes that his or her death is imminent—a "dying declaration"—is allowed in court even though it is hearsay.[47] The rules of most courts also allow hearsay when the person who made the statement is unavailable to be questioned in court or when the statement is particularly important to the argument being made by one side. Consequently, an admission of guilt by the defendant is often permitted even when it falls under the strict definition of hearsay.[48]

Competence and Reliability of Witnesses The rules of evidence include certain restrictions and qualifications pertaining to witnesses. Witnesses must have sufficient mental competence to understand the significance of testifying under oath. They must also be reliable in the sense that they are able to give a clear and unadulterated description of the events in question. For example, during the murder trial of Robert Blake mentioned earlier, defense attorneys severely damaged the credibility of Ronny "Duffy" Hambleton, who testified that he had been solicited by Blake to kill his wife. Hambleton, as it turned out, had smoked, snorted, and eaten so much of the drug methamphetamine that he experienced hallucinations, a revelation that generally would not instill a jury with confidence in a witness's reliability.[49]

Cross-Examination

After the prosecutor has directly examined her or his witnesses, the defense attorney is given the chance to question the same witnesses. The Sixth Amendment states, "In all criminal prosecutions, the accused shall enjoy the right . . . to be confronted with witnesses against him." In practical terms, this gives the accused, through his or her attorneys, the right to cross-examine witnesses. **Cross-examination** refers to the questioning of an opposing witness during trial, and both sides of a case are allowed to do so (see Figure 10.2 on the following page).

Cross-examination allows the attorneys to test the truthfulness of opposing witnesses and usually entails efforts to create doubt in the jurors' minds that the witness is reliable. Cross-examination is also linked to the problems presented by hearsay evidence. When a witness offers hearsay, the person making the original remarks is not in the court and therefore cannot be cross-examined. If such testimony were allowed, the defendant's Sixth Amendment right to confront witnesses against him or her would be violated.

After the defense has cross-examined a prosecution witness, the prosecutor may want to reestablish any reliability that might have been lost. The prosecutor can do so by again questioning the witness, a process known as *redirect examination*. Following the redirect examination, the defense attorney will be given the opportunity for *recross-examination*, or to ask further questions of prosecution witnesses. Thus, each side has two opportunities to question a witness. The attorneys need not do so, but only after each side has been offered the opportunity will the trial move on to the next witness or the next stage.

Motion for a Directed Verdict

After the prosecutor has finished presenting evidence against the defendant, the government will inform the court that it has rested the people's case. At this point, the defense may make a **motion for a directed verdict** (now also known as a *motion for*

CourtTV is a cable television channel that offers continuous coverage of the most important criminal trials of the day. Find its Web site, which offers news on current and classic trials, by clicking on *Web Links* under *Chapter Resources* at **www.cjinaction.com**.

Cross-Examination
The questioning of an opposing witness during trial.

Motion for a Directed Verdict
A motion requesting that the court grant judgment in favor of the defense on the ground that the prosecution has not produced sufficient evidence to support the state's claim.

FIGURE 10.2

The Cross-Examination

In the so-called Boston Nanny case, nineteen-year-old British *au pair* Louise Woodward was charged with second degree murder of an infant left in her care. Prosecutors tried to convince the jury that Woodward was a temperamental teenager who became frustrated with caring for a sick child and "snapped." The defense claimed that the brain hemorrhage that killed the child was actually the delayed result of another accident that had occurred several weeks earlier.

Detective Sergeant William Byrne, who interviewed Woodward following the boy's death, testified that she claimed to have dropped the infant on a towel on the bathroom floor, and that the infant "may have banged his head on the floor where it meets the tub." On cross-examination, defense counsel tried to clarify exactly what Woodward, who denied making such statements, had told the police officer.

DEFENSE: You asked her, "What do you mean by 'drop him on the floor,'" and her answer was, "I was angry."

DETECTIVE SERGEANT BYRNE: Yes, sir.

DEFENSE: So she wasn't telling you, according to your testimony, that "I dropped him by accident."

DETECTIVE SERGEANT BYRNE: No, sir.

DEFENSE: She wasn't saying, "I tripped and he fell."

DETECTIVE SERGEANT BYRNE: No, sir.

DEFENSE: She wasn't saying, "He slipped out of my hands."

DETECTIVE SERGEANT BYRNE: No, sir.

DEFENSE: You're saying that she told you that she did this on purpose.

DETECTIVE SERGEANT BYRNE: She was angry, sir.

DEFENSE: Okay. That's what she meant by "angry," according to you, right, that she did this on purpose.

DETECTIVE SERGEANT BYRNE: She didn't say that she did it on purpose.

DEFENSE: But you understood that to mean that she did it on purpose.

DETECTIVE SERGEANT BYRNE: That was my feeling.

In this case, the cross-examination may have hurt the defendant, as Detective Sergeant Byrne was able to reassert his belief that Woodward was responsible for the death. In fact, the Boston jury did convict Woodward, though the trial judge later overturned the conviction.

judgment as a matter of law in federal courts). Through this motion, the defense is basically saying that the prosecution has not offered enough evidence to prove that the accused is guilty beyond a reasonable doubt. If the judge grants this motion, which rarely occurs, then a judgment will be entered in favor of the defendant, and the trial is over.

The Defendant's Case

Assuming that the motion for a directed verdict is denied, the defense attorney may offer the defendant's case. Because the burden is on the state to prove the accused's guilt, the defense is not required to offer any case at all. It can simply "rest" without calling any witnesses or producing any real evidence and ask the jury to judge the merits of the case on what it has seen and heard from the prosecution.

Placing the Defendant on the Stand If the defense does present a case, its first—and often most important—decision is whether the defendant will take the stand in her or his own defense. Because of the Fifth Amendment protection against self-incrimination, the defendant is not required to testify. Therefore, the defense attorney must make a judgment call. He or she may want to place the defendant on the stand if the defendant is likely to appear sympathetic to the jury or is well spoken and able to aid the defense's case. With a less sympathetic or less effective defendant, the defense attorney may decide that exposing the defendant before the jury presents too large a risk. Also, if the defendant testifies, she or he is open to cross-examination under oath from the prosecutor. In any case, remember that the prosecution cannot comment on a defendant's refusal to testify.[50]

Creating a Reasonable Doubt Defense lawyers most commonly defend their clients by attempting to expose weaknesses in the prosecutor's case. Remember that if the defense attorney can create reasonable doubt concerning the client's guilt in the mind of just a single juror, the defendant has a good chance of gaining an acquittal or at least a *hung jury,* a circumstance explained later in the chapter.

The photo above was shown as an exhibit in the murder trial of John William King, who was charged with dragging an African American named James Byrd, Jr., to his death behind a pickup truck. Jurors were shown a number of photos of images tattooed on King's body, including one that showed a black man hanging from a tree. Do you agree with prosecutors that the intricate racist, satanic, and neo-Nazi tattoos covering King's body helped prove motive, intent, and state of mind? Or do you agree with the defense attorney who said that the tattoos do not necessarily make King a racist?

Even if the prosecution can present seemingly strong evidence, a defense attorney may succeed by creating reasonable doubt. In an illustrative case, Jason Korey bragged to his friends that he had shot and killed Joseph Brucker in Pittsburgh, Pennsylvania, and a great deal of circumstantial evidence linked Korey to the killing. The police, however, could find no direct evidence: they could not link Korey to the murder weapon, nor could they match his footprints to those found at the crime scene. Michael Foglia, Korey's defense attorney, explained his client's bragging as a ploy to gain attention from his friends. Though this explanation may strike some as unlikely, in the absence of physical evidence it did create doubt in the jurors' minds, and Korey was acquitted.

This strategy is also very effective in cases that essentially rely on the word of the defendant against the word of the victim. In sexual-assault cases, for example, if the defense attorneys can create doubt about the victim's credibility—in other words, raise the possibility that he or she is lying—then they may prevail at trial. According to the Alcohol and Rape Study, carried out by researchers at Rutgers University and the University of New Hampshire, juries acquit about 90 percent of the time when the defendant says the sex was consensual and there is evidence that the alleged victim was drinking alcohol before the incident in question.[51] (The *Criminal Justice in Action* feature at the end of this chapter explores issues concerning evidence in sexual-assault cases in more detail.)

Other Defense Strategies The defense can choose among a number of strategies to generate reasonable doubt in the jurors' minds. It can present an *alibi defense,* by submitting evidence that the accused was not at or near the scene of the crime at the time the crime was committed. Another option is to attempt an *affirmative defense,* by presenting additional facts to the ones offered by the prosecution. Possible affirmative defenses, which we discussed in detail in Chapter 4, include the following:

1 Self-defense   2 Insanity   3 Duress   4 Entrapment

With an affirmative defense strategy, the defense attempts to prove that the defendant should be found not guilty because of extenuating circumstances surrounding the crime. An affirmative strategy can be difficult to carry out because it forces the defense to prove the veracity of its own evidence, not simply disprove the evidence offered by the prosecution.

The defense is often willing to admit that a certain criminal act took place, especially if the defendant has already confessed. In this case, the primary question of the trial becomes not whether the defendant is guilty, but what the defendant is guilty of. In these situations, the defense strategy focuses on obtaining the lightest possible penalty for the defendant. As we saw in the last chapter, this strategy is responsible for the high percentage of proceedings that end in plea bargains.

Rebuttal and Surrebuttal

After the defense closes its case, the prosecution is permitted to bring new evidence forward that was not used during its initial presentation to the jury. This is called the

> "I'm trusting in the Lord and a good lawyer."
> —Oliver North, U.S. Marine officer, after being
> indicted for obstruction of justice (1986)

rebuttal stage of the trial. When the rebuttal stage is finished, the defense is given the opportunity to cross-examine the prosecution's new witnesses and introduce new witnesses of its own. This final act is part of the *surrebuttal.* After these stages have been completed, the defense may offer another motion for a directed verdict, asking the judge summarily to find in the defendant's favor. If this motion is rejected, and it almost always is, the case is closed, and the opposing sides offer their closing arguments.

Closing Arguments

In their **closing arguments,** the attorneys summarize their presentations and argue one final time for their respective cases. In most states, the defense attorney goes first, and then the prosecutor. (In Colorado, Kentucky, and Missouri, the order is reversed.) An effective closing argument includes all of the major points that support the government's or the defense's case. It also emphasizes the shortcomings of the opposing party's case. Jurors will view a closing argument with some skepticism if it merely recites the central points of a party's claim or defense without also responding to the unfavorable facts or issues raised by the other side. Of course, neither attorney wants to focus too much on the other side's position, but the elements of the opposing position do need to be acknowledged and their flaws highlighted. (For an example of opposing closing arguments, see Figure 10.3.)

One danger in the closing arguments is that an attorney will become too emotional and make remarks that are later deemed by appellate courts to be prejudicial. Once both attorneys have completed their remarks, the case is submitted to the jury, and the attorneys' role in the trial is, for the moment, complete.

THE FINAL STEPS OF THE TRIAL AND POSTCONVICTION PROCEDURES

After closing arguments, the outcome of the trial is in the hands of the jury. In this section, we examine the efforts to give jurors the means necessary to make informed decisions about the guilt or innocence of the accused. We will also look at the posttrial motions that can occur when the defense feels that the jurors, prosecution, or trial judge made errors that necessitate remedial legal action.

Jury Instructions

Before the jurors begin their deliberations, the judge gives the jury a **charge,** summing up the case and instructing the jurors on the rules of law that apply to the issues in the case. These charges, also called jury instructions, are usually prepared during a special

Rebuttal
Evidence given to counteract or disprove evidence presented by the opposing party.

Closing Arguments
Arguments made by each side's attorney after the cases for the plaintiff and defendant have been presented.

Charge
The judge's instructions to the jury following the attorneys' closing arguments; the charge sets forth the rules of law that the jury must apply in reaching its decision, or verdict.

FIGURE 10.3

Closing Arguments

Lee Boyd Malvo was charged with two counts of capital murder in connection with the sniper attacks that terrified the Washington, D.C., area in the early 2000s. As the trial progressed, it became clear the defense was trying to convince the jury that young Malvo was under the influence of his partner, John Muhammad, and therefore was not responsible for his actions. The prosecution, in contrast, emphasized Boyd's sanity and his reasoned choice to collaborate with Muhammad. These themes are evident in both sides' closing arguments, excerpts of which are provided here.

For the defense, attorney Michael S. Arif: "Understand what [Malvo] told you [in the confessions to police] is not believable. Frankly, it's bull. It's nonsense. It's not real. What he wants to do is take the blame on himself. He's putting it on himself. Why? Why does he want to do that? We've told you he was indoctrinated. We've told you he was protecting his father. Not his real father, but this John Muhammad. Why? Because this was the father he knew."

For the prosecution, Fairfax County Commonwealth Attorney Robert F. Horan, Jr.: "Members of the jury, there can be no doubt, reasonable or otherwise, that [Malvo] is the shooter of both Linda Franklin and Dean Meyers. He said he was. We have the mental-health crowd coming and saying don't believe that. Believe something else. If you believe the mental-health experts the defense presented, they are telling you he's insane, he doesn't know right from wrong, he doesn't know the nature, consequences, and character of his acts, but believe him when he said he was the spotter. Believe this insane man when he said he was the spotter."

The jury eventually found Malvo guilty, and he is now serving a life sentence at Red Onion Prison in Southwest Virginia.

charging conference involving the judge and the trial attorneys. In this conference, the attorneys suggest the instructions they would like to see be sent to the jurors, but the judge makes the final decision as to the charges submitted.[52] If the defense attorney disagrees with the charges sent to the jury, he or she can enter an objection, thereby setting the stage for a possible appeal.

The Judge's Role The judge usually begins by explaining basic legal principles, such as the need to find the defendant guilty beyond a reasonable doubt. Then the jury instructions narrow to the specifics of the case at hand, and the judge explains to the jurors what facts the prosecution must have proved to obtain a conviction. If the defense strategy centers on an affirmative defense such as insanity or entrapment, the judge will discuss the relevant legal principles that the defense must have proved to obtain an acquittal. The final segment of the charges discusses possible verdicts. These always include "guilty" and "not guilty," but some cases also allow for the jury to find "guilt by reason of insanity" or "guilty but mentally ill." Juries are often charged with determining the seriousness of the crime as well, such as deciding whether a homicide is murder in the first degree, murder in the second degree, or manslaughter.

Understanding the Instructions A serious problem with jury instructions is that jurors often do not seem to understand them.[53] This is hardly surprising, as most average Americans do not have the education or legal background to understand the somewhat unfathomable jargon of the law. One study came to the unfortunate conclusion that juries that received no instructions whatsoever were basically as well equipped— or poorly equipped, as the case may be—as juries that did receive instructions.[54]

One solution is to simplify the language of the jury instructions. This idea, however, has met resistance among legal professionals, who are accustomed to "legalese" and do not wish to change. Another suggestion is for the judge to give the jury its instructions before *and* after the trial. In this way, some of the legal concepts would be

Verdict

A formal decision made by the jury.

Hung Jury

A jury whose members are so irreconcilably divided in their opinions that they cannot reach a verdict.

introduced before the evidence and narratives are established, giving jurors a chance to comprehend the issues involved before they are overwhelmed by the evidence in a complicated case.

Jury Deliberation

After receiving the charge, the jury begins its deliberations. Jury deliberation is a somewhat mysterious process, as it takes place in complete seclusion. In extreme cases, the judge will order that the jury be *sequestered,* or isolated from the public, during the trial and deliberation stages of the proceedings. Sequestration is used when deliberations are expected to be lengthy, or the trial is attracting a high amount of interest and the judge wants to keep the jury from being unduly influenced. Juries are usually sequestered in hotels and kept under the watch and guard of officers of the court. The importance of *total* sequestration is reflected in a 2005 Colorado Supreme Court decision to overturn the death penalty of a man who was sentenced after the jurors consulted a Bible during deliberations. The court held that the Bible constituted an improper outside influence and a reliance on a "higher authority."[55]

Most of what is known about how a jury deliberates comes from mock trials or interviews with jurors after the verdict has been reached. A general picture of the deliberation process can be constructed from this research. It shows that the romantic notion of jurors with high-minded ideals of justice making eloquent speeches is, for the most part, not the reality. In approximately three out of every ten cases, the initial vote by the jury led to a unanimous decision. In 90 percent of the remaining cases, the majority eventually dictated the decision.[56] (To learn how a popular television show has affected jury deliberations, see the feature *CJ and the Media—The* "CSI *Effect.*")

The Verdict

Once it has reached a decision, the jury issues a **verdict.** The most common verdicts are guilty and not guilty, though, as we have seen, juries may signify different degrees of guilt if instructed to do so. Following the announcement of a guilty or not guilty verdict, the jurors are discharged, and the jury trial proceedings are finished. (See Figure 10.4 for a review of the steps of a jury trial.)

The Hung Jury When a jury in a criminal trial is unable to agree on a unanimous verdict—or a majority in certain states—it returns with no decision. This is known as a **hung jury.** After the trauma of a trial, a hung jury is often unsatisfactory to the partic-

FIGURE 10.4
The Steps of a Jury Trial

The " *CSI* Effect"

Prosecutors in Maricopa County (Arizona) thought they had an easy conviction on their hands. A witness, who testified in court, saw the defendant leaving a commercial office building carrying a stolen stereo. Police arrested the man a few minutes later and found tools commonly used in burglaries in his car. The jurors, however, were not satisfied. Why, they wondered, weren't any of the defendant's fingerprints lifted from the scene of the alleged crime inside the building? Deciding that the police "didn't do enough," the jury voted to acquit.

The Maricopa County prosecutors were victims of the "*CSI* effect," another example of how the fictional world of the media can affect the real world of the criminal justice system. The phenomenon takes its name from the popular television series, *CSI: Crime Scene Investigation,* which, along with two spin-offs, draws more than 40 million viewers a week. The *CSI* shows follow different teams of crime-lab technicians as they use forensic technology to solve at least two violent crimes a week. According to many prosecutors, the problem (which is not a problem at all if you happen to be a defense attorney) is that the shows have fostered unrealistic notions as to what forensic science can accomplish as part of a criminal investigation. Consequently, juries have become much more interested in, and demanding of, the use of "supertechnology" to solve cases. One of the jurors who voted to acquit actor Robert Blake of the murder of his wife (see page 324) admitted afterwards, "I just expected so much more" from the prosecution because of the television shows.

PERCEPTION VERSUS REALITY

In reality, the kind of physical evidence used to solve crimes on *CSI* is often not available to prosecutors, who must instead rely on witnesses and circumstantial evidence. The show also severely distorts how a crime lab functions: *CSI* technicians seem to be able to get the results of a DNA sample in hours, if not minutes, but real DNA labs are so overburdened that the procedure can take weeks, if not months. Furthermore, while perfect fingerprints are routinely taken from all types of surfaces on *CSI*, the actual collection of fingerprints is a frustrating process, characterized by smudged prints and slick or bumpy surfaces.

MORE LABWORK NEEDED

Many prosecutors have accepted that juries are more demanding and have begun to cater to their need for *CSI*-type evidence. In Arizona, for example, DNA profiling requests to the State Department of Safety crime labs increased 333 percent from 1999, when the show debuted, to 2004. In the same time period, requests for blood analysis rose 133 percent, trace evidence analysis 75 percent, and latent fingerprint examinations 39 percent. Despite all of the headaches it has caused, the "*CSI* effect" has benefited prosecutors in at least one way. "Talking about science in the courtroom used to be like talking about geometry—a real turnoff," says one expert. "Now that there's this almost obsession with the [*CSI*] shows, you can talk to jurors about [scientific evidence] and just see from the looks on their faces that they find it fascinating."

Dr. Alexx Woods (Khandi Alexander) and Lieutenant Horatio Caine (David Caruso) examine the evidence on *CSI: Miami.*

Photo by Bill Inoshita/CBS Photo Archive via Getty Images

ipants of the trial. After a hung jury was announced in the trial of Jeremy Morse, a white Inglewood (California) police officer who had been caught on videotape beating a black teenager, someone in the courtroom shouted out, "There's no justice here."[57]

A judge can do little to reverse a hung jury, considering that "no decision" is just as legitimate a verdict as guilty or not guilty. In some states, if there are only a few dissenters to the majority view, a judge can send the jury back to the jury room under a

Allen Charge

An instruction by a judge to a deadlocked jury with only a few dissenters that asks the jurors in the minority to reconsider the majority opinion.

Jury Nullification

An acquittal of a defendant by a jury even though the evidence presented and the judge's instructions indicate that the defendant is guilty.

Appeal

The process of seeking a higher court's review of a lower court's decision for the purpose of correcting or changing the lower court's judgment or decision.

Double Jeopardy

To twice place at risk (jeopardize) a person's life or liberty. The Fifth Amendment to the U.S. Constitution prohibits a second prosecution for the same criminal offense.

set of rules set forth more than a century ago by the Supreme Court in *Allen v. United States* (1896).[58] The **Allen Charge,** as this instruction is called, asks the jurors in the minority to reconsider the majority opinion. Many jurisdictions do not allow *Allen* Charges on the ground that they improperly coerce jurors with the minority opinion to change their minds.[59]

For all of the attention they receive, hung juries are relatively rare. Juries are unable to come to a decision in only about 6 percent of all cases.[60] Furthermore, juries may be more lenient (or easy to "trick") than is generally perceived; one study found that juries were six times more likely than judges (in bench trials) to acquit a person who turns out to be guilty.[61]

Jury Nullification The last statistic points to a growing concern of a number of criminal justice observers: the question of whether the jury's verdict is always based on the proper legal principles. This question deals with the controversial subject of **jury nullification,** which occurs when jurors "nullify" the law by acquitting a defendant who may be guilty according to the instruction given to them by the court. In other words, the jury acquits *in spite of* the evidence, rather than *because of* the evidence.[62] The specter of jury nullification is most often raised in cases that involve issues on which jurors may have strong ideological opinions, such as race, the death penalty, assisted suicide, or drug offenses. The not guilty verdict in O. J. Simpson's 1995 criminal trial was widely seen as an example of jury nullification, with jurors swayed by the racially based arguments of the defense rather than the facts of the case.

Many observers believe jury nullification is counter to the principles of American law because it allows a jury to "play by its own rules." Others, however, feel that jurors are within their rights when they question not only the facts in the case before them, but also the merits of the laws that the court is asking them to enforce. This argument has been made since the earliest days of the American legal system, when John Adams (1735–1826) said that a juror has not only a right, but a duty, "to find the verdict according to his own best understanding, judgment, and conscience, though in direct opposition to the direction of the court."[63] By this reasoning, jurors who feel that a particular law is unjust, or that the penalty for a law is too severe, are justified in nullifying a guilty verdict.

Appeals

Even if a defendant is found guilty, the trial process is not necessarily over. In our criminal justice system, a person convicted of a crime has a right to appeal. An **appeal** is the process of seeking a higher court's review of a lower court's decision for the purpose of correcting or changing the lower court's judgment. Any defendant who loses a case in a trial court cannot automatically appeal the conviction. The defendant normally must first be able to show that the trial court acted improperly on a question of law. Common reasons for appeals include the introduction of tainted evidence by the prosecution or faulty jury instructions delivered by the trial judge. In federal courts, about 16 percent of criminal convictions are appealed.[64]

Double Jeopardy The appeals process is available only to the defense. If a jury finds the accused not guilty, the prosecution cannot appeal to have the decision reversed. To do so would infringe on the defendant's Fifth Amendment rights against multiple trials for the same offense. This guarantee against being tried a second time for the same crime is known as protection from **double jeopardy.**

The Limits of Double Jeopardy The prohibition against double jeopardy means that once a criminal defendant is found not guilty of a particular crime, the government may not reindict the person and retry him or her for the same crime. The basic idea behind the double jeopardy clause, in the words of Supreme Court Justice Hugo Black, is that the state should not be allowed to

> make repeated attempts to convict an individual for an alleged offense, thereby subjecting him to embarrassment, expense, and ordeal and compelling him to live in a continuing state of anxiety and insecurity, as well as enhancing the possibility that though innocent he may be found guilty.[65]

AP Photo/Jim McKnight

On May 6, 2002, Court of Appeals Chief Judge Judith S. Kaye and Judge Howard A. Levine enter the New York State Court of Appeals to hear arguments as to whether Darrel K. Harris should be executed by the state. The court of appeals eventually overturned Harris's death sentence. Six of the seven judges found that he had been unfairly forced to choose between exercising his constitutional rights under the Fifth and Sixth Amendments and pleading guilty to a lesser charge that was not punishable by execution. How does Harris's case show the important role that appeals courts play in the criminal justice system?

The bar against double jeopardy does not preclude a *civil* suit's being brought against the same person by a crime victim to recover damages. For example, in 1982 Karen Ely was convicted of helping to kill her husband, Raymond Ely, in Rensselaer, New York. More than two decades later, in 2004, Raymond's sister, Barbara Bizzi, won a $7 million wrongful death suit against Karen, who was still in prison. This was not considered double jeopardy because the second suit involved a civil claim, not a criminal one. Therefore, Karen Ely was not charged with committing the same *crime* twice.

The Possibility and Risk of Retrial Additionally, a state's prosecution of a crime will not prevent a separate federal prosecution of the same crime, and vice versa; that is, a defendant found not guilty of violating a state law can be tried in federal court for the same act, if the act is also defined as a crime under federal law. Furthermore, as we saw in Chapter 8 with the example of Washington, D.C., area sniper John Allen Muhammad, double jeopardy does not preclude different states from prosecuting the same person for multiple crimes that take place in different jurisdictions.

Note that a hung jury is *not* an acquittal for purposes of double jeopardy. So, if a jury is deadlocked, the government is free to seek a new trial. The United States Supreme Court reiterated this principle in *Sattazahn v. Pennsylvania* (2003),[66] a case involving a defendant who was convicted of murder but then had a hung jury in the

penalty phase of his trial—resulting in an automatic sentence of life in prison rather than execution. The defendant appealed the initial conviction and won a new trial. When he was convicted a second time, the state once again sought the death penalty and suc-

> "Appeal: In law, to put the dice into the box for another throw."
>
> —Ambrose Bierce, American author (c. 1900)

ceeded. The Court held that as no acquittal had taken place in the sentencing phase of the first trial, double jeopardy protections were irrelevant.

The Appeal Process There are two basic reasons for the appeal process. The first is to correct an error made during the initial trial. The second is to review policy. Because of this second function, the appellate courts are an important part of the flexible nature of the criminal justice system. When existing law has ceased to be effective or no longer reflects the values of society, an appellate court can effectively change the law through its decisions and the precedents that it sets.[67] A classic example was the *Miranda v. Arizona* decision, which, although it failed to change the fate of the defendant (he was found guilty on retrial), had a far-reaching impact on custodial interrogation of suspects.

Habeas Corpus
An order that requires correctional officials to bring an inmate before a court or a judge and explain why he or she is being held in prison.

It is also important to understand that once the appeal process begins, the defendant is no longer presumed innocent. The burden of proof has shifted, and the defendant is obligated to prove that her or his conviction should be overturned. The method of filing an appeal differs slightly among the fifty states and the federal government, but the six basic steps are similar enough for summarization in Figure 10.5.

For the most part, defendants are not required to exercise their right to appeal. The one exception is in the case of the death sentence. Given the seriousness of capital punishment, the defendant is required to appeal the case, regardless of his or her wishes.

Habeas Corpus

The 1980s and early 1990s saw a rise in a postconviction process known as **habeas corpus** (Latin for "you have the body"). *Habeas corpus* is a judicial order that literally commands a corrections official to bring a prisoner before a federal court so that the court can hear the person's claim that he or she is being held illegally. A writ of *habeas corpus* differs from an appeal in several respects. First, it can be filed only by someone who is imprisoned. Second, it can address only constitutional issues, not technical errors. Thus, an inmate can file a *habeas corpus* petition claiming that the conditions of her or his imprisonment constitute cruel and unusual punishment, but not that the judge provided the jury with improper instructions during the trial. (Peter Sakarias, discussed in this chapter's introductory segment, filed a successful *habeas corpus* petition with the California Supreme Court. In it, he claimed that the prosecutor's contradictory theories of Viivi Piirisild's murder violated his due process rights.)

The most aggressive move to limit *habeas corpus* review in recent years has come from Congress. In 1996, motivated by the politically popular goal of shortening the

---

FIGURE 10.5

The Steps of an Appeal

1. Within a specific period of time—usually between thirty and ninety days—the defendant must file a *notice of appeal.* This is a short written statement outlining the basis of the appeal.

2. The appellant, or losing party in the lower court, must then transfer the trial court record to the appellate court. This record contains items of the case file, including exhibits, and a transcript of the testimony.

3. Next, the briefs must be filed. A *brief* is a written argument that presents the party's legal arguments and precedents to support these arguments. Both the appellant and the winning prosecutorial team must submit briefs to the appellate court.

4. The briefs are followed by *oral arguments,* in which attorneys from both sides appear before the appellate court panel to state their positions. In oral arguments, the judge or judges ask questions of the attorneys to clarify certain points or voice a particular disagreement.

5. After the oral arguments, the judges retire to deliberate the case. After a decision has been made, one or more of the judges prepare the *written opinion.* (This process is described in Chapter 8 in more detail.) A judge who disagrees with the majority opinion may write a *dissenting opinion.*

6. Finally, the court holds a disposition in which it announces the next step for the case. The court can *uphold* the decision of the lower court, or it can *modify* the lower court decision by changing a part of it but not the whole. The lower court's decision can be *reversed,* or set aside, or the appellate court can *reverse* and *remand* the case, meaning that the lower court's decision is overturned and the matter is sent back for further proceedings. Or, the appellate court may simply *remand* the case without overturning it.

time between conviction and execution in death penalty cases, Congress passed the Antiterrorism and Effective Death Penalty Act, which placed a one-year time limit on filing a *habeas corpus* petition and restricted a federal court's ability to overturn a state court's criminal conviction.[68] Many observers felt that if this legislation was challenged, the United States Supreme Court would not uphold it on the basis that Article I of the Constitution limits Congress's ability to suspend *habeas corpus*.[69]

The Court was given the chance to do so almost immediately when Georgia inmate Ellis Wayne Felker challenged the new law, claiming it unconstitutionally limited the appeals of convicted murderers. Felker had been found guilty of rape and murder in 1983 and sentenced to die, but he had managed to elude the death penalty through *habeas corpus* petitions. In a unanimous decision, the Court rejected Felker's claim and upheld the act,[70] setting the stage for further erosion of *habeas corpus* in the future.

Rape Shield Laws

One of the cardinal rules of the courtroom is that evidence is admissible so long as it is relevant and not unfairly prejudicial. Of course, all evidence should be prejudicial to some degree—the main reason lawyers introduce it is to prejudice the jury in favor of their own arguments and against those of their opponents. The key point is that evidence must not be *unfairly* prejudicial. As we close this chapter, we will examine the controversial role of evidence in rape cases, an area where politicians, judges, and attorneys have been battling over the ever-elusive concept of "fairness" for decades, with no end to the struggle in sight.

The "Chastity Requirement"

Almost one hundred years ago, a Texas appeals court questioned the trustworthiness of a woman who claimed to have been sexually assaulted. The possibility that she "was in the habit of bestowing carnal favors indiscriminately upon men," said the court, "would certainly have had a very strong bearing upon her credibility as a witness."[71] Around the same time, the Iowa Supreme Court held that "voluntary sexual relations . . . may and should have been considered as substantive proof that, whatever the act done, it was done with the consent" of the accuser.[72] The message was clear: if a woman had been sexually active, she "assumed the risk" that she would be sexually assaulted and did not deserve the trust or protection of the law.

These attitudes—labeled the "chastity requirement" by Professor Michelle Anderson of the Villanova University School of Law[73]—have historically made the courtroom a hostile environment for victims of sexual assault. According to Anderson and numerous other experts, rape victims who were perceived by juries to be sexually virtuous were much more likely to be believed than those who had been sexually active. If a woman had consented to sex before, so the line of thought went, she was more likely to do so again. Consequently, defense attorneys inevitably and successfully focused on the accuser's sexual past, convincing juries that consent had been given in the present instance by establishing a pattern of consent in past ones. Rather than expose their private lives to this kind of scrutiny, many women decided not to bring charges against their attackers.[74]

State and Federal Legislation (with Exceptions)

In an attempt to keep sexual-assault judicial proceedings from being little more than morality trials of the accuser, in 1974 Michigan passed the first **rape shield law** in the United States. The statute kept specific evidence, reputation evidence, and opinion evidence of the victim's previous sexual conduct out of the courtroom, except under certain circumstances.[75] Today, every state but Arizona has a rape shield law. (In Arizona, well-established case law, rather than a state statute, declares evidence of the accuser's "unchastity" inadmissible.[76]) In 1978, the U.S. Congress also imposed a rape shield law in federal courts with Federal Rule of Evidence 412.[77]

Rape shield laws have two general goals: (1) to encourage victims to report incidents of sexual assault by protecting their privacy, and (2) to ensure that defendants are convicted or acquitted based on the relevant evidence, not the prejudices of the jury. Though few would dispute the worthiness of these objectives, many observers—particularly defense attorneys—argued vigorously that proposed rape shield laws would be not only unfair toward defendants, but also unconstitutional. The Sixth Amendment gives all defendants the right to confront their accusers and to bring forth witnesses in their favor. By limiting these rights, the critics contended, a rape shield law would leave defendants in sexual-assault cases at the mercy of juries that would not know all of the facts surrounding a case.

To allay these fears, every rape shield law contains certain exceptions that allow the defense to use evidence of the accuser's prior sexual conduct to undermine the credibility of her or his testimony. For example, Federal Rule of Evidence 412 states that evidence of "other sexual behavior" or the "sexual disposition" of a rape complainant is inadmissible *except* when it is offered

1 to prove that a person other than the accused was the source of semen, injury, or other physical evidence;

Rape Shield Law

A state or federal law that disallows any evidence of an alleged sexual-assault victim's prior sexual conduct to be used against her or him in a criminal trial. These laws are designed to spare the victim the humiliation of irrelevant references to past sexual behavior that may improperly influence the jury.

2 to prove consent *and* involves previous sexual behavior by the alleged victim with the person accused of sexual misconduct; or

3 to show that the exclusion of the evidence would violate the constitutional rights of the defendant.[78]

All of the state rape shield laws include identical or similar exceptions.

Judging the Evidence

Many observers feel that the exceptions have effectively "gutted" rape shield laws by giving defense attorneys a number of ways to avoid the statutes' protective measures.[79] An example of how these exceptions operate can be seen in a North Carolina case involving a woman who accused two men of raping her in the back seat of a car.[80] Both defendants claimed the sexual activity was consensual. Relying on North Carolina's rape shield law, the trial court *excluded* three pieces of evidence offered by the defense: First, that a person had witnessed the accuser flirting aggressively with numerous men at a local club, "feeling on them and stuff like that." Second, that the accuser had openly tried to seduce the older brother of one of the defendants and have sex with him in a car. And, third, that another person had seen the accuser sitting on a soda crate in front of two men, one of whom was zipping up his pants.[81] At trial, the jury convicted both defendants of second degree rape.

On appeal, however, a North Carolina appellate court reversed the decision. One of the exceptions to the state's rape shield law allows the defense to establish a pattern of prior sexual conduct with third parties that might explain how a defendant would have a reasonable but mistaken belief that the accuser consented to sex.[82] The appellate court ruled that the trial court should have admitted the excluded evidence because this evidence "suggests that the prosecuting witness was the initiator, the aggressor, in her sexual encounters."[83] Thus, the appellate court explained, the defendants could have plausibly thought she consented to sex in the car because they had seen her behave similarly in other circumstances.

The Bryant Case

Decisions such as the one made by the North Carolina appellate court have led some to wonder if the situation for sexual-assault victims has actually improved since the

Professional basketball player Kobe Bryant, left, is reassured by defense attorney Pamela Mackey during a hearing in Eagle, Colorado. Bryant was charged with felony sexual assault against a nineteen-year-old; she claimed he forced her to have sex, while Bryant insisted that the sex was consensual.

advent of rape shield laws. Numerous studies show that the "chastity requirement" is still a prejudicial influence that works to the advantage of defense attorneys who manage to get evidence of prior sexual acts before the jury.[84] In 2003, the New Jersey Supreme Court ruled that an exception to the state's rape shield law allowed juries to hear about all of the alleged victim's past sexual activity, including flirting, that involved the person accused of committing rape—a decision the United States Supreme Court declined to consider.[85] Furthermore, since only 16 percent of those who have been sexually assaulted report the crime to police, the laws do not appear to have encouraged rape victims to come forward to authorities.[86]

For many, the "final straw" concerning rape shield laws came when basketball star Kobe Bryant was charged with a Class 3 felony sexual assault after a sexual encounter with an employee of the Lodge & Spa resort in Cordillera, Colorado, on June 30, 2003. Bryant insisted the sex was consensual. His alleged victim countered that he forced her by putting his hand around her throat and bending her over a chair. Although the stated purpose of rape shield laws is to protect the accuser's privacy, the law meant little in the face of media attention and several mistakes by court employees. As one commentator said, "it took me less than five minutes at my computer to learn [the woman's] name, address, and phone number."[87]

Furthermore, it became apparent very early in the proceedings that previous sexual activity of Bryant's accuser would be an issue at trial. During an evidentiary hearing, one of his defense attorneys asked an expert witness if the accuser's vaginal injuries—which she said were caused by Bryant—were "consistent with someone who had sex with three different men in three days."[88] The Colorado rape shield law gives trial judges a large amount of discretion in deciding whether evidence of a woman's prior sexual conduct will unfairly prejudice the jury.[89] In this case, Judge W. Terry Ruckriegle ruled that the jury could hear about previous sexual encounters to counter the prosecution's claim that Bryant had been the cause of her injuries. Perhaps wary of how the "chastity requirement" (see page 338) might affect her case, Bryant's alleged victim eventually refused to cooperate with prosecutors, who were forced to drop the charges against the basketball star. In the minds of many observers, Colorado might as well have had no rape shield law for all the protection the statute provided this woman.[90]

A Drastic Response

Supporters of legislation to protect rape victims insist that the laws do what they are supposed to: balance the rights of the accuser and the rights of the accused, who, they point out, faces severe punishment if found guilty and must be given every chance to present a vigorous defense. Others feel the laws need major reform. Legal expert Cristina Carmody Tilley, for one, believes that rape shield laws should be done away with all together.[91] She thinks that facts related to the accuser's previous sexual acts with the defendant or anybody else should be treated like any other evidence. That is, they should be admitted unless they are unfairly prejudicial. In Tilley's opinion, the focus should ultimately shift from the accuser's state of mind to her or his actions. In other words, juries should not have to determine whether "no" meant "yes," but whether the alleged victim ever indicated "no" in the first place.

Making Sense of Rape Shield Laws

1 Do you agree with Cristina Carmody Tilley that rape shield laws should be abolished? What would be the ramifications of such a policy?

2 Kobe Bryant's lawyers argued that rape shield laws are inherently unfair because they limit the admissibility of the alleged victim's sexual history but place no limits on the defendant's sexual history. Explain why you agree or disagree with this statement.

3 Should evidence that an alleged rape victim has a history of prostitution be admissible under Federal Rule of Evidence 412? Why or why not?

Chapter Summary

1 **Identify the basic protections enjoyed by criminal defendants in the United States.** According to the Sixth Amendment, a criminal defendant has the right to a speedy and public trial by an impartial jury in the physical location where the crime was committed. Additionally, a person accused of a crime must be informed of the nature of the crime and be confronted with the witnesses against him or her. Further, the accused must be able to summon witnesses in her or his favor and have the assistance of counsel.

2 **List the three requirements of the Speedy Trial Act of 1974.** In federal court, those accused of crimes must experience (a) no more than thirty days between arrest and indictment; (b) no more than ten days between indictment and arraignment; and (c) no more than sixty days between arraignment and trial. Of course, extra time is allowed for hearings on pretrial motions, mental competency examinations, and other procedural actions.

3 **Explain what "taking the Fifth" really means.** The Fifth Amendment states that no person "shall be compelled in any criminal case to be a witness against himself." Thus, defendants do not have to testify if their testimony would implicate them in the crime. Witnesses may refuse to testify on this same ground. (Witnesses, though, are often granted immunity and thereafter can no longer take the Fifth.) In the United States, silence on the part of a defendant cannot be used by the jury in forming its opinion about guilt or innocence.

4 **List the requirements normally imposed on potential jurors.** They must be (a) citizens of the United States; (b) over eighteen years of age; (c) free of felony convictions; (d) of the necessary health to function on a jury; (e) sufficiently intelligent to understand the issues at trial; and (f) able to read, write, and comprehend the English language.

STORIES FROM THE STREET

Go to the *Stories from the Street* feature at **www.cjinaction.com** to hear Larry Gaines tell insightful stories related to this chapter and his experiences in the field.

5 Contrast challenges for cause and peremptory challenges during *voir dire.* A challenge for cause occurs when an attorney provides the court with a legally justifiable reason why a potential juror should be excluded; for example, because the juror does not speak English. In contrast, peremptory challenges do not require any justification by the attorney and are usually limited to a small number. They cannot, however, be based, even implicitly, on race or gender.

6 List the standard steps in a criminal jury trial. (a) Opening statements by the prosecutor and the defense attorney; (b) presentation of evidence, usually in the form of questioning by the prosecutor, known as direct examination; (c) cross-examination by the defense attorney of the same witnesses; (d) at the end of the prosecutor's presentation of evidence, motion for a directed verdict by the defense (also called a motion for judgment as a matter of law in the federal courts), which is normally denied by the judge; (e) presentation of the defendant's case, which may include placing the defendant on the stand and direct examination of the defense's witnesses; (f) cross-examination by the prosecutor; (g) after the defense closes its case, rebuttal by the prosecution, which may involve new evidence that was not used initially by the prosecution; (h) cross-examination of the prosecution's new witnesses by the defense and introduction of new witnesses of its own, called the surrebuttal; (i) closing arguments by both the defense and the prosecution; (j) the charging of the jury by the judge, during which the judge sums up the case and instructs the jurors on the rules of law that apply; (k) jury deliberations; and (l) presentation of the verdict.

7 Explain the difference between testimony and real evidence; between lay witnesses and expert witnesses; and between direct and circumstantial evidence. Testimony consists of statements by competent witnesses, whereas real evidence includes physical items that affect the case; a lay witness is an "average person," whereas an expert witness speaks with the authority of one who has professional training, advanced knowledge, or substantial experience in a specialized area; direct evidence is evidence presented by witnesses as opposed to circumstantial evidence, which can create an inference that a fact exists, but does not directly establish the fact.

8 List possible affirmative defenses. (a) Self-defense, (b) insanity, (c) duress, and (d) entrapment.

9 Delineate circumstances in which a criminal defendant may in fact be tried a second time for the same act. A defendant who is acquitted in a criminal trial may be sued in a civil case for essentially the same act. When an act is a crime under both state and federal law, a defendant who is acquitted in state court may be tried in federal court for the same act, and vice versa.

10 List the six basic steps of an appeal. (a) The filing of a notice of appeal; (b) the transfer of the trial court record to the appellate court; (c) the filing of briefs; (d) the presentation of oral arguments; (e) the deliberation of the appellate judges who then prepare a written opinion; and (f) the announcement of the judges—upholding the decision of the lower court, modifying part of the decision, reversing the decision, or reversing and remanding the decision to the trial court.

Key Terms

acquittal 313
Allen Charge 334
appeal 334
authentication 326
bench trial 313
beyond a reasonable
  doubt 314
challenge for cause 317
charge 330

circumstantial evidence 324
closing arguments 330
cross-examination 327
direct evidence 324
direct examination 326
double jeopardy 334
evidence 322
expert witness 323
habeas corpus 336

hearsay 326
hung jury 332
jury nullification 334
jury trial 313
lay witness 322
master jury list 316
motion for a directed
  verdict 327
opening statements 322

peremptory challenges 318
rape shield law 338
real evidence 322
rebuttal 330
relevant evidence 324
testimony 322
venire 317
verdict 332
voir dire 317

Questions for Critical Analysis

1 If a defendant waives his or her right to a jury trial, what type of trial then takes place?

2 Why is there a higher standard of proof in criminal cases than in civil cases?

3 What danger lies in a defense attorney's or prosecutor's decision to present an opening statement to the jury?

4 Under what circumstances may evidence be excluded?

5 How does an attorney authenticate evidence presented?

6 Are there exceptions to the hearsay rule, and if so, what are they?

7 Why might a defense attorney not want to call the defendant to the stand to testify?

8 What is usually the major problem with the jury instructions that judges present prior to jury deliberations?

9 What steps can a judge take if the jury does not come to a decision on the defendant's guilt or innocence?

10 Under what circumstances can a person ask for *habeas corpus* review of her or his case?

Test Preparation Online

ⓒ Criminal JusticeNow

Go to **www.cjinaction.com** and click on *Criminal JusticeNow* for access to this powerful online study tool. You will get a *personalized study plan* based on your responses to a diagnostic pretest. Once you have mastered the material with the help of interactive learning tools, video clips with questions, an integrated e-book, and more, you can take a posttest to confirm you are ready to move on to the next chapter.

ⓒ Book Companion Web Site

At the book companion Web site (**www.cjinaction.com**), you will find many resources in addition to *Criminal JusticeNow* to aid you in studying for your exams. For example, under *Chapter Resources,* you will find the *Chapter Outline, Chapter Summary, Flashcards, Glossary, Learning Objectives, Lecture Presentations, Concept Builder, Essay Questions,* and a *Tutorial Chapter Quiz.* You can also test yourself with interactive *Online Reviews* of each chapter section. Check out the *Web Links* to access the Web sites mentioned in the text, as well as many others. You can also access recent perspectives by clicking on *CJ in the News* and *Terrorism Update* under *Course Resources.*

Suggested Readings

Langbein, John, *The Origins of the Adversary Criminal Trial,* New York: Oxford University Press, 2005. Believe it or not, at one time lawyers played almost no role in the criminal trial. Until the end of the seventeenth century, English custom—which forms the basis for modern American law—prohibited defendants from being represented by counsel, and lawyers hardly ever appeared on behalf of the prosecution. Instead, the trial was a forum where the defendant was expected to answer the charges himself (or herself) without any attorneys to muddle the situation. Only the sheer brazenness of witnesses for the prosecution, who were often criminals themselves intent on lying their way to a more lenient punishment, finally convinced English judges that lawyers were needed for purposes of cross-examination. Langbein, a professor at Yale Law School, uses this and other anecdotes to trace the evolution of the criminal trial from a defendant-focused procedure to the present battleground between prosecution and defense.

Spence, Gerry, *The Smoking Gun: Day by Day through a Shocking Murder Trial with Gerry Spence,* New York: Scribner, 2003. Spence, one of the nation's best-known defense attorneys, takes his readers on a detailed voyage through a criminal trial. The defendants are Sandy Jones and her son, who have been charged with murdering a real estate developer on their Oregon farm. The trial develops into a classic battle between Jones, a poor woman, and the "powers that be" in the community who seem convinced of her guilt regardless of any evidence to the contrary. Spence jumps into his role as a voluntary member of Jones's defense team, and this book follows his efforts as he struggles with two different judges and lead prosecutors. The author is particularly insightful as he describes how he selects the jury and the reasoning behind his questioning of witnesses.

Notes

1. Muara Dolan, "California Court Rules against Prosecutors," *Los Angeles Times* (March 4, 2005), B1.
2. *In re Waidla,* Cal. SC S102401 (2005).
3. *In re Sakarias,* Cal. SC S082299 (2005).
4. Jerome Frank, *Courts on Trial: Myth and Reality in American Justice* (New York: Atheneum, 1969), 14–33.
5. William L. Prosser, *Handbook of the Law of Torts,* 2d ed. (St. Paul, MN: West Publishing Co., 1955), 7.
6. David L. Cook, Steven R. Schlesinger, Thomas J. Bak, and William T. Rule II, "Criminal Caseload in U.S. District Courts: More than Meets the Eye," *American University Law Review* 44 (June 1995), 44.
7. 407 U.S. 514 (1972).
8. Roger Misner, *Speedy Trials: Federal and State Practice* (Charlottesville, VA: The Michie Co., 1983).
9. L. Stuart Ditzen, "Suspects' Release Stuns City Lawyers: Seven Murder Defendants Were Set Free on a Speedy-Trial Violation," *Philadelphia Inquirer* (August 6, 2004), B1.
10. 18 U.S.C. Section 3161.
11. 391 U.S. 145 (1968).
12. *Blanton v. Las Vegas,* 489 U.S. 538 (1989).
13. *Williams v. Florida,* 399 U.S. 102 (1970).
14. 435 U.S. 223 (1978).
15. *Johnson v. Louisiana,* 406 U.S. 356 (1972); and *Apodaca v. Oregon,* 406 U.S. 404 (1972).
16. 332 U.S. 46 (1947).
17. Barton L. Ingraham, "The Right of Silence, the Presumption of Innocence, the Burden of Proof, and a Modest Proposal," *Journal of Criminal Law and Criminology* 85 (1994), 559–595.
18. 397 U.S. 358 (1970).
19. James P. Levine, "The Impact of Local Political Cultures on Jury Verdicts," *Criminal Justice Journal* 14 (1992), 163–164.
20. *State v. Gonzales,* No. CR-99-139 (N.M. January 19, 2000).
21. Kate Zernike, "Trial Will Weigh Matters of Intent of Betrayed Wife Who Killed Her Husband," *New York Times* (January 24, 2003), A16.
22. *Lockhart v. McCree,* 476 U.S. 162 (1986).

23. *Witherspoon v. Illinois,* 391 U.S. 510 (1968).
24. John Kaplan and Jon R. Waltz, *The Trial of Jack Ruby* (New York: Macmillan, 1965), 91–94.
25. Jeremy W. Barber, "The Jury Is Still Out," *American Criminal Law Review* 31 (Summer 1994), 1225–1252.
26. 380 U.S. 224 (1965).
27. 476 U.S. 79 (1986).
28. Eric L. Muller, "Solving the *Batson* Paradox: Harmless Error, Jury Representation, and the Sixth Amendment," *Yale Law Journal* 106 (October 1996), 93.
29. 499 U.S. 400 (1991).
30. 502 U.S. 1056 (1992).
31. *Miller-El v. Cockrell,* 537 U.S. 322 (2003).
32. *Miller-El v. Dretke,* 361 F.3d 894 (5th Cir. 2004); and *Miller-El v. Dretke,* ___ U.S. ___ (2005).
33. Karen L. Cipriani, "The Numbers Don't Add Up: Challenging the Premise of *J.E.B. v. Alabama,*" *American Criminal Law Review* 31 (Summer 1994), 1253–1277.
34. 511 U.S. 127 (1994).
35. Harry Kalven and Hans Zeisel, *The American Jury* (Boston: Little, Brown, 1966), 163–167.
36. Douglas D. Koski, "Testing the Story Model of Juror Decision Making," *Sex Offender Law* (June/July 2003), 53–58.
37. Nancy Pennington and Reid Hastie, "The Story Model for Juror Decision Making," in *Inside the Juror: The Psychology of Juror Decision Making* (Cambridge, MA: Harvard University Press, 1983), 192, 194–195.
38. 424 U.S. 600 (1976).
39. Federal Rule of Evidence 703.
40. Richard A. Epstein, "Judicial Control over Expert Testimony: Of Deference and Education," *Northwestern University Law Review* 87 (1993), 1156.
41. L. Timothy Perrin, "Expert Witnesses under Rules 703 and 803(4) of the Federal Rules of Evidence: Separating the Wheat from the Chaff," *Indiana Law Journal* 72 (Fall 1997), 939.
42. Andrew Blankstein and Jean Guccione, "Actor Robert Blake Acquitted in Shooting Death of His Wife," *Los Angeles Times* (March 17, 2005), A1.
43. Thomas J. Reed, "Trial by Propensity: Admission of Other Criminal Acts Evidenced in Federal Criminal Trials," *University of Cincinnati Law Review* 50 (1981), 713.
44. *Ibid.*
45. *People v. Zackowitz,* 254 N.Y. 192 (1930).
46. Charles McCormick, *Handbook on Evidence* (St. Paul, MN: West Publishing Co., 1987), Chapter 1.
47. Federal Rules of Procedure, Rule 804(b)(2).
48. Arthur Best, *Evidence: Examples and Explanations,* 4th ed. (New York: Aspen Law & Business, 2001), 89–90.
49. Andrew Blankstein, "Blake Witness Meth Use Described," *Los Angeles Times* (February 17, 2005), B5.
50. *Griffin v. California,* 380 U.S. 609 (1965).
51. Douglas D. Koski, "Alcohol and Rape Study," *Criminal Law Bulletin* 38 (2002), 21–159.
52. Roger LeRoy Miller and Mary S. Urisko, *West's Paralegal Today,* 3d ed. (St. Paul, MN: West Publishing Co., 2003), 443.
53. Firoz Dattu, "Illustrated Jury Instructions," *Judicature* 82 (September/October 1998), 79.
54. Walter J. Steele, Jr., and Elizabeth Thornburg, "Jury Instructions: A Persistent Failure to Communicate," *Judicature* 74 (1991), 249–254.
55. *People v. Harlan,* 109 P.3d 616 (Colo. 2005).
56. David W. Broeder, "The University of Chicago Jury Project," *Nebraska Law Review* 38 (1959), 744–760.
57. Robert Jablon, "Hung Jury Declared in Police Brutality Trial," *San Diego Union-Tribune* (July 30, 2003), A3.
58. 164 U.S. 492 (1896).
59. *United States v. Fioravanti,* 412 F.2d 407 (3d Cir. 1969).
60. National Center for State Courts, *Are Hung Juries a Problem?* (Washington, D.C.: U.S. Department of Justice, 2002), 1.
61. Joseph L. Gastwirth and Michael D. Sinclair, "Diagnostic Test Methodology in the Design and Analysis of Judge-Jury Agreement Studies," *Jurimetrics Journal* 39 (Fall 1998), 59.
62. Peter Western, "The Three Faces of Double Jeopardy: Reflections on Government Appeals of Criminal Sentences," *Michigan Law Review* 78 (1980), 1001–1002.
63. Quoted in Jeffrey Abramson, *We, the Jury: The Jury System and the Ideal of Democracy* (New York: Basic Books, 1994), 250.
64. Bureau of Justice Statistics, *Federal Criminal Appeals, 1999 with Trends 1985–1999* (Washington, D.C.: U.S. Department of Justice, April 2001), 1.
65. *Green v. United States,* 355 U.S. 184 (1957).
66. 537 U.S. 101 (2003).
67. David W. Neubauer, *America's Courts and the Criminal Justice System,* 5th ed. (Belmont, CA: Wadsworth Publishing Co. 1996), 254.
68. 28 U.S.C. Section 2254(d)(1).
69. F. Martin Tieber, "Federal *Habeas Corpus* Law and Practice—The Antiterrorism and Effective Death Penalty Act of 1996," *Michigan Bar Journal* 77 (January 1998), 50.
70. *Felker v. Turpin,* 518 U.S. 1051 (1996).
71. *Calhoun v. State,* 214 S.W. 335, 339 (Tex.Crim. App. 1919).
72. *State v. Johnson,* 133 N.W. 115 (Iowa 1911).
73. Michelle J. Anderson, "From Chastity Requirement to Sexuality License: Sexual Consent and a New Rape Shield Law," *George Washington Law Review* (February 2002), 51.
74. *Ibid.,* 60
75. Mich. Comp. Laws Ann. Section 750.520j (West 1991).
76. *State ex rel. Pope v. Superior Court,* 545 P.2d 946, 953 (Ariz. 1996).
77. Federal Rule of Evidence, 412(a)(1)–(2).
78. *Ibid.,* 412(b)(1)(A)–(C).
79. Michelle J. Anderson, "Time to Reform Rape Shield Laws," *Criminal Justice* (Summer 2004), 14, 16.
80. *State v. Shoffner,* 302 S.E.2d 830 (N.C. Ct.App. 1983).
81. *Ibid.,* 832.

82. N.C. Gen. Stat. Section 8C-1, R. 412 (1999).

83. *State v. Shoffner*, 832.

84. Regina A. Schuller and Marc A. Klippenstine, "The Impact of Sexual Complainant Sexual History Evidence on Jurors' Decision," *Psychology, Public Policy, and Law* (September 2004), 321–342.

85. *State v. Garron*, 827 A.2d 243 (N.J. 2003).

86. Patrick O'Driscoll, "Bryant Defense Ignites Debate," *USA Today* (October 13, 2003), 3A.

87. Susan Estrich, "Rape Shield Laws Aren't Foolproof," *USA Today* (July 28, 2003), 13A.

88. O'Driscoll.

89. Colo. Rev. Stat. Section 18-3-407 (2000).

90. Lorraine Dusky, "Bryant Lawyer Is Using Dirty Tactics," *Newsday* (March 4, 2004), A51.

91. Cristina Carmody Tilley, "A Feminist Repudiation of the Rape Shield Laws," *Drake Law Review* (2002), 45–80.

CHAPTER ELEVEN

Punishment and Sentencing

Chapter outline

- The Purpose of Sentencing
- The Structure of Sentencing
- Individualized Justice and the Judge
- Inconsistencies in Sentencing
- Sentencing Reform
- Capital Punishment—The Ultimate Sentence
- Criminal Justice in Action—The Gender Factor

Chapter objectives

After reading this chapter, you should be able to:

1 List and contrast the four basic philosophical reasons for sentencing criminals.
2 Contrast indeterminate with determinate sentencing.
3 Explain why there is a difference between a sentence imposed by a judge and the actual sentence carried out by the prisoner.
4 List the six forms of punishment.
5 State who has input into the sentencing decision and list the factors that determine a sentence.
6 Explain some of the reasons why sentencing reform has occurred.
7 Describe sentencing guidelines and explain how two recent Supreme Court rulings have affected them.
8 Identify the arguments for and against the use of victim impact statements during sentencing hearings.
9 Outline the Supreme Court rulings on capital punishment.

Criminal JusticeNow

Optimize your study time and master key chapter concepts with *Criminal JusticeNow*, an online study tool that provides you with a *personalized study plan*. Check out the "Test Preparation Online" section at the end of the chapter for additional information.

Dealing with Drunk Driving

By the time Daniel Lanzaro left

Giants Stadium in East Rutherford, New Jersey, he had downed fourteen beers. Despite his drunken state, Lanzaro got behind the wheel of his pickup truck and headed home. On the way, he swerved across a double yellow line and struck the car of the Verni family. As a result of the accident, two-year-old Antonio Verni was paralyzed from the neck down for life. On August 9, 2003, a superior court judge in Hackensack, New Jersey, sentenced Lanzaro to five years in prison.

Three days earlier and fifty miles to the east, in Central Islip, New York, Michele April also faced a sentencing hearing. She had killed one man and badly hurt another when driving while intoxicated. Unlike Lanzaro, however, April did not receive any prison or jail time. Instead, she was sentenced to 280 hours of community service.

The wreck of a car that had been carrying one of the more than 17,000 people killed each year in this country by drunk drivers.

Given that drunk driving accidents are the leading cause of death in the United States for people under the age of thirty-one and account for nearly 40 percent of all traffic fatalities, one might ask why April got off with the proverbial "slap on the wrist." Furthermore, how could she and Lanzaro, who committed similar crimes, be given such disparate punishments?

Because each state has the authority to pass its own drunk driving laws, there are at least fifty different

answers to the question of how we should punish intoxicated drivers. In New Jersey, prosecutors were able to charge Daniel Lanzaro with aggravated assault—a felony. In New York, because Michele April was not speeding or driving outside her lane when she hit her victims, she had not engaged in criminally negligent or reckless conduct and thus could be found guilty only of a misdemeanor.

Is it possible to argue that either New York or New Jersey is "better" at penalizing drunk drivers? Punishment and sentencing present some of the most complex issues of the criminal justice system. One scholar has even asserted:

> There is no such thing as "accurate" sentencing; there are only sentences that are more or less just, more or less effective. Nothing in the recent or distant history of sentencing reform suggests that anything approaching perfection is attainable.[1]

In this chapter, we will discuss the various attempts to "perfect" the practice of sentencing over the past century and explore the ramifications of these efforts for the American criminal justice system. Whereas previous chapters have concentrated on the prosecutor and defense attorney, this one will spotlight the judge and his or her role in making the sentencing decision. We will particularly focus on recent national and state efforts to limit judicial discretion in this area, a trend that has had the overall effect of producing harsher sentences for many offenders. Finally, we will examine the issues surrounding the death penalty, a controversial subject that forces us to confront the

◐ CONCEPT BUILDER

Deterrence is a common justification for many crime policies and a main goal of sentencing. Does deterrence work? Visit **www.cjinaction.com** for an interactive exploration of this key topic.

basic truth of sentencing: the way we punish criminals says a great deal about the kind of people we are.[2]

THE PURPOSE OF SENTENCING

Professor Herbert Packer has said that punishing criminals serves two ultimate purposes: the "deserved infliction of suffering on evil doers" and "the prevention of crime."[3] Even this straightforward assessment raises several questions. How does one determine the sort of punishment that is "deserved"? How can we be sure that certain penalties "prevent" crime? Should criminals be punished solely for the good of society, or should their well-being also be taken into consideration? Sentencing laws indicate how any given group of people has answered these questions, but do not tell us why they were answered in that manner. To understand why, we must first consider the four basic philosophical reasons for sentencing—retribution, deterrence, incapacitation, and rehabilitation.

Retribution

The oldest and most common justification for punishing someone is that he or she "deserved it"—as the Old Testament states, "an eye for an eye and a tooth for a tooth." Under a system of justice that favors **retribution,** a wrongdoer who has freely chosen to violate society's rules must be punished for the infraction. Retribution relies on the principle of **just deserts,** which holds that the severity of the punishment must be in proportion to the severity of the crime. Retributive justice is not the same as *revenge.* Whereas revenge implies that the wrongdoer is punished only with the aim of satisfying a victim or victims, retribution is more concerned with the needs of society as a whole.

The *principle of willful wrongdoing* is central to the idea of retribution; that is, society is morally justified in punishing someone only if that person was aware that he or she committed a crime. Therefore, animals, children, and the mentally incapacitated are not responsible for criminal action, even though they may be a threat to the community.[4] Furthermore, the principles of retribution reject any wide-reaching social benefit as a goal of punishment. The philosopher Immanuel Kant, an early proponent of retributivism, believed that punishment by a court

> can never be inflicted merely as a means to promote some other good for the criminal himself or for civil society. It must always be inflicted upon him only because he has committed a crime. For a man can never be treated merely as a means to the purposes of another.[5]

In other words, punishment is an end in itself and cannot be justified by any future good that may result from a criminal's suffering.

One problem with retributive ideas of justice lies in proportionality. Whether or not one agrees with the death penalty, the principle behind it is easy to fathom: the punishment (death) fits the crime (death). But what about the theft of an automobile? How does one fairly determine the amount of time the thief must spend in prison? Should the type of car or the wealth of the car owner matter? Theories of retribution often have a difficult time providing answers to such questions.[6]

Deterrence

The concept of **deterrence** (as well as incapacitation and rehabilitation) takes the opposite approach: rather than seeking only to punish the wrongdoer, the goal of sentencing should be to prevent future crimes. By "setting an example," society is sending

Retribution
The philosophy that those who commit criminal acts should be punished based on the severity of the crime and that no other factors need be considered.

Just Deserts
A sanctioning philosophy based on the assertion that criminals deserve to be punished for breaking society's rules. The severity of the punishment should be determined by no other factor than the severity of the crime.

Deterrence
The strategy of preventing crime through the threat of punishment. Assumes that potential criminals will weigh the costs of punishment versus the benefits of the criminal act; therefore, punishments should be severe.

On June 6, 2005, Mark Hacking wipes away a tear as a Utah judge sentences him to six years to life for the first degree murder of his wife, Lori. Hacking had shot Lori in the head while she was asleep and dumped her body in the trash. Why does society demand that offenders such as Hacking receive harsh punishments?

Douglas C. Pizac/Getty Images

Singapore—A Utilitarian Oasis

Suppose one were to ask Immanuel Kant and Jeremy Bentham the following question: Is the death penalty a justifiable punishment for illegally selling marijuana? Kant, a proponent of the "principle of equity," would answer no; such a punishment would be too harsh for the crime. Bentham, however, might not agree. If the ultimate goal of punishment is to deter people from committing future crimes, then a literal reading of Bentham's utilitarian theory would seem to support severe penalties for seemingly minor criminal behavior.

Singapore, a nation-city of three million people in Southeast Asia, leans toward Bentham rather than Kant in its sentencing theories. According to Singapore law, the selling of any drug—including marijuana—carries a mandatory death sentence by hanging, as do murder and the use of a firearm in committing or attempting to commit a crime. Someone caught smoking marijuana is sentenced to a ten-year prison term. Citizens who litter are fined the equivalent of $1,000, with similar penalties imposed for chewing gum and failing to flush a public toilet. Vandals are sentenced to up to three years in prison and (as American teenager Michael Fay learned in the mid-1990s) are subject to caning.

Many observers criticize Singapore, claiming its strict laws violate human rights. Indeed, according to the human rights group Amnesty International, the country has the highest capital punishment rate in the world, with most of the executions taking place for drug trafficking. But Singaporeans point to one of the world's lowest crime rates as justification for their system. The year after robbery with a firearm was deemed punishable by death, for example, not one such incident took place in the city. Singapore officials also point out that the United States—which consistently criticizes human rights abuses in other nations—has the highest violent crime rate and the most citizens in prison of any country in the West.

FOR CRITICAL ANALYSIS
It is important to note that Singapore is a democracy, and many, if not most, of its citizens support its law enforcement principles. How do you think the American public would react if given the chance to vote on implementing similarly harsh punishments for crime in this country?

a message to potential criminals that certain actions will not be tolerated. Jeremy Bentham, a nineteenth-century British reformer who first articulated the principles of deterrence, felt that retribution was counterproductive because it does not serve the community. (See Chapter 2 to review Bentham's utilitarian theories.) He believed that a person should be punished only when doing so was in society's best interests and that the severity of the punishment should be based on its deterrent value, not on the severity of the crime.[7] (See the feature *International CJ—Singapore: A Utilitarian Oasis.*)

Deterrence can take two forms: general and specific. The basic idea of *general deterrence* is that by punishing one person, others will be dissuaded from committing a similar crime. *Specific deterrence* assumes that an individual, after being punished once for a certain act, will be less likely to repeat that act because she or he does not want to be punished again.[8] Both forms of deterrence have proved problematic in practice. General deterrence assumes that a person commits a crime only after a rational decision-making process, in which he or she implicitly weighs the benefits of the crime against the possible costs of the punishment. This is not necessarily the case, especially for young offenders who tend to value the immediate rewards of crime over the possible future consequences.[9] Specific deterrence, for its part, seems to be contradicted by the fact that a relatively small number of habitual offenders are responsible for the majority of certain criminal acts.[10]

Another criticism of deterrence is that for most crimes, wrongdoers are unlikely to be caught, sentenced, and imprisoned. A study by Texas A&M economist Morgan Reynolds found that, after factoring in the low likelihood of capture and imprisonment, the average statistically expected stay in prison is only 4.8 days for an act of burglary, 60.5 days for rape, and 1.8 years for murder.[11] Thus, in gen-

"Men are not hanged for stealing horses, but that horses may not be stolen."
—Marquis de Halifax, *Political Thoughts and Reflections* (1750)

eral, potential criminals have less to fear from the criminal justice system than one might expect. Professors Paul H. Robinson of Northwestern University School of Law and John M. Darley of Princeton University note that this low probability of punishment could be offset by making the punishment so severe that even the slightest chance of apprehension could act as a deterrent—for example, an eighty-five-year prison term for shoplifting or the loss of a hand for burglary.[12] Our society is, however, unwilling to allow for this possibility.

Incapacitation

"Wicked people exist," said James Q. Wilson. "Nothing avails except to set them apart from innocent people."[13] Wilson's blunt statement summarizes the justification for **incapacitation** as a form of punishment. As a purely practical matter, incarcerating criminals guarantees that they will not be a danger to society, at least for the length of their prison terms. To a certain extent, the death penalty is justified in terms of incapacitation, as it prevents the offender from committing any future crimes.

Several studies do support incapacitation's efficacy as a crime-fighting tool. Criminologist Isaac Ehrlich of the University of Chicago estimated that a 1 percent increase in sentence length will produce a 1 percent decrease in crime rates.[14] Another Chicago professor, Steve Levitt, has noticed a trend that further supports incapacitation. He found that violent crime rates rise in communities where inmate litigation over prison overcrowding has forced the early release of some inmates and a subsequent drop in the prison population.[15]

Incapacitation as a theory of punishment suffers from several weaknesses, however. Unlike retribution, it offers no proportionality with regard to a particular crime. Giving a burglar a life sentence would certainly assure that she or he would not commit another burglary. Does that justify such a severe penalty? Furthermore, incarceration protects society only until the criminal is freed. Many studies have shown that, on release, offenders may actually be more likely to commit crimes than before they were imprisoned.[16] In that case, incapacitation may increase the likelihood of crime, rather than diminish it.

Some observers believe that strategies of *selective incapacitation* should be favored over strategies of *collective incapacitation* to solve this problem. With collective incapacitation, all offenders who have committed a similar crime are imprisoned for the same time period, whereas selective incapacitation provides longer sentences for individuals, such as career criminals, who are judged more likely to commit further crimes if and when they are released.[17] The problem with selective incapacitation, however, lies in the difficulty of predicting just who is at the greatest risk to commit future crimes. Studies have shown that with even the most effective methods the predictions are correct less than half of the time.[18]

Rehabilitation

For most of the past century, **rehabilitation** has been seen as the most "humane" goal of punishment. This line of thinking reflects the view that crime is a "social phenomenon" caused not by the inherent criminality of a person, but by factors in that person's surroundings. By removing wrongdoers from their environment and intervening to change their values and personalities, the rehabilitative model suggests, criminals can be "treated" and possibly even "cured" of their proclivities toward crime.

For most of the past two decades, the American criminal justice system has been characterized by a notable rejection of many of the precepts of rehabilitation in favor of retributive, deterrent, and incapacitating sentencing strategies that "get tough on crime." Recently, however, more jurisdictions are turning to rehabilitation as a cost-effective

Incapacitation
A strategy for preventing crime by detaining wrongdoers in prison, thereby separating them from the community and reducing criminal opportunities.

Rehabilitation
The philosophy that society is best served when wrongdoers are provided the resources needed to eliminate criminality from their behavioral pattern rather than simply being punished.

In 2005, former Tyco chief executive officer Dennis Kozlowski, shown here entering the New York State Supreme Court in Manhattan, was sentenced to eight to twenty-five years for grand larceny, fraud, and numerous other charges. Kozlowski had used millions of dollars of the corporation's money to fund a lavish lifestyle, including $1 million for a toga party celebrating his wife's fortieth birthday. What is the purpose of handing down harsh punishments for nonviolent crimes such as white-collar crime?

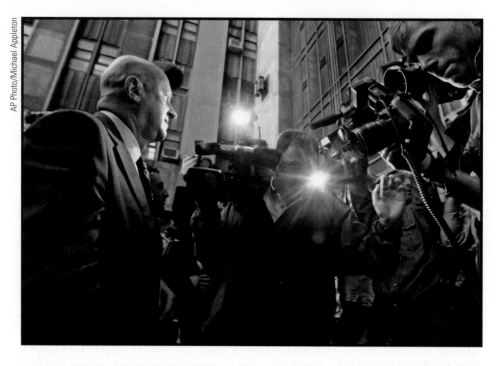

AP Photo/Michael Appleton

(and, possibly, crime-reducing) alternative to punishment, a topic that we will explore more fully in the next chapter. Furthermore, the American public may be more accepting of rehabilitative principles than many elected officials think. A survey by the Public Policy Forum found that only 46 percent of those polled favored spending more funds on punishment than rehabilitation, while 65 percent wanted to create alternatives to prison for nonviolent offenders and 63 percent wanted better drug and alcohol treatment for lawbreakers.[19]

Nevertheless, it would be a mistake to separate these four philosophies. For the most part, a society's overall sentencing direction is influenced by all four theories, with political and social factors determining which one is predominant at any given time.

THE STRUCTURE OF SENTENCING

Philosophy not only is integral to explaining *why* we punish criminals, but also influences *how* we do so. The history of criminal sentencing in the United States has been characterized by shifts in institutional power among the three branches of the government. When public opinion moves toward more severe strategies of retribution, deterrence, and incapacitation, *legislatures* have responded by asserting their power over determining sentencing guidelines. In contrast, periods of rehabilitative justice are marked by a transfer of this power to the *judicial* and *administrative* branches.

Legislative Sentencing Authority

Because legislatures are responsible for making law, these bodies are also initially responsible for passing the criminal codes that determine the length of sentences.

Indeterminate Sentencing For most of the twentieth century, goals of rehabilitation dominated the criminal justice system, and legislatures were more likely to enact **indeterminate sentencing** policies. Penal codes with indeterminate sentences set a minimum and maximum amount of time that a person must spend in prison. For

Indeterminate Sentencing
An indeterminate term of incarceration in which a judge determines the minimum and maximum terms of imprisonment. When the minimum term is reached, the prisoner becomes eligible to be paroled.

example, the indeterminate sentence for aggravated assault could be three to nine years, or six to twelve years, or twenty years to life. Within these parameters, a judge can prescribe a particular term, after which an administrative body known as the *parole board* decides at what point the offender is to be released. A prisoner is aware that he or she is eligible for *parole* as soon as the minimum time has been served and that good behavior can further shorten the sentence.

Determinate Sentencing Disillusionment with the ideals of rehabilitation has led to **determinate sentencing,** or fixed sentencing. As the name implies, in determinate sentencing an offender serves exactly the amount of time to which she or he is sentenced (minus "good time," described below). For example, if the legislature deems that the punishment for a first-time armed robber is ten years, then the judge has no choice but to impose a sentence of ten years, and the criminal will serve ten years minus good time before being freed.

"Good Time" and Truth in Sentencing Often, the amount of time prescribed by a judge bears little relation to the amount of time the offender actually spends behind bars. In states with indeterminate sentencing, parole boards have broad powers to release prisoners once they have served the minimum portion of their sentence. Furthermore, all but four states offer prisoners the opportunity to reduce their sentences by doing **"good time"**—or behaving well—as determined by prison administrators. (See Figure 11.1 for an idea of the effects of good-time regulations and other early-release programs.)

Sentence-reduction programs promote discipline within a correctional institution and reduce overcrowding; therefore, many prison officials welcome them. The public, however, may react negatively to news that a violent criminal has served a shorter term than ordered by a judge and pressure elected officials to "do something." In Illinois, for example, some inmates were serving less than half their sentences by receiving a one-day reduction in their term for each day of "good time." Under pressure from victims' groups, the state legislature passed a **truth-in-sentencing law** that requires murderers and others convicted of serious crimes to complete at least 85 percent of their sentences with no time off for good behavior.[20] Today, forty states have instituted some form of truth-in-sentencing laws, though the future of such statutes is in doubt due to numerous challenges on constitutional grounds and the pressure of overflowing prisons.

Determinate Sentencing
A period of incarceration that is fixed by a sentencing authority and cannot be reduced by judges or other corrections officials.

"Good Time"
A reduction in time served by prisoners based on good behavior, conformity to rules, and other positive actions.

Truth-in-Sentencing Laws
Legislative attempts to assure that convicts will serve approximately the terms to which they were initially sentenced.

Conviction Offense	Sentence length (in months)
Murder/manslaughter	225 / 142
Rape	132 / 90
Robbery	91 / 53
Assault	54 / 36
Burglary	50 / 24
Drug trafficking	55 / 24

■ Average Prison Sentence
■ Estimated Time in Prison

FIGURE 11.1

Average Sentence Length and Estimated Time to Be Served in State Prison

Source: Bureau of Justice Statistics, *Felony Sentences in State Courts, 2002* (Washington, D.C.: U.S. Department of Justice, December 2004), Table 4, page 5.

Judicial Sentencing Authority

Determinate sentencing is a direct encroachment on the long-recognized power of judges to make the final decision on sentencing. Historically, the judge bore most of the responsibility for choosing the proper sentence within the guidelines set by the legislature.[21] In the twentieth century, this power was reinforced by the rehabilitative ethic. Each offender, it was believed, has a different set of problems and should therefore receive a sentence tailored to her or his particular circumstances. Legislators have generally accepted a judge as the most qualified person to choose the proper punishment.

Between 1880 and 1899, seven states passed indeterminate sentencing laws, and in the next dozen years, another twenty-one followed suit. By the 1960s, every state in the nation allowed its judges the freedom of operating under an indeterminate sentencing system.[22] In the 1970s, however, criticism of indeterminate sentencing began to grow. Marvin E. Frankel, a former federal district judge in New York, gained a great deal of attention when he described sentencing authority as "unchecked" and "terrifying and intolerable for a society that professes devotion to a rule of law."[23] As we shall see, the 1980s and 1990s saw numerous attempts on both the state and federal levels to limit this judicial discretion.

Administrative Sentencing Authority

Parole is a condition of early release in which a prisoner is released from a correctional facility but is not freed from the legal custody and supervision of the state. Generally, after an inmate has been released on parole, he or she is supervised by a parole officer for a specified amount of time. The decision of whether to parole an inmate lies with the parole board. Parole is a crucial aspect of the criminal justice system and will be discussed in detail in Chapter 14.

For now, it is important to understand the role rehabilitation theories play in *administrative sentencing authority*. The formation in 1910 of the U.S. Parole Commission and similar commissions in the fifty states implied that the judge, though a legal expert, was not trained to determine when an inmate had been rehabilitated. Therefore, the sentencing power should be given to experts in human behavior, who were qualified to determine whether a convict was fit to return to society.[24] The recent repudiation of rehabilitation principles has not spared these administrative bodies; since 1976, fourteen states and the federal government have abolished traditional parole for their prisoners.[25] (See *Mastering Concepts—Who Has the Responsibility to Determine Sentences?*)

INDIVIDUALIZED JUSTICE AND THE JUDGE

During the pretrial procedures and the trial itself, the judge's role is somewhat passive and reactive. She or he is a primarily a "procedural watchdog," assuring that the rights of the defendant are not infringed on while the prosecutor and defense attorney dictate the course of action.

At a traditional sentencing hearing, however, the judge is no longer an arbiter between the parties. She or he is now called on to exercise the ultimate authority of the state in determining the defendant's fate.

From the 1930s to the 1970s, when theories of rehabilitation held sway over the criminal justice system, indeterminate sentencing practices were guided by the theory of "individualized justice." Just as a physician gives specific treatment to individual patients depending on their particular health needs, the hypothesis goes, a judge needs

Who Has the Responsibility to Determine Sentences?

Three different sentencing authorities determine the amount of time a person who has been convicted of a felony will spend in prison: legislatures, judges, and officials of the executive branch (governor's office). The process through which these three groups influence the sentencing process is summarized below.

First Step: Legislators Pass Laws

Federal and state legislators are responsible for creating and updating the criminal codes that define how the law will punish those who commit crimes. Legislatures specify the terms of imprisonment in two different ways:

- By passing *indeterminate sentencing laws.* These laws designate a maximum and minimum amount of time that a person who commits a specific crime must spend in prison—one to three years, five to ten years, and so on.
- By passing *determinate sentencing laws.* These laws designate a fixed amount of time that a person who commits a specific crime must spend in prison—seven years, for example, instead of five to ten.

If lawmakers feel that the other two bodies—judges and officials of the executive branch—are being too lenient in their sentencing decisions, they can pass truth-in-sentencing laws that require convicts to serve the amount of time indicated in criminal codes.

Second Step: Judges Impose Sentences

Judges have the authority to choose among the sentencing options provided by legislatures. They are expected to consider all of the circumstances that surround a case and decide the length of the sentence based on these circumstances. (There are a few exceptions to this judicial authority. Only a jury, for example, can decide whether to impose the death penalty.)

Third Step: Executive Officials Set the Date of Release

Although judges impose the sentence, officials of the executive branch are responsible for deciding the extent to which a prisoner will serve his or her entire sentence. Most prisoners do not serve their maximum possible terms of imprisonment. Parole boards, appointed in most states by the governor, decide whether an inmate is eligible for *parole*—the conditional release of a prisoner before his or her sentence has been served. Executive officials also determine whether an inmate will have his or her sentence reduced because of *"good time,"* which is awarded for good behavior and participation in various treatment, vocational, and educational programs. (Remember, however, that legislatures can restrict parole and good-time provisions.)

to consider the specific circumstances of each individual offender in choosing the best form of punishment. Taking the analogy one step further, just as the diagnosis of a qualified physician should not be questioned, a qualified judge should have absolute discretion in making the sentencing decision. *Judicial discretion* rests on the assumption that a judge should be given ample leeway in determining punishments that fit both the crime and the criminal.[26] As we shall see later in the chapter, the growth of determinate sentencing has severely restricted judicial discretion in many jurisdictions.

Forms of Punishment

Within whatever legislative restrictions apply, the sentencing judge has a number of options when it comes to choosing the proper form of punishment. These sentences, or *dispositions*, include:

1. *Capital punishment.* Reserved normally for those who commit first degree murder under aggravated circumstances, capital punishment, or the death penalty, is a sentencing option in thirty-eight states and in federal courts.

2. *Imprisonment.* Whether for the purpose of retribution, deterrence, incapacitation, or rehabilitation, a common form of punishment in American history has been imprisonment. In fact, it is used so commonly today that judges—and legislators—are having to take factors such as prison overcrowding into consideration when making sentencing decisions. The issues surrounding imprisonment will be discussed in Chapters 13 and 14.

U.S. District Judge Charles Pickering of Mississippi, pictured here, showed the power of the bench in the case of Daniel Swan, who had been sentenced to seven years in prison for burning a cross on the front lawn of a biracial couple in Walthall County, Mississippi. Pickering believed that the punishment was too harsh and went to great lengths to convince prosecutors to reduce the sentence to twenty-seven months. Should judges be able to have such a profound impact on the sentencing process? Why or why not?

3) *Probation.* One of the effects of prison overcrowding has been a sharp rise in the use of probation, in which an offender is permitted to live in the community under supervision and is not incarcerated. (Probation is covered in Chapter 12.) *Alternative sanctions* (also discussed in Chapter 12) combine probation with other dispositions such as electronic monitoring, house arrest, boot camps, and shock incarceration.

4) *Fines.* Fines can be levied by judges in addition to incarceration and probation or independently of other forms of punishment. When a fine is the full extent of the punishment, it usually reflects the judge's belief that the offender is not a threat to the community and does not need to be imprisoned or supervised. In some instances, mostly involving drug offenders, a judge can order the seizure of an offender's property, such as his or her home.

5) *Restitution and community service.* Whereas fines are payable to the government, restitution and community service are seen as reparations to the injured party or to the community. Restitution is a direct payment to the victim or victims of a crime; community service consists of "good works"—such as cleaning up highway litter or tutoring disadvantaged youths—that benefit the entire community.

6) *Restorative justice.* Where the offender has committed a less serious crime, many judges are turning to restorative justice to provide a remedy. At the heart of restorative justice is the apology. So, for example, a judge in Texas required a teenager who had vandalized thirteen schools to go to each school and apologize to the students and faculty. In many such cases, victims appreciate the expression of remorse, and offenders are thankful for a chance to "set things right."[27] Restorative justice focuses more on "healing" the harm that a crime does to individual relationships and the community than on punishing the offender. (For information on a form of restorative justice practiced in Native American jurisdictions in the United States, see the feature *Outside the Box—Navajo Peacemaker Courts.*)

In some jurisdictions, judges have a great deal of discretionary power and can impose sentences that do not fall into any of these categories. In Florida, for example, judges have the option of ordering *chemical castration,* or the use of drugs to lower sex drive, for a first conviction for sexual battery. The same legislation requires the punishment for a second conviction for that offense.[28] In practice, however, the Florida judiciary ordered only six offenders to be chemically castrated between 1997 and 2005, even though more than 2,300 sexual battery convictions occurred during that time.[29] Apparently, even when given the power to do so, many judges are hesitant to step outside their area of expertise—in this instance, into the realm of psychology and science.

The Sentencing Process

The decision of how to punish a wrongdoer is the end result of what Yale Law School professor Kate Stith and federal appeals court judge José A. Cabranes call the "sentencing ritual."[30] The two main participants in this ritual are the judge and the defendant, but prosecutors, defense attorneys, and probation officers also play a role in the proceedings.

OUTSIDE THE BOX

Navajo Peacemaker Courts

When the Navajo returned to their native lands in 1892 after being forcibly relocated to Fort Sumner, New Mexico, by the U.S. Army during the "Long Walk" twenty-eight years earlier, the federal government operated the criminal courts on tribal property. In 1959, the Navajo Nation, which extends across several southwestern states, took control of its court system, which was still patterned after the American model and, in the words of one Navajo, had "little meaning for us in the Navajo way." Now, the tribe's judicial system is returning to the "Navajo way" in the form of Peacemaker courts. These courts reflect the traditional function of Navajo criminal law, which strives not so much to punish wrongdoers as to use community participation to resolve the issues behind the wrongdoing.

RESTORING HARMONY

The American concept of "crime" is referred to in Navajo culture as "disharmony." Disharmony is caused by *nayee*, which can be translated as "anything that gets in the way of a person living her or his life," such as depression, poverty, illness, or problems in a personal relationship. Therefore, the goal of Peacemaker courts is to restore harmony by bringing the offender back into the proper relationship with other members of the family and community who have been harmed by his or her actions. In contrast, as we have seen, American courts operate under an adversarial system that encourages conflict between the parties involved.

A Peacemaker court is "resided" over by a *naat'aani*, a respected member of the community. The *naat'aani* gathers the parties to the dispute and their relatives in a room and facilitates a process of "talking out." During the conversation, the group discusses the episode and decides what steps should be taken to resolve the problem. The *naat'aani* then gives a kind of lecture that spells out the community values that relate to the dispute. Next, the victim can request restitution or reparation. Rather than punishing the individual, a successful resolution aims at achieving *hozho nahasadli*, or a return to good relations and harmony for those involved.

In 1992, its first year, the Peacemaker court heard only forty-two cases. Today, there are more than three hundred Peacemaker courts in the seven districts of the Navajo Nation, and they hear more than two thousand cases a year. Most of these cases involve alcohol-related crimes such as domestic violence, property damage, and child abuse and are referred to the Peacemaker court by a Navajo district court.

FOR CRITICAL ANALYSIS

Under the umbrella term *community justice*, a number of American courts—mostly dealing with low-level drug crimes and misdemeanors—have adopted some of the methods of the Peacemaker courts. What aspects, if any, of the Navajo criminal justice system do you think could be usefully integrated into the "mainstream" criminal justice system?

Individualized justice requires that the judge consider all the relevant circumstances in making sentencing decisions. Therefore, judicial discretion is often tantamount to *informed* discretion—without the aid of the other members of the courtroom work group, the judge would not have sufficient information to make the proper sentencing choice.

The Presentence Investigative Report For judges operating under various states' indeterminate sentencing guidelines, information in the **presentence investigative report** is a valuable component of the sentencing ritual. Compiled by a probation officer, the report describes the crime in question, notes the suffering of any victims, and lists the defendant's prior offenses (as well as any alleged but uncharged criminal activity). The report also contains a range of personal data such as family background, work history, education, and community activities—information that is not admissible as evidence during trial. In putting together the presentence investigative report, the probation officer is supposed to gain a "feel" for the defendant and communicate these impressions of the offender to the judge.

The report also includes a sentencing recommendation. In the past, this aspect has been criticized as giving probation officers too much power in the sentencing process, because lazy judges would simply rely on the recommendation in determining punishment.[31] Consequently, as we shall see, many jurisdictions have moved to limit the influence of the presentence investigative report.

Presentence Investigative Report
An investigative report on an offender's background that assists a judge in determining the proper sentence.

"Real Offense"
The actual offense committed, as opposed to the charge levied by a prosecutor as the result of a plea bargain. Judges who make sentencing decisions based on the real offense are often seen as undermining the plea bargain process.

The Prosecutor and Defense Attorney To a certain extent, the adversary process does not end when the guilt of the defendant has been established. Both the prosecutor and the defense attorney are interviewed in the process of preparing the presentence investigative report, and both will try to present a version of the facts consistent with their own sentencing goals. The defense attorney in particular has a duty to make sure that the information contained in the report is accurate and not prejudicial toward his or her client. Depending on the norms of any particular courtroom work group, prosecutors and defense attorneys may petition the judge directly for certain sentences. Note that this process is not always adversarial. As we saw in Chapter 9, in some instances the prosecutor will advocate leniency and may join the defense attorney in requesting a short term of imprisonment, probation, or some form of intermediate sanction.[32]

Factors of Sentencing

The sentencing ritual strongly lends itself to the concept of individualized justice. With inputs—sometimes conflicting—from the prosecutor, attorney, and probation officer, the judge can be reasonably sure of getting the "full picture" of the crime and the criminal. In making the final decision, however, most judges consider two factors above all others: the seriousness of the crime and any mitigating or aggravating circumstances.

The Seriousness of the Crime As would be expected, the seriousness of the crime is the primary factor in a judge's sentencing decisions. The more serious the crime, the harsher the punishment, for society demands no less. (See Figure 11.2.) Each judge has his or her own methods of determining the seriousness of the offense. Many judges simply consider the "conviction offense"; that is, they base their sentence on the crime for which the defendant was convicted.

Other judges—some mandated by statute—focus instead on the **"real offense"** in determining the punishment. The "real offense" is based on the actual behavior of the defendant, regardless of the official conviction. For example, through a plea bargain, a defendant may plead guilty to simple assault when in fact he hit his victim in the face with a baseball bat. A judge, after reading the presentence investigative report, could decide to sentence the defendant as if he had committed aggravated assault, which is the "real" offense. Though many prosecutors and defense attorneys are opposed to "real offense" procedures, which can render a plea bargain meaningless, there is a growing belief in criminal justice circles that they bring a measure of fairness to the sentencing decision.[33]

Mitigating and Aggravating Circumstances Consider the case of Marcos Mascarenas of Questa, New Mexico, who was responsible for the death of his six-month-old son by "shaken baby syndrome." Mascarenas had an intelligence quotient (IQ) of 90 and purportedly was not aware of the harm he was doing when he shook the baby. The judge in his case, Peggy Nelson, expressed frustration that she was forced to sentence the defendant to prison for a minimum of twelve years under state law. Because of his lack of mental capacity, the judge felt that Mascarenas did not deserve the punishment he received. In many situations, circumstances surrounding the crime may prompt a judge to adjust a sentence so that it more accurately reflects the totality of the crime. Judge

FIGURE 11.2
Average Maximum Sentences for Selected Crimes in State and Federal Courts

Source: Bureau of Justice Statistics, *Felony Sentences in State Courts, 2002* (Washington, D.C.: U.S. Department of Justice, December 2004), 3.

Crime	Average Maximum Sentence (in months)
Murder	217 (State) / 109 (Federal)
Sexual assault	78 (State) / 96 (Federal)
Robbery	79 (State) / 91 (Federal)
Aggravated assault	37 (State) / 38 (Federal)
Burglary	36 (State) / 33 (Federal)
Motor vehicle theft	18 (State) / 31 (Federal)
Drug trafficking	38 (State) / 76 (Federal)
Drug possession	22 (State) / 79 (Federal)

Nelson considered Mascarenas's lack of mental capacity a *mitigating circumstance,* and given the opportunity, she would have given him a lesser punishment. There are other **mitigating circumstances,** or those circumstances that allow a lighter sentence to be handed down. They can include a defendant's youth or the fact that the defendant was coerced into committing the crime. In contrast, **aggravating circumstances** such as a prior record, blatant disregard for safety, or the use of a weapon can lead a judge to inflict a harsher penalty than might otherwise be the case (see Figure 11.3).

Judicial Philosophy Most states spell out mitigating and aggravating circumstances in statutes, but there is room for judicial discretion in applying the law to particular cases. Judges are not uniform, or even consistent, in their opinions concerning which circumstances are mitigating or aggravating. One judge may believe that a fourteen-year-old is not fully responsible for his or her actions, while another may believe that teenagers should be treated as adults. Those judges who support rehabilitative theories of criminal justice have been found to give more lenient sentences than those who subscribe to theories of deterrence and incapacitation.[34] Furthermore, judges can have different philosophies with regard to different crimes, handing down, for example, harsh penalties for domestic abusers while showing leniency toward drug offenders.

> **Mitigating Circumstances**
> Any circumstances accompanying the commission of a crime that may justify a lighter sentence.
>
> **Aggravating Circumstances**
> Any circumstances accompanying the commission of a crime that may justify a harsher sentence.

INCONSISTENCIES IN SENTENCING

For some, the natural differences in judicial philosophies, when combined with a lack of institutional control, raise important questions. Why should a bank robber in South Carolina receive a different sentence than a bank robber in Michigan? Even federal indeterminate sentencing guidelines seem overly vague: a bank robber can receive a prison term from one day to twenty years, depending almost entirely on the judge.[35] Furthermore, if judges have freedom to use their discretion, do they not also have the freedom to misuse it?

Purported improper judicial discretion is often the first reason given for two phenomena that plague the criminal justice system: *sentencing disparity* and *sentencing*

FIGURE 11.3

Aggravating and Mitigating Circumstances

Aggravating Circumstances
- An offense involved multiple participants and the offender was the leader of the group.
- A victim was particularly vulnerable.
- A victim was treated with particular cruelty for which an offender should be held responsible.
- The offense involved injury or threatened violence to others and was committed to gratify an offender's desire for pleasure or excitement.
- The degree of bodily harm caused, attempted, threatened, or foreseen by an offender was substantially greater than average for the given offense.
- The degree of economic harm caused, attempted, threatened, or foreseen by an offender was substantially greater than average for the given offense.
- The amount of contraband materials possessed by the offender or under the offender's control was substantially greater than average for the given offense.

Mitigating Circumstances
- An offender acted under strong provocation, or other circumstances in the relationship between the offender and the victim make the offender's behavior less serious and therefore less deserving of punishment.
- An offender played a minor or passive role in the offense or participated under circumstances of coercion or duress.
- An offender, because of youth or physical or mental impairment, lacked substantial capacity for judgment when the offense was committed.

Source: *ABA Standards for Criminal Justice Sentencing* (Washington, D.C.: American Bar Association, 1994), 47, 52–53.

discrimination. Though the two terms are often used interchangeably, they describe different statistical occurrences—the causes of which are debatable.

Sentencing Disparity

Sentencing Disparity
A situation in which those convicted of similar crimes do not receive similar sentences.

Sentencing Discrimination
A situation in which the length of a sentence appears to be influenced by a defendant's race, gender, economic status, or other factor not directly related to the crime he or she committed.

Justice would seem to demand that those who commit similar crimes should receive similar punishments. **Sentencing disparity** occurs when this expectation is not met in one of three ways:

1 Criminals receive similar sentences for different crimes of unequal seriousness.
2 Criminals receive different sentences for similar crimes.
3 Mitigating or aggravating circumstances have a disproportionate effect on sentences. Prosecutors, for example, reward drug dealers who inform on their associates with lesser sentences. As a result, low-level drug sellers, who have no information to trade for reduced sentences, often spend more time in prison than their better-informed bosses.[36]

A number of different explanations have been offered to explain sentencing disparity. Two of these involve geography and courtroom norms.

Geographic Disparities For wrongdoers, the amount of time spent in prison often depends as much on where the crime was committed as on the crime itself. A comparison of the sentences for drug trafficking reveals that someone convicted of the crime in the Northern District of California faces an average of 74 months in prison, whereas a similar offender in Iowa can expect an average of 120 months.[37] The average sentences imposed in the Fifth Circuit, which includes Louisiana, Mississippi, and Texas, are considerably harsher than those in the Ninth Circuit, comprising most of the western states: 155 months longer for murder, 24 months longer for robbery, and 16 months longer for firearms violations.[38] Such disparities can be attributed to a number of different factors, including local attitudes toward crime and available financial resources to cover the expenses of incarceration.

Courthouse Norms The norms established by individual courtroom work groups can also lead to sentencing disparities. For nearly a century, scholars have been producing studies that point to different sentencing tendencies of different judges for similar crimes. A Department of Justice survey concluded that more than 20 percent of sentencing disparities can be directly attributed to the propensity of a particular judge to give harsh or lenient sentences.[39]

Sentencing Discrimination

Sentencing discrimination occurs when disparities can be attributed to extralegal variables such as the defendant's gender, race, or economic standing.

The "Punishment Penalty" At first glance, racial discrimination would seem to be rampant in sentencing practices. Research by Cassia Spohn and David Holleran of the University of Nebraska at Omaha suggests that minorities pay a "punishment penalty" when it comes to sentencing.[40] In Chicago, Spohn and Holleran found that convicted African Americans were 12.1 percent more likely to go to prison than convicted whites, and convicted Hispanics were 15.3 percent more likely. In Miami, Hispanics were 10.3 percent more likely to be imprisoned than either blacks or whites.[41] Nationwide, in 2004 nearly half of all inmates in state and federal prisons were African American, even though that minority group makes up only about 13 percent of the country's population.[42]

Interestingly, Spohn and Holleran found that the rate of imprisonment rose significantly for minorities who were young and unemployed. This led them to conclude that the disparities between races were not the result of "conscious" discrimination on the part of the sentencing judges. Rather, faced with limited time to make decisions and limited information about the offenders, the judges would resort to stereotypes, considering not just race, but age and unemployment as well.[43] (This research addresses the need for diversity among judges, discussed in Chapter 8.)

Furthermore, Spohn and Holleran found that none of the offender characteristics (race, age, employment) had an effect on the *length* of the prison sentence,[44] a result that is corroborated by national statistics. According to the Bureau of Justice Statistics, the average prison sentence handed out to blacks and whites in state courts was virtually the same. Indeed, with some crimes, such as murder, whites on average received longer sentences.[45]

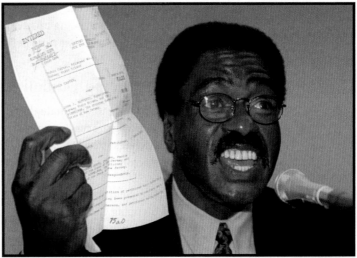

Prizefighter Rubin "Hurricane" Carter was convicted in 1966 of a triple murder in New Jersey and sentenced to life. In 1985, he was exonerated. Today, he heads the Association in Defense of the Wrongly Convicted. At one conference he stated, "There is no separation between being on death row or being held unjustly for the rest of your life. Prison is death." What might be the cost to society if no sentences of life imprisonment were ever handed out?

Hispanics and Sentencing Unfortunately, the federal data did not include Hispanics. Other studies, such as one conducted in Pennsylvania by Darrell Steffensmeier of Pennsylvania State University and Stephen DeMuth of Bowling Green State University, suggest that Hispanics receive harsher penalties than either whites or blacks.[46] Explanations for this finding vary. Some believe that the harsher sentences result from the "threat" posed by Hispanics as the most recent large immigrant group to change the ethnic outlook of the United States.[47] Steffensmeier and DeMuth suggest several other possibilities, including language barriers that put Hispanics at a disadvantage in court proceedings, for example, by making it difficult for them to understand what is offered in a plea bargain. A cultural emphasis on loyalty among Hispanics may also limit the number of sentencing "breaks" they get by informing on criminal associates.[48] (For a discussion of trends in sentencing women, see the feature *Criminal Justice in Action—The Gender Factor* at the end of this chapter.)

SENTENCING REFORM

Judicial discretion, then, appears to be a double-edged sword. Although it allows judges to impose a wide variety of sentences to fit specific criminal situations, it appears to fail to rein in a judge's subjective biases, which can lead to disparity and perhaps discrimination. Critics of judicial discretion believe that its costs (the lack of equality) outweigh its benefits (providing individualized justice). As Columbia law professor John C. Coffee noted:

> If we wish the sentencing judge to treat "like cases alike," a more inappropriate technique for the presentation could hardly be found than one that stresses a novelistic portrayal of each offender and thereby overloads the decisionmaker in a welter of detail.[49]

In other words, Professor Coffee feels that judges are given too much information in the sentencing process, making it impossible for them to be consistent in their decisions. It follows that limiting judicial discretion would not only simplify the process but lessen the opportunity for disparity or discrimination. Since the 1970s, this

Daniel Leroy Crocker, shown here at his sentencing at the Johnson County courthouse in Olathe, Kansas, confessed to smothering nineteen-year-old Tracy Fesquez after sexually assaulting the sleeping woman. Crocker was sentenced to only twenty years in prison with eligibility for parole in just ten years. This lenient sentence was based on the fact that he was never a suspect in the case. Rather, he eventually admitted to the murder, based on his religious faith. Should the reason Crocker voluntarily confessed affect his sentence?

attitude has spread through state and federal legislatures, causing more extensive changes in sentencing procedures than in any other area of the American criminal justice system over that time period.

Sentencing Guidelines

In an effort to eliminate the inequities of disparity by removing judicial bias from the sentencing process, many states and the federal government have turned to **sentencing guidelines,** which require judges to dispense legislatively determined sentences based on factors such as the seriousness of the crime and the offender's prior record.

State Sentencing Guidelines In 1978, Minnesota became the first state to create a Sentencing Guidelines Commission with a mandate to construct and monitor the use of a determinate sentencing structure. The Minnesota Commission left no doubt as to the philosophical justification for the new sentencing statutes, stating unconditionally that retribution was its primary goal.[50] Today, about twenty states employ some form of sentencing guidelines with similar goals.

In general, these guidelines remove discretionary power from state judges by turning sentencing into a mathematical exercise. Members of the courtroom work group are guided by a *grid,* which helps them determine the proper sentence. Figure 11.4 shows the grid established by the Oregon Sentencing Commission. As with the grids used by most states, one axis ranks the type of crime, while the other refers to the offender's criminal history. In Oregon, each of roughly fifty felonies is ranked in seriousness for use with the grid.

For example, Burglary I is assigned a crime seriousness level of 9 if it involved the use of a deadly weapon, level 8 if the dwelling was occupied at the time of the crime, and so on. The state's crime history grid ranks the offender based on prior felonies and misdemeanors, with various points accrued on the basis of the seriousness of the prior crime. Of the ninety-nine cells in Oregon's grid, fifty-three "presume" prison terms and forty-six "presume" probationary sentences. The judge cannot deviate from these guidelines except under certain circumstances, which we will explore shortly.

Federal Sentencing Guidelines In 1984, Congress passed the Sentencing Reform Act (SRA),[51] paving the way for federal sentencing guidelines that went into effect in 1987. Similar in many respects to the state guidelines, the SRA also eliminated parole for federal prisoners and severely limited early release from prison due to good behavior.[52] Furthermore, the act changed the sentencing role of U.S. probation officers. No longer would they be allowed to "suggest" the terms of punishment in presentence investigative reports. Instead, they are simply called on to calculate the presumptive sentence based on the federal sentencing guidelines grid.[53] The impact of the new law has been dramatic: the average federal prison sentence today is fifty months, more than twice as long as in 1984.[54]

Judicial Departures Even in their haste to limit a judge's power, legislators realized that sentencing guidelines could not be expected to cover every possible criminal situation. Therefore, both state and federal sentencing guidelines allow an "escape hatch" of limited judicial discretion known as a **departure.** The SRA has a proviso that a judge may "depart" from the presumptive sentencing range if a case involves aggravating or mitigating circumstances that are not adequately covered in the guidelines. For example, suppose two men are involved in the robbery of a liquor store, and during court proceedings it becomes clear that one of them forced his partner to take part in the crime by threatening physical harm. In this case, a federal judge could reduce the accomplice's sentence because he committed the crime under "duress," a factor that is not accounted for in the sentencing guidelines.

Sentencing Guidelines
Legislatively determined guidelines that judges are required to follow when sentencing those convicted of specific crimes. These guidelines limit judicial discretion.

Departure
A stipulation in many federal and state sentencing guidelines that allows a judge to adjust his or her sentencing decision based on the special circumstances of a particular case.

FIGURE 11.4
Oregon's
Sentencing Guidelines

Post-Prison Supervision	Crime		A — Three or more person felonies / Multiple (3+) felony person offender	B — Two person felonies, adult or juvenile / Repeat (2) felony person offender	C — One person felony, plus one or more adult or juvenile non-person felony / Single (1) felony person with felony non-person offender	D — One adult or juvenile person felony and no other felony / Single (1) felony person offender	E — Four or more adult non-person felonies / Multiple (4+) felony non-person offender	F — Two or three adult non-person felonies / Repeat (2–3) felony non-person offender	G — 4 or more adult A misdo's, or 1 adult non-person felony, or 3 or more juvenile non-person felonies / Significant minor criminal record	H — No more than 3 adult A misdo's, or no more than 2 juvenile non-person felonies / Minor criminal record	I — No juvenile felony or adult A misdemeanors / Minor misdemeanor or no criminal record	Probation Term
	Murder	11	225–269	196–224	178–194	149–177	149–177	135–148	129–134	122–128	120–121	
	Manslaughter I, Assault I, Rape I, Arson I	10	121–130	116–120	111–115	91–110	81–90	71–80	66–70	61–65	58–60	5 years
3 years	Rape I, Assault I, Kidnapping II, Arson I, Burglary I, Robbery I	9	66–72	61–65	56–60	51–55	46–50	41–45	39–40	37–38	34–36	
	Manslaughter II, Sexual Abuse I, Assault II, Rape II, Using Child in Display of Sexual Conduct, Drugs-Minors, Cult/Mftr/Delivery, Compelling Prostitution, Negligent Homicide	8	41–45	35–40	29–34	27–28	25–26	23–24	21–22	19–20	16–18	Opt probation
	Extortion, Coercion, Supplying Contraband, Escape I	7	31–36	25–30	21–24	19–20	16–18	180 / 90	180 / 90	180 / 90	180 / 90	3 years
	Robbery II, Assault III, Rape III, Bribe Receiving, Intimidation, Property Crimes (more than $50,000), Drug Possession	6	25–30	19–24	15–18	13–14	10–12	180 / 90	180 / 90	180 / 90	180 / 90	
2 years	Robbery II, Theft by Receiving, Trafficking Stolen Vehicles, Property Crimes ($10,000–$49,999)	5	15–16	13–14	11–12	9–10	6–8	180 / 90	120 / 60	120 / 60	120 / 60	2 years
	FTA I, Custodial Interference II, Property Crimes ($5,000–$9,999), Drugs-Cult/Mftr/Delivery	4	10 / 10	8–9	120 / 60	120 / 60	120 / 60	120 / 60	120 / 60	120 / 60	120 / 60	
	Abandon Child, Abuse of Corpse, Criminal Nonsupport, Property Crimes, ($1,000–$4,999)	3	120 / 60	120 / 60	120 / 60	120 / 60	120 / 60	120 / 60	90 / 30	90 / 30	90 / 30	
1 year	Dealing Child Pornography, Violation of Wildlife Laws, Welfare Fraud, Property Crimes (less than $1,000)	2	90 / 30	90 / 30	90 / 30	90 / 30	90 / 30	90 / 30	90 / 30	90 / 30	90 / 30	18 mos.
	Altering Research, Habitual Offender Violation, Bigamy, Paramilitary Activity, Drugs–Possession	1	90 / 30	90 / 30	90 / 30	90 / 30	90 / 30	90 / 30	90 / 30	90 / 30	90 / 30	

● In light green blocks, numbers are presumptive prison sentences expressed as a range of months.

● In blue blocks, upper number is the maximum number of days of punishment (incarceration or community corrections) that may be imposed; lower number is the maximum number of jail days only that may be imposed.

Judges do not have unlimited access to departures, however. Any such decision must be justified in writing, and both the prosecution and the defense may appeal a judicial departure. In 1989, the Court of Appeals for the First Circuit ruled that departures must be measured on the basis of the circumstances and facts of the case and the reasonableness of the judge's decision.[55] (See the feature *You Be the Judge—What's the Sentence?* on the following page.)

YOU BE THE JUDGE

What's the Sentence?

THE FACTS
Twenty-three-year-old law school student Angela attended the rehearsal dinner for a friend's wedding. At the event, she took part in a series of toasts. Driving back to her home in Seattle, Washington, in her Porsche, Angela ran a red light and collided with another vehicle. The occupant of the other car suffered a broken neck. Angela had a blood alcohol level of 0.16 percent (the legal limit was 0.10 percent at the time and has since been lowered to 0.08 percent) and pled guilty to vehicular assault.

THE LAW
Under Washington State's Sentencing Reform Act (SRA), vehicular assault is considered a "violent offense" and categorized as a "most serious" Level IV felony. Under the SRA presumptive sentencing guidelines, Angela, who had no previous offense, could be sentenced to between three and nine months in jail.

YOUR DECISION
Angela's lawyer presented the trial court with a number of arguments aimed at lowering her sentence, including her lack of a prior record, her history of charitable work, her sincere sense of regret, and her family background, which made it unlikely she would commit any further crimes. What sentence would you give Angela?

[To see how the Washington trial court ruled in this case, go to Example 11.1 in Appendix B.]

Mandatory Sentencing Guidelines

The **United States Sentencing Commission** is an independent agency in the judicial branch that establishes sentencing policies for federal courts. To visit its Web site, click on *Web Links* under *Chapter Resources* at **www.cjinaction.com**.

In an attempt to close even the limited loophole of judicial discretion offered by departures, politicians (often urged on by their constituents) have passed sentencing laws even more contrary to the idea of individualized justice. These **mandatory (minimum) sentencing guidelines** further limit a judge's power to deviate from determinate sentencing laws by setting firm standards for certain crimes. Forty-six states have mandatory sentencing laws for crimes such as selling drugs, driving under the influence of alcohol, and committing any crime with a dangerous weapon. In Alabama, for example, any person caught selling drugs must spend at least two years in prison, with five years added to the sentence if the sale takes place within three miles of a school or housing project.[56] Similarly, Congress has set mandatory minimum sentences for more than one hundred crimes, mostly drug offenses.

Habitual Offender Laws **Habitual offender laws** are a form of mandatory sentencing that has become increasingly popular over the past decade. Also known as "three-strikes-and-you're-out" laws, these statutes require that any person convicted of a third felony must serve a lengthy prison sentence. The crime does not have to be of a violent or dangerous nature. Under Washington's habitual offender law, for example, a "persistent offender" is automatically sentenced to life even if the third felony offense happens to be "vehicular assault" (an automobile accident that causes injury), unarmed robbery, or attempted arson, among other lesser felonies.[57] Today, twenty-three states and the federal government employ "three-strikes" statutes, with varying degrees of severity.

"Three Strikes" in Court The United States Supreme Court paved the way for these "three-strikes" laws when it ruled in *Rummel v. Estelle* (1980)[58] that Texas's habitual offender statute did not constitute "cruel and unusual punishment." Basically, the Court gave each state the freedom to legislate such laws in the manner that it deems proper. Twenty-three years later, in *Lockyer v. Andrade* (2003),[59] the Court upheld California's

Mandatory Sentencing Guidelines
Statutorily determined punishments that must be applied to those who are convicted of specific crimes.

Habitual Offender Laws
Statutes that require lengthy prison sentences for those who are convicted of multiple felonies.

"three-strikes" law. The California statute allows prosecutors to seek penalties up to life imprisonment without parole on conviction of any third felony, including for nonviolent crimes. Leandro Andrade received fifty years in prison for stealing $153 worth of videotapes, his fourth felony conviction. A federal appeals court overturned the sentence, agreeing with Andrade's attorneys that it violated Eighth Amendment protections against cruel and unusual punishment.[60]

In a bitterly divided 5–4 decision, the Court reversed. Justice Sandra Day O'Connor, writing for the majority, stated that the sentence was not so "objectively" unreasonable that it violated the Constitution.[61] In his dissent, Justice David H. Souter countered that "[i]f Andrade's sentence is not grossly disproportionate, the principle has no meaning."[62] Basically, the justices who upheld the law said that if the California legislature—and by extension the California voters—felt that the law was reasonable, then the judicial branch was in no position to disagree. For all the publicity they receive, "three-strikes" laws are underused in most jurisdictions. As of 2004, only three states had more than 400 convicts serving terms under "three-strikes" legislation—California had 42,322; Florida, 1,628; and Georgia, 7,631.[63]

Opposition to Determinate Sentencing

Just as indeterminate sentencing produced outrageous examples of judicial discretion, so determinate sentencing has given its opponents fodder for criticism. Examples of mandatory sentencing "gone wild" usually involve such disproportionate sentences as the life term imposed on a teenager for stealing a cell phone. Determinate sentencing, complained one observer, has "shown that there are things worse than disparity: rigidity, extreme severity, irrationality."[64] Among the staunchest opponents of the new sentencing measures have been members of the courtroom work group, who have seen the laws transform their well-established procedural norms.

The *Blakely* Decision As might be expected, judges, for the most part, have not welcomed the reduction in their discretionary powers. University of Minnesota law professor Michael Tonry has written that sentencing guidelines are the most "disliked sentencing reform initiative in the history of the United States" among judges.[65] Federal judges have called the guidelines "a farce," a "dismal failure," and "out of whack."[66] According to the U.S. Sentencing Commission, judges have shown their displeasure with the rules by "downward departing" in approximately 20 percent of all the sentences they hand out.[67] Indeed, then U.S. Attorney General John Ashcroft became so frustrated with the high incidence of downward departures that in 2003 he ordered the U.S. Department of Justice to keep track of federal judges who give more lenient sentences than those provided for in the sentencing guidelines. Although such an action can have little practical effect on federal judges, who, as we learned in Chapter 8, are appointed for life, it was criticized in many judicial quarters as an attempt to intimidate them into compliance.[68]

Undoubtedly, then, many judges were pleasantly surprised when the United States Supreme Court threw sentencing guidelines into doubt with its unexpected ruling in *Blakely v. Washington* (2004).[69] The case involved a Washington trial judge's decision under state sentencing guidelines to add an extra thirty-seven months to a kidnapping sentence because the defendant acted with "deliberate cruelty." The Court overturned the sentence, holding that by allowing *judges* to make findings that increase a defendant's penalty, Washington's system violated the defendant's Sixth Amendment right to trial by jury. The Court held that only a *jury* can make such a finding—in this case, the jury would have had to decide whether the accused acted with "deliberate cruelty."

AP Photo/Department of Corrections

Leandro Andrade, pictured here, unsuccessfully challenged California's "three-strikes" law. Under the state law, Andrade was sentenced to fifty years in prison without possibility of parole for stealing $153 worth of videocassettes—the lengthy sentence coming because of his previous convictions for the "serious" felony of residential burglary. What effect do you think the knowledge that a third felony conviction will lead to a long sentence has on those people already found guilty of two such crimes?

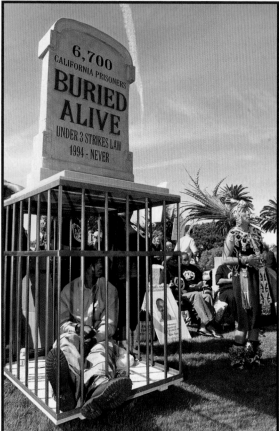

6,700
CALIFORNIA PRISONERS
BURIED
ALIVE
UNDER 3 STRIKES LAW
1994 - NEVER

Outside a federal building in Los Angeles, activist Corey Nasario sits inside a makeshift cell to protest the thousands of California prisoners who have been imprisoned under the state's "three-strikes" law. The vast majority of these prisoners have never committed a violent crime, yet they will spend from twenty-five years to life behind bars. What are the arguments for and against the contention that such "three-strikes" laws violate the Eighth Amendment's prohibition of cruel and unusual punishment?

Although the *Blakely* decision effectively nullified the sentencing guidelines of seven states, its greatest impact was on the federal sentencing guidelines that had been in place for twenty years. Indeed, the ruling caused something akin to panic among federal court officials, who feared that it might invalidate as many as 270,000 recent sentences in which a judge had made a sentencing decision.[70] Furthermore, given the complexity of the federal guidelines, many worried that juries would be forced to make dozens of extra decisions that would add hours, if not days, to trials: a routine federal robbery case can require as many as twenty separate sentencing determinations. In short, the *Blakely* ruling threw the federal court system into turmoil.

The *Booker* Decision The Supreme Court addressed the problems created by its *Blakely* ruling with another surprising pronouncement. In *United States v. Booker* (2005),[71] the Court held that the federal sentencing guidelines were merely "advisory," not "mandatory," in effect restoring to federal judges the individualized discretion they enjoyed before 1984. Using legal reasoning based more on convenience than logic, the Court seemed to be saying that all the sentences handed down under the federal guidelines in the past were valid because judges had merely been following Congress's "advice" (even if they did not know it at the time).

Most critics of determinate sentencing hailed the ruling, whatever its inspiration, for shifting the balance of power in the sentencing process back to the judiciary.[72] The judges may not have much time to relish their newfound freedom, however. The *Booker* decision does not limit Congress's ability to pass mandatory *minimum* sentences that still must be followed by judges, and several members of Congress have already indicated a willingness to take this very step.[73] In addition, prosecutors may respond by charging defendants with more serious crimes, therefore guaranteeing harsher sentences either as part of a plea bargain or at trial.

Sentencing and the Jury

The Supreme Court's *Blakely* decision reflects a trend toward giving juries more power in the sentencing process. Two other recent cases—both of which, like the *Blakely* ruling, turned on the Court's interpretation of the Sixth Amendment right to trial by jury—have greatly increased the importance of juries in sentencing hearings. The first, *Apprendi v. New Jersey* (2000),[74] involved a New Jersey hate crime statute that allowed judges to increase the penalty for any crime if they decided that it was committed with the purpose of intimidating a person because of his or her race. The Court found the law unconstitutional and held that any fact that increases a sentence beyond the legal maximum must be proved beyond a reasonable doubt to the satisfaction of the jury. Then, in *Ring v. Arizona* (2002),[75] the Court ruled that Arizona's death penalty procedure was unconstitutional because the judge, and not a jury, decided whether the defendant would be executed. The decision directly voided the death penalty procedures in five states that gave the judge the ultimate power over the "life or death" sentencing decision, a subject we will explore in great detail in the next section.

Only six states (Arkansas, Kentucky, Missouri, Oklahoma, Texas, and Virginia) allow juries, rather than the judge, to make the sentencing decision when the death penalty is not an option. In these states, the judge gives the jury instructions on the range of penalties available, and then the jury makes the final decision.[76] Juries have traditionally been assigned a relatively small role in felony sentencing largely out of concern that jurors' lack of experience and legal expertise will lead to improper verdicts and sentencing disparity.[77] When sentencing by juries is allowed, the practice is popular with prosecutors because jurors are more likely than judges to give harsher sentences in noncapital cases, particularly for drug crimes, sex abuse, and theft. Consequently, defendants facing sentencing juries are more likely to plea bargain to ensure that they do not receive a lengthy sentence.[78]

Victim Impact Evidence

Many prosecutors also feel they benefit from another recent reform of American courtroom procedure: the increased involvement of victims and victims' families in the sentencing process. As we saw in Chapter 2, crime victims traditionally were banished to the peripheries of the criminal justice system. This situation has changed dramatically with the emergence of the victims' rights movement over the past few decades. Victims are now given the opportunity to testify—in person or through written testimony—during sentencing hearings about the suffering they experienced as the result of the crime. These **victim impact statements (VIS)** have proved extremely controversial, however, and even the Supreme Court has had a difficult time determining whether they cause more harm than good.

Balancing the Process Every state and federal government has some form of victim impact legislation. In general, these laws allow a victim (or victims) to tell his or her "side of the story" to the sentencing body, be it a judge, jury, or parole officer. In non-murder cases, the victim can personally describe the physical, financial, and emotional impact of the crime. When the charge is murder or manslaughter, relatives or friends can give personal details about the victim and describe the effects of her or his death. In almost all instances, the goal of the VIS is to increase the harshness of the sentence.

Most of the debate surrounding the VIS centers on its use in the sentencing phases of death penalty cases. Supporters point out that the defendant has always been allowed to present character evidence in the hopes of dissuading a judge or jury from capital punishment. In the sentencing phase of Scott Peterson's trial, referenced in Chapter 1, the defense called thirty-nine witnesses, including Peterson's mother and father, in an ultimately futile effort to convince the jury that Peterson did not deserve to be executed.[79] According to some, a VIS balances the equation by giving survivors a voice in the process. Presenting a VIS is also said to have psychological benefits for victims, who are no longer forced to sit in silence as decisions that affect their lives are made by others.[80] Finally, on a purely practical level, a VIS may help judges and juries make informed sentencing decisions by providing them with an understanding of all of the consequences of the crime.

The Risks of Victim Evidence Opponents of the use of a VIS claim that it interjects dangerously prejudicial evidence into the sentencing process, which should be governed by reason, not emotion. The inflammatory nature of VIS, they say, may distract judges and juries from the facts of the case, which should be the only basis for a sentence.[81] Furthermore, critics contend that VIS introduces the idea of "social value" into the courtroom. In other words, judges and juries may feel compelled to base the punishment on the "social value" of the victim (his or her standing in the community, role as an family member, and so on) rather than the circumstances of the crime.

In 1987, the United States Supreme Court sided with the opponents of VIS, holding that such evidence is "irrelevant to a capital sentencing decision" and "creates a constitutionally unacceptable risk that the jury may impose the death penalty"

Victim Impact Statement (VIS) A statement to the sentencing body (judge, jury, or parole board) in which the victim is given the opportunity to describe how the crime has affected her or him. The general purpose of the statement is to convince the sentencing party to hand down a harsher punishment than might otherwise be the case.

FIGURE 11.5

Victim Impact Statements in Action

According to the U.S. Supreme Court, victim impact statements are admissible as long as they are relevant and do not unfairly prejudice the jury against the defendant. In their discretion, however, judges often allow seemingly inflammatory victim impact evidence during sentencing hearings. For example the Oklahoma Court of Criminal Appeals deemed that the following statement, given by the daughter of a murder victim, was admissible.

"I think the only fair punishment for him is he should be confined in a small area, someone three or four times his size should come into that confined area and beat him, cause him pain. I think he should have to beg for his life. I thing he should have to crawl in his own blood. And he should have to crawl to get away from his attacker. I think he should suffer, suffer, suffer. But you know, even if he's put to death, he won't suffer; you know he will have a painless death. We can't do anything to him that will cause him the kind of pain that has been caused to our mother and us . . . . Mother raised us to be kind and forgiving, but we can't forgive this and we want him killed."

Source: *Williams v. State*, 947 P.2d 1074 (Okla. Crim. App. 1997).

arbitrarily.[82] Just four years later, however, in *Payne v. Tennessee* (1991),[83] the Court (with several new justices) modified its ruling, finding that a VIS is not *always* inadmissible and that its prejudicial effects must be determined on a case-by-case basis just as with any other type of evidence. (See Figure 11.5 for an example of a VIS that was ruled not to be prejudicial.)

Several years after the *Payne* decision, Bryan Myers of the University of North Carolina at Wilmington and Jack Arbuthnot of Ohio University decided to test the prejudicial impact of the testimony in question. They ran simulated court proceedings with two groups of mock jurors: one group heard a "family member" give a VIS similar to the one presented by the victim's grandmother during Payne's sentencing hearing, while the other group did not. Of those mock jurors who ultimately voted for the death penalty, 67 percent had heard the VIS; in contrast, only 30 percent of those who did not hear it voted to execute the defendant.[84]

CAPITAL PUNISHMENT— THE ULTIMATE SENTENCE

"You do not know how hard it is to let a human being die," Abraham Lincoln (1809–1865) once said, "when you feel that a stroke of your pen will save him." Despite these misgivings, during his four years in office Lincoln approved the execution of 267 soldiers, including those who had slept at their posts.[85] Our sixteenth president's ambivalence toward **capital punishment** is reflected in America's continuing struggle to reconcile the penalty of death with the morals and values of society. Capital punishment has played a role in sentencing since the earliest days of the Republic and—having survived a brief period of abolition between 1972 and 1976—continues to enjoy public support.

Still, few topics in the criminal justice system inspire such heated debate. Death penalty opponents such as legal expert Stephen Bright wonder whether "there comes a time when a society gets beyond some of the more primitive forms of punishment."[86] They point out that two dozen countries have abolished the death penalty since 1985 and that the United States is the only Western democracy that continues the practice. Critics also claim that a process whose subjects are chosen by "luck and money and

Capital Punishment
The use of the death penalty to punish wrongdoers for certain crimes.

race" cannot serve the interests of justice.[87] Proponents believe that the death penalty serves as the ultimate deterrent for violent criminal behavior and that the criminals who are put to death are the "worst of the worst" and deserve their fate.

Today, just under 3,500 convicts are living on "death row" in American prisons, meaning they have been sentenced to death and are awaiting execution. In the 1940s, as many as two hundred people were put to death in the United States in one year; as Figure 11.6 shows, the most recent high-water mark was ninety-eight in 1999. Despite declines since then, states and the federal government are currently executing convicts at a rate not seen in five decades. Consequently, the questions that surround the death penalty—Is it fair? Is it humane? Does it deter crime?—will continue to inflame both its supporters and its detractors.

The American Tradition of Capital Punishment

"Before there were prisons" in the American tradition, points out social psychologist Mark Costanzo, "there was the penalty of death."[88] The first person executed by an American colonial government—taking its cue from the homeland of England, where capital punishment was widespread—was George Kendall, who was shot to death by a firing squad in Virginia for spying for Spain in 1608.[89] Since Kendall, more than 18,000 Americans have been legally executed as punishment for their crimes.

Capital Punishment in the Seventeenth and Eighteenth Centuries In studying capital punishment in the colonies and the early days of the United States, one is struck by two aspects of the practice: the variety of crimes that were punished by death, and the public nature of the executions. During the 1600s, colonists were put to death for the crime of murder, but also for witchcraft, blasphemy, sodomy, and adultery. In the 1700s, citizens were executed for robbery, forgery, and illegally cutting down a tree.[90] These executions by hanging, beheading, or firing squad regularly took place in the town square or common area and were attended by the public. In fact, by modern standards the death penalty was often carried out in an overly gruesome manner in an attempt to deter criminal behavior by members of the audience. In 1710, a Virginia court ordered the bodies of two slaves who had been hanged for inciting rebellion to be cut up and displayed in various parts of the colony to keep "other Slaves from entering into such dangerous Conspiracys."[91]

The practice of public executions continued unabated until the 1830s, when reformers instigated the first widespread movement to abolish capital punishment.

FIGURE 11.6
Executions in the United States, 1976 to 2004

Source: Death Penalty Information Center.

Prisoners Executed Under Civil Authority

To See or Not to See?

In the low-budget, low-quality film *Citizen Verdict* (2003), an unscrupulous television producer (played by notorious television host Jerry Springer) arranges for the ultimate pay-per-view event: an execution. Although no real network has been so bold as to suggest such a broadcast, public interest in televised executions does exist. Two-thirds of those polled by Harris Interactive indicated that they support the idea of televising executions, and 21 percent said that they would pay to watch Osama bin Laden put to death.

There is also a good deal of ideological support for televising executions from both supporters and critics of the death penalty. Proponents believe that public viewing of executions adds to their deterrent value. Opponents believe that by "hiding" executions, the government prevents people from seeing how gruesome they really are. These critics are convinced that if the public were allowed to witness these events, support for the death penalty would drop dramatically.

Evidence in support of such a theory is hard to find, however. In fact, human curiosity seems to drive large numbers of people to horrific events, whether they are televised or not. In 1837, when support for capital punishment was as high as it is today, 20,000 spectators gathered in Philadelphia to watch the hanging of the pirate James Moran. More than 160 years later, in 1999, Florida Supreme Court Justice Leander J. Shaw, Jr., placed photos of the electrocution of Allen Lee "Tiny" Davis on the court's Web site to highlight the brutality of the electric chair. (The photos showed Davis hemorrhaging blood from his nose onto his white prison shirt.) The site received so many hits in such a short period of time that it crashed. Such incidents lend credence to the rea-

Allen Lee Davis was executed on July 8, 1999. Photos of his gruesome death, during which blood flowed freely from his nose, were posted on the Internet. What effect do you think the broadcasting of executions such as Davis's would have on public opinion concerning the death penalty in this country?

sons most often given by prison officials when refusing media requests to bring cameras into the execution chamber: the privacy rights of the convict and the need to preserve the "solemnity of executions."

Government officials in northeastern states, aware that public executions provided death penalty opponents with opportunities to protest, passed a number of laws limiting the number of witnesses at an execution and requiring law enforcement officers to set up enclosures for the event. Furthermore, a desire to "civilize" the execution process moved it indoors, transforming it from a public spectacle to a sober action of the state.[92] The last public execution in the United States took place in Missouri in 1937. (See the feature *CJ and the Media—To See or Not to See?*)

> "Let's do it."
>
> —convicted murderer Gary Gilmore, shortly before his execution by a Utah firing squad (1977)

Methods of Execution The desire to civilize executions can also be seen in the evolution of the methods used to carry out the death sentence. Hanging was considered a more humane form of execution than other methods adopted from England, which including drawing and quartering and boiling the subject alive, and was the primary means of carrying out the death sentence in the United States until the end of the nineteenth century. (Indeed, the "long drop" method, in which the subject was hung from a greater height to ensure that death came from breaking the neck rather than strangulation, resulted from the reform movement in the 1830s and 1840s.) The 1890s saw the introduction of electrocution as a less painful method of execution than hanging, and in 1890 in Auburn Prison, New York, William Kemmler became the first American to die in an electric chair.

The "chair" remained the primary form of execution until 1977, when Oklahoma became the first state to adopt lethal injection. Today, almost all of the thirty-eight states that allow the death penalty employ lethal injection; the condemned convict is given a sedative, followed by a combination of drugs administered intravenously. Fifteen states authorize two different methods of execution, meaning that electrocution (nine states), lethal gas (four states), hanging (four states), and the firing squad (four states) are still used from time to time.[93]

See the Web sites of the **Death Penalty Information Center** and **Pro-Death Penalty.com** for opposing views on capital punishment. Find these Web sites by clicking on *Web Links* under *Chapter Resources* at **www.cjinaction.com**.

The Death Penalty and the Supreme Court

In 1890, William Kemmler challenged his sentence to die in New York's new electric chair (for murdering his mistress) on the grounds that electrocution infringed on his Eighth Amendment rights against cruel and unusual punishment.[94] Kemmler's challenge is historically significant in that it did not challenge the death penalty itself as being cruel and unusual, but only the method by which it was carried out. Many constitutional scholars believe that the framers never questioned the necessity of capital punishment, as long as due process is followed in determining the guilt of the suspect.[95] Accordingly, the Supreme Court rejected Kemmler's challenge, stating that:

> Punishments are cruel when they involve torture or a lingering death; but the punishment of death is not cruel, within the meaning of that word as used in the Constitution. It implies there something inhuman and barbarous, something more than the mere extinguishment of life.[96]

Thus, the Court set a standard that it has followed to this day. No *method* of execution has ever been found to be unconstitutional by the Supreme Court.

Weems v. United States   For nearly eight decades following its decision regarding *Kemmler,* the Supreme Court was silent on the question of whether capital punishment was constitutional. In *Weems v. United States* (1910),[97] however, the Court did make a ruling that would significantly affect the debate on the death penalty. *Weems* concerned a defendant who had been sentenced to fifteen years of hard labor, a heavy fine, and a number of other penalties for the relatively minor crime of falsifying official records. The Court overturned the sentence, ruling that the penalty was too harsh considering the nature of the offense. Ultimately, in the *Weems* decision, the Court set three important precedents concerning sentencing:

1 Cruel and unusual punishment is defined by the changing norms and standards of society and therefore is not based on historical interpretations.

2 Courts may decide whether a punishment is unnecessarily cruel with regard to physical pain.

3 Courts may decide whether a punishment is unnecessarily cruel with regard to psychological pain.[98]

Furman v. Georgia   In 1971, three cases challenging the death penalty as "cruel and unusual" were brought before the Supreme Court. Again, these cases did not question the death penalty itself as cruel and unusual. Instead, they raised the argument that capital punishment was imposed arbitrarily; that is, the death penalty was unconstitutional because there were no recognizable standards under which it could or could not be imposed.

In *Furman v. Georgia* (1972),[99] the lead case, the Supreme Court issued a very complex ruling on this issue. By a 5–4 margin, the Court essentially agreed that the death

Gary Gilmore is led to a Provo, Utah, court on December 1, 1976. Less than two months later, Gilmore became the first American executed under a new bifurcated system adopted by a number of states in the mid-1970s. Why did the United States Supreme Court put a halt to executions in this country in 1972?

penalty violated the Eighth Amendment. Only two of those in the majority (Justices Marshall and Brennan), however, were willing to state that capital punishment was blatantly unconstitutional. The other three (Justices Douglas, Stewart, and White) took the narrower view that the sentence was unconstitutional as practiced by the states. Justice Potter Stewart was particularly eloquent on the subject, stating that the sentence of death was so arbitrary as to be comparable to "being struck by lightning."[100] In its decision, therefore, the Court did not rule that the death penalty inherently violated the Eighth Amendment's protection against cruel and unusual punishment or the Fourteenth Amendment's guarantee of due process, only that it did so as practiced by the states. So, although *Furman* invalidated the death penalty for over six hundred offenders on death row at the time, it also provided the states with a window of opportunity to bring their death penalty statutes up to constitutional standards.

The Bifurcated Process By 1976, thirty-five states had done just that, attempting to comply with *Furman* by either making the death penalty mandatory for certain offenses or adopting elaborate procedures to ensure that standards of due process were upheld during the sentencing process. The ten states that attempted the mandatory route found their statutes invalidated for a second time in 1976, when, in *Woodson v. North Carolina*,[101] the Supreme Court ruled that such laws failed to allow for different circumstances in different cases.

The remaining twenty-five states adopted an alternate means of satisfying the questions raised in *Furman* by establishing a two-stage, or *bifurcated*, procedure for capital cases. In the first stage, a jury determines the guilt or innocence of the defendant for a crime that has statutorily been determined to be punishable by death. If the defendant is found guilty, the jury reconvenes in the second stage and considers all relevant evidence to decide whether the death sentence is in fact warranted. Therefore, even if a jury were to find the defendant guilty of a crime, such as first degree murder, that *may be* punishable by death, in the second stage it could decide that the circumstances surrounding the crime justified only a punishment of life in prison. The circumstances that justify the death penalty can vary from state to state. In Colorado, for example, the seventeen aggravating factors include deliberately killing a woman knowing that she is pregnant.[102] (See *Mastering Concepts—The Bifurcated Death Penalty Process.*)

Gregg v. Georgia In *Gregg v. Georgia* (1976),[103] the Supreme Court ruled in favor of Georgia's new bifurcated process, stating that the state's legislative guidelines removed the ability of a jury to "wantonly and freakishly impose the death penalty." The Court upheld similar procedures in Texas and Florida, establishing a model for all states to follow that would assure them protection from lawsuits based on Eighth Amendment grounds. On January 17, 1977, Gary Mark Gilmore became the first American executed (by Utah) under the new laws, and today thirty-eight states and the federal government have capital punishment laws based on the guidelines established by *Gregg*. (Note that state governments are responsible for almost all executions in this country. The executions of Timothy McVeigh and Juan Raul Garza in 2001 were the first death sentences carried out by the federal government since 1963.)

The Court reaffirmed the important role of the jury in death penalties in *Ring v. Arizona* (2002).[104] The case involved Arizona's bifurcated process: after the jury determined a defendant's guilt or innocence, it would be dismissed, and the judge would decide whether execution was warranted. As mentioned earlier, the Court found that this procedure violated the defendant's Sixth Amendment right to a jury trial; juries

MASTERING CONCEPTS

The Bifurcated Death Penalty Process

The Bifurcated Model Trial

By judge → Not guilty or guilty of lesser offense

Guilty verdict

Sentencing hearing before jury empaneled for sentence determination

By jury → Not guilty or guilty of lesser offense

Guilty verdict

Sentencing hearing before jury empaneled for sentence determination

must be involved in *both* stages of the bifurcated process. The decision invalidated death penalty laws in Arizona, Colorado, Idaho, Montana, and Nebraska, forcing legislatures in those states to hastily revamp their procedures.

Mitigating Circumstances   Several mitigating circumstances will prevent a defendant found guilty of first degree murder from receiving the death penalty.

Insanity   In 1986, the United States Supreme Court held that the Constitution prohibits the execution of a person who is insane. The Court failed to provide a test for insanity other than Justice Lewis F. Powell's statement that the Eighth Amendment "forbids the execution only of those who are unaware of the punishment they are about to suffer and why they are to suffer it."[105] Consequently, each state must come up with its own definition of "insanity" for death penalty purposes. A state may also force convicts on death row to take medication that will make them sane enough to be aware of the punishment they are about to suffer and why they are about to suffer it.[106]

Mentally Handicapped   The Supreme Court's recent change of mind on the question of whether a mentally handicapped convict may be put to death underscores the continuing importance of the *Weems* test. In 1989, the Court rejected the argument that execution of a mentally handicapped person was "cruel and unusual" under the Eighth Amendment.[107] At that time, only two states barred execution of the mentally handicapped. Today, eighteen states have such laws, and the Court has decided that this increased number reflects "changing norms and standards of society." In *Atkins v. Virginia* (2002),[108] the Court used the *Weems* test as the main rationale for barring the execution of the mentally handicapped.

Age   Following the *Atkins* case, many observers, including four Supreme Court justices, hoped that the same reasoning would be applied to the question of whether convicts who committed the relevant crime when they were juveniles may be executed.

> "We didn't feel she should get the death penalty. When you're on Death Row, you're there so long with nothing to bother you. In jail, she'll be with murderers and rapists. We thought the death penalty would be too easy for her."
>
> —Jodi Dotts, explaining her decision to ask the prosecutor not to seek capital punishment for her daughter's killer (1999)

CJ IN FOCUS/LANDMARK CASE

Roper v. Simmons

When he was seventeen years old, Christopher Simmons abducted Shirley Crook, used duct tape to cover her eyes and mouth and bind her hands, and threw her to her death in a river. Although he bragged to his friends that he would "get away with it" because he was a minor, he was found guilty of murder and sentenced to death by a Missouri court. After the United States Supreme Court held, in *Atkins v. Virginia* (2002), that "evolving standards of decency" rendered the execution of mentally retarded persons unconstitutional, Simmons appealed his own sentence on similar grounds, pointing to his juvenile status at the time of the crime. The Missouri Supreme Court agreed and overturned his death sentence, stating that, in light of the *Atkins* ruling, the United States Supreme Court's support for juvenile executions in *Stanford v. Kentucky* (1989) was no longer valid. On appeal, the U.S. Supreme Court had to decide whether to follow its own precedent or that of the Missouri Supreme Court.

Roper v. Simmons
United States Supreme Court
125 S.Ct. 1183 (2005)
http://laws.findlaw.com/us/000/03-633.html

In the words of the court . . .
Justice KENNEDY, majority opinion

* * * *

The evidence of national consensus against the death penalty for juveniles is similar, and in some respects parallel, to the evidence *Atkins* held sufficient to demonstrate a national consensus against the death penalty for the mentally retarded. * * * [I]n this case, thirty States prohibit the juvenile death penalty, comprising twelve that have rejected the death penalty altogether and eighteen that maintain it but, by express provision or judicial interpretation, exclude juveniles from its reach. * * * In the present case, too, even in the twenty States without a formal prohibition on executing juveniles, the practice is infrequent.

* * * *

Three general differences between juveniles under 18 and adults demonstrate that juvenile offenders cannot with reliability be classified among the worst offenders. First, as any parent knows and as the scientific and sociological studies * * * tend to confirm, "[a] lack of maturity and an underdeveloped sense of responsibility are found in youth more often than in adults and are more understandable among the young. These qualities often result in impetuous and ill-considered actions and decisions * * * ." In recognition of the comparative immaturity and irresponsibility of juveniles, almost every State prohibits those under eighteen years of age from voting, serving on juries, or marrying without parental consent.

The second area of difference is that juveniles are more vulnerable or susceptible to negative influences and outside pressures, including peer pressure. * * * The third broad difference is that the character of a juvenile is not as well formed as that of an adult. The personality traits of juveniles are more transitory, less fixed.

These differences render suspect any conclusion that a juvenile falls among the worst offenders. * * * Retribution is not proportional if the law's most severe penalty is imposed on one whose culpability or blameworthiness is diminished, to a substantial degree, by reason of youth and immaturity.

DECISION
The Court found that, applying the Eighth Amendment in light of "evolving standards of decency," the execution of offenders who were under the age of eighteen when their crimes were committed was cruel and unusual punishment and therefore unconstitutional. The Missouri Supreme Court's decision to overturn Simmons's death penalty was, therefore, upheld.

FOR CRITICAL ANALYSIS
In the majority decision, Justice Kennedy noted that since 1990 Iran, Pakistan, Saudi Arabia, Yemen, Nigeria, the Democratic Republic of Congo, and China have disavowed the death penalty for juveniles, leaving the United States "alone in a world that has turned its face" against the practice. What effect, if any, should international customs have on American criminal law?

For more information and activities related to this case, click on Landmark Cases *under* Book Resources *at* **www.cjinaction.com.**

These hopes were realized in 2005 when the Court issued its *Roper v. Simmons* decision, which effectively ended the execution of those who committed crimes as juveniles.[109] As in the *Atkins* case, the Court relied on the "evolving standards of decency" test, noting that a majority of the states, as well as every other civilized nation, prohibited the execution of offenders who committed their crimes before the age of eighteen. (See the feature *CJ in Focus—Landmark Cases:* Roper v. Simmons.) The *Roper* ruling required that seventy-two convicted murderers in twelve states be resentenced and took the death penalty "off the table" for dozens of pending cases in which prosecutors were seeking capital punishment for juvenile criminal acts.

Debating the Sentence of Death

Of the topics covered in this textbook, few inspire the passion of argument that can be found concerning the death penalty. Many advocates believe that execution is "just deserts" for those who commit heinous crimes. In the words of Ernest van den Haag, death is the "only fitting retribution for murder that I can think of."[110] Opponents worry that retribution is simply another word for vengeance and that "the use of the death penalty by the state will increase the acceptance of revenge in our society and will give official sanction to a climate of violence."[111] As the debate over capital punishment continues, it tends to focus on several key issues: deterrence, incapacitation, fallibility, arbitrariness, constitutionality, and discrimination.

Deterrence Those advocates of the death penalty who wish to show that the practice benefits society often turn to the idea of deterrence. In other words, they believe that by executing convicted criminals, the criminal justice system discourages potential criminals from committing similar violent acts. (When people speak of "deterrence" with regard to the death penalty, they are usually referring to general deterrence rather than specific deterrence.) Deterrence was the primary justification for the frequent public executions carried out in this country before the 1830s and for the brutality of those events. Many social scientists claim that there is little valid statistical proof of the deterrent effect of capital punishment. Nonetheless, in 1975, Isaac Ehrlich, an economist at the University of Chicago, attempted to find some by focusing on the relationship between different jurisdictions' homicide rates and the percentage of those convicted of murder who were actually executed. According to Ehrlich, each additional execution that would have taken place between 1933 and 1967 could have saved the lives of as many as eight murder victims.[112] Ehrlich's results, though widely hailed at the time of their release, remain controversial; they have not been duplicated to the satisfaction of some scholars, and numerous subsequent studies have found that execution rates appear to have little effect on homicide rates. In fact, the latest major study on the issue, released by criminal justice professors Lisa Stolzenberg and Stewart J. D'Alessio of Florida International University in 2004, found no evidence that the number of executions had any effect on the incidence of murder in the Houston, Texas, area over a five-year period.[113]

In the end, the deterrence debate follows a familiar pattern. Opponents of the death penalty claim that murderers rarely consider the consequences of their act, and therefore it makes no difference whether capital punishment exists or not. Proponents counter that this proves the death penalty's deterrent value, because if the murderers *had* considered the possibility of execution, they would *not* have committed the crime.

Incapacitation In one sense, capital punishment acts as the ultimate deterrent by rendering those executed incapable of committing further crimes. A study done by Paul Cassell and Stephen Markman analyzed the records of 52,000 state inmates doing time for murder and found that 810 of them had been previously convicted for the same crime. These 810 recidivists had killed 821 people after being released from prison the first time.[114] If, hypothetically, the death penalty was mandatory for those convicted of murder, then 821 innocent lives would have been saved in Cassell and Markman's example, and thousands of others among the general population. Such projections seem to show that by incapacitating dangerous criminals, capital punishment could provide society with measurable benefits.

Fallibility The incapacitation justification for capital punishment, however, rests on two questionable assumptions: (1) every convicted murderer is likely to recidivate; and (2) the criminal justice system is *infallible*. In other words, the system never convicts

⊙ GREATDEBATES

Does the death penalty deter murder? For many, this is the central question of the capital punishment debate. To better understand the issues of deterrence and the death penalty, click on *Great Debates* under *Book Resources* at **www.cjinaction.com**.

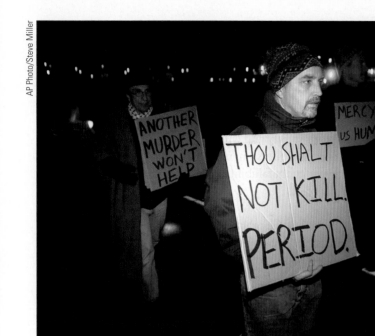

Protesters march outside the Osborn Correctional Institution in Somers, Connecticut, in opposition to the death sentence for Michael Ross, who had confessed to the rape and murder of eight young women and requested to die. On May 13, 2005, Ross became the first person to be executed in New England in forty-five years. What are the arguments for and against allowing an offender to "volunteer" for his or her capital punishment?

someone who is actually not guilty. According to the Death Penalty Information Center, however, between 1976, when the Supreme Court reinstated capital punishment, and June 2005, 119 American men and women who had been convicted of capital crimes and sentenced to death were later found to be innocent. Over that same time period, 972 executions took place, meaning that for every eight convicts put to death since *Gregg*, one death row inmate has been found innocent.[115]

There are several explanations for this relatively high rate of error in capital cases. First, police and prosecutors are often under a great deal of public pressure to solve violent crimes and may be overzealous in arresting and prosecuting suspects. Such was the case with Rolando Cruz, who spent a decade on Illinois's death row for the rape and murder of a ten-year-old girl. Even after another man named Brian Dugan confessed to the crime and DNA testing linked Dugan to the crime scene, prosecutors still insisted that Cruz was the culprit. Only after a police officer admitted that he lied under oath concerning Cruz's "confession" was Cruz declared not guilty.[116]

Outright lying by persons involved in capital cases contributes to false convictions as well. Professors Hugo Bedau of Tufts University and Michael Radelet of the University of Florida found that one-third of wrongful capital convictions resulted from "jailhouse snitches" who perjured themselves by telling the court that they overheard a confession by the defendant. In addition, false confessions and faulty eyewitness identifications were found to be responsible for two of every seven wrongful convictions.[117] The single factor that contributes the most to the criminal justice system's fallibility, however, is widely believed to be unsatisfactory legal representation. Many states and counties cannot or will not allocate adequate funds for death penalty cases, meaning that indigent capital defendants are often provided with a less-than-vigorous defense. During a double homicide trial in Vinton County, Ohio, for example, public defenders for Gregory McKnight presented one witness on their client's behalf while prosecutors called forty against him. After a relatively short—two and a half weeks—trial, McKnight was convicted and sentenced to death.[118]

Arbitrariness One of the reasons it is so difficult to determine the deterrent effect of the death penalty is that it is rarely meted out. Despite the bifurcated process required by *Furman*, a certain amount of arbitrariness appears to remain in the system. Comparing the number of murders known by police to the number of executions, the chances of a murderer being executed are approximately 1,000 to 1.[119]

The chances of a defendant in a capital trial being sentenced to death seem to depend heavily on, as we have just seen, the quality of the defense counsel and the jurisdiction where the crime was committed. A Columbia University study, headed by Professor James Liebman, reported that of the 4,578 death sentences handed down between 1973 and 1995, two-thirds were reversed on appeal. About 37 percent of the reversals occurred because of incompetent lawyering.[120] Furthermore, as Figure 11.7 shows, a convict's chances of being executed are strongly influenced by geography. Six states (Texas, Virginia, Oklahoma, Missouri, Florida, and Georgia) account for nearly two-thirds of all executions, while twelve states and the District of Columbia do not provide for capital punishment within their borders. Therefore, a person on trial for first degree murder in New Mexico has a much better chance of avoiding execution than someone who has committed the same crime in Texas. Dramatic differences can even exist within the same state. Further research by Professor Liebman and his associates showed that the death sentence was handed down in 93 of 1,000 homicides in Lexington County, South Carolina. Richland County, South Carolina, only a few miles away, had a rate of 9 per 1,000.[121] Accordingly, Professor Hugo Bedau compares those who are executed to "losers in an arbitrary lottery."[122]

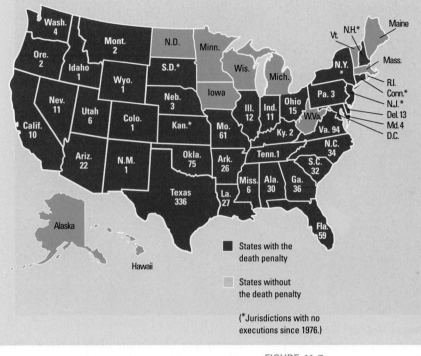

FIGURE 11.7
Executions by State, 1976–2004

Not all observers of the criminal justice system agree with Professor Bedau's assessment. In responding to the first Columbia University study mentioned above, James Q. Wilson points out that its authors do not claim that any innocent people have actually been executed.[123] Instead, Wilson suggests, the system is designed to give convicted murderers every chance to prove their innocence. In the *Gregg* case, the Supreme Court interpreted the Fourteenth Amendment as requiring "meaningful appellate review" for anybody found guilty of a capital crime.[124] In other words, the case of any defendant sentenced to death must automatically be reviewed by a higher court. To decrease the chances that the death sentence will be imposed "in a freakish manner," to use the Court's phrase, the appeals process in capital cases usually lasts twelve years. Thus, Wilson notes, the death penalty is actually quite rare: of the 4,578 death sentences considered in the Columbia University study, only 313 led to executions.[125]

Still Cruel and Unusual Finally, many observers believe that the Supreme Court should revisit the idea of the death penalty as cruel and unusual punishment, given the changing standards of society provided for in the *Weems* decision discussed earlier. Even lethal injection, critics point out, may cause undue suffering. Some medical experts believe that pancuronium bromide, one of the chemicals used in the process, only paralyzes its subjects, rendering them unable to speak or cry out in pain as they suffocate to death.[126] In the latest ruling on the subject, however, a Kentucky judge upheld the procedure as falling within "contemporary norms and societal standards," ruling only that prison officials could not insert the drugs directly into the offender's neck.[127]

Developments in Louisiana may cause the Supreme Court to revisit another Eighth Amendment issue. In 1977, the Court held that the death penalty could not be imposed for rape, labeling as "cruel and unusual" a punishment that is not proportionate to the crime.[128] In 2003, however, a Louisiana court sentenced Patrick O. Kennedy to be executed for raping an eight-year-old girl. If the state supreme court upholds the sentence, the question of whether the death penalty can be applied to crimes other than murder may once again come before the highest court in the land.

Gregory McKnight is comforted by his attorney in a Vinton County (Ohio) common pleas court. Even though McKnight was convicted of aggravated murder, which is punishable by execution, the judge in his case initially ruled that McKnight was not eligible for the death penalty because Vinton County did not have the funds to provide him with an adequate defense. The judge later rescinded this ruling, and McKnight was sentenced to death. What role, if any, should the level of representation by the defense attorney play in a court's decision to execute a convict?

Discriminatory Effect and the Death Penalty

Whether or not capital punishment is imposed arbitrarily, some observers claim that it is not done without bias. Of the 972 prisoners executed in the United States between 1976 and the summer of 2005, 34 percent were African American, even though that minority group made up only about 12 percent of the national population during that time span.[129] Today, 42 percent of all inmates on death row are black; thus, the black proportion of the death row population is more than triple the black proportion of the population.

The Race of the Victim Another set of statistics also continues to be problematic. African Americans are approximately four times more likely to receive the death penalty if their victim is white than if he or she is black.[130] A study of death penalty cases in North Carolina found that the odds of getting a death sentence for convicts of any race increased three and a half times if the victim was white rather than black.[131] In fact, although less than half of murder victims are white, four out of every five executions involve white victims (see Figure 11.8). More recent data also suggest that minority defendants charged with murdering white victims are much more likely than others to be erroneously convicted of capital offenses.[132]

In *McCleskey v. Kemp* (1987),[133] the defense attorney for an African American sentenced to death for killing a white police officer used similar statistics to challenge Georgia's death penalty law. A study of two thousand Georgia murder cases showed that although African Americans were the victims of six out of every ten murders in the state, over 80 percent of the cases in which death was imposed involved murders of whites.[134] In a 5–4 decision, the United States Supreme Court rejected the defense's claims, ruling that statistical evidence did not prove discriminatory intent on the part of Georgia's lawmakers.

The Income of the Victim One of the reasons the study was unpersuasive in the *McKleskey* case is that statistics, as we noted in Chapter 3, are often imperfect tools to measure trends. Even though the studies mentioned above show that race has an effect on the probability of receiving the death penalty, to prove discrimination from a legal standpoint, race must be the *only* determinant. Thus, a study must show that race, and not other factors such as the severity of the crime, the criminal history of the defendant, and the quality of the defense attorney, was the determining factor.[135]

Furthermore, some experts contend that the wealth, and not the race, of the defendant is the most important factor in death penalty cases. This hypothesis is based on the truism that adequate representation lessens the probability of being sentenced to death, and adequate representation is expensive.[136] Research by William M. Holmes of the Criminal Justice Center at the University of Massachusetts in Boston found that race did not account for wrongful convictions in capital cases. A much more important factor, according to Holmes, was education level, which correlates strongly with income.[137]

The Immediate Future of the Death Penalty

As Figure 11.6 on page 369 made clear, the number of executions carried out each year in the United States has decreased dramatically since 1999. Other statistics also indicate a decline in death penalty activity. In 2004, only 125 people were sentenced to death, down from 144 in 2003 and, more significantly, 320 in 1996.[138] State death rows are also shrinking, albeit slowly.[139]

Reasons for the Decline in Executions We have already addressed many of the reasons for the diminishing presence of executions in the criminal justice system. With its decisions in the *Atkins* (2002) and *Roper* (2005) cases, the Supreme Court removed the possibility that hundreds of mentally handicapped and juvenile offenders could be sentenced to death.[140] Furthermore, thirty-six of the thirty-eight states (the exceptions being New Mexico and Texas) that allow for the death penalty now permit juries to impose a sentence of life in prison without parole as an alternative to death. In response, more juries seem to be choosing the life sentence; in 2003, fifteen out of sixteen federal juries refused to impose the death penalty on convicted murderers.[141] For this reason, many experts believe that the Supreme Court's *Ring* (2002)[142] ruling ensuring that juries, and not judges, will make the death sentence decision will dissuade prosecutors from seeking capital punishment.[143] Finally, as we saw earlier, new evidence uncovered by DNA technology has resulted in the exoneration of numerous death row inmates over the past several decades, a trend that will certainly continue.

Fairness Concerns Does this mean society's "standards of decency" are changing to the point that the death sentence is in danger of being abolished? Probably not. Despite its decisions in the first half of the 2000s, the Supreme Court has shown no interest in holding that the death penalty itself is unconstitutional. Although public support for the death penalty has been steadily dropping since the mid-1990s, a Gallup poll taken in 2005 showed that 74 percent of Americans still favor the practice. Other surveys have found a different worry: that the death penalty must be administered fairly. A number of steps have been taken to allay these concerns. Some states have begun to put aside funds for more effective defense counsel in capital cases. In 2004, the U.S. Congress made $25 million available to the states to ensure postconviction DNA testing for individuals on death row.[144] Indeed, the tenor of the death penalty debate seems to have shifted. The main focus is no longer on the morality of executions, but rather on how the sentence of death can be made fairer.

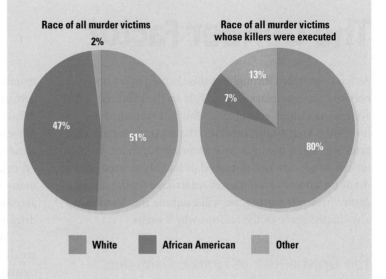

Race of all murder victims

2% · 47% · 51%

Race of all murder victims whose killers were executed

13% · 7% · 80%

White | African American | Other

FIGURE 11.8

Race and the Death Penalty

As these two graphs show, a disproportionate percentage of executed murderers had white victims.

Source: U.S. Bureau of Justice Statistics.

The Gender Factor

As has been noted throughout this chapter, many observers believe that race plays a large role in the criminal justice system's decisions concerning who gets punished and for how long. Statistically, however, the most important characteristic when it comes to sentencing is gender. Women, on the whole, are not punished as harshly as men, and in many instances the differences are striking. In this *Criminal Justice in Action* feature, we will examine the "gender gap" and discuss some of the reasons why it exists.

The Drastic Rise in Female Offenders

As was noted in Chapter 1, women account for a small fraction of this country's criminal offenders. Only 12 percent of the national jail population and 7 percent of the national prison population are female, and in 2004 only 24 percent of all arrests involved women.[145] These statistics, however, fail to convey the startling rate at which the female presence in the criminal justice system has been increasing. In 1970, there were about 6,000 women in federal and state prisons; today, there are nearly 100,000. Between 1991 and 2004, the number of women incarcerated in this country more than doubled, and the number of women arrested increased by 42 percent.[146]

There is little support in the academic community for any idea that the basic nature of American women has changed over the past thirty years. Freda Adler, a professor of criminal justice at Rutgers University, uses the "liberation hypothesis" to partially explain the increase in female arrestees and inmates.[147] This theory holds that as women become more and more equal in society as a whole, their opportunities to commit crimes will increase as well. "You can't embezzle if you're not near funds," Professor Adler notes. "You can't get involved in a fight at the bar if you're not allowed in the bar."[148] Criminologist Meda Chesney-Lind believes that the "get tough" attitude among politicians and law enforcement agencies has been the main contributor to increased rates of female criminality. "Simply put," she says, "it appears that the criminal justice system is now more willing to incarcerate women."[149]

Women and the "War on Drugs"

A closer look at the offenses for which women are sent to prison and jail supports Chesney-Lind's thesis. The vast majority of women are prosecuted for nonviolent crimes, usually drug-related offenses. In fact, drug offenses account for nearly two-thirds of the women sent to federal prison each year (violent crimes account for less than 2 percent).[150] The habitual offender statutes and mandatory sentences for drug crimes that have accompanied the "war on drugs" have been particularly influential. In the 1980s, many of the women now in prison would not have been arrested or would have received light sentences for their drug-related wrongdoing.

When women commit violent crimes, the patterns are distinct as well. Research conducted by social psychologists Angela Browne and Kirk R. Williams shows that when women do kill, the victim is usually an intimate male partner. Moreover, a woman is likely to kill in response to physical aggression or threats of physical aggression by her partner.[151]

The "New Female Criminal"

As the last sentence suggests, not only are the criminal patterns of women distinct from those of their male counterparts, but the reasons behind the crime are different as well. According to Jane Roberts Chapman, the "new female criminal" is a single mother with children, who commits property crimes out of need or abuses drugs as an avenue of escape from her difficult situation.[152] Two-thirds of all female prisoners are mothers, and nearly 37 percent describe themselves as the "primary caregiver" of their children (meaning they do not have a partner to share the

In 2003, Clara Harris was sentenced to twenty years in prison for murder. She could have received a life term, but a Houston jury decided on the lesser punishment, finding her to have been in an anguished mental state when she repeatedly ran over her husband—who had been committing adultery—with a car.

AP Photo/Buster Dean, Pool

responsibility).[153] Chapman predicts that if the number of single mothers living below the poverty line increases, female crime rates will rise accordingly.

Using information found in presentencing investigative reports, feminist criminologist Kathleen Daly has identified several distinct pathways to crime that women follow.[154] The *harmed-and-harming woman,* for example, suffered from abuse and neglect as a child, which in turn led her to "act out" and be labeled a "problem child." As an adult, this woman reacts to difficult situations with violence. The *battered woman,* in contrast, does not necessarily have a history of childhood abuse, but uses violence to defend herself against an abusive partner. Similarly, the *drug-connected woman* does not have a criminal past, but has become involved in a relationship—either with a partner or with a child—characterized by drug use. A drug-connected woman might, for example, let her son use their home as a place to sell drugs or turn to street crime to support a boyfriend or husband's drug habit.

The Chivalry Effect

Few people would argue that race or ethnicity should be a factor in sentencing decisions. The system should be "color-blind." But what about women—should the system be "gender-blind" as well? On a policy level, at least, Congress answered that question in the Sentencing Reform Act of 1984, which emphasized the ideal of gender-neutral sentencing.[155] In practice, however, this is not the case. Women who are convicted of crimes are less likely to go to prison than men, and those who are incarcerated tend to

serve shorter sentences (see Figure 11.9). One study attributes these differences to the elements of female criminality: in property crimes, women are usually accessories, and in violent crimes, women are usually reacting to physical abuse. In both cases, the mitigating circumstances would lead to lesser punishment.[156] Wider evidence suggests, however, that a *chivalry effect,* the idea that women should be treated more leniently than men, plays a large part in the decisions of prosecutors, judges, and juries.

Data compiled by the U.S. Sentencing Commission show that prosecutors are more likely to offer women beneficial plea bargains.[157] Several self-reported studies have shown that judges may treat female defendants more "gently" than male ones and that judges are influenced by mitigating factors such as marital status and family background with women that they would ignore with men.[158] As for juries, their leniency toward women can be most clearly seen in death penalty cases. Though women account for 13 percent of all murder arrests, they represent only 1.3 percent of those prisoners on death row. According to Karen Jo Koonan, an Oakland (California) jury consultant, jurors do not want to believe that a woman, in her role as nurturer, could also be a cold-blooded killer.[159]

Is Chivalry Dead?

There are signs, however, that some of these attitudes are changing. Overall, chivalry appears to be dying. Twenty-five years ago, almost two-thirds of all women sentenced in federal court were given probation, and, as mentioned

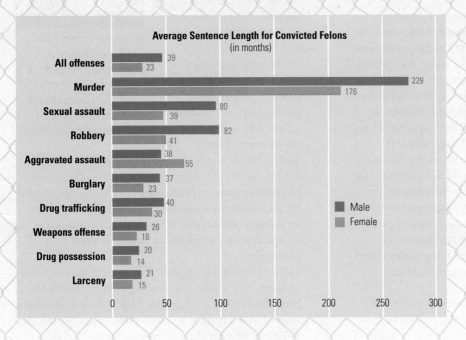

Average Sentence Length for Convicted Felons
(in months)

Offense	Male	Female
All offenses	39	23
Murder	229	176
Sexual assault	80	39
Robbery	82	41
Aggravated assault	38	55
Burglary	37	23
Drug trafficking	40	30
Weapons offense	26	18
Drug possession	20	14
Larceny	21	15

FIGURE 11.9
Sentence Length by Gender

Source: Bureau of Justice Statistics, *State Court Sentencing of Convicted Felons, 2002* (Washington, D.C.: U.S. Department of Justice, May 2005), Table 2.6.

before, the female presence in prison was negligible.[160] Between 1976 and 1997, only one woman was executed in the United States; since 1998, nine have been put to death. And, it must be noted, the chivalry effect was never in effect for African American women. In Florida, for example, black women are nine times more likely to be sentenced as habitual offenders for drug-related offenses than white women.[161]

Is there an argument to be made in favor of the chivalry effect? In fact, some observers are now supporting judicial leniency for women and claim that gender-neutral sentencing exacts a heavy price on society. By separating increasing numbers of nonviolent female offenders from their children, the sentencing guidelines often shift the cost of caring for these children to the taxpayer through social service programs.[162] Furthermore, by increasing the chances that the children themselves will have emotional problems due to lack of an active parent, such laws increase the probability that they will become delinquent. Instead of sending nonviolent offenders who are pregnant or have children to jail or prison, the argument goes, the correctional system should place them in community-based programs where they can continue to care for their offspring.

Making Sense of the Gender Gap in Punishment and Sentencing

1 Do you believe that sentencing should be gender neutral? What are the arguments for and against giving women more lenient sentences for nonviolent crimes?

2 To what extent should a judge consider the motivation behind a crime committed by a woman (self-defense, did it for boyfriend, and so on) as a mitigating circumstance? What might be the result if judges did this more often?

3 Give some reasons to explain why so few women are on death row. Why do you think society seems to be uncomfortable with the idea of sentencing a woman to be executed? Do you think that there are some crimes a woman could commit that a judge or jury might be *more* likely to punish with the death sentence?

Chapter Summary

1 List and contrast the four basic philosophical reasons for sentencing criminals. (a) Retribution, (b) deterrence, (c) incapacitation, and (d) rehabilitation. Under the principle of retributive justice, the severity of the punishment is in proportion to the severity of the crime. Punishment is an end in itself. In contrast, the deterrence approach seeks to prevent future crimes by setting an example. Such punishment is based on its deterrent value and not necessarily on the severity of the crime. The incapacitation theory of punishment simply argues that a criminal in prison cannot impose further harm on society. In contrast, the rehabilitation theory believes that criminals can be rehabilitated in the appropriate prison environment.

2 Contrast indeterminate with determinate sentencing. Indeterminate sentencing follows from legislative penal codes that set minimum and maximum amounts of incarceration time; determinate sentencing carries a fixed amount of time, although this may be reduced for "good time."

3 Explain why there is a difference between a sentence imposed by a judge and the actual sentence carried out by the prisoner. Although judges may decide on indeterminate sentencing, thereafter it is parole boards that

decide when prisoners will be released after the minimum sentence is served.

4 List the six forms of punishment. (a) Capital (death sentence), (b) imprisonment, (c) probation, (d) fines, (e) restitution and community service, and (f) restorative justice.

5 State who has input into the sentencing decision and list the factors that determine a sentence. The prosecutor, defense attorney, probation officer, and judge provide inputs. The factors considered in sentencing are (a) the seriousness of the crime, (b) mitigating circumstances, (c) aggravating circumstances, and (d) judicial philosophy.

6 Explain some of the reasons why sentencing reform has occurred. One reason is sentencing disparity, which has been seen both on a geographic basis and on a courtroom basis (due to a particular judge's philosophy). Sentencing discrimination has also occurred on the basis of defendants' gender, race, or economic standing. An additional

STORIES FROM THE STREET

Go to the *Stories from the Street* feature at **www.cjinaction.com** to hear Larry Gaines tell insightful stories related to this chapter and his experiences in the field.

reason for sentencing reform has been a general desire to "get tough on crime."

7   Describe sentencing guidelines and explain how two recent Supreme Court rulings have affected them. Sentencing guidelines are legislative restrictions on judicial discretion. The guidelines require judges to remain within certain boundaries when choosing a punishment. In 2004, the Supreme Court invalidated state sentencing guidelines that allowed the judge, and not the jury, to make determinations of fact that affected the length of the sentence. In 2005, the Court held that federal sentencing guidelines were "advisory," not "mandatory," thus returning some sentencing discretion to judges.

8   Identify the arguments for and against the use of victim impact statements during sentencing hearings. Proponents of victim impact statements believe that they allow victims to provide character evidence in the same manner as defendants have always been allowed to do and

that they give victims a therapeutic "voice" in the sentencing process. Opponents argue that the statements bring unacceptable levels of emotion into the courtroom and encourage judges and juries to make sentencing decisions based on the "social value" of the victim rather than the facts of the case.

9   Outline the Supreme Court rulings on capital punishment. In 1967, the Supreme Court placed a hold on all scheduled executions. In 1972, the Court invalidated the death penalty in states that imposed it because the way it was practiced violated the Eighth and Fourteenth Amendments. By 1976, thirty-five states had changed their death penalty statutes to comply with the Supreme Court ruling. The Supreme Court then declared mandatory death penalty statutes invalid, but established a bifurcated process that involves two steps. Today, thirty-eight states have adopted this process and provide for legally acceptable capital punishment.

Key Terms

like 3 strikes law

- aggravating circumstances   359
- capital punishment   368
- departure   362
- determinate sentencing   353
- deterrence   349
- "good time"   353
- habitual offender laws   364
- incapacitation   351
- indeterminate sentencing   352
- just deserts   349
- mandatory sentencing guidelines   364
- mitigating circumstances   359
- presentence investigative report   357 - *PSI*
- "real offense"   358
- rehabilitation   351
- retribution   349
- sentencing discrimination   360
- sentencing disparity   360
- sentencing guidelines   362
- truth-in-sentencing laws   353
- victim impact statement (VIS)   367

Questions for Critical Analysis

1   What is the difference between general deterrence and specific deterrence?
2   Why is rehabilitation seen as the most "humane" form of punishment?
3   What are truth-in-sentencing laws, and why are they popular among victims' rights advocates?
4   Why do those who believe in "individualized justice" compare the proper role of a judge in the sentencing process to that of a medical doctor?
5   How do "real offense" procedures effectively render plea bargains meaningless?

6   What is the difference between sentencing disparity and sentencing discrimination?
7   Under what circumstances can a federal judge depart from the federal sentencing guidelines?
8   What is the "bifurcated process," and how did it come to be the standard for state death penalty procedure?
9   What are some of the arguments in favor of the death penalty? What are some of the arguments against it?
10   What is the likelihood that the death penalty will be abolished in the near future? Explain your answer.

Test Preparation Online

Criminal JusticeNow

Go to **www.cjinaction.com** and click on *Criminal JusticeNow* for access to this powerful online study tool. You will get a *personalized study plan* based on your responses to a diagnostic pretest. Once you have mastered the material with the help of interactive learning tools, video clips with questions, an integrated e-book, and more, you can take a posttest to confirm you are ready to move on to the next chapter.

Book Companion Web Site

At the book companion Web site (**www.cjinaction.com**), you will find many resources in addition to *Criminal JusticeNow* to aid you in studying for your exams. For example, under *Chapter Resources*, you will find the *Chapter Outline, Chapter Summary, Flashcards, Glossary, Learning Objectives, Lecture Presentations, Concept Builder, Essay Questions,* and a *Tutorial Chapter Quiz.* You can also test yourself with interactive *Online Reviews* of each chapter section. Check out the *Web Links* to access the Web sites mentioned in the text, as well as many others. You can also access recent perspectives by clicking on *CJ in the News* and *Terrorism Update* under *Course Resources.*

Suggested Reading

Junkin, Tim, *Bloodsworth: The True Story of the First Death Row Inmate Exonerated by DNA,* Chapel Hill, NC: Algonquin Books of Chapel Hill, 2004. In 1984, Kirk Bloodsworth was charged, tried, and convicted of the rape and murder of a nine-year-old girl. He spent time on Maryland's death row, having been sentenced to die in the state's gas chamber. After a successful appeal, his punishment was reduced to two life sentences. In total, Bloodsworth spent nine years in prison before being freed by DNA evidence that proved another person committed the crimes. One would expect Bloodsworth to be bitter, but he is not. With the help of author Junkin, Bloodsworth expresses forgiveness toward a criminal justice system that can be lazy, ineffective, and incompetent, but rarely acts with malice. His story details the pitfalls in our capital punishment system while offering hope that, with more attention to human error, they can be avoided.

Zimring, Franklin E., *The Contradictions of American Capital Punishment,* New York: Oxford University Press, 2003. One of the country's leading criminologists examines why Americans are so determined to keep the death penalty, even though nearly every other developed nation in the world has decried the practice as barbaric. Zimring's conclusions are, to say the least, unsettling. He shows that while public support for capital punishment is fairly uniform across the United States, almost all executions take place in a few states in the South and Southwest. These same states, Zimring notes, are where the lynching of African Americans and other forms of vigilante violence were most prevalent in our nation's history. The author also explores how these vigilante values have clashed with another American tradition—mistrust of government—to create the lengthy appeals process that ensures that more inmates on death row die of old age than by execution.

Notes

1. David Yellen, "Just Deserts and Lenient Prosecutors: The Flawed Case for Real Offense Sentencing," *Northwestern University Law Review* 91 (Summer 1997), 1434.
2. Brian Forst, "Prosecution and Sentencing," in *Crime,* ed. James Q. Wilson and Joan Petersilia (San Francisco: ICS Press, 1995), 386.
3. Herbert L. Packer, "Justification for Criminal Punishment," in *The Limits of Criminal Sanction* (Palo Alto, CA: Stanford University Press, 1968), 36–37.
4. Jami L. Anderson, "Reciprocity as a Justification for Retributivism," *Criminal Justice Ethics* (Winter/Spring 1997), 13–14.
5. Immanuel Kant, *Metaphysical First Principles of the Doctrine of Right,* trans. Mary Gregor (Cambridge, UK: Cambridge University Press, 1991), 331.
6. Harold Pepinsky and Paul Jesilow, *Myths That Cause Crime* (Cabin John, MD: Seven Locks Press, 1984).
7. Jeremy Bentham, *An Introduction to the Principles of Morals and Legislation 1789* (New York: Hafner Publishing Corp., 1961).
8. Forst, 376.
9. John J. DiIulio, Jr., "Help Wanted: Economists, Crime, and Public Policy," *Journal of Economic Perspectives* 10 (1996), 3, 16–17.
10. Sue T. Reid, *Crime and Criminology,* 7th ed. (New York: Holt, Rinehart, and Winston, 1995), 352.
11. Morgan O. Reynolds, *Why Does Crime Pay?* (Dallas, TX: National Center for Policy Analysis Backgrounder #110, 1990), 5.
12. Paul H. Robinson and John M. Darley, "The Utility of Desert," *Northwestern University Law Review* 91 (Winter 1997), 453.
13. James Q. Wilson, *Thinking about Crime* (New York: Basic Books, 1975), 235.
14. Isaac Ehrlich, "Participation in Illegitimate Activities: A Theoretical and Empirical Investigation," *Journal of Political Economy* 81 (May/June 1973), 521–564.
15. Steve Levitt, "The Effect of Prison Population Size on Crime Rates," *Quarterly Journal of Economics* 111 (May 1996), 319.
16. Todd Clear, *Harm in Punishment* (Boston: Northeastern University Press, 1980).
17. Franklin E. Zimring and Gordon Hawkins, *Incapacitation: Penal Confinement and Restraint of Crime* (New York: Oxford University Press, 1995), 60–70.
18. Jan Chaiken, Marcia Chaiken, and William Rhodes, "Predicting Violent Behavior and Classifying Violent Offenders," in *Understanding and Preventing Violence,* ed. Albert J. Reiss, Jr., and Jeffrey A. Roth (Washington, D.C.: National Academy Press, 1994).
19. Public Policy Forum, "Prevention Advocated More Than Punishment in PPF Survey," *Research Brief* (February 12, 2001), 7.
20. Gregory W. O'Reilly, "Truth-in-Sentencing: Illinois Adds Yet Another Layer of 'Reform' to Its Complicated Code of Corrections," *Loyola University of Chicago Law Journal* (Summer 1996), 986, 999–1000.
21. Arthur W. Campbell, *Law of Sentencing* (Rochester, NY: Lawyers Cooperative Publishing Co., 1978), 9.
22. Marvin Zalman, "The Rise and Fall of the Indeterminate Sentence," *Wayne Law Review* 24 (1977), 45, 52.
23. Marvin E. Frankel, *Criminal Sentences: Law without Order* (New York: Hill & Wang, 1972), 5.
24. Jessica Mitford, *Kind and Usual Punishment* (New York: Alfred A. Knopf, 1973), 80–83.
25. Bureau of Justice Statistics, *Truth in Sentencing in State Prisons* (Washington, D.C.: Department of Justice, 1999).

26. Paul W. Keve, *Crime Control and Justice in America: Searching for Facts and Answers* (Chicago: American Library Association, 1995), 77.

27. Harry Mika, Mary Achilles, Ellen Halbert, Lorraine Stutzman Amstutz, and Howard Zehr, "Listening to Victims—A Critique of Restorative Justice Policy and Practice in the United States," *Federal Probation* (June 2004), 32.

28. Fla. Stat. Section 794.0235(1)(a) (1997).

29. David Royse, "Sex Offenders: Chemical Castration Law Has Seldom Been Enforced," *Miami Herald* (June 1, 2005), B10.

30. Kate Stith and José A. Cabranes, "Judging under the Federal Sentencing Guidelines," *Northwestern University Law Review* 91 (Summer 1997), 1247.

31. Mark M. Lanier and Claud H. Miller III, "Attitudes and Practices of Federal Probation Officers towards Pre-Plea/Trial Investigative Report Policy," *Crime & Delinquency* 41 (July 1995), 365–366.

32. Stith and Cabranes, 1247.

33. Julie R. O'Sullivan, "In Defense of the U.S. Sentencing Guidelines Modified Real-Offense System," *Northwestern University Law Review* 91 (1997), 1342.

34. Brian Forst and Charles Wellford, "Punishment and Sentencing: Developing Sentencing Guidelines Empirically from Principles of Punishment," *Rutgers Law Review* 33 (1981).

35. 18 U.S.C. Section 2113(a) (1994).

36. Bob Barr and Eric Sterling, "The War on Drugs: Fighting Crime or Wasting Time?" *American Criminal Law Review* (Fall 2001), 1545.

37. Office of Policy Analysis, United States Sentencing Commission, 2002.

38. *Ibid.*

39. U.S.C.C.A.N. 3182, 3228 (1984).

40. Cassia Spohn and David Holleran, "The Imprisonment Penalty Paid by Young, Unemployed Black and Hispanic Male Offenders," *Criminology* 35 (2000), 281.

41. *Ibid.,* 297.

42. Bureau of Justice Statistics, *Prisoners in 2004* (Washington, D.C.: U.S. Department of Justice, December 2004), x.

43. Spohn and Holleran, 301.

44. *Ibid.,* 291.

45. Bureau of Justice Statistics, *State Court Sentencing of Convicted Felons, 2003* (Washington, D.C.: U.S. Department of Justice, May 2005), Table 2.7.

46. Darrell Steffensmeier and Stephen DeMuth, "Ethnicity and Judges' Sentencing Decisions: Hispanic-Black-White Comparisons," *Criminology* 39 (2001), 145.

47. *Ibid.*

48. *Ibid.,* 167.

49. John C. Coffee, "Repressed Issues of Sentencing," *Georgetown Law Journal 66* (1978), 987.

50. J. S. Bainbridge, Jr., "The Return of Retribution," *ABA Journal* (May 1985), 63.

51. Pub. L. No. 98–473, 98 Stat. 1987, codified as amended at 18 U.S.C. Sections 3551–3742 and 28 U.S.C. Sections 991–998 (1988).

52. Julia L. Black, "The Constitutionality of Federal Sentences Imposed under the Sentencing Reform Act of 1984 after *Mistretta v. United States*," *Iowa Law Review* 75 (March 1990), 767.

53. Roger Haines, Kevin Cole, and Jennifer Wole, *Federal Sentencing Guidelines Handbook* (New York: McGraw-Hill, 1994), 3.

54. *Fifteen Years of Guidelines Sentencing: An Assessment of How Well the Federal Criminal Justice System Is Achieving the Goals of Sentencing Reform* (Washington, D.C.: U.S. Sentencing Commission, November 2004), 46.

55. *United States v. Diaz-Villafane*, 874 F.2d 43, 49 (1st Cir. 1989).

56. Alabama Code 1975 Section 20–2–79.

57. Washington Rev. Code Ann. Section 9.94A.030.

58. 445 U.S. 263 (1980).

59. *Lockyer v. Andrade*, 538 U.S. 63 (2003).

60. *Lockyer v. Andrade*, 270 F.3d 743 (2001).

61. 538 U.S. 63, 76.

62. *Ibid.,* 83.

63. Ryan S. King and Marc Mauer, *Aging behind Bars: "Three Strikes" Seven Years Later* (Washington, D.C.: The Sentencing Project, August 2001), 3.

64. Yellen, 1434.

65. Michael Tonry, "The Failure of the U.S. Sentencing Commission's Guidelines," *Crime & Delinquency* 39 (1993), 131–149.

66. Erik Luna, *Misguided Guidelines: A Critique of Federal Sentencing* (Washington, D.C.: Cato Institute, 2002), 3.

67. *2003 Annual Report* (Washington, D.C.: U.S. Sentencing Commission, 2004), 37.

68. Richard Willing, "Judges Go Soft on Sentences More Often," *USA Today* (August 28, 2003), 1A.

69. 542 U.S. 1174 (2004).

70. Adam Liptak, "Sentencing Decision's Reach Is Far and Wide," *New York Times* (June 27, 2004), 14.

71. 125 S.Ct. 738 (2005).

72. David G. Savage, "Judges Freed from Sentencing Rules," *Los Angeles Times* (January 13, 2005), A1.

73. David D. Kirkpatrick, "Congress Rekindles Battle on Mandatory Sentences," *New York Times* (May 11, 2005), A16.

74. 530 U.S. 466 (2000).

75. 536 U.S. 584 (2002).

76. Nancy J. King and Roosevelt L. Noble, "Felony Jury Sentencing in Practice: A Three-State Study," *Vanderbilt Law Review* (2004), 886.

77. Jena Iontcheva, "Jury Sentencing as Democratic Practice," *Virginia Law Review* (April 2003), 325.

78. King and Noble, 895.

79. John Ritter, "Jury Begins Deliberating Peterson's Fate," *USA Today* (December 10, 2004), 3A.

80. Edna Erez, "Victim Voice, Impact Statements, and Sentencing: Integrating Restorative Justice and Therapeutic Jurisprudence Principles in Adversarial Proceedings," *Criminal Law Bulletin* (September/October 2004), 495.

81. Bryan Myers and Edith Greene, "Prejudicial Nature of Impact Statements," *Psychology, Public Policy, and Law* (December 2004), 493.

82. *Booth v. Maryland,* 482 U.S. 496, 503 (1987).

83. 501 U.S. 808 (1991).

84. Bryan Myers and Jack Arbuthnot, "The Effects of Victim Impact Evidence on the Verdicts and Sentencing Judgments of Mock Jurors," *Journal of Offender Rehabilitation* (1999), 95–112.

85. Walter Berns, "Abraham Lincoln (Book Review)," *Commentary* (January 1, 1996), 70.

86. Comments made at the Georgetown Law Center, "The Modern View of Capital Punishment," *American Criminal Law Review* 34 (Summer 1997), 1353.

87. David Bruck, quoted in Bill Rankin, "Fairness of the Death Penalty Is Still on Trial," *Atlanta Constitution-Journal* (July 29, 1997), A13.

88. Mark Costanzo, *Just Revenge: Costs and Consequences of the Death Penalty* (New York: St. Martin's Press, 1997), 11.

89. Randall Coyne and Lyn Entzeroth, *Capital Punishment and the Judicial Process* (Durham, NC: Carolina Academic Press, 1994), 2.

90. Jeffrey C. Matura, "When Will It Stop? The Use of the Death Penalty for Non-Homicide Crimes," *Journal of Legislation* 24 (1998), 249.

91. Thorsten Sellin, "The Philadelphia Gibbet Iron," *Journal of Criminal Law, Criminology, and Police Science* 46 (1955), 19.

92. G. Mark Mamantov, "The Executioner's Song: Is There a Right to Listen?" *Virginia Law Review* 69 (March 1983), 373.

93. Bureau of Justice Statistics, *Capital Punishment, 2003* (Washington, D.C.: U.S. Department of Justice, November 2004), 4.

94. Larry C. Berkson, *The Concept of Cruel and Unusual Punishment* (Lexington, MA: Lexington Books, 1975), 43.

95. John P. Cunningham, "Death in the Federal Courts: Expectations and Realities of the Federal Death Penalty Act of 1994," *University of Richmond Law Review* 32 (May 1998), 939.

96. *In re Kemmler,* 136 U.S. 447 (1890).

97. 217 U.S. 349 (1910).

98. Pamela S. Nagy, "Hang by the Neck until Dead: The Resurgence of Cruel and Unusual Punishment in the 1990s," *Pacific Law Journal* 26 (October 1994), 85.

99. 408 U.S. 238 (1972).

100. 408 U.S. 309 (1972) (Stewart, concurring).

101. 428 U.S. 280 (1976).

102. 102. C.R.S. 18.1.3-1201(5)(f) and (p) (2003).

103. 428 U.S. 153 (1976).

104. 536 U.S. 584 (2002).

105. *Ford v. Wainwright,* 477 U.S. 399, 422 (1986).

106. Neil A. Lewis, "Judges Let Stand Ruling That Allows Forcibly Drugging an Inmate before Execution," *New York Times* (October 7, 2003), A14.

107. *Penry v. Lynaugh,* 492 U.S. 302 (1989).

108. 536 U.S. 304 (2002).

109. 125 S.Ct. 1183 (2005).

110. Ernest van den Haag, "The Ultimate Punishment: A Defense," *Harvard Law Review* 99 (1986), 1669.

111. *The Death Penalty: The Religious Community Calls for Abolition* (pamphlet published by the National Coalition to Abolish the Death Penalty and the National Interreligious Task Force on Criminal Justice, 1988), 48.

112. Isaac Ehrlich, "The Deterrent Effect of Capital Punishment: A Question of Life and Death," *American Economic Review* 65 (June 1975), 397–417.

113. Lisa Stolzenberg and Stewart J. D'Alessio, "Capital Punishment, Execution Publicity, and Murder in Houston, Texas," *Journal of Criminal Law and Criminology* (Winter 2004), 351–379.

114. Stephen Markman and Paul Cassell, "Protecting the Innocent: A Response to the Bedau-Radelet Study," *Stanford Law Review* 41 (1988), 153.

115. **http://www.deathpenaltyinfo.org**.

116. Joseph F. Shapiro, "The Wrong Men on Death Row," *U.S. News & World Report* (November 9, 1998), 26.

117. Hugo Adam Bedau and Michael L. Radelet, "Miscarriages of Justice in Potentially Capital Cases," *Stanford Law Review* 40 (1987), 21–23.

118. Frank Hinchey, "McKnight Gets Death Penalty," *Columbus Dispatch* (October 26, 2002), A1.

119. John J. DiIulio, "Abolish the Death Penalty, Officially," *Wall Street Journal* (December 15, 1997), A23.

120. James S. Liebman, Jeffrey Fagan, and Valeria West, "A Broken System: Error Rates in Capital Cases, 1973–1995," (2000), **http://www.justice.policy.net/jpreport**.

121. James S. Liebman, Andrew Gelman, Garth Davies, Jeffrey Fagan, Valerie West, and Alexandra Kiss, *A Broken System, Part II: Why There Is So Much Error in Capital Cases, and What Can Be Done about It* (Washington, D.C.: Criminal Justice Reform Education Fund, 2002), 348.

122. Quoted in Walter Berns and Joseph Bessette, "Why the Death Penalty Is Fair," *Wall Street Journal* (January 9, 1998), A16.

123. James Q. Wilson, "What Death-Penalty Errors?" *New York Times* (July 10, 2000), A19.

124. *Gregg v. Georgia,* 428 U.S. 153, 195 (1976).

125. Wilson, "What Death-Penalty Errors?"

126. Adam Liptak, "On Death Row, a Battle Over the Fatal Cocktail," *New York Times* (September 16, 2004), A14.

127. Beth Musgrave, "Judge Upholds Lethal Injection," *Lexington Herald-Leader* (July 9, 2005), A1.

128. *Coker v. Georgia,* 433 U.S. 584 (1977).

129. See **http://www.deathpenaltyinfo.org/article. php?scid=5&did=184**.

130. Janice Joseph, "Young, Black, and Sentenced to Die: Black Males and the Death Penalty," *Challenge: A Journal of*

Research on African American Men 7 (December 1996), 68.

131. Isaac Utah and John Charles Boger, *Race and the Death Penalty in North Carolina* (Raleigh, NC: The Common Sense Foundation, 2001).

132. Talia Roitberg Harmon, "Race for Your Life: An Analysis of the Role of Race in Erroneous Capital Convictions," *Criminal Justice Review* (Spring 2004), 76–94.

133. 481 U.S. 279 (1987).

134. David C. Baldus, George Woodworth, and Charles A. Pulaski, *Equal Justice and the Death Penalty: A Legal and Empirical Analysis* (Boston: Northeastern University Press, 1990), 140–197, 306.

135. Laura Argys and Naci Mocan, *Who Shall Live and Who Shall Die? An Analysis of Prisoners on Death Row in the United States* (Cambridge, MA: National Bureau of Economic Research, February 2003), 22.

136. *Ibid.,* 8.

137. William M. Holmes, "Who Are the Wrongly Convicted on Death Row?" in *Wrongly Convicted: When Justice Fails,* ed. Saundra Westervelt and John Humphrey (Piscataway, NJ: Rutgers University Press, 2001).

138. Bureau of Justice Statistics, *Capital Punishment, 2003,* 14.

139. "Justice Dept. Reports a 30-Year Low in Death Sentences, and Fewer Inmates on Death Row," *New York Times* (November 15, 2004), A12.

140. 536 U.S. 304 (2002); and 125 S.Ct. 1183 (2005).

141. Adam Liptak, "Juries Reject Death Penalty in Nearly All Federal Trials," *New York Times* (July 15, 2003), A12.

142. 536 U.S. 584 (2002).

143. A. J. Flick, "Juries Add New Complexities to Death Cases," *Tucson (Arizona) Citizen* (March 21, 2005), 1A.

144. Innocence Protection Act of 2004, Pub. L. No. 108-405, Sections 401–432.

145. Federal Bureau of Investigation, *Crime in the United States, 2004* (Washington, D.C.: U.S. Department of Justice, 2005), Table 42, page 297.

146. Bureau of Justice Statistics, *Prison and Jail Inmates at Midyear 2004* (Washington, D.C.: U.S. Department of Justice, 2004), 5 and *Ibid.*

147. Freda Adler, *Sisters in Crime: The Rise of the New Female Criminal* (New York: McGraw-Hill, 1975), 95.

148. Barry Yoeman, "Violent Tendencies: Crime by Women Has Skyrocketed in Recent Years," *Chicago Tribune* (March 15, 2000), 3.

149. Meda Chesney-Lind, "Patriarchy, Prisons, and Jails: A Critical Look at Trends in Women's Incarceration," *Prison Journal* (Spring/Summer 1991), 57.

150. Bureau of Justice Statistics, *Sourcebook of Criminal Justice Statistics* (Washington, D.C.: U.S. Department of Justice, 2004), Table 6.53.

151. Angela Browne and Kirk R. Williams, "Exploring the Effect of Resource Availability and the Likelihood of Female-Perpetrated Homicides," *Law and Society Review* 23 (1989), 75–94.

152. Jane Roberts Chapman, *Economic Realities and Female Crimes* (Lexington, MA: Lexington Books, 1980).

153. Bureau of Justice Statistics, *Incarcerated Parents and Their Children* (Washington, D.C.: U.S. Department of Justice, August 2000), 2, 4.

154. Kathleen Daly, "Women's Pathways to Felony Court: Feminist Theory of Lawbreaking and Problems of Representation," *Review of Law and Women's Studies* 2 (1992), 11–52.

155. 28 U.S.C. Section 991 (1994).

156. Clarice Feinmen, *Women in the Criminal Justice System,* 3d ed. (Westport, CT: Praeger, 1994), 35.

157. Ilene H. Nagel and Barry L. Johnson, "The Role of Gender in a Structured Sentencing System: Equal Treatment, Policy Choices, and the Sentencing of Female Offenders under the United States Sentencing Guidelines," *Journal of Criminal Law and Criminology* 85 (1994), 181–190.

158. Darrell Steffensmeir, John Kramer, and Cathy Streifel, "Gender and Imprisonment Decisions," *Criminology* 31 (1993), 411.

159. Quoted in Raymond Smith, "Death Penalty Rare for Women," *Press-Enterprise* (Riverside, California) (July 30, 1998), A12.

160. Elizabeth F. Moulds, "Chivalry and Paternalism: Disparities of Treatment in the Criminal Justice System," in *Women, Crime, and Justice,* ed. Susan Datesman and Frank Scarpitti (New York: Oxford University Press, 1980), 286–287.

161. Charles Crawford, "Sentencing in Florida," *Criminology* 38 (February 2000), 277.

162. Myrna S. Raeder, "Gender and Sentencing: Single Moms, Battered Women, and Other Sex-Based Anomalies in the Gender-Free World of the Federal Sentencing Guidelines," *Pepperdine Law Review* 20 (1993), 14.

CHAPTER TWELVE

Probation and Community Corrections

Chapter outline

- The Justification for Community Corrections
- Probation: Doing Time in the Community
- Intermediate Sanctions
- The Paradox of Community Corrections
- Criminal Justice in Action—Drug Courts: Rehab Revisited

Chapter objectives

After reading this chapter, you should be able to:

1 Explain the justifications for community-based corrections programs.

2 Indicate when probation started to fall out of favor, and explain why.

3 Explain several alternative sentencing arrangements that combine probation with incarceration.

4 Specify the conditions under which an offender is most likely to be denied probation.

5 Describe the three general categories of conditions placed on a probationer.

6 Explain why probation officers' work has become more dangerous.

7 Explain the three stages of probation revocation.

8 List the five sentencing options for a judge besides imprisonment and probation.

9 Contrast day reporting centers with intensive supervision probation.

10 List the three levels of home monitoring.

Criminal JusticeNow

Optimize your study time and master key chapter concepts with *Criminal JusticeNow*, an online study tool that provides you with a *personalized study plan.* Check out the "Test Preparation Online" section at the end of the chapter for additional information.

A Light Rap for 50 Cent?

Chad Jackson's appearance at the Hippodrome nightclub in Springfield, Massachusetts, on May 8, 2004, was a pleasant surprise. The rapper, better known as 50 Cent, was not supposed to perform that night. By the end of the evening, however, many of the audience members wished Jackson had stayed home. In the middle of the show, someone allegedly threw a water bottle onto the stage, striking the entertainer in the head. Jackson retaliated, leaping into the crowd and starting a melee that took security and local police an hour to quell. Two women suffered injuries after Jackson "walked over them," and another said the rapper had punched her in the face.

As a result of the incident, Jackson was charged with three counts of assault and battery. Although he could have been imprisoned for two and a half years for each count under Massachusetts law, Springfield District Court Judge Robert F. Kumor, Jr., accepted a plea bargain under which Jackson was to serve two years' probation, pay $3,000 in court costs, cover his victims' medical bills, and produce an educational antiviolence public service announcement. During the probationary period,

Rapper 50 Cent was sentenced to two years' probation for an incident at a Massachusetts nightclub for which he was charged with three counts of assault and battery.

the judge required Jackson to undergo random tests to make sure he was not using drugs and prohibited him from carrying a gun in Massachusetts. Finally, having learned during the court proceedings that Jackson had a nine-year-old son, Judge Kumor scolded the defendant, remarking, "You better think about how you want that boy to grow up to be a man."

Jackson's sentence sparked skepticism, as many felt he had been "let off easy" because of his fame and high-priced defense attorney. In fact, Judge Kumor was hardly breaking new ground. Defendants found guilty of crimes far more serious than assault and battery are routinely given probation in this country. A system that initially gave judges the discretion to show leniency to first-time, minor offenders increasingly allows those who have committed serious crimes to serve their time in the community rather than prison or jail. Nearly one out of every four probationers has been convicted of a violent felony such as assault or rape.[1]

Ironically, the trend toward probation can be partly attributed to the "get tough" approach to crime that has emerged in public policy. Campaigns to crack down on drunk drivers, the "war on drugs," harsher sentencing statutes, and limitations on judicial discretion have placed intense pressure on the American corrections infrastructure. Even with unprecedented rates of prison and jail construction, there is simply not enough space to incarcerate all the new criminals. In addition, the rising costs of

ⓒ CONCEPTBUILDER

Reintegration of offenders into the community is a common strategy for rehabilitative programs utilized by community corrections. Visit **www.cjinaction.com** for an interactive exploration of this key topic.

imprisonment have made it fiscally impossible for many jurisdictions to house their inmates. The result: more than 4 million adults are under the supervision of state and federal probation organizations—a figure growing at a rate of 3 percent each year.[2]

In this chapter, we will discuss the strengths and weaknesses of probation and other community sanctions such as intensive probation, fines, boot camps, electronic monitoring, and home confinement. Given the scarcity of prison resources, decisions made today concerning community-based punishment will affect the criminal justice system for decades to come.

THE JUSTIFICATION FOR COMMUNITY CORRECTIONS

In the court of popular opinion, retribution and crime control take precedence over community-based correctional programs. America, says University of Minnesota law professor Michael Tonry, is preoccupied with the "absolute severity of punishment" and the "widespread view that only imprisonment counts."[3] Mandatory sentencing guidelines and "three-strikes" laws are theoretically opposed to community-based corrections.[4] To a certain degree, correctional programs that are administered in the community are considered a less severe, and therefore less worthy, alternative to imprisonment. (See the feature *CJ in Focus—The Balancing Act: Children and the Commercial Sex Industry* on the following page.)

Reintegration

Supporters of probation and intermediate sanctions reject such views as not only shortsighted, but also contradictory to the aims of the corrections system. A very small percentage of all convicted offenders have committed crimes that warrant capital punishment or life imprisonment. Most, at some point, will return to the community. Consequently, according to one group of experts, the task of the corrections system

> includes building or rebuilding solid ties between the offender and the community, integrating or reintegrating the offender into community life—restoring family ties, obtaining employment and an education, securing in the larger sense a place for the offender in the routine functioning of society.[5]

Considering that some studies have shown higher recidivism rates for offenders who are subjected to prison culture, a frequent justification of community-based corrections is that they help to reintegrate the offender into society.

Reintegration has a strong theoretical basis in rehabilitative theories of punishment. An offender is generally considered to be "rehabilitated" when he or she no longer represents a threat to other members of the community and therefore is believed to be fit to live in that community. In the context of this chapter and the two that follow, it will also be helpful to see reintegration as a process through which corrections officials such as probation and parole officers provide the offender with incentives to follow the rules of society. In doing so, the corrections system must constantly balance the rights of the individual offender against the rights of law-abiding members of the community.

Diversion

Another justification for community-based corrections, based on practical considerations, is **diversion.** As you are already aware, most criminal offenses fall into the category of "petty," and it is practically impossible, as well as unnecessary, to imprison

The **Sentencing Project** is a nonprofit organization that promotes reduced reliance on incarceration and alternative forms of sentencing. To visit its Web site, click on *Web Links* under *Chapter Resources* at **www.cjinaction.com**.

Reintegration
A goal of corrections that focuses on preparing the offender for a return to the community unmarred by further criminal behavior.

Diversion
In the context of corrections, a strategy to divert those offenders who qualify away from prison and jail and toward community-based and intermediate sanctions.

Children and the Commercial Sex Industry

The number of girls and boys under the age of eighteen who sell their bodies for sex in this country is very difficult to determine. A three-year study by researchers at the University of Pennsylvania arrived at 400,000, but other estimates have been both significantly higher and lower. Apart from pure statistics, the issue presents a number of challenges for the criminal justice system, which has not yet figured out what to do with these juveniles. Although many social service providers contend that they need counseling and treatment rather than punishment, most law enforcement agencies continue to regard them as criminals. Hence, police officers arrest them and judges put them in jail.

According to Katherine E. Mullen, a Legal Aid lawyer in New York City who works with child prostitutes, the results are disastrous. "The tragedy," she says, "is that they are victims, and because we treat them like criminals, they never heal, they never trust, and no wonder they go back out and do it again." Indeed, child prostitutes often come from similar backgrounds: a poor home life with abusive parents that leads to flight and homelessness, where the sex industry is the only means of survival. Many of these boys and girls are "brainwashed," in the words of one expert, by protectors/pimps and need very specialized mental health services to break free from the lifestyle.

Needless to say, such services are expensive and thus unavailable in most parts of the country. Judges often have no choice but to lock up the young offenders. Furthermore, because child prostitutes often come across as anti-authoritarian and disrespectful in a courtroom setting, they do not elicit much sympathy from the judges who decide their fate. Prosecutors, for their part, frequently argue that the juveniles need the "tough love" of a detention facility. As one put it, stints in correctional facilities force child prostitutes to "face up to where they are in their lives and what they have done."

G. Paul Burnett/*The New York Times*

A young woman using the alias "Quiana," right, speaks about the effects of juvenile prostitution at a New York City Council hearing.

A DIFFERENT APPROACH

In one area of the country, however, law enforcement is trying a new strategy in dealing with these children. Police departments in San Francisco, Oakland, and San Jose, California, have begun to form task forces designed to identify and help juvenile sex workers. "We always looked at them as prostitutes," says Sergeant Nick Battaglia of the San Jose police child exploitation detail. "We'd arrest them and lock them up. Now we see them as victims being exploited."

FOR CRITICAL ANALYSIS

Should the criminal justice system treat juvenile prostitutes differently than adult prostitutes? How might society benefit from counseling "sexually exploited children," as they are called by many social workers, rather than punishing them?

every offender for every offense. Community-based corrections are an important means of diverting criminals to alternative modes of punishment so that scarce incarceration resources are consumed by only the most dangerous criminals. In his "strainer" analogy, corrections expert Paul H. Hahn likens this process to the workings of a kitchen strainer. With each "shake" of the corrections "strainer," the less serious offenders are diverted from incarceration. At the end, only the most serious convicts remain to be sent to prison.[6] (The concept of diversion is closely linked to that of selective incapacitation, mentioned in Chapter 11.)

The diversionary role of community-based punishments has become more pronounced as prisons and jails have filled up over the past three decades. In fact, probationers now account for nearly two-thirds of all adults in the American corrections systems (see Figure 12.1 on p. 394). According to the U.S. Department of Justice, on any single day, nearly 2 percent of all adult citizens are under probation supervision.[7]

The "Low-Cost Alternative"

Not all of the recent expansion of community corrections can be attributed to acceptance of its theoretical underpinnings. Many politicians and criminal justice officials who do not look favorably on ideas such as reintegration and diversion have embraced programs to keep nonviolent offenders out of prison. The reason is simple: money, or rather, its lack. Many of the tough sentencing laws discussed in the last chapter were passed during the 1990s, when state governments were in good financial positions. By the mid-2000s, state budgets came under strain, and state officials were looking to lighten the load by cutting down on corrections costs.

In the first part of this decade, about twenty-five states eliminated mandatory minimums and "truth-in-sentencing" laws with an eye toward financial savings. In Michigan, for example, some of the nation's most stringent mandatory sentencing laws contributed to an increase of 15,000 inmates and an $800 million spike in the state's Department of Corrections budget during the 1990s.[8] In 2002, a Republican governor and Republican-controlled state legislature eliminated most of Michigan's mandatory sentences and gave judges more discretion in sentencing. According to the *Detroit Free Press,* the new laws saved the Michigan corrections system $41 million in 2003 alone.[9]

"Three-strikes" laws have also felt the effects of budget restraints. Washington, the first state to pass such a law, effectively repealed it in 2002 by shortening sentences for drug offenders and offering more public funds for predetention drug treatment programs.[10] In California, where "three-strikes" laws have had the most effect, voters passed Proposition 36 in 2000.[11] The initiative, which allows drug offenders to choose between treatment and incarceration, is projected to eventually save $100 million to $150 million in annual prison costs and divert 36,000 nonviolent offenders from corrections facilities.[12] (For more information on the growing popularity of "rehab justice," see the *Criminal Justice in Action* feature at the end of this chapter.)

PROBATION: DOING TIME IN THE COMMUNITY

As Figure 12.1 shows, **probation** is the most common form of punishment in the United States. Although it is administered differently in various jurisdictions, probation can be generally defined as

> the legal status of an offender who, after being convicted of a crime, has been directed by the sentencing court to remain in the community under the supervision of a probation service for a designated period of time and subject to certain conditions imposed by the court or by law.[13]

The theory behind probation is that certain offenders, having been found guilty of a crime, can be more economically and humanely treated by placing them under controls while still allowing them to live in the community. One of the advantages of probation has been that it provides for the rehabilitation of the offender while saving society the costs of incarceration. Despite probation's widespread use, certain participants in the criminal justice system question its ability to reach its rehabilitative goals. Critics point to the immense number of probationers and the fact that many of them are violent felons as evidence that the system is "out of control." Supporters contend that nothing is wrong with probation in principle, but admit that its execution must be adjusted to meet the goals of modern corrections.[14]

Probation
A criminal sanction in which a convict is allowed to remain in the community rather than be imprisoned as long as she or he follows certain conditions set by the court.

FIGURE 12.1

Probation in
American Corrections

As you can see, the number of
Americans on probation more
than tripled between 1980 and
2003 (matching the growth rate
of prison and jail populations).

Source: Department of Justice Statistics,
*Probation and Parole in the United
States, 2003* (Washington, D.C.: U.S.
Department of Justice, July 2004), 1.

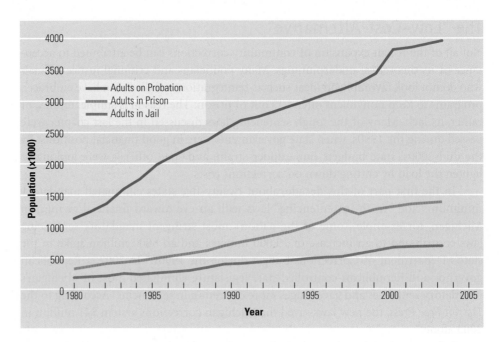

Judicial Reprieve
Temporary relief or the
postponement of a sentence on the
authority of a judge. In the United
States, the judicial power to offer a
reprieve has been limited by the
Supreme Court.

In 2004, Joseph Smith was charged
with the abduction and murder of
Carlie Brucia in Sarasota, Florida.
In the decade before Brucia's death,
Smith had been arrested at least
thirteen times in Florida, never
spending longer than fourteen
months in prison. When not
incarcerated, Smith was usually on
probation, as he was at the time of
Brucia's murder. How does a case
such as Smith's leave the probation
system open to criticism?

REUTERS/The Sarasota County Sheriff's Office/Landov

The Roots of Probation

In its earliest forms, probation was based on a desire to inject leniency into an often
harsh criminal justice system. Nineteenth-century English judges had the power to
issue **judicial reprieves,** or to suspend sentences for a certain amount of time, on the
condition of continued good behavior on the part of the defendant. This practice was
adopted in the United States, albeit in a different form. American judges used their
reprieve power to suspend the imposition of a penalty indefinitely, so long as the
offender did not commit a second crime. If another crime was committed, the offender
could be punished for both crimes.

In *Ex parte United States* (1916),[15] the United States Supreme Court ruled that
such indefinite reprieves were unconstitutional because they limited the ability of the
legislative and administrative branches to make and enforce sentencing laws. With this
diversion option removed, judges increasingly turned to the model of probation first
established in Massachusetts eighty years earlier.

John Augustus and the Origins of Probation The roots of probation can be directly
traced to a Boston shoemaker named John Augustus. In 1841, Augustus, a religious
person with considerable wealth, offered to post bail for a man charged with drunkenness. Augustus persuaded the judge to defer sentencing for three weeks, during which
time the offender would be in his custody. At the end of this probationary period, the
offender was able to convince the judge that he had been reformed and received a fine
instead of incarceration.

During the next eighteen years until his death, Augustus bailed out and supervised nearly 1,800 persons in lieu of confinement in the Boston House of Corrections.
He carefully screened potential probationers, researching their personal backgrounds
before deciding whether to include them in his caseload. Generally, Augustus accepted
only first offenders of otherwise good character. During the probationary period, he
helped his charges find employment and lodging and aided them in obtaining an education.[16] Augustus can be credited with nearly every aspect of modern probation, from
the name itself (from the Latin term *probatio,* or a "period of governing or trial"), to
presentence investigations, to supervision, to revocation.

Augustus's work was continued by a group of volunteer "probation officers" who
strived to rescue youths from the dangers of imprisonment. In 1869, the state of

Massachusetts passed a law that allowed for probation of juveniles and, nine years later, provided for paid probation officers to be hired by Boston's criminal courts. The law limited probation to "such persons as may reasonably be expected to be reformed without punishment." By 1891, Massachusetts had established the first statewide probation program.[17]

The Evolution of Probation Even as probation systems have been adopted in each of the fifty states and the federal government, the basic conflict between "help" and "punishment" has dominated the context of probation. When both criminal justice practitioners and the public hold the rehabilitative model in favor, as was the case for most of the first half of the twentieth century, probation is generally considered a valuable aspect of treatment. When, however, retributive goals come to the fore, probation is seen as being in need of reform, as has been the case in the United States since the mid-1970s. (It should be noted, though, that the number of Americans on probation has continued to grow even as its theoretical underpinnings are being challenged.)

Sentencing Choices and Probation

Probation is basically an "arrangement" between sentencing authorities and the offender. In traditional probation, the offender agrees to comply with certain terms for a specified amount of time in return for serving the sentence in the community. One of the primary benefits for the offender, besides not getting sent to a correctional facility, is that the length of the probationary period is usually considerably shorter than the length of a prison term (see Figure 12.2).

The "traditional" form of probation is not, however, the only arrangement that can be made. A judge can forgo probation altogether by handing down a **suspended sentence.** A descendant of the judicial reprieve discussed earlier, a suspended sentence places no conditions or supervision on the offender. He or she remains free for a certain length of time, but the judge keeps the option of revoking the suspended sentence and remanding the offender to prison or jail if circumstances call for such action.

Alternative Sentencing Arrangements Judges can also combine probation with incarceration. Such sentencing arrangements include:

- *Split sentences.* In **split sentence probation,** also known as *shock probation,* the offender is sentenced to a specific amount of time in prison or jail, to be followed by a period of probation.
- *Shock incarceration.* In this arrangement, an offender is sentenced to prison or jail with the understanding that after a period of time, she or he may petition the court to be released on probation. Shock incarceration is discussed more fully later in the chapter.
- *Intermittent incarceration.* With intermittent incarceration, the offender spends a certain amount of time each week, usually during the weekend, in a jail, workhouse, or other government institution.

Suspended Sentence
A judicially imposed condition in which an offender is sentenced after being convicted of a crime, but is not required to begin serving the sentence immediately. The judge may revoke the suspended sentence and remit the offender to prison or jail if he or she does not comply with certain conditions.

Split Sentence Probation
A sentence that consists of incarceration in a prison or jail, followed by a probationary period in the community.

FIGURE 12.2
Average Length of Sentence: Prison versus Probation

As you can see, the average probation sentence is much shorter than the average prison sentence for most crimes.

Source: Bureau of Justice Statistics, *Felony Sentences in State Courts, 2002* (Washington, D.C.: U.S. Department of Justice, December 2004), 4.

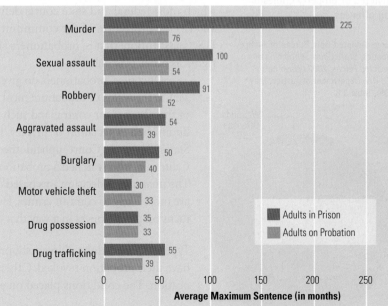

	Adults in Prison	Adults on Probation
Murder	225	76
Sexual assault	100	54
Robbery	91	52
Aggravated assault	54	39
Burglary	50	40
Motor vehicle theft	30	33
Drug possession	35	33
Drug trafficking	55	39

Average Maximum Sentence (in months)

Split sentences have become increasingly popular with judges, as they combine the "treatment" aspects of probation with the "punishment" aspects of incarceration. According to the Department of Justice, nearly 30 percent of all convicted felons receive split sentences.[18]

Eligibility for Probation Not every offender is eligible for probation. In Bell County, Texas, for example, juries can recommend probation only for assessed prison sentences of ten years or less. Generally, research has shown that offenders are most likely to be denied probation if they:

- Are convicted on multiple charges.
- Were on probation or parole at the time of the arrest.
- Have two or more prior convictions.
- Are addicted to narcotics.
- Seriously injured the victim of the crime.
- Used a weapon during the commission of the crime.[19]

As might be expected, the chances of a felon being sentenced to probation are highly dependent on the seriousness of the crime he or she has committed (see Figure 12.3).

Conditions of Probation

As part of the decision to sentence an offender to probation, a judge may also set conditions of probation. These conditions represent a "contract" between the judge and the offender, in which the latter agrees that if she or he does not follow certain rules, probation may be revoked (see Figure 12.4). The probation officer usually recommends the conditions of probation, but judges also have the power to set any terms they believe to be necessary.

Principles of Probation This power is far-reaching, and a judge's personal philosophy is often reflected in the probation conditions that are set. In *In re Quirk* (1998),[20] for example, the Louisiana Supreme Court upheld the ability of a trial judge to impose church attendance as a condition of probation. Though judges have a great deal of discretion in setting the conditions of probation, they do operate under several guiding principles. First, the conditions must be related to the dual purposes of probation, which most federal and state courts define as (1) the rehabilitation of the probationer and (2) the protection of the community. Second, the conditions must not violate the U.S. Constitution; that is, probationers are generally entitled to the same constitutional rights as other prisoners.[21]

Of course, probationers do give up certain constitutional rights when they consent to the terms of probation; most probationers, for example, agree to spot checks of their homes for contraband such as drugs or weapons, and they therefore have a diminished expectation of privacy. In *United States v. Knights* (2001),[22] the United States Supreme Court upheld the actions of deputy sheriffs in Napa County, California, who searched a probationer's home without a warrant or probable cause. The unanimous decision was based on the premise that because those on probation are more likely to commit crimes, law enforcement agents "may therefore justifiably focus on probationers in a way that [they do] not on the ordinary citizen."[23]

Types of Conditions Obviously, probationers who break the law are very likely to have their probation revoked. Other, less serious infractions may also result in revocation. The conditions placed on a probationer fall into three general categories:

- *Standard conditions,* which are imposed on all probationers. These include reporting regularly to the probation officer, notifying the agency of any

FIGURE 12.3
Adults on Probation by Felony Conviction Type

As you see here, the majority of adults on probation were convicted of property crimes or drug offenses.

Source: Adapted from Bureau of Justice Statistics, *State Court Sentencing of Convicted Felons, 2002* (Washington, D.C.: U.S. Department of Justice, May 2005), Table 3.6.

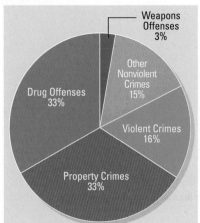

Weapons Offenses 3%
Other Nonviolent Crimes 15%
Drug Offenses 33%
Violent Crimes 16%
Property Crimes 33%

FIGURE 12.4
Conditions of Probation

**CONDITIONS OF PROBATION
UNITED STATES DISTRICT COURT
FOR THE DISTRICT OF COLUMBIA**

To   No. 84-417

Address: 1440 N St., N.W., #10, Wash., D.C.

In accordance with authority conferred by the United States Probation Law, you have been placed on probation this date, January 25, 2006 for a period of one year by the Hon. Louis F. Oberdorfer, United States District Judge, sitting in and for this District Court at Washington, D.C.

CONDITIONS OF PROBATION

It is the order of the Court that you shall comply with the following conditions of probation:

(1) You shall refrain from violation of any law (federal, state, and local). You shall get in touch immediately with your probation officer if arrested or questioned by a law-enforcement officer.

(2) You shall associate only with law-abiding persons and maintain reasonable hours.

(3) You shall work regularly at a lawful occupation and support your legal dependents, if any, to the best of your ability. When out of work you shall notify your probation officer at once. You shall consult him prior to job changes.

(4) You shall not leave the judicial district without permission of the probation officer.

(5) You shall notify your probation officer immediately of any change in your place of residence.

(6) You shall follow the probation officer's instructions.

(7) You shall report to the probation officer as directed.

(8) You shall not possess a firearm (handgun or rifle) for any reason.

The special conditions ordered by the Court are as follows:

Imposition of sentence suspended, one year probation, Fine of $75 on each count.

I understand that the Court may change the conditions of probation, reduce or extend the period of probation, and at any time during the probation period or within the maximum probation period of 5 years permitted by law, may issue a warrant and revoke probation for a violation occurring during the probation period.

I have read or had read to me the above conditions of probation. I fully understand them and I will abide by them.

(Signed)   1/25/06

You will report as follows: Probationer Date

As directed by your Probation Officer

(Signed)   2/5/06

U.S. Probation Officer Date

change of address, not leaving the jurisdiction without permission, and remaining employed.

- *Punitive conditions,* which usually reflect the seriousness of the offense and are intended to increase the punishment of the offender. Such conditions include fines, community service, restitution, drug testing, and home confinement (discussed later).

- *Treatment conditions,* which are imposed to reverse patterns of self-destructive behavior. Data show that more than 40 percent of probationers were required to undergo drug or alcohol treatment as part of their sentences, and an additional 18 percent were ordered to seek other kinds of treatment such as anger-control therapy.[24] (Figure 12.5 on the following page shows a typical set of conditions for adult felony probationers.)

Some observers feel that judges have too much discretion in imposing overly restrictive conditions that no person, much less one who has exhibited antisocial tendencies, could meet. Citing prohibitions on drinking liquor, gambling, and associating with "undesirables," as well as requirements such as meeting early curfews, University of Delaware professor Carl B. Klockars claims that if probation rules were taken

FIGURE 12.5

Basic Conditions of Felony Probation in Hunt County, Texas

The probationer shall:

1. Not commit any new offenses. If this occurs, the probationer must notify his or her probation officer within forty-eight hours.

2. Not use illegal drugs and/or alcohol or become intoxicated by any substance.

3. Submit to random urinalysis testing to verify that there is no illegal drug use and reimburse the probation department for the costs of the testing.

4. Not associate with others on probation, parole, or people of questionable character.

5. Reimburse the probation department for costs of supervision and the County for all court costs.

6. Stay within Hunt County unless granted permission to leave for a time specified by the Court or probation officer.

7. Keep the probation officer notified of the current address, employment, and phone number and notify the probation officer of any change in this information *before* you make the change.

8. Obtain a high school diploma or equivalency within one year of his or her probation or show proof that he or she has achieved this level of education.

9. Maintain stable employment to the extent possible and, if not employed, provide the probation officer with verifiable documentation of attempts to find work.

10. Not own or possess any firearm at any time during the probationary period and, depending on the type of probation, the probationer may not be allowed by federal law to own or possess any firearm for the rest of his or her life.

Source: Hunt County (Texas) Community Supervision and Corrections Department.

seriously, "very few probationers would complete their terms without violation."[25] As more than eight out of ten federal probationers do complete their terms successfully, Klockars's statement suggests that either probation officers are unable to determine that violations are taking place, or many of them are exercising a great deal of discretion in reporting minor probation violations. Or, perhaps, the officers realize that violating probationers for every single "slip-up" is unrealistic and would add to the already immense problem of jail and prison overcrowding.

The Supervisory Role of the Probation Officer

The probation officer has two basic roles. The first is investigative and consists of conducting the presentence investigation (PSI), which was discussed in Chapter 11. The second is supervisory and begins as soon as the offender has been sentenced to probation. In smaller probation agencies, individual officers perform both tasks. In larger jurisdictions, the trend has been toward separating the responsibilities, with *investigating officers* handling the PSI and *line officers* concentrating on supervision.

Supervisory policies vary and are often a reflection of whether the authority to administer probation services is *decentralized* (under local, judicial control) or *centralized* (under state, administrative control). In any circumstance, however, certain basic principles of supervision apply. Starting with a preliminary interview, the probation officer establishes a relationship with the offender. This relationship is based on the mutual goal of both parties: the successful completion of the probationary period. Just because the line officer and the offender have the same goal, however, does not mean that probation is necessarily marked by excessive cooperation.

The Use of Authority The ideal probation officer–offender relationship is based on trust. In reality, this trust does not often exist. Any incentive an offender might have to be completely truthful with a line officer is marred by one simple fact: self-reported wrongdoing can be used to revoke probation. Even probation officers whose primary mission is to rehabilitate are under institutional pressure to punish their clients for violating conditions of probation. One officer deals with this situation by telling his clients

> that I'm here to help them, to get them a job, and whatever else I can do. But I tell them too that I have a family to support and that if they get too far off track, I can't afford to put my job on the line for them. I'm going to have to violate them.[26]

In the absence of trust, most probation officers rely on their **authority** to guide an offender successfully through the sentence. An officer's authority, or ability to influence a person's actions without resorting to force, is based not only on her or his power to revoke probation, but also on a number of lesser sanctions. For example, if a probationer fails to attend a required alcohol treatment program, the officer can place him or her in a "lockup," or detention center, overnight. To be successful, a probation officer must establish this authority early in the relationship; it is the primary tool in persuading the probationer to behave in a manner acceptable to the community.[27]

Authority
The power designated to an agent of the law over a person who has broken the law.

The Offender's Perspective The public perception of probationers is that they are lucky not to be in prison or jail and should be grateful for receiving a "second chance." Although they may not describe their situation in that way, many probationers are willing to comply with the terms of their sentences, if for no other reason than to avoid any further punishments. Such offenders can make a line officer's supervision duties relatively simple.

By the same token, as we discussed in Chapter 2, criminal behavior is often predicated on a lack of respect for authority. This outlook does not coincide with the supervisory aspects of probation. According to the Department of Justice, in any given month, 61 percent of offenders have a face-to-face meeting with their supervisors in a probation office, at home, at work, or in another setting. Another 25 percent were in contact through the mail or over the phone.[28] Furthermore, to follow the conditions of probation, convicts may have to discontinue activities that they find enjoyable, such as going to a bar for a drink on Saturday night. Consequently, some probationers consider supervision as akin to "baby-sitting" and resist the strict controls placed on them by the government.

The Changing Environment of the Probation Officer To some extent, today's probation officers function similarly to John Augustus's volunteers. They spend a great deal of time in the community, working with businesses, churches, schools, and neighborhood groups on behalf of their charges.

Nevertheless, the profession has seen considerable changes over the past three decades. As noted earlier, probation is being offered to more offenders with violent criminal histories than in the past. Inevitably, this has changed the job description of the probation officer, who must increasingly act as a law enforcement agent rather than concentrating on the rehabilitation of clients. Probation officers now conduct surveillance and search and seizure operations, administer drug tests, and accompany police officers on high-risk law enforcement assignments.[29] Consequently, the work has become more dangerous. According to the National Institute of Corrections, more than half of the probation officers who directly supervise wrongdoers have been victims of a "hazardous incident" that endangered their safety.[30]

As a result, many probation officers are seeking permission to carry guns on the job. Several years ago, for example, the Arizona Probation Officer Association convinced state authorities that probation officers should be able to wield firearms if they so desire. Making a similar argument, Los Angeles probation officer Janis Jones said,

See the **Corrections Connection** for information on the corrections industry, including community corrections. Find its Web site by clicking on *Web Links* under *Chapter Resources* at **www.cjinaction.com**.

Scott T. Ballock
U.S. Probation Officer

Scott T. Ballock

As a federal probation officer, I work for the United States District Court in the District of Nevada (Las Vegas office). U.S. probation officers serve as officers of the court and as agents of the U.S. Parole Commission. We are responsible for the supervision of all persons conditionally released to the community by the courts, the Parole Commission, the Federal Bureau of Prisons, and military authorities. Being released "conditionally" to the community means that in exchange for allowing an offender to remain in the community, the court expects him or her to meet certain standards and goals. These include remaining law abiding and drug free, working, supporting family members, repaying victims, perhaps performing volunteer work for the community, and making other improvements in his or her life.

Supervising offenders in the community, our mission is to execute the court's sentence, control risk, and promote law-abiding behavior. In order to meet these goals, probation officers must become very knowledgeable about an offender's activities and lifestyle. We do so by meeting with him or her on a regular basis in the community, conducting unannounced home inspections, speaking regularly with his or her family, friends, neighbors, and employers, and—when necessary—conducting surveillance or warrantless searches of his or her home and vehicle.

I am often asked whether probation officers are law enforcement officers or social workers. We are both. Responsible for protecting the public, we are also charged with promoting positive change among our probationers and parolees. Half of our day may be spent following an offender through the city to learn if he is engaged in illegal activities, while the second half is spent counseling offenders, helping them prepare résumés, or referring them to local social-service agencies for further assistance. Our dual role is an especially challenging aspect of the job.

Fortunately, we have the guidance of our boss, the sentencing judge. I used to think that justice was dispensed routinely and methodically with little consideration given to the impact of a sentence. Having worked for several judges, however, I have learned that sentences are carefully crafted and well thought out. Probation officers and judges are genuinely concerned about the welfare of the people who appear before them. If offenders have a substance abuse problem, they'll be offered treatment. If they are lacking in job skills, a judge may order successful completion of a vocational training program.

We recognize that a prison sentence is a very costly proposition, to both the offender and the community. A decision to send or return a person to a prison setting is a serious matter, and great lengths are taken to first effect positive change. I think even those we supervise come to realize this. It's not infrequent that a person I've spent months trying to help, and who ultimately fails and is sent back to prison, extends his hand to thank me for trying—even as he's being led away by the U.S. marshals.

Go to the Careers in Criminal Justice Interactive CD *for more profiles in the field of criminal justice.*

"We're not in the '70s anymore. We're not dealing with little dope dealers on the corner selling nickel bags of marijuana." Jones, whose unit collects about a dozen guns a week, added, "These guys are into hard-core, heavy firepower to protect their interests. You feel totally vulnerable [without a gun]."[31] In the federal probation system, eighty-three of the ninety-four federal judicial districts permit their probation officers to carry firearms.

Revocation of Probation

The probation period can end in one of two ways. Either the probationer successfully fulfills the conditions of the sentence, or the probationer misbehaves and probation is revoked, resulting in a prison or jail term. The decision of whether to revoke after a **technical violation**—such as failing to report a change of address or testing positive for drug use—is often a "judgment call" by the probation officer and therefore the focus of controversy.

Revocation Trends In the past, a technical violation almost always led to revocation. Today, many probation officers will take that step only if they believe the technical vio-

Technical Violation

An action taken by a probationer that, although not criminal, breaks the terms of probation as designated by the court; can result in the revocation of probation and a return to prison or jail.

lation in question represents a danger to the community. At the same time, the public's more punitive attitude, along with improved drug-testing methods, has increased the number of conditions under which probationers are placed and, consequently, the odds that they will violate one of those conditions.

In the 1980s and 1990s, to a certain extent, these two trends negated each other: between 1987 and 1996, there was almost no change in the percentage (between 75 and 80 percent) of offenders who successfully completed their probation terms.[32] In the past few years, however, this rate has dropped. In 2003, only 59 percent of probationers completed their terms without revocation.[33] Because revocation results in incarceration, it can make a significant contribution to prison and jail overcrowding. In Texas, for example, about one-third of prison admissions are for probation revocations.[34]

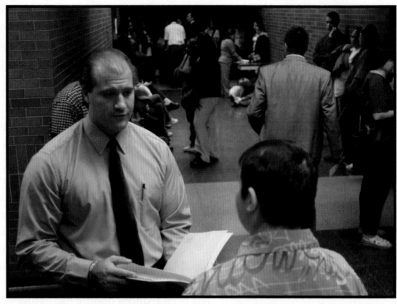

Juvenile Court Probation Officer Michael J. Manteria, left, consults with a probationer at the Hampden County Hall of Justice in Springfield, Massachusetts. The ideal probation officer–probationer relationship is based on trust, but often probation officers must rely on their authority to do their jobs correctly. Why is trust often so difficult to achieve between probation officers and offenders?

The Revocation Process Probationers do not enjoy the same rights as other members of society. In *Griffin v. Wisconsin* (1987),[35] the Supreme Court ruled that probationers have only "conditional liberty" that is dependent "on observance of special restrictions." As long as the restrictions assure that a probationer works toward rehabilitation and does not harm the community, the Court allows the probationer's privacy to be restricted in a manner it would not accept otherwise.

The Supreme Court has not stripped probationers of all due process rights, however. In *Mempa v. Rhay* (1967),[36] the Court ruled that probationers were entitled to an attorney during the revocation process. Then, in *Morrissey v. Brewer* (1972) and *Gagnon v. Scarpelli* (1973),[37] the Court established a three-stage procedure by which the "limited" due process rights of probationers must be protected in potential revocation situations:

- *The preliminary hearing.* In this appearance before a "disinterested person" (often a judge), the facts of the violation or arrest are presented, and it is determined whether probable cause for revoking probation exists. This hearing can be waived by the probationer.
- *The revocation hearing.* During this hearing, the probation agency presents evidence to support its claim of violation, and the probationer can attempt to refute this evidence. The probationer has the right to know the charges being brought against him or her. Furthermore, probationers can testify on their own behalf and present witnesses in their favor, as well as confront and cross-examine adverse witnesses. A "neutral and detached" body must hear the evidence and rule in favor of the probation agency or the offender.
- *Revocation sentencing.* If the presiding body rules against the probationer, then the judge must decide whether to impose incarceration and for what length of time. In a revocation hearing dealing with technical violations, the judge will often reimpose probation with stricter terms or intermediate sanctions.

In effect, this is a "bare-bones" approach to due process. Most of the rules of evidence that govern regular trials do not play a role in revocation hearings. Probation officers are not, for example, required to read offenders *Miranda* rights when questioning them about crimes that may have been committed during probation. In *Minnesota v. Murphy* (1984),[38] the Supreme Court ruled that a meeting between probation officer and client does not equal custody and, therefore, the Fifth Amendment protection against self-incrimination does not apply.

Does Probation Work?

To address the question of whether probation is effective, one must first establish its purpose. Should the probation system be designed to rehabilitate offenders? Is it primarily a method of surveillance and control? Should probation's role in the criminal justice system be to reduce pressure on prison and jail populations? Each of these aspects of probation has its supporters and critics. Indeed, the only consensus among supporters of probation is that the system is severely underfunded. As many states face growing budget deficits, spending for probation agencies has at best remained stagnant and, in many instances, has been reduced despite increasing probation populations.

> "I try to get in the field two to three nights a week to see my offenders. It's really the only way to stop trouble before it happens. Otherwise, it's a free-for-all."
>
> —Kevin Dudley, Salt Lake City probation officer (1997)

The Caseload Dilemma As a result of these low budgets, say observers, probation agencies do not have the resources to provide full services to all offenders. Patrick A. Langan of the U.S. Department of Justice estimates that fully half of this country's probationers do not comply with the conditions of their sentences. The problem, contends Langan and many of his colleagues, is that probation officers have such large caseloads that they cannot rigorously enforce the conditions imposed on many of their clients.[39]

Unlike a prison cell, a probation officer can always take on "just one more" offender/client. As there is no accepted standard for determining optimal caseloads, probation officers can find themselves responsible for supervising an extremely large number of convicts. One official interviewed by Professors Charles Linder and Robert L. Bonn at John Jay College of Criminal Justice admitted to having 6,500 clients supervised by four probation officers.[40] Though data vary from state to state, Professor Joan Petersilia of the University of California at Irvine estimates that, on average, each probation officer in the United States has a caseload of 175 offenders.[41] Another study found that 20 percent of adult *felony* probationers had no personal contact with their probation officers whatsoever.[42]

Recidivism and Probation Such statistics fuel the popular belief that probation allows dangerous felons to roam the streets and commit new crimes at will. This perception is not entirely accurate. In fact, the majority of probationers complete their terms without being arrested (which does not necessarily mean that they did not commit a new offense). Low rearrest rates are not surprising, given that many of those on probation are first-time, low-risk offenders. Furthermore, a controlled comparison of the recidivism rates of 511 probationers and 511 offenders released from prison found that probation can be at least as effective as incarceration, if not more so. Seventy-two percent of the prisoners were rearrested and 47 percent were imprisoned, while only 38 percent of the probationers were rearrested and 31 percent incarcerated.[43]

A more recent comparison of drug offenders in Kansas City, Missouri, found that those who went to prison were 2.3 times more likely to be charged with a new offense than those on probation and 2.2 times more likely than the probationers to be sent back to a correctional facility.[44]

By the same token, there is no question that probationers do commit numerous crimes. Researchers John DiIulio, John Walters, and William Bennett have written that convicted offenders living in the community "do tremendous numbers of serious crimes, including a frightening fraction of all murders."[45] They found that, in one year, probation violators were convicted of nearly 6,500 homicides, more than 7,000 rapes, about 10,000 assaults, and 17,000 robberies.[46]

Risk Assessment Management
Many reformers reject the notion that large caseloads are to blame for the inadequacies of the supervision system. These critics believe that probation agencies have failed to direct their limited resources efficiently. In other words, they have failed to devote more supervisory controls to the relatively small percentage of offenders who run the highest risk of recidivism and pose the greatest threat to the community.

In 1981, the National Institute of Corrections developed a "model system" of case management to address these concerns. Based on the notion that some offenders require

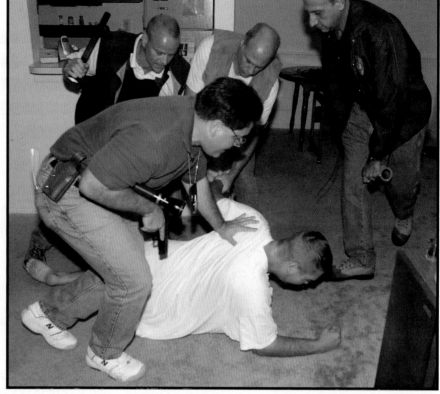

Three probation officers and a sheriff's deputy take down a probation violator during a roundup in Tampa, Florida. When an offender violates the terms of probation, his or her status can be revoked, and he or she can be sent to jail or prison. Whether to revoke probation is often a "judgment call" by the probation officer. What might be some reasons that a probation officer would not revoke an offender's probation even though that person has committed a violation?

more attention than others, the model provides probation officers with statistical methods—based on the type of crime committed—to identify these offenders.[47] Within a decade, nearly every probation system in the nation was using similar classification devices to determine the level of supervision based on *risk assessment*.[48]

Basically, risk assessment management strategies determine the offender's threat to the community and the level of supervision required to lessen that threat.[49] In doing so, the probation officer or other officer of the court considers several factors, such as the offender's record of committing violent crimes; previous performance in probation, parole, or other community-based corrections programs; previous experience in jail or prison; and substance abuse or anger-management problems. (See Figure 12.6 on the following page for two factors that have proved helpful.) In general, those offenders who are believed to pose the greatest threat to the community are labeled "maximum" risk and subjected to the highest level of supervision. Offenders who have not committed violent crimes or are deemed "medium" or "minimum" risks for other reasons are subjected to less supervision, thus freeing probation officers to deal with their most dangerous clients. This risk assessment model has two benefits: (1) in keeping with "just deserts," those who have committed more serious crimes are subject to more restrictive probationary terms, and (2) it prioritizes community protection.

INTERMEDIATE SANCTIONS

During the 1960s and 1970s, many probation departments experimented with smaller caseloads under a management program known as *intensive supervision probation (ISP)*. These programs were discontinued when research showed that offenders in ISP had similar rearrest rates and more technical violations than those under regular supervision.[50] ISP was resurrected by the state of Georgia in 1982, however, with a different mandate. The state, experiencing prison crowding and a limited corrections

FIGURE 12.6

Risk Factors for Probation Revocation

Risk assessment management strategies require corrections officials to allocate scarce resources to those probationers who have the greatest chance of revocation. As this figure shows, two helpful indicators are the seriousness of the probationer's initial offense and his or her level of education.

Source: Bureau of Justice Statistics, *Compendium of Federal Justice Statistics, 2002* (Washington, D.C.: U.S. Department of Justice, September 2004), Figures 7.2 and 7.3.

budget, saw ISP as an alternative sanction for offenders who would have otherwise gone to prison. Georgia's version of ISP has been adopted in some measure by all fifty states, and it is at the vanguard of a movement to use **intermediate sanctions** to a greater degree in the American corrections system.

Many observers feel that the most widely used sentencing options—imprisonment and probation—fail to reflect the immense diversity of crimes and criminals. Intermediate sanctions provide a number of additional sentencing options for those wrongdoers who require stricter supervision than that supplied by probation, but for whom imprisonment would be unduly harsh and counterproductive.[51] The intermediate sanctions discussed in this section are designed to match the specific punishment and treatment of an individual offender with a corrections program that reflects that offender's situation.

Dozens of different variations of intermediate sanctions are handed down each year. To cover the spectrum succinctly, two general categories of such sanctions will be discussed in this section: those administered primarily by the courts and those administered primarily by probation departments, including day reporting centers, ISP programs, shock incarceration, and home confinement. Remember that none of these sanctions are exclusive; they are often combined with imprisonment and probation, and with each other.

Judicially Administered Intermediate Sanctions

Intermediate Sanctions
Sanctions that are more restrictive than probation and less restrictive than imprisonment. Intended to alleviate pressure on overcrowded corrections facilities and understaffed probation departments.

The lack of sentencing options is most frustrating for the person who, in the majority of cases, does the sentencing: the judge. Consequently, when judges are given the discretion to "color" a punishment with intermediate sanctions, they will often do so. Besides imprisonment and probation (and, to a lesser extent, other intermediate sanctions), a judge has five sentencing options:

1 Fines

2 Community service

3 Restitution

4 Forfeiture

5 Pretrial diversion programs

Fines, community service, and restitution were discussed in Chapter 11. In the context of intermediate sanctions, it is important to remember that these punishments are generally combined with incarceration or probation. For that reason, some critics feel the retributive or deterrent impact of such punishments is severely limited. Many European countries, in contrast, rely heavily on fines as the sole sanctions for a variety of crimes. (See *International CJ— Swedish Day-Fines* on p. 406.)

Two gang members perform their court-ordered community service under the watchful eye of a supervisor. Community service is one of a number of intermediate sanctions used to punish offenders instead of probation or incarceration. Why might corrections officials support the increased use of intermediate sanctions?

Forfeiture In 1970, Congress passed the Racketeer Influenced and Corrupt Organizations Act (RICO) in an attempt to prevent the use of legitimate business enterprises as shields for organized crime.[52] As amended, RICO and other statutes give judges the ability to implement forfeiture proceedings in certain criminal cases. **Forfeiture** refers to a process by which the government seizes property gained from or used in criminal activity. For example, if a person is convicted for smuggling cocaine into the United States from South America, a judge can order the seizure of not only the narcotics, but also the speedboat the offender used to deliver the drugs to a pickup point off the coast of South Florida. In *Bennis v. Michigan* (1996),[53] the Supreme Court ruled that a person's home or car could be forfeited even if the owner was unaware that it was connected to illegal activity.

Once property is forfeited, the government has several options. It can sell the property, with the proceeds going to the state and/or federal government law enforcement agencies involved in the seizure. Alternatively, the government agency can use the property directly in further crime-fighting efforts or award it to a third party, such as an informant. Forfeiture has proved highly profitable: federal law enforcement agencies impound close to $1 billion worth of contraband and property from alleged criminals each year.

Pretrial Diversion Programs Not every criminal violation requires the courtroom process. Consequently, some judges have the discretion to order an offender into a **pretrial diversion program** during the preliminary hearing. (Prosecutors can also offer an offender the opportunity to join such a program in return for reducing or dropping the initial charges.) These programs represent an "interruption" of the criminal proceedings and are generally reserved for young or first-time offenders who have been arrested on charges of illegal drug use, child or spousal abuse, or sexual misconduct. Pretrial diversion programs usually include extensive counseling, often in a treatment center. If the offender successfully follows the conditions of the program, the criminal charges are dropped.

Day Reporting Centers

First used in Great Britain, **day reporting centers** are mainly tools to reduce jail and prison overcrowding. Although the offenders are allowed to remain in the community, they must spend all or part of each day at a reporting center. To a certain extent, being

Forfeiture
The process by which the government seizes private property attached to criminal activity.

Pretrial Diversion Program
An alternative to trial offered by a judge or prosecutor, in which the offender agrees to participate in a specified counseling or treatment program in return for withdrawal of the charges.

Day Reporting Center
A community-based corrections center to which offenders report on a daily basis for purposes of treatment, education, and incapacitation.

Swedish Day-Fines

Few ideals are cherished as highly in our criminal justice system as equality. Most Americans take it for granted that individuals guilty of identical crimes should face identical punishments. From an economic perspective, however, this emphasis on equality renders our system decidedly *unequal*. Take two citizens, one a millionaire investment banker and the other a checkout clerk earning the minimum wage. Driving home from work one afternoon, each is caught by a traffic officer doing 80 miles per hour in a 55-mile-per-hour zone. The fine for this offense is $150. This amount, though equal for both, has different consequences: it represents mere pocket change for the investment banker, but a significant chunk out of the checkout clerk's weekly paycheck.

Restricted by a "tariff system" that sets specific amounts for specific crimes, regardless of the financial situation of the convict, American judges often refrain from using fines as a primary sanction. They either assume that poor offenders cannot afford the fine or worry that a fine will allow wealthier offenders to "buy" their way out of a punishment.

PAYING FOR CRIME

In searching for a way to make fines more effective sanctions, many reformers have seized on the concept of the "day-fine," as practiced in Sweden and several other European countries. In this system, which was established in the 1920s and 1930s, the fine amount is linked to the monetary value of the offender's daily income. Depending on the seriousness of the crime, a Swedish wrongdoer will be sentenced to between 30 and 150 days or, as combined punishment for multiple crimes, up to 200 days. Each day, the offender is required to pay the equivalent of one-third of her or his daily discretionary income (as established by the Prosecutor General's Office) to the court. Consequently, the day-fine system not only reflects the degree of the crime, but ensures that the economic burden will be equal for those with different means.

Swedish police and prosecutors can levy day-fines without court involvement. Consequently, plea bargaining is nonexistent, and more than 80 percent of all offenders are sentenced to intermediate sanctions without a trial. The remaining cases receive full trials, with an acquittal rate of only 6 percent, compared to roughly 30 percent in the United States.

FOR CRITICAL ANALYSIS

Do you think a "day-fine" system would be feasible in the United States? Why might it be difficult to implement in this country?

---

sentenced to a day reporting center is an extreme form of supervision. With offenders under a single roof, they are much more easily controlled and supervised. Government officials are also attracted by the economics of these alternative programs. For example, taxpayers pay $12 per day for an offender at the day reporting center in Morrow, Georgia, compared to $45 per day to house an inmate in a state prison.[54]

Day reporting centers are instruments of rehabilitation as well. They often feature treatment programs for drug and alcohol abusers and provide counseling for a number of psychological problems, such as depression and anger management. Many of those found guilty in the Roanoke (Virginia) Drug Court, for example, are ordered to participate in a year-long day reporting program. At the center, offenders meet with probation officers, submit to urine tests, and attend counseling and education programs, such as parenting and life-skills classes. After the year has passed, if the offender has completed the program to the satisfaction of the judge and found employment, the charges will be dropped.

Given that each day reporting center is unique, it is difficult to evaluate the success of this particular intermediate sanction. In general, however, the centers appear to have a limited impact on recidivism rates unless they include strong therapeutic programs.[55] For example, only 3.2 percent of those who successfully completed the Roanoke program, which stresses rehabilitation, are convicted of another felony offense.[56] By contrast, in West Virginia, where funds for treatment are limited, day reporting centers have a 15 percent recidivism rate, only slightly lower than the 18 percent rate for all probationers.[57]

Intensive Supervision Probation

As stated previously, **intensive supervision probation (ISP)** offers a more restrictive alternative to regular probation, with higher levels of face-to-face contact between offenders and officers, drug testing, and electronic surveillance. Different jurisdictions have different methods of determining who is eligible for ISP. In New Jersey, for example, violent offenders may not be placed in the program, while a majority of states limit ISP to those who do not have prior probation violations. The frequency of officer-client contact also varies widely.

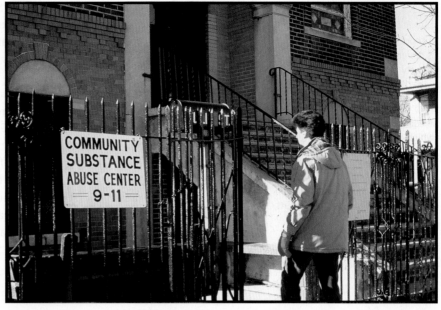

PhotoEdit/Jeff Greenberg

Judges and prosecutors may, in certain cases, give offenders the chance to attend pretrial diversion programs. Offered by caregiving facilities such as the community substance abuse center pictured here, these programs provide a chance to treat the causes behind criminal behavior without sending the offender to prison or jail. Do pretrial diversion programs "punish" offenders? If not, can they be justified as part of the corrections system?

Intensive supervision has two primary functions: (1) to *divert* offenders from overcrowded prisons or jails, and (2) to place these offenders under higher levels of *control,* as befits the risk they pose to the community. Researchers have had difficulty, however, in determining whether ISP is succeeding in these two areas. Any diversion benefits of ISP programs have tended to be offset by the stricter sentencing guidelines discussed in Chapter 11.[58] Furthermore, a number of studies have found that ISP clients have higher violation rates than traditional probationers.[59] One theory is that ISP "causes" these high failure rates—greater supervision increases the chances that an offender will be caught breaking conditions of probation.

In addition, as with other intermediate sanctions, the success of ISP programs seems to relate directly to the rigor with which they are carried out. In the New Jersey program, which is considered one of the most effective in the nation, ISP officers are equipped with cell phones, beepers, laptop computers, and automobiles. They have caseloads of only twenty offenders (compared to 115 for other probation officers in the state) and average thirty-one contacts with each client per month. The results have been striking: graduates of the program have only a 10 percent recidivism rate after five years, whereas two-thirds of state prisoners are rearrested within three years of release.[60] Whatever its results, ISP is viable in today's political landscape because it satisfies the public's desire for stricter controls on convicts, while providing intermediate sanctions options for judges, prosecutors, and corrections administrators.

Shock Incarceration

Before the concept of intermediate sanctions was widely recognized in the criminal justice community, "Scared Straight" programs were used by some jurisdictions with the express purpose of deterring further criminal activity by juveniles and first-time offenders. The original Scared Straight was developed by the Lifers Group at Rahway State Prison (now East Jersey State Prison) in New Jersey in the mid-1970s. Consisting of about forty inmates serving sentences from twenty-five years to life, the Lifers Group would oversee juvenile offenders who had not yet been incarcerated but were considered "at risk" during a short stint (between 30 and 120 days) in the prison. The hope, as the program's name indicates, was that by getting a taste of the brutalities of daily prison life, the offender would be shocked into a crime-free existence.

Intensive Supervision Probation (ISP)
A punishment-oriented form of probation in which the offender is placed under stricter and more frequent surveillance and control than conventional probation by probation officers with limited caseloads.

Shock Incarceration
A short period of incarceration that is designed to deter further criminal activity by "shocking" the offender with the hardships of imprisonment.

Home Confinement
A community-based sanction in which offenders serve their terms of incarceration in their homes.

Electronic Monitoring
A technique of probation supervision in which the offender's whereabouts, though not his or her actions, are kept under surveillance by an electronic device; often used in conjunction with home confinement.

A form of **shock incarceration,** Scared Straight programs generally fell out of favor in the 1980s, though several states, including Nevada, still employ them. Critics contended that the programs seemed to have no discernible effect on recidivism rates and thus needlessly exposed minor offenders to mental and physical cruelties from hardened criminals.[61]

Boot camps are another form of shock incarceration that has declined in popularity in the face of rising costs and inconclusive results. Modeled on military basic training, the programs emphasize strict discipline, manual labor, and physical training. They are designed to instill self-responsibility and self-respect, thereby lessening the chances that the offender will return to a life of crime on release. At their peak of popularity in the mid-1990s, state and federal boot camps housed more than 7,000 inmates. In 2005, however, the Federal Bureau of Prisons announced plans to close down its three boot camps, following the lead of numerous states that have been unwilling to foot the bill for programs that have had no measurable effect on recidivism rates.[62]

Home Confinement and Electronic Monitoring

Various forms of **home confinement**—in which offenders serve their sentences not in a government institution but at home—have existed for centuries. It has often served, and continues to do so, as a method of political control, used by totalitarian regimes to isolate and silence dissidents. For example, the military government of Myanmar (Burma) has confined Nobel Peace laureate Aung San Suu Kyi to her home for years at a time since she won an election for leadership of that country in 1990.

For purposes of general law enforcement, home confinement was impractical until relatively recently. After all, one could not expect offenders to "promise" to stay at home, and the personnel costs of guarding them were prohibitive. In the 1980s, however, with the advent of **electronic monitoring,** or using technology to "guard" the prisoner, home confinement became more viable. Today, all fifty states and the federal government have home monitoring programs with about 120,000 offenders participating at any one time.[63]

The Levels of Home Monitoring and Their Benefits Home monitoring has three general levels of restriction:

1 *Curfew,* which requires offenders to be in their homes at specific hours each day, usually at night.
2 *Home detention,* which requires that offenders remain home at all times, with exceptions being made for education, employment, counseling, or other specified activities such as the purchase of food or, in some instances, attendance at religious ceremonies.
3 *Home incarceration,* which requires the offender to remain home at all times, save for medical emergencies.

Under ideal circumstances, home confinement serves many of the goals of intermediate sanctions. It protects the community. It saves public funds and space in correctional facilities by keeping convicts out of institutional incarceration. It meets public expectations of punishment for criminals. Uniquely, home confinement also recognizes that convicts, despite their crimes, play important roles in the community, and allows them to continue in those roles. An offender, for example, may be given permission to leave confinement to care for elderly parents.

Home confinement is also lauded for giving sentencing officials the freedom to match the punishment with the needs of the offender. In Missouri, for instance, the conditions of detention for a musician required him to remain at home during the day,

CJ AND TECHNOLOGY

Satellite Tracking: The Next Step in Electronic Monitoring

As we have already discussed, all intermediate sanctions entail a certain amount of risk. In electronic monitoring, as with other sanctions, this risk is compounded by the fact that the success of the program depends on the offender's commitment to "play by the rules." If the offender decides to leave the area of confinement, the signaling device will emit an alarm, alerting the police of the infraction but giving them no clues as to where the person is going.

A new breakthrough in electronic monitoring may provide the solution to this problem. Pro Tech Monitoring, Inc., a Palm Harbor (Florida) company, has developed a system that uses federal government satellites to monitor an offender's movements from above. Under this system, each subject will carry a "smart box" along with an ankle bracelet. The "smart box" contains a tracking device and is programmed with information about the offender's geographic restrictions. A Global Positioning System (GPS) satellite monitors the offender's movements and notifies the police if she or he violates conditional boundaries. So, for example, if a pedophile approaches an "off-limits" junior high school, the

satellite warning system would alert police of the person's present location.

This system is particularly alluring for economic reasons. In Florida, where more than 600 probationers and parolees are "on the box," it costs $60 a day to house someone in a state prison, compared with $8 to $12 a day for surveillance using the GPS device. Offenders may prefer this form of punishment as well. "You know you are being monitored, you know you are being watched," said one. "But if I had to choose prison or the box, I choose the box."

IN THE FUTURE

As satellite tracking technology becomes more advanced, corrections agencies will have the ability to keep an "electronic eye" on convicts at all times, calling up a visual image whenever necessary.

For more information on satellite tracking and other CJ technologies, click on Web Links *under* Book Resources *at* **www.cjinaction.com.**

but allowed him to continue his career at night. In addition, he was obliged to make antidrug statements before each performance, to be verified by the manager at whichever club he appeared.

Types of Electronic Monitoring According to some reports, the inspiration for electronic monitoring was a *Spiderman* comic book in which the hero was trailed by the use of an electronic device on his arm. In 1979, a New Mexico judge named Jack Love, having read the comic, convinced an executive at Honeywell, Inc., to begin developing similar technology to supervise convicts.[64]

Two major types of electronic monitoring have grown out of Love's initial concept. The first is a "programmed contact" program, in which the offender is contacted periodically by telephone or beeper to verify his or her whereabouts. Verification is obtained via a computer that uses voice or visual identification techniques or by requiring the offender to enter a code in an electronic box when called. The second is a "continuously signaling" device, worn around the convict's wrist, ankle, or neck. A transmitter in the device sends out a continuous signal to a "receiver-dialer" device located in the offender's dwelling. If the receiver device does not detect a signal from the transmitter, it informs a central computer, and the police are notified.[65] (For advances in this field, see the feature *CJ and Technology—Satellite Tracking: The Next Step in Electronic Monitoring.*)

Effectiveness of Home Confinement As might be expected, technical problems can limit the effectiveness of an electronic monitoring device. So can tampering by the offender. In 2005, for example, a fourteen-year-old girl in Princeton, West Virginia, who was under house arrest on charges of murdering her father, managed to escape after cutting the electronic monitoring device off her ankle and gluing it on a cat. The possibility of such problems will decrease as tamper-resistant monitoring devices are

Offenders who are confined to their homes are often monitored by an electronic device that fits around the ankle. A transmitter in the device sends a continuous signal to a receiver, also located within the home. If this signal is broken—that is, the offender moves outside the range of the device—the police are automatically notified. What are some of the drawbacks of this form of electronic monitoring?

perfected. One such device reacts to the application of heat, which normally loosens some transmitters, by contracting; if enough heat is applied, the offender's circulation will be cut off.[66]

Because most participants in home confinement programs are low-risk offenders, their recidivism rates are quite low. Joan Petersilia found that most home confinement programs report rearrest rates of less than 5 percent.[67] The data are less supportive when measuring how many offenders broke the conditions of confinement. In Indiana, over 40 percent of participants had at least one violation, and between one-third and one-half failed to complete the program.[68]

One concern about home confinement is that offenders are often required to defray program costs, which can be as high as $100 per week. Consequently, those who cannot afford to pay for electronic monitoring may not be eligible. Furthermore, families of offenders confined to the home can experience high levels of stress and a loss of privacy.[69] In general, however, those who successfully complete a home confinement term seem to benefit in areas such as obtaining and holding employment.[70]

Widening the Net

As mentioned above, most of the convicts chosen for intermediate sanctions are low-risk offenders. From the point of view of the corrections official doing the choosing, this makes sense. Such offenders are less likely to commit crimes and attract negative publicity. This selection strategy, however, appears to invalidate one of the primary reasons intermediate sanctions exist: to reduce prison and jail populations. If most of the offenders in intermediate sanctions programs would otherwise have received probation, then the effect on these populations is nullified. Indeed, studies have shown this to be the case.[71]

At the same time, such selection processes broaden the reach of the corrections system. In other words, they increase rather than decrease the amount of control the state exerts over the individual. Suppose a person is arrested for a misdemeanor such as shoplifting and, under normal circumstances, would receive probation. With access to intermediate sanctions, the judge may add a period of home confinement to the sentence. Critics contend that such practices **widen the net** of the corrections system by augmenting the number of citizens who are under the control and surveillance of the state and also *strengthen the net* by increasing the government's power to intervene in the lives of its citizens.[72]

Widen the Net
The criticism that intermediate sanctions designed to divert offenders from prison actually increase the number of citizens who are under the control and surveillance of the American corrections system.

THE PARADOX OF COMMUNITY CORRECTIONS

Despite their many benefits, including cost savings, treatment options, and the ability to divert hundreds of thousands of nonviolent wrongdoers from prisons and jails, community-based corrections programs suffer from a basic paradox: the more effectively offenders are controlled, the more likely they are to be caught violating the terms of their conditional release. As you may have noticed, the community supervision programs discussed in this chapter are "graded" according to rates of recidivism and revocation, with low levels of each reflecting a successful program. Increased control and surveillance, however, will necessarily raise the level of violations, thus increasing the probability that any single violation will be discovered. Therefore, as factors such as the number of conditions placed on probationers and the technological proficiency of electronic monitoring devices increase, so, too, will the number of offenders who fail to meet the conditions of their community-based punishment.

One observer calls this the "quicksand" effect of increased surveillance. Instead of helping offenders leave the corrections system, increased surveillance pulls them more deeply into it.[73] The quicksand effect can be quite strong, according to researchers Barbara Sims of Sam Houston State University and Mark Jones of East Carolina University. In a study of North Carolina corrections data, Sims and Jones found that 26 percent of the probationers whose probation terms were revoked had been guilty of violations such as failing a single drug test. The researchers believe this strategy is overly punitive—anybody who has tried to quit smoking is aware of the difficulties of breaking an addiction.[74]

Drug Courts: Rehab Revisited

Few would have predicted that judges would be at the forefront of a revolution in American corrections. After all, as we saw in the last chapter, the bench has lost much of its sentencing power to legislatures and juries over the past few decades. Nobody, however, was in a better position to observe one of the unintended side effects of the "war on drugs": courts overwhelmed by petty offenders with addiction problems who were caught in a closed loop of arrest, imprisonment, release, rearrest, and imprisonment again. In this *Criminal Justice in Action* feature, we will see how frustration with this "revolving door" syndrome inspired judges to create a new form of community corrections, reinserting the ideals of rehabilitation into the criminal justice system in the process.

A New Kind of Court

Vincent Sweeting was trying to explain to Miami-Dade (Florida) Circuit Judge Jeffrey Rosinek why he had just tested positive for cocaine. "I broke up with my girlfriend," Sweeting said. "I was emotionally hurt." Judge Rosinek was not impressed. "If it's not perfect next time, you're going to jail," he announced.[75] Sweeting's lawyer did not object because the lawyer was not in the building. Judge Rosinek and Sweeting were in the Miami-Dade Drug Court, where the normal rules of the courtroom do not apply. Drug courts reject the adversarial model and focus instead on a single problem—the addiction of the defendant. These programs offer certain offenders the choice to participate in a relatively new form of community-based therapy rather than proceed with more traditional sentencing. If they choose to attend drug court, they place themselves in the hands of a judge who will enforce a mixture of treatment and sanctions in an attempt to cure their addiction. On successful completion of the program, offenders are usually rewarded by having all charges against them dropped.

The connection between crime and drugs, which we will explore in more detail in Chapter 16, has been well established; one recent study of arrestees in New York City found

that 81 percent tested positive for at least one illegal substance.[76] Drug courts operate on the assumption that by reducing a criminal addict's drug use, his or her drug-fueled criminal activity will also be reduced. Another potential benefit is that the process may divert nonviolent offenders from the nation's overcrowded corrections facilities.

Judge Gerald Weatherington of the Florida Eleventh Judicial Circuit founded the nation's first drug court in Miami in 1989. Since then, consistently low recidivism rates by those who complete the programs have spurred interest in drug courts to impressive levels. Today, nearly two thousand such courts have been established nationwide, many by judges following in Judge Weatherington's footsteps. "Drug courts are literally becoming a way of doing business," notes C. West Huddleston III, director of the National Drug Court Institute.[77]

The Treatment Program

Though the specific procedures of drug courts vary widely from jurisdiction to jurisdiction, most of them follow a general pattern. Either after arrest or on conviction, the offender is given the option of entering a drug court pro-

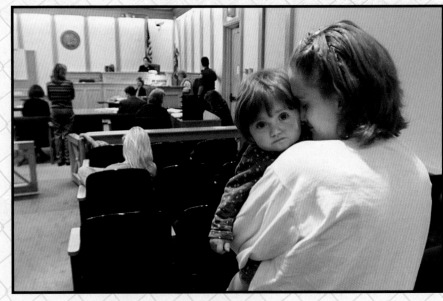

Amanda Nagel, who had been arrested on a methamphetamine charge, hugs her nine-month-old daughter, Alexis, while waiting to appear before a judge in the Placer County (California) Drug Court.

AP Photo/Rich Pedroncelli

gram or continuing through the standard courtroom procedure. Once the offender decides to pursue addiction treatment, she or he enters into a kind of "contract" with the drug court judge. This agreement stipulates that the offender will follow a rehabilitation program designed and enforced by the judge and abide by any punishments that the judge may find necessary. The program almost always includes frequent court appearances, random drug tests to ensure total abstinence, and counseling, in addition to any other requirements the court may impose. In Delaware, for example, drug court participants must obtain steady employment, find a stable home, and acquire a high school general equivalency degree (if applicable).[78]

Not all offenders are eligible for drug court programs. Prosecutors generally screen out anybody with a record of violent crimes, and many jurisdictions refuse to admit anyone charged with or convicted of drug dealing rather than drug use. Furthermore, though the underlying crime does not necessarily have to involve drugs, most drug courts require that the offender prove that he or she is an addict in order to participate.[79]

Judicial Activism

A truly remarkable aspect of drug courts is the role played by the judge. Instead of concentrating on the offender's innocence or guilt, a drug court judge focuses on his or her treatment and rehabilitation. The judge abandons any semblance of neutrality—so crucial in other courtroom settings—and acts solely in the participant's best interest. Furthermore, in contrast to the heavily regulated procedure of criminal trials, few hard-and-fast rules govern a drug court judge's actions. Each one has the freedom to shape the treatment program to the individual needs of the offender.[80]

In practice, many drug court judges adopt a "carrot and stick" approach, offering encouragement and praise when the offender keeps on-program and warnings and punishments when he or she does not. One drug court judge even compared the process to "training a pet."[81] The judges have some very heavy "sticks" with which to threaten participants. Failure to comply with the conditions of the program may lead to increased supervision (such as intensive probation or electronic monitoring), extra counseling, or, in drastic cases, short periods of incarceration.[82] If the participant fails to comply in a meaningful way with the program, the judge can revoke the "contract" and return the offender to the prosecutor. Given this incentive system, it is not surprising that those defendants facing more serious charges and longer prison terms are more likely to successfully complete a drug court program.[83]

Too Good to Be True?

Numerous studies attest to the success of drug courts, at least in terms of recidivism rates. Researchers from the Center for Court Innovation recently compared reconviction rates of participants in six New York drug court programs with those of offenders with similar backgrounds who did not participate in such programs. The recidivism rate of the participants was 29 percent lower than that of their nonparticipating counterparts.[84] A larger study conducted by the National Institute of Justice produced almost identical results.[85] The administration of President George W. Bush was impressed enough to offer more than $60 million in federal funds for drug court development in 2004. By 2005, 165 DUI (driving under the influence) courts had been created to apply similar treatment strategies to the problem of drunk driving.

Not everyone, however, is convinced that drug courts are fulfilling their promise. Recall that one of the goals of community corrections is to divert offenders from incarceration. Eric J. Miller, an associate law professor at Western New England College, points out that, because of the screening process, most offenders offered the chance to enter drug courts would not have been sentenced to prison terms anyway. Virtually all of them would have received probation or, at most, a brief jail term (certainly shorter than drug court programs, which can last as long as three years).[86] Consequently, although drug courts may benefit individuals by helping them conquer their addictions, there is no evidence that the programs have actually reduced the prison population. Thus, the goal of diversion is better served by innovations such as the Drug Treatment Alternative-to-Prison program in Brooklyn, New York, which *only* accepts offenders who would otherwise find themselves behind bars.[87]

Making Sense of Drug Courts

1 How might drug courts reduce the prison population even though most of their participants are nonviolent drug offenders who would otherwise have been sentenced to probation?

2 Review the concept of net widening on page 410. In what ways do drug courts have a net-widening effect of their own?

3 The United States Supreme Court has held that the government may not pass a law that criminalizes drug addiction. Make the argument that drug courts are inconsistent with this ruling.

Chapter Summary

1 Explain the justifications for community-based corrections programs. The first justification involves reintegration of the offender into society. Reintegration restores family ties, encourages employment and education, and secures a place for the offender in the routine functioning of society. The other justification involves diversion; by diverting criminals to alternative modes of punishment, further overcrowding of jail and prison facilities can be avoided, as can the costs of incarcerating the offenders.

2 Indicate when probation started to fall out of favor, and explain why. When both criminal justice practitioners and the public held the rehabilitative model in favor, probation was generally considered a valuable aspect of this treatment. Since about the 1950s and more seriously since the mid-1970s, retributive goals have become more important, and probation has fallen out of favor in some criminal justice circles. Nonetheless, two-thirds of those involved in the American corrections system are on probation at any given time.

3 Explain several alternative sentencing arrangements that combine probation with incarceration. In addition to a suspended sentence, which is in fact a judicial reprieve, there are three general types of sentencing arrangements: (a) split sentence probation, in which the judge specifies a certain time in jail or prison followed by a certain time on probation; (b) shock incarceration, in which a judge sentences an offender to be incarcerated, but allows that person to petition the court to be released on probation; and (c) intermittent incarceration, in which an offender spends a certain amount of time each week in jail or in a halfway house or another government institution.

4 Specify the conditions under which an offender is most likely to be denied probation. The offender (a) has been convicted of multiple charges, (b) was on probation or parole when arrested, (c) has two or more prior convictions, (d) is addicted to narcotics, (e) seriously injured the victim of the crime, or (f) used a weapon while committing the crime.

5 Describe the three general categories of conditions placed on a probationer. (a) Standard conditions, such as requiring that the probationer notify the agency of a change of address, not leave the jurisdiction without permission, and remain employed; (b) punitive conditions, such as restitution, community service, and home confinement; and (c) treatment conditions, such as required drug or alcohol treatment.

6 Explain why probation officers' work has become more dangerous. One reason is that probation is increasingly offered to felons, even those who have committed violent crimes. Additionally, because there are more guns on the streets, a probationer is more likely to be armed.

7 Explain the three stages of probation revocation. (a) The preliminary hearing, which usually takes place before a judge, during which the facts of the probation violation are presented; (b) the revocation hearing, during which the claims of the violation are presented as well as any refutation by the probationer; and (c) revocation sentencing, during which a judge decides what to do with the probationer convicted of violating the terms of probation.

8 List the five sentencing options for a judge besides imprisonment and probation. (a) Fines, (b) community service, (c) restitution, (d) forfeiture, and (e) pretrial diversion programs.

9 Contrast day reporting centers with intensive supervision probation. In a day reporting center, the offender is allowed to remain in the community, but must spend all or part of each day at the reporting center. While at the center, offenders meet with probation officers, submit to drug tests, and attend counseling and education programs. In contrast, with intensive supervision probation (ISP), more restrictions are imposed, and there is more face-to-face contact between offenders and probation officers. ISP may also include electronic surveillance.

10 List the three levels of home monitoring. (a) Curfew, which requires that the offender be at home during specified hours; (b) home detention, which requires that the offender be at home except for education, employment, and counseling; and (c) home incarceration, which requires that the offender be at home at all times except for medical emergencies.

STORIES FROM THE STREET

Go to the *Stories from the Street* feature at **www.cjinaction.com** to hear Larry Gaines tell insightful stories related to this chapter and his experiences in the field.

Key Terms

authority 399
day reporting centers 405
✓ diversion 391
✓ electronic monitoring 408
✓ forfeiture 405

✓ home confinement 408
intensive supervision probation (ISP) 407
✓ intermediate sanctions 404
judicial reprieve 394

pretrial diversion program 405
✓ probation 393
✓ reintegration 391
shock incarceration 408

✓ split sentence probation 395
✓ suspended sentence 395
✓ technical violation 400
widen the net 410

& same as probation

Questions for Critical Analysis

1 What is the major reason that probationers account for nearly two-thirds of all adults in the American corrections system?

2 Why have many "tough on crime" politicians embraced community corrections?

3 Why did the Supreme Court rule against indefinite reprieves?

4 Why can law enforcement agents search a probationer's home without a warrant or probable cause?

5 Why don't probationers have all constitutionally defined due process rights during revocation procedures?

6 Is the small number of probation officers a reason that recidivism is high?

7 What happens to property that is forfeited by a convicted criminal?

8 What is the purpose of day reporting centers?

9 "Home confinement is only for rich criminals." Comment.

10 What does the term *widening the net* mean, and why is it important today?

Test Preparation Online

Criminal JusticeNow

Go to **www.cjinaction.com** and click on *Criminal JusticeNow* for access to this powerful online study tool. You will get a *personalized study plan* based on your responses to a diagnostic pretest. Once you have mastered the material with the help of interactive learning tools, video clips with questions, an integrated e-book, and more, you can take a posttest to confirm you are ready to move on to the next chapter.

Book Companion Web Site

At the book companion Web site (**www.cjinaction.com**), you will find many resources in addition to *Criminal JusticeNow* to aid you in studying for your exams. For example, under *Chapter Resources*, you will find the *Chapter Outline, Chapter Summary, Flashcards, Glossary, Learning Objectives, Lecture Presentations, Concept Builder, Essay Questions,* and a *Tutorial Chapter Quiz.* You can also test yourself with interactive *Online Reviews* of each chapter section. Check out the *Web Links* to access the Web sites mentioned in the text, as well as many others. You can also access recent perspectives by clicking on *CJ in the News* and *Terrorism Update* under *Course Resources.*

Suggested Readings

Festervan, Earlene, *Survival Guide for New Probation Officers,* Lanham, MD: American Correctional Association, 2000. This no-nonsense guide for new—or potential—probation officers is sponsored by the American Correctional Association. It addresses the pressing issues in a profession that has undergone dramatic changes over the past few decades: the ethics of probation, maintaining a relationship with clients, officer safety, court work, and the perils of paperwork. With the number of Americans on probation and parole surpassing four million, the demand for officers in this field is growing; this publication offers a "leg up" into the world of probation.

Jacobson, Michael, *Downsizing Prisons: How to Reduce Crime and End Mass Incarceration,* New York: New York University Press, 2005. As the title of his book advertises, Jacobson boldly claims to have the blueprint for meeting two of the criminal justice system's most challenging goals: reducing crime and easing the inmate population explosion. If anyone can offer valuable insight into these subjects, it is Jacobson, who served as commissioner of the New York City Departments of Correction and Probation in the mid-1990s. During that time, crime rates in the city dropped dramatically, as did the number of inmates in city jails. Arguing that the United States cannot afford the continuing rise in its general prison population, Jacobson describes how some of the strategies that worked in New York City could work on a nationwide basis as well. These tactics include the repeal of mandatory minimum sentencing and "three-strikes" laws, less stringent probation and parole conditions (and thus fewer revocations), and more drug treatment programs for low-level offenders.

Notes

1. Bureau of Justice Statistics, *Probation and Parole in the United States, 2003* (Washington, D.C.: U.S. Department of Justice, July 2004), Table 4, page 4.
2. *Ibid.,* 1.
3. Michael Tonry, *Sentencing Matters* (New York: Oxford Press, 1996), 28.
4. Todd Clear and Anthony Braga, "Community Corrections," in *Crime,* ed. James Q. Wilson and Joan Petersilia (San Francisco: ICS Press, 1995), 444.
5. Corrections Task Force of the President's Commission on Law Enforcement and Administration of Justice (1967).

6. Paul H. Hahn, *Emerging Criminal Justice: Three Pillars for a Proactive Justice System* (Thousand Oaks, CA: Sage Publications, 1998), 106–108.

7. *Probation and Parole in the United States, 2003*, 1.

8. Press Release, Families Against Mandatory Minimums, "Historic Michigan 'Smart on Crime' Sentencing Reforms Save Taxpayers $41 Million in 2003" (February 24, 2003).

9. *Ibid.*

10. Fox Butterfield, "With Cash Tight, States Reassess Long Jail Terms," *New York Times* (November 11, 2003), A1.

11. Daniel Abrahamson and Jaffer Abbasin, "SACPA's Sophomore Year: The Second Annual Review of Proposition 36 in California's Criminal Courts," *California Criminal Defense Practice Reporter* (October 2003), 517.

12. *Ibid.*, 524.

13. Paul W. Keve, *Crime Control and Justice in America* (Chicago: American Library Association, 1995), 183.

14. Andrew R. Klein, *Alternative Sentencing, Intermediate Sanctions and Probation*, 2d ed. (Cincinnati: Anderson Publishing Co., 1997), 72.

15. 242 U.S. 27 (1916).

16. Joan Petersilia, "Probation in the United States," *Perspectives* (Spring 1998), 32–33.

17. Barry A. Krisberg and James F. Austin, "The Unmet Promise of Alternatives to Incarceration," in John Kaplan, Jerome H. Skolnick, and Malcolm M. Feeley, *Criminal Justice*, 5th ed. (Westbury, NY: The Foundation Press, 1991), 537.

18. Bureau of Justice Statistics, *State Court Sentencing of Convicted Felons, 2002* (Washington, D.C.: U.S. Department of Justice, May 2005), Table 3.2.

19. Joan Petersilia and Susan Turner, *Prison versus Probation in California: Implications for Crime and Offender Recidivism* (Santa Monica, CA: Rand Corporation, 1986).

20. 705 So.2d 172 (La. 1997).

21. Neil P. Cohen and James J. Gobert, *The Law of Probation and Parole* (Colorado Springs, CO: Shepard's/McGraw-Hill, 1983), Section 5.01, 183–184; Section 5.03, 191–192.

22. 534 U.S. 112 (2001).

23. *Ibid.*, 113.

24. Bureau of Justice Statistics, *Substance Abuse and Treatment for Adults on Probation, 1995* (Washington, D.C.: U.S. Department of Justice, March 1998), 11.

25. Carl B. Klockars, Jr., "A Theory of Probation Supervision," *Journal of Criminal Law, Criminology, and Police Science* 63 (1972), 550–557.

26. *Ibid.*, 551.

27. Hahn, 116–118.

28. "Most Probationers Have Contact with Probation Officers," *Crime and Justice International* (March 1998), 23.

29. Shawn E. Small, "Arming Probation Officers: Enhancing Public Confidence and Officer Safety," *Federal Probation* (December 2001), 25.

30. National Institute of Corrections, *New Approaches to Staff Safety* (Washington, D.C.: U.S. Department of Justice, March 2003), 16.

31. Nicholas Riccardi, "Probation Dept. Divided over Rule Prohibiting Guns," *Los Angeles Times* (January 2, 1999), B1.

32. Bureau of Justice Statistics, *Special Report, Federal Offenders under Community Supervisions, 1987–1996* (Washington, D.C.: U.S. Department of Justice, August 1998), Table 6, page 5.

33. *Probation and Parole in the United States, 2003*, Table 4, page 4.

34. "Put the Prison Bed Idea to Rest," *Dallas Morning News* (January 19, 2001), A28.

35. 483 U.S. 868, 874 (1987).

36. 389 U.S. 128 (1967).

37. *Morrissey v. Brewer*, 408 U.S. 471 (1972); and *Gagnon v. Scarpelli*, 411 U.S. 778 (1973).

38. 465 U.S. 420 (1984).

39. Quoted in John J. DiIulio, Jr., "Reinventing Parole and Probation," *Brookings Review* 5 (Spring 1997), 43.

40. Charles Linder and Robert L. Bonn, "Probation Officer Victimization and Fieldwork Practices: Results of a National Study," *Federal Probation* (June 1996), 16.

41. Joan Petersilia, "Community Corrections," in *Crime: Public Policies for Crime Control*, ed. James Q. Wilson and Joan Petersilia (Oakland, CA: ICS Press, 2002) 483–508.

42. Patrick Langan and M. Cunniff, "Recidivism of Felons on Probation, 1986–89," *Special Report* (Washington, D.C.: U.S. Department of Justice, 1992).

43. Petersilia and Turner, vii.

44. Cassia Spohn and David Holleran, "The Effect of Imprisonment on Recidivism Rates of Felony Offenders: A Focus on Drug Offenders," *Criminology* (May 1, 2002), 329–357.

45. William J. Bennett, John J. DiIulio, and John P. Walters, *Body Count: Moral Poverty and How to Win America's War against Crime and Drugs* (New York: Simon & Schuster, 1996), 105.

46. *Ibid.*

47. James M. Byrne and Linda M. Kelly, *Restructuring Probation as an Intermediate Sanction: An Evaluation of the Massachusetts Intensive Probation Supervision Program* (Washington, D.C.: National Institute of Justice, 1989).

48. Todd R. Clear and George F. Cole, *American Corrections*, 4th ed. (Belmont, CA: Wadsworth Publishing Co., 1997), 179.

49. John P. Storm, "What United States Probation Officers Do," *Federal Probation* (March 1997), 13.

50. Robert M. Carter and Leslie T. Wilkins, "Caseloads: Some Conceptual Models," in *Probation, Parole, and Community Corrections*, ed. Robert M. Carter and Leslie T. Wilkins (New York: Wiley & Sons, 1976), 391–401.

51. Norval Morris and Michael Tonry, *Between Prison and Probation: Intermediate Punishments in a Rational Sentencing System* (Oxford, UK: Oxford University Press, 1990).

52. 18 U.S.C. Sections 1961–1968.

53. 516 U.S. 442 (1996).

54. Kathy Jefcoats, "Criminal Justice Centers: Day Reporting Site Opens," *Atlanta Journal-Constitution* (April 7, 2005), 1.

55. Adele Harrell, Ojmarrh Mitchell, Alex Hirst, Douglas Marlowe, and Jeffrey Merrill, "Breaking the Cycle of Drugs and Crime: Findings from the Birmingham BTC Demonstration," *Criminology and Public Policy* (March 2002), 189–216.

56. Modern State Drug Court Legislation Committee, *Model State Drug Court Legislation: Model Drug Offender Accountability and Treatment Act* (Alexandria, VA: National Drug Court Institute, May 2004), 42.

57. Vada Mossavat, "Alternative to Area Jails Considered," *Charleston Gazette & Daily Mail* (May 21, 2002), P1A.

58. Betsy Fulton, Edward J. Latessa, Amy Stichman, and Lawrence F. Travis, "The State of ISP: Research and Policy Implications," *Federal Probation* (December 1997), 65.

59. Benjamin Steiner, "Treatment Retention: A Theory of Post-Release Supervision for the Substance Abusing Offender," *Federal Probation* (December 2004), 24.

60. Kate Coscarelli, "A Model Program for Model Prisoners," *(Newark, New Jersey) Star Ledger* (February 24, 2004), 25.

61. U.S. Department of Heath and Human Services, "Youth Violence: A Report of the Surgeon General," at **http://www.surgeongeneral.gov/library/youthviolence/chapter5/sec6.html**.

62. Richard Willing, "U.S. Prisons to End Boot Camp Program," *USA Today* (February 2, 2005), 1A.

63. Margaret M. Conway, ed., "2002 Electronic Monitoring Survey," in *Journal of Offender Monitoring* (Kingston, NJ: Civic Research Institute, 2002).

64. Josh Kurtz, "New Growth in a Captive Market," *New York Times* (December 31, 1989), 12.

65. Edna Erez, Peter R. Ibarra, and Norman A. Lurie, "Electronic Monitoring of Domestic Violence Cases—A Study of Two Bilateral Programs," *Federal Probation* (June 2004), 15–20.

66. Russell Carlisle, "Electronic Monitoring as an Alternative Sentencing Tool," *Georgia State Bar Journal* 24 (1988), 132.

67. Joan Petersilia, *Expanding Options for Criminal Sentencing* (Santa Monica, CA: Rand Corporation, 1987).

68. Terry Baumer and Robert Mendelsohn, "Electronically Monitored Home Confinement: Does It Work?" in *Smart Sentencing: The Emergence of Intermediate Sanctions,* ed. James M. Byrne, Arthur Lurigio, and Joan Petersilia (Newbury Park, CA: Sage, 1992).

69. Joseph B. Vaughn, "Planning for Change: The Use of Electronic Monitoring as a Correctional Alternative," in *Intermediate Punishments: Intensive Supervision, Home Confinement, and Electronic Surveillance,* ed. Belinda R. McCarthy (Monsey, NY: Criminal Justice Press, 1987), 158.

70. Terry Baumer and Robert Mendelsohn, *The Electronic Monitoring of Nonviolent Convicted Felons* (Washington, D.C.: National Institute of Justice, 1992).

71. Michael Tonry and Mary Lynch, "Intermediate Sanctions," in *Crime and Justice,* vol. 20, ed. Michael Tonry (Chicago: University of Chicago Press, 1996), 99.

72. Dennis Palumbo, Mary Clifford, and Zoann K. Snyder-Joy, "From Net Widening to Intermediate Sanctions: The Transformation of Alternatives to Incarceration from Benevolence to Malevolence," in *Smart Sentencing: The Emergence of Intermediate Sanctions,* ed. James M. Byrne, Arthur Lurigio, and Joan Petersilia (Newbury Park, CA: Sage, 1992), 231.

73. Keve, 207.

74. Barbara Sims and Mark Jones, "Predicting Success or Failure on Probation: Factors Associated with Felony Probation Outcomes," *Crime & Delinquency* (July 1997), 314–327.

75. Jay Weaver, "Drug Court Wins Top Praise," *Miami Herald* (February 24, 2005), B1.

76. Charles J. Hynes, "Prosecution Backs Alternatives to Prison for Drug Addicts," *Criminal Justice* (Summer 2004), 29, citing *Arrestee Drug Abuse Monitoring Program Annualized Site Report for Manhattan, New York.*

77. Quoted in "Drug Courts Rapidly Increasing Nationwide," *Providence Journal Bulletin* (May 31, 2005), B1.

78. Del. Code Ann. Tit. 11, Section 4332 (2001).

79. Peggy Fulton Hora, William G. Schma, and John T. A. Rosenthal, "Therapeutic Jurisprudence and the Drug Treatment Court Movement: Revolutionizing the Criminal Justice System's Response to Drug Abuse and Crime in America," *Notre Dame Law Review* (1999), 507–508.

80. James L. Nolan, Jr., *Reinventing Justice: The American Drug Court Movement* (Princeton, NJ: Princeton University Press, 2001), 141.

81. Stephen C. Cooper, "The Carrot and the Stick: How Effective Sanctions and Incentives Succeed in Overcoming Addiction," *Michigan Bar Journal* (January 2003), 23.

82. Lynne M. Brennan, "Drug Courts: A New Beginning for Non-Violent Drug-Addicted Offenders—An End to Cruel and Unusual Punishment," *Hamline Law Review* (1998), 380.

83. Michael Rempel, Dana Fox-Kralstein, and Amanda Cissner, "Drug Courts: An Effective Treatment Alternative," *Criminal Justice* (Summer 2004), 35.

84. Ibid., 34–38.

85. John Roman, Wendy Townsend, and Avinash Singh Bhati, *Recidivism Rates for Drug Court Graduates: Nationally Based Estimates, Final Report* (Washington, D.C.: Urban Institute and Caliber Associates, July 2003), 27–42.

86. Eric J. Miller, "Embracing Addiction: Drug Courts and the False Promise of Judicial Interventionism," *Ohio State Law Journal* (2004), 1479–1576.

87. Hynes, 29–33.

CHAPTER THIRTEEN

Prisons and Jails

Cook County Department of Correction
Division IX Maximum Security Dormito

Chapter outline

- A Short History of American Prisons
- The Prison Population Bomb
- The Role of Prisons in Society
- Types of Prisons
- Prison Administration
- The Emergence of Private Prisons
- Jails
- The Consequences of Our High Rates of Incarceration
- Criminal Justice in Action—The End of the Line: Supermax Prisons

Chapter objectives

After reading this chapter, you should be able to:

1. Contrast the Pennsylvania and the New York penitentiary theories of the 1800s.
2. List the factors that have caused the prison population to grow dramatically in the last several decades.
3. Explain the three general models of prisons.
4. List and briefly explain the four types of prisons.
5. Contrast formal with informal prison management systems.
6. List the reasons why private prisons can often be run more cheaply than public ones.
7. Summarize the distinction between jails and prisons, and indicate the importance of jails in the American correctional system.
8. Explain how jails are administered.
9. Indicate the difference between traditional jail design and new-generation jail design.
10. Indicate some of the consequences of our high rates of incarceration.

Criminal JusticeNow

Optimize your study time and master key chapter concepts with *Criminal JusticeNow*, an online study tool that provides you with a *personalized study plan*. Check out the "Test Preparation Online" section at the end of the chapter for additional information.

The Largest Corrections System in the World

Sir Henry Alfred McCardie, the famed

English jurist, once said, "Trying a man is easy, as easy as falling off a log, compared with deciding what to do with him when he has been found guilty." In the American criminal justice system, to a certain extent, the decision has been simplified: many of the guilty go behind bars. The United States has the largest corrections system in the world. One out of every 138 Americans is in a federal or state prison or in a local jail. By 2004, the number of inmates in American prisons and jails had surpassed 2.2 million. The United States now locks up six times as many of its citizens as Canada does, and seven times as many as most European democracies. In fact, recent years have seen this country move past Russia to lay claim to the title of "the world's leading incarcerator."

For the most part, this high rate of imprisonment is a product of the past thirty years. From the 1920s until 1970, America's incarceration rate remained fairly stable at 110 per 100,000. Over the past three and a half decades, the jail and prison population of the United States increased by nearly 700 percent. There is, it must be noted, some evidence that the growth rate of the nation's incarcerated population is beginning to slow down. The average annual growth of the nation's prison

Inside Tutwiler Women's Prison in Wetumpka, Alabama, a handful of the more than 2.2 million inmates incarcerated in the United States pass time.

population dropped from 6.7 percent in 1995 to 1.9 percent in 2004; the 1.1 percent growth rate in 2001 was the lowest in three decades. Some corrections experts believe that this slowed growth is a result of the decline in crime rates in the 1990s: with fewer people committing crimes, fewer people will go to prison. Others point to a number of new state laws under which those convicted of drug possession are sent to treatment programs rather than prison or jail, a trend we discussed in the previous chapter.

A few years of slower growth cannot reverse a decades-long trend, however. The American corrections system remains a massive institution.[1] Throughout the course of this textbook, we have discussed many of the social and political factors that help explain the prison population "boom" of the past thirty years.

In this chapter and the next, we turn our attention to the incarceration system itself. This chapter focuses on the history and organizational structures of prisons (which generally hold those who have committed serious felonies for long periods of time) and jails (which generally hold those who have committed less serious felonies and misdemeanors, and those awaiting trial, for short periods of time). Though the two terms are often used interchangeably, they refer to two very different institutions, each with its own responsibilities and its own set of seemingly unsolvable problems.

420

A SHORT HISTORY OF AMERICAN PRISONS

Today, we view prisons as instruments of punishment; the loss of freedom imposed on inmates is society's retribution for the crimes they have committed. This has not always been the function of incarceration. The prisons of eighteenth-century England, known as "bridewells" after London's Bridewell Palace, actually had little to do with punishment. These facilities were mainly used to hold debtors or those awaiting trial, execution, or banishment from the community. (In many ways, as shall be made clear, these facilities resemble the modern jail.) English courts generally imposed one of two sanctions on convicted felons: they turned them loose, or they executed them.[2] To be sure, most felons were released, pardoned either by the court or the clergy after receiving a whipping or a branding.

The correctional system in the American colonies differed very little from that of their motherland. If anything, colonial administrators were more likely to use corporal punishment than their English counterparts, and the death penalty was not uncommon in early America. The one dissenter was William Penn, who adopted the "Great Law" in Pennsylvania in 1682. Based on Quaker ideals of humanity and rehabilitation, this criminal code forbade the use of torture and mutilation as forms of punishment; instead, felons were ordered to pay restitution of property or goods to their victims. If the felons did not have sufficient property to make restitution, they were placed in a prison, which was primarily a "workhouse."[3] The death penalty was still allowed under the "Great Law," but only in cases of premeditated murder. Penn proved to be an exception, however, and the path to reform was much slower in the colonies than in England.

Walnut Street Prison: The First Penitentiary

On Penn's death in 1718, the "Great Law" was rescinded in favor of a harsher criminal code, similar to those of the other colonies. At the time of the American Revolution, however, the Quakers were instrumental in the first broad swing of the incarceration pendulum from punishment to rehabilitation. In 1776, Pennsylvania passed legislation ordering that offenders be reformed through treatment and discipline rather than simply beaten or executed.[4] Several states, including Massachusetts and New York, quickly followed Pennsylvania's example.

Pennsylvania continued its reformist ways by opening the country's first **penitentiary** in a wing of Philadelphia's Walnut Street Jail in 1790. The penitentiary operated on the assumption that silence and labor provided the best hope of rehabilitating the criminal spirit. Remaining silent would force the prisoners to think about their crimes, and eventually the weight of conscience would lead to repentance. At the same time, enforced labor would attack the problem of idleness—regarded as the main cause of crime by penologists of the time.[5] Consequently, inmates at Walnut Street were isolated from one another in solitary rooms and kept busy with constant menial chores.

Eventually, the penitentiary at Walnut Street succumbed to the same problems that continue to plague institutions of confinement: overcrowding and excessive costs. As an influx of inmates forced more than one person to be housed in a room, silence became a nearly impossible condition. By the early 1800s, officials could not find work for all of the convicts, so many were left idle.

Penitentiary
An early form of correctional facility that emphasized separating inmates from society and from each other so that they would have an environment in which to reflect on their wrongdoing and ponder their reformation.

The Great Penitentiary Rivalry: Pennsylvania versus New York

The apparent lack of success at Walnut Street did little to dampen enthusiasm for the penitentiary concept. Throughout the first half of the nineteenth century, a number of states reacted to prison overcrowding by constructing new penitentiaries. Each state tended to have its own peculiar twist on the roles of silence and labor, and two such

FIGURE 13.1

The Eastern Penitentiary

The Eastern Penitentiary opened in 1829 with the controversial goal of changing the behavior of inmates instead of merely punishing them. An important component of this goal was the layout of the facility. As you can see, the Eastern Penitentiary was designed in the form of a "wagon wheel," known today as the radial style. The back-to-back cells in each "spoke" of the wheel faced outward from the center to limit contact between inmates. About three hundred prisons worldwide have been built based on this design.

systems—those of Pennsylvania and New York—emerged to shape the debate over the most effective way to run a prison.

The Pennsylvania System After the failure of Walnut Street, Pennsylvania constructed two new prisons: the Western Penitentiary near Pittsburgh (opened in 1826) and the Eastern Penitentiary in Cherry Hill, near Philadelphia (1829). The Pennsylvania system took the concept of silence as a virtue to new extremes. Based on the idea of **separate confinement,** these penitentiaries were constructed with back-to-back cells facing both outward and inward. (See Figure 13.1 for the layout of the original Eastern Penitentiary.) To spare each inmate from the corrupting influence of the others, prisoners worked, slept, and ate alone in their cells. Their only contact with other human beings came in the form of religious instruction from a visiting clergyman or prison official.[6]

The New York System If Pennsylvania's prisons were designed to transform wrongdoers into honest citizens, those in New York focused on obedience. When New York's Newgate Prison (built in 1791) became overcrowded, the state authorized the construction of Auburn Prison, which opened in 1816. Auburn initially operated under many of the same assumptions that guided the penitentiary at Walnut Street. Solitary confinement, however, seemed to lead to an inordinate amount of sickness, insanity, and even suicide among inmates, and it was abandoned in 1822. Nine years later, Elam Lynds became warden at Auburn and instilled the **congregate system,** also known as the Auburn system. Like Pennsylvania's separate confinement system, the congregate system was based on silence and labor. At Auburn, however, inmates worked and ate together, with silence enforced by prison guards.[7]

If either state can be said to have "won" the debate, it was New York. The Auburn system proved more popular, and a majority of the new prisons built during the first half of the nineteenth century followed New York's lead, though mainly for economic reasons rather than philosophical ones. New York's penitentiaries were cheaper to build because they did not require so much space. Furthermore, inmates in New York were employed in workshops, whereas those in Pennsylvania toiled alone in their cells. Consequently, the Auburn system was better positioned to exploit prison labor in the early years of widespread factory production.

The Reformers and the Progressives

The Auburn system did not go unchallenged. In the 1870s, a group of reformers argued that fixed sentences, imposed silence, and isolation did nothing to improve prisoners; they proposed that penal institutions should offer the promise of early release as a prime tool for rehabilitation. Echoing the views of the Quakers a century earlier, the reformers presented an ideology that would heavily influence American corrections for the next century.

This "new penology" was put into practice at New York's Elmira Reformatory in 1876. At Elmira, good behavior was rewarded by early release and misbehavior was punished with extended time under a three-grade system of classification. On entering the institution, the offender was assigned a grade of 2. If the inmate followed the rules and completed work and school assignments, after six months he was moved up to grade 1, the necessary grade for release. If, however, the inmate broke institutional rules, he was lowered to grade 3. A grade 3 inmate needed to behave properly for three months before he could return to grade 2 and begin to work back toward grade 1 and eventual release.[8]

Separate Confinement
A nineteenth-century penitentiary system developed in Pennsylvania in which inmates were kept separate from each other at all times, with daily activities taking place in individual cells.

Congregate System
A nineteenth-century penitentiary system developed in New York in which inmates were kept in separate cells during the night but worked together in the daytime under a code of enforced silence.

Although other penal institutions did not adopt the Elmira model, its theories came into prominence in the first two decades of the twentieth century thanks to the Progressive movement in criminal justice. The Progressives—linked to the positivist school of criminology discussed in Chapter 2—believed that criminal behavior was caused by social, economic, and biological factors and, therefore, a corrections system should have a goal of treatment, not punishment. Consequently, they trumpeted a **medical model** for prisons, which held that institutions should offer a variety of programs and therapies to cure inmates of their "ills," whatever the root causes. The Progressives were greatly responsible for the spread of indeterminate sentences (Chapter 11), probation (Chapter 12), community sanctions (Chapter 12), and parole (Chapter 14) in the first half of the twentieth century.

Inmates of Elmira State Prison in New York attend a presentation at the prison auditorium. Zebulon Brockway, the superintendent at Elmira, believed that criminals were an "inferior class" of human being and should be treated as society's defectives. Thus, mental exercises designed to improve the inmates' minds were part of the prison routine at Elmira. To what extent do you believe that treatment should be a part of the incarceration of criminals?

The Reassertion of Punishment

Even though the Progressives had a great influence on the corrections system as a whole, their theories had little impact on the prisons themselves, many of which had been constructed in the nineteenth century and were impervious to change. More important, prison administrators usually did not agree with the Progressives and their followers, so the day-to-day lives of most inmates varied little from the congregate system of Auburn Prison.

Academic attitudes began to shift toward the prison administrators in the mid-1960s. Then, in 1974, the publication of Robert Martinson's famous "What Works?" essay provided critics of the medical model with statistical evidence that rehabilitation efforts did nothing to lower recidivism rates.[9] This is not to say that Martinson's findings went unchallenged. A number of rebuttals arguing that rehabilitative programs could be successful appeared immediately after the publication of "What Works?"[10] In fact, Martinson himself retracted most of his claims in a little-noticed article published five years after his initial report.[11] Attempts by Martinson and others to "set the record straight" went largely unnoticed, however, as a sharp rise in crime in the early 1970s led many criminologists and politicians to champion "get tough" measures to deal with criminals they now considered "incurable." By the end of the 1980s, the legislative, judicial, and administrative strategies that we have discussed throughout this text had positioned the United States for an explosion in inmate populations and prison construction unparalleled in the nation's history.

THE PRISON POPULATION BOMB

Medical Model
A model of corrections in which the psychological and biological roots of an inmate's criminal behavior are identified and treated.

The number of Americans in prison or jail has almost tripled since 1985 and is continuing to rise, though at a slower rate, as mentioned earlier (see Figure 13.2 on p. 424). These numbers are not only dramatic, but also, say some observers, inexplicable, given the

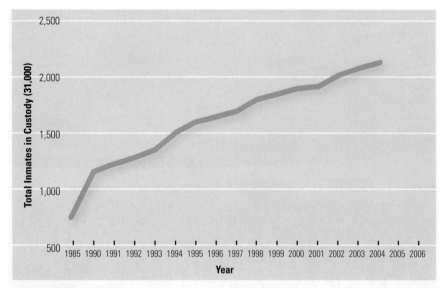

FIGURE 13.2

The Inmate Population of the United States

The total number of inmates in custody in the United States has risen from 744,208 in 1985 to 2,267,787 in 2004.

Source: Bureau of Justice Statistics, *Prisoners in 2004* (Washington, D.C.: U.S. Department of Justice, October 2005).

The **Federal Bureau of Prisons** is the largest incarceration system in the United States. Find its Web site by clicking on *Web Links* under *Chapter Resources* at **www.cjinaction.com**.

overall crime picture in the United States. In the 1990s, violent and property crime rates dropped; yet the number of inmates continued to rise. According to accepted theory, rising incarceration rates should be the result of a rise in crime, leaving one expert to comment that America's prison population is "defying gravity."[12] (See the feature *CJ in Focus—Myth versus Reality: Does Placing Criminals in Prison Reduce Crime?*)

Factors in Prison Population Growth

Much of the growth in the number of Americans behind bars can be attributed to the enhancement and stricter enforcement of the nation's drug laws. There are more people in prison and jail for drug offenses today than there were for all offenses in the early 1970s.[13] In 1980, about 19,000 drug offenders were incarcerated in state prisons and 4,800 drug offenders were in federal prisons. Twenty-one years later, state prisons contained more than 246,000 inmates who had been arrested for drug offenses,[14] and by 2004, the number of drug offenders in federal prisons had risen to nearly 78,000, representing about 55 percent of all inmates in those facilities.[15]

Other reasons for the growth in incarcerated populations include:

- *Increased probability of incarceration.* Simply stated, the chance of someone who is arrested going to prison today is much greater than it was twenty years ago. Most of this growth took place in the 1980s, when the likelihood of incarceration in a state prison after arrest increased fivefold for drug offenses, threefold for weapons offenses, and twofold for crimes such as sexual assault, burglary, auto theft, and larceny.[16] For federal crimes, the proportion of defendants being sent to prison rose from 54 percent in 1988 to 75 percent in 2002.[17]

- *Inmates serving more time for each crime.* After the Sentencing Reform Act of 1984, the length of time served by federal convicts for their crimes rose significantly. As noted in Chapter 11, in the fifteen years after the law went into effect, the average time served by inmates in federal prisons rose to fifty months—an increase of more than 50 percent.[18] For drug offenders, the average amount of time served in federal prison escalated from 39.3 months to 62.4 months, while the average prison term for weapons offenses grew from 32.4 months to 64.5 months.[19] State sentencing reform statutes and "truth-in-sentencing" laws have had similar consequences. In the thirty-two states that require their inmates to serve at least 85 percent of their sentences, for example, violent offenders are expected to spend an average of fifteen months more in prison than violent offenders in states without such laws.[20]

- *Federal prison growth.* Thanks in part to federal sentencing policy, the federal prison system is now the largest in the country with more than 180,000 inmates. In fact, since 1995 the federal prison population has risen at a rate more than double that of state prisons (90 percent to 26 percent).[21] Besides the increase in federal drug offenders already mentioned, this growth can be attributed to efforts by Presidents Bill Clinton and George W. Bush to

Does Placing Criminals in Prison Reduce Crime?

Violent crime rates in the United States have been stable or declining in recent years. At the same time, as Figure 13.3 shows, the rate at which Americans have been imprisoned has climbed precipitously. The correlation between these two trends has become the subject of much discussion among crime experts.

THE MYTH

A popular view of incarceration is that "a thug in jail can't shoot your sister." Obviously, a prison inmate is incapable of doing any further harm to the community. By extension, then, as the number of criminals behind bars increases, the crime rate should drop accordingly.

THE REALITY

Numerous studies have shown that this is not always the case. Between 1985 and 1995, the prison population in the United States almost doubled, yet the number of all major violent crimes also increased. A study released in 2000 by the Sentencing Project, a research group in Washington, found that states that increased the number of prison inmates the most in the 1990s actually had less reduction in crime than those states with below-average increases in incarceration over the same time period. Over the past decade, the rate of imprisonment has risen much more slowly in New York than in California, yet California's crime rate has been significantly higher than New York's during that time period. Such statistics may indicate that other factors (particularly the social factors discussed in Chapter 2) play a more significant role in crime rates than the number of criminals who are incapacitated.

Allen J. Beck, a statistician with the Bureau of Justice Statistics, thinks that sentencing policies may explain the apparent lack of positive correlation between rates of imprisonment and crime in general. He points out that even though the number of arrests has been dropping in the United States since 1993, the chances of imprisonment and lengthy prison terms have increased, thanks to mandatory minimum, truth-in-sentencing, and habitual offender laws.

Few observers would suggest that imprisonment rates have *no* effect on crime rates. Indeed, many think that efforts to keep more offenders in prison for longer periods of time are directly responsible for dropping crime rates. A number of criminologists, however, caution that the relationship between the prison population and crime rates is not fully understood and that public policymakers should not make laws on the assumption that more prisoners equals less crime.

FOR CRITICAL ANALYSIS

Some criminologists believe that certain inmates become hard-core criminals after being exposed to prison culture and, therefore, commit more crimes after release than they would have if they had never been incarcerated in the first place. If this theory is correct, what would be the implications for the relationship between crime rates and incarceration rates?

FIGURE 13.3

Comparing Crime Rates and Incarceration Rates

Source: Federal Bureau of Investigation and Bureau of Justice Statistics.

The Ouachita River Correctional Unit in Malvern, Arkansas, opened in August 2003. The facility's 361 beds were filled immediately, but state corrections officials say more prison construction is needed to accommodate an inmate population that grows by fifteen to twenty people a day.

As the name implies, **PrisonSucks.com** is highly critical of what it calls the "crime control industry." Find this Web site by clicking on *Web Links* under *Chapter Resources* at **www.cjinaction.com**.

federalize gun possession crimes: from 1995 to 2001, the number of inmates sent to federal prisons for such crimes jumped by 68 percent.[22] Over that same time period, immigration law offenders increased by 133 percent; by 2003, they represented more than 10 percent of all federal inmates,[23] a situation we will discuss in more detail in Chapter 17.

• *Rising incarceration rates of women.* In 1981, 14,000 women were prisoners in federal and state institutions; by 2004, the number had grown to over 104,000. Women still account for only 7 percent of all prisoners nationwide, but their rates of imprisonment are growing twice as rapidly as those of men.[24]

The Prison Construction Boom

The escalation in the prisoner population has brought with it an increased demand for new prisons. In 1980, the U.S. Bureau of Prisons had a budget of $330 million and operated forty-four prisons. Today, its budget is nearly $5 billion and there are 103 federal prisons. Over the past twenty-five years, the number of state prisons has increased from fewer than six hundred to more than one thousand.[25] In 1971, total corrections construction spending was $2.3 billion; today, it is over $60 billion.[26] These costs have pushed corrections budgets to unprecedented levels. Eight states spend in excess of $1 billion each year on corrections-related services.[27] Indeed, for many states, the single largest item in their budgets is correctional expenditures. In the absence of politically unpopular tax increases, legislators are thereby forced to find another revenue source to pay for the new prisons. Thus, the opportunity cost of prison construction can be great—every dollar that goes to build a prison is a dollar that cannot be used to fund education programs, health care, and other social programs.

Legislative efforts have kept prison construction well financed. The 1994 Crime Bill allocated $10 billion in grants for the construction of new incarceration facilities through 2000.[28] Forty-five states are required by law and/or court order to keep crowding in prisons and jails below a certain level; therefore, as the number of inmates continues to increase, state corrections agencies are forced to build new facilities or find alternative forms of punishment such as the community-based sanctions discussed in Chapter 12.

"To assert in any case that a man must be absolutely cut off from society because he is absolutely evil amounts to saying that society is absolutely good, and no one in his right mind will believe this today."
—Albert Camus, French author (1961)

THE ROLE OF PRISONS IN SOCIETY

The demands placed on penal institutions are hardly limited to providing economic benefits for the communities in which they are located. As University of Connecticut sociologist Charles Logan once noted,

Americans expect prisons to "correct the incorrigible, rehabilitate the wretched . . . restrain the dangerous, and punish the wicked."[29] Basically, prisons exist to make society a safer place. Whether this is to be achieved through retribution, deterrence, incapacitation, or rehabilitation—the four justifications of corrections introduced in Chapter 11—depends on the operating philosophy of the individual penal institution.

Three general models of prisons have emerged to describe the different schools of thought behind prison organization:

- The *custodial model* is based on the assumption that prisoners are incarcerated for reasons of incapacitation, deterrence, and retribution. All decisions within the prison—such as what form of recreation to provide the inmates—are made with an eye toward security and discipline, and the daily routine of the inmates is highly controlled. The custodial model has dominated the most restrictive prisons in the United States since the 1930s.

- The *rehabilitation model* stresses the ideals of individualized treatment that we discussed in Chapter 11. Security concerns are often secondary to the well-being of the individual inmate, and a number of treatment programs are offered to aid prisoners in changing their criminal and antisocial behavior. The rehabilitation model came into prominence during the 1950s and enjoyed widespread popularity until it began to lose general acceptance in the 1970s and 1980s.

- In the *reintegration model*, the correctional institution serves as a training ground for the inmate to prepare for existence in the community. Prisons that have adopted this model give the prisoners more responsibility during incarceration and offer halfway houses and work programs (both discussed in Chapter 14) to help them reintegrate into society. This model is becoming more influential, as corrections officials react to problems such as prison overcrowding.[30]

Competing views of the prison's role in society are at odds with these three "ideal" perspectives. Professor Alfred Blumstein argues that prisons create new criminals, especially with regard to nonviolent drug offenders. Not only do these nonviolent felons become socialized to the criminal lifestyle while in prison, but the stigma of incarceration makes it more difficult for them to obtain employment on release. Their only means of sustenance "on the outside" is to apply the criminal methods they learned in prison.[31] A study by criminal justice professors Cassia Spohn of the University of Nebraska and David Holleran of East Tennessee State University found that convicted drug offenders who were sentenced to prison were 2.2 times more likely to be incarcerated for a new offense than those sentenced to probation.[32]

TYPES OF PRISONS

Prison administrators have long been aware of the need to separate different kinds of offenders. In federal prisons, this led to a system with six levels based on the security needs of the inmates, from level 1 facilities with the lowest amount of security to level 6 with the harshest security measures. (Many states also use the six-level system, an example of which can be seen in Figure 13.4 on the next page.) To simplify matters, most observers refer to correctional facilities as being one of three levels—minimum, medium, or maximum. A fourth level—the supermaximum-security prison, known as the "supermax"—is relatively rare and extremely controversial due to its hyperharsh methods of punishing and controlling the most dangerous prisoners. (See the feature *Criminal Justice in Action—The End of the Line: Supermax Prisons* at the end of the chapter.)

FIGURE 13.4

Security Levels in Virginia

The security levels of correctional facilities in Virginia are graded from level 1 to level 6. As you can see, level 1 facilities are for those inmates who pose the least amount of risk to fellow inmates, staff members, and themselves. Level 6 facilities are for those who are considered the most dangerous by the Virginia Department of Corrections.

Level	Restrictions
Level 1-Low	No Murder I or II, Robbery, Sex-Related crime, Kidnapping/abduction, Felonious Assault (current or prior), Flight/Escape, Carjacking, Malicious Wounding, No Escape Risk, No Disruptive Behavior
Level 1-High	No Murder I or II, Sex offense, Kidnap/Abduction, Escape history. No Disruptive Behavior for at least past 24 months.
Level 2	For initial assignment only. No escape history for past 5 years. No disruptive behavior for at least past 24 months prior to transfer to any less secure facility.
Level 3	Single, Multiple and Life + sentences. Must have served 20 consecutive years on sentence. No disruptive behavior for past 24 months for a transfer to any less secure facility.
Level 4	Single, Multiple and Life + sentences. No disruptive behavior for past 24 months for a transfer to any less secure facility.
Level 5	Same as level 4.
Level 6	Single, Multiple and Life + sentences. PROFILE OF INMATES: Disruptive, Assaultive, Severe Behavior Problems; Predatory-type behavior; Escape Risks; No disruptive behavior for past 24 months for a transfer to any less secure facility.

Source: Virginia Department of Corrections.

Maximum-Security Prisons

In a certain sense, the classification of prisoners today owes a debt to the three-grade system developed at the Elmira Penitentiary, discussed earlier in the chapter. Once wrongdoers enter a corrections facility, they are constantly graded on behavior. Those who serve "good time," as we have seen, are often rewarded with early release. Those who compile extensive misconduct records are usually housed, along with violent and repeat offenders, in **maximum-security prisons.** The names of these institutions—Folsom, San Quentin, Sing Sing, Attica—conjure up foreboding images of concrete and steel jungles, with good reason.

Maximum-security prisons are designed with full attention to security and surveillance. In these institutions, inmates' lives are programmed in a militaristic fashion to keep them from escaping or from harming themselves or the prison staff. About a quarter of the prisons in the United States are classified as maximum security, and these institutions house about 16 percent of the country's prisoners.

The Design Maximum-security prisons tend to be large—holding more than a thousand inmates—and they have similar features. The entire operation is usually surrounded by concrete walls that stand twenty to thirty feet high and have also been sunk deep into the ground to deter tunnel escapes; fences reinforced with razor-ribbon barbed wire that can be electrically charged may supplement or replace these barriers. The prison walls are studded with watchtowers, from which guards armed with shotguns and rifles survey the movement of prisoners below. The designs of these facilities, though similar, are not uniform. Though correctional facilities built using the radial design pioneered by the Eastern State Penitentiary still exist, several other designs have

Maximum-Security Prison
A correctional institution designed and organized to control and discipline dangerous felons, as well as prevent escape, with intense supervision, cement walls, and electronic, barbed wire fences.

become prominent in more recently constructed institutions. For an overview of these designs, including the radial design, see Figure 13.5.

Inmates live in cells, most of them with similar dimensions to those found in the I-Max maximum-security prison for women in Topeka, Kansas: eight feet by fourteen feet with cinder block walls.[33] The space contains bunks, a toilet, a sink, and possibly a cabinet or closet. Cells are located in rows of *cell blocks*, each of which forms its own security unit, set off by a series of gates and bars. A maximum-security institution is essentially a collection of numerous cell blocks, each constituting its own prison within a prison.

FIGURE 13.5

Prison Designs

The Radial Design

The radial design has been utilized since the early nineteenth century. The "wagon wheel"–like form of the structure was created with the dual goals of separation and control. Inmates are separated from each other in their cells on the "spokes" of the wheel, and prison officials can control the activities of the inmates from the control center in the "hub" of the wheel.

The Courtyard Style

In the courtyard-style prison, a courtyard replaces the transportation function of the "pole" in the telephone-pole prison. The prison buildings form a square around the courtyard, and to get from one part of the facility to another, the inmates go across the courtyard. In a number of these facilities, the recreational area, mess hall, and school are located in the courtyard.

The Telephone-Pole Design

The main feature of the telephone-pole design is a long central corridor that serves as a means for transporting inmates from one part of the facility to another. Branching off from this main corridor are the functional areas of the facility: housing, food services, workshops, treatment program rooms, etc. Prison officials survey the entire facility from the central "pole" and can shut off the various "arms" when necessary for security reasons. The majority of maximum-security prisons in the United States were constructed using this design blueprint.

The Campus Style

Some of the newer minimum-security prisons have adopted the campus style, a style that had previously been used in correctional facilities for women and juveniles. Like a college campus, housing units are scattered among functional units such as the dining room, recreation area, and treatment centers. The benefit of the campus style is that individual buildings can be used for different functions, making the operation more flexible. Due to concerns that the campus style provides less security than the other designs discussed, it is used for the most part only for medium- and minimum-security prisons.

Source: Text adapted from Todd R. Clear and George F. Cole, *American Corrections*, 4th ed. (Belmont, CA: Wadsworth Publishing Company, 1997), 255–256.

This photograph shows the stark and austere quality of the Condemned Inmates Housing Adjustment Center (death row) at California's San Quentin Prison. Maximum-security prisons such as San Quentin are designed with one overriding concern in mind: control of inmates. Examine the photo and identify the various features of this area of San Quentin that show the facility's emphasis on security.

Inmates' lives are dominated by security measures. Whenever they move from one area of the prison to another, they do so in groups and under the watchful eye of armed correctional guards. Television surveillance cameras may be used to monitor their every move, even when sleeping, showering, or using the toilet. They are subject to frequent pat-downs or strip searches at the guards' discretion. Constant "head counts" assure that every inmate is where he or she should be. Tower guards—many of whom have orders to shoot to kill in the case of a disturbance or escape attempt—constantly look down on the inmates as they move around outdoor areas of the facility.

Technology has added significantly to the power an institution holds over the individual prisoner. Walk-through metal detectors and X-ray body scanners can detect weapons or other contraband hidden on the body of an inmate. Ground-penetrating radar allows the correctional staff to search courtyards for buried items. Prison officials expect that within the next decade, electronic eye scans and noninvasive skin patches will be available to determine whether a prisoner has been using drugs.

Aging Foundations The advancing age of many maximum-security prisons is a major concern today. Given their size and the expense involved in their construction, these institutions were built to last, and many have achieved that goal. Fifty-four prisons constructed before 1900 are still in use. Illinois's Menard Correctional Center, for example, began operating in 1878 and experiences constant difficulties with outdated electrical and plumbing systems.

Besides being inconvenient for staff and inmates, aging penal institutions increase the possibility of the most dangerous of all security situations: the escape. Six prisoners were able to tunnel out of the century-old State Correctional Institution near Pittsburgh, Pennsylvania, by drilling through the prison wall with a hydraulic jack. Though the escapees were eventually recaptured, state officials immediately budgeted $135.5 million for a new maximum-security prison that would have better sight lines from guard towers and enable corrections officers to exact more control over the inmates.[34]

Medium- and Minimum-Security Prisons

Medium-security prisons hold about 35 percent of the prison population and minimum-security prisons 49 percent. Inmates at **medium-security prisons** have for the most part committed less serious crimes than those housed in maximum-security prisons and are not considered high risks for escaping or causing harm. Consequently, medium-security institutions are not designed for control to the same extent as maximum-security prisons and have a more relaxed atmosphere. These facilities also offer more educational and treatment programs and allow for more contact between inmates. Medium-security prisons are rarely walled, relying instead on high fences. Prisoners have more freedom of movement within the structures, and the levels of surveillance are much lower. Living quarters are less restrictive as well—many of the newer medium-security prisons provide dormitory housing.

Medium-Security Prison
A correctional institution that houses less dangerous inmates and therefore uses less restrictive measures to avoid violence and escapes.

A **minimum-security prison** seems at first glance to be more like a college campus than an incarceration facility. Most of the inmates at these institutions are first-time offenders, nonviolent, and well behaved and include a high percentage of white-collar criminals. Indeed, inmates are often transferred to minimum-security prisons as a reward for good behavior in other facilities. Therefore, security measures are lax compared even to medium-security prisons. Unlike medium-security institutions, minimum-security prisons do not have armed guards. Prisoners are allowed amenities such as television sets and computers in their rooms, they enjoy freedom of movement, and they are allowed off prison grounds for educational or employment purposes to a much greater extent than those held in more restrictive facilities. (Danbury Women's Prison—where television personality Martha Stewart spent more than five months in 2004 and 2005—has a law library, a track, and a gymnasium that is used for Dancersize, Pilates, and yoga classes.) Some critics have likened minimum-security prisons to "country clubs," but in the corrections system, everything is relative. A minimum-security prison may seem like a vacation spot when compared to the horrors of Sing Sing, but it still represents a restriction of personal freedom and separates the inmate from the outside world.

Security measures—including television surveillance, pat-downs, and the constant attention of correctional officers in towers (pictured above)—dominate the lives of inmates in maximum-security prisons. How do guard towers contribute to the overall security of a prison facility? What might be some of the limitations of the guard tower as a security device?

PRISON ADMINISTRATION

The security level of the institution generally determines the specific methods by which a prison is managed. There are, however, general goals of prison administration, summarized by Charles Logan as follows:

> The mission of a prison is to keep prisoners—to keep them in, keep them safe, keep them in line, keep them healthy, and keep them busy—and to do it with fairness, without undue suffering and as efficiently as possible.[35]

Considering the environment of a prison—an enclosed world inhabited by people who are generally violent and angry and would rather be anywhere else—Logan's mission statement may be highly Utopian. A prison staff must supervise the daily routines of hundreds or thousands of inmates, a duty that includes providing them with meals, education, vocational programs, and different forms of leisure. The smooth operation of this supervision is made more difficult—if not, at times, impossible—by budgetary restrictions, overcrowding, and continual inmate turnover.

The implications of mismanagement are severe. While studying a series of prison riots, sociologists Bert Useem and Peter Kimball found that breakdowns in managerial control commonly preceded such acts of mass violence.[36] During the 1970s, for example, conditions in the State Penitentiary in New Mexico deteriorated significantly; inmates who had become well organized and comfortable with their daily routines increasingly became the targets of harsh treatment from the prison staff, while at the same time a reduction in structured activities left prison life "painfully boring."[37] The result, in 1980, was one of the most violent prison riots in the nation's history. (To learn how new monitoring systems are helping prison administrators manage and control prison populations, see the feature *CJ and Technology—The Electronic Head Count* on the following page.)

Minimum-Security Prison
A correctional institution designed to allow inmates, most of whom pose low security risks, a great deal of freedom of movement and contact with the outside world.

CJ AND TECHNOLOGY

The Electronic Head Count

In Chapter 12, we saw how monitoring devices have changed the face of community corrections. Similar technology, though not as widespread, is beginning to have an equally dramatic effect on prison management. Called TSI PRISM, the monitoring equipment acts as a high-tech head count: inmates wear bracelets, while corrections officers wear small, pagerlike devices. Guided by a series of radio transmitters and receivers, the system is able to pinpoint the location of inmates and guards within twenty feet. Every two seconds, radio signals "search out" where each inmate and guard is, and relay this information to a central computer. On-screen, the inmate shows up as a yellow dot and the corrections officer as a blue dot on a grid of the prison. Administrators can quickly determine which inmates and officers are represented by each dot, and all movements are stored in a database for future reference, if necessary. "It completely revolutionizes a prison because you know where everyone is—not approximately but exactly where they are," says an official at the National Institute of Justice.

In 2002, a new maximum-security juvenile prison in Michigan was outfitted with PRISM. The hope is that PRISM will end the "guessing games" that inevitably follow charges of assault—either physical or sexual—by one juvenile against another. With its tracing abilities, the system will allow corrections officials to immediately determine whether the accuser is telling the truth. "It's almost like having a videotape" of the attack, noted one official, "because you can track who was there." The bracelet is also tamper resistant, so if an inmate tries to remove it or damage it in any way, an alarm is immediately sent to the central computer system.

IN THE FUTURE

Electronic monitoring experts predict that systems such as PRISM will soon be "customized" to fit the needs of any specific prison population. So, for example, if officials are aware that two rival

AP Photo/Fred Greaves

Vincent Campos (above), a correctional officer at Calipatria State Prison in California, monitors inmates using the TSI PRISM system. Inmates wear electronic wrist bands so that their movements can be tracked at all times.

gangs exist, PRISM can be programmed to trigger an alarm when individual gang members come in close contact with each other. The bracelets could also be linked to satellite tracking systems, helping locate escaped convicts who manage to get outside the boundaries of the prison's radio transmitters.

For more information on electronic monitoring of inmates and other CJ technologies, click on Crime and Technology *under* Book Resources *at* **www.cjinaction.com**.

Formal Prison Management

In some respects, the management structure of a prison is similar to that of a police department, as discussed in Chapter 5. Both systems rely on a hierarchical (top-down) *chain of command* to increase personal responsibility. Both assign different employees to specific tasks, though prison managers have much more direct control over their subordinates than do police managers. The main difference is that police departments have a *continuity of purpose* that is sometimes lacking in prison organizations. All members of a police force are, at least theoretically, working to reduce crime and apprehend criminals. In a prison, this continuity is less evident. An employee in the prison laundry service and one who works in the visiting center have little in common. In some cases, employees may even have cross-purposes: a prison guard may want to punish an inmate, while a counselor in the treatment center may want to rehabilitate her or him.

Consequently, a strong hierarchy is crucial for any prison management team that hopes to meet Charles Logan's expectations. As Figure 13.6 shows, the **warden** (also

Warden
The prison official who is ultimately responsible for the organization and performance of a correctional facility.

Warden

Assistant Warden: Custody	Assistant Warden: Management	Assistant Warden: Programs	Assistant Warden: Industry and Agriculture
1. Security	1. Budget	1. Treatment Programs	1. Prison Work Programs
2. Guard Forces	2. Accounting	2. Medical Services	2. Prison Farm Programs
3. Training	3. Purchasing	3. Mental Health	
4. Safety	4. Warehouse	4. Recreation	
5. Prisoner Discipline	5. Commissary	5. Classification	
6. Investigations	6. Food Service	6. Volunteers	
7. Visiting Schedules	7. Clothing and Laundry	7. Religious Services	
	8. Grounds Maintenance		

FIGURE 13.6
Organizational Chart for a Typical Correctional Facility

known as a superintendent) is ultimately responsible for the operation of a prison. He or she oversees deputy wardens, who in turn manage the various organizational lines of the institution. The custodial employees, who deal directly with the inmates and make up more than half of a prison's staff, operate under a militaristic hierarchy, with a line of command passing from the deputy warden to the captain to the corrections officer.

Informal Prison Management

Within the confines of the management structure, the personal philosophy of an administrator plays a significant role in prison management. Tara Gray and Jon'a F. Meyer of New Mexico State University illustrate this point by contrasting two influential prison administrators of the 1960s and 1970s.[38] George Beto, director of corrections in Texas for ten years, espoused the *control model* of administration, and Tom Murton, an Arkansas warden depicted in the 1980 film *Brubaker*, preferred the *participation model*.

Beto felt that by forcing inmates to abide by stringent prison rules, he was preparing them to follow the rules of society when they were released. Consequently, Texas prisons under Beto were tightly controlled. Infractions such as talking in a loud voice were summarily—and, some said, cruelly—punished. Because Texas had only about half as many prison guards per convict as other states, Beto made widespread use of a practice in which selected inmates known as "building tenders" were given the status of guards or overseers in return for certain privileges. Building tenders had been employed in the South for nearly fifty years, and in many cases these inmate guards were more brutal than their state-employed counterparts.

In contrast, Murton felt that

> Inmates cannot learn to dance by having their legs tied together. The only way to prepare them for life in a democracy is to expose them to democracy while they are incarcerated.[39]

In keeping with this philosophy, Murton allowed the inmates to govern some aspects of their prison lives. For example, he established inmate councils whose leaders were elected by the prisoners themselves. These councils were responsible for controlling inmate violence and making decisions such as who would be allowed to leave the prison on furlough. One criminologist, after visiting Murton's prison, stated that his theories would lead to a "renaissance in corrections."

The prediction failed to come true, not necessarily because Murton's ideas were invalid, but because the philosophy was rejected. Contemporary management practices frown on giving such power to inmates. As for Beto's system, building tenders were discontinued following the Texas prison reform lawsuit *Ruiz v. Estelle* (1977).[40] The fact that neither Beto's inmate guards nor Murton's inmate councils have survived suggests that prison management is an inherently conservative field. Most wardens have their hands full simply trying to run the prison, without attempting to "change the system"—even if the courts would let them.

THE EMERGENCE OF PRIVATE PRISONS

In addition to all the other pressures placed on wardens and other prison administrators, they must operate within a budget assigned to them by an overseeing governmental agency. Today, the great majority of all prisons are under the control of federal and state governments, but government-run prisons have not always been the rule. In the nineteenth century, some correctional facilities were not under the control of the state. In fact, the entire Texas prison system was privately operated from 1872 to the late 1880s. For most of the twentieth century, however, **private prisons,** or prisons run by private business firms to make a profit, could not be found in the United States.

That is certainly not the case today. With corrections exhibiting all appearances of, in the words of one observer, "a recession-proof industry," the American business community eagerly entered the market in the late 1980s and 1990s.[41] Fourteen private corrections firms operate more than two hundred facilities across the United States. The two largest corrections companies, Corrections Corporation of America (CCA) and The GEO Group, Inc., have contracted to supervise more than 60,000 inmates. In 1997, the Federal Bureau of Prisons awarded the first contract paying a private company to operate one of its prisons—the GEO Group received $88 million to run the Taft Correctional Institution in Taft, California. Today, the GEO Group operates twenty-one federal corrections facilities. By 2004, private penal institutions housed almost 100,000 inmates, representing 6.6 percent of all inmates in the state and federal corrections systems.[42]

Why Privatize?

It would be a mistake to automatically assume that private prisons are less expensive to run than public ones.[43] The incentive to privatize is, however, primarily financial.

Cost Efficiency In the 1980s and 1990s, a number of states and cities saved operating costs by transferring government-run services such as garbage collection and road maintenance to the private sector. Similarly, private prisons can often be run more cheaply and efficiently than public ones for the following reasons:

- *Labor costs.* The wages of public employees account for nearly two-thirds of a prison's operating expenses. Although private corrections firms pay base salaries comparable to those enjoyed by public prison employees, their nonunionized staffs receive lower levels of overtime payments, workers' compensation claims, sick leave, and health-care insurance.

- *Competitive bidding.* Because of the profit motive, private corrections firms have an incentive to buy goods and services at the lowest possible price.

- *Less red tape.* Private corrections firms are not part of the government bureaucracy and therefore do not have to contend with the massive amount of paperwork that can clog government organizations.[44]

When the Arizona Department of Corrections compared three private prisons with fifteen public ones in the state, researchers found that the cost per day of incarcer-

Penny Lucero
Warden

Courtesy Penny Lucero

Penny Lucero

As warden of the New Mexico Women's Correctional Facility, I have executive oversight of the management and operation of the nation's first privately managed, multi-custody state prison. I became interested in corrections as a result of the employment opportunities made available with the state. When I entered the job market, I had received my undergraduate degree in psychology and completed work toward my graduate degree from New Mexico State University.

My corrections career began in 1981 with the New Mexico Department of Corrections, where I held a series of progressively more responsible positions, including training officer, ACA accreditation manager, and chief classification officer. In 1985, I became the first woman to be promoted to the rank of assistant warden at a male prison in New Mexico. In order to expand my experience to include juvenile corrections, I took the position of deputy superintendent at the Youth Diagnostic Center and New Mexico Girls' School.

Although I left corrections for a while to manage my own business, I realized that my true career had become corrections. Being my own boss had its "pros," but the "cons" had won my heart; I wanted to dedicate my energy, expertise, and leadership to corrections. Fortunately, Corrections Corporation of America was opening the new women's prison in Grants, and I was quickly recruited as a member of the management team. Joining this team of experienced corrections professionals is what I claim to be the catalyst that propelled me to the highest executive level of institutional leadership. The management team included three well-established professionals: two retired wardens from the New Mexico system and one nationally recognized warden of a female prison. All three became friends and mentors, always encouraging me to excel.

Working with adult female offenders and for a private company were both new experiences for me. The opening of the New Mexico Women's Correctional Facility was the first time the state had provided a purpose-built staffed and programmed facility specifically for female offenders. As program director, I had the opportunity to develop a wide array of state-of-the-art programs and services that would help prepare the women for a successful return to their communities.

As warden, I consider my major responsibilities to be maintaining a healthful, positive, safe, and mutually respectful environment for staff and inmates; establishing a working relationship with outside communities in order to assist with public education about offenders and the mutual benefit of working with them on release; participating in civic and professional organizations and encouraging the staff to do so; ensuring that the New Mexico Women's Correctional Facility meets established national correctional standards; and staying current on new management, program, and technology trends that can assist me in maintaining the standards of excellence established at the facility.

Prisons have changed dramatically over the past two decades. No longer "closed" communities where "outsiders" are unwelcome, they have become an extension of society, welcoming daily interaction with local citizens, elected officials, researchers, student interns, and volunteers in order to create a more normalized environment. Equally important is the commitment to assist offenders in preparing for a lawful return to society. To that end, correctional administrators are eager to recruit and retain creative, thoughtful, and industrious employees for rewarding careers in a lifetime of service to society.

Go to the Careers in Criminal Justice Interactive CD *for more profiles in the field of criminal justice.*

---

ating one person was $40.88 at a private facility and $45.85 at a public institution, a savings of 10.8 percent for private institutions.[45] A similar survey in Florida revealed not only that housing inmates in private prisons reduced the daily price tag by 10.5 percent, but that construction costs were 24 percent lower for private prisons than public ones.[46]

Overcrowding and Outsourcing Private prisons are becoming increasingly attractive to state governments faced with the competing pressures of tight budgets and overcrowded corrections facilities. Lacking the funds to alleviate overcrowding by building more prisons, state officials are turning to the private institutions for help. Often, the private prison is out of state, which leads to the "outsourcing" of inmates. In 2004, for example, Arizona shipped 1,200 prisoners to CCA facilities in Oklahoma because it had no room for them in its own corrections system.[47]

Quality of Service Executives at corrections firms claim that because their contracts can be canceled for poor performance, private prisons have a greater incentive to provide higher-quality service than their public counterparts. At least one study, conducted by Charles Logan, supports this contention. Logan found that, according to statistical data and staff surveys, a private women's prison in New Mexico outperformed a state prison and a federal prison in a number of areas such as security, safety, living conditions, and management.[48] One reason a private prison might be expected to perform better than a public one is that the latter enjoys some immunity from civil liability suits. In other words, an aggrieved inmate can more easily sue a private prison in a civil court.[49]

The Argument against Private Prisons

Significantly, in Logan's study mentioned above, the inmates themselves gave the private prison lower scores than did the staff members. Opponents of private prisons worry that, despite the assurances of corporate executives, private corrections companies will "cut corners" to save costs, denying inmates important security guarantees in the process.

Financial Concerns These criticisms find some support in the anecdotal evidence. U.S. District Judge Sam Bell of the Northern District of Ohio, for example, ordered CCA to devise a classification system to divert dangerous offenders after two inmates were killed and eleven others injured in a spate of stabbings at the company's medium-security facility in Youngstown, Ohio.[50] In 2004, Arizona recalled some of its inmates from Oklahoma after a racially motivated riot at a CCA facility in Watonga during which hundreds of prisoners attacked each other with fire extinguishers and baseball bats. Later that year, a female inmate at a private prison in Nashville, Tennessee, died from a violent head wound—an incident that led to a local police investigation of four CCA employees.[51] Research conducted by Curtis R. Blakely of the University of South Alabama and Vic W. Bumphus of the University of Tennessee at Chattanooga found that a prisoner in a private corrections facility was twice as likely to be assaulted by a fellow inmate as a prisoner in a public one.[52]

Furthermore, some observers note, if a private corrections firm receives a fee from the state for each inmate housed in its facility, does that not give management an incentive to increase the amount of time each prisoner serves? Though government parole boards make the final decision on an inmate's release from private prisons, the company could manipulate misconduct and good behavior reports to maximize time served and, by extension, higher profits.[53]

Philosophical Concerns Other critics see private prisons as inherently unjust, even if they do save tax dollars or provide enhanced services. These observers believe that corrections is not simply another industry, like garbage collection or road maintenance, and that only the government has the authority to punish. In the words of University of Pennsylvania criminologist John DiIulio:

> It is precisely because corrections involves the deprivation of liberty, precisely because it involves the legally sanctioned exercise of coercion by some citizens over others, that it must remain wholly within public hands.[54]

The Future of Privatization in the Corrections Industry

Critics of private correctional facilities still hope to slow, and eventually stop, their growth. They believe that private prisons are constitutional contradictions and offer Article I of the U.S. Constitution as support. That passage states that "legislative powers herein granted shall be vested in a Congress of the United States." These powers include the authority to define penal codes and to determine the punishments that will be handed out for breaking federal law. Therefore, a strict interpretation of the Constitution appears to prohibit the passing of this authority from the federal government to a private company.[55]

If the growth of private prisons and jails does slow, however, it appears that the motivation will be economic, not constitutional. For most of the past two decades, the primary clients for the private corrections industry have been state governments. In fact, six states (Alaska, Hawaii, Montana, New Mexico, Oklahoma, and Wyoming) house more than a quarter of their inmates in private facilities.[56] In the past few years, however, state corrections officials have been more reluctant to expend scarce resources on private prison services. In fact, since 2000 very few states have negotiated new contracts with private corrections firms, and several, including California, North Carolina, and Arkansas, have reduced their reliance on private incarceration.[57]

Although these developments have caused financial hardship for the private corrections industry (especially CCA, which almost went bankrupt in the early 2000s), it has found "a source of salvation" in the federal government.[58] As noted earlier, tougher drug and immigration laws have increased the number of federal prisoners dramatically, and the federal Bureau of Prisons has turned to private prisons to expand its capacity. New federal contracts valued at more than $100 million seem likely to ensure the health of the private prison industry for the foreseeable future.[59]

An unidentified prisoner is rushed to the emergency room in Cushing, Oklahoma, after a March 2005 riot at the Cimarron Correction Facility left one inmate dead and thirteen others injured. About fifty gang members at the prison, operated privately by the Corrections Corporation of America, had attacked each other with bats and other gym equipment. What are some of the arguments against sending inmates to a privately run prison?

JAILS

Although prisons and prison issues dominate the public discourse on corrections, there is an argument to be made that jails are the dominant penal institutions in the United States. In general, a prison is a facility designed to house people convicted of felonies for lengthy periods of time, while a **jail** is authorized to hold pretrial detainees and offenders who have committed misdemeanors. On any given day, about 714,000 inmates are in jail in this country, and approximately 7 million Americans spend at least a day in jail each year. Furthermore, the jail population has increased by more than 40 percent since 1995.[60] Yet jail funding is often the lowest priority for the tight budgets of local governments, leading to severe overcrowding and other dismal conditions.

Many observers see this negligence as having far-reaching consequences for criminal justice. Jail is often the first contact that citizens have with the corrections system. It is at this point that treatment and counseling have the best chance to deter future criminal behavior.[61] By failing to take advantage of this opportunity, says Professor Frank Zimring of the Earl Warren Legal Institute at the University of California at Berkeley, corrections officials have created a situation in which "today's jail folk are tomorrow's prisoners."[62]

Jail
A facility, usually operated by county government, used to hold persons awaiting trial or those who have been found guilty of misdemeanors.

AP Photo/The Brazosport Facts

Local sheriffs' deputies strike an inmate of the Brazoria County Detention Center in Clute, Texas, with a baton. After viewing the video from which this scene was taken, the FBI began an investigation into possible civil rights violations at the jail. Guard-on-inmate violence is only one of the problems plaguing the nation's jails, others being inmate-on-inmate violence, poor living conditions, and inadequate health-care facilities. Yet jail problems do not receive nearly the same attention as prison issues. Why might this be the case?

The Function of Jails

Until the eighteenth century, all penal institutions existed primarily to hold those charged with a crime until their trial. Although jails still serve this purpose, they have evolved to play a number of different roles in the corrections system. According to the Department of Justice, these roles include the following:

• Holding those convicted of misdemeanors.

• Receiving individuals pending arraignment and holding them while awaiting trial (if they cannot post bail), conviction, or sentencing.

• Temporarily detaining juveniles pending transfer to juvenile authorities.

• Holding the mentally ill pending transfer to health facilities.

• Detaining those who have violated conditions of probation or parole and those who have "jumped" bail.

• Housing inmates awaiting transfer to federal or state prisons.

• Operating community-based corrections programs such as home confinement and electronic monitoring.

Increasingly, jails are also called on to handle the overflow from saturated state and federal prisons. In Texas, for example, corrections officials were forced to rent a thousand county jail cells to house inmates for whom no space was available in state prisons.[63]

According to sociologist John Irwin, the unofficial purpose of the jail is to manage society's "rabble," so-called because

> [they] are not well integrated into conventional society, they are not members of conventional social organizations, they have few ties to conventional social networks, and they are carriers of unconventional values and beliefs.[64]

In Irwin's opinion, "rabble" who act violently are arrested and sent to prison. The jail is reserved for merely offensive rabble, whose primary threat to society lies in their failure to conform to its behavioral norms. This concept has been used by some critics of American corrections to explain the disproportionate number of poor and minority groups who may be found in the nation's jails at any time.

The Jail Population

About 88 percent of jail inmates in the United States are male. As in other areas of corrections, however, women are becoming more numerous. Since 1995, the adult female jail population has grown at an annual rate of 7 percent, compared to 4.2 percent for males.[65] Jails also follow the general corrections pattern in that, as mentioned, a disproportionate number of their inmates are members of minority groups. (For an overview of the characteristics of the jail population, see Figure 13.7.)

Pretrial Detainees A significant number—about 30 percent—of those detained in jails technically are not prisoners. They are **pretrial detainees** who have been arrested by the police and, for a variety of reasons that we discussed in Chapter 9, are unable to post bail. Pretrial detainees are, in many ways, walking legal contradictions. According to the U.S. Constitution, they are innocent until proven guilty. At the same time, by

Pretrial Detainees
Individuals who cannot post bail after arrest or are not released on their own recognizance and are therefore forced to spend the time prior to their trial incarcerated in jail.

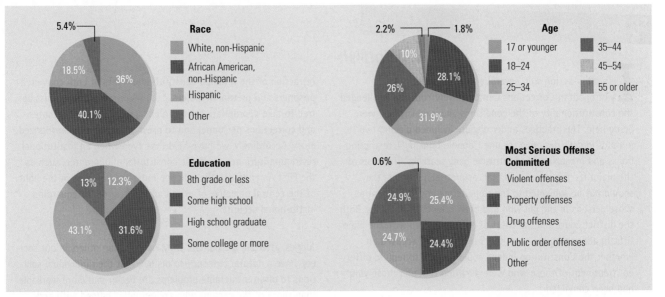

FIGURE 13.7

The Characteristics of America's Jail Population

Source: Bureau of Justice Statistics, *Profile of Jail Inmates, 2002* (Washington, D.C.: U.S. Department of Justice, July 2004), 1–4.

being incarcerated while awaiting trial, they are denied a number of personal freedoms and are subjected to the poor conditions of many jails. In 1979, the Supreme Court rejected the notion that this situation is inherently unfair by refusing to give pretrial detainees greater legal protections than sentenced jail inmates have.[66] (See the feature *CJ in Focus—Landmark Cases:* Bell v. Wolfish on the next page.)

Sentenced Jail Inmates According to the Department of Justice, 60 percent of those in jail have been convicted of their current charges.[67] In other words, they have been found guilty of a crime, usually a misdemeanor, and sentenced to time in jail. The typical jail term lasts between thirty and ninety days, and rarely does a prisoner spend more than one year in jail for any single crime. Often, a judge will credit the length of time the convict has spent in detention waiting for trial—known as **time served**—toward his or her sentence. This practice acknowledges two realities of jails:

1 Terms are generally too short to allow the prisoner to gain any benefit (that is, rehabilitation) from the jail's often limited or nonexistent treatment facilities. Therefore, the jail term can serve no other purpose than to punish the wrong-doer. (Judges who believe jail time can serve purposes of deterrence and incapacitation may not agree with this line of reasoning.)

2 Jails are chronically overcrowded, and judges need to clear space for new offenders.

Other Jail Inmates Pretrial detainees and misdemeanants make up the vast majority of the jail population. As mentioned earlier, jail inmates also include felons either waiting for transfer or assigned to jails because of prison overcrowding, probation and parole violators, the mentally ill, and juveniles. In addition, jails can hold those who require incarceration but do not "fit" anywhere else. A material witness or an attorney in a trial who refuses to follow the judge's instructions may, for example, be held in contempt of court and sent to jail.

Jail Administration

Of the nearly 3,300 jails in the United States, more than 2,700 are operated on a county level by an elected sheriff. Most of the remaining 600 are under the control of municipalities, although eight state governments (Alaska, Connecticut, Delaware, Hawaii, Maine, Rhode Island, Texas, and Vermont) manage jails.

Time Served

The period of time a person denied bail has spent in jail prior to his or her trial. If the suspect is found guilty and sentenced to a jail or prison term, the judge will often lessen the duration of the sentence based on the amount of time served as a pretrial detainee.

Bell v. Wolfish

In a class-action suit, several pretrial detainees in the Metropolitan Corrections Center in New York City challenged the constitutionality of the conditions under which they were being held. The practices under dispute included placing two inmates in cells designed for one ("double bunking"), restricting books and magazines, and intrusive body searches. The basis of the plaintiffs' argument was that, as pretrial detainees, they should not be subjected to the same terms of confinement as those persons in the jail who had been convicted of crimes. Both the district court and the court of appeals agreed with the plaintiffs. In addressing the case, the Supreme Court focused on whether the Constitution indeed could be seen to require different treatment of those who were awaiting trial and those who had been convicted.

> Bell v. Wolfish
> United States Supreme Court
> 441 U.S. 520 (1979)
> http://laws.findlaw.com/US/441/520.html

IN THE WORDS OF THE COURT . . .
Justice REHNQUIST, majority opinion

* * * *

The presumption of innocence is a doctrine that allocates the burden of proof in criminal trials; * * * . But it has no application to a determination of the rights of a pretrial detainee during confinement before his trial has even begun.

* * * *

[T]he Government concededly may detain [a person] to ensure his presence at trial and may subject him to the restrictions and conditions of the detention facility so long as those conditions and restrictions do not amount to punishment, or otherwise violate the Constitution. * * * Whether it be called a jail, a prison, or a custodial center, the purpose of the facility is to detain. Loss of freedom of choice and privacy are inherent incidents of confinement in such a facility. And the fact that such detention interferes with the detainee's understandable desire to live as comfortably as possible and with as little restraint as possible during confinement does not convert the conditions or restrictions of detention into "punishment."

* * * *

[M]aintaining institutional security and preserving internal order and discipline are essential goals that may require limitation or retraction of the retained constitutional rights of both convicted prisoners and pretrial detainees. * * * Prison officials must be free to take appropriate action to ensure the safety of inmates and corrections personnel and to prevent escape or unauthorized entry. Accordingly, we have held that even when an institutional restriction infringes a specific constitutional guarantee, such as the First Amendment, the practice must be evaluated in the light of the central objective of prison administration, safeguarding institutional security.

* * * *

Judges, after all, are human. They, no less than others in our society, have a natural tendency to believe that their individual solutions to often intractable problems are better and more workable than those of the persons who are actually charged with and trained in the running of the particular institution under examination. But under the Constitution, the first question to be answered is not whose plan is best, but in what branch of the Government is lodged the authority to initially devise the plan. This does not mean that constitutional rights are not to be scrupulously observed. It does mean, however, that the inquiry of federal courts into prison management must be limited to the issue of whether a particular system violates any prohibition of the Constitution or, in the case of a federal prison, a statute. The wide range of "judgment calls" that meet constitutional and statutory requirements are confided to officials outside of the Judicial Branch of Government.

DECISION
The Court reversed the ruling of the court of appeals, holding that the possible innocence of pretrial detainees does not prevent corrections officials from taking any steps necessary to manage jails and maintain security. In a larger sense, the *Bell* decision is seen as giving corrections officials a great deal of freedom in making decisions without interference from the courts.

FOR CRITICAL ANALYSIS
Which constitutional principles apply to the arguments being made in *Bell v. Wolfish?* How much weight does the Court give these principles in light of the need to maintain security in correctional facilities?

For more information and activities related to this case, click on Landmark Cases *under* Book Resources *at* **www.cjinaction.com.**

The "Burden" of Jail Administration Given that the public's opinion of jails ranges from negative to indifferent, some sheriffs neglect their jail management duties. Instead, they focus on high-visibility issues such as placing more law enforcement officers on the streets and improving security in schools. In fact, a jail usually receives publicity only after an escape or an incident in which inmates are abused by jailers.

Despite some sheriffs' general apathy toward jails, few would be willing to give up their management duties. As troublesome as they may be, jails can be useful in other ways. The sheriff appoints a jail administrator, or deputy sheriff, to oversee the day-to-day operations of the facility. The sheriff also has the power to hire other staff members, such as deputy jailers. The sheriff may award these jobs to people who helped her or him get elected, and, in return, jail staffers can prove helpful to the sheriff in future elections.

The Challenges of Overcrowding In many ways, the sheriff is placed in an untenable position when it comes to jail overcrowding. He or she has little control over the number of people who are sent to jail; that power resides with prosecutors and judges. Yet the jail is expected to find space to hold all comers, regardless of its capacity. A sheriff from Kane County, Utah, describes the situation:

Courtesy National Corrections Corporation

The linear design is similar to that of a hospital in which long rows of rooms are placed along a corridor. To carry out her or his surveillance duties, the custodial officer must either look down the corridor, or walk down it and peer into the windows of the individual cells. What sorts of risks are inherent in this type of jail design?

> We have people who should get sixty or ninety days, and they just do a weekend and we kick them out. Unless we get a real habitual abuser, we have no choice but to set them free. Most of the time we're pretty sure they will be back in a couple of days with a new offense.[68]

One way to alleviate overcrowding is to build more jails. The problem, however, is what economists call supply creating its own demand; that is, the number of jail inmates seems to expand to meet the number of available beds. In the twelve months leading up to June 30, 2004, the nation's jails added nearly 20,000 new beds in an effort to meet demand. During that same time period, the jail inmate population in the United States grew by more than 22,500. Today, U.S. jails are filled to 94 percent of their capacity, and twenty of the nation's fifty largest jails have an occupancy rate of greater than 100 percent.[69] In 2004, overcrowding at the Los Angeles County Jail became so severe that the sheriff's department was forced to release more than 63,000 jail inmates before they had served their full terms.[70]

New-Generation Jails

The boom in jail construction has been accompanied by a growing realization that simply adding bed space is not sufficient to deal with the problems endemic to the facilities. These problems include high suicide rates, an influx of mentally ill inmates, high drug use, and violence and rape. In other words, *how* the jail is built is just as important as *why* it is built. Over the past thirty years, the trend in jail construction has moved away from a traditional design toward a structure known as the new-generation jail.

The Traditional Design For most of the nation's history, the architecture of a jail was secondary to its purpose of keeping inmates safely locked away. Consequently, most jails in the United States continue to resemble those from the days of the Walnut Street Jail in Philadelphia. In this *traditional,* or *linear design,* jail cells are located along a corridor (see the photo above). To supervise the inmates while they are in their cells, correctional staff members must walk up and down the corridor; thus, the number of prisoners they can see at any one time is severely limited. With this limited supervision, inmates can more easily break institutional rules.

The harsh environment and lack of supervision inherent in the traditional design have been found to contribute to inmates' antisocial behavior. The prisoners spend most of their free time isolated and devoid of social control, and they have a tendency

New-Generation Jail
A type of jail that is distinguished architecturally from its predecessors by a design that encourages interaction between inmates and jailers and that offers greater opportunities for treatment.

Podular Design
The architectural style of the new-generation jail. Each "pod" consists of between twelve and twenty-four one-person cells and a communal "day-room" to allow for social interaction.

Direct Supervision Approach
A process of prison and jail administration in which correctional officers are in continuous physical contact with inmates during the day.

to respond with hostility.[71] Given that most jail inmates are released after a short period of confinement, many observers feel that the traditional design can pose a threat to the community by "creating" citizens who are more disposed toward violence on release than when they entered the jail.

Podular Design In the 1970s, the Federal Bureau of Prisons (BOP) decided to upgrade the traditional design based on the motto "If you can't rehabilitate, at least do no harm."[72] The BOP implemented a new management philosophy in designing three Metropolitan Correctional Centers in Chicago, New York, and San Diego. The National Institute of Corrections designated these three facilities **new-generation jails** to distinguish them from the older models.[73]

The new-generation jails differ significantly from their predecessors. The layout of the new facilities makes it easier for the staff to monitor cell-confined inmates. The basic structure of the new-generation jail is based on a **podular design.** Each "pod" contains "living units" for individual prisoners. These units, instead of lining up along a straight corridor, are often situated in a triangle so that a staff member in the center of the triangle has visual access to nearly all the cells. Daily activities such as eating and showering take place in the pod, which also has an outdoor exercise area. Treatment facilities are also located in the pod, allowing greater access for the inmates. A new wing of the Pima County jail in Arizona has even installed two-way video monitors in the rooms so that inmates will not have to leave the pod to receive visitors. Furthermore, the surroundings are not as harsh as in the older jails. Cells have comfortable furniture, rugs, and windows, and a communal "day-room" has televisions, radios, and telephones.[74]

Direct Supervision Approach The podular design also enables a new-generation jail to be managed using a **direct supervision approach.**[75] One or more jail officers are stationed in the living area of the pod and are therefore in constant interaction with all prisoners in that particular pod (see the photo below). Some new-generation jails even provide a desk in the center of the living area, which sends a very different message to the prisoners than the traditional control booth. Theoretically, jail officials who have constant contact with inmates will be able to stem misconduct quickly and efficiently and will also be able to recognize "danger signs" from individual inmates and stop outbursts before they occur.

In a direct supervision jail, the custodial officer is stationed at an in-pod control terminal. From this point, he or she has visual contact with all inmates and can communicate with inmates quickly and easily. During the day, inmates stay in the open area and are allowed in their cells only when given permission. The officer locks the door to the cells from his or her control terminal. How would the behavior of inmates in a direct supervision jail differ from that of inmates in a traditional, linear jail?

Courtesy National Corrections Corporation

Overcoming Initial Apprehension At first, the new-generation jails provoked a great deal of skepticism, as they were seen as inherently "soft" for criminals. A number of empirical results, however, seem to speak to the success of podular design and direct supervision. One study measured inmate behavior in an adult detention facility before and after it was converted to a direct supervision jail. The researchers found a "dramatic reduction" in the number of assaults, batteries, attempted suicides, sex offenses, possession of weapons, and escapees.[76] Today, nearly two hundred new-generation jails are in operation or under construction.

THE CONSEQUENCES OF OUR HIGH RATES OF INCARCERATION

For many observers, especially those who support the crime control theory of criminal justice, America's high rate of incarceration has contributed significantly to the drop in the country's crime rates.[77] At the heart of this belief is the fact, which we discussed in Chapter 2, that most crimes are committed by a relatively small group of repeat offenders. Several studies have tried to corroborate this viewpoint, with varying results—estimates of the number of crimes committed each year by habitual offenders range from three to 187.[78] If one accepts the higher estimate, each year a repeat offender spends in prison prevents a significant number of criminal acts.

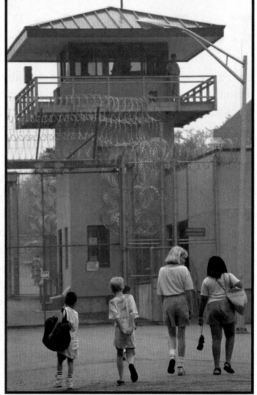

About half a million children in the United States, including the three pictured above, can see their mothers only by visiting them in prison or jail. What are some of the possible consequences of this separation?

Criminologists, however, note the negative consequences of America's growing prison and jail population. For one, incarceration can have severe social consequences for communities and the families that make up those communities. When a parent is imprisoned, her or his children will often suffer financial hardships, reduced supervision and discipline, and a general deterioration of the family structure.[79] These factors are used to explain the fact that children of convicts are more likely to become involved in delinquent behavior. Our high rates of incarceration also deny one of the basic rights of American democracy—the right to vote—to a large segment of the citizenry. (A number of states and the federal government *disenfranchise,* or take away the ability to vote, from those convicted of felonies. Some states do not, however.) This has a disproportionate impact on minority groups, weakening their voice in the democratic debate. Today, 8.6 percent of African American men between the ages of twenty-five and twenty-nine are in prison, compared to 2.5 percent of Hispanic men and 1.2 percent of white men in the same age group.[80] With more black men behind bars than enrolled in the nation's colleges and universities, Marc Mauer of the Sentencing Project believes that the "ripple effect on their communities and on the next generation of kids, growing up with their fathers in prison, will certainly be with us for at least a generation."[81]

Whether the American incarceration situation is "good" or "bad" depends to a large extent on one's personal philosophy. In the end, it is difficult to do a definitive cost-benefit analysis for each person incarcerated, weighing the benefits of preventing crimes that might (or might not) have been committed by an inmate against the costs to the convict's family and society. One thing that can be stated with some certainty is that, even with the growing interest in diversion and rehabilitation described in the previous chapter, the increase in prison and jail populations will continue in the foreseeable future.

The End of the Line: Supermax Prisons

On Easter Sunday 1993, inmates at a maximum-security prison in Lucasville, Ohio, seized control of an entire cell block and held it for eleven days. During the extended rioting, one correctional officer and nine inmates were killed; afterward the state spent nearly $80 million on prison repairs, investigations, and lawsuits. The Easter riot had a profound effect on the state's prison system. Within five years, Ohio had added seven new penal institutions and doubled the budget of the Department of Rehabilitation and Corrections. The centerpiece of the new efforts was the Ohio State Penitentiary in Youngstown. At its opening in the spring of 1998, the Youngstown facility was celebrated by officials as one of the nation's latest **supermax** (short for supermaximum-security) **prisons.** In this *Criminal Justice in Action* feature, we will examine these "intense" corrections facilities, condemned by critics as inhumane and lauded by supporters as the ultimate in "get tough" incarceration.

"The Worst of the Worst"

About thirty states and the Federal Bureau of Prisons (BOP) operate supermax prisons, which are supposedly reserved for the "worst of the worst." Inmates are not sent to such facilities by a sentencing court; instead, commitment to a supermax prison is usually the result of misbehavior within a penal institution. As Figure 13.8 shows, the murder or attempted murder of a fellow inmate was the most common reason for commitment to the BOP's U.S. Penitentiary Administrative Maximum (ADX) in Florence, Colorado.

The main purpose of a supermax prison is to strictly control the inmates' movement, thereby limiting (or eliminating) situations that could lead to breakdowns in discipline. The conditions in California's Security Housing Unit (SHU) at Pelican Bay State Prison are representative of most supermax institutions. Prisoners are confined to their one-person cells for twenty-two and a half hours each day under video camera surveillance; they receive meals through a slot in the door. The cells measure eight by ten feet in size and are windowless.

Supermax Prison

A correctional facility reserved for those inmates who have extensive records of misconduct in maximum-security prisons; characterized by extremely strict control and supervision over the inmates, including extensive use of solitary confinement.

FIGURE 13.8

Reasons for Transfer to a Supermax Prison

Rarely are offenders sent directly to a supermax facility by a court. For the most part, they are transferred there because of misbehavior in another correctional facility. This figure shows the reason inmates were transferred to the most secure facility operated by the Federal Bureau of Prisons: the U.S. Penitentiary Administrative Maximum (ADX) in Florence, Colorado.

Reason for Transfer	Percent
Murder or attempted murder of a fellow inmate	20
Assault of a fellow inmate with a weapon	18
Assault of a staff member	16
Escape attempt	10
Involved in riot	5
Judicial order	3
Other*	28

*Includes attempted murder of a staff member, involvement in a work or food strike, taking a staff member hostage, introducing drugs into a correctional facility, and involvement in gang activity.
Source: Gregory L. Hershberger, "To the Max: Supermax Facilities Provide Prison Administrators with More Security Options," *Corrections Today* 60 (February 1, 1998), 54.

No decorations of any kind are permitted on the white walls.[82]

For the ninety minutes each day the inmates are allowed out of their cells (compared to twelve to sixteen hours in regular maximum-security prisons), they may either shower or exercise in an enclosed, concrete "yard" covered by plastic mesh. Prisoners are strip-searched before and after leaving their cells, and placed in waist restraints and handcuffs on their way to and from the "yard" and showers. They can have a limited number of books or magazines in their cells and, if they can afford it, a television or radio.[83]

Removing the most violent and problematic inmates from the general prison population is seen as a key to modern prison management. Because those inmates transferred to supermax facilities are more likely to be impulsive and unpredictable and to have a gang affiliation, their absence is believed to create a safer environment for other inmates and the correctional staff. Furthermore, prison administrators use the supermax as a disciplinary tool—problematic inmates may change their behavior if they fear being transferred.[84]

Marion— The First Supermax

The precursor of today's supermax was San Francisco's Alcatraz Prison. Opening in 1932 on Alcatraz Island in San Francisco Bay, the maximum-security prison was populated by the most dangerous and disruptive federal convicts. Alcatraz was closed in 1963—mainly due to the expense of operating an island prison. For most of the next two decades, the BOP used the **dispersion** model for placing the most hazardous inmates. In other words, the department dispersed its "hard-core" offenders to various federal prisons around the country, hoping the general inmate population would assimilate them.[85]

By the late 1970s, it became apparent that this strategy was not functioning as planned. The "hard cores" continued to act violently, endangering other inmates and correctional employees. Then, in October 1983, two staff members and an inmate were murdered within a week at the federal prison in Marion, Illinois. Prison officials instituted a **lockdown,** in which all inmates are confined to their cells, and social activities such as meals, recreational sports, and treatment programs are canceled. Lockdowns are considered temporary, "cooling-off" measures, but officials at Marion decided to leave the conditions in effect indefinitely, creating the first supermax prison. The supermax is based on the model of **consolidation:** all high-risk inmates are placed in a single institution, which is administered with a focus on complete control.[86]

A typical supermax prison cell at the ADX outside Florence, Colorado. The cell is 8 feet 8 inches x 12 feet 3 inches, and contains a stainless steel mirror and a 12-inch black-and-white television set, as well as a concrete desk, stool, and bed that are permanently fixed to the floor. The small window has no view.

Bob Daemmrich/CORBIS/Sygma

Dispersion

A corrections model in which high-risk inmates are spread throughout the general prison population, in the hopes that they will be absorbed without causing misconduct problems.

Lockdown

A disciplinary action taken by prison officials in which all inmates are ordered to their quarters and nonessential prison activities are suspended.

Consolidation

A corrections model in which the inmates who pose the highest security risk are housed in a single facility to separate them from the general prison population.

The New-Generation Supermax

At first, the consolidation model led federal and state officials to construct supermax facilities on existing prison grounds. Over the past decade, however, the trend has been toward building new penal institutions, expressly designed with the goals of the supermax in mind. The Closed Maximum Security Correctional Center (CMAX) in Tamms, Illinois, for example, is designed around inmate housing pods (much like the new-generation jails mentioned earlier in the chapter). Each pod contains sixty cells on two levels, arranged around a control station with complete visual access. CMAX is designed so that an inmate never leaves his pod; medical facilities, library cells, and recreational areas are located within its boundaries.

All inmate movement in the pod takes place on the lower level, while armed security staff patrol the upper level. These guards can see through the upper-level flooring grid, allowing them to closely monitor any activity below. Furthermore, officials can control circulation by sealing off portions of the facility at will.[87] These new-generation supermax prisons also strive to limit contact between staff and inmates through technology. Automatic doors, intercoms, and electronic surveillance cameras have reduced the exposure of guards to inmates at most of the new facilities.

Senseless Suffering?

Many prison officials support the proliferation of supermax prisons because they provide increased security for the most dangerous inmates. Observers believe that as the inmate population becomes aware of these new facilities, their harsh reputation will deter convicts from misbehaving for fear of transfer to a supermax.

The supermax has aroused a number of criticisms, however. Amnesty International and other human rights groups assert that the facilities violate international standards of proper treatment for prisoners. At Wisconsin's Supermax Correctional Institution, for example, the cells are illuminated twenty-four hours a day and, because they have no air-conditioning or windows, average temperatures during the summer top 100 degrees.[88] Opponents also contend that the "worst of the worst" argument used by prison officials to justify the harsh conditions at supermax institutions often is not valid. They claim that these facilities are frequently used as "dumping grounds" for troublesome inmates and the mentally ill. In the early 2000s, 23 percent of the inmates at the Wallens Ridge supermax in Virginia were serving sentences of five years or less, many for nonviolent crimes such as drug offenses or burglary.[89]

These statistics highlight another problem with the supermax: most of the inmates will eventually reenter society with a host of psychological problems they did not have before being sentenced. While studying prisoners at California's Pelican Bay facility, a Harvard University psychiatrist found that 80 percent suffered from what he called "SHU [security housing unit] syndrome," a condition brought on by long periods of isolation.[90] Further research on "SHU syndrome" shows that supermax inmates manifest a number of psychological problems, including massive anxiety, hallucinations, hyperresponsiveness to external stimuli, and acute confusion.[91]

The United States Supreme Court has never ruled on whether these conditions violate the Eighth Amendment's prohibition against cruel and unusual punishment. In 2005, however, the Court did find that inmates faced "atypical hardships" in a supermax and therefore prison administrators could not send an offender to one of these facilities without providing minimal levels of due process.[92] This decision effectively requires officials who wish to transfer inmates to a supermax facility to grant them a hearing so that they can dispute the reasons for the proposed transfer.

Making Sense of Supermax Prisons

1 Explain the thinking behind the dispersion and consolidation models of dealing with highly dangerous inmates. Why is the supermax prison considered to be an example of the consolidation model?

2 Summarize the arguments for and against the supermax prison. Which side do you fall on, and why?

3 Do you feel that supermax prisons infringe on inmates' Eighth Amendment right to be free from "cruel and unusual punishment"? What other information about how supermax prisons are operated might you need to know before you answer?

Chapter Summary

1 Contrast the Pennsylvania and the New York penitentiary theories of the 1800s. Basically, the Pennsylvania system imposed total silence on its prisoners. Based on the concept of separate confinement, penitentiaries were constructed with back-to-back cells facing both outward and inward. Prisoners worked, slept, and ate alone in their cells. In contrast, New York used the congregate system; silence was imposed, but inmates worked and ate together.

2 List the factors that have caused the prison population to grow dramatically in the last several decades. (a) The enhancement and stricter enforcement of the nation's drug laws; (b) increased probability of incarceration; (c) inmates serving more time for each crime; (d) federal prison growth; and (e) rising incarceration rates for women.

3 Explain the three general models of prisons. (a) The custodial model assumes the prisoner is incarcerated for reasons of incapacitation, deterrence, and retribution. (b) The rehabilitation model puts security concerns second and the well-being of the individual inmate first. As a consequence, treatment programs are offered to prisoners. (c) The reintegration model sees the correctional institution as a training ground for preparing convicts to reenter society.

4 List and briefly explain the four types of prisons. (a) Maximum-security prisons, which are designed mainly with security and surveillance in mind. Such prisons are usually large and consist of cell blocks, each of which is set off by a series of gates and bars. (b) Medium-security prisons, which offer considerably more educational and treatment programs and allow more contact between inmates. Such prisons are rarely walled, but rather are surrounded by high fences. (c) Minimum-security prisons, which permit prisoners to have television sets and computers and often allow them to leave the grounds for educational and employment purposes. (d) Supermaximum-security (supermax) pris-

STORIES FROM THE STREET

Go to the *Stories from the Street* feature at **www.cjinaction.com** to hear Larry Gaines tell insightful stories related to this chapter and his experiences in the field.

ons, in which prisoners are confined to one-person cells for up to twenty-two and a half hours per day under constant video camera surveillance.

5 **Contrast formal with informal prison management systems.** A formal system is militaristic with a hierarchical (top-down) chain of command; the warden (or superintendent) is on top, then deputy wardens, and last, custodial employees. The informal prison management system depends on the philosophy of the warden, or superintendent, and may even allow for inmate councils and inmate "guards."

6 **List the reasons why private prisons can often be run more cheaply than public ones.** (a) Labor costs are lower because private prison employees are nonunionized and receive lower levels of overtime payments, sick leave, and health care. (b) Competitive bidding requires the operators of private prisons to buy goods and services at the lowest possible prices. (c) There is less red tape in a private prison facility.

7 **Summarize the distinction between jails and prisons, and indicate the importance of jails in the American correctional system.** Generally, a prison is for those convicted of felonies who will serve lengthy periods of incarceration, whereas a jail is for those who have been convicted of misdemeanors and will serve less than a year of incarceration. A jail also (a) receives individuals pending arraignment and holds them while awaiting trial, conviction, or sentencing; (b) temporarily holds juveniles pending transfer to juvenile authorities; (c) holds the mentally ill pending transfer to health facilities;

(d) detains those who have violated probation or parole and those who have "jumped" bail; and (e) houses those awaiting transfer to federal or state prisons. Approximately 7 million Americans spend time in jail each year.

8 **Explain how jails are administered.** Most jails are operated at the county level by an elected sheriff, although about 20 percent are under the control of municipalities and eight states manage jails themselves. Sheriffs appoint jail administrators (deputy sheriffs) as well as deputy jailers.

9 **Indicate the difference between traditional jail design and new-generation jail design.** A traditional design is linear, with jail cells located along a corridor. Such a physical structure is rather cold with an emphasis on iron and steel fixtures that are not easily broken. New-generation jails, in contrast, use a podular design, with the "pods" often arranged in a triangle. Each cell has furniture, rugs, and windows, and there are communal "day-rooms" with televisions, radios, and telephones.

10 **Indicate some of the consequences of our high rates of incarceration.** (a) Some people believe that the reduction in the country's crime rate is a direct result of increased incarceration rates; (b) others believe that high incarceration rates are having increasing negative social consequences, such as financial hardships, reduced supervision and discipline of children, and a general deterioration of the family structure when one parent is in prison; and (c) more money spent on prisons has taken away money for other public services, such as education.

Key Terms

congregate system 422
consolidation 445
direct supervision approach 442
dispersion 445
jail 437
lockdown 445
maximum-security prison 428
medical model 423
medium-security prison 430
minimum-security prison 431
new-generation jails 442
penitentiary 421
podular design 442
pretrial detainees 438
private prisons 434
separate confinement 422
supermax prison 444
time served 439
warden 432

diff bet. jail & prison

Questions for Critical Analysis

1 Explain the benefit of nonfixed sentences coupled with the possibility of early release.
2 How did the Elmira Reformatory classify prisoners? How did the system work?
3 Crime rates are falling, yet prison populations are rising. Why?
4 What are several reasons why prison construction continues to increase?
5 The chain of command in prisons and police departments appears quite similar, yet there is a big difference. What is it?
6 Why have private prisons grown over the last decade?
7 Why are jails so important in the American corrections system?
8 Most sheriffs are quite apathetic toward the job of running jails, yet they do not want to give up their management duties. Why not?
9 In the first two decades after the closing of Alcatraz, what method did the Bureau of Prisons use in dealing with its most dangerous inmates? Was the method successful?

Test Preparation Online

Criminal JusticeNow

Go to **www.cjinaction.com** and click on *Criminal JusticeNow* for access to this powerful online study tool. You will get a *personalized study plan* based on your responses to a diagnostic pretest. Once you have mastered the material with the help of interactive learning tools, video clips with questions, an integrated e-book, and more, you can take a posttest to confirm you are ready to move on to the next chapter.

Book Companion Web Site

At the book companion Web site (**www.cjinaction.com**), you will find many resources in addition to *Criminal JusticeNow* to aid you in studying for your exams. For example, under *Chapter Resources*, you will find the *Chapter Outline, Chapter Summary, Flashcards, Glossary, Learning Objectives, Lecture Presentations, Concept Builder, Essay Questions*, and a *Tutorial Chapter Quiz*. You can also test yourself with interactive *Online Reviews* of each chapter section. Check out the *Web Links* to access the Web sites mentioned in the text, as well as many others. You can also access recent perspectives by clicking on *CJ in the News* and *Terrorism Update* under *Course Resources*.

Suggested Readings

Applebaum, Anne, *Gulag: A History,* New York: Doubleday, 2003. As the U.S. incarceration rate has risen to historic levels, many comparisons have been made to the Gulag system that operated under the Communist dictatorship of the Soviet Union. This book should dispel the notion that the American corrections system, whatever its problems, is comparable to that wide network of prison labor camps. From 1928 to the death of Soviet leader Joseph Stalin in 1953, Applebaum estimates that 18 million people passed through the Gulag camps, with about 4.5 million perishing there. Through painstaking research and interviews with survivors, the author provides a vivid look at how the prisoners lived, worked, slept, ate, and died.

Braman, Donald, *Doing Time on the Outside: Incarceration and Family Life in Urban America*, Ann Arbor, MI: University of Michigan Press, 2004. The math is simple: with more than two million Americans in prison and jail, many millions of loved ones are suffering the shame and hardship of having a family member behind bars. In this book, Braman provides one of the first large-scale investigations into the effects of incarceration on those on the outside. Through the stories of spouses, children, and parents, the author makes a forceful argument that, rather than protecting communities, mass incarceration is destroying some of them. He also raises an interesting question about the purpose of incarceration—by separating offenders from the area where they committed their crimes, are we preventing them from taking full responsibility for the harm they have done?

Notes

1. Bureau of Justice Statistics, *Prisoners in 2004* (Washington, D.C.: U.S. Department of Justice, October 2005), 1.
2. James M. Beattie, *Crime and the Courts in England, 1660–1800* (Princeton, NJ: Princeton University Press, 1986), 506–507.
3. Samuel Walker, *Popular Justice* (New York: Oxford University Press, 1980), 11.
4. Michael Meranze, *Laboratories of Virtue: Punishment, Revolution, and Authority in Philadelphia, 1760–1835* (Chapel Hill, NC: University of North Carolina Press, 1996), 55.
5. Negley K. Teeters, *The Cradle of the Penitentiary: The Walnut Street Jail at Philadelphia, 1773–1835* (Philadelphia: 1955), 30.
6. Negley K. Teeters and John D. Shearer, *The Prison at Philadelphia's Cherry Hill* (New York: Columbia University Press, 1957), 142–143.
7. Henry Calvin Mohler, "Convict Labor Policies," *Journal of the American Institute of Criminal Law and Criminology* 15 (1925), 556–557.
8. Zebulon Brockway, *Fifty Years of Prison Service* (Montclair, NJ: Patterson Smith, 1969), 400–401.
9. Robert Martinson, "What Works? Questions and Answers about Prison Reform," *Public Interest* 35 (Spring 1974), 22.
10. See Ted Palmer, "Martinson Revisited," *Journal of Research on Crime and Delinquency* (1975), 133; and Paul Gendreau

and Bob Ross, "Effective Correctional Treatment: Bibliotherapy for Cynics," *Crime & Delinquency* 25 (1979), 499.
11. Robert Martinson, "New Findings, New Views: A Note of Caution Regarding Sentencing Reform," *Hofstra Law Review* 7 (1979), 243.
12. Fox Butterfield, "'Defying Gravity,' Inmate Population Climbs," *New York Times* (January 19, 1998), A10.
13. *Ibid.*
14. Bureau of Justice Statistics, *Prisoners in 2002* (Washington, D.C.: U.S. Department of Justice, July 2003), Table 15, page 10.
15. Bureau of Justice Statistics, *Sourcebook of Criminal Justice Statistics Online,* at **http://www.albany.edu/sourcebook/pdf/t654.pdf**.
16. Allen J. Beck, "Growth, Change, and Stability in the U.S. Prison Population, 1980–1995," *Corrections Management Quarterly* (Spring 1997), 9–10.
17. Bureau of Justice Statistics, *Federal Criminal Case Processing, 2002* (Washington, D.C.: U.S. Department of Justice, January 2005), 1.
18. *Fifteen Years of Guidelines Sentencing: An Assessment of How Well the Federal Criminal Justice System Is Achieving the Goals of Sentencing Reform* (Washington, D.C.: U.S. Sentencing Commission, November 2004), 46.

19. Bureau of Justice Statistics, *Federal Criminal Case Processing, 2002,* 1.
20. Bureau of Justice Statistics, *Truth in Sentencing in State Prisons* (Washington, D.C.: U.S. Department of Justice, 1999), 7.
21. *Prisoners in 2004,* 2.
22. Bureau of Justice Statistics, *Prisoners in 2002* (Washington, D.C.: U.S. Department of Justice, July 2003), 11.
23. *Sourcebook of Criminal Justice Statistics, 2003* (Washington, D.C.: Bureau of Justice Statistics, 2004), Table 5.56, page 519.
24. *Prisoners in 2004,* 4.
25. Sarah Lawrence and Jeremy Travis, *The New Landscape of Imprisonment: Mapping America's Prison Expansion* (Washington, D.C.: Urban Institute Justice Policy Center, 2004), 2.
26. Bureau of Justice Statistics, *Justice Expenditure and Employment in the United States* (Washington, D.C.: U.S. Department of Justice, May 2004), 1.
27. *Sourcebook of Criminal Justice Statistics, 2001* (Washington, D.C.: Bureau of Justice Statistics, 2002), Table 1.9.
28. Holly Idelson, "Republican Crime Bills Take a 'Get Tougher' Approach," *Congressional Quarterly Weekly Report* 53 (1995), 211.
29. Charles H. Logan, *Criminal Justice Performance Measures in Prisons* (Washington, D.C.: U.S. Department of Justice, 1993), 5.
30. Todd R. Clear and George F. Cole, *American Corrections,* 4th ed. (Belmont, CA: Wadsworth Publishing Co., 1997), 245–246.
31. Alfred Blumstein, "Prisons," in *Crime,* ed. James Q. Wilson and Joan Petersilia (San Francisco: ICS Press, 1995), 392.
32. Cassia Spohn and David Holleran, "The Effect of Imprisonment on Recidivism Rates of Felony Offenders: A Focus on Drug Offenders," *Criminology* (May 1, 2002), 329–357.
33. Tony Izzo, "I-Max Awaits Green," *Kansas City Star* (May 26, 1996), A1.
34. "Pennsylvania Plans New Prison to Replace Site of Tunnel Escape," *Corrections Journal* (February 9, 1998), 6.
35. Charles H. Logan, "Well Kept: Comparing Quality of Confinement in a Public and Private Prison," *Journal of Criminal Law and Criminology* 83 (1992), 580.
36. Bert Useem and Peter Kimball, *Stages of Siege: U.S. Prison Riots, 1971–1986* (New York: Oxford University Press, 1989).
37. Bert Useem, "Disorganization and the New Mexico Prison Riot of 1980," *American Sociology Review* 50 (1985), 685.
38. Tara Gray and Jon'a F. Meyer, "Prison Administration: Inmate Participation versus the Control Model," in *Correction Contexts: Contemporary and Classical Readings,* ed. James W. Marquart and Jonathan R. Sorenson (Los Angeles: Roxbury Publishing Co., 1997), 203–211.
39. *Ibid.,* 208.
40. 550 F.2d 238 (5th Cir. 1977); *cert.* denied, 460 U.S. 1042 (1983).
41. "A Recession-Proof Industry," *Economist* (November 15, 1997), 28.
42. *Prisoners in 2004,* 5.
43. James Austin and Garry Coventry, *Emerging Issues on Privatized Prisons* (Washington, D.C.: Bureau of Justice Assistance, 2001), iii.
44. "A Tale of Two Systems: Cost, Quality, and Accountability in Private Prisons," *Harvard Law Review* (May 2002), 1872.
45. *Public-Private Prisons Comparison* (Phoenix, AZ: Arizona Department of Corrections, 2000), 47.
46. *Private Prison Review* (Tallahassee, FL: Office of Program Policy Analysis and Government Accountability, 2000), 5.
47. Barrett Marson, "Some Ariz. Inmates Being Returned to State," *Arizona Daily Star* (July 3, 2004), A6.
48. Logan, "Well Kept," 577.
49. Richard C. Brister, "Changing of the Guard: A Case for Privatization of Texas Prisons," *The Prison Journal* 76 (September 1996), 322–323.
50. "Private Prison Is Ordered to Screen Dangerous Inmates," *Corrections Journal* (March 9, 1998), 5.
51. Sean Kelly, "Riot Reignites Debate over Private Prisons," *Denver Post* (July 22, 2004), A6.
52. Curtis R. Blakely and Vic W. Bumphus, "Private and Public Sector Prisons," *Federal Probation* (June 2004), 27.
53. Richard L. Lippke, "Thinking about Private Prisons," *Criminal Justice Ethics* (Winter/Spring 1997), 32.
54. John DiIulio, "Prisons, Profits, and the Public Good: The Privatization of Corrections," in *Criminal Justice Center Bulletin* (Huntsville, TX: Sam Houston State University, 1986).
55. Ira P. Robbins, "Privatization of Prisons, Privatization of Corrections: Defining the Issues," *Vanderbilt Law Review* 40 (1987), 823.
56. *Prisoners in 2004,* 5.
57. Amy Cheung, *Prison Privatization and the Use of Incarceration* (Washington, D.C.: The Sentencing Project, 2002), 3.
58. *Ibid.*
59. Getahn Ward, "CCA Awarded Georgia Prison Contract," *(Nashville) Tennessean* (May 31, 2002), A7.
60. Bureau of Justice Statistics, *Prison and Jail Inmates at Midyear 2004* (Washington, D.C.: U.S. Department of Justice, April 2005), 8.
61. Arthur Wallenstein, "Jail Crowding: Bringing the Issue to the Corrections Center Stage," *Corrections Today* (December 1996), 76–81.
62. Quoted in Butterfield, "Defying Gravity."
63. "State to Rent County Jails for Inmates," *UPI Online* (February 5, 1998).
64. John Irwin, *The Jail: Managing the Underclass in American Society* (Berkeley, CA: University of California Press, 1985), 2.
65. Bureau of Justice Statistics, *Prison and Jail Inmates at Midyear 2004* (Washington, D.C.: U.S. Department of Justice, April 2005), 8.
66. 441 U.S. 520 (1979).
67. *Prison and Jail Inmates at Midyear 2004,* 9.

68. Quoted in Greg Burton, "Jail Builders Race to Keep Up with Demand," *Salt Lake City Tribune* (May 6, 1998), N31.

69. *Prison and Jail Inmates at Midyear 2004*, 8–9.

70. Jeffrey L. Rabin, "63,332 Inmates Released Early," *Los Angeles Times* (October 28, 2004), B3.

71. John J. Gibbs, "Environmental Congruence and Symptoms of Psychopathology: A Further Exploration of the Effects of Exposure to the Jail Environment," *Criminal Justice and Behavior* 18 (1991), 351–374.

72. Richard Weiner, William Frazier, and Jay Farbstein, "Building Better Jails," *Psychology Today* (June 1987), 40.

73. R. L. Miller, "New Generation Justice Facilities: The Case for Direct Supervision," *Architectural Technology* 12 (1985), 6–7.

74. Gerald J. Bayens, Jimmy J. Williams, and John Ortiz Smykla, "Jail Type and Inmate Behavior: A Longitudinal Analysis," *Federal Probation* (September 1997), 54.

75. Linda L. Zupan, *Jails: Reform and the New Generation Philosophy* (Cincinnati, OH: Anderson Publishing Co., 1991).

76. Bayens, Williams, and Smykla.

77. Dan Seligman, "Lock 'Em Up," *Forbes* (May 23, 2005), 216–217.

78. Franklin E. Zimring and Gordon Hawkins, *Incapacitation: Penal Confinement and the Restraint of Crime* (New York: Oxford University Press, 1995), 38, 40, 145.

79. Todd R. Clear and Dina R. Rose, "A Thug in Jail Can't Shoot Your Sister: The Unintended Consequences of Incarceration," paper presented to the American Sociological Association (August 18, 1996).

80. *Prisoners in 2004*, 8.

81. Quoted in Fox Butterfield, "Study Finds 2.6% Increase in U.S. Prison Population," *New York Times* (July 28, 2003), A8.

82. Charles A. Pettigrew, "Technology and the Eighth Amendment: The Problem of Supermax Prisons," *North Carolina Journal of Law and Technology* (Fall 2002), 195.

83. "Facts about Pelican Bay's SHU," *California Prisoner* (December 1991).

84. Jeffrey Endicott, Jerry Berge, and Gary McCaughtry, "Prison Wardens Push for 'Supermax' Prison," *Wisconsin State Journal* (February 12, 1996), 5A.

85. Gregory L. Hershberger, "To the Max," *Corrections Today* (February 1998), 55.

86. *Ibid.*, 55–56.

87. Robert A. Sheppard, Jeffrey G. Geiger, and George Welborn, "Closed Maximum Security: The Illinois Supermax," *Corrections Today* (July 1996), 4.

88. *Jones'El et al. v. Berge and Lichter,* 164 F.Supp.2d 1096 (2001).

89. Craig Timberg, "Documents Show Use of Force at Wallens Ridge," *Washington Post* (July 31, 2001), B1.

90. Robert Perkinson, "Shackled Justice: Florence Federal Penitentiary and the New Politics of Punishment," *Social Justice* (Fall 1994), 117–123.

91. Terry Kupers, *Prison Madness: The Mental Health Crisis behind Bars and What We Must Do about It* (San Francisco: Jossey-Bass, 1999), 56–64.

92. *Wilkinson v. Austin,* 545 U.S. ___ (2005).

Behind Bars:
The Life of an Inmate

Chapter outline

- Prison Culture
- Prison Violence
- Inside a Women's Prison
- Correctional Officers and Discipline
- Protecting Prisoners' Rights
- Parole and Release from Prison
- Reentry into Society
- Criminal Justice in Action—Protecting the Community from Sex Offenders

Chapter objectives

After reading this chapter, you should be able to:

1 Explain the concept of prison as a total institution.
2 Describe the possible patterns of inmate behavior, which are driven by the inmate's personality and values.
3 Indicate some of the reasons for violent behavior in prisons.
4 List and briefly explain the six general job categories among correctional officers.
5 Contrast the hands-off doctrine of prisoner law with the hands-on approach.
6 Contrast probation, parole, mandatory release, pardon, and furlough.
7 Describe truth-in-sentencing laws and their goals.
8 Describe typical conditions of parole.
9 Explain the goal of prisoner reentry programs.
10 Indicate typical conditions for release for a paroled child molester.

Criminal JusticeNow

Optimize your study time and master key chapter concepts with *Criminal JusticeNow*, an online study tool that provides you with a *personalized study plan*. Check out the "Test Preparation Online" section at the end of the chapter for additional information.

The "No Frills" Movement

Five days in the Los Angeles County Jail may not seem like an overly harsh punishment, but for Ki Chul Hong it was a death sentence. Rival gang members stabbed Hong, who had been convicted of prostitution, thirty-six times before wrapping his body in sheets and dumping it in a laundry trolley. Hong's murder was the fifth in a seven-month period at the jail in 2004. Other victims included Raul Tinejero, strangled for testifying against his attacker; Steven Pendegrast, a mentally ill inmate killed by two cell mates drunk on contraband wine; and Kristopher Frye, stabbed during a race riot that began over the use of a telephone.

Today's penal institutions are often characterized by "grindingly dull routine interrupted by occasional flashes of violence and brutality." The situation is even worse in overcrowded establishments such as the Los Angeles jail, which often crams six inmates into each small cell, forcing two to sleep on the floor near a leaking toilet. "You keep putting rats in a box, and pretty soon those rats are going to go off and kill each other," remarked one California correctional officer. A "no

A cell block at the Men's Central Jail in Los Angeles, which has been widely critized for its inhumane living conditions.

frills" movement in public policy and prison management has further succeeded in removing many of the comforts from inmates' lives. Many state prisons ban weightlifting, televisions, radios, adult magazines, and conjugal visits. All states and the federal government have limited smoking in their correctional facilities to some extent, and many institutions spend less than $3 per day per inmate on meals.

Life behind bars has long been predicated on the *principle of least eligibility*, which holds that the least advantaged members of outside society should lead a better existence than any person living in prison or jail.[1] As the "no frills" movement shows, the idea that incarceration is not punishment enough, and that daily life itself must be an arduous trial for prisoners, is particularly popular at the moment. Many critics, however, feel that the treatment of prisoners has become increasingly inhumane and, indeed, unconstitutional. At one time or another over the past two decades, the federal government, nearly every state government, and countless local authorities have been under court order to improve living conditions in their penal institutions.[2]

In this chapter, we look at some of the factors that influence the quality of life in America's prisons and jails. To that end, we will discuss the ramifications of violence in prison, the role played by correctional officers, efforts by prisoners and prisoners' rights advocates to improve conditions, and several other issues that are at the forefront of prison debate today. To start, we must understand the forces that shape prison culture and how those forces affect the overall operation of the correctional facility.

PRISON CULTURE

Any institution—whether a school, a bank, or a police department—has an organizational culture; that is, a set of values that help the people in the organization understand what actions are acceptable and what actions are unacceptable.[3] According to a theory put forth by the influential sociologist Erving Goffman, prison cultures are unique because prisons are **total institutions** that encompass every aspect of an inmate's life. Unlike a student or a bank teller, a prisoner cannot leave the institution or have any meaningful interaction with outside communities. Others arrange every aspect of daily life, and all prisoners are required to follow this schedule in exactly the same manner.[4]

Inmates develop their own argot, or language (see Figure 14.1). They create their own economy, which, in the absence of currency, is based on the barter of valued items such as food, contraband, and sexual favors. They establish methods of determining power, many of which, as we shall see, involve violence. Isolated and heavily regulated, prisoners create a social world that is, out of both necessity and design, separate from the outside world.[5]

Total Institution

An institution, such as a prison, that provides all of the necessities for existence to those who live within its boundaries.

FIGURE 14.1

Prison Slang

Ace-duce. Best friend.

All day. Life sentence, as in "he's doing all day."

Big bitch. A felon who has been convicted under habitual criminal laws that carry a mandatory life sentence.

Catch a ride. To ask a friend with drugs to get you high, as in "Hey, man, can I catch a ride?"

Catch a square. To prepare to fight, as in "you'd better catch a square."

Chi-mo, also chester, baby-raper, short eyes. Child molester.

Click up. To join a gang.

Deck. Pack of cigarettes.

Ding. A term of derision for a mentally deranged prisoner.

Fish. A new arrival who does not yet know the rules of the prison culture.

Gangster, or monster. HIV/AIDS. As in "watch out for that guy, he's got the gangster."

Hacks, also hogs, snouts, pigs, cops, bulls, screws. Correctional officers.

Herb. Weak inmate.

The hole. Solitary confinement.

Jigger. An inmate who stands watch while an illegal act is taking place.

Luv, luv. Doing well, as in "living luv, luv."

Mule. A person who smuggles drugs into the correctional facility.

Nazi low rider. A member of a white prison gang.

Old school. A prisoner who is seen as having values from the "old days" in prisons, when more respect was given to fellow prisoners.

On the leg. A prisoner who is seen as being overly friendly with prison staff.

Pepsi generation. The newer, younger inmates who are seen as having no respect for the old school ways of the prison.

Pitcher. A sexually aggressive, dominant inmate.

Playing on ass. Gambling without having any cash, as in "if you lose, it's your ass."

Punk. A derogatory term referring to a homosexual or weak-willed person.

Rapo. Anyone imprisoned on a sex offense.

Riding leg. An inmate who is friendly with staff in order to receive preferential treatment.

Split your wig. A quick punch to the head.

Stick. A marijuana joint.

T-jones. An inmate's mother or parents, as in "I got a letter from my T-jones."

Wolf ticket. To "talk tough" without the will to back it up, as in, "he's selling wolf tickets," or "he's making a lot of noise but doesn't have the guts to stand up for himself."

Prisoners also use rhyming slang in order to make their conversations confusing to newcomers or outsiders. In rhyming slang, "bees and money" could mean "honey," "oh my dear" could mean "beer," and so on.

Sources: Adapted from much larger glossaries found at www.halcyon.com/scripts/dante/cgi-pvt and www.wco.com/~aerick/lingo.htm.

Who Is in Prison?

Prisonization

The socialization process through which a new inmate learns the accepted norms and values of the prison population.

The culture of any prison is heavily influenced by its inmates; their values, beliefs, and experiences in the outside world will be reflected in the social order that exists behind bars. In Chapter 2, we noted that a majority of Americans commit at least one crime that could technically send them to prison. In reality, slightly more than 5 percent will be confined in a state or federal prison during their lifetimes. That percentage is considerably higher for male members of minority groups: according to the U.S. Department of Justice, about one in three African American males and one in six Hispanic males, as compared to one in seventeen white males, are likely to go to prison during their lifetimes.[6]

The prison population is not static. The past two decades have seen the incarceration rates of women and minority groups rise sharply. Furthermore, the arrest patterns of inmates have changed over that time period. A prisoner today is much more likely to have been incarcerated on drug charges than was the case in the 1980s.[7] The most significant shift in the prison population, however, involves age. While the majority of inmates are still under thirty-four years old, as you can see in Figure 14.2 the number of offenders over the age of forty has increased dramatically during the past ten years. A number of factors have contributed to this upsurge, including "get tough on crime" measures that impose mandatory terms and longer sentences (discussed in Chapter 11), high rates of recidivism, higher levels of murder and sex crimes committed by older offenders, and the aging of the U.S. population as a whole.[8] (To learn how this demographic swing has had a particularly burdensome effect on corrections budgets, see the feature *CJ in Focus—A Question of Ethics: The Costs of Growing Old in Prison.*)

Adapting to Prison Society

On arriving at prison, each convict attends an orientation session and receives a "Resident's Handbook." The handbook provides information such as meal and official count times, disciplinary regulations, and visitation guidelines. The norms and values of the prison society, however, cannot be communicated by the staff or learned from a handbook. As first described by Donald Clemmer in his classic 1940 work, *The Prison Community*, the process of **prisonization**—or adaptation to the prison culture—advances as the inmate gradually understands what constitutes acceptable behavior in the institution, as defined not by the prison officials but by other inmates.[9]

In studying prisonization, criminologists have focused on two areas: how prisoners change their behavior to adapt to life behind bars, and how life behind bars has changed because of inmate behavior. Sociologist John Irwin has identified several patterns of inmate behavior, each one driven by the inmate's personality and values:

1 Professional criminals adapt to prison by "doing time." In other words, they follow the rules and generally do whatever is necessary to speed up their release so that they can continue their chosen careers.

2 Some convicts, mostly state-raised youths or those frequently incarcerated in juvenile detention centers, are more comfortable inside prison than outside. These inmates serve time by "jailing," or establishing themselves in the power structure of prison culture.

FIGURE 14.2
The Aging Prison Population

Source: Bureau of Justice Statistics, *Prisoners in 2003* (Washington, D.C.: U.S. Department of Justice, November 2004), Table 10, page 8.

The Costs of Growing Old in Prison

Before they enter the medical profession, most physicians take the Hippocratic Oath, in which they promise to treat every patient to the best of their ability—no matter what kind of person that patient may be. Prison administrators take no such vow, but thanks to the general aging of the prison population, they are increasingly forced to provide free medical care to society's least sympathetic sufferers.

According to the best estimates, about 40 percent of prisoners over the age of forty-five have serious medical problems, including diabetes, emphysema, hypertension, heart disease, lung cancer, and other cancers. In 1976, the United States Supreme Court ruled that prisoners have the right to "adequate" medical care, which has been interpreted to mean the same level of care they would receive if they were not behind bars. According to Dr. Michael A. Grodin, director of medical ethics at the Boston University School of Medicine and Public Health, "[B]ecause someone is incarcerated, we have a higher obligation to provide them with care because we have deprived them of their liberty."

HEALTH-CARE HEADACHES

Free health care for inmates has not proved so popular in the court of public opinion. Victims' rights groups complained loudly in 2002 when a convicted armed robber received a $1 million heart transplant at the Stanford Medical Center in California. Similar protests were heard three years later when treatment of an imprisoned heroin addict cost Connecticut taxpayers about $1.1 million. Meanwhile, prison budgets are straining under the financial pressures created by growing numbers of old and infirm inmates, who are three times more expensive to care for than younger prisoners. In Massachusetts, the department of corrections' medical budget jumped from $39 million in 1995 to $69 million in 2005, while the cost of providing health care for Arizona's prisoners rose by $36 million over that same time period. Nationally, spending on prison health care increased by 78 percent over the past decade.

Given that elderly inmates tend to have the lowest recidivism rates, some criminologists have suggested that the corrections system should institute a form of "medical parole," in which older prisoners with health problems are transferred to a form of house arrest. But, with many of these convicts serving time for violent crimes, this option has proved to be politically unfeasible. Instead, sixteen states have set up separate facilities to house older and sicker inmates in the hope that providing constant care will prevent more serious, and more expensive, medical emergencies.

FOR CRITICAL ANALYSIS

To what extent does society have an ethical obligation to provide health care to inmates? What role, if any, should cost play in determining a prisoner's right to receive treatment?

---

3   Other inmates take advantage of prison resources such as libraries or drug treatment programs by "gleaning," or working to improve themselves to prepare for a return to society.

4   Finally, "disorganized" criminals exist on the fringes of prison society. These inmates may have mental impairments or low levels of intelligence and find it impossible to adapt to prison culture on any level.[10]

The process of categorizing prisoners has a theoretical basis, but it serves a practical purpose as well, allowing administrators to reasonably predict how different inmates will act in certain situations. An inmate who is "doing time" generally does not present the same security risk as one who is "jailing."

PRISON VIOLENCE

A prison is a dangerous place to live. Prison culture is predicated on violence; one observer calls the modern institution an "unstable and violent jungle."[11] Prison guards use the threat of violence (and, at times, its reality) to control the inmate population. Among the prisoners, violence is used to establish power and dominance. Often, this violence leads to death. About one hundred inmates are murdered by fellow inmates each year, and about 26,000 inmate-on-inmate assaults take place annually.

Violence in Prison Culture

Until the 1970s, prison culture emphasized "noninterference" and did not support inmate-on-inmate violence. Prison "elders" would themselves punish any of their peers who showed a proclivity toward assaulting fellow inmates. Today, in contrast, violence is used to establish the prisoner hierarchy by separating the powerful from the weak. Humboldt State University's Lee H. Bowker has identified several other reasons for violent behavior:

- It provides a deterrent against being victimized, as a reputation for violence may eliminate an inmate as a target of assault.
- It enhances self-image in an environment that does not respect other attributes, such as intelligence.
- In the case of rape, it gives sexual relief.
- It serves as a means of acquiring material goods through extortion or outright robbery.[12]

The **deprivation model** can be used to explain the high level of prison violence. According to this model, the stressful and oppressive conditions of prison life lead to aggressive behavior on the part of inmates. When conditions such as overcrowding worsen, prison researcher Stephen C. Light found that inmate misconduct often increases.[13] In these circumstances, the violent behavior may not have any express purpose—it may just be a means of relieving tension.[14]

Riots

The deprivation model is helpful, though less convincing, in searching for the roots of collective violence. As far back as the 1930s, Frank Tannenbaum noted that harsh prison conditions can cause tension to build among inmates until it eventually explodes in the form of mass violence.[15] Living conditions in prisons are fairly constant, however, so how can the seemingly spontaneous outbreak of prison riots be explained?

Researchers have addressed these inconsistencies with the concept of **relative deprivation,** a theory that focuses on the gap between what is expected in a certain situation and what is achieved. Peter C. Kratcoski has argued that because prisoners enjoy such meager privileges to begin with, any further deprivation can spark disorder.[16] A number of criminologists, including Bert Useem in his studies made in the wake of a major riot at the Penitentiary of New Mexico in 1980, have noted that collective violence occurs in response to heightened measures of security at corrections facilities.[17] Thus, the violence occurs in response to an additional reduction in freedom for inmates, who enjoy very little freedom to begin with.

Riots, which have been defined as situations in which a number of prisoners are beyond institutional control for a significant amount of time,[18] are relatively rare. Because of their explosive nature and potential for high casualties, however, riots have a unique ability to focus public attention on prison conditions. The collective violence that took place in 1971 at Attica Prison in upstate New York has been described as a turning point in the history of American corrections because it alerted citizens to the situation in correctional facilities and spurred the prisoners' rights movement.[19]

The Spectrum of Violence The Attica Prison riot lasted five days in September 1971. Nearly half of the institution's 2,500 inmates seized control of most of the prison, holding thirty-eight correctional officers as hostages. In large measure, the riot was a reac-

Defrocked Catholic priest John Geoghan was strangled to death by another inmate at the maximum-security Souza-Baranowski Correctional Center in Shirley, Massachusetts. At the time of his 2003 murder, Geoghan was serving a nine- to ten-year sentence for groping a ten-year-old boy. What are some of the reasons that violence is prevalent in prison culture?

AP Photo/Michael; Dwyer, Pool

tion to the punitive atmosphere in Attica; during negotiations to end the standoff, one inmate complained, "We are men, we are not beasts and we will not be beaten or driven as such."[20] The talks ended abruptly when New York state troopers raided the prison grounds, killing thirty-nine inmates and wounding eighty-eight others. In the wake of the riot, however, New York Governor Nelson Rockefeller called for "radical reforms" in the state's corrections system, and twenty-four of the prisoners' original demands for such things as better food, more programs, and due process for disciplinary action were met.

The Attica riot has, however, proved to be the exception to the rule. Most riots are disorganized, and the participants have no political agenda. The incidents are marked by extreme levels of inmate-on-inmate violence and can often be attributed, at least in part, to poor living conditions and incompetent prison administration. The worst disturbance in the past forty years, for example, took place at the Penitentiary of New Mexico in Santa Fe in 1980. Prisoners killed thirty-three of their fellow inmates, and nearly two hundred others were tortured, beaten, and raped. The levels of violence—including the use of blowtorches on genitals—shocked the public. Two weeks *before* the riot, an outside consultant had warned that New Mexico prison officials were playing "Russian roulette with the lives of inmates" by failing to properly staff and train the personnel at the state's penal institutions.[21]

Issues of Race and Ethnicity The night before the Attica riot erupted, inmates yelled "[g]et a good night's sleep, whitey. Sleep tight, because tomorrow's the day." Officers in the prison were known to refer to their batons as "nigger sticks."[22] Race plays a major role in prison life, and prison violence is often an outlet for racial tension. As prison populations have changed over the past three decades, with African Americans and Hispanics becoming the majority in many penal institutions, issues of race and ethnicity have become increasingly important to prison administrators and researchers. (See the feature *You Be the Judge—Prison Segregation* on the next page.)

> "I've seen seven stabbings, about six bashings, and three self-mutilations. Two hangings, one attempted hanging, any number of overdoses. And that's only me, in just seventy days."
>
> —Anonymous jail inmate (1998)

As early as the 1950s, researchers were noticing different group structures in inmate life. At that time, for example, prisoners at California's Soledad Prison informally segregated themselves according to geography as well as race: Tejanos (Mexicans raised in Texas), Chicanos, blacks from California, blacks from the South and Southwest, and the majority whites all formed separate social worlds.[23]

Leo Carroll, professor of sociology at the University of Rhode Island, has written extensively on how today's prisoners are "balkanized," with race determining nearly every aspect of an inmate's life, including friends, job assignments, and cell location.[24] Carroll's research has also shown how minority groups in prison have seized on race to help form their prison identities.[25] In many instances, racial and ethnic identification is the primary focus of prison gangs, or cliques of inmates linked to illegal and violent activities such as prostitution, extortion, drug selling, gambling, and loan sharking. Though the stereotypical gang is composed of African Americans or Hispanics, in truth the array of different racial and ethnic prison groups is extensive. One of the most far-reaching and violent groups, for example, is the Aryan Brotherhood, or the Brand, a white supremacist gang that has transformed itself into a major criminal organization over the past fifteen years.[26] Regardless of make-up, however, gangs share the same purpose:

YOU BE THE JUDGE

Prison Segregation

THE FACTS

State X has an unwritten policy of assigning all new and transferred prisoners to cell mates of the same race and ethnicity for the first sixty days of incarceration. The state not only segregates African Americans, whites, and Hispanics in this manner but also keeps Japanese and Chinese inmates separate, as well as Laotians, Vietnamese, Cambodians, and Filipinos. Prison officials say the sixty-day segregation period allows them to determine the threat level posed by each new inmate. They claim that the policy is a necessary measure to prevent violence caused by racial gangs.

THE LAW

A government body is not permitted to make policy decisions based on race or ethnicity unless it can prove that there is no other way to "further compelling government interests."

YOUR DECISION

State X argues that it has a compelling interest in preventing racial violence in its prisons. Yet, no other state segregates its inmates in this manner. Neither does the federal government. Should prison officials be allowed to classify inmates based on race?

[To see how the United States Supreme Court ruled in a similar case, go to Example 14.1 in Appendix B.]

Their members have done in prison what many people do elsewhere when they feel personally powerless, threatened, and vulnerable: They align themselves with others, organize to fight back, and enhance their own status and control through their connection to a more powerful group.[27]

Rape

In contrast to riots, the problem of sexual assault in prisons receives very little attention from media sources. This can be partly attributed to the ambiguity of the subject: that rape occurs in prisons and jails is undisputed, but determining exactly how widespread the problem is has proved difficult. Prison officials, aware that any sexual contact is prohibited in most penal institutions, are often unwilling to provide realistic figures for fear of negative publicity. Even when they are willing, they may be unable to do so. Most inmates are ashamed of being rape victims and refuse to report instances of sexual assault. Consequently, it has been difficult to come up with consistent statistics for sexual assault in prison. While research published in *The Prison Journal* stated that about 21 percent of all inmates in four states had been sexually assaulted,[28] self-reported data gathered by the Human Rights Watch revealed that one in three inmates has been raped.[29]

Whatever the figures, prison rape, like all rape, is considered primarily an act of violence rather than sex. Inmates subject to rape ("punks") are near the bottom of the prison power structure and, in some instances, may accept rape by one particularly powerful inmate in return for protection from others.[30] Abused inmates often suffer from rape trauma syndrome and a host of other psychological ailments, including suicidal tendencies. Many prisons do not offer sufficient medical treatment for rape victims, nor does the prison staff take the necessary measures to protect obvious targets of rape— young, slightly built, nonviolent offenders. Furthermore, corrections officials are rarely held liable for inmate-on-inmate violence. To address the problem of prison rape, in 2003 the U.S. Congress passed the Prison Rape Elimination Act. The new legislation requires annual federal and state surveys of sexual assaults in prison, provides federal funds to train and educate corrections staff about rape, and encourages greater prosecution of prison rapists.[31]

INSIDE A WOMEN'S PRISON

When the first women's prison in the United States opened in 1839 on the grounds of New York's Sing Sing institution, the focus was on rehabilitation. Prisoners were groomed for a return to society

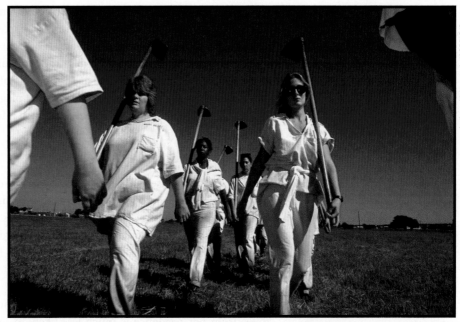

Inmates at a women's prison in Gatesville, Texas, prepare for work detail. Today, nearly 100,000 women are incarcerated in the United States, up from about 70,000 in 1995. Almost one hundred prisons in this country house only female inmates, compared to more than one thousand male correctional facilities.

with classes on reading, knitting, and sewing. Early women's reformatories had few locks or bars, and several contained nurseries for the inmates' young children.[32] Today, the situation is dramatically different. "Women's institutions are literally men's institutions, only we pull out the urinals," remarks Meda Chesney-Lind, a criminologist at the University of Hawaii.[33] Given the different circumstances surrounding male and female incarceration, this uniformity has had serious consequences for those who find themselves housed in one of the nearly one hundred women's prisons in this country.

Characteristics of Female Inmates

Although most research concerning the American corrections system focuses on male inmates and men's prisons, enough data exist to provide a portrait of women behind bars. The majority of female inmates are members of racial or ethnic minorities between the ages of twenty-five and forty-four.[34] Most have been incarcerated for a nonviolent drug or property crime[35] (see Figure 14.3). Only four in ten report having had full-time employment at the time of arrest, and nearly 30 percent were on welfare before incarceration, compared to just under 8 percent for male inmates.[36]

The single factor that most distinguishes female prisoners from their male counterparts is a history of physical or sexual abuse. A self-report study conducted by the

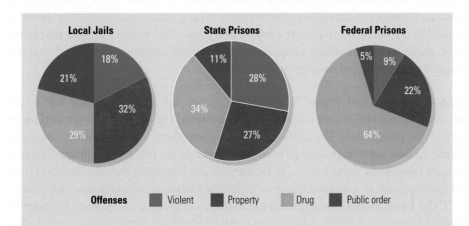

FIGURE 14.3

Offenses of Women in Jail and Prison

Sources: Bureau of Justice Statistics, *Sourcebook of Criminal Justice*, 3d ed. (Washington, D.C.: U.S. Department of Justice, 2003), 495, 519; and Bureau of Justice Statistics, *Special Report: Women Offenders* (Washington, D.C.: U.S. Department of Justice, December 1999), Table 15, page 6.

federal government indicates that 55 percent of female jail inmates have been abused at some point in their lives, compared to only 13 percent of male jail inmates.[37] Fifty-seven percent of women in state prisons and 40 percent of women in federal prisons report some form of past abuse; both figures are significantly higher than those for male prisoners.[38] Health experts believe that these levels of abuse are related to the significant amount of drug and/or alcohol addiction that plagues the female prison population, as well as to the mental illness problems that such addictions can cause or exacerbate.[39]

The Motherhood Problem

Drug and alcohol use within a women's prison can be a function of the anger and depression many inmates experience due to being separated from their children. An estimated seven out of every ten female prisoners have at least one minor child; more than 1.3 million American children have incarcerated mothers.[40] Given the scarcity of women's correctional facilities, inmates are often housed at great distances from their children. One study found that almost two-thirds of women in federal prison are more than five hundred miles from their homes.[41]

Further research indicates that an inmate who serves her sentence more than fifty miles from her residence is much less likely to receive phone calls or personal visits from family members. For most inmates and their families, the costs of "staying in touch" are too high.[42] This kind of separation can have serious consequences for the children of inmates. When a father goes to prison, his children are likely to live with their mother. When a mother is incarcerated, however, her children are likely to live with other relatives or, in about 10 percent of the cases, be sent to foster care.[43] Only three prisons in the United States—all in New York—allow inmates to have their infant children live with them, and even in these facilities nursery privileges end once the child is eighteen months old.[44]

Violence in Women's Prisons

There are no federal maximum- or medium-security women's prisons. Any female inmate that requires a high level of security is housed in a special unit of a men's prison. This does not mean, of course, that women's prisons are free of violence.

Inmate-on-Inmate Violence Compared to men's prisons, women's prisons have relatively low levels of physical aggression. Gang activity and violence do occur, but most incidents involve conflicts over personal relationships and do not play a large a role in daily prison life.[45] A recent survey of three women's prisons found that the amount of sexual coercion varies greatly from institution to institution and that only one out of every five such incidents could be classified as sexual assault or rape. Most of the unwanted contact involved "forceful sexual touching." Not surprisingly, the research showed that there is more inmate-on-inmate violence in women's prisons that house large numbers of offenders arrested for committing serious crimes and that are plagued by security and management problems.[46]

Sexual Violence and Prison Staff In the survey just mentioned, only half of the reports of sexual victimization involved other inmates. The other half implicated members of the prison staff. The problem of male correctional officers sexually assaulting female inmates has attracted much more attention over the past decade, primarily due to lawsuits brought by the prisoners. In recent years, such lawsuits have touched off criminal investigations in a number of states, including Alabama, Louisiana, and New Jersey.

The worst abuses, however, appear to have occurred in Michigan. A report by Human Rights Watch first brought to light problems of rape, impregnation, forced abortions, privacy violations, and retaliation in the state's corrections system nearly ten years ago.[47] Since the report's release, nearly 250 female inmates have sued the Michigan state government because of alleged sexual harassment by correctional officers. Court documents in these cases reveal serious lapses in the state corrections system's hiring practices; many officers assigned to guard female inmates in Michigan had records of criminal activity and domestic abuse.[48] For some, the solution to this problem seems clear: hire more female correctional officers and prohibit male guards from working in women's prisons.[49] In the past, however, male correctional officers have successfully sued in the courts to block such policies as discriminating against them on the basis of gender.[50]

The Pseudo-Family

As in male facilities, a system of prisonization is evident in women's prisons. The adaptation process in the female institution, however, relies on tightly knit cliques of prisoners that mimic the traditional family structure. The more experienced convicts adopt the role of the "father" or "mother" and act as parent figures for younger, inexperienced "sons" or "daughters." Inmates choose their roles depending on appearance, personality, and background. As in "real" families, prison female families restrict sexual contact between members, relying on each other primarily for emotional support.[51]

> "I know not whether Laws be right
> Or whether Laws be wrong;
> All that we know who live in gaol
> Is that the wall is strong;
> And that each day is like a year,
> A year whose days are long."
> —Oscar Wilde, Irish playwright, author (1898)

Homosexuality often manifests itself in a women's prison through the formation of another traditional family model: the monogamous couple. One member of the couple chooses the role of the husband, and the other becomes the wife.[52] In general, sex between inmates plays a different role in women's prisons than in men's prisons. In the latter, rape is considered an act of aggression and power rather than sex, and "true" homosexuals are relegated to the lowest rungs of the social hierarchy. By contrast, women who engage in sexual activity in prison are not automatically labeled homosexual, and lesbians are not hampered in their social-climbing efforts.[53]

Researchers have also found that female inmates share a great deal more than their male counterparts. In a men's prison, self-sufficiency and autonomy are valued, whereas in women's prisons members of cliques and families allocate cosmetics, foods, clothes, and other goods.[54] (One observer points out that this greater tendency to share may be attributed to the fact that women are allowed more personal belongings in prison than men are.[55])

CORRECTIONAL OFFICERS AND DISCIPLINE

Under model circumstances, the presence of correctional officers—the standard term used to describe prison guards—would mitigate the levels of violence in American correctional institutions. To a large extent, this is indeed the case; without correctional officers, the prison would be a place of anarchy. But in the highly regulated, oppressive environment of the prison, correctional officers must use the threat of violence, if not actual violence, to instill discipline and keep order. Thus, the relationship between prison staff and inmates is marked by mutual distrust. Consider the two following statements, the first made by a correctional officer and the second by a prisoner:

> [My job is to] protect, feed, and try to educate scum who raped and brutalized women and children . . . who, if I turn my back, will go into their cell, wrap a blanket around their cellmate's legs, and threaten to beat or rape him if he doesn't give sex, carry contraband, or fork over radios, money, or other goods willingly. And they'll stick a shank in me tomorrow if they think they can get away with it.[56]

The pigs in the state and federal prisons . . . treat me so violently, I cannot possibly imagine a time I could ever have anything but the deepest, aching, searing hatred for them. I can't begin to tell you what they do to me. If I were weaker by a hair, they would destroy me.[57]

The **U.S. Department of Labor** offers information about a career as a correctional officer. Find its Web site by clicking on *Web Links* under *Chapter Resources* at **www.cjinaction.com**.

It may be difficult for an outsider to understand the emotions that fuel such sentiments. French philosopher Michael Foucault points out that discipline, both in prison and in the general community, is a means of social organization as well as punishment.[58] Discipline is imposed when a person behaves in a manner that is contrary to the values of the dominant social group. Correctional officers and inmates have different concepts of the ideal structure of prison society, and, as the two quotations above demonstrate, this conflict generates intense feelings of fear and hatred, which often lead to violence.

Rank and Duties of Correctional Officers

After seven convicts escaped from the Connally Unit in Kenedy, Texas, several years ago, much of the blame fell on the custodial staff. Security at the facility had been extremely lax, with officers failing to properly identify individuals before opening gates, leaving prison vehicles unattended on the premises, and allowing unsupervised prisoners to work in a maintenance room. To avoid such problems and promote efficiency, in most prisons each correctional officer has a clearly delineated rank and duty. The custodial staff at most prisons is organized according to four general ranks—captain, lieutenant, sergeant, and officer. In keeping with the militaristic model, captains are primarily administrators who deal directly with the warden on custodial issues. Lieutenants are the disciplinarians of the prison, responsible for policing and transporting the inmates. Sergeants oversee platoons of officers in specific parts of the prison, such as various cell blocks or work spaces.

Lucien X. Lombardo, professor of sociology and criminal justice at Old Dominion University, has identified six general job categories among correctional officers:[59]

1 *Block officers.* These employees supervise cell blocks containing as many as four hundred inmates, as well as the correctional officers on block guard duty. In general, the block officer is responsible for the "well-being" of the inmates. He or she makes sure the inmates do not harm themselves or other prisoners and also acts as something of a camp counselor, dispensing advice and seeing that inmates understand and follow the rules of the facility.

2 *Work detail supervisors.* In many penal institutions, the inmates work in the cafeteria, the prison store, the laundry, and other areas. Work detail supervisors oversee small groups of inmates as they perform these tasks.

3 *Industrial shop and school officers.* These officers perform maintenance and security functions in workshop and educational programs. Their primary responsibility is to make sure that inmates are on time for these programs and do not cause any disturbances during the sessions.

4 *Yard officers.* Officers who work the prison yard usually have the least seniority, befitting the assignment's reputation as dangerous and stressful. These officers must be constantly on alert for breaches in prison discipline or regulations in the relatively unstructured environment of the prison yard.

5 *Tower guards.* These officers spend their entire shifts, which usually last eight hours, in isolated, silent posts high above the grounds of the facility. Although their only means of communication are walkie-talkies or cellular devices, the safety benefits of the position can outweigh the loneliness that comes with the job.

Robert M. Lucas
Corrections Facility Commander

My interest in the corrections field grew out of the need to be involved in solving problems associated with crime and punishment. I began my career as a law enforcement deputy. On completion of my undergraduate studies I sought experience in the counseling and programs aspects of detention. Ultimately I became interested in the management of jails and decided to become a sworn detention officer. My career path has given me a unique perspective from having experience in three major components of criminal justice: law enforcement, detention, and programs. Throughout my career I have continued my education as a corrections professional; my accomplishments include a master of arts degree in criminal justice from the University of South Florida, and I am a graduate of the Southern Police Institute's administrative officers course.

I am currently assigned as a facility commander in a 1,714-bed direct supervision jail. The facility is divided into two factions: housing and central intake. Central intake encompasses all facets of booking as well as the classification and records bureau. There is a combined total of approximately 300 sworn and civilian employees assigned to this multidimensional command and responsible for the processing and booking of over 62,000 inmates in 1998. Additionally, my command must ensure that inmates make all required court appearances and that all transfers or releases are proper and within established releasing standards. My most important duties are ensuring that staff are properly trained; that staff are assigned to functions which guarantee security is maintained at the highest level; and that all inmates are treated in accordance with local, state, and federal standards.

A defining incident in my career was being involved in the mass arrest of 186 individuals as a result of a demonstration. As an assistant tactical commander, I was responsible for remote booking, security, crowd control, and the coordination of inmate transportation to the central jail facility. The incident was significant from two aspects: 1) the dynamics and logistics involved in the arrest, detainment, and booking of a large number of individuals in a short period of time; and 2) the awareness of the importance of a cooperative effort between law enforcement and detention. A number of problems were immediately evident in the arrest and processing of this large number of inmates, includ-

Courtesy Robert M. Lucas

Robert M. Lucas

ing security, site location, feeding, sanitation, and medical care for those in need. As is typical with most agencies, the booking process was normally accomplished in a secure facility separate from any outside disruptive factors. The remote booking exposed the staff to dissidents and necessitated the initial processing of the inmates in a temporary booking area without normal security.

This incident clearly displayed the talents and abilities of the detention staff assigned to the tactical unit. The members functioned as a disciplined team and demonstrated to law enforcement peers that members of the detention staff were capable and anxious to work together toward common goals. Subsequent to that mass arrest, the detention tactical unit has worked in tandem with law enforcement in training exercises, support for crowd control during a Super Bowl game, preparation for natural disasters, search for missing persons, and the development of an honor guard in which representatives from detention and law enforcement routinely perform together at funerals, civic events, dedications, and public demonstrations.

I feel the qualities essential to the corrections field are those common to most fields, such as a desire to perform at a high level of standards, a commitment to personal growth through change and development, and facing each task as a challenge as opposed to a problem. The management and operation of any detention facility is taxing, and it challenges the abilities, knowledge, and experience of those in supervisory roles. Staff are expected to fulfill a number of roles and encounter any number of problems or emergencies daily. The jail practitioner of today must be well versed in all aspects of the jail operation and applicable laws and standards, and be able to address problems associated with expanding inmate populations, construction needs, and specialized inmate categories.

Go to the Careers in Criminal Justice Interactive CD *for more profiles in the field of criminal justice.*

6 *Administrative building assignments.* Officers who hold these positions provide security at prison gates, oversee visitation procedures, act as liaisons for civilians, and handle administrative tasks such as processing the paperwork when an inmate is transferred from another institution.

One benefit of the prison boom has been economic, as prisons infuse money and jobs into the regions where they are located. These regions are often rural and poor. In upstate New York's North County, for example, the average worker earns about $20,000 a year; the correctional officers at North County's Clinton Prison, shown above, earn an average of $40,000. Working as a correctional officer is one of the few ways that residents of North County who do not have a college degree can enjoy a middle-class life. Furthermore, as prisons are recessionproof, job security among correctional officers is higher than in most other local industries. Why, despite these benefits, does the profession of correctional officer continue to have a negative image?

Discipline

As Erving Goffman noted in his essay on the "total institution," in the general society adults are rarely placed in a position where they are "punished" as a child would be.[60] Therefore, the strict disciplinary measures imposed on prisoners come as something of a shock and can provoke strong defensive reactions. Correctional officers who must deal with these responses often find that disciplining inmates is the most difficult and stressful aspect of their job.

The Severity of Sanctions The prisoners' manual lists the types of behavior that can result in disciplinary action. An institutional disciplinary committee decides the sanctions for specific types of misconduct. These sanctions include loss of privileges such as visiting and recreational opportunities for minor infractions, as well as more serious punishments for major infractions. The most severe sanction is *solitary confinement*, also known as administrative or punitive segregation, in which an inmate is removed from the general prison population and placed alone in a cell. Under certain circumstances, this form of punishment can violate the Eighth Amendment's prohibition against "cruel and unusual punishment"—if the cell is too small (less than five by seven feet), the length of confinement is too long, or the prisoner is deprived of necessary warmth and "modesty."[61] Otherwise, solitary confinement is an effective and widely used practice. In Florida, 7.4 percent of the state's prisoners are in solitary confinement at any given time, and three other states (Illinois, New York, and Texas) keep more than 6 percent of their prisoners separated from other inmates in this manner.[62]

Discipline and Discretion For the most part, the judicial system has not greatly restricted disciplinary actions in prison. Generally, correctional officers are given the same discretionary powers as police officers (discussed in Chapter 5) to use their experience to determine when force is warranted. In *Whitley v. Albers* (1986),[63] the Supreme Court held that the use of force by prison officials violates an inmate's Eighth Amendment protections only if the force amounts to "the unnecessary and wanton infliction of pain." Excessive force can be considered "necessary" if the legitimate security interests of the penal institution are at stake. Consequently, an appeals court ruled that when officers at a Maryland prison formed an "extraction team" to remove the leader of a riot from his cell, beating him in the process, the use of force was justified given the situation.[64]

In contrast, in *Hudson v. McMillan* (1992)[65] the Supreme Court ruled that minor injuries suffered by a convict at the hands of a correctional officer following an argument did violate the inmate's rights, because there was no security concern at the time of the incident. In other words, the issue is not *how much* force was used, but whether the officer used the force as part of a good faith effort to restore discipline or acted "maliciously and sadistically" to cause harm. This "malicious and sadistic" standard has been difficult for aggrieved prisoners to meet; in the ten years following the *Hudson* decision, only about 20 percent of excessive force lawsuits against correctional officials were successful.[66]

PROTECTING PRISONERS' RIGHTS

The general attitude of the law toward inmates is summed up by the Thirteenth Amendment to the U.S. Constitution:

> Neither slavery nor involuntary servitude, except as a punishment for crime whereof the party shall have been duly convicted, shall exist within the United States.

In other words, inmates do not have the same guaranteed rights as other Americans. For most of the nation's history, courts have followed the spirit of this amendment by applying the **"hands-off" doctrine** of prisoner law. This (unwritten) doctrine assumes that the care of inmates should be left to prison officials and that it is not the place of judges to intervene in penal administrative matters.

In the 1960s, as disenfranchised groups from all parts of society began to insist on their constitutional rights, prisoners did so as well. Movement leaders demanded, and received, fuller recognition of prisoners' rights and greater access to American courts. It would be difficult, however, to label the movement a complete success. As one observer notes, "conditions of confinement in many American prisons have deteriorated during the same time period in which judicial recognition and concern for prisoners' legal rights dramatically increased."[67]

The "Hands-On" Approach

The end of the "hands-off" period can be dated to the Supreme Court's decision in *Cooper v. Pate* (1964).[68] In this case, Cooper, an inmate at the Illinois State Penitentiary, filed a petition for relief under the Civil Rights Act of 1871, stating that he had a First Amendment right to purchase reading material about the Black Muslim movement. The Court, overturning rulings of several lower courts, held that the act did protect the constitutional rights of prisoners. This decision effectively allowed inmates to file civil lawsuits under Title 42 of the United States Code, Section 1983—known simply as Section 1983— if they felt that a prison or jail was denying their civil rights. An inmate who has been beaten by a correctional officer, for example, can bring a Section 1983 suit against the penal institution for denial of Eighth Amendment protection from cruel and unusual punishment.

Symbolically, the Supreme Court's declaration in *Wolff v. McDonnell* (1974)[69] that "[t]here is no iron curtain drawn between the Constitution and the prisons of this country" was just as significant as the *Cooper* ruling. It signaled to civil rights lawyers that the Court would no longer follow the "hands-off" doctrine. The case had practical overtones as well, establishing that prisoners have a right to the following basic due process procedures when being disciplined by a penal institution:

- A fair hearing.
- Written notice at least twenty-four hours in advance of the hearing.
- An opportunity to speak at the hearing (though not to be represented by counsel during the hearing).
- An opportunity to call witnesses (unless doing so jeopardizes prison security).
- A written statement detailing the final decision and reasons for that decision.

In the 1970s, the prisoners' rights movement also led to Court decisions establishing an inmate's constitutional right to practice non-"mainstream" religions,[70] to send and receive uncensored mail,[71] and to spend no more than thirty consecutive days in solitary confinement.[72] In 2005, in a case brought by a Wiccan and a Satanist, the Court solidified its support for the free practice of religion in correctional facilities by upholding a federal law requiring prisons to

"Hands-Off" Doctrine
The unwritten judicial policy that favors noninterference by the courts in the administration of prisons and jails.

Roderick Johnson, pictured below, filed a lawsuit against the Texas Department of Corrections alleging that prison officials refused to protect him when he was sold as a "sex slave" by other inmates and raped hundreds of times at the Allred Unit facility in Iowa Park. Under what circumstances can inmates expect courts to address unbearable living conditions?

© Brandon McKelvey/Daily Texan

INTERNATIONAL CJ

Terrorist Breeding Grounds?

When José Emilio Suarez Trashorras went into a Spanish prison for a drug offense, he was neither particularly religious nor politically active. The same could be said for Jamal Ahmidan, who was also serving time in the same facility after being convicted of a similarly petty crime. By the time Trashorras and Ahmidan left the prison, however, they had embraced radical Islamic beliefs and were quickly recruited by Takfir wa al-Hijra, a Moroccan terrorist organization. Several years later, the two ex-convicts helped carry out the March 11, 2004, bombing attack on the Madrid subway system that killed 191 commuters and left hundreds more injured.

Law enforcement and prison officials throughout Europe are increasingly wary of the threat posed by terrorist recruitment in their prisons and jails. Over the past two decades, the wealthy nations of Western Europe have experienced an influx of immigrants, a large number of whom are from Turkey and other countries with significant Muslim populations. Given the low socioeconomic status of many of these immigrants, it is not surprising that they also make up a growing percentage of European prison populations. Because those who are detained or arrested for terrorist-related crimes are not separated from other inmates in most European correctional facilities, many experts fear that fundamentalist militants take advantage of the situation to proselytize and enlist new members.

Trashorras and Ahmidan are not the only examples of this phenomenon. Richard Reid, who tried to blow up a commercial airliner en route from Paris to Miami, Florida, in 2001 with a shoe bomb, converted to Islam while at a juvenile detention center in London. A militant Islamist serving time for credit-card fraud convinced several of his fellow inmates to aid him in an ultimately unsuccessful attempt to blow up Spain's main counter-terrorism court in 2004. José Padilla, detained several years ago for his role in an alleged plot to detonate a "dirty bomb" in the United States, is believed to have discovered Islam in a South Florida jail. "It's in prison where political operatives recruit specialists whom they need to run their networks—specialists in fraudulent documents, arms trafficking, etc.," says Belgian terrorism expert Alain Grignard. "The prisons of today are producing the terrorists of tomorrow."

FOR CRITICAL ANALYSIS

Padilla's apparent jailhouse conversion to a radical form of Islam drew attention to the possibility of organized terrorist recruitment operations in U.S. prisons and jails. Even though no concrete evidence of such activity has been produced, Federal Bureau of Investigation director Robert Mueller recently told the U.S. Senate that prisons are a "fertile ground" for terrorist exploitation. Under what circumstances do you think that American prison officials should be able to restrict religious activities such as Muslim prayer meetings in the interests of national security?

---

accommodate the practice and beliefs of all inmates.[73] (This commitment to freedom of religion in prisons and jails has caused some concern in homeland security circles, as you can see in the feature *International CJ—Terrorist Breeding Grounds?*)

Limiting Prisoners' Rights

Despite these successes, not all proponents of prisoners' rights feel that the courts have entirely abandoned the "hands-off" doctrine. Instead, they believe that by establishing standards of "deliberate indifference" and "identifiable human needs," court rulings have merely provided penal institutions with legally acceptable methods of denying prisoners' constitutional protections.

"Deliberate Indifference"
A standard that must be met by inmates trying to prove that their Eighth Amendment rights were violated by a correctional facility. It occurs when prison officials are aware of harmful conditions of confinement but fail to take steps to remedy those conditions.

"Deliberate Indifference" In the 1976 case *Estelle v. Gamble*,[74] the Supreme Court established the **"deliberate indifference"** standard. Specifically, Justice Thurgood Marshall wrote that prison officials violated a convict's Eighth Amendment rights if they deliberately failed to provide him or her with necessary medical care. At the time, the decision was hailed as a victory for prisoners' rights, and it continues to ensure that a certain level of health care is provided. Defining "deliberate" has proved difficult, however. Does it mean that prison officials "should have known" that an inmate was placed in harm's way, or does it mean that prison officials purposefully placed the inmate in that position?

The "Purpose" Requirement In subsequent decisions, the Supreme Court appears to have accepted the latter interpretation. In ruling on two separate 1986 cases, for example, the Court held that "simple negligence" was not acceptable grounds for a Section 1983 civil suit, and that a prison official's behavior was actionable only if it was done "maliciously or sadistically for the very purpose of causing harm."[75] As it is quite difficult to prove in court a person's state of mind, the "deliberate negligence" standard has become a formidable one for prisoners to meet.

In *Wilson v. Seiter* (1991),[76] for example, Pearly L. Wilson filed a Section 1983 suit alleging that certain conditions of his confinement—including overcrowding; excessive noise; inadequate heating, cooling, and ventilation; and unsanitary bathroom and dining facilities—were cruel and unusual. The Supreme Court ruled against Wilson, stating that he had failed to prove that these conditions, even if they existed, were the result of "deliberate indifference" on the part of prison officials. Three years later, in a case concerning a transsexual inmate who was placed in the general population of a federal prison and subsequently beaten and raped, the Court narrowed the definition of "deliberate" even further. Though ruling in favor of the inmate, it held that the prison official must both be aware of the facts that create a potential for harm and also *draw the conclusion* that those facts will lead to harm.[77]

"Identifiable Human Needs" The *Wilson* decision created another standard for determining Eighth Amendment violations that has drawn criticism from civil rights lawyers. It asserted that a prisoner must show that the institution has denied her or him a basic human need such as food, warmth, or exercise.[78] The Court failed, however, to mention any other needs besides these three, forcing other courts to interpret **"identifiable human needs"** for themselves. Taking a similar slant, in *Sandin v. Conner* (1995),[79] the Court ruled that inmates have rights to due process in disciplinary matters only when the punishment imposes "atypical or significant hardships in relation to ordinary incidents of prison life." This standard usually applies only when the punishment affects the length of a sentence, but in 2005 the Court did follow the *Sandin* ruling in holding that inmates transferred to a supermax prison have the right to a hearing because conditions in those facilities (discussed in Chapter 13) reach the level of atypical and significant hardship.[80]

PAROLE AND RELEASE FROM PRISON

At any given time, more than 750,000 Americans are living in the community on **parole,** or the *conditional* release of a prisoner after a portion of his or her sentence has been served. Parole allows the corrections system to continue to supervise an offender who is no longer incarcerated. As long as parolees follow the conditions of their parole, they are allowed to finish their terms outside the prison. If parolees break the terms of their early release, however, they face the risk of being returned to a penal institution.

According to Todd Clear and George F. Cole, parole is based on three concepts:

1 *Grace.* The prisoner has no right to be given an early release, but the government has granted her or him that privilege.

2 *Contract of consent.* The government and the parolee enter into an arrangement whereby the latter agrees to abide by certain conditions in return for continued freedom.

3 *Custody.* Technically, though no longer incarcerated, the parolee is still the responsibility of the state. Parole is an extension of corrections.[81] (The phonetic and administrative similarities between probation and parole can be confusing. See *Mastering Concepts—Probation versus Parole* on p. 470 for clarification.)

"Identifiable Human Needs"
The basic human necessities that correctional facilities are required by the Constitution to provide to inmates. Beyond food, warmth, and exercise, the court system has been unable to establish exactly what these needs are.

Parole
The conditional release of an inmate before his or her sentence has expired. The remainder of the sentence is served in the community under the supervision of correctional (parole) officers, and the offender can be returned to incarceration if he or she breaks the conditions of parole, as determined by a parole board.

MASTERING CONCEPTS

Probation versus Parole

Probation and parole have many aspects in common. In fact, probation and parole are so similar that many jurisdictions combine them into a single agency. There are, however, some important distinctions between the two systems, as noted below.

Because of these differences, many observers believe that probation and parole should not be combined in the same agency, though limited financial resources will assure that many jurisdictions will continue to do so.

	PROBATION	PAROLE
Basic Definition	An alternative to imprisonment in which a person who has been convicted of a crime is allowed to serve his or her sentence in the community subject to certain conditions and supervision by a probation officer.	An early release from a correctional facility as determined by an administrative body (the parole board), in which the convicted offender is given the chance to spend the remainder of his or her sentence under supervision in the community.
Timing	The offender is sentenced to a probationary term in place of a prison or jail term. If the offender breaks the conditions of probation, he or she is sent to prison or jail. Therefore, probation occurs *before* imprisonment.	Parole is a form of early release. Therefore, parole occurs *after* an offender has spent time behind bars.
Authority	Probation falls under the domain of the judiciary. In other words, judges make the decision whether to send a convicted offender to prison or jail or to give her or him a sentence of probation. If a person violates the terms of probation, a judge ultimately decides whether she or he should be sent to a correctional facility as punishment.	Parole falls under the domain of an administrative body (often appointed by an executive such as a state governor) known as the parole board. The parole board determines whether the prisoner is qualified for early release, and under which conditions he or she will be allowed to remain in the community. When a parolee violates the conditions of parole, the parole board must decide whether to send him or her back to prison. (Although they may be asked to make recommendations to the parole board, judges generally are *not* involved in the parole decision.)
Characteristics of Offenders	As a number of studies have shown, probationers are normally less involved in the criminal lifestyle. Most of them are first-time offenders who have committed nonviolent crimes.	Many parolees have spent months or even years in prison and, besides abiding by conditions of parole, must make the difficult transition to "life on the outside."

Because of good-time credits and parole, most prisoners do not serve their entire sentence in prison. In fact, the average felon serves only about half of the term handed down by the court.

Other Types of Prison Release

Parole, a conditional release, is the most common form of release, but it is not the only one (see Figure 14.4). Prisoners receive an unconditional release when they have completed the terms of their sentence and no longer require incarceration or supervision. One form of unconditional release is **mandatory release** (also known as "maxing out"), which occurs when an inmate has served the maximum amount of time on the initial sentence, minus reductions for good-time credits.

Another, quite rare unconditional release is a **pardon,** a form of executive clemency. The president (on the federal level) and the governor (on the state level) can

Mandatory Release
Release from prison that occurs when an offender has served the length of his or her sentence, with time taken off for good behavior.

Pardon
An act of executive clemency that overturns a conviction and erases mention of the crime from the person's criminal record.

grant a pardon, or forgive a convict's criminal punishment. Most states have a board of pardons—affiliated with the parole board—which makes recommendations to the governor in cases in which it believes a pardon is warranted. Most pardons involve obvious miscarriages of justice, though sometimes a governor will pardon an individual to remove the stain of conviction from his or her criminal record.

Certain *temporary releases* also exist. Some inmates, who qualify by exhibiting good behavior and generally proving that they do not represent a risk to society, are allowed to leave the prison on **furlough** for a certain amount of time, usually between a day and a week. At times, a furlough is granted because of a family emergency, such as a funeral. Furloughs can be particularly helpful for an inmate who is nearing release and can use them to ease the readjustment period.

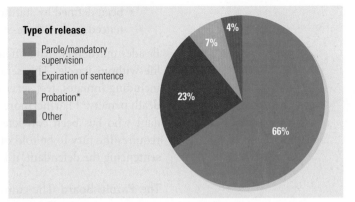

Type of release
- Parole/mandatory supervision
- Expiration of sentence
- Probation*
- Other

4%
7%
23%
66%

*As the second step in a split sentence.

FIGURE 14.4
Release from State and Federal Correctional Facilities

Source: Adapted from Bureau of Justice Statistics, *Correctional Populations in the United States, 1998* (Washington, D.C.: U.S. Department of Justice, 2002), Table 5.13.

Discretionary Release

As you may recall from Chapter 11, corrections systems are classified by sentencing procedure—indeterminate or determinate. Indeterminate sentencing occurs when the legislature sets a range of punishments for particular crimes, and the judge and the parole board exercise discretion in determining the actual length of the prison term. For that reason, states with indeterminate sentencing are said to have systems of **discretionary release.** Until the mid-1970s, all states and the federal government operated in this manner.

Eligibility for Parole Under indeterminate sentencing, parole is not a right but a privilege. This is a crucial point, as it establishes the terms of the relationship between the inmate and the corrections authorities during the parole process. In *Greenholtz v. Inmates of the Nebraska Penal and Correctional Complex* (1979),[82] the Supreme Court ruled that inmates do not have a constitutionally protected right to expect parole, thereby giving states the freedom to set their own standards for determining parole eligibility. In most states that have retained indeterminate sentencing, a prisoner is eligible to be considered for parole release after serving a legislatively determined percentage of the minimum sentence—usually one-half or two-thirds—less any good time or other credits.

Contrary to what is depicted in many films and television shows, a convict does not "apply" for parole. An inmate's case automatically comes up before the parole board a certain number of days—often ninety—before she or he is eligible for parole. The date of eligibility depends on statutory requirements, the terms of the sentence, and the behavior of the inmate in prison. The board has an eligibility report prepared, which provides information on the various factors that must be considered in making the decision. The board also reviews the case file to acquaint itself with the original crime and conducts an interview with the inmate. At some point before the eligibility date, the entire board, or a subcommittee of the board, votes on whether parole will be granted.

Not all convicts are eligible for parole. Many states have a sentencing system in which offenders who have committed the most serious crimes receive life terms without the possibility of early release. In general, life-without-parole is reserved for those offenders who have

- committed capital, or first degree, murder;
- committed serious offenses other than murder; or

Furlough

Temporary release from a prison for purposes of vocational or educational training, to ease the shock of release, or for personal reasons.

Discretionary Release

The release of an inmate into a community supervision program at the discretion of the parole board within limits set by state or federal law.

• been defined by statute as habitual, or repeat, offenders, such as those sentenced under "three-strikes" laws.[83]

Besides murderers, drug offenders and sex offenders are most commonly targeted for life-without-parole. The sentence is fraught with controversy, as many observers, including inmates, feel serving life-without-parole is a crueler punishment than the death penalty.[84] Furthermore, the Supreme Court has ruled that when a capital defendant who has been convicted of murder will be ineligible for parole, due process requires the jury to be told of this fact.[85] In other words, the jury must know that, in sentencing the defendant, it has a choice between execution and life-without-parole.

The Parole Board The cumulative efforts of the police, the courtroom work group, and correctional officials lead to a single question in most cases: When should an offender be released?[86] This is a difficult question and is often left to the **parole board** to answer. When members of the parole board make what in retrospect was a mistake, they quickly draw the attention of the media, the public, and the courts.

According to the American Correctional Association, the parole board has four basic roles:

1 To decide which offenders should be placed on parole.
2 To determine the conditions of parole and aid in the continuing supervision of the parolee.
3 To discharge the offender when the conditions of parole have been met.
4 If a violation occurs, to determine whether parole privileges should be revoked.[87]

Most parole boards are small, made up of five to seven members. In many jurisdictions, board members' terms are limited to between four and six years. The requirements for board members vary. Nearly half the states have no prerequisites, while others require a bachelor's degree or some expertise in the field of criminal justice.

Parole boards are either affiliated with government agencies or act as independent bodies. In the first instance, board members are usually members of the correctional staff appointed by the state department of corrections. In contrast, independent parole boards are made up of citizens from the community who have been chosen for the post by a government official, usually the governor. Because most states with independent boards have no specific criteria for the members, critics believe that these boards tend to be "politicized" by the appointment of members—who have limited knowledge of the criminal justice system—as a return for political favors.[88]

The Parole Hearing In a system that uses discretionary parole, the actual release decision is made at a **parole grant hearing.** During this hearing, the entire board or a subcommittee reviews relevant information on the convict. Sometimes, but not always, the offender is interviewed. Because the board members have only limited knowledge of each offender, key players in the case are often notified in advance of the parole hearing and asked to provide comments and recommendations. These participants include the sentencing judge, the attorneys at the trial, the victims, and any law enforcement officers who may be involved.[89] After these preparations, the typical parole hearing itself is very short—usually lasting just a few minutes.

If parole is denied, the entire process is replayed at the next "action date," which depends on the nature of the offender's crimes and all relevant laws. In 2004, for example, Leslie Van Houten was denied parole for the fifteenth time. Van Houten was convicted of murder in 1969 for the role she played in the gruesome Beverly Hills, California, killing of pregnant actress Sharon Tate and six others under the direction of Charles Manson. While in prison, Van Houten—who claims that she played a minimal role in the murders—has earned bachelor's and master's degrees and has never

Parole Board
A body of appointed civilians that decides whether a convict should be granted conditional release before the end of his or her sentence.

Parole Grant Hearing
A hearing in which the entire parole board or a subcommittee reviews information, meets the offender, and hears testimony from relevant witnesses to determine whether to grant parole.

had a disciplinary report filed against her. Families of the victims continue to petition the California Board of Prison Terms to keep her incarcerated. Although the board has said Van Houten's chances improve with each hearing, most observers believe she will never be released. (Manson himself has been denied parole nine times and stated during his last hearing in 1997 that he did not want to be released.) In some states, the parole board is required to give written reasons for denying parole, and some jurisdictions give the inmate, prosecution, or victims the option to appeal the board's decision.

The Emergence of Mandatory Release

The legitimacy of discretionary release relies to a certain extent on the perception of parole decisions by offenders, victims, and the general public. Like judicial discretion (as we discussed in Chapter 11), parole board discretion is criticized when the decisions are seen as arbitrary and unfair and lead to rampant disparity in the release dates of similar offenders.[90] Proponents of discretionary release argue that parole boards must tailor their decisions to the individual case, but such protestations seem to be undermined by the raw data: research done by the Bureau of Justice Statistics has found that most offenders were serving less than a third of their sentences in the early 1990s.[91]

As Michael Tonry noted, such statistics gave the impression that parole board members "tossed darts at a dartboard" to determine who should be released, and when.[92] As a result of this criticism, twenty-seven states have now implemented determinate sentencing systems, which set minimum mandatory terms without possibility of parole. These systems provide for *mandatory release*, in which offenders leave incarceration when their sentences have expired, minus adjustments made for good time.

Truth in Sentencing The move toward mandatory release has come partly at the urging of the federal government. The federal sentencing guidelines that went into effect in 1987 required those who were convicted in federal courts to serve at least 85 percent of their terms.[93] Federal crime bills in 1994 and 1995 encouraged states to adopt this truth-in-sentencing (previously mentioned in Chapter 11) approach by making federal aid for prison construction conditional on the passage of such laws.[94] Twenty-nine states have done just that, while fourteen others feature less stringent truth-in-sentencing statutes.[95]

Truth in sentencing is an umbrella term that covers a number of different state and federal statutes. In general, these laws have the following goals:

- To restore "truth" to the sentencing process by eliminating situations in which offenders are released by a parole board after serving less than the minimum term to which they were sentenced.

- To increase the percentage of the term that is actually served in prison, with the purpose of reducing crime by keeping convicts imprisoned for a longer period.

- To control the use of prison space by giving corrections officials the benefit of predictable terms and policymakers advance notice of the impact that sentencing statutes will have on prison populations.[96]

Note that fourteen states and the federal government have officially "abolished" parole. For the most part, however, these states simply emphasize prison terms that are "truthful," not necessarily "longer." Therefore, in Louisiana—noted for its harsh

Andrew Lichtenstein/CORBIS/Sygma

In August 2003, Kathy Boudin was released on parole after serving twenty-two years in prison for her role in an armored-car robbery and shootout that left three persons, including two police officers, dead. Despite opposition from the victims' families, the New York Parole Board decided that Boudin's work with AIDS sufferers and incarcerated mothers at the Bedford Hill Correctional Facility warranted her early release. What effect should such good works have on the parole decision when, as in this case, the initial crime was of a "serious and brutal nature"?

sentencing practices—violent offenders who serve only 50 percent of their term spend more time in prison than do prisoners in many states that have "abolished" parole.[97]

Parole Guidelines One of the most popular methods of ensuring truth in sentencing is the use of **parole guidelines.** Similar to sentencing guidelines (see Chapter 11), parole guidelines attempt to measure a potential parolee's risk of recidivism by considering factors such as the original offense, criminal history, behavior in prison, past employment, substance abuse, and performance under any previous periods of parole or probation. Inmates who score positively in these areas are considered less likely to pose a danger to society and have a better chance of obtaining an early release date.

Parole Supervision

The term *parole* has two meanings. The first, as we have seen, refers to the establishment of a release date. The second relates to the continuing supervision of convicted felons after they have been released from prison.

Conditions of Parole Many of the procedures and issues of parole supervision are similar to those of probation supervision. Like probationers, when parolees are granted parole, they are placed under the supervision of correctional officers and required to follow certain conditions. Some of these conditions are fairly uniform. All parolees, for example, must comply with the law, and they are generally responsible for reporting to their parole officer at certain intervals. The frequency of these visits, along with the other terms of parole, is spelled out in the **parole contract,** which sets out the agreement between the state and the paroled offender. Under the terms of the contract, the state agrees to release the inmate under certain conditions, and the future parolee agrees to follow these conditions.

Each jurisdiction has its own standard parole contract, although the parole board can add specific provisions if it sees the need (see Figure 14.5). Besides common restrictions, such as no drug use, no association with known felons, and no change of address without notifying authorities, parolees have on occasion been ordered to lose weight and even to undergo chemical castration.

Parole plans are not always so one sided. In some instances, prison authorities will agree to help the parolee find employment and a place to live during the supervision period. **Work release programs** are usually available for low-risk prisoners nearing the end of their sentences. Inmates on work release programs must either return to the correctional facility in the evening or live in community residential facilities, known as **halfway houses.** These facilities, also available to other parolees and those who have finished their sentences, are often remodeled hotels or private homes. They provide a less institutional living environment than a prison or jail for a small number of inmates (usually between ten and twenty-five).

Parole Officers The correctional agent assigned the responsibility of supervising parolees is the parole officer. In many respects, the parole officer's relationship with the parolee mirrors that of the probation officer and the probationer (see Chapter 12); in fact, many municipal and state departments of corrections combine the two posts to create probation/parole officers. Parole officers are required to enforce the conditions of parole and initiate revocation hearings when these conditions are not met. Furthermore, a parole officer is expected to help the parolee readjust to life outside the

Parole Guidelines
Employed to remove discretion from the parole process, these guidelines attempt to measure the risks of an offender recidivating, and then use these measurements to determine whether early release will be granted and under what conditions.

Parole Contract
An agreement between the state and the offender that establishes the conditions under which the latter will be allowed to serve the remainder of her or his prison term in the community.

Work Release Program
Temporary release of convicts from prison for purposes of employment. The offenders may spend their days on the job, but must return to the correctional facility at night and during the weekend.

Halfway House
A community-based form of early release that places inmates in residential centers and allows them to reintegrate with society.

> ## "Johnny plus alcohol plus women equals trouble."
>
> —Excerpt from 1976 parole report on Johnny Robert Eggers, who was released on parole five different times before stabbing a female teenager to death in 1994

FIGURE 14.5

Standard Conditions of Parole

1. Upon my release I will report to my parole officer as directed and follow the parole officer's instructions.
2. I will report to my parole officer in person and in writing whenever and wherever the parole officer directs.
3. I agree that the parole officer has the right to visit my residence or place of employment at any reasonable time.
4. I will seek, obtain, and maintain employment throughout my parole term, or perform community service as directed by my parole officer.
5. I will notify my parole officer prior to any changes in my place of residence, in my place of employment, or of any change in my marital status.
6. I will notify my parole officer within 48 hours if at any time I am arrested for any offense.
7. I will not at any time have firearms, ammunition, or any other weapon in my possession or under my control.

8. I will obey all laws, and to the best of my ability, fulfill all my legal obligations, including payment of all applicable child support and alimony orders.
9. I will not leave the state of _____ without prior permission of my parole officer.
10. I will not at any time, use, or have in my possession or control, any illegal drug or narcotic.
11. I will not at any time have contact or affiliation with any street gangs or with any members thereof.
12. Your release on parole is based upon the conclusion of the parole panel that there is a reasonable probability that you will live and remain at liberty without violating the law and that your release is not incompatible with the welfare of society. In the event that you engage in conduct in the future which renders this conclusion no longer valid, then your parole will be revoked or modified accordingly.

Source: Connecticut Board of Parole.

correctional institution by helping her or him find a place to live and a job, and seeing that she or he receives any treatment or rehabilitation that may be necessary.

According to Todd Clear of Florida State University and Edward Latessa of the University of Cincinnati, the major role conflict for parole officers is whether to be a law enforcement officer or a social worker.[98] In other words, parole officers are constantly required to choose between the good of the community and the good of the paroled offender. In one study of parole officer stress and burnout, researchers found that more than 60 percent of the officers interviewed felt uncertain about how to balance these two requirements.[99] To be sure, some parole officers focus entirely on protecting the community and see the welfare of the client as a secondary concern.

A growing number of parole experts, however, believe that parole officers should act as agents of change, meaning that they should try to change the offender's behavior and not simply focus on controlling it. This entails that the parole officer establish strong bonds of trust and commitment with the parolee by taking what could be called a parental attitude to the officer-client relationship.[100]

Parole Revocation If convicts follow the conditions of their parole until the *maximum expiration date,* or the date on which their sentence ends, then they are discharged from supervision. A large number—about 36 percent, according to the latest research—return to incarceration before their maximum expiration date, most because they were convicted of a new offense or had their parole revoked (see Figure 14.6 on the following page). **Parole revocation** is similar in many aspects to probation revocation. If the parolee commits a new crime, then a return to prison is very likely. If, however, the individual breaks a condition of parole, known as a *technical violation,* the parole authorities have discretion as to whether revocation proceedings should be initiated. An example of a technical violation would be failure to report a change in address to parole authorities. As with probation revocation, many observers believe that those who commit technical violations should not be imprisoned, as they have not committed a crime.

Until 1972, parole officers had the power to arbitrarily revoke parole status for technical violations. A parolee who was returned to prison had little or no recourse. In

Parole Revocation
When a parolee breaks the conditions of parole, the process of withdrawing parole and returning the person to prison.

FIGURE 14.6
Terminating Parole

As you can see, more than half of all parolees successfully complete their terms of parole. The rest are either returned to incarceration, or have their supervision terminated for administrative reasons such as death or the parole officer's discretion.

Source: Bureau of Justice Statistics, *Compendium of Federal Justice Statistics, 2002* (Washington, D.C.: U.S. Department of Justice, September 2004), Table 7.8, page 100.

Morrissey v. Brewer (1972),[101] the Supreme Court changed this by holding that a parolee has a "liberty interest" in remaining on parole. In other words, before parolees can be deprived of their liberty, they must be afforded a measure of due process at a parole revocation hearing.

Although this hearing does not provide the same due process protections as a criminal trial, the parolee does have the right to be notified of the charges, to present witnesses, to speak in his or her defense, and to question any hostile witnesses (so long as such questioning would not place them in danger). In the first stage of the hearing, the parole board determines whether there is probable cause that a violation occurred. Then, the board decides whether to return the parolee to prison.

REENTRY INTO SOCIETY

After Jerry B. Hobbs was arrested for brutally murdering Laura, his eight-year-old daughter, and her nine-year-old friend on Mother's Day, 2005, in Zion, Illinois, much was made of the fact that he had been released from prison only weeks before the killings. Hobbs had just completed a two-year sentence stemming from an incident in which he chased Laura's mother around a trailer park with a chain saw. Ex-convicts such as Hobbs present a crucial challenge for the criminal justice system. Each year, over 600,000 persons leave prison and return to the community—six times more than were reentering society in 1970.[102]

What steps can be taken to lessen the possibility that these ex-convicts will continue to harm society following their release? Efforts to answer that question have focused on programs that help inmates make the transition from prison to the "outside." In past years, these programs would have come under the general heading of "rehabilitation," but today corrections officials and criminologists refer to them as part of the strategy of **prisoner reentry.** The concept of reentry has come to mean many things to many people; for our purposes, keep in mind the words of Joan Petersilia of the University of California at Irvine, who defines *reentry* as encompassing "all activities and programming conducted to prepare ex-convicts to return safely to the community and to live as law abiding citizens."[103]

Barriers to Reentry

Perhaps the largest obstacle to successful prisoner reentry is the simple truth that life behind bars is very different from life on the outside. As one inmate explains, the "rules" of prison survival are hardly compatible with good citizenship:

> An unexpected smile could mean trouble. A man in uniform was not a friend. Being kind was a weakness. Viciousness and recklessness were to be respected and admired.[104]

Prisoner Reentry

A corrections strategy designed to prepare inmates for a successful return to the community and to reduce their criminal activity after release.

The prison environment also insulates inmates. They are not required to make the day-to-day decisions that characterize a normal existence beyond prison bars. Depending on the length of incarceration, a released inmate must adjust to an array of economic, technological, and social changes that took place while she or he was behind bars; common acts such as using an ATM or pumping gas may be completely alien to someone who has just completed a long prison term.

Other obstacles hamper reentry efforts. Housing can be difficult to secure, as many private property owners refuse to rent to someone with a criminal record, and federal and state laws restrict public housing options for ex-convicts. A criminal past also limits the ability to find employment, as does the lack of job skills of someone who has spent a significant portion of his or her life in prison. These economic barriers can be complicated by the physical and mental condition of the freed convict. We have already discussed the high incidence of substance abuse among prisoners (Chapter 12) and the health-care needs of aging inmates. In addition, one recent study concluded that as many as one in five Americans in jail or prison is seriously mentally ill.[105]

All of these problems conspire to make successful reentry difficult to achieve. (Figure 14.7 on the following page provides a list of rights that are now or have in the past been denied to convicts once they return to the community.) Perhaps it is not surprising that research conducted by the Bureau of Justice Statistics projects that 67 percent of all ex-prisoners will be rearrested and 40 percent will be returned to prison or jail within three years of their release dates.[106]

Reentry in Action

One ex-inmate compared the experience of being released to entering a "dark room, knowing that there are steps in front of you and waiting to fall."[107] Reentry programs try to shed some light on the more difficult aspects of leaving prison. Although there is no single model for reentry programs, most either (1) specifically focus on the transition from prison to the community or (2) involve a treatment curriculum within the prison that continues after release.[108] The majority of reentry programs include job training and work release programs, continuing education and prerelease "life skills" classes, drug treatment, and a residency period at a halfway house. (A typical "life skills" class includes topics such as finding and keeping a job, locating a residence, understanding family responsibilities, and budgeting.)

As the philosophy of prisoner reentry becomes more widely accepted, corrections officials are becoming more creative at finding ways to prepare inmates for the return to society. Today, more than 10,000 prisoners work directly for about 250 private companies; both numbers are significantly higher than a decade ago.[109] Several correctional facilities are experimenting with "moral education" programs geared toward improving a convict's decision-making skills.[110] Other prisons are forming partnerships with religious organizations to provide spiritual guidance in preparation for reentry.[111] A number of jurisdictions have established "therapeutic communities," or residential treatment programs that house convicts for as long as eighteen months after their release. The therapeutic community offers residents the opportunity to "resocialize" themselves outside the prison environment while at the same time providing them with drug treatment programs, anger management classes, and other important

Dennis, left, and his sponsor, Jamal, right, are residents of the Walden House, a drug and alcohol treatment center located in San Francisco's Mission District. California officials are increasingly looking to therapeutic communities such as Walden House as reentry options for nonviolent drug offenders. Why are reentry programs generally not created with violent offenders in mind?

AP Photo/Jakub Mosur

FIGURE 14.7

The Limited Rights of Convicts

In some states, convicted offenders are denied the right to vote, the reasoning being that they do not have the required honesty and proper values to be allowed to participate in the voting process. Although such restrictions have been lifted in most states, convicted offenders still face other limits on their rights in some jurisdictions.

In many jurisdictions, convicts do not have the right to:

- Hold public office
- Be employed in the public sector
- Live in public housing
- Own firearms
- Serve on a jury
- Have automobile and life insurance
- Adopt children
- Receive welfare or food stamps
- Be eligible for student loans
- Have custody of their children

The **Urban Institute** is a nonprofit research organization that focuses on many different aspects of corrections policy. To visit its site dedicated to prisoner reentry, click on *Web Links* under *Chapter Resources* at **www.cjinaction.com**.

resources. (See the feature *Outside the Box—The Delancey Street Foundation* for information about the nation's most highly acclaimed therapeutic community.)

Evaluating Reentry Programs

The success of prisoner reentry programs is, for the most part, measured by levels of recidivism. As with the other treatment and diversion programs discussed over the past two chapters, the data consistently show lower levels of rearrest and reimprisonment for those who participate in reentry activities.[112]

Beyond Recidivism A number of criminologists believe that the corrections community needs to look beyond recidivism to determine the effectiveness of reentry. As Joan Petersilia points out, the ultimate goal of reentry is the reintegration of an offender into his or her community, "which clearly includes more than remaining arrest-free for a specified time period."[113] Petersilia suggests that future research should focus on whether the reentry efforts increase client sobriety and participation in various treatment programs, involvement in family and community activities, and other indicators of a successful return to society.

Political Considerations In addition, if prison officials focus only on keeping recidivism rates low, they will be less likely to allow those inmates who run the highest risks of reoffending to participate. Many jurisdictions, for example, do not allow sex offenders to participate in reentry programs, even though these offenders would benefit greatly and their eventual return to society causes a great deal of community anxiety.[114] (See the feature *Criminal Justice in Action—Protecting the Community from Sex Offenders* at the end of the chapter.)

Indeed, fear of the political fallout that occurs whenever a released inmate commits a heinous crime continues to play a large role in release policies. For example, when Arnold Schwarzenegger took office as California's governor in 2003, he vowed to fix the state's parole system, which had been labeled a "$1 billion failure." Schwarzenegger promised to increase the amount of drug treatment, job training, and counseling convicts received while on parole. As late as February 2005, the governor was still touting his administration's support of widespread community-based reentry programs. By April of that year, however, criticism from victim rights' groups and low approval ratings had convinced Schwarzenegger to "scrap" much of his reform plan, and once again large numbers of nonviolent parole violators in California are being returned to prison.

The Delancey Street Foundation

The Delancey Street Restaurant in San Francisco offers panoramic views of the Embarcadero, an eclectic menu (featuring matzo-ball soup, spanakopita, and Szechuan noodles), and reasonable prices. The most unique aspect of this establishment, however, is the staff: every waiter, cook, and busboy (or girl) is a former criminal working without pay. The restaurant operates under the auspices of the Delancey Street Foundation, a self-supporting rehabilitation program for five hundred former inmates in the Bay area.

Founded in 1971 by Mimi Silbert, the Delancey Street Foundation predates many of today's reentry efforts by at least three decades. Silbert believes that the main problem with most prisoner rehabilitation programs is that they focus on only one aspect of reentry, such as drug abuse, education, or employability. At Delancey Street, residents learn three skills simultaneously by working at one or more of the Foundation's "training schools," which include the restaurant, a café, a moving company, a car service, and an annual Christmas tree sale. Each participant is also required to earn a high school equivalency diploma (if necessary) and has the opportunity to take classes toward a bachelor of arts degree from San Francisco State University. In addition, all residents take a pledge to remain drug and alcohol free as long as they remain in the program.

Delancey Street is based on the idea that the residents will support and teach each other; therefore, it has no counselors, therapists, or social workers. More than 14,000 people have successfully completed the program, with many of the graduates moving into private business or public service; one was even elected to the San Francisco Board of Supervisors. To those who believe that the Foundation represents a "soft on crime" philosophy, Silbert responds that each resident puts in twelve- to fifteen-hour days at the various training schools, not counting homework. The easiest life for convicts, she points out, is often back in prison, where the government takes care of them. "What is hard on criminals," Silbert says, "is to insist that they be accountable, that they work hard, and that they give back."

FOR CRITICAL ANALYSIS

Why might an organization such as the Delancey Street Foundation be more successful at reentry than a more traditional program that provides separate drug treatment or education to ex-convicts who have returned to their homes?

Protecting the Community from Sex Offenders

In the summer of 1994, seven-year-old Megan Kanka of Hamilton Township, New Jersey, was raped and murdered by a twice-convicted pedophile (an adult sexually attracted to children) who had moved into her neighborhood after being released from prison on parole. The next year, in response to public outrage, the state passed a series of laws known collectively as the New Jersey Sexual Offender Registration Act, or "Megan's Law."[115] Today, all fifty states and the federal government have passed their own versions of Megan's Law, which require local law authorities to alert the public when a sex offender has been released in the community. Hailed by victims' rights groups and reviled by civil libertarians, these laws—which are the focus of this *Criminal Justice in Action* feature—have been the topic of much controversy.

Active and Passive Notification

No two of these laws have exactly the same provisions, but all are designed with the goal of allowing the public to learn the identities of convicted sex offenders living in their midst. The incentive to institute such laws was enhanced in 1996 when Congress passed its own Megan's Law, which requires a state to provide communities with relevant information on sex offenders as a condition of receiving federal anticrime funds.[116] In 2000, Congress passed another law requiring sexual offenders to report their status to college administrations if they are enrolled at the school or if they have a job on campus.[117] By October 2002, all colleges had to give the public access to this information.

In general, these laws demand that a paroled sexual offender notify local law enforcement authorities on taking up residence in a state. This registration process must be renewed every time the parolee changes address. The process of community notification by the authorities has two models. The "active" model requires that they directly notify the community or community representatives. This often takes the form of bulletins or posters, distributed and posted within a certain distance from the offender's home. In the "passive" model, information on sex offenders must be open and available for public scrutiny. In California, for example, the state has created a CD-ROM that provides the names, photos, and ZIP codes of tens of thousands of the state's released sex offenders.

In some instances, convicts must notify authorities themselves. Paroled sex offenders in Georgia are required to present themselves to both the sheriff and the superintendent of the public school district where they plan to reside.[118] Generally, sex offenders are supervised by parole officers and are subject to the same threat of revocation as other parolees. Paroled child molesters usually have the following conditions of release:

- Must have no contact with children under the age of sixteen.
- Must continue psychiatric treatment.
- Must receive permission from their parole officers to change residence.
- Must stay a certain distance from schools or parks where children are present.
- Cannot own toys that may be used to lure children.
- Cannot have a job or participate in any activity that involves children.

In some cases, after release from incarceration, sex offenders must return to the county where they committed their

Judge Manuel Banales ordered twenty-one registered sex offenders in Corpus Christi, Texas, to place signs similar to the one pictured here in their front yards. Do you think this unfairly infringes on the privacy rights of the sex offenders? Or, are such steps justified to protect children who live nearby?

AP Photo/*Corpus Christi Caller–Times*, Paul Iverson

crimes. Nearly 500,000 convicted sex offenders have been required to register through one of these methods across the United States.

Legal Issues

In nearly every jurisdiction, Megan's Laws have been challenged as unconstitutional. The common theme among these court cases is that Megan's Laws represent a form of "punishment" and as such violate state and federal constitutional prohibitions against double jeopardy and cruel and unusual punishment. In other words, by forcing sex offenders to register in expectation of a crime they have yet to commit, these laws operate in opposition to the principle that persons are innocent until proven guilty. Furthermore, because of the scrutiny that is certain to fall on a pedophile whose past crimes have been broadcast to the community, offenders have filed suit claiming that the laws unconstitutionally invade their privacy.[119]

With two recent decisions, the United States Supreme Court signaled that it was going to give the states a great deal of leeway in managing sex offenders. In *Smith v. Doe* (2003),[120] the Court held that Alaska's sex offender law did not violate the *ex post facto* clause of the Constitution even though it required two men who had completed their prison sentences before its passage to register. (For a review of this clause, go to page 114.) The Court noted that even though some of the ramifications of Megan's Laws are punitive, their general purpose is remedial and, therefore, *ex post facto* protections do not apply.

The other case, *Connecticut Department of Public Safety v. Doe* (2003),[121] concerned a convicted sex offender's claim that he was denied his due process rights when the state posted his name and address on the Internet without first holding a hearing to determine whether he was still a threat to the community. The Court rejected this argument: because Connecticut requires *all* sex offenders to register and places information about *all* of them on the Web, the law is not unfair. In other words, the relative dangerousness of any individual offender is irrelevant.

System Failure?

Although Megan's Laws have survived numerous legal challenges, the reputation of registration efforts has been tarnished by a series of highly publicized sex offender crimes committed during the past few years. In 2003, authorities found the body of college student Dru Sjodin in a ravine; she was allegedly abducted and murdered by convicted sex offender Alfonso Rodriguez. In 2005, sex offenders murdered two Florida girls—nine-year-old Jessica Lunsford and thirteen-year-old Sarah Lunde—and ten-year-old Iowan Jetseta Gage. That same year in Idaho, another sex offender, Joseph Duncan, bludgeoned several members of eight-year-old Shasta Groene's family to death before kidnapping the girl, who was eventually rescued by law enforcement agents.

The perpetrators of these crimes had one thing in common: they were all registered as sex offenders. Joseph Duncan, in fact, had an outstanding arrest for failing to reregister as a high-risk offender and was facing charges of molesting another boy when he kidnapped Groene. Joseph Couey, who killed Jessica Lunsford in Florida, worked on a construction site at his victim's school and failed to inform the state when he moved into her neighborhood. As one Florida lawmaker put it, "The current 'honor system' of having each offender check in with local law enforcement has proven itself ineffective in tracking sexual predators."[122]

Indeed, according to victims' rights groups, as many as a quarter of the country's half million registered sex offenders are "missing"—in other words, local police departments do not know their exact locations.[123] Many law enforcement agencies simply lack the resources to monitor all of the sex offenders in their jurisdictions, and while some departments are starting to assign extra officers to sex offender squads, most continue to give priority to other crime-fighting duties.

Getting Tougher on Sex Offenders

Dean A. Schwartzmiller is believed to have molested hundreds of boys over a thirty-five-year period before being apprehended in 2005. The criminal justice system's apparent failure to identify, treat, and monitor sex offenders such as Schwartzmiller has led to frustration among federal and state politicians. "The issue is, what can you do short of putting them all in prison for the rest of their lives?" complained one policymaker.[124]

Some states are trying to expand the reach of their Megan's Laws. In both New York and Pennsylvania, for example, all rapists (of minors *and* adults), "pimps," and child pornographers must register as sex offenders.[125] Massachusetts authorities now require Level 3 Sex Offenders (those considered the most likely to recidivate) to include the addresses of partners and relatives in their registration information. Other states have addressed the problem by changing their criminal codes. In 2005, Florida passed the Jessica Lunsford Act, the strictest sex offender law in the nation. This legislation sets a mandatory sentence of at least twenty-five years for any person convicted of molesting a child under the age of twelve and requires that these offenders wear global satellite tracking devices for the rest of their lives on release from prison.[126]

Legislators and prison officials have found another way to keep sex offenders incarcerated for lengthy periods of time. In about twenty states, sexual offenders can be sent to another, noncorrectional facility (such as a psychiatric hospital) after serving their prison or jail terms. Indeed, in the wake of Dru Sjodin's death, her home state of North Dakota vastly increased the number of sex offenders eligible for "civil confinement." This strategy was upheld in 2001 by the United States Supreme Court, which rejected a rapist's claim that Washington prison officials violated his Fifth Amendment rights against double jeopardy (see page 334) by locking him up for twelve years in a health-care facility after the end of his prison term.[127] A year later, however, the Court did limit a state's ability to civilly confine sexual offenders, ruling that there must "be proof of serious difficulty in controlling [the convict's] behavior" for such confinement to be constitutional.[128]

Making Sense of Sex Offender Laws

1 What are the two "rights" that legislators must weigh in passing Megan's Laws? Do you agree that the rights of the community outweigh the rights of the individual offender? Explain your answer.

2 One of the primary justifications for Megan's Laws is that sex offenders have a high rate of recidivism. In other words, because they are unlikely to be "cured," these ex-convicts need to have greater restrictions placed on them than other criminals. Do you have any concerns about this reasoning? How do recent data released by the U.S. Department of Justice showing that sex offenders are less likely to be rearrested after release from prison than robbers, car thieves, and arsonists affect your opinion of Megan's Laws?

3 Some states and local communities post lists of convicted sex offenders, with photos, on the Internet. Is this a fair method of notification, or is it too intrusive on the privacy of the felon? Why?

Chapter Summary

1 Explain the concept of prison as a total institution. Though many people spend time in partial institutions—schools, companies where they work, and religious organizations—only in prison is every aspect of an inmate's life controlled, and that is why prisons are called total institutions. Every detail for every prisoner is fully prescribed and managed.

2 Describe the possible patterns of inmate behavior, which are driven by the inmate's personality and values. (a) Professional criminals adapt to prison by "doing time" and follow the rules in order to get out quickly. (b) Those who are "jailing" establish themselves within the power structure of prison culture. These are often veterans of juvenile detention centers and other prisons. (c) Those who are "gleaning" are working to improve themselves for return to society. (d) "Disorganized" criminals have mental impairments or low IQs and therefore are unable to adapt to prison culture.

3 Indicate some of the reasons for violent behavior in prisons. (a) To separate the powerful from the weak and to establish a prisoner hierarchy; (b) to minimize one's own probability of being a target of assault; (c) to enhance one's self-image; (d) to obtain sexual relief; and (e) to obtain material goods through extortion or robbery.

4 List and briefly explain the six general job categories among correctional officers. (a) Block officers, who supervise cell blocks or are on block guard duty; (b) work detail supervisors, who oversee the cafeteria, prison store, and laundry, for example; (c) industrial shop and school officers, who generally oversee workshop and educational programs; (d) yard officers, who patrol the prison yard when prisoners are allowed there; (e) tower guards, who work in isolation; and (f) those who hold administrative building assignments, such as prison gate guards, overseers of visitation procedures, and so on.

5 Contrast the hands-off doctrine of prisoner law with the hands-on approach. The hands-off doctrine assumes that the care of prisoners should be left entirely to prison officials and that it is not the place of judges to intervene. In contrast, the hands-on philosophy started in 1964 after the Supreme Court decision in *Cooper v. Pate*. Prisoners have been able to file civil lawsuits, called Section 1983 petitions, when they feel their civil rights have been violated.

6 Contrast probation, parole, mandatory release, pardon, and furlough. Probation is an alternative to incarceration. Parole is an early release program for those incarcerated. Mandatory release occurs when the inmate has served the maximum time for her or his initial sentence minus good-time credits. A pardon can be given only by the

STORIES FROM THE STREET

Go to the *Stories from the Street* feature at **www.cjinaction.com** to hear Larry Gaines tell insightful stories related to this chapter and his experiences in the field.

president or one of the fifty governors. Furlough is a temporary release while in jail or prison.

7 **Describe truth-in-sentencing laws and their goals.** Such laws make more transparent the actual time that a convicted criminal will serve in jail or prison. The goals are (a) to restore "truth" to the sentencing process; (b) to increase the percentage of the term that is actually served in prison in order to reduce crime by keeping convicts "off the streets" for a longer period; and (c) to better control the use of prison space by giving corrections officials predictable terms and policymakers advance notice of potential overcrowding.

8 **Describe typical conditions of parole.** Parolees must not use drugs, not associate with known felons, not change their addresses without notifying authorities, and report to their parole officer at specified intervals. (The latter is usually specified in the parole contract.)

9 **Explain the goal of prisoner reentry programs.** Based on the ideals of rehabilitation, these programs have two main objectives: (a) to prepare a prisoner for a successful return to the community, and (b) to protect the community by reducing the chances that the ex-convict will continue her or his criminal activity after release from prison.

10 **Indicate typical conditions for release for a paroled child molester.** (a) Have no contact with children under the age of sixteen; (b) continue psychiatric treatment; (c) obtain permission from a parole officer to change residence; (d) keep away from schools or parks where children are present; (e) cannot own toys that may be used to lure children; and (f) cannot have a job or participate in any activity that involves children.

Key Terms

"deliberate indifference" 468
deprivation model 458
discretionary release 471
furlough 471
halfway house 474
"hands-off" doctrine 467

"identifiable human
    needs" 469
mandatory release 470
pardon 470
parole 469
parole board 472

parole contract 479
parole grant hearing 472
parole guidelines 474
parole revocation 475
prisoner reentry 476
prisonization 456

relative deprivation 458
total institution 455
work release program 474

Questions for Critical Analysis

1 Why is the principle of least eligibility relevant in today's political environment?
2 How does the deprivation model seek to explain prison violence?
3 How does the inmate culture differ in men's prisons and women's prisons?
4 What is the most demanding job assignment in the correctional institution hierarchy?
5 What has caused a reduction in the amount of discretion that parole boards have?

6 Who are some of the individuals asked to provide comments and recommendations for a parole grant hearing?
7 When a parolee is caught committing a crime, what typically tends to happen, and why?
8 How do reentry programs prepare convicts for their return to the community after being released from prison?
9 Why do civil libertarians criticize Megan's Laws?

Test Preparation Online

Criminal JusticeNow

Go to **www.cjinaction.com** and click on *Criminal JusticeNow* for access to this powerful online study tool. You will get a *personalized study plan* based on your responses to a diagnostic pretest. Once you have mastered the material with the help of interactive learning tools, video clips with questions, an integrated e-book, and more, you can take a posttest to confirm you are ready to move on to the next chapter.

Book Companion Web Site

At the book companion Web site (**www.cjinaction.com**), you will find many resources in addition to *Criminal JusticeNow* to aid you in studying for your exams. For example, under *Chapter Resources*, you will find the *Chapter Outline, Chapter Summary, Flashcards, Glossary, Learning Objectives, Lecture Presentations, Concept Builder, Essay Questions,* and a *Tutorial Chapter Quiz.* You can also test yourself with interactive *Online Reviews* of each chapter section. Check out the *Web Links* to access the Web sites mentioned in the text, as well as many others. You can also access recent perspectives by clicking on *CJ in the News* and *Terrorism Update* under *Course Resources.*

Suggested Readings

Lerner, Jimmy, *You Got Nothing Coming: Notes from a Prison Fish*, New York: Broadway Books, 2002. The author killed a man in Las Vegas and was convicted of voluntary manslaughter. He is now serving time in the Nevada state prison system. A memoir of Lerner's first year behind bars, this book is a lively, graphic, and often funny recounting of what it's like to be a newcomer in prison.

Petersilia, Joan, *When Prisoners Come Home: Parole and Prisoner Reentry*, New York: Oxford University Press, 2003. William Weld, who served as governor of Massachusetts for most of the 1990s, once declared that the prison experience should be a "tour through the circles of hell" in which inmates learn nothing more than "the joys of busting rocks." This attitude prevailed among corrections officials during that decade, and, according to Petersilia, a criminology professor at the University of California at Irvine and former president of the American Society of Criminology, the nation is now paying the price. As Petersilia points out, "No one is more dangerous than a criminal who has no incentive to straighten himself out while in prison and who returns to society without . . . a plan." American prisons are now churning more than 600,000 inmates back to the community each year, and many of them are in worse shape and have worse prospects than when they entered. In this book, Petersilia provides a blueprint for how the United States can start to extricate itself from this very difficult situation.

Notes

1. Edward W. Sieh, "Less Eligibility: The Upper Limits of Penal Policy," *Criminal Justice Policy Review* 3 (1989), 159.
2. Edward L. Rubin and Malcolm M. Feeley, "Judicial Policy Making and Litigation against the Government," *University of Pennsylvania Journal of Constitutional Law* (April 2003), 617.
3. Gregory Moorhead and Ricky W. Griffin, *Organizational Behavior*, 2d ed. (Boston: Houghton Mifflin, 1989), 497.
4. Erving Goffman, "On the Characteristics of Total Institutions," in *Asylums: Essays on the Social Situation of Mental Patients and Other Inmates* (New York: Doubleday, 1961), 6.
5. Justin Brooks, "How Can We Sleep While the Beds Are Burning: The Tumultuous Prison Culture of Attica Flourishes in American Prisons Twenty-five Years Later," *Syracuse Law Journal* 47 (1996), 159.
6. Bureau of Justice Statistics, *Prevalence of Imprisonment in the U.S. Population, 1974–2001* (Washington, D.C.: U.S. Department of Justice, August 2003), 1.
7. Bureau of Justice Statistics, *Prisoners in 2002* (Washington, D.C.: U.S. Department of Justice, 2003), Table 15, page 10.
8. Robert Aday, *Aging Prisoners: Crisis in American Corrections* (Westport, CT: Praeger, 2003), 1–5.
9. Donald Clemmer, *The Prison Community* (Boston: Christopher, 1940).
10. John Irwin, *Prisons in Turmoil* (Boston: Little, Brown, 1980), 67.
11. Robert Johnson, *Hard Time: Understanding and Reforming the Prison*, 2d ed. (Belmont, CA: Wadsworth Publishing Company, 1996), 133.
12. Lee H. Bowker, *Prison Victimization* (New York: Elsevier, 1981), 31–33.
13. Stephen C. Light, "The Severity of Assaults on Prison Officers: A Contextual Analysis," *Social Science Quarterly* 71 (1990), 267–284.
14. Lee H. Bowker, "An Essay on Prison Violence," in *Prison Violence in America*, ed. Michael Braswell, Steven Dillingham, and Reid Montgomery, Jr. (Cincinnati, OH: Anderson Publishing Co., 1985), 7–18.
15. Frank Tannenbaum, *Crime and Community* (Boston: Ginn & Co., 1938).
16. Randy Martin and Sherwood Zimmerman, "A Typology of the Causes of Prison Riots and an Analytical Extension to the 1986 Virginia Riot," *Justice Quarterly* 7 (1990), 711–737.
17. Bert Useem, "Disorganization and the New Mexico Prison Riot of 1980," *American Sociological Review* 50 (1985), 677–688.
18. Bert Useem and Peter Kimball, *State of Siege: U.S. Prison Riots 1971–1984* (New York: Oxford University Press, 1989), 4.
19. Stuart B. Klein, "Prisoners' Rights to Physical and Mental Health Care: A Modern Expansion of the Eighth Amendment's Cruel and Unusual Punishment Clause," *Fordham University Law Journal* 7 (1978), 1.
20. Herman Badillo and Milton Haynes, *A Bill of No Rights: Attica and the American Prison System* (New York: Outerbridge & Lazard, 1972), 42.
21. Michael S. Serrill and Peter Katel, "New Mexico: The Anatomy of a Riot," *Corrections Magazine* (April 1980), 6–7.
22. Badillo and Haynes, 26.
23. Irwin, 47.
24. Leo Carroll, "Race, Ethnicity, and the Social Order of the Prison," in *The Pains of Imprisonment*, ed. R. Johnson and H. Toch (Beverly Hills, CA: Sage, 1982).
25. Leo Carroll, *Hacks, Blacks, and Cons: Race Relations in a Maximum-Security Prison* (Lexington, MA: Lexington Books, 1988), 78.
26. David Grann, "The Brand," *The New Yorker* (February 16 and 23, 2004), 157–171.
27. Craig Haney, "Psychology and the Limits to Prison Pain," *Psychology, Public Policy, and Law* 3 (December 1977), 499.
28. Robert W. Dumond, "Inmate Sexual Assault," *Prison Journal* 80 (December 2000), 407.

29. Human Rights Watch, "World Report 2000—United States."

30. James E. Robertson, "The Prison Rape Elimination Act of 2003: A Primer," *Criminal Law Bulletin* (May/June 2004), 270–273.

31. Bureau of Justice Statistics, *Data Collections for the Prison Rape Elimination Act of 2003* (Washington, D.C.: U.S. Department of Justice, June 30, 2004), 1.

32. Christina Rathbone, "Locked In," *Boston Globe* (May 29, 2005), D1.

33. Quoted in Alexandra Marks, "Martha Checks in Today," *Seattle Times* (October 8, 2004), A8.

34. Bureau of Justice Statistics, *Special Report: Women Offenders* (Washington, D.C.: U.S. Department of Justice, December 1999), 7.

35. *Sourcebook of Criminal Justice Statistics Online* at **http://www.albany.edu/sourcebook/pdf/t653.pdf**.

36. *Special Report: Women Offenders*, 8.

37. Bureau of Justice Statistics, *Profile of Jail Inmates, 2002* (Washington, D.C.: U.S. Department of Justice, July 2004), 10.

38. Bureau of Justice Statistics, *Prior Abuse Reported by Inmates and Probationers* (Washington, D.C.: U.S. Department of Justice, April 1999), 2.

39. *Caught in the Net: The Impact of Drug Policies on Women and Families* (Washington, D.C.: American Civil Liberties Union, 2004), 18–19.

40. *Special Report: Women Offenders*, 8.

41. Kelly Bedard and Eric Helland, "Location of Women's Prisons and the Deterrent Effect of 'Harder' Time," *International Review of Law and Economics* (June 2004), 152.

42. *Ibid.*

43. *Caught in the Net*, 49–50.

44. Jessica Y. Kim, "In-Prison Day Care: A Correctional Alternative for Women Offenders," *Cardozo Women's Law Journal* (2001), 221.

45. Candace Kruttschnitt and Rosemary Gartner, "Women's Imprisonment," *Crime and Justice* (2003), 1.

46. "Sexual Coercion Reported by Women in Three Midwestern Prisons," *Journal of Sex Research* (August 2002), 217–227.

47. *All Too Familiar: Sexual Abuse of Women in U.S. State Prisons* (New York: Human Rights Watch, 1996).

48. Melvin Claxton, Ronald J. Hansen, and Norman Sinclair, "Guards Assault Female Inmates," *Detroit News* (May 22, 2005), 1.

49. Jennifer A. Segal, "Family Ties and Federal Sentencing: A Critique of the Literature," *Federal Sentencing Reporter* (2001), 258.

50. Iman R. Soliman, "Male Officers in Women's Prisons: The Need for Segregation of Officers in Certain Positions," *Texas Journal of Women and the Law* (Fall 2000), 45.

51. Andi Rierden, *The Farm: Life inside a Women's Prison* (Amherst, MA: University of Massachusetts Press, 1997), 23–26.

52. Esther Heffermn, *Making It in Prison: The Square, the Cool, and the Life* (New York: Wiley, 1972), 91.

53. Leanne F. Alarid, "Female Inmate Subcultures," in *Corrections Contexts: Contemporary and Classical Readings,* ed. James W. Marquart and Jonathan R. Sorenson (Los Angeles: Roxbury Publishing Co., 1997), 136–137.

54. James G. Fox, *Organizational and Racial Conflict in Maximum Security Prisons* (Lexington, MA: Lexington Books, 1982).

55. Lee H. Bowker, "Gender Differences in Prisoner Subcultures," in *Women and Crime in America,* ed. Lee H. Bowker (New York: Macmillan, 1981), 409–419.

56. Quoted in John J. DiIlulio, Jr., *No Escape: The Future of American Corrections* (New York: Basic Books, 1991), 268.

57. Jack Henry Abbott, *In the Belly of the Beast* (New York: Vintage Books, 1991), 54.

58. Michael Foucault, *Discipline and Punish: The Birth of the Prison* (New York: Pantheon Books, 1977), 128.

59. Lucien X. Lombardo, *Guards Imprisoned: Correctional Officers at Work* (Cincinnati, OH: Anderson Publishing Co., 1989), 51–71.

60. Goffman, 7.

61. *Berch v. Stahl,* 373 F.Supp. 412 (1974).

62. Kevin Johnson, "After Years of Solitary, Freedom Is Hard to Grasp," *USA Today* (June 9, 2005), 2A.

63. 475 U.S. 312 (1986).

64. *Stanley v. Hejirika,* 134 F.3d 629 (4th Cir. 1998).

65. 503 U.S. 1 (1992).

66. Darrell L. Ross, "Assessing *Hudson v. McMillan* Ten Years Later," *Criminal Law Bulletin* (September/October 2004), 508.

67. Haney, 499.

68. 378 U.S. 546 (1964).

69. 418 U.S. 539 (1974).

70. *Cruz v. Beto,* 405 U.S. 319 (1972).

71. *Procunier v. Martinez,* 416 U.S. 396 (1974).

72. *Hutto v. Finney,* 437 U.S. 678 (1978).

73. *Cutter v. Wilkinson,* 544 U.S. ___ (2005).

74. 429 U.S. 97 (1976).

75. *Daniels v. Williams,* 474 U.S. 327 (1986); and *Whitley v. Albers,* 475 U.S. 312 (1986).

76. 501 U.S. 296 (1991).

77. *Farmer v. Brennan,* 511 U.S. 825 (1994).

78. 501 U.S. 294, 304 (1991).

79. 515 U.S. 472 (1995).

80. *Wilkinson v. Austin,* 545 U.S. ___ (2005).

81. Todd R. Clear and George F. Cole, *American Corrections,* 4th ed. (Belmont, CA: Wadsworth Pubishing Co., 1997), 416.

82. 442 U.S. 1 (1979).

83. Danya W. Blair, "A Matter of Life and Death: Why Life without Parole Should Be a Sentencing Option in Texas," *American Journal of Criminal Law* 22 (Fall 1994), 191.

84. Julian H. Wright, Jr., "Life-without-Parole: An Alternative to Death or Not Much of a Life at All?" *Vanderbilt Law Review* 43 (March 1990), 529.

85. *Simmons v. South Carolina,* 512 U.S. 154 (1994).

86. Victoria J. Palacios, "Go and Sin No More: Rationality and Release Decisions by Parole Boards," *South Carolina Law Review* 45 (Spring 1994), 567.

87. William Parker, *Parole: Origins, Development, Current Practices, and Statutes* (College Park, MD: American Correctional Association, 1972), 26.

88. Susan Blaustein, "Witness to Another Execution," *Harper's Magazine* (May 1994), 57.

89. Mike A. Cable, "Limiting Parole: Required Consideration of Statements and Recommendations Received by the Parole Board," *Pacific Law Journal* 28 (Spring 1997), 778.

90. Andrew Von Hirsch and Kathleen J. Hanrahan, *The Question of Parole: Retention, Reform, or Abolition* (Cambridge, MA: Ballinger Publishing Co., 1979), 4.

91. Bureau of Justice Statistics, *Bulletin* (Washington, D.C.: U.S. Department of Justice, January 1995), 2.

92. Michael Tonry, "Twenty Years of Sentencing Reform: Steps Forward, Steps Backward," *Judicature* 78 (January/February 1995), 169.

93. Comprehensive Crime Control Act of 1984, Pub. L. No. 98-473, Section 217(a), 98 Stat. 1837, 2017 (1984), codified as amended at 28 U.S.C. Sections 991–998 (1988).

94. 42 U.S.C.A. Sections 13701–13709.

95. William J. Sabol, Katherine Rosich, Kamala Malik Kane, David P. Kirk, and Glenn Durbin, *The Influences of Truth-in-Sentencing Reforms on Changes in States' Sentencing Practices and Prison Populations* (Washington, D.C.: National Institute of Justice, April 2002), 8.

96. Marc Mauer, "The Truth about Truth in Sentencing," *Corrections Today* (February 1, 1996), S1.

97. *Ibid.*

98. Todd R. Clear and Edward Latessa, "Probation Officer Roles in Intensive Supervision: Surveillance versus Treatment," *Justice Quarterly* 10 (1993), 441–462.

99. J. T. Whitehead and C. A. Lindquist, "Job Stress and Burnout among Probation/Parole Officers: Perceptions and Causal Factors," *International Journal of Offender Therapy and Comparative Criminology* 29 (1985), 109–119.

100. Betsy Fulton, Amy Stichman, Lawrence Travis, and Edward Latessa, "Moderating Probation and Parole Officers' Attitudes to Achieve Desired Outcomes," *Prison Journal* (September 1, 1997), 295.

101. 408 U.S. 471 (1972).

102. Joan Petersilia, "What Works in Prisoner Reentry," *Federal Probation* (September 2004), 4.

103. Joan Petersilia, *When Prisoners Come Home: Parole and Prisoner Reentry* (New York: Oxford University Press, 2003), 39.

104. Victor Hassine, *Life without Parole: Living in Prison Today,* ed. Thomas J. Bernard and Richard McCleary (Los Angeles: Roxbury Publishing Co., 1996), 12.

105. *Ill Equipped: U.S. Prisons and Offenders with Mental Illness* (New York: Human Rights Watch, 2003).

106. Bureau of Justice Statistics, *Recidivism of Sex Offenders Released from Prison in 1994* (Washington, D.C.: U.S. Department of Justice, November 2003), 2.

107. Johnson, "After Years of Solitary."

108. Richard P. Seiter and Karen R. Kadela, "Prisoner Reentry: What Works, What Doesn't, and What's Promising," *Crime & Delinquency* (2003), 360–388.

109. Nicholas Stein, "Business behind Bars," *Fortune* (September 15, 2003), 163.

110. Lindsay A. Phillips, "Evaluating the Effects of a Brief Program for Moral Education in a County Jail," *Journal of Offender Rehabilitation* (2004), 59–72.

111. John Leland, "Offering Ministry, and Early Release, to Prisoners," *New York Times* (June 10, 2004), A1.

112. Petersilia, "What Works in Prisoner Reentry."

113. *Ibid.,* 7.

114. James M. Byrne, "Targeting for Reentry: Inclusion/Exclusion Criteria across Eight Model Programs," *Federal Probation* (September 2004), 53.

115. N.J. Rev. Stat. Section 2C:7-8(c) (1995).

116. Megan's Law, Pub. L. No. 104-145, 110 Stat. 1345 (1996).

117. 20 U.S.C. Section 1094(c)(3)(B) (2000).

118. Ga. Code Ann. Section 42-9-44.1(b)(1).

119. Tara L. Wayt, "Megan's Law: A Violation of the Right to Privacy?" *Temple Political and Civil Rights Law Review* 6 (Fall 1996/Spring 1997), 139.

120. 538 U.S. 84 (2003).

121. 538 U.S. 1 (2003).

122. "Problems Still Linger with Megan's Laws," *Law Enforcement News* (May 2004), 12.

123. Abby Goodnough, "After 2 Cases in Florida, Crackdown on Molesters," *New York Times* (May 1, 2005), 18.

124. *Ibid.*

125. "The Net Widens," *The Economist* (April 2, 2005), 28.

126. Sect. 1012.465 F.S. (as amended, 2005).

127. *Seling v. Young,* 531 U.S. 250 (2001).

128. *Kansas v. Crane,* 534 U.S. 407, 415 (2002).

CHAPTER FIFTEEN

The Juvenile Justice System

Chapter outline

- The Evolution of American Juvenile Justice
- Determining Delinquency Today
- First Contact: Delinquents and the Police
- Pretrial Procedures in Juvenile Justice
- Juveniles on Trial
- Juvenile Corrections
- Recent Trends in Juvenile Delinquency
- Factors in Juvenile Delinquency
- Keeping Juvenile Delinquency under Control
- Criminal Justice in Action—The Bully Problem

Chapter objectives

After reading this chapter, you should be able to:

1 Describe the child-saving movement and its relationship to the doctrine of *parens patriae.*

2 List the four major differences between juvenile courts and adult courts.

3 Identify and briefly describe the single most important Supreme Court case with respect to juvenile justice.

4 List the factors that normally determine what police do with juvenile offenders.

5 Describe the four primary stages of pretrial juvenile justice procedure.

6 Explain the distinction between an adjudicatory hearing and a disposition hearing.

7 List the four categories of residential treatment programs.

8 Describe the one variable that always correlates highly with juvenile crime rates.

9 Indicate some of the reasons why youths join gangs.

Criminal JusticeNow

Optimize your study time and master key chapter concepts with *Criminal JusticeNow,* an online study tool that provides you with a *personalized study plan.* Check out the "Test Preparation Online" section at the end of the chapter for additional information.

Old Enough to Do the Crime . . .

Nobody seemed to think

that Lionel Tate deserved the punishment that he got. Tate was twelve years old when he killed his six-year-old playmate Tiffany Eunick, apparently while imitating the violent moves of a professional wrestler he had seen on television. The jurors at his trial found that although Tate did not mean to kill Tiffany, he did mean to hurt her and, therefore, he was guilty of first degree murder under Florida law. Even for someone of Tate's tender years, this conviction carried a mandatory sentence of life in prison without parole.

Three years after Tate was convicted, the prosecutor in the case stated that a sentence "without hope of rehabilitation" for such a young boy was too harsh. One of the jurors said that she would never have agreed to the conviction if she had known the consequences. "This is no solution," said another juror. "The problem is with the system." In 2003, a Florida appeals court ordered a new trial because of errors made by Tate's original defense attorneys. Before the trial could be held, Tate agreed to a plea bargain under which he pleaded guilty to second degree murder and was sentenced to three years in juvenile prison. Because he had already served almost this long, the sentence essentially amounted to "time served," allowing him to be freed in 2004.

Five years after being convicted of first degree murder for killing a six-year-old family friend, Lionel Tate finds himself back in a Fort Lauderdale, Florida, courtroom on charges that he was linked to the armed robbery of a pizza deliveryman.

Then, in the spring of 2005, a pizza deliveryman claimed that Tate, now eighteen years old, robbed him at gunpoint. While in jail awaiting a probation hearing triggered by this incident, he smashed a cell window with a plastic box. Broward County (Florida) prosecutors proceeded to charge him with criminal mischief. As a result of these alleged offenses, Tate faced a return to prison—perhaps for life.

The controversy over Lionel Tate underscores a debate that goes to the heart of the American juvenile justice system, which has been both hailed as one of the "greatest social inventions of modern times" and criticized for "failing to protect either the legal rights of the juvenile offenders or the public on whom they prey."[1] The question: Should criminal acts by youths be given the same weight as those committed by adults or be seen as "mistakes" that can be "corrected" by the state?

For most of its century-long history, the system was dominated by the latter philosophy; only recently have opposing views summarized by the sound bite "old enough to do the crime, old enough to do the time" gained widespread acceptance—a change reflected in political trends. Over the past two decades, nearly every state has changed its laws to make it easier to try juveniles as adults, representing a shift toward harsher

CONCEPTBUILDER

The term *delinquency* is generally reserved for violators of the law who are below a certain age. Visit **www.cjinaction.com** for an interactive exploration of this key topic.

measures in a juvenile system that generally acts as a "compromise between rehabilitation and punishment, treatment and custody."[2]

In this chapter, we will discuss the successes and failures of this compromise and examine the aspects of the juvenile justice system that differentiate it from the criminal justice system. As you will see, observers on both sides of the "rehabilitation versus punishment" debate find many flaws with the present system; some have even begun to call for its dismantling. Others blame social problems such as racism, poverty, and a culture dominated by images of violence for creating a system that no government agency or policy can effectively control.[3]

THE EVOLUTION OF AMERICAN JUVENILE JUSTICE

In a recent poll, almost 60 percent of Americans indicated that they favored trying violent youths in adult criminal court instead of juvenile courts, which were perceived as too lenient.[4] To a certain degree, such opinions reflect a desire to return the focus of the American juvenile justice system toward punishment and incapacitation, as was the case at the beginning of the nineteenth century. At that time, juvenile offenders were treated the same as adult offenders—they were judged by the same courts and sentenced to the same severe penalties. This situation began to change in the early 1800s, as urbanization and industrialization created an immigrant underclass that was, at least in the eyes of certain reformers, predisposed to deviant activity. Certain members of the Progressive movement, known as the child savers, began to take steps to "save" children from these circumstances, introducing the idea of rehabilitating delinquents in the process.

> "This is a cultural virus. We have to ask ourselves what kind of children we are raising."
>
> —Bill Owens, Colorado governor, following the massacre of fourteen classmates and one teacher by two students at Columbine High School in Littleton, Colorado (1999)

The Child-Saving Movement

In general, the child savers favored the doctrine of **parens patriae,** which holds that the state has not only a right but a duty to care for children who are neglected, delinquent, or in some other way disadvantaged. Juvenile offenders, the child savers believed, required treatment, not punishment, and they were horrified at the thought of placing children in prisons with hardened adult criminals. In 1967, then Supreme Court Justice Abe Fortas said of the child savers:

> They believed that society's role was not to ascertain whether the child was "guilty" or "innocent," but "What is he, how has he become what he is, and what had best be done in his interest and in the interest of the state to save him from a downward career." The child—essentially good, as they saw it—was made "to feel that he is the object of [the government's] care and solicitude," not that he was under arrest or on trial.[5]

Child-saving organizations convinced local legislatures to pass laws that allowed them to take control of children who exhibited criminal tendencies or had been neglected by their parents. To separate these children from the environment in which they were raised, the organizations created a number of institutions, the best known of which was New York's House of Refuge. Opening in 1825, the House of Refuge implemented many of the same reformist measures popular in the penitentiaries of the time, meaning that its charges were subjected to the healthful influences of hard study and labor. Although the House of Refuge was criticized for its harsh discipline (which

Parens Patriae

A doctrine that holds that the state has a responsibility to look after the well-being of children and to assume the role of parent if necessary.

CORBIS

An illustration detailing the daily activities in the New York House of Refuge that appeared in *Harper's Weekly* in 1868. The House of Refuge was created in 1825 as a result of reformers' outrage that children who broke the law were treated the same as adults. The purpose of the House was to receive "all such children as shall be taken up or committed as vagrants, or convicted of criminal offenses." As you can see, the children were put to work at a number of different tasks, such as making shoes and hoop skirts. They also attended four hours of school every day. Judging from this illustration, how would you characterize the philosophy behind the House of Refuge?

Status Offender

A juvenile who has been found to have engaged in behavior deemed unacceptable for those under a certain, statutorily determined age.

Juvenile Delinquency

Behavior that is illegal under federal or state law that has been committed by a person who is under an age limit specified by statute.

caused many boys to run away), similar institutions sprang up throughout the Northeast during the middle of the nineteenth century.

The Illinois Juvenile Court

The efforts of the child savers culminated with the passage of the Illinois Juvenile Court Act in 1899. The Illinois legislature created the first court specifically for juveniles, guided by the principles of *parens patriae* and based on the concepts that children are not fully responsible for criminal conduct and are capable of being rehabilitated.[6]

The Illinois Juvenile Court and those in other states that followed in its path were (and, in many cases, remain) drastically different from adult courts:

- *No juries.* The matter was decided by judges who wore regular clothes instead of black robes and sat at a table with the other participants rather than behind a bench. Because the primary focus of the court was on the child and not the crime, the judge had wide discretion in disposing of each case.
- *Different terminology.* To reduce the stigma of criminal proceedings, "petitions" were issued instead of "warrants"; the children were not "defendants," but "respondents"; they were not "found guilty" but "adjudicated delinquent."
- *No adversarial relationship.* Instead of trying to determine guilt or innocence, the parties involved in the juvenile court worked together in the best interests of the child, with the emphasis on rehabilitation rather than punishment.
- *Confidentiality.* To avoid "saddling" the child with a criminal past, juvenile court hearings and records were kept sealed, and the proceedings were closed to the public.

By 1945, every state had a juvenile court system modeled after the first Illinois court. For the most part, these courts were able to operate without interference until the 1960s and the onset of the juvenile rights movement.

After the first juvenile court was established in Illinois, the Chicago Bar Association described its purpose as, in part, to "exercise the same tender solicitude and care over its neglected wards that a wise and loving parent would exercise with reference to his [or her] own children under similar circumstances."[7] In other words, the state was given the responsibility of caring for those minors whose behavior seemed to show that they could not be controlled by their parents. As a result, many **status offenders** found themselves in the early houses of refuge and continue to be placed in state-run facilities today. Also known as "children (or minors, youths, and the like) in need of supervision," status offenders have exhibited behavior—such as violating curfew, truancy (skipping school), and alcohol consumption—that is considered illegal only if an offender is below a specified age (see Figure 15.1). In contrast, **juvenile delinquency** refers to conduct that would be criminal if committed by an adult.

Constitutional Protections and the Juvenile Court

Though the ideal of the juvenile court seemed to offer the "best of both worlds" for juvenile offenders, in reality the lack of procedural protections led to many children being arbitrarily punished not only for crimes, but for status offenses. Juvenile judges were treating all violators similarly, which led to many status offenders being incarcerated in the same institutions as violent delinquents. In response to a wave of lawsuits demanding due process rights for juveniles, the Supreme Court issued several rulings in the 1960s and 1970s that significantly changed the juvenile justice system.

Kent v. United States   The first decision to extend due process rights to children in juvenile courts was *Kent v. United States* (1966).[8] The case concerned sixteen-year-old Morris Kent, who had been arrested for breaking into a woman's house, stealing her purse, and raping her. Because Kent was on juvenile probation, the state sought to transfer his trial for the crime to an adult court (a process to be discussed later in the chapter). Without giving any reasons for his decision, the juvenile judge consented to this judicial waiver, and Kent was sentenced in the adult court to a thirty- to ninety-year prison term. The Supreme Court overturned the sentence, ruling that juveniles have a right to counsel and a hearing in any instance in which the juvenile judge is considering sending the case to an adult court. The Court stated that, in jurisdiction waiver cases, a child receives "the worst of both worlds," getting neither the "protections accorded to adults" nor the "solicitous care and regenerative treatment" offered in the juvenile system.[9]

In re Gault   The *Kent* decision provided the groundwork for *In re Gault* one year later. Considered by many the single most important case concerning juvenile justice, *In re Gault* involved a fifteen-year-old boy who was arrested for allegedly making a lewd phone call while on probation.[10] (See the feature *CJ in Focus—Landmark Cases:* In re Gault on the following page.) In its decision, the Supreme Court held that juveniles are entitled to many of the same due process rights granted to adult offenders, including notice of charges, the right to counsel, the privilege against self-incrimination, and the right to confront and cross-examine witnesses.

Other Important Court Decisions   Over the next ten years, the Supreme Court handed down three more important rulings on juvenile court procedure. *In re Winship* (1970)[11] required the government to prove "beyond a reasonable doubt" that a juvenile had committed an act of delinquency, raising the burden of proof from a "preponderance of the evidence." In *Breed v. Jones* (1975),[12] the Court held that the Fifth Amendment's double jeopardy clause prevented a juvenile from being tried in an adult court for a crime that had already been adjudicated in juvenile court. In contrast, *McKeiver v. Pennsylvania* (1971)[13] represented the one instance in which the Court did not move the juvenile court further toward the adult model. It ruled that the Constitution did not give juveniles the right to a jury trial.

DETERMINING DELINQUENCY TODAY

In the eyes of many observers, the net effect of the Supreme Court decisions during the 1966–1975 period was to move juvenile justice away from the ideals of the child savers and toward a formalized system that is often indistinguishable from its adult counterpart. But, though the Court has recognized that minors possess certain constitutional rights, it has failed to dictate at what age these rights should be granted and at what age minors are to be held criminally responsible for delinquent actions. Consequently, the legal status of children in the United States varies depending on where they live, with each state making its own policy decisions on the crucial questions of age and competency.

FIGURE 15.1

Status Offenses

A status offense is an act that, if committed by a juvenile, is considered grounds for apprehension and perhaps state custody. The same act, if committed by an adult, does not warrant law enforcement action.

1. Smoking cigarettes
2. Drinking alcohol
3. Being truant (skipping school)
4. Disobeying teachers
5. Running away from home
6. Violating curfew
7. Participating in sexual activity
8. Using profane language

In re Gault

In 1964, fifteen-year-old Gerald Gault and a friend were arrested for making lewd telephone calls to a neighbor in Gila County, Arizona. Gault, who was on probation, was placed under custody with no notice given to his parents. The juvenile court in his district held a series of informal hearings to determine Gault's punishment. During these hearings, no records were kept, Gault was not afforded the right to counsel, and the complaining witness was never made available for questioning. At the close of the hearing, the judge sentenced Gault to remain in Arizona's State Industrial School until the age of twenty-one. The defendant filed a writ of *habeas corpus,* claiming that he had been denied due process rights at his hearing. The Arizona Supreme Court affirmed the dismissal of this writ, ruling that the proceedings did not infringe on Gault's due process rights, a matter eventually taken up by the United States Supreme Court.

In re Gault
United States Supreme Court
387 U.S. 1 (1967)
http://laws.findlaw.com/US/387/1.htm

In the words of the court . . .
Justice FORTAS, majority opinion

* * * *

From the inception of the juvenile court system, wide differences have been tolerated—indeed insisted upon—between the procedural rights accorded to adults and those of juveniles. In practically all jurisdictions, there are rights granted to adults which are withheld from juveniles.

* * * *

Accordingly, the highest motives and most enlightened impulses led to a peculiar system for juveniles, unknown to our law in any comparable context. The constitutional and theoretical basis for this peculiar system is—to say the least—debatable. And in practice, as we remarked in the *Kent* case, the results have not been entirely satisfactory. * * * The absence of substantive standards has not necessarily meant that children receive careful, compassionate, individualized treatment. The absence of procedural rules based upon constitutional principle has not always produced fair, efficient, and effective procedures. Departures from

established principles of due process have frequently resulted not in enlightened procedure, but in arbitrariness.

* * * *

Ultimately, however, we confront the reality of that portion of the Juvenile Court process with which we deal in this case. A boy is charged with misconduct. The boy is committed to an institution where he may be restrained of liberty for years. It is of no constitutional consequence—and of limited practical meaning—that the institution to which he is committed is called an Industrial School. The fact of the matter is that, however euphemistic the title, a "receiving home" or an "industrial school" for juveniles is an institution of confinement in which the child is incarcerated for a greater or lesser time. His world becomes "a building with whitewashed walls, regimented routine and institutional hours . . . ." Instead of mother and father and sisters and brothers and friends and classmates, his world is peopled by guards, custodians, state employees, and "delinquents" confined with him for anything from waywardness to rape and homicide. In view of this, it would be extraordinary if our Constitution did not require the procedural regularity and the exercise of care implied in the phrase "due process." Under our Constitution, the condition of being a boy does not justify a kangaroo court.

* * * *

DECISION

The Court held that juveniles were entitled to the basic procedural safeguards afforded by the Fourteenth Amendment, including the right to advance notice of charges, the right to counsel, the right to confront and cross-examine witnesses, and the privilege against self-incrimination. The decision marked a turning point in juvenile justice in this country: no longer would informality and paternalism be the guiding principles of juvenile courts. Instead, due process would dictate the adjudication process, much as in an adult court.

FOR CRITICAL ANALYSIS

What might be some of the negative consequences of the *In re Gault* decision for juveniles charged with committing delinquent acts?

For more information and activities related to this case, click on Landmark Cases under Book Resources at **www.cjinaction.com**.

The Age Question

In 2005, a nine-year-old stabbed and killed her eleven-year-old friend during a playtime dispute in a Brooklyn, New York, apartment. When the girl was charged with juvenile murder, some in the community expressed surprise. "She's just a child," remarked the victim's aunt. "What can you do?"[14]

This question is answered in different ways by different jurisdictions. Under common law, a child under the age of seven was considered to lack the requisite *mens rea* to commit a crime (that is, he or she did not possess the mental capacity to understand the consequences of his or her action). Also under common law, a child between the ages of seven and fourteen could use the defense of infancy (being a minor) to plead innocent. On attaining fourteen years of age, the youth was considered an adult and treated accordingly.[15]

Today, as Figure 15.2 shows, twenty-four states and the District of Columbia do not have age restrictions on prosecuting juveniles as adults. Indeed, many states require juveniles who commit violent felonies such as murder, rape, or armed robbery to be waived to adult courts. (Because the Brooklyn girl mentioned in the previous paragraph did not meet New York's age limit for her offenses, she could not be sentenced to more than eighteen months in a juvenile facility.) When juveniles in a state without such a requirement commit a serious crime, they are given a "limited" sentence, usually meaning they cannot remain incarcerated in juvenile detention centers past their eighteenth or twenty-first birthday.

The Competency Question

One of the precepts of *parens patriae* was the assumption that children are not legally competent and must, in the absence of parental care, be protected by the state. In today's juvenile justice environment, however, the question of a minor's competency to make informed decisions about criminal actions is far more complicated.

Most researchers believe that by the age of fourteen, an adolescent has the same ability to make a competent decision as does an adult.[16] Nevertheless, according to some observers, a juvenile's ability to theoretically understand the difference between "right" and "wrong" does not mean that she or he should be held to the same standards of competency as an adult. A study released in 2003 by the Research Network on Adolescent Development and Juvenile Justice found that 33 percent of juvenile defendants in criminal courts had the same low level of understanding of legal matters as mentally ill adults who had been found incompetent to stand trial.[17]

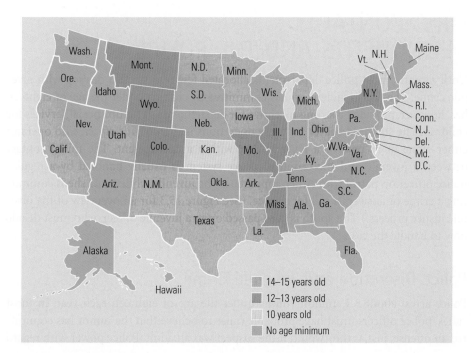

FIGURE 15.2

The Minimum Age at Which a Juvenile Can Be Tried as an Adult

Source: Office of Juvenile Justice and Delinquency Prevention.

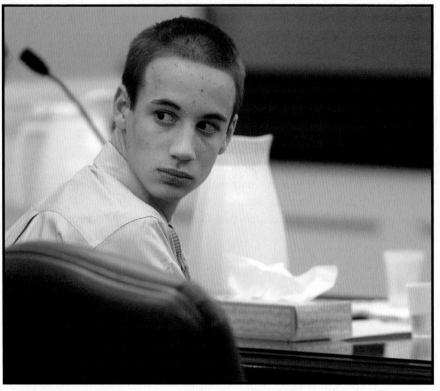

Christopher Pittman was twelve years old when he killed his grandparents with a shotgun and burned down their house outside Chester, South Carolina. Shown here on the first day of his murder trial in 2005, the fifteen-year-old was eventually found guilty on two counts of murder and sentenced to thirty years in prison. The defense claimed that Pittman was not responsible for his actions because he was under the influence of the antidepressant Zoloft at the time of the murders. Should an offender's age be taken into account when determining his or her ability to form criminal intent?

Legal psychologist Richard E. Redding believes that:

> adolescents' lack of life experience may limit their real-world decision-making ability. Whether we call it wisdom, judgment, or common sense, adolescents may not have nearly enough.[18]

Juveniles are generally more impulsive, more likely to engage in risky behavior, and less likely to calculate the long-term consequences of any particular action. Furthermore, adolescents are far more likely to respond to peer pressure than are adults. The desire for acceptance and approval may drive them to commit crimes; juveniles are arrested as part of a group at much higher rates than adults.[19]

The "diminished culpability" of juveniles was one of the reasons given by the United States Supreme Court in its landmark decision in *Roper v. Simmons* (2005)[20] to forbid the execution of offenders who were under the age of eighteen when they committed their crimes. In his majority opinion, Justice Anthony Kennedy wrote that because minors cannot fully comprehend the consequences of their actions, the two main justifications for the death penalty—retribution and deterrence—do not "work" with juvenile wrongdoers.[21] (To review this important decision, see pages 373–374.)

FIRST CONTACT: DELINQUENTS AND THE POLICE

Until recently, most police departments allocated few resources to dealing with juvenile crime. The rise in violent crimes committed by citizens under the age of eighteen has, however, provided a strong incentive for departments to set up special services for children. The standard bearer for these operations is the *juvenile officer,* who operates either alone or as part of a juvenile unit within a department. The initial contact between a juvenile and the criminal justice system is usually handled by a regular police officer on patrol who either apprehends the juvenile while he or she is committing a crime or answers a call for service. (See Figure 15.3 for an overview of the juvenile justice process.) The youth is then passed on to a juvenile officer, who must decide how to handle the case.

Police Discretion and Juvenile Crime

Police arrest about 2.3 million youths under the age of eighteen each year. In most states, police officers must have probable cause to believe that the minor has committed an offense, just as they would if the suspect was an adult. Police power with regard

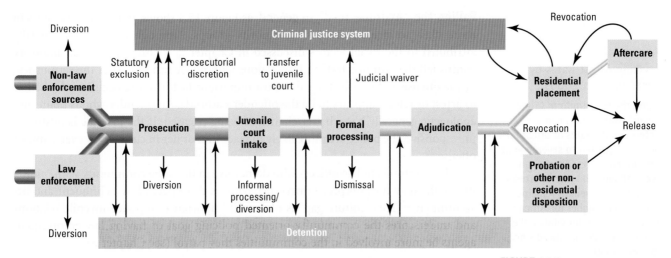

FIGURE 15.3
The Juvenile Justice Process
This diagram shows the possible tracks that a young person may take after her or his first contact with the juvenile justice system (usually a police officer).

Source: Office of Juvenile Justice and Delinquency Prevention.

to juveniles is greater than with adults, however, because police can take youths into custody for status offenses such as possession of alcohol or truancy. In these cases, the officer is acting *in loco parentis,* or in the place of the parent. The officer's role is not necessarily to punish the youths, but to protect them from harmful behavior.

Low-Visibility Decision Making Police officers also have a great deal of discretion in deciding what to do with juveniles who have committed crimes or status offenses. Juvenile justice expert Joseph Goldstein labels this discretionary power **low-visibility decision making** because it relies on factors that the public is generally not in a position to understand or criticize. When a grave offense has taken place, a police officer may decide to formally arrest the juvenile, send him or her to juvenile court, or place the youth under the care of a social-service organization. About 85 percent of the cases in juvenile courts are referred by police.[22] In less serious situations, the officer may simply issue a warning or take the offender to the police station and release the child into the custody of her or his parents.

In making these discretionary decisions, police generally consider the following factors:

- The nature of the child's offense.
- The offender's past history of involvement with the juvenile justice system.
- The setting in which the offense took place.
- The ability and willingness of the child's parents to take disciplinary action.
- The attitude of the offender.
- The offender's race and gender.

Arrests and Minority Youths As in other areas of the criminal justice system, members of minority groups are disproportionately represented in juvenile arrests. The violent crime arrest rate for African American juveniles is about four times that for white juveniles, and the property arrest crime rate for black juveniles is double that of whites. Furthermore, African American juveniles are referred to juvenile court twice as often as their white peers.[23]

A great deal of research, much of it contradictory, has been done to determine whether these statistics reflect inherent racism in the juvenile justice system or if social factors are to blame.[24] The latest large-scale study, performed by federal government crime researchers Carl E. Pope and Howard Snyder using the National Incident-Based Reporting System (see page 75), found that nonwhite offenders were no more likely to be arrested for the same delinquent behavior than were white offenders.[25]

Low-Visibility Decision Making
A term used to describe the discretionary power police have in determining what to do with misbehaving juveniles. For the most part, this power goes unchallenged and unnoticed by citizens.

Failing the "Attitude Test" In general, as Figure 15.4 shows, police officers do seem more likely to arrest members of minority groups. Although this may be partially attributed to the social factors discussed in Chapter 2, it also appears that minority youths fail the "attitude test" in interactions with police officers. After the seriousness of the offense and past history, the most important factor in the decision of whether to arrest or release appears to be the offender's attitude. An offender who is polite and apologetic generally has a better chance of being released. If the juvenile is hostile or unresponsive, the police are more likely to place him or her in custody for even a minor offense.[26]

Furthermore, police officers who do not live in the same community with minority youths may misinterpret normal behavior as disrespectful or delinquent and act accordingly.[27] This "culture gap" is of crucial importance to police-juvenile relations and underscores the community-oriented policing goal of having law enforcement agents be more involved in the communities they patrol (see Chapter 6).

Juveniles and the Constitution

The privacy and *Miranda* rights of juveniles are protected during contact with law enforcement officers, though not to the same extent as for adults. In most jurisdictions, the Fourth Amendment ban against unreasonable searches and seizures and Fifth Amendment safeguards against custodial self-incrimination apply to juveniles. In other words, juvenile court judges cannot use illegally seized evidence in juvenile hearings, and police must read youths their *Miranda* rights after arrest.

Searches and Students Such rights are not absolute, however. In *New Jersey v. T.L.O.* (1985),[28] the Supreme Court held that school officials may search a student on mere "reasonable suspicion" that he or she has violated school regulations or laws. The Court justified this lower standard—most searches require probable cause—on the grounds of maintaining school discipline and the *in loco parentis* doctrine.[29] In 1995, the Court further strengthened school officials' ability to search students by upholding a random drug-testing policy for high school athletes.[30] Seven years later, in *Board of Education v. Earls* (2002),[31] the Court allowed similar testing of students participating in any extracurricular activities.

***Miranda* Warnings** In *Fare v. Michael C.* (1979),[32] the Supreme Court clarified law enforcement officials' responsibilities with regard to *Miranda* warnings and juveniles. The case involved a boy who had been arrested on suspicion of murder. After being read his rights, the youth asked to speak to his probation officer. The request was denied. The boy eventually confessed to the crime. The Court ruled that juveniles may waive their right to protection against self-incrimination and that admissions made to the police in the absence of counsel are admissible. Then, in 2004, the Court seemed to blur any constitutional distinction between juveniles and adults for *Miranda* purposes by ruling that a trial court does not need to consider the defendant's age in determining whether a "reasonable person" would think she or he is in custody.[33] (See pages 224–230 for a review of the *Miranda* procedure.)

FIGURE 15.4

Juvenile Arrest Rates by Race, 1980 to 2000s

Using the FBI's Uniform Crime Report, statisticians can determine the rates of arrest for persons aged ten to seventeen in the United States. As you can see, although the rate of arrests per 100,000 juveniles remains considerably higher for African Americans than for whites, the discrepancy has narrowed since the mid-1990s.

Source: Office of Juvenile Justice and Delinquency Prevention.

This does not mean that juvenile status is completely irrelevant in these situations. Remember that any statement to the police must be given voluntarily. Thus, courts can look at the defendant's age in determining whether he or she was unfairly coerced into speaking.[34] As can be seen in the feature *CJ in Focus—A Question of Ethics: Interrogating Children* on the next page, police can be taking a chance by relying on the testimony of young suspects and witnesses.

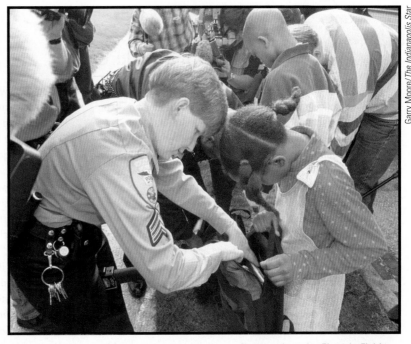

Garry Moore/The Indianapolis Star

PRETRIAL PROCEDURES IN JUVENILE JUSTICE

After arrest and before the start of the trial, various decision makers are provided the opportunity to determine how the juvenile justice system will dispose of each case. The offender may be diverted to a social-services program or detained in a juvenile lockup facility. In the most serious cases, the youth may even be transferred to adult court. To ensure due process during pretrial procedures, offenders and their families may retain an attorney or have one appointed by the court. The four primary stages of this critical period—intake, diversion, waiver, and detention—are discussed below.

Intake

If, following arrest, a police officer feels the offender warrants the attention of the juvenile justice process, the officer will refer the youth to juvenile court. As noted earlier, the juvenile court receives the majority of its respondents from the police, though parents, relatives, welfare agencies, and school officials may also refer juveniles. Once this step has been taken, a complaint is filed with a special division of the juvenile court, and the **intake** process begins. During intake, an official of the juvenile court—usually a probation officer, but sometimes a judge—must decide, in effect, what to do with the offender. The screening official has several options during intake.

1 Simply dismiss the case, releasing the offender without taking any further action.
2 Divert the offender to a social-services program, such as drug rehabilitation or anger management.
3 File a **petition** for a formal court hearing.
4 Transfer the case to an adult court where the offender will be tried as an adult.

The intake process is changing in several very important ways. In particular, the influence of prosecutors on the fate of the juvenile wrongdoer is growing significantly. In the past, the primary responsibility for providing a juvenile judge with a recommendation on how the case should be handled was left to probation personnel. Even though the judge handed down the final decision, in most cases she or he followed the recommendation of a probation officer as to whether the juvenile should take part in a formal court hearing. This approach, indicative of a system that favors rehabilitation, is being replaced in some jurisdictions.

As second-grader Ejuanda Fields exits the school bus that takes her to Indianapolis Public School 84, Indianapolis Public Schools Police Sergeant Kelly Browning checks her backpack for weapons and drugs. Do you believe that students should have the same privacy protections against searches as everybody else? What reasons can be given for denying them those protections?

Intake

Following referral of a juvenile to juvenile court by a police officer or other concerned party, the process by which an official of the court must decide whether to file a petition, release the juvenile, or place the juvenile under some other form of supervision.

Petition

The document filed with a juvenile court alleging that the juvenile is a delinquent or a status offender and asking the court to either hear the case or transfer it to an adult court.

Interrogating Children

The seven-year-old boy had been brought to the Wentworth Area police headquarters in Chicago for questioning in connection with the murder of Ryan Harris. Two weeks earlier, the beaten and sexually assaulted body of the eleven-year-old girl had been found lying in a lot behind an abandoned building. Two Chicago detectives took the boy into an empty room and asked him if he knew what a lie was. "You should never lie," he answered. Each detective took one of the boy's hands and then asked him about Harris. The seven-year-old admitted throwing a brick at the girl and knocking her off her bicycle, and then dragging her body into the weeds with the help of an eight-year-old friend. After checking the story with the friend, the police detained the boys and classified the case of Ryan Harris as "Cleared/Closed by Arrest."

Because of the age of the assailants and the brutality of the murder, the case immediately attracted the attention of the national media. Consequently, the spotlight was just as bright several weeks later, when the police abruptly released the two suspects. A forensic examination had found semen—that boys so young could not have produced—on the girl's torn underwear. Questions immediately arose concerning the Chicago police's interrogation techniques. Why had both boys been questioned at various times without the presence of counsel or even their parents? Both boys had waived their *Miranda* rights, but how could those so young understand the concept or consequences of such

an act? Why weren't obvious disparities between the two boys' stories given more attention, such as the contention by the eight-year-old that Harris was dead before she was hit in the head with the brick?

The Chicago police denied that they had bent any rules in gaining the confessions. In fact, a parent or guardian is not required by law to be present when police advise juvenile suspects of their constitutional rights—police must only make a "reasonable attempt" to contact parents, after which they can question the child. *Miranda* rights must be read only if the youth is "in custody," meaning that he or she does not feel free to leave. Finally, if a child "spontaneously confesses," as did the seven-year-old, *Miranda* warnings are not required.

To avoid situations such as occurred in Chicago, many police departments are considering digitally recording all interrogations of juveniles. Some observers are even suggesting that all interrogations of juveniles *must* take place in the presence of a parent or counsel.

FOR CRITICAL ANALYSIS

How reliable are the statements of juveniles, especially those as young as the boys in the Harris case? Regardless of the law, how should police approach the interrogation of children who may not fully understand the concept of constitutional rights?

Pretrial Diversion

To a certain extent, the juvenile justice system started as a diversionary program with the goal of diverting children from the punitive adult court to the more rehabilitative juvenile court.[35] By the 1960s, many observers felt that juvenile courts had lost sight of this early mandate and were badly in need of reform. One specific target for criticism was the growing number of status offenders—40 percent of all children in the system—who were being punished even though they had not committed a truly delinquent act.

The idea of diverting certain children, including status and first-time offenders, from the juvenile court system to nonjudicial community agencies was encouraged by the President's Commission on Law Enforcement and Administration of Justice in 1967.[36] Seven years later, Congress passed the Juvenile Justice and Delinquency Prevention (JJDP) Act, which ordered the development of methods "to divert juveniles from the traditional juvenile justice system."[37] Within a few years, hundreds of diversion programs had been put into effect. Today, **diversion** refers to the process of removing low-risk offenders from the formal juvenile justice system by placing them in community-based rehabilitation programs.

Diversion programs vary widely, but fall into three general categories:

1 *Probation.* In this program, the juvenile is returned to the community, but placed under the supervision of a juvenile probation officer. If the youth breaks the conditions of probation, he or she can be returned to the formal juvenile system.

Diversion
The removal of an alleged juvenile delinquent from the formal criminal or juvenile justice system and the referral of that person to a treatment or rehabilitation program.

2 *Treatment and aid.* Many juveniles have behavioral or medical conditions that contribute to their delinquent behavior, and many diversion programs offer remedial education, drug and alcohol treatment, and other forms of counseling to alleviate these problems.

3 *Restitution.* In these programs, the offender "repays" her or his victim, either directly or, in the case of community service, symbolically.[38]

Proponents of diversion programs include many labeling theorists (see Chapter 2), who believe that contact with the formal juvenile justice system "labels" the youth a delinquent, which leads to further delinquent behavior.

Transfer to Adult Court

One side effect of diversionary programs is that the youths who remain in the juvenile courts are more likely to be seen as "hardened" and less amenable to rehabilitation. This, in turn, increases the likelihood that the offender will be transferred to an adult court, a process in which the juvenile court waives jurisdiction over the youth. As the American juvenile justice system has shifted away from ideals of treatment and toward punishment, transfer to adult court has been one of the most popular means of "getting tough" on delinquents.

Methods of Transfer Juveniles are most commonly transferred to adult court through **judicial waiver.** In all states except New York and Nebraska, the juvenile judge is the official who determines whether jurisdiction over a minor offender should be waived to adult court. The judge formulates this ruling by taking into consideration the offender's age, the nature of the offense, and any criminal history.

Thirty-four states have taken the waiver responsibility out of judicial hands through **automatic transfer,** also known as *legislative waiver.* In these states, the legislatures have designated certain conditions—usually involving serious crimes such as murder and rape—under which a juvenile case is automatically "kicked up" to adult court. In Rhode Island, for example, a juvenile aged sixteen or older with two prior felony adjudications will automatically be transferred on being accused of a third felony.[39] Ten states allow for **prosecutorial waiver,** in which juvenile court judges are allowed to waive jurisdiction when certain age and offense conditions are met. In general, no matter what the process, those juveniles who commit violent felonies are most likely to be transferred to an adult court (see Figure 15.5).

In twenty-four states, criminal court judges also have the freedom to send juveniles who were transferred to adult court back to juvenile court. Known as *reverse transfer* statutes, these laws are designed to provide judges with a measure of discretion even when automatic transfer takes place.[40]

Consequences of Transfer When transfer laws were first enacted, observers worried that judges in adult courts would tend to give juveniles more lenient sentences than adults who had committed the same crime. This "leniency gap" does not appear to exist. Indeed, critics of transfer laws insist that adult courts are *too* severe on juveniles. The most recent study on the subject, carried out by Megan C. Kurlychek of the University of South Carolina and Brian D. Johnson of the University of Maryland, compared the sentencing outcomes of juveniles and young adults over a three-year period in Pennsylvania. The research showed that "transferred" juveniles were more likely to be sent to

Judicial Waiver

The process in which the juvenile judge, based on the facts of the case at hand, decides that the alleged offender should be transferred to adult court.

Automatic Transfer

The process by which a juvenile is transferred to adult court as a matter of state law. In some states, for example, a juvenile who is suspected of murder is automatically transferred to adult court.

Prosecutorial Waiver

A procedure in which juvenile court judges have the discretion to transfer a juvenile case to adult court, when certain predetermined conditions as to the seriousness of the offense and the age of the offender are met.

FIGURE 15.5

Felony Arrest Charges for Juveniles Transferred to Adult Criminal Courts

Two out of every three juveniles transferred to adult criminal court under suspicion of committing a felony were charged with a violent offense. The data shown here were collected in criminal courts located in forty of the largest urban counties in the United States.

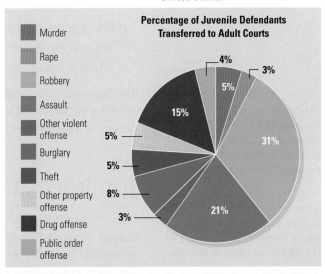

Source: Bureau of Justice Statistics, *Juvenile Felony Defendants in Criminal Courts* (Washington, D.C.: U.S. Department of Justice, May 2003), Table 2, page 2.

AP Photo/Morry Gash

Thirteen-year-old Artieas Shanks, pictured here, was originally charged as an adult for his part in the beating death of Charlie Young, Jr., in Milwaukee, Wisconsin. Eventually, however, he reached a plea bargain with prosecutors allowing him to be found delinquent rather than pleading guilty to a felony. In 2003 his case was sent to Children's Court, and he was sentenced as a juvenile to two years in the custody of the Wisconsin Department of Youth Services. How might this "reverse transfer" benefit Shanks?

prison than young adults and received sentences 81 percent longer than their similarly aged counterparts.[41]

Furthermore, a number of observers believe that juveniles tried in adult courts have higher recidivism rates than those who are tried in juvenile courts. Comparing juveniles who were transferred to adult prisons for nonviolent crimes and adults in the same facilities for nonviolent crimes, the *Arizona Republic* found that the juvenile inmates were four times more likely than the adults to commit a violent crime after release.[42] Another survey found that, over the short term, 30 percent of transferred offenders were rearrested after release, compared to 19 percent of those processed in the juvenile court system.[43] "You can learn a whole lot more bad things in here than good," said one juvenile inmate from his cell in an Arizona adult prison.[44]

Detention

Once the decision has been made that the offender will face adjudication in a juvenile court, the intake official must decide what to do with him or her until the start of the trial. Generally, the juvenile is released into the custody of parents or a guardian—most jurisdictions favor this practice in lieu of setting money bail for youths. The intake officer may also place the offender in **detention,** or temporary custody in a secure facility, until the disposition process begins. Once a juvenile has been detained, most jurisdictions require that a **detention hearing** be held within twenty-four hours. During this hearing, the offender has several due process safeguards, including the right to counsel, the right against self-incrimination, and the right to cross-examine and confront witnesses.

In justifying its decision to detain, the court will usually address one of three issues:

1 Whether the child poses a danger to the community.

2 Whether the child will return for the adjudication process.

3 Whether detention will provide protection for the child.

The Supreme Court upheld the practice of preventive detention (see Chapter 9) for juveniles in *Schall v. Martin* (1984)[45] by ruling that youths can be detained if they are deemed a "risk" to the safety of the community or to their own welfare.

Detention

The temporary custody of a juvenile in a state facility after a petition has been filed and before the adjudicatory process begins.

Detention Hearing

A hearing to determine whether a juvenile should be detained, or remain detained, while waiting for the adjudicatory process to begin.

JUVENILES ON TRIAL

Over the past thirty-five years, the one constant in the juvenile justice system has been change. Supreme Court rulings in the wake of *In re Gault* (1967) have increased the procedural formality and the overriding punitive philosophy of the juvenile court. Diversion policies have worked to remove many status offenders from the juvenile

MASTERING CONCEPTS

The Juvenile Justice System versus the Criminal Justice System

When the juvenile justice system first began in the United States, its participants saw it as being separate from the adult criminal justice system. Indeed, the two systems remain separate in many ways. There are, however, a number of similarities between juvenile and adult justice. Here, we summarize both the similarities and the differences.

SIMILARITIES
• The right to receive the *Miranda* warning
• Procedural protections when making an admission of guilt
• Prosecutors and defense attorneys play equally important roles
• The right to be represented by counsel at the crucial stages of the trial process
• Access to plea bargains
• The right to a hearing and an appeal
• The standard of evidence is proof beyond a reasonable doubt
• Both can be placed on probation by the judge
• Both can be held before adjudication if the judge believes them to be a threat to the community
• Following trial, both can be sentenced to community supervision

DIFFERENCES	Juvenile System	Adult System
Purpose	Rehabilitation of the offender	Punishment
Arrest	Juveniles can be arrested for acts (status offenses) that are not criminal for adults	Adults can be arrested only for acts made illegal by the relevant criminal code
Wrongdoing	Considered a "delinquent act"	A crime
Proceedings	Informal, closed to public	Formal and regimented; open to public
Information	Courts may NOT release information to the press	Courts MUST release information to the press
Parents	Play significant role	Play no role
Release	Into parent/guardian custody	May post bail when justified
Jury trial	In most, but not all, states, juveniles do NOT have this right	All adults have this right
Searches	Juveniles can be searched in school without probable cause	No adult can be searched without probable cause
Records	Juvenile's record is sealed at age of majority	Adult's criminal record is permanent
Sentencing	Juveniles are placed in separate facilities from adults	Adults are placed in county jails or state prisons
Death penalty	No death penalty	Death penalty for certain serious crimes under certain circumstances

court's jurisdiction, and waiver policies assure that the most violent juveniles are tried as adults. Some observers feel these adjustments have "criminalized" the juvenile court, effectively rendering it indistinguishable both theoretically and practically from adult courts.[46]

Along with a number of his colleagues, law professor Barry C. Feld thinks that the juvenile court has become obsolete and should be abolished. Feld believes the changes noted above have "transformed the juvenile court from its original model as a social service agency into a deficient second-rate criminal court that provides young people with neither positive treatment nor criminal procedural justice."[47] Indeed, juvenile hearings do proceed along many of the same lines as the adult criminal court, with similar due process protections and rules of evidence (though minors do not enjoy the right to a jury trial). As the *Mastering Concepts* feature above explains, however, juvenile justice proceedings may still be distinguished from the adult system of criminal justice, and these differences are evident in the adjudication and disposition of the juvenile trial.

Adjudication

During the adjudication stage of the juvenile justice process, a hearing is held to determine whether the offender is delinquent or in need of some form of court supervision. Most state juvenile codes dictate a specific set of procedures that must be followed during the **adjudicatory hearing,** with the goal of providing the respondent with "the essentials of due process and fair treatment." Consequently, the respondent in an adjudicatory hearing has the right to notice of charges, counsel, confrontation and cross-examination, and the privilege against self-incrimination. Furthermore, "proof beyond a reasonable doubt" must be established to find the child delinquent. When the child admits guilt—that is, admits to the charges of the initial petition—the judge must ensure that the admission was voluntary.

The increased presence of defense attorneys in juvenile courts has had a significant impact on juvenile adjudication. Aspects of the adversarial system have become increasingly apparent in juvenile courts, as has the practice of plea bargaining. To a certain extent, however, juvenile trials have retained the informal atmosphere that characterized pre–*In re Gault* proceedings. Respondents and their families often waive the due process rights provided by the Supreme Court at the suggestion of a juvenile probation officer or judge. One study of Minnesota juvenile courts found that no counsel was present in 50 percent of that state's adjudicatory hearings.[48]

At the close of the adjudicatory hearing, the judge is generally required to rule on the legal issues and evidence that have been presented. Based on this ruling, the judge determines whether the respondent is delinquent or in need of court supervision. Alternatively, the judge can dismiss the case based on a lack of evidence. It is important to remember that finding a child to be delinquent is *not* the same as convicting an adult of a crime. A delinquent does not face the same restrictions, such as those concerning the right to vote and to run for political office, as do adult convicts in some states (discussed in Chapter 14).

Disposition

Once a juvenile has been adjudicated delinquent, the judge must decide what steps will be taken toward treatment and/or punishment. Most states provide for a *bifurcated process* in which a separate **disposition hearing** follows the adjudicatory hearing. Depending on state law, the juvenile may be entitled to counsel at the disposition hearing.

Sentencing Juveniles In an adult trial, the sentencing phase is primarily concerned with the "needs" of the community to be protected from the convict. In contrast, a juvenile judge uses the disposition hearing to determine a sentence that will serve the "needs" of the child. For assistance in this crucial process, the judge will order the probation department to gather information on the juvenile and present it in the form of a **predisposition report.** The report usually contains information concerning the respondent's family background, the facts surrounding the delinquent act, and interviews with social workers, teachers, and other important figures in the child's life.

Judicial Discretion In keeping with the rehabilitative tradition of the juvenile justice system, many judges have a great deal of discretion in choosing one of several disposition possibilities. Generally, the choice is among incarceration in a juvenile correctional facility, probation, or community treatment. In most cases, seriousness of the offense is the primary factor used in determining whether to incarcerate a juvenile, though history of delinquency, family situation, and the offender's attitude are all relevant. Some research suggests that race plays a significant role in disposition—that minority delinquents are more likely to be incarcerated than their white counterparts.[49]

CAREERS IN CJ

Cathy Wasserman
Public Defender: Juvenile Courts

Grandpa had always said I could talk my way out of the electric chair. So when a friend in college suggested applying to law school, I thought, yes, why not? I attended Seton Hall Law in Newark, New Jersey, where I participated in the Juvenile Justice Clinic for two and a half semesters. This experience representing delinquents, coupled with a childhood of being raised on *Perry Mason,* as well as a law clerkship with a Superior Court judge, helped me to recognize my strong interest in criminal law. The forum of pleading my case in open court seemed like the only place to be.

Following my clerkship, I was hired by the office of the public defender. Working for the P.D. is the fastest way to be in command of your own cases and to appear in court on all kinds of matters, particularly trials. My caseload consisted of clients charged with everything from fourth degree theft to armed robbery. The first year and a half, I represented adults. Then I went to the appellate section, where I wrote briefs for two and a half years. I enjoyed the treasure hunt of looking for the cases to support my arguments. I also enjoyed presenting those arguments to the appellate division panels. However, I found I missed being in court on a daily basis and dealing with clients in person. Thus, when the opportunity to transfer to another trial region arose, I grabbed it and began representing juveniles once again.

Every day I enter court prepared to do battle for a youngster who in all likelihood is not cognizant of how at risk his or her freedom is. Initially, my most important responsibility is to interview my client and his family to gain their trust, obtain information about the child, and learn their version of the facts in the case. I gather all the evidence provided by the State, review it carefully, and conduct my own investigations. Following a careful review of all the evidence available, weighing all the strengths and weaknesses in the case, and considering whether any trial would be before a judge rather than a jury, I discuss the options, risks, and penalties with my client. Whether we go to trial or negotiate a plea agreement, my duties are to be an effective attorney for the child. However, once we face a sentence, I must also become a social worker as I attempt to fashion the least restrictive disposition from the myriad of sentencing alternatives. It is this array of options and the court's discretion to impose

them which most clearly distinguishes the juvenile system from its adult counterpart.

Courtesy Cathy Wasserman

Cathy Wasserman

Some of the most challenging cases of my career have involved representing children the State is seeking to have referred to adult court. In New Jersey, there is a presumption of referral where a juvenile is charged with the most serious offenses and is fourteen years of age or older. The discretion to file for referral lies solely in the hands of the prosecutor. There are few tasks more difficult than having to tell a fourteen-year-old, who had a fight in which someone died, that he could be spending the next thirty years of his life in an adult jail. I faced this very scenario a number of years ago. In that particular case, H. T. had no prior involvement with the system and did not inflict the fatal wound. Worse, the confession he gave to the police to "help" himself was the main evidence against him. Although the State's psychiatrist agreed with the defense expert that the boy could be rehabilitated in the juvenile system, the State pressed on. The pressure and emotional toll on me as counsel was enormous. I struggled to construct arguments out of the jigsaw puzzle of facts and the kid's life. I was confidante, commander, and adviser to not only my client in custody but also to his family. Contrary to the norm in waiver cases, H. T. prevailed. This case helped me to recognize how important my role can be in the life of a child.

I am an impassioned advocate for children because I believe most offenders should be allowed to survive childhood and adolescence without permanently damaging their prospects for a positive future. My skills as an attorney and negotiator give my clients the opportunity to rise above their acts, often committed through poor judgment, due to inexperience, or by succumbing to peer pressure. Occasionally, I make a significant difference in the life of a youngster.

Go to the Careers in Criminal Justice Interactive CD *for more profiles in the field of criminal justice.*

Further indication of the treatment goals of juvenile courts can be found in the indeterminate sentencing practices that, until recently, dominated disposition. Under this system, correctional administrators were given the freedom to decide when a delinquent had been sufficiently rehabilitated and could be released. In a clear indication of the shift toward the crime control model, today nearly half of the states have enacted determinate or minimum mandatory sentencing laws that cover convicted juvenile offenders. Such statutes shift the focus of disposition from the treatment needs of the delinquent to society's desire to punish and incapacitate.[50]

JUVENILE CORRECTIONS

In general, juvenile corrections are based on the concept of **graduated sanctions**—that is, the severity of the punishment should fit the crime. Consequently, status and first-time offenders are diverted or placed on probation, repeat offenders find themselves in intensive community supervision or treatment programs, and serious and violent offenders are placed in correctional facilities.[51] As society's expectations of the juvenile justice system have changed, so have the characteristics of its corrections programs. In some cities, for example, juvenile probation officers join police officers on the beat. Because the former are not bound by the same search and seizure restrictions as other law enforcement officials, this interdepartmental teamwork provides more opportunities to fight youth crime aggressively. Juvenile correctional facilities are also changing their operations to reflect public mandates that they both reform and punish. Also, note that as of 2004, almost 2,500 juveniles were serving time in state adult prisons—half as many as a decade earlier.[52]

Probation and Residential Treatment Programs

The most common form of juvenile corrections is probation—35 percent of all delinquency cases disposed of by juvenile courts result in conditional diversion. The majority of all adjudicated delinquents (nearly 58 percent) will never receive a disposition more severe than being placed on probation.[53] These statistics reflect a general understanding among juvenile court judges and other officials that removing a child from her or his home should be considered primarily as a last resort.

The organization of juvenile probation is very similar to adult probation (see Chapter 12), and juvenile probationers are increasingly subjected to electronic monitoring and other supervisory tactics. The main difference between the two programs lies in the attitude toward the offender. Adult probation officers have an overriding responsibility to protect the community from the probationer, while juvenile probation officers are expected to take the role of a mentor or a concerned relative in looking after the needs of the child.

When intensive supervision must be instituted, youths can be placed in **residential treatment programs.** These programs, run by either probation departments or social-service organizations, provide treatment in a nonsecure living facility. Residential treatment programs can be divided into four categories:

1 *Foster care programs,* in which the juvenile lives with a couple who act as surrogate parents.

2 *Group homes,* which generally house between twelve and fifteen youths and provide treatment, counseling, and educational services by a professional staff.

3 *Family group homes,* which combine aspects of foster care and group homes, meaning that a single family, rather than a group of professionals, looks after the needs of the offenders.

Until recently, young people who misbehaved in California juvenile corrections facilities were placed in steel cages such as the one shown here. In 2005, officials phased out the cages as part of a large-scale attempt to improve the state juvenile justice system's image, which suffered in the wake of widespread reports of violence by corrections officials, gang warfare, and corruption. How might steel cages undermine the purpose of the juvenile justice system?

Monica Almeida/The New York Times

4 *Rural programs,* which include wilderness camps, farms, and ranches where between thirty and fifty children are placed in an environment that provides recreational activities and treatment programs.[54]

Institutionalizing Juveniles

More than 130,000 American youths (up from 30,000 at the end of the 1970s) are incarcerated in public and private juvenile correctional facilities in the United States.[55] Most of these juveniles have committed crimes against people or property, but a significant number (about 16 percent) have been incarcerated because of other factors, such as familial neglect or mental incapacity.

The most restrictive of these facilities—referred to as **training schools**—are similar in many aspects to adult prisons and jails. In theory, training schools differ from adult prisons and jails in their efforts to treat and rehabilitate young offenders. In practice, although many juvenile facilities do uphold this traditional justification for incarcerating children, a number do not.

Juveniles leave corrections facilities through an early release program or because they have served the length of their sentences. Juvenile corrections officials recognize that many of these children, like adults, need assistance readjusting to the outside world. Consequently, released juveniles are often placed in *aftercare* programs. Based on the same philosophy that drives the prisoner reentry movement (discussed in the last chapter), aftercare programs are designed to offer services for the juveniles, while at the same time supervising them to reduce the chances of recidivism. The ideal aftercare program includes community support groups, aid in finding and keeping employment, and continued monitoring to assure that the juvenile is able to deal with the demands of freedom.[56] (See the feature *Outside the Box—Young Women's Support Project* on p. 508.)

RECENT TRENDS IN JUVENILE DELINQUENCY

When asked, juveniles will admit to a wide range of illegal or dangerous behavior, including carrying weapons, getting involved in physical fights, driving after drinking alcohol, and stealing or deliberately damaging school property.[57] Have juvenile law enforcement efforts, juvenile courts, and juvenile corrections been effective in controlling and preventing this kind of misbehavior, as well as more serious acts?

To answer this question, many observers turn to the Federal Bureau of Investigation's Uniform Crime Report (UCR), initially covered in Chapter 3. Because the UCR breaks down arrest statistics by age of the arrestee, it has been considered the primary source of information on the presence of juveniles in America's justice system. This does not mean, however, that the UCR is completely reliable when it comes to measuring juvenile delinquency. The process measures only those juveniles who were caught and therefore does not accurately reflect all delinquent acts in any given year. Furthermore, it measures the number of arrests but not the number of arrestees, meaning that—due to repeat offenders—the number of juveniles actually in the system could be below the number of juvenile arrests.

Delinquency by the Numbers

With these cautions in mind, UCR findings are quite clear as to the extent of the juvenile delinquency problem in the United States today. In 2004, juveniles accounted for 15.6 percent of violent crime arrests and 15.9 percent of criminal

The **National Center for Juvenile Justice** is a valuable source for juvenile delinquency information and data. Find its Web site by clicking on *Web Links* under *Chapter Resources* at **www.cjinaction.com**.

Training Schools
Correctional institutions for juveniles found to be delinquent or status offenders.

Young Women's Support Project

On probation for a drug charge, sixteen-year-old Joy was returned to the King County Youth Detention Center in Seattle, Washington, after a fight at home. According to Laura Culberg, that may have been the best thing that could have happened to her. "They keep coming back to detention because they don't have anyone to support them," says Culberg. In juvenile detention (or "juvie"), however, Joy and about three hundred other girls have access to the Young Women's Support Project, a series of workshops run by Culberg that address a number of issues facing delinquent girls.

Culberg's ultimate goal is to change the defeatist perspective of girls who come through the juvenile justice system. The workshops are not unlike pep talks, in that Culberg and her female volunteer assistants try to improve the girls' self-esteem. The sessions also concentrate on sensitive subjects—such as birth control, rape, sexually transmitted diseases, and eating disorders—that many young women do not feel comfortable discussing with male counselors. In addition, Culberg directs sessions designed to teach the girls how to keep themselves out of trouble when they are sent back home. Each girl is asked to create a "stay out of juvie map" with a detailed plan on how she plans to achieve her goals once released.

The Young Women's Support Project is one of the few programs in the country that focuses on female delinquents. Many observers hope it becomes a model for similar programs in other areas, considering that young women are committing an increasing amount of juvenile crime. Over the past two decades, the arrest rate for girls has increased at twice the rate for boys, and girls now comprise almost 30 percent of the juvenile justice system's population.

FOR CRITICAL ANALYSIS
Why do you think that programs such as the Young Women's Support Project are so rare?

activity arrests in general.[58] According to the 2004 UCR, juveniles were responsible for

- 10.6 percent of all murder arrests;
- 13.7 percent of all aggravated assault arrests;
- 16.2 percent of all forcible rapes;
- 23.1 percent of all weapons arrests;
- 23.4 percent of all robbery arrests;
- 27.5 percent of all property crimes; and
- 11.1 percent of all drug offenses.

Is Juvenile Crime Leveling Off?

A recent poll found that more than 70 percent of parents felt that a shooting was likely at their child's school.[59] Although, as we will see in the *Criminal Justice in Action* feature at the end of this chapter, school crime is a serious problem, the high visibility of violence on campus tends to skew public perceptions of juvenile offending. In fact, crime against students on school grounds dropped by more than 50 percent between 1992 and 2002,[60] and as Figure 15.6 shows, after a dramatic rise in the mid-1990s, juvenile arrest rates have been steadily dropping for about a decade.

Violent Crime Trends Between 1993 and 2003, the juvenile arrest rate for violent crimes dropped 29 percent. The juvenile murder rate fell 64 percent in the 1990s, settling at levels not seen since the 1960s.[61] Incidences of juvenile robbery, burglary, and motor vehicle theft have seen similar downturns. Although juvenile arrest rates for some crimes, such as fraud, embezzlement, and driving under the influence, are still rising, the overall situation is not nearly as bleak as it was at the height of the youth crime wave in the mid-1990s.

Reasons for the Decline Although the theory is not universally accepted, many observers see the rise and decline of juvenile arrests as mirroring the rise and decline of crack cocaine.[62] When inner-city youths took advantage of the economic opportunities offered by the crack trade in the 1980s, they found they needed to protect themselves against rival dealers. This led to the proliferation of firearms among juveniles, as well as the formation of violent youth gangs. As the crack "epidemic" has slowed in recent years, so have arrest and violent crime rates for juveniles.

Other theories have been put forth as well. Some observers point to the increase in police action against "quality-of-life" crimes such as loitering, which they believe stops juveniles before they have a chance to commit more serious crimes. Furthermore, many schools have adopted "zero-tolerance" policies that punish students harshly for bringing weapons or drugs onto school grounds. (To see other steps schools are taking to make themselves safer, see the feature *CJ and Technology—The Electronic Hall Monitor* on the next page.) Richard Curtis, a professor of anthropology at John Jay College of Criminal Justice in New York, thinks young Americans have learned from the examples of friends and relatives. "They saw the toll that the whole epidemic of drugs . . . had taken on their families and peers, and they didn't want to go there," says Curtis.[63]

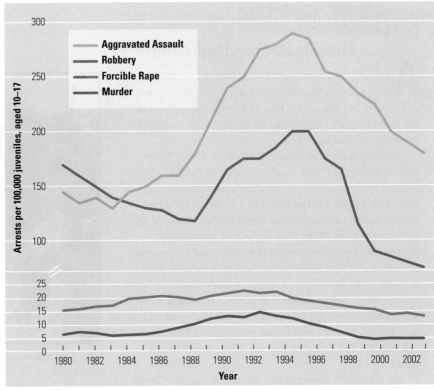

FIGURE 15.6
Arrest Rates of Juveniles, 1980 to 2000s

After rising dramatically from 1985 to 1994, arrest rates for juveniles began to fall.

Source: Office of Juvenile Justice and Delinquency Prevention.

Girls in the Juvenile Justice System

Though overall rates of juvenile offending have been dropping, one particular group of juveniles has become more involved in the juvenile justice system than ever before. Just as we saw earlier in this textbook that women are the fasting-growing segment of the adult prison population, girls are becoming more and more visible in the institutions that punish juvenile delinquency and crime.

A Growing Presence Although girls have for the most part been treated more harshly than boys for status offenses,[64] a "chivalry effect" (see page 381) has traditionally existed in other areas of the juvenile justice system. In the past, police were likely to arrest offending boys while allowing girls to go home to the care of their families for similar behavior. This is no longer the case. Between 1995 and 2004, arrests of juvenile boys dropped 27 percent while arrests of juvenile girls fell by only 7 percent.[65] More young females are also being brought into juvenile court. Between 1985 and 2000, the overall number of cases involving girls grew at an average rate of 4 percent per year—double the growth rate for boys over that same time period.[66]

Family-Based Delinquency Criminologists disagree on whether increasing arrest rates for female juveniles reflect a change in behavior or a change in law enforcement practices. A significant amount of data support the latter proposal, especially research

CJ AND TECHNOLOGY

The Electronic Hall Monitor

Americans are accustomed to being watched. Surveillance cameras are commonplace in banks, stores, office lobbies, and airports. But how about schools? Increasingly, the student hall monitor is being replaced by the electronic eye—or even better, dozens of electronic eyes.

Following the lead of colleagues across the United States, officials at Mansfield High, located just outside Boston, recently installed fourteen cameras in the school's halls and entryways. A video feed is piped into two television monitors in the school office, allowing administrators to watch and record a great deal of student activity. During their first year of operation, the devices were primarily successful in recording and consequently preventing acts of petty vandalism. Their main purpose, however, is to "create an atmosphere of safety," says principal Peter Deftos. In other words, Deftos and other proponents of using cameras in schools believe they will protect against acts of violence such as occurred in Columbine High School in Colorado in 1999, when two students shot and killed fourteen fellow students and a teacher.

Not everyone is convinced that the cameras can be effective in deterring such shootings. First, because of privacy concerns schools will generally not place cameras in bathrooms or classrooms, thereby severely limiting their scope and effectiveness. Second, just because school officials may be able to see a student with a gun walking down the hall, there is no guarantee that the official will be able to stop that student from committing a crime. In fact, Columbine High was equipped with hall cameras at the time of the tragedy.

IN THE FUTURE

What if law enforcement officers, as well as school officials, could monitor the hallways? Safewatch is a real-time video monitoring system that allows the police to view the images from as many as ten cameras at one time on a Web browser. To protect student and teacher privacy, systems such as Safewatch remain dormant

AP Photo/Jefferson County Sheriff's Department

Surveillance cameras in Columbine High School in Littleton, Colorado, show Eric Harris, left, and Dylan Klebold during their April 20, 1999, shooting spree in which they killed fourteen students and one teacher.

until activated by a trigger such as a 911 call, somewhat limiting their effectiveness in preventing a student or intruder from initiating a violent event. Because almost all police stations, as well as many police cars, are equipped with computer screens, however, officers responding to a crisis at a school would have the invaluable advantage of an electronic eye on the events within. "We could use the cameras to see inside the building before we sent in officers," said one police official. "It could save lives."

For more information on school surveillance systems and other CJ technologies, click on Crime and Technology *under* Book Resources *at* **www.cjinaction.com**.

---

showing that police are much more likely to make arrests in situations involving domestic violence than they were even a decade ago. Experts have found that girls are four times more apt to fight with parents or siblings than are boys, who usually engage in violent encounters with strangers. Consequently, a large percentage of female juvenile arrests for assault arise out of family disputes—arrests that until relatively recently would not have been made.[67]

Evidence also shows that law enforcement agents continue to treat girls more harshly for status offenses. More girls than boys are arrested for the status offense of running away from home, for example, even though studies show that male and female juveniles run away from home with equal frequency.[68] Criminologists who focus on issues of gender hypothesize that such behavior is considered normal for boys, but is seen as deviant for girls and therefore more deserving of punishment.[69]

FACTORS IN JUVENILE DELINQUENCY

In one of the most influential studies in the field of criminology, Professor Marvin Wolfgang found that 6 percent of all boys in any given cohort (group of persons who share similar characteristics) will become a chronic offender, defined as someone who is arrested five or more times before his eighteenth birthday. Furthermore, Wolfgang found that these chronic offenders were responsible for half of all crimes and two-thirds of all violent crimes within the cohort.[70] Does this "6 percent rule" mean that no matter what steps society takes, six out of every hundred juveniles are "bad seeds" and will act delinquently? Or does it point to a situation in which a small percentage of children may be more likely to commit crimes under certain circumstances?

Most criminologists favor the second interpretation. It is generally believed that a number of "risk factors" are linked to delinquent activity (see Figure 15.7). Researchers have found a number of statistical trends that show certain youths to be at higher risk for antisocial behavior. For example, juvenile delinquency appears to be linked to family structure—adolescents from single-parent families are much more likely to exhibit delinquent behavior than those who live with both biological, married parents.[71] High school dropouts also seem to be at greater risk of becoming part of Wolfgang's 6 percent; 70 percent of all adults in prison in the United States failed to complete the twelfth grade.[72] In this section, we will discuss the four factors that are most commonly used to explain juvenile criminal behavior and violent crime rates: age, substance abuse, family problems, and gangs.

The Age–Crime Relationship

Crime statistics are fairly conclusive on one point: the older a person is, the less likely he or she will exhibit criminal behavior. According to many criminologists, particularly Travis Hirschi and Michael Gottfredson, age is the one constant factor in criminal behavior, more important than gender, race, intelligence, or class.[73] Any group of at-risk persons—whether they be high school dropouts or (as we shall see) the children of abusive parents—will commit fewer crimes as they grow older. This process is known as **aging out.**

Another view sees the **age of onset,** or the age at which the youth begins delinquent behavior, as a consistent predictor of future criminal behavior. One study compared recidivism rates between juveniles first judged to be delinquent before the age of fifteen and those first adjudicated delinquent after the age of fifteen. Of the seventy-one subjects who made up the first group, 32 percent became chronic offenders. Of the sixty-five who made up the second group, none became chronic offenders.[74] Furthermore, according to the Office of Juvenile Justice and Delinquency Prevention, the earlier a youth enters the juvenile justice system, the more likely he or she will become a violent offender.[75] This research suggests that juvenile justice resources should be concentrated on the youngest offenders, with the goal of preventing crime and reducing the long-term risks for society.

Aging Out
A term used to explain the fact that criminal activity declines with age.

Age of Onset
The age at which a juvenile first exhibits delinquent behavior. The earlier the age of onset, according to some observers, the greater the chance a person will become a career offender.

FIGURE 15.7

Risk Factors for Juvenile Delinquency

The characteristics listed here are generally accepted as "risk factors" for juvenile delinquency. In other words, if one or more of these factors are present in a juvenile's life, he or she has a greater chance of exhibiting delinquent behavior—though such behavior is by no means a certainty.

Family
- Broken home/lack of parental role model
- Parental or sibling drug/alcohol abuse
- Extreme economic deprivation
- Family members in a gang

School
- Academic frustration/failure
- Learning disability
- Negative labeling by teachers
- Disciplinary problems

Community
- Social disorganization (refer to Chapter 2)
- Presence of gangs in the community
- Presence of obvious drug use in the community
- Availability of firearms
- High crime/constant feeling of danger
- Lack of social and economic opportunities

Peers
- Delinquent friends
- Friends who use drugs or are members of gangs
- Lack of "positive" peer pressure

Individual
- Tendency toward aggressive behavior
- Inability to concentrate or focus/easily bored/hyperactive
- Alcohol or drug use
- Fatalistic/pessimistic viewpoint

Child Abuse
Mistreatment of children by causing physical, emotional, or sexual damage without any plausible explanation, such as an accident.

Child Neglect
A form of child abuse in which the child is denied certain necessities such as shelter, food, care, and love. Neglect is justification for a government agency to assume responsibility for a child in place of the parents or legal guardian.

Two female juvenile offenders make their beds in their room at the Orange County Youth Guidance Center in Orange, California. According to data gathered by the National Council of Crime and Delinquency, 75 percent of all girls institutionalized by the California juvenile justice system reported regular use of drugs, including alcohol, starting around the age of fourteen.

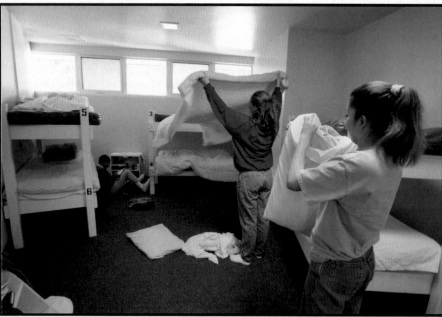

Substance Abuse

As we have seen throughout this textbook and will see again in the next chapter, substance abuse plays a strong role in criminal behavior for adults. The same can certainly be said for juveniles. According to the National Survey on Drug Use and Health (NSDUH), nearly 11 million Americans under the age of twenty consume alcohol on a regular basis, increasing the probability that they will experience academic problems, drop out of school, or commit acts of *vandalism* (the willful destruction of property).[76] The health consequences of this level of underage drinking are staggering: alcohol is a factor in between 50 and 65 percent of all teenage suicides, and nearly 2,500 youths are killed each year in alcohol-related automobile crashes. Furthermore, the NSDUH shows that nearly 11 percent of those between the ages of twelve and seventeen are current drug users, placing them at risk for delinquency.[77]

There are some signs, however, that use of illegal drugs and alcohol is declining. The Monitoring the Future survey, carried out annually by the University of Michigan's Institute for Social Research, found that cigarette smoking, alcohol intake, and use of illegal drugs by teenagers all decreased in 2002, the first time this had happened in the survey's twenty-seven-year history; furthermore, they continued to drop through 2004.[78] A similar trend can be found in drug- and alcohol-related arrests. From 1995 to 2004, for example, juvenile arrests for drunkenness decreased 30 percent.[79] And, although arrests for drug abuse violations continued to increase until the late 1990s, they fell 6.3 percent between 2000 and 2004.[80]

There is little doubt, however, that substance abuse still plays a major role in juvenile delinquency and crime. Thirteen percent of all juvenile arrests involve a drug-related crime. About 60 percent of juveniles in correctional facilities admit to regular drug use, and 50 percent say that they were under the influence of drugs or alcohol at the time they committed the offense that led to their incarceration.[81] The impact seems even greater on female juveniles: 75 percent of young women incarcerated in juvenile facilities report regular drug and alcohol use—starting at the age of fourteen—and one study found that 87 percent of female teenage offenders need substance abuse treatment.[82]

Child Abuse and Neglect

Abuse by parents also plays a substantial role in juvenile delinquency. **Child abuse** can be broadly defined as the infliction of physical or emotional damage on a child, while **child neglect** refers to deprivations—of love, shelter, food, proper care—children undergo by their parents. A significant portion (estimates can range from 40 percent[83] to 88 percent[84]) of parents who mistreat their children are believed to be under the influence of illegal drugs or alcohol.

Children in homes characterized by violence or neglect suffer from a variety of physical, emotional, and mental health problems at a much greater rate than their peers.[85] This, in turn, increases their chances of engaging in delinquent behavior. A report issued by the Arizona Supreme Court, for example, indicated that 73 percent of children between the ages of fourteen and seventeen whose parents had records of abuse in 2002 had also been sent to juvenile court for delinquency that year.[86] Another survey of violent juveniles showed that 75 percent had suffered severe abuse by a family member, 80 percent had witnessed violence in their homes, 33 percent had a sibling with a criminal record, and 25 percent had at least one parent who abused drugs or alcohol.[87]

Cathy Spatz Widom, a professor of criminal justice and psychology at the State University of New York at Albany, compared the arrest records of two groups of subjects—one made up of 908 cases of substantiated parental abuse and neglect and the other made up of 667 children who had not been abused or neglected. Widom found that those who had been abused or neglected were 53 percent more likely to be arrested as juveniles than those who had not.[88]

Gangs

When youths cannot find the stability and support they require in the family structure, they will often turn to their peers. This is just one explanation for why juveniles join **youth gangs.** Although jurisdictions may have varying definitions, for general purposes a youth gang is viewed as a group of three or more persons who (1) self-identify themselves as an entity separate from the community by special clothing, vocabulary, hand signals, and names and (2) engage in criminal activity. Although the first gangs may have appeared at the time of the American Revolution in the 1780s, there have been four periods of major gang activity in American history: the late 1800s, the 1920s, the 1960s, and the present. According to an exhaustive survey of law enforcement agencies, there are probably around 25,000 gangs with more than 720,000 members in the United States.[89]

Who Joins Gangs?

The average gang member is seventeen to eighteen years old, though members tend to be older in cities with long traditions of gang activity such as Chicago and Los Angeles.[90] Although it is difficult to determine with any certainty the make-up of gangs as a whole, one recent self-reported survey found that 47 percent of all gang members in the United States are Hispanic, 31 percent are African American, 13 percent are white, and 7 percent are Asian, with the remaining 2 percent belonging to other racial or ethnic backgrounds.[91] Though gangs tend to have racial or ethnic characteristics—that is, one group predominates in each gang—many researchers do not believe that race or ethnicity is the dominant factor in gang membership. Instead, gang members seem to come from lower-class or working-class communities, mostly in urban areas but with an increasing number from the suburbs and rural counties. In addition, researchers are finding that adolescents who will eventually join a gang display significantly higher levels of delinquent behavior than those who will never become involved in gang activity.[92]

Why Do Youths Join Gangs?

Gang membership often appears to be linked with status in the community. This tends to be true of both males and females. Many teenagers, feeling alienated from their families and communities, join gangs for the social relationships and the sense of identity a gang can provide.[93]

Gang membership is seen as a necessity for a number of youths, especially those who live in high-crime neighborhoods—joining a gang is a form of protection against violence from other gangs. Excitement is another attraction of the gang life, as is the economic incentive of enjoying the profits from illegal gang activities such as dealing drugs or robbery.[94] Finally, some teenagers are literally forced to join gangs by the threat of violence from gang members.

Youth Gangs
Self-formed groups of youths with several identifiable characteristics, including a gang name and other recognizable symbols, a geographic territory, a leadership structure, a meeting pattern, and participation in illegal activities.

GREAT DEBATES
Some observers feel that popular culture is another "risk factor" and bears some of the blame for delinquent behavior in juveniles. To better understand this controversial issue, click on *Great Debates* under *Book Resources* at **www.cjinaction.com.**

The **National Youth Gang Center** is a government-sponsored organization that researches the problems caused by gangs and proposes methods of solving them. Find its Web site by clicking on *Web Links* under *Chapter Resources* at **www.cjinaction.com.**

Gangs and Crime To a certain extent, the violent and criminal behavior of youths has been exaggerated by information sources such as the media. In proportion to all gang activities, violence is a rare event; youth gang members spend most of their time "hanging out" and taking part in other normal adolescent behavior.[95] That having been said, gang members are responsible for a disproportionate amount of violent and nonviolent criminal acts by juveniles. As we saw in Chapter 1, traditional gang activities such as using and trafficking in drugs, protecting their territory in "turf battles," and graffiti/vandalism all contribute to high crime rates among members.

> "My homeboys became my family—the older ones were father figures. Each time I shot someone, each time I put another gun on the set, each time I successfully recruited a combat soldier, I was congratulated by my older homeboys."
>
> —Sanyka Shakur, former gang member (1993)

Nationwide, youth gang homicides rose from 692 in 1999 to 1,232 in 2004.[96] One-fifth of all murders in New Jersey are gang related, and more than half the annual homicides in Chicago and Los Angeles are attributed to gang violence.[97] Statistics also show high levels of gang involvement in aggravated assault, larceny, and motor vehicle theft, while 42 percent of all youth gangs are believed to be involved in drug sales.[98] Furthermore, a recent study of criminal behavior among juveniles in Seattle found that gang members were considerably more likely to commit crimes than at-risk youths who shared many characteristics with gang members but were not affiliated with any gang (see Figure 15.8).[99] The gang members in Seattle were also much more likely to own firearms or to have friends who owned firearms.

Guns

It is hardly surprising that the gang members in Seattle were much more likely to own firearms or to have friends who did. Studies have shown that youths who are members of gangs are three times as likely to own a handgun as those who are not.[100] Gang members are also much more likely to believe that they need a gun for protection and to be involved in gun-related crimes.[101]

The harmful link between juveniles and guns is hardly limited to gang members, however. Indeed, one explanation for the increase in youth violence in the late 1980s and early 1990s points to the unprecedented access minors had to illegal weapons during that time. According to Carnegie Mellon's Alfred Blumstein:

> [Y]outh have always fought with each other. But when it's a battle with fists, the dynamics run much more slowly. With a gun, it evolves very rapidly, too fast for a third party to intervene. That also raises the stakes and encourages others to arm themselves, thereby triggering a preemptive strike: "I better get him before he gets me."[102]

In fact, the correlation between access to guns and juvenile homicide rates is striking. The juvenile arrest rate for weapons violations doubled between 1987 and 1993. By 1994, 82 percent of all homicides committed by juveniles involved a handgun. Then, as the homicide rate began to drop, so did the arrest rate for weapons offenses, and many experts believe that the downward trend in juvenile homicide arrests can be traced largely to a decline in firearm usage.[103]

Despite these encouraging trends, guns are still widespread in youth culture. A recent survey by the Josephson Institute of Ethics found that 47 percent of high school and 22 percent of middle school students said they could obtain

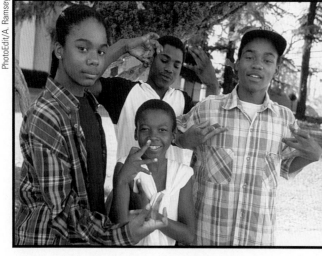

Along with wearing "colors," speaking in code, and marking their turf with graffiti, gangs use hand signals to differentiate themselves from other gangs and to strengthen the social bonds among gang members, such as the Crips of the San Fernando Valley (California), pictured here. A number of communities have tried to limit gang activity by forbidding such expressions of unity, including barring gang members from appearing in public together.

PhotoEdit/A. Ramsey

a gun if they felt the need.[104] Nearly 26,000 juveniles were arrested for gun-related crimes in 2004.[105]

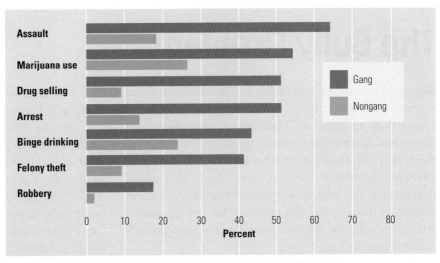

KEEPING JUVENILE DELINQUENCY UNDER CONTROL

Though the decrease in juvenile crime over the past few years has been welcome, many criminologists and law enforcement officials have expressed concern that this recent drop in youth crime will lead to a sense of complacency among their colleagues. Any such decline, they believe, should be seen in the context of the immense growth in delinquency since 1985. Furthermore, the factors we have just discussed—substance abuse by adults and adolescents, child abuse and neglect, guns, and gang membership—continue to plague juveniles.

The Office of the Surgeon General, which produced a far-reaching report on juvenile violence several years ago, also cautions that the "war against youth crime" has not been won. Even as crime statistics have shown a decrease since 1994, self-reports of violent offending show no decline at all. In other words, when researchers ask juveniles about their violent behavior, the answers suggest that delinquency and youth crime are still quite high, leading the report to conclude that "the rise and fall in arrest rates are set against a backdrop of ongoing violent behavior."[106]

Three general strategies are being put in place to deal with juvenile delinquency—and its possible increase—in the near future. The first, transfer to adult court, was discussed earlier in the chapter and is based on the notion that harsher punishments will deter juvenile crime. The second, known as *social-control regulation,* aims to prevent crime by changing behavior without addressing underlying causes. Examples of social-control regulation would be

- *Juvenile curfews,* which restrict the movements of minors during certain hours, usually after dark. Juvenile arrests for curfew violations and loitering nearly doubled between 1991 and 2004.[107]
- *Parental responsibility statutes,* which make parents responsible in some way for the offenses of their children. At present, forty-four states have enacted these statutes; seventeen of these states hold the parents *criminally* liable for their children's actions, punishing them with fines, community service, and even jail time.

The third method of juvenile delinquency prevention can be found in community-based programs that attempt to improve the chances that at-risk youth will not turn to crime. These programs may try to educate children about the dangers of drugs and crime, or they may counsel parents who abuse their children. Today, nearly a thousand private and public groups hold after-school workshops to prevent youth violence. Though the results of community-based efforts are difficult, if not impossible, to measure—it cannot be assumed that children would have become delinquent if they did not participate—they are generally considered a crucial element in keeping youth crime under control.

FIGURE 15.8
Comparison of Gang and Nongang Delinquent Behavior

Taking self-reported surveys of subjects aged thirteen to eighteen in the Seattle area, researchers for the Office of Juvenile Justice and Delinquency Prevention found that gang members were much more likely to exhibit delinquent behavior.

Source: Karl G. Hill, Christina Lui, and J. David Hawkins, *Early Precursors of Gang Membership: A Study of Seattle Youth* (Washington, D.C.: Office of Juvenile Justice and Delinquency Prevention, December 2001), Figure 1, page 2.

The Bully Problem

Students between the ages of five and nineteen are about seventy times more likely to be murdered away from school than on campus.[108] Because of their sensational nature and the inevitable media coverage that goes with them, however, shootings at schools tend to focus public attention on juvenile offenders more than other types of delinquency and adolescent violent behavior. As we will discuss in this feature, this attention has led to intense scrutiny of behavior that is as common on school grounds as homicides are rare.

Pathway to a Shooting

Sixteen-year-old Jeff Weise started the killing spree on March 21, 2005, at the home of his grandfather, Daryl Lussier, a tribal police officer for the Red Lake Nation of northern Minnesota. After shooting Lussier and a companion, Weise took his grandfather's squad car and drove the short distance to Red Lake High School, where he was a student. In just under nine minutes, the sophomore proceeded to murder five students, a teacher, and a security guard before placing a shotgun to his chin and committing suicide.

As the small, isolated community of Chippewa Indians came to grips with the tragedy, some questioned how local authorities had failed to see, in the words of one expert, the "classic signs of a pathway leading to a shooting."[109] These "classic signs" included Weise's previous psychiatric treatment, his drawings of bloody bodies and guns (often shared with classmates), and a short story about a violent school rampage by a single gunman that he posted on the Internet. Furthermore, Weise had been a frequent target of taunting at the high school because of his "goth" style of dress and loner tendencies. The reports of bullying brought back memories of the fatal shootings six years earlier at Columbine High School near Littleton, Colorado. There, two students who claimed to have been

Students from Red Lake Senior High School in Red Lake, Minnesota, place ritual tobacco at a makeshift memorial for the victims of a shooting spree by student Jeff Weise in March 2005.

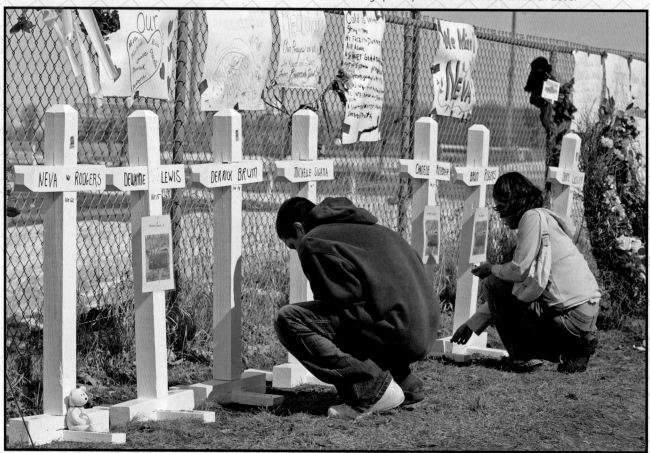

AP Photo/Ann Heisenfelt

mistreated by their peers killed fourteen classmates and a teacher.

Other incidents also seem to point to a connection between bullying and violent, retaliatory behavior. Michael Carneal, who killed three students and injured five others at his high school in West Paducah, Kentucky, in 1997, had been called a "faggot" by his classmates. After Charles Williams killed two students and wounded thirteen others in a 2001 shooting at Santana High School in Santee, California, his father said that other students had burned his son with cigarette lighters, snapped him with wet towels, and twice slammed him against a tree. In a study of school shootings from 1974 to 2000 conducted by the U.S. Secret Service, revenge was cited as a motive more than half the time.[110]

Taking on Bullies

The first large-scale national study of bullying in American schools was released in 2001, about six weeks after the killings at Santana High. Of nearly 16,000 students interviewed, 10.6 percent reported being bullied "sometimes" or "weekly," and 13 percent admitted to having bullied others. About 6 percent said they had been both the targets and the perpetrators of bullying. The bullying seemed to be most intense among the younger students: the researchers found that about a quarter of all middle school children had been involved in behavior that included threats, ridicule, name calling, punching, slapping, and taunting.[111]

These figures came as no surprise to many observers, who see bullying as a normal, if unfortunate, aspect of growing up. In the wake of the Columbine High tragedy, however, both schools and legislators have taken measures to, if not eliminate the behavior, at least keep it from leading to violence. Hundreds of schools have instituted "zero-tolerance" policies that impose harsh penalties on what in the past might have been seen as unthreatening behavior. A third grader in Hudson, Ohio, for example, was suspended from school for writing the words "You will die an honorable death" during a fortune-cookie writing project, while a seven-year-old Cincinnati elementary student was suspended for bringing a cap gun on the school bus. Many school authorities have banned the game of dodgeball, which experts say fosters overly aggressive behavior and stigmatizes less athletic students.[112]

In 2005, lawmakers in Arizona, Tennessee, and Virginia passed antibullying legislation, bringing the total of states that have codified measures to prevent this behavior to nineteen.[113] These state laws are similar, generally requiring local school districts to draw up policies aimed at stopping student bullying and directing officials to notify parents of any such behavior at their child's school.

Warning Signs

Some experts criticize such policies and laws as an over-simplification of the problem of school violence. One clinical psychologist pointed out that if bullying were the actual cause of such incidents, "we would have millions of school shootings each year."[114] Instead, bullying appears to be only one piece of the puzzle, which includes violence and instability in the home, depression, violence in the culture at large, and the availability of firearms.

In fact, the best way to stem school violence seems to be to convince students to take threats of violence by their peers seriously. One student wounded by Weise in Minnesota said the troubled youth spoke often of launching an attack on the school, and the boy's interest in guns and violence was well known among members of the student body. About a week after the shootings, federal officials arrested Louis Jourdain, another Red Lake High student, who apparently helped Weise plan the assault but told law enforcement agents that he never thought his friend would go through with the scheme. This is apparently typical behavior in such cases. The U.S. Secret Service found that in almost three-quarters of the school shootings that have taken place in this country since 1974, the shooters told someone what they were going to do.[115] Within three days after the killings at Santana High, eight other juveniles in southern California were arrested when students alerted law enforcement authorities of their plans for "copycat" violence.

The Illusion of Safety?

Why did the students at Red Lake High School keep silent about the seemingly obvious threat posed by Weise? The answer may lie in a government study that measured fear of crime in schools. The report found that twice as many African American and Hispanic students as white students are afraid of school violence.[116] Although the study did not include Native Americans, the residents of Red Lake seemed similarly confident that they were insulated from such violence. "Usually this happens in places like Columbine, white schools, always somewhere else," said one local. "We never hear that in our community."[117]

This lack of fear points to a crucial fact concerning school violence: even though minority youths living in low-income, urban areas have much higher rates of victimization, the majority of all school shootings take place in rural or suburban areas and are perpetrated by white students. Since the mid-1990s, when crime at inner-city schools reached its peak, many such schools have hired security guards and adopted other safety measures such as metal detectors. It is highly unlikely, for example, that Weise could have easily carried his guns into Ballou High School, which is located in a high-crime area of Washington, D.C. At Ballou High, students must pass through a metal detector each time they enter the school and are constantly under observation by security guards.

Another explanation is that guns are not considered as dangerous in rural areas as in metropolitan ones. Whereas a teenager carrying a gun near Ballou High would set off a certain number of warning bells, it is relatively common for rural youths to have firearms for hunting and target practice. Indeed, Weise appeared to have no problem finding his grandfather's .40-caliber handgun and 12-gauge shotgun—the two firearms he eventually used on his victims and then himself.

Making Sense of the Bully Problem and School Violence

1 A number of school districts have implemented "snitch" programs that pay students for reporting on classmates who carry guns on campus or otherwise violate school rules. What is your opinion of such programs as measures to prevent school crime?

2 What would be your main concerns if you were to set up a policy against bullying at schools? Do you think any policy or plan could effectively stop such behavior?

3 Do you favor "zero-tolerance" plans that punish any hint of violent or illegal behavior at schools? What are the advantages and drawbacks of such plans?

Chapter Summary

1 **Describe the child-saving movement and its relationship to the doctrine of** *parens patriae.* Under the doctrine of *parens patriae,* the state has a right and a duty to care for neglected, delinquent, or disadvantaged children. The child-saving movement, based on the doctrine of *parens patriae,* started in the 1800s. Its followers believed that juvenile offenders require treatment rather than punishment.

2 **List the four major differences between juvenile courts and adult courts.** (a) No juries, (b) different terminology, (c) limited adversarial relationship, and (d) confidentiality.

3 **Identify and briefly describe the single most important Supreme Court case with respect to juvenile justice.** The case was *In re Gault,* decided by the Supreme Court in 1967. In this case a minor was arrested for allegedly making an obscene phone call. His parents were not notified. They were not present during the juvenile court judge's decision-making process. In this case, the Supreme Court held that juveniles are entitled to many of the same due process rights granted to adult offenders, including notice of charges, the right to counsel, the privilege against self-incrimination, and the right to confront and cross-examine witnesses.

4 **List the factors that normally determine what police do with juvenile offenders.** The arresting police officers consider (a) the nature of the offense, (b) the youthful offender's past criminal history, (c) the setting in which the offense took place, (d) whether the parents can take disciplinary action, (e) the attitude of the offender, and (f) the offender's race and gender.

5 **Describe the four primary stages of pretrial juvenile justice procedure.** (a) Intake, in which an official of the juvenile court engages in a screening process to determine what to do with the youthful offender; (b) pretrial diversion, which may consist of probation, treatment and aid, and/or restitution; (c) jurisdictional waiver to an adult court, in which case the youth leaves the juvenile justice system; and (d) some type of detention, in which the youth is held until the disposition process begins.

6 **Explain the distinction between an adjudicatory hearing and a disposition hearing.** An adjudicatory hearing is essentially the "trial." Defense attorneys may be present during the adjudicatory hearing in juvenile courts. In many states, once adjudication has occurred, there is a separate disposition hearing that is similar to the sentencing phase in an adult court. At this point, the court, often aided by a predisposition report, determines the sentence that serves the "needs" of the child.

7 **List the four categories of residential treatment programs.** Foster care, group homes, family group homes, and rural programs such as wilderness camps, farms, and ranches.

STORIES FROM THE STREET

Go to the *Stories from the Street* feature at **www.cjinaction.com** to hear Larry Gaines tell insightful stories related to this chapter and his experiences in the field.

8 Describe the one variable that always correlates highly with juvenile crime rates. The older a person is, the less likely he or she will exhibit criminal behavior. This process is known as aging out. Thus, persons in any at-risk group will commit fewer crimes as they get older.

9 Indicate some of the reasons why youths join gangs. Some alienated teenagers join gangs for the social relationships and the sense of identity that gangs can provide. Youths living in high-crime neighborhoods join gangs as a form of protection. The excitement of belonging to a gang is another reason to join.

Key Terms

adjudicatory hearing 504	detention hearing 502
age of onset 511	disposition hearing 504
aging out 511	diversion 500
automatic transfer 501	graduated sanctions 506
child abuse 512	intake 499
child neglect 512	judicial waiver 501
detention 502	juvenile delinquency 492

low-visibility decision making 497	residential treatment programs 506
parens patriae 491	status offender 492
petition 499	training schools 507
predisposition report 504	youth gangs 513
prosecutorial waiver 501	

Questions for Critical Analysis

1 In spite of the constitutional safeguards given to juvenile defendants by the Supreme Court decision in *In re Gault,* only 50 percent of juvenile defendants have lawyers. Why?

2 Why is the discretion given to police officers over juveniles called low-visibility decision making?

3 Is probable cause necessary before a search can legally be conducted in a school setting? Why or why not?

4 Under what conditions in certain states is a juvenile automatically transferred to the adult court system?

5 The presence of defense attorneys in juvenile courts has led to what changes? In what way have these changes made juvenile courts resemble adult courts?

6 What distinguishes the sentencing phase in juvenile versus adult courts?

7 Why is the age of onset an important factor in predicting juvenile criminal behavior?

8 What has been the relationship between alcohol and drug abuse and juvenile offenders?

9 What has been the statistical relationship between armed gang members and juvenile violent crime?

Test Preparation Online

Criminal JusticeNow

Go to **www.cjinaction.com** and click on *Criminal JusticeNow* for access to this powerful online study tool. You will get a *personalized study plan* based on your responses to a diagnostic pretest. Once you have mastered the material with the help of interactive learning tools, video clips with questions, an integrated e-book, and more, you can take a posttest to confirm you are ready to move on to the next chapter.

Book Companion Web Site

At the book companion Web site (**www.cjinaction.com**), you will find many resources in addition to *Criminal JusticeNow* to aid you in studying for your exams. For example, under *Chapter Resources,* you will find the *Chapter Outline, Chapter Summary, Flashcards, Glossary, Learning Objectives, Lecture Presentations, Concept Builder, Essay Questions,* and a *Tutorial Chapter Quiz.* You can also test yourself with interactive *Online Reviews* of each chapter section. Check out the *Web Links* to access the Web sites mentioned in the text, as well as many others. You can also access recent perspectives by clicking on *CJ in the News* and *Terrorism Update* under *Course Resources.*

Suggested Readings

Rodriguez, Joseph, and Neill Bernstein, *Juvenile,* New York: PowerHouse Books, 2004. As a teenager, Joseph Rodriguez found himself locked up in New York's infamous Rikers Island jail on a drug charge. He relied on photography as a means of "escape," and in this book he turns the camera's eye on the difficult world he left behind. The ninety-one black-and-white photographs in this collection focus on the offenders, judges, attorneys, probation officers, and social workers who make up the California juvenile court system. Although *Juvenile* contains only a minimal amount of text, the photos speak volumes about the problems that plague American juvenile justice.

Salzman, Mark, *True Notebooks,* New York: Knopf, 2003. When novelist Salzman was approached to teach a writing course at Central Juvenile Hall, a detention center for "high-risk" juvenile offenders in Los Angeles, he agreed—with reservations. Salzman soon warmed to his task, however, and this book reflects his experiences with his pupils, most of whom were waiting to be sent to juvenile correctional facilities or adult prisons. Their writing is often as bleak as their situations, but it does offer a clear picture of the life of a juvenile offender, including what it is like to be facing life behind bars.

Notes

1. Peter W. Greenwood, "Juvenile Crime and Juvenile Justice," in *Crime*, ed. James Q. Wilson and Joan Petersilia (San Francisco: ICS Press, 1995), 91.

2. Jennifer M. O'Connor and Lucinda K. Treat, "Getting Smart about Getting Tough: Juvenile Justice and the Possibility of Progressive Reform," *American Criminal Law Review* 33 (Summer 1996), 1299.

3. Eric K. Klein, "Dennis the Menace or Billy the Kid: An Analysis of the Role of Transfer to Criminal Court in Juvenile Justice," *American Criminal Law Review* 35 (Winter 1998), 371.

4. *Sourcebook of Criminal Justice Statistics Online* at **http://www.albany.edu/sourcebook/pdf/t20006.pdf**.

5. *In re Gault,* 387 U.S. 15 (1967).

6. Samuel Davis, *The Rights of Juveniles: The Juvenile Justice System,* 2d ed. (New York: C. Boardman Co., 1995), Section 1.2.

7. Cited in Anthony Platt, *The Child Savers* (Chicago: University of Chicago Press, 1969), 119.

8. 383 U.S. 541 (1966).

9. *Ibid.,* 556.

10. 387 U.S. 1 (1967).

11. 397 U.S. 358 (1970).

12. 421 U.S. 519 (1975).

13. 403 U.S. 528 (1971).

14. Luis Perez, Deborah S. Morris, and Rocco Parascandola, "'She's Just a Little Girl,'" *Newsday* (June 1, 2005), A3.

15. Andrew Walkover, "The Infancy Defense in the New Juvenile Court," *UCLA Law Review* 31 (1984), 509–513.

16. Gary B. Melton, "Toward 'Personhood' for Adolescents: Autonomy and Privacy as Values in Public Policy," *American Psychology* 38 (1983), 99–100.

17. Research Network on Adolescent Development and Juvenile Justice, *Youth on Trial: A Developmental Perspective on Juvenile Justice* (Chicago: John D. & Catherine T. MacArthur Foundation, 2003), 1.

18. Richard E. Redding, "Juveniles Transferred to Criminal Court: Legal Reform Proposals Based on Social Science Research," *Utah Law Review* (1997), 709.

19. Howard N. Snyder and Melissa Sickmund, *Juvenile Offenders and Victims: A National Report* (Washington, D.C.: U.S. Department of Justice, 1995), 47.

20. 125 S.Ct. 1183 (2005).

21. *Ibid.,* 1198.

22. Office of Juvenile Justice and Delinquency Prevention, *Juveniles in Court* (Washington, D.C.: U.S. Department of Justice, June 2003), 2.

23. *Ibid.,* 15.

24. Carl E. Pope and Howard N. Snyder, *Race as a Factor in Juvenile Arrests* (Washington, D.C.: Office of Juvenile Justice and Delinquency Prevention, April 2003), 1.

25. *Ibid.,* 4.

26. Sarah Lee Browning, "Race and Getting Hassled by the Police: A Research Note," *Police Studies* 17 (1994), 3.

27. George S. Bridges and Sara Steen, "Racial Disparities in Official Assessments of Juvenile Offenders," *American Sociological Review* 63 (1998), 554.

28. 469 U.S. 325 (1985).

29. *Ibid.,* 348.

30. *Vernonia School District v. Acton,* 515 U.S. 646 (1995).

31. 536 U.S. 822 (2002).

32. 422 U.S. 23 (1979).

33. *Yarborough v. Alvarado,* 124 S.Ct. 2140 (2004).

34. *Schneckloth v. Bustamonte,* 412 U.S. 218 (1973).

35. Frederick Ward, Jr., "Prevention and Diversion in the United States," in *The Changing Faces of Juvenile Justice,* ed. V. Lorne Stewart (New York: New York University Press, 1978), 43.

36. President's Commission on Law Enforcement and Administration of Justice, *Task Force Report: Juvenile Delinquency and Youth Crime* (Washington, D.C.: U.S. Government Printing Office, 1967).

37. 42 U.S.C. Sections 5601–5778 (1974).

38. S'Lee Arthur Hinshaw II, "Juvenile Diversion: An Alternative to Juvenile Court," *Journal of Dispute Resolution* (1993), 305.

39. Rhode Island Gen. Laws Section 14-1-7.1 (1994 and Supp. 1996).

40. David S. Tanenhaus and Steven A. Drizin, "'Owing to the Extreme Youth of the Accused': The Changing Legal Response to Homicide," *Journal of Criminal Law and Criminology* (Spring/Summer 2002), 641.

41. Megan C. Kurlychek and Brian D. Johnson, "The Juvenile Penalty: A Comparison of Juvenile and Young Adult Sentencing Outcomes in Criminal Court," *Criminology* (May 2004), 485–517.

42. Judi Villa, "Adult Prisons Harden Teens," *Arizona Republic* (November 14, 2004), A1.

43. Donna Bishop and Charles Frazier, "Consequences of Transfer," in *The Changing Borders of Juvenile Justice: Transfer of Adolescents to Adult Court,* ed. Jeffrey Fagan and Franklin E. Zimring (Chicago: University of Chicago Press, 2000), 237.

44. Villa, A27.

45. 467 U.S. 253 (1984).

46. Barry C. Feld, "Criminalizing the American Juvenile Court," *Crime and Justice* 17 (1993), 227–254.

47. Barry C. Feld, "Abolish the Juvenile Court," *Journal of Criminal Law and Criminology* 88 (Fall 1997), 68.

48. Barry C. Feld, "Violent Youth and Public Policy: A Case Study of Juvenile Justice Law Reform," *Minnesota Law Review* 79 (May 1995), 965.

49. *Juveniles in Court,* 27.

50. Jullianne P. Sheffer, "Serious and Habitual Juvenile Offender Statutes: Reconciling Punishment and Rehabilitation within the Juvenile Justice System," *Vanderbilt Law Review* 48 (1995), 500–506.

51. Eric R. Lotke, "Youth Homicide: Keeping Perspective on How Many Children Kill," *Valparaiso University Law Review* 31 (Spring 1997), 395.

52. Bureau of Justice Statistics, *Prison and Jail Inmates at Midyear 2004* (Washington, D.C.: U.S. Department of Justice, April 2005), 5.

53. *Juveniles in Court*, 22.

54. Melissa Sickmund and Howard N. Snyder, *Juvenile Offenders and Victims: 1999 National Report* (Washington, D.C.: Office of Juvenile Justice and Delinquency Prevention, 1999), 182.

55. Melissa Sickmund, *Juveniles in Corrections* (Washington, D.C.: Office of Juvenile Justice and Delinquency Prevention, June 2004), 4.

56. Douglas Young, "First Count to Ten: Innovation and Implementation in Juvenile Reintegration Programs," *Federal Probation* (September 2004), 70.

57. *Surveillance Summaries: Youth Risk Behavior Surveillance—United States, 2001* (Washington, D.C.: Centers for Disease Control and Prevention, June 28, 2002).

58. Federal Bureau of Investigation, *Crime in the United States, 2004* (Washington, D.C.: U.S. Department of Justice, 2005), Table 38, page 290.

59. Lori Dorfman and Vincent Schiraldi, "Media Delinquency," *Star-Ledger, NJ* (April 20, 2001), 19.

60. National Center for Education Statistics and Bureau of Justice Statistics, *Indicators of School Crime and Safety: 2004* (Washington, D.C.: U.S. Department of Education and U.S. Department of Justice, November 2004), Table 2.1, page 11.

61. Howard N. Snyder, *Juvenile Arrests, 2002* (Washington, D.C.: Office of Juvenile Justice and Delinquency Prevention, November 2004), 3.

62. Alfred Blumstein, "Youth Violence, Guns, and Illicit Drug Markets," *NIJ Research Journal* (Washington, D.C.: National Institute of Justice, 1995).

63. Angie Cannon, "Kids Just Say No to Violence," *U.S. News & World Report* (November 1, 1999), 42.

64. Kimberly Kempf-Leonard and Lisa Sample, "Disparity Based on Sex: Is Gender-Specific Treatment Warranted?" *Justice Quarterly* 17 (2000), 89–128.

65. *Crime in the United States, 2004,* Table 33, page 285.

66. National Center for Juvenile Justice, *Juvenile Court Statistics 2000* (Washington, D.C.: Office of Juvenile Justice and Delinquency Prevention, December 2004), 12.

67. Meda Chesney-Lind, "Are Girls Closing the Gender Gap in Violence?" *Criminal Justice* (Spring 2001), 20.

68. Sickmund and Snyder, 58.

69. Meda Chesney-Lind, *The Female Offender: Girls, Women, and Crime* (Thousand Oaks, CA: Sage Publications, 1997).

70. Marvin E. Wolfgang, *From Boy to Man, From Delinquency to Crime* (Chicago: University of Chicago Press, 1987).

71. Stephen Demuth and Susan L. Brown, "Family Structure, Family Process, and Adolescent Delinquency: The Significance of Parental Absence versus Parental Gender," *Journal of Research in Crime and Delinquency* (February 2004), 69–76.

72. Bureau of Justice Statistics, *Education and Correctional Trends* (Washington, D.C.: U.S. Department of Justice, January 2003), 1.

73. Travis Hirschi and Michael Gottfredson, "Age and the Explanation of Crime," *American Journal of Sociology* 89 (1982), 552–584.

74. David P. Farrington, "Offending from 10 to 25 Years of Age," in *Prospective Studies of Crime and Delinquency,* ed. Katherine Teilmann Van Dusen and Sarnoff A. Mednick (Boston: Kluwer-Nijhoff Publishers, 1983), 17.

75. *Juveniles in Court*, 29.

76. Substance Abuse and Mental Health Services Administration, *Overview of Findings from the 2003 National Survey on Drug Use and Health* (Rockville, MD: Office of Applied Studies, 2004), 14.

77. *Ibid.*, 3.

78. National Institute on Drug Abuse, *Monitoring the Future: National Results on Adolescent Drug Use: Overview of Key Findings 2004* (Washington, D.C.: U.S. Department of Heath and Human Services, April 2005), 3.

79. *Crime in the United States, 2004,* Table 32, page 284.

80. *Ibid.*, Table 34, page 286.

81. Lisette Blumhardt, "In the Best Interests of the Child: Juvenile Justice or Adult Retribution?" *University of Hawaii Law Review* (Winter 2000), 341.

82. National Mental Health Association, "Mental Health and Adolescent Girls in the Justice System" at **http://www. nmha.org/children/justjuv/girlsjj.cfm.**

83. *Collaboration, Coordination, and Cooperation: Helping Children Affected by Parental Addiction and Family Violence* (New York: Children of Alcoholics Foundation, 1996).

84. Ching-Tung Lung and Deborah Daro, *Current Trends in Child Abuse Reporting and Fatalities: The Results of the 1997 Annual Fifty-State Survey* (Chicago: National Committee to Prevent Child Abuse, 1998).

85. Polly E. Bijur, Matthew Kurzon, Mary Overpeck, and Peter C. Scheidt, "Parental Alcohol Use, Problem Drinking, and Child Injuries," *Journal of the American Medical Association* 267 (1992), 3166–3171.

86. Joyesha Chesnick, "Child Abuse, Crime Linked," *Arizona Daily Star* (December 3, 2004), B1.

87. Grover Trask, "Defusing the Teenage Time Bomb," *Prosecutor* (March/April 1997), 29.

88. Cathy Spatz Widom, *The Cycle of Violence* (Washington, D.C.: National Institute of Justice, October 1992).

89. Office of Juvenile Justice and Delinquency Prevention, *Highlights of the 2000 National Youth Gang Survey* (Washington, D.C.: U.S. Department of Justice, 2002), 1.

90. G. David Curry and Scott H. Decker, *Confronting Gangs: Crime and the Community* (Los Angeles: Roxbury, 1998).

91. Arlen Egly, Jr., *Highlights of the 1999 National Youth Gang Survey* (Washington, D.C.: Office of Juvenile Justice and Delinquency Prevention, November 2000), 1.

92. Rachel A. Gordon, Benjamin B. Lahey, Eriko Kawai, Rolf Loeber, and Magda Stouthamer-Loeber, "Antisocial Behavior and Youth Gang Membership: Selection and Socialization," *Criminology* (February 1, 2004), 55–89.

93. Marjorie S. Zatz, "Voices from the Barrio: Chicano Gangs, Families, and Communities," *Criminology* (May 31, 2000), 369.

94. Scott H. Decker and B. Van Winkle, *Life in the Gang: Family, Friends, and Violence* (New York: Cambridge University Press, 1996).

95. Sara R. Battin, Karl G. Hill, Robert D. Abbott, Richard F. Catalano, and J. David Hawkins, "The Contribution of Gang Membership to Delinquency beyond Delinquent Friends," *Criminology* 36 (1998), 93–115.

96. Marilyn Rauber, "First Lady Takes on Gang Violence," *Richmond Times Dispatch* (March 6, 2005), A11.

97. *Ibid.;* and Lauren O. Kidd, "Gang Activity Growing in N.J.," *Asbury Park Press* (July 1, 2005), A3.

98. Office of Juvenile Justice and Delinquency Prevention, *1998 Youth Gang Survey* (Washington, D.C.: U.S. Department of Justice, 1999), Table 34.

99. Karl G. Hill, Christina Lui, and J. David Hawkins, *Early Precursors of Gang Membership: A Study of Seattle Youth* (Washington, D.C.: Office of Juvenile Justice and Delinquency Prevention, December 2001).

100. Joseph F. Sheley and James D. Wright, *In the Line of Fire: Youth, Guns, and Violence in Urban America* (Hawthorne, NY: Aldine De Gruyter, 1995), 100.

101. Beth Bjerregaard and Alan J. Lizotte, "Gun Ownership and Gang Membership," *Journal of Criminal Law and Criminology* 86 (1995), 49.

102. Quoted in Gracie Bond Staples, "Guns in School," *Fort Worth Star-Telegram* (June 3, 1998), 1.

103. Office of Juvenile Justice and Delinquency Prevention, *1999 National Report Series: Juvenile Justice Bulletin—Kids and Guns* (Washington, D.C.: U.S. Department of Justice, March 2000), 4.

104. *Ethics of American Youth* (Marina del Rey, CA: Josephson Institute of Ethics, 2001).

105. *Crime in the United States, 2004,* Table 32, page 284.

106. Delbert Elliot, Norma J. Hatot, Paul Sirovatka, and Blair B. Potter, eds., *Youth Violence: A Report to the Surgeon General* (Washington, D.C.: U.S. Department of Health and Human Services, 2001), Chapter 2, Section 1.

107. Federal Bureau of Investigation, *Crime in the United States, 2000* (Washington, D.C.: U.S. Department of Justice, 2001), Table 32, page 220; and *Crime in the United States, 2004,* Table 32, page 284.

108. *Indicators of School Crime and Safety: 2004,* 6.

109. Monica Davey and Jodi Wilgoren, "Signs of Danger Were Missed in a Troubled Teenager's Life," *New York Times* (March 24, 2005), A14.

110. U.S. Secret Service, *The Final Report and Findings of the Safe School Initiative: Implications for the Prevention of School Attacks in the United States* (Washington, D.C.: U.S. Department of Education, May 2002), 24.

111. Tonja R. Nansel, Mary Overpeck, Ramani S. Pilla, W. June Ruan, Bruce Simons-Morton, and Peter Scheidt, "Bullying Behaviors among U.S. Youth," *Journal of the American Medical Association* 285 (April 25, 2001), 2094.

112. Natalie Angier, "Bully for You: Why Push Comes to Shove," *New York Times* (May 20, 2001), Section 4, page 1.

113. Sherry Anne Rubiano, "Anti-Bully Law Will Soon Go into Effect," *Arizona Republic* (July 3, 2005), B6.

114. Michael Janofsky, "Bill on Student Bullying Is Considered in Colorado," *New York Times* (March 19, 2001), A10.

115. U.S. Secret Service, 21.

116. National Center for Education Statistics, *Indicators of School Crime and Safety* (Washington, D.C.: U.S. Department of Education, October 2000), Table 13.2.

117. Jodi Wilgoren, "Shooting Rampage by Student Leaves 10 Dead on Reservation," *New York Times* (March 22, 2005), A1.

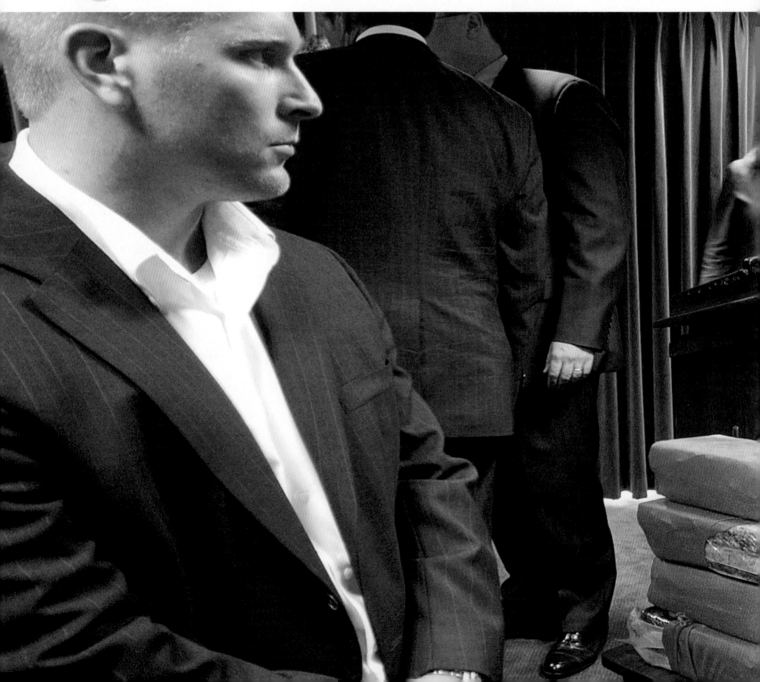

CHAPTER SIXTEEN

The Ongoing War against Illegal Drugs

Chapter outline

- Drugs Defined
- Outlawing Drugs
- The Abuse of Drugs
- Fighting the War on Drugs
- Alternatives to Proscription
- Public Support for the War on Drugs
- Criminal Justice in Action—The Global Drug War

Chapter objectives

After reading this chapter, you should be able to:

1 Explain why the criminal law concepts of *mala in se* and *mala prohibita* are necessary to understand drug laws.

2 Tell what happened to alcohol use and murder rates during Prohibition.

3 List the three factors in the learning process that cause first-time drug users to become habitual users.

4 Explain the 20-80 Rule as it applies to the use of psychoactives.

5 Contrast the medical model of addiction with the criminal model of addiction.

6 List federal agencies involved in drug law enforcement.

7 Summarize the three main legislative strategies to reduce illegal drug use.

8 Explain the *iron law of substitution.*

9 Identify some of the reasons law enforcement agencies may be likely to target members of minority groups when enforcing drug laws.

10 Outline the three major arguments against legalization.

Criminal JusticeNow

Optimize your study time and master key chapter concepts with *Criminal JusticeNow*, an online study tool that provides you with a *personalized study plan.* Check out the "Test Preparation Online" section at the end of the chapter for additional information.

The Meth "Monster"

Residents of Crothersville, Indiana (population 1,541), knew that they had a problem on their hands. First, police raided a house located right beside the town school. Then, an explosion blew off the roof of a building next to the funeral home. The worst, however, came on January 26, 2005, when ten-year-old Katlyn Collman accidentally stumbled into a ramshackle apartment that had been converted into a methamphetamine lab. Her lifeless body, hands tied behind her back, was found five days later in a creek.

Methamphetamine—also known as speed or crank—is a highly addictive stimulant to the central nervous system. The drug, which can be smoked, swallowed, or injected, produces feelings of increased energy and euphoria but also leads to violent behavior, anxiety, and confusion. It is cheap and easy to make in a home lab using the ingredients of common cold medicines and farm chemicals. Consequently, the drug has become a "scourge" in the poor rural areas of states such as Indiana. In 2004, the Drug Enforcement Administration (DEA) raided nearly 16,000 methamphetamine labs in the United States, up from about 10,000 in 2000. In 2005, a majority of the nation's sheriffs listed it as their leading drug problem.

The secondary effects of methamphetamine are also dramatic. Children who have been taken away from par-

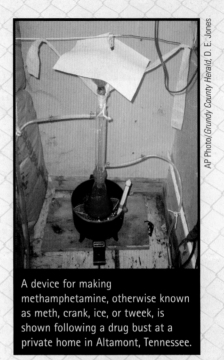

A device for making methamphetamine, otherwise known as meth, crank, ice, or tweek, is shown following a drug bust at a private home in Altamont, Tennessee.

AP Photo/Grundy County Herald, D. E. Jones

ents caught using or making the drug, known as "meth orphans," are overwhelming foster homes and social services in many states. Meth labs cause more than 200 explosions and fires each year, and the federal government spends nearly $30 million to dispose of the dangerous waste materials generated by the drug's production. Dentists are reporting an epidemic of "meth mouth," a form of rapid gum and tooth decay found in methamphetamine users. "It is a monster," said Reverend John Pierce of the First Baptist Church in Crothersville after Katlyn's murder. "We just didn't know what kind of monster it was before."

The awesome impact of drugs on the criminal justice system has been evident throughout this textbook. In the Crothersville area, law enforcement officials estimate that as much as 90 percent of crime is tied to illegal drugs.[1] Nationally, according to one recent study, about 75 percent of all arrestees test positive for illegal drugs or alcohol when they are booked at the police station.[2] Nearly half a million of the two million Americans behind bars were arrested for selling or using a banned substance. The illegal drug trade in the United States has reached $160 billion per year; worldwide the industry amounts to $600 billion annually. Federal, state, and local governments spend over $40 billion a year for drug control, yet two leading indicators of law enforcement success—

526

illegal drug price and availability—show little improvement. The effects of drugs and alcohol on society as a whole are also apparent. Three-fourths of all foster children are from families with drug- or alcohol-addicted parents. The nation's businesses lose 500 million workdays a year to alcoholism, and half of all workplace fatalities are linked to drugs and alcohol. By the ninth grade, 67 percent of all adolescents have consumed alcohol, 48 percent have smoked cigarettes, and 30 percent have used marijuana.[3]

For many Americans, these numbers call for greater enforcement of drug laws. They believe that illegal drugs are an insidious presence on the country's social and cultural landscape and support drastic measures for eradication. According to at least one New York narcotics officer, however, such efforts are as effective as "a gnat biting a horse's behind."[4] In this chapter, we will try to determine whether the officer's pessimism is warranted by examining the United States' century-long struggle against illicit drugs. We will also discuss the tactics of the continuing "war on drugs," as well as assertions that such a war should never have been declared and can never be won. We will start by asking a deceptively simple question at the center of the debate: What is a drug?

DRUGS DEFINED

To use the broadest possible definition, a **drug** is any substance that modifies biological, psychological, or social behavior.[5] In popular terminology, however, the word *drug* has a more specific connotation. When people speak of the "drug" problem, or the war on "drugs," or "drug" abuse, they are referring specifically to illegal drugs. To be even more precise, they are referring to illegal **psychoactive drugs,** which affect the brain and alter consciousness or perception. Almost all the drugs that concern the criminal justice system are psychoactive.

Types of Psychoactives

Psychoactives can be classified by their effects on the central nervous system. The different types of psychoactives are explained in the following overview.[6]

Opiates For more than six thousand years, humans have extracted **opiates** from the seed pod of the opium poppy. In harvesting the substance, the pod is sliced open, releasing a milky sap. The sap dries to form a resin called *opium*. Opium and its derivatives have the ability to block pain receptors in the brain and therefore have a variety of medical uses. The substance also produces a feeling of euphoria and reduction of anxiety, which explains its popularity as a pleasure drug.

Opiates may be ingested orally, smoked, sniffed, or injected. It is generally believed that opium smoking was brought to the United States in the mid–nineteenth century by Chinese laborers. The opium derivatives *morphine* and *codeine* were not fully utilized for medicinal purposes until 1853, when the perfection of the hypodermic syringe allowed delivery of the drugs directly into the bloodstream. Morphine was so widely used as a painkiller in the American Civil War (1861–1865) that many infantrymen became addicted—morphine addiction became known as the "soldier's disease." *Heroin,* a substitute for codeine and morphine, was created by Bayer Laboratories and marketed following the Civil War as nonaddictive. In fact, heroin—more fat soluble and therefore able to reach the brain more quickly—is two to three times more potent than morphine.

Stimulants Acting on both the central nervous system (the spinal cord and the brain) and the peripheral nervous system (the muscles, glands, organs, and fibers that carry

Drug
Any substance that modifies behavior; in particular, an illegal substance with those properties.

Psychoactive Drugs
Chemicals that affect the brain, causing changes in emotions, perceptions, and behavior.

Opiates
Drugs containing opium or its derivatives; have the effects of dulling sensations including pain and anxiety, producing a feeling of euphoria, and causing general inaction.

sensory information to the brain), **stimulants** produce feelings of well-being and mood elevation. The stimulant *cocaine* is the active ingredient in the South American coca plant. It is isolated from the leaves by soaking them in a mixture of water, potassium carbonate, and a petroleum product such as kerosene. The resulting paste is then dried and purified into a white powder, which can be snorted, or the paste itself can be smoked. In the 1970s, "freebasing"—a process in which the drug is vaporized and inhaled—became popular among cocaine users because it produced a more intense high. A cheaper, less complex method of freebasing led to the production of *crack cocaine* in the 1980s.

Amphetamine, originally developed in the 1920s to treat asthma sufferers, was found to be a stimulant in the 1930s and prescribed to narcoleptics, or individuals who involuntarily fall asleep during waking hours. The drug was dispensed to soldiers in World War II to keep them alert during combat, which led to its popularization as a nonmedical substance that could be taken in pill form, via inhalants, or intravenously. *Nicotine,* a naturally occurring substance in the tobacco plant, and *caffeine,* found in coffee, tea, and soft drinks, are also stimulants.

Marijuana The cannabis plant is the source of *marijuana,* the most widely used illegal drug in the United States today. Marijuana is a mixture produced by grinding the leaves and stem of the plant. Delta-9-tetrahydrocannabinol (THC), the active ingredient in marijuana, is rapidly absorbed from the surface of the lungs when the mixture is smoked, producing effects of mild sedation, euphoria, and, in rare cases, hallucination in the user. The Spanish probably imported cannabis to Central and South America in the sixteenth century because its strong fibers can be used to make rope. The plant is easily grown and cultivated (to the point where it has been called a weed), which has contributed to its widespread use.

Hallucinogens A wide variety of plants and other natural products can be classified as **hallucinogens,** or substances that intensify sensory perception and in the process bring about hallucinations. The best-known hallucinogen is called *LSD,* after the substance lysergic acid diethylamide from which it is made. Synthesized in 1938, LSD rose in popularity during the 1960s as part of the then-prevailing youth culture. Only minuscule amounts of LSD (less than two-thousandths of a gram per kilogram of body weight) are needed to induce a hallucinatory state. Other hallucinogens include *PCP (phencyclidine), mescaline* (taken from the peyote cactus), and *psilocybin* (taken from wild mushrooms). In the 1980s, new forms of hallucinogens known as *designer drugs* arrived. Produced by modifying the chemical structure of amphetamines, these drugs, which include Ecstasy, GHB, and "Foxy Methoxy," take on hallucinogenic properties.

Sedatives **Sedatives** are able to reduce anxiety or induce sleep by depressing functions of the brain. Also known as "sleeping pills," *barbiturates* were the most popular form of sedatives in the first half of the twentieth century. Today, a different class of sedative, the *benzodiazepines,* has captured the market, with millions of prescriptions for Valium and Xanax being dispensed every year.

Stimulants
Drugs such as cocaine or amphetamine that stimulate the central nervous system, thereby quickening motor functions of the body.

Hallucinogens
Drugs that cause the user to experience alterations in sensory experiences, or hallucinations.

Sedatives
Drugs that slow the signals sent from the brain to other parts of the body, thereby inducing sleep or reducing anxiety.

U.S. Customs agents stand guard by more than one thousand pounds of the drug Ecstasy—valued at $40 million—at the U.S. Customs House in Los Angeles, California. Ecstasy typically induces feelings of increased energy and euphoria, but in high doses the drug can sharply increase body temperature and, in some instances, can lead to death by hyperthermia—a condition in which skeletal muscle breaks down and organs fail due to overheating.

AP Photo/Nick Ut

Alcohol The most widely used drug in the United States, *alcohol,* in the form of alcoholic beverages, is consumed at least occasionally by approximately two-thirds of adult Americans.[7] Alcohol is unique in the sense that it acts as both a stimulant and a sedative, initially giving the user a feeling of euphoria before beginning to act as a depressant.

Illicit and Licit Drugs

Most people do not consider alcohol—or nicotine or caffeine, for that matter—to be a drug. In one survey, for example, 95 percent of adults recognized heroin as a drug, but only 39 percent and 29 percent identified alcohol and nicotine, respectively, as drugs.[8] To a certain extent, then, the definition of drugs has been equated with **illicit drugs,** or those drugs whose sale and use have been made illegal. **Licit** (legal) **drugs** such as alcohol, caffeine, and nicotine are seen not as drugs, but as socially acceptable substances, if used in moderation and not by children. Furthermore, the common use of drugs for medical purposes—Americans spend approximately $235 billion for prescription drugs and billions more for over-the-counter drugs each year—is seen as enhancing our quality of life.[9]

Distinguishing between Licit and Illicit Drugs Sometimes the line between licit and illicit is difficult to draw. According to the National Center on Addiction and Substance Abuse, more than 15.1 million Americans abuse prescription drugs such as Vicodin, Valium, and Ritalin. By comparison, approximately 5.9 million use cocaine and 300,000 use heroin.[10] Law enforcement agents also report a growing black market trade in OxyContin, a prescription drug used by terminal cancer patients to ease pain.

Why has society prohibited the use of certain drugs, while allowing the use of others? The answer cannot be found in measuring the risk of harm caused by the substances. Both licit and illicit drugs, if abused, can have serious consequences for the health of the user. Hospital emergency rooms are reporting a dramatic increase in the number of children who overdose on common, over-the-counter cold medicines such as Robitussin, which contain an ingredient (dextromethorphan) that can produce hallucinations and loss of motor control.[11] About 1,400 students between the ages of eighteen and twenty-four die each year from alcohol-related incidents such as motor vehicle accidents.[12]

Nor is illegality linked to the addictive quality of the drug. According to the American Medical Association, nicotine is the most addictive substance, with over two-thirds of people who smoke cigarettes becoming addicted.[13] The next most addictive drug is heroin, followed by cocaine, alcohol, amphetamines, and marijuana, in that order. The drug most widely associated with violent behavior, especially domestic violence, is alcohol.[14] One professor of preventive medicine has concluded that "there are no scientific . . . or medical bases on which the legal distinctions between various drugs are made."[15]

Society and the Law If drug laws are not based on science or medicine, on what are they based? To understand in part how the distinctions are made between illegal and legal drugs, we must turn to the concepts of criminal acts that are considered *mala in se,* or inherently evil, and *mala prohibita,* or deemed evil by the laws of society. From our discussion in Chapter 3, you will recall that acts such as murder and rape are *mala in se,* whereas those such as prostitution and gambling are *mala prohibita.* Taking a *mala prohibitum* view, certain drugs are characterized as illicit while others are not because of the presiding societal norms and values.

Samantha Spady, a nineteen-year-old student at Colorado State University, died of alcohol poisoning in September 2004. Four other American college students drank themselves to death that month, leading many to call for stricter measures against underage alcohol consumption on the nation's campuses.

Illicit Drugs
Certain drugs or substances whose use or sale has been declared illegal.

Licit Drugs
Legal drugs or substances, such as alcohol, coffee, and tobacco.

Society's norms and values are reflected in its laws, and the primary law for determining illicit drugs in the United States is the Controlled Substances Act (CSA), which is part of the Comprehensive Drug Abuse Prevention and Control Act of 1970.[16] The CSA specifies five hierarchical categories for drugs and the penalties for the manufacture, sale, distribution, possession, or consumption of these drugs, based on the substances' medical use, potential for abuse, and addictive qualities (see Figure 16.1). The CSA explicitly excludes "distilled spirits, wine, malt beverages, and tobacco" from the legal definition of a "controlled substance."[17] Therefore, alcohol and tobacco are legal not because they have pharmacological effects that are considerably different, or safer, than those of illicit drugs, but rather because the law, as supported by society, says so.[18] (For a further discussion of the politics behind drug classification, see the feature *CJ in Focus—The Balancing Act: Steroids versus Supplements*.)

> "Let us not forget who we are. Drug abuse is a repudiation of everything America is."
>
> —Ronald Reagan, former U.S. president (1986)

OUTLAWING DRUGS

Government policies to limit and outlaw narcotics have a long and varied history, both in the United States and in other parts of the world. Nonetheless, drugs were not always regulated in this country to the extent that they are today. The general attitude of American society toward drugs has changed over the past century. With the notable exception of alcohol, many drugs were considered useful, medicinal substances in the 1800s. Cocaine was promoted as a remedy for tuberculosis, whooping cough, and asthma. Coca-Cola, introduced in 1886, was marketed as providing the benefits of coca without the dangers of alcohol. Opium was labeled "God's Own Medicine," and opiates were prescribed for a number of different ailments, including rheumatism, food poisoning, dysentery, and lockjaw.[19]

FIGURE 16.1

Schedules of Narcotics as Defined by the Federal Controlled Substances Act

The Comprehensive Drug Abuse Prevention and Control Act of 1970 continues to be the basis for the regulation of drugs in the United States. Substances named by the act were placed under direct regulation of the Drug Enforcement Administration (DEA). The act "ranks" drugs from I to V, with Schedule I drugs being the most heavily controlled and carrying the most severe penalties for abuse.

	CRITERIA	EXAMPLES
Schedule I	Drugs with high abuse potential that are lacking therapeutic utility or adequate safety for use under medical supervision.	Marijuana, heroin, LSD, peyote, PCP, mescaline
Schedule II	Drugs with high abuse potential that are accepted in current medical practice despite high physical and psychological dependence potential.	Opium, cocaine, morphine, Benzedrine, methadone, methamphetamine
Schedule III	Drugs with moderate abuse potential that are utilized in current medical practice despite dependence potential.	Barbiturates, amphetamine
Schedule IV	Drugs with low abuse potential that are accepted in current medical practice despite limited dependence potential.	Valium, Darvon, phenobarbital
Schedule V	Drugs with minimal abuse potential that are used in current medical practice despite limited dependence potential.	Cough medicine with small amounts of narcotic

Source: The Comprehensive Drug Abuse Prevention and Control Act of 1970.

CJ IN FOCUS / THE BALANCING ACT

Steroids versus Supplements

In 1990, Congress passed the Anabolic Steroids Act, which designated certain steroids as Schedule III drugs under the Controlled Substances Act (CSA) and imposed severe penalties for their unauthorized sale or possession. The CSA broadly defines an "anabolic steroid" as "any drug or hormonal substance" that "promotes muscle growth." Many members of Congress felt they had no choice but to regulate anabolic steroids in this manner; considerable scientific evidence showed that, when misused, anabolic steroids could be directly linked to serious liver, heart, and kidney problems.

Although steroids have been banished to the black market, consumers looking for "help" in improving their athletic ability or physical appearance are not lacking in choices. The dietary supplement market includes numerous products that purport to provide the same benefits as anabolic steroids without the health risks. To qualify as a "dietary supplement" under federal law, a substance must contain ingredients (except for tobacco) that occur "naturally," such as vitamins, minerals, amino acids, and herbs, and be taken by mouth as a pill, capsule, liquid, or tablet. Such products are quite popular—Americans spend $3 billion on dietary supplements each year, and an estimated one million youths between the ages of twelve and seventeen are users.

RISKS INVOLVED

The only problem is that, like steroids, dietary supplements can cause serious health problems under certain circumstances. Androstenedione, or "andro," which became popular after baseball player Mark McGwire acknowledged using it in the late 1990s, has been banned by many sports leagues due to its similarity in molecular structure to an anabolic steroid. Some doctors believe that the amino acid creatine, one of the most popular supplements, can cause renal failure. In 2003, the Food and Drug Administration finally banned sales of the weight-loss supplement ephedra after it was linked to the death of Baltimore Orioles pitcher Steve Bechler—the ninety-second person believed to have died as a result of ingesting the substance, which one expert likened to "low-grade speed."

Why does the federal government classify anabolic steroids in the same category as amphetamines and barbiturates but allow dietary supplements to be sold to anyone over the counter? Most observers point to intense lobbying of Congress by dietary supplement manufacturers in the late 1980s and early 1990s. These efforts led to the Dietary Supplement Health and Education Act of 1994, which essentially ended all government regulation of supplements. Thus, when it comes to supplements, there is only one rule: *caveat emptor* ("buyer beware").

FOR CRITICAL ANALYSIS

Even if there is little scientific evidence that dietary supplements deliver the results promised on their labels, most are harmless unless used improperly. Do you think the federal government should place tighter restrictions on supplements? To what extent should the government be expected to "protect consumers from themselves" when it comes to dietary supplements, steroids, or any drug?

Under the U.S. Constitution, the states assumed responsibility for regulating and controlling the health profession, including pharmacological products. For most of the nineteenth century, the states chose to impose no controls whatsoever in this area.[20] As a result, the United States led the Western world in opium and morphine consumption and was, in Edward Brecher's words, a "dope fiend's paradise."[21] To the extent that addiction was seen as a problem, concern was primarily focused on drug use by middle-class housewives, who were prohibited from drinking alcohol by the social customs of the day.

The Harrison Act

America's first comprehensive antidrug legislation, the Harrison Narcotic Drug Act of 1914,[22] was primarily a political act, driven by foreign policy concerns rather than by medical or criminal ones. The United States had recently colonized the Philippines, an island nation with a considerable opium-smuggling problem. At the same time, China had started a campaign against opium use in an attempt to modernize and wean its citizens off the drug. This campaign relied a great deal on limiting the drug supply in outside markets, which included the Philippines. Partly to control rampant opium smuggling in its new territory and partly to appease the Chinese government, which had been complaining about treatment of Chinese nationals in America, the United States led an international effort to combat *narcotics* trafficking.[23] (Narcotics are a class of drugs derived from the opium poppy and include opium, heroin, and morphine.)

These efforts culminated in the Hague Convention of 1912, in which twelve countries, including the United States, agreed to outlaw the international nonmedical opium trade. Certain American politicians—embarrassed that the United States was a signatory to an international trafficking ban without having a similar domestic law—urged Congress to pass legislation prohibiting the nonmedical use of narcotics. The resulting Harrison Act of 1914 banned the importation, sale, or possession of narcotics outside proper medical channels. To accomplish this goal, the act empowered the Internal Revenue Service to strictly control the sale of narcotics by placing a tax on such transfers—any such transfer that did not result in the tax being paid and was not authorized by an accredited physician became *de facto* illegal.

Interestingly, cocaine was included in the substances covered by the Harrison Act, even though it is not a narcotic (that is, it derives from the coca plant, not from opium poppies). Some historians believe that cocaine was willfully misclassified because of its usefulness as a propaganda tool to combat the apathetic views on drug criminalization held by many legislators.[24] The antidrug reformer Dr. Hamilton Wright, for example, informed Congress that "cocaine is often the direct incentive to the crime of rape . . . [in] the South and other sections of the country."[25]

The National Prohibition Act

In contrast to the *laissez-faire* attitude toward most drugs, the nineteenth century saw an active antialcohol movement. Between 1850 and 1855, thirteen states passed statutes prohibiting alcohol within their borders. Though all but five had repealed such legislation within a decade, public sentiment against the evils of alcohol remained strong. Finally, in 1919, the passage of the National Prohibition Act (also known as the Volstead Act), which became the Eighteenth Amendment to the U.S. Constitution, made it illegal to manufacture, sell, and transport alcoholic beverages in the United States.

This period of **Prohibition** remains a crucial component in the debate over a society's proper response to the problem of addictive substances. For almost fourteen years until the Eighteenth Amendment was repealed by the Twenty-first Amendment, both the costs and benefits of prohibition policies were evident. Alcoholism and health problems attendant to alcohol use—such as death from cirrhosis of the liver—declined during Prohibition.[26] At the same time, the enormous profits to be made from illegally transporting and selling alcoholic beverages—a bottle of gin that sold for $1 in Ontario, Canada, was worth $6 across the border in Detroit—provided gangsters such as Al Capone sufficient incentive to use violent measures to protect their underground markets. Nationwide, the murder rate reached record levels.

The spread of lawlessness and corruption eventually turned public opinion against Prohibition, and the law was repealed in 1933. As might be predicted, alcoholism and alcohol-related abuses rose, while violent crime rates dropped. In fact, the country's murder rate declined for eleven consecutive years after the repeal of Prohibition.[27]

The Marijuana Tax Act

Four years after Prohibition ended, Congress passed the Marijuana Tax Act, which outlawed the sale, possession, and use of marijuana.[28] The new law effectively added marijuana to the Harrison Act's list of illicit drugs. The

Two sisters, Florence Friermuth and Susie Friermuth Duffing, pose after being arrested for illegally producing "moonshine" alcohol on their family farm near St. Paul, Minnesota, in 1921. What incentives did people have to manufacture, transport, and sell alcohol during the period of Prohibition?

© Minnesota Historical Society/CORBIS

timing of the law was not a coincidence. Though its euphoria-inducing effects were well known during the nineteenth century and the early part of the twentieth century, marijuana was primarily used as a remedy for ailments such as asthma.[29]

It was not until the 1920s that marijuana (still legal) began to be widely used for recreational purposes, in many cases as a replacement for criminalized alcoholic beverages.[30] During that decade, a number of states began to pass laws prohibiting the sale or use of marijuana, based primarily on concerns that the drug caused users to commit violent crimes. This worry was also the basis for the passage of the national law, and the image of the violent "dope fiend" dominated government efforts to increase restrictions on marijuana use into the 1950s.[31]

The Gateway Drug

Few people still believe that marijuana leads to violence; all available evidence shows that marijuana inhibits, rather than causes, aggressive behavior. Yet more people are arrested for marijuana-related crimes today than for those associated with any other drug (see Figure 16.2). The reason for restrictions against marijuana use is fairly straightforward: although marijuana does not directly lead to violence, use of the drug may have serious repercussions. First of all, those who smoke marijuana may suffer negative health consequences. Heavy marijuana use can damage the part of the brain that is crucial for learning and memory, and smoked marijuana contains twice as many carcinogens (agents that lead to cancer) as does smoked tobacco.[32]

Second, some members of the criminal justice system, as well as the scientific community, regard marijuana as a "gateway" drug that leads the user to experiment with, and possibly become addicted to, "harder" illegal substances. These observers feel that a person who uses marijuana will become socialized to the drug culture and more readily use cocaine and heroin. Though they are not universally accepted, a number of studies support this theory. The latest involved 311 sets of same-gender twins, including 136 identical twins, in which just one twin had smoked marijuana before the age of seventeen. The early marijuana smokers were found to be five times more likely than their siblings to use "harder" drugs, most commonly cocaine and other stimulants.[33] Researchers warned, however, that such findings do not prove that smoking marijuana somehow changes the user's brain to make him or her crave stronger drugs; many other factors could explain the correlation. The statistics are notable nonetheless, given that nearly 50 percent of all American high school seniors have experimented with marijuana.[34]

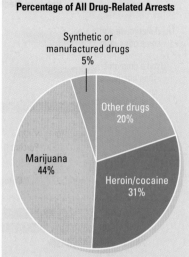

Percentage of All Drug-Related Arrests

- Synthetic or manufactured drugs 5%
- Other drugs 20%
- Marijuana 44%
- Heroin/cocaine 31%

FIGURE 16.2
Distribution of Arrests by Drug Violation

Approximately 1.7 million arrests for drug abuse violations were made in the United States in 2004. As you can see, more of these arrests concerned marijuana than any other illegal drug.

Source: Federal Bureau of Investigation, *Crime in the United States, 2004* (Washington, D.C.: U.S. Department of Justice, 2005), 278.

> "Drug misuse is not a disease, it is a decision, like the decision to step out in front of a moving car. You would call that not a disease but an error of judgment."
>
> —Philip K. Dick, American author (1977)

THE ABUSE OF DRUGS

Do we need the federal government to be so vigilant in enforcing drug laws? How you answer this question probably depends on how widespread you believe the problem of illicit drug use is.

Drug Use Examined

The main source of drug use data is the National Survey on Drug Use and Health, conducted annually by the National Institute on Drug Abuse (see Figure 16.3 on p. 534). According to the survey, only 7.9 percent of those surveyed had used an illicit drug in

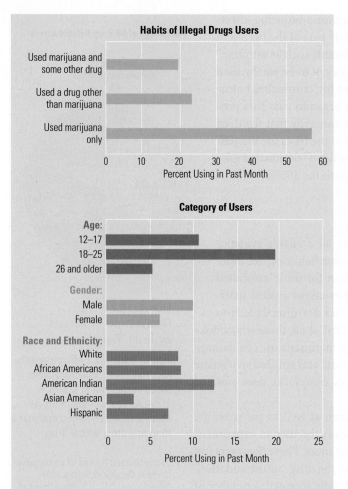

Habits of Illegal Drugs Users

Category of Users

FIGURE 16.3.
Drug Use in
the United States

According to the National Survey
on Drug Use and Health,
approximately 19 million
Americans, or 7.9 percent, can be
considered "illicit drug users." As
you can see, most of these people
used marijuana instead of other,
stronger drugs. Furthermore,
eighteen- to twenty-five-year-
olds were more likely to have
used drugs than any other
segment of the population.

Source: National Survey on Drug Use
and Health, 2004.

Drug Abuse
The use of drugs that results in
physical or psychological problems
for the user, as well as disruption
of personal relationships and
employment.

the past month. Even so, this means that a significant number of Americans—19.1 million—are regularly using illegal drugs, and the figure mushrooms when one considers licit substances such as alcohol (121 million users) and tobacco (70.3 million users).[35]

The Criminology of Drug Use At first glance, the reason people use psychoactive drugs is obvious: such drugs give the user pleasure and provide a temporary escape for those who may feel tension or anxiety. Ultimately, however, such explanations are unsatisfactory because they fail to explain why some people use drugs while others do not. Several theories, some of which were discussed in Chapter 2, have been formulated to explain drug use. *Social disorganization theory* holds that rapid social change can cause people to become disaffiliated from mainstream society, causing them to turn to drugs. *Subculture theory,* particularly as applied to adolescents, sees drug use as the result of peer pressure. *Control theory* hypothesizes that a lack of social control, as provided by units such as the family or school, can lead to antisocial activity such as drug use.

Drugs and the "Learning Process" Focusing on the question of why first-time drug users become habitual users (especially given that the first experience is often a negative one), sociologist Howard Becker sees three factors in the "learning process." He believes first-time users:

1 Learn the techniques of drug use.
2 Learn to perceive the pleasurable effects of drug use.
3 Learn to enjoy the social experience of taking drugs.[36]

Becker's assumptions are evident in a growing belief that positive images of drug use in popular culture "teach" adolescents that such behavior is not only acceptable but desirable. The entertainment industry, in particular, has been criticized for glamorizing various forms of drug use.

Drug Addiction and Dependency

Another theory rests on the assumption that some people possess overly sensitive drug receptors in their brains and are therefore biologically disposed toward drug use.[37] Though there is little conclusive evidence that biological factors can explain initial drug experimentation, science has provided a great deal of insight into patterns of drug use. In particular, it has aided in understanding the difference between drug *use* and drug *abuse*. **Drug abuse** can be defined as the use of any drug—licit or illicit—that causes either physiological or psychological harm to the abuser or to third parties. Just as most people who drink beer or wine avoid abusing that drug, most users of controlled substances are not abusers. For most drugs, only between 7 and 20 percent of all users suffer from compulsive abuse.[38]

Despite their small numbers, drug abusers have a disparate impact on the drug market. The 20 percent of Americans, for example, who drink the most consume more than 80 percent of all alcoholic beverages sold in the United States. The data are similar for illicit substance abusers, leading to the conclusion that, to a large extent, abusers and addicts sustain the market for drugs.

Addiction Basics The most extreme abusers are addicted, or physically dependent on a drug. To understand the basics of addiction and physical dependence, one must understand the role of *dopamine* in the brain.[39] Dopamine is responsible for delivering pleasure signals to brain nerve endings in response to behavior—such as eating good food or engaging in sex—that makes us feel good. The bloodstream delivers drugs to the area of the brain that produces dopamine, thereby triggering a large amount of the neurotransmitter. Over time, the continued use of drugs physically changes the nerve endings, called receptors. To continue operating in the presence of large amounts of dopamine, the receptors become less sensitive, meaning that greater amounts of any particular drug are required to create the amount of dopamine needed for the same level of pleasure. When the supply of the drug is cut off, the brain strongly feels the lack of dopamine stimulation, and the abuser will suffer symptoms of withdrawal until the receptors readjust.

Addiction and physical dependence are interrelated, though not exactly the same. Those who are physically dependent on a drug suffer withdrawal symptoms when they stop using it, but after a certain time period they are generally able to emerge without further craving. Addicts, in contrast, continue to feel a need for the drug long after withdrawal symptoms have passed. Though some evidence suggests that certain people are genetically predisposed to alcoholism,[40] researchers are still striving to determine whether some people are more likely to become addicts than others for biological reasons.

The Medical Model of Addiction Since the late nineteenth century, the treatment and rehabilitation of addiction have played a role in determining the attitude society takes toward criminal drug abusers. Those who followed, and follow, the **medical model of addiction** believe that addicts are not criminals, but mentally or physically ill individuals who are forced into acts of petty crime to "feed their habit." Those who believe in the "enslavement theory of addiction" advocate treating addiction as a disease and hold that society should not punish addicts but attempt to rehabilitate them, as would be done for any other patients.[41]

The Drug–Crime Relationship

Although a number of organizations, including the American Medical Association, recognize alcoholism and other forms of drug dependence as diseases, the criminal justice system tends to favor the **criminal model of addiction** over the medical model. The criminal model holds that drug abusers and addicts endanger society with their behavior and should be treated the same as any other citizens who commit crimes.[42] (See Figure 16.4 on p. 536 for research results on drug and alcohol use by criminals.)

Research Efforts The argument that drug use is an intricate part of criminal culture has been made since the 1920s. In the mid-1970s, the newly created National Institute on Drug Abuse and the National Institute of Justice estimated the number of arrestees and prisoners who used illicit drugs (mostly heroin and marijuana) at between 15 percent and 40 percent.[43] Later studies further cemented the drug-crime relationship. In the early 1990s, a team of researchers in Miami, Florida, interviewed 699 cocaine users and found that nearly 92 percent had criminal histories and 41.5 percent had participated in robberies. Furthermore, each member of the test group had committed hundreds of crimes in the ninety days before being interviewed (nearly 93 percent of the

Medical Model of Addiction
An approach to drug addiction that treats drug abuse as a mental illness and focuses on treating and rehabilitating offenders rather than punishing them.

Criminal Model of Addiction
An approach to drug abuse that holds that drug offenders harm society by their actions to the same extent as other criminals and should face the same punitive sanctions.

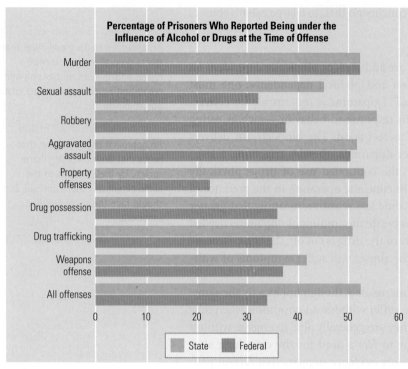

FIGURE 16.4
Committing Crime
under the Influence
of Drugs and Alcohol

For most crime categories, more than half of state prisoners and about one-third of federal prisoners said that they were under the influence of either drugs or alcohol when they committed the crime for which they were arrested.

Source: Adapted from Bureau of Justice Statistics, *Substance Abuse and Treatment, State and Federal Prisoners, 1997* (Washington, D.C.: U.S. Department of Justice, January 1999), Table 1, page 3.

crimes involved retail drug sales).[44] Today, about 56 percent of the inmates in federal prisons were incarcerated for a drug offense.[45]

Epidemiologist Paul Goldstein has devised three models to explain the relationship between drugs and crime:

- The *psychopharmacological model* holds that individuals act violently or criminally as a direct result of the drugs they have ingested.
- The *economically impulsive model* holds that drug abusers commit crimes to get the money to purchase drugs. According to the U.S. Department of Justice, 16 percent of jail inmates said that they committed the crimes for which they were incarcerated in order to get money to buy drugs.[46]
- The *systemic model* suggests that violence is a by-product of the interpersonal relationships within the drug-using community, such as when a dealer is assaulted by a buyer for selling "bad" drugs.[47]

The strength of the drug-crime relationship has provided justification for increased law enforcement efforts to criminalize drug use to punish offenders of controlled substance laws. Indeed, the connection was cited as the reason overall crime rates fell in the mid-1990s, in conjunction with a similar downturn in the use of crack cocaine.[48]

Other Explanations Some observers, however, have questioned the conclusion that drug use causes crime. Instead, they contend, drug use and criminal activity both reflect the same willingness to deviate from established norms among certain members of society, labeled by sociologists as the *criminal subculture*.[49]

Furthermore, many believe that the violent and property crimes associated with illicit drugs take place "not because the drugs are drugs [but because] the drugs are illegal."[50] Seventy years ago, when alcohol was illegal in this country, the criminal gangs that controlled the alcohol trade used methods of violence similar to those associated with today's drug gangs. The fact that we

> no longer have drive-by shooting, turf wars and "cement shoes" in the alcohol business [is due to the fact that] alcohol today is legal—not because alcohol no longer intoxicates people, not because alcohol is no longer addicting, and not because alcohol dealers have suddenly developed a social conscience.[51]

FIGHTING THE WAR ON DRUGS

The consumption of most illicit drugs is preceded by an act of voluntary exchange: a willing seller provides a willing buyer with the drug of choice. When a government decides to prohibit voluntary exchange, its officials must decide whether to target the seller or the buyer. For the past four decades, the American government has decided to focus on the seller, or supplier; therefore, the "war on drugs" is generally predicated on the idea of **supply-side enforcement.** As Figure 16.5 shows, the largest portion of the 2006 federal drug control budget is going to law enforcement agencies, which are primarily concerned with reducing the supply of illegal drugs in this country. Treatment and prevention programs, which target the buyer by trying to reduce demand for illegal drugs, receive 39 percent of the budget, up from only 27 percent in 2003.

Law Enforcement Efforts

Federal, state, and local law agencies share responsibility for carrying out supply-side enforcement. In 1973, the federal Drug Enforcement Administration (DEA) was formed to restrict the supply of controlled substances through coordination with state and local agencies. Today, the DEA has more than four thousand officers and often works in tandem with local law enforcement agencies. The Controlled Substances Act gave the Federal Bureau of Investigation (FBI) concurrent jurisdiction with the DEA for domestic drug law enforcement. Along with the DEA and FBI, U.S. Customs and Border Protection, U.S. Customs, U.S. Coast Guard, U.S. Border Patrol, and branches of the U.S. military work to stem the flow of illegal drugs from other countries into the United States. Called *interdiction,* this process is discussed at length in the feature *Criminal Justice in Action—The Global Drug War* at the end of this chapter.

Most arrests for drug law violations take place at the local and state levels. About 90 percent of local law enforcement agencies regularly enforce drug laws, and in large U.S. cities (population of 250,000 or more), police departments assign an average of 123 officers to special drug units.[52] In general, the goals of local police with regard to illegal drug activity are as follows:

- To reduce the gang violence associated with the illegal drug trade.
- To control the street crimes committed by illegal drug users.
- To improve the quality of life in communities plagued by illegal drug use.
- To deter minors from using illegal drugs.
- To improve the physical, social, and economic well-being of illegal drug users.[53]

To accomplish these goals, police use tactics such as crackdowns, raids, and surveillance, discussed in Chapter 5. Since 1990, the federal government has contributed to regional antidrug efforts through its High Intensity Drug Trafficking Areas (HIDTA) program. The program provides $225 million to help fund task forces made up of federal, state, and local law enforcement agents in areas that are considered "hotbeds" of illegal drug activity. Initially, these efforts focused mostly on large cities such as New York and Los Angeles and on the U.S.-Mexican border. In the past five years, however, HIDTA has spread to rural areas overwhelmed by the methamphetamine problem described at the beginning of this chapter.

Legislative Efforts

Lawmakers have also taken measures to stop the spread of methamphetamine. By the summer of 2005, more than a dozen states had placed limits on access to cold medicines such as Sudafed and Claritin that contain pseudophedrine—a key ingredient in the production of the drug. Federal and state legislators have generally been willing, if not eager, to fortify existing drug laws. One Texas politician proposed cutting off a

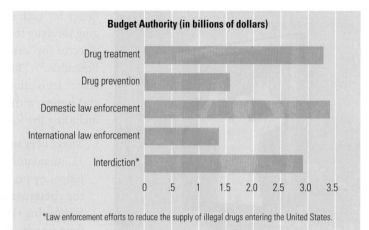

Budget Authority (in billions of dollars)

*Law enforcement efforts to reduce the supply of illegal drugs entering the United States.

FIGURE 16.5
Federal Drug Control Budget, 2006

The federal drug control budget for 2006 was triple the federal drug control budget of 1989. As you can see, the single largest item on the budget is domestic law enforcement.

Source: Office of National Drug Control Policy, *National Drug Control Strategy: 2005 Annual Report* (Washington, D.C.: Executive Office of the President, 2005).

Supply-Side Enforcement
The law enforcement strategy of combating the use of illegal drugs by concentrating on the suppliers of the drugs rather than the buyers. Thus, agents will focus on a single drug dealer rather than on his or her many clients.

NYT Pictures/Librado Romero

Drug smugglers use a variety of different methods to avoid interdiction efforts. One that is becoming increasingly popular is paying poor men and women to swallow thumb-sized pellets of heroin wrapped in the cutoff fingers of surgical gloves. The body scanner shown here is being used in many international airports to stop this form of smuggling. According to one customs official, these searches focus on "high-risk flights" from "high-risk countries." How can such an attitude lead to complaints of racial and ethnic bias?

Asset Forfeiture Law
A statute that allows law enforcement agents to seize any equipment used in manufacturing, storing, or transporting illicit drugs and any profits or property gained from the sale of the drugs, as well as the drugs themselves.

finger for each drug conviction. A peer from Delaware suggested flogging for drug felons, and William Bennett, former National Drug Policy director (or "drug czar"), voiced the opinion that drug dealers should be beheaded.[54] Though none of these propositions was taken seriously, recent legislation has provided law enforcement officers, prosecutors, and judges with a varied array of "weapons" to combat drug offenses, including the following:

- *Mandatory minimum sentencing laws.* As we discussed in Chapter 11, mandatory minimum sentencing laws remove discretion from judges by predetermining the prison term for a crime depending on the circumstances surrounding that crime. In 1986, the Federal Sentencing Guidelines established minimum sentences for those found guilty of breaking federal drug laws. Federal law also provides that someone convicted of possessing or distributing one gram of crack cocaine will receive the same punishment as someone possessing or distributing one hundred grams of powder cocaine.[55] Furthermore, nearly every state has, at one point, passed its own mandatory minimum sentencing law for drug-related crimes.

- *Asset forfeiture laws.* An **asset forfeiture law** authorizes federal or state governments to seize contraband, drug manufacturing and storage equipment, and any item used to transport drugs. The goal of these laws is to combat the spread of drugs not only by arresting the traffickers but also by confiscating the material used in the illegal operation. Federal and local law enforcement agencies seize more than $1 billion worth of cash and property each year under drug forfeiture statutes.

- *Child-protection laws.* To protect children from drug use and drug users, many legislatures have increased the penalties for drug offenses that involve minors. Under federal law, for example, any person convicted of selling a controlled substance to a person under eighteen years of age is subject to a sentence of up to twice the term and fine that would otherwise be authorized.

Recently, many states have begun to retreat from some of these tougher measures. In 2005, New York lawmakers voted to soften the state's drug laws, considered among the toughest in the nation. Previously, New York judges were required to sentence many first-time offenders to fifteen years to life in prison. Today, the same offenses bring an eight- to twenty-year term. Furthermore, mandated sentences for certain nonviolent offenders decreased from fifty-four months to three years.[56] In softening its drug laws, New York was following a trend. Between 1996 and 2002, forty-six states passed laws to ease penalties for drug offenses; the new laws provide for treatment instead of incarceration, permit those convicted of drug crimes to be eligible for public-assistance programs, or, as we shall discuss later in the chapter, allow marijuana use for medical reasons.[57]

Prospects for Success

A study of homicides in New York offered the following breakdown of drug-related murders: they were overwhelmingly the result of the drug trade (74 percent), not of someone acting violently while under the influence of drugs or of someone killing to get the money to purchase drugs.[58] Such data raise a central question about the nation's current illegal drug policy: Do drugs laws cause more harm than illegal drugs?

Critics of American drug policy believe the answer is yes—that the "cure" of enforcement is worse than the "disease" of drug use. They offer a number of reasons for their stand, as summarized by Douglas N. Husak, professor of philosophy and law at Rutgers University:

- The drug trade has created opportunities for a black market to flourish, which has greatly benefited organized crime. By keeping the prices of illegal drugs higher than they would be otherwise, law enforcement has provided a "subsidy" for drug dealers.
- The enormous profits have made corruption of law enforcement officials inevitable.
- Because the quality of illegal drugs is not regulated, consumers face risks of medical complications from "bad" drugs.
- Drugs are expensive not because of their production costs, but because of their illegality. Heroin is approximately one hundred times more expensive and cocaine twenty times more expensive than they would be if the drugs were legal. As a result, users commit property crimes to obtain the funds necessary to purchase the drugs.
- Millions of otherwise law-abiding Americans have been labeled "criminals" because of drug use, with consequences throughout the criminal justice system.[59]

If this list represents some of the drawbacks of America's drug policy, what have been its benefits? Have supply-side enforcement tactics been successful? To answer that question, we must turn to the issue of illicit drug supply and price.

Reducing the Supply of Illegal Drugs

It is very difficult to "measure" the success of drug enforcement policies. After all, neither the sellers nor the buyers are eager to report their activities to official sources. If authorities are not certain of the total amount of drugs being manufactured and sold, then they can only guess as to the overall effect of their efforts. There is, however, a way to gauge these efforts: the price of illegal drugs on the street. This measurement is based on two assumptions:

1 If law enforcement agents are successful in incapacitating those who grow, refine, transport, and sell drugs, the amount of drugs available should drop. When the supply of a resource that many people want—whether it be diamonds, baseball cards, or drugs—decreases, the price should rise.

2 When authorities seize drugs and destroy the means of manufacturing and distributing them by arresting people in the drug business and confiscating equipment, drug lords must spend resources to rebuild their operations. If it become more expensive to make and distribute drugs, the dealers will pass these costs on to their customers, and the price should rise.

Therefore, if the price of illegal drugs is rising, then law enforcement agents know that they are having the desired impact. In reality, the opposite

The **U.S. Drug Enforcement Administration** is the nation's leading law enforcement agency in the fight against illegal drugs. To visit its Web site, click on *Web Links* under *Chapter Resources* at **www.cjinaction.com**.

A sheriff's car marks the site of a drug bust in Hazard, Kentucky. Many drug trafficking "enterprises" have moved their operations from large cities to more rural areas. Why might drug dealers make the move from the city to the country, and what challenges does this trend present to rural law enforcement agencies?

AP Photo/*Lexington Herald-Leader*, Mark Cornelison

is taking place. According to many observers, the street price of illegal drugs has dropped dramatically since the beginning of the "war on drugs." According to the federal government, the price of a gram of cocaine was $272 in 1981 and roughly $51 in 2003. The price of a gram of heroin dropped even more dramatically, from nearly $1,974 in 1981 to $362 in 2003.[60] The price of marijuana has increased slightly, but the drug is much more potent than it was two decades ago, meaning that consumers are getting a more powerful product for relatively the same price.

The Substitution Effect Further complicating supply-side enforcement is the *iron law of substitution,* which holds that successful efforts to restrict the supply of one drug will lead to increased production and consumption of a substitute. As a corollary of this "law," whenever a drug is made illegal, more potent forms of the drug will drive less potent forms out of the market. Producers have a profit incentive to provide consumers with "more bang for the buck."[61] The smaller the "package," the less risk involved for both suppliers and consumers. Hence, it did not make economic sense to ship and sell beer when all alcohol was illegal.[62] During Prohibition, for example, America changed from a predominantly beer-drinking society to a hard-liquor one. Hard liquor can be more easily concealed because it has a greater potency and thus smaller quantities are needed for the same effect.

The identical process has been played out with cocaine replacing marijuana in the 1970s and crack replacing powder cocaine in the 1980s. Today, successful law enforcement efforts to reduce crack production have led to a resurgence in the use of methamphetamine. Since September 11, 2001, improvements in airport security have made it more difficult to smuggle Ecstasy into the country from Europe, forcing teens and young adults to turn to cheaper, more readily available prescription drugs such as OxyContin and Vicodin and inhalants such as paint thinner. The consequence of this substitution effect is that although law enforcement efforts may reduce the supply of a particular illicit drug in a particular place, they have been unsuccessful in reducing the supply of all illicit drugs on the national market.

The Darwinian Trafficker The substitution effect applies to drug suppliers as well as the illegal drugs themselves. For every "drug kingpin" or dealer that law enforcement manages to incarcerate, others are willing to take his or her place. The reason: few industries can match the profit incentive of the illegal drug market. In fact, successful apprehension of drug dealers may lead to what Jerome H. Skolnick calls "the Darwinian trafficker dilemma." According to Skolnick, law enforcement efforts succeed in capturing the marginal traffickers and dealers, leaving the most violent and efficient ones to dominate the market.[63] (The term *Darwinian* refers to the doctrine of English naturalist Charles Darwin [1809–1882]. Darwin believed that living things change and adapt to their environments. Consequently, any characteristic of an individual that allows it to better adapt to its environment will increase its chances of survival, as well as the chances of its offspring.)

Illegal Drugs and America's Inner Cities

For many, the negative consequences of our drug policy are most evident in low-income neighborhoods across the United States. The social and economic conditions of the inner cities seem designed to foster both illegal drug sellers and drug buyers. For those inner-city residents with ambition, mainstream educational and employment opportunities are less available. The only way to gain wealth and status seems to be through the drug trade. "Ambitious, energetic, inner-city youth are attracted to the underground economy precisely because they believe in the rags-to-riches American

Who Is Using Drugs?

llegal drug abuse in the United States follows certain demographic patterns. In other words, people are more or less likely to abuse illegal drugs depending on factors such as their age, gender, race, or economic status. These patterns, however, do not necessarily match the expectations of many Americans.

THE MYTH

The stereotypical drug abuser is an uneducated, unemployed minority male living in a large city. This image is perpetuated by media coverage of drug use, which focuses on America's inner cities.

THE REALITY

The only aspect of the stereotype that is clearly supported by statistics is that drug abusers tend to be male. In 2004, according to the National Survey on Drug Use and Health, 9.9 percent of American men, compared to 6.1 percent of women, were users of illicit drugs. As for race, the study found that about 70 percent of all users were white, 13 percent African American, and 10 percent Hispanic. These findings closely resemble those of prior years. Furthermore, eight of every ten illegal drug users are employed, and 75 percent of the demand for illegal drugs comes from middle-class users living in the suburbs.

As with many statistics, however, these do not tell the entire story of drug use. Though the overall number of white drug users dwarfs black users, the percentage of all African Americans who use drugs (8.7 percent) is slightly higher than for whites (8.1 percent). Furthermore, the negative consequences of drug use—loss of employment, family dislocation, overdose, death—are much greater for minorities than for whites. Researcher Jeffrey Kallan found that black males were almost twice as likely to die from illegal drug-related causes as whites.

FOR CRITICAL ANALYSIS

Kallan also found that people who have never been married have a significantly higher chance of dying from illegal drug use than those who have been married. What conclusion concerning illegal drug use and risky behavior can you draw from this finding? Also, what factors could explain higher mortality rates among African American users than white users?

dream," notes anthropologist Phillipe Bourgeois.[64] Other residents of poor neighborhoods may react to their surrounding with despair, indifference, and a sense that the future holds no hope. (See the discussion of *anomie* theory in Chapter 2.) Such people are at high risk of turning to the induced euphoria of drug use to escape their surroundings.

The Ideal Environment To a certain extent, then, inner cities are ideal environments for illegal drug activity and risky behavior. Law enforcement officers often react to this by converging on poor neighborhoods, where they make a disproportionate number of drug-related arrests. Because statistics tend to show that the majority of American drug users do not live in poor neighborhoods (see the feature *CJ in Focus—Myth Versus Reality: Who Is Using Drugs?*), critics see these arrest rates as evidence of police bias.

Police Motivation It is true that African Americans make up a high proportion of those charged and incarcerated for drug offenses. The targeting of inner cities for drug arrests may, however, be the result of selective enforcement rather than overt racism. Because of the low-income levels of those areas, residents are unlikely to hire expensive legal help to contest police action. A faulty drug arrest in a middle-class or wealthy neighborhood

> is apt to earn the police an expensive and embarrassing lawsuit by the wronged individual. The same mistake inflicted on the resident of an inner city will likely produce little more than a futile voice complaint. Quite simply, the inner city is an expedient locale for police to rack up impressive arrest numbers, with little fear for consequences if mistakes are made.[65]

Furthermore, because inner-city residents are often disconnected from the political process, elected officials will not suffer any negative consequences if they single out such areas for "get tough" police action.

ALTERNATIVES TO PROSCRIPTION

Considering the economic and social costs of "zero-tolerance" drug policies, many observers have called for liberalization of the nation's controlled substances laws. In general, these alternatives to proscription fall into two broad categories: legalization and decriminalization.

Legalization

Believing that drug laws create worse evils than they solve, and that these same laws can never reduce illicit drug demand, some observers believe that illicit drugs should be made legal. In its most extreme form, **legalization** refers to the removal of all criminal sanctions on the sale and production of all psychoactive substances—with the exception of restrictions on sales to children.[66] Some see such a move as a panacea for many of the problems of the criminal justice system. Others, however, believe legalization is a risky proposition with consequences that cannot be predicted.

The Benefits of Legalization Certain proponents of legalization cite the "peace dividend" that would come with the end of the "war on drugs." On the one hand, law enforcement agencies could eliminate costly drug enforcement programs. On the other hand, the state would reap a windfall in taxes on the controlled sale of substances previously available only on the black market. One Harvard University economist has estimated that the net economic gain to the United States for legalizing marijuana alone would be between $10.1 billion and $13.9 billion each year.[67] Other predicted benefits of legalization include:

- The reduction in drug prices to competitive levels, which means drug abusers and addicts would no longer require large sums of money to finance their drug use. This would reduce, if not eliminate (given the examples of alcohol and cigarettes), the need to steal money or engage in prostitution to acquire sufficient funds to cover one's habit.
- The end of violent crime associated with drug dealing, as black market organizations would be put out of business or forced to rely on less profitable criminal activities.
- A more efficient criminal justice system, as scarce law enforcement resources would be diverted away from drug offenses toward violent crimes, and the pressure on both overloaded court dockets and overcrowded prisons would be alleviated.[68]

Furthermore, as economist Milton Friedman has observed, legalization would improve the living conditions both in America's inner cities and in drug-producing nations, whose corrupt political and law enforcement systems and high levels of violence can be attributed, at least in part, to America's demand for illicit drugs.[69]

Arguments against Legalization Many observers insist that such a policy would cause more problems than it would solve. Given what we know about the "gateway effect," discussed earlier, they ask, how could we as a society justify making it easier for young people to obtain drugs? As an example, they point to cigarettes. Although tobacco products are generally prohibited to those under eighteen years of age, most teenagers find little to stop them from smoking if they so desire. In general, opponents of legalization rely on three arguments, summarized by drug abuse researchers James A. Inciardi and Duane C. McBride:

- *The public-health and behavioral consequences argument.* If drugs such as marijuana, cocaine, and heroin were legalized, more people would use and abuse them. The abuse of these and other illicit drugs does negatively affect users' health, and the consequences could be significant. It is estimated that cigarette- and alcohol-related illnesses cause the deaths of 440,000 and 105,000 Americans each year, respectively.

- *The expanded-market argument.* Even with the restrictions imposed by government regulations, American alcohol and tobacco companies spend $5 billion a year on advertising. The goal of this advertising is to expand the market for their products, and one could assume the same would occur with legalized drugs. Furthermore, just as minors can often obtain cigarettes or alcoholic beverages, they are likely to have access to other legalized drugs.

- *The drugs and violence argument.* The United States already has a problem with alcohol-related violence. Although some drugs, notably marijuana, do not provoke aggressive behavior, others such as cocaine and certain hallucinogens do.[70]

Decriminalization
A policy that combines the elimination of criminal penalties on drug use with restrictions to discourage use such as high taxes and limitations on advertising of drugs.

Another argument against legalization warns that we do not know what the exact consequence of such an action would be. What happens if drugs are legalized and the results are unacceptable? Once instituted, legalization would be difficult to rescind. Finally, it would be a mistake to say that antidrug efforts have been a complete failure. Use of marijuana, inhalants, and hallucinogens among teenagers—the primary target of efforts to reduce substance abuse—reached the lowest levels in a decade in 2004.[71]

Decriminalization

"It would be strange," writes UCLA policy studies professor Mark Kleiman, "if one could not devise a set of laws and programs tighter than the light taxes and poorly enforced age restrictions applied to alcohol, yet much looser than the virtually total prohibition now applied to marijuana."[72] Kleiman, along with many other observers, advocates a middle ground between legalization and prohibition, generally known as **decriminalization.** In general, a decriminalization policy would:

- Place high taxes on the substance in question.
- Severely limit promotion of the substance, while using tax proceeds to finance public relations campaigns warning of its health risks.
- Restrict the sellers of the substance through governmental licensing.
- Restrict buyers by age and through strict sanctions for any public harm caused by abuse of the substance.[73]

Decriminalization at Home and Abroad At times, decriminalization has had support in the United States. In 1972, for example, the Presidential Commission on Marijuana and Drug Abuse recommended the decriminalization of marijuana. In 2001, the Nevada legislature decriminalized small amounts of the drug.[74] A year later the state held a ballot initiative to legalize possession of up to three ounces of marijuana, but the measure was soundly defeated.

A number of western European countries have adopted decriminalization policies, most notably the Netherlands, which has decriminalized "soft drugs" such as marijuana and hashish. Within the past few years, both Britain and Portugal have also limited or even eliminated criminal

In Amsterdam, a customer smokes a marijuana cigarette in a coffeehouse. Law enforcement agencies generally turn a blind eye to cannabis use in these establishments, some two thousand of which are in operation in the city. This lax attitude encourages marijuana users from countries with harsher laws to flock to Amsterdam and has caused many neighbors of the Netherlands to criticize its policies as contributing to drug use throughout northern Europe. What do you think would be the consequences if an American city or state took a similar stance on marijuana use?

Daniel Giry/CORBIS/Sygma

The Border Dispute

According to a high-ranking Canadian government official, the Canadian and U.S. governments have the same goal of "zero use of marijuana." The Canadian government, in his opinion, is more realistic because it is willing to admit that—with 100,000 Canadians using the drug daily—efforts to combat marijuana use have failed. New legislation proposed by the Canadian Parliament in 2004 reflects this reality. Under the proposed law, possession of half an ounce or less of marijuana would be punishable by a $150 fine (about $115 in U.S. currency), and the offender would not be given a criminal record. In other words, in Canada the punishment for possession of small amounts of pot would be essentially the same as for a speeding ticket.

Government officials in the United States expressed outrage at Canada's plans to relax its marijuana laws. "Marijuana is the most abused drug in our country," complained a spokesperson for the U.S. Drug Enforcement Administration. "For Canada to decriminalize or legitimize marijuana means a greater availability of marijuana in Canada, which is going to cause individuals and

organizations to try and smuggle the drug into the United States."

In fact, since security on the U.S.-Canadian border was tightened in the wake of the September 11, 2001, terrorist attacks, the amount of marijuana seized by U.S. Customs agents has quadrupled. If the proposed legislation becomes law, U.S. officials warn that it would mean "more customs, more border patrols, more DEA," which would severely disrupt the $1 billion in legal trade that takes place every day along the four-thousand-mile border between the United States and Canada.

FOR CRITICAL ANALYSIS

Canadian officials have gone to great lengths to assure the U.S. government that the proposed legislation does not reflect a "softening" attitude toward illegal drugs. Indeed, the legislation would also increase the maximum sentence for those caught growing marijuana from seven years to fourteen years. What is the reasoning behind a strategy of punishing producers of drugs harshly while letting users off with the equivalent of a traffic ticket?

---

penalties for certain types of drug use. In 2004, much to the dismay of the U.S. government, Canadian lawmakers introduced legislation that would decriminalize possession of small amounts of marijuana. (For more information on this situation, see the feature *International CJ—The Border Dispute*.)

Medical Marijuana To a certain extent, a number of states have already decriminalized marijuana use under certain circumstances. Since 1996, Alaska, Arizona, California, Colorado, Hawaii, Maine, Maryland, Nevada, Oregon, Vermont, and Washington have passed voter initiatives that allow for the *medical use* of marijuana. For the most part, these laws allow people suffering from certain medical conditions to grow and possess marijuana as long as they have permission from a doctor to do so.

Medical marijuana laws have placed these states in direct conflict with the federal government, which does not recognize *any* legal uses of marijuana, designated a Schedule I illicit drug by the Controlled Substances Act. In *Gonzales v. Raich* (2005),[75] the United States Supreme Court came down on the side of the federal government, ruling that Congress may prohibit the production and possession of marijuana used solely for medical purposes, regardless of state law. The Court's decision, however, turned on the issue of federal regulation of state-level economic activity rather than the validity of the medical marijuana laws themselves. Indeed, in his majority opinion Justice John Paul Stevens expressed sympathy with the plaintiffs in the case—two women who used marijuana to ease their suffering from various ailments—and suggested that supporters of medical marijuana should take their cause to "the halls of Congress."[76]

As a practical matter, it does not appear that the *Raich* decision will have much impact. The ruling did not overturn the state laws, which means that state officials will not be forced to prosecute patients who use medical marijuana. Furthermore, the likelihood of federal law enforcement agencies expending resources to combat small-scale marijuana operations is small; between 1996 and 2005, the federal government prose-

Drug Watch International and Reform Coordination Network have differing views on the legalization of drugs. Find their Web sites by clicking on *Web Links* under *Chapter Resources* at **www.cjinaction.com**.

cuted fewer than twenty medical marijuana cases.[77] Nevertheless, the administration of President George W. Bush continues to steadfastly oppose any decriminalization of marijuana, arguing that such a policy would only increase overall criminal activity linked with the drug. As if to make that point, several weeks after the *Raich* decision, the Drug Enforcement Administration raided a medical marijuana club in San Francisco that was a "front" for a large-scale distribution network with more than $17 million in sales over a two-year period.

PUBLIC SUPPORT FOR THE WAR ON DRUGS

In certain countries such as Singapore and Malaysia, the sale of minuscule amounts of illicit drugs—as little as half an ounce of heroin or a hundred grams of marijuana—carries the death penalty. Despite little evidence that a majority of Americans would favor such strict penalties (though they would certainly lessen the sale of drugs if applied uniformly), public opinion polls show that we would rather continue the "war on drugs" than liberalize drug policy. A recent poll conducted by the Pew Research Center for People and the Press found that although most Americans agree that U.S. antidrug efforts have failed, they support the continuation and expansion of such efforts.[78]

These survey results show that most Americans view the war on drugs as a moral issue rather than a legal, economic, or health-related one. Some observers blame this on the media, which they say overplay issues of crime and violence instead of addiction and treatment when dealing with the drug problem. Others point out that, having started a "war" on drugs, to reduce law enforcement efforts would constitute a "surrender," an act with which Americans have never been comfortable. Whatever the reason, it seems clear that as long as our society considers illegal drugs a major danger to community values, the government will continue to take great efforts to eradicate them.

The Global Drug War

In this chapter, we have focused mostly on domestic efforts to stop the consumption and sale of illegal drugs. The problem, however, is hardly limited to our national boundaries. A high percentage of the heroin, cocaine, marijuana, and amphetamines seized in the United States was smuggled across the Mexican border, mostly coming from sources in Central and South America. Southeast Asia has been a major source of illegal drugs in the past, and Africa is expected to be one in the future. The international illegal drug trade has been infiltrated by *narcoterrorists*, who finance their terrorist activities by participating in the drug trade. The ease with which funds can be transferred from country to country has contributed to *money laundering*, in which drug dealers convert illegally gained profits to cash using foreign businesses and banks. As we conclude this chapter, we will take a closer look at the challenges presented by the globalization of the illegal drug trade.

The Balloon Principle

If the United States is in fact engaged in a "war" on illegal drugs, it should come as no surprise that the U.S.S. *Curts* participated in the largest seizure of cocaine ever. On September 17, 2004, the Navy frigate intercepted the *Lina Maria* just southwest of the Galapagos Islands in the Pacific Ocean. A Coast Guard team boarded the shrimping vessel and found 29,000 pounds of cocaine (street value: more than $1.3 billion) in a sealed ballast tank. Several days later, in the same area another frigate, the U.S.S. *Crommelin*, stopped another fishing boat, the *San José*. Another Coast Guard team boarded it and found 26,000 pounds of the drug hidden under packs of ice.

Though large, the two seizures were not in themselves extraordinary. In 2004, the Coast Guard confiscated more than 240,000 pounds of cocaine.[79] The significance of the incidents was the route by which the boats were entering American territory. For the past three decades, South American drug trafficking organizations have primarily smuggled their contraband into the United States across the Mexican border or through the Caribbean corridor. Enhanced border security since the September 11, 2001, terrorist attacks and increased DEA operations in the Caribbean, however, have forced the smugglers to look for new avenues: both the *Lina Maria* and the *San José* were headed from Colombia to the U.S. West Coast.

When you press your finger on a balloon, the air inside pushes the balloon outward somewhere else. This *balloon principle* applies to the "war on drugs" as well. As can be seen from the above example, when law enforcement agents place pressure on one segment of the illicit drug trade, the market shifts to compensate. Given the overall scope of the international illegal drug market—estimated by the United Nations to have $600 billion in annual revenues, or 8 percent of total international trade—the balloon principle represents the single largest impediment to efforts to stop, or even slow, the flow of illegal drugs into the United States.

Interdiction Efforts

These efforts are extensive. Each year, almost $3 billion of federal funds go to interdiction programs. In the early 1980s, Vice President George H. W. Bush coordinated the National Narcotics Border Interdiction System, which linked the four military branches (Air Force, Navy, Army, and Marines) with local and federal law enforcement agencies to combat drug trafficking. The "militarization" of interdiction can be seen in the Navy's cooperation with the Coast Guard and in efforts such as Operation Blast Furnace, during which U.S. Army Blackhawk helicopters attempted to destroy coca production labs in the South American country of Bolivia. In 1989, the U.S. military invaded Panama to arrest its president, Manuel Noriega, for violating federal drug trafficking laws.

The federal government also directs large amounts of foreign aid to *source-zone* countries, where illicit drugs are produced, with the understanding that the funds are to be used to enhance local law enforcement efforts and provide alternative sources of income for drug-producing citizens. In recent years, the most significant efforts in this area have focused on Colombia. Since 1999, the United States has spent more than $3.3 billion to eradicate cocaine production in this South American country and has provided the Colombian government with more than eighty helicopters and fixed-wing aircraft to destroy coca crops. This strategy has resulted in the devastation of more than 1.3 million acres of coca plants.

Despite this massive movement of government resources, the balloon principle has severely limited the effectiveness of the antidrug campaign in Colombia. Before aerial fumigation began, coca production was

Spectators in Kandahar, Afghanistan, watch as local police burn more than 650 pounds of opium and hashish. Afghanistan is the world's leading source for opium and heroin, and U.S. officials believe that proceeds from the sale of these drugs have been used to support international terrorism.

There are a number of reasons for this phenomenon. First, law enforcement agents seize only a small percentage of the illegal drugs that enter this country—10 percent, according to the Coast Guard.[82] Second, the supply of drugs is expanding rapidly; estimates are that the world production of cocaine has more than doubled over the past decade, and the supply of heroin has more than tripled. In other words, while the finger pressure on the balloon remains weak, the size of the balloon is rapidly expanding.

Third, the profits to be made in the illegal drug trade are often astounding. For instance, a kilogram of the high-grade heroin known as China White that can be purchased for $2,500 in the Southeast Asian country of Myanmar (formerly Burma) will sell for $200,000 in New York City.[83] Consequently, people are willing to take great risks to get illegal drugs into the United States and western Europe.

A Matter of Climate and Economy

The coca bush, whose leaves provide the raw material for cocaine, is averse to below-freezing temperatures, but otherwise it will flourish in any climate that receives between 40 and 240 inches of rain annually. The opium poppy requires mild, sunny, and drier conditions, but the marijuana plant literally grows like a weed and can be found on every continent except Antarctica. Figure 16.6 (p. 548) lists the countries that are primarily responsible for producing and exporting the drugs that can be made using these three plants.

Illegal drug production depends on more than climate, however. As Figure 16.6 also shows, the major producers of coca, opium, and cannabis are among the world's materially poorest nations. The people who live in these countries have an economic incentive to grow illicit crops, and their governments do not have the resources to restrict the practice. In Afghanistan, for example, farmers can earn ten times more from a plot (about eight-tenths of an acre) of opium poppies than from a legal crop such as wheat.[84] This general poverty restricts the United States' ability to offer foreign aid as an inducement to reduce production of illicit crops. The annual opium crop in Afghanistan is worth almost $3 billion, which represents about one-third of the national economy and dwarfs the $1.2 billion in annual American foreign aid.[85] Finally, because law enforcement agents and government officials earn such low wages in these countries, they are more susceptible to corruption. Mexican police in the border town of Matamoros, for example, earn less than cab drivers and must buy their own bullets, making them easy targets for the bribes of drug traffickers.[86]

widespread in only twelve Colombian states. Today, the crop has spread to twenty-three states, making it much more difficult to control.[80] In addition, drug traffickers have moved their crop production into neighboring countries, particularly Peru. Furthermore, Colombian farmers are shifting from coca plants to opium poppies, which are easier to grow in areas hidden from the view of crop-dusting airplanes. Colombia is now the source of 50 percent of the heroin in the United States.[81]

Greater Supply, Low Prices

The goal of interdiction is to reduce the supply of illegal drugs entering the United States, thereby raising the prices of the substances that do reach American streets. In fact, as noted earlier in the chapter, illegal drug prices have actually *dropped* as interdiction efforts have increased.

FIGURE 16.6

Global Illicit Drug Production

According to the U.S. State Department, the countries indicated below are the world's major producers of opium, coca, and marijuana for export. Consequently, they are the focus of American interdiction efforts.

OPIUM	COCA
Myanmar	Colombia
Laos	Brazil
Thailand	Peru
Vietnam	Ecuador
Afghanistan	MARIJUANA
Pakistan	Mexico
India	Colombia
Iran	Jamaica
Colombia	
Mexico	

Source: U.S. Department of State.

The Connection between the Drug Trade and Terrorism

The phenomenon of narcoterrorism is well documented. Guerrilla armies that engage in terrorism often rely on drug trafficking as their main source of income. The DEA has determined, for example, that Hezbollah—the militant Shiite group based in Lebanon that was responsible for the truck bombing of a U.S. Marine base in Beirut in 1983—has been using illegal drug profits to finance its operations for decades.[87] Since September 11, 2001, however, the practice has taken center stage. In 2004, Representative Mark Steven Kirk, a Republican from Illinois, asserted that Osama bin Laden funds his al Qaeda terrorist organization with $28 million in profits from drug trafficking operations in Pakistan and Afghanistan.[88] "Lawlessness that breeds terrorism is also a fertile ground for the drug trafficking that supports terrorism," said one government official. "To surrender to either of these threats is to surrender to both."[89]

Some observers believe that the connection is not quite so simple. A series of television advertisements produced by the federal government that aired in 2002 came under heavy criticism for exploiting the tragedy of September 11, 2001, as antidrug propaganda. In the ads, teenagers and young adults admitted to buying illegal drugs and expressed remorse for having, at the same time, supported international terrorism. "I helped blow up a building," said one actor. As the Drug Policy Alliance pointed out at the time, federal authorities have yet to produce any evidence that proceeds from drug sales in the United States have gone to al Qaeda or any other Middle Eastern terrorist organization.[90]

Making Sense of the Global Drug War

1 Should U.S. policymakers continue to see the drug program as a domestic problem? In other words, should we focus on decreasing the demand for illegal narcotics in the United States rather than trying to stem the supply from other countries? Why or why not?

2 Explain the different ways the "balloon principle" affects efforts to keep illegal drugs from entering this country.

3 According to one critic of U.S. drug policy, "If helping to put money in the pockets of drug dealers is akin to aiding terrorist causes, then by continuing to drive up the price of drugs the U.S. government is the biggest supporter of terrorism." Explain the rationale behind this assertion. Exaggeration aside, do you think there is any merit to the statement?

Chapter Summary

1 Explain why the criminal law concepts of *mala in se* and *mala prohibita* are necessary to understand drug laws. Because there are no clear-cut differences in risk of harm among certain psychoactives, to understand which are legal and which are illegal one must look to which drugs are considered *mala prohibita,* or inherently evil, depending on presiding societal norms and values. Basically, whatever psychoactives are deemed illegal by the Controlled Substances Act of 1970 and its amendments are therefore prohibited.

2 Tell what happened to alcohol use and murder rates during Prohibition. Alcohol abuse fell during most of the almost fourteen years of Prohibition, whereas violent crime and especially murder rates increased dramatically. After Prohibition was repealed, these two trends reversed themselves.

STORIES FROM THE STREET

Go to the *Stories from the Street* feature at **www.cjinaction.com** to hear Larry Gaines tell insightful stories related to this chapter and his experiences in the field.

3 List the three factors in the learning process that cause first-time drug users to become habitual users. (a) They learn the techniques of drug use, (b) they learn to perceive the pleasurable effects of drug use, and (c) they learn to enjoy the social experience of taking drugs.

4 Explain the 20–80 Rule as it applies to the use of psychoactives. For most psychoactives, 20 percent of users consume about 80 percent of the total amount used.

5 Contrast the medical model of addiction with the criminal model of addiction. Those who support the former believe that addicts are not criminals but rather are mentally or physically ill individuals who are forced into acts of petty crime to "feed their habit." Those in favor of the criminal model of addiction believe that abusers and addicts endanger society with their behavior and should be treated like any other citizens who commit crimes.

6 List federal agencies involved in drug law enforcement. The Drug Enforcement Administration (DEA), Federal Bureau of Investigation (FBI), U.S. Customs and Border Protection, U.S. Customs, U.S. Coast Guard, U.S. Border Patrol, and branches of the U.S. military.

7 Summarize the three main legislative strategies to reduce illegal drug use. (a) Mandatory minimum sentencing laws predetermine the prison sentence for individuals convicted of drug-related crimes; (b) asset forfeiture laws authorize law enforcement agencies to seize cash, equipment, and property used to produce and transport illegal drugs; and (c) child-protection laws increase the penalties for drug-related crimes when they involve minors.

8 Explain the *iron law of substitution.* Successful efforts to restrict the supply of one drug will lead to increased production and consumption of substitutes. The corollary to this "law" is that when a drug is made illegal, more potent forms of the drug drive less potent forms out of the market.

9 Identify some of the reasons law enforcement agencies may be likely to target members of minority groups when enforcing drug laws. Although sometimes attributed to racism, the high incidence of drug arrests in inner cities might be the result of selective enforcement. Residents of low-income neighborhoods are often unable to hire expensive lawyers to contest police action. Also, elected officials will probably not suffer negative publicity if they single out inner cities for "get tough" law enforcement strategies.

10 Outline the three major arguments against legalization. (a) Legalization would lead to increased use and abuse of the newly legalized drugs; (b) the market for newly legalized drugs would expand through advertising and word of mouth; and (c) violence would increase with the use of newly legalized drugs.

Key Terms

asset forfeiture law 538	drug abuse 534	medical model of	sedatives 528
criminal model of	hallucinogens 528	addiction 535	stimulants 528
addiction 535	illicit drugs 529	opiates 527	supply-side enforcement 537
decriminalization 543	legalization 542	Prohibition 532	
drug 527	licit drugs 529	psychoactive drugs 527	

Questions for Critical Analysis

1 On what basis is a distinction made between licit and illicit drugs?

2 Why did the murder rate rise during Prohibition and fall thereafter?

3 What role does dopamine play in the chemistry of addiction?

4 What are some of the reasons that illegal drug trafficking has grown so consistently?

5 What should happen to the price of successfully interdicted drugs, and why?

6 Why have we observed a resurgence in the use of methamphetamines ("crank")?

7 What is the distinction between legalization of illicit drugs and decriminalization?

8 How does the balloon principle apply to the war on drugs?

9 Why are the major illegal drug production areas found in the world's materially poorest nations?

Test Preparation Online

Criminal JusticeNow

Go to **www.cjinaction.com** and click on *Criminal JusticeNow* for access to this powerful online study tool. You will get a *personalized study plan* based on your responses to a diagnostic pretest. Once you have mastered the material with the help of interactive learning tools, video clips with questions, an integrated e-book, and more, you can take a posttest to confirm you are ready to move on to the next chapter.

Book Companion Web Site

At the book companion Web site (**www.cjinaction.com**), you will find many resources in addition to *Criminal JusticeNow* to aid you in studying for your exams. For example, under *Chapter Resources,* you will find the *Chapter Outline, Chapter Summary, Flashcards, Glossary, Learning Objectives, Lecture Presentations, Concept Builder, Essay Questions,* and a *Tutorial Chapter Quiz.* You can also test yourself with interactive *Online Reviews* of each chapter section. Check out the *Web Links* to access the Web sites mentioned in the text, as well as many others. You can also access recent perspectives by clicking on *CJ in the News* and *Terrorism Update* under *Course Resources.*

Suggested Readings

Chepesiuk, Ron, *The Bullet or the Bribe: Taking Down Colombia's Cali Drug Cartel,* Westport, CT: Praeger Publishers, 2003. The Cali Cartel, based in Colombia, was once the world's largest cocaine supplier, generating $8 billion a year in sales in the early 1990s. This book details the strategies employed by Colombian and U.S. law enforcement agencies to combat and ultimately dismantle the organization. In the process, author Chepesiuk offers insights into the history of international drug trafficking, organized crime, and the consequences of U.S. drug policy.

Torgoff, Martin, *Can't Find My Way Home: America in the Great Stoned Age, 1945–2000,* New York: Simon & Schuster, 2004. To understand the role of illicit drugs in the criminal justice system, it is important to understand their role in American popular culture. In this book, Torgoff offers an "everything you ever wanted to know" exploration of the drug culture—in both its mainstream and its underground forms—of the last century. The author's goal is to chronicle our country's use of drugs "without sensationalizing, apologizing, moralizing, or demonizing." By mixing elements of history, sociology, tabloid sensationalism, and memoir, he largely succeeds.

Notes

1. Jodi Wilgoren, "Too Late for Katie, Town Tackles a Drug's Scourge," *New York Times* (February 10, 2005), A1.
2. Arrestee Drug Abuse Monitoring Program, *Drug and Alcohol Use and Related Matters among Arrestees 2003* (Washington, D.C.: National Institute of Justice, 2005), 7, 22.
3. Rocky Mountain Behavioral Science Institute, *American Drug & Alcohol Survey,* available at **http://www.rmbsi.com/whatis.html**.
4. Quoted in Jerome H. Skolnick, "Rethinking the Drug Problem," in *Drugs, Crime, and Justice,* ed. Larry K. Gaines and Peter B. Kraska (Prospect Heights, IL: Waveland Press, 1997), 404.
5. Weldon Witters, Peter Venturelli, and Glen Hanson, *Drugs and Society,* 3d ed. (Boston: Jones & Bartlett, 1992), 4.
6. James E. Royce and David Scratchley, *Alcoholism and Other Drug Problems* (New York: Free Press, 1996), Chapters 1, 2, and 5.
7. National Center for Health Statistics, *Health, United States, 2004* (Washington, D.C.: Centers for Disease Control and Prevention, 2004), Table 66, page 235.
8. Referred to in Douglas N. Husak, *Drugs and Rights* (New York: Cambridge University Press, 2002), 21.
9. Marguerite Higgins, "Aging America Fuels Drug Industry," *Washington Times* (March 27, 2005), A1.
10. *Under the Counter: The Diversion and Abuse of Controlled Prescription Drugs in the U.S.* (New York: National Center on Addiction and Substance Abuse at Columbia University, July 2005), i–ii.
11. Donna Leinwand, "Latest Trend in Drug Abuse: Youths Risk Death for Cough-Remedy High," *USA Today* (December 29, 2003), 1A.
12. Task Force of the National Advisory Council on Alcohol Abuse and Alcoholism, *A Call to Action: Changing the Culture of Drinking at U.S. Colleges* (Washington, D.C.: National Institutes of Health, 2002), 4.
13. John Slade, "Health Consequences of Smoking: Nicotine Addiction," *Hearings before the Subcommittee on Health and the Environment of the House Committee on Energy and Commerce* (Washington, D.C.: U.S. Government Printing Office, 1988), 163–164.
14. Ethan Nadelmann, "Should We Legalize Drugs? History Answers: Yes," *American Heritage* (February/March 1993), 41.
15. Steven Jonas, "Solving the Drug Problem: A Public Health Approach to the Reduction of the Use and Abuse of Both Legal and Illegal Recreational Drugs," *Hofstra Law Review* 18 (1990), 753.
16. Codified as amended at 21 U.S.C. Sections 801–966 (1994).
17. Uniform Controlled Substances Act (1994), Section 201(h).
18. Husak, 25.
19. David F. Musto, *The American Disease: Origins of Narcotic Control* (New York: Oxford University Press, 1987), 1.
20. David F. Musto, "Opium, Cocaine, and Marijuana in American History," in *Drugs, Crime, and Justice,* ed. Larry K. Gaines and Peter B. Kraska (Prospect Heights, IL: Waveland Press, 1997), 22.

21. Edward M. Brecher, *Licit and Illicit Drugs* (Boston: Little, Brown, 1972), 3.

22. 38 Stat. 785 (1923).

23. Musto, "Opium, Cocaine, and Marijuana," 28–35.

24. Franklin E. Zimring and Gordon Hawkins, *The Search for Rational Drug Control* (New York: Cambridge University Press, 1992), 58–61.

25. Quoted in Erik Grant Luna, "Our Vietnam: The Prohibition Apocalypse," *DePaul Law Review* 46 (Winter 1997), 483.

26. P. Aaron and David F. Musto, "Temperance and Prohibition in America: A Historical Overview," in *Alcohol and Public Policy: Beyond the Shadow of Prohibition,* ed. Mark H. Moore and Dean R. Gerstein (Washington, D.C.: National Academy Press, 1981), 165.

27. Daniel K. Benjamin and Roger L. Miller, *Undoing Drugs: Beyond Legalization* (New York: Basic Books, 1991), 21.

28. 26 U.S.C.A. Section 4742(a)(2)(1937).

29. Zimring and Hawkins, 70.

30. Brecher, 409.

31. Duane C. McBride and Clyde B. McCoy, "The Drugs-Crime Relationship: An Analytical Framework," in *Drugs, Crime, and Justice,* ed. Larry K. Gaines and Peter B. Kraska (Prospect Heights, IL: Waveland Press, 1997), 91–92.

32. Gabriel G. Nahas and Nicholas A. Pace, "Marijuana as Chemotherapy Aid Poses Hazards," *New York Times* (December 4, 1993), 20.

33. Michael T. Lynskey, Andrew C. Heath, Kathleen K. Bucholz, Wendy S. Slutske, Pamela A. F. Madden, Elliot C. Nelson, Dixie J. Statham, and Nicholas G. Martin, "Escalation of Drug Use in Early-Onset Cannabis Users vs Co-twin Controls," *Journal of the American Medical Association* (January 22, 2003), 427–433.

34. National Institute of Drug Abuse, *Monitoring the Future: National Results on Adolescent Drug Use; Overview of Key Findings, 2002* (Washington, D.C.: U.S. Department of Health and Human Services, 2003), 8.

35. Substance Abuse and Mental Health Services Administration, *National Survey on Drug Use and Health, 2004* (Washington, D.C.: National Institute on Drug Abuse, 2005), 11, 23, 33.

36. Howard S. Becker, *Outsiders: Studies in the Sociology of Deviance* (New York: Free Press, 1966).

37. Meyer Glantz and Roy Pickens, "Introduction and Overview," in *Vulnerability to Drug Abuse,* ed. Meyer Glantz and Roy Pickens (Washington, D.C.: American Psychological Association, 1992), 29–32.

38. Peter B. Kraska, "The Unmentionable Alternative: The Need for and the Argument against the Decriminalization of Drug Laws," in *Drugs, Crime, and the Criminal Justice System,* ed. Ralph Weisheit (Cincinnati, OH: Anderson Publishing, 1990).

39. Anthony A. Grace, "The Tonic/Phasal Model of Dopamine System Regulation," *Drug and Alcohol Dependence* 37 (1995), 111.

40. Lawrence K. Altman, "Scientists See a Link between Alcoholism and a Specific Gene," *New York Times* (April 18, 1990), A1.

41. James A. Inciardi, *The War on Drugs: Heroin, Cocaine, and Public Policy* (Palo Alto, CA: Mayfield, 1986), 148.

42. *Ibid.,* 106.

43. Duane C. McBride, "The Relationship between Type of Drug Use and Arrest Charge in an Arrested Population," in *Drug Use and Crime* (Springfield, VA: National Technical Information Service, 1976), 409–418.

44. James A. Inciardi, Duane C. McBride, H. Virginia McCoy, and Dale D. Chitwood, "Recent Research on the Crack-Cocaine/Crime Connection," in *Studies in Crime and Crime Prevention* (Stockholm, Sweden: National Council for Crime Prevention), 63–82.

45. Bureau of Justice Statistics, *Federal Criminal Case Processing, 2002* (Washington, D.C.: U.S. Department of Justice, January 2005), 5.

46. Bureau of Justice Statistics, *Substance Dependence, Abuse, and Treatment of Jail Inmates, 2002* (Washington, D.C.: U.S. Department of Justice, July 2005), 7.

47. Paul J. Goldstein, "The Drugs/Violence Nexus: A Tripartite Conceptual Framework," *Journal of Drug Issues* 15 (1985), 493–506.

48. James Alan Fox and Jack Levin, *The Will to Kill: Making Sense of Senseless Murder* (Needham Heights, MA: Allyn & Bacon, 2001).

49. McBride and McCoy, 99.

50. Benjamin and Miller, 110.

51. *Ibid.,* 110–111.

52. Bureau of Justice Statistics, *Police Departments in Large Cities, 1990–2000* (Washington, D.C.: U.S. Department of Justice, May 2002), 7.

53. Mark H. Moore and Mark A. R. Kleiman, "The Police and Drugs," in *Drugs, Crime, and Justice,* ed. Larry K. Gaines and Peter B. Kraska (Prospect Heights, IL: Waveland Press, 1997), 229.

54. Quoted in Husak, 13.

55. United States Sentencing Commission Guidelines Manual, Section 2D1.(c) (1994).

56. "NYS Finally Eases Harsh 1970s Drug Laws," *Law Enforcement News* (February 2005), 4.

57. Bill Piper, Matthew Briggs, Katharine Huffman, and Rebecca Lubot-Conk, *State of the States: Drug Policy Reforms, 1996–2002* (New York: Drug Policy Alliance, September 2003), i.

58. Paul J. Goldstein, "Crack and Homicide in New York City, 1988: A Conceptually Based Event Analysis," *Contemporary Drug Problems* 16 (1989), 662.

59. Husak, 53–58.

60. John M. Walsh, "Are We There Yet? Measuring Progress in the U.S. War on Drugs in Latin America," *Drug War Monitor* (December 2004), 4.

61. Steven B. Duke, "Drug Prohibition: An Unnatural Disaster," *Connecticut Law Review* 27 (Winter 1995), 571.

62. Skolnick, 414.

63. *Ibid.,* 412.

64. Phillipe Bourgeois, "Just Another Night on Crack Street," *New York Times Magazine* (November 12, 1989), 63.

65. Benjamin and Miller, 66.

66. Ethan A. Nadelmann, "The Case for Legalization," *Public Interest* (Summer 1992), 5.

67. Jeffrey A. Miron, "The Budgetary Implications of Marijuana Prohibition" (June 2005), available at **http://www.prohibitioncosts.org/mironreport.html**.

68. James A. Inciardi and Duane C. McBride, "Debating the Legalization of Drugs," in *Handbook of Drug Control in the United States,* ed. James A. Inciardi (New York: Greenwood Press, 1990), 285–289.

69. Milton Friedman, "A Quarter-Century Later, 'War on Drugs' Is Still Misguided," *Seattle Post-Intelligencer* (January 15, 1998), A11.

70. Inciardi and McBride, 289–294.

71. Substance Abuse and Mental Health Services Administration, *National Survey on Drug Use and Health, 2004* (Washington, D.C.: National Institute on Drug Abuse, 2005); and Megan Fromm, "Parent Corps to Help Curb Drug Use," *Washington Times* (July 15, 2004), A9.

72. Mark A. R. Kleiman, "Neither Prohibition nor Legalization: Grudging Toleration in Drug Control Policy," in *Drug Use and Drug Policy,* ed. Marilyn McShane and Frank P. Williams III (New York: Garland Publishing, 1997), 180.

73. *Ibid.,* 186–190.

74. A.B. 453, 2001 Leg., 71st Sess. (Nev. 2001).

75. 545 U.S. ___ (2005).

76. *Ibid.*

77. Dean C. Murphy, "Drug's Users Say Ruling Won't End Their Efforts," *New York Times* (June 7, 2005), A14.

78. The Pew Research Center for People and the Press, "Interdiction and Incarceration Still Top Remedies," March 21, 2001, at **http://people-press.org/reports/display.php3?ReportID=16**.

79. Elaine de Valle and Brooke Prescott, "Coast Guard Sets Drug Arrest Record," *Miami Herald* (September 28, 2005), 3B.

80. David E. Sanger and Juan Forero, "Bush, in Colombia, Promises More Aid," *New York Times* (November 23, 2004), A3.

81. Joel Brinkley, "Anti-Drug Gains in Colombia Don't Reduce Flow to U.S.," *New York Times* (April 28, 2005), A3.

82. Jamie Thompson, "Coast Guard Picks Up Pace," *St. Petersburg Times* (August 9, 2004), 1A.

83. Matthew Brzezinski, "Re-Engineering the Drug Business," *New York Times Magazine* (September 4, 2003), 27.

84. N. C. Aizenman, "Apparent Success Creates Challenges for Country's Poor," *San Jose Mercury News* (February 9, 2005), A12.

85. Carlotta Gall, "Afghan Poppy Growing Reaches Record Level, U.N. Says," *New York Times* (November 19, 2004), A3.

86. Ginger Thompson, "Corruption Hampers Mexican Police in Border Drug War," *New York Times* (July 5, 2005), A3.

87. Deborah J. Daniels, "The Challenge of Domestic Terrorism to American Criminal Justice," *Corrections Today* (December 1, 2002), 66.

88. Rowan Scarborough, "Heroin Traffic Finances bin Laden," *Washington Times* (December 6, 2004), A1.

89. Thomas Ginsberg, "One Country, Two Wars," *Seattle Times* (December 23, 2002), A3.

90. Cathy Young, "Drugs and Terrorism and Insulting Ads," *Boston Globe* (January 13, 2002), A11.

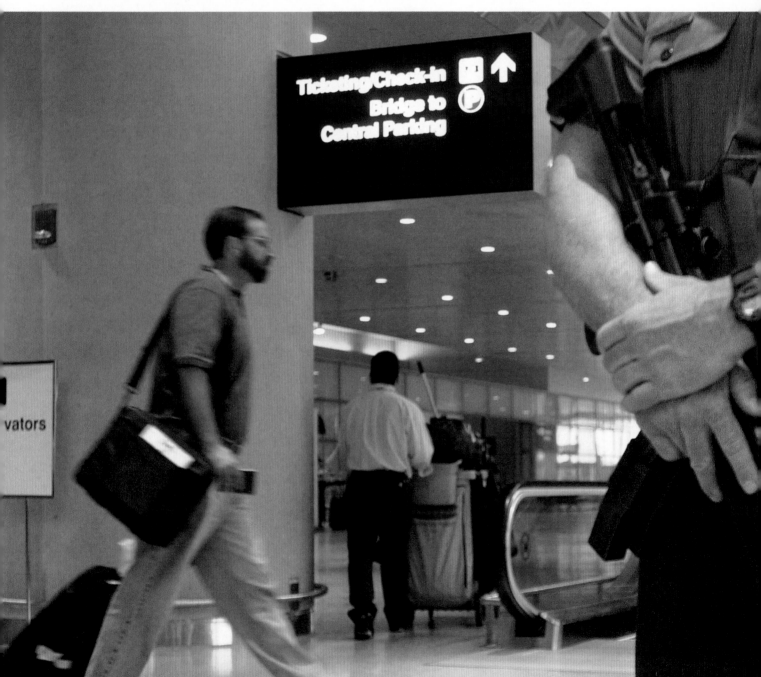

CHAPTER SEVENTEEN

Terrorism, Cyber Crime, and the Future

Chapter outline

- Law Enforcement and the "War" on Terrorism
- The Double-Edged Sword: Security versus Civil Liberties
- Cyber Crime
- Criminal Justice: Looking to the Future
- Criminal Justice in Action—Border Insecurity

Chapter objectives

After reading this chapter, you should be able to:

1 Explain why the Antiterrorism and Effective Death Penalty Act of 1996 (AEDPA) is an important legal tool against potential terrorists.

2 Describe the primary goals of an intelligence agency and indicate how it differs from an agency that focuses solely on law enforcement.

3 List some of the ways federal law enforcement can use aspects of immigration law to fight terrorism.

4 Indicate the three amendments to the U.S. Constitution that are cited most often by critics of the USA PATRIOT Act of 2001, and briefly explain why.

5 Explain how military tribunals differ from federal courts with respect to trials of suspected terrorists.

6 Distinguish cyber crime from "traditional" crime.

7 Explain the activities and purposes of most hackers.

8 Outline the three major reasons that the Internet is conducive to juvenile cyber crime.

9 Describe the challenges to enforcing online gambling laws.

10 Indicate some reasons why the database is seen as an important crime-fighting tool for the future of law enforcement.

Criminal JusticeNow

Optimize your study time and master key chapter concepts with *Criminal JusticeNow,* an online study tool that provides you with a *personalized study plan.* Check out the "Test Preparation Online" section at the end of the chapter for additional information.

Safety Checks

Early on the morning of July 7, 2005, New York City Police Commissioner Raymond W. Kelly learned of a terrorist attack in London, England. Four bombs had struck that city's public transportation system—three in underground trains and one on a bus—killing fifty-six commuters and wounding more than seven hundred others. Within two hours, Kelly made a dramatic decision: police officers would begin random checks of passengers' bags in New York's own mass transit system. The commissioner had been considering this course of action since the winter of 2004, when similar blasts in Moscow, Russia, and Madrid, Spain, took hundreds of lives, but he had been uncertain about how New Yorkers would receive such measures. "The reality is," Kelly said, "you need an event such as London for people to realize this is a procedure put in place for their safety."

In general, American courts—both of criminal justice and of public opinion—have looked with mistrust at random searches. Judges and citizens alike are fiercely protective of individual privacy, and issues of racial profiling (discussed in Chapter 7) continue to trouble minority groups. The search process in New York's subways, buses, and commuter trains was designed to alle-

New York Police Officer Russell King searches the bag of a commuter at the 42nd Street Port Authority subway station.

viate these concerns. Police officers randomly selected one out of every five travelers without regard for race, ethnicity, or age. Furthermore, passengers could choose not to cooperate, with the only consequence being denial of access to transportation services. During the first week of the operation, police searched about 20,000 commuters with only one arrest—for possession of illegal fireworks. Despite the lack of any immediate, tangible results, passengers seemed to welcome the extra police presence. "Every little bit helps," said one woman whose purse had just been checked. "Searches are just a new part of the commute."

Several weeks after the July 7 terrorist attacks, London police officers shot and killed a Brazilian national who had been acting suspiciously at the Stockwell Underground Station. When he turned out to be innocent of any wrongdoing, British government officials admitted their error but justified their "shoot first" policy as necessary during what Metropolitan Police Commissioner Ian Blair called "fantastically difficult times."[1] The new challenges of fighting terrorism have brought about a shift in the criminal justice systems of Great Britain, the United States, and many other nations as well. The goal is no longer to solve crimes after they have occurred, but rather to prevent them from happening in the first place. Peter Ahearn, head of the Buffalo (New York) office of the Federal Bureau of Investigation (FBI), described the strategy as follows: "If we don't know for sure they're going to do something, or not, we need to make sure that we prevent anything they may be planning, whether or not we know or don't know about it."[2]

Though Ahearn's strategy may seem somewhat confusing, it accurately represents the brave new world of law enforcement. Because of what journalist Fareed Zakaria has called the "democratization of violence," threats to the safety of Americans are coming from an ever-expanding array of sources. Pointing out that Osama bin Laden gained technical knowledge for his biological weapons program by downloading documents from the Internet, Zakaria notes, "Today, if you want to find sources for anthrax, recipes for poison, or methods to weaponize chemicals, all you need is a good [Web] search engine."[3] In this final chapter, we will explore the impact terrorism and computer crimes have had on the criminal justice system and consider how these and other developments will affect the immediate future of law enforcement.

LAW ENFORCEMENT AND THE "WAR" ON TERRORISM

In Chapter 4, we learned that criminal law generally requires intent and action; that is, a person must have both intended to commit a crime and taken some steps toward doing so. In most cases, criminal law also requires that a harm has been done and that the criminal act caused the harm. Consequently, the criminal justice system is structured to prove that these elements exist in any particular case, and the police and the courts spend a great deal of time trying to piece together events that have already taken place.

Combating terrorism requires, in contrast, that illegal acts be stopped before they occur. As the September 11, 2001, attacks dramatically showed, we cannot afford to wait for terrorists to strike and then retroactively bring them to justice. The criminal justice system must, therefore, change in a fundamental way if it is to protect Americans effectively from terrorism. Whether this change is possible or, in some instances, desirable is perhaps the most important question in law enforcement today.

Prosecuting Terrorism

In 2003, federal agents arrested six young Muslim men from the small town of Lackawanna, New York. According to court records, a man named Kamal Derwish recruited the so-called Lackawanna Six to take part in an al Qaeda boot camp in Afghanistan just before September 11, 2001. At this camp, they were trained in weapons use, learning to operate rocket-propelled grenade launchers and firearms such as Kalashnikov machine guns, .9-millimeter handguns, and M-16 rifles. They were also exposed to anti-American propaganda films and lectures. Sahim Alwan, one of the "Six," met with Osama bin Laden three times and delivered a videotape to al Qaeda operatives in Pakistan. The six men eventually pled guilty to supporting terrorism.

There was no evidence, however, that any of them had prior knowledge of the September 11, 2001, attacks, although they did hear rumors of "martyr operations" while at the camp. Furthermore, there was no evidence that they supported such operations.[4] In the end, what crimes had they committed? What harm had they caused?

Federal Law and Terrorism The "Lackawanna Six" were prosecuted under the **Antiterrorism and Effective Death Penalty Act of 1996 (AEDPA).** Passed by Congress in response to the 1995 truck bombing of the Alfred P. Murrah Federal Building in Oklahoma City, Oklahoma, this law makes it a crime to provide "material support or resources" to any group that the United States has designated a "terrorist organization."[5] The AEDPA is a critical legal tool in efforts to combat terrorism, as it permits law

CONCEPT BUILDER

Anonymity is necessary for criminals to perpetrate their crimes without being apprehended. Does any one type of crime depend more on anonymity? Visit **www.cjinaction.com** for an interactive exploration of how such anonymity affects crime policies.

The **Terrorism Research Center** serves as a clearinghouse for information concerning law enforcement and the "war" on terrorism. Find its Web site by clicking on *Web Links* under *Chapter Resources* at **www.cjinaction.com**.

Antiterrorism and Effective Death Penalty Act of 1996 (AEDPA)

Legislation giving federal law enforcement officers the power to arrest and prosecute any individual who provides "material support or resources" to a "terrorist organization."

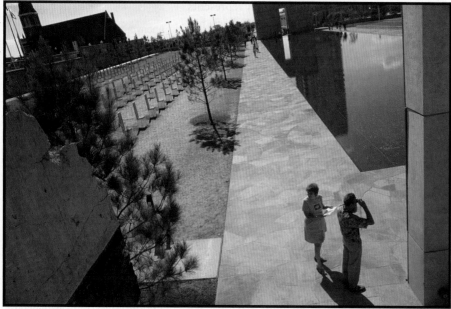

Visitors walk past the reflecting pool at the Oklahoma City National Memorial. On April 19, 1995, Timothy McVeigh exploded a truck bomb outside the Alfred P. Murrah Federal Building in Oklahoma City, killing 168 people in what was at the time the largest terrorist attack on American soil. In response, Congress passed the Antiterrorism and Effective Death Penalty Act (AEDPA). How is the AEDPA being used to combat terrorism in the wake of the events of September 11, 2001?

enforcement agents to arrest suspects even though no crime, in the traditional sense of the word, has taken place and no evident harm has been caused. In the words of former Attorney General John Ashcroft, the act allows the government to "prevent first, prosecute second."[6]

The Criminal Justice System and Terrorism The AEDPA is an important part of America's *criminal justice model* response to terrorism. Under this model, terrorism is treated like any other crime, and the law enforcement, court, and correctional systems work together to deter terrorist activity through the threat of arrest and punishment.[7] Before September 11, 2001, the criminal justice model was our primary response to terrorist activity on American soil. In 1993, for example, a car bomb exploded in the basement of the World Trade Center in New York City, killing six people and injuring more than one thousand. Following an intense investigation, law enforcement agents were able to identify and apprehend the members of the fundamentalist Islamic group responsible for the act. Foreign governments provided aid in the worldwide search for the suspects. In fact, police in Pakistan arrested Ramzi Yousef, who planned the bombing, and handed him over to U.S. authorities to stand trial in this country. Though one suspect remains at large, the remaining perpetrators were tried, convicted, and sentenced in the U.S. District Court for the Southern District of New York.[8]

There is no doubt that the criminal justice system has been a very active participant in the efforts against terrorism. In the years since the September 11 attacks, federal prosecutors have won more than one hundred convictions in terrorism cases. Almost all of these convictions, however, were for relatively minor acts, such as providing material support (as in the case of the "Lackawanna Six"), rather than for actual terrorism. To a certain degree, the criminal justice system is at a disadvantage in the "war" against terrorism because it offers little protection against large-scale attacks, especially when the terrorists are willing to commit suicide in the process and are therefore impervious to deterrence. After-the-fact punishment, no matter how harsh, of someone who may be responsible for hundreds or thousands of deaths also strikes many as irrelevant in light of the damage that has already been done.[9]

Preventing Terrorism

A growing number of experts believe that the *intelligence model,* rather than the criminal justice model, should be the nation's blueprint for combating terrorism. The intelligence model regards terrorist activities as threats to the security of the state rather than as criminal acts.[10] Instead of attempting to deter wrongdoing with the threat of arrest and punishment, the goal of an intelligence investigation is to gather information that will keep the wrongdoing from happening in the first place.

Failure to Communicate Today, it is evident that intelligence gathering has not been a strong point of the U.S. law enforcement community. The FBI, in particular, has come under withering criticism for its perceived inability to protect the nation against terrorist threats. In 2004, the chair of an independent congressional panel (the "9/11 Commission") investigating the September 11 attacks said of the agency, "It failed and it failed and it failed and it failed."[11]

During the months prior to September 11, the FBI and other government agencies uncovered a number of clues that, in retrospect, pointed to a major terrorist incident. For example, in July 2001, an FBI agent based in Phoenix, Arizona, sent a memo to his superiors warning that Osama bin Laden—considered the mastermind behind the attacks on New York City and the Washington, D.C., area—had been sending operatives to flight training schools in the United States. Several of those American-trained operatives ultimately piloted the airplanes used in the attacks, but officials at FBI headquarters in Washington, D.C., did not see the memo until after September 11. Furthermore, although the Central Intelligence Agency (CIA) suspected as early as March 2000 that Khalid al-Midhar and Nawaf Alhazmi had ties to al Qaeda, the agency did not share this information with the FBI and other federal agencies until three weeks before the attacks. Consequently, as the CIA does not operate extensively within U.S. borders, nothing was done to limit the movements of these two men on American soil, and both men were on the plane that crashed into the Pentagon.[12]

A Change in Attitude At the root of these problems was the relatively low priority given to terrorism by federal law enforcement officials before September 11, 2001. In the summer of 2001, only 6 percent of FBI agents were assigned to counterterrorism. On September 10, 2001, the Department of Justice proposed to cut $65 million from a counterterrorism program that provides local and state law enforcement agencies with training and equipment. That same day, the department refused to endorse a request by the FBI for $58 million to hire four hundred new employees, including agents, analysts, and translators, to combat terrorism. Indeed, within the FBI, the terrorism "beat" was seen as less glamorous than other assignments such as bank robbery and police corruption.[13]

Needless to say, this is no longer the situation. In 2005, the federal government spent almost $50 billion to fight domestic terrorism, with $3 billion going to the FBI and Department of Justice.[14] The FBI has increased the number of agents assigned to terrorism from 535 to nearly 3,000, moving personnel from nonterrorism investigations such as narcotics and white-collar crime in the process. (See Figure 17.1.)

FIGURE 17.1

Funding for Homeland Security, 2005

The Department of Homeland Security is the lead government agency for fighting terrorism. As this figure shows, however, it is not the only one. Other agencies, such as the Department of Justice (which oversees the FBI), also expend considerable resources in the "war" on terrorism.

Source: Congressional Budget Office.

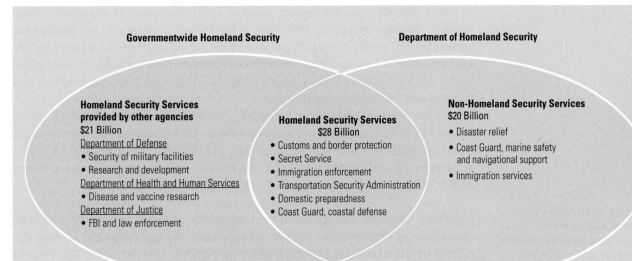

Governmentwide Homeland Security

Department of Homeland Security

Homeland Security Services provided by other agencies
$21 Billion
Department of Defense
• Security of military facilities
• Research and development
Department of Health and Human Services
• Disease and vaccine research
Department of Justice
• FBI and law enforcement

Homeland Security Services
$28 Billion
• Customs and border protection
• Secret Service
• Immigration enforcement
• Transportation Security Administration
• Domestic preparedness
• Coast Guard, coastal defense

Non-Homeland Security Services
$20 Billion
• Disaster relief
• Coast Guard, marine safety and navigational support
• Immigration services

British Intelligence

Perhaps the most remarkable thing about MI5, the British domestic intelligence agency, is that for most of its history, it did not officially exist. Although the agency was formed in 1909 to protect English ports against German spies, no statute was ever passed to give it authority. In the eyes of the law, its employees were simply "ordinary citizens with no powers greater than anyone else" who happened to spend their time gathering intelligence in "defense of the Realm."

Britain was forced to draw up legislation recognizing MI5 (the *MI* stands for "military intelligence") in 1988, but the agency retains many of its shadowy aspects. MI5 agents have far-reaching surveillance powers to gather information about groups that may threaten Britain's security, including the ability to intercept communications, use informants and moles to infiltrate suspicious organizations, and electronically eavesdrop on a suspect's telephone calls and e-mails. Once the information is gathered, MI5 passes it on to the police. According to its Web site, MI5 cannot detain or arrest its targets, but seeks to "gain the advantage over [them] by covertly obtaining information."

In the wake of MI5's success in uncovering several terrorist plots, including one involving stores of the deadly toxin ricin in several London apartments, a number of U.S. politicians and policy observers called for an "MI5 solution" to problems in the American intelligence community. They wanted to "break down the walls" that seemed to separate the crime-fighting FBI from the intelligence-gathering CIA with a new agency modeled after MI5.

Tom Ridge, the first U.S. secretary of homeland security, visited MI5's London headquarters, but he rejected the idea of an MI-like U.S. agency because of a rather large obstacle: the U.S. Constitution. MI5 agents can, for example, search any property as long as a superior agrees—there is no need to prove that any crime has been or will be committed. The ricin bust mentioned earlier was partly the result of e-mail monitoring that would have violated the Fourth Amendment to the U.S. Constitution. Furthermore, MI5's activities are not subject to judicial review, meaning that it is very difficult for citizens who may be unfairly targeted to seek help. Finally, some critics worry that a domestic spy agency modeled on MI5 would mark a return to the days when J. Edgar Hoover headed the FBI (from 1924 to 1972) and investigated citizens simply for speaking out against the government. Among Hoover's targets: civil rights leader Martin Luther King, Jr., and musician John Lennon.

FOR CRITICAL ANALYSIS

What steps could be taken to make sure that a domestic intelligence agency patterned after MI5 would not infringe on the constitutional rights of Americans?

Cultural Changes Though the larger budget and personnel reorganization will undoubtedly improve the FBI's ability to combat terrorism, the agency's problems went deeper than mere lack of resources. Philip D. Zelikow, the executive director of the 9/11 Commission, observed that FBI agents "don't ask questions the way an intelligence agent would ask questions. The FBI agent is typically interested in the facts of an event [whereas] an intelligence agent is really interested in a person's whole world."[15] In other words, to shift from a federal police agency to an **intelligence agency,** the FBI would have to change its very nature. As noted earlier, a police agency works to solve crimes that have already been committed; in contrast, an intelligence agency works to prevent crimes by gathering information on potential criminals and criminal acts "in the planning stage."

At one point in 2004, several members of the 9/11 Commission were even calling for the FBI to be "split" into two separate entities. In this scheme, one agency would retain its jurisdiction over traditional crimes, and the other would become an intelligence agency based on the model of Great Britain's MI5.[16] (For a discussion of this agency, see the feature *International CJ—British Intelligence* above.)

Structural Changes Though the FBI has apparently survived the initial bout of criticism following the September 11, 2001, attacks intact, the agency has had to make significant structural changes. In 2002, it added the National Joint Terrorism Task Force to its operational configuration. This organization acts as a clearinghouse for information gathered by eighty-four terrorist task forces spread across the United States. FBI agents

Intelligence Agency
An agency that is primarily concerned with gathering information on potential criminals and criminal acts in order to prevent crimes from occurring.

are also becoming involved in intelligence gathering that was primarily the domain of local police and fire departments prior to September 11, 2001. In the summer of 2003, for example, two Washington, D.C.–based FBI agents were sent to investigate the possibility that someone had spread gasoline around an office building with the intention of starting a fire. As it turned out, the call was a false alarm caused by gas fumes from a car in the building's parking garage. "We no longer treat anything as routine," said J. Roger Morrison, who heads the National Joint Terrorism Task Force. "There's no threat, no complaint, no bit of information that's not addressed immediately."[17]

Then, in 2005, President George W. Bush ordered the creation of the National Security Service, a new division within the FBI that will be responsible for the agency's intelligence-gathering activities. The restructuring resonated in law enforcement circles because the head of this new service will answer not only to the director of the FBI but also to the director of the Office of National Intelligence, another new government agency. The move was fiercely resisted by many in the FBI, who did not appreciate the idea of an "outsider" having any authority over agency doings. The Bush administration, however, insisted that one person—the director of national intelligence—must have access to the intelligence work of all federal agencies to break down the barriers that hindered the free flow of such information in the past.[18]

Some critics worry that these changes will simply add another level of bureaucracy to an intelligence community already plagued by communication problems.[19] Meanwhile, FBI officials insist that the agency's ability to gather, analyze, and disseminate intelligence has improved greatly over the past five years. Maureen Baginksi, the director of the agency's Office of Intelligence, points out that every FBI field office now has a "field intelligence person" who is responsible for reviewing all "investigative product" and making sure that any important information is immediately shared with relevant law enforcement authorities. Under this system, Baginski believes, intelligence such as the infamous 2001 "Phoenix memo" discussed earlier, which was ignored because it did not have any connection to criminal wrongdoing, will receive proper attention.[20]

Challenges for Local Law Enforcement

Even if the FBI *can* effectively protect the nation against terrorist attacks, *should* it be doing so? A number of politicians wonder whether the agency's new focus on terrorism has caused it to neglect its other crime-fighting duties. A study by the Government Accountability Office found that drug enforcement efforts by the FBI "diminished significantly" after September 11, 2001, with criminal referrals and prosecutions for federal drug crimes dropping about 15 percent by 2003.[21] Furthermore, local police officials believe that the FBI, by removing itself to some extent from the realm of traditional crime, has increased the burden on already shorthanded local police departments.

An Overwhelming Situation In the aftermath of September 11, 2001, the budgetary and personnel resources of many state and city police departments were overwhelmed by the new security demands. The city of Boston found itself spending $100,000 a week on police overtime as officers responded to terrorism-related calls. Memphis city officials stationed officers at twenty-eight locations considered potential terrorist targets, including three bridges on the Mississippi River, at considerable additional cost. The human toll of fatigue and stress on individual officers caught between the need to provide counterterrorism security and fight traditional crimes has also been significant.[22]

> "I think a good case could be made that this is war, and we're part of the front-line troops."
>
> —John Timoney, Philadelphia police commissioner, commenting on the role of local police in combating terrorism (2001)

"This is it, point blank: The infrastructure cannot continue to support this substantive an increase of calls [regarding terrorism fears]," said Police Chief Theron Bowman of Arlington, Texas. "At the local level, we can't do it, and it's impacting our ability to deliver the same level of service for other noncrime-related things."[23] In Philadelphia, the number of drug-related murders increased 50 percent in the first month after September 11, 2001, a development attributed to the decision to move a number of narcotics detectives to uniformed patrols of city streets.[24]

Federal Help, or the Lack Thereof In the long run, local police departments will need the aid of federal law enforcement agencies to prepare adequately for terrorism prevention. To a certain extent, this aid has been forthcoming. FBI personnel have trained almost 30,000 state and local law enforcement officers to act as "first responders" to a terrorist attack involving chemical, biological, or nuclear weapons. Between 2002 and 2005, the federal government provided about $9 billion to state and local law enforcement agencies for training and equipment such as biohazard suits and "terrorist-proof" communications systems.

For many, however, these efforts are insufficient. A 2003 report by the Council on Foreign Relations estimated that $125 billion in subsidies would be required for "first responders" such as local police, fire, and health officials.[25] That same year, the Homeland Security Preparedness Survey, distributed to more than 17,000 state, local, tribal, and federal law enforcement agencies by the International Association of Chiefs of Police, revealed high levels of dissatisfaction. Seventy-one percent of those responding indicated that their agency was either "somewhat" or "not at all" prepared to prevent a terrorist attack; 94 percent identified "critical incident response" training as their most urgent need.[26]

Local officials have also expressed frustration at the lack of federal aid for protecting metropolitan transit systems. When the New York Police Department deployed hundreds of officers to do random checks of commuters in 2005, the price tag was around $1.9 million a week in overtime pay. Most cities, however, do not have the budget or personnel to provide that level of protection for passengers on their subways, trains, and buses. Even though 10 million commuters use transit systems every day in the United States, the federal government has not seemed particularly concerned about increasing security on the nation's railways. One week after the London bombings described in the introduction to this chapter, the U.S. Senate voted to reduce funding for transit security by $50 million.[27]

Cooperation, or the Lack Thereof Another area of concern for many local police officials is the lack of communication with federal agencies on terrorism-related subjects. In 2003, for example, Las Vegas police and sheriff's officials reacted angrily after the FBI failed to warn them of a potential danger—a videotape of the MGM Grand Hotel in the Nevada city had been found among other material belonging to an alleged terrorist cell in Dearborn, Michigan. Frustration

In 2003, an emergency responder, wearing protective clothing, examines several "victims" during a training exercise at a Massachusetts Bay Transit Authority train station in Cambridge, Massachusetts. The drill allowed local emergency personnel to work with the Massachusetts State Police and other law enforcement agencies in preparation for a possible bioterrorism attack.

AP Photo/Angela Rowlings

over such incidents spurred police chiefs from a dozen of the nation's largest cities to create an informal information-sharing network in 2005. In announcing the new system, Los Angeles Police Chief William J. Bratton said that the joint terrorism task forces discussed earlier were oriented toward gathering information rather than providing local police departments with useful, "real-time" intelligence. "We're used to things breaking very quickly and have to respond quickly," said Chief Bratton. "We don't have the luxury of waiting."[28]

Hamilton County (Ohio) Sheriff Simon Leis is even blunter in his assessment of the problem. "The work we do here we can do better without being tied down by the federal bureaucracy," he insists. "I'm not highly excited about joining task forces with federal authorities."[29] Federal law officials, while recognizing the importance of greater cooperation with metropolitan police units, do face a dilemma when it comes to sharing intelligence with them: most local law enforcement agents do not have the security clearance to handle classified information. Few would disagree, though, that continued efforts to better coordinate all of the nation's law enforcement agencies will be a crucial aspect of the "war" on terrorism.

Alien

A person who is not a citizen of a given country and therefore may not enjoy the same protections as citizens of that country.

Immigration Violations

Infractions of U.S. immigration laws, such as failing to comply with the terms of a visa, for which the punishment is often removal from the United States.

The Role of Immigration Law

One area in which local police departments have been willing to take on *more* responsibility is the enforcement of immigration laws. As noted in Chapter 5, the federal government has granted local law enforcement officers in Florida and Alabama the authority to enforce immigration laws, and numerous other jurisdictions are seeking similar powers. In Orange County, California, Sheriff Mike Carona sees it as "another law enforcement tool to take bad guys off the street."[30]

Means for Removal Even before September 11, 2001, federal agents and federal courts were using immigration laws to apprehend criminal offenders. The Illegal Immigration Reform and Responsibility Act of 1996 increased the range of crimes for which certain **aliens**—people living in the United States who are not U.S. citizens—could be deported from this country.[31] As a result, the number of noncitizen immigration offenders in federal prisons increased from just over 4,400 in 1996 to more than 13,100 in 2000.[32] Over the same period, as Figure 17.2 shows, the number of noncitizens deported from the United States because of violations grew significantly as well. Many of these aliens make easy targets for law enforcement officers because they often do not have valid *visas,* the papers given to foreigners by the U.S. State Department allowing them to be in the United States for a particular purpose.

Fewer Restrictions Whereas terrorism charges, as we will see in the next section, are often difficult to prosecute, immigration laws offer fewer procedural protections to noncitizens apprehended for **immigration violations** than are available under criminal laws in general. Such violations include staying in the United States longer than the time specified on the visa, remaining in the country after the purpose for which the visa was issued has expired (for example, visitors on student visas must leave as soon as they have completed their studies), and crossing U.S.

FIGURE 17.2

Aliens Removed from the United States after Conviction, 1992 to 2000s

Under U.S. immigration laws, aliens may be removed from the country after being convicted of a number of different crimes. Following passage of the Illegal Immigration Reform and Reponsibility Act of 1996, federal law enforcement involvement in immigration law increased, as did the number of aliens removed because of criminal convictions, as this graph shows.

Source: Bureau of Citizenship and Immigration Services, *2002 Statistical Yearbook* (Washington, D.C.: U.S. Department of Homeland Security, 2003), 19.

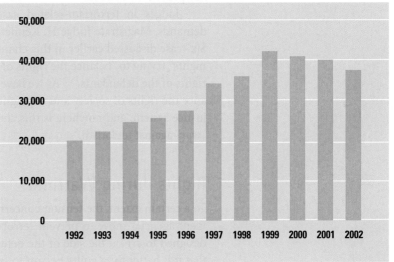

borders without obtaining a visa. Law enforcement agents do not have to meet the probable cause requirement (discussed in Chapter 7) when stopping a noncitizen for a violation of immigration law.[33] Furthermore, immigration arrestees are not guaranteed court-appointed counsel,[34] and federal law allows a person suspected of violating immigration law to be held for seven days before immigration or criminal charges are filed, and then indefinitely thereafter.[35]

Officials at the Department of Homeland Security's U.S. Immigration and Customs Enforcement (ICE) agency credit immigration laws for allowing them to apprehend dangerous terrorism suspects legally and quickly. In 2003, for example, immigration officials detained Somali-born Nuradin Hamdi for an immigration violation; a year later, he was indicted for conspiring with an al Qaeda agent to blow up a shopping mall in Columbus, Ohio. Between 2003 and 2005, the federal government filed five hundred immigration charges as part of its national security investigations—a number that critics of ICE policies call excessive given that few of these suspects were found to have any connection to terrorist activities.[36] (For a more in-depth discussion of the connection between immigration laws and terrorism, see the *Criminal Justice in Action* feature at the end of this chapter.)

THE DOUBLE-EDGED SWORD: SECURITY VERSUS CIVIL LIBERTIES

The day after the September 11, 2001, terrorist attacks, President George W. Bush pledged that "we will not allow this enemy to win the war by changing our way of life or restricting our freedoms."[37] There is little doubt, however, that the Bush administration has adopted the crime control model in its approach to the "war" on terrorism. As you may recall from Chapter 1, in the crime control model the criminal justice system must be quick and efficient, with the courts operating on a "presumption of guilt," hampered as little as possible by the protection of individual rights.

In the interests of greater security, Americans appear willing to relinquish some personal freedoms: overwhelming majorities have indicated that they favor increased searches of people and their possessions at airports, office buildings, and other places.[38] At the same time, far smaller percentages are willing to accept monitoring of phone calls and Internet use,[39] and widespread criticism of the USA PATRIOT Act of 2001 for infringing on civil liberties led to efforts to prevent the renewal of some of its key provisions in 2005.

Judges in terrorism-related cases have also felt the pressure of conflicting demands. Magistrate Judge H. Kenneth Schroeder, Jr., who oversaw the "Lackawanna Six" case discussed earlier in this chapter, said he spent "some pretty restless, sleepless nights" trying to "balance the rights of the people of the community to be safe and the rights of the defendants."[40] As we have seen throughout this textbook, the need to balance the rights of society and the rights of the individual is a constant in the criminal justice system, and nowhere is this challenge more fraught with difficulty than in the "war" against terrorism.

Rights during Wartime

To a certain extent, the tension concerning civil liberties that has arisen as law enforcement agencies move to prevent terrorism is inevitable. The criminal justice system is designed to err on the side of the defendant; that is, it operates under the assumption that it is better for a guilty person to go free than for an innocent one to be convicted.

Furthermore, criminal justice is a deliberative process: no matter how heinous the crime or certain the suspect's guilt, criminal law requires that certain procedures be followed.

These same rules do not apply, however, in a war, even an undeclared one such as the "war" on terrorism. The goal of a military operation is to destroy the enemy's forces, not to capture them and bring them to justice. The idea that an intelligence officer, having apprehended a terrorist suspect, should be required to read that person his or her *Miranda* rights, which include the right to remain silent and to be represented by counsel, strikes many as "ludicrous and highly counterproductive."[41] One senior military official—stationed in Afghanistan—believes the U.S. counterterrorism strategy should be as follows: "[A]s long as they want to send them here, we will kill them here. If they want to go somewhere else, we will kill them there."[42] Obviously, under the U.S. Constitution, law enforcement officials cannot take a similar view.

> "As terrible as 9/11 was, it didn't repeal the Constitution."
>
> —Rosemary S. Pooler, U.S. circuit judge (2003)

"Necessary and Appropriate Force" To a certain extent, democracies are the perfect target for terrorist activities. The freedoms available to people in the United States—freedom of speech, freedom of association, freedom of movement—make it much easier for terrorists and their supporters to operate in "enemy territory." Furthermore, a free press allows those with political goals to communicate the reasons behind an attack or action—a crucial aspect of the terrorist agenda. Finally, as already noted, the emphasis on the rights of the accused in the American criminal justice system often makes it difficult to investigate and prosecute terrorists.[43] (See the feature *CJ in Focus—The Balancing Act: Free Speech in the Age of Terrorism* on the next page.)

It is not surprising, therefore, that the first impulse in Washington, D.C., after September 11, 2001, was to "level the playing field." Within seven days, the U.S. Congress had authorized the president "to use all necessary and appropriate force" against those responsible for the attacks,[44] and within six weeks, it had passed the USA PATRIOT Act providing law enforcement with extra tools to fight terrorism. Though both measures were generally applauded at the time, in the intervening years many have begun to question whether they give the federal government too much power.

With his "necessary and appropriate force" authorization as justification, President George W. Bush ordered the U.S. Department of Defense to designate certain terrorist suspects as **enemy combatants.** This action caused consternation among constitutional scholars, for once suspects are given this label, they lose the right to a court hearing and representation by counsel. In the wake of September 11, 2001, hundreds of suspects were detained as enemy combatants, including several American citizens. According to Georgetown University law professor David Cole, this practice goes against one of the basic tenets of criminal law: all suspects must be treated equally. "When [federal officials] feel they can win a criminal case, they'll go the criminal route," says Cole. "Where they feel they can't, where they don't have the evidence," the officials will turn to military alternatives such as enemy combatant status.[45] As Figure 17.3 on page 567 shows, this can lead to inconsistency in the legal treatment of terrorist suspects.

Legislative Response As mentioned earlier, a major lightning rod for those who oppose the Bush administration's approach to fighting terrorism has been the USA PATRIOT Act. Critics of the act, such as Democratic Senator Russell Feingold of Wisconsin, believe that it has allowed enemies of the United States "to win this battle without firing a shot."[46]

In particular, opponents of the legislation focus on two of its provisions. The first allows law enforcement agents to search a person's home without notifying him or her beforehand.[47] The second grants the government authority to demand personal

Enemy Combatant
A label given to certain persons suspected of terrorist activities by the U.S. government. Persons given this designation lose a number of rights provided by the U.S. Constitution.

Free Speech in the Age of Terrorism

The First Amendment to the U.S. Constitution states, in part, that Congress "shall make no law . . . abridging the freedom of speech." In other words, the government cannot pass a law that criminalizes words alone, even if those words are violent or hateful. In some circumstances, however, words have an impact that is harmful to an individual or society—the famous example being a person falsely shouting "fire" in a crowded theater. In 1969, the United States Supreme Court established a three-part test to distinguish between speech that is constitutionally protected and speech that can be punished as "criminal conduct." According to the Court, speech can be prosecuted if (1) the speaker's intent was to incite criminal action, (2) the speaker was likely to succeed, and (3) the action would pose a risk of imminent harm.

The issue of criminalizing speech has come to the forefront in recent years as part of the overall "war" against terrorism. American law enforcement officials and courts are having to work out how far they can go in limiting speech that supports terrorism without violating the First Amendment. In 2005, a federal judge in Virginia sentenced Ali al-Timimi, a Muslim scholar, to life in prison for inciting his followers to wage war against the United States. In the weeks after September 11, 2001, Al-Timimi had met with several young men in his apartment and called for a "holy war" and "violent jihad." He also told them that U.S. forces in Afghanistan were "legitimate targets." Some of the young men eventually traveled to Pakistan to train with the terrorist organization Lashkar-e-Taiba, although none of them ever took up arms against American troops.

The prosecutors successfully argued that al-Timimi's statements not only advocated unlawful conduct, which is constitutionally protected speech, but also encouraged imminent unlawful acts, which is not. "This is not a case about speech; this was a case about intent," said Judge Leonie K. Brinkema. Even when combating terrorism, however, law enforcement agents cannot go too far. In 2004, an Idaho jury acquitted graduate student Sami Omar al-Hussayen, who had been indicted for violating a section of the USA PATRIOT Act that makes it a crime to provide "expert advice or assistance" to terrorists. Al-Hussayen had used his Internet skills to set up a Web site that was used for propaganda purposes by several Middle Eastern terrorist organizations. "He never spoke a word supporting terrorists," said one juror in explaining the verdict. "He just did what a university or a television station does—he posted the stuff." That same year, a federal district judge in Los Angeles struck down the "expert advice or assistance" section of the USA PATRIOT Act for being so vague that it could be applied to speech protected by the First Amendment.

FOR CRITICAL ANALYSIS

In defending the "expert advice or assistance" clause of the USA PATRIOT Act, one government official said, "Americans are threatened as much by the person who teaches a terrorist to build a bomb as by the one who pushes the button." What is your opinion of this statement? Under what circumstances could teaching a terrorist to build a bomb be a crime under the Supreme Court's three-pronged test?

records from businesses, medical offices, and other entities (including, to the dismay of some, libraries) as part of terrorism investigations.[48] Neither of these provisions has been used extensively—only about 150 "delayed notification" search warrants and thirty-five "library" searches had taken place as of the summer of 2005.[49] Nonetheless, five states and nearly four hundred communities have passed resolutions condemning the provisions and the legislation in the general.

In the following sections, we will examine how the USA PATRIOT Act and several related government regulations intersect with the U.S. Constitution, particularly the Fourth, Fifth, and Sixth Amendments. We will also examine some of the justifications for these laws, as well as the complaints of those such as Senator Feingold who believe that they betray the spirit, if not the letter, of the Constitution.

The Fourth Amendment and Monitoring Communications

The Fourth Amendment protects against unreasonable searches and seizures. According to the United States Supreme Court, the purpose of this amendment is to "prevent arbitrary and oppressive interference by enforcement officials with the privacy and personal security of individuals."[50] In practice, this has meant that a "neutral

	JOHN WALKER LINDH	YASER ESAM HAMDI	JOSE PADILLA	ZACARIAS MOUSSAOUI	RICHARD REID
Citizenship	U.S.	U.S.	U.S.	French	British
When taken into custody	November 2001	November 2001	May 2002	August 2001	December 2001
Charged with	Conspiracy to kill Americans, providing material support and resources to terrorist organization al Qaeda.	No charges filed. Held as "enemy combatant" after being captured as member of Taliban forces in Afghanistan.	Held as "enemy combatant" for three years with no charges filed. Indicted in 2005 for taking part in a U.S.-based terrorism conspiracy.	Participating in an al Qaeda conspiracy, including the September 11, 2001, attacks and other planned terrorist acts in the United States.	Attempted murder and use of weapon of mass destruction for trying to detonate a bomb in his shoe on a commercial airline flight from Paris, France, to Miami, Florida.
Access to counsel?	Yes	No	Yes	Yes	Yes
Outcome of proceedings	Pled guilty in federal court, sentenced to twenty years in prison.	Released by U.S. government in September 2004 without being charged with any crime.	As of December 2005, awaiting trial in the Miami (Florida) Federal Detention Center.	Pled guilty to six terrorism conspiracy charges in federal court in April 2005.	Found guilty in federal court and sentenced to life in prison.

FIGURE 17.3
Legal Treatment of Terrorist Suspects

As this summary shows, there is no single strategy in dealing with terrorist suspects. Two of these suspects who are American citizens are being held without access to an attorney, while two aliens were provided with the protections of civilian courts.

and detached" judge must, in most circumstances, decide whether a search of a suspect's person or property is warranted.[51]

The USA PATRIOT Act and Searches The need for judicial approval before a search in terrorism cases came under quick criticism following the September 11, 2001, attacks. During the summer of that year, FBI agents in Minnesota had arrested Zacarias Moussaoui for immigration violations and sought a warrant to search his apartment and his laptop computer. Because FBI officials felt the agents had not established Moussaoui's involvement in terrorist activities, they did not ask a judge for a warrant until after September 11. According to a congressional report, the information on Moussaoui's computer would have helped to provide a "veritable blueprint for 9/11."[52]

In response, several sections of the USA PATRIOT Act make it easier for law enforcement agents to conduct searches. Previously, for example, if American intelligence agents wanted to monitor communications (telephones, e-mail, voice mail) to gather "foreign intelligence," they needed a court order based on probable cause that a crime had taken place or was about to take place. The USA PATRIOT Act amends the law to allow the FBI to obtain warrants for "terrorism" investigations, "chemical weapons" investigations, or "computer fraud and abuse" investigations as long as agents can prove that such actions have a "significant purpose."[53] In other words, no proof of criminal activity need be provided.

The USA PATRIOT Act and Surveillance The USA PATRIOT Act also provides federal agents with "roving surveillance authority," allowing them to continue monitoring a terrorist suspect on the strength of an original warrant even if the suspect moves into another jurisdiction.[54] Previously, agents were required to obtain a new warrant from a judge in the new jurisdiction. Furthermore, the legislation makes it much easier for law enforcement agents to avoid the notification requirements of search warrants, meaning that a person whose home has been the target of a search and whose voice mails or computer records have been seized may not be informed of these activities until weeks after they have taken place.[55]

Experts worry that the USA PATRIOT Act makes it too easy for law enforcement agents and prosecutors to gather evidence. They warn that police may abuse the act by claiming that they need a warrant to gather foreign intelligence when, in fact, the goal of the investigation is nonterrorist criminal activity. Finally, because these warrants are obtained from special intelligence courts, they cannot be challenged—a crucial aspect of the adversarial process.[56]

The Fifth Amendment and Indefinite Detention

The Fifth Amendment holds that no person shall be deprived of life, liberty, or property without due process of law. As we discussed in Chapter 4, to a large extent criminal law is designed to ensure that those charged with a crime are guaranteed due process. The question of how the due process clause applies to noncitizens or enemy combatants has not, however, been resolved. The USA PATRIOT Act requires the U.S. attorney general to take into custody any alien that he or she has "reasonable grounds" to believe has engaged in activity that "endangers the national security of the United States." If the alien is charged with a criminal offense, the government can hold her or him for seven days without filing charges. If the alien is in custody for an immigration violation, the Constitution does not apply, and that person can be held indefinitely.[57]

The U.S. government has come under a great deal of international criticism for its policy regarding its detention center at the U.S. Naval Base at Guantánamo Bay, Cuba. The prison camp there has been used to detain more than six hundred prisoners captured during the American-led invasion of Afghanistan in 2001. Most of the detainees are either members of al Qaeda or fought for the Taliban. Because these detainees were seized during a military campaign and are not American citizens, the Fifth Amendment was not believed to apply to their incarceration. (Indeed, one prisoner who was discovered to have been born in the United States was transferred to a Navy prison in Norfolk, Virginia.)

Many experts believe, however, that under international law they should be considered "prisoners of war" and accorded a number of rights under agreements signed by the United States—including the right to either a timely trial for war crimes or release.[58] The U.S. government has, instead, labeled them unlawful combatants and insisted that they may be held until the end of

Detainees in orange jumpsuits sit in a holding area at the U.S. Naval Base at Guantánamo Bay, Cuba. The base is serving as a holding facility for hundreds of suspected al Qaeda and Taliban operatives captured during U.S. military operations in Afghanistan. The U.S. government considers the detainees to be "unlawful combatants" and has denied them legal representation and the right to trial. Under what amendment(s) are such rights guaranteed to American citizens? Do you think non-American citizens who are in the custody of the U.S. military should be protected by our Constitution? Why or why not?

© Reuters NewMedia, Inc./CORBIS

hostilities. Given the vague nature of "hostilities" under present circumstances, critics point out that those held at Guantánamo Bay could be detained without being charged and without access to legal representation for years.[59]

The Sixth Amendment and Trial Rights

As you will recall from Chapter 10, the Sixth Amendment guarantees the right to the assistance of counsel. Some argue that antiterrorism regulations restrict this right by inhibiting both the privacy that is assured in the attorney-client relationship and the ability to obtain the aid of a lawyer in the first place.

Limiting Counsel The United States Supreme Court has consistently held that the attorney-client privilege (see Chapter 9) is protected by the Constitution, even after the client's death.[60] In 2001, the U.S. Department of Justice imposed a new requirement on federal correctional facilities: all conversations between prisoners and their attorneys would be subject to monitoring if there is "reasonable suspicion" that the communication would be used to "further or facilitate" terrorist activities.[61] Like the provisions of the USA PATRIOT Act discussed above, this regulation does away with procedural safeguards that were designed to protect the due process rights of a suspect or prisoner. Previously, a judge could allow such monitoring only after the government presented probable cause that criminal activity was occurring. Critics of the regulation also point out that there is no judicial review of the decision to monitor these communications, essentially giving the government free rein to infringe on an important right.[62]

Of course, one must have an attorney before the privilege can go into effect. Most of the aliens and enemy combatants detained during the investigation of the September 11 attacks had difficulty obtaining counsel, and in some instances, they were denied access to their attorneys. Some of those arrested since 2001 have also been denied access to counsel. For example, federal authorities refused to let American citizen José Padilla speak to his lawyer for more than two years after he was arrested in May 2002 and taken into custody as an enemy combatant because of alleged ties to the al Qaeda terrorist network. Again, attorneys for the U.S. government deny that such treatment is illegal, as the suspects are either being held for immigration violations or have been designated enemy combatants and, therefore, are not under the protection of the Constitution.

Military Tribunals Perhaps the most controversial step taken by the Bush administration was a presidential order stating that suspected terrorists would be tried in tribunals operated by the U.S. military, and not by civilian courts (described in Chapter 8).[63] In these military proceedings, there is no right to a trial by jury, as guaranteed by the Sixth Amendment. Instead, a panel of military officers acts in the place of a judge and jury and decides questions of "both fact and law." The traditional rules of evidence (see Chapter 10) do not apply; instead, any evidence is admissible if, in the opinion of the tribunal, it would help a reasonable person decide the issue at hand. Furthermore, only two-thirds of the panel must agree to convict, in contrast to the unanimous jury required in criminal trials.[64] (See Figure 17.4 on the next page for a list of the differences between military tribunals and regular criminal courts.)

Proponents of military tribunals raise a number of concerns with trying accused terrorists in civilian courts. Primarily, they believe that it would be difficult to protect classified information in an "open" court. They also worry that an accused terrorist might escape conviction on a "technicality" in a regular criminal court.[65] Of course, for critics of these measures, the lack of constitutional protections for the defendant is precisely the problem with military tribunals, as well as with many of the other legal weapons the federal government has given itself to combat terrorism.

Rules Comparison: Federal Criminal Courts and Military Tribunals

In 2002, the Bush administration announced the procedural rules for military tribunals. These special courts will primarily be used to try terrorist suspects captured during military operations in Afghanistan and Iraq. These tribunals do not provide the same safeguards for defendants as do civilian courts, although the standard of proof for conviction is the same.

	FEDERAL COURT	MILITARY TRIBUNAL
Right to counsel	Defendant chooses an attorney, or, if the defendant cannot afford to pay for his or her defense, the government will provide counsel at no cost.	A military attorney is provided. Defendants can replace this attorney with a different military attorney of their own choosing or pay for a civilian attorney.
Standard of proof	Guilt beyond a reasonable doubt.	Guilt beyond a reasonable doubt.
Vote required for verdict	Unanimous to convict and impose penalty.	Two-thirds vote required to convict. Decision to impose death penalty must be unanimous.
Composition of jury	Twelve civilians.	Three to seven military officers. Seven members are required for death penalty cases.
Rules of evidence	Federal rules of evidence, including limits on hearsay. (See Chapter 10.)	Evidence is admissible if it would "have probative value to a reasonable person."
Appeals	U.S. court of appeals and then the United States Supreme Court.	Review panel appointed by the secretary of defense. Panel members may be military officers or civilians temporarily appointed as officers.

The Courts Respond

As we have seen throughout this textbook, the court system plays the role of final arbiter when it comes to balancing rights in the criminal justice system. This has been the case with counterterrorism measures as well, and the results have been somewhat surprising. Historically, the courts have assumed a deferential position to the federal government in times of crisis and military action. One of the most shameful moments in the United States Supreme Court's past came in 1944 when it upheld President Franklin D. Roosevelt's decision to "relocate" 110,000 Japanese Americans to prison camps during World War II.[66] In its rulings concerning the "war" on terrorism, however, the Court has not been so willing to follow the adage, "In wartime, law is silent."

Limiting Government Power Any predictions that the Supreme Court would continue its pattern of deference to the federal government on national security matters were dispelled over the course of two days in June 2004. At that time, the Court handed down three decisions concerning some of the policies of the Bush administration discussed earlier in this section. One case, *Rasul v. Bush* (2004),[67] involved the authority of U.S. courts to decide whether the noncitizen detainees in Guantánamo Bay could be held indefinitely without judicial review of their cases. The federal government argued that U.S. courts had no jurisdiction in the matter because the detainees were not American citizens and Guantánamo Bay was not American soil. The Court rejected this line of reasoning and ruled that, for due process purposes, the naval base in Cuba was to be considered U.S. territory. The decision opened the door for more than two hundred detainees to file *habeas corpus* petitions challenging their imprisonment. (For a review of *habeas corpus,* see page 336.)

Another case concerned the fate of Yaser Hamdi, an American citizen who was captured in Afghanistan in 2001. Designated an enemy combatant, Hamdi was held by the U.S. military in solitary confinement for two years—first in Guantánamo Bay, then in naval brigs in Virginia and South Carolina. Hamdi's father filed a *habeas corpus* petition on his son's behalf, claiming that his detention without charges, trial, or access to counsel constituted a due process violation. In *Hamdi v. Rumsfeld* (2004), the Court held that Hamdi, as an American citizen, was entitled to an explanation of his enemy combatant status and a "fair opportunity" to rebut the status before a neutral decision maker.[68] (See the feature *CJ in Focus—Landmark Cases:* Hamdi v. Rumsfeld on p. 572.) Rather than provide Hamdi with this opportunity, the Department of Justice decided to release the suspect and deport him to Saudi Arabia.

A Return to Deference The third case, involving the military's ability to hold enemy combatant José Padilla in a manner similar to Yaser Hamdi, was sent back to the lower courts because the defendant's attorney filed the claim in the wrong state.[69] Following the Supreme Court's lead in the *Hamdi* ruling, U.S. District Court Judge Henry F. Floyd ruled that the federal government must either charge Padilla with a crime or release him. In September 2005, however, a three-judge panel of the U.S. Court of Appeals for the Fourth Circuit reversed Judge Floyd's opinion. In its ruling, the panel stated that the president has authority to detain Padilla, or any other enemy combatant associated with al Qaeda, indefinitely.[70]

This is not the only indication that deference has not completely vanished from the judicial landscape. Also in 2005, a three-judge panel of the U.S. Court of Appeals for the District of Columbia ruled that congressional authorization to use "all necessary and appropriate force" justified utilizing military tribunals to try suspected terrorists held at Guantánamo Bay.[71] The tribunals had been suspended during the dispute, and immediately after the panel's decision, the Pentagon announced that the proceedings would resume. It is likely, however, that this case will eventually be decided by the Supreme Court as well, giving the high court another opportunity to influence the "war" on terrorism.

CYBER CRIME

In the days after the September 11, 2001, attacks, federal investigators had a difficult time determining the identities of the individuals who had hijacked the commercial airplanes. As it turned out, the hijackers had covered their tracks by stealing the identities of random individuals off the Internet and opening credit and bank accounts under the new names. There are other links between terrorism and the World Wide Web. A number of terrorist organizations operate Web sites to proselytize and raise funds. The FBI has publicly expressed concerns that information available on the Internet about energy infrastructures, water systems, uranium storage systems, and nuclear facilities might be used to the advantage of terrorist plotters. Federal law enforcement officials have found evidence that al Qaeda planned to breach computer networks operated by the U.S. military and commercial banks, and both government and private officials acknowledge the threat of cyberterrorism.[72]

Hamdi v. Rumsfeld

In 2001, Northern Alliance forces captured American citizen Yaser Esam Hamdi in Afghanistan and turned him over to the U.S. military. The federal government accused Hamdi of fighting on the side of the Taliban, labeled him an "enemy combatant," and detained him without a trial or access to a lawyer. When Hamdi (through his father) filed a writ of *habeas corpus* claiming that his detention was unconstitutional, the Bush administration countered that the president had the right to use extraordinary measures to protect the nation from terrorism. The Fourth Circuit Court of Appeals ruled in favor of the government, holding that courts should defer to the president and Congress in times of "overseas conflict." The United States Supreme Court accepted the executive branch's power to designate a person an "enemy combatant" under certain circumstances, but took issue with the lower court's view that the judiciary has no role in protecting the rights of citizens during wartime.

Hamdi v. Rumsfeld
United States Supreme Court
124 S.Ct. 2633 (2004)
http://laws.findlaw.com/us/000/03-6696.html

IN THE WORDS OF THE COURT . . .
Justice O'CONNOR, plurality opinion

* * * *

It is beyond question that substantial interests lie on both sides of the scale in this case. Hamdi's "private interest . . . affected by the official action," is the most elemental of liberty interests—the interest in being free from physical detention by one's own government.

* * * *

On the other side of the scale are the weighty and sensitive governmental interests in ensuring that those who have in fact fought with the enemy during a war do not return to battle against the United States. [T]he law of war and the realities of combat may render such detentions both necessary and appropriate, and our due process analysis need not blink at those realities. Without doubt, our Constitution recognizes that core strategic matters of warmaking belong in the hands of those who are best positioned and most politically accountable for making them.

* * * *

Striking the proper constitutional balance here is of great importance to the Nation during this period of ongoing combat. But it is equally vital that our calculus not give short shrift to the values that this country holds dear or to the privilege that is American citizenship. It is during our most challenging and uncertain moments that our Nation's commitment to due process is most severely tested; and it is in those times that we must preserve our commitment at home to the principles for which we fight abroad.

* * * *

We therefore hold that a citizen-detainee seeking to challenge his classification as an enemy combatant must receive notice of the factual basis for his classification, and a fair opportunity to rebut the Government's factual assertions before a neutral decisionmaker.

* * * *

In so holding, we necessarily reject the Government's assertion that separation of powers principles mandate a heavily circumscribed role for the courts in such circumstances. * * * We have long since made clear that a state of war is not a blank check for the President when it comes to the rights of the Nation's citizens.

DECISION

The Court reversed the appellate court's ruling and ordered the federal government to give Hamdi the opportunity to challenge his status as an enemy combatant in court. The *Hamdi* decision reflects the Court's refusal to automatically defer to the president or Congress on questions of national security.

FOR CRITICAL ANALYSIS

In his dissenting opinion, Justice Clarence Thomas stated that he and the other justices "lack the expertise and capacity to second guess" the president's decisions concerning Hamdi. Why might the president have more "expertise and capacity" to make national security determinations than a judge? Why might it be important for the courts to pass judgment on the president's actions during times of crisis?

For more information and activities related to this case, click on Landmark Cases under Book Resources at www.cjinaction.com.

Crime and the Internet

Computer Crime
Any wrongful act that is directed against computers and computer parts or that involves wrongful use or abuse of computers or software.

Cyberterrorism is, without question, a top concern for law enforcement. Most illegal activity on the Internet, however, is done for economic gain, not for ideological reasons. We will now examine the growing world of **computer crime,** which can be defined as any act that is directed against computers and computer parts, that uses computers as instruments of crime, or that involves computers and constitutes some form of abuse. A number of white-collar crimes, discussed in Chapter 1, such as fraud, embezzlement, and the theft of intellectual property, are now committed with the aid of computers and are thus considered computer crimes. As we discuss this illegal activity, we will be using the term **cyber crime,** which covers any criminal activity occurring in the virtual community of the Internet.

It is very difficult, if not impossible, to tell how much cyber crime actually takes place. Often, people will never know that they have been the victims of a cyber crime. Furthermore, businesses sometimes do not report such crimes for fear of losing customer confidence. Nonetheless, reliable information on specific areas of cyber crime can be obtained from agencies such as the Internet Security Alliance, the

National Institute for Standards and Technology, and the National Infrastructure Protection Center. We will rely on these sources for a great deal of the information in this section.

Cyber Crimes against Persons and Property

Most cyber crimes are not "new" crimes. Rather, they are existing crimes in which the Internet is the instrument of wrongdoing. When, for example, Dera Marie Jones posted an online message threatening to kill Michael Schiavo, who decided to have his brain-damaged wife's feeding tube removed in 2005, she was charged with transmitting in interstate commerce a communication containing a threat to injure a person.[73] The charge would have been the same if she had sent the message via regular mail or over the telephone. The challenge for law enforcement is to apply traditional laws, which were designed to protect persons from physical harm or to safeguard their physical property, to crimes committed in cyberspace. Here, we look at several types of activity that constitute "updated" crimes against persons and property—online consumer fraud, cyber theft, and cyberstalking.

Cyber Consumer Fraud The expanding world of e-commerce (buying and selling that takes place in cyberspace) has created many benefits for consumers. It has also led to some challenging problems, including fraud conducted via the Internet. In general, fraud is any misrepresentation knowingly made with the intention of deceiving another and on which a reasonable person would and does rely to her or his detriment. **Cyber fraud,** then, is fraud committed over the Internet. Scams that were once conducted solely by mail or phone can now be found online, and new technology has led to increasingly more creative ways to commit fraud. In 2003, for example, a California couple was indicted for operating a fraudulent online dating scheme in which they posed as Russian or Ukrainian women. Over three years, the pair stole $600,000 from nearly four hundred male victims.

No one knows the full extent of cyber fraud, but indications are that it is increasing with the growing use of the Internet. In 2000, the FBI and the National White

Cyber Crime
A crime that occurs online, in the virtual community of the Internet, as opposed to in the physical world.

Cyber Fraud
Any misrepresentation knowingly made over the Internet with the intention of deceiving another and on which a reasonable person would and does rely to his or her detriment.

Collar Crime Center formed the Internet Fraud Complaint Center (IFCC). In its first six months of operation, the IFCC received nearly 20,000 complaints and referred more than a quarter of them to law enforcement agencies for possible investigation.[74] In 2004, the organization, renamed the Internet Crime Complaint Center (IC3), received more than 200,000 complaints of fraud involving total losses of $68 million.[75]

Online Auction Fraud According to research conducted by the IC3, online auction fraud remains a widely reported form of consumer fraud on the Internet.[76] In its most basic form, online auction fraud is a simple process. A person puts up an expensive item for auction, on either a legitimate or a fake auction site, and then refuses to send the product after receiving payment. Or, as a variation, the wrongdoer may provide the purchaser with an item that is worth less than the one offered in the auction.

Online Retail Fraud Somewhat similar to online auction fraud is online retail fraud, in which consumers pay directly (without bidding) for items that are never delivered. Because most online consumers will purchase items only from reputable, brand-name sites, criminals have had to take advantage of some of the complexities of cyberspace to lure unknowing customers.

Again, though determining the actual extent of online sales fraud is difficult, the anecdotal evidence suggests it is a substantial problem. Virginian Jeremy Jaymes grossed more than $750,000 per week selling nonexistent or worthless products such as "penny stock pickers" and Internet history erasers. By the time he was arrested in 2004, he had amassed an estimated $24 million from his various fraudulent schemes. Perhaps the longest-running Internet fraud is the "Nigerian letter fraud scam." In this scheme, targets are sent e-mails promising them a percentage if they will send money to help fictitious officials from the African country transfer millions of nonexistent dollars to Western banks. The scam was recently updated to reflect current events, with con artists sending out e-mails asking for financial help in retrieving the fortune of a loved one who had perished in the deadly Indian Ocean tsunami of December 2004.

Cyber Theft In cyberspace, thieves are not subject to the physical limitations of the "real" world. A thief can steal data stored in a networked computer with network access from anywhere on the globe. Only the speed of the connection and the thief's computer equipment limit the quantity of data that can be stolen. This freedom has led to a marked increase in **identity theft,** which occurs when the wrongdoer steals a form of identification—such as a name, date of birth, or Social Security number—and uses the information to access the victim's financial resources. This crime existed to a certain extent before widespread use of the Internet. Thieves would "steal" calling-card numbers by watching people using public telephones, or they would rifle through garbage to find bank account or credit-card numbers. The identity thief would then use the calling-card or credit-card number or withdraw funds from the victim's account until the theft was discovered.

Stealing Information The Internet has, however, turned identity theft into perhaps the fastest-growing financial crime in the United States. Primarily, it provides those who steal information offline with an easy medium for using items such as stolen credit-card numbers or e-mail addresses while protected by anonymity. Also, frequent Web surfers may be providing a wealth of information about themselves without knowing it. Many Web sites use "cookies" to collect data on those who visit their sites. The data can include the areas of the site the user visits and the links the user clicks on. Furthermore, Web browsers often store information such as the consumer's name and e-mail address. Finally, every time a purchase is made online, the item is linked to the purchaser's name, allowing Web retailers to amass a database of who is buying what.

Identity Theft
The theft of identity information, such as a person's name, driver's license number, or Social Security number. The information is then usually used to access the victim's financial resources.

As more consumers are discovering, information that can be collected can be stolen. A study released by the Federal Trade Commission (FTC) reported that 27.3 million consumers were victims of identity theft between 1998 and 2003. The FTC estimated the cost at $5 billion to consumers and $48 billion to businesses and financial institutions such as banks and credit unions.[77] (See Figure 17.5.)

Phishing The newest form of identity theft, known as *phishing,* has added a different wrinkle to the practice. In a phishing attack, the perpetrators "fish" for financial data and passwords from consumers by posing as a legitimate business such as a bank or credit-card company. The "phisher" sends an e-mail asking the recipient to "update" or "confirm" vital information, often with the threat that an account or some other service will be discontinued if the information is not provided. Once the unsuspecting target enters the information, the phisher can use it to masquerade as the person or to drain his or her bank or credit account. Although the true incidence of phishing is probably incalculable, one study estimates that 57 million people receive at least one fraudulent e-mail each year, and the 3 percent who actually provide their personal data in response lose more than $1 billion annually.[78]

Cyberstalking California passed the first stalking law in 1990, in response to the murders of six women by men who had harassed them. The law made it a crime to harass or follow a person while making a "credible threat" that puts the person in reasonable fear for her or his safety or the safety of the person's immediate family. Today, forty-five states have passed laws that criminalize **cyberstalking,** which involves stalkers who find their victims through Internet chat rooms, Usenet groups and other bulletin boards, and e-mail. Some of the legislation requires a direct threat for prosecution, but Arizona's statute requires only that a victim be "seriously alarmed" or "annoyed."[79]

FIGURE 17.5
Fraudulent Activities Online

In 2004, the Federal Trade Commission received 635,173 reports of online fraud. As the graph shows, the largest number of these reports concerned identity theft.

Source: Consumer Sentinel and Identity Theft Data Clearinghouse, *National and State Trends in Fraud & Identity Theft, January–December 2004* (Washington, D.C.: Federal Trade Commission, February 2005), 5.

Cyber Crimes in the Business World

Just as cyberspace can be a dangerous place for consumers, it presents a number of hazards for businesses that wish to offer their services on the Internet. The same circumstances that enable companies to reach a wide number of consumers also leave them vulnerable to cyber crime. In 2005, an unknown person was able to gain access to computerized records at CardSystems Solutions, a company in Tucson, Arizona, that processes credit-card transactions for small Internet businesses. The breach exposed 40 million credit-card numbers.

Hackers The person who "broke into" CardSystems' database to steal the credit-card numbers was a hacker. A **hacker** is someone who uses one computer to break into another. Hackers who break into computers without authorization often commit cyber theft. In many cases, however, a hacker's principal aim is to prove how smart she or he is by gaining access to others' password-protected computers and causing data errors. German teenager Sven Jaschan, for example, received a twenty-one-month suspended sentence in 2005 for creating and spreading the Sasser worm through the Internet. A **worm** is a software program that is capable of reproducing itself as it spreads from one computer to the next. The Sasser worm, which prompted hundreds of thousands of computers to continually "crash" and reboot, caused millions of dollars' worth of

Cyberstalking
The crime of stalking, committed in cyberspace. Generally, stalking consists of harassing a person and putting that person in reasonable fear for his or her safety or the safety of the person's immediate family.

Hacker
A person who uses one computer to break into another.

Worm
A computer program that can automatically replicate itself over a network such as the Internet and interfere with the normal use of a computer. A worm does not need to be attached to an existing file to move from one network to another.

Virus
A computer program that can replicate itself over a network such as the Internet and interfere with the normal use of a computer. A virus cannot exist as a separate entity and must attach itself to another program to move through a network.

damage worldwide. German prosecutors believe, however, that Jaschan's motive was to gain renown as a programmer, and, in fact, just before his arrest the young man had created a new version of the Sasser worm designed to defuse the original one.

The Scope of the Problem At the same time the Sasser worm was winding its way through the World Wide Web, a virus called "Scob" was declared one of the most harmful computer programs ever. Like a worm, a **virus** reproduces itself, but unlike a worm, it must be attached to an "infected" host file to travel from one computer network to another. Scob improved on previous viruses by "lurking" on Web sites and then transferring itself to the hard drives of persons who visited the infected sites.

Though the hackers and other "techies" who create worms and viruses are often romanticized as youthful rebels, they cause significant damage. A destructive program such as the Scob virus often overloads a company's computer system, making e-mail and many other functions impossible until it is "cleaned out of the system." This cleansing process can cost between $100,000 and $5 million a day, depending on the size of the company affected. One computer-security firm estimates that the damage caused by Scob and other viruses may amount to as much as $55 billion a year worldwide, including clean-up costs and lost productivity.[80]

The Computer Crime and Security Survey polled 700 companies and large government institutions and found that 65 percent had suffered security breaches through computer-based means in 2004. Eighty percent suffered losses because of the breaches, costing more than $130 million to correct.[81] These numbers are actually down from previous years, a trend that analysts attribute to three factors: (1) more businesses are taking steps to protect their computer systems; (2) Internet wrongdoers are shifting their focus to identity theft, an easier and more profitable enterprise; and (3) many corporations refuse to report security breaches to law enforcement agencies because of negative publicity and possible loss of customers.[82]

Juvenile Cyber Crime Several years ago, a series of "hack attacks" were launched at some of the largest Internet companies, including Amazon.com and eBay. The sites either froze or significantly slowed down, causing nearly $2 billion in damage for the parent companies. While the FBI was searching for the hacker, one of its investigation chiefs joked that the companies' computer systems were so vulnerable that any fifteen-year-old with technological know-how could break into them.

> "There is a segment in society that views the unleashing of computer viruses as a challenge, a game. Far from it; it is a serious crime."
>
> —Robert J. Cleary, lead prosecutor for the U.S. attorney's office, New Jersey (1997)

As it turned out, the FBI agent was only a year off. The culprit was a sixteen-year-old Canadian high school dropout who was employed as a kitchen worker in Montreal when he was arrested. The teenager, who went by the moniker of Mafiaboy, had uploaded software programs on Web sites in Europe and South Korea, from which he bombarded the American companies with e-mails.

According to Assistant U.S. Attorney Joseph V. DeMarco, it should come as no surprise that Mafiaboy could cause so much damage. DeMarco believes that there are three main reasons why cyber crime is clearly suited to the habits and limitations of juveniles:

- *The enormous technological capacities of personal computers.* Most juvenile delinquents will never commit crimes more serious than shoplifting and other forms of petty theft. Advanced computer equipment and software, however, give these youth the ability to carry out complex criminal fraud and hacking schemes without leaving their bedrooms. Thus, computer technology has given juveniles the ability to "commit offenses that are disproportionate to their age." In addition, about 87 percent of all children have access to the Internet at home, at school, or through a library.[83]

- *The anonymity of the Internet.* The physical world denies juveniles the ability to commit many crimes. It would be very difficult, for example, for a fifteen-year-old to run a fraudulent auction in the flesh. The Internet, however, allows young people to depict themselves as adults, thereby opening up a number of criminal possibilities that would otherwise be denied to them. Furthermore, the lack of a driver's license or the wealth necessary to travel does not limit a cyber juvenile delinquent's ability to commit far-reaching offenses, as we saw in the case of Mafiaboy.

- *The acceptance of hacking in youth culture.* A recent poll of nearly 50,000 elementary and middle school students conducted by Scholastic, Inc., found that nearly half of them did not consider hacking to be a crime.[84] Thus, DeMarco believes, there is an "ethical deficit" when it comes to youth and computer crimes: juveniles who would never consider robbery or burglary are not troubled by the prospect of committing cyber crimes.[85]

The Spread of Spam Businesses and individuals alike are targets of *spam,* or unsolicited "junk e-mails" that flood virtual mailboxes with advertisements, solicitations, and other messages. Considered relatively harmless in the early days of the Internet's popularity, by 2004 spam accounted for 65 percent of all e-mails.[86] Far from being harmless, the unwanted files can wreak havoc on business operations.

Responding to complaints from overwhelmed constituents, a number of jurisdictions have started to pass antispamming laws. In 2005, Jeremy Jaymes (mentioned earlier in the chapter) was sentenced to nine years in prison for violating Virginia's antispam law, which bars people from sending bulk e-mail that is unsolicited and has a masked origin. Jaymes was sending close to 10 million such e-mails a day. In 2003, Congress passed the Controlling the Assault of Non-Solicited Pornography and Marketing Act (CAN-SPAM), which requires all unsolicited e-mails to be labeled and to include opt-out provisions and the sender's physical address.[87] Despite these efforts, spam continues to grow and evolve, with frequent users of instant messaging increasingly becoming the target of "spim," so called because it attacks IM services.

Pirating Intellectual Property Online Most people think of wealth in terms of houses, land, cars, stocks, and bonds. Wealth, however, also includes **intellectual property,** which consists of the products that result from intellectual, creative processes. The government provides various forms of protection for intellectual property such as copyrights and patents. These protections ensure that a person who writes a book or a song or creates a software program is financially rewarded if that product is sold in the marketplace.

Intellectual property such as books, films, music, and software is vulnerable to "piracy"—the unauthorized copying and use of the property. In the past, copying intellectual products was time consuming, and the quality of the pirated copies was clearly inferior. In today's online world, however, things have changed. Simply clicking a mouse can now reproduce millions of unauthorized copies, and pirated duplicates of copyrighted works obtained via the Internet are often exactly the same as the original, or close to it.

The Business Software Alliance estimates that 35 percent of all business software is pirated, costing software makers more than $32 billion in 2004.[88] The International Federation of the Phonographic Industry

Jeremy Jaymes was the first person in the United States to be convicted of a felony for illegal spamming. In 2005, a Virginia judge sentenced him to nine years in prison for his wrongdoing. Why is spamming a criminal act deserving of such serious punishment?

AP Photo/Loudoun County Sheriff's Office

believes that 34 percent of recorded music is pirated.[89] In the United States, digital pirates can be prosecuted under the No Electronic Theft Act[90] and the Digital Millennium Copyright Act.[91] In 2005, the entertainment industry celebrated the United States Supreme Court's decision in *MGM v. Grokster*.[92] The ruling provided film and music companies with the ability to file piracy lawsuits against Internet file-sharing Web sites that market software used primarily to illegally download intellectual property.

Cyber Crimes against the Community

One of the greatest challenges cyberspace presents for law enforcement is how to enforce laws governing activities that are prohibited under certain circumstances but are not always illegal. Such laws generally reflect the will of the community, which recognizes behavior as acceptable under some circumstances and unacceptable under others. Thus, while it is legal in many areas to sell a pornographic video to a fifty-year-old, it is never legal to sell the same item to a fifteen-year-old. Similarly, placing a bet on a football game with a bookmaker in Las Vegas, Nevada, is legal, but doing the same thing with a bookmaker in Cleveland, Ohio, is not. Of course, in cyberspace it is often impossible to know whether the customer buying porn is aged fifty or fifteen, or if the person placing the bet is from Las Vegas or Cleveland.

Consequently, the Internet has been a boon to both the pornography and the gambling industries. According to the Internet Filter Review, 12 percent of all Web sites (4.2 million) have pornographic content, and these sites generate $2.5 billion in revenues a year.[93] Though no general figures are available, the Internet has undoubtedly also been a boon to those who produce and sell material depicting sexually explicit conduct involving a child—child pornography. Because it is so difficult to track Web-based child pornographers, courts and lawmakers have had a difficult time controlling the dissemination of this material via the Internet.

In 2004, $7.5 billion was wagered online, and that figure is expected to exceed $18 billion by 2010.[94] In some states, certain forms of gambling, such as casino gambling or betting on horse and dog racing, are legal. This presents a legal quandary: Can citizens in a state that does not allow gambling place online bets to a Web site located in a state that does? After all, states have no constitutional authority over activities that take place in other states. Complicating the problem is the fact that many Internet sites are located outside the United States in countries where Internet gambling is legal, and no state government has power over activities that take place in other countries.

Fighting Cyber Crime

Why not just pass a law that makes gambling in cyberspace illegal? In fact, six states—Illinois, Louisiana, Nevada, Oregon, South Dakota, and Wisconsin—have specifically banned Internet gambling, and Congress is considering a similar step. Simply passing a law, however, does not guarantee that the law will be effectively enforced. With hundreds of millions of users reaching every corner of the globe, transferring unimaginable

Officials at the headquarters of World Wide Web Casinos in Antigua demonstrate some of their activities. Technology allows Internet users from all over the world to gamble online through companies outside the United States such as World Wide Web Casinos. World Wide Web Casinos has claimed that using its service "cannot be illegal because, despite their origination, bets will technically be placed on the computer at our offshore land-based casino site that is legally licensed and taxed by the host government." Is this statement correct?

AP Photo/Jack Dempsey

amounts of information almost instantaneously, the Internet has proved resistant to regulation. In the past, the U.S. government has generally adopted a "hands-off" attitude toward the Internet to promote the free flow of ideas and encourage the growth of electronic commerce. The terrorist attacks of September 11, 2001, seem to have changed this attitude.

Jurisdictional Challenges Regardless of what type of cyber crime is being investigated, law enforcement agencies are often frustrated by problems of jurisdiction (explained more fully in Chapter 8). Jurisdiction is primarily based on physical geography—each country, state, and nation has jurisdiction, or authority, over crimes that occur within its boundaries. The Internet, however, destroys these traditional notions because geographic boundaries simply do not exist in cyberspace.

To see how this can affect law enforcement efforts, let's consider a hypothetical cyberstalking case. Phil, who lives in State A, has been sending e-mails containing graphic sexual threats to Stephanie, who lives in State B. Where has the crime taken place? Which police department has authority to arrest Phil, and which court system has authority to try him? To further complicate matters, what if State A has not yet added cyberstalking to its criminal code, while State B has? Does that mean that Phil has not committed a crime in his home state, but has committed one in Stephanie's?

Federal Law Enforcement and Cyber Crime Of course, federal law enforcement agencies have jurisdiction over all federal crimes, no matter in which state they may take place. Because of this freedom from jurisdictional restraints, the federal government has traditionally taken the lead in law enforcement efforts against cyber crime. This is not to say that little cyber crime prevention occurs on the local level. Most major metropolitan police departments have created special units to fight cyber crime. In general, however, only a handful of local police and sheriffs' departments have the resources to support a squad of cyber investigators.[95]

The Federal Bureau of Investigation As the primary crime-fighting unit of the federal government, the FBI has taken the lead in law enforcement efforts against cyber crime. The FBI has the primary responsibility for enforcing all federal criminal statutes involving computer crimes. (See Figure 17.6 on the next page for a rundown of these laws.) In 1998, the Bureau oversaw the creation of the National Infrastructure Protection Center (NIPC), a Washington, D.C.–based agency charged with detecting and investigating cyber threats concerning the country's "critical infrastructures," such as transportation, energy, telecommunications, and financial networks.[96] Four years later, FBI Director Robert Mueller ordered the creation of a cyber division, which consolidated the agency's efforts against computer crime under a single command structure. Today, cyber crime is the FBI's third-highest priority (after counterterrorism and counterintelligence), and each of the bureau's fifty-six field divisions has at least one agent who focuses solely on crimes committed on the Internet.

The United States Secret Service The USA PATRIOT Act greatly increased the Secret Service's role in fighting cyber crime. In the legal arena, the legislation gave the agency jurisidiction over some of the crimes listed in 18 U.S.C. Section 1030 (see Figure 17.6).[97] The Secret Service was authorized to develop a national network of electronic crime task forces based on the New York Electronic Crime Task Force, a collaboration among federal, state, and local law enforcement officers and a wide range of corporate sponsors. The Secret Service is also engaging in increasingly aggressive tactics against cyber crime. In 2003, it launched Operation Firewall to combat credit- and debit-card fraud online. During the investigation, the Secret Service became the first law enforcement agency to

Cyberangels is an organization designed to assist people who need help online—whether they are being cyberstalked, harassed, or otherwise victimized by cyber criminals. To visit its Web site, click on *Web Links* under Chapter Resources at **www.cjinaction.com**.

FIGURE 17.6

Federal Laws and Computer Crime

18 U.S.C. Section 1030—It is a crime to do any of the following to and/or by means of a computer used by a financial institution, used by the federal government, or used in interstate or foreign commerce or communication:

1. gain unauthorized entry into a government computer and thereby discover information which is intended to remain confidential, information which the perpetrator either unlawfully discloses to someone not authorized to receive it or retains in violation of the law;

2. gain unauthorized entry to a computer and thereby gain access to information to which the perpetrator is not entitled to have access;

3. gain unauthorized access to a computer and thereby further the perpetration of a fraud;

4. cause damage to a computer as the result either of gaining unauthorized access to it or of inserting a program, code, or information into the computer;

5. transmit, in interstate or foreign commerce, a threat to cause damage to a computer in order to extort money or property from a person or other legal entity.

6. traffic, with intent to defraud, in passwords which either permit unauthorized access to a government computer or affect interstate or foreign commerce; or

7. transmit in interstate or foreign commerce any threat to cause damage to a protected computer with intent to extort something of value.

18 U.S.C. Section 1462—It is a crime to use a computer to import obscene material into the United States.

18 U.S.C. Section 1463—It is a crime to transport obscene material in interstate or foreign commerce.

18 U.S.C. Section 2251—It is a crime to employ a minor or induce a minor to participate in making a visual depiction of a sexually explicit act if the depiction was created using materials that had been transported (including the transportation by computer) in interstate or foreign commerce.

18 U.S.C. Section 2252—It is a crime to transport child pornography in interstate or foreign commerce.

18 U.S.C. Section 1028—It is a crime to produce, transfer, or possess a device, including a computer, that is intended to be used to falsify identification documents.

Many traditional crimes encompass the use of a computer as well; for example, threatening the president's life or infringing a copyright.

Sources: Susan W. Brenner, "State Cybercrime Legislation in the United States of America: A Survey," *Richmond Journal of Law and Technology* 7 (Winter 2001), 1–5; Heather Jacobson and Rebecca Green, "Computer Crimes," *American Criminal Law Review* (Spring 2002), 280–284; and Computer Fraud and Abuse Act, 18 U.S.C. Section 1030.

wiretap a private computer network. By 2005, with the help of the FBI, Operation Firewall had gathered evidence against four hundred suspects in five different countries.[98]

Private Efforts to Combat Cyber Crime The fact remains, however, that the federal government has very little regulatory oversight over the Internet. Hence, it has little choice but to rely on the voluntary efforts of private companies to secure their computer infrastructures. Although many federal officials do not believe private companies are being sufficiently diligent in this area, the fear of being "hacked" has spurred a billion-dollar industry that helps clients—either individuals or businesses—protect the integrity of their computer systems. Because every computer hooked up to the Internet is a potential security breach, these experts help devise elaborate and ever-changing password systems to ensure that only authorized users access data. They also install protective software such as firewalls and antivirus software, which can limit outside access to a computer or network. Because cyber criminals are constantly updating their technology, cyberspace security firms help their clients do the same with their defensive systems.

Perhaps the most successful and controversial way to protect computer information is to encrypt it. Through **encryption,** a message (plaintext) is transformed into something (ciphertext) that only the sender and receiver can understand. Unless a third party is able to "break the code," the information will stay secure. Encryption is particularly useful in protecting e-mails. Indeed, until recently the most widely used encryption program, known as P.G.P. for Pretty Good Privacy, was considered unbreakable. Several years ago, however, two cryptologists announced that the program may be flawed and would require a software fix called a "patch" to restore consumer confidence.

Encryption

The process by which a message is transmitted into a form or code that the sender and receiver intend third parties not to understand.

CAREERS IN CJ

David Hendron
Investigator, High Technology Crime Task Force

One of the most challenging aspects of my job on the High Technology Crime Task Force in San Diego County is the technological sophistication of the cyber criminals. They use all the tricks imaginable. As a result, it can take tremendous patience to solve a case. For example, I've been working on one case for almost three years that involves a small group of people selling counterfeit software over several states, at a cost to the public of some $20 million.

These kinds of difficult investigations can involve hundreds of legal processes, such as grand jury subpoenas, search warrants, etc. I also have to make sure that I investigate suspect computers and networks in a way that complies with the search and seizure laws, while dealing with evidence that may be encrypted or hidden or protected in some way. For example, evidence may be linked to software time-bombs, Trojan horses, or other destruction devices. Also, the cyber criminals are very hard to find since they resort to aliases, phony addresses, and dead-end cell phone accounts. But the challenges are also what make it especially satisfying to see these individuals standing before a judge and jury.

My first job in law enforcement was with the San Diego County Marshall's office (now in the Sheriff's Department)—and they hired me just after I left the Navy. I eventually moved up the ranks to become a detective with the San Diego Police Department. My interest in computer forensics was just developing when I worked on an assignment with the U.S. Secret Service. That assignment made me realize that this was the area I wanted to pursue.

The case involved a man studying for his master's degree who was accused of plagiarizing his thesis. Apparently, he hid a gun in the lab and when he was brought before a team of professors to address their suspicions, he suddenly pulled out the gun and shot all three. Tragically, they all died. As part of the investigation, I

did an extensive investigation of the suspect's computer and not only did I find copies of the thesis buried in different spots, but photo scans of the gun used in the shooting. This evidence helped convince jurors that the murders were premeditated, rather than the result of an impulsive rage or temporary insanity.

After this case, I decided I wanted to stay in high tech for the rest of my career in law enforcement. I've learned much on the job, but have also taken additional courses, and have a CRCD certificate (Certified Forensic Computer Examiner) that I earned through the International Association of Computer Investigative Specialists (IACIS).

A key ingredient to being successful as an investigator of cyber crimes is patience. You need to sift through mountains of data and go down many blind alleys before you can finally piece together the puzzle. Often the hours are long, and the demands on your time great. In addition, it's important that you can be self-directed and self-motivated because often no one but you is as deeply immersed in an individual case.

If you're interested in this field, you should focus on developing your knowledge and understanding of computers, as well as making sure you have a good background in criminal justice. In particular, you should gain understanding of so-called white-collar crime since that is the foundation of most cyber crime.

Go to the Careers in Criminal Justice Interactive CD *for a video interview with David Hendron and for other profiles in the field of criminal justice.*

David Hendron

Courtesy of David Hendron

CRIMINAL JUSTICE:
LOOKING TO THE FUTURE

Some observers feel that the massive amount of illegal activity that occurs on the Internet is a sign of an inherent weakness that could be exploited by cyberterrorists. Richard A. Clarke, a former cyber security adviser for the U.S. Department of Homeland Security, warns of a possible "digital Pearl Harbor."[99] Cyber crime expert Chris Rouland believes the nation has been "lucky" that the authors of the viruses and worms that have caused so much economic damage were not "terribly malicious with their intent." Rouland points out that with minor changes, the Blaster worm could have "shut down major pieces of infrastructure."[100]

Others insist that such fears are overstated. A simulation of a possible "digital Pearl Harbor" carried out by the U.S. Naval War College determined that, though a

Electronic fingerprint scanners such as the one shown above are an important part of the U.S. Department of Homeland Security's efforts to tighten security at entry points to the United States. The equipment allows border inspectors to check the identities of foreign visitors by comparing their fingerprints to the fingerprints of those on terrorist watch lists.

Web-based attack on America could cause serious damage, anyone attempting such an attack would need five years of preparation and $200 million of funding.[101] As we have seen, much cheaper, easier, and similarly effective terrorist methods exist.

This does not mean, of course, that law enforcement agencies or private companies should be lax in protecting against possible security breaches on the Internet. Without question, the immediate future of the criminal justice system will be characterized by a focus on counterterrorism. These efforts are sure to inspire new technologies and strategies that will affect crime fighting beyond the sphere of terrorism.

Reemerging Technology: The Database

We have discussed a number of technologies in this textbook, from infrared sensors that can "see" through walls to satellites that can track criminals from thousands of miles above the earth. For many criminal justice experts, however, the most promising new crime-fighting technology has existed for years: the database.

"Talking" Computers In July 2001, a police officer in South Hackensack, New Jersey, ran a check on the license plate of a suspicious automobile parked outside a local hotel. He was told that the vehicle was registered to Nawaf Alhazmi, a guest at the hotel. He was not told, however, that the CIA was searching for Alhazmi, who had ties to the al Qaeda network; the officer's local police department and the federal agency had no means to communicate with each other. Several months later, Alhazmi was on American Airlines Flight 77, which crashed into the Pentagon.

Almost every law enforcement agency in the United States, from the FBI to small local police departments, stores information concerning its crime-fighting activities. As the above example shows, however, the trick is to figure out a way for these various databases to "talk" to each other. Today, Alhazmi's link to international terrorism would have a much better chance of being discovered, thanks to the Statewide Information Management System (SIMS), which has been in use in New Jersey since 2004. SIMS is a network connecting computer databases from local, state, and federal law enforcement agencies via secure telephone lines. The service has two sections—one for gangs, drug trafficking, and organized crime, and the other for counterterrorism. Local police officers can enter information on any incident that relates to one of these areas, and the data are immediately sent to the relevant state and federal agencies, including the FBI's Joint Terrorism Task Force, for review.[102]

Database Developments The largest local information database is in New York City, where the DataShare system stores all information concerning offenders gathered from the New York Police Department, the district attorney's office, local courts, and a number of other agencies. The data are available to law enforcement officers at the click of a mouse. About a decade ago, scientists at the University of Arizona's Artificial Intelligence Lab formulated a computer code that creates "search engines" for law enforcement agencies. This code, called Coplink, allows police departments to enter names, weapons, and other elements of criminal behavior into a database that provides matches for similar crimes in other areas of the country. In 2005, Coplink was being used in more than one hundred jurisdictions.

"Smart" Cards of the Near Future In 2005, Congress passed the REAL ID Act, which proposes to create a database that will contain information on every adult American citizen who drives a car.[103] The legislation "requests" that states change the way that they issue driver's licenses. Under the new rules, state licensing offices will have to verify the identity of every person who applies for a new license or renews an old one and ensure that he or she is a U.S. citizen. The new driver's license will include much of the same information as today's version, but each card will also contain a "smart chip" that will allow government officials to retrieve more detailed information, such as fingerprints or employment history. (See Figure 17.7 for more information on these requirements.)

Under the terms of the REAL ID Act, by 2008 anybody wishing to use federally regulated services such as airplanes, national parks, trains, and federal courthouses will have to possess the new driver's license or a state-issued identification card containing the same information. Each state is also required to create and maintain a database containing all information printed on its driver's licenses and make these records available to other states. The data must also be accessible by police and the federal government. Federal law enforcement officials hope these measures will make it more difficult for illegal aliens to obtain driver's licenses through fraudulent means.

Privacy Rights and Fears

Critics of the REAL ID Act doubt that it will provide much protection against forged or fake identification cards. But their primary concerns involve privacy: the system would create a massive database with information on every American over the age of sixteen, accessible by the federal government, possibly by private enterprise, and, in the worst-case scenario, by hackers. As we learned in Chapter 7, even though privacy as a fundamental right is not explicitly mentioned in the U.S. Constitution, the United

FIGURE 17.7
The Driver's License of the Future

Source: The REAL ID Act of 2005.

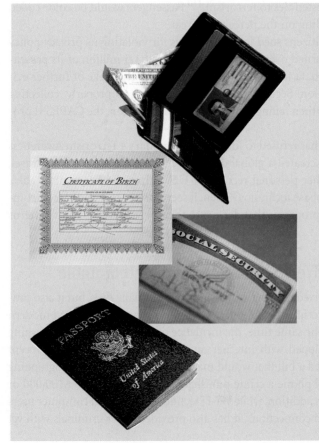

In 2005, Congress passed the REAL ID Act, which will change the way states issue driver's licenses by 2008. Federal officials hope that these changes will make it more difficult for noncitizens wishing to commit terrorist acts on U.S. soil to obtain driver's licenses by fraudulent means.

Before issuing a driver's license, the state must verify the identity of the applicant with the following:
- A photo identity card (or nonphoto identity card) that includes the person's full legal name and date of birth.
- Documentation showing the person's date of birth, such as a birth certificate.
- Proof of a person's Social Security number.
- Documentation showing the person's full name and principal residence address.
- Proof that the person (a) is a citizen or national of the United States, or (b) is an alien lawfully admitted to the United States.

Each new driver's license must contain:
- The person's full legal name.
- The person's date of birth.
- The person's gender.
- The person's driver's license or identification card number.
- The person's digital photograph.
- The person's signature.
- Physical security features to prevent tampering, counterfeiting, or duplication.
- Common machine-readable technology with minimum data requirements (a "smart chip").

States Supreme Court has found that some aspects of privacy, including personal information, are constitutionally protected.[104] Furthermore, Congress has passed legislation preventing certain information, such as financial data, from being released without the person's consent.[105]

Public Concerns Provisions of the USA PATRIOT Act do allow for increased monitoring of financial and educational records.[106] Large segments of the American public, however, do not seem as eager as the federal government to sacrifice their privacy in the name of greater security. In 2002, the Florida Department of Law Enforcement developed a program called the Multistate Anti-Terrorism Information Exchange—dubbed Matrix—that gave police departments access to commercial data such as property and automobile ownership, domain names, insurance information, and past addresses. So, for example, with Matrix it would be possible for police officers to download the identity of every male who owns a red Ford pickup truck within a twenty-mile radius of a suspicious event.[107]

At its inception, Matrix linked databases in thirteen different states. The program, however, inspired harsh criticism from civil libertarians, who called it "profoundly un-American,"[108] and law enforcement agents alike. "It's scary," said one Florida police officer. "I mean, I can call up everything about you, your pictures and pictures of your neighbor."[109] By the spring of 2005, public complaints had forced nine states to back out of the project, and it was discontinued. Though Florida continues to use the system, the new "Matrix lite" no longer includes financial and insurance information.

Data-Mining Dilemmas The force of public opinion has also had an impact on federal efforts to use the database as a crime-fighting tool. Several years ago, the federal government started the Computer Assisted Prescreening System, known as CAPPS II. The plan was to create a system that would analyze passengers' past travel reservations, housing information, credit history, and family connections to determine if they represented a pattern that suggested ties to terrorism.[110] Passengers would be color coded green, yellow, or red, depending on the perceived threat.

In 2003, several angry citizens sued JetBlue Airways for violating its privacy policy after the company secretly turned over information on about 1.5 million of its passengers to an agency compiling data for CAPPS II. A year later, in the wake of further evidence that the Transportation Security Administration was improperly collecting information on travelers and then failing to protect that information, the CAPPS II program was discontinued.

Furthermore, Congress has refused to fund the U.S. military's Terrorism Awareness Program, which would have created a global data-surveillance system to collect travel, credit-card, medical, and other personal records of U.S. citizens and foreigners alike. Whatever the benefits of database technology, then, it seems that Americans are uncomfortable with "data-mining" programs that delve into their private lives to find patterns of terrorism.

Developments and Trends: Predictably Unpredictable

Technology, inevitably, is a mixed blessing. It may improve our daily lives, but it also provides fresh opportunities for crime. Cell phones, for instance, have transformed modern life for many Americans. At the same time, the incidence of viruses, spam, and phishing schemes on cell phones equipped with Internet capabilities has skyrocketed in recent years. Congress has considered a bill that would make the unauthorized photographing of a naked person with a cell phone a crime punishable by a fine of up to $100,000 or one year in prison, or both. In addition, while Wi-Fi technology has freed computer users from the hassle of land-based connections, it has also provided cyber criminals with yet another means to cover their tracks, as they "steal" wireless Internet signals from unsuspecting victims.

As these examples show, the criminal justice system is not static. The landscape of law enforcement, the courts, and corrections is constantly changing and providing new challenges for those who make criminal justice their life's work. In this textbook, we have identified a number of these challenges, with terrorism being the most obvious. Other trends are also having a significant impact, however, including:

- The use of DNA evidence to convict and exonerate.
- The efforts to curb the costs of state prisons and jails, either by providing alternatives to incarceration or through the early release of those already serving time.
- The move to treat juvenile delinquents as adult offenders.
- The use of immigration law to combat drug trafficking and terrorism.

According to industry estimates, more than 80 percent of the mobile phones sold in the United States are equipped with cameras. What privacy concerns does this new technology raise? What kind of laws should be passed to make sure that cell phone cameras are not misused?

These developments and countless others mean that the criminal justice system ten years from now will not be exactly the same as the one you have learned about in this textbook. This course has, however, provided you with a strong grasp of the fundamentals of criminal justice and hopefully has inspired you to consider a career in one of the most exciting and challenging fields of the twenty-first century.

Border Insecurity

In its final report on the events that led up to September 11, 2001, the National Commission on Terrorist Attacks Upon the United States had plenty of blame to spread around. Poor airport security, poor performance by the FBI and other domestic law enforcement agencies, and poor intelligence gathering by the CIA were all highlighted as causes for concern and needed reform. The commission seemed particularly disturbed, however, at the ease with which proven and potential terrorists could enter the United States. "Protecting borders was not a national security issue before 9/11," the report remarked, with a hint of disbelief.[111] There is little doubt that the link between terrorism and immigration has become an "issue" since the terrorist attacks. In this *Criminal Justice in Action* feature, we discuss whether our national security has improved as a result.

The Mexican Connection

Somewhere between eight million and nine million illegal aliens live in the United States. The vast majority pose no threat to our national security and have come to this country for no other reason than to make a better life for themselves and their families. That having been said, the connection between illegal aliens and terrorism in this country is undeniable. Since 1993, forty-eight persons of foreign origin have committed terrorist acts on American soil; twenty-two of them had violated immigration laws.[112]

In the years since September 11, 2001, the federal government has expended massive resources to keep illegal aliens from entering the United States on airplanes. Many experts believe, however, that such efforts should be directed closer to the ground. Border Patrol agents apprehend only one-third of the estimated three million people who illegally cross this country's 2,000-mile-long border with Mexico each year.[113] National security officials worry that these odds are too tempting for terrorist organizations to resist. In August 2004, shortly after the Border Patrol apprehended two terrorist suspects at a checkpoint on the border, the FBI issued an alert warning that al Qaeda officials might attempt to enter the United States through Mexico. "These terrorists are smart," says Richard Shultz, an international security expert at Tufts University in Medford, Massachusetts. "They study these issues and

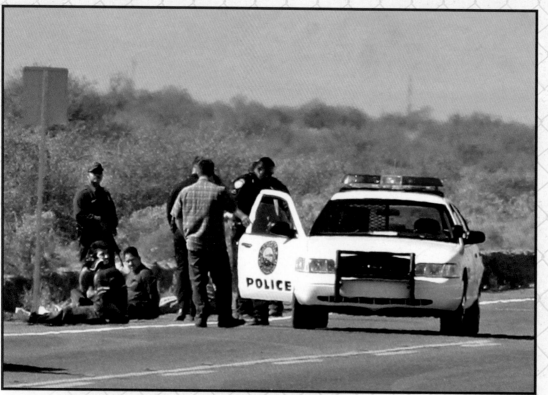

AP Photo/N. Scott Trimble

Police officers watch over four men taken into custody in connection with a roadside shooting in Arizona. Four people were killed in the incident, which involved the transportation of illegal immigrants across the Mexican border. Violent crime associated with immigrant smuggling skyrocketed in the mid-2000s, a reflection of the high profits to be made by "people traffickers" in the Southwest United States.

learn from one other. And one way in is right through the southern security perimeter."[114]

Sidestepping the Law

On March 1, 2005, Lebanese national Mahmoud Youssef Kourani pled guilty to providing material support to the Middle Eastern terrorist organization Hezbollah. Three years earlier, Kourani had paid a *coyote*—a person who smuggles illegal immigrants across the U.S.-Mexican border for a fee—to get him into the United States. These smuggling networks are of particular concern to federal officials, who realize that it would be very difficult for those unfamiliar with the harsh, desert conditions of the southern border region to make a crossing on their own. In 2005, Deputy Secretary of Homeland Security David Loy told Congress, "Several al Qaeda leaders believe operatives can pay their way into the country through Mexico."[115]

The complexities of immigration law provide another loophole through which potential terrorists can make their way into the United States. Almost all Mexicans who try to enter the United States surreptitiously do so in order to find work, which is not, according to federal law, a valid reason for entry. There are, however, a number of valid reasons for non-Mexicans to cross the border and enter this country. For example, the alien may be eligible for *asylum* in the United States because of mistreatment by the government in his or her homeland. Consequently, while Mexicans without proper visas are automatically turned back at the border, undocumented citizens of other countries (known as "other than Mexicans," or OTMs) may be allowed in, on the condition that they appear before an immigration judge at a later date.

In 2004, 44,000 OTMs entered the United States under this policy, called "catch and release" by its critics. The problem: nearly 90 percent of the OTMs failed to apear at their immigration hearings, meaning that they had become fugitives within U.S. borders.[116] It seems obvious that, in the words of one observer, "the honor system has failed."[117] The worry, of course, is that potential terrorists could pose as OTMs and easily pass through a border checkpoint.

A Logistical Nightmare

No matter what various schemes are utilized, the main problem in stemming the flow of illegal immigrants—terrorists or otherwise—from Mexico is logistics. The border stretches for 2,000 miles, much of it an uninhabited desert wasteland marked only by the Rio Grande. Even with 11,000 border agents (an increase of 1,300 since September 11, 2001) and physical barriers such as checkpoint stations, tall barbed-wire fences, and roadblocks in the most populated areas, effectively policing this immense expanse of land is practically impossible. "When you crack down in one area, they're going to try to exploit weaknesses in another area," says T. J. Bonner, president of the National Border Patrol Council.[118]

Technology has provided some relief to the overburdened Border Patrol. In the past few years, the agency has made use of remote video cameras, underground sensors, unmanned aircraft, and radiation detectors to locate border crossers. Databases, as discussed earlier in this chapter, have also been helpful. Border Patrol agents now have the technological ability to match fingerprints lifted from detained illegal immigrants against the FBI's national criminal database. Between May and December 2004, agents apprehended 30,000 illegal immigrants with U.S. criminal records, up from only 2,600 during the same period in 2002, before the technology had been made available.[119]

The federal government has also decided to close the loophole created by its "catch and release" policy. In 2004, the Department of Homeland Security (DHS) gave Border Patrol agents the power to deport OTMs found within one hundred miles of Mexico without giving them the opportunity to appear in immigration court.[120] The DHS is coordinating with local police departments along the border in efforts to apprehend illegal aliens and has set up a special force of about eighty law enforcement agents to hunt down immigrant fugitives in the country's interior.

Looking North

Despite these efforts, there is no evidence that the flow of illegal immigrants across the U.S.-Mexican border has slowed. Equally disturbing is the possibility that such efforts may be a poor use of time and resources, at least as far as the "war" on terrorism is concerned. For all the attention being paid to the U.S. border with Mexico, our border with Canada could be a more inviting entry point for potential terrorists. Canada has a much more liberal immigration policy than the United States; refugees from countries such as Pakistan and Iraq can gain entry without a passport or a background check and can move freely within the country until their asylum hearings. According to various law enforcement agencies, as many as fifty international terrorist groups operate in Canada, including al Qaeda and the Armed Islamic Group—both linked to Osama bin Laden. It would be relatively easy for operatives from these groups to get into the United States: our border with Canada measures 4,000 miles, twice as long as the border with Mexico, yet it is staffed with fewer than half as many Customs and Border Patrol agents.[121] "I believe the [Canadian-American] border is so far out of control that we don't even have an idea how far out of control it is," said one Border Patrol officer.[122]

Finally, it is worth noting that hardly any of the illegal immigrants involved in terrorist incidents on American soil (and none of the 9/11 hijackers) entered the country illegally via either the Mexican or the Canadian border. Rather, most of them entered legally with a valid business or tourist visa. Their status changed from "legal" to "illegal" after they violated the terms of their visas, usually by remaining in the United States past the expiration date. This suggests that database systems such as US-VISIT, which electronically monitors visa holders from certain countries during their stay in the United States, may be the most effective "border patrol" devices in America's arsenal against terrorism.[123]

Making Sense of America's Borders and Terrorism

1   Why do you think security problems at the U.S.-Mexican border receive so much more law enforcement and government attention than the weaknesses at the U.S.-Canadian border?

2   Several commentators have suggested building a security fence, or "wall," along the entire length of the U.S.-Mexican border. Others have proposed that the U.S. military should be given the responsibility of patrolling our borders. What is your opinion of these recommendations?

3   Do you think that illegal aliens who make their way into the United States should enjoy the protections of the U.S. Constitution? Explain your answer.

Chapter Summary

1   **Explain why the Antiterrorism and Effective Death Penalty Act of 1996 (AEDPA) is an important legal tool against potential terrorists.** The AEDPA allows federal law enforcement officials to prosecute those suspected of providing "material support or resources" to any group that the U.S. government has designated a "terrorist organization." The act permits the arrest of a suspect who has not yet committed a criminal act, thereby allowing for preventive measures not usually available under criminal law.

2   **Describe the primary goals of an intelligence agency and indicate how it differs from an agency that focuses solely on law enforcement.** The primary goal of an intelligence agency is to prevent crime by gathering information on potential illegal acts before they occur. In contrast, a law enforcement agency devotes its resources to solving crimes that have already occurred and bringing those who committed those crimes to justice.

3   **List some of the ways federal law enforcement can use aspects of immigration law to fight terrorism.** Immigration law provides fewer procedural protections to suspected wrongdoers than does criminal law: (a) federal agents do not need to meet the probable cause requirement when detaining someone on suspicion of an immigration violation; (b) those arrested for violating immigration law are not guaranteed counsel; and (c) federal law allows a person suspected of violating immigration law to be held for seven days before being charged.

4   **Indicate the three amendments to the U.S. Constitution that are cited most often by critics of the USA PATRIOT** Act of 2001, and briefly explain why. (a) Critics see the act as infringing on the Fourth Amendment because it gives the federal government broader powers to monitor and search those suspected of supporting terrorism. (b) Critics believe the act allows for the indefinite detention of suspects in breach of the due process clause of the Fifth Amendment. (c) The USA PATRIOT Act and other government directives are seen as restricting the rights to counsel and a fair trial guaranteed by the Sixth Amendment.

5   **Explain how military tribunals differ from federal courts with respect to trials of suspected terrorists.** A defendant before a military tribunal does not enjoy the right to trial by jury; instead, a panel of military officers makes decisions of guilt and innocence. The traditional rules of evidence do not apply in military tribunals, which operate under a much more lenient standard of what evidence is allowed against the defendant. Also, military tribunals do not have to reach a unanimous verdict—only two-thirds of the panel must agree to find guilt.

6   **Distinguish cyber crime from "traditional" crime.** Most cyber crimes are not "new" types of crimes. Rather, they are traditional crimes committed in cyberspace. Perpetrators of cyber crimes are often aided by certain aspects of the Internet, such as its ability to cloak the

STORIES FROM THE STREET

Go to the *Stories from the Street* feature at **www.cjinaction.com** to hear Larry Gaines tell insightful stories related to this chapter and his experiences in the field.

user's identity and its effectiveness as a conduit for transferring—or stealing—large amounts of information very quickly.

7 **Explain the activities and purposes of most hackers.** A hacker is someone who uses one computer to gain access to another computer. Sometimes a hacker's goal is to commit cyber theft. In many cases, however, a hacker's principal aim is to "show off" the ease with she or he can break into protected computer systems and cause errors.

8 **Outline the three major reasons that the Internet is conducive to juvenile cyber crime.** (a) Advanced computer equipment and software allow juveniles to commit crimes without leaving their homes; (b) the anonymity of cyberspace allows young people to commit crimes such as theft that would otherwise be almost impossible, given the limitations of size, money, and experience; and (c) hacking and other cyber crimes are often not recognized as unethical in youth culture.

9 **Describe the challenges to enforcing online gambling laws.** Although gambling is generally illegal in this country, almost anybody with a credit card can gamble online, regardless of his or her age or place of residence. Furthermore, many Internet gambling sites are physically based outside the United States, limiting the authority, or jurisdiction, of American law enforcement agencies and courts to control their actions.

10 **Indicate some reasons why the database is seen as an important crime-fighting tool for the future of law enforcement.** Almost every law enforcement agency in the United States keeps and updates a database with information on crimes, arrests, and other aspects of law enforcement in its jurisdiction. If law enforcement officers had the means to access the databases of other agencies and government organizations, it would allow them to "tap into" a wealth of crime information, aiding their investigative and preventive efforts immeasurably.

Key Terms

alien 563
Antiterrorism and Effective Death Penalty Act of 1996 (AEDPA) 557
computer crime 572
cyber crime 573
cyber fraud 573
cyberstalking 575
encryption 580
enemy combatant 565
hacker 575
identity theft 574
immigration violations 563
intellectual property 577
intelligence agency 560
virus 576
worm 575

Questions for Critical Analysis

1 What is the "big cultural change" that the FBI is facing in the aftermath of the September 11, 2001, terrorist attacks?

2 What are some of the problems that local police departments face in their counterterrorism efforts? Why do many local police chiefs feel the federal government has hampered, rather than helped, these efforts?

3 Has the United States Supreme Court been deferential to the federal government when it comes to the civil liberties of terrorism suspects? Support your answer by discussing the Court's decisions in several recent cases.

4 Why does the nature of online communication make it difficult to identify and prosecute those who commit cyber crimes?

5 How are the goals of a military operation different from those of a law enforcement investigation?

6 Why has the U.S. government been criticized for holding suspected terrorists at the U.S. Naval Base at Guantánamo Bay, Cuba? On what constitutional principle is this criticism based?

7 Consider the following situation: Melissa Chin is the sheriff of Jackson County, Missouri, population 1,434. Sheriff Chin has only two deputies at her disposal. Mae Brown, a resident of Jackson County, is receiving threatening e-mails from someone who has the cyberspace name of johndoe1313. Mae is certain that the sender is actually Matthew Green, her ex-husband. Matthew lives in Wilson County, Louisiana. What are some of the jurisdictional problems Sheriff Chin may face in investigating Matthew's possible involvement in cyberstalking? What are some of the practical problems Sheriff Chin may encounter? How might she solve these problems?

8 How does encryption help protect information delivered via the Internet? Is this method foolproof?

9 Why have database programs such as Matrix and CAPPS II been discontinued despite their potential for preventing traditional crimes and terrorism?

Test Preparation Online

Criminal JusticeNow

Go to **www.cjinaction.com** and click on *Criminal JusticeNow* for access to this powerful online study tool. You will get a *personalized study plan* based on your responses to a diagnostic pretest. Once you have mastered the material with the help of interactive learning tools, video clips with questions, an integrated e-book, and more, you can take a posttest to confirm you are ready to move on to the next chapter.

Book Companion Web Site

At the book companion Web site (**www.cjinaction.com**), you will find many resources in addition to *Criminal JusticeNow* to aid you in studying for your exams. For example, under *Chapter Resources,* you will find the *Chapter Outline, Chapter Summary, Flashcards, Glossary, Learning Objectives, Lecture Presentations, Concept Builder, Essay Questions,* and a *Tutorial Chapter Quiz.* You can also test yourself with interactive *Online Reviews* of each chapter section. Check out the *Web Links* to access the Web sites mentioned in the text, as well as many others. You can also access recent perspectives by clicking on *CJ in the News* and *Terrorism Update* under *Course Resources.*

Suggested Readings

Mitnick, Kevin D., and William L. Simon, *The Art of Intrusion: The Real Stories behind the Exploits of Hackers, Intruders, and Deceivers,* Indianapolis, IN: Wiley Publishers, 2005. One of the most notorious hackers of the 1990s, Mitnick went straight after his release from prison in 2002 and became a computer-security consultant. He also became an author, and in this, his second book, Mitnick brings together ten stories of true computer crimes, using his expertise to make clear why and how they happened. The accounts, with titles such as "Hacking the Casinos for a Million Bucks" and "The Robin Hood Hacker," also provide a "how-to" guide for computer users, with Mitnick explaining how each crime could and should have been prevented. The author remains under a federal gag order that forbids him to disclose details of his own crimes, so, for now, these accounts of others' exploits will have to suffice.

Rosen, Jeffrey, *The Naked Crowd: Reclaiming Security and Freedom in an Anxious Age,* New York: Random House, 2004. "Americans are perfectly happy to violate their own privacy, and those of strangers, as long as they have an illusion of control over the conditions under which the violation occurs," writes Rosen, a professor at the George Washington University Law School in Washington, D.C. In Rosen's opinion, the key word of this sentence is *illusion.* Americans seem to think that feeling safe is the same as being safe, and the author uses this polemic to put them straight. Although Rosen's argument that, in today's world of reality television and bloggers, we need to expose our personal lives in order to gain trust in the realm of national security seems a bit forced, the book does provide valuable insight into how our collective national psyche has responded to the amorphous threat of terror.

Notes

1. Reuters, "U.K. Police Defend Shoot-to-Kill after Mistake," at **http://msnbc.msn.com/id/8655541.**
2. Matthew Purdy and Lowell Bergman, "Unclear Danger: Inside the Lackawanna Terror Case," *New York Times* (October 12, 2003), Section 1, page 1.
3. Fareed Zakaria, *Illiberal Democracy at Home and Abroad* (New York: W. W. Norton, 2003), 15.
4. Purdy and Bergman.
5. 18 U.S.C. Section 2339B(a)(1)(1996).
6. John Ashcroft, Testimony before the Senate Committee on the Judiciary, 107th Congress (September 25, 2001), available at **http://www.usdoj.gov/ag/testimony/2001/0925AttorneyGeneralJohnAshcroftTestimonybeforetheSenateCommitteeontheJudiciary.htm.**
7. Arunabha Bhoumik, "Democratic Responses to Terrorism: A Comparative Study of the United States, Israel, and India," *Denver Journal of International Law and Policy* (Spring 2005), 285.
8. *United States v. Salameh,* 152 F.3d 88 (2d Cir. 1998).
9. Bhoumik.
10. *Ibid.*
11. Quoted in Philip Shenon and Eric Lichtblau, "FBI Assailed for Its Handling of Terror Risks," *New York Times* (April 14, 2004), A1.
12. Eric Lichtblau, "New Details Put FBI's Actions under Scrutiny," *New York Times* (April 12, 2004), A1.
13. David Johnston and Don Van Natta, Jr., "Wary of Risk, Slow to Adapt, FBI Stumbles in Terror War," *New York Times* (June 2, 2002), Section 1, page 24.
14. Congressional Budget Office, *Federal Funding for Homeland Security: An Update* (July 20, 2005), 1, 5.
15. Quoted in Else Walsh, "Learning to Spy," *New Yorker* (November 8, 2004), 96.
16. Richard Shelby, statements made during an appearance on *FOX News,* December 1, 2002.
17. Quoted in Toni Locy, "Anti-Terror Crew Chases Leads Big and Small," *USA Today* (October 8, 2003), 10A.
18. Douglas Jehl, "Bush to Create New Unit in FBI for Intelligence," *New York Times* (June 30, 2005), A1.
19. Dan Eggen, "Center to Assess Terrorist Threat: New Operation to Be Housed at CIA for Now," *Washington Post* (May 1, 2003), A10.
20. Walsh, 101.
21. David M. Walker, *FBI Reorganization: Progress Made in Efforts to Reform, but Major Challenges Continue* (Washington, D.C.: General Accounting Office, June 2003), 17–18.
22. Office of Community Oriented Policing Services, *Local Law Enforcement Responds to Terrorism* (Washington, D.C.: U.S. Department of Justice, 2002), 3.
23. Quoted in Jennifer Nislow, "Local Police Suffer Strain of Stretched Resources," *Law Enforcement News* (October 31, 2001), 11.
24. Kevin Sack, "Focus on Terror Creates Burden for the Police," *New York Times* (October 28, 2001), B4.
25. Warren Rudman, Richard A. Clarke, and Jamie F. Metzl, *Emergency Responders: Drastically Underfunded, Dangerously Unprepared* (New York: Council on Foreign Relations, 2003), 13.
26. "Unanswered Prayers: Police Officials Say Anti-Terror Needs Are Still Unmet," *Law Enforcement News* (September 15–31, 2003), 1.

27. Samantha Young, "Washington Digest: Senate OKs Homeland Security Bill," *Las Vegas Review-Journal* (July 17, 2005), 4B.

28. Quoted in John M. Broder, "Police Chiefs Moving to Share Terror Data," *New York Times* (July 29, 2005), A12.

29. Quoted in Dan Horn, "Law Enforcement Agencies Butting Heads," *Cincinnati Enquirer* (March 27, 2005), 1.

30. Quoted in Ben Fox, "More Police Agencies Seek to Enforce Immigration Laws," *Arizona Daily Star* (April 25, 2005), A1.

31. Pub. L. No. 104-208, 110 Stat. 3009 (1996).

32. Bureau of Justice Statistics, *Immigration Offenders in the Federal Criminal Justice System* (Washington, D.C.: U.S. Department of Justice, 2002), 3.

33. *United States v. Martinez-Fuerte*, 428 U.S. 543, 566–567 (1976).

34. 8 U.S.C. Section 1362 (2000).

35. 8 U.S.C. Section 287.3 (2001).

36. Mary Beth Sheridan, "Immigration Law as Anti-Terrorism Tool," *Washington Post* (June 13, 2005), A1.

37. "Remarks by the President in Photo Opportunity with National Security Team," The White House, Office of the Press Secretary at **http://www.whitehouse.gov/news/releases/2001/09/20010912-4.html**.

38. "Polls: Trade Some Freedom for Security," *Law Enforcement News* (September 15, 2001), 1.

39. *Ibid.*

40. Susan Sachs, "Murky Lives, Fateful Trip in Buffalo Terrorism Case," *New York Times* (September 20, 2002), A1.

41. Ronald J. Sievert, "War on Terrorism or Global Law Enforcement Operation?" *Notre Dame Law Review* (January 2003), 319.

42. Quoted in Michael Elliot, "Inside the Battle of Shah-i-Kot," *Time* (March 18, 2002), 38–39.

43. Bhoumik.

44. Authorization for Use of Military Force, Pub. L. No. 107-40, 115 Stat. 224 (2001).

45. Quoted in Katharine Q. Seelye, "War on Terror Makes for Odd Twists in the Justice System," *New York Times* (June 23, 2002), Section 1, page 16.

46. Quoted in John Cloud, "Hitting the Wall," *Time* (November 5, 2001), 70.

47. Uniting and Strengthening America by Providing Appropriate Tools Required to Intercept and Obstruct Terrorism Act, Pub. L. No. 107-56, Section 213 (2001).

48. USA PATRIOT Act, Pub. L. No. 107-56, Section 215 (2001).

49. Mark Sherman, "Officials Urge Patriot Act Renewal," *Cincinnati Post* (April 5, 2005), A2.

50. *INS v. Delgado*, 466 U.S. 215 (1983).

51. *Johnson v. United States*, 333 U.S. 13–14 (1948).

52. Philip Shenon, "Senate Report on Pre–9/11 Failure Tells of Bungling at FBI," *New York Times* (August 28, 2002), A14.

53. USA PATRIOT Act, Pub. L. No. 107-56, Sections 201–202, 115 Stat. 272, 278 (2001).

54. USA PATRIOT Act, Section 206 (amending Section 105(c)(2)(B) of Foreign Intelligence Surveillance Act).

55. USA PATRIOT Act, Section 213.

56. Michael Hill, "Life, Liberty, and the Pursuit of Terrorists," *Baltimore Sun* (November 2, 2003), 1C.

57. USA PATRIOT Act, Section 412.

58. Geneva Convention Relative to the Treatment of Prisoners of War, 75 U.N.T.S. 287 Art. 84 (August 12, 1949).

59. Jamie Fellner, "Double Standards," *International Herald Tribune* (March 31, 2002), at **http://hrw.org/editorials/2003/us033103.htm**.

60. *Swidler & Berlin v. United States*, 524 U.S. 410 (1998).

61. 28 C.F.R. 501.3(d) (as amended, 2001).

62. American Civil Liberties Union, "Regarding Eavesdropping on Confidential Attorney-Client Communications," in Scott H. Decker, Leanne F. Alarid, and Charles M. Katz, eds., *Controversies in Criminal Justice* (Los Angeles: Roxbury Publishing Co., 2003), 85–93.

63. Military Order of November 11, 2001, "Detention, Treatment, and Trial of Certain Non-Citizens in the War against Terror," 66 *Federal Register* 57,833 (November 13, 2001).

64. *Military Commission Order No. 1* (Washington, D.C.: U.S. Department of Defense, March 21, 2002).

65. Spencer J. Crona and Neal A. Richardson, "Justice for War Criminals of Invisible Armies: A New Legal and Military Approach to Terrorism," *Oklahoma City University Law Review* 21 (1996), 371–374.

66. *Korematsu v. United States*, 323 U.S. 214 (1944).

67. 124 S.Ct. 2686 (2004).

68. 124 S.Ct. 2633 (2004).

69. *Rumsfeld v. Padilla*, 124 S.Ct. 2711 (2004).

70. *Padilla v. Hanft*, ___ F.3d ___ (4th Cir. 2005).

71. Rowan Scarborough, "Military Tribunals to Begin for Gitmo Detainees," *Washington Times* (July 19, 2005), A3.

72. Deborah J. Daniels, "The Challenge of Domestic Terrorism to American Criminal Justice," *Corrections Today* (December 1, 2002).

73. "Woman Accused of Threatening to Kill Michael Schiavo," *Chicago Sun Times* (April 7, 2005), 36.

74. Internet Fraud Complaint Center, *IFCC 2001 Internet Fraud Report: January 1, 2001–December 31, 2001* (Washington, D.C.: Federal Bureau of Investigation and National White Collar Crime Center, 2003), 5.

75. Internet Crime Complaint Center, *IC3 2004 Internet Fraud Crime Report, January 1, 2004–December 31, 2004* (Washington, D.C.: National White Collar Crime Center and Federal Bureau of Investigation, 2005), 3.

76. *Ibid.*

77. Federal Trade Commission, *Identity Theft Survey Report* (McLean, VA: Synovate, September 2003), 7.

78. Jim Middlemiss, "Gone Phishing," *Wall Street & Technology* (August 2004), 38.

79. Arizona Revised Statute Ann. Section 2921(E) (West Supp. 1997).

80. April Terreri, "Securing Your Company's Data," *Business NH Magazine* (September 1, 2004), 24.

81. Lawrence A. Gordon, Martin P. Loeb, William Lucyshyn, and Robert Richardson, *2005 CSI/FBI Computer Crime*

and Security Survey (San Francisco: Computer Security Institute, 2005), 7.

82. *Ibid.*

83. Amanda Lenhart, Mary Madden, and Paul Hitlin, *Teens and Technology* (Washington, D.C.: Pew Internet and American Life Project, July 27, 2005), ii.

84. Joseph V. DeMarco, *It's Not Just Fun and "War Games"— Juveniles and Computer Crimes* (Washington, D.C.: U.S. Department of Justice, 2001).

85. *Ibid.*

86. Saul Hansell, "Junk E-Mail and Fraud Are Focus of Crackdown," *New York Times* (August 25, 2004), C1.

87. 15 U.S.C. Sections 7701–7713 (2003).

88. *Second Annual BSA and IDC Global Software Piracy Study* (Washington, D.C.: Business Software Alliance, May 2005), 2, 5.

89. *The Recording Industry 2005 Commercial Piracy Report* (London: International Federation of the Phonographic Industry, June 2005), 4.

90. 18 U.S.C. Section 23199(c) (1998).

91. 17 U.S.C. Sections 2301 *et seq.* (1998).

92. 534 U.S. ___ (2005).

93. Internet Filter Review, "Internet Pornography Statistics," at **http://internet-filter-review.toptenreviews.com/ internet-pornography-statistics.html**.

94. Jeffrey Sparshott, "WTO Lets U.S. Limit Internet Gambling," *Washington Times* (April 8, 2005), C8.

95. Alison Gerber, "Police Perplexed in Dealing with Cybercrime," *USA Today* (August 29, 2000), 5A.

96. Thomas T. Kubic, "Statement for the Record on the FBI's Perspective on the Cyber Crime Problem," delivered before the House Committee on the Judiciary Subcommittee on Crime (June 12, 2001).

97. Heather Jacobson and Rebecca Green, "Computer Crimes," *American Criminal Law Review* (Spring 2002), 283.

98. Brian Grow, "Hacker Hunters," *BusinessWeek* (May 30, 2005), 80–82.

99. Quoted in Amy Harmon, "As Digital Vandals Disrupt the Internet, a Call for Oversight," *New York Times* (September 1, 2003), A1.

100. Quoted in Frank James, "Teen Held in Net Attack, but Bigger Fears Remain," *Chicago Tribune* (August 30, 2003), 1.

101. "The Mouse That Might Roar," *Economist* (October 26, 2002), 19.

102. "Network Links Watchful Eyes around State," *New Jersey Record* (August 26, 2004), A1.

103. Pub. L. No. 109-13 (2005).

104. *Katz v. United States,* 389 U.S. 347, 350–351 (1967).

105. Privacy Act of 1974, 5 U.S.C. Section 552(a) (1999).

106. USA PATRIOT Act, Sections 355, 356, 358, 507.

107. "Matrix Resurrected: Florida Looks at Successor to Anticrime Database," *Law Enforcement News* (July 2005), 4.

108. *Ibid.*

109. Quoted in Robert O'Harrow, Jr., "U.S. Backs Florida's New Counterterrorism Database," *Washington Post* (August 6, 2003), A1.

110. Robert O'Harrow, Jr., "Profiling System Advances," *International Herald Tribune* (December 26, 2002), 9.

111. Executive Summary, *The Final Report of the National Commission on Terrorist Attacks Upon the United States,* quoted in "9/11 Commission Says Former INS Not Seen as Counterterrorism Tool before Attacks, Should Be in the Future," *Interpreter Releases* (August 9, 2004), 1048.

112. Chadwick M. Graham, "Defeating an Invisible Enemy: The Western Superpowers' Efforts to Combat Terrorism by Fighting Illegal Immigration," *Transnational Law & Contemporary Problems* (Fall 2004), 286.

113. Mimi Hall, "Despite New Technology, Border Patrol Overwhelmed," *USA Today* (February 23, 2005), 10A.

114. Quoted in Faye Bowers, "U.S.-Mexican Border as a Terror Risk," *Christian Science Monitor* (March 22, 2005), 1.

115. Hall.

116. Frank James, "U.S. Tracks Immigrants with Device," *Chicago Tribune* (April 4, 2005), A1.

117. *Ibid.*

118. Quoted in Hall.

119. Richard Marosi, "Criminals at the Border Thwarted by Their Own Hands," *Los Angeles Times* (February 19, 2005), A1.

120. Rachel L. Swarns, "U.S. to Give Border Patrol Agents the Power to Deport Illegal Aliens," *New York Times* (August 11, 2004), A1.

121. Melissa Blair, "Terrorism, America's Porous Borders, and the Role of the Invasion Clause Post-9/11/2001," *Marquette Law Review* (Fall 2003), 167.

122. Michelle Malkin, *Invasion: How America Still Welcomes Terrorists, Criminals, and Other Foreign Menaces to Our Shores* (Washington, D.C.: Regnery, 2002), 165.

123. Graham, 285.

Appendix A

THE CONSTITUTION OF THE UNITED STATES

PREAMBLE

We the People of the United States, in Order to form a more perfect Union, establish Justice, insure domestic Tranquility, provide for the common defence, promote the general Welfare, and secure the Blessings of Liberty to ourselves and our Posterity, do ordain and establish this Constitution for the United States of America.

ARTICLE I

Section 1. All legislative Powers herein granted shall be vested in a Congress of the United States, which shall consist of a Senate and House of Representatives.

Section 2. The House of Representatives shall be composed of Members chosen every second Year by the People of the several States, and the Electors in each State shall have the Qualifications requisite for Electors of the most numerous Branch of the State Legislature.

No Person shall be a Representative who shall not have attained to the Age of twenty five Years, and been seven Years a Citizen of the United States, and who shall not, when elected, be an Inhabitant of that State in which he shall be chosen.

Representatives and direct Taxes shall be apportioned among the several States which may be included within this Union, according to their respective Numbers, which shall be determined by adding to the whole Number of free Persons, including those bound to Service for a Term of Years, and excluding Indians not taxed, three fifths of all other Persons. The actual Enumeration shall be made within three Years after the first Meeting of the Congress of the United States, and within every subsequent Term of ten Years, in such Manner as they shall by Law direct. The Number of Representatives shall not exceed one for every thirty Thousand, but each State shall have at Least one Representative; and until such enumeration shall be made, the State of New Hampshire shall be entitled to chuse three, Massachusetts eight, Rhode Island and Providence Plantations one, Connecticut five, New York six, New Jersey four, Pennsylvania eight, Delaware one, Maryland six, Virginia ten, North Carolina five, South Carolina five, and Georgia three.

When vacancies happen in the Representation from any State, the Executive Authority thereof shall issue Writs of Election to fill such Vacancies.

The House of Representatives shall chuse their Speaker and other Officers; and shall have the sole Power of Impeachment.

Section 3. The Senate of the United States shall be composed of two Senators from each State, chosen by the Legislature thereof, for six Years; and each Senator shall have one Vote.

Immediately after they shall be assembled in Consequence of the first Election, they shall be divided as equally as may be into three Classes. The Seats of the Senators of the first Class shall be vacated at the Expiration of the second Year, of the second Class at the Expiration of the fourth Year, and of the third Class at the Expiration of the sixth Year, so that one third may be chosen every second Year; and if Vacancies happen by Resignation, or otherwise, during the Recess of the Legislature of any State, the Executive thereof may make temporary Appointments until the next Meeting of the Legislature, which shall then fill such Vacancies.

No Person shall be a Senator who shall not have attained to the Age of thirty Years, and been nine Years a Citizen of the United States, and who shall not, when elected, be an Inhabitant of that State for which he shall be chosen.

The Vice President of the United States shall be President of the Senate, but shall have no Vote, unless they be equally divided.

The Senate shall chuse their other Officers, and also a President pro tempore, in the Absence of the Vice President, or when he shall exercise the Office of President of the United States.

The Senate shall have the sole Power to try all Impeachments. When sitting for that Purpose, they shall be on Oath or Affirmation. When the President of the United States is tried, the Chief Justice shall preside: And no Person shall be convicted without the Concurrence of two thirds of the Members present.

Judgment in Cases of Impeachment shall not extend further than to removal from Office, and disqualification to hold and enjoy any Office of honor, Trust, or Profit under the United States: but the Party convicted shall nevertheless be liable and subject to Indictment, Trial, Judgment, and Punishment, according to Law.

Section 4. The Times, Places and Manner of holding Elections for Senators and Representatives, shall be prescribed in each State by the Legislature thereof; but the Congress may at any time by Law make or alter such Regulations, except as to the Places of chusing Senators.

The Congress shall assemble at least once in every Year, and such Meeting shall be on the first Monday in December, unless they shall by Law appoint a different Day.

Section 5. Each House shall be the Judge of the Elections, Returns, and Qualifications of its own Members, and a Majority of each shall constitute a Quorum to do Business; but a smaller Number may adjourn from day to day, and may be authorized to compel the Attendance of absent Members, in such Manner, and under such Penalties as each House may provide.

Each House may determine the Rules of its Proceedings, punish its Members for disorderly Behavior, and, with the Concurrence of two thirds, expel a Member.

Each House shall keep a Journal of its Proceedings, and from time to time publish the same, excepting such Parts as may in their Judgment require Secrecy; and the Yeas and Nays of the Members of either House on any question shall, at the Desire of one fifth of those Present, be entered on the Journal.

Neither House, during the Session of Congress, shall, without the Consent of the other, adjourn for more than three days, nor to any other Place than that in which the two Houses shall be sitting.

Section 6. The Senators and Representatives shall receive a Compensation for their Services, to be ascertained by Law, and paid out of the Treasury of the United States. They shall in all Cases, except Treason, Felony and Breach of the Peace, be privileged from Arrest during their Attendance at the Session of their respective Houses, and in going to and returning from the same; and for any Speech or Debate in either House, they shall not be questioned in any other Place.

No Senator or Representative shall, during the Time for which he was elected, be appointed to any civil Office under the Authority of the United States, which shall have been created, or the Emoluments whereof shall have been increased during such time; and no Person holding any Office under the United States, shall be a Member of either House during his Continuance in Office.

Section 7. All Bills for raising Revenue shall originate in the House of Representatives; but the Senate may propose or concur with Amendments as on other Bills.

Every Bill which shall have passed the House of Representatives and the Senate, shall, before it become a Law, be presented to the President of the United States; If he approve he shall sign it, but if not he shall return it, with his Objections to the House in which it shall have originated, who shall enter the Objections at large on their Journal, and proceed to reconsider it. If after such Reconsideration two thirds of that House shall agree to pass the Bill, it shall be sent together with the Objections, to the other House, by which it shall likewise be reconsidered, and if approved by two thirds of that House, it shall become a Law. But in all such Cases the Votes of both Houses shall be determined by Yeas and Nays, and the Names of the Persons voting for and against the Bill shall be entered on the Journal of each House respectively. If any Bill shall not be returned by the President within ten Days (Sundays excepted) after it shall have been presented to him, the Same shall be a Law, in like Manner as if he had signed it, unless the Congress by their Adjournment prevent its Return in which Case it shall not be a Law.

Every Order, Resolution, or Vote, to which the Concurrence of the Senate and House of Representatives may be necessary (except on a question of Adjournment) shall be presented to the President of the United States; and before the Same shall take Effect, shall be approved by him, or being disapproved by him, shall be repassed by two thirds of the Senate and House of Representatives, according to the Rules and Limitations prescribed in the Case of a Bill.

Section 8. The Congress shall have Power To lay and collect Taxes, Duties, Imposts and Excises, to pay the Debts and provide for the common Defence and general Welfare of the United States; but all Duties, Imposts and Excises shall be uniform throughout the United States;

To borrow Money on the credit of the United States;

To regulate Commerce with foreign Nations, and among the several States, and with the Indian Tribes;

To establish an uniform Rule of Naturalization, and uniform Laws on the subject of Bankruptcies throughout the United States;

To coin Money, regulate the Value thereof, and of foreign Coin, and fix the Standard of Weights and Measures;

To provide for the Punishment of counterfeiting the Securities and current Coin of the United States;

To establish Post Offices and post Roads;

To promote the Progress of Science and useful Arts, by securing for limited Times to Authors and Inventors the exclusive Right to their respective Writings and Discoveries;

To constitute Tribunals inferior to the supreme Court;

To define and punish Piracies and Felonies committed on the high Seas, and Offenses against the Law of Nations;

To declare War, grant Letters of Marque and Reprisal, and make Rules concerning Captures on Land and Water;

To raise and support Armies, but no Appropriation of Money to that Use shall be for a longer Term than two Years;

To provide and maintain a Navy;

To make Rules for the Government and Regulation of the land and naval Forces;

To provide for calling forth the Militia to execute the Laws of the Union, suppress Insurrections and repel Invasions;

To provide for organizing, arming, and disciplining, the Militia, and for governing such Part of them as may be employed in the Service of the United States, reserving to the States respectively, the Appointment of the Officers, and the Authority of training the Militia according to the discipline prescribed by Congress;

To exercise exclusive Legislation in all Cases whatsoever, over such District (not exceeding ten Miles square) as may, by Cession of particular States, and the Acceptance of Congress, become the Seat of the Government of the United States, and to exercise like Authority over all Places purchased by the Consent of the Legislature of the State in which the Same shall be, for the Erection of Forts, Magazines, Arsenals, dock-Yards, and other needful Buildings;—And

To make all Laws which shall be necessary and proper for carrying into Execution the foregoing Powers, and all other Powers vested by this Constitution in the Government of the United States, or in any Department or Officer thereof.

Section 9. The Migration or Importation of such Persons as any of the States now existing shall think proper to admit, shall not be prohibited by the Congress prior to the Year one thousand eight hundred and eight, but a Tax or duty may be imposed on such Importation, not exceeding ten dollars for each Person.

The privilege of the Writ of Habeas Corpus shall not be suspended, unless when in Cases of Rebellion or Invasion the public Safety may require it.

No Bill of Attainder or ex post facto Law shall be passed.

No Capitation, or other direct, Tax shall be laid, unless in Proportion to the Census or Enumeration herein before directed to be taken.

No Tax or Duty shall be laid on Articles exported from any State.

No Preference shall be given by any Regulation of Commerce or Revenue to the Ports of one State over those of another: nor shall Vessels bound to, or from, one State be obliged to enter, clear, or pay Duties in another.

No Money shall be drawn from the Treasury, but in Consequence of Appropriations made by Law; and a regular Statement and Account of the Receipts and Expenditures of all public Money shall be published from time to time.

No Title of Nobility shall be granted by the United States: And no Person holding any Office of Profit or Trust under them, shall, without the Consent of the Congress, accept of any present, Emolument, Office, or Title, of any kind whatever, from any King, Prince, or foreign State.

Section 10. No State shall enter into any Treaty, Alliance, or Confederation; grant Letters of Marque and Reprisal; coin Money; emit Bills of Credit; make any Thing but gold and silver Coin a Tender in Payment of Debts; pass any Bill of Attainder, ex post facto Law, or Law impairing the Obligation of Contracts, or grant any Title of Nobility.

No State shall, without the Consent of the Congress, lay any Imposts or Duties on Imports or Exports, except what may be absolutely necessary for executing its inspection Laws: and the net Produce of all Duties and Imposts, laid by any State on Imports or Exports, shall be for the Use of the Treasury of the

United States; and all such Laws shall be subject to the Revision and Controul of the Congress.

No State shall, without the Consent of Congress, lay any Duty of Tonnage, keep Troops, or Ships of War in time of Peace, enter into any Agreement or Compact with another State, or with a foreign Power, or engage in War, unless actually invaded, or in such imminent Danger as will not admit of delay.

ARTICLE II

Section 1.   The executive Power shall be vested in a President of the United States of America. He shall hold his Office during the Term of four Years, and, together with the Vice President, chosen for the same Term, be elected, as follows:

Each State shall appoint, in such Manner as the Legislature thereof may direct, a Number of Electors, equal to the whole Number of Senators and Representatives to which the State may be entitled in the Congress; but no Senator or Representative, or Person holding an Office of Trust or Profit under the United States, shall be appointed an Elector.

The Electors shall meet in their respective States, and vote by Ballot for two Persons, of whom one at least shall not be an Inhabitant of the same State with themselves. And they shall make a List of all the Persons voted for, and of the Number of Votes for each; which List they shall sign and certify, and transmit sealed to the Seat of the Government of the United States, directed to the President of the Senate. The President of the Senate shall, in the Presence of the Senate and House of Representatives, open all the Certificates, and the Votes shall then be counted. The Person having the greatest Number of Votes shall be the President, if such Number be a Majority of the whole Number of Electors appointed; and if there be more than one who have such Majority, and have an equal Number of Votes, then the House of Representatives shall immediately chuse by Ballot one of them for President; and if no Person have a Majority, then from the five highest on the List the said House shall in like Manner chuse the President. But in chusing the President, the Votes shall be taken by States, the Representation from each State having one Vote; A quorum for this Purpose shall consist of a Member or Members from two thirds of the States, and a Majority of all the States shall be necessary to a Choice. In every Case, after the Choice of the President, the Person having the greater Number of Votes of the Electors shall be the Vice President. But if there should

remain two or more who have equal Votes, the Senate shall chuse from them by Ballot the Vice President.

The Congress may determine the Time of chusing the Electors, and the Day on which they shall give their Votes; which Day shall be the same throughout the United States.

No person except a natural born Citizen, or a Citizen of the United States, at the time of the Adoption of this Constitution, shall be eligible to the Office of President; neither shall any Person be eligible to that Office who shall not have attained to the Age of thirty five Years, and been fourteen Years a Resident within the United States.

In Case of the Removal of the President from Office, or of his Death, Resignation or Inability to discharge the Powers and Duties of the said Office, the same shall devolve on the Vice President, and the Congress may by Law provide for the Case of Removal, Death, Resignation or Inability, both of the President and Vice President, declaring what Officer shall then act as President, and such Officer shall act accordingly, until the Disability be removed, or a President shall be elected.

The President shall, at stated Times, receive for his Services, a Compensation, which shall neither be increased nor diminished during the Period for which he shall have been elected, and he shall not receive within that Period any other Emolument from the United States, or any of them.

Before he enter on the Execution of his Office, he shall take the following Oath or Affirmation: "I do solemnly swear (or affirm) that I will faithfully execute the Office of President of the United States, and will to the best of my Ability, preserve, protect and defend the Constitution of the United States."

Section 2.   The President shall be Commander in Chief of the Army and Navy of the United States, and of the Militia of the several States, when called into the actual Service of the United States; he may require the Opinion, in writing, of the principal Officer in each of the executive Departments, upon any Subject relating to the Duties of their respective Offices, and he shall have Power to grant Reprieves and Pardons for Offenses against the United States, except in Cases of Impeachment.

He shall have Power, by and with the Advice and Consent of the Senate to make Treaties, provided two thirds of the Senators present concur; and he shall nominate, and by and with the Advice and Consent of the Senate, shall appoint Ambassadors, other public Ministers and Consuls, Judges of the supreme Court, and all other Officers of the United States, whose Appointments are not herein otherwise provided for, and which shall be established by Law; but the Congress may by Law vest the Appointment of such inferior Officers, as they think proper, in the President alone, in the Courts of Law, or in the Heads of Departments.

The President shall have Power to fill up all Vacancies that may happen during the Recess of the Senate, by granting Commissions which shall expire at the End of their next Session.

Section 3.   He shall from time to time give to the Congress Information of the State of the Union, and recommend to their Consideration such Measures as he shall judge necessary and expedient; he may, on extraordinary Occasions, convene both Houses, or either of them, and in Case of Disagreement between them, with Respect to the Time of Adjournment, he may adjourn them to such Time as he shall think proper; he shall receive Ambassadors and other public Ministers; he shall take Care that the Laws be faithfully executed, and shall Commission all the Officers of the United States.

Section 4.   The President, Vice President and all civil Officers of the United States, shall be removed from Office on Impeachment for, and Conviction of, Treason, Bribery, or other high Crimes and Misdemeanors.

ARTICLE III

Section 1.   The judicial Power of the United States, shall be vested in one supreme Court, and in such inferior Courts as the Congress may from time to time ordain and establish. The Judges, both of the supreme and inferior Courts, shall hold their Offices during good Behaviour, and shall, at stated Times, receive for their Services a Compensation, which shall not be diminished during their Continuance in Office.

Section 2.   The judicial Power shall extend to all Cases, in Law and Equity, arising under this Constitution, the Laws of the United States, and Treaties made, or which shall be made, under their Authority;—to all Cases affecting Ambassadors, other public Ministers and Consuls;—to all Cases of admiralty and maritime Jurisdiction;—to Controversies to which the United States shall be a Party;—to Controversies between two or more States;—between a State and Citizens of another State;—between Citizens of different States;—between Citizens of the same State claiming Lands under Grants of different States, and between a State, or the Citizens thereof, and foreign States, Citizens or Subjects.

In all Cases affecting Ambassadors, other public Ministers and Consuls, and those in which a State shall be a Party, the supreme Court shall have original Jurisdiction. In all the other Cases before mentioned, the supreme Court shall have appellate Jurisdiction, both as to Law and Fact, with such Exceptions, and under such Regulations as the Congress shall make.

The Trial of all Crimes, except in Cases of Impeachment, shall be by Jury; and such Trial shall be held in the State where the said Crimes shall have been committed; but when not committed within any State, the Trial shall be at such Place or Places as the Congress may by Law have directed.

Section 3.   Treason against the United States, shall consist only in levying War against them, or, in adhering to their Enemies, giving them Aid and Comfort. No Person shall be convicted of Treason unless on the Testimony of two Witnesses to the same overt Act, or on Confession in open Court.

The Congress shall have Power to declare the Punishment of Treason, but no Attainder of Treason shall work Corruption of Blood, or Forfeiture except during the Life of the Person attainted.

ARTICLE IV

Section 1.   Full Faith and Credit shall be given in each State to the public Acts, Records, and judicial Proceedings of every other State. And the Congress may by general Laws prescribe the Manner in which such Acts, Records and Proceedings shall be proved, and the Effect thereof.

Section 2.   The Citizens of each State shall be entitled to all Privileges and Immunities of Citizens in the several States.

A Person charged in any State with Treason, Felony, or other Crime, who shall flee from Justice, and be found in another State, shall on Demand of the executive Authority of the State from which he fled, be delivered up, to be removed to the State having Jurisdiction of the Crime.

No Person held to Service or Labour in one State, under the Laws thereof, escaping into another, shall, in Consequence of any Law or Regulation therein, be discharged from such Service or Labour, but shall be delivered up on Claim of the Party to whom such Service or Labour may be due.

Section 3. New States may be admitted by the Congress into this Union; but no new State shall be formed or erected within the Jurisdiction of any other State; nor any State be formed by the Junction of two or more States, or Parts of States, without the Consent of the Legislatures of the States concerned as well as of the Congress.

The Congress shall have Power to dispose of and make all needful Rules and Regulations respecting the Territory or other Property belonging to the United States; and nothing in this Constitution shall be so construed as to Prejudice any Claims of the United States, or of any particular State.

Section 4. The United States shall guarantee to every State in this Union a Republican Form of Government, and shall protect each of them against Invasion; and on Application of the Legislature, or of the Executive (when the Legislature cannot be convened) against domestic Violence.

ARTICLE V

The Congress, whenever two thirds of both Houses shall deem it necessary, shall propose Amendments to this Constitution, or, on the Application of the Legislatures of two thirds of the several States, shall call a Convention for proposing Amendments, which, in either Case, shall be valid to all Intents and Purposes, as part of this Constitution, when ratified by the Legislatures of three fourths of the several States, or by Conventions in three fourths thereof, as the one or the other Mode of Ratification may be proposed by the Congress; Provided that no Amendment which may be made prior to the Year One thousand eight hundred and eight shall in any Manner affect the first and fourth Clauses in the Ninth Section of the first Article; and that no State, without its Consent, shall be deprived of its equal Suffrage in the Senate.

ARTICLE VI

All Debts contracted and Engagements entered into, before the Adoption of this Constitution shall be as valid against the United States under this Constitution, as under the Confederation.

This Constitution, and the Laws of the United States which shall be made in Pursuance thereof; and all Treaties made, or which shall be made, under the Authority of the United States, shall be the supreme Law of the Land; and the Judges in every State shall be bound thereby, any Thing in the Constitution or Laws of any State to the Contrary notwithstanding.

The Senators and Representatives before mentioned, and the Members of the several State Legislatures, and all executive and judicial Officers, both of the United States and of the several States, shall be bound by Oath or Affirmation, to support this Constitution; but no religious Test shall ever be required as a Qualification to any Office or public Trust under the United States.

ARTICLE VII

The Ratification of the Conventions of nine States shall be sufficient for the Establishment of this Constitution between the States so ratifying the Same.

AMENDMENT I [1791]

Congress shall make no law respecting an establishment of religion, or prohibiting the free exercise thereof; or abridging the freedom of speech, or of the press; or the right of the people peaceably to assembly, and to petition the Government for a redress of grievances.

AMENDMENT II [1791]

A well regulated Militia, being necessary to the security of a free State, the right of the people to keep and bear Arms, shall not be infringed.

AMENDMENT III [1791]

No Soldier shall, in time of peace be quartered in any house, without the consent of the Owner, nor in time of war, but in a manner to be prescribed by law.

AMENDMENT IV [1791]

The right of the people to be secure in their persons, houses, papers, and effects, against unreasonable searches and seizures, shall not be violated, and no Warrants shall issue, but upon probable cause, supported by Oath or affirmation, and particularly describing the place to be searched, and the persons or things to be seized.

AMENDMENT V [1791]

No person shall be held to answer for a capital, or otherwise infamous crime, unless on a presentment or indictment of a Grand Jury, except in cases arising in the land or naval forces, or in the Militia, when in actual service in time of War or public danger; nor shall any person be subject for the same offence to be twice put in jeopardy of life or limb; nor shall be compelled in any criminal case to be a witness against himself, nor be deprived of life, liberty, or property, without due process of law; nor shall private property be taken for public use, without just compensation.

Amendment VI [1791]

In all criminal prosecutions, the accused shall enjoy the right to a speedy and public trial, by an impartial jury of the State and district wherein the crime shall have been committed, which district shall have been previously ascertained by law, and to be informed of the nature and cause of the accusation; to be confronted with the witnesses against him; to have compulsory process for obtaining witnesses in his favor, and to have the Assistance of Counsel for his defence.

Amendment VII [1791]

In Suits at common law, where the value in controversy shall exceed twenty dollars, the right of trial by jury shall be preserved, and no fact tried by jury, shall be otherwise reexamined in any Court of the United States, than according to the rules of the common law.

Amendment VIII [1791]

Excessive bail shall not be required, nor excessive fines imposed, nor cruel and unusual punishments inflicted.

Amendment IX [1791]

The enumeration in the Constitution, of certain rights, shall not be construed to deny or disparage others retained by the people.

Amendment X [1791]

The powers not delegated to the United States by the Constitution, nor prohibited by it to the States, are reserved to the States respectively, or to the people.

Amendment XI [1798]

The Judicial power of the United States shall not be construed to extend to any suit in law or equity, commenced or prosecuted against one of the United States by Citizens of another State, or by Citizens or Subjects of any Foreign State.

Amendment XII [1804]

The Electors shall meet in their respective states, and vote by ballot for President and Vice-President, one of whom, at least, shall not be an inhabitant of the same state with themselves; they shall name in their ballots the person voted for as President, and in distinct ballots the person voted for as Vice-President, and they shall make distinct lists of all persons voted for as President, and of all persons voted for as Vice-President, and of the number of votes for each, which lists they shall sign and certify, and transmit sealed to the seat of the government of the United States, directed to the President of the Senate;—The President of the Senate shall, in the presence of the Senate and House of Representatives, open all the certificates and the votes shall then be counted;—The person having the greatest number of votes for President, shall be the President, if such number be a majority of the whole number of Electors appointed; and if no person have such majority, then from the persons having the highest numbers not exceeding three on the list of those voted for as President, the House of Representatives shall choose immediately, by ballot, the President. But in choosing the President, the votes shall be taken by states, the representation from each state having one vote; a quorum for this purpose shall consist of a member or members from two-thirds of the states, and a majority of all states shall be necessary to a choice. And if the House of Representatives shall not choose a President whenever the right of choice shall devolve upon them, before the fourth day of March next following, then the Vice-President shall act as President, as in the case of the death or other constitutional disability of the President.—The person having the greatest number of votes as Vice-President, shall be the Vice-President, if such number be a majority of the whole number of Electors appointed, and if no person have a majority, then from the two highest numbers on the list, the Senate shall choose the Vice-President; a quorum for the purpose shall consist of two-thirds of the whole number of Senators, and a majority of the whole number shall be necessary to a choice. But no person constitutionally ineligible to the office of President shall be eligible to that of Vice-President of the United States.

Amendment XIII [1865]

Section 1. Neither slavery nor involuntary servitude, except as a punishment for crime whereof the party shall have been duly convicted, shall exist within the United States, or any place subject to their jurisdiction.

Section 2.   Congress shall have power to enforce this article by appropriate legislation.

AMENDMENT XIV [1868]

Section 1.   All persons born or naturalized in the United States, and subject to the jurisdiction thereof, are citizens of the United States and of the State wherein they reside. No State shall make or enforce any law which shall abridge the privileges or immunities of citizens of the United States; nor shall any State deprive any person of life, liberty, or property, without due process of law; nor deny to any person within its jurisdiction the equal protection of the laws.

Section 2.   Representatives shall be apportioned among the several States according to their respective numbers, counting the whole number of persons in each State, excluding Indians not taxed. But when the right to vote at any election for the choice of electors for President and Vice President of the United States, Representatives in Congress, the Executive and Judicial officers of a State, or the members of the Legislature thereof, is denied to any of the male inhabitants of such State, being twenty-one years of age, and citizens of the United States, or in any way abridged, except for participation in rebellion, or other crime, the basis of representation therein shall be reduced in the proportion which the number of such male citizens shall bear to the whole number of male citizens twenty-one years of age in such State.

Section 3.   No person shall be a Senator or Representative in Congress, or elector of President and Vice President, or hold any office, civil or military, under the United States, or under any State, who having previously taken an oath, as a member of Congress, or as an officer of the United States, or as a member of any State legislature, or as an executive or judicial officer of any State, to support the Constitution of the United States, shall have engaged in insurrection or rebellion against the same, or given aid or comfort to the enemies thereof. But Congress may by a vote of two-thirds of each House, remove such disability.

Section 4.   The validity of the public debt of the United States, authorized by law, including debts incurred for payment of pensions and bounties for services in suppressing insurrection or rebellion, shall not be questioned. But neither the United States nor any State shall assume or pay any debt or obligation incurred in aid of insurrection or rebellion against the United States, or any claim for the loss or emancipation of any slave; but all such debts, obligations and claims shall be held illegal and void.

Section 5.   The Congress shall have power to enforce, by appropriate legislation, the provisions of this article.

AMENDMENT XV [1870]

Section 1.   The right of citizens of the United States to vote shall not be denied or abridged by the United States or by any State on account of race, color, or previous condition of servitude.

Section 2.   The Congress shall have power to enforce this article by appropriate legislation.

AMENDMENT XVI [1913]

The Congress shall have power to lay and collect taxes on incomes, from whatever source derived, without apportionment among the several States, and without regard to any census or enumeration.

AMENDMENT XVII [1913]

Section 1.   The Senate of the United States shall be composed of two Senators from each State, elected by the people thereof, for six years; and each Senator shall have one vote. The electors in each State shall have the qualifications requisite for electors of the most numerous branch of the State legislatures.

Section 2.   When vacancies happen in the representation of any State in the Senate, the executive authority of such State shall issue writs of election to fill such vacancies: *Provided,* That the legislature of any State may empower the executive thereof to make temporary appointments until the people fill the vacancies by election as the legislature may direct.

Section 3.   This amendment shall not be so construed as to affect the election or term of any Senator chosen before it becomes valid as part of the Constitution.

AMENDMENT XVIII [1919]

Section 1.   After one year from the ratification of this article the manufacture, sale, or transportation of intoxicating liquors within, the importation thereof into, or the exportation thereof from the United States and all territory subject to the jurisdiction thereof for beverage purposes is hereby prohibited.

Section 2.   The Congress and the several States shall have concurrent power to enforce this article by appropriate legislation.

Section 3. This article shall be inoperative unless it shall have been ratified as an amendment to the Constitution by the legislatures of the several States, as provided in the Constitution, within seven years from the date of the submission hereof to the States by the Congress.

AMENDMENT XIX [1920]

Section 1. The right of citizens of the United States to vote shall not be denied or abridged by the United States or by any State on account of sex.

Section 2. Congress shall have power to enforce this article by appropriate legislation.

AMENDMENT XX [1933]

Section 1. The terms of the President and Vice President shall end at noon on the 20th day of January, and the terms of Senators and Representatives at noon on the 3d day of January, of the years in which such terms would have ended if this article had not been ratified; and the terms of their successors shall then begin.

Section 2. The Congress shall assemble at least once in every year, and such meeting shall begin at noon on the 3d day of January, unless they shall by law appoint a different day.

Section 3. If, at the time fixed for the beginning of the term of the President, the President elect shall have died, the Vice President elect shall become President. If the President shall not have been chosen before the time fixed for the beginning of his term, or if the President elect shall have failed to qualify, then the Vice President elect shall act as President until a President shall have qualified; and the Congress may by law provide for the case wherein neither a President elect nor a Vice President elect shall have qualified, declaring who shall then act as President, or the manner in which one who is to act shall be selected, and such person shall act accordingly until a President or Vice President shall have qualified.

Section 4. The Congress may by law provide for the case of the death of any of the persons from whom the House of Representatives may choose a President whenever the right of choice shall have devolved upon them, and for the case of the death of any of the persons from whom the Senate may choose a Vice President whenever the right of choice shall have devolved upon them.

Section 5. Sections 1 and 2 shall take effect on the 15th day of October following the ratification of this article.

Section 6. This article shall be inoperative unless it shall have been ratified as an amendment to the Constitution by the legislatures of three-fourths of the several States within seven years from the date of its submission.

AMENDMENT XXI [1933]

Section 1. The eighteenth article of amendment to the Constitution of the United States is hereby repealed.

Section 2. The transportation or importation into any State, Territory, or possession of the United States for delivery or use therein of intoxicating liquors, in violation of the laws thereof, is hereby prohibited.

Section 3. This article shall be inoperative unless it shall have been ratified as an amendment to the Constitution by conventions in the several States, as provided in the Constitution, within seven years from the date of the submission hereof to the States by the Congress.

AMENDMENT XXII [1951]

Section 1. No person shall be elected to the office of the President more than twice, and no person who has held the office of President, or acted as President, for more than two years of a term to which some other person was elected President shall be elected to the office of President more than once. But this Article shall not apply to any person holding the office of President when this Article was proposed by the Congress, and shall not prevent any person who may be holding the office of President, or acting as President, during the term within which this Article becomes operative from holding the office of President or acting as President during the remainder of such term.

Section 2. This article shall be inoperative unless it shall have been ratified as an amendment to the Constitution by the legislatures of three-fourths of the several States within seven years from the date of its submission to the States by the Congress.

AMENDMENT XXIII [1961]

Section 1. The District constituting the seat of Government of the United States shall appoint in such manner as the Congress may direct:

A number of electors of President and Vice President equal to the whole number of Senators and

Representatives in Congress to which the District would be entitled if it were a State, but in no event more than the least populous state; they shall be in addition to those appointed by the states, but they shall be considered, for the purposes of the election of President and Vice President, to be electors appointed by a state; and they shall meet in the District and perform such duties as provided by the twelfth article of amendment.

Section 2. The Congress shall have power to enforce this article by appropriate legislation.

AMENDMENT XXIV [1964]

Section 1. The right of citizens of the United States to vote in any primary or other election for President or Vice President, for electors for President or Vice President, or for Senator or Representative in Congress, shall not be denied or abridged by the United States, or any State by reason of failure to pay any poll tax or other tax.

Section 2. The Congress shall have power to enforce this article by appropriate legislation.

AMENDMENT XXV [1967]

Section 1. In case of the removal of the President from office or of his death or resignation, the Vice President shall become President.

Section 2. Whenever there is a vacancy in the office of the Vice President, the President shall nominate a Vice President who shall take office upon confirmation by a majority vote of both Houses of Congress.

Section 3. Whenever the President transmits to the President pro tempore of the Senate and the Speaker of the House of Representatives his written declaration that he is unable to discharge the powers and duties of his office, and until he transmits to them a written declaration to the contrary, such powers and duties shall be discharged by the Vice President as Acting President.

Section 4. Whenever the Vice President and a majority of either the principal officers of the executive departments or of such other body as Congress may by law provide, transmit to the President pro tempore of the Senate and the Speaker of the House of

Representatives their written declaration that the President is unable to discharge the powers and duties of his office, the Vice President shall immediately assume the powers and duties of the office as Acting President.

Thereafter, when the President transmits to the President pro tempore of the Senate and the Speaker of the House of Representatives his written declaration that no inability exists, he shall resume the powers and duties of his office unless the Vice President and a majority of either the principal officers of the executive department or of such other body as Congress may by law provide, transmit within four days to the President pro tempore of the Senate and the Speaker of the House of Representatives their written declaration that the President is unable to discharge the powers and duties of his office. Thereupon Congress shall decide the issue, assembling within forty-eight hours for that purpose if not in session. If the Congress, within twenty-one days after receipt of the latter written declaration, or, if Congress is not in session, within twenty-one days after Congress is required to assemble, determines by two-thirds vote of both Houses that the President is unable to discharge the powers and duties of his office, the Vice President shall continue to discharge the same as Acting President; otherwise, the President shall resume the powers and duties of his office.

AMENDMENT XXVI [1971]

Section 1. The right of citizens of the United States, who are eighteen years of age or older, to vote shall not be denied or abridged by the United States or by any State on account of age.

Section 2. The Congress shall have power to enforce this article by appropriate legislation.

AMENDMENT XXVII [1992]

No law, varying the compensation for the services of the Senators and Representatives, shall take effect, until an election of Representatives shall have intervened.

Appendix B

4.1 The court refused to throw out the charges. Although Emil was unconscious at the time his car struck the schoolgirls, he had earlier made the decision to get behind the wheel despite the knowledge that he suffered from epileptic seizures. In other words, the *actus reus* in this crime was not Emil's driving into the girls, but his decision to drive in the first place. That decision was certainly voluntary and therefore satisfies the requirements of *actus reus*. Note that if Emil had never had an epileptic seizure before, and had no idea that he suffered from that malady, the court's decision would probably have been different. Source: *People v. Decina,* 138 N.E.2d 799 (1956). A briefed (summarized) version of this case can be found at **http://www.lectlaw.com/files/lws50.htm**. Scroll down the list to the case title to view the brief.

4.2 A jury found that Bernhard had reasonably believed that he was in danger of being physically attacked and that he acted reasonably to protect himself given what he thought was going to happen. Therefore, he was acquitted of all charges, save for one minor weapons violation. The case was very controversial, as many observers felt that the fact that Bernhard was white and his "assailants" were African American influenced the jury's decision. In other words, the jury might have felt that Bernhard's fear was reasonable only because of the racial make-up of the four young men. Source: *People v. Goetz,* 506 N.Y.S.2d 18 (1986). More information about this trial can be found at **http://en.wikipedia.org/wiki/Bernhard_Goetz**.

6.1 The Court, while recognizing that this case belonged in the gray area "between excessive and acceptable force," threw out Haugen's lawsuit against Officer Brosseau. It ruled that even though Brosseau was erroneous in her belief that Haugen (who was unarmed and not wanted for any violent crimes) was a threat to others in the vicinity, her actions were rea-

sonable given the fact that he was a "disturbed felon, set on avoiding capture." The decision signals the Court's desire that judges give police officers the benefit of the doubt in "reasonable force" cases, and makes it very difficult to file a suit against law enforcement agents after questionable shootings. Source: *Brosseau v. Haugen,* 543 U.S. __ (2005). The full text of this case can be found online at **http://laws.findlaw.com/us/000/03-1261.html**.

7.1 The Court ruled that the evidence was valid and could be presented against Harold. If the police officers had known, or should have known, that the third floor contained two apartments before they entered Harold's residence, then they would have been required to search only Larry's lodging. But, the Court said, "honest mistakes" by police officers do not equal an "unreasonable search" under the Fourth Amendment. Source: *Maryland v. Garrison,* 480 U.S. 79 (1987). The full text of this case can be found online at **http://laws.lp.findlaw.com/getcase/us/480/79.html**.

9.1 The court ruled that Noel was indigent and therefore had a right to free counsel, despite the fact that he owned a car worth more than potential lawyer's fees. The court reasoned that defendants should not be expected to sell necessities such as homes or cars in order to pay for a lawyer when they are obviously living on a low income. If Noel had owned a luxury automobile, the court probably would have ruled differently: people do not have a "fundamental right" to expensive automobiles, only those that get them from Point A to Point B. Source: *State v. Mickle,* 525 P.2d 1108 (1974).

10.1 The appeals court found that the prosecution had provided a "race-neutral" reason for dismissing Rev. Robert Cook and affirmed the defendant's conviction. The court agreed that religion-based professionals such as pastors, ministers, and rabbis tend to be more sympathetic and that the trial court's decision to uphold the challenge was not "clearly erroneous." The subtext of this challenge is evident: the defendant's attorney felt that the fact that Rev. Robert Cook was a pastor was only a pretense to challenging his presence on the jury. The real reason was his race. This decision underscores a problem with the Supreme Court's ruling that peremptory challenges cannot be based on race: as long as attorneys can come up with another plausible reason for the challenge, members of racial minorities will continue to be discriminated against during *voir dire*. Source: Adam Liptak, "Court Rules That Lawyers May Keep Clergy Off Juries," *New York Times* (October 13, 2002), Section 1, page 31.

11.1   The trial judge, swayed by the arguments of the defendant's lawyer, sentenced Angela to eighty-nine days of community service and one day in jail. The Washington Supreme Court, however, overruled the sentence, saying that the trial judge's light sentence was not justified given the facts of the case. The

Supreme Court said it was up to the state legislature, and not individual judges, to decide whether an "altruistic background" can be used as a reason for leniency. Source: "High Court Says Judge Can't Levy Light Sentence," *Seattle Times* (June 24, 1995), A10.

14.1   The Court ruled that California could not continue its policy of assigning inmates to racially segregated cells unless the state could prove there was no other way of preventing racial gang violence. As this would be very difficult to do, the decision essentially ended the practice. The Court decided not to defer to prison officials' expertise and judgment in this instance, forcefully arguing that racial classifications may actually cause violence by reinforcing the idea that members of different racial groups represent a danger to one another. Source: *Johnson v. California*, 125 S.Ct. 1141 (2005). The full text of this case can be found online at **http://laws.findlaw.com/us/000/03-636.html**.

Appendix C

TABLE OF CASES

Glossary

A

Acquittal A declaration following a trial that the individual accused of the crime is innocent in the eyes of the law and thus absolved from the charges.

Actus Reus (pronounced *ak*-tus *ray*-uhs) A guilty (prohibited) act. The commission of a prohibited act is one of the two essential elements required for criminal liability, the other element being the intent to commit a crime.

Adjudicatory Hearing The process through which a juvenile court determines whether there is sufficient evidence to support the initial petition.

Administrative Law The body of law created by administrative agencies (in the form of rules, regulations, orders, and decisions) in order to carry out their duties and responsibilities.

Adversary System A legal system in which the prosecution and defense are opponents, or adversaries, and present their cases in the light most favorable to themselves. The court arrives at a just solution based on the evidence presented by the contestants and determines who wins and who loses.

Affidavit A written statement of facts, confirmed by the oath or affirmation of the party making it and made before a person having the authority to administer the oath or affirmation.

Age of Onset The age at which a juvenile first exhibits delinquent behavior. The earlier the age of onset, according to some observers, the greater the chance a person will become a career offender.

Aggravating Circumstances Any circumstances accompanying the commission of a crime that may justify a harsher sentence.

Aging Out A term used to explain the fact that criminal activity declines with age.

Alien A person who is not a citizen of a given country and therefore may not enjoy the same protections as citizens of that country.

***Allen* Charge** An instruction by a judge to a deadlocked jury with only a few dissenters that asks the jurors in the minority to reconsider the majority opinion.

Anomie A condition in which the individual suffers from the breakdown or absence of social norms. According to this theory, this condition occurs when a person is disconnected from these norms or rejects them as inconsistent with his or her personal goals.

Antiterrorism and Effective Death Penalty Act of 1996 (AEDPA) Legislation giving federal law enforcement officers the power to arrest and prosecute any individual who provides "material support or resources" to a "terrorist organization."

Appeal The process of seeking a higher court's review of a lower court's decision for the purpose of correcting or changing the lower court's judgment or decision.

Appellate Courts Courts that review decisions made by lower courts, such as trial courts. Also known as courts of appeals.

Arraignment A court proceeding in which the suspect is formally charged with the criminal offense stated in the indictment. The suspect enters a plea (guilty, not guilty, *nolo contendere*) in response.

Arrest To take into custody a person suspected of criminal activity. Police may use only reasonable levels of force in making an arrest.

Arrest Warrant A written order, based on probable cause and issued by a judge or magistrate, commanding that the person named on the warrant be arrested by the police.

Asset Forfeiture Law A statute that allows law enforcement agents to seize any equipment used in manufacturing, storing, or transporting illicit drugs and any profits or property gained from the sale of the drugs, as well as the drugs themselves.

Attorney General The chief law officer of a state; also, the chief law officer of the nation.

Attorney-Client Privilege A rule of evidence requiring that communications between a client and his or her attorney be kept confidential, unless the client consents to disclosure.

Authentication Establishing the genuineness of an item that is to be introduced as evidence in a trial.

Authority The power designated to an agent of the law over a person who has broken the law.

Automatic Transfer The process by which a juvenile is transferred to adult court as a matter of state law. In some states, for example, a juvenile who is suspected of murder is automatically transferred to adult court.

B

Bail The amount or conditions set by the court to ensure that an individual accused of a crime will appear for further criminal proceedings. If the accused person provides bail, whether in cash or by means of a bail bond, then she or he is released from jail.

Bail Bondsperson A businessperson who agrees, for a fee, to pay the bail amount if the accused fails to appear in court as ordered.

Bench Trial A trial conducted without a jury, in which a judge makes the determination of the defendant's guilt or innocence.

Beyond a Reasonable Doubt The standard used to determine the guilt or innocence of a person charged with a crime. To be guilty of a crime, a suspect must be proved guilty "beyond and to the exclusion of a reasonable doubt."

Bill of Rights The first ten amendments to the U.S. Constitution.

Blue Curtain A metaphorical term used to refer to the value placed on secrecy and the general mistrust of the outside world shared by many police officers.

Booking The process of entering a suspect's name, offense, and arrival time into the police log following her or his arrest.

***Boykin* Form** A form that must be completed by a defendant who pleads guilty; the defendant states that she or he has done so voluntarily and with full comprehension of the consequences.

Broken Windows Theory Wilson and Kelling's theory that a neighborhood in disrepair signals that criminal activity is tolerated in the area. Thus, by cracking down on quality-of-life crimes, police can reclaim the neighborhood and encourage law-abiding citizens to live and work there.

Bureaucracy A hierarchically structured administrative organization that carries out specific functions.

C

Capital Punishment The use of the death penalty to punish wrongdoers for certain crimes.

Case Attrition The process through which prosecutors, by deciding whether or not to prosecute each person arrested, effect an overall reduction in the number of persons prosecuted. As a result, the number of persons convicted and sentenced is much smaller than the number of persons arrested.

Case Law The rules of law announced in court decisions. Case law includes the aggregate of reported cases that interpret judicial precedents, statutes, regulations, and constitutional provisions.

Challenge for Cause A *voir dire* challenge for which an attorney states the reason why a prospective juror should not be included on the jury.

Charge The judge's instructions to the jury following the attorneys' closing arguments; the charge sets forth the rules of law that the jury must apply in reaching its decision, or verdict.

Child Abuse Mistreatment of children by causing physical, emotional, or sexual damage without any plausible explanation, such as an accident.

Child Neglect A form of child abuse in which the child is denied certain necessities such as shelter, food, care, and love. Neglect is justification for a government agency to assume responsibility for a child in place of the parents or legal guardian.

Choice Theory A school of criminology that holds that wrongdoers act as if they weigh the possible benefits of criminal or delinquent activity against the expected costs of being apprehended. When the benefits are greater than the expected costs, the offender will make a rational choice to commit a crime or delinquent act.

Chronic Offender A delinquent or criminal who commits multiple offenses and is considered part of a small group of wrongdoers who are responsible for a majority of the antisocial activity in any given community.

Circumstantial Evidence Indirect evidence that is offered to establish, by inference, the likelihood of a fact that is in question.

Citizen Oversight The process by which citizens review complaints brought against individual police officers or police departments. The citizens often do not have the power to discipline misconduct, but can recommend that action be taken by police administrators.

Civil Law The branch of law dealing with the definition and enforcement of all private or public rights, as opposed to criminal matters.

Classical Criminology A school of criminology based on the belief that individuals have free will to engage in any behavior, including criminal behavior. To deter criminal behavior, society must hold wrongdoers responsible for their actions by punishing them.

Closing Arguments Arguments made by each side's attorney after the cases for the plaintiff and defendant have been presented.

Common Law The body of law developed from custom or judicial decisions in English and U.S. courts and not attributable to a legislature.

Community Policing A policing philosophy that emphasizes community support for and cooperation with the police in preventing crime. Community policing stresses a police role that is less centralized and more proactive than reform-era policing strategies.

Computer Crime Any wrongful act that is directed against computers and computer parts or that involves wrongful use or abuse of computers or software.

Concurring Opinions Separate opinions prepared by judges who support the decision of the majority of the court but who want to make or clarify a particular point or to voice disapproval of the grounds on which the decision was made.

Confidential Informant (CI) A human source for police who provides information concerning illegal activity in which he or she is involved.

Conflict Model A criminal justice model in which the content of criminal law is determined by the groups that hold economic, political, and social power in a community.

Congregate System A nineteenth-century penitentiary system developed in New York in which inmates were kept in separate cells during the night but worked together in the daytime under a code of enforced silence.

Consensus Model A criminal justice model in which the majority of citizens in a society share the same values and beliefs. Criminal acts are those acts that conflict with these values and beliefs and are deemed harmful to society.

Consent Searches Searches by police that are made after the subject of the search has agreed to the action. In these situations, consent, if given of free will, validates a warrantless search.

Consolidation A corrections model in which the inmates who pose the highest security risk are housed in a single facility to separate them from the general prison population.

Constitutional Law Law based on the U.S. Constitution and the constitutions of the various states.

Control Theory A series of theories that assume that all individuals have the potential for criminal behavior, but are restrained by the damage that such actions would do to their relationships with family, friends, and members of the community. Criminality occurs when these bonds are broken or nonexistent.

Coroner The medical examiner of a county, usually elected by popular vote.

Corpus Delicti The body of circumstances that must exist for a criminal act to have occurred.

Courtroom Work Group The social organization consisting of the judge, prosecutor, defense attorney, and other court workers. The relationships among these persons have a far-reaching impact on the day-to-day operations of any court.

Crime Control Model A criminal justice model that places primary emphasis on the right of society to be protected from crime and violent criminals. Crime control values emphasize speed and efficiency in the criminal justice process; the benefits of lower crime rates outweigh any possible costs to individual rights.

Criminal Model of Addiction An approach to drug abuse that holds that drug offenders harm society by their actions to the same extent as other criminals and should face the same punitive sanctions.

Criminology The scientific study of crime and the causes of criminal behavior.

Cross-Examination The questioning of an opposing witness during trial.

Cultural Deviance Theory A branch of social structure theory based on the assumption that members of certain subcultures reject the values of the dominant culture through deviant behavior patterns.

Custodial Interrogation The questioning of a suspect after that person has been taken in custody. In this situation, the suspect must be read his or her *Miranda* rights before interrogation can begin.

Custody The forceful detention of a person, or the perception that a person is not free to leave the immediate vicinity.

Cyber Crime A crime that occurs online, in the virtual community of the Internet, as opposed to the physical world.

Cyber Fraud Any misrepresentation knowingly made over the Internet with the intention of deceiving another and on which a reasonable person would and does rely to his or her detriment.

Cyber Stalking The crime of stalking, committed in cyberspace. Generally, stalking consists of harassing a person and putting that person in reasonable fear for his or her safety or the safety of the person's immediate family.

D

Dark Figure of Crime A term used to describe the actual amount of crime that takes place. The "figure" is "dark," or impossible to detect, because a great number of crimes are never reported to the police.

Day Reporting Center A community-based corrections center to which offenders report on a daily basis for purposes of treatment, education, and incapacitation.

Deadly Force Force applied by a police officer that is likely or intended to cause death.

Decriminalization A policy that combines the elimination of criminal penalties on drug use with restrictions to discourage use such as high taxes and limitations on advertising of drugs.

Defense Attorney The lawyer representing the defendant.

Delegation of Authority The principles of command on which most police departments are based; personnel take orders from and are responsible to those in positions of power directly above them.

"Deliberate Indifference" A standard that must be met by inmates trying to prove that their Eighth Amendment rights were violated by a correctional facility. It occurs when prison officials are aware of harmful conditions of confinement but fail to take steps to remedy those conditions.

Departure A stipulation in many federal and state sentencing guidelines that allows a judge to adjust his or her sentencing decision based on the special circumstances of a particular case.

Deprivation Model A theory that inmate aggression is the result of the frustration inmates feel at being deprived of freedom, consumer goods, sex, and other staples of life outside the institution.

Detective The primary police investigator of crimes.

Detention The temporary custody of a juvenile in a state facility after a petition has been filed and before the adjudicatory process begins.

Detention Hearing A hearing to determine whether a juvenile should be detained, or remain detained, while waiting for the adjudicatory process to begin.

Determinate Sentencing A period of incarceration that is fixed by a sentencing authority and cannot be reduced by judges or other corrections officials.

Deterrence The strategy of preventing crime through the threat of punishment. Assumes that potential criminals will weigh the costs of punishments versus the benefits of the criminal act; therefore, punishments should be severe.

Deviance Behavior that is considered to go against the norms established by society.

Differential Response A strategy for answering calls for service in which response time is adapted to the seriousness of the call.

Direct Evidence Evidence that establishes the existence of a fact that is in question without relying on inference.

Direct Examination The examination of a witness by the attorney who calls the witness to the stand to testify.

Direct Supervision Approach A process of prison and jail administration in which correctional officers are in continuous physical contact with inmates during the day.

Directed Patrol Patrol strategies that are designed to respond to a specific criminal activity at a specific time.

Discovery Formal investigation prior to trial. During discovery, the defense uses various methods to obtain information from the prosecution to prepare for trial.

Discretion The ability of individuals in the criminal justice system to make operational decisions based on personal judgment instead of formal rules or official information.

Discretionary Release The release of an inmate into a community supervision program at the discretion of the parole board within limits set by state or federal law.

Dispersion A corrections model in which high-risk inmates are spread throughout the general prison population, in the hopes that they will be absorbed without causing misconduct problems.

Disposition Hearing Similar to the sentencing hearing for adults, a hearing in which the juvenile judge or officer decides the appropriate punishment for a youth found to be delinquent or a status offender.

Dissenting Opinions Separate opinions in which judges disagree with the conclusion reached by the majority of the court and expand on their own views about the case.

Diversion In the context of corrections, a strategy to divert those offenders who qualify away from prison and jail and toward community-based and intermediate sanctions.

Diversion The removal of an alleged juvenile delinquent from the formal criminal or juvenile justice system and the referral of that person to a treatment or rehabilitation program.

Docket The list of cases entered on a court's calendar and thus scheduled to be heard by the court.

Double Jeopardy To twice place at risk (jeopardize) a person's life or liberty. The Fifth Amendment to the U.S. Constitution prohibits a second prosecution for the same criminal offense.

Drug Any substance that modifies behavior; in particular, an illegal substance with those properties.

Drug Abuse The use of drugs that results in physical or psychological problems for the user, as well as disruption of personal relationships and employment.

Dual Court System The separate but interrelated court system of the United States, made up of the courts on the national level and the courts on the state level.

Due Process Clause The provisions of the Fifth and Fourteenth Amendments to the Constitution that guarantee that no person shall be deprived of life, liberty, or property without due process of law. Similar clauses are found in most state constitutions.

Due Process Model A criminal justice model that places primacy on the right of the individual to be protected from the power of the government. Due process values hold that the state must prove a person's guilt within the confines of a process designed to safeguard personal liberties as enumerated in the Bill of Rights.

Duress Unlawful pressure brought to bear on a person, causing the person to perform an act that he or she would not otherwise perform.

Durham **Rule** A test of criminal responsibility adopted in a 1954 case: "an accused is not criminally responsible if his unlawful act was the product of mental disease or mental defect."

Duty The moral sense of a police officer that she or he should apply authority in a certain manner.

E

Electronic Monitoring A technique of probation supervision in which the offender's whereabouts, though not his or her actions, are kept under surveillance by an electronic device; often used in conjunction with home confinement.

Encryption The process by which a message is transmitted into a form or code that the sender and receiver intend third parties not to understand.

Enemy Combatant A label given to certain persons suspected of terrorist activities by the U.S. government. Persons given this designation lose a number of rights provided by the U.S. Constitution.

Entrapment A defense in which the defendant claims that he or she was induced by a public official—usually an undercover agent or police officer—to commit a crime that he or she would otherwise not have committed.

Ethics The rules or standards of behavior governing a profession; aimed at ensuring the fairness and rightness of actions.

Evidence Anything that is used to prove the existence or nonexistence of a fact.

Exclusionary Rule A rule under which any evidence that is obtained in violation of the accused's rights under the Fourth, Fifth, and Sixth Amendments, as well as any evidence derived from illegally obtained evidence, will not be admissible in criminal court.

Exigent Circumstances Situations that require extralegal or exceptional actions by the police. In these circumstances, police officers are justified in not following procedural rules, such as those pertaining to search and arrest warrants.

Expert Witness A witness with professional training or substantial experience qualifying her or him to testify on a certain subject.

F

Federal Bureau of Investigation (FBI) The branch of the Department of Justice responsible for investigating violations of federal law. The bureau also collects national crime statistics and provides training and other forms of aid to local law enforcement agencies.

Federalism A form of government in which a written constitution provides for a division of powers between a central government and several regional governments. In the United States, the division of powers between the federal government and the fifty states is established by the Constitution.

Felony A serious crime punishable by death or by imprisonment in a federal or state corrections facility for more than a year.

Field Training The segment of a police recruit's training in which he or she is removed from the classroom and placed on the beat, under the supervision of a senior officer.

Forfeiture The process by which the government seizes private property attached to criminal activity.

Frisk A pat-down or minimal search by police to discover weapons; conducted for the express purpose of protecting the officer or other citizens, and not to find evidence of illegal substances for use in a trial.

Fruit of the Poisoned Tree Evidence that is acquired through the use of illegally obtained evidence and is therefore inadmissible in court.

Furlough Temporary release from a prison for purposes of vocational or educational training, to ease the shock of release, or for personal reasons.

G

General Patrol Patrol strategies that rely on police officers monitoring a certain area with the goal of detecting crimes in progress or preventing crime due to their presence. Also known as random or preventive patrol.

"Good Faith" Exception The legal principle, established through court decisions, that evidence obtained with the use of a technically faulty search warrant is admissible during trial if the police acted in good faith when they sought the warrant from a judge.

"Good Time" A reduction in time served by prisoners based on good behavior, conformity to rules, and other positive actions.

Graduated Sanctions The practical theory in juvenile corrections that a delinquent or status offender should receive a punishment that matches in seriousness the severity of the wrongdoing.

Grand Jury The group of citizens called to decide whether probable cause exists to believe that a suspect committed the crime with which she or he has been charged.

H

Habeas Corpus An order that requires correctional officials to bring an inmate before a court or a judge and explain why he or she is being held in prison.

Habitual Offender Laws Statutes that require lengthy prison sentences for those who are convicted of multiple felonies.

Hacker A person who uses one computer to break into another.

Halfway House A community-based form of early release that places inmates in residential centers and allows them to reintegrate with society.

Hallucinogens Drugs that cause the user to experience alterations in sensory experiences, or hallucinations.

"Hands-Off" Doctrine The unwritten judicial policy that favors noninterference by the courts in the administration of prisons and jails.

Harm Reduction A drug policy based not on reducing use of illicit drugs but on reducing the crime and health problems associated with drug use.

Hate Crime Law A statute that provides for greater sanctions against those who commit crimes motivated by animosity against an individual or a group based on race, ethnicity, religion, gender, sexual orientation, disability, or age.

Hearsay An oral or written statement made by an out-of-court declarant that is later offered in court by a witness (not the declarant) concerning a matter before the court. Hearsay usually is not admissible as evidence.

Home Confinement A community-based sanction in which offenders serve their terms of incarceration in their homes.

Hot Spots Concentrated areas of high criminal activity that draw a directed police response.

Hung Jury A jury whose members are so irreconcilably divided in their opinions that they cannot reach a verdict.

I

"Identifiable Human Needs" The basic human necessities that correctional facilities are required by the Constitution to provide to inmates. Beyond food, warmth, and exercise, the court system has been unable to establish exactly what these needs are.

Identity Theft The theft of identity information, such as name, driver's license number, or Social Security number. The information is then usually used to access the victim's financial resources.

Illicit Drugs Certain drugs or substances whose use or sale has been declared illegal.

Immigration Violations Infractions of U.S. immigration laws, such as failing to comply with the terms of a visa, for which the punishment is often removal from the United States.

Impeached As authorized by Article I of the Constitution, impeachment is voted on by the House of Representatives and then sent to the Senate for a vote to remove the president, vice president, or civil officers (such as federal judges) of the United States.

Incapacitation A strategy for preventing crime by detaining wrongdoers in prison, thereby separating them from the community and reducing criminal opportunities.

Inchoate Offenses Conduct deemed criminal without actual harm being done, provided that the harm that would have occurred is one the law tries to prevent.

Incident-Driven Policing A reactive approach to policing that emphasizes a speedy response to calls for service.

Indeterminate Sentencing An indeterminate term of incarceration in which a judge determines the minimum and maximum terms of imprisonment. When the minimum term is reached, the prisoner becomes eligible to be paroled.

Index Crimes Those crimes reported annually by the FBI in its Uniform Crime Report. Index crimes include murder, rape, robbery, aggravated assault, burglary, larceny, motor vehicle theft, and arson. Also known as Part I offenses.

Indictment A charge or written accusation, issued by a grand jury, that probable cause exists to believe that a named person has committed a crime.

"Inevitable Discovery" Exception The legal principle that illegally obtained evidence can be admitted in court if police using lawful means would have "inevitably" discovered it.

Information The formal charge against the accused issued by the prosecutor after a preliminary hearing has found probable cause.

Initial Appearance An accused's first appearance before a judge or magistrate following arrest; during the appearance, the defendant is informed of the charges, advised of the right to counsel, told the amount of bail, and given a date for the preliminary hearing.

Insanity A defense for criminal liability that asserts a lack of criminal responsibility. According to the law, a person cannot have the requisite state of mind to commit a crime if she or he did not know at the time of the act that it was wrong, or did not know the nature and quality of the act.

Intake Following referral of a juvenile to juvenile court by a police officer or other concerned party, the process by which an official of the court must decide whether to file a petition, release the juvenile, or place the juvenile under some other form of supervision.

Intellectual Property Property resulting from intellectual, creative processes.

Intelligence Agency An agency that is primarily concerned with gathering information on potential criminals and criminal acts in order to prevent crimes from occurring.

Intensive Supervision Probation (ISP) A punishment-oriented form of probation in which the offender is placed under stricter and more frequent surveillance and control by probation officers with limited caseloads.

Intermediate Sanctions Sanctions that are more restrictive than probation and less restrictive than imprisonment. Intended to alleviate pressure on overcrowded corrections facilities and understaffed probation departments.

Internal Affairs Unit (IAU) A division within a police department that receives and investigates complaints of wrongdoing by police officers.

Interrogation The direct questioning of a suspect to gather evidence of criminal activity and try to gain a confession.

Intoxication A defense for criminal liability in which the defendant claims that the taking of intoxicants rendered him or her unable to form the requisite intent to commit a criminal act.

Irresistible Impulse Test A test for the insanity defense under which a defendant who knew his or her action was wrong may still be found insane if he or she was nonetheless unable, as a result of a mental deficiency, to control the urge to complete it.

J

Jail A facility, usually operated by county government, used to hold persons awaiting trial or those who have been found guilty of misdemeanors.

Judicial Misconduct A general term describing behavior that diminishes public confidence in the judiciary. This behavior includes obviously illegal acts, such as bribery, and conduct that gives the appearance of impropriety, such as consorting with known felons.

Judicial Reprieve Temporary relief or the postponement of a sentence on the authority of a judge. In the United States, the judicial power to offer a reprieve has been limited by the Supreme Court.

Judicial Waiver The process in which the juvenile judge, based on the facts of the case at hand, decides that the alleged offender should be transferred to adult court.

Jurisdiction The authority of a court to hear and decide cases within an area of the law or a geographical territory.

Jury Nullification An acquittal of a defendant by a jury even though the evidence presented and the judge's instructions indicate that the defendant is guilty.

Jury Trial A trial before a judge and a jury.

Just Deserts A sanctioning philosophy based on the assertion that criminals deserve to be punished for breaking society's rules. The severity of the punishment should be determined by no other factor than the severity of the crime.

Justice of the Peace Established in fourteenth-century England, a government official who oversaw various aspects of local law enforcement. The post eventually became strictly identified with judicial matters.

Juvenile Delinquency Behavior that is illegal under federal or state law that has been committed by a person who is under an age limit specified by statute.

L

Labeling Theory The hypothesis that society creates crime and criminals by labeling certain behavior and certain people as deviant. The stigma that results from this social process excludes a person from the community, thereby increasing the chances that she or he will adopt the label as her or his identity and engage in a pattern of criminal behavior.

Lay Witness A witness who can truthfully and accurately testify on a fact in question without having specialized training or knowledge; an ordinary witness.

Learning Theory The hypothesis that delinquents and criminals must be taught both the practical and emotional skills necessary to partake in illegal activity.

Legalization The elimination or modification of federal and state laws that prohibit the manufacture, use, and sale of illegal drugs.

Licit Drugs Legal drugs or substances, such as alcohol, coffee, and tobacco.

Life Course Criminology The study of crime based on the belief that behavioral patterns developed in childhood can predict delinquent and criminal behavior later in life.

Lockdown A disciplinary action taken by prison officials in which all inmates are ordered to their quarters and nonessential prison activities are suspended.

Low-Visibility Decision Making A term used to describe the discretionary power police have in determining what to do with misbehaving juveniles. For the most part, this power goes unchallenged and unnoticed by citizens.

M

M'Naughten Rule A common law test of criminal responsibility derived from *M'Naughten's* case in 1843 that relies on the defendant's inability to distinguish right from wrong.

Magistrate A public civil officer or official with limited judicial authority within a particular geographical area, such as the authority to issue an arrest warrant.

Mala in Se A descriptive term for acts that are inherently wrong, regardless of whether they are prohibited by law.

Mala Prohibita A descriptive term for acts that are made illegal by criminal statute and are not necessarily wrong in and of themselves.

Mandatory Release Release from prison that occurs when an offender has served the length of his or her sentence, with time taken off for good behavior.

Mandatory Sentencing Guidelines Statutorily determined punishments that must be applied to those who are convicted of specific crimes.

Master Jury List The list of citizens in a court's district from which a jury can be selected; often compiled from voter-registration lists, driver's license lists, and other sources.

Maximum-Security Prison A correctional institution designed and organized to control and discipline dangerous felons, as well as prevent escape, with intense supervision, cement walls, and electronic, barbed wire fences.

Medical Model A model of corrections in which the psychological and biological roots of an inmate's criminal behavior are identified and treated.

Medical Model of Addiction An approach to drug addiction that treats drug abuse as a mental illness and focuses on treating and rehabilitating offenders rather than punishing them.

Medium-Security Prison A correctional institution that houses less dangerous inmates and therefore uses less restrictive measures to avoid violence and escapes.

Mens Rea (pronounced *mehns* ray-uh) Mental state, or intent. A wrongful mental state is as necessary as a wrongful act to establish criminal liability.

Minimum-Security Prison A correctional institution designed to allow inmates, most of whom pose low security risks, a great deal of freedom of movement and contact with the outside world.

Miranda Rights The constitutional rights of accused persons taken into custody by law enforcement officials. Following the United States Supreme Court's decision in *Miranda v. Arizona*, on taking an accused person into custody, the arresting officer must inform the person of certain constitutional rights, such as the right to remain silent and the right to counsel.

Misdemeanor Any crime that is not a felony; punishable by a fine or by confinement for up to a year.

Missouri Plan A method of selecting judges that combines appointment and election. Under the plan, the state governor or another government official selects judges from a group of nominees chosen by a nonpartisan committee. After a year on the bench, the judges face a popular election to determine whether the public wishes to keep them in office.

Mitigating Circumstances Any circumstances accompanying the commission of a crime that may justify a lighter sentence.

Motion for a Directed Verdict A motion requesting that the court grant judgment in favor of the defense on the ground that the prosecution has not produced sufficient evidence to support the state's claim.

N

Necessity A defense against criminal liability in which the defendant asserts that circumstances required her or him to commit an illegal act.

Negligence A failure to exercise the standard of care that a reasonable person would exercise in similar circumstances.

New-Generation Jail A type of jail that is distinguished architecturally from its predecessors by a design that encourages interaction between inmates and jailers and that offers greater opportunities for treatment.

Nolo Contendere Latin for "I will not contest it." A criminal defendant's plea, in which he or she chooses not to challenge, or contest, the charges brought by the government. Although the defendant may still be sentenced or fined, the plea neither admits nor denies guilt.

Nonpartisan Elections Elections in which candidates are presented on the ballot without any party affiliation.

O

Opening Statements The attorneys' statements to the jury at the beginning of the trial. Each side briefly outlines the evidence that will be offered during the trial and the legal theory that will be pursued.

Opiates Drugs containing opium or its derivatives; have the effects of dulling sensations including pain and anxiety, producing a feeling of euphoria, and causing general inaction.

Opinion A statement by the court expressing the reasons for its decision in a case.

Oral Arguments The verbal arguments presented in person by attorneys to an appellate court. Each attorney presents reasons why the court should rule in his or her client's favor.

Organized Crime A conspiratorial relationship between any number of persons engaged in the market for illegal goods or services, such as illicit drugs or firearms.

P

Pardon An act of executive clemency that overturns a conviction and erases mention of the crime from the person's criminal record.

Parens Patriae A doctrine that holds that the state has a responsibility to look after the well-being of children and to assume the role of parent if necessary.

Parole The conditional release of an inmate before his or her sentence has expired. The remainder of the sentence is served in the community under the supervision of correctional (parole) officers, and the offender can be returned to incarceration if he or she breaks the conditions of parole, as determined by a parole board.

Parole Board A body of appointed civilians that decides whether a convict should be granted conditional release before the end of his or her sentence.

Parole Contract An agreement between the state and the offender that establishes the conditions under which the latter will be allowed to serve the remainder of her or his prison term in the community.

Parole Grant Hearing A hearing in which the entire parole board or a subcommittee reviews information, meets the offender, and hears testimony from relevant witnesses to determine whether to grant parole.

Parole Guidelines Employed to remove discretion from the parole process, these guidelines attempt to measure the risks of an offender recidivating, and then use these measurements to determine whether early release will be granted and under what conditions.

Parole Revocation When a parolee breaks the conditions of parole, the process of withdrawing parole and returning the person to prison.

Part II Offenses All crimes recorded by the FBI that do not fall into the category of Part I offenses. Include both misdemeanors and felonies.

Partisan Elections Elections in which candidates are affiliated with and receive support from political parties; the candidates are listed in conjunction with their party on the ballot.

Patronage System A form of corruption in which the political party in power hires and promotes police officers, receiving job-related "favors" in return.

Penitentiary An early form of correctional facility that emphasized separating inmates from society and from each other so that they would have an environment in which to reflect on their wrongdoing and ponder their reformation.

Peremptory Challenges *Voir dire* challenges to exclude potential jurors from serving on the jury without any supporting reason or cause.

Petition The document filed with a juvenile court alleging that the juvenile is a delinquent or a status offender, and asking the court to either hear the case or transfer it to an adult court.

Plain View Doctrine The legal principle that objects in plain view of a law enforcement agent who has the right to be in a position to have that view may be seized without a warrant and introduced as evidence.

Plea Bargaining The process by which the accused and the prosecutor work out a mutually satisfactory conclusion to the case, subject to court approval. Usually, plea bargaining involves the defendant's pleading guilty to a lesser offense in return for a lighter sentence.

Podular Design The architectural style of the new-generation jail. Each "pod" consists of between twelve and twenty-four one-person cells and a communal "day-room" to allow for social interaction.

Police Corruption The abuse of authority by a law enforcement officer for personal gain.

Police Cynicism The suspicion that citizens are weak, corrupt, and dangerous. This outlook is the result of a police officer being constantly exposed to civilians at their worst and can negatively affect the officer's performance.

Police Subculture The values and perceptions that are shared by members of a police department and, to a certain extent, by all law enforcement agents. These values and perceptions are shaped by the unique and isolated existence of the police officer.

Positivism A school of social science that sees criminal and delinquent behavior as the result of biological, psychological, and social forces. Because wrongdoers are driven to deviancy by external factors, they should not be punished but treated to lessen the influence of those factors.

Precedent A court decision that furnishes an example of authority for deciding subsequent cases involving similar facts.

Predisposition Report A report prepared during the disposition process that provides the judge with relevant background material to aid in the disposition decision.

Preliminary Hearing An initial hearing in which a magistrate decides if there is probable cause to believe that the defendant committed the crime with which he or she is charged.

Presentence Investigative Report An investigative report on an offender's background that assists a judge in determining the proper sentence.

Presumptive Sentencing A sentencing strategy in which legislators set the average sentence that should be served for any particular crime, leaving judges with the ability to shorten or lengthen the sentence based on the circumstances of each case.

Pretrial Detainees Individuals who cannot post bail after arrest and are therefore forced to spend the time prior to their trial incarcerated in jail.

Pretrial Diversion Program An alternative to trial offered by a judge or prosecutor, in which the offender agrees to participate in a specified counseling or treatment program in return for withdrawal of the charges.

Preventive Detention The retention of an accused person in custody due to fears that she or he will commit a crime if released before trial.

Prisoner Reentry A corrections strategy designed to prepare inmates for a successful return to the community and to reduce their criminal activity after release.

Prisonization The socialization process through which a new inmate learns the accepted norms and values of the prison population.

Private Prisons Correctional facilities operated by private corporations instead of the government and, therefore, reliant on profit for survival.

Private Security The practice of private corporations or individuals offering services traditionally performed by police officers.

Probable Cause Reasonable grounds to believe the existence of facts warranting certain actions, such as the search or arrest of a person.

Probation A criminal sanction in which a convict is allowed to remain in the community rather than be imprisoned as long as she or he follows certain conditions set by the court.

Problem-Solving Policing A policing philosophy that requires police to identify potential criminal activity and develop strategies to prevent or respond to that activity.

Procedural Criminal Law Rules that define the manner in which the rights and duties of individuals may be enforced.

Procedural Due Process A provision in the Constitution that states that the law must be carried out in a fair and orderly manner.

Professional Model A style of policing advocated by August Vollmer and O. W. Wilson that emphasizes centralized police organizations, increased use of technology, and a limitation of police discretion through regulations and guidelines.

Prohibition A period in American history, lasting from the passage of the Eighteenth Amendment in 1919 until its repeal in 1933, during which the production and consumption of alcohol were prohibited by federal law.

Property Crime Crimes committed against property, including larceny/theft, burglary, and arson.

Prosecutorial Waiver A procedure in which juvenile court judges have the discretion to transfer a juvenile case to adult court, when certain predetermined conditions as to the seriousness of the offense and the age of the offender are met.

Psychoactive Drugs Chemicals that affect the brain, causing changes in emotions, perceptions, and behavior.

Public Defenders Court-appointed attorneys who are paid by the state to represent defendants who are unable to hire private counsel.

Public Order Crime Behavior that has been labeled criminal because it is contrary to shared social values, customs, and norms.

Public Prosecutors Individuals, acting as trial lawyers, who initiate and conduct cases in the government's name and on behalf of the people.

R

Rape Shield Law A state or federal law that disallows any evidence of an alleged sexual-assault victim's prior sexual conduct to be used against her or him in a criminal trial. These laws are designed to spare the victim the humiliation of irrelevant references to past sexual behavior that may improperly influence the jury.

Real Evidence Evidence that is brought into court and seen by the jury, as opposed to evidence that is described for a jury.

"Real Offense" The actual offense committed, as opposed to the charge levied by a prosecutor as the result of a plea bargain. Judges who make sentencing decisions based on the real offense are often seen as undermining the plea bargain process.

Reasonable Force The degree of force that is appropriate to protect the police officer or other citizens and is not excessive.

Rebuttal Evidence given to counteract or disprove evidence presented by the opposing party.

Rehabilitation The philosophy that society is best served when wrongdoers are not simply punished, but provided the resources needed to eliminate criminality from their behavioral patterns.

Reintegration A goal of corrections that focuses on preparing the offender for a return to the community unmarred by further criminal behavior.

Relative Deprivation The theory that inmate aggression is caused when freedoms and services that the inmate has come to accept as normal are decreased or eliminated.

Release on Recognizance (ROR) A judge's order that releases an accused from jail with the understanding that he or she will return for further proceedings of his or her own will; used instead of setting a monetary bond.

Relevant Evidence Evidence tending to make a fact in question more or less probable than it would be without the evidence. Only relevant evidence is admissible in court.

Residential Treatment Programs Government-run facilities for juveniles whose offenses are not deemed serious enough to warrant incarceration in a training school.

Response Time A measurement of police efficiency based on the rapidity with which calls for service are answered.

Retribution The philosophy that those who commit criminal acts should be punished based on the severity of the crime and that no other factors need be considered.

Rule of Four A rule of the United States Supreme Court that the Court will not issue a writ of *certiorari* unless at least four justices approve of the decision to hear the case.

S

Search The process by which police examine a person or property to find evidence that will be used to prove guilt in a criminal trial.

Search Warrant A written order, based on probable cause and issued by a judge or magistrate, commanding that police officers or criminal investigators search a specific person, place, or property to obtain evidence.

Searches and Seizures The legal term, as found in the Fourth Amendment of the U.S. Constitution, that generally refers to the searching for and the confiscating of evidence by law enforcement agents.

Searches Incidental to Arrests Searches for weapons and evidence of persons who have just been arrested. The fruit of such searches is admissible if any items found are within the immediate vicinity or control of the suspect.

Sedatives Drugs that slow the signals sent from the brain to other parts of the body, thereby inducing sleep or reducing anxiety.

Seizure The forcible taking of a person or property in response to a violation of the law.

Self-Defense The legally recognized privilege to protect one's self or property from injury by another. The privilege of self-defense protects only acts that are reasonably necessary to protect one's self or property.

Self-Reported Surveys A method of gathering crime data that relies on participants to reveal and detail their own criminal or delinquent behavior.

Sentencing Discrimination A situation in which the length of a sentence appears to be influenced by a defendant's race, gender, economic status, or other factor not directly related to the crime he or she committed.

Sentencing Disparity A situation in which those convicted of similar crimes do not receive similar sentences.

Sentencing Guidelines Legislatively determined guidelines that judges are required to follow when sentencing those convicted of specific crimes. These guidelines limit judicial discretion.

Separate Confinement A nineteenth-century penitentiary system developed in Pennsylvania in which inmates were kept separate from each other at all times, with daily activities taking place in individual cells.

Sheriff The primary law enforcement officer in a county, usually elected to the post by a popular vote.

Shire-Reeve The chief law enforcement officer in an early English shire, or county. The forerunner of the modern sheriff.

Shock Incarceration A short period of incarceration that is designed to deter further criminal activity by "shocking" the offender with the hardships of imprisonment.

Social Conflict Theories A school of criminology that views criminal behavior as the result of class conflict. Certain behavior is labeled illegal not because it is inherently criminal, but because the ruling class has an economic or social interest in restricting such behavior in order to protect the status quo.

Social Disorganization Theory The theory that deviant behavior is more likely in communities where social institutions such as the family, schools, and criminal justice system fail to exert control over the population.

Social Process Theories A school of criminology that considers criminal behavior to be the predictable result of a person's interaction with his or her environment. According to these theories, everybody has the potential for wrongdoing. Those who act on this potential are conditioned to do so by family or peer groups, or institutions such as the media.

Social Reality of Crime The theory that criminal laws are designed by those in power (the rich) to help them keep power at the expense of those who do not have power (the poor). This would explain, for example, why the punishment for white-collar crime, mostly committed by members of the upper and middle classes, is less severe than the punishment for property and violent crimes, mostly committed by members of the lower class.

Socialization The process through which a police officer is taught the values and expected behavior of the police subculture.

Specialty Courts Lower courts that have jurisdiction over one specific area of criminal activity, such as illegal drugs or domestic violence.

Split Sentence Probation A sentence that consists of incarceration in a prison or jail, followed by a probationary period in the community.

Stare Decisis (pronounced *ster*-ay dih-*si-ses*) A common law doctrine under which judges are obligated to follow the precedents established under prior decisions.

Status Offender A juvenile who has been found to have engaged in behavior deemed unacceptable for those under a certain, statutorily determined age.

Statutory Law The body of law enacted by legislative bodies.

Stimulants Drugs such as cocaine or amphetamine that stimulate the central nervous system, thereby quickening motor functions of the body.

Stop A brief detention of a person by law enforcement agents for questioning. The agents must have a reasonable suspicion of the person before making a stop.

Strain Theory The assumption that crime is the result of frustration felt by individuals who cannot reach their financial and personal goals through legitimate means.

Strict Liability Certain crimes, such as traffic violations, in which the defendant is guilty regardless of her or his state of mind at the time of the act.

Subculture A group exhibiting certain values and behavior patterns that distinguish it from the dominant culture.

Substantial Capacity Test From the Model Penal Code, a test that states that a person is not responsible for criminal behavior if when committing the act "as a result of mental disease or defect he lacks substantial capacity either to appreciate the wrongfulness of his conduct or to conform his conduct to the requirements of the law."

Substantive Criminal Law Law that defines the rights and duties of individuals with respect to each other.

Substantive Due Process The constitutional requirement that laws used in accusing and convicting persons of crimes must be fair.

Supermax Prison A correctional facility reserved for those inmates who have extensive records of misconduct in maximum-security prisons; characterized by extremely strict control and supervision over the inmates, including extensive use of solitary confinement.

Supply-Side Enforcement The law enforcement strategy of combating the use of illegal drugs by concentrating on the suppliers of the drugs rather than the buyers. Thus, agents will focus on a single drug dealer rather than on his or her many clients.

Suspended Sentence A judicially imposed condition in which an offender is sentenced after being convicted of a crime, but is not required to begin the sentence immediately. The judge may revoke the suspended sentence and remit the offender to prison or jail if he or she does not follow certain conditions.

T

Technical Violation An action taken by a probationer that, although not criminal, breaks the terms of probation as designated by the court; can result in the revocation of probation and a return to prison or jail.

Ten Percent Cash Bail An alternative to traditional bail in which defendants may gain pretrial release by posting 10 percent of their bond amount to the court instead of seeking a bail bondsperson.

Terrorism The use or threat of violence to achieve political objectives.

Testimony Verbal evidence given by witnesses under oath.

Theory of Differential Association Sutherland's theory that criminality is the result of the values an individual is exposed to by family, friends, and other members of the community. When these values favor deviant behavior over conventional norms, criminal activity is more likely.

Time Served The period of time a person denied bail has spent in jail prior to his or her trial. If the suspect is found guilty and sentenced to a jail or prison term, the judge will often lessen the duration of the sentence based on the amount of time served as a pretrial detainee.

Tithing System In Anglo-Saxon England, a system of law enforcement in which groups of ten families, known as tithings, were collectively responsible for law and order within their groups.

Total Institution An institution, such as a prison, that provides all of the necessities for existence to those who live within its boundaries.

Training Schools Correctional institutions for juveniles found to be delinquent or status offenders.

Trial Courts Courts in which most cases usually begin and in which questions of fact are examined.

Truth-in-Sentencing Laws Legislative attempts to assure that convicts will serve approximately the terms to which they were initially sentenced.

U

Uniform Crime Report (UCR) An annual report compiled by the FBI to give an indication of criminal activity in the United States. The FBI collects data from local, state, and federal law enforcement agencies in preparing this report.

Utilitarianism An approach to ethical reasoning in which the "correct" decision is the one that results in the greatest amount of good for the greatest number of people affected by that decision.

V

Venire The group of citizens from which the jury is selected.

Verdict A formal decision made by the jury.

Victim Impact Statement (VIS) A statement to the sentencing body (judge, jury, or parole board) in which the victim is given the opportunity to describe how the crime has affected her or him. The general purpose of the statement is to convince the sentencing party to hand down a harsher punishment than might otherwise be the case.

Victimology A school of criminology that studies why certain people are the victims of crimes and the optimal role for victims in the criminal justice system.

Victim Surveys A method of gathering crime data that directly surveys participants to determine their experiences as victims of crime.

Violent Crime Crimes committed against persons, including murder, rape, assault and battery, and robbery.

Virus A computer program that can replicate itself over a network such as the Internet and interfere with the normal use of a computer. A virus cannot exist as a separate entity and must attach itself to another program to move through a network.

Voir Dire The preliminary questions that the trial attorneys ask prospective jurors to determine whether they are biased or have any connection with the defendant or a witness.

W

Warden The prison official who is ultimately responsible for the organization and performance of a correctional facility.

Warrantless Arrest An arrest made without first seeking a warrant for the action; permitted under certain circumstances, such as when the arresting officer has witnessed the crime or has a reasonable belief that the suspect has committed a felony.

"Wedding Cake" Model A wedding cake–shaped model that explains why different cases receive different treatment in the criminal justice system. The cases at the "top" of the cake receive the most attention and have the greatest effect on public perception of criminal justice, while those cases at the "bottom" are disposed of quickly and virtually ignored by the media.

White-Collar Crime Nonviolent crimes committed by corporations and individuals to gain a personal or business advantage.

Widen the Net The criticism that intermediate sanctions designed to divert offenders from prison actually increase the number of citizens who are under the control and surveillance of the American corrections system.

Work Release Program Temporary release of convicts from prison for purposes of employment. The offenders may spend their days on the job, but must return to the correctional facility at night and during the weekend.

Worm A computer program that can automatically replicate itself over a network such as the Internet and interfere with the normal use of a computer. A worm can exist as a separate entity.

Writ of *Certiorari* A request from a higher court asking a lower court for the record of a case. In essence, the request signals the higher court's willingness to review the case.

Y

Youth Gangs Self-formed groups of youths with several identifiable characteristics, including a gang name and other recognizable symbols, a geographic territory, a leadership structure, a meeting pattern, and participation in illegal activities.

Index